Human Resource Management

Tenth Edition

John M. Ivancevich

*Cullen Professor of Organizational
Behavior and Management,
C.T. Bauer College of Business,
University of Houston*

**McGraw-Hill
Irwin**

Boston   Burr Ridge, IL   Dubuque, IA   Madison, WI   New York
San Francisco   St. Louis   Bangkok   Bogotá   Caracas   Kuala Lumpur
Lisbon   London   Madrid   Mexico City   Milan   Montreal   New Delhi
Santiago   Seoul   Singapore   Sydney   Taipei   Toronto

McGraw-Hill
Irwin

HUMAN RESOURCE MANAGEMENT

Published by McGraw-Hill/Irwin, a business unit of The McGraw-Hill Companies, Inc., 1221 Avenue of the Americas, New York, NY, 10020. Copyright © 2007 by The McGraw-Hill Companies, Inc. All rights reserved. No part of this publication may be reproduced or distributed in any form or by any means, or stored in a database or retrieval system, without the prior written consent of The McGraw-Hill Companies, Inc., including, but not limited to, in any network or other electronic storage or transmission, or broadcast for distance learning.

Some ancillaries, including electronic and print components, may not be available to customers outside the United States.

This book is printed on acid-free paper.

3 4 5 6 7 8 9 0 QPD/QPD 0 9 8 7

ISBN 978-0-07-313711-7
MHID 10: 0-07-313711-1

Editorial director: *John E. Biernat*
Executive editor: *John Weimeister*
Editorial assistant: *Heather Darr*
Associate marketing manager: *Margaret A. Beamer*
Senior media producer: *Damian Moshak*
Project manager: *Dana M. Pauley*
Production supervisor: *Gina Hangos*
Senior designer: *Adam Rooke*
Senior media project manager: *Susan Lombardi*
Cover design: *Jillian Lindner*
Typeface: *10/12 Sabon*
Compositor: *International Typesetting & Composition*
Printer: *Quebecor Word Dubuque Inc.*

Library of Congress Cataloging-in-Publication Data

Ivancevich, John M.
    Human resource management /John M. Ivancevich.—10th ed.
      p. cm.
    Includes index.
     ISBN-13: 978-0-07-313711-7 (alk. paper)
     ISBN-10: 0-07-313711-1 (alk. paper)
     1. Personnel management. 2. Personnel management—Case studies. I. Title.
HF5549.I88 2007
    658.3—dc22
                                                               2005058379

www.mhhe.com

To:
Dana Louise Ivancevich
Our sun, mountain, and water

Preface

The strategic role of human resource management in organizations is now an accepted viewpoint. Managers are aware that HRM is a function that must play a vital role in the success of organizations. HRM is no longer an afterthought, a limited service, or a unit to be tolerated. It is an active participant in charting the strategic course an organization must take to remain competitive, productive, and efficient.

This Tenth Edition of *Human Resource Management*—like the earlier editions—takes a managerial orientation; that is, HRM is viewed as relevant to managers in every unit, project, or team. Managers constantly face HRM issues, challenges, and decision making. Each manager must be a human resource problem solver and diagnostician who can deftly apply HRM concepts, procedures, models, tools, and techniques. This book pays attention to the application of HRM approaches in real organizational settings and situations. Realism, currentness, understanding, and critical thinking are cornerstones in each edition of this text.

Human resource management is clearly needed in all organizations. Its focal point is people; people are the lifeblood of organizations. Without them, there is no need for computer systems, compensation plans, mission statements, programs, strategic planning, or procedures. Because HRM activities involve people, the activities must be finely tuned, properly implemented, and continuously monitored to achieve desired outcomes. The uniqueness of HRM lies in its emphasis on people in work settings and its concern for the well-being and comfort of the human resources in an organization. This edition focuses on (1) managers and leaders with the responsibility to optimize performance and do what is ethically correct; (2) employees (e.g., engineers, clerks, software programmers, designers, machinists, chemists, teachers, nurses) who perform the work and (3) HRM specialists who advise, support, and aid managers and nonmanagers in their work.

Students and faculty identify readability as a key strength of this book. This book also remains current, thorough, and relevant. But it was never intended to be an encyclopedia or a compendium of human resource management tools, laws, or ideas. Instead, the intent was to provide a book that instructors and students could learn from and that would stimulate their own ideas, while keeping them up to date on HRM theory and practice.

Pedagogical Features

In order to make the book relevant, interesting, scholarly, and practical, a number of pedagogical procedures were adopted and strengthened with each new edition. Each chapter contains most of the following elements:

- Brief list of *behavioral learning objectives* and an outline of the chapter.
- *Career Challenge*—a short situation emphasizing applied HRM techniques and issues that introduces each chapter and is further developed at various points in the chapter and at its conclusion.
- *HR Journal*—a brief news story or best-in-class example about an actual company, technique, or group of people.
- *HRMemo*—a margin item that highlights a statistic, fact, historical point, or relevant piece of information.
- The most *recent statistics* and data available on topics covered in the chapter.
- *Chapter summary*—a handy, concise reference to the chapter's main points.
- List of *key terms* (plus a comprehensive glossary of key terms at the end of the book).

- *Questions for Review and Discussion.*
- *HRM Legal Adviser*—a brief legal point, case, or fact tied to the content of the chapter. Managers must be familiar with legal factors and the law.
- *Application case(s) and/or experiential exercises*—reflecting HRM issues, concerns, and problems faced in organizations of various sizes and in a wide array of industries.
- Use of a *video case* and discussion questions to integrate material relevant to the participation section of the book in each of the five parts.

Parts and Appendixes

The Tenth Edition consists of five parts, divided into 17 chapters, and four appendixes. Appendix A is at the end of Chapter 1 and discusses careers in HRM. Appendix B, "Measuring Human Resource Activities," was originally prepared by Jac Fitz-Enz, Ph.D., president of the Saratoga Institute. It spells out the reasons why measurement is important and how a measurement system for the HRM unit can be developed and styled. Appendix C, "Sources of Information about Human Resource Management: Where to Find Facts and Figures," was originally prepared by Paul N. Keaton of the University of Wisconsin, LaCrosse, and has been updated for this edition. This appendix provides valuable sources of information that are useful in HRM. Appendix D, "Career Planning," was prepared by the author of the text. It examines important steps involved in career planning that each person must accept responsibility for and initiate at the appropriate time. Each reader of the book must become actively involved in his or her own career plan.

New and Strengthened Content Features

Each new edition involves major revisions, additions, deletions, and rewriting. Comments by instructors, students, practitioners, researchers, consultants, legal experts, and colleagues are each taken seriously so that the Tenth Edition is better, fresher, more valuable, and current. It is estimated that over 2,000 changes were made in this edition. Instead of detailing these changes, mention of a select few will set the tone for your own perusal.

- More small and medium-sized company examples are included.
- Increased discussion of global issues, ethical issues, and technology and family/life balance issues are included throughout the book.
- The law and its impact on HRM is introduced to illustrate why managers must be up to date and knowledgeable about legal matters.
- The end-of-chapter element called "HRM Legal Advisor" illustrates the importance of understanding the legal rights of employees and employers.
- The most up-to-date reference and illustrative materials are incorporated. This is a book for the 21st century. However, when earlier citations were the best available, they remained. Recent citations are not always the best or the most relevant.
- A greater emphasis on managerial responsibilities and actions pertaining to HRM activities is woven throughout the content and chapter elements.

Students Guide to the Internet/World Wide Web

While most students are well acquainted with computers, a revolution is under way in how to use them. If you link computers together, each can have its own software and data, but can take advantage of the resources of the network. For any course or program you take, you have at your fingertips and at the convenience of a "click" information, data, statistics, historical factors, and an endless array of content.

You can increase your understanding of human resource management by using the tips and recommended address sites in each chapter to link to other pods of information that will further extend your understanding. The Internet and World Wide Web (WWW) have provided this wonderful opportunity to students.

The Internet

The Internet was created nearly 30 years ago as a project of the U.S. Department of Defense, specifically, the Defense Advanced Research Projects Administration, or DARPA. Its goal was to provide a way for widely separated computers to transfer information and data and to make these data communications as robust and reliable as possible. DARPA wanted to make a network that was smart enough to recover on its own from problems such as power failures and interruptions in communication lines.

Eventually, the government dropped the idea that its network was only useful for defense-related projects, and the network became known as *Arpanet*. The government then began connecting many of the country's universities to the network. Since then, generations of students have studied, used, and improved what we now call the *Internet*.

Although the Internet began as a government research project and was funded by tax dollars for years, the government is not involved in it anymore. It might still be one of the largest single users of the Internet, but it no longer funds new development or supports any of the costs associated with maintaining the network. The Internet is completely self-sufficient.

About 10 years ago, the Internet was still relatively unknown outside of the scientific and technical communities. That has changed dramatically in just a short time. After two decades of development and improvements, the Internet has exploded into the mainstream.

People were initially attracted to the Internet because it connected them to the world at large. They could exchange electronic mail, participate in discussions (via Usenet newsgroups), and easily exchange programs and data with others around the world using the Internet's file-transfer facilities.

Technically, the Internet isn't a network of computers—it's a network of networks. Local networks throughout the world are tied together by wires, telephone lines, fiber-optic cables, microwave transmissions, and satellites in orbit. But the details of how data get from one computer on the Internet to another are invisible to the user.

The Internet is dramatically different from online services such as America Online. These companies sell access to their computers; think of them as gigantic bulletin board systems owned and operated by a company. What you see and what you can do with them are limited to what they allow you to see and do. To avoid losing their entire memberships to the Internet, these services have found it necessary to offer access to the Internet and the World Wide Web. They determine which parts of the Internet you can access, however, and some of them charge extra for Internet access, even for sending e-mail to an Internet address.

The World Wide Web

For all its technological wonder, the Internet has suffered for years from a reputation of being difficult to learn, hard to use, and downright homely compared to the sexy interfaces of bulletin board systems, online services, and most of the software people use on personal computers.

Part of the reason for the Web's huge and rapid success is that it's easy to use: It's as simple as clicking a mouse button. In the front of each chapter you will be provided with addresses that you can enter and then simply click to find the information you want or need.

Just as you need an e-mail address so people can communicate with you, files on the Internet need an address so people can access them. A file's address is known as its *Uniform Resource Locator* or *URL*. Each chapter has URLs that will link to specific information associated to human resource issues, concerns, challenges, or opportunities.

The first page of any site is called the *home page*. The "home page" is simply a starting point. You will need a browser, a program that permits you to visit different URLs on the Internet/World Wide Web. Two of the most widely used browsers are Internet Explorer or Netscape Navigator. They are the Coke and Pepsi of browsers. A browser displays a document from the Internet on your computer screen.

Another key to the Web's magic is its simplicity. Web "pages" are simply files residing on the hundreds of thousands of computers connected to the Internet. To "serve" the pages when they're requested by a browser, all a computer needs is another simple program called a *Web server*. The Web server just waits and listens for requests from Web browsers. When a request comes in, it finds the requested file and sends it back to the browser.

Search Engines

Getting information is made easier if you know the URL of the Web site that contains what you want. But what if you don't know the URL? Don't worry—all you need to use is a search engine. A *search engine* is a Web site that enables you to enter a query and provides a list of hyperlinks (text or graphics that when clicked take you to a different page on the same site or to a completely different site). Some of the better known and used search engines are:

www.google.com

www.yahoo.com

www.msn.com

Type the URL of a search engine in the address bar of your Web browser (Explorer or Netscape) and press *enter.* You can take it from there by clicking and/or typing in some words that describe what you are looking for and then pressing *enter.* Don't be surprised if your search for human resource management information turns up hundreds or even thousands of Web pages. Since the Internet/World Wide Web is expanding and changing every day, you need to keep your favorite URLs current.

The Internet/World Wide Web will serve you well in this and in other courses. As you use this invaluable resource more, you will become more comfortable and proficient. Think of the Internet/World Wide Web as your own personal tutor that can be used when you need to improve your understanding of an HRM issue, topic, subject, or situation.

Contributions of a Colleague

Robert (Rob) Konopaske, assistant professor of management at Florida Atlantic University, contributed significantly to the development and presentation of chapters, pedagogy, and revision work on this Tenth Edition. He made suggestions, introduced creative examples, worked on chapters, responded to reviewers' comments, and discussed with the author ways to improve the student and instructor friendliness of the book. As an accomplished and experienced educator, researcher, and practitioner, Rob is superb and meticulous in what he contributes to this book.

Instructor's Resource Materials

A complete set of instructor's resource materials is available with this text. The instructional materials have been carefully updated and revised to complement the Tenth Edition.

Instructor's Manual and Test Bank

For each chapter, the instructor's manual contains a list of learning objectives; a chapter synopsis; a summary of the Career Challenge; presentation notes; teaching tips; answers to questions for review and discussion; suggestions for additional questions, term paper topics, and a group project; case and/or exercise notes; and answers to case questions. The test bank consists of approximately 1,600 true/false, multiple-choice, and essay questions. Each question is classified according to level of difficulty and includes a text page reference.

Computerized Testing Software (Windows)

The most recent version of McGraw-Hill's test-generation software, this program includes advanced features such as allowing the instructor to add and edit questions online, save and reload tests, create up to 99 versions of each test, attach graphics to questions, import and export ASCII files, and select questions based on type, level of difficulty, or key word. The program allows password protection of saved test and question databases and is networkable.

Videos (ISBN 13: 9780073137148; ISBN 10: 0073137146)

The text consists of five parts, each of which has a corresponding video clip.
Part 1—Learn how the success of Von Maur Department Stores is based on their exceptional HRM department.
Part 2—Check out MonsterBoard.com and the role of the Internet for recruitment.
Part 3—Find out how Southwest Airlines achieves exceptional service by rewarding their employees for giving it.
Part 4—Learn why training and development is important to Arthur Andersen.
Part 5—See how Saturn has changed the way labor and management work together.

Web site (ISBN 13: 9780073137124; ISBN 10: 007313712X)
www.mhhe.com/ivancevich10e

Students—Visit the Student Resources section for everything from up-to-date real-world HRM material to a Career Corner, which provides tips for finding a job and creating a resume.
Instructors—Access the Web site for the Instructor Resources section. Find updated teaching materials, a link to our MORE Supersite, and downloadable supplements.

Acknowledgments

Helpful comments were provided for each edition by outstanding reviewers, many of whose ideas and recommendations were used. Their promptness, tact, and knowledge of HRM were certainly appreciated. The lead reviewers for the Tenth Edition were:

Tracy Miller
University of Dayton

Kathleen Premo
St. Bonaventure University

James D. Proffitt
Illinois College

The following faculty members also provided extensive market information on the HRM discipline in general. They are to be commended for their time and effort in providing us with feedback.

David A. Ainscow
National University

Benigno Alicea
University of Puerto Rico

Barry Armandi
SLTNY-Old Westbury

Tim Barnett
Louisiana Tech

Steven Bershire
Alaska Pacific University

Vicky K. Black
Oakland City University

Teresa Brady
Holy Family College

John C. Bucelato
Hampton University

John F. Burgess
Concordia University

G. W. Bush
Brandeis University

Charles Cambridge
California State University-Chico

Anne Cowden
California State University-Sacramento

Janette Dozier
Tulane University

Nilgun Dungan
Minot State University

Norb Elbert
Bellarmine College

Richard J. Erickson
Southern College

Karl M. Everett
Webster University

Michael Feldstein
Peace College

Robert J. Forbes
Oakland University

Robert Gatewood
University of Georgia

C. Josef Ghosn
Atlantic Union College

Perry Haan
Wilmington College

E. C. Hamm
Tidewater Community College

Carol Harvey
Assumption College

Nancy Hess
Bloomsburg University

Paul E. T. Jensen
Northwestern Polytechnic University

Harriet Kandelman
Barat College

George J. Karl III
Southern College

Paul N. Keaton
University of Wisconsin-LaCrosse

Kenneth A. Kovach
University of Maryland

Leo A. Lennon
Webster University
Barry University

Robert Lewellen
Peru State College

Jerry Madkins
Tarleton State University

Daniel S. Marrone
SUNY-Farmingdate

Norman Mermetstein
Touro College

Linda Merrill
SUNY-Stony Brook

Kenneth Mitchell
Harris-Stowe State College

Jonathan S. Monat
California State University-Long Beach

William Muller
University of Northern Iowa

Charles Noty
Roosevelt University

Allen Ogheneiobo
Miles College

Michael W. Popejoy
Palm Beach Atlantic College

Charles Rarick
Transylvania University

Dennis Rhodes
Drake University

Rajib Sanyal
Trenton State College

Michael Soltys
Allentown College

Diane M. Stagg
Parks College

David B. Stephens
Utah State University

Saia Swanepoet
Tednikan Prekna-South Africa

Dave Wilderman
Wabash Valley College

Carolyn Wiley
The University of Tennessee-Chattanooga

Douglas S. Woundy
Virginia Military Institute

Peggy Adams is the organizer (home-based and virtual); administrative assistant, locator of data, word processing wizard, and interpreter of my numerous revisions. This revision would be incomplete without Peggy's prompt, accurate, and creative work, patience, experience, and tolerance. Peggy always makes my revision work pleasant, productive, and invaluable. She is a consummate professional who has enabled the author to meet deadlines, complete thorough revisions, and provide top quality materials to the publisher. I sincerely thank her for being a part of my team and working so hard to complete the revision of this book on time and with a pleasant smile.

Brief Contents

Preface iv

PART ONE
Introduction to Human Resource Management and the Environment 1

1 Human Resource Management 2

2 A Strategic Management Approach to Human Resource Management 30

3 Equal Employment Opportunity: Legal Aspects of Human Resource Management 65

4 Global Human Resource Management 96

PART TWO
Acquiring Human Resources 127

5 Human Resource Planning and Alignment 128

6 Job Analysis and Design 150

7 Recruitment 185

8 Selection 213

PART THREE
Rewarding Human Resources 249

9 Performance Evaluation and Management 250

10 Compensation: An Overview 293

11 Compensation: Methods and Policies 325

12 Employee Benefits and Services 355

PART FOUR
Developing Human Resources 391

13 Training and Development 392

14 Career Planning and Development 440

PART FIVE
Labor-Management Relations and Promoting Safety and Health 481

15 Labor Relations and Collective Bargaining 482

16 Managing Employee Discipline 518

17 Promoting Safety and Health 546

APPENDIXES 579

GLOSSARY 603

INDEXES 614

Contents

Preface iv

PART ONE
INTRODUCTION TO HUMAN
RESOURCE MANAGEMENT
AND THE ENVIRONMENT 1

Chapter 1
Human Resource Management 2

A Brief History of Human Resource
Management 5
Strategic Importance of HRM 7
HRM and Organizational Effectiveness 9
Objectives of the HRM Function 10
    Helping the Organization Reach Its Goals 11
    Efficiently Employing the Skills and Abilities
    of the Workforce 11
    Providing Well-Trained and Well-Motivated
    Employees 12
    Increasing Employees' Job Satisfaction and
    Self-Actualization 12
    Achieving Quality of Work Life 12
    Communicating HRM Policies to
    All Employees 12
    Maintaining Ethical Policies and Socially
    Responsible Behavior 13
    Managing Change 13
    Managing Increased Urgency and
    Faster Cycle Time 13
Who Performs HRM Activities 14
    Outsourcing 14
    The Interaction of Operating and
    HR Managers 15
    HRM's Place in Management 16
HR Department Operations 16
    HRM Strategy 16
    Clarifying Meaningful HRM Objectives 17
    HRM Policy 19
    HRM Procedures 19
    Organization of an HR Department 19
Plan of the Book 21
Summary 22
Key Terms 22
Questions for Review and Discussion 23
Notes 23

Application Case 1-1
    The Human Resource Manager and Managing
    Multiple Responsibilities 25
Appendix A
    Careers in HRM 28

Chapter 2
A Strategic Management Approach to
Human Resource Management 30

A Model to Organize HRM 33
How to Take a Diagnosic Approach to HRM 34
External Environmental Influences 35
    Government Law and Regulations 35
    The Union 36
    Economic Conditions 36
    Competitiveness 38
    Composition and Diversity of the Labor Force 38
    Geographic Location of the Organization 42
Internal Environmental Influences 43
    Strategy 44
    Goals 45
    Organization Culture 45
    Nature of the Task 46
    Work Group 47
    Leader's Style and Experience 48
Strategic HRM: An Important Key to Success 48
Strategic Challenges Facing HRM 49
    Technology 49
    Diversity: Building a Competitive Workforce 50
    Caliber of the Workforce 54
    Organizational Restructuring and Downsizing 54
    Contingent Workers 55
People and the HRM Diagnostic Framework 56
    Abilities of Employees 56
    Employees' Attitudes and Preferences 56
    Motivation of Employees 56
    Personality of Employees 57
Desirable End Results 57
Summary 58
Key Terms 60
Questions for Review and Discussion 60
Notes 60
Exercise 2-1
    Dissecting the ARDM Model and Its Application 62
Application Case 2-1
    Best Buy's Approach to Outsourcing 63

Chapter 3
Equal Employment Opportunity: Legal Aspects of Human Resource Management 65

How Did EEO Emerge? 68
    Societal Values and EEO 68
    Economic Status of Minorities: Before 1964 69
    The Government 69
Equal Employment Opportunity Laws: Content and Court Interpretations 69
    Title VII of the 1964 Civil Rights Act 69
    Title VII and Sexual Harassment 72
    Title VII and Pregnancy Discrimination 74
    Title VII and Religious Minorities 74
    Title VII and "English-Only" Rules 74
    Civil Rights Act of 1991 75
    Executive Order 11246 (1965) 76
    Equal Pay Act of 1963 76
    Age Discrimination in Employment Act of 1967 (ADEA) 76
    Americans with Disabilities Act of 1990 (ADA) 77
    State Laws 79
Enforcing the Law 79
    Equal Employment Opportunity Commission (EEOC) 79
    The Courts 80
Affirmative Action in Organizations 82
    What Is Affirmative Action? 82
    Voluntary Affirmative Action Plans 82
    Involuntary Affirmative Action Plans 82
    Update on Affirmative Action 84
Summary 86
Key Terms 87
Questions for Review and Discussion 87
HRM Legal Advisor 87
Notes 88
Exercise 3-1
    Dissecting the Diagnostic Model and Its Application 90
Application Case 3-1
    Meeting the Challenge of Sexual Harassment 93

Chapter 4
Global Human Resource Management 96

A Global Perspective 98
    The Cultural Nature of Global HRM 100
    The Concept of "Fit" in Global HRM 101
    Multinational and Global Corporations 101

The Expatriate Manager in the Multinational Corporation 103
    Selecting the Expatriate Manager 103
    Culture Shock and the Expatriate Manager 105
    Training the Expatriate Manager 106
    Compensating the Expatriate Manager 109
Host Country Nationals and the Global Corporation 110
    A Note on Global Corporate Boards of Directors 111
The Legal and Ethical Climate of Global HRM 111
Labor Relations and the International Corporation 113
Summary 115
Key Terms 116
Questions for Review and Discussion 116
HRM Legal Advisor 116
Notes 117
Exercise 4-1
    Development of Global Managers 121
Exercise 4-2
    Avoiding Costly International HRM Mistakes 121
Application Case 4-1
    Solving the Labor Dilemma in a Joint Venture in Japan 123
Application Case 4-2
    Toyota in France: Culture Clash? 124
Video Case
    Southwest Airlines: Competing through People 125

PART TWO
ACQUIRING HUMAN RESOURCES 127

Chapter 5
Human Resource Planning and Alignment 128

Human Resource Planning 129
Strategic and Human Resource Planning 130
The HR Planning Process 131
    Situation Analysis and Environmental Scanning 131
    Forecasting Demand for Employees 131
    Analyzing the Current Supply of Employees 135
    Action Decisions in Human Resource Planning 137
Human Resource Information Systems 139
    Employees' Privacy, Identity Theft, and HRIS 141
Summary 142
Key Terms 143
Questions for Review and Discussion 143

HRM Legal Advisor   144
Notes   144
Application Case 5-1
   Human Resource Planning and Virtual Human
   Resource Management   148

Chapter 6
Job Analysis and Design   150

The Vocabulary of Job Analysis   152
The Steps in Job Analysis   152
The Uses of Job Analysis   153
Who Should Conduct the Job Analysis?   154
The Use of Charts   154
Methods of Data Collection   155
   Observation   156
   Interviews   156
   Questionnaires   159
   Job Incumbent Diary or Log   159
   Which Method to Use?   159
Specific Quantitative Techniques   160
   Functional Job Analysis   160
   Position Analysis Questionnaire   162
   Management Position Description
   Questionnaire   164
Job Descriptions and Specifications   165
   Job Analysis and Strategic Human Resource
   Management   168
   Job Analysis and Employee Competencies   169
Job Design   169
   Scientific Management and the Mechanistic
   Approach   170
   Job Enrichment: A Motivational Approach   171
   Work-Family Balance and Job Design   172
   Job Design: The Next Challenge   174
Summary   175
Key Terms   175
Questions for Review and Discussion   176
HRM Legal Advisor   176
Notes   177
Application Case 6-1
   Job Analysis: Assistant Store Managers at Today's
   Fashion   182
Application Case 6-2
   Job Analysis and Maternity Leave: Calming the
   Boss's and Co-workers' Nerves   183

Chapter 7
Recruitment   185

External Influences   188
   Government and Union Restrictions   188
   Labor Market Conditions   189
   Composition of Labor Force and Location of
   Organization   190
Interactions of the Recruit and the Organization   190
   The Organization's View of Recruiting   190
   The Potential Employee's View of
   Recruiting   191
Methods of Recruiting   193
   Internal Recruiting   193
   External Recruiting   194
Realistic Job Previews   200
Alternatives to Recruitment   201
   Overtime   201
   Outsourcing   201
   Temporary Employment   201
Cost-Benefit Analysis of Recruiting   202
Summary   203
Key Terms   204
Questions for Review and Discussion   204
HRM Legal Advisor   204
Notes   205
Exercise 7-1
   Netiquette: Effectively Communicating with
   E-Mail   208
Application Case 7-1
   So Long to the Sunday Classifieds   209
Application Case 7-2
   Are New Recruits Looking for Work-Life
   Balance?   211

Chapter 8
Selection   213

Influences on the Selection Process   214
   Environmental Circumstances Influencing
   Selection   214
Selection Criteria   216
   Categories of Criteria   216
   Reliability and Validity of Selection Criteria   218
The Selection Process   221
   Step 1: Preliminary Screening   221
   Step 2: Employment Interview   224
   Step 3: Employment Tests   228
   Step 4: Reference Checks and
   Recommendations   232
   Step 5: Physical Examinations   233
Selection of Managers   234
Cost-Benefit Analysis for the Selection
Decision   237
Summary   237
Key Terms   238

Questions for Review and Discussion   238
HRM Legal Advisor   239
Notes   240
Exercise 8-1
    Posting Your Resume Online   243
Application Case 8-1
    *Bechtel Power Corporation's Use of Objective
    Welding Tests   244*
Application Case 8-2
    Are Traditional Resumes Gone Forever?   245
Video Case
    *Creative Staffing Solutions: A Pipeline of
    Human Assets   246*

PART THREE
REWARDING HUMAN RESOURCES   249

Chapter 9
Performance Evaluation
and Management   250

The Case for Using Formal Evaluation   253
    Purposes of Evaluation   253
    Performance Evaluation and the Law   254
Format of Evaluation   256
    Establish Criteria   256
    *Set Policies on Who Evaluates, When,
    and How Often   257*
Selected Evaluation Techniques   260
    Individual Evaluation Methods   260
    Multiple-Person Evaluation Methods   266
    Management by Objectives   268
    Which Technique to Use   270
Potential Problems in Performance Evaluations   271
    Opposition to Evaluation   271
    System Design and Operating Problems   272
    Rater Problems   272
    Eliminating Rater Errors   275
    Avoiding Problems with Employees   275
The Feedback Interview   276
Summary   279
Key Terms   280
Questions for Review and Discussion   280
HRM Legal Advisor   280
Notes   281
Exercise 9-1
    *Selecting and Appraising Administrative Assistants
    at Row Engineering   283*
Application Case 9-1
    *Evaluating Store Managers at
    Bridgestone/Firestone Tire & Rubber   287*

Application Case 9-2
    The Politics of Performance Appraisal   290

Chapter 10
Compensation: An Overview   293

Objective of Compensation   295
External Influences on Compensation   295
    The Labor Market and Compensation   295
    Economic Conditions and Compensation   298
    Government Influences and Compensation   298
    Union Influences and Compensation   302
Internal Influences on Compensation   303
    The Labor Budget   303
    Who Makes Compensation Decisions   303
Compensation and Motivation   304
    Pay and Motivation   304
    Pay and Employees' Satisfaction   306
    Pay and Employees' Productivity   306
Compensation Decisions   308
    The Pay-Level Decision   308
    Pay Surveys   309
    The Pay Structure Decision   311
    Delayering and Broadbanding   316
    The Individual Pay Decision   316
Summary   317
Key Terms   318
Questions for Review and Discussion   318
HRM Legal Advisor   318
Notes   319
Application Case 10-1
    The Comparable Worth Debate   322

Chapter 11
Compensation: Methods and Policies   325

Determination of Individual Pay   327
Methods of Payment   328
    Flat Rates   328
    Payment for Time Worked   328
    Variable Pay: Incentive Compensation   329
    Ownership   339
    People-Based Pay   340
    Executive Pay   341
Issues in Compensation Administration   343
    Pay Secrecy or Openness   343
    Pay Security   344
    Pay Compression   345
Summary   345
Key Terms   346
Questions for Discussion and Review   347
HRM Legal Advisor   347

Notes   348
Application Case 11-1
   Customizing Bonus Pay Plans   351

Chapter 12
Employee Benefits and Services   355

Background   357
   *Why Do Employers Offer Benefits and
   Services?   357*
   Who Makes Decisions about Benefits?   357
Mandated Benefits Programs   359
   Unemployment Insurance   359
   Social Security   360
   Workers' Compensation   362
Voluntary Benefits   364
   Compensation for Time Off   365
   Paid Holidays   365
   Paid Vacations   366
   International Vacation Benefits   366
   Personal Time Off   367
   Sick Leave   367
   Family Leave   368
   Maternity and Parental Leave   368
   Employer-Purchased Insurance   369
   Health Insurance   369
   Life Insurance   371
   Disability Income Replacement Insurance   371
Income in Retirement   372
   Retirement Income from Savings and Work   372
   Individual Retirement Accounts (IRAs)   372
   SEP (Simplified Employee Pension) IRAs   372
   401(k) Plans   372
   Private Pensions   373
Employee Services   375
   Stock Ownership Plans   375
   Education Programs   375
   Preretirement Programs   375
   Child Care   375
   Elder Care   375
   Financial Services   376
   Social and Recreational Programs   376
Flexible Benefits Plans and Reimbursement
Accounts   376
Managing an Effective Benefits Program   377
   *Step 1: Set Objectives and Strategy for
   Benefits   378*
   Step 2: Involve Participants and Unions   378
   Step 3: Communicate Benefits   378
   Step 4: Monitor Costs Closely   379
Cost-Benefit Analysis of Benefits   379

Summary   379
Key Terms   380
Questions for Review and Discussion   380
HRM Legal Advisor   381
Notes   382
Application Case 12-1
   Benefits Are Vanishing   384
Video Case
   Budget Rent-a-Car and International   387

PART FOUR
DEVELOPING HUMAN
RESOURCES   391

Chapter 13
Training and Development   392

Introduction to Orientation   394
   Goals of Orientation   394
   Who Orients New Employees?   395
   Orientation Follow-Up   398
Introduction to Training   399
   Goals of Training   399
   Learning Theory and Training   400
   "Learning Organizations"   401
   Training Activities   401
Managing the Training Program   403
   Determining Needs and Objectives   403
   Choosing Trainers and Trainees   407
Training and Development Instructional
Methods   408
   On-the-Job Training   408
   Case Method   409
   Role Playing   410
   In-Basket Technique   410
   Management Games   410
   Behavior Modeling   411
   Outdoor-Oriented Programs   412
   *Which Training and/or Development Approach
   Should Be Used?   412*
Management Development: An Overview   418
   What Is Management Development?   418
Development: Individual Techniques   419
   Goal Setting   419
   Behavior Modification   421
Development: Team Building   425
Development: An Organizationwide Technique   426
   Total Quality Management (TQM)   426
Evaluation of Training and Development   427
   Criteria for Evaluation   430
   A Matrix Guide for Evaluation   431

Summary   433
Key Terms   433
Questions for Review and Discussion   434
HRM Legal Advisor   434
Notes   435
Exercise 13-1
   Assessing Training Needs   438
Application Case 13-1
   *Dunkin' Donuts and Domino's Pizza: Training
   for Quality and Hustle   438*

Chapter 14
Career Planning and Development   440

The Concept of Career   442
   Career Stages   444
   Career Choices   448
Career Development: A Commitment   451
Career Development for Recent Hires   451
   Causes of Early Career Difficulties   452
   *How to Counteract Early Career
   Problems   453*
Career Development during Midcareer   454
   The Midcareer Plateau   455
   *How to Counteract Midcareer
   Problems   455*
   Preretirement Problems   459
   *How to Minimize Retirement Adjustment
   Problems   459*
Career Planning and Pathing   460
   Career Planning   461
   Career Pathing   463
Career Development Programs: Problems
and Issues   463
   *Integrating Career Development and Workforce
   Planning   464*
   Managing Dual Careers   464
   *Career Planning and Equal Employment
   Opportunity   466*
   Downsizing and Job Loss   466
Summary   471
Key Terms   472
Questions for Review and Discussion   472
HRM Legal Advisor   472
Notes   473
Exercise 14-1
   My Career Audit   475
Application Case 14-1
   The Dual-Career Couple   476
Video Case
   Hot Jobs.com   479

PART FIVE
LABOR-MANAGEMENT RELATIONS AND PROMOTING SAFETY AND HEALTH   481

Chapter 15
Labor Relations and Collective Bargaining   482

Early Collective Action and Union Formation   486
Labor Legislation Overview   486
   National Labor Relations Act (Wagner Act)   487
   *Labor Management Relations Act
   (Taft-Hartley Act)   488*
   *Labor–Management Reporting and Disclosure Act
   (Landrum-Griffin Act)   488*
Structure and Management of Unions   489
   Federation of Unions   489
   Intermediate Union Bodies   489
   National Unions   489
   Local Unions   489
The Union Organizing Campaign   490
   *Authorization Card Campaign and Union
   Certification   490*
Union Security   491
   Levels of Union Security   491
   Right-to-Work Requirements   493
Public Employee Associations   493
   Background   493
   Public Sector Labor Legislation   493
Collective Bargaining   494
   Prenegotiation   495
   Selecting the Negotiators   495
   Developing a Bargaining Strategy   496
   Using the Best Tactics   496
   Reaching a Formal Contractual Agreement   497
   Contract Ratification   498
Failure to Reach Agreement   498
   Strikes   498
   Lockouts   499
   Permanent Replacements   500
   Third Party Intervention   500
Administering the Contract   501
   Discipline   501
   Grievances   501
   Arbitration   502
The Changing Climate of Unionization in the
United States   503
   Union Membership Trends   504
   Global Unionization   504
   Union Organizing Trends   506

Summary   507
Key Terms   508
Questions for Review and Discussion   509
HRM Legal Advisor   509
Notes   510
Exercise 15-1
    Reporting on Labor Unions   512
Exercise 15-2
    Union–Management Contract Negotiation   512
Application Case 15-1
    *The Union's Demand for Recognition
    and Bargaining Rights*   515

Chapter 16
Managing Employee Discipline   518

Categories of Difficult Employees   520
    Category 1: Ineffective Employees   521
    *Category 2: Alcoholic and Substance-Abusing
    Employees*   521
    *Category 3: Participants in Theft, Fraud, and
    Other Illegal Acts*   523
    Category 4: Rule Violators   529
The Discipline Process   531
Approaches to Discipline   532
    The Hot Stove Rule   532
    Progressive Discipline   533
    Positive Discipline   534
The Disciplinary Interview: A Constructive
Approach   534
Legal Challenges to Discipline and
Termination   535
    Employment at Will   536
    Alternative Dispute Resolution   537
Summary   539
Key Terms   540
Questions for Review and Discussion   540
HRM Legal Advisor   540
Notes   541
Exercise 16-1
    Making Difficult Decisions   543
Application Case 16-1
    The Case for and against Drug Testing   544

Chapter 17
Promoting Safety and Health   546

Background   547
Causes of Work-Related Accidents
and Illnesses   550
Who Is Involved with Safety and Health?   552
Governmental Responses to Safety and Health
Problems   553
    OSHA Safety Standards   555
    OSHA Inspections   555
    OSHA Record Keeping and Reporting   556
    OSHA: A Report Card   557
Organizational Responses to Safety and Health
Issues   558
    Safety Design and Preventive Approaches   558
    *Inspection, Reporting, and Accident
    Research*   558
    Safety Training and Motivation Programs   559
Preventive Health Programs: A Wellness
Approach   559
Safety and Health Issues   562
    Stress Management   562
    Violence in the Workplace   564
    Indoor Environmental Quality (IEQ)   565
    HIV-AIDS in the Workplace   566
    Cumulative Trauma Disorders (CTDs)   568
Evaluation of Safety and Health Programs   569
Summary   570
Key Terms   571
Questions for Review and Discussion   571
Notes   571
Exercise 17-1
    Preparing for an OSHA Inspection   574
Application Case 17-1
    Campus Food Systems   575
Video Case
    *OSHA and Unions versus Manufacturers: Is
    Workplace Ergonomics a Problem?*   577

Appendix B
Measuring Human Resource Activities   579

Appendix C
**Sources of Information about Human
Resource Management: Where to Find Facts
and Figures   585**

Appendix D
Career Planning   593

Glossary   603

Name Index   614

Company Index   623

Subject Index   626

Part 1

Introduction to Human Resource Management and the Environment

Human resource management (HRM) is the effective management of people at work. HRM examines what can or should be done to make working people more productive and satisfied. This book has been written for individuals interested in learning about people working within organizations. Its goal is to help develop more effective managers and staff specialists who work directly with the human resources of organizations.

Part One consists of four chapters. Chapter 1, "Human Resource Management," introduces the reader to HRM and careers in HRM. The diagnostic approach is introduced in Chapter 2, "A Strategic Management Approach to Human Resource Management." Chapter 2 also reviews behavioral science perspectives on managing people and shows how knowledge of these can be used to influence employee effectiveness. In addition, the chapter discusses the ways managers use knowledge of environmental factors—the work setting, technological change, globalization, government regulations, and union requirements—to influence employee performance. Chapter 3, "Equal Employment Opportunity: Legal Aspects of Human Resource Management," describes the influences of the legal environment on HRM. A number of major laws and regulations are discussed in this chapter, as well as throughout the book. Chapter 4, "Global Human Resource Management," discusses HRM in the new era of globalization. The "global enterprise" and the interdependence of nations have become a reality. Global markets, mass markets, and market freedom have fostered an international interest in managing human resources.

Chapter 1

Human Resource Management

Learning Objectives

After studying this chapter you should be able to:

1. **Define** the *term human resource management.*
2. **Describe** the strategic importance of human resource management (HRM) activities performed in organizations.
3. **Explain** what career opportunities are available in the HRM field.
4. **Discuss** the role that specialists and operating managers *play* in performing HRM activities.
5. **List** the main objectives pursued by HRM units in organizations.

Internet/Web Resources

General Sites

www.amazon.com
www.blackboard.com
www.fastcompany.com
www.barnesandnoble.com
www.gartner.com
www.google.com
www.hotwired.com
www.lawgic.com
www.trainingmag.com
www.trainlink.com

Company Sites

www.chevron.com
www.dole.com
www.martinmarietta.com
www.monsanto.com

Don Brokop has, over the past nine years, proved himself an outstanding shift supervisor at the Melody Machine Products Corp. plant in South Chicago. He has worked every shift, likes people, and recently was the winner of the Outstanding Plant Manager award. Don, now 38 years old, is beginning to look closely at his career plans. He believes that he needs to gain some experience in jobs other than production.

Last week a position opened at the plant for an assistant director of human resources. At first, Don gave no thought to the position, but later he asked his boss, Marty Fogestrom, about it. Marty encouraged Don to think his plans through and to consider whether he wanted to work in the area of human resource management.

Don talked with plant colleagues about the new position, looked over the want ads in the *Chicago Tribune*, read *The Wall Street Journal, Fast Company, Inc., Business 2.0, HR Magazine, Workforce,* and *Fortune,* and found a number of interesting news items concerning human resource management. He discovered that many different careers existed in this field. He realized that he had not really understood the job done by Melody's department of human resources. What struck him most was that issues, problems, and challenges concerning people are what human resources are about.

Here are a few of the news items that caught his eye:[1]

- Over 10 years ago, at the height of another economic downturn, Ben Cheever lost his job as an editor at *Reader's Digest.* He decided to write a book (*Selling Ben Cheever: Back to Square One in a Service Economy.*) In response to his sudden job loss he offered advice to those faced with a job market. A few of Ben's pearls of wisdom are (1) you are not your job title, (2) get past the shame barrier, (3) keep in touch with those in your network, and (4) always have a plan. In a nutshell—don't be shy; don't be ashamed, take action with confidence.

- The Web is a great place for HR managers and those interested in HRM to find suggestions, best-in-class examples, and resources. A few favorite sites of those in the know are www.hr.com, www.webhire.com, and www.cyfe.com.umn.edu/work.html. Russell J. Campenello is a user of these sites and from his position of "Chief People Officer" of Nervewire, Inc., he points people to human capital-oriented Web sites.

- Training is a must HRM activity. In good and bad economic times the top firms stick with training and the message it sends about valuing people. Some of the top annual training budgets are found at IBM—$1 billion; Ford Motor—$500 million; Intel—$319 million; and Boeing—$250 million. Companies continue to stress the importance of training as a competitive business advantage.

- The number of companies offering employees online access to HR functions such as benefits enrollment, family status changes, and changes to 401(k) contributions is increasing. A survey conducted by Towers Perrin indicated 60 percent of employers reported that they allow employees to complete their benefits enrollment and to perform other HR functions online. These findings show a 30 to 50 percent increase across companies in one year.

- Many companies praise the benefits of telecommuting (employees who work at home on a regular basis) such as lower real estate costs, reduced turnover, increased productivity, and an increased ability to comply with workplace laws (e.g., Americans with Disabilities Act and Family and Medical Leave Act). However, a study of managers and employees by Boston College Center for Work & Family found some telecommuting disadvantages. It found that telecommuters work more, rate their work/life balance satisfaction lower, believe they have worse relationships with their managers and co-workers, and are less committed to their job. The pros and cons of telecommuting need to be studied over long time periods.

- In Australia, companies that have an HR director serving on their executive committee tend to be more successful than those that do not. A study of the 50 largest Australian

(continued on next page)

companies reported more than twice the median growth in earnings per share than those without such an HR presence. When strategic HR knowledge and authority sits on the board, there is more focus on people issues. A similar study in Great Britain found higher profitability in firms that had HR representatives on their boards of directors than those that did not.

- Don Tapscott, internationally recognized consultant, has been talking about a new economy based on knowledge for years. Microsoft, he says, has almost missed the environmental shift. The firm's management was clinging to the view that it was a PC (personal computer) firm, ignoring the Net and its potential. It was not money that turned Microsoft around but human capital (knowledge). Brain power is what Tapscott claims saved Microsoft and makes it a major force in the 21st century economy.

Don Brokop thought about his recent conversations, his career plans, the news stories, and the challenges of moving from production to human resource management. He thought his experience in first-line management would be helpful if he was fortunate enough to land the job, but he wondered if he was qualified for this kind of job. Otherwise, he was confident and considered his college education and experience invaluable. He wanted new challenges. Then he learned through the grapevine that the job was his if he wanted to make the move. (If you were Don, would you be likely to make this kind of career shift? Don's decision will be presented at the end of this chapter.)

People, human resources, making organizations more aware of human resources, being in the people business—these words and thoughts are common in modern society. Don Brokop is considering the challenges associated with this new wave of professional treatment and concern for people within organizations. Organizations are definitely in the people business: Don certainly saw this after only a quick review of a few news stories.

This book will focus on people and optimizing performance in organizational settings. The entire book will be concerned with the employees of organizations—the clerks, technicians, software engineers, product designers, supervisors, managers, and executives. Large, medium, and small organizations, such as IBM (www.ibm.com), Kroger Supermarkets (www.kroger.com), Procter & Gamble (www.pg.com), Merck-Medco (www.merck-medco.com), CVS Pharmacies (www.cvs.com), eBay (www.ebay.com), and GAP (www.gap.com), understand clearly that to grow, prosper, and remain healthy, they must optimize the return on investment of all resources—financial and human.

When an organization is really concerned about people, its total philosophy, culture, and orientation will reflect this belief. In this book, **human resource management (HRM)** is specifically charged with programs concerned with people—the employees. Human resource management is the function performed in organizations that facilitates the most effective use of people (employees) to achieve organizational and individual goals. Whether a human resource management function or department even exists in a firm, every manager must be concerned with people.

Terms such as *personnel, human resource management, industrial relations,* and *employee development* are used by different individuals to describe the unit, department, or group concerned about people. The term *human resource management* is now widely used, though some people still refer to a *personnel department.* In order to be current, the term *human resource management* will be used throughout the book. It is a term that reflects the increased concern both society and organizations have for people. Today, employees—the human resource—demand more of their jobs and respond favorably to management activities that give them greater control of their lives.[2]

Human resource management (HRM) consists of numerous activities, including

1. Equal employment opportunity (EEO) compliance.
2. Job analysis.
3. Human resource planning.
4. Employee recruitment, selection, motivation, and orientation.
5. Performance evaluation and compensation.
6. Training and development.
7. Labor relations.
8. Safety, health, and wellness.

These activities are topics of various chapters in this book. They also appear as elements in the model of the HRM function that is used to illustrate the importance of being diagnostic. (This model is described in Chapter 2.)

The following four descriptions of the HRM unit should be stressed at the outset:

1. *It is action-oriented* Effective HRM focuses on action rather than on record keeping, written procedure, or rules. Certainly, HRM uses rules, records, and policies, but it stresses action. HRM emphasizes the solution of employment problems to help achieve organizational objectives and facilitate employees' development and satisfaction.
2. *It is people-oriented* Whenever possible, HRM treats each employee as an individual and offers services and programs to meet the individual's needs. McDonald's, the fast-food chain, has gone so far as to give an executive the title vice president of individuality.
3. *It is globally oriented* HRM is a globally oriented function or activity; it is being practiced efficiently and continuously in Mexico, Poland, and Hong Kong. Many organizations around the world treat people fairly, with respect, and with sensitivity. Thus, American practitioners can review best-in-class HRM practices in Brazil to determine if some principles can be applied or modified to work in the United States.
4. *It is future-oriented* Effective HRM is concerned with helping an organization achieve its objectives in the future by providing for competent, well-motivated employees. Thus, human resources need to be incorporated into an organization's long-term strategic plans.

The following HR Journal of Malden Mills Company captures HRM at the peak of effectiveness. This company did not allow a devastating fire to shut it down. Staffed by people of many nations of the world, the company, with the help of a people-oriented leader, Aaron Feuerstein, showed tenacity, dedication, and loyalty in their decision to rebuild.

A Brief History of Human Resource Management

The history of HRM can be traced to England, where masons, carpenters, leather workers, and other craftspeople organized themselves into guilds. They used their unity to improve their work conditions.[3]

The field further developed with the arrival of the Industrial Revolution in the latter part of the 18th century, which laid the basis for a new and complex industrial society. In simple terms, the Industrial Revolution began with the substitution of steam power and machinery for time-consuming hand labor. Working conditions, social patterns, and the division of labor were significantly altered. A new kind of employee—a boss, who wasn't necessarily the owner, as had usually been the case in the past—became a power broker in the new factory system. With these changes also came a widening gap between workers and owners.

HR Journal   *Malden Mills*

Article after article, television programs, and commentary have continued for years about managerial greed, corruption, and unethical behavior. One manager's story, however, serves as a shining model of caring for people and really meaning it when you state that human assets are the most important factor in an organization. This is the story of Aaron Feuerstein, a real manager of human resources.

On the evening of December 11, 1995, an explosion occurred at the Malden Mills plant in Lawrence, Massachusetts. Approximately 300 employees were working when the fire broke out around 7:50 P.M. As is turned out, 22 workers were rushed to several local hospitals.

Malden Mills was founded in 1906 by Aaron Feuerstein's grandfather. The $300 million-a-year manufacturing company is best known for its high-quality surface-finished fabrics, Polarfleece® and Polartec®.

The story of Malden Mills has focused on Aaron Feuerstein and how he eschewed the option of taking insurance money from the fire and closing his plant. Instead, the third-generation owner opted to pay 1,400 displaced employees for three months, extend their health benefits for nine months, and rebuild the plant—all at a personal cost of $15 million. He has since received worldwide praise for his do-right deeds.

What many don't hear about, however, are the incredible efforts of Malden's HRM team: how it galvanized Malden's corporate and community resources at critical junctures since Massachusetts' largest fire. For its achievements, Malden Mills received the *Workforce Magazine* Optimas Award for Managing Change. Says Feuerstein: "The tremendous amount of change in the past few years makes me once again recognize HRM's strength and courage. At Malden Mills, we have self-confidence to change without fear."

Feuerstein's vow to rebuild Malden sounded the trumpet. On the day after the fire, Feuerstein made his unexpected announcement to pay his employees' salaries and benefits. Workers wept as he declared his commitment. Meanwhile, HRM shifted into high gear with a crisis team—the foundation of which was actually laid before the fire. It was composed of Feuerstein, three other executives, and representatives from each department. The team met daily to discuss the status of those injured, to assess the immediate needs of Malden employees, to set up a communications and workers' training center, to call upon community resources—even to collect Christmas presents for the children of Malden's corporate family.

As workers waited for the new state-of-the-art mill to be completed, they learned the computer skills that would be required to run the new machines. In less than a year, more than 600 employees completed courses at the internal communications center or at outside training facilities. Malden's center has received praise from former Secretary of Labor Robert Reich as a national role model for employee training and development.

Clearly, what began as a traumatic event rallied the company and community—if not others worldwide. HRM received calls from out-of-state employers offering jobs to Malden's displaced workers. Their reputation as skilled and committed employees brought forth myriad offers. Of the 1,400 displaced employees, more than 90 percent of them returned to work.

Since the fire Malden Mill has fallen on some hard financial times. The company continues to struggle financially, but the story of what Aaron Feuerstein did for his employees after the fire is still a bright light in the firm's history. His legacy is an example of how one person wanted his family business to create jobs, help the economy of the community, and be ethical and moral in making difficult choices. He succeeded in creating an inspiring legacy for managers in any country or industry.

Source: "Malden Mills Senior Management Team" (January 27, 2005), *Corporate News;* "The Mensch of Malden Mill" (July 6, 2003), CBS News; Kathy Skala (March 1999), "Balancing the Human Equation," *Workforce,* pp. 54–59.

Scientific management and welfare work represent two concurrent approaches that began in the 19th century and, along with industrial psychology, merged during the era of the world wars.[4] Scientific management represented an effort to deal with inefficiencies in labor and management primarily through work methods, time and motion study, and specialization. Industrial psychology represented the application of psychological principles toward increasing the ability of workers to perform efficiently and effectively.

The renowned father of scientific management was Frederick W. Taylor. An engineer at Midvale Steel Works in Philadelphia from 1878 to 1890, he studied worker efficiency and attempted to discover the "one best way" and the one fastest way to do a job. He summarized scientific management as (1) science, not rules of thumb; (2) harmony, not discord; (3) cooperation, not individualism; and (4) maximum output, not restricted output.[5]

Whereas scientific management focused on the job and efficiencies, industrial psychology focused on the worker and individual differences. The maximum well-being of the worker was the focus of industrial psychology. Hugo Munsterberg and his book *Psychology and Industrial Efficiency* initiated in 1913 the field of industrial psychology.[6] The book served as a stimulus and model for the development of the field in the United States and Europe.

The drastic changes in technology, the growth of organizations, the rise of unions, and government concern and intervention concerning working people resulted in the development of personnel departments. There is no specific date assigned to the appearance of the first personnel department, but around the 1920s more and more organizations seemed to take note of and do something about the conflict between employees and management.[7] Early personnel administrators were called *welfare secretaries*. Their job was to bridge the gap between management and operator (worker); in other words, they were to speak to workers in their own language and then recommend to management what had to be done to get the best results from employees.

Another early contributor to HRM was called the *human relations* movement. Two Harvard researchers, Elton Mayo and Fritz Roelthisberger, incorporated human factors into work. This movement began as a result of a series of studies conducted at the Hawthorne facility of Western Electric in Chicago between 1924 and 1933. The purpose of the studies was to determine the effects of illumination on workers and their output. The studies pointed out the importance of the social interaction and work group on output and satisfaction. The human relations movement eventually, around the mid-1960s, became a branch of and a contributor to the field of organizational behavior.[8]

The early history of personnel still obscures the importance of the HRM function to management. Until the 1960s, the personnel function was considered to be concerned only with blue-collar or operating employees. It was viewed as a record-keeping unit that handed out 25-year tenure pins and coordinated the annual company picnic. Peter Drucker, a respected management scholar and consultant, made a statement about personnel management that reflected its blue-collar orientation. Drucker stated that the job of personnel was "partly a file clerk's job, partly a housekeeping job, partly a social worker's job, and partly firefighting, heading off union trouble."[9]

Strategic Importance of HRM

The HRM function today is concerned with much more than simple filing, housekeeping, and record keeping.[10] When HRM strategies are integrated within the organization, HRM plays a major role in clarifying the firm's human resource problems and develops solutions to them. It is oriented toward action, the individual, worldwide interdependence, and the future. Today it would be difficult to imagine any organization achieving and sustaining effectiveness without efficient HRM programs and activities. The strategic and competitive advantage importance of HRM to the survival of an organization will become clearer as we move into the book.[11]

Strategic HRM differs significantly from traditional HRM. Exhibit 1-1 shows that the main responsibility for managing human resources in a traditional arrangement rests with specialists in a division (large companies) or team. In a strategic approach the main responsibility for people management rests with any individual who is in direct contact with them or a line manager. Thus, any individual in an organization who has responsibility for people is a human resource manager in addition to his or her regular position.

EXHIBIT 1-1
Traditional HRM and Strategic HRM Characteristics

	Traditional HRM	Strategic HRM
Responsibility for human resources and management	Specialists	Line managers
Objective	Better performance	Improved understanding and strategic use of human assets
Role of HRM area	Respond to needs	Lead, inspire, understand
Time focus	Short-term results	Short, intermediate, long-term
Control	Rules, policies, position power	Flexible, based on human resources
Culture	Bureaucratic, top-down, centralization	Open, participative, empowerment
Major emphasis	Following the rules	Developing people
Accountability	Cost centers	Investment in human assets

For years the HRM function had not been linked to the corporate profit margin or what is referred to as the *bottom line.* The role of HRM in the firm's strategic plan and overall strategy was usually couched in fuzzy terms and abstractions. HRM was merely a tagalong unit with people-oriented plans, not a major part of planning or strategic thinking.

Despite the appeal that strategic HRM is important, many organizations have had a difficult time adopting a strategic perspective. They take a short-run approach and focus only on current performance. This is not surprising given the emphasis by Wall Street and many stockholders on achieving attractive quarterly performance results.

Second, many human resource managers do not have a strategic perspective. They are narrowly trained and educated and primarily pay attention to their area of expertise—compensation, labor law, performance evaluation, and other HR areas. They have insufficient knowledge of finance, accounting, marketing, and production.

Third, most executives simply categorize HRM in a traditional manner. They fail to see how HRM can contribute to strategic initiatives, goals, and programs.

Finally, it is difficult to develop metrics for HRM activities. Placing values on and tracking HRM programs is difficult. For example, the measures of effectiveness for health wellness programs are not easy to develop and discuss. Thus, providing funds to programs that have less measurable results is difficult to implement.

Today, because of the recognition of the crucial importance of people, HRM in an increasing number of organizations has become a major player in developing strategic plans.[12] Organizational and human resource plans and strategies are inextricably linked. The HRM strategies must reflect clearly the organization's strategy regarding people, profit, and overall effectiveness. The human resource manager, like all managers, is expected to play a crucial role in improving the skills of employees and the firm's profitability. In essence, HRM in a growing number of organizations is now viewed as a "profit center" and not simply a "cost center."

The strategic importance of HRM means that a number of key concepts must be applied. Some of these concepts are

- Analyzing and solving problems from a profit-oriented, not just a service-oriented, point of view.
- Assessing and interpreting costs or benefits of such HRM issues as productivity, salaries and benefits, recruitment, training, absenteeism, overseas relocation, layoffs, meetings, and attitude surveys.

- Using planning models that include realistic, challenging, specific, and meaningful goals.
- Preparing reports on HRM solutions to problems encountered by the firm.
- Training the human resources staff and emphasizing the strategic importance of HRM and the importance of contributing to the firm's profits.

The increased strategic importance of HRM means that human resource specialists must show managers that they contribute to the goals and mission of the firm.[13] The actions, language, and performance of the HRM function must be measured, precisely communicated, and evaluated. The new strategic positioning of HRM means that accountability must be taken seriously and the investment in human assets is the focal point.

The era of accountability for HRM has resulted from concerns about productivity, from widespread downsizing and redesigning of organizations, from the need to effectively manage an increasingly diverse workforce, and from the need to effectively use all the resources of an organization to compete in an increasingly complex and competitive world.[14]

The HRM function today is much more integrated and strategically involved. The importance of recruiting, selecting, training, developing, rewarding, compensating, and motivating the workforce is recognized and practiced by managers in every unit and functional area of an institution. HRM and every other function must work together to achieve the level of organizational effectiveness required to compete locally and internationally.

If the HRM function is to be successful, managers in other functions must be knowledgeable and involved. Managers play a major role in setting the direction, tone, and effectiveness of the relationship between the employees, the firm, and the work performed. Managers must understand that carrying out HRM activities and programs is strategically vital. Without managerial participation, there are likely to be major human resource problems. Richard Kovacevich (currently CEO at Wells Fargo) was CEO of Norwest, a large financial service firm that merged with Wells Fargo Bank. When the merger occurred he described managerial job responsibilities: to influence the hearts and minds of our people, consistent with the culture of Norwest, so they care more about our business than competitors care about theirs.[15]

HRM and Organizational Effectiveness

HRM activities play a major role in ensuring that an organization will survive and prosper. Organizational effectiveness or ineffectiveness is described in this book in terms of such criteria and components as performance, legal compliance, employee satisfaction, absenteeism, turnover, training effectiveness and return on investment, grievance rates, and accident rates. In order for a firm to survive and prosper and earn a profit, reasonable goals in each of these components must be achieved.[16] In most organizations, effectiveness is measured by the balance of such complementary characteristics as reaching goals, employing the skills and abilities of employees efficiently, and ensuring the influx and retention of well-trained and motivated employees.

Around the world, managers are beginning to recognize that human resources deserve attention because they are a significant factor in top-management strategic decisions that guide the organization's future operations. Three crucial elements are needed for firms to be effective: (1) mission and strategy, (2) organizational structure, and (3) HRM.[17] However, it is important to remember that people do the work and create the ideas that allow the organization to survive. Even the most capital-intensive, best-structured organizations need people to run them.

People limit or enhance the strengths and weaknesses of an organization. Current changes in the environment are often related to changes in human resources, such as shifts in the composition, education, and attitudes of employees. The HRM function should provide for or respond to these changes.

The changes experienced by organizations around the world include growing global competition; rapidly expanding technologies; increased demand for individual, team, and organizational competencies; faster cycle times; increasing legal and compliance scrutiny; and higher customer expectations. These changes combined with the realization that the performance of a firm's human assets must be managed, led, and coached have resulted in the need for more strategic planning and modern leadership practices. The mechanized or routine-oriented workforce is giving way to a more knowledge-based, information-rich workforce.[18]

One problem top management has in making strategic planning decisions regarding people is that all other resources are evaluated in terms of money, and at present, in most organizations, people are not. There has been a push toward human resources accounting, which would place dollar values on the human assets of organizations.[19] Professional sports teams, such as the New York Yankees (www.yankees.com), Los Angeles Lakers (www.nba.com/lakers), and New England Patriots (www.patriots.com), place a dollar value on athletes. They then depreciate these values over the course of time.

If the objectives of the HRM function are to be accomplished, top managers will have to treat the human resources of the organization as the key to effectiveness. To do this—to accomplish the important objectives of HRM—management must regard the development of superior human resources as an essential competitive requirement that needs careful planning, hard work, and evaluation.

An increasing number of studies conducted in the United States and in other countries across industries from high to low technology firms emphasize the importance of people.[20] There is now evidence that shows that implementing high performance management practices results in profitability gains, stock price increases, and higher company survival rates. One study of 968 firms found that a 1 standard deviation increase in the use of "people-first" practices is associated with a 7.05 percent decrease in turnover, $27,044 more in sales, and $18,641 and $3,814 more in market value and profits.[21] Another study found that a 1 standard deviation improvement in human resource practices was associated with a $41,000 increase in shareholder wealth per employee.[22]

Similar results of people-first improvements were found in German industrial firms. Investing time, energy, and resources in people was associated with stock market performance increases.[23]

Based on the available research and analyses, we can specify some of the people-first practices that have contributed to the positive research findings. Each of these practices will be covered later in the book: employment security; selective hiring; self-managed teams; compensation linked to performance; training; and the sharing of performance, strategy, and operational information, data, and measures.[24]

Objectives of the HRM Function

The contributions HRM makes to organizational effectiveness include the following:

- Helping the organization reach its goals.
- Employing the skills and abilities of the workforce efficiently.
- Providing the organization with well-trained and well-motivated employees.
- Increasing to the fullest the employee's job satisfaction and self-actualization. Developing and maintaining a quality of work life that makes employment in the organization desirable.

HR Journal   *Generation Y: Get Ready at Work*

generation Y

Employers are now facing a new workforce pool of candidates referred to as generation Y. They are also called the *millennials* or *echo boomers*. Individuals born between 1980 and 2000 make up generation Y. About one-quarter of new immigrants to the United States are also a part of this 80 million strong generation.

Generation Y members are used to making and spending money on iPods, TiVos, and other technologies. They tend to be skeptical customers, somewhat distrusting, and are independent. For the HRM area this means that company materials, including Web sites, will need to offer potential hirees easy, independent access to information that generation Ys can evaluate.

Research shows that 23 percent of generation X (born between 1966 and 1979), like generation Y, do not identify with a religious denomination or don't believe in God. This is more than twice the number of nonbelievers among baby boomers, or those born between 1946 and 1965.

The introduction of generation Y into the workplace raises the possibility of cooperation and conflict. For both generation Y and generation X, working together will be a challenging task. To prepare for generation Ys, managers should consider the following practices:

1. Always provide full disclosure.
2. Create customized career paths.
3. Provide more public praise.
4. Encourage the use of mentors.
5. Provide access to innovative technology.
6. Allow for input into job-related decisions.

These are a few management pointers for working with a large new generation that is beginning to enter the workforce.

Source: Cheryl Wetzstein (April 12, 2005), "Generation Y Embraces Choice, Redefines Religion," *Washington Times;* "The New Workforce: Generation Y" (Summer 2001), *Workplace Visions,* pp. 1–8.

- Communicating HRM policies to all employees.
- Helping to maintain ethical policies and socially responsible behavior.
- Managing change to the mutual advantage of individuals, groups, the enterprise, and the public.

Helping the Organization Reach Its Goals

Bruce R. Elly, vice president of personnel at Pfizer, Inc., expresses the role of the HRM function this way:

> The HR function is a very key portion of the organization today. That message is coming across consistently in surveys of CEOs. So far, the emphasis has been on doing things right. The real jump in effectiveness will come when the focus is first placed on doing the right things. I can't imagine how HR functions without thoroughly knowing the business issues of its organization. Every business issue has HR implications.[25]

→ Efficiently Employing the Skills and Abilities of the Workforce

Clyde Benedict, the chief personnel officer for Integon Corporation, stated this purpose somewhat differently. He said the purpose is "to make people's strengths productive, and to benefit customers, stockholders, and employees. I believe this is the purpose Walt Disney had in mind when he said his greatest accomplishment was to build the Disney organization with its own people."

The HR Journal points out that a new generation Y wave of employees is entering the workforce. Managing their skills and abilities will require some preparation and consideration of their similarities and differences with other generations.

→ Providing Well-Trained and Well-Motivated Employees

This is a measure of effectiveness for HRM. David Babcock, chairman of the board and chief executive officer of the May Company, phrases this purpose as "building and protecting the most valuable asset of the enterprise: people."

Norman Augustine, chairman of Martin Marietta, is specific about how to motivate people when he states, "If you want to improve performance, people must see justice in the rewards you give. Reward good results, but don't reward people who don't perform. Make the goals clear, and how they are measured, with no room for side issues like whether someone's a nice person."[26]

HRM's effectiveness measure—its chief effectiveness measure, anyway—is to provide the right people at the right phase of performing a job, at the right time for the organization.

→ Increasing Employees' Job Satisfaction and Self-Actualization

Thus far, the emphasis has been on the organization's needs. But unlike computers or cash balances, employees have feelings. For employees to be productive, they must feel that the job is right for their abilities and that they are being treated equitably. For many employees, the job is a major source of personal identity. Most of us spend the majority of our waking hours at work and getting to and from work. Thus, our identity is tied closely to our job.

Satisfied employees are not *automatically* more productive. However, unsatisfied employees do tend to quit more often, to be absent more frequently, and to produce lower-quality work than satisfied workers. Nevertheless, both satisfied and dissatisfied employees may perform equally in quantitative terms, such as processing the same number of insurance claims per hour.

→ Achieving Quality of Work Life

This purpose is closely related to the previous one. Quality of work life is a somewhat general concept, referring to several aspects of the job experience. These include such factors as management and supervisory style, freedom and autonomy to make decisions on the job, satisfactory physical surroundings, job safety, satisfactory working hours, and meaningful tasks. Basically, a sound quality of work life (QWL) program assumes that a job and the work environment should be structured to meet as many of the worker's needs as possible.

Jac Fitz-Enz, the past president of Saratoga Institute (www.saratogainstitute.com), believes that American business has done a good job of dealing with many organizational inefficiencies, such as poor productivity, spiraling benefits costs, and poor quality.[27] He believes that people need to have a stake in their work and that employees will respond when employers pay attention to their personal needs and their work situations. He cites the example of Tandem Computers, which builds a strong bond between the development of a good QWL and the retention of employees. He states that, at Tandem, "the critical difference seems to be trust. . . . Technology and trust have turned Tandem into a miniversion of the global village." Tandem has paid attention to the personal and social situation of each employee, and, as a consequence, it has one of the lowest turnover rates in the Silicon Valley.

→ Communicating HRM Policies to All Employees

Chuck Kelly, director of human resources of a small manufacturing firm, expressed this objective as follows: "We can't afford not to communicate our programs, policies, and procedures fully. There are effective, personal development and legal reasons why everyone in the firm has to be HRM-knowledgeable. Communicating HRM programs does not just happen; a manager has to work at it constantly." HRM's responsibility is "to communicate in the fullest possible sense both in tapping ideas, opinions, and feelings of customers, noncustomers, regulators, and other external publics, and in understanding the views of internal human resources. The other facet of this responsibility is communicating managerial decisions to relevant publics in their own language."

Closely related to communication within the organization is representation of the organization to those outside: trade unions and local, state, and federal government bodies that pass laws and issue regulations affecting HRM. The HRM department must also communicate effectively with other top-management people (e.g., marketing, production, and research and development) to illustrate what it can offer these areas in the form of support, counsel, and techniques, and to increase its contribution to the overall strategic mission and goals of the organization.

Maintaining Ethical Policies and Socially Responsible Behavior

The human resource manager plays an important role in showing by example that each employee is important and will be treated ethically. That is, any activity engaged in by the HRM area will be fair, truthful, and honorable; people will not be discriminated against, and all of their basic rights will be protected. These ethical principles should apply to all activities in the HRM area.

IBM received the 2004 Best Corporate Citizen award because they pay attention to customers, shareholders, the communities where they do business, and employees. The technology giant with over 330,000 employees working in 164 countries received the award for progressive diversity policies, serving women and minorities, and giving back to communities. IBM doesn't rely on giving only money. Its annual philanthropic donations are over $125 million. Only about 30 percent is cash. The remainder is technology and technical services.[28]

IBM, through its handling of challenging issues such as creating a diverse and productive work environment and giving back to the community, impresses stakeholders and competitors. It serves as an example of how policies and behavior are recognized and appreciated.

Managing Change

In the past decade, there have been rapid, turbulent, and often strained developments in the relationship between employers and employees. New trends and changes have occurred in telecommuting, outsourcing HRM practices, family medical leave, child care, spouse-relocation assistance, pay for skills, benefit cost-sharing, union–management negotiations, testing, and many other HRM areas of interest. Nearly all of these trends and changes can be traced to the emergence of new lifestyles and an aging population.[29]

What these changes mean to HR managers is that new, flexible approaches must be initiated and used effectively without jeopardizing the survival of the organization. HR managers must cope with trends and changes while still contributing to the organization.

Managing Increased Urgency and Faster Cycle Time

Today firms place a growing emphasis on speed and urgency. The ability to increase customer service, the development of new products or services for the market, and the training and education of technicians, managers, and astute decision makers are thought of in terms of cycle time.[30] Frameworks for cycle time reduction focus on effective management not only of products and services, but also of human resources. Faster cycle times to train, educate, and assign managers; solve sexual harassment complaints; recruit and select the most talented people; and improve the firm's image are becoming important milestones for organizations.

Organizational learning provides a framework for increasing cycle time. Key areas within this framework are leadership behaviors, a culture that encourages and rewards learning, and an emphasis on learning to work more efficiently, quickly, and confidently.

Quicker and more flexible decision making and an increased sense of empowerment are also emphasized in firms using a learning framework.

Foreign and domestic competition, technological changes, and the emergence of new opportunities encouraged faster, more urgent management behaviors. A leisurely pace of conducting business is a thing of the past. The 40-hour workweek is outdated. At firms like Microsoft, Intel, Novell, and Goldman Sachs, 60- to 80-hour weeks are both the norm and the expectation. Fed Ex has a policy that every customer or employee query is answered the day it is asked. At Chaparral Steel, employees are encouraged to learn every job in their department. This learning approach enhances flexibility and provides employees with opportunities to be challenged.

The pressures to increase learning and reduce cycle time, while at the same time reducing costs and expenses, are today's competitive realities. If firms are to remain competitive, HRM activities performed by specialists and operating managers are going to have to be in sync with the firm's environment. This environment demands speed, urgency, top quality, and high-value products and services.[31]

These are the most significant and widely accepted HRM objectives. There are, of course, other objectives and different ways of stating them. But these can serve as guidelines for the HRM function in organizations. Effective HR departments set specific, measurable objectives to be accomplished within specified time limits.

Who Performs HRM Activities

Delegation of HRM duties has changed over time. In most organizations two groups perform HRM activities: HR manager-specialists and operating managers. Operating managers (supervisors, department heads, vice presidents) are involved in HRM activities because they are responsible for effective utilization of *all* the resources at their disposal. The human resource is a very special kind of resource. If it is improperly managed, effectiveness declines more quickly than with other resources. And in all but the most capital-intensive organizations, the investment in people has more effect on organizational effectiveness than resources such as money, materials, and equipment.

Therefore, operating managers spend considerable time managing people. Just as an operating manager is personally responsible if a machine breaks down and production drops, he or she must see to the training, performance, and satisfaction of employees. Research indicates that a large part of an operating manager's day is spent in unscheduled and scheduled meetings, telephone conversations, and solving problems that have a direct impact on people. The manager, through constant contact with many different people, attempts to solve problems, reach decisions, and prevent future difficulties.[32]

Smaller organizations usually have no HR unit, so the operating managers have many HRM responsibilities, such as scheduling work, recruitment and selection, and compensating people. As the organization increases in size, the operating manager's work is divided up, and some of it becomes specialized. HRM is one such specialized function. Usually the manager of a unit first assigns an assistant to coordinate certain HRM matters. HR specialists are employed in organizations with about 100 to 150 employees, and an HR department is typically created when the number of employees reaches 200 to 500, depending on the nature of the organization.

→ Outsourcing

Outsourcing, or contracting with a vendor to perform on a recurring basis an HRM activity previously performed by a firm, is growing in popularity. The market for outsourced services (which includes HRM activities) was over $200 billion in 2000. A study of 1,700 organizations estimated that 53 percent planned to outsource some HRM activities. The drivers of increased outsourcing include downsizing, rapid growth or decline of business, globalization, increased competition, and restructuring.[33]

Some executives assume that outsourcing some HRM activities is a competitive advantage. It is assumed that outsourcing can reduce costs, improve flexibility, and permit the hiring of specialized expertise. The choice to outsource some, all, or none of the HRM activities is being made with little empirical support.[34] However, outsourcing is likely to continue as decision makers search for ways to improve the financial and operating performance of firms.

The Interaction of Operating and HR Managers

With two groups of people (operating managers and HR specialists) making HRM decisions, there can be conflict.[35] Conflict occurs because operating and HR managers sometimes differ on who has authority for what decisions, or there may be other differences between operating and HR managers. They have different orientations, called *line* and *staff,* which have different objectives. A *staff* person typically supports the primary functions such as marketing and production by providing advice, counsel, and information. The picture of organizational life portrayed by a textbook assumes that the staff does not wield direct authority over the line manager. Line managers have the authority to make final decisions concerning their operations. However, the specific distinction between line and staff is not as clear-cut in actual organizations. More often than not, members of the HR unit have much to say about various programs and activities. Consider recruitment and selection practices and the crucial role played by HR specialists. Line managers are generally not familiar with the legal requirements concerning recruitment and selection. Therefore, they welcome the HR experts' involvement and direct authority in making final decisions.

The conflict between HR employees and operating managers is most pressing when there must be joint decisions on such issues as discipline, physical working conditions, termination, transfer, promotion, and employment planning. Research indicates that operating managers and HR specialists differ on how much authority employees should have over job design, labor relations, organizational planning, and certain rewards, such as bonuses and promotions.[36]

In the last decade, sweeping changes in business, globalization, technology, and demography have changed not only the role of HRM, but the role of operating managers as well. Line managers now have greater responsibilities, managing more people and/or bigger projects. Steve McElfresh, CEO of a consulting firm, explains: "Before, line managers were masters of routine. Now they must be masters of change." In addition, research shows that people don't leave companies; they leave managers. Because operating managers are expected to do so much, they realize more than before that HRM can help them do a better job.

However, there is still tension and conflict between some HRM units and operating managers. Lilly Eng, a line manager at All State Insurance, stated, "In many respects, HRM is viewed as a company policeman who many managers get tired of being told no." Others also tell stories of HRM inflexibility and overattention to detail.

Suggestions on how to improve the HRM and operating manager relationship abound. A few plead for HRM to analyze every HRM activity and show what it offers to the organization in terms of added value. HRM units are also encouraged to understand the business so they can become strategic partners with line managers. HRM specialists are requested to seek out operating managers. They are also asked to help managers avoid problems. Being more flexible and open to the ideas of others is a recommendation that applies to both HRM and operating managers.[37]

HRMEMO
Needed
Competencies

According to the "Official End-of-the-Millennium State-of-HR Survey" conducted by Workforce, *HR professionals believe the following competencies will be needed to optimize HRM activities:*

1. *Communication skills*
2. *Problem solving*
3. *Leadership*
4. *Recruiting/ staffing*
5. *Employment law*
6. *Training and development*
7. *Technology*
8. *Forecasting*
9. *Compensation design*
10. *Benefits design/ administrative*
11. *Accounting/ finance*
12. *Record keeping*

Source: Linda Davidson (August 1999), "Top 12 Future HR Competencies," *Workforce,* p. 73.

HRM's Place in Management

An increasing number of firms recognize that the HR department has a responsibility to be a proactive, integral component of management and the strategic planning process.[38] This new emphasis does not replace the competence required in counseling, consulting, industrial relations, or managerial control systems. Instead, it is an orientation that states that an HR department must do more than simply sit and listen when strategic management plans are nurtured and developed. The department must determine a strategic direction for its own activities that will make it a proactive arm of the management team. To accomplish this new role, HRM must ascertain specific organizational needs for the use of its competence, evaluate the use and satisfaction among other departments, and educate management and employees about the availability and use of HRM services. The long-range goal of any HRM strategic plan must be to build on the firm's strengths.

The theoretical work in business strategy has given a boost to the importance of HRM in creating a firm's sustained competitive advantage.[39] Organizations can develop a competitive advantage over other firms only by creating value in a way that is rare and difficult for competitors to imitate. Unlike capital investments, patents, or technology, a properly functioning HRM system is an invisible asset that creates value when it is so embedded in the firm's operational systems that it enhances the organization's capabilities.[40] The compensation system, training opportunities, diversity management programs, and other programs planned, implemented, and evaluated by HRM must become so important and so effective that any unit within the firm knows they are needed for the firm to be successful. This is what is meant by HRM's competitive advantage.

As HRM executives play an increasingly dominant role at the organization's strategic planning table, they must continually educate the members of other departments or units about the human resource implications of various decisions.[41] Thus, the HR executive must be familiar with other aspects of the organization—investments, advertising, marketing, production control, computer utilization, research, and development. It is crucial to know the business.

HR Department Operations

Both the makeup and the procedure of HR departments have changed over time. HR units vary by size and sector, but most organizations keep them small. One study found that in the largest headquarters unit there were 150 people.[42]

The number of HR specialists in relation to the number of operating employees, or the *personnel ratio,* varies in different industries. According to one study, the national average is 1 HR specialist per 100 employees. Some industries—construction, agriculture, retail and wholesale trade, and services—have fewer personnel specialists than the average. Others—public utilities, durable goods manufacturing, banking, insurance, and government—have an above-average ratio.

HRM Strategy

A firm's **HRM strategy** is the pattern or plan that integrates the major objectives, policies, and procedures into a cohesive whole. A well-formulated HRM strategy will help aggregate and allocate a firm's resources into a unique entity on the basis of its internal strengths and weaknesses, changes in the environment, and the anticipated actions of competitors.

Samsung is South Korea's largest chaebol (industrial group) with annual sales of over $102 billion. The firm consists of 14 companies ranging from manufacturing companies to service firms. The company is the world's number 1 maker of computer memory chips. It employs over 201,000 people.

Samsung believes that people are the future of the company. Samsung employees recognize their duties as members of a global society to exert their full potential and contribute to the betterment of society.

Samsung's success depends upon its employees. Customer satisfaction and sustainable corporate growth can only be ensured when employees are supported and fulfilled. Company policy has long dictated that employees be guaranteed respect, fair treatment, rewards for competence, and opportunities for personal growth in a supportive environment. The firm strongly believes that training and development of its employees helps the firm accomplish its strategy accomplishment indicators—customer satisfaction and sustainable corporate growth.[43]

Clarifying Meaningful HRM Objectives

The *objectives* of an organization or department are the goals it seeks to achieve—its reason for existence. Eight objectives of the HRM function have already been pointed out, but most of these objectives were stated in very general terms.

To help the organization achieve these objectives, more specific statements are developed in larger, most middle-sized, and some smaller organizations. For example, suppose that one of a number of **HRM objectives** is to increase employees' satisfaction with opportunities for advancement.

How can this objective be achieved? First, management must measure employees' satisfaction with advancement opportunities. Management could design an attitude survey to ask employees how satisfied they are with facets of their jobs. The key issue is to determine the degree of job satisfaction associated with advancement opportunities. Next, the organization could use the survey information to develop plans to correct any deficiencies in satisfaction with advancement opportunities. These plans are called *policies* and *procedures* or rules. Exhibit 1-2, which illustrates the relationship between objectives, policies, and rules, indicates that objectives are the most general factor. For example, maintaining a

EXHIBIT 1-2

Relationship between Strategy, Objectives, Policies, and Rules

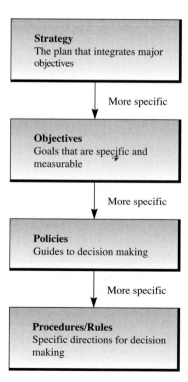

Strategy
The plan that integrates major objectives

More specific

Objectives
Goals that are specific and measurable

More specific

Policies
Guides to decision making

More specific

Procedures/Rules
Specific directions for decision making

HR Journal   *A Day in the Life of a Vice President of Human Resources, Sue Hagen*

Sue Hagen, 37, has what she calls "a great but somewhat mixed-up job." Her primary role is that of vice president of HR for Dole Food Co., Inc.'s (www.dole.com) operating groups, which includes providing support for the business units, including training, staffing, and employee relations. The other hat she wears is corporate HR director for the company's corporate campus based in Westlake Village, California, which houses about 250 people in two buildings—it includes the support group staff, packaged goods staff, and the fresh fruit division (primarily the banana business), including salespeople. On this side, she's responsible for general HR policy, health and welfare programs, plan design, communication (including the HR intranet site), and salaried payroll issues for the firm's North American operations. She also interacts with divisional HR groups and international HR operations. The corporate philosophy for many years has been to have as small a corporate staff as possible—so there are only about 80 true corporate employees, she says. "It's a highly decentralized company."

The company is set up more from a regional standpoint than from a product line standpoint. The organizational structure includes four divisions: North America, Asia, Latin America, and Europe, with regional managers assigned to each. Each division has its own HR organization that supports it.

A quick look at Sue's day.

5:30 A.M.

Sue's already out the door for an early morning, before-work run.

7:05 A.M.

Sue arrives at the office earlier than usual this morning after taking Friday off for a personal day. She's a big believer in work/life balance, which spills over into her HR philosophy and the programs she's helped develop for Dole, where she's worked for the past 13 years. She catches up on e-mail and voice-mail after her long weekend. "I used to get about 50 calls a day," says Sue. "As for e-mail, I get 100 e-mails every day."

8:00 A.M.

Sue attends a meeting led by Peter M. Nolan, the division president. Each executive gives an update for his or her area. They discuss Thailand operations, pineapple sales, a customer database, the upcoming peach harvest, who their "Broker of the Year" was, and a recent promotion. When it's her turn, Sue discusses a current problem with payroll accruals, then goes on to

add that soon Dole employees will be able to access their 401 (k) information and make changes to their own accounts through their vendor's new Web site.

9:20 A.M.

Sue meets with the HR administrative assistant, Heidi Hintz, in her office. Heidi's one of 16 people that Sue manages directly or indirectly. After reviewing Sue's schedule for the week, they discuss Dole's wellness program called "Healthy Lifestyles" and their HR-sponsored "Lunch & Learn" seminars.

11:05 A.M.

Sue walks over to the payroll department to meet with David Dale, Nashawn Smith, and Soccoro Garcia about a payroll problem with some expats' paychecks. It seems their accounting system was incorrectly withholding the wrong amount of "hypotax." Sue later explains that they were referring to federal taxes that Dole employees living outside the United States (but still American citizens) must pay on their wages each year, even if they're working elsewhere. Dole helps employees estimate "hypothetical tax"—and withholds the amount.

11:50 A.M.

Sue walks across the street to a local Chinese restaurant. She explains that she often doesn't take a formal lunch. She usually grabs something to eat quickly and gets back to work.

1:30 P.M.

Sue returns to her office and makes more phone calls. She receives a call from someone at Levi Strauss who aims to organize a coalition of employers to look at "living wages" and other self-sufficiency issues for workers overseas. Sue makes a call to one of Dole's corporate attorneys to discuss drawing up a contract that would bind an employee to Dole for a certain time if they arrange and pay for the costs involved in helping the employee establish permanent residency.

2:05 P.M.

Sue walks to the office of Henry Cassity, the director of purchasing. She tells him about an employee survey she's implementing (the company's first of that type).

2:35 P.M.

One door down from Sue's office, Jacqueline Hill, human resources consultant, has been comparing

HR Journal   *A Day in the Life of a Vice President of Human Resources, Sue Hagen (concluded)*

compensation data against industry norms for two particular employees. Sue walks to her office to discuss what she's found out and whether the two employees should be eligible to participate in the executive bonus plan.

3:05 P.M.

Sue pops into George Horne's office at the end of the hall. George is a Dole vice president who oversees HR. They discuss a job candidate for one of the company's high-level positions, then talk about transitioning HRM's support from the information systems group upstairs during a move to a new building. They talk about confidentiality and security issues, and how to back up the system during the interim. Sue then shows George data on total executive compensation

for the past three years, which reveals variances in target comp and actual comp.

4:10 P.M.

Sue spends the rest of her afternoon returning phone calls and e-mails, verifying vacation accruals, checking on the hypotax problem, and hunting for a consultant for the divisional design study,

6:10 P.M.

Sue makes the short trip home, and goes for another run. Then she spends a quiet evening fixing dinner and relaxing.

Source: Adapted from Jennifer Laabs (June 1999), "A Day in the Life of Sue Hagen: HR Models Work/Life Balance at Dole," *Workforce,* pp. 78–80.

high level of job satisfaction for employees is an objective. An organization makes an objective more specific by developing policies.

→ HRM Policy

A **policy** is a general guide that expresses limits within which action should occur. Policies are developed from past problem areas or for potential problem areas that management considers important enough to warrant policy development. Policies free managers from having to make decisions in areas in which they have less competence or on matters with which they do not wish to become involved. Policies ensure some consistency in behavior and allow managers to concentrate on decisions in which they have the most experience and knowledge.

After the broadest policies are developed, some organizations develop procedures and rules. These are more specific plans that limit the choices of managers and employees, as Exhibit 1-2 shows. Procedures and rules are developed for the same reasons as policies.

→ HRM Procedures

A **procedure** or rule is a specific direction to action. It tells a manager how to do a particular activity. In large organizations, procedures are collected and put into manuals, usually called *standard operating procedures* (SOPs).

Organizations must be careful to have consistent decision making that flows from a well-developed, but not excessive, set of policies and procedures. Some organizations, in effect, eliminate managerial initiative by trying to develop policies and procedures for everything. Procedures should be developed only for the most vital areas.

→ Organization of an HR Department

In most organizations, the chief HR executive reports to the top manager—in larger firms, perhaps to an executive vice president. Exhibit 1-3 shows the way HRM is organized in a large insurance business. The vice president of human resources has responsibility and authority for all HRM activities within the firm.

EXHIBIT 1-3   Organization of HRM in a Large Insurance Company

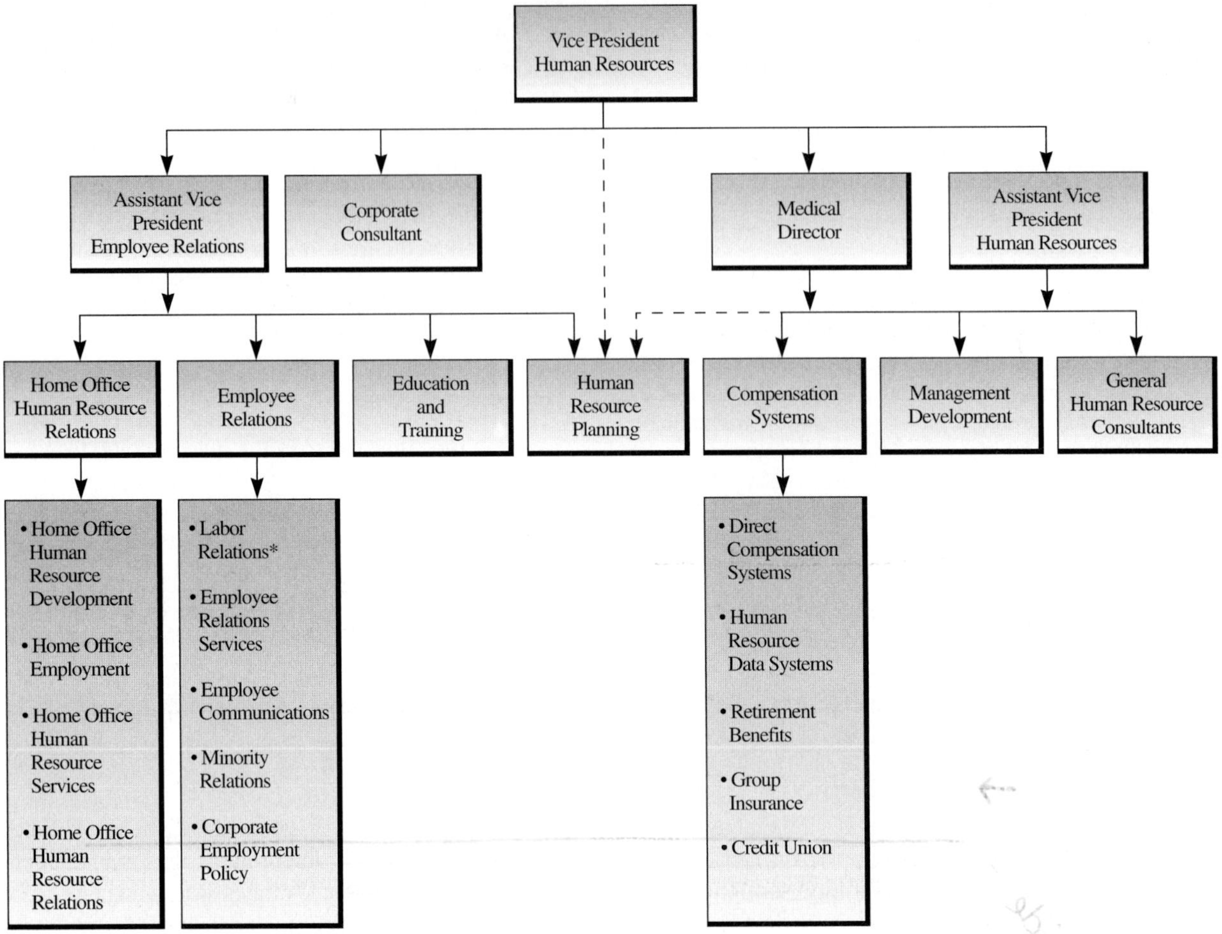

*Manager of function is also assigned general human resource consultant responsibilities.

In medium-sized organizations (500 to 5,000 employees) and smaller organizations (under 500 employees), HRM and other functions, such as public relations, may be part of a single department.

Thirty percent of all HR managers work for local, state, and federal governments. The legislature and the governor set policy for departments, subject to review by the courts, and then appoint an HR commission that is headed by an HR officer. This central HR unit is a policy-making body that serves a policy, advisory, and regulatory purpose similar to that of the home office HR unit of a business. At the federal level, this personnel commission is called the U.S. Office of Personnel Management (www.opm.gov).

In nonprofit organizations, such as hospitals and universities, HRM typically is a unit in the business office. More will be said in Chapter 2 about differences in HRM work in these three settings. HR specialists are usually located at the headquarters of an organization, but larger organizations may divide the HRM function. Usually the largest group is at headquarters, but HR advisers may be stationed at unit and divisional levels. In this case, the headquarters unit consists of specialists or experts on certain topics and advisers to top management, while the unit-level HR people are generalists who advise operating managers.

Don Brokop is ready to make an important career decision. He now understands the role that human resource management plays at Melody. He can see that HRM is important not only to his firm, but also to society. The people business is the job of all managers in an organization. Don has decided to accept the assistant director position and to become involved on a full-time basis with HRM activities.

The activities that Don will learn about firsthand are what this book is about. As you learn more about HRM, think about Don Brokop and how he stepped from the operating level of management into the HR role in the Melody plant. His on-the-job training will be invaluable in his personal growth and development. However, Don will also have to supplement this firsthand experience with reading and self-learning. Your job now is to dig into the type of reading and self-learning that Don will use to make himself a more successful HRM practitioner.

There are, of course, other decisions that could be made in this situation. What would you have decided if you were Don?

Plan of the Book

This book is designed to show how HR departments work, to discuss the importance of HR activities in organizations of any size, to describe the challenges that exist for HR department employees, and to show clearly that operating managers must be aware of and able to implement HRM tools, procedures, and policies. *Every manager* must be able to utilize the

EXHIBIT 1-4 Organization of Human Resource Management

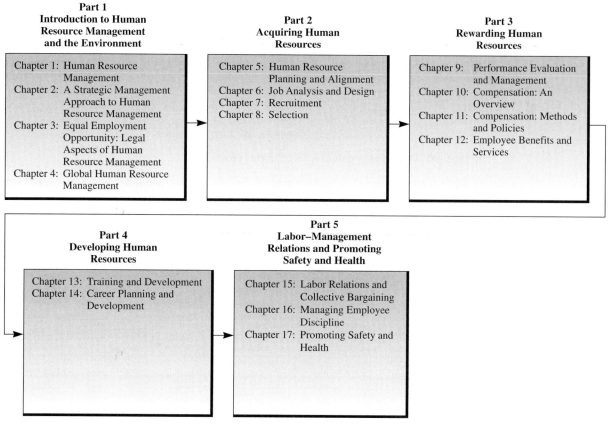

Part 1
Introduction to Human Resource Management and the Environment

Chapter 1: Human Resource Management
Chapter 2: A Strategic Management Approach to Human Resource Management
Chapter 3: Equal Employment Opportunity: Legal Aspects of Human Resource Management
Chapter 4: Global Human Resource Management

Part 2
Acquiring Human Resources

Chapter 5: Human Resource Planning and Alignment
Chapter 6: Job Analysis and Design
Chapter 7: Recruitment
Chapter 8: Selection

Part 3
Rewarding Human Resources

Chapter 9: Performance Evaluation and Management
Chapter 10: Compensation: An Overview
Chapter 11: Compensation: Methods and Policies
Chapter 12: Employee Benefits and Services

Part 4
Developing Human Resources

Chapter 13: Training and Development
Chapter 14: Career Planning and Development

Part 5
Labor–Management Relations and Promoting Safety and Health

Chapter 15: Labor Relations and Collective Bargaining
Chapter 16: Managing Employee Discipline
Chapter 17: Promoting Safety and Health

human assets they are responsible for in the most optimal way to help achieve the firm's goals. The operating managers are closest to employees; and their competency in executing HRM techniques, programs, and policies will be tested on how effective each is in practice.

The chapters begin with a Career Challenge vignette, an example from a real organization that describes an HRM problem or issue. Solving the problem or issue is an HRM activity or a manager's decision. This activity is explained, and then how the activity is carried out is discussed.

Each chapter includes a diagnostic analysis of the activity being discussed. HRM activities are affected by many different factors, such as the types of people employed, organized labor, and government. Solving HRM problems demands consideration of all these factors. The theme of strategy and diagnosis will be thoroughly examined in Chapter 2.

For each HRM activity, suggestions are given for the techniques, tools, and approaches available to solve the problem, with an evaluation of when each tool is most useful and tips on how to use it well. When feasible, the various HRM activities are evaluated using a cost-benefit approach. Since HRM must compete with requests for other resources (machinery, advertising, buildings, and so on), the expenditures and investments in the organization's people must be justified in terms of costs and benefits.

The chapter summary sections review the major points in each chapter. The organization of the book's chapters is presented in Exhibit 1-4. The five parts and 17 chapters cover HRM activities that need to be performed to achieve acceptable levels of organization effectiveness and employee development.

Summary

This chapter (and all others in the text) concludes with a list of statements summarizing the most important concepts covered in the chapter. You can use this list to review your understanding of the HRM process, HRM activities, and what operating managers will need to effectively implement the HR manager's job.

In your introduction to this field, HRM has been defined as the function or unit in organizations that facilitates the most effective utilization of human resources to achieve the objectives of both the organization and the employees. This introduction has described some of the characteristics of HR managers and a number of approaches to the organization and operation of HR units. It has concluded with a brief description of how the material in this book is organized and the devices used to present it. A special appendix to this chapter describes typical careers in HRM, suggests ways HR specialists can achieve greater professionalism, and briefly describes accreditation procedures.

To summarize the major points covered in this chapter:

1. HRM is action-oriented, individual-oriented, globally oriented, and future-oriented. It focuses on satisfying the needs of individuals at work.
2. HRM is a necessary function. Effectively performed, it can make the crucial difference between successful and unsuccessful organizations.
3. One of the challenges faced in HRM is that many decisions require input from both operating managers and HR specialists.
4. This dual purpose can lead to conflict, or it can result in more effective HRM decisions.

HRM is one of the most challenging and exciting functions in an organization. This book has been written to help you face these challenges more effectively since many of you will become managers who must use and apply HRM activities, tools, and policies. Every manager is involved, in some way, with HRM.

Key Terms

HRM objectives, *p. 17*
HRM policy, *p. 19*
HRM procedures, *p. 19*
HRM strategy, *p. 16*
Human resource management (HRM), *p. 4*

Questions for Review and Discussion

1. Why is the HR department playing a more significant role in organizational strategic planning processes today than it did 20 years ago?

2. Why is it correct to conclude that all managers are involved in the human resource management function and implementing HRM activities and programs?

3. How has increased globalization influenced the way HRM is practiced in the United States?

4. Why has the HRM function increased in stature and influence in many organizations?

5. Do accreditation procedures make the HRM field professional? In other words, are lawyers, doctors, and HRM managers all professionals?

6. What difficulties would an HRM executive face in assessing and then communicating the contribution of his or her area to the company profit margin?

7. The book proposes that Peter Drucker is incorrect when he states that work in HRM is nothing more than the work of a file clerk. What has happened in the world of work to make his statement false?

8. Why is it necessary for the HRM area to clearly communicate human resource policies?

9. Why should even very small firms (with 10 to 100 employees) be concerned about HRM?

10. What do you think about Dan Brokop's decision to accept the position of assistant director in HR?

Notes

1. Pamela Babcock (April 2005), "Find What Workers Want." *HR Magazine;* Adelle Waldman (March 24, 2005), "Making a Good Last Impression," *Wall Street Journal Online;* Erin White and Kris Maher (April 19, 2005), "Web-Site Suffix.jobs Is Added in Hopes It Is Easier to Find One," *Wall Street Journal,* p. 34; "GOODBYE to Pay for No Performance" (April 11, 2005), *Wall Street Journal,* p. R1.

2. D. Ulrich and N. Smallwood (June 2004), "Capitalizing on Capabilities," *Harvard Business Review,* pp. 119–127.

3. Paul Evans, Vladimir Pucik, and Jean-Louis Barsoux (2002), *The Global Challenge: Frameworks for International Human Resource Management* (Burr Ridge: Irwin/McGraw-Hill).

4. Frederick W. Taylor (1947), *The Principles of Scientific Management* (Mineola, NY: Dover Publications).

5. Frederick W. Taylor (1998), *The Principles of Scientific Management* (New York: Harper).

6. Hugo Munsterberg (1913), *Psychology and Industrial Efficiency* (Boston: Houghton-Mifflin).

7. Henry Eilbert (Autumn 1959), "The Development of Personnel Management in the United States," *Business History Review,* pp. 345–64.

8. B. E. Kaufman (1993), *The Origins and Evolution of the Field of Industrial Relations in the United States* (Ithaca, NY: Industrial Relations Press).

9. Fred K. Foulkes (March–April 1975), "The Expanding Role of the Personnel Function," *Harvard Business Review,* pp. 71–72.

10. Tim Hatcher (Spring 2005), "Research Integrity: Ensuring Trust in the Academy," *Human Resource Development Quarterly,* pp. 1–5.

11. Diane E. Johnson (March 2005), "Theorizing about the Impact of Strategic Human Resource Management," *Human Resource Management Review,* pp. 1–18.

12. Patricia Ordonez de Pablos (2005), "Strategic Human Resource Management and Organizational Competitiveness: The Importance of Fit and Flexibility," *International Journal of Human Resource Development,* Vol. 5, p. 1.

13. Linda Holbeche (2002), *Aligning Human Resources and Business Strateg* (Woburn, MA: Butterworth-Heinemann).

14. "Workplace Diversity: Leveraging the Power of Difference for Competitive Advantage" (June 2005), *HR Magazine,* pp. 1–9.

15. A. Pasternack, Shelley S. Keller, and Albert J. Visco (Second Quarter 1997), "The Triumph of People Power and the New Economy," *Strategy & Business,* pp. 50–56.

16. Edward E. Lawler, III (Summer 2005), "From Human Resource Management to Organizational Effectiveness," *Human Resource Management*, pp. 165–169.

17. Eleni Stavrou-Costea (2005), "The Challenges of Human Resource Management towards Organizational Effectiveness," *Journal of European Industrial Training,* Vol. 29, pp. 112–134.

18. Jurgen Kluge and Wolfram Stein (2001), *Knowledge Unplugged: The McKinsey and Company Global Survey on Knowledge Management* (New York: Palgrave-McMillan).

19. Thomas A. Stewart (2001), *The Wealth of Knowledge* (New York: Doubleday).

20. Neil Longley (Spring 2005), "The Role of Performance Volatility in Pricing Human Assets: Adapting the Capital Asset Pricing Model to Salary Determination in the National Hockey League," *Journal of Business & Economics,* pp. 1–17.

21. Mark A. Huselid (June 1995), "The Impact of Human Resource Management Practices on Turnover, Productivity, and Corporate Financial Performance," *Academy of Management Journal,* pp. 647–672.

22. M. A. Huselid and B. E. Becker (Unpublished paper, 1997), "The Impact of High Performance Work Systems, Implementation Effectiveness, and Alignment with Strategy on Shareholder Wealth," Rutgers University, New Brunswick, NJ, pp. 18–19.

23. L. Blimes, K. Wetzker, and P. Xhonneux (February 1997), "Value in Human Resources," *Financial Times,* p. 10.

24. "A Fitting Role" (June 2005), *HR Magazine,* pp. 54–60.

25. Thomasino Rendero (August 1990), "HR Panel Takes a Look Ahead," *Personnel,* p. 24.

26. "Justice: the Leader's Job" (March 1993), *Success,* p. 45.

27. Jac Fitz-Enz (2000), *The ROI of Human Capital: Measuring the Economic Value of Employee Performance* (New York: AMACOM).

28. Fifteenth Annual Corporate Citizenship Awards, June 2004.

29. Mike Losey, Dave Ulrich, and Sue Meisinger (eds.) (2005), *The Future of Human Resource Management: 64 Thought Leaders Explore the Critical HR Issues of Today and Tomorrow* (New York: John Wiley).

30. Mark A. Huselid, Brian E. Becker, and Richard W. Beatty (2005), *The Workforce Scorecard: Managing Human Capital to Execute Strategy* (Boston, MA: Harvard Business School Press).

31. *Harvard Business Review on Business and the Environment* (2002) (Cambridge, MA: Harvard Business School Press).

32. Larry Bossidy, with Charles Burck and Ram Charan (2002), *Execution: The Discipline of Getting Things Done* (New York: Crown Publishing Group).

33. Edward E. Lawler, Dave Ulrich, Jac Fitz-enz, James Madden, and Regina Maruca (2004), *Human Resources Business Process Outsourcing* (San Francisco: Jossey-Bass).

34. Ibid.

35. Daniel Druckman (2005), *Doing Research: Methods of Inquiry for Conflict Analysis* (Thousand Oaks, CA: Sage).

36. Ibid.

37. Robert C. Prezrosi (2005), *The Pfeffer 2004: Annual of Human Resource Management* (New York: Pfefffer & Co.).

38. Carter Pate and Harlan Platt (2002), *The Phoenix Effect: Revitalizing Strategies No Business Can Do Without* (New York: John Wiley).

39. Hugh Bucknall (2005), *Magic Numbers for Human Resource Management* (New York: John Wiley).

40. Jack J. Phillips and Patricia Pullman Phillips (2005), *Proving the Value of HR: How and Why to Calculate ROI* (Washington, DC: Society for Human Resource Management).

41. Ibid.

42. Human Resource Activities, Budgets, and Staffs (2001) (Washington, DC: The Bureau of National Affairs).

43. Samsung Group Web site (June 6, 2005), www.samsung.com/corporate/human.html.

44. See www.shrm.org for analysis of Society for Human Resource Management.

Application Case 1-1

The Human Resource Manager and Managing Multiple Responsibilities

At 7:30 A.M. on Monday, Sam Lennox, human resource manager of the Lakeview plant of Supreme Textile Corporation, pulled out of his suburban home and headed for work. It was a beautiful day; the sun was shining in a bright blue sky, and a cool breeze was blowing. The plant was about nine miles away and the 15-minute ride gave Sam an opportunity to think about business problems without interruption.

Supreme Textile Corporation owned and operated five plants: one yarn-spinning operations, two knitting plants, and two apparel-making operations. Supreme enjoyed a national reputation for high-quality products, specializing in men's sports shirts. Corporate headquarters was located in Twin-Cities adjacent to two of the plant operations. The Hillsville, Eastern, and Lakeview plants were 100 to 200 miles distant. Each employed 70 to 100 people. About 250 employees were located in Twin-Cities.

Sam had started with Supreme's Eastern plant after college. He progressed rapidly through several staff positions. He then served two years as a night foreman. He became known for his ability to organize a "smooth team," never having a grievance procedure brought against him. While his productivity figures were not outstanding, he was given credit by many people in the company for being the person who prevented the union from successfully organizing the Eastern plant. As a result, he was promoted to assistant personnel manager.

Sam's progress was noted by Glen Johnson, corporate vice president of personnel. Glen transferred Sam to the Lakeview plant, which was having some personnel problems, as a special staff assistant. Six months later he was made personnel manager when the incumbent suddenly resigned. Sam had been able to work out most of the problems and was beginning to think about how to put together a first-rate personnel program.

Sam was in fine spirits as his car picked up speed, and the hum of the tires on the newly paved highway faded into the background. He said to himself, "This is the day I'm really going to get things done."

He began to run through the day's work, first one project, then another, trying to establish priorities. After a few minutes, he decided that the management by objectives (MBO) program was probably the most important. He frowned for a moment as he recalled that on Friday, Glen Johnson had asked him if he had given the project any further thought. He had been meaning to get to work on this idea for over three months, but something else always seemed to crop up. "I haven't had much time to sit down and really work it out," he said to himself. "I'd better hit this one today for sure." With that, he began to break down the objectives, procedures, and installation steps. "It's about time," he told himself. "This idea should have been followed up long ago." Sam remembered that he and Johnson had discussed it over a year ago when they had both attended a seminar on MBO. They had agreed it was a good idea, and when Sam moved to the Lakeview plant, they decided to try to install it there. They both realized it would be met with resistance by some of the plant managers.

A blast from a passing horn startled him, but his thoughts quickly returned to other projects he was determined to get under way. He started to think about ideas he had for supervisory training programs. He also needed to simplify the employee record system. Not only was the present system awkward, but key information was often lacking. There were also a number of nagging carryover employee grievance problems. Some of this involved weak supervisors, some poor working conditions, and some poor communications and morale. There were a few other projects he couldn't recall offhand, but he could tend to them after lunch, if not before. "Yes, sir," he said to himself, "this is a day to really get rolling."

Sam's thoughts were interrupted as he pulled into the parking lot. He knew something was wrong as Al Noren, the stockroom foreman, met him by the loading dock. "A great morning, Al," Sam greeted him cheerfully.

"Not so good, Sam, my new man isn't in this morning," Al growled.

"Have you heard from him?" asked Sam.

"No, I haven't," replied Al.

Sam frowned. "Better call him," he said.

Al hesitated for a moment before replying, "Okay, Sam, but can you find me a man? I have two cars to unload today."

As Sam turned to leave, he called, "I'll call you in half an hour, Al," and headed for his office.

When he walked into the personnel office, there were several plant employees huddled around his secretary, Terry. They were complaining that there was an error in their paychecks. After checking their files and calling payroll twice, he found that an automatic pay increase had not been picked up properly. He finally got everyone settled down.

He sat down at his desk, which was opposite Terry and two other clerks. One of the clerks brought him a big pile of mail. He asked her to get him some office supplies and started to open the mail. The phone rang; it was the plant manager, asking him about finding a new secretary. As Sam sat listening to all the problems the manager had with secretaries, he thought, "Fussbudget." He started to call a couple of foremen to see if they had someone to fill in for Al in the stockroom when he was interrupted by one of his clerks asking him to check over several termination reports. He was trying to decide whether any of these represented trouble spots when the phone rang again. Glen Johnson was on the other end. With an obvious edge to his voice, he asked, "I've heard rumblings about some of the grievance we can't seem to solve. What about it?" Sam responded that he hadn't had time, but would get to it. There followed a series of questions. The conversation ended with, "Sam, you really need to get after those problems." Sam sighed. Terry was at his desk asking him to approve a couple of rate changes.

Several job applicants came into the office as a result of want ads the company had run over the weekend. There was a buzz as the applications and interview progressed. Sam started to help out, and was talking with one applicant when Cecil Hardy came in. Cecil was the plant engineer, who liked to stop by to chat and have a cup of coffee. He was approaching retirement and today wanted to talk about the company's pension benefits. He also described in detail a round of golf he had played Sunday afternoon. Sam had played golf when he was in school and enjoyed an occasional game with Cecil.

It was suddenly 10:45 and time to go to a staff meeting to discuss quality control. Sam wasn't awfully interested, but the plant manager wanted all the department heads at staff meetings. "They always drag on so long, and we get off on things that don't seem real important to all of us," Sam reflected as he headed toward the conference room.

Sam went to lunch with a friend who owned a plastics fabrication business. He called an hour ahead to say he wanted to discuss a major medical package that had been proposed by an insurance company. They drove across town to a new restaurant.

When Sam returned at about 2 P.M., the office was busy again with job applicants. He suddenly remembered the replacement stock clerk. "Too late now," he mused. He sat down and began to assemble the files relating to the grievances. The production superintendent called to discuss his need for several production people. He wanted experienced people and wasn't happy with some of the prospects Sam's department had sent him. Sam took a break to get a soft drink from the storage room. He noticed that some of the confidential employee files had been pulled out and not returned. As he straightened them out he thought, "I wonder who did this?"

Sam returned to his desk to find a Boy Scout troop selling advertisements in a program for a rally they were putting on. This was one of the odd tasks Sam had been assigned by the plant manager. As the afternoon wore on, Sam became increasingly irritated at not being able to make much progress with the grievances. "Trouble is," he thought, "I'm not sure what should be done about the Sally Foster and Curt Davis cases."

At 4:45 the personnel manager at the Eastern plant called to ask about some employee matters Sam had handled when he was there. When he finished, it was 5:30 and he was the only one left in the office. Sam was tired. He put on his coat and headed toward the parking lot. He ran into Al Noren, who was also heading for his car. "Thanks for the stock clerk," Al grumbled as he drove off.

With both eyes on the traffic, Sam reviewed the day he had just completed. "Busy?" he asked himself. "Too much so—but did I accomplish anything?" His mind raced over the day's activities. *Yes* and *no* seemed to be the answer. "There was the usual routine, the same as any other day. The personnel function kept going, and we must have hired several new people. Any creative or special project work done?" Sam grimaced as he reluctantly answered, "No."

With a feeling of guilt, he probed further. "Am I a manager? I'm paid like one, I'm respected like one, and I have a responsible assignment with the necessary authority to carry it out. Yet some of the greatest values a company derives from a manager are creative thinking and accomplishments. You need some time for thinking. Today was like most other days; I did little, if any, creative work. The projects that I so enthusiastically planned to work on this morning are exactly as they were last week. What's more, I have no guarantee that tomorrow will bring me any closer to their completion. There must be an answer."

Sam continued, "Night work? Yes occasionally. This is understood. But I've been doing too much of this lately. I owe my wife and family some of my time. When you come down to it, they are the people for whom I'm really working. If I am forced to spend much more time away from them, I'm not meeting my own personal objectives. What about church work? Should I eliminate that? I spend a lot of time on it, but I feel I owe God some time, too. Besides, I believe I'm making a worthwhile contribution. Perhaps I can squeeze a little time from my fraternal activities. But where does recreation fit in?"

Sam groped for the solution. By this time, he had turned off the highway onto the side street leading from his home—the problem still uppermost in his mind. "I guess I really don't know the answer," he told himself as he pulled into his driveway. "This morning, everything seemed so simple, but now . . ." His son ran toward the car, calling out, "Mommy, Daddy's home."

Discussion Questions

1. Human resource management consists of numerous activities. What areas were illustrated by Sam's schedule on this particular day?
2. List the areas of ineffective management and time robbers that are affecting Sam.
3. Discuss Sam's career progress. Is he now promotable?

1. problem solver.   Labor relations
   job interviews

2. Drinkin coffee and talkin about golf.

3. No. Time management is an issue.

Appendix  A

Careers in HRM

Most HR managers have college degrees and have taken courses across a number of discipline areas. College training includes courses such as HRM, compensation administration, HRM problems, labor law and legislation, and collective bargaining. Those who want to become more specialized can join associations—such as the American Society for Human Resource Management, previously called the American Society for Personnel Administrators (ASPA)—attend meetings, read professional journals, or seek accreditation. The Society for Human Resource Management (www.shrm.org) has over 165,000 members and more than 500 local chapters and members in more than 120 countries.

HR employees generally are paid comparably to other business school graduates at the supervisory and middle-management levels. At top-management levels, they sometimes are paid slightly less than operating vice presidents. Current average salaries of HR specialists and executives are presented in Exhibit 1A-1. The career ladder opportunities in various HR positions are also shown. For example, an entry level HRM position would result in an average salary of $35,000. Working up the career ladder in this area could result in a position as the top organizational development and training manager earning $105,000.

An HR professional can enter the field through different types of positions. One way is to become an HR manager for a small unit of a large organization. Remember Don Brokop at the beginning and end of this chapter? This is what he would be doing if he accepted the Melody Machine Products plant position.

Accreditation

One move to increase the professionalism of HR executives is the Society of Human Resource Management Accreditation Program. SHRM has set up an Accreditation Institute to offer HR executives the opportunity to be accredited as specialists (in a functional area such as employment, placement and HR planning, training and development, compensation and benefits, health, safety and security, employee and labor relations, and personnel research) or generalists (multiple specialties). Accreditation requires passing a series of examinations developed by the Psychological Corporation of New York. Tests are given by SHRM in these HRM activity areas.[44]

- Management practices
- Selection and placement
- Training and development
- Compensation and benefits
- Employee and labor relations

The American Society for Training and Development (www.astd.org) is made up of over 70,000 members who are concerned with the training and development of human resources. The ASTD professional development committee is working to identify the competencies needed to master training and development activities.

EXHIBIT 1A-1   Sample Salaries in Human Resource Management

Source: Bureau of National Affairs, Inc., Washington, DC, for 1996, 1999, 2001, and 2004. Inflation adjustment = 3 percent per year.

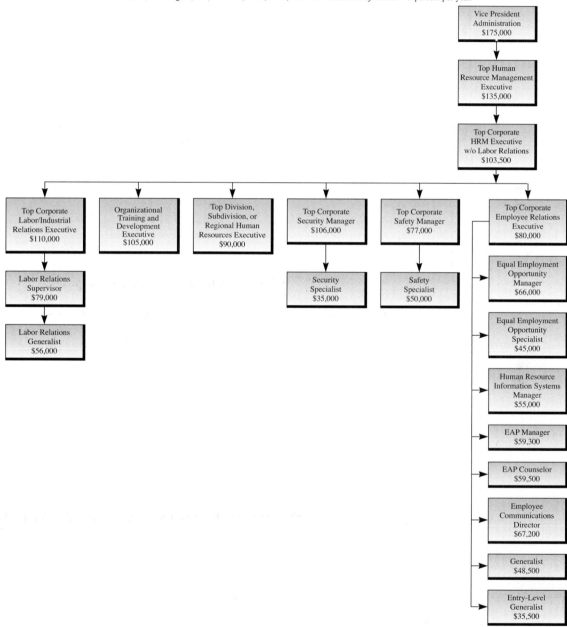

Chapter  2

A Strategic Management Approach to Human Resource Management

Learning Objectives

After studying this chapter you should be able to:

1. **Describe** how a ARDM model can be used to organize, examine, and solve "people problems."
2. **Explain** the difference between external and internal environmental forces that affect HRM problems.
3. **Discuss** the role that HRM can play in accomplishing an organization's strategic plan.
4. **Identify** how HRM activities contribute to a firm's productivity.

Internet/Web Resources

General Sites

www.bizweb.com

www.eeoc.gov

www.astd.org

www.workforceonline.com

Company Sites

www.aetna.com

www.catalytica.com

www.cocacola.com

www.dttus.com

www.gs.com

www.eeoc.gov

www.honda.com

www.ibm.com

www.merck.com

www.microsoft.com

www.mmm.com

www.toyota.com

Martha Wilson is the newly appointed manager of the National Pancake House in Fort Lauderdale, Florida, which is known for its beach area. Officially, the restaurant is known as Unit 827; National is a large chain. Martha believes that if she does a good job managing 827 she has an excellent chance to be promoted at National. She is also thinking about opening her own restaurant someday.

Martha entered National's management training program after completing college at a small liberal arts school. The focus of the training program was technical. Martha learned all about the equipment of a typical National restaurant. She also learned about National's finance and accounting system, theft control, and advertising. She was taught a great deal about National's goals for the firm and for Unit 827. The topics included sales goals, financial return, cleanliness, customer service, and so on.

She has been at 827 three weeks now and is adjusting pretty well. She is not reaching all the goals National set up for her yet, but she feels she will do so in time. She often wishes the training program had taught her more about the people part of the success equation. Her college courses were not much help to her on this either.

This problem was on her mind as she sat in her office one morning staring at her paperwork over a cup of coffee. She was thinking of the two cooks on duty, Lenny and Harry. Lenny Melvina is about 24. He's been with National as a cook for almost six years. He finished high school locally. It's the only job he's ever had. He arrives on time, works hard, and leaves on time. He's never absent except for perhaps one day a year for illness.

Everyone likes Lenny: the other help, his managers, the customers. It's easy to see why. He does his job well and in a friendly manner. For example, today Martha watched Lenny deal with a customer. National has a policy that second helpings are free. A girl, about 13, came up to Lenny and asked for seconds. He asked her in a friendly manner how many more pancakes she wanted. She said, "Oh, I don't know, one or two."

Instead of having her wait at the serving line, he suggested that she be seated and said he'd bring her the pancakes. He delivered a plate with three pancakes on it that looked like this:

The customer and her family were very pleased with his effort to please her and give them a little joke too. They told Martha they'd come back again.

The other cook is Harry Bennis. Harry is about 19. He didn't finish high school. He's worked at National for two years. Harry is tolerated rather than liked. Most of his coworkers tend to ignore him. He rarely says anything beyond the minimum to co-workers, bosses, and customers. He is often late or absent. In about 1 case in 10, his food is sent back. He's not surly, but not too pleasant either. He's not bad enough to fire, but not good enough to be pleased with.

Martha wonders why there are these differences between Lenny and Harry, and what, if anything, she can do about it. It affects her now because she must hire a cook. Business at 827 has been growing faster than usual, even for this busy season. So the staff needs to be expanded to include at least one new cook. Martha wonders how she can be sure to choose a person like Lenny, not another Harry.

(continued on next page)

It's also raise time. She doesn't have enough money to give everyone a raise. To hire a new cook, she may have to pay close to what she pays Lenny, because few cooks are out of work at present. Yet company policy says she must pay senior people like Lenny more. And if things weren't already complicated enough, the pay must be above the government minimum wage.

Many of the employees at 827 told Martha they wanted more pay because the job wasn't pleasant: The stove was hot, and they had to deal with the public. What should she do? To help her make an intelligent, effective decision, she went to visit a friend, Amy Adams, who had majored in human resource management. Amy spent an afternoon with Martha explaining how to deal with the four personnel problems Martha faced (employee satisfaction, performance, selection, and pay) by understanding how three sets of factors affect HRM and organizational effectiveness:

- People.
- The internal and external environment of the organization.
- The organization, task, work group, and leadership.

Think about how Martha must diagnose the present situation and work with people at the restaurant.

As mentioned in Chapter 1 the role of HRM in organizations has been changing significantly in the past decade. Organizations that continue to utilize HRM as a necessary record-keeping and largely clerical function are forgoing the contributions human resource management can make to a firm's performance and end results. Taking a strategic HRM approach requires a greater focus on strategic thinking and processes. It means placing the management of human resources as a top priority and also integrating HRM with the company's strategy, mission, and goals.

Strategic HRM is defined as the development and implementation of human resource processes to enhance and facilitate the achievement of the organization's strategic objectives. An organization's strategy is linked to human resource processes by developing organizational objectives that impact how people should be managed effectively.

There is no single idea or best way to manage people. There are some good, generalizable practices, but there is no perfect system. Management must have an understanding that HRM can make significant contributions to end results if it is a part of the strategic planning from the outset. The most important theme is that strategic HRM requires the proper alignment of human resources with the firm's overall strategy. If an organization's human resource processes are not in sync with its vision, mission, and goals, there will typically be significant problems.

In general, strategic management is a process by which an organization works to determine what needs to be done to accomplish priority objectives, and how they will be achieved. Senior leaders generally examine the full resources of an organization and its environment to determine an optimal fit to achieve desired end results. In many cases a three- to five-year time line is used, with annual monitoring and modification of the strategic plan. In a straightforward explanation, strategy means determining how an organization intends to achieve its goals. The strategic choices may need to include consideration and inclusion of the appropriate HR processes. In best cases, the HR strategy will result in a better fit between the organization's strategy and individual HRM policies and programs (e.g., recruitment, selection, outsourcing, telecommuting, performance evaluation, compensation).

Martha Wilson in the opening career challenge is not engaged in making an organization strategy choice. She is, however, engaged in making an appropriate HRM choice.

She is involved in making the most optimal choice to help National Pancake House achieve its strategic goals or end results. She is performing the hard work of decision making faced by most managers. Her choices should be in alignment with the National Pancake House strategic plan. By using a model or framework to aid her in making decisions Martha can be more confident and prepared to diagnose, choose, or prescribe a solution, implement the choice, and then evaluate how good the choice was in terms of solving the problem.

A Model to Organize HRM

When you're experiencing pain and must see a physician, you are typically asked a number of questions. Where do you hurt? When did the pain start? What does the pain feel like— is it sharp or dull? The doctor examines you and may also run a number of tests. The doctor is diagnosing the problem by examination and observation. After making a diagnosis, the physician will prescribe medicine or a course of action. In most cases the patient will implement the prescription, and the doctor will evaluate how the prescription is working.

The problem faced by Martha at National Pancake House could also be examined through a careful diagnosis. The ARDM (A = acquiring, R = rewarding, D = developing, and M = maintaining and protecting) human resource management *model* might help her. The ARDM model with a strategic (overall, broad) focus can help operating managers home in on a set of relevant factors; it offers a map that aids a person in seeing the whole picture or parts of the picture. The three factors that Martha was concerned about (people, the internal and external environment, and the organization itself) would be included as parts of the ARDM approach.

Exhibit 2-1 presents the ARDM model that will serve as a reference point in each chapter. The model emphasizes some of the major external and internal environmental

EXHIBIT 2-1   The ARDM Model for Human Resource Management

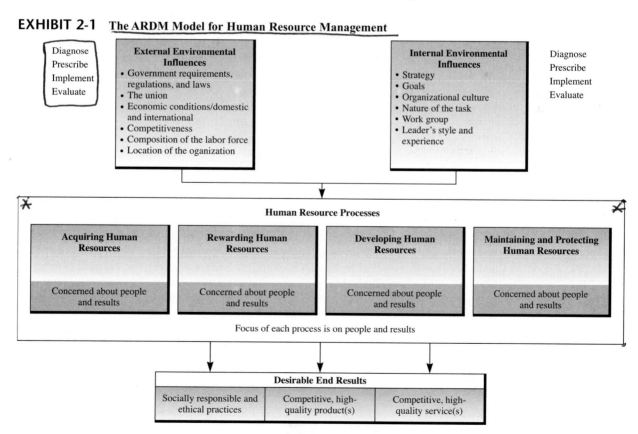

influences that directly or indirectly affect the match between HRM activities and people.

Diagnosis, prescription, implementation, and evaluation are important in achieving the eight HRM objectives presented in Chapter 1. Again, it should be pointed out that a significant reason for the eventual success of any HRM activity is that the organization's employees are the best qualified and are performing jobs that suit their needs, skills, and abilities. Matching people and activities to accomplish desirable goals is easier with a diagnostic approach. Of course, the ARDM model shown in Exhibit 2-1 can't include every important environmental influence, HRM activity, or criterion for effectiveness. Instead, it provides an orderly and manageable picture of what HRM activities intend to accomplish.

How to Take a Diagnosic Approach to HRM

The ARDM model includes four specific steps to be taken by managers: (1) diagnosis, (2) prescription, (3) implementation, and (4) evaluation.[1] Managers typically diagnose a work situation by observing and identifying the key factors. For example, why is Harry always late for work? Using a diagnostic approach to answer the question will show how the four steps are applied. Over a period of time, Harry has acquired a reputation for being late. Being late would, of course, be observed; the crucial question is why? There may be a personal reason, a job-related reason, or some other kind of explanation. Various management and HR theories may help the manager diagnose Harry's tardiness, as may many observational techniques such as interviews, surveys, or group meetings. Once a diagnosis is completed, a prescription is made to translate the diagnosis into action.

Suppose that the diagnosis indicated that Harry is dissatisfied with his job. Therefore, a solution might be to find Harry a more suitable job. If, however, it was determined that Harry had a substance abuse problem, then a different prescription would be needed to correct the behavior. Most human resource problems have no single correct prescription, because of the complexity of behaviors, emotions, and attitudes. Solutions to a problem may range from changing the design of a job to altering the performance evaluation system to providing training to changing the compensation system for the job. Familiarity with a full range of ways to address a problem is a valuable contribution that HRM experts can make. There are many different HRM programs and techniques for managers to consider in addressing a problem.

Implementing a solution is the next step in the diagnostic approach. Changing the way Harry is compensated may correct the problem. However, can a compensation system solely for Harry's use be implemented? Deciding when, how, and whether a solution can be implemented is a complex set of considerations that managers face.

Finally, any solution that is implemented must be evaluated. Has Harry's tardiness been corrected? Evaluation tells managers how and whether to improve the diagnosis, prescription, and implementation steps.

The ARDM model provides the four major anchor points (e.g., acquiring human resources) to be the centerpiece of effective HRM. If an organization teaches its members how to focus on each anchor point A, R, D, and M plus the environment, it is likely to achieve socially responsible, ethical behaviors and competitive, high-quality products and services. The ARDM model calls for thorough, timely, and systematic review of each situation.[2]

Deloitte Touche Tohmatsu, a large accounting firm with over $1.5 billion worldwide revenue, used its own ARDM model to retain more female accountants. By the mid-1980s, 50 percent of Deloitte's new hires at the professional level were female. For 2005 Deloitte set a goal that 25 percent of the partners promoted would be women, up from the 22 percent in 2001. This goal has been accomplished.

Top Deloitte managers *diagnosed* the shortage of women problem and situation and launched the Women's Initiative. Women were being precluded from advancement, and many decided to leave Deloitte in the late 1980s. Management *prescribed* and *implemented* an aggressive campaign to address the male-dominated advancement culture and to provide mentors and role models for female professionals. The prescription also included support programs to allow women to better balance work and family responsibilities. Also, workshops on "Men and Women as Colleagues" became mandatory for all 5,000 Deloitte managers and partners.

Deloitte monitored and evaluated the implemented programs and reported significant improvements. More highly talented women were staying with the firm. The number of female managers, female senior managers, and female partners increased significantly.

Deloitte diagnosed a problem and prescribed, implemented, and evaluated a solution concerning the hiring, retention, and promotion of more female professionals. The firm clearly understands the importance of diagnosis. Deloitte blazed a new trail for its professional women and now other firms have instituted similar programs by using their own approaches to diagnosis, prescription, implementation, and evaluation.

External Environmental Influences

Exhibit 2-1 shows that HRM processes in an organization do not operate in a vacuum. They are influenced by and influence the external environment (outside the organization) and internal environment (inside the organization). On the one hand, **external environmental influences**—such as government laws and regulations, union procedures and requirements, economic conditions, and the labor force—have a significant impact on HRM processes. On the other hand, the HR planning of a firm must operate within guidelines, limits of available resources, and competencies produced by the organization. HRM is one important function among other internal functions, including finance, accounting, research and development, marketing, and production. The interaction of these internal programs sets the tone of the entire organizational system.

At the National Pancake House, Martha's HRM problems are aggravated by external environmental factors. Remember that Martha is faced with a tight labor market and government wage legislation. Let's look at some external environmental factors.

Government Law and Regulations

A powerful external environmental influence is government law and regulations, which affect organizations directly. Federal regulations influence HRM activities, policies, and programs. When an organization makes decisions about hiring, promotion, managing diversity, performance evaluation, downsizing, and discipline, it must weigh the impact of government regulations.

The government regulates and influences some aspects of HRM more directly than others. Major areas of legislation and regulation include:

Equal employment opportunity and human rights legislation, which directly affects recruiting, selection, evaluation, and promotion, and indirectly affects employment planning, orientation, career planning, training, and development.

Employment of illegal aliens.

Discrimination based on sex, age, and disability.

Compensation regulation, which affects pay, hours of work, unemployment, and similar conditions.

Benefits regulation, which affects pensions and retirement.

Workers' compensation and safety laws, which affect health and safety.

Labor relations laws and regulations, which affect the conduct of collective bargaining.

Privacy laws.

Government regulation has increased substantially. In 1940 the U.S. Department of Labor administered 18 regulatory programs; in 2004 it administered more than 135.[4] And that is just *one* government agency affecting managers and the activities of the HR department.

John Dunlop lists a number of the problems government regulation imposes on management.[5] All of these make the operating and HR managers' job more difficult:

- Regulation encourages simplistic thinking on complicated issues. Small enterprises are treated like large ones. Different industries are regulated alike.
- Designing and administering regulations is an incredibly complex task, leading to very slow decision making.
- Regulation does not encourage mutual accommodation but rather leads to complicated legal maneuvering.
- Many regulations are out of date and serve little social purpose, yet they are not eliminated.
- There is increasing evidence of regulatory overlap and contradictions among different regulatory agencies.

To cope with increasing governmental control, management has tried to influence the passage of relevant legislation and the way it is administered. Managements have sued to determine the constitutionality of many of the laws. When such efforts fail to influence the process as management prefers, it has learned to adapt its HRM policies.

The Union

The presence of a union directly affects most aspects of HRM—recruiting, selection, performance evaluation, promotion, compensation, and benefits, among others. These effects will be discussed later in the book. Chapter 15 focuses directly on relations with labor unions.

A *union* is an organization that represents the interests of employees on such issues as working conditions, wages and salaries, fringe benefits, employees' rights, grievance processes, and work hours. Unions differ, just as people and other organizations differ. There are cooperative unions and combative unions, just as there are sensitive organizations and socially irresponsible organizations. Those familiar with union history are aware of the kind of toughness a James Hoffa or a John L. Lewis can bring to the employment scene. The union leadership of the Air Line Pilots Association; State, Local, and Municipal Workers; Baseball Players Association; and others is not so well known because they have different bargaining styles and philosophies.

At one time, unions were concentrated in a few sectors of the economy, such as mining and manufacturing, and were influential in only a few sections of the United States, primarily the highly industrialized areas. But the fastest-growing sectors for unions in the United States are the public sector and the third sector. It is no longer useful to think of the unionized employee as a blue-collar factory worker. Engineers, nurses, teachers, secretaries, salespersons, college professors, professional football players, and even physicians belong to unions. In sum, unions often play a significant role in HRM programs.[6]

Economic Conditions

Two aspects of economic conditions affect HRM programs: productivity and the work sector of the organization.

Cooperative union
Combative union

Productivity

Data, empirical evidence, and general opinion indicate that the productivity of employees is an important part of a nation's general economic condition. Managers are concerned with productivity because they feel it is a representative indicator of the overall efficiency of an organization. **Productivity** is defined as output of goods and services per unit of input of resources used in a production process.[7] *Inputs,* as applied in the measurement of productivity, are expressions of the physical or dollar amount of several elements used in producing a good or a service, including labor, capital, materials, fuel, and energy.

Before productivity can be effectively managed and improved, it must be measured. This can be done by isolating the outputs—division by division, department by department, work team by work team, individual by individual, or product line by product line. Next, the costs that went into producing the output must be determined, including labor (salaries, bonuses, fringes), heating, lighting, and capital.[8] Then, using the previous year as a baseline period, the manager must compare the current year's figures with those of the previous year. Some period of comparison is needed to make necessary adjustments. While improving productivity is a worthy goal, managers should lay the groundwork for measuring and monitoring productivity before they rush into changes.

Productivity measures are crude and subject to short-term error. But over the long run, productivity measures can present a trend. Productivity in the United States slid in the 1970s to an annual rate of increase of about 2.0 percent. In 1994–2004, however, productivity began to increase annually and averaged about 3.1 percent. The Japanese averaged productivity rates in the 1960s and 1970s of about 6.0 percent annually. The Japanese and German economic infrastructures were destroyed in World War II, and postwar gains until about 1980 were dramatic. The American worker still is the most productive, but Japan, Korea, and other nations have narrowed the gap.[9]

Some suggested solutions for increasing productivity include reducing government controls, developing more favorable income tax incentives to invest in new plants and equipment, and reindustrializing the entire business-industrial complex (such as plants and equipment). These suggested solutions have both proponents and opponents.[10] For example, there are many citizens who believe that reducing or eliminating legislative controls will adversely affect the quality of life and society for decades to come. Toxic waste, radiation, air pollution, and other forms of destruction must be carefully controlled.

On the other hand, managers can influence productivity by the sound application of HRM programs. Specific activities and practices can improve individual performance and consequently organizational productivity. Managers can through diagnosis, prescription, implementation, and evaluation help employees achieve their optimum level of productivity. Also, recruitment and selection techniques can be used to attract and hire the best performers. Motivational and compensation techniques can be used to retain employees and improve job performance. Training and development can improve job performance or rectify deficiencies in skill and competency, in turn increasing performance.

The Work Sector of the Organization

The ARDM model in Exhibit 2-1 does not consider the work sector in which the organization is located. This was omitted so that the model could remain relatively uncluttered.

About 60 percent of professional HR specialists work in the *private sector,* consisting of businesses owned by individuals, families, and stockholders; while 30 percent of all HR employees in the United States work in the *public sector,* which is that part of the economy owned and operated by the government. Many economists define other institutions that are neither governmental nor profit-oriented as the *third sector.* Examples of these institutions are museums, symphony orchestras, private schools and colleges, not-for-profit hospitals and nursing homes, and voluntary organizations such as churches and social clubs. About 10 percent of HR specialists and employees work in the third sector.

In general, private sector and third sector HRM are structured similarly. Hospitals have different internal organization problems from most businesses, though. For example, the presence of three hierarchies—physicians, administrators, and the board of trustees (representing the public)—can lead to conflicts. Pressures from third party payers such as Blue Cross or Medicare can lead to other conflicts. Hospitals employ professional groups that zealously guard their "rights," and this also leads to conflict. Structurally, HRM work in the private and third sectors is similar, but because of organizational differences, jobs in HRM vary.

HRM in the public sector is fundamentally different from HRM in the other two sectors because it varies structurally. The public manager faces a different world; in fact, a manager who moves from the private or third sector to the public sector will find the HRM role much more complicated. HRM in the public sector generally is under much more direct outside pressure. Politicians, the general public, pressure groups, and reporters influence the HR manager much more in the public sector than in private business or the third sector.

Competitiveness

At the macroeconomic level, the term *competitiveness* is defined as the degree to which a nation can, under free and fair market conditions, produce goods and services that meet the test of international markets while simultaneously maintaining or expanding the real incomes of its citizens.[11]

If you substitute the word *organization* for *nation,* and the word *employees* for *citizens,* you would have a definition of *organizational competitiveness.*

At the organizational level, competitiveness is an important issue.[12] How effectively do the workers produce the product? How good is the quality of the services or goods provided? Can employees handle new technology and produce the product at lower costs? Does the firm have the human resources needed to increase the size of the manufacturing facility to handle global demand? Will the push to work harder and faster raise turnover, absenteeism, and the number of defects?

An increasing amount of research suggests that the way organizations implement and modify their HRM activities can provide them with competitive advantages. A *competitive advantage* is defined as having a superior marketplace position relative to competitors.[13] Sustainable competitive advantage requires a firm to deal effectively with employees, customers, suppliers, and all competitors. Pfeffer identified 16 HRM activities that he recommends to enhance and sustain a firm's competitive advantages.[14] Exhibit 2-2 briefly describes these activities.

Sustaining competitive advantage is extremely difficult over long periods. Competitors, by learning about other firms, can also adopt and, in some cases, improve on successful HRM activities.[15] Although it is difficult for competitors to have total access to a firm's HRM policies, programs, and approaches, it is possible to learn through laid-off employees, customers, communication materials, and other procedures what a company does in the HRM area. If a firm has a strong culture noted for the fair, equitable, and productive treatment of human resources, it will be less susceptible to losing all or any of its competitive advantage. Certainly, a few HRM activities can be copied, but the imitation of an entire culture and system of HRM is extremely difficult.[16]

Composition and Diversity of the Labor Force

The labor force of the United States comprises all people age 16 years or older who are not in the military and who are employed or seeking work. As of 2004 there were over

EXHIBIT 2-2
HRM Activities That Can Enhance and Sustain Competitive Advantage

Source: Adapted from Jeffrey Pfeffer (1994), *Competitive Advantage through People* (Boston: Harvard Business School Press).

1. *Employment security* A guarantee of employment stating that no employee will be laid off for lack of work. Provides a signal to employees of long-term commitment by the organization to the workforce.
2. *Selectivity in recruiting* Carefully selecting the right employees in the right way. On average, a highly qualified employee produces twice as much as a poorly qualified one.
3. *High wages* Wages that are higher than that required by the market (i.e., higher than that paid by competitors). High wages tend to attract better qualified applicants, make turnover less likely, and send a message that the firm values its employees.
4. *Incentive pay* Allowing employees who are responsible for enhanced levels of performance and profitability to share in the benefits. Employees consider such a practice fair and just.
5. *Employee ownership* Giving employees ownership interests in the organization by providing them with such things as shares of company stock and profit-sharing programs.
6. *Information sharing* Providing employees with information about operations, productivity, and profitability.
7. *Participation and empowerment* Encouraging the decentralization of decision making and broader worker participation and empowerment in controlling the work process.
8. *Teams and job redesign* The use of interdisciplinary teams that coordinate and monitor their own work. Teams exert a powerful influence on individuals by setting norms regarding appropriate work quantity and quality.
9. *Training as skill development* Providing workers with the skills necessary to do their jobs. Training not only ensures that employees and managers can perform their jobs competently, but also demonstrates the firm's commitment to its employees.
10. *Cross-utilization and cross training* Train people to perform several different tasks. Having people do multiple jobs can make work more interesting and provides management with greater flexibility in scheduling work.
11. *Symbolic egalitarianism* Equal treatment of employees by such actions as eliminating executive dining rooms and reserved parking spaces.
12. *Wage compression* Reducing the size of pay differences among employees.
13. *Promotion from within* Filling job vacancies by promoting employees from jobs at a lower organizational level.
14. *Long-term perspective* The organization must realize that achieving competitive advantage through the workforce takes time to accomplish, and thus requires a long-term perspective.
15. *Measurement of practices* Organizations should measure such things as employee attitudes, the success of various programs and initiatives, and employee performance levels.
16. *Overarching philosophy* Having an underlying management philosophy that connects various individual practices into a coherent whole.

146 million Americans in the workforces; by 2012, the labor force is projected to be over 162 million.[17] These data suggest a slowing in the growth rate of the labor force in the next decade. Other changes projected by the Bureau of Labor Statistics (BLS) are reported in the *Monthly Labor Review*, which carefully tracks trends in the available labor supply.[18]

Exhibit 2-3 presents an overall view of the civilian labor force in terms of sex, age, race, and Hispanic origin for 2002–2012.

Women

In 2002 about 47 percent of the full-time U.S. workforce consisted of women. The number of married women in the labor force has increased 235 percent since 1947, while the number of married male employees has increased by only 30 percent.[19]

Although women are supposed to have equal job opportunities, it is difficult to argue with the facts of discrimination against women in the workplace. There are some signs, however, that by the year 2006 more women will be found in professional jobs: college

EXHIBIT 2-3   Civilian Labor Force by Sex, Age, Race 1992, 2002 and Growth Projected to 2012

Source: *Civilian Labor Force,* Washington, DC: U.S. Department of Labor, February 11, 2004.

				Change			
	Level			Number		Percent	
Group	1992	2002	2012	1992 to 2002	2002 to 2012	1992 to 2002	2002 to 2012
Total, 16 years and older	128,105	144,863	162,269	14,429	17,406	11.3	12.0
Men	69,964	77,500	85,252	6,088	7,751	8.7	10.0
Women	58,141	67,363	77,017	8,340	9,654	14.3	14.3
One race							
White	108,837	120,150	130,358	9,732	10,208	8.9	8.5
Black or African American	14,162	16,564	19,765	2,672	3,201	18.9	19.3
Asian	5,106	5,948	8,971	2,024	3,022	39.6	50.8
Hispanic or Latino	11,338	17,942	23,785	4,862	5,843	42.9	32.6

teachers, lawyers, physicians, and accountants. Women are landing more professional jobs that require advanced education. For example, 46 percent of the recipients of accounting degrees and 45 percent of business majors are women.[20]

Minorities

The situation for racial and ethnic minorities in the United States is similar to that for women. Large numbers of Hispanics, African Americans, and Native Americans are employed in low-skill, low-paying jobs, and few are in high-status, high-paying jobs.[21]

Historically, the most recent immigrant groups took the lowest-level jobs offered. In the early 1900s this was true of the Irish, Polish, Serbs, Croatians, and Jews. One difference between immigrant groups and other minorities—like African Americans, Hispanics, and Native Americans—is that the minority groups were living in the United States long before the immigrants arrived. Native Americans have been in the United States before the time of "discovery," as were many of the Hispanics in the Southwest, and African Americans since the mid-1700s. They have not advanced to the degree that the immigrants have, however. Native Americans were kept on reservations, and Hispanics remained in the areas that once belonged to the Mexican Republic (except for the Cuban and Puerto Rican immigrants, who came much later). Most African Americans worked in southern agriculture until relatively recently. These minorities represent about 13 percent of the population of the United States. They have been less educated than the majority, although recent programs have attempted to improve this situation.

Older Employees

About 13 percent of the labor force currently is 55 years or older. In 2006 about 17 percent, or over 23 million, of the workforce is 55 or older.

Probably one of the most difficult employment problems today is the older employee who loses a job through no personal fault. In some cases, employers assume that because a person is older he or she is less qualified to work and less able to adapt to changes. Also, benefit plans (which may amount to one-third of base compensation) are set up in such a way that it costs more to employ older people (the cost of insurance premiums is higher).[22]

HR Journal *Women: A New Revolution*

In spite of glass ceilings, outright hostility, and discrimination, women are making progress and climbing corporate ladders. The pressures on women to succeed in careers as mothers, and as spouses are significant. The lure of entrepreneurship is strong among women because instead of fighting their way to the top they can establish and operate their own business.

Sally Heigesen, author of *Everyday Revolutionaries: Working Women and the Transformation of American Life* (Doubleday, 1998), may have come up with the best way yet to make sense of the pressures on working women. Heigesen's book explains the twin effects of women's widespread entry into the workplace over the last 30 years: First it transformed the economy and society; then it transformed the women. To show just how much the world has changed, Heigesen juxtaposes her thoughts with William Whyte's *Organization Man*, Whyte's celebrated 1956 study of the wing-tipped, gray-suited archetype of corporate conformity homed in on junior executives living in the bedroom community of Park Forest, Illinois. For her look at everyday revolutionaries, Heigesen conducted hundreds of interviews with the inhabitants of nearby Naperville, Illinois. The residents of Whyte's Park Forest were mostly married, Republican, and Protestant; they bought the same cars, watched the same television shows, and subscribed to the same magazines. Naperville residents form a "postmodern pastiche" marked by demographic variety, ethnic diversity, and a profusion of niche lifestyles.

In almost every respect, the 1950s Organization Man is a perfect foil for the 2000s Hyperkinetic Woman. He embodied an absolute faith in large organizations, an overriding homogeneity, and a sense of leisure and unhurried ease. His paradigm—life as a progression through predictable stages—has no relevance in a community where only 18 percent of households feature a dad at work and a mom at home with the children. Faced with increasing complexity and a squeeze on their time, the women of Naperville lead every trend of new-economy work—from entrepreneurialism to project work to careers punctuated by periods of education.

What makes the book compelling is Heigesen's ability to convey a sociologist's argument in a storyteller's voice. In *Everyday Revolutionaries*, Heigesen mixes the real-life pathos of Naperville's "improvising chorus" with a clear-eyed analysis of how the experiences of these women fit into a larger cultural landscape. In so doing, she breathes life into the now-standard themes of work and life in the new economy.

In addition, she avoids predictability. Heigesen's answer to the book's implicit question—What are these women revolutionaries after?—is remarkable and unexpected. What they are looking for, she suggests, are "new vernaculars of work and life that seek to reconcile the demands of personal ambition with the need for embeddedness in family and community." In other words, these revolutionaries part company with the women warriors of the last generation. Instead, their real kinship is with the bloomer girls, suffragettes, and immigrant women of the late 19th century. Their ultimate quest, according to Heigesen, is to "make the whole world homelike."

Source: Susan J. Wells (June 2001), "A Female Executive Is Hard to Find," *HR Managers*, pp. 41–49; and Polly LaBarre (February 1998), "The Starbucks Sisterhood," *Fast Company*, p. 66.

An important fact to remember is that each person ages at a different rate. As we grow older, we lose some of our faculties. This process is ongoing: Rarely is a swimmer better than in his or her midteens, for example. The key, then, is to match employees with jobs. Older workers may be less efficient on some jobs requiring quick physical response rates. But speed or response is more important for a race driver or airline pilot than for a stock analyst or social worker.

Most studies indicate that even for jobs requiring physical work, employees over 45 do not have more accidents than younger employees. Older employees also have the same or lower rates of absenteeism—at least until age 55. The worst accident rate observed in one study was for employees under 35 years old.[23] When total performance is considered (including factors such as speed, accuracy, judgment, and loyalty), the older employee has been found to be at least as effective as the younger one.

EXHIBIT 2-4   **Ten Fastest-Growing Occupations, 2002–2012**

Source: "Occupational Employment Projections" (February 2004), *Monthly Labor Review.*

Standard Occupation Classification Code and Title	Employment		Change		Most Significant Source of Postsecondary Education and Training
	2002	2012	Number	Percent	
1. Medical assistants	365	579	215	59	Moderate-term on-the-job training
2. Network systems and data communication analysts	186	292	106	57	Bachelor's degree
3. Physician assistants	63	94	31	49	Bachelor's degree
4. Social and human service assistants	305	454	149	49	Moderate-term on-the-job training
5. Home health aides	580	859	279	48	Short-term on-the-job training
6. Medical records and health information technicians	147	216	69	47	Associate's degree
7. Physical therapist aides	37	54	17	46	Short-term on-the-job training
8. Computer software engineers, applications	394	573	179	46	Bachelor's degree
9. Computer software engineers, systems software	281	409	128	45	Bachelor's degree
10. Physical therapist assistants	50	73	22	45	Associate's degree

Employment Projection

The 10 fastest-growing occupations for an increasingly diverse workforce are presented in Exhibit 2-4. Technology-based occupations will have the greatest growth in opportunities for well-educated and well-trained applicants.

Geographic Location of the Organization

The location of the organization influences the kinds of people it hires and the HRM activities it conducts. A hospital, plant, university, or government bureau located in a rural area confronts different conditions than one located in an urban area. For example, the workforce in a rural area might be more willing to accept a bureaucratic organization style. Recruiting and selection in rural areas will be different in that there may be fewer applicants. Yet the organization may find a larger proportion of hirable workers ingrained with the work ethic.

An urban location might be advantageous for recruiting and holding professional workers. Urban locations provide a bigger labor force but generally call for higher wages. Late shifts may be a problem because workers may not feel safe at night in the parking lots or going home.

Geographic location, therefore, influences the kinds of workers available to staff the organization. The location or setting is extremely significant for companies operating in other countries. The employees may speak a different language, practice different religions, have different attitudes toward work, and so on. Let's consider some of the major differences between home-based and multinational organizations.

Educational Factors

Examples include the number of skilled employees available, attitudes toward education, and literacy level. Educational deficiencies in some countries can lead to a scarcity of qualified employees, as well as a lack of educational facilities to upgrade potential employees.

Behavioral Factors

Societies differ in factors such as attitudes toward wealth and profits, managerial roles, and authority.

Legal-Political Factors

Laws and political structures differ and can encourage or discourage private enterprises. Nations also differ in degree of political stability. Some countries are very nationalistic (even xenophobic) in their business practices. Such countries can require local ownership of organizations or, if they are so inclined, expropriate foreign concerns.

Economic Factors

Economies differ in basic structure, inflation rate, constraints on ownership, and the like. The nations of the world can be divided into three economic categories: fully developed, developing, and less developed. The fully developed nations include the United States, Canada, Australia, Japan, and most European countries (the United Kingdom, Germany, France, Belgium, Luxembourg, the Netherlands, Switzerland, Italy, Sweden, Denmark, Norway, Finland). In these countries, managers will find fewer differences in educational, behavioral, economic, and legal-political factors than they are likely to encounter in developing or less developed countries.

The developing nations are those that are well along in economic development but cannot yet be said to be fully developed. Examples include Brazil, Mexico, Argentina, Venezuela, Spain, Nigeria, India, and Eastern Europe.

Third world nations—the less developed countries—are the most difficult to work in because of significant constraints in terms of education, economic system, political structure, and the general infrastructure. The remaining 180 or so countries in the world are in this group. A sample list would include Afghanistan, Ethiopia, Bolivia, and Pakistan.

To be successful abroad, managers must learn all they can about the countries in which they will be working. There are many sources of this kind of information. Knowledge of differences among nations in (1) educational, (2) behavioral, (3) legal-political, and (4) economic factors is essential for managerial success abroad. It is equally important (and more difficult) for the enterprise to obtain managers with proper attitudes toward other countries and their cultures. A manager with the wrong set of attitudes may try to transfer North American ways of doing things directly to the host country, without considering the constraints in these four factors. The more significant the differences, the more likely they are to cause problems for the unperceptive manager.

In sum, the physical location of the organization (rural or urban, at home or abroad) can have a significant impact on how HRM programs are used and which activities are conducted. The manager using a diagnostic orientation will be better able to closely examine, consider, and understand the complexities involved with different physical locations.

Internal Environmental Influences

The **internal environmental influences** listed in Exhibit 2-1 (strategy, goals, organization culture, nature of the task, work group, and leader's style and experience) involve characteristics and factors that are found within the organization. Let's examine how each of these influences affects the HRM program.

HR Journal   *Achieving Work-Life Balance*

The Families and Work Institute's Business Work-Life Study (BWLS) and National Study of the Changing Workforce (NSCW) found that employees with more supportive workplaces are more likely than other workers to have:

- Higher levels of job satisfaction.
- More commitment to their companies.
- A stronger intention to remain with their companies.

Additionally, they found that when employees' personal and family well-being is compromised by work, employees experience more negative spillover from home to work, which diminishes job performance.

First Tennessee National Corporation treats work-life issues as a strategic issue. They have found that customer service and productivity have improved when the firm started to introduce flexible work hours, reduced work schedules, telecommuting, and other programs.

Aetna Life & Casualty halved the rate of resignations among new mothers by extending its unpaid parental leave to six months, saving it $1 million a year in hiring and training costs.

Ernst & Young has implemented programs through its Office for Retention that address work-life balance issues. Included are programs that provide:

- Child care at or near the worksite.
- Job sharing.
- Sick care for children and employees.

- On-site summer camp.
- Training supervisors to respond to work-family needs of employees.
- Concierge services to assist employees with a wide variety of errands from dry cleaning to making dinner reservations.

Abbott Laboratories strives to attract and retain the highest skill-level employees. The company is committed to work-life programs, recreation activities, adoption assistance, paternity leave, tuition assistance, and alternative work arrangements. Abbott has typically been voted one of the best places to work for all types of employees.

The organizations that have developed work-life balance programs have found happier and more productive employees. There are, however, many companies that still have not investigated, implemented, or experimented with work-life balance programs. Apparently, many firms and managers believe that bringing about work-life balance is a personal problem and not an organizational issue.

Source: See Abbott Laboratories (accessed June 10, 2005), "Work Life Programs at http://abbott.com/career/work_life_programs.cfm; Patricia Digh (May–June 2001), "Achieving Work-Life Balance for Employees," *Mosaics*, pp. 1–4; and Rhona Rapoport, Lotte Bailyn, Joyce K. Fletcher, and Bettye H. Pruit (2001), *Advancing beyond Work-Family Balance: Advancing Gender Equity and Workplace Performance* (San Francisco: Jossey-Bass).

Strategy

A **strategy** indicates what an organization's key executives hope to accomplish in the long run.[24] As a plan, a strategy takes the firm into the area of competition in the environment and into alignment with the resources of the firm.

For example, Apple Computer's early success was due to high alignment of its strategy, structure, people, and management. People were "empowered through Apple technology." The Apple workforce believed that the company's technology and ideas were superior to all others. But then competitors and deviation from a high-end technology strategy resulted in protest, discontent, and political infighting. Apple did not adapt, and it lost profit margin and had to lay off large numbers of employees.

There are companies that believe that the long-term success of their firms is linked to helping their employees achieve a work-life balance. These companies have instituted programs designed to help employees feel safe and better about such issues as child care, families, and home life. The above HR Journal illustrates how and what firms are doing at the strategic level with regard to work-life balance.

SMART goals

Specific
Measurable
Attainable
Realistic
Trackable

Goals

The goals of organizations differ within and among departments. All departments probably have goals that include employee satisfaction, survival, and adaptability to change. The differences arise in the *importance* the decision makers place on the different goals. In some organizations, profit is of such major importance that other goals, such as increased employee satisfaction, are not well developed. In these organizations where profits take precedence, HRM goals involving the human resources are paid only minimal attention. The result of such negligence is typically problems in the effectiveness area of the diagnostic model (e.g., high absenteeism, performance decrements, high grievance rates). In other organizations, HRM-related goals are highly regarded by decision makers. Thus, how much the HRM function is valued and how it is implemented are affected by these goals.

Diversity refers to any mixture of themes characterized by differences and similarities. The public is accustomed to thinking of diversity in terms of workforce demographics, but diversity in organizations is much more than just demographics. It is important not only to address the issue of how people differ but also to understand similarities.[25] All human beings share some commonalities. Today more and more firms realize that when they deal with the diversity of the workforce, they are focusing on the collective picture of differences and similarities.

Wisconsin Power and Light has established a specific goal-based diversity management program.[26] The program includes addressing differences and similarities in race, gender, age, physical and mental abilities, education, lifestyle, and background. The firm expects its future workforce to be more diverse but to be focused on respecting and valuing the differences and similarities among its employees. The firm has implemented companywide diversity training using a six-step approach: (1) forming a diversity steering team, (2) creating a diversity training team, (3) selecting a diversity training project manager, (4) completing a cultural audit, (5) designing a training program, and (6) implementing and evaluating the training. The goal at Wisconsin Power and Light is to highlight, respect, and value differences and similarities throughout the organization.

Organization Culture

Organization culture refers to a system of shared meaning held by members that distinguishes the organization from other organizations.[27] The essence of a firm's culture is shown by the firm's way of doing business, the manner in which it treats customers and employees, the extent of autonomy or freedom that exists in the departments or offices, and the degree of loyalty expressed by employees about the firm. Organization culture represents the perceptions held by the organization's employees. Is there a sense of shared value? Is there a common value system held by employees? These are the kinds of questions asked to arrive at a picture of the firm's culture.[28]

There is no one "best" culture for the development of human resources. The culture at Neiman Marcus is different from the one found at Foley's Department Stores. Culture can be strong or weak; a firm with values shared by a large majority of the employees is said to have a strong culture. Japanese companies like Sony, Honda, and Toyota are often cited as firms with strong cultures. IBM, 3M, and Merck are examples of firms with strong cultures in the United States.

Culture can have an impact on the behavior, productivity, and expectations of employees. It provides a benchmark of the standards of performance among employees. For example, it can provide clear guidelines on attendance, punctuality, concern about quality, and customer service.

Catalytica is a 120-employee, $10 million annual sales organization in New Jersey that produces technologies to eliminate or reduce pollution during the manufacturing process. This firm has a powerful culture that it attempts to display while recruiting all potential new employees. The interviewee is asked to talk for about 35 minutes on any topic of interest to him or her. Catalytica employees want to see the recruit in action presenting a favorite topic.[29] Later in the day, the candidate is escorted to meetings with four or five employees. The next day there are meetings with two or more people. The employees who have met the candidate then meet to evaluate how the candidate would fit into the culture of Catalytica. The rituals, style, and ethical standards of the firm are known to the interviewers; Catalytica wants people who can blend with its already existing culture and make a contribution. The company operates in teams, and loners would have a difficult time contributing. Culture at Catalytica is so vital to the firm that it sets the tone for interviewing every job candidate.

Nature of the Task

Many experts believe that the task to be performed is one of the two most vital factors affecting HRM. They describe HRM as the effective matching of the nature of the task (job) with the nature of the employee performing the task.[30]

There are perhaps unlimited similarities and differences among jobs that attract or repel workers and influence the meaning of work for them. Some of the most significant are the following:

Degree of knowledge and ability to use information technology Advantages in informational and computer technology have resulted in a need for employees with the skill to use these technologies. Instead of physical lifting and moving as requirements of a task, the use of "knowledge skills" has become significant. "Knowledge workers" are now expected to plan, decide, and solve problems using databases, computer programs, and other technology-driven information sources (e.g., Internet and intranet).[31]

Degree of empowerment Empowering employees to complete job tasks means that power or authority to make relevant and meaningful decisions is delegated. In fact, the empowered worker can complete his or her job task because he or she has information, knowledge, and power.[32]

Degree of physical exertion required Contrast the job of ditch digger with that of a computer programmer. In general, most people prefer work involving minimal physical exertion. Some companies, like 3M, believe that working with the mind is better for curing productivity problems than working with the back.

Degree of environmental unpleasantness Contrast the environment of a coal miner with that of a bank teller. People generally prefer physically pleasant and safe conditions.

Physical location of work Some jobs require outside work; others, inside work. Contrast the job of a telephone craftsperson during the winter in Minnesota with that of a disk jockey. Some jobs require the employee to stay in one place. Others permit moving about. Contrast the job of an employee on an assembly line with that of a traveling sales representative. There are individual differences in preference for physical location.

Time dimension of work Some jobs require short periods of intense effort; others require long hours of less taxing work. In some jobs, such as automobile assembly, the work is continuous; in others, such as toll booth operation, it is intermittent.

Human interaction on the job Some jobs require interaction with others. Contrast the position of a radar operator in an isolated location who rarely sees anyone else with that of a receptionist in a busy city hall.

Degree of variety in the task The amount of freedom and responsibility a person has on the job determines the degree of *autonomy* provided for in the work. Contrast the autonomy of a college professor with that of an assembly-line worker.

Task identity The degree of wholeness in a job—the feeling of completing a whole job as opposed to contributing to only a portion of a job—is its *task identity*. Contrast the job of an auto assembler with that of a tax accountant.

Task differences and job design Because jobs are not created by nature, engineers and specialists can create jobs with varying attention to the characteristics described here. There are a number of approaches to those aspects of job design that affect variety, autonomy, task identity, and similar job factors. These approaches will be covered in Chapter 6.

How do these task factors affect HRM-type decisions? They obviously affect recruiting and selection, since employees will probably be more satisfied and productive if their preferences are met. As we mentioned, few jobs match all preferences exactly. With jobs that are difficult, dirty, or in smoky or hot environments, the manager must provide additional incentives (more pay, shorter hours, or priority in vacations) because few people prefer such jobs. Or the manager may try to find employees who can handle the conditions better.

Work Group

Groups play a major role in the life of an individual. You probably belong to family, friendship, and student groups. Once a person joins an organization, his or her experiences are largely influenced by a work group.

A **work group** consists of two or more people who consider themselves a group, who are interdependent with one another for the accomplishment of a purpose, and who communicate and interact with one another on a more or less continuous basis. In many cases (but not always), they work next to each other.

An effective group is one in which:

- Members function and act as a team.
- Members participate fully in group discussion.
- Group goals are clearly developed.
- Resources are adequate to accomplish group goals.
- Members furnish many useful suggestions leading to achievement of goals.

Most effective work groups are small (research indicates that 7 to 14 members is a good range), and their members have eye contact and work closely together. Effective groups also generally have stable membership, and their members have similar backgrounds. Their membership is composed of persons who depend on the group to satisfy their needs.[33]

Although the effective group supports management and the organization's goals, it can also work against them. This is usually the case when the group perceives the organization's goals as being in conflict with its own. If the work group is effective and works with management, the manager's job is easier, and objectives are more likely to be achieved. If the group is working against the manager, an effort must be made to change the group's norms and behavior by the use of the manager's leadership and the manager's power to reward discipline and by the transfer of some group members.

Work groups are directly related to the success of HRM activities. If a work group opposes HRM programs, it can ruin them. Examples of programs that can be successes or failure depending on the support or resistance they receive from work groups include incentive compensation, profit sharing, safety, and labor relations. Operational and HR managers who desire success in such programs should at least consider permitting work-group participation in designing and implementing HRM.

Leader's Style and Experience

The experience and leadership style of the operating manager or leader directly affect HRM activities because many, if not most, programs must be implemented at the work-unit level. Thus, the operating manager or leader is a crucial link in the HRM function.

Leaders must orchestrate the distinctive skills, experiences, personalities, and motives of individuals. Leaders also must facilitate the interactions that occur within work groups. In his or her role, a leader provides direction, encouragement, and authority to evoke desired behaviors.[34] In addition, leaders reinforce desirable behavior so that it is sustained and enhanced. The leader is an important source of knowledge about the tasks, the organization, and the HRM policies, programs, and goals. The experience and operating style of a leader will influence which HRM programs are communicated, implemented, and effective.

Strategic HRM: An Important Key to Success

As indicated in Chapter 1, HR managers are becoming more involved in formulating and implementing strategy in the organization. Exhibit 2-5 presents the three levels of strategy—strategic, managerial, and operational—as they apply to four specific HRM activities.

EXHIBIT 2-5   Human Resource Activities by Level

Level	Employee Selection/Placement	Rewards (Pay and Benefits)	Appraisal	Development
Strategic (long term)	Specify the characteristics of people needed to run business over long term Examine labor force trends Analyze immigration flows into the country	Establish reward program that will be competitive with domestic and international competitors Establish reward system that is linked to strategic goals	Determine the level and type of performance that are crucial for the growth of the firm Develop equitable performance criteria Link appraisal to accomplishment of long-term objectives	Plan development experiences for staff Plan development program with flexibility necessary to adjust to change
Managerial (medium term)	Make longitudinal validation of selection criteria Develop recruitment marketing plan Develop approach to build labor resource pool	Set up five-year compensation progression plans for individuals Set up cafeteria-type benefits menu Set up retirement packages	Validate systems that relate current conditions and future needs Establish assessment centers for development Use annual or more frequent appraisal system	Establish general management development program Provide for organizational development Encourage self-development
Operational (short term)	Prepare staffing plans Prepare recruitment plans Review performance of workers daily	Administer wage and salary program Administer wage and salary program Administer benefits packages	Use annual or more frequent appraisal system Use day-to-day performance review systems	Use specific job-skill training Use specific job-skill training Use on-the-job training Use Web-based training on a 24/7 basis

The efforts to formulate and implement sound HRM strategies at the three levels presented in Exhibit 2-5 are designed to achieve desirable end results such as high-quality products and services and socially responsible behavior. In other words, sound strategies are intended to result in growth, profits, and survival.

Strategic planning by an organization leads to informed, purposeful actions. By articulating a clear common vision of why the organization exists, now and in the future, a strategic plan provides direction and a cornerstone for making important HRM decisions. Planning HRM activities expands awareness of possibilities, identifies strengths and weaknesses, reveals opportunities, and points to the need to evaluate the probable impact of internal and external forces.

A well-designed organizational strategic plan permits the HR department to be better prepared to cope with changes in both the internal and the external environments presented in Exhibit 2-1. The idea of incorporating HRM activities and plans into the organization's strategic plan is not new. Each organization can adopt a specific form of strategy that best fits its goals, environment, resources, and people. Matching an organization's strategic plan, its employees' characteristics, and its HRM activities is important for achieving desirable organizational end results—competitive products and competitive services.

The days of viewing the HRM function or unit as only a highly specialized and technical staff activity are over. Human resources are vitally important to the firm's success, and the HRM function must be involved in all aspects of an organization's operation. Employees must perform at an optimal level so that the overall strategy and goals can be achieved. The HR unit must make everyday contributions to the organization. Thus, HRM programs must be comprehensive, adapted to the organization's culture, and responsive to employee needs. This means that management creativity and action must be exerted to match an organization's overall strategy with its HRM programs, activities, and talents.

Strategic Challenges Facing HRM

Surveys of HRM practitioners, researchers, and generalists and national meetings of the American Management Association, Human Resources Conference, and the Human Resource Planning Society all point to a number of strategic challenges facing the field.[35] Global competition has become so intense that HRM professionals are now being asked by their firms to optimize the skills, talents, and creativity of every employee. This strategic challenge and a number of others described here will serve to set the tone for the remainder of the book. In each case, HRM practitioners are being asked to utilize the human assets of the firm more effectively. Failure to do so will probably mean that the firm cannot compete in the globally interconnected world.

① Technology

The much heralded "information age" has arrived swiftly.[36] Its arrival has impacted jobs, the way business is conducted, and the need for more knowledge workers. The trends of the technology revolution are recognizable as the following:

1. *Growth in knowledge needs* World trade is growing over three times faster in knowledge-intensive goods and services such as biomedicine, robotics, and engineering.
2. *Shift in human competencies* Some predict that by 2015 almost all net employment growth will be in knowledge workers.
3. *Global market connection* Technology is dissolving borders and creating an interconnected marketplace.

4. *Business streamlining* Easy to use communication, electronic mail, electronic conferencing, and databases are creating instantaneous dissemination of data to make better decisions to geographically dispersed workers.

5. *Rapid response* Technology permits quick communications, which allows faster decision making. In Tokyo, Coca-Cola automatically informs distributors when inventory is low.

6. *Quicker innovation* Teams of marketing, engineering, and production personnel working in parallel with computer-provided files, data, and information develop products faster. Every stage—product conception, design, development, and manufacturing—is accredited through the use of electronic technology resources.

7. *Quality improvement* The concept of building quality into the entire process of making, marketing, and servicing is enhanced by computer monitoring systems and through robotics.

8. *Industrial Revolution* Prior to the Industrial Revolution most people worked either close to or in their homes. However, mass production technologies changed this and people began to travel to work locations or factories. Today, with increased computer technology, there is a move for many to work from their homes, or engage in what is referred to as *telework* or telecommuting. It is estimated that over 23.5 million U.S. workers now telecommute. Telecommuting raises a number of HRM issues that need to be answered, such as how will performance be monitored, how should telecommuters be rewarded, how can telecommuters be made to feel like they are part of the team, and how can telecommuters be mentored?

Diversity: Building a Competitive Workforce

There is no doubt that the American workforce is changing in dramatic ways. There is a much slower increase in the total number of Caucasian (white) workers than there are of other groups, especially Hispanic or Latino.

Two decades ago the American workforce was predominately white and male: In 2006, white males represent less than 40 percent of the workforce. One of the reasons white males no longer dominate the workforce is that women have entered the workforce in record numbers. By 2008, about 60 percent of adult American women, or almost half of the American workforce, will be female.[37]

The number of Hispanic, Asian, and older workers will continue to increase. The baby boomers (those born between 1946 and 1963), or 76 million people, are staying in the workforce longer. Meanwhile, generation X (those born between 1964 and 1981) are vying for jobs held onto by older workers. The potential conflict between these two large groups is likely to increase. According to the Bureau of Labor Statistics, by 2008 about 18 percent of the workforce will be older than 55.[38]

The changing look, age, and needs of the workforce have resulted in more concern about child care, elder care, and training in understanding diversity. High-quality day care has made it easier for women to help raise a family and also begin a productive career. Unfortunately, however, although the need for child care is obvious, only about 5 or 6 percent of employers provide day care assistance.[39]

Improved understanding of diversity (differences and similarities) also seems to be an obvious need, yet most firms fail to invest the time, resources, and energy needed to become "diversity friendly." A few success stories about diversity management are beginning to appear in the literature and serve as the best examples for practice.

- United Airlines experienced an increase in Spanish-speaking travelers when it installed a Spanish-speaking telephone reservation line.
- Avon Products had significant revenue growth after it hired African American, Hispanic American, and Asian American sales and marketing personnel.

HR Journal *Remote Workforce Doing Real Work*

Old habits die hard and many managers fail to embrace telecommuting. They still believe that commitment to working in a central and permanent location is valuable. The "surveillance type" manager thrives on being able to see employees. Telecommuting arrangements do not allow "real time," continuous management observation. In spite of some managerial resistance to telecommuting the approach is being used by more organizations each year.

Mark Dane, 53, VP of engineering and operations at HireSystems, Inc., in Waltham, Massachusetts, discusses the firm's remote workforce.

"HireSystems works with its customers to search, organize, track, and process resumes. All of that is done on the Web by more than 150 employees, 130 of whom work at home. They process 2 million resumes a year for demanding customers, such as Goldman Sachs and Microsoft. How do we tap into the flexibility of a remote workforce, while maintaining quality, efficiency, and fast turnaround? Plus, how do we organize work to meet the needs of our at-home employees, while satisfying our customers, whose demands for our services can spike dramatically and unpredictably?

"It's easy to see the benefits of a remote workforce: We don't have lots of real estate or a 'bull pen' of grumpy people sitting at workstations. We've built our company around people who can work where they want and how they want.

"What's less visible are the challenges. We have all of the problems of a big, complex data-processing center, compounded by the fact that nobody's here! There's no way to practice 'management by walking around,' no way to see whether folks are stressed.

"It's in the systems. All the work our people do is Web-based, so we use the Web as an extension of our office. While people enter data, we're tracking their work in real time. That way, we monitor the quality and accuracy of what they're doing.

"One way we monitor quality is to seed the stuff that people are processing with bad data. People know we do that, and they know that if they correct these 'test' documents, they get a bonus. Since they never know which documents are tests, they treat all their work as if it has bonus potential.

"So far, the system has been working well. After working with new people for five weeks, our turnover rate has been less than 5 percent. Our goal, over the next several years, is to process 16 million resumes annually."

The International Telework Association and Council (ITAC) estimates that 241 million employed Americans worked from home at least one day per month in 2004. The ITAC forecasts over 40 million teleworkers in the United States by 2010. The greatest number of teleworkers occurred in medium-size businesses like HireSystems.

Source: "U.S. Telework Scene: Stats and Facts," InnoVisions Canada; www.ncca/studies/US.html (June 7, 2005); Susan J. Wells (October 2001), "Making Telecommuting Work," *HRM Magazine*, pp. 34–45; Lisa Chadderhorn (September 1999), "Remote Workforce, Real Work," *Fast Company*, p. 62; and P. Coy (April 6, 1998), "Home Sweet Office," *BusinessWeek*, p. 30.

- Pillsbury Company and Kraft General Foods both recorded access to more of the African American and Hispanic American markets after increasing the number of sales and advertising professionals from these ethnic-racial groups.

Another interesting story that illustrates the positive aspects of being diversity-friendly is present in the HR Journal. The story describes the case of Aurora Archer.

An increasing number of empirically based studies are illustrating that diversity-friendly strategies can have a significant impact on end results, such as being considered socially responsible and earning a favorable return on the products and services provided to consumers.[40]

While diversity is a top corporate priority at Ford Motor Company, the real nuts-and-bolts diversity work is being carried out at the local level, within Ford's divisions. Ford's Marketing, Sales, and Service organization (MS&S), for example, has made a substantial commitment to diversity as a way to differentiate itself from its competition and in response to an increasingly diverse consumer marketplace.

MS&S has developed a strategic communication plan that enlisted senior management to lead by example and teach employees why diversity is critical to Ford's success. The first

HR Journal *A Rising Star*

Aurora knows she's lucky to have made it out of the barrios of south San Antonio and into the boardroom. She grew up amidst gangs and crushing poverty. And the job descriptions of some former high school classmates include prostitute and drug dealer.

Given the hand Aurora was dealt, it seemed unlikely that a career as a corporate executive was ever in the cards. "My way out was an education," says the self-assured mother of two. "That was cemented in my head by my parents."

Today Aurora is a rising star in the tech industry, working as director of global marketing communications for Hewlett-Packard in Houston. And she got there by working hard and seizing opportunities. For instance, prior to her employment at HP, she used her fluency in Spanish to work with a group launching subsidiaries in several Spanish-speaking countries. "I got to see the establishment of an operation from the ground up," says Aurora, who was recently named one of Houston's top women in technology by the Association for Women in Computing.

Now this bilingual star oversees communications for three different organizations that market HP products. Improving HP's efforts to reach out to its customers requires Aurora to communicate with colleagues from Latin America to Europe to Asia practically around the clock. Though the job is challenging, "it can't compare to the hardships my parents went through," she says.

Her African American father and Mexican immigrant mother toiled for years as domestic help, enduring abusive employers and working for menial wages. When Aurora and her older sister, Violeta Babic-Archer, reached their teen years, their parents decided to become live-in help, moving the family above the garage of the home where they worked in a tony San Antonio neighborhood so the girls could get a better high school education.

"My parents set the bar really high for us," says Aurora, who went on to graduate with a bachelor's degree in business from Syracuse University. "My mother used to say, 'Dime con Quien andas y te diré quien eres': Tell me who you're hanging out with and I'll tell you who you are," she recalls.

Because her responsibilities are at a worldwide level, Aurora's hours follow the sun wherever it rises. She starts her day as early as 4:00 A.M., when she's heading to the gym and trying to get some "me time." Before most people have had their first morning cup of coffee she is already dressed, showered, and sporting a wireless telephone headset as she takes conference calls from colleagues around the globe to discuss such things as project status and marketing requirements. Her laptop stays within reach as she moves from room to room, preparing her family for their day before she heads to the office.

Source: Adapted from Denise DiFulco, "How She Does It," www.workingmother.com/june05_hpstory1.html.

phase of the plan centered on five half-hour modules, each of which forms the basis of a monthly discussion led by managers and supervisors for their staff. Each module is accompanied by a video and a set of comprehensive instruction materials so that all 5,500 people in MS&S receive a consistent message from the 250 senior managers. Modules deal with such topics as leadership behaviors, tips for excelling in diverse work environments, how diverse teams function most effectively, and the role of work-life balance in diversity.[41]

To strengthen the link between diversity and the bottom line, Aetna, a global provider of health and financial services products, has put into effect a diversity stewardship structure that places responsibility for managing diversity squarely in the hands of senior line managers. At the top of this structure is Aetna's executive diversity steward, a position that rotates every two years among the presidents of Aetna's three major business units. The current diversity steward Thomas McInerney, is president of Aetna Retirement Services. "This structure means we have Aetna's chairman telling his business line presidents that they have not only business responsibility for diversity, but also a companywide responsibility," says Alfonso Martinez, vice president, diversity, and national director, Latino business development.

The Aetna Emerging Leaders Program is designed to groom the next generation of leaders by guiding participants through a rigorous multiyear development plan. One of the goals is to build wide-ranging diversity into Aetna's talent base. Candidates must have five to seven years of work experience either within Aetna or from outside; external candidates are usually recruited from MBA programs.

The program guides participants through a series of 12- to 24-month assignments in different areas of the business. According to Orlene Weyland, program director, "This program is different because it's highly individualized, and it reaches people early in their careers. Each candidate receives coaching, education, mentoring, and a career path developed from a mindful point of view."

For Emerging Leader Ricardo M. Berckemeyer, who is in his first assignment in the Aetna International unit, the program's focus on mapping a career path is key. "A lot of young people get frustrated because they don't see a clear career path or where they're going. This program gives you that advantage—it's a great motivational tool." Berckemeyer looks forward to developing a network of fellow emerging leaders who will be able to rely on one another in the future. "Ten years from now, I'll be able to pick up the phone and speak freely about the issues I'm facing and how these colleagues might help."

Addressing diversity on a global level is also critical at IBM, where the global diversity theme is "None of us is as strong as all of us." Diversity at IBM is being leveraged worldwide through a system of diversity councils and task forces.

IBM's 48 diversity councils operate in geographic areas around the world, including Latin America, Asia Pacific, Europe, and several U.S. sites. Their purpose is to advise management in their region on diversity issues.

Work-life balance is one of six global workforce challenges being addressed by IBM's Global Diversity Council. The other challenges are the global marketplace, cultural awareness/acceptance, diversity of the management team, advancement of women, and integration of people with disabilities.

Diversity-unfriendly examples still emerge, however—showing that much more needs to be done within organizations and across society. Texaco, Inc., tape-recorded a group of executives who were discussing the shredding of documents relevant to a race-discrimination lawsuit and using vulgar racial epithets while talking about African American employees. Texaco claimed that the racial remarks caught on the tape were an isolated incident, but some experts claim that racism is widespread in the oil industry. Almost as disturbing as the racial epithets—from a legal and ethical standpoint—are Texaco management's comments about withholding or shredding documents. The tapes revealed Texaco managers discussing how they would purge all accounts and documents pertaining to minority hiring practices. Such destruction of documents has become a hot topic in legal circles.

Texaco settled the race-discrimination lawsuit for $176.1 million (for the six plaintiffs).[42] In addition, as pressures from outside the firm were increased, Texaco established some ambitious hiring goals for minorities and women and pledged to increase purchases from minority firms.

Texaco in the past decade has made significant progress in hiring more minorities and women, increasing the number of African American owned gasoline stations, and increasing the number of female and male managers and executives. The company's image in the marketplace is still not as bright as before the discrimination settlement, but it is improving.[43]

Workforce diversity is a reality that influences every HRM area and issue from strategic planning to recruitment to training to health. There is a steadily growing body of empirical evidence that managing diversity is becoming a necessary part of the job responsibilities of managers. There is no one best way or best formula available with regard to managing the increasing diversity of the workforce. However, there is likely to be increased demand to find fair, ethical, and prompt ways to manage diversity.

Caliber of the Workforce

Recruiting and developing skilled labor are important for any company concerned about competitiveness, productivity, quality, and managing a diverse workforce effectively. Chemical Bank of New York reports that it has to interview 40 job applicants for every one found suitable for training as a bank teller.[44] NYNEX reports that it has had to carefully screen and test 60,000 applicants to fill 3,000 open positions. The mismatch between jobs and applicants—high-skill job demands and the lack of qualifications among job applicants—is documented in a list of reports and statistics.[45] Since a growing number of jobs will require more education and higher levels of language, math, and reasoning skills than current ones, HRM practitioners and specialists will have to communicate this to educators, parents, and community leaders. A shortage of skilled talent can damage any firm's competitive position. Strategic human resource planning models will have to carefully weigh deficiencies in skills and shortages of skills.

The **"skills gap"** must be faced not only by HRM. In fact, the entire society will have to face the consequences of not having the workforce needed to compete in the global economy. Strategic planning to reduce the skills gap in a firm's workforce, however, is a serious issue facing HRM.

Organizational Restructuring and Downsizing

The endless stream of headlines and news stories about restructuring and downsizing could fill page after page.[46] A few facts about downsizing:

1. About half of all firms downsizing end up with at least as many employees again within a few years' time.
2. Downsizing in manufacturing is nothing new and has been occurring since 1967. Manufacturing is only about 15 percent of the downsizing story. Retailing and services have been upsizing considerably for the past decade.
3. Downsizing is positively correlated with the degree of foreign competition in a sector. A logical proposition is that downsizing does encourage firms to reduce their costs.
4. Downsizing firms tend to increase their profits in the short run but not their productivity.
5. Downsizing commonly leads to lower compensation/wages within the downsizing firm.

Restructuring means changing the reporting and authority relationships within a firm. In restructuring, a layer of a firm's hierarchy may be eliminated, reporting relationships may be changed, or a new subsidiary may be created to conduct business in a new market location. **Downsizing** is a term used to designate a reduction in a company's workforce. The percentage of firms that downsize has actually decreased in the past five years (2000–2004) versus the previous five years (1995–1999). But despite the decrease in downsizing activity, it is likely that increased competition, excessive costs, and interest in improving share value will mean that downsizing will be a fact of life for thousands of firms and millions of workers for years.[47]

Downsizing has a human face in that people are laid off, friends and colleagues are given new job responsibilities, and feelings of trust and job security are threatened. The emotional impact of being laid off or of having a colleague laid off can result in stress-related health problems.[48] There is a growing sense that job security is a thing of the past. Stories and statistical data about downsizing suggest that job security has declined as layoffs spread from industry to industry. Job tenure has declined the most for employees without a high school education.[49]

Contingent Workers

There are permanent or full-time employees and another category, referred to as **contingent workers.** The category of contingent employees includes temporaries, part-timers, contract or leased workers (outsources), and other individuals who are hired to handle extra job tasks or workloads. Contingent employees are becoming a widespread part of the staffing mix of firms.

The number of contingent workers increased steadily from the early 1970s through 2004. This group is expected to grow by more than 4 percent annually for the remainder of the 1990s.[50] More than 230 million people were classified as being contingent employees at some time in 2004.[51] The industries with the highest growth rate of contingent workers are health service, residential care, retail, and data processing and computer services.

Part-timers (as the term implies) put in fewer hours than full-time employees. The part-time employee usually receives fewer fringe benefits and often has a flexible work schedule. A 20-hour workweek or less is often the regular schedule of a part-timer. The Bureau of Labor Statistics defines a full-time job as working 35 hours or more per week. There are over 90 million workers who have the following work schedules: they work full time on a primary job and also hold one or more part-time jobs; they combine several part-time jobs to make up a full-time workweek; or they combine jobs with varying hours to make up a full-time workweek.

Microsoft employs over 6,000 temporary employees. These employees are excluded from benefits and stock option plans that Microsoft's 19,000 regular U.S. workers receive. The Microsoft temps have expressed feelings of being treated as second-class citizens, which is underscored by the orange ID badges they wear versus the blue ones regular employees wear. One fear at Microsoft is that union organization efforts could gain a foothold as long as temporary employees hold feelings of being second class.

Outsourcing is the practice of hiring another firm to complete work that is important and must be done efficiently. A growing number of firms are outsourcing HRM activities. The outsource firm provides the employees to complete the job. This type of activity is also called *employee leasing.* Today there are about 2,500 professional employee organizations (PEOs). They are growing in popularity because they can save a firm money, reduce its risks, improve its efficiency, and allow it to focus on its core business operations. An estimated 2.5 million workers call PEOs their primary employer.[52]

PEOs not only provide employees but also perform a variety of human resource services, including the administration of payrolls, unemployment insurance, workers' compensation, and compliance with payroll taxes. PEOs can provide job descriptions, employee manuals, and employee assistance programs (EAPs), and administer a firm's compliance with existing laws and regulations.

Servo Corp of America, a commercial aerospace firm based in Hicksville, New York, leases all of its 58 employees from the Alcott Corp. In 1994 Servo had 250 employees and a three-person HRM staff. Then the firm sold its major product line and reduced its employees to 50. The three-person HRM department wasn't needed. In 1996 Servo leased all of its employees and HRM activities from Alcott. The firm could no longer afford to maintain its HRM unit but still needed HRM services.

The obvious question is: Are PEOs a threat to in-house HRM activities and professionals? For some small and medium-size firms, the PEO will remain an option to be cost-analyzed. PEOs today are serving primarily small firms with fewer than 50 employees. This is simply an option and is not likely to replace a majority of HRM professionals. In fact, some HRM professionals could migrate more to this type of employment, since their expertise and experience are needed. Outsourcing and employee leasing are options available to firms exploring the full-time, part-time, and contract opportunities available in staffing jobs and meeting the needs of the company.

People and the HRM Diagnostic Framework

People, the employees—the human resource element—are the most important concern in the diagnostic model. Simply putting together HRM activities without paying attention to employees' characteristics would be ill-advised. The most carefully designed and implemented HRM activity may backfire because adjustments for individual differences were not built into the program. In the Career Challenge earlier in the chapter, Martha is attempting to understand why Lenny and Harry behave differently on the job at the National Pancake House. She will discover that people differ in many characteristics. Lenny and Harry differ in their abilities, attitudes, and preferences. They also have different styles, intellectual capacities, and ways of doing the job.

Abilities of Employees

Some differences in employees affecting HRM programs are due to differences in abilities. Abilities or skills can be classified as mechanical, motor coordination, mental, or creative. According to many psychologists, some abilities are a result of genetic factors that are rarely subject to change through training. Examples of these differences are finger dexterity and response time. Other abilities, such as interpersonal skills and leadership, are more subject to change. People learn abilities at home, at school, and at work; their present inventories of abilities are at least partly a consequence of this past learning.

The importance of a manager's understanding of differences in employees' abilities is emphasized by the example of Harry at National Pancake. Does he lack the abilities to do the job? If it appears that Harry's problem is in fact ability, Martha would have at least two options. One is training, whereby Harry's aptitudes would be developed into the ability needed for the job. The other is placement, whereby Harry could be transferred to another job, such as busboy or cashier.

Do you think Harry's problem is a problem of ability?

Employees' Attitudes and Preferences

How an individual thinks, feels, and behaves with regard to work and the place of work forms an important attitude. An *attitude* is a characteristic and usually long-lasting way of thinking, feeling, and behaving toward an object, idea, person, or group of persons. A *preference* is a type of attitude that evaluates an object, idea, or person in a positive or negative way.

People are motivated by powerful emotional forces, and work provides an opportunity for the expression of both aggressive and pleasure-seeking drives. Besides offering a way to channel energy, work also provides the person with income, a justification for existence, and the opportunity to achieve self-esteem and self-worth. The amount of energy directed toward work is related to the amount directed to family, interpersonal relations, and recreation.

What kind of attitudes about work do Lenny and Harry have?

Motivation of Employees

Motivation is the set of attitudes that predisposes a person to act in a specific goal-directed way. Motivation is thus an inner state that energizes, channels, and sustains human behavior to achieve goals. *Work motivation* is concerned with those attitudes that channel a person's behavior toward work and away from recreation or other areas of life. The motivation to work is likely to change as other life activities change.

A number of theories have attempted to explain work motivation. The theories differ in their assumptions about how rational people are and about the degree to which the conscious and the unconscious mind direct behavior. Most of these theories have received some research support, but none has been overwhelmingly substantiated. At the moment, attention is focused on the importance of individual motivation in achieving organizational and individual goals.

How will knowledge of employees' motivation help a person be a more effective manager of people? As with work attitudes, a manager who can determine what the work motivations of the employees are will make more effective HRM decisions. For employees who appear to be work-oriented and motivated toward working hard, incentive compensation systems will probably lead to higher productivity and higher-quality work. Those who are consciously motivated to do a better job benefit from performance evaluation techniques such as management by objectives. Managers who can determine or predict how employees are motivated can create the work environment that will most optimally sustain the motivation.

Personality of Employees

Personality is the characteristic way a person thinks and behaves in adjusting to his or her environment. It includes the person's traits, values, motives, genetic blueprints, attitudes, emotional reactivity, abilities, self-image, and intelligence. It also includes the person's visible behavior patterns. Each employee has a unique personality. Because of this, it is highly unlikely that a single set of HRM activities or leadership approaches will be equally successful for all employees.

Behavioral scientists have found the following:

1. The employee, as a person, is both rational and intuitive—emotional in makeup and behavior. Therefore, his or her choices and behavior are a consequence of rational (conscious) and emotional (unconscious) influences. Choices are occasionally entirely influenced in one way or the other, but most behavior is influenced in both ways.
2. A person acts in response to internal inclinations and choices and environmental influences.
3. Each person is unique and acts and thinks in a certain way because of
   - The personality the person develops.
   - The abilities the person has or learns.
   - The attitudes and preferences the person has or develops.
   - The motives the person has or develops.

This section has touched briefly on some relevant concepts from the behavioral sciences that will be developed further in later chapters. Theory and research indicate that the nature of the employee has a great influence on HRM decisions. The effective manager realizes that the employee's nature is a crucial variable in HRM activities and organizational effectiveness. The implications of this knowledge of human behavior for the various HRM activities will become more obvious as we move further into this book.

Desirable End Results

As Exhibit 2-1 shows, the desired end results of sound and effective HRM are socially responsible and ethical behavior and high-quality, competitive products or services. In applying the diagnostic model, HRM must make decisions and solve problems in a way that is both socially responsible and ethically sound, while helping the firm satisfy its customers and its employees.

The theories, principles, and lessons found in this book should indicate that managing human resources is a demanding job. However, it is also an exciting challenge. As you apply the diagnostic model and learn more about HRM, reflect a moment on these comments:

> Research shows that organizational effectiveness is critically influenced by human resource (HR) management practices. Improvements in productivity, quality, and customer satisfaction do not occur simply through changes in accounting systems or technology; rather they typically depend on changes in multiple management systems. Changes in staffing, training, and compensation form an integral part of a coordinated change effort. Because HR management systems are critical drivers of behavior, they must be in alignment with other management systems. Otherwise, change efforts are met with resistance and often fail. In short, it is very difficult to improve organizational performance without paying attention to HR management. Accordingly, the HR department must be a central player in a company's competitive efforts.[53]

Now, after learning about the diagnostic model, let's find out what happened at National Pancake House 827. The conclusion of this chapter's Career Challenge on the opposite page will show you how Martha worked on the problem and solved the mystery of Harry's behavior.

Summary

The main objective of this chapter has been to introduce you to the diagnostic model to help diagnose HR problems and prescribe, implement, and evaluate solutions. This chapter also briefly reviews some concepts from the behavioral sciences to show you how they apply to HRM decisions. It further examines two other aspects of the environment of the HRM function: the physical location of the organization in a labor market and the work sector in which it is located. This book has been written on the assumption that HRM programs are more likely to be effective if the manager or specialist follows a diagnostic approach.

To summarize the major points covered in this chapter:

1. A sound HRM program can contribute to organizational end results such as socially responsible and ethical behavior and high-quality, competitive products and services.

2. The diagnostic approach suggests that before you choose an HRM program you should examine the nature of the employees, the external and internal environmental influences on the organization, and organizational factors. These factors act as moderating variables in HRM decisions, and HRM activities are influenced by them.

3. Various factors in the external environment—such as government regulations, unionization of employees, and competitive pressure—also exert strong influences on the HRM function.

4. Understanding the characteristics and composition of the labor force is important when designing an HRM program.

5. HRM has become a strategic area and is now recognized as important in creating and implementing the overall strategies of a firm. Specific strategic challenges facing both HRM and the firm include global competition, productivity and quality, workforce diversity, and the caliber of the workforce.

6. The work sector in which the organization is operating—public, private, or third—determines the complexity, strategic importance, and power of HRM as a function and the activities operating managers must implement.

7. Organizational factors—including goals, organization culture, the nature of the task, the makeup of the work group, and the leader's style and experience—must be taken into account to maximize the effectiveness of HRM.

8. An attitude is a characteristic and usually long-lasting way of thinking, feeling, and behaving. A preference is a type of attitude that evaluates an object, idea, or person in a positive or negative way.

Martha picked up her cup of coffee and thought: "Amy helped me a lot. But it's my job to figure out what to do." She wondered what factors could cause the differences between Lenny and Harry. It could be personality differences. Lenny is an outgoing person, and Harry tends to be introverted. There are some differences in abilities. Lenny is more agile. He uses his hands well. Harry seems a bit clumsier. And Lenny is more experienced—he's been on the job four years longer than Harry.

Lenny and Harry have the same leader and work group. They do the same task at the same time. The environment is the same. These factors couldn't cause the differences.

This narrows the option down to differences in motivation and attitude. Was there a good match of interests and abilities with the job? Martha decided to discuss the issues formally with Harry. Later that day, she invited Harry to have a chat with her.

Martha   Harry, this is the first chance I've had to chat with you for very long. How do you like it at National by now?

Harry   It's OK. It's a job.

Martha   Is there anything we can do to make it better than just a job for you?

Harry   Not really, jobs are jobs. They're all the same.

Martha   All of them? Did you ever have a dream about what you wanted to do?

Harry   Sure. I've always wanted to be a disk jockey, but I hated school. So I quit. Then I got married, and I'm locked in. I can go back to school and make it.

Martha   I didn't know you wanted to go back to school. I'm sure you could go to night school.

Harry   I might be ready for that now.

Martha   If I can help by scheduling you differently, let me know. People should get all the schooling they can. And who knows? You could go on to be assistant manager here—or even a disk jockey.

After talking with Martha, Harry did go back to school. His work improved, as did his willingness to be friendlier with co-workers and customers. Martha's chats became more frequent with all the employees, including Harry. Harry did graduate from high school and now is an assistant manager for National. He's very happy in his job.

What about Lenny? He's chief cook at 827. He's had several opportunities to become assistant manager, but he loves his work and has refused to be transferred. As Lenny put it, "I've found my niche. I do my job, then go to the beach. No worries. And I get to talk to lots of nice people."

What about the new cook? The pay issues had to be settled first. Martha contacted the home office, emphasizing that business had been steadily increasing at 827. When she told them that she needed more money to hire an extra cook to handle the increased business, they gave her more, but not enough to completely satisfy everyone.

Instead of hiding this fact from the rest of her employees, Martha explained the situation and asked them for their suggestions. Their solution was to help her recruit a cook with some experience, but one who would not demand so high a salary that their raises would be eliminated. All of the employees asked their friends for leads to fill the vacancy. Martha called guidance counselors at schools and the state employment service.

Within a week, Martha had hired Dan, a friend of Harry's. Lenny, Harry, and all the other employees liked him very much, and he worked out well as the third cook. Besides that, employees' satisfaction improved all around. Not only could Martha pay Dan what he expected as a beginning wage, but all the other employees got a slight increase in pay, too.

Key Terms

contingent workers, *p. 54*
diversity, *p. 45*
downsizing, *p. 54*
external environmental
influences, *p. 35*

internal environmental
influences, *p. 43*
motivation, *p. 56*
outsourcing, *p. 55*
personality, *p. 57*

productivity, *p. 37*
restructuring, *p. 54*
skills gap, *p. 54*
strategy, *p. 44*
work group, *p. 47*

Questions for Review and Discussion

1. How is the work of HR practitioners and operating managers similar to that of physicians who must conduct a diagnosis before treating a patient?
2. The productivity of the workforce is essential for the success of an organization. What HRM activities and programs can impact productivity?
3. Historically HRM activities were developed and implemented by a department or functional unit. Today, however, operating managers are in the forefront in applying and modifying HRM tools and activities. Why has the shift in application occurred?
4. What role does education play in the fastest-growing occupations?
5. Why must external environmental forces be considered in the design of an HRM program?
6. Explain the reasons why today HRM is playing an increasing role in an organization's strategy over that it did 10 years ago.
7. Why would some believe that professional employee organizations (PEOs) result in an increase in the demand for HRM professionals instead of a decrease in a demand for them?
8. Small firms, like large enterprises, must engage in developing clearly stated strategic plans. Why?
9. What are the implications for a society with an aging workforce?
10. Was Martha's leadership style at National Pancake House 827 effective? Why?

Notes

1. John M. Ivancevich and Michael T. Matteson (2002), *Organizational Behavior and Management* (Burr Ridge, IL: McGraw-Hill/Irwin), pp. 21–23.
2. Ibid.
3. U.S. Department of Labor estimates provided on telephone and in e-mail dialogue (June 1, 2005).
4. U.S. Department of Labor estimates per telephone discussion (June 7, 2005).
5. Ruth Milkman and Kim Voss (2004), *Rebuilding Labor: Organizing and Organizers in the New Union Movement* (New York: ILR Press).
6. www.blsgovdata is updated on productivity and costs continuously. See latest 2005 Productivity and Costs documents (June 9, 2005).
7. Ibid.
8. Ibid.
9. John M. Ivancevich, Peter Lorenzi, Steven Skinner, and Philip B. Crosby (1997), *Management: Quality and Competitiveness* (Burr Ridge, IL: Irwin), pp. 80–81.
10. Dail L. Fields (2002), *Taking the Measure of Work* (New York: Sage).
11. Yossi Sheffi (2005), *The Resilient Enterprise: Overcoming Vulnerability for Competitive Advantage* (Boston: MIT Press).
12. Willie E. Hopkins, Shirley A. Hopkins, and Paul Mallette (2005), *Aligning Organizational Subcultures for Competitive Advantage* (New York: Basic Books).
13. Allen I. Kraut and Abraham K. Korman (eds.) (1999), *Evolving Practices in Human Resource Management: Responses to a Changing World* (San Francisco: Jossey-Bass).
14. Ibid.
15. Paul Gollen (2005), *Strategic HRM* (Thousand Oaks, CA: Sage).
16. U.S. Bureau of Labor Statistics, Workforce Data in Tables, February 2004.
17. Ibid.
18. Ibid.

19. Ibid.

20. Ibid.

21. Frank J. Bitzer (2005), *Benefit Facts 2005* (New York: National Underwriter Co.).

22. Susan Drake, Michelle Gulman, and Sara Roberts (2005), *Light Their Fire: Using Internal Marketing to Ignite Employee Performance and Wow Your Customers* (Chicago: Dearborn Trade).

23. Gollen, op.cit.

24. Rosabeth Moss Kanter (Winter 2002), "Strategy as Improvisational Theater," *MIT Sloan Management Review,* pp. 76–82.

25. Kenneth Prewitt (Winter 2002), "Demography, Diversity, and Democracy: The 2000 Census Story," *The Brookings Review,* pp. 6–9.

26. Kim S. Cameron and Robert E. Quinn (2005), *Diagnosing and Changing Organizational Culture: Based on the Competing Values Framework* (San Francisco: Jossey-Bass).

27. Ibid.

28. Gerhard Apfelthaler, Helen J. Muller, and Robert R. Rehder (Summer 2006), "Corporate Global Culture as a Competitive Advantage: Learning from Germany and Japan in Alabama and Austria," *Journal of World Business,* pp. 108–118.

29. James L. Gibson, John M. Ivancevich, James H. Donnelly, and Robert Konopaske (2006), *Organizations: Behavior, Structure, Processes* (Burr Ridge, IL: McGraw-Hill).

30. John P. Wilson (ed.) (2005), *Human Resource Development: Learning and Training for Individuals and Organizations* (New York: Kogan Page).

31. Ray W. Coye and James A. Belohav (March 1995), "An Exploratory Analysis of Employee Participation," *Group and Organization Management,* pp. 4–17.

32. John M. Ivancevich and William Lidwell (2004), *Guidelines for Excellence in Management* (Cincinnati: Southwestern).

33. Marlene E. Turner (ed.) (2001), *Groups at Work: Theory and Research* (Mahwah, NJ: LEA).

34. For example see www.hrps.org/index.html, accessed June 9, 2005.

35. Henry C. Lucas, Jr. (1999), *Information Technology and the Productivity Paradox* (New York: Oxford University Press); and Deborah L. Duarte and Nancy Tennant Snyder (1999), *Mastering Virtual Teams* (San Francisco: Jossey-Bass).

36. U.S. Bureau of Labor, accessed June 10, 2005.

37. Peter Skerry (Winter 2002), "Beyond Sushiology: Does Diversity Work?" *The Brookings Review,* pp. 20–23.

38. Hank Karp, Connie Fuller, and Danilo Sirias (2002), *Bridging the Boomer-Xer Gap* (Palo Alto, CA: Davies-Black).

39. Michalle Mor Barak (2005), *Managing Diversity: Toward a Globally Inclusive Workplace* (Thousand Oaks, CA: Sage).

40. "Diversity: The Bottom Line" (May 3, 1999), *BusinessWeek* Diversity Insert, pp. 1–28.

41. Geoffrey Colvin (July 19, 1999), "The 50 Best Companies for Asians, Black, and Hispanics," *Fortune*, pp. 53–70.

42. Mike France and Tim Smart (November 18, 1996), "The Ugly Talk on the Texaco Tape," *BusinessWeek,* p. 58.

43. Bari-Ellen Roberts and Jack E. White (1999), *Roberts v. Texaco: A True Story of Race and Corporate America* (New York: William Morrow).

44. Allison Bruce (May 29, 2005), "Employees Are Demanding More Job Skills, Education," *Knight Ridder Tribune Business News,* p. 1.

45. Julie Brisbee (June 8, 2005), "GM Cutbacks Fuel Fears Here; 25 Thousand Layoffs Set," *Knight Ridder Tribune Business News,* p. 1.

46. Stephanie Thompson (March 7, 2005), "Kraft CEO Pledges a Faster Culture," *Crain's Chicago Business,* p. 19.

47. Carolyn Hirschman (April 2001), "The Kindest Cut," *HR Magazine.*

48. Bruce, op. cit.

49. J. Weber (January 19, 2004), "Not Just a Temporary Lift," *BusinessWeek*.

50. "The Lure of Free Agents" (January 2000), *Workplace Visions*, pp. 1–3.

51. *Contingent Employment Law Journal* (2002) (New York: REW Associates).

52. Bill Leonard (December 2001), "A Job Well Done," *HR Magazine*.

53. Richard A. Swanson and Elwood F. Holton, III (2001), *Foundations of Human Resource Development*, San Francisco: Berrett-Koehler.

EXERCISE 2-1

DISSECTING THE ARDM MODEL AND ITS APPLICATION

Objective The objective of this exercise is to have students examine in detail the main model used for studying HRM.

Set Up the Exercise

1. Each student is to individually examine the various parts of Exhibit 2-1. Note the three main parts of HRM programs: activities, people, and criteria for effectiveness.

2. Set up groups of four students each. Each student is to take one of the following hypothetical organizational types: a large manufacturing firm, a medium-size community hospital (350 beds), a government agency such as the Equal Employment Opportunity Commission, or a small mom-and-pop department store with 10 full-time and 15 part-time employees.

3. Each student is to develop an analysis of the type of environmental influences, and of the HRM activities, human characteristics, criteria, and results that pertain to his or her type of organization. Thus, each group will have four separate analyses to prepare. The analyses should use Exhibit 2-1 as the reference point.

4. Students will bring their analyses to a group meeting for discussion and to compare similarities and differences.
   a. What are the criteria used in the different organizations?
   b. What factors affect the end results?
   c. What environmental forces are important for the various organizations?

A Learning Note

This exercise will require individual and group work. It should show that the ARDM model (Exhibit 2-1) can be applied to large, medium-size, and small organizations.

Application Case 2-1

Best Buy's Approach to Outsourcing

HRM outsourcing may seem frightening for those who believe it means cutting HR jobs and authority. But one company's journey into business process outsourcing (BPO) has taken its own tack—outsourcing to reposition HR skills to support a companywide quest to achieve outstanding customer service.

In the initiative that Best Buy has undertaken with Accenture HR, its BPO partner, outsourcing can be seen not as "shipping HR away," but as incorporating it more completely as a corporate function.

Randall Ross, vice president, human resources, Best Buy (Minneapolis; www.bestbuy.com), and Diane Shelgren, COO, North America, Accenture HR Services (Chicago; www.accenturehrservices.com), described their long-term contract and how it's working.

Best Buy has more than 750 stores in the United States and Canada and more than 90,000 employees. It sells consumer electronics, personal computers, entertainment software, and appliances.

To ensure the organization's success in this highly competitive environment, Best Buy has developed a "customer-centric" corporate philosophy. Its strategy, according to Ross, is to "identify and eliminate work that takes time and focus away from connecting with and serving our customers." The organization intends to "do things quicker, smarter, at a lower cost—and with a clearer focus."

To reach its goal, Best Buy is using several tactics, including setting priorities, reallocating resources, leveraging outside expertise, forming strategic partnerships for activities that are not directly "customer facing," and developing standard change-management processes.

HRM was seen as central to the enhanced focus on employees in terms of strategic impact, cultural change, and getting the best from employees. Best Buy sought the best from HRM too, from anticipated improvement and employee contact support. The company wanted to increase its ability to deliver effective and consistent HR services, to make sure new business strategies could obtain support quickly and with flexibility, and to improve performance and service delivery through aligning technologies with business processes.

Goals for HRM services included:

- Making access to services simpler and easier via a Web portal, a customer contact center, and real-time resolution of issues.

- Using HRM technology to support "one-stop shopping" data integrity and consistency, integration of the Web site and contact center, and identification of trends, risks, and opportunities.

- Creating a transparent and seamless HRM experience for employees and managers via customized solutions, and an HRM experience that reflected Best Buy's culture.

- Implementing strong risk management through consistent guidelines and processes, case management and documentation, empowered internal HRM staff, and proactive policy development, review, and application.

To arrive at the ends described, Best Buy established an outsource service delivery option in its Minneapolis headquarters, plus limited local presence. Services to be delivered were rewards (benefits and compensation), payroll, staffing, performance management, HRM generalist support, employee relations and ethics, and HRM technology/applications management.

Best Buy chose Accenture HRM for a variety of reasons, including an existing relationship, the company's understanding of Best Buy's culture, and its ability to meet Best Buy's needs. The outsource operation assumed responsibilities for these services and part of the ranks of HRM generalists. Accenture HR also integrated third party vendor management for all contracts that fell within the scope of its responsibilities.

In the first year of the arrangement, a new service center was established in Minneapolis, and more than 100 Best Buy employees were moved to the outsource operation. The "phased in" approach to transition capabilities includes:

- The move from a "staffing" department to "talent discovery and acquisition."
- The deployment of a case-management tool for HR technology.

- The launch of a new recruitment software package.
- The creation of a new contact center for service delivery that begins operations this year.

Among the goals planned for this year are portal and benefits integration, establishment of policies, reporting, and salary administration, and compensation.

Best Buy believes it is ahead of the curve. More and more firms are outsourcing HRM activities and entire functions. One survey indicated that among large companies, 94 percent of the firms outsource at least one HRM activity or function.

The most commonly outsourced functions are:

- Outplacement—91%
- Employee assistance programs—89%
- Compensation plans—83%
- Pension plans—68%

Discussion Question

1. What is the significance of changing a title of a department from "staffing" to "talent discovery and acquisition"?
2. Why would Best Buy continue to use or drop using outsourcing services of a firm such as Accenture?
3. Would you assign total responsibility to the vendor (Accenture) for the design, implementation, and strategic direction of a HRM function? Explain.

Source: "An Outsourcing Plan That Builds on Internal HR Strengths," *HRFocus*, May 2005 and Kathy Gurchiek, "Record Growth In Outsourcing of HR Functions," *HR Magazine,* June 2005, pp. 1 and 38.

Chapter 3

Equal Employment Opportunity: Legal Aspects of Human Resource Management

Learning Objectives

After studying this chapter you should be able to:

1. **Determine** three major reasons why equal employment opportunity (EEO) programs have evolved.

2. **Describe** two major criteria used to determine EEO and affirmative action compliance or noncompliance.

3. **Explain** what is meant by the term *discrimination*.

4. **List** the enforcement agencies responsible for administering Title VII of the Civil Rights Act, Executive Order 11246, and the Americans with Disabilities Act.

5. **Outline** how an organization can implement an affirmative action program.

Internet/Web Resources

General Sites
http://www.eeoc.gov
http://www.fjc.gov/
http://www.statelocalgov.net/
http://www.uslaw.com
http://www.disability.gov

Company Sites
www.ford.com
http://www.mitsubishi-motors.co.jp/
    inter/entrance.html
http://www.dennys.com
http://www.fedex.com

Career Challenge

Hugo Gerbold, the director of human resource management at Reliable Insurance, is sitting in his office, thinking. The problem is equal employment opportunity. Reliable is a medium-size company in Milwaukee that specializes in homeowners', auto, and, to a lesser extent, life and health insurance. As is typical of firms of this type, the top-management team members are all white, are in their 50s, and have been with the firm all their careers. The composition of the workforce is as follows:

- Sales representatives—98 percent white males, the rest white females and African American males.
- Underwriters—98 percent white males, 2 percent white females. Claims agents—90 percent white males, 8 percent white females, 2 percent African American males.
- Clerical staff—90 percent white females, 10 percent African American females.
- Other administrative personnel, such as computer programmers, marketing staff, and security—95 percent white males, 5 percent white females.

Reliable is located in an area where at least 35 percent of the labor force is African American.

Hugo knows that many firms just like Reliable have been ordered to set up affirmative action plans. At a recent conference, Reliable's lawyers devoted much time to discussing the laws and recent cases. This had prompted Hugo to visit the company president, Gregory Inness.

Gregory, 64 years old and a lawyer by training, did not give Hugo much hope that things were going to change at Reliable with regard to equal employment opportunities.

It is a few days after the meeting. Hugo has just received a call from a professor at one of the local universities. The professor had encouraged Osanna Kenley to apply at Reliable for a management trainee position that had been advertised. She had been discouraged by the HRM department because, they said, she was a liberal arts major. She'd also been told there were no positions. In fact, the company had just hired a white male for a trainee position. Somehow she found out about this.

The professor informed Hugo that Osanna was going to file a complaint against the firm with the Equal Employment Opportunity Commission (EEOC). He suggested that Hugo talk with her before she went to the EEOC. In fact, she is on her way over to see Hugo right now.

Hugo and Osanna have a pleasant talk, but it is clear that she would like Reliable to be open to all applicants, even if she personally does not get a job there. He arranges to see Gregory right after Osanna leaves.

Hugo   Gregory, remember how I was just talking about equal employment opportunities? Well, we may have a case on our hands. And remember the insurance company that just paid out $15 million in back pay and had to hire its fair share of minorities as a result?

Gregory Well, maybe we should hire this young woman. That ought to take care of the problem, won't it?

Hugo   No, it won't. We'd better establish minority recruitment, retention, and promotion programs now.

Hugo then explains the legal details of recent court cases on affirmative action.

The impact of law on HRM is indicative of the development of all laws governing business and societal activities. Today it is common for patients to sue doctors and consumers to sue manufacturers of faulty products; children even sue parents for not being supportive and nurturing. In 1960, there were about 59,000 civil suits filed in United States district courts. In 2004, there were 281,338.[1]

HR Journal Test   *Are You Aware of the Law?*

Listed below are a few questions that can determine your present state of understanding of the law. Try them out now and when you complete the chapter, look them over again. The correct answers are at the end of this chapter.

Yes   No   1.   The EEO laws provide clear definitions and distinctions about what constitutes illegal discrimination.

Yes   No   2.   If an organization can prove that only *men* can carry out a job's duties (bona fide occupational qualification), it precludes someone from suing on the grounds of discrimination.

Yes   No   3.   A group of men are passing around a *Playboy* magazine that a female employee notices. She files a complaint of sexual harassment. Is her complaint acceptable?

Yes   No   4.   An employer that knowingly hires an employee who is not authorized by law can be fined.

Yes   No   5.   An employer is exempt from paying an employee such as a repair person for time spent waiting to get called—even if the time is spent reading a novel, watching television, or napping.

Yes   No   6.   An employer must accept any accommodation an employee with a serious religious belief has regarding time, date, and place of work.

Yes   No   7.   An organization in downsizing lays off more workers (they are older) with higher salaries to cut costs. This is a violation of the Age Discrimination in Employment Act.

Yes   No   8.   Requiring employees to speak only English to English-only customers is in violation of discrimination law.

Yes   No   9.   An employer *must* find reasonable accommodations for an employee who must take prescription medication to treat a disability.

Yes   No   10.   A sales clerk who makes demeaning comments about female customers to co-workers can be charged with sexual harassment.

Although suits by consumers against manufacturers of defective products account for a large proportion of the increased litigation, suits by employees or job candidates against employers are increasing rapidly.[2] Therefore, it is in the best interest of the organization for the HRM unit to develop policies and procedures that comply with the law. The best way to begin studying the relationship between HRM and the law is to devote time and attention to **equal employment opportunity (EEO).** No other regulatory area has so thoroughly affected HRM. EEO has implications for almost every activity in HRM: hiring, recruiting, training, terminating, compensating, evaluating, planning, disciplining, and collective bargaining.[3] EEO programs are implemented by employers to prevent employment discrimination in the workplace or to take remedial action to offset employment discrimination.

EEO cuts across every HRM activity, and this means that HR officials and managers in every function of the organization are involved. Top managers must get involved in EEO issues and programs to make sure that the organization complies with the law, avoids fines, and establishes a discrimination-free workplace. Operating managers must assist by changing their attitudes about protected-category employees and by helping all employees adjust to the changes EEO brings to the workplace.

The HR Journal presented above will test your initial understanding of the law and various aspects of employment. Try it now before you progress further in the chapter.

How Did EEO Emerge?

The three main factors that led to the development of EEO were (1) changes in societal values, (2) the economic status of women and minorities, and (3) the emerging role of government regulation. These are briefly discussed in this section. Regulations and laws are then discussed more fully in the remaining sections of the chapter.

Societal Values and EEO

Throughout history, Western society has accepted the principle that people should be rewarded according to the worth of their contributions. When the United States became a nation, that principle was embodied in the American dream: the idea that any individual, through hard work, could advance from the most humble origins to the highest station, according to the worth of her or his contributions. Such opportunity was everyone's birthright. To this day the American dream, with its emphasis on merit rather than privilege, is widely accepted.

Another value that has encouraged equal opportunity is the profit motive. Nondiscrimination makes good business sense. If a company gives opportunities only to white males, it cuts itself off from the vast reservoir of human talent made up of women and minorities. Moreover, it adds to such societal problems as poverty, crime, high taxes, and civic disorder, which also hurt the business community.

Until the early 1960s, it was not unusual for many people, while believing in the American dream of rewards based on merit, to also believe that African Americans (and other minorities) had their "place"—a place largely cut off from the rewards that the majority received. This apparent contradiction in beliefs was a dilemma, observed as early as in the 1940s by the distinguished Swedish economist Gunnar Myrdal in his studies for the Carnegie Corporation of race relations in the United States. African Americans were often excluded from schools, public accommodations, jobs, and voting; and economic realities for African Americans belied the ideals of the American dream.[4]

The differences between American ideals and American realities lent special significance to the civil rights conflict of the 1960s. The conflict is often said to have begun in Montgomery, Alabama, on December 1, 1955, when Rosa Parks, an African American department store worker in her 50s, was arrested for refusing to give up her bus seat to a white man. Out of that single act of protest emerged a previously unthinkable act—a bus boycott by African Americans. At the center of the boycott was a loosely knit group called the Montgomery Improvement Association, which chose as its leader a young minister who was in town, Dr. Martin Luther King, Jr.

Demonstrations, marches, and confrontations with the police captured headlines throughout the early 1960s. Reports on television included scenes of civil rights demonstrators being attacked with cattle prods, dogs, and fire hoses. These events shocked the public into recognition that infringements of civil rights were a serious social problem in the United States. Gradually, overt discrimination declined and recognition of the problems faced by minorities grew. The business community shared in this attitude change, voluntarily supporting such EEO-related efforts as the National Alliance of Businessmen.

As Congress turned its attention to civil rights, laws were passed prohibiting discrimination in education, voting, public accommodations, and the administration of federal programs, as well as discrimination in employment. The civil rights movement was instrumental in raising congressional concern and stimulating the passage of this legislation.

Economic Status of Minorities: Before 1964

Undeniable economic inequality helped focus national attention on employment as a specific area of discrimination. Unemployment figures for African Americans were twice as high as for whites, and they were higher still among nonwhite youth. While African Americans accounted for only 10 percent of the labor force, they represented 20 percent of total unemployment and nearly 30 percent of long-term unemployment. Moreover, in 1961, only one-half of African American men worked steadily at full-time jobs, as opposed to two-thirds of white men. African Americans were three times as likely as whites to work less than full time. Similar statistical differences existed for other minorities, such as Hispanics and Native Americans.[5]

The inequalities are especially striking in the income comparisons between African Americans and whites. In 1962, the average family income for African Americans was $3,000, compared with nearly $6,000 for whites. More important, the relative position of African Americans had been worsening during the preceding 10 years. Family income of African Americans was only 52 percent of family income of whites in 1962, but it had been 57 percent of whites' family income in 1952. These inequalities could not be attributed entirely to differences in education level between African Americans and whites. The average income of an African American high school graduate was lower than the average income of a white elementary school graduate.[6]

The Government

Organizations spend billions of dollars to comply with federal regulations and direct most of the duties associated with compliance to their HR departments. The growing requirements of equal employment opportunity laws constitute a large portion of human resource managers' compliance responsibilities. The growth of equal employment opportunity has given employees specific rights in their relationship with their employers. Employees' rights were not widely publicized or seen as front-page news prior to the early 1970s. Now it seems that a key story appears daily dealing with employees' rights, equal opportunity, or diversity.

Equal Employment Opportunity Laws: Content and Court Interpretations

Title VII of the 1964 Civil Rights Act[7]

Title VII of the 1964 Civil Rights Act prohibits covered entities from discriminating against employees on the basis of race, color, religion, sex, or national origin. The act prohibits discrimination with regard to any employment condition including hiring, firing, promotion, transfer, compensation, and training programs. Entities which Title VII prohibits from discriminating include private employers with 15 or more employees; labor organizations with 15 or more members; employment agencies; and federal, state, and local government employers. Title VII specifically exempts private membership clubs other than labor unions and Native American tribes from coverage. Additionally, religious organizations are allowed to base selection decisions on religion in some cases.

[handwritten margin note: exempts organizations private membership clubs]

Discrimination: Current Legal Definitions

Because Title VII and other EEO laws have not provided definitions of illegal discrimination, this task has fallen upon courts. Judges have arrived at definitions by examining the statutes' legislative history to gain insight into the social problems Congress hoped the laws would solve. For Title VII, the history of the civil rights conflict clearly identifies the problems: economic inequality and the denial of employment opportunities to minorities. In interpreting Title VII and other EEO laws, courts have held that both intentional (disparate treatment) and unintentional (disparate impact) acts of covered entities may constitute illegal employment discriminations.[8]

Disparate Treatment

Intentional discrimination labeled as **disparate treatment** occurs when employers apply different standards or treatment to different groups of employees or applicants based upon a protected category (e.g., race, color, religion, sex, national origin). In *McDonnell Douglas* v. *Green,*[9] the U.S. Supreme Court set forth a shifting burden-of-proof standard for analyzing disparate treatment cases. To prove that intentional discrimination occurred, the person filing the suit (plaintiff) must first establish a *prima facie* case proving the following four elements:

1. He or she belongs to a protected class;
2. He or she applied or was considered for a job for which he or she was qualified;
3. He or she suffered an adverse employment action (was not hired, etc.); and
4. The position remained open and the employer continued to seek applicants with qualifications similar to those of the plaintiff.

Although the *McDonnell Douglas* case dealt with employee selection, the *prima facie* elements can be modified for application to other employment contexts such as termination, discipline, and compensation. Upon establishing a *prima facie* case, a presumption of employment discrimination is created. The burden of proof then shifts to the employer (defendant) for rebuttal. The employer may satisfy its burden of proof at this stage by articulating a legitimate nondiscriminatory reason for its actions or by proving that a protected category is a **"bona fide occupational qualification" (BFOQ).** Specifically, Title VII states that organizations may hire employees based upon "religion, sex, or national origin in those certain instances where religion, sex, or national origin is a bona fide occupational qualification reasonably necessary to the normal operation of that particular business or enterprise."[10]

Courts have applied the BFOQ defense very narrowly. Supreme Court cases concerning BFOQ indicate that overall, the defense is most likely to be accepted when exclusion of a protected group relates to the ability to safely perform a job, particularly when the safety of third parties is at risk. For example, in *Dothard* v. *Rawlinson,*[11] the court held that a prison housing male sex offenders could refuse to hire female guards based upon the threat to third parties created by a possible loss of control. However, sex was not a valid BFOQ in *International Union, UAW* v. *Johnson Controls, Inc.*[12] In this case, the battery manufacturing company implemented a fetal protection policy which prohibited fertile female employees from holding positions that exposed them to lead. The court held that although lead exposure could endanger the health of a fetus that may be conceived, sex or pregnancy in this situation did not interfere with the employees' ability to perform the job.

In addition to safety, a BFOQ defense may also be upheld for customer preferences in narrow situations related to authenticity (e.g., actors, actresses, models) and privacy (bathroom attendants). Generally, however, the courts have rejected companies' claims of BFOQ due to customer preference. For example, in *Diaz* v. *Pan Am. World Airways,*[13] sex was not a valid BFOQ for the position of flight attendant. The airline offered the following rationale for excluding men from flight attendant positions:

- *Passengers' preferences* Surveys showed that passengers preferred women as flight attendants.
- *Psychological needs* A clinical psychologist testified that women, simply because they were women, could provide comfort and reassurance to passengers better than men could.
- *Feasibility* An industrial psychologist testified that sex was the best practical screening device in determining whom to hire for the position.

Disparate Impact

Disparate impact or unintentional discrimination occurs when a racially neutral employment practice has the effect of disproportionately excluding a group based upon a protected category. The Supreme Court expanded the definition of illegal discrimination in 1971 to include disparate impact in the case of *Griggs* v. *Duke Power* Co.[14] Willie Griggs was an applicant for a job as a coal handler at the Duke Power Company. Duke required coal handlers to be high school graduates and receive a satisfactory score on two aptitude tests. Griggs claimed that these requirements were unfairly discriminatory in that they resulted in a disproportionate number of African Americans being disqualified and were not related to the job. In ruling for Griggs, the Supreme Court held that Duke failed to demonstrate that the selection criteria were job-related.

The concept of disparate impact discrimination was further clarified by subsequent Supreme Court cases and was codified by Congress in the 1991 Civil Rights Act. Title VII, as amended by the 1991 Civil Rights Act, states that a disparate impact claim is established if the following conditions are met:

1. A complaining party demonstrates that a respondent uses a particular employment practice that causes a disparate impact on the basis of race, color, religion, sex, or national origin; and either

2. The respondent fails to demonstrate that the challenged practice is job related for the position in question and consistent with business necessity; or

3. The respondent refuses to adopt an alternative employment practice.[15]

To demonstrate disparate impact under condition (1) above, a plaintiff must identify a specific employment practice when possible to separate the employer's practices, and show that it results in a significantly higher percentage of a protected group in the available population being rejected for employment, placement, or promotion. One method of evaluating whether such a disparity exists is called the **four-fifths rule.**[16] This rule states that discrimination typically occurs if the selection rate for one group is less than 80 percent of the selection rate for another group. Thus to avoid adverse impact, if 20 out of 100 white applicants were selected, at least 16 (4/5, or 80 percent of 20) nonwhite applicants should be selected.

If a plaintiff proves that a disparate impact exists, an organization may then defend its employment practices by showing validation or business necessity. The EEOC's Uniform Guidelines on Employee Selection Procedures provides a detailed description of test validation. Specific validation methods are discussed further in Chapter 8. If the defendant successfully demonstrates business necessity, the plaintiff may prevail by proving that the defendant refused to adopt an alternative practice. This condition was introduced by the Supreme Court in *Albermarle Paper Co.* v. *Moody,*[17] stating that a plaintiff may demonstrate that an employer's test is a pretext for discrimination by showing "that other tests or selection devices, without a similarly undesirable racial effect, would also serve the employer's legitimate interest in efficient and trustworthy workmanship."[18] The Supreme Court noted in *Watson* v. *Fort Worth Bank and Trust*[19] that cost, burdens, and effectiveness are factors that may be used to evaluate alternative practices.

Retaliation

Title VII as well as other federal legislation including the Age Discrimination in Employment Act (ADEA), the Americans with Disabilities Act (ADA), and the Equal Pay Act (EPA) prohibit **retaliation** against employees who oppose discriminatory practices or participate in a protected investigation, proceeding, or hearing. Retaliation claims filed with the EEOC have risen significantly over the past decade increasing from 7,900 in 1991 to over 22,000 in 2004.[20] These claims can be quite costly since employees may seek compensatory and punitive damages for organizations' retaliatory actions. The EEOC recently issued guidance in a compliance manual which outlines the three essential elements of a retaliation claim: protected employee activity, adverse action by an organization, and a causal connection between the protected activity and adverse action.[21]

Employee activities that are considered protected include opposition to discrimination and participation in a protected proceeding. Opposition is protected if the employee's manner of opposition is reasonable and if the employee has a reasonable good faith belief that the opposed employment practice was discriminatory. According to the EEOC, the following are examples of protected opposition:

- Threatening to file a charge or other formal complaint alleging discrimination;
- Complaining to anyone about alleged discrimination against oneself or others;
- Refusing to obey an order because of a reasonable belief that it is discriminatory; and
- Requesting a reasonable accommodation for a disability or religion.

Protected participation activities include "filing a charge, testifying, assisting, or participating in any manner in an investigation, proceeding, or hearing"[22] under Title VII, ADEA, ADA, and EPA. These activities are protected regardless of whether underlying discrimination claims are valid. Notably, employees are protected against retaliation for participation activities involving claims against current as well as former employers.

Adverse employment actions which may be considered retaliatory include termination, denial of promotion, denial of job benefits, refusal to hire, demotion, suspension, threats, reprimands, negative evaluations, harassment, and limiting access to internal complaint or grievance procedures. In 1997, the Supreme Court ruled that employers are also prohibited from engaging in postemployment retaliation such as providing negative job references with retaliatory motives.[23]

Both direct and circumstantial evidence may be used to prove that a causal connection exists between adverse employment actions and protected employee activities. Direct evidence typically consists of written or oral statements expressing a retaliatory motive. Circumstantially, a causal connection may be inferred if "the adverse action occurred shortly after the protected activity, and the person who undertook the adverse action was aware of the complainant's protected activity before taking the action."[24]

Title VII and Sexual Harassment

The well-publicized sexual harassment allegations made by Anita Hill against Clarence Thomas during Thomas's Supreme Court nomination hearings and sexual harassment charges by a female naval officer against the Tailhook Association caught the attention of the nation in the early 1990s. Enforcement statistics provided by the EEOC indicate that since this time, sexual harassment claims filed with the agency have steadily increased, rising from 10,532 in 1992 to 13,136 in 2004.[25] In pursuing sexual harassment claims, the EEOC has recently reached some high-profile multi-million-dollar settlements. In 1999, Ford Motor Company agreed to pay $7.5 million to compensate women subjected to sexual harassment at two of its Chicago plants. In the largest sexual harassment settlement to date, Mitsubishi Motors agreed to pay $34 million in 1998 to women who were harassed at Mitsubishi's Normal, Illinois, plant.[26]

Sexual harassment is considered a form of sex discrimination under Title VII of the Civil Rights Act of 1964 and is actionable when it occurs between same as well as opposite sex individuals. There are two forms of sexual harassment, *quid pro quo* and *hostile work environment*. Quid pro quo harassment is the exchange of sexual favors for job benefits (e.g., the promise of a salary increase for a private dinner date), while hostile work environment is the creation of an offensive working environment.

Quid Pro Quo

According to the EEOC, employers are always liable for quid pro quo sexual harassment because a supervisor's acts involving tangible job detriments are viewed as acts of the employer.[27] The following five elements, provided in *Pease* v. *Alford Photo Industries, Inc.,*[28] must exist for the plaintiff to successfully prove quid pro quo harassment:

1. Plaintiff is a member of a protected class;
2. Plaintiff was subjected to unwelcome sexual harassment in the form of sexual advances or requests for sexual favors from a supervisor or individual with authority over the plaintiff;
3. Harassment complained of was based on sex;
4. Submission to the unwelcome advances was an express or implied condition for receiving some form of job benefits, or refusal to submit to sexual demands resulted in a tangible job detriment; and
5. Employer knew or should have known of the harassment.

Hostile Work Environment

Hostile work environment as a form of sexual harassment was first recognized by the U.S. Supreme Court in the case of *Meritor Savings Bank* v. *Vinson.*[29] In this case, the Supreme Court held that Title VII does not require a tangible job detriment for sexual harassment to be actionable, stating that unwelcome conduct constituting hostile work environment harassment must be "sufficiently severe or pervasive to alter the conditions of the victim's employment and create an abusive working environment." Examples of such conduct may include making sexually oriented jokes or comments, displaying sexually oriented calendars or posters, and touching of a sexual nature.

The distinction between hostile work environment and quid pro quo sexual harassment is important for determining employer liability. Employers can be liable for hostile work environment harassment caused by a supervisor, other employees, or third parties (e.g., customers and vendors) if the employer knew or should have known of the harassing conduct and failed to take appropriate corrective action.[30] Generally, an employer may fulfill its duty to prevent or remedy hostile work environment harassment by developing an antiharassment policy, promptly and thoroughly investigating harassment allegations, and properly disciplining offenders.[31]

Recent Developments

Recent U.S. Supreme Court decisions have highlighted the importance of effective human resource policies prohibiting sexual harassment in the workplace. Employers must be concerned about and take appropriate action against sexual harassment. In the cases of *Faragher* v. *City of Boca Raton* and *Burlington Industries* v. *Ellerth,*[32] both decided in 1998, the Supreme Court held that employers are vicariously liable for sexual harassment by a supervisor who has authority over the harassed employee. The court also established the following two-part affirmative defense that employers may assert if the harassment resulted in no tangible loss: (a) the employer exercised reasonable care to prevent and correct promptly any sexually harassing behavior, and (b) the plaintiff employee unreasonably failed to take advantage of any preventive or corrective opportunities provided by the employer or to avoid harm otherwise. This defense is not available to employers if the employee failed to complain due to a reasonable fear of retaliation.

In light of these decisions, it is now critical for organizations to update and strengthen their antiharassment policies to include the following components:

- Specific definitions and prohibition of sexual harassment.
- Strong prohibitions of retaliation for reporting allegations of harassment.

- Multiple channels for making complaints.
- Assurances of prompt investigations and appropriate remedial actions.
- Provisions for confidentiality and privacy.[33]

Title VII and Pregnancy Discrimination

The **Pregnancy Discrimination Act of 1978**[34] amended Title VII to protect pregnant women from employment discrimination. The act prohibits employers from discrimination in providing benefits such as vacation time, sick leave, and health insurance. Employers must allow women to work until their pregnancy results in physical disability that interferes with their job performance and is the same level of disability that would cause workers with other medical problems to have to stop working. Employers must also allow employees to return to work after childbirth on the same basis as for other disabilities.

Title VII and Religious Minorities

The number of religious discrimination cases filed with the EEOC has been increasing in recent years. In 2004 alone, the agency received 2,466 religion-based claims and resolved 85,000 claims in its caseload.[35] The focus of religious discrimination cases has been on hours of work and working conditions. The cases largely concern employers telling employees to work on days or at times that conflict with their religious beliefs—at regular times or on overtime. For example, employees who are Orthodox Jews, Seventh Day Adventists, or members of the Worldwide Church of God cannot work from sunset Friday through sundown Saturday. Although it is still lower than it was in the 1950s, religious participation has been steadily increasing since 1987, and policies on religion in the workplace are becoming quite common.

Wal-Mart reached a settlement with an employee who claimed that he was forced to quit his job after refusing to work on Sunday, his Sabbath.[36] The case settlement was startling in that Wal-Mart agreed to:

- Provide training on discrimination at a meeting of all Wal-Mart managers and give managers a handout that specifically addressed religious discrimination.
- Send 30 to 40 regional trainers into Wal-Mart stores to train assistant managers, support-team managers, and hourly supervisors on discrimination laws and employees' rights to have their religious beliefs reasonably accommodated.
- Prepare a training manual on the topic of scheduling and staffing to be used in the company's computer-based learning program.

The change in attitudes about Arab Americans and Muslims post–September 11, 2001, is pointed out in the HR Journal.

Title VII and "English-Only" Rules

A rising number of organizations are implementing "English-only" rules, requiring employees to exclusively speak English in the workplace. Organizations supporting English-only rules claim that they are needed to promote harmony among employees, effective communication and supervision, and safe working conditions.[37] When applied too broadly, however, these rules create controversy among employees and may result in claims of disparate impact national origin discrimination.

The EEOC's Guidelines on Discrimination Because of National Origin presume that English-only rules violate Title VII unless justified by a business necessity such as safety considerations.[38] Federal courts, however, have not consistently adopted this perspective. In *Garcia* v. *Gloor*[39] the Fifth Circuit upheld an English-only rule which applied to bilingual employees and allowed exceptions for employee breaks and communications with

HR Journal   *Arab Americans and Harassment*

Mohamed claims that his dismissal was the result of profiling a Muslim who happens to have the same first name as the most wanted man in the world. Arab Americans are increasingly filing complaints about alleged harassment and discrimination. Since the tragedies of September 11, 2001, there has been an uneasiness and a heightened wariness of anyone who is or appears to be Arab or Muslim.

Targeted Arabs and Muslims are claiming that employee possessions are being examined. Employers claim they have a responsibility to know who is working for them. Many in the Arab American communities believe that companies are now being too careful.

The bulk of Arab American and Muslim discrimination charges are based on:

- Being dismissed after being questioned.
- Not being accommodated for daily prayer and foot-washing rituals.
- Bans on turbans and head scarves.
- Religious and racial slurs by co-workers on the job.

Some of these complaints have turned into lawsuits as employers and the country deal with post–September 11 attitudes, emotions, and caution.

One police official, a tactical officer with the Chicago Police Department, has sued for discrimination. Nail Majid filed the lawsuit claiming his superior participated in harassment or turned a blind eye when it occurred. He claims he faced offensive and intimidating stories about Arabs on a daily basis. Fellow officers made fun of his religious practices, his holidays, the food he ate, the way his name was pronounced, and the fact that he could speak Arabic.

Majid's attorney said the nation has addressed issues of discrimination against blacks, Hispanics, and women. Since 9/11, he said, Arabs have become the primary target.

Those who track Muslims and Arab Americans in law enforcement say the kind of case brought by Majid is an isolated incident. There is no evidence of a pattern of or widespread discrimination against officers in U.S. police stations.

Source: "Town Hall Brings Arab Americans and FBI Officials Together" (April 8, 2005), Arab Institute, www.aaiusa.org/townhall0404.htm, accessed June 10, 2005; Frances & Donnelly (November 3, 2003), "Metro Arabs, Muslims Suffer Harassment, Hatred," *Detroit News;* Michelle Conlin (December 3, 2001), "Taking Precautions—or Harassing Workers?" *BusinessWeek,* p. 84.

Spanish-speaking customers. The Ninth Circuit reached a similar decision in *Garcia* v. *Spun Steak.*[40] Spun Steak implemented an English-only rule after some workers complained that they were being harassed and insulted in a language they could not understand. The rule allowed bilingual employees to speak Spanish during breaks and lunch periods but urged them not to use their fluency in other languages to humiliate co-workers. The court upheld Spun Steak's rule, finding that the plaintiffs, whose spoken language was a matter of choice, were unable to prove a disparate impact on the terms, conditions, or privileges of employment of a protected class.

Civil Rights Act of 1991[41]

On November 21, 1991, the **Civil Rights Act of 1991** (CRA 1991) became law, amending Title VII. The legislative history of the act indicated that Congress wished to provide additional remedies to deter harassment and intentional employment discrimination, to codify some disparate impact discrimination concepts, and to expand the scope of existing EEO statutes. The major provisions of CRA 1991 are summarized below:

- Allows plaintiffs to seek compensatory and punitive damages when an organization engages in intentional discrimination with malice or reckless indifference.
- Allows plaintiffs to demand a jury trial for claims involving intentional discrimination.

- Codified disparate impact concepts in accordance with the law prior to *Wards Cove Packing* Co. v. *Antonio*,[42] reversing the Supreme Court's decision in that case.
- Prohibited adjusting test scores or using different cutoff scores on the basis of a protected category.
- Clarified the concept of mixed motive in disparate treatment cases, stating that when a plaintiff proves intentional discrimination but the respondent proves that it would have taken the same action for a legitimate reason, the plaintiff may recover only declaratory and injunctive relief, and attorney's fees.
- Extended the coverage of Title VII and the ADA to U.S. citizens employed by covered entities operating in foreign countries.
- Charged the EEOC with the tasks of providing technical assistance training, education, and outreach.
- Expanded the coverage of Title VII to the House of Representatives and agencies of the legislative branch.
- Encouraged the use of alternative dispute resolution including negotiation, facilitation, mediation, fact-finding minitrials, and arbitration to resolve employment discrimination disputes.

Executive Order 11246 (1965)[43]

Executive Order 11246, issued by President Lyndon B. Johnson in 1965, prohibits employment discrimination on the basis of race, color, religion, sex, or national origin by federal contractors, subcontractors, and federally assisted construction contracts. While Executive Order 11246 prohibits the same actions as Title VII does, it carries the additional requirement that contractors must develop a written plan of affirmative action and establish numerical goals and timetables to achieve integration and equal opportunity.

Equal Pay Act of 1963[44]

Congress passed the **Equal Pay Act** (EPA) as an amendment to the Fair Labor Standards Act to eliminate wage differentials between men and women performing the same work in organizations. The EPA states:

> No employer having employees subject to any provisions of this section shall discriminate, within any establishment in which such employees are employed, between employees on the basis of sex by paying wages to employees in such establishment at a rate less than the rate at which he pays wages to employees of the opposite sex in such establishment for equal work on jobs the performance of which requires equal skill, effort, and responsibility, and which are performed under similar working conditions, except where such payment is made pursuant to (i) a seniority system; (ii) a merit system; (iii) a system which measures earnings by quantity or quality of production; or (iv) a differential based on any other factor other than sex.

Age Discrimination in Employment Act of 1967 (ADEA)[45]

The ADEA protects individuals 40 years of age and older from employment discrimination based upon their age. In 2004, EEOC received 17,837 charges of age discrimination, resolved 15,792 cases, and recovered $60 million in monetary benefits for charging parties. The act covers the actions of private employers with 20 or more employees, employment agencies, labor organizations with at least 25 members, as well as federal, state, and local governments. As in Title VII, Native American tribes are exempt from coverage. Proving disparate treatment claims of age discrimination parallels the process described for Title VII claims. However, some courts have recently held that disparate impact claims for age discrimination are not available under the ADEA.[46]

Reductions in force (RIFs) associated with organizational downsizing have emerged as a major issue in age discrimination cases. Financial concerns underlying downsizing tend to result in the termination of higher paid employees who often are the more experienced, older workers. Plaintiffs may defend the termination of protected employees with legitimate reasons other than age such as performance. However, employees may overcome this defense by demonstrating that the stated reason was a pretext for discrimination. This was displayed in the case of *Brown* v. *Delaware and Hudson Railway Co.*[47]

Delaware and Hudson Railway Co. was sold to Canadian Pacific Railroad, at which time the plaintiffs were terminated. A month later, Canadian Pacific set up a sales and marketing department and hired nine people, all of whom were younger than the plaintiffs. Four months later, Delaware and Hudson bought the company back, kept the sales and marketing unit, and did not hire any of the plaintiffs. The court ruled that age discrimination had occurred because:

- The railroad hired younger, less experienced workers with qualifications that were not superior to those of the plaintiffs.
- The railroad did not consider any of the plaintiffs for the new department, despite the company's knowledge that the plaintiffs had training and experience in sales and marketing.
- Canadian Pacific never reviewed the plaintiffs' resumes, because of their ages.
- Canadian Pacific did not offer a job in the sales and marketing department to anyone over the age of 50.
- The plaintiffs' ages were discussed at company meetings prior to their termination.

A number of barriers face older workers in many organizations. Some are a matter of company economics, others a matter of management attitudes and stereotypes.[48] The economic reasons include the added expense of funding pensions for older workers and the increased premiums necessary for health and life insurance plans. The attitude problems are more difficult to pin down. Perhaps some managers feel that older workers lose their faculties, becoming less effective on the job. There are, however, advantages to hiring older workers: lower turnover, greater consciousness of safety, longer work experience, more maturity, and more loyalty to the enterprises.[49] McDonald's capitalizes on these advantages and actively recruits older workers. The firm decided to permit older workers to proceed at their own pace, provide them with experts they can consult with, and then get out of their way and let them work.[50] McDonald's is very satisfied with their older workers' productivity, attendance, and attitudes.

Americans with Disabilities Act of 1990 (ADA)[51]

The legislative history of the ADA indicates that prior to its passage, over 43 million Americans had one or more physical or mental disabilities and that the number of Americans with disabilities would increase as our population aged. Findings of Congress further indicated that society had historically isolated the disabled and that individuals with disabilities continue to experience discrimination, often without legal recourse. Title I of the ADA was passed to protect individuals with disabilities from discrimination in the workplace.

Covered Entities and Protected Individuals

The ADA prohibits discrimination against qualified individuals with disabilities on the basis of those disabilities "in regard to job application procedures, the hiring, advancement, or discharge of employees, employee compensation, job training, and other terms, conditions, and privileges of employment" by private sector employers with 15 or more employees, state and local government employers, and the U.S. Congress. Additional requirements for federal government employers as well as contractors with federal contracts exceeding 2,500 are contained in the **Rehabilitation Act of 1973,**[52] which was the first major piece of federal legislation prohibiting disability discrimination. Both the Rehabilitation Act and the ADA define an individual with a disability as someone who:

1. Has a physical or mental impairment that substantially limits one or more of the major life activities;

2. Has a record of such an impairment; or

3. Is regarded as having such an impairment.

Examples of physical impairments which courts have considered to be disabilities are visual and hearing impairments, cancer, and HIV/AIDS.[53] Mental impairments may include major depression, bipolar disorder, anxiety disorders, schizophrenia, and personality disorders.[54]

Reasonable Accommodations

The ADA states that employers must make reasonable accommodations for the known disabilities of a qualified individual with a disability. A qualified individual with a disability is an individual with a disability who, with or without reasonable accommodation, can perform the essential functions of a job. Organizations are not required to make disability accommodations if doing so would create undue hardship for the employer.

According to the act, reasonable accommodations may include making existing facilities accessible, restructuring jobs, modifying work schedules, reassigning employees, and providing readers or interpreters. Research indicates that more than 50 percent of these accommodations may cost employers virtually nothing while about 30 percent may cost less than $500.[55] The cost of providing accommodations is one factor in making individualized determinations regarding whether an undue hardship exists. Other factors include financial resources of the facility and of the employer, number of employees, effects of expenses and resources, the impact of accommodations on operations, and type of operation of the employer including the composition, structure, and functions of the workforce.

Ongoing Developments

The issue of who is considered disabled under the ADA was recently addressed by the U.S. Supreme Court, which reviewed three cases involving correctable conditions. Overall, these three cases, each decided by the Supreme Court on June 22, 1999, narrowed the definition of a disability under the ADA by excluding correctable conditions such as visual impairments and high blood pressure. In *Sutton et al.* v. *United Airlines,*[56] twin sisters were rejected as commercial airline pilots because they failed to meet a minimum uncorrected vision requirement. The Supreme Court upheld lower court rulings and held that the sisters were not disabled under the ADA because their visual impairments could be fully corrected. Similarly, in the case of *Albertsons, Inc.* v. *Kirkingburg,*[57] a truck driver was discharged for failing to meet the Department of Transportation's (DOT) vision standards for commercial truck drivers. The Supreme Court ruled that because the employee's brain had subconsciously compensated for his visual impairment, he did not suffer from an impairment that substantially limited his ability to perform a major life activity. In another case involving DOT standards, a mechanic was discharged when the company learned that the employee's blood pressure exceeded minimum health certification requirements. The Supreme Court ruled in *Murphy* v. *United Parcel Service Inc.*[58] that the employee was not disabled under the ADA because, when medicated, his hypertension did not substantially limit a major life activity. Lower courts which must now apply these rulings to subsequent cases are beginning to address questions regarding the amount of control provided by corrective measures. The issue of whether corrective measures must fully control an impairment to preclude ADA coverage remains unclear.[59]

State Laws

Virtually every state also has some form of equal employment law.[60] In 41 states, plus the District of Columbia and Puerto Rico, there are comprehensive "fair employment" laws similar to Title VII. In fact, some of these state laws antedate Title VII. If a state's law is strong enough, charges of discrimination brought under Title VII are turned over by the federal government to the state fair employment practices agency, which has the first chance at investigating.

Enforcing the Law

Most laws regarding discrimination in employment provide enforcement agencies that issue the regulations that affect HR administrators directly. The units of government most responsible for enforcing the regulations considered in this chapter are the U.S. **Equal Employment Opportunity Commission (EEOC),** which enforces Title VII, the Civil Rights Act of 1991, the Equal Pay Act, the Age Discrimination in Employment Act, and the Americans with Disabilities Act; and the Office of Federal Contract Compliance Programs (OFCCP), which enforces Executive Order 11246. Federal courts play the role of enforcing and interpreting EEO laws.

Equal Employment Opportunity Commission (EEOC)[61]

Title VII originally gave EEOC the rather limited powers of resolving charges of discrimination and interpreting the meaning of Title VII. Later, in 1972, Congress gave EEOC the power to bring lawsuits against employers in the federal courts, but the agency still does not have the power to issue directly enforceable orders, as many other federal agencies have. Thus, EEOC cannot order an employer to discontinue a discriminatory practice, nor can it direct an employer to give back pay to victims of discrimination. However, the EEOC has won on these issues in out-of-court settlements, and it has made effective use of the limited powers it does have.

EEOC has the power to:

1. Require employers to report employment statistics. Typically, they do so by completing a form called EEO-1 each year (see Exhibit 3-1).
2. Process charges of discrimination, as follows:
   - Preinvestigation division interviews the complainants.
   - Investigation division collects facts from all parties concerned.
   - If there seems to be substance to the charge, the EEOC tries to work out an out-of-court settlement through conciliation.
   - If conciliation fails, the EEOC can sue the employer.

The complaint processing steps involving the EEOC are presented in Exhibit 3-1. The specific steps in the process must occur within the following time limit: Any person has 180 days from the occurrences of the discriminatory act to file a charge with the EEOC or with the state or local EEO agency.

Is the EEOC effective? In its fiscal year 2001, the EEOC resolved 90,106 claims in its caseload, received 80,840 new charges, filed 431 lawsuits, and won $247.8 million in monetary benefits for charging parties.[62] However, a substantial backlog of cases remains. The agency has recently implemented a mediation program as an alternative to

EXHIBIT 3-1
EEOC Complaint Steps and Actions

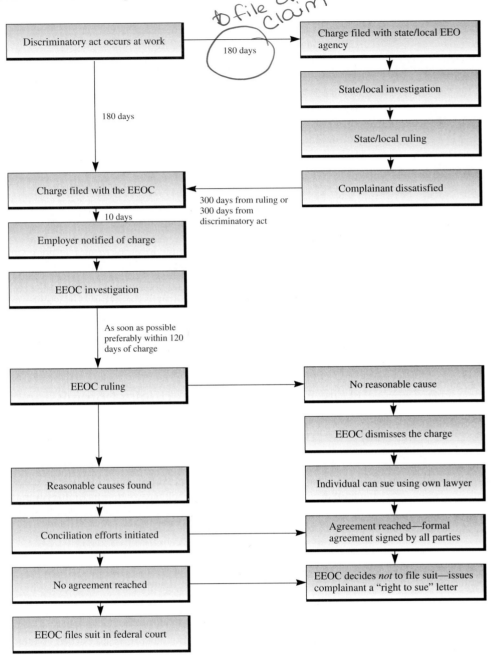

the more time-consuming traditional investigative process.[63] The mediation program began in 1991 with a pilot test in the agency's Philadelphia, New Orleans, Houston, and Washington field offices. The success of this pilot program led to the establishment of an Alternative Dispute Resolution (ADR) task force which recommended full implementation of the program in 1994. Today, each district office has a mediation program in place which utilizes a combination of both internal and external mediation.

The Courts

Besides federal and state agencies, the courts are constantly interpreting the laws, and rulings sometimes conflict.[64] Appellate courts then reconcile any conflicts. All the employment

EXHIBIT 3-2
Legal Courses for Complaints against an Employer's HRM Policies

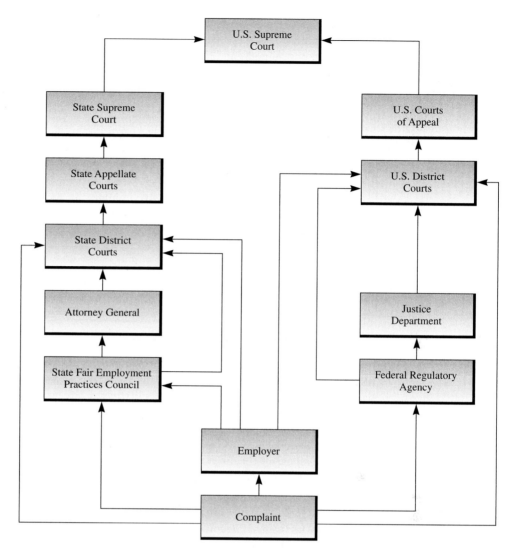

discrimination laws provide for court enforcement, often as a last resort if agency enforcement fails. With regard to Title VII, the federal courts are frequently involved in two ways: settling disputes between the EEOC and employers over such things as access to company records, and deciding the merits of discrimination charges when out-of-court conciliation efforts fail. The possible legal routes for complaints against an employer's HRM activities are presented in Exhibit 3-2.

With regard to enforcement by the courts, legal maneuvering often makes the picture confusing, largely because every step of the process can be appealed. And with three parties involved—the EEOC, the plaintiff, and the defendant—appeals are commonplace. All these possibilities for trial, appeal, retrial, and even appeal of the retrial can cause several years' delay before an issue is settled. When that delay is added to the delay created by EEOC's processing of the charge, the result is discouraging to the parties involved.

Once a final court decision is reached in a Title VII case, it can provide drastic remedies: back pay, hiring quotas, reinstatement of employees, immediate promotion of employees, abolition of testing programs, or creation of special recruitment or training programs.[65] In a class action suit against Georgia Power Company that sought back pay and jobs for

African American employees and applicants, the court ordered the company to set aside $1.75 million for back pay and another $388,925 for other purposes. Moreover, the court imposed numerical goals and timetables for employment of African Americans in various job classes. If Georgia Power failed to meet the goals, then the court order provided for mandatory hiring ratios: One African American was to be hired for each white until the goal percentages were reached. Other courts have ordered companies to give employees seniority credit for the time they have been discriminatorily denied employment.[66]

Many court orders are not so drastic, however. Much depends, of course, on the facts surrounding the case. One important factor is whether the employer is making any voluntary efforts to comply with antidiscrimination laws. If the company shows evidence of successfully pursuing an affirmative action plan, the court may decide to impose less stringent measures. The proper implementation of voluntary as well as involuntary affirmative action plans is discussed further in the next section of the chapter.

Affirmative Action in Organizations

What Is Affirmative Action?

Affirmative action has been defined as "those actions appropriate to overcome the effects of past or present practices, policies, or other barriers to equal employment opportunity."[67] The most controversial interpretation of affirmative action is that it grants special treatment to some individuals to the detriment of others. The legality of special treatment depends in part on whether the affirmative action is involuntary (mandated by law or court-ordered) or voluntary. As previously discussed, any employer having a contract with the federal government of at least $50,000 and employing at least 50 individuals must have an affirmative action plan (AAP) in writing. Although not all employers are required to have an AAP, some have elected to implement affirmative action as an indication of being a socially responsible business. By having an AAP, the organization suggests to the public and the courts that it is attempting to deal with discrimination.

Voluntary Affirmative Action Plans

In the case of *United Steelworkers of America* v. *Weber* (1979),[68] the Supreme Court addressed the use of affirmative action in training program admissions and held that Title VII does allow organizations to implement voluntary AAPs. The permissible characteristics of voluntary plans were further clarified by the court in *Johnson v. Transportation Agency* (1987).[69] In this case, the defendant promoted Diane Joyce to the position of road dispatcher even though a male candidate, Paul Johnson, received higher ratings by a panel of interviewers. The court upheld the defendant's voluntary AAP, which played a role in Ms. Joyce's promotion because of an absence of women in road dispatcher positions. The Supreme Court's decisions in these two cases established the following criteria necessary for lawful voluntary AAPs in organizations:

- The AAP must exist to eliminate past imbalances based upon a protected group category.
- The AAP must not unnecessarily trammel the rights of the majority.
- The plan must be temporary.
- The plan must not provide for set-aside positions.

Involuntary Affirmative Action Plans

The OFCCP issued Revised Order No. 4, which suggests the format and parts of an AAP. The following steps are an integral part of an affirmative action plan.

HR Journal   *Denny's: A Firm Changing Its Spots?*

In 1993, Denny's settled a federal suit for discriminating against African American customers in California. By 1995, Denny's had paid $54 million to 295,000 aggrieved customers and their lawyers. After the settlement Denny's practiced aggressive affirmative action and was becoming a model of a multiculturally sensitive leader in diversity management. In 1996, minorities held 20 percent of the jobs below vice president, and by the end of 1998, there were 126 African American owned restaurants, versus only one in 1993.

Upon arriving at the firm, Denny's CEO Jim Adamson declared that he was "going to do everything possible to provide better jobs for women and minorities." He added, "And I will fire you if you discriminate." Adamson devised a four-part strategy to implant cultural diversity.

1. He loosened up the corporate culture.
2. He made diversity a performance criterion for all managers.
3. He required the entire Denny's staff to attend workshops on racial sensitivity.
4. He continually spoke about and promoted diversity.

Nelson Marchioli, Denny's CEO in 2003, stated that "we take claims of discrimination very seriously at Denny's. We long ago adopted a zero tolerance approach to such incidents. If we find that any allegation of discrimination has merit, we take swift and forceful action."

Denny's continues to put a public face on its affirmative action efforts. Newspaper ads and other print promotions depicting customers or employees were required to feature a minimum of 30 percent African American or other "identifiable" nonwhite persons.

In January 1999, Denny's parent company Advantica Restaurant Group, Inc., announced its upcoming $2 million television campaign promoting racial diversity. On the same day of the announcement, a group of 17 Hispanic customers and 1 white customer filed a lawsuit alleging that they were discriminated against at a Denny's restaurant in Santa Clara County. Also in 1999, a court awarded $300 in damages to each of six African American and three white prison guards who were told by a Denny's manager in a Miami restaurant that they did not "look right together." Denny's executives continued to respond in 2005 by emphasizing the company's zero tolerance for discrimination and promising appropriate remedial action upon proof of discrimination.

Ray Hood has been Denny's chief diversity officer for over a decade and he continually, aggressively challenges any accusations that are presented. Some believe that, after a poor start, Denny's continues to make strides in becoming a leader in addressing discrimination problems.

Source: Adapted from Denny's Web site www.corporate-ir.net story on "About Denny's" (April 29, 2005); Sara Nathan (August 20, 1999), "Discrimination Lawsuits," *USA Today*, p. 1B; Todd Henneman (January 13,1999), "Denny's Sued by Bay Area Latinos," The *San Francisco Chronicle*, p. A4; Fay Rice (May 13, 1996), "Denny's Changes Its Spots," *Fortune*, pp. 133–142; "Is Affirmative Action Obsolete?" (October 1995), *Training and Development*, p. 20; Charlene Marmer Soloman (August 1995), "What You Need to Know about Affirmative Action," *Personnel Journal*, pp. 56–67.

Step 1: Analyze Underrepresentation and Availability

AT&T found a problem simply by examining the sex composition of its job classes: There were almost no women in outside-crafts positions. But how great was the extent of underrepresentation? Many organizations find the answer to this question in the statistics compiled for affirmative action plans by state labor departments, which show the number of women and minorities in each of 10 or 20 broad occupational groups. Others use the overall population figures compiled by the United States Census. Both sets of data are readily available from the appropriate government agencies. In addition, some larger firms are investing in sophisticated labor market studies to arrive at a more accurate estimate of availability. Of course, any set of statistics is open to criticism. Many employers strive to collect statistics that put them in the best light. While some may argue that such a strategy is manipulative, it often does succeed in reducing pressure from enforcement agencies. Employers are likely to continue using it until a generally accepted statistical definition of availability emerges.

Step 2: Set Goals

Once the statistics are agreed upon, the organization sets goals to help achieve greater minority representation in the job in question. The EEO goals have to be realistic, and they have to be attainable without discriminating against those in the majority. Nevertheless, while good availability statistics help make goals realistic, there is no way to be sure that goals will not discriminate in reverse unless the means by which the company seeks to attain them are carefully planned.

Step 3: Specify How Goals Are to Be Attained

If the means used to attain AAP goals are to be nondiscriminatory against white males, management should find out the causes of underrepresentation of women and minorities in the company's workforce. Otherwise, it will not know what discriminatory employment practices must be changed in order to increase representation without preferential treatment of women and minorities. For example, the underrepresentation of women in a certain job class may be caused by a company's reputation for being rough on women or by a policy that unnecessarily schedules work shifts so that parents cannot meet family responsibilities. If management knows the cause, it can attempt to increase the representation of women by working on its public image and by exploring the possibility of retiming the shifts. But if management doesn't know, it may attempt to increase the representation of women by lowering the requirements for women applying from the outside or by granting transfers to women employees while refusing to grant them to more qualified male employees. Not only would this increase the risk of discrimination charges from white males, but it would also contribute to problems with morale and foster resentment against women in the company.

At AT&T, 24 reverse discrimination cases eventually went to court. In one case, the union claimed that reverse discrimination resulted from promotion policies favoring qualified women and minorities. A district court and an appeals court ruled against the union and supported preferential treatment and quotas. The courts reasoned that such treatment was justified to correct the abuses of past discrimination.

The AT&T case illustrates that even a large company (at the time of the initial court case, AT&T employed 980,000) can take specific action to alleviate discrimination. AT&T took these steps.

- It tried to change the image of outside-crafts employees from male to gender-neutral by advertising, public relations, and relationships with guidance counselors.
- It redesigned the jobs so that women could perform them more easily.
- It provided detailed information to the Department of Labor on the status of the AAP. The information provided exceeded what is ordinarily required by federal rules.[70]

Update on Affirmative Action

In 1995 the Supreme Court fueled the debate over affirmative action with its decision in *Adarand Constructors Inc.* v. *Peña*. In this case, Adarand submitted the lowest bid for a Department of Transportation job, but a minority-owned business was awarded the subcontract under a program that sets aside 5 percent of federal funding for businesses deemed "economically and socially disadvantaged."[71] While the court did not rule directly on whether reverse discrimination had occurred, it did hold that any governmental action based on race should be subjected to strict judicial scrutiny to ensure that the personal right to equal protection under the law is not infringed.

The *Adarand* decision has not affected contractors' obligation to make good faith affirmative action efforts. In 1995 the Department of Justice issued an opinion letter distinguishing programs and laws such as Executive Order 11246 (which requires federal

Hugo Gerbold has just returned from his discussion with Gregory Inness, company president. Gregory seemed impressed with Hugo's presentation, but he still seemed to doubt that more women and minorities would "fit in" at Reliable. Hugo had pointed out that the EEOC and the courts wouldn't think much of this reasoning. He wondered if Gregory would take the next step in instituting an EEO plan at Reliable Insurance.

Hugo decided to be ready, just in case. He prepared an EEO program designed to focus on the areas where he felt Reliable was in the worst shape. He prepared a list of current employees, primarily in the clerical ranks, who could be promoted to underwriters and claims agents. These promotions could increase female representation in better jobs fairly quickly. They would require training, but it could be done.

To get minorities represented fairly in all categories would require special recruiting efforts. Hugo prepared a plan to increase Reliable's recruiting efforts in all categories of employment. The plan was drawn up to protect the position of current white male employees and applicants. In no case would a person be hired with fewer qualifications than white male applicants.

Luckily, Reliable was growing and was hiring more people as it expanded. Attrition would also open positions in most lower-level managerial, professional, and sales positions.

After spending quite a bit of time developing the plan, Hugo waited. When he didn't hear from Gregory, he made an appointment to see the president.

Hugo Gregory, you recall we discussed the EEO issue. We hired Osanna, but that's as far as our effort went. I've prepared an EEO . . .

Gregory Hugo, after we discussed it, I checked with the rest of the management. We feel we're OK as is. We don't want to upset our local workforce with an EEO plan. Now, about the pay plan for next year . . .

And that was that. Hugo took his EEO plan and placed it in a folder in his desk drawer.

Six months later, another female employee, Dot Greene, filed a complaint. The EEOC came to investigate, and the investigators indicated that Reliable had not taken the necessary steps to eliminate job discrimination. The company was instructed to develop an EEO plan to correct the problem.

government contractors to take affirmative action) from the type of programs prone to preferences, numerical quotas, and percentages, such as that examined in *Adarand*.

Another important affirmative action case was *Hopwood* v. *State of Texas*.[72] The case was filed by four white applicants to the University of Texas Law School who alleged that they had not been admitted because of the school's affirmative action program. After a two-week trial in 1994, the district court ruled that the law school's affirmative action program was unconstitutional because separate admission committees were used to review minority and nonminority applicants.

The 1996 United States Court of Appeals for the Fifth Circuit decided that the University of Texas Law School's affirmative action plan unconstitutionally discriminated against whites and nonpreferred minorities.[73] The court held that the classification of persons on the basis of race for the purpose of diversity frustrates rather than promotes the constitutional goals of equal protection.

Although the Fifth Circuit ruling applies to only the states of Texas, Louisiana, and Mississippi, it will be closely examined in other parts of the country. At the heart of the court's decision is a question of importance to institutions of higher education throughout the United States: Is diversity of the student body a compelling interest that justifies taking race into account in deciding which applicants to admit?[74]

The U.S. Supreme Court chose not to stop enforcement of California's Proposition 209, which prohibits the use of affirmative action in college admissions, state and local government employment, and state contract awards.[75] California state courts face a growing docket of cases requiring them to apply and interpret the law.[76] Although the long-term effects of Proposition 209 remain unclear, the California State University system already reports declines in numbers of minority faculty.[77] Other states are now closely examining issues of equal employment opportunity and affirmative action, paying close attention to the aftermath of Proposition 209 and the *Hopwood* decision.[78]

Summary

This chapter has focused on EEO programs designed to eliminate bias in HRM programs. The role of EEO and the law as a significant force in shaping HRM policies and programs is now an accepted fact in society. The law, executive orders, and the court's interpretations will continue to influence every phase of HRM programs and activities. This influence will become clearer as specific HRM activities are discussed in Chapters 4 through 17. This chapter provides only the general theme of the importance of the law in HRM. The remaining chapters will at times spell out specifically how the law affects HRM.

To summarize the major points covered in this chapter:

1. Equal employment opportunity is one of the most significant activities in the HRM function today.
2. The three main influences on the development of EEO were
   a. Changes in societal values.
   b. The economic status of women and minorities.
   c. The emerging role of government regulation.
3. Laws prohibiting employment discrimination that were discussed in this chapter include
   a. Title VII of the 1964 Civil Rights Act.
   b. Executive Order 11246
   c. Age Discrimination Act.
   d. Pregnancy Discrimination Act.
   e. Americans with Disabilities Act of 1990.
   f. Civil Rights Act of 1991.
4. Two different definitions of discrimination have been arrived at by the courts over the years:
   a. Disparate treatment.
   b. Disparate impact.
5. The criterion for compliance with EEO and affirmative action can theoretically be reduced to two questions:
   a. Does an employment practice have unequal or adverse impact on the groups (race, color, sex, religion, or national origin) covered by the law?
   b. Is that practice job-related or otherwise necessary to the organization?
6. The government unit most responsible for enforcing EEO regulations is the U.S. Equal Employment Opportunity Commission (EEOC)—Title VII.
7. Courts are constantly interpreting the laws governing EEO. Owing to numerous appeals, an EEO complaint can take years to reach settlement.
8. EEO planning can be used as a preventive action to reduce the likelihood of employment discrimination charges and to ensure equal employment opportunities for applicants and employees.
9. Affirmative action plans may be either voluntary or involuntary. Characteristics necessary for a lawful voluntary plan include
   a. Implemented to eliminate discrimination.
   b. Cannot trammel the rights of the majority.
   c. Temporary.
   d. No set-asides permitted.

Key Terms

affirmative action, *p. 82*
Age Discrimination in Employment Act of 1967 (amended 1978 and 1986), *p. 76*
Americans with Disabilities Act, 1990, *p. 77*
bona fide occupational qualification (BFOQ), *p. 70*

Civil Rights Act of 1964, Title VII, *p. 71*
Civil Rights Act of 1991, *p. 75*
disparate impact, *p. 71*
disparate treatment, *p. 70*
Equal Employment Opportunity Commission (EEOC), *p. 79*
equal employment opportunity (EEO) programs, *p. 67*

Equal Pay Act, *p. 76*
four-fifths rule, *p. 71*
Pregnancy Discrimination Act of 1978, *p. 74*
Rehabilitation Act of 1973, *p. 78*
retaliation, *p. 71*
sexual harassment, *p. 72*

Questions for Review and Discussion

1. The ADA could be a very costly law for employers to comply with in terms of making reasonable accommodations. What could be some of the costs that employers must bear?
2. Do you believe that Muslims working in the United States need legal protection against retaliation? Why?
3. What could be some of the effects of being discriminated against because of race, sex, or age?
4. Examine the equal opportunity laws of another country, such as France, Japan, or Libya. Are laws in other countries as much a concern for HRM specialists as they are in the United States?
5. What can managers do to minimize their chance of litigation and of being found negligent with regard to sexual harassment?
6. Why is the decision in *Griggs* v. *Duke Power Company* considered a landmark?
7. In a workplace with a diverse workforce, how could an English-only rule create lower morale, poorer communication, and lower productivity?
8. What is meant by the term *bona fide occupational qualification* (BFOQ)?
9. Should the rulings in *Faragher* v. *City of Boca Raton* be considered significant for the HRM area of an organization?
10. Affirmative action has become a political, economic, and emotional issue. What are some of the reasonable arguments in favor of and opposed to affirmative action?

HRM Legal Advisor

Based on *Torres* v. *Pisano,* 116 F.3d 625 (Second Cir 1997).

The Plaintiff's Allegations and Requests

Jenice Torres began working as an administrative secretary for New York University's (NYU) Dental Center in 1990. Ms. Torres alleged that during her employment at the Dental Center, her supervisor, Eugene Coe, engaged in harassing behaviors toward her including derogatory remarks about her gender and race; insulting comments about her body, her sexual behavior, and her pregnancy; sexual innuendoes toward her; and indications to other employees that he wanted to have sex with her. From 1990 until 1993, Ms. Torres did not inform NYU's management or her union of the harassment and filed no formal harassment complaints. Leonard Pisano, assistant director of maintenance of academic facilities at NYU, learned of the harassing behavior from another employee in September of 1993 and immediately met with Ms. Torres to discuss the situation. He suggested at the meeting and again in late 1993 that Ms. Torres file an internal formal written complaint. Ms. Torres submitted an initial complaint on February 23, 1994, in which she generally criticized Mr. Coe, but described only a few specific harassing behaviors. The complaint ended with a request that Mr. Pisano keep her allegations confidential until they spoke at a later date. As requested by Mr. Pisano, she sent a second letter three days later which described the alleged harassment in more detail. Mr. Pisano then met with Ms. Torres in March of 1994, at which time she again requested that he keep her allegations confidential. Additionally, Ms. Torres indicated in a phone conversation with Mr. Pisano that she did not want him to take any action and that she just wanted someone to talk to. Would you honor Ms. Torres' requests for confidentiality? What action would you take at this point?

The Defendant's Response and Plaintiff's Discrimination Claim

Mr. Pisano took no action until June of 1994. At this time, he invited Ms. Torres to meet with Stephen Heller, NYU's assistant vice president for administrative services. Upon hearing her allegations of harassment, Mr. Heller referred Ms. Torres to counseling and transferred her to Mr. Pisano's office where she would no longer be in contact with Mr. Coe. Ms. Torres then filed a claim of discrimination with the EEOC. In September of 1994, Mr. Coe was discharged following NYU's investigation of the harassment. In October, Ms. Torres was granted a transfer to a departmental secretary position at NYU and was given a $6,500 per year raise. In March of 1995, Ms. Torres filed a discrimination suit against Coe, Pisano, Heller, and NYU in federal court. How do you think the court ruled? Should NYU be held liable for Coe's harassing behavior? Did Pisano react appropriately in honoring Ms. Torres' confidentiality request?

The Court's Decision

In June of 1997, the U.S. Court of Appeals for the Second Circuit affirmed a lower court decision in favor of NYU. Although the court found that a hostile work environment did indeed exist and that NYU knew of its existence, NYU was not liable for the harassment. Employer liability for hostile work environment sexual harassment requires negligence in failing to act reasonably to address the harassment. The appeals court opinion stated that Mr. Pisano's failure to act was reasonable given the plaintiff's repeated confidentiality requests. The court indicated that company liability for requested inaction could be found in other cases where inaction may lead to serious physical or psychological harm or where only one of a number of harassed employees requests that no action be taken.

Notes

1. www.uscourts.gov/caseload2004/tables/COOMarch04.pdf, accessed June 11, 2005.
2. N. Peter Lareau et al. (2004), *Labor and Employment Law* (New York: Matthew Bender).
3. Lisa Guerin and Amy Del Po (2004), *Everyday Employment Law: The Basics* (Berkeley, CA: Nolo).
4. Gunnar Myrdal (1944), *An American Dilemma: The Negro Problem and American Democracy* (New York: Harper and Row).
5. Charles Silverman (1964), *Crisis in Black and White* (New York: Random House).
6. St. Clair Drake (1966), "The Social and Economic Status of the Negro in the United States," in Talcoot Parsons and Kenneth B. Clark (eds.), *The Negro American* (Boston: Houghton Mifflin), pp. 3–46.
7. Title VII of the 1964 Civil Rights Act, http://www.eeoc.gov/laws/vii.html.
8. *Federal Laws Prohibiting Employment Discrimination* (1998) (Rosemount, Minnesota: Data Research, Inc.).
9. *McDonnell Douglas v. Green* (1973), 411 U.S. 792.
10. Title VII of the 1964 Civil Rights Act, 42 U.S.C. 2000e-2(e).
11. *Dothard v. Rawlinson* (1977), 433 U.S. 321.
12. *International Union* (1991), *UAW v. John Controls, Inc.,* 499 U.S. 187.
13. *Diaz v. Pan Am. World Airways* (1971), 442 F.2d 385 (Fifth Cir.), *cert., Denied,* 404 U.S. 950.
14. *Griggs v. Duke Power Co.,* 401 U.S. 424, 1971.
15. 42 U.S.C. 2000e-2(k).
16. EEOC Uniform Guidelines on Employee Selection Procedures, http://www.uniformguidelines.com/uniformguidelines.html
17. *Albemarle Paper Co. v. Moody,* 422 U.S. 405, 1975.
18. Ibid.

19. *Watson v. Forth Worth Bank and Trust,* 487 U.S. 977, 1988.

20. EEOC Charge Statistics, http://www.eeoc.gov/stats/charges.html, accessed June 11, 2005.

21. EEOC Compliance Manual, http://www.eeoc.gov/policy/compliance.html.

22. Ibid.

23. *Robinson v. Shell Oil Co.,* 117 S.Ct. 843, 1997.

24. EEOC Compliance Manual, http://www.eeoc.gov/policy/compliance.html.

25. EEOC Enforcement Statistic, http://www.eeoc.gov/docs/.

26. *Financial Times* (September 8, 1999), "Ford Settles $7.5 MM Case over Sexual Harassment," p. 27.

27. EEOC Enforcement Guidance, http://www.eeoc.gov/stats/harass.html.

28. *Pease v. Alford Photo Industries, Inc.,* 667 F.Supp. 1188 , W.D.Tenn. 1987.

29. *Meritor Savings Bank v. Vinson,* 477 U.S. 57, 1986.

30. EEOC Guidelines on Discrimination Because of Sex, http://www.access.gpo.gov/nara/cfr/waisidx_99/29cfr1604_99.html.

31. Clara Bingham and Laura Leedy Gunsler (2002), *Class Action* (New York: Doubleday).

32. 1998 U.S. Lexis 4216; 1998 U.S. Lexis 4217.

33. Joseph Kizza (2002), *Ethical and Social Issues in the Information Age* (New York: Springer-Verlag).

34. Title VII of the 1964 Civil Rights Act, http://www.eeoc.gov/laws/vii.html.

35. EEOC Enforcement Statistics, http://www.eeoc.gov/laws/religion.html.

36. Maureen Minehan (January 1996), "Time to Promote Religious Tolerance," *HR Focus,* pp. 12–13.

37. Eric Matusewitch (December 30, 1998), "English-Only Rules Come Under Fire," *The Legal Intelligencer,* p. 7.

38. EEOC Guidelines on Discrimination Because of National Origin, http://www.access.gpo.gov/nara/cfr/waisidx/29cfr1606.html.

39. *Garcia v. Gloor,* 618 F.2d 264, Fifth Cir. 1980, *cert.* Denied, 449 U.S. 1113, 1981.

40. *Garcia v. Spun Steak,* 998 F.2d 264, Ninth Cir. 1993.

41. Civil Rights Act of 1991, http://www.eeoc.gov/laws/cra91.html.

42. *Wards Cove Packing Co. v. Antonio,* 490 U.S. 642, 1989.

43. Executive Order 11246, http://www.dol.gov/dol/esa/public/regs/statutes/ofccp/eo11246.htm.

44. Equal Pay Act of 1963, http://www.eeoc.gov/laws/epa.html.

45. Age Discrimination in Employment Act of 1967, http://www.eeoc.gov/laws/epa.html.

46. *Mullin v. Raytheon Co.,* 164 F.3d 696, First Cir. 1999.

47. Fair Empl. Prac. Cas. (BNA) 345 (E.D. Pa. 1992).

48. Michel Marmot (2005), *The Status Syndrome: How Social Standing Affects Our Health and Longevity* (New York: Henry Holt).

49. Ronald J. Burke and Cary L. Cooper (2005), *Reinventing HRM* (London: Taylor & Francis).

50. Dan Coughlin (2005), *Corporate Catalysts* (New York: Career Press).

51. Americans with Disabilities Act of 1990, http://www.eeoc.gov/laws/ada.html.

52. Rehabilitation Act of 1973, http://eeoc.gov/laws/rehab.html.

53. Peter Baldwin (2005), *Disease and Democracy: The Industrialized World Faces AIDS* (Berkeley, CA: University of California).

54. Charles H. Fleischer (2005), *HR for Small Business* (New York: Sourcebooks).

55. Barbara Gamble Magill (July 1997), "ADA Accommodations Don't Have to Break the Bank," *HR Magazine,* pp. 84–88.

56. *Sutton et al. v. United Airlines,* No. 97–143.

57. *Albertsons v. Kirkingburg,* No. 98–591.

58. *Murphy v. United Parcel Service,* No. 97–1992.
59. Shannon P. Duffy (July 21, 1999), "Judge: Jury Should Decide Some ADA Cases If Treatment Doesn't Fully Control Disability," *The Legal Intelligencer.*
60. State and Local Governments, http://www.loc.gov/global/state/stategov.html.
61. U.S. Equal Employment Opportunity Commission, http://www.eeoc.gov/.
62. Enforcement Statistics and Litigation, http://www.eeoc.gov/stats/index.html.
63. History of EEOC Mediation Program, http://www.eeoc.gov/mediate/history/html.
64. Office of Federal Contract Compliance Programs, http://www.dol.gov/dol/esa/public/ofcp_org.htm.
65. Christopher Thomlins (ed.) (2005), *The United States Supreme Court: The Pursuit of Justice,* (New York: Houghton Mifflin).
66. *Teamsters Union,* U.S. 14 EPD, 7579, 1979.
67. Steven M. Cahn (ed.) (2002), *The Affirmative Action Debate* (New York: Routledge).
68. *United Steelworkers of America v. Weber,* 433 U.S. 193, 1979.
69. *Johnson v. Transportation Agency,* 480 U.S. 616, 1987.
70. Terry H. Anderson (2005), *The Pursuit of Fairness: A History of Affirmative Action* (New York: Oxford University).
71. Gary Glaser, Edmund Cook Jr., and Sandra Pearlman (April 1996), "Affirmative Action: The Scrutiny Intensified," *HR Focus,* p. 5.
72. *Hopwood v. State of Texas,* 861 F. Supp.551, W.D. Tex. 1994.
73. *Hopwood v. State of Texas,* 78 F.3d 932, 948, Fifth Cir. 1996.
74. Anderson, op. cit.
75. Ward Connerly (2001), *My Fight against Race Preferences* (New York: Encounter Books).
76. Harriet Chiang (September 2, 1999), "High Court to Take Its First Look at Prop. 201," *The San Francisco Chronicle,* p. A22.
77. Alison Schneider (November 20, 1998), "What Has Happened to Faculty Diversity in California?"*Chronicle of Higher Education,* pp. A10–A12.
78. Audrey Magnusen and Katherine Naff (Summer 1998), "Proposition 209: The Death Knell for Affirmative Action?" *Public Manager,* pp. 37–40.

EXERCISE 3-1 DISSECTING THE DIAGNOSTIC MODEL AND ITS APPLICATION

Objective
The purpose of this exercise is to understand the requirements for bona fide occupational qualification (BFOQ).

Background
Title VII of the Civil Rights Act of 1964 has stated that it is unlawful for an employer to discriminate against a person in any condition of employment because of race, religion, color, national origin, or sex. As with most rules, however, there are exceptions. Regarding Title VII, one exception to the rule is termed a bona fide occupational qualification (BFOQ). With the BFOQ provision, Congress has stated that it is not unlawful to utilize certain personal characteristics in employment (such as sex) in situations where that particular characteristic is necessary to meet the normal operation of the business. The BFOQ is not intended, however, to serve as a loophole for resistant organizations that want to flout the Equal Employment Opportunity Commission (EEOC) requirements. The EEOC believes that the BFOQ provision should be "interpreted narrowly" and places the burden of proof for justifying the BFOQ squarely upon the organization.

Want Ads

A number of hypothetical situations in which an organization has advertised for an employee of a particular race, color, religion, sex, or national origin are presented. In your opinion, do these particular situations warrant a BFOQ? Read each description carefully and indicate whether you think a BFOQ is warranted.

Broadway Actress   Finally a chance to make it big on stage. A company needs four young, liberal-minded females to star in sophisticated adult play off Broadway. The appearance of the person to fit the part is important.

> Apply in person at
>> Off Broadway
>> Stage Forum
>> New York, NY

BFOQ warranted? YES_____ NO_____
Why? _____

Digital Equipment Assembler   Need females to assemble intricate computer equipment. Must have excellent hand-eye coordination and dexterity. No experience necessary—we train.

> Apply in person at
>> Rayco Digital Equipment Co.
>> Third Street
>> New Albany, IN

(The owner attended a recent convention of computer manufacturers and heard an industrial psychologist say that a number of sophisticated research studies have shown that women are much more dexterous than men and therefore make better assemblers of intricate parts and equipment.)

BFOQ warranted? YES_____ NO_____
Why? _____

Sales Representative   Large title manufacturer needs aggressive salesperson to cover Texas region. Prefer male with extensive title-selling experience.

> Send résumé to
>> Rachman Title
>> Trans Street
>> Houston, TX

BFOQ warranted? YES_____ NO_____
Why? _____

Flight Attendant   Regional airline needs young, attractive female to fly West Coast routes. Must pass height and weight requirements.

> Apply at
>> Flightly Airlines
>> Mesa Boulevard
>> San Diego, CA

(The human resource director had conducted a study showing that the airline's passengers—mostly male—show a strong preference for attractive female flight attendants. Additionally, the firm's consulting psychologist stated that the airline cabin represents a unique environment in which the psychological needs of passengers are better attended to by females than males.)

BFOQ warranted? YES_____ NO_____
Why? _____

Warehouseman   Small lumber company needs six men to replace striking warehouse-men. Job involves lifting and carrying heavy lumber products. Excellent pay and benefits. Apply in person at

    Knothole Lumber Company
    Bark and Splinter Streets
    Macon, GA

BFOQ warranted? YES_____ NO_____
Why? _____

Prison Guard   Need self-confident, muscular, and experienced male facility guard. Must be able to work effectively with others in a potentially violent, dangerous environment.

    Send résumé to
        District Attorney for Penal System
        Illinois Board of Corrections
        Springfield, IL

BFOQ warranted? YES_____ NO_____
Why? _____

Mechanic   Large auto dealer needs several men for light mechanic work. Experienced only need apply. Must have own tools.

    Apply in person at
        Friendly Frank's Foreign Imports
        Michigan Avenue
        Evanston, IL

(The owner informally surveyed the other mechanics about the new employees. They emphatically stated, "We don't want to work around women!" In addition, the owner noted that state law requires separate restrooms for each sex, and that there was only one restroom in the shop. Building another restroom would require a large expenditure, and the space wasn't available.)

BFOQ warranted? YES_____ NO_____
Why? _____

Women's High School Basketball Coach   Coed high school looking for proven female basketball coach. Head coaching experience needed; ability to work with young women 14–18 years old is important. Need at least an undergraduate college degree.

    Apply in person at
        Pasadena High School
        Main Street
        Pasadena, TX

BFOQ warranted? YES_____ NO_____
Why? _____

A final question: Is it legal for publishers to place ads in the paper on the basis of sex, such as "Help Wanted—Male" and Help Wanted—Female"?

Application Case 3-1

Meeting the Challenge of Sexual Harassment

At an office of Goldman, Sachs and Company in Boston, some male employees allegedly pasted photos of bare-breasted women on company newsletters, next to biographies of new female employees (suggesting that the photos were pictures of the new staff members). Copies of the newsletters were circulated around the office. Sexist literature such as "The Smart Man's Creed or Why Beer Is Better Than Women" ("After you've had a beer, the bottle is still worth a dime") was allegedly also distributed. Kristine Utley, a former Goldman sales associate, has made these allegations in a suit charging that the environment at Goldman, Sachs constitutes sexual harassment. Fired for refusing a transfer to a New York office, she is suing to gain reinstatement and damages and to eliminate the harassment.

Joanne Barbetta has filed a similar suit seeking damages for harassment caused by an environment that she asserted "was poisoning my system." Ms. Barbetta reports that during her tenure as a clerk at Chemlawn, male employees circulated pornographic magazines and pinup posters. She viewed a slide presentation that included suggestive pictures (e.g., a nude woman) put there, according to management, "to keep the guys awake." After these experiences and continual breast-grabbing by a male employee, Ms. Barbetta quit.

Marie Regab, formerly an 18-year employee of Air France, has filed similar charges concerning the Washington office where she worked as a salesperson. She alleges that several characteristics of the office environment combined to create harassment, including propositions by one of her bosses, circulation of *Playboy* and *Penthouse* magazines in the office, and open discussion of sexual activity by male employees. "It was sickening and an insult to women in the office," she claims. Ms. Regab was fired; she is suing to gain reinstatement, for $1.5 million in damages, and to eliminate the harassment in the office.

These three situations are examples of a growing number of suits being filed by women who charge that a sexist environment in the workplace constitutes sexual harassment and that their employers are therefore liable. Plaintiff actions in this area have been fueled by the Supreme Court's ruling that sexist behavior that creates an "intimidating, hostile, or offensive working environment" is sexual harassment and violates Title VII of the 1964 Civil Rights Act.

The Court's ruling has spurred an increasing number of companies to act to prevent sexual harassment in the workplace and to deal with it effectively when the problem occurs. Other factors have also triggered company action. Employers are realizing that the costs of harassment can be high in terms of lowered productivity, absenteeism, and turnover. One study of female employees in the federal government concluded that the government loses about $200 million each year to the effects of sexual harassment. Costs can also be high if an employee sues. Even if the plaintiff opts for an out-of-court settlement, the costs of these settlements are often in six figures, and it's the company that pays. Companies are also realizing that sexual harassment is a very real issue in today's workplace; from 20 to over 50 percent of working women have experienced sexual harassment (and so have at least 15 percent of male employees).

Thus, companies are tackling the issue; the more effective strategies developed so far contain four primary features:

1. Training programs that educate employees concerning the meaning of sexual harassment and the behaviors that constitute a hostile and harassing workplace: Training is especially important simply because men and women often differ in their perception of what constitutes harassment. Most

Written originally by Kim Stewart and adopted from Joseph Pereira (February 10, 1988), "Women Allege Sexist Atmosphere in Office Constitutes Harassment" *The Wall Street Journal*, p. 19; Cathy Trost (August 28, 1986), "With Problem More Visible, Firms Crack Down on Sexual Harassment," *The Wall Street Journal*, p. 19; Walter Kiechet III (September 14, 1987) "The High Cost of Sexual Harassment," *Fortune*, p, 147ff; and Moriso Manley (May 1987), "Dealing with Sexual Harassment," *Inc.*, p. 145ff. Also see Louise F Fitzgerald (October 1993), "Sexual Harassment: Violence against Women in the Workplace," *American Psychologist*, pp. 1070–1076.

training is in the form of seminars and workshops, often with films and videos. Philip Morris USA conducts a mandatory training program for its field managers that includes viewing a video called "Shades of Gray." General Motors conducts an awareness seminar for employees and offers this benchmark for judging the appropriateness of office conduct: "Would you be embarrassed to see your remarks or behavior in the newspaper or described to your own family?"

Du Pont has developed one of the most comprehensive antiharassment programs in business (begun in 1981). Recently, the corporation added a $500,000 course on personal safety, rape, and harassment prevention primarily for its female employees (many of whom are moving into traditionally male jobs at Du Pont such as agricultural products sales). The course offers no-nonsense advice on how to handle a harasser. For example, if a male customer fondles a woman's knee, Du Pont advises that she "firmly remove his hand . . . and then say, 'Let's pretend this didn't happen.'" If she receives a verbal proposition, Du Pont advises that she say, "No, I wouldn't want our business relationship to be jeopardized in any way." About 1,600 employees have completed the course.

Like General Motors, Du Pont offers its employees a guideline for evaluating their behavior. Said a Du Pont spokesman, "We tell people, it's harassment when something starts bothering somebody."

Some other companies provide advice concerning how to handle harassment. One popular piece of advice: Document the incident as soon as possible by describing on paper what happened in full detail and talking to someone informally about the incident. A relatively mild case of harassment can be handled by talking to the harasser, explaining what he or she did, how it made you feel, and telling the harasser to stop. In a more serious situation, communicating these points via a certified letter sent to the harasser, with the victim keeping a copy, is often recommended (and reportedly proves to be quite effective).

2. An internal complaint procedure: Ideally, the procedure provides for fast action and confidentiality and ensures that the employee can report the problem to a manager who is not involved in the harassment. Some companies encourage employees to report a problem to their immediate supervisor but also designate an individual (often a woman) in the HR department as someone employees can speak with in cases where the immediate supervisor is involved in the problem. To ensure speedy action, some companies require that an investigation begin within 24 hours after the harassment complaint has been reported. Ideally, the procedure also stipulates how investigations will be conducted.

3. Speedy, corrective action that solves the problem: If the investigation supports the employee's claims, corrective action is quickly taken. Such action can range from simply talking to the harasser to discharge, depending on the severity of the offense. One federal agency requires offending employees to publicly apologize to the individuals they've harassed. Staffing changes also sometimes occur. One New York bank faced a problem of a highly talented male executive who generated much profit for the bank—and also several costly EEOC complaints from his secretaries. The bank solved the problem by assigning the executive an all-male secretarial staff. Corrective action is particularly important because it communicates to both victims and potential offenders that harassment will not be tolerated.

4. A written and communicated antiharassment policy. The written policy is documented and distributed to all employees. The policy contains a definition of harassment, the company's position prohibiting harassment, the grievance procedure, and penalties.

While a growing number of companies are implementing antiharassment policies, the courts have yet to establish a consistent record concerning the issue of "hostile environment" as illegal harassment. For example, a federal district court in Michigan dismissed a claim by Vivienne Rabidue that sexual posters and obscene language in her office at Osceola Refining Co. constituted illegal sexual harassment.

However, Joanne Barbetta has won the first round of her court battle with Chemlawn. The judge hearing her complaint rejected Chemlawn's motion to dismiss the suit; he has ordered Ms. Barbetta's case to trial. Chemlawn is expected to present a vigorous defense, asserting that the men involved in the newsletter incident have been disciplined and that the situations Ms. Barbetta cites fall far short of creating a hostile, harassing environment because they occurred "over the course of two years."

Discussion Questions

1. Assume that you are an HR executive for a company that manufactures and sells agricultural products (for example, fertilizers and grain feeds). The company's workforce of 1,200 employees is 70 percent male and 30 percent female. Drawing from this case and the chapter content, develop an antiharassment policy and program. What are the major challenges you see in implementing the program?

2. Many experts assert that reported cases of sexual harassment represent only a small percentage of the total number of incidents that actually occur in the workplace. If their assertion is true, why do so many cases go unreported? How would your HRM policy on harassment address this situation?

3. As research indicates, people differ widely in their perceptions of sexual harassment. What is a harmless remark to one individual can be an annoying, even infuriating insult to another. In your view, what separates harmless conduct from harassing behavior? In the same vein, when does a sexist environment become a hostile, harassing one?

HR Journal Test Answers

Answers to HR Journal on page 67, "Are You Aware of the Law?"

1. No	6. No
2. Yes	7. No
3. Yes	8. No
4. Yes	9. No
5. Yes	10. Yes

Chapter 4

Global Human Resource Management

Learning Objectives

After studying this chapter, you should be able to:

1. **Describe** the drivers behind globalization in the early 21st century.

2. **Discuss** the role that culture plays in determining the effective use of human resource management practices in a global organization.

3. **Identify** critical HRM issues faced by multinational and global organizations when they conduct business in the international marketplace.

Internet/Web Resources

General Sites
www.expatexchange.com

www.ilo.org

www.odei.gov/cia/publications/factbook/index.html

www.mexicomaquila.com

www.gmacglobalrelocation.com

www.shrm.org

globalgateway.monster.com

Company Sites
www.globaldynamics.com

www.nortel.com

www.bp.com

www.dell.com

www.ballygaming.com

www.nestle.com

www.unilever.com

www.fiat.com

www.volvo.com

Career Challenge

Boswell Technologies is a computer software development firm located in Akron, Ohio. Michael Carl, vice president for human resources at Boswell Technologies, has just returned from San Benedetto, Italy. It seems that Boswell is soon going to become Boswell International. The company has just acquired a successful software firm located in San Benedetto. The purpose of the acquisition was to quickly allow Boswell to become a premier supplier of new and innovative computer software in Europe.

On his first day back in Ohio, Michael has been called into the office of Boswell's president, David Randolf, to give a status report.

David Well, Mike? How soon can we get our management team into place over there in Italy and phase out their current staff? I've heard how slow and inefficient Italian businesses are, and I don't want to waste time getting our company's policies in action. Maybe we can get a head start on the European competition with good old American know-how.

Michael It's not going to be that easy, Dave. I think it might be a mistake to send our people. The Italians have an excellent sense of how we should try to run operations in Europe. I am concerned that some of our HRM policies might not work as well in Europe.

David What do you mean, our HRM policies won't work? We've been very successful here in Ohio and have even been singled out for our training and compensation programs. Of course they'll work. I don't care whether we are in Ohio or Rome; business is still business.

Michael If we do send some of our people, who should go?

David Mike, the international operation is our future. Let's send our best performers for a year or two to be sure we get the job done right the first time. Let's send them as soon as possible, too. They have the skills and know-how. All they need is the chance.

Michael But what about the costs?

David Costs? We can't be talking about that much money, can we? Airline tickets, room, and board? That should not run more than a few thousand dollars for each person we send. The new markets we tap into will give us a quick payback.

Despite occasional protests and other evidence of antiglobalization backlash, integration of the world's economies and the globalization of business continue unabated at the beginning of the 21st century.[1] Evidence of globalization can be inferred from several different macroeconomic indicators. First, international trade is growing at a more rapid rate than world output. Over the past 50 years, trade flows have increased 17-fold while real output has expanded by only a factor of 6.[2]

Second, foreign direct investment (FDI) flows, though experiencing some decreases since 2001, are making a strong comeback with global flows of FDI reaching over U.S.$1.7 trillion in 2003. The world's 61,000 transnational corporations, along with their 900,000 affiliates, consider FDI as the main force in global economic integration.[3]

Third, the number of cross-border interfirm agreements, another indicator of globalization, has risen dramatically during the past two decades. Defined as joint ventures, licensing, subcontracting, franchising, marketing, manufacturing, research and development, and exploration, cross-border interfirm agreements reached record levels in recent years.[4]

Finally, social, economic, and political developments throughout the world have contributed to dramatic changes in the way global business is conducted. Such changes include the growth in offshoring, the development of regional trade agreements such as the North

American Free Trade Agreement (NAFTA), the emergence of a more economically powerful European Union (EU), the continued opening of China to trade and foreign investment, and the growth in influence of such supranational entities as the E.U. Parliament and the World Trade Organization (WTO).

The trend toward greater economic integration has led to a dramatic increase in the amount of competition for American businesses both abroad and in the U.S. domestic market. In the early 1960s, American firms produced over 40 percent of the world's output. By the late 1990s, U.S. share of world output slipped to 20.8 percent.[5] Domestically, American businesses are facing more foreign competition than in the past. This trend continued throughout the 1990s and does not show signs of slowing in the 21st century. One international management scholar summed it up this way: "Today, at the beginning of the 21st century, global competition is serious, pervasive, and here to stay."[6]

How will firms survive in such a competitive, global environment? The *people factor* can help make a significant difference. Firms need to strengthen their presence, involvement, and relative positions in the domestic and global marketplace by utilizing their global human resources in a manner that helps them establish and sustain competitive advantage.[7]

A Global Perspective

The external environment is one of the most important influences on HRM activities for the international organization. Each country in which the international organization operates will have its own laws, business customs, and workforce characteristics. In addition, the international organization must constantly be aware of the political climate of each country in which it is located. Changes that can affect the organization occur very rapidly.

Although an organization that is expanding into international markets is faced with many problems when it decides to become global, the "people challenge" might, in fact, be the most difficult. In a survey, 57 percent of the top executives who were asked about globalization indicated that acquiring a competent workforce was the factor most critical to success.[8] More specifically, another survey of top international human resource executives indicated that there are several key challenges related to international HR effectiveness.[9] These seven critical HRM issues are summarized in Exhibit 4-1. As will be shown later in this chapter, dealing effectively with these issues requires a global human resource management perspective.

Global human resource management (GHRM) refers to the policies and practices related to managing people in an internationally oriented organization. Although GHRM includes the same functions as domestic HRM, there are many unique aspects to human resource management in the international organization.

The purpose of this chapter is to explain the unique character of GHRM and to provide a framework for understanding the effects of national, cultural, and global business differences on effective HRM practices.

EXHIBIT 4-1
HRM Challenges for Multinational Corporations

Source: GMAC Global Relocation Services, National Foreign Trade Council, and SHRM Global Forum (2004), *Global Relocation Trends 2003/2004 Survey Report.*

Human Resource Challenge	Percentage Reporting as High Priority
Finding suitable candidates	73%
Intercultural understanding	55
Career management	45
Employee retention	44
Adjusting to environment	42
Partner dissatisfaction	41
Relocation reluctance	36

EXHIBIT 4-2
International Comparison of Labor Costs

Source: Bureau of Labor Statistics (2003).

There are many reasons that an organization might expand its operations beyond its domestic boundaries, but all are intended to help achieve the end results outlined in the diagnostic model: satisfied employees and competitive products and services. The specific reasons include searching for new or broader markets, acquiring new and more efficient manufacturing technology, and taking advantage of large, inexpensive labor forces located in other countries. Exhibit 4-2 shows how much less expensive it can be for a typical manufacturing operation to locate some of its production outside (e.g., Mexico) of nations with high labor costs, such as the United States and Japan.

One way in which many corporations located in high-labor-cost countries are utilizing this untapped labor supply is through maquiladora factories along the border between the United States and Mexico. The *maquiladoras* are Mexican assembly plants that are used by international companies for routine production processes. They are sometimes called "twin plants" because many of them are associated with large research and development operations located just inside the United States.[10]

The maquiladoras, most of which are owned by American, Japanese, and Korean manufacturing organizations, save these corporations millions of dollars each year in labor costs. The savings easily offset any potential increase in shipping costs that the organizations might incur.

After a couple of sluggish years following the slowdown of the U.S. economy in 2001, the maquiladora industry is once again showing signs of strong growth. In June 2004, approximately 2,900 plants exported goods worth a total of $7.72 billion. In addition, over 55,000 new jobs were added during the first half of 2004. Over 90 percent of these manufactured and assembled goods—including everything from automobiles, computers, and refrigerators—are exported into the United States.[11] The impact of the twin plants along the U.S.–Mexico border is indisputable.

Mexico is not the only area popular with American firms that want to develop cooperative business relationships; nor is a search for less expensive labor the only driving force behind such relationships. One reason that Intel built a manufacturing facility in Limerick, Ireland, was that certain targeted businesses are guaranteed that their tax rate will not increase beyond 10 percent until the year 2010.[12]

Foreign direct investment in developed countries and regions like the United States, the European Union, and Japan has decreased since 2001, but is still a very important source for each of their economies. For example, in 2003, the United States received approximately $30 billion; the European Union, $95 billion; and Japan, $6 billion in foreign direct investment from other countries. In contrast to the 1990s, developing countries in

Africa, Asia, and the Pacific are seeing increases in the amount of foreign direct investment they received in 2003 over the previous year.[13]

The Cultural Nature of Global HRM

Most HR professionals no longer question that there are important cultural differences between nations that might influence the effectiveness of HRM policies and practices. The real issue is understanding these differences and ensuring that HRM and the cultural orientation of workers are congruent with one another.

Several models of how culture influences work behavior exist. Perhaps the most widely recognized is Hofstede's "theory of the cultural relativity of organizational practices."[14] Hofstede argues that national cultural differences are not changing much at all, even though more superficial work-related norms and values might be. As a result, he feels that national culture will continue to have a strong influence on the effectiveness of various business practices.

According to Hofstede, cultures differ in at least five ways that may have important implications for understanding business.[15] The five dimensions are:

1. *Individualism versus collectivism* Cultures differ in terms of the relationship of a person to his or her "family." In some societies, such as Peru and Taiwan, the group's achievement and well-being will be emphasized over the individual's. In contrast, individualistic societies like the United States and Australia place more emphasis on individual actions, accomplishments, and goals.

2. *Power distance* Cultures also vary in their view of power relationships. Human inequality is almost inevitable, but cultures with a high "power distance" emphasize these differences. For example, symbols of power and authority such as large offices, titles, and so on are usually found in a culture with a high power distance. In a culture with a low power distance, there is less emphasis on such displays. In German corporations, the concepts of codetermination and worker councils are common. Giving employees genuine input into important decisions is an organizational practice typical of low-power-distance cultures.

3. *Avoidance of uncertainty* Another inevitability is not knowing what the future holds. Cultures like Japan and Portugal with a high avoidance of uncertainty attempt to predict, control, and influence future events, while cultures with a low avoidance of uncertainty are more willing to take things day by day. To the extent that control reduces uncertainty, the rigid use of managerial control systems is more likely to be found in organizations in high-uncertainty-avoidance cultures.

4. *Masculinity* The fourth dimension (which was the last one in Hofstede's original work) refers to the division of roles for males and females that a particular culture imposes. Masculine cultures have strict sex roles; feminine cultures have less well-defined roles. From an organizational perspective, masculine cultures like Austria and Japan might tend to be less supportive of efforts to integrate women into upper-level management than feminine cultures found in Norway and Sweden.

5. *Long-term versus short-term orientation* This fifth dimension was not included in Hofstede's original work but was added later as a result of studies involving Chinese values. It generally refers to the extent to which cultures think in terms of the future (the long term) or in terms of more immediate events (the short term).

Virtually every aspect of HRM can be influenced by cultural differences along one or more of these dimensions. For example, there is evidence that national differences in uncertainty avoidance and power distance can affect the extensiveness of organizational selection practices.[16] Similarly, differences in individualism and collectivism can affect the overall success that a training program has on culturally diverse audiences.[17]

The Concept of "Fit" in Global HRM

When an organization structures its HRM policies for international operations, it should consider cultural differences through the concept of "fit." *Fit* refers to the degree that HRM policies are congruent with the strategic international plan of the organization and with the work-related values of foreign culture.[18]

For an organization to be successful in the international marketplace, it must be concerned with this fit from both an internal and an external perspective. *Internal fit* is concerned with making sure that HRM policies facilitate the work values and motivations of employees. Policies must be structured in ways that allow headquarters and foreign subsidiaries to interact without sacrificing efficiency.

External fit, on the other hand, refers to the degree to which HRM matches the context in which the organization is operating. In this regard, HRM is critical to international operations because of its effects on cross-cultural interaction.[19] To be effective, the organization must understand the cultural and socioeconomic environments of the foreign subsidiary.[20]

Multinational and Global Corporations

Although the terms are sometimes treated as the same, there are distinctions between a **multinational corporation** and a **global corporation** that have important HRM implications. Multinational corporations (MNCs) are usually found in the early stages of an internationalization strategy. An MNC has operations in many different nations, but each is viewed as a relatively separate enterprise. Within each country, the operations of the MNC strongly resemble a miniature version of the parent company in terms of structure, product lines, and procedures. Each separate enterprise within the MNC will be responsible for adapting the company's products to the local culture, but most significant control remains either with the company's home offices or in the hands of an expatriate from the home country. However, most of the employees and managers will tend to be from the host country as MNCs utilize polycentric staffing practices. This is especially true in the earliest stages of internationalization.

In contrast to the MNC, the global corporation (GC) is structured so that national boundaries disappear; this leads to staffing practices in which the organization hires the best people for jobs irrespective of national origin. This is referred to as a global or geocentric staffing approach. The GC sees the world as its labor source as well as its marketplace. Thus, the global corporation will locate an operation wherever it can accomplish its goals in the most cost-effective way. The true global corporation like Coco-Cola, Nestlé, or McDonald's, also believes in a world market for its products.[21] This leads to a very different strategy of managing international operations because each subsidiary of the company isn't restricted to serving only the local culture. Moreover, the national affiliation of an employee becomes less important than his or her particular area of expertise as people are frequently moved across national boundaries to meet the current needs of the organization.[22]

GHRM in the early 21st century will be a challenging task for both an MNC and a GC. Many of the problems that the MNC and GC will face are the same; others are unique to one or the other. Exhibit 4-3 illustrates the major focus of GHRM processes for these two different international perspectives.

Generally speaking, there are three sources of employees for an international assignment. For key managerial and technical positions, all three sources of workers are frequently used in international organizations. Which source is used the most depends, however, on the GHRM perspective of the company. The organization might choose to hire

> **Host country nationals (HCNs),** who are employees from the local population. Sometimes they are referred to as *local nationals.* An employee from Riyadh employed by an American firm operating in Saudi Arabia would be considered a host country national.

EXHIBIT 4-3   **HRM Focus for Multinational and Global Corporations**

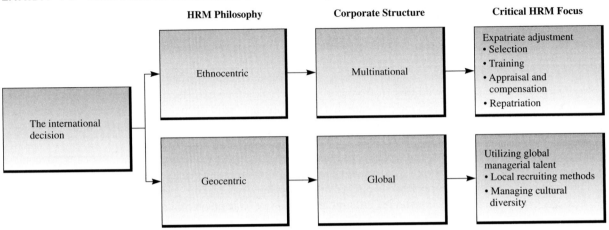

Parent country nationals (PCNs), who are sent from the country in which the organization is headquartered. These people are usually referred to as expatriates. An American manager on assignment in Saudi Arabia is an expatriate or parent country national.

Third country nationals (TCNs), who are from a country other than where the parent organization's headquarters or operations are located. If the American firm employed a manager from Great Britain at facilities in Saudi Arabia, he or she would be considered a third country national.

If the company is an MNC, especially one that is in the early stages of becoming an international enterprise, it will probably take a relatively **ethnocentric perspective** by trying to use the HRM policies from the home country with at best minor adaptations. The new, ethnocentric multinational organization generally believes that all key personnel should be PCNs because it believes that its ways of doing things are superior to those of other cultures.

The tendency to be ethnocentric is strong for new and even for many well-established foreign organizations conducting business in the United States, especially the Japanese. Virtually every executive-level position in Japanese-owned businesses in the United States is occupied by a Japanese national. Only about 31 percent of the senior management positions in such firms are occupied by American managers. More commonly, local nationals are used for specific functions such as a liaison, but Japanese organizations have a reputation for showing little regard for the career development of these persons. In contrast, foreign companies in Japan hire local Japanese managers for nearly 80 percent of their management needs.[23]

In contrast to the ethnocentric perspective, a mature MNC or a true global corporation will tend to have more of a **geocentric orientation** to HRM. It will begin seeing the world as its labor market and, therefore, will hire key personnel from wherever they are available. The geocentric organization will ignore national boundaries for staffing its overseas operations.

Regardless of its overall strategy, the single biggest HR challenge facing any globally oriented corporation is finding competent expatriate managers.[24] Traditionally, an **expatriate manager** is a manager who is on a foreign assignment from the corporation's home nation. In today's global economy, however, corporations are beginning to understand that relocation overseas can be equally troublesome for the parent country national.

Thus, the real challenge for GHRM will be to capitalize on the diversity of a global workforce without suppressing each nation's desire to maintain its own cultural heritage.

Perhaps the biggest mistake unsuccessful global organizations make is to assume that there is "one best way" to structure HRM policies and practices. For example, as many as 120 critical differences between Japanese and American workplace norms that might affect HRM policies have been identified. Many of these revolve around HRM policies related to feedback and performance evaluation methods, lines of authority, and information management.[25] Therefore, trying to apply HRM principles that work well in one work environment may not lead to the same degree of success in another.

The Expatriate Manager in the Multinational Corporation

As mentioned previously, managing the expatriate's adjustment process is a primary focus of GHRM for the multinational corporation. The difficulty of this task has increased in recent years, for several reasons. First, multinationals have shifted more and more of their sales and production to countries closer to their worldwide markets. Thus, they are doing business in record numbers of different nations and cultures. Second, there is a slow but steady increase in the use of host country and third country management, with a concurrent increase in the number of "inpats" found in large multinationals. An inpat is a foreign manager on assignment in the parent country headquarters. Research indicates that these persons can also have a difficult time adapting to their new surroundings,[26] so their adjustment must also be a priority for the global HR manager.

When these statistics are coupled with the results of recent surveys indicating that a majority of multinationals actually plan to increase their use of expatriates (especially those on short-term and traveling global assignments) in the coming years,[27] it is obvious that expatriates will play crucial roles in many of the world's largest international employers. It is, in fact, estimated that approximately 80 percent of all middle- to large-size companies use expatriates.[28] For example, Northern Telecom has doubled the number of expatriates it employs since the early 1990s; it now has 450 people on extended (3- to 5-year) assignments, with an additional 300 people on international assignments of shorter durations.[29]

Despite the importance of expatriate managers in international business, many companies are apparently not yet effectively selecting and preparing their employees for overseas assignments. Though estimates of the failure rates (or premature return) of American expatriates are often exaggerated or misquoted, there is sufficient research evidence to suggest that on average, American expatriates fail more often than do their Japanese and European counterparts.[30] This should not come as a surprise when considering the results of a recent study of 134 multinational firms with a combined total of 31,000 expatriates, which found that only 60 percent of companies provide cross-cultural training for their overseas assignees.[31] These findings were corroborated by the results of a comparable research study of 270 European firms that employ over 65,000 expatriates.[32]

Selecting the Expatriate Manager

Exhibit 4-4 lists the factors that seem to be most commonly associated with expatriates' success and failure. It is obvious from the list that selection for expatriate assignments will be an extremely complex and sensitive task. Many of the factors that are related to a successful expatriate assignment will be difficult to measure, and the managers' level of success in domestic operations may have very little to do with their success overseas. One of the major reasons that expatriate failure rates are so high for many American companies is that these companies continue to believe that a manager's domestic performance will always be related to his or her overseas performance. As a result, many expatriates believe that too little attention is being paid to numerous other critical factors during the selection process.[33]

EXHIBIT 4-4
Expatriate Managers' Success and Failure

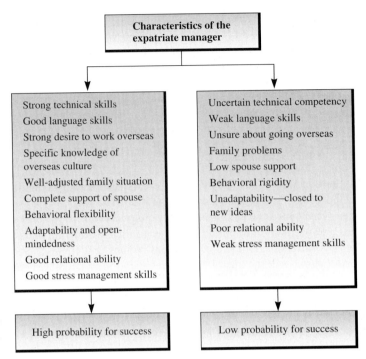

HRMEMO

The proportion of women among American expatriates has inched upward over the past several years. Estimates are that approximately 18 percent of U.S. expatriates are female. Many attribute this relatively low percentage to bias selection practices that are influenced by outdated beliefs that women are less interested in overseas assignments and that they will not be treated with the same amount of respect from members of the host country.

Sources: GMAC Global Relocation Services, National Foreign Trade Council, and SHRM Global Forum (2004), *Global Relocation Trends 2003/2004 Survey Report;* Hilary Harris (March–April 2002), "Think International Manager, Think Male," *Thunderbird International Business Review,* pp. 175–203; Kathryn Tyler (2001), "Don't Fence Her In," *HRMagazine,* pp. 69–77; Linda Stroh, Arup Varma, and Stacey Valy-Durbin (Fall 2000), "Why Are Women Left at Home: Are They Unwilling to Go on International Assignments?" *Journal of World Business,* pp. 241–255.

While technical competency is obviously important, expatriate manager selection should focus on at least three other major categories of skills:

1. Manager's self-image—levels of self-confidence, self-esteem, and ability to cope with stress.
2. Manager's normal way of interacting with others—interpersonal style and sensitivity to nonverbal communication.
3. Manager's perceptual orientation—ability to tolerate uncertainty, open-mindedness, and acceptance of cultural differences.[34]

Thus, as Exhibit 4-4 shows, the first key to finding a successful expatriate is a selection process that accurately determines who is culturally flexible and adaptable, has a supportive family situation, and is motivated to accept the overseas assignment.

The role of the expatriate's family should never be underestimated when making decisions about overseas assignments. Research indicates that when the spouse and/or family adjusts to the new culture, it can significantly affect the expatriate's performance.[35] Some evidence even suggests that a spouse's inability to adjust to the overseas assignment is the single most common factor in expatriates' failures.[36] For an expatriate with children, worries over schooling and leisure activities can add to the stress associated with the assignment. Eventually, if these worries are not resolved, the assignment might end with an early return of the expatriate to his or her parent country.

Family support for the expatriate can be improved if family members are directly involved in the decision-making process. Fortunately, it appears that many companies now understand how important this can be. Not only are family members interviewed during the selection process, but many international companies now include family members in training programs and systematically use the knowledge and experience that family members who have been on international assignments have gained through their experiences.[37]

One of the more difficult family issues to deal with during the process of selecting and training expatriate managers is the realities of dual career marriages in the United States.

HR Journal — *Rapid Response Expatriates: The New Generation of Global Managers*

Expatriate managers have become an integral part of the global marketplace. Historically, organizations have needed qualified managers willing to travel overseas regardless of the cost. And the costs of traditional expatriate managers have been well documented, easily running two to three times more than a domestic peer. Now, however, organizations are increasingly cost conscious when they assess the usefulness of international assignees. As a result, a new generation of expatriate manager is emerging. Today, there are record numbers of short-term assignment expatriates stationed around the globe. Organizations are also employing "just-in-time" expatriates, managers with specialized skills who are hired for assignments of limited duration.

A number of potential advantages are associated with the new generation expatriate. First, organizations find that short-term assignments are more attractive to a significant number of managers who otherwise would opt out of an international assignment. Second, when structured properly, these assignments create much less stress and strain on the expatriate's family, frequently requiring no relocation. Third, the organization may identify and arrange for the transfer of a short-term expatriate much more quickly than for the traditional expatriate. Toward this end, the Internet has become an invaluable tool. By posting global assignments on the World Wide Web, organizations can quickly identify qualified candidates from a much larger pool than parent country national managers alone. In today's

business environment, rapid response can be the difference between winners and losers bidding for lucrative overseas contracts. And last, but certainly not least, short-term assignments prove to be substantially less costly overall to the organization than more traditional assignments. The savings stem from a number of factors including lower foreign service premiums, reduced relocation costs, and perhaps, most important, dramatically lower turnover and failure rates.

A new generation of expatriate is clearly on the business horizon. Experts warn, however, that not all overseas projects can be handled effectively by the short-termers. More traditional expatriates will still be needed in the foreseeable future, but the new perspective on global management is clearly changing the nature of expatriate recruitment, selection, and placement.

Sources: Robert Konopaske, Chet Robie, and John M. Ivancevich (March 2005), "A Preliminary Model of Spouse Influence on Managerial Global Assignment Willingness," *The International Journal of Human Resource Management*, Vol. 16, Iss. 3, pp. 405–426; Helene Mayerhofer, Linley C. Hartmann, Gabriela Michelitsch-Riedl, and Iris Kollinger (December 2004), "Flexpatriate Assignments: A Neglected Issue in Global Staffing," *The International Journal of Human Resource Management*, Vol.15, Iss. 8, pp. 1371–1389; Siobhan Cummins (October 2000), "Short-Term Assignments: Combining Employer and Employee Interests," *Benefits & Compensation International*, pp. 8–12.

As a result of this trend, organizations are becoming more actively involved in career assistance for expatriates' spouses, especially since issues regarding spouses' careers are the most frequently cited reason that qualified managers turn down an international assignment.[38]

A company can do several things to enhance the expatriate manager's motivation to accept and do well in an international assignment. Attractive compensation programs can help. Perhaps more important, however, is providing comprehensive predeparture training[39] and making sure that the assignment is perceived as beneficial to the manager's long-term career objectives.[40]

Culture Shock and the Expatriate Manager

A trip to a foreign culture can cause tourists and expatriate managers alike to go through a predictable series of reactions to their unfamiliar surroundings. Exhibit 4-5 illustrates the cycle of these reactions. First, there is a period of fascination, where all of the different aspects of the culture are viewed with interest and curiosity. This first reaction to a new culture is generally a positive experience.

Next, however, comes a period known as **culture shock.** Culture shock refers to the frustration and confusion that result from being constantly subjected to strange and unfamiliar

EXHIBIT 4-5
The Culture Shock Cycle

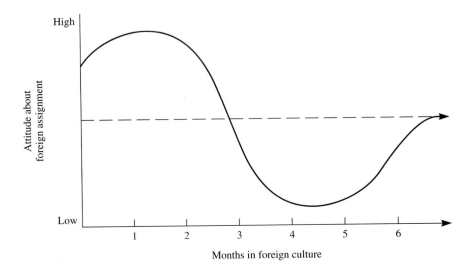

cues about what to do and how to get it done.[41] Notice, in Exhibit 4-5, that culture shock does not typically occur during the earliest days of a trip overseas. Thus, while many expatriate managers' assignments begin very positively, their experiences often turn negative soon after.

The final stage of coping with a new culture is adaptation. During this stage, the expatriate has made reasonable adjustments to the new culture and is able to deal effectively with it. Although this stage seldom returns the expatriate to the heights of excitement that he or she first experienced, a successful transition to a new culture does return the expatriate to manageable levels of a "normal" lifestyle.

So, how can HR help the expatriate to deal effectively with the inevitable frustrations of culture shock? The answer obviously begins with preparation. Successful expatriates *want* to live and work overseas.[42] Forcing a manager to accept an extended assignment in a new culture and disrupting his or her family structure will inevitably result in failure.

Language skills are also invaluable to the future expatriate. Some experts suggest, in fact, that fluency in the host country's language is the single most important aid the expatriate has for dealing with the multitude of business challenges that await.[43]

A comprehensive approach to the international assignment also includes preparation for the host country personnel that will be working with the newly arrived expatriate. His or her culture will be as unfamiliar to the host country nationals as theirs is to the expatriate.[44] And without their cooperation the expatriate's efforts are destined for failure.

Another important step is to prepare the expatriate and his or her family for *reverse culture shock,* which can affect these individuals after they return to their home country and culture.[45] For example, the returning expatriate, having changed while abroad, finds that he or she no longer fits well with the company culture and seeks alternative employment. Also, reverse culture shock can affect the spouse when they find out that their career cannot be restarted immediately without networking for a job and upgrading some of the skills that may have become outdated while living overseas.

Training the Expatriate Manager

Once the groundwork for a successful overseas assignment has been laid by choosing expatriates who have good chances of succeeding, the next step toward ensuring success is for the organization to properly train and prepare these managers for their upcoming assignments. As with selection, training programs for expatriate managers need to focus on issues that are not typically dealt with in domestic training programs.

EXHIBIT 4-6
Cross-Cultural Training and Consulting Companies

The following are companies that provide cross-cultural training, consulting, and other services for global assignees. For more information, please visit the following Web site: http://www.shrmglobal.org/function/xculture.asp.

Cendant Intercultural (http://www.cendantintercultural.com/)

Cendant Intercultural is an international training and consulting firm, specializing in international human resources support services. The firm's primary service areas are global workforce development and international assignment support services, such as cross-cultural training, destination services, assessment and selection, and repatriation workshops. Cendant Intercultural has trainers, associates, and destination services representatives in over 100 countries worldwide.

Berlitz International, Inc. (http://www.berlitz.com)

Berlitz, provider of international language training services, offers customized language instructions, cross-cultural training, translation, and interpretation services through 400 offices worldwide, including more than 70 in the United States and Canada. Private, semiprivate, and group programs are available, and the Total Immersion Program delivers conversational proficiency in as little as 2 to 6 weeks. Certain Berlitz courses are recommended for college credits by the American Council on Education.

Farnham Castle (http://www.farnhamcastle.com)

For 50 years the castle has been the home of the world renowned Farnham Castle International Briefing and Conference Centre, providing intercultural training to employees of the world's leading companies as well as U.K. and overseas governments. In addition, specific programs are available in intercultural management, country and business briefings, repatriation, and intensive language training.

Global Dynamics (http://www.global-dynamics.com)

Global Dynamics Inc. is a leading provider of cross-cultural management, expatriate, team building, and marketing solutions designed to meet the global needs of multinational corporations. In addition to having an in-depth Knowledge Management Resource Center, Global Dynamics offers a variety of cross-cultural programs that are designed to enhance the effectiveness of all persons whose work brings them into contact with people from other countries. Some of the more popular programs include Working Globally, Living and Working Internationally and in the United States, Executive Coaching, International Team Building, Virtual Teamwork, Effective Electronic Communications for Global Business, Change Management, Project Management and Country Specific Programs, and a variety of language and repatriate programs.

Sietar International (http://www.sietar.org)

Sietar International is an international professional organization for managers, consultants, and educators who are involved in facilitating contact, exchange, and integration for students, trainees, migrants, and professional personnel operating in a host culture different from their own. Members include educators at primary, secondary and third level whose subject areas include languages, geography, civics, international relations, or conflict resolution; administrators and faculty of study abroad and foreign student programs; third world development administrators and trainers; international business and language trainers; and intercultural exchange facilitators. Publication: *Communique—International Journal of Intercultural Relations.*

Intercultural training does seem to improve the chances for success on an overseas assignment.[46] According to Tung,[47] there are two primary determinants of how much and what kind of training expatriate managers should receive. These are the level of contact with the host culture that the expatriate will encounter and the degree of dissimilarity between the home and host cultures. As either of these increases, the expatriate will require more in-depth training for the overseas assignment.

As can be seen in Exhibit 4-6, expatriate training can involve three different phases, and each phase has specific objectives for helping the expatriate to be successful.

EXHIBIT 4-7
Expatriates' Self-Awareness; Being Prepared for Culture Shock

Source: Adapted from Philip R. Harris and Robert T. Moran (1991), "So You're Going Abroad Survey," in *Managing Cultural Differences*, 3rd ed. (Houston: Gulf Publishing).

Prospective global managers should prepare satisfactory answers to the following questions before going on an overseas assignment:

1. Can we expect to encounter any anti-Americanism? What about the threat of terrorism?
2. How will living abroad affect me and my family?
3. What will my spouse do in terms of work and home life?
4. Are my children prepared for living abroad?
5. What assistance and support will be available to us?
6. What will happen to our home and other personal property while we are gone?
7. What arrangements can be made for family pets?
8. How will we handle health care while we are overseas?
9. What security measures should we take?
10. What kinds of recreational opportunities are available?
11. Will language barriers present problems for me?
12. What is the proper form of dress for various occasions?
13. How will we handle transportation at the overseas location?
14. What kinds of food can we expect to eat?

Predeparture training includes the critical activities of preparing the expatriate for the overseas assignment. Its purpose is to reduce the amount of culture shock that the manager and his or her family encounter by familiarizing them with the host country. It also helps to increase the expatriate manager's commitment to the parent organization, perhaps also leading to higher performance.[48]

Self-awareness is an important aspect of successfully preparing for an international assignment. Assessment techniques such as those presented in Exhibit 4-7 can be very helpful to the expatriate. Responding to these kinds of questions can help the manager know where he or she is most likely to encounter the ill effects of culture shock. This kind of advance preparation can go a long way toward reducing the negative effects of being transplanted to a new culture.

The second phase of the training program occurs at the host country site. In other words, training does not stop just because the manager has his or her boarding pass in hand. Language training continues to be a priority during this phase of training. In addition, mentoring relationships have proved to be very effective tools for training expatriates. For many organizations that have several expatriates at the same overseas location, local support groups have developed to help the entire family of a newly arriving expatriate.

Many experts suggest that one method for helping the expatriate manager to cope with a new culture is to get him or her involved with daily experiences as soon as possible.[49]

The final phase of an integrated expatriate training program occurs when the manager prepares to return to the parent country. The process of being reintegrated into domestic operations is referred to as repatriation. And, while too many organizations assume that **repatriation** is a straightforward matter, evidence suggests that it can be even more frustrating than the culture shock experienced by the expatriate during the overseas assignment. The reality of repatriation is that managers returning home after an overseas assignment are more likely to leave the parent organization than their domestic counterparts, due in large part to a mismatch between the expatriate's expectations and the reality of life at the home offices.[50] Surveys indicate that not only do many expatriates experience the "out of sight, out of mind" syndrome, but a sizable number believe that they have actually lost ground to their domestic peers in terms of career advancement.[51] Considering the fact that 68 percent of firms do not provide postassignment guarantees, it's not surprising to learn that only 40 percent of returning expatriates were unsure whether international assignments lead to enhanced promotion opportunities within their companies.[52] This may help explain why 82 percent of expatriates believe that their companies are not doing enough to keep their careers on track after an international assignment.[53]

As is the case in domestic career management, an organization can help managers deal with such issues if it actively plans how the international assignment will fit with the expatriate manager's career aspirations. To do so, companies should identify prospective international managers early in their careers. In fact, many companies who are now committed to the international marketplace realize that every hire should be treated as a prospective global employee. Interest in and propensity for accepting an international assignment has become a routine part of recruitment.[54]

Compensating the Expatriate Manager

Maintaining an expatriate manager on an overseas assignment is very expensive. Estimates are that a middle- to upper-level expatriate can cost an organization anywhere from two to three times what it costs to maintain him or her on a domestic assignment.[55] These higher costs are often due to the compensation practices of many multinational organizations. One of the most popular international compensation approaches for U.S., European, and Japanese firms is known as the *balance-sheet approach*. The objective here is to ensure that the expatriate maintains a similar standard of living (i.e., is "kept whole") as in the home country and to ensure employee mobility by providing some financial incentives to accept the global assignment. The major components include assistance with home and host country income taxes, host country housing, goods and services (e.g., food, clothing, medical care), and a reserve for contributions to savings, benefits, pensions, and the like.

In addition, expatriates are often provided with a variety of "extras" as incentives for relocation and to make sure they are able to maintain their home country standard of living. According to Milkovich and Newman,[56] there are three broad categories of allowances:

1. *Financial* Examples include company-paid children's education allowance, home leave allowance, mobility premium, and assignment completion bonuses.
2. *Social adjustment* Rest and relaxation leave, language and cross-cultural training, club memberships, and assistance with locating a new home.
3. *Family support* Child care providers, assistance locating spousal employment, and assistance locating schools for children.

One of the most popular financial allowances, expatriate premiums, sometimes referred to as "foreign service premiums," are adjustments made to the expatriate manager's base salary for the inconvenience that an international assignment causes both the manager and his or her family.[57] Foreign service premiums usually vary in size according to the perceived hardship that the host culture causes. For example, foreign service premiums paid to American expatriates at Amoco (BP) range from nothing for an assignment in Canada to 25 percent for an assignment in Thailand to a full 50 percent if the expatriate is stationed in Azerbaijan.

The actual cost of living in many foreign settings is extremely high. The five most expensive cities in the world include Tokyo, London, Moscow, Osaka, and Hong Kong.[58] The expatriate's compensation will usually include a cost-of-living premium to offset these differences. These premiums might be further supplemented with a home maintenance allowance, a home furnishings allowance, assistance with maintaining or selling the expatriate's home before leaving for the overseas assignment, transportation differential allowances, educational allowances, and hardship premiums in difficult or hazardous environments.

When all of the costs incurred with an expatriate are added together, a company is faced with spending as much as five times the manager's domestic salary to maintain him or her and the family overseas for just one year.[59] To combat these costs, some firms have shifted to using more short-term assignees.[60] Interestingly, even short-term expatriate assignments can be expensive for companies as illustrated in Exhibit 4-8.

EXHIBIT 4-8
Sample Costs* of a Short-Term Expatriate in London

Source: Adapted from Runzheimer International Short-Term Assignment Report (June 25, 2002), www.runzheimer.com.

Monthly Expenses	Accompanied (2-bedroom, 2 adults)	Unaccompanied (1-bedroom, 1 adult)
Housing:		
Apartment rental	U.S. $3,718	U.S. $2,091
Furniture rental	included	included
Utilities	included	included
Maid service	included	included
Food:		
Food at home	253	156
Food out of home	1,271	635
Car:		
Rental	1,742	1,742
Fuel	244	244
Miscellaneous:		
Personal	148	99
Laundry	195	117
Total monthly living expenses:	$7,571	$5,084
Total annual living expenses:	$90,852	$61,008

*Costs (in U.S. dollars) subject to change based on British pound–U.S. dollar exchange rate.

In spite of the costs, many corporations continue to rely heavily on short- and long-term expatriate managers. The importance of expatriates can be summed up by the comments of John Pepper, chairman of the board of Procter and Gamble, who believes that international assignments were one of the most powerful development experiences in shaping him as an effective global leader.[61]

Host Country Nationals and the Global Corporation

When an organization begins to operate as a global rather than a multinational corporation, the use of expatriate managers will decrease. Part of the desire to limit the use of expatriates stems directly from the high cost of sending managers and their families on international assignments. Organizations are also beginning to understand, however, that managers who are host country nationals have distinct advantages over expatriates in terms of cultural sensitivity and understanding local employees' motivations and needs. In order to train and develop its future Chinese managers, Motorola has established its own corporate university in China.[62] Other companies have turned over more of the key managerial positions in their foreign operations to host country and even third country nationals. When Dell Computer built its new manufacturing plant in Ireland, for example, it hired an Irish managing director immediately.[63] To solve its management problem, Las Vegas–based Bally Gaming International hired former East Germans who had lived in Russia for many years to manage its majority-owned Russian joint ventures.[64] However, many companies still have strong reservations about using HCNs. Some of the reasons most frequently mentioned for not using locals are (1) concern that the locals will not adopt the parent company's culture and management system, (2) concern about the level of commitment to the organization that locals may have, (3) concern that HCNs may not have the expertise that expatriates have, and (4) concern about how effective communication will be between the host country and home offices.

Careful recruitment, selection, and training can reduce or eliminate many of the potential problems with using HCNs. Current estimates suggest that American corporations, for example, employ approximately 5.4 million foreign workers in overseas operations, but although many developing nations welcome foreign investments, they also want their own citizens to begin occupying more critical managerial positions in foreign-owned companies.[65] Thus, it is essential for global HR professionals to understand that training for international assignments is a two-sided coin—train the expatriate to be more culturally sensitive, and train the host country manager to be prepared to accept greater responsibility.

Noel Tichy and his colleagues describe one of the most elaborate selection and training systems designed to help global managers bridge their cultural differences.[66] The program, referred to as the Global Leadership Program (GLP), is an intense leadership development program whose purpose is to facilitate communication and teamwork among culturally diverse executives. The integrated training experience involves both off-site and on-the-job training methods and even involves many physical "Outward Bound" kinds of activities. One of the first classes of managers to be trained in the GLP brought together upper-level executives from America, Europe, and Asia. The results reported by Tichy and his colleagues are quite encouraging and suggest that cultural barriers can be effectively eliminated in the global corporation of the future.

When an organization recruits HCNs, it should not assume that the same sources that it uses for domestic applicants will be effective. Its HRM policies will definitely have to be more flexible, and the organization will have to strive for a reasonable fit between these policies and cultural values.[67]

Several suggestions can improve the effectiveness of HCN recruiting efforts. Overall, the best advice is for the organization to follow the example of other companies doing business in a particular country. Try to use the same methods and sources as the host country organizations.[68] Specifically, a recruiting liaison can help with the details of the process. Recruitment ads should be written in ways that are consistent with local custom and jargon so there are no misunderstandings. In addition, so the company can get the best picture of an applicant's qualifications, HCNs should be allowed to use their native language during interviews.[69]

A Note on Global Corporate Boards of Directors

In spite of the movement toward global corporations in today's business world, the boards of directors of most major American corporations have been slow to include foreign members. In a survey of 589 American corporations, only 24 percent of the manufacturing firms, 14 percent of the financial firms, and 9 percent of other nonfinancial firms had a global representative on their boards. And while major Japanese corporations continue to share this ethnocentrism with regard to corporate boards, European companies are progressing more quickly. Nestlé, Unilever, Fiat, and Volvo all have global representation on their boards.[70]

The Legal and Ethical Climate of Global HRM

When an organization decides to become an international enterprise, it will be confronted with new and potentially unique standards of legal and ethical conduct. International business is conducted in a maze of international trade agreements, parent country laws, and host country regulation of foreign enterprises. In addition, many decisions that might challenge an organization's normal standards of ethical conduct may be encountered. For example, environmental regulation is weaker in many countries around the world than it is in the United States. Since relaxed environmental controls can allow an organization to operate at lower cost, management philosophy about protecting the environment will inevitably have to be dealt with. Should the organization continue to meet or exceed standards used in the United States, or should it merely attempt to meet less stringent foreign standards?

Other business practices that are considered unethical or illegal in the United States might be considered part of the normal conduct of business in other countries. "Gift giving" is a common practice in many parts of the world. Unfortunately, in situations where there is a conflict of interest, such gift giving can be considered bribery in the United States. The Congress of the United States was so concerned with this particular issue that it passed the **Foreign Corrupt Practices Act of 1977 (FCPA).**

The purpose of the FCPA was to make it illegal for employees of American corporations to induce foreign officials, by offering monetary or other payments, to use their influence to gain an unfair competitive advantage for the organization. However, it does not prohibit payments made to minor officials if the payments are intended to get the official to provide normal clerical services (e.g., processing paperwork at a customs office) in a more timely fashion. This kind of "greasing" is common in many countries, but such payments are probably not a violation of the FCPA, since they do not have a corrupt intent. At the same time, many forms of payment that are not illegal in the host country might very well be considered violations.[71]

Another legal area in which many HR professionals from American corporations will find substantial differences from country to country is employment discrimination. Although equal opportunity employment is, unfortunately, not yet a reality in all American corporations, we do have some of the more stringent antidiscrimination laws affecting HR activities such as recruitment, selection, training, and compensation. As detailed in Chapter 3, there are numerous laws designed to regulate how organizations can and should make such decisions. Many countries around the world have not, however, attempted to create this kind of enforcement.

The differences that exist can create many problems for the HR manager thrown into a new cultural and legal arena. Host country managers may not understand or accept the standards of conduct that the expatriate manager has become accustomed to. One thing is, however, very clear. The Civil Rights Act of 1991, which prohibits discrimination on the basis of sex, race, religion, color, and national origin, applies to American corporations' overseas operations.

Doing business overseas can also create ethical dilemmas related to the potential conflict that exists between profits and the preservation of basic human rights. Perhaps the most famous case where business, morality, and politics clashed was in the disengagement of most American corporations from South Africa during the era of apartheid. Today, similar ethical dilemmas occur around the globe in developing countries where child labor is abused and working conditions for adults may be abysmal. It is, in fact, a significant issue for the maquiladoras that were discussed earlier in the chapter. On one hand, the maquiladoras provide an attractive opportunity for otherwise impoverished people to earn a living.[72] Unfortunately, the other side of the maquiladoras sometimes reveals widespread safety and health problems at these foreign-owned sites.[73]

Resolving ethical dilemmas of this kind is not a simple task. Is it worse for an organization to be associated with labor abuses or to not invest at all in developing nations? To help answer some of these questions during apartheid in South Africa, the Reverend Leon Sullivan articulated six principles to promote racial equality in employment practices. (See Exhibit 4-9.) Reverend Sullivan was the first African American to serve on General Motors' board of directors. In that role, he was able to influence the direction of corporate America through his **"Sullivan Principles,"** as they are now known. The basic tenets of the principles were designed to eliminate oppressive racism in South African business.[74] This was perhaps the first major attempt by a large U.S. corporation to codify ethics in international business.

EXHIBIT 4-9
The Sullivan Principles

Source: *See* www.sullivanprinciples.org.

- Nonsegregation of the races in all work facilities.
- Equal and fair employment practices for all employees.
- Equal pay for all employees performing equal work.
- Training programs to prepare, in substantial numbers, blacks and other nonwhites for supervisory and technical jobs.
- Increasing the number of blacks and other nonwhite minorities in management.
- Improving the quality of employees' lives outside the work environment.

HR Journal *Outsourcing: Does It Create or Replace Jobs in the Global Marketplace?*

There's a good chance that you recently have seen a nightly newscast or a newspaper article reporting that another U.S. company is "offshoring" or "outsourcing" part of its back-office or computer operations to a vendor in an international location like India. The trend is real. More and more firms are sending a part of their operations—software development, call centers, payroll, loan and insurance claims processing, and the like—to an offshore location. Firms like General Electric, Oracle, and Prudential engage in offshore activities. Opponents of offshoring argue that such decisions cost Americans their jobs. These critics claim that bottom-line oriented American executives are too willing to lay off Americans in order to save some money in labor costs (since an individual working at a call center in Bangalore, India, makes considerably less than her counterpart in Cleveland, Ohio). They contend that exporting jobs will have the unintended effects of increasing unemployment and transferring wealth to workers in other countries.

Do the statistics support these claims? The data provide mixed results. On one hand, companies that provide outsourcing services in India like Infosys Technologies Ltd., Wipro Ltd., and Tata Consultancy Services have experienced very rapid growth within recent years. These and other companies make up part of the $3.5 billion call center and back-office industry in India. This high-growth (and high-profit) industry has led to a recent wave of acquisitions, including IBM, which agreed to pay $150 million for Daksh eServices, the third largest call center and back-office service provider with revenues of $60 million. In a similar move, Citigroup is increasing its ownership stake in another Indian outsourcing firm, e-Serve International Ltd. Certainly, one could argue that such trends will lead to job growth for Indian workers, most likely at a cost of American jobs.

On the other hand, proponents of free trade argue that outsourcing is an economically healthy and acceptable practice that should be allowed to flourish. These individuals point out that such free trade practices have led to job growth and profits for U.S. organizations that provide such services as legal work, computer programming, telecommunications, banking, engineering, management consulting, and other private services to the world market. The U.S. Commerce Department reported in March of 2004 that the value of such U.S. exports of services had reached $131 billion. This far exceeds the amount of outsourcing of such private services as call centers and data processing operations to other countries ($77 billion as of March 2004). In 2003, U.S. organizations collectively posted a $54 billion trade surplus in private services with the rest of the world. In essence, U.S. companies that successfully sell services to the rest of the world are much more likely to be able to grow their businesses and employ larger numbers of U.S. employees. In addition to the trade surplus argument, proponents of free trade point to the number of Indian companies that have set up large operations in the United States. For example, Tata Consultancy Services has established 47 worksites in the United States to serve customers that include American Express Co., Citigroup Inc., ChevronTexaco Corp., and Eli Lilly & Co. This translates to the creation of more U.S. jobs.

In sum, outsourcing/offshoring is a controversial business practice that represents one aspect of how the globalization of business across national borders is occurring in today's global economy. In order to be effective, managers should understand how globalization impacts their domestic operations and influences the effective management of their human resources around the globe.

Sources: Julie Forster (June 27, 2004), "Universities Begin to Offer Courses on Offshoring," *Knight Ridder Tribune Business News*, p.1; Manjeet Kripalani and Steve Hamm (April 26, 2004), "Merger Fever Breaks Out in Bangalore," *BusinessWeek*, Iss. 3880, p. 56; Joanna Slater (April 8, 2004), "IBM to Buy Indian Call-Center Firm," *Wall Street Journal*, p. B6; Jay Solomon and Elena Cherney (April 1, 2004), "A Global Journal Report: Outsourcing to India Sees a Twist," *Wall Street Journal*, p. A2; Michael M. Phillips (March 15, 2004), "More Work Is Outsourced to U.S. Than Away from It, Data Show," *Wall Street Journal*, p. A2.

Labor Relations and the International Corporation

Both multinational and global corporations encounter a variety of labor relations issues that are different from purely domestic operations. There are many differences in the structure of unions and the influence that they have over an organization's operations worldwide.

After reading this chapter, David now knows how difficult it can be to become an international corporation. He also knows that there are cultural differences among nations that influence how business is conducted and what HRM practices will work. Finally, he has a real sense of just how expensive it can be to send an expatriate manager overseas and how difficult it is to prepare someone to be successful in the overseas assignment.

In their next meeting, David tells Michael that he has reconsidered and decided that more careful study of the situation should be done before making any final management team decisions. Both agree, however, that one or two key people from Ohio should undoubtedly be assigned to the European operation at least long enough for a successful transition to occur.

David   So, whom should we send, Mike? There are several people who have the technical skills to do the job.

Michael   We need to finish our assessments before I can give you an answer. At least we now know what characteristics to focus on. And please don't forget that you authorized money to establish the expatriate manager training program we talked about.

David   Stop worrying—you've got the money. Just give me some expatriates who are prepared for the challenges ahead.

Coupled with these differences are labor laws that will be virtually unique to every nation in which an organization wishes to do business.

Internationally, there are many important differences in labor–management relationships from those typically found in the United States. In Mexico, for example, management places much less emphasis on details of written contracts than it would in the United States. Culturally, the Mexican worker tends to believe in and rely on informal agreements with management more than many American unions do.[75]

Differences in how much participation employees are entitled to in setting HRM policies are another critical area for the global human resource manager to understand. If an organization tries to impose policies and procedures on workers who are used to making HRM decisions along with management, then the imposed policies will be met with resistance. Thus, before establishing operations in a different country, one important task for the global HR manager is to research the local labor relations climate.

There are many important differences in employee participation under the American labor relations system and the labor relations systems in other countries. While it is beyond the scope of this chapter to outline all of these, several examples should help to reinforce the need for understanding local labor relations before an organization becomes an MNC or a GC.

Employee codetermination is a legally guaranteed right in Germany. German law gives employees three different degrees of participation, depending on the issue in question. German worker councils merely have to be informed and consulted for most economic decisions. But they are allowed to participate in decisions such as dismissals, work procedures, and the design of the workplace. At an even greater level of involvement, worker councils have approval rights over decisions such as working hours, training programs, and safety regulations.[76]

Labor relations in South Korea's giant industrial firms, the chaebol, are an entirely different matter. The chaebol are South Korea's enormous conglomerates such as Hyundai and Samsung. To understand their size, consider that their 2004 sales were approximately equal to 7 percent of South Korea's GNP.

Labor relations in the chaebol are characterized by the philosophy of ruling with an iron fist. The chaebol control every aspect of the workers' lives, including much of their nonworking time. For example, as recently as 1987, many Korean corporations dictated proper nonworking dress for women and acceptable hair-styles for men. At work, laborers were not given a work schedule but were expected to be available whenever they were needed and to work long overtime hours without notice.[77]

Government regulation of business is another area where the American firm will encounter vastly different systems around the world. For example, in Singapore, there is a National Wages Council that sets guidelines for annual wage adjustments; work stoppages are nearly impossible because of governmental controls; and legislation regulates working conditions to a great extent.[78]

It should be obvious that there is no simple solution to the labor relations problems that MNCs and GCs are confronted with. Nor is there any simple solution for unions that must deal with these corporations. The response of labor has been to try to establish global organizations to represent labor. These International Trade Secretariats have yet to succeed because MNCs tend to have considerable financial resources and readily available alternative sources of labor. At the same time, labor has made some progress in presenting its global reactions to MNCs and GCs. For example, as the European Union becomes more unified, labor is getting prepared with its own organizations, such as the European Trade Union Confederation. And the International Labor Organization has adopted a code for labor relations policies in MNC dealings.[79]

Summary

This chapter has discussed the critical issues faced by organizations that conduct international business. Global human resource management is an important component of an organization's success in a global marketplace. For an organization to become a successful international enterprise, it must be sure that its HRM policies can accommodate a culturally diverse workforce. As students learn more about HRM, including selection, training, appraisal, and compensation, they should become capable of adapting and then applying principles of domestic HRM to an international organization.

To summarize the major points covered in this chapter:

1. International business continues to grow at a remarkable rate. In the coming years, a majority of corporations will have internationalized to one degree or another.
2. Any attempt to become an international organization must include a systematic evaluation of how HRM will adapt to the diverse cultural backgrounds of employees.
3. There are three sources of employees for an international organization:
   a. Parent country nationals (PCNs).
   b. Host country nationals (HCNs).
   c. Third country nationals (TCNs).
4. An ethnocentric corporation tends to view its HRM policies as the best method for dealing with employees and therefore relies on PCNs to fill key managerial and technical positions in its overseas operations.
5. In contrast, a geocentric corporation ignores national boundaries in favor of managerial expertise when filling key positions in the organization.
6. Currently, failure rates among expatriate managers are very high in many American corporations. The major reasons for the high failure rates are
   a. Selection processes that focus too much on technical skills and too little on cultural factors.
   b. Lack of systematic training for the overseas assignments.
   c. Too little involvement of family members in the selection decision.
   d. Lack of clear expectations about the role of the overseas assignment in the manager's career plans.
7. Family adjustment plays a critical role in an expatriate manager's success overseas.
8. The cost of keeping an expatriate manager on an overseas assignment can be as much as three times the cost of maintaining that same manager on a domestic assignment.

9. An important part of an expatriate manager's training should be an overview of the legal and ethical issues that are likely to be encountered on the overseas assignment.

10. Labor unions have begun to form international organizations to negotiate with the growing number of multinational and global corporations. To date, these international unions have met with only limited success.

Key Terms

culture shock, *p. 105*
ethnocentric HRM perspective, *p. 102*
expatriate manager, *p. 102*
Foreign Corrupt Practices Act of 1977 (FCPA), *p. 111*
geocentric HRM orientation, *p. 102*

global corporation, *p. 101*
global human resource management, *p. 98*
host country national (HCN), *p. 101*
multinational corporation, *p. 101*

parent country national (PCN), *p. 102*
repatriation, *p. 108*
Sullivan Principles, *p. 112*
third country national (TCN), *p. 102*

Questions for Review and Discussion

1. Identify and describe three macroeconomic drivers behind globalization.

2. What are the HRM differences between an ethnocentric and a geocentric organization? How do these influence staffing decisions for international assignments?

3. In addition to having good technical skills, what other skills should an expatriate have in order to be successful in an international assignment?

4. What types of information should be included in cross-cultural training for expatriates? Should spouses and family members be included in the training?

5. What is culture shock? When does it occur? What can be done to reduce its negative effects?

6. Where would you place yourself on each of the five work-related cultural dimensions identified by Hofstede? (e.g., high on individualism)?

7. Discuss the advantages and disadvantages of using PCNs and HCNs for filling key managerial and technical positions in an international organization.

8. Why are so many multinational companies using short-term international assignments (less than 1 year in length)? Should they do away with the long-term assignments altogether? Why or why not?

9. What is the Foreign Corrupt Practices Act of 1977? How can it affect HRM policies?

10. What are the Sullivan Principles? How have they helped organizations understand the ethical issues they face when conducting business in foreign cultures?

HRM Legal Advisor

Based on *Kunihiko Iwata* v. *Stryker Corporation and Matsumoto Medical Instruments Inc.,* 59 F. Supp. 2d 600 (U.S. District Court, Northern District of Texas 1999).

The Facts

Mr. Iwata is a Japanese citizen who served as the chairman and president of Matsumoto from October 1, 1996, through November 6, 1997. Matsumoto, a Japanese subsidiary of Stryker, is a distributor of medical products exclusively in Japan. Mr. Iwata was living in the United States as a resident alien when he was hired by Matsumoto, then moved back to Japan to serve as the company's president. He lived in Japan until he was dismissed by Matsumoto in November 1997. At this time, Mr. Iwata moved back to the United States as a resident alien and filed a Title VII suit claiming race and national origin discrimination as well as retaliation and an Age Discrimination in Employment Act (ADEA) suit claiming age discrimination. The defendants, Stryker and Matsumoto, have challenged the district court's subject matter jurisdiction to hear the case. Does the Civil Rights Act of

1991 allow extraterritorial application of Title VII and ADEA? Is Mr. Iwata a covered employee, and is the foreign subsidiary Matsumoto a covered employer?

The Court's Decision

The U.S. District Court for the Northern District of Texas found that it did not have subject-matter jurisdiction over Mr. Iwata's claims. The Civil Rights Act of 1991, which amended Title VII of the 1964 Civil Rights Act, states that "with respect to employment in a foreign country, such term (employee) includes an individual who is a citizen of the United States." Language in the ADEA which defines covered employees is identical. Because Mr. Iwata was at no time a citizen of the United States, the court concluded that Mr. Iwata was not a protected employee under Title VII or the ADEA. Thus, the court found it unnecessary to determine whether Title VII or the ADEA covered the actions of Matsumoto.

Human Resource Implications

Because of the extraterritorial coverage included in the Civil Rights Act of 1991, global human resource management has become more complex. With respect to foreign employment, Title VII covers American citizens employed outside of the United States by U.S. companies or their foreign subsidiaries. The Civil Rights Act of 1991 further specifies that foreign subsidiaries are covered if an American company "controls" the subsidiary through interrelated operations, common management, centralized control of labor relations, or common ownership or financial control. Companies should carefully analyze the status of employees and subsidiaries to determine whether they are covered by U.S. EEO laws.

Source: Amy B. Ganci (December 29, 2004), "Wading In: How GCs Can Minimize Their Companies' Overseas Employment Liability," *ALM Properties*, p. 4.

Notes

1. Robert Konopaske and John M. Ivancevich (2004), *Global Management and Organizational Behavior* (New York: McGraw-Hill/Irwin).
2. Charles W. L. Hill (2004), *International Business: Competing in the Global Marketplace,* 5th ed. (Boston: Irwin/McGraw-Hill), p. 5.
3. United Nations Conference on Trade and Development (2004), *World Investment Report* (New York and Geneva).
4. Nancy Adler (2002), *International Dimensions of Organizational Behavior,* 4th ed. (Cincinnati: South-Western), p. 4.
5. United Nations Conference on Trade and Development (1997), *World Investment Report* (New York and Geneva).
6. Adler, op. cit.
7. David P. Lepak and Scott A. Snell (1990), "The Human Resource Architecture: Toward a Theory of Human Capital Allocation and Development," *Academy of Management Review,* Vol. 24, Iss. 1, pp. 31–49; Jay Barney (1991), "Firm Resources and Sustained Competitive Advantage," *Journal of Management,* pp. 99–120; Randall Schuler and Nikolai Rogovsky (1998), "Understanding Compensation Practice Variations across Firms: The Impact of National Culture," *Journal of International Business Studies,* pp. 159–177.
8. Robin Tierney (December 1993), "Sites," *World Trade: 1994 Going Global Guide from A to Z,* pp. 86–87.
9. GMAC Global Relocation Services, National Foreign Trade Council, and SHRM Global Forum (2004), *Global Relocation Trends 2003/2004 Survey Report.*
10. Meena Thiruvengadam (March 23, 2005), "Maquiladoras' Employment Rebounding," *Knight Ridder Tribune Business News,* p. 1.
11. Geri Smith (August 16, 2004), "Made in the Maquilas—Again," *BusinessWeek,* p. 45.
12. Tierney, op. cit., p. 87.
13. United Nations Conference on Trade and Development (2004), *World Investment Report* (New York and Geneva).

14. Geert Hofstede (1984), *Culture's Consequences: International Differences in Work-Related Values* (Newbury Park, CA: Sage Publishing).

15. Geert Hofstede (February 1993), "Cultural Constraints in Management Theories," *Academy of Management Executive,* pp. 81–94.

16. Ann Marie Ryan, Lynn McFarland, Helen Baron, and Ron Page (Summer 1999), "An International Look at Selection Practices: Nation and Culture as Explanations for Variability in Practice," *Personnel Psychology,* pp. 359–391.

17. Seyyed Babak Alavi and John McCormick (2004), "A Cross-Cultural Analysis of the Effectiveness of the Learning Organization Model in School Contexts," *The International Journal of Education Management,* Vol. 18, Iss. 6, pp. 408–416. William Weech (January 2001), "Training across Cultures: What to Expect," *Training & Development,* pp. 62–64.

18. John F. Milliman, Mary Ann Von Glinow, and Maria Nathan (April 1991), "Organizational Life Cycles and Strategic International Human Resource Management in Multinational Companies: Implications for Congruence Theory," *Academy of Management Review,* pp. 318–339.

19. J. Stewart Black, Hal B. Gregersen, and Mark E. Mendenhall (1992), *Global Assignments: Successfully Expatriating and Repatriating International Managers* (San Francisco, CA: Jossey-Bass Publishing).

20. Patricia Ordonez de Pablos (2005), "Strategic Human Resource Management and Organizational Competitiveness: The Importance of Fit and Flexibility," *International Journal of Human Resources Development and Management*, Vol. 5, Iss.1, pp. 1–14; John F. Milliman and Mary Ann Von Glinow (1991), "Strategic International Human Resources: Prescriptions for MNC Success," in Kendrith Rowland (ed.), *Research in Personnel and Human Resources Management,* Supplement 2 (Greenwich, CT: JAI Press), pp. 21–35.

21. Gail Dutton (March 2005), "Is 'Brand America' Going to Be an Endangered Species in World Markets?" *World Trade*, Vol. 18, Iss. 3, pp. 26–31; Paul W. Beamish, J. Peter Killing, Donald J. LeCraw, and Allen J. Morrison (1994), *International Management: Text and Cases,* 2nd ed. (Burr Ridge, IL: Irwin), pp. 143–157; and Preston Townley (January–February 1990), "Global Business in the Next Decade," *Across the Board,* pp. 13–19.

22. David J. Cherrington and Laura Zaugg Middleton (June 1995), "An Introduction to Global Business Issues," *HRMagazine,* pp. 124–130.

23. Susan Moffatt (December 3, 1990), "Should You Work for the Japanese?" *Fortune,* pp. 107ff.

24. GMAC Global Relocation Services, National Foreign Trade Council, and SHRM Global Forum (2004), *Global Relocation Trends 2003/2004 Survey Report;* Michael S. Schell and Charlene Marmer Solomon (1997), *Capitalizing on the Global Workforce* (Chicago: Irwin), p. 148.

25. Roblyn Simeon (2001), "Top Team Characteristics and the Business Strategies of Japanese Firms," *Corporate Governance,* pp. 4–12; "East Meets West: An Interview with Clifford Clarke" (October 1990), *Training and Development Journal,* pp. 43–47.

26. Michael Harvey and Milorad M. Novicevic (November 2004), "The Development of Political Skill and Political Capital by Global Leaders through Global Assignments," *International Journal of Human Resource Management,* Vol. 15, Iss. 7, pp. 1173–1188; Caroll Lachnit (August 2001), "Low-Cost Tips for Successful Inpatriation," *Workforce,* pp. 42–47; Michael Harvey and Helen Fung (2000), "Inpatriate Managers: The Need for Realistic Relocation Reviews," *International Journal of Management,* pp. 151–159; Carla Joinson (April 1999), "The Impact of 'Inpats,'" *HRMagazine,* pp. S4–S10.

27. GMAC, op cit., p. 30.

28. J. Stewart Black and Hal B. Gregersen (March–April 1999), "The Right Way to Manage Expats," *Harvard Business Review,* pp. 52–63.

29. Shirley R. Fishman (Spring 1996), "Developing a Global Workforce," *The Canadian Business Review,* pp. 18–21.

30. Anne-Wil Harzing (February 2002), "Are Our Referencing Errors Undermining Our Scholarship and Credibility? The Case of Expatriate Failure Rates," *Journal of Organizational Behavior,* pp. 127–148; Rosalie Tung (1982), "Selecting and Training Procedures of the U.S.,

European, and Japanese Multinationals," *California Management Review,* pp. 51–71; Rosalie Tung (1981), "Selecting and Training of Personnel for Overseas Assignments," *Columbia Journal of World Business*, Vol. 16, Iss. 7, pp. 68–78.

31. GMAC Global Relocation Services, National Foreign Trade Council, and SHRM Global Forum (2004), *Global Relocation Trends 2003/2004 Survey Report.*

32. PricewaterhouseCoopers (1999), *International Assignments: European Policy and Practices.*

33. Mary A. Gowan and Carlos Ochoa (Spring 1998), "Parent-Country National Selection for the Maquiladora Industry in Mexico: Results of a Pilot Study," *Journal of Managerial Issues,* pp. 103–118.

34. Marvina Shilling (July 1993), "Avoid Expatriate Culture Shock," *HRMagazine,* pp. 58–63.

35. Alexander T. Mohr and Simone Klein (November 2004), "Exploring the Adjustment of American Expatriate Spouses in Germany," *The International Journal of Human Resource Management,* Vol. 15, Iss. 7, pp. 1189–1206; Paula M. Caligiuri, MaryAnne M. Hyland, Aparna Joshi, and Allon S. Bross (August 1998), "Testing a Theoretical Model for Examining the Relationship between Family Adjustment and Expatriate's Work Adjustment," *Journal of Applied Psychology,* Vol. 83, Iss. 4, pp. 598–614.

36. Winfred Arthur Jr. and Winston Bennett Jr. (Spring 1995), "The International Assignee: The Relative Importance of Factors Perceived to Contribute to Success," *Personnel Psychology,* pp. 99–114.

37. Rensia Melles (March 2004), "Lost in Translation," *Canadian HR Reporter,* Vol. 17, Iss. 5, pp. 14–15; Charlene Solomon (July 1996), "Expats Say: Help Make Us Mobile," *Personnel Journal,* pp. 47–52.

38. Jan Selmer and Alicia S. M. Leung (2003), Provision and Adequacy of Corporate Support to Male Expatriate Spouses: An Exploratory Study," *Personnel Review,* Vol. 32, Iss. 1, pp. 9–22; Kimmo Riusala and Vesa Suutari (2000), "Expatriation and Careers: Perspectives of Expatriates and Spouses," *Career Development,* pp. 81–90.

39. Hal B. Gregersen and J. Stewart Black (March 1992), "Antecedents to Commitment to a Parent Company and a Foreign Operation," *Academy of Management Journal,* pp. 65–90.

40. Earl Naumann (January 1993), "Organizational Predictors of Expatriate Job Satisfaction," *Journal of International Business Studies,* pp. 61–80.

41. Robert Konopaske and John M. Ivancevich, op cit., p. 346; Kalervo Oberg (1960), "Culture Shock: Adjustment to New Cultural Environments," *Practical Anthropology,* pp. 177–182.

42. Graham Hall (July 25, 1996), "Surviving Life in a Foreign Environment," *Personnel Management,* p. 31.

43. Arno Haslberger (2005), "Facets and Dimensions of Cross-Cultural Adaptation: Refining the Tools," *Personnel Review,* Vol. 34, Iss. 1, pp. 85–109; Rebecca Marschan, Denice Welch, and Lawrence Welch (October 1997), "Language: The Forgotten Factor in Multinational Management," *European Management Journal,* pp. 591–598.

44. Charles M. Vance and Peter Smith Ring (Winter 1994), "Preparing the Host Country Workforce for Expatriate Managers: The Neglected Other Side of the Coin," *Human Resource Development Quarterly,* pp. 337–352.

45. Jane Simms (March 2004), "A Leap of Faith . . . ," *Human Resources,* pp. 56–59.

46. Rita Bennett, Anne Aston, and Tracy Colquhoun (Summer–Fall 2000), "Cross-Cultural Training: A Critical Step in Ensuring the Success of International Assignments," *Human Resource Management,* pp. 239–250; J. Kline Harrison (Fall 1994), "Developing Successful Expatriate Managers: A Framework for the Structural Design and Strategic Alignment of Cross-Cultural Training Programs," *Human Resource Planning,* pp. 17–35.

47. Tung, op. cit., pp. 51–71.

48. Gregersen and Black, op. cit., pp. 65–90.

49. Jan Selmer (2001), "The Preference for Predeparture or Postarrival Cross-Cultural Training—An Exploratory Approach," *Journal of Managerial Psychology,* pp. 50–62; Gary Topchik (January 1995), "Cures for Culture Shock," *Training and Development,* p. 58.

50. Annette B. Bossard and Richard B. Peterson (February 2005), "The Repatriate Experience as Seen by American Expatriates," *Journal of World Business*, Vol. 40, Iss. 1, pp. 9–28; Linda K. Stroh, Hal B. Gregersen, and J. Stewart Black (Summer 1998), "Closing the Gap: Expectations versus Reality among Repatriates," *Journal of World Business,* pp. 111–124.

51. Douglas Allen and Sharon Alvarez (Winter 1998), "Empowering Expatriates and Organizations to Improve Repatriation Effectiveness," *Human Resource Planning,* pp. 29–39.

52. GMAC Global Relocation Services, National Foreign Trade Council, and SHRM Global Forum, op. cit., p. 49.

53. Jacqueline Hauser (February 1999), "Managing Expatriates' Careers," *HR Focus,* pp. 11–12.

54. Shannon Peters Talbott (March 1996), "Building a Global Workforce Starts with Recruitment," *Personnel Journal,* pp. 9–11.

55. Black and Gregersen, op. cit., pp. 52–63.

56. George T. Milkovich and Jerry Newman (2005), *Compensation,* 8th ed. (New York: McGraw-Hill/Irwin).

57. Black, Gregersen, and Mendenhall, op. cit., p. 184.

58. Kathy Chu (June 17, 2004), "U.S. Companies Send Fewer Workers Overseas," *The Wall Street Journal,* p. D2.

59. Van Pelt, op. Cit., p. 40.

60. *The Economist* (April 23, 2005), "Business: In Search of Stealth; Expatriate Workers," Vol. 375, Iss. 8423, p. 78.

61. Christopher Bingham, Teppo Felin, and J. Stewart Black (Summer–Fall 2000), "An Interview with John Pepper: What It Takes to Be a Global Leader," *Human Resource Management,* pp. 287–292.

62. Sue Shaw (2005), "The Corporate University: Global or Local Phenomenon?" *Journal of European Industrial Training*, Vol. 29, Iss. 1, pp. 21–40.

63. Robin Tierney (December 1993), "Hiring," in *World Trade: 1994 Going Global Guide from A to Z,* pp. 38–41.

64. Mel Mandell (December 1993), "Excellence," in *World Trade: 1994 Going Global Guide from A to Z,* pp. 26–29.

65. Charlene Solomon (March 1995), "Learning to Manage Host-Country Nationals," *Personnel Journal,* pp. 60–67.

66. Noel M. Tichy, Michael I. Brimm, Ram Charan, and Hiroraka Takeuchi (1992), "Leadership Development as a Lever for Global Transformation," in Vladimir Pucik, Noel M. Tichy, and Carole K. Barnett (eds.), *Globalizing Management: Creating and Leading the Competitive Organization* (New York: Wiley), pp. 47–60.

67. Dennis R. Briscoe and Randall S. Schuler (2004), *International Human Resource Management* (London: Routledge, Taylor & Francis).

68. George M. Taoka and Don R. Beeman (1991), *International Business: Environments, Institutions, and Operations* (New York: Harper-Collins), pp. 518–519.

69. Keith Allen (October 1989), "Making the Right Choices in International Recruiting," *Personnel Management,* pp. 56–59.

70. Konstantin Richter (August 25, 1999), "Europe's Boards Begin a Trend-Growing Pattern in Business Prompts Firms to Seek Diversity in Directors," *The Wall Street Journal,* p.1; John Thackray (January–February 1990), "Foreigners on Board?" *Across the Board,* pp. 11–12.

71. Michael Litka (1988), *International Dimensions of the Legal Environment of Business* (Boston: PWS-Kent), pp. 82–83.

72. Geri Smith (March 7, 2005), "It's Hot South of the Border," *BusinessWeek,* Iss. 3923, p. 32; John Sargent and Linda Matthews (January 1999), "Exploitation or Choice? Exploring the Relative Attractiveness of Employment in the Maquiladoras," *Journal of Business Ethics,* pp. 213–227.

73. S. L. Smith (February 1998), "Maquiladora Workers,"*Occupational Hazards,* pp. 26–27.

74. http://horizonmag.com/8/principles.asp.

75. Charles R. Greer and Gregory K. Stephens (Spring 1996), "Employee Relations Issues for U.S. Companies in Mexico," pp. 121–145.

76. Peter Conrad and Rudiger Pieper (1990), "Human Resource Management in the Federal Republic of Germany," in Rudiger Pieper (ed.), *Human Resource Management: An International Comparison* (Berlin: Walter de Gruyter), pp. 109–139.

77. Robert P. Kearney (April 1991), "Managing Mr. Kim," *Across the Board,* pp. 40–46.

78. Dahlia Hackman and Brian Kleiner (1990), "The Nature of Effective Management in Singapore," *Leadership and Organization Development Journal.*

79. International Labor Organization, http://www.us.ilo.org/aboutilo/index.html#declaration.

EXERCISE 4-1

DEVELOPMENT OF GLOBAL MANAGERS

Objective
The exercise is designed to have students review and consider the goals of various developmental approaches used by organizations.

Set Up the Exercise
Review the six approaches (a – f) used to develop global managers in the table in Exhibit 4A-1. Answer the following for each approach.

1. What can the firm accomplish with the approach used?
2. What would the cost-benefit analysis for each approach illustrate?
3. How do your answers to questions 1 and 2 compare with those of other students?
4. Why are students' responses different?

EXHIBIT 4A-1
Developing Global Managers

Source: J. S. Lublin (March 31, 1992), "Young Managers Learn Global Skills," *The Wall Street Journal.*

Company	Program
a. American Express Co.'s travel-related services unit	Gives American business students summer jobs in which they work outside the United States for up to 10 weeks. Also transfers junior managers with at least two years' experience to other countries.
b. Colgate-Palmolive Co.	Trains about 15 recent college graduates each year for 15 to 24 months prior to multiple overseas job stints.
c. General Electric Co.'s aircraft-engine unit	Will expose selected midlevel engineers and managers to foreign language and cross-cultural training even though not all will live abroad.
d. Honda of America Manufacturing Inc.	Has sent about 42 American supervisors and managers to the parent company in Tokyo for up to three years after preparing them with six months of Japanese language lessons, cultural training, and lifestyle orientation during work hours.
e. PepsiCo Inc.'s international beverage division	Brings about 25 young foreign managers a year to the United States for one-year assignments in bottling plants.
f. Raychem Corp.	Assigns relatively inexperienced Asian employees (from clerks through middle managers) to the United States for six months to two years.

EXERCISE 4-2   AVOIDING COSTLY INTERNATIONAL HRM MISTAKES

Objective
This exercise is designed to have students use the Internet to uncover mistakes that multinational corporations have made while managing their human resources around the world.

Instructions
Students should read the exercise below, conduct research on the Internet, prepare a one-page report, and then in groups of three to four, discuss the findings with their colleagues in class.

Exercise
Parent (or Headquarters) companies have experienced difficulties adjusting to host-nation management practices. Examples of blunders being made by American, Japanese, French, British, and Swedish firms have continued to make news for decades. For example, a Japanese company doing business in Indonesia hired primarily Bataks, members of an ethnic group with characteristics similar to the Japanese. Other Indonesians, however, resented this hiring practice, viewed it as discriminatory, and forced the company to change its policy.

As an assignment, students should use their favorite search engine on the Internet to collect examples of three blunders or problems that companies and organizations have encountered when addressing management practices in a host country and prepare a one-page summary on each of these examples for discussion with class colleagues.

Source: Adapted from Robert Konopaske and John M. Ivancevich (2004), "Global Labor Relations IQ," *Global Management and Organizational Behavior* (Boston: McGraw-Hill/Irwin), p. 413.

Application Case 4-1

Solving the Labor Dilemma in a Joint Venture in Japan

John has found himself with a critical labor shortage, and he doesn't know exactly how to solve his problem. John is the founder, president, and CEO of a small manufacturing firm, Johnsco Electronics. The company has approximately 300 employees in its home state of Tennessee. Recently, it was approached by a major Japanese automobile manufacturing company about a possible joint venture in which Johnsco could retain majority ownership. The opportunity seemed attractive, so John agreed to build and operate a plant outside of Tokyo. The plant is expected to employ around 500 workers to fabricate and assemble computer components for new automobiles.

John had recently discovered the extremely high cost of maintaining a significant number of expatriate managers in a city with a cost of living as high as Tokyo. Thus, he had agreed to the joint venture expecting to use mostly his host country nationals for the new facility. Unfortunately, John is having problems staffing many of the essential positions. First, he was not aware that equal employment opportunity laws would apply to his international operation. Since John supplies the federal government with certain military components, his hiring practices are scrutinized to see whether minorities and women are appropriately represented in his workforce. Only recently did John discover that few if any Japanese women ever move into managerial positions in Japan. He's confused about how to balance his obligations under United States law, local customs in Tokyo, and the high cost of using expatriates.

John was led to believe that there would be a large supply of inexpensive labor throughout Asia. He had heard that multinational organizations acquire very inexpensive labor by relying heavily on women to staff labor-intensive production jobs. Culturally, he'd heard, these people defer to authority and are willing to work long, tedious hours. Once again, however, he discovered that Japan has strict policies prohibiting foreign labor. In fact, nearly 15,000 undocumented aliens were arrested in Tokyo each year while attempting to find work.

The Japanese liaison to Johnsco has told John that Japan's workforce is aging even more rapidly than the workforce in the United States. Historically, Japanese companies have been dominated by seniority systems that encourage older workers to remain with a single firm until retirement. There are also fewer young, semiskilled workers, because of the ever-increasing percentages of Japanese children who attend college. For example, over half of the more than 4 million Japanese blue-collar workers in construction-related fields are older than 50. John is confused about the implications of these facts for his ability to staff the Tokyo operation; he wonders about problems with his company-sponsored retirement programs. And, to add one last problem, John's American plant is almost entirely unionized. The union steward expects two things: (1) any good promotional opportunities created by the international joint venture must give union members the first right of accepting a transfer; and (2) host country nationals who are hired in Japan should be covered by the same union contract as the workers in the United States.

John's enthusiasm over the opportunity to work closely with one of the most powerful automobile makers in the world has diminished. But the agreement is signed, and John now wonders how he can ever get the Tokyo operation off the ground, let alone make a profit, without violating local customs or American laws.

Discussion Questions

1. What steps can you suggest that might help John solve his labor problems for the new plant in Tokyo?
2. How could he persuade either the union or his joint venture partner to help him with this problem?
3. What types of cultural training, both here and in Japan, might be necessary for John's new venture to be successful?
4. What could John have done differently to eliminate some of his current labor problems?

Source: Adapted from material contained in Naohiro Ogawa, G. W. Jones, and J. G. Williamson (eds.) (1993), *Human Resources in Development along the Asia-Pacific Rim* (Singapore: Oxford University Press).

Application Case 4-2

Toyota in France: Culture Clash?

Hiroaki Watanabe, the Japanese general manager of the first major Toyota plant in Valenciennes, France (and in continental Europe), has a lot at stake. He is in charge of a modern and efficient $570 million Toyota Motor factory designed to manufacture the Yaris, a subcompact car. The plant was designed to employ 2,000 workers. Currently, there are about 200 Japanese managers and 150 Japanese trainers on staff. The remaining employees are mostly French. Culturally speaking, there were many potential areas of conflict between the Japanese and French customs. For example, the plant holds calisthenics at 8:00 A.M. every morning to avoid starting off the day "cold" and being more prone to injuries. This is a common Japanese practice that is not frequently done in France. Also, the plant does not serve wine at lunch, a common practice in other French organizations. As is common in other Japanese firms, blue and gray windbreaker jackets are made available with the word "Toyota" on the back and the employee's name on the front.

To help bridge these and other potential cultural gaps, the leadership of the venture needs to understand the potential cultural clashes that these issues can cause. How did Mr. Watanabe prepare himself for this high-profile assignment? Although fluent in English, he decided that he would learn French and as much about French culture as possible. After all, the vast majority of workers at the plant would be from northern France. To prepare himself, he traveled to France as a tourist and visited the Toyota plant in Canada. He conducted interviews in French, with assistance of an interpreter, in order to improve his language skills.

Are his efforts succeeding? Toyota had high hopes for this first major undertaking in continental Europe. Its goal was to increase its market share that was 3.7 percent in 2001, less than half its share in the United States in that year. In 2004, Toyota surpassed this goal by achieving a 5.3 percent market share in Europe, higher than both Mercedes and Audi. The French employees at the Toyota plant have a lot at stake when one considers that the Valenciennes area, a former coal and steel region, suffers from high unemployment with the closing of many companies in heavy industry over the past 20 years. To underscore the importance of Toyota to this region, more than 30,000 people applied for the 2,000 jobs at the factory when it first opened its doors.

Discussion Questions

1. What potential conflicts could arise between the Japanese managers/trainers and the French employees? Explain.
2. What do you think of Mr. Watanabe's approach to preparing himself for French culture? Do you think that his approach would be useful for American managers? Why or why not?
3. What kind of organizational culture did Mr. Watanabe want to establish at the factory in Valenciennes, France? Do you think he'll try to manage the plant just like a Toyota factory in Tokyo? Why or why not?
4. What implications are there for the French employees of the plant if its good fortune takes a turn for the worse, and the factory consequently shuts its doors? Explain.

Source: Gail Edmondson and Adeline Bonnet (June 7, 2004), "Toyota's New Traction in Europe: Stylish Models and an Innovative Factory Have Renault, Fiat, and Others Worried," *BusinessWeek*, Iss. 3886, pp. 64–65; John Tagliabue (February 25, 2001), "At a French Factory, Culture Is a Two-Way Street," *The New York Times*, section 3, p. 4.

Video Case

Southwest Airlines: Competing through People

For some organizations, the slogan "focus on customers" is merely a slogan. At Southwest Airlines, however, it is a daily goal. Consider an elderly woman on her way to cancer therapy, alone with no one to care or help. A Southwest Airlines agent befriends her and spends two weeks driving her around the strange city, helping her through a crisis. Or consider the passenger on an Oklahoma City flight headed to an important business meeting with no necktie. Flight attendant Jennifer Smith manages to find him a tie before the flight has even landed.

Southwest Airlines is an organization that has built its business and corporate culture around the tenets of total quality management and customer service. Focus on the customer, employee involvement and empowerment, and continuous improvement are the company's strategic focus. Frequent fliers are asked to assist personnel managers in interviewing and selecting prospective flight attendants. Focus groups are used to help measure passenger response to new services and to help generate new ideas for improving current services. It is no surprise that the company won the DOT's triple crown for best on-time performance, best baggage handling, and fewest customer complaints every year from 1992 through 1996. Then, on April 20, 1998, the airline learned it had won the Airline Quality Rating for the third year in a row. To make the story even more remarkable, the company has managed to make a profit every year since 1973 despite at least two major industry turndowns during the same time. While competitors were laying off over 120,000 employees, Southwest Airlines was hiring, year after year. From three airplanes in 1972, it has grown to over 280 in 1999.

Herb Kelleher: The Heart and Soul of Southwest Airlines

From its beginning, Herb Kelleher has been the guiding force behind Southwest Airline's phenomenal story. His efforts have paid off not only in profits for the company, but in 1999 Kelleher was named the "Chief Executive of the Year" by *Chief Executive magazine.* His approach has always been different from other major airlines. Although reservations and ticketing are done in advance of a flight, seating occurs on a first-come, first-served basis. Turnaround times are kept to an industry low of 15 minutes with the help of pilots and crew who clean and restock the planes. The airline is famous for its "peanut" fares matched by its inflight food services consisting almost entirely of peanuts. The average meal cost for a passenger on other airlines is $5.00 per person; on Southwest it is $.20.

Corporate Philosophy, Culture, and HRM Practices

How does Southwest maintain its unique, cost-effective position? In an industry in which antagonistic labor–management relations are common, how does Southwest build cooperation with a workforce that is 85 percent unionized? Led by Kelleher, the corporation has developed a culture that treats employees the same way that it treats its passengers. By listening, being responsive, and involving employees in decision making, Southwest has developed some of the best employee–management relations in the industry. The company has, after all, never had a labor strike.

Sources: "Air Herb's Secret Weapon" (July–August, 1999), *Chief Executive,* pp. 32–42; "Chief Executive of the Year" (July–August, 1999), *Chief Executive,* p. 32; "How Herb Keeps Southwest Hopping" (June 1999), *Money,* pp. 61–62; Joanne Cole (May 1998), "Flying High at Southwest," *HR Focus,* p. 8; Jennifer Laubs (June 1998), "Southwest Airlines Credits Employees for Winning Quality Award," *Workforce,* pp. 13–14.

According to Elizabeth Pedrick Sartain, vice president of people (and the company's top HRM person), Southwest's corporate culture makes the airline unique. The company's philosophy is that people should have fun at work, another one of Kelleher's influences. According to Sartain, the company hires "attitudes" and then builds upon that foundation. The company's reputation makes selectivity possible. In 1998, Southwest received 141,710 applications yet only hired 4,115 new employees. This large labor pool allows the company to hire employees who most closely fit the company's culture—in which they are asked to use their own judgment and to go beyond "the job description."

Kelleher's "fun at work" philosophy can be seen in the way employees work, dress, and act. But Kelleher himself sets the example. He once sent an entire elementary school class on a round-trip flight from Dallas to Austin because the children had never had an opportunity to fly. Then, when his mechanics on the late night shift felt left out because they couldn't attend many of the company's social functions, Kelleher threw them a private barbeque with himself and several of the pilots as cooks. Then, of course, there is the company tradition of always wearing black on Herb's birthday. Although safety is never compromised, the "have fun" attitude carries right onto the airplanes and involves passengers as well. Safety instructions might be given with an accompanying country and western tune. Or there might be an occasional greeting from inside one of the overhead cargo bins as the flight attendants prepare the plane for its next leg. It is definitely not coincidental that employees' births, deaths, marriages, and promotions are acknowledged by Herb or that the headquarters is covered with pictures of employee gatherings and celebrations.

According to Colleen Barrett, her position as executive vice president for customers is the second ranking officer in the company. She has been with Kelleher for most of the history of Southwest and has helped to permeate his philosophies throughout the company. About hiring new pilots, for example, she says, "We don't care if you're the best pilot in the USAF, if you condescend to a secretary, you won't get hired." Again, the sense of the organization is that it employs and values people, not robots. Letting people be themselves is another key to Southwest's success. Once you let people be themselves, the next step is to make sure they understand that the company cares. In one way or another, all 27,000 employees at Southwest hear from the CEO several times a year. So who do you think the company credits for its string of awards? Yes, that's right. Its people! Everyone from the pilots, flight attendants, mechanics, ramp workers, agents, and so on.

Discussion Questions

1. How has Southwest Airlines dealt with the competitive challenges in the airline industry? What human resource and strategic practices have helped the company to maintain its growth?

2. What special role has corporate culture played in contributing to Southwest Airline's successes?

3. What aspects of work life at Southwest do you think you would most enjoy and least enjoy? Why?

4. Do you think that Kelleher's "fun at work" philosophy could work equally well in any other company? Why?

5. Is Southwest's success more a function of good HR practices or good business practices? Can good business strategy survive without equally good HR strategy?

Acquiring Human Resources

Part Two consists of four chapters. Chapter 5, "Human Resource Planning and Alignment," emphasizes the important role of planning in an organization's overall human resource strategy. In Chapter 6, "Job Analysis and Design," methods for analyzing and describing jobs are discussed and critiqued. Numerous approaches to recruitment, as well as currently popular alternatives to recruitment, are presented in Chapter 7, "Recruitment." In Chapter 8, "Selection," the various steps in the selection process are presented and several alternative methods of selection are described.

5

Human Resource Planning and Alignment

Learning Objectives

After studying this chapter, you should be able to:

1. **Discuss** the importance of human resources planning in organizations and **describe** the critical linkages that exist between strategic planning and human resources planning.

2. **Describe** how managers forecast demand for and analyze the supply of employees in the organization.

3. **List four** forecasting techniques that are used in human resource planning.

4. **Define** the terms *skills inventory, succession planning,* and *replacement chart.*

5. **Identify** reasons why a computerized human resource planning system could be useful to an organization.

Internet/Web Resources

General Sites

www.ajb.dni.us

www.sireport.com

www.hrps.org/index.html

www.bls.gov

Company Sites

www.cessna.textron.com

www.chevron.com

www.apple.com

www.prudential.com

www.hewitt.com

www.aol.com

www.unilever.com

www.rand.com

www.spss.com

www.sas.com

www.pg.com

www.ibm.com

www.amp.com

www.dbm.com

www.internationalpaper.com

www.bellhelicopter.com

www.merck.com

www.mci.com

www.phillips66.com

www.att.com

www.monsanto.com

"What do you mean, we're going to lose the government contract?" asked the company president, Ted Sloane.

"We're going to lose it," said the human resource management vice president, Anne Wilson. "We don't have trained personnel to meet the contract specifications. We have to furnish records to show that we have enough employees with the right technical qualifications who meet the government's equal employment opportunity goals. I don't have those kinds of records available at a moment's notice. You know I asked you to let me set up a human resource information system (HRIS). Why didn't we get around to it?"

Ted didn't know what Anne had in mind. Everything he ever heard about computer systems suggested that they were expensive and complex. Now he wanted to learn more about HRISs.

Experiences like Ted's are common, and, as the complexity of doing business increases, they are probably going to become more common. Today, more than ever, success in business is dependent on being able to react quickly to opportunities that arise. More than ever, organizations must have accurate, rapid access to information about both the supply of and the demand for human resources and be prepared to deal with any surplus or shortage that may come about. Predicting future needs for human resources and using existing resources effectively are the basic issues addressed in this chapter.

Human resource planning (HR planning) is both a process and a set of plans.[1] It is how organizations assess the future supply of and demand for human resources. In addition, an effective HR plan also provides mechanisms to eliminate any gaps that may exist between supply and demand. Thus, HR planning determines the numbers and types of employees to be recruited into the organization or phased out of it. Dynamic by nature, the HR planning process often requires periodic readjustments as labor market conditions change.

Human Resource Planning

One of the most significant factors affecting planning involves the goals of the controlling interests in the organization. If planning and effective utilization of human resources are not a significant goal for the organization, employment planning will not be performed formally, or it will be done in a slipshod manner. If the goals of top management include stable growth, employment planning will be less important than if the goals include rapid expansion, diversification, or other factors with a significant impact on future employment needs.

Changing demographics in the United States are an important factor that will continue to influence the future composition of the workforce. From 2003 to 2008, the U.S. Department of Labor projects that the two fastest growing demographic groups, Asians and Hispanics, will join the labor force at rates of 44.0 and 36.0 percent, respectively. As a comparison, white non-Hispanics are expected to increase at a much slower rate of 9.0 percent. Another important change includes the aging of the workforce. Over that same 5-year period, an increase of 51.7 percent is expected in the 55- to 64-year-old category; while the second highest growth category, the 65 and older group, is expected to increase by 29.6 percent (U.S. Department of Labor, 2003).[2]

Government policies are another important factor in planning. Requirements for equal employment opportunity and promotion call for more HR planning for women and other employees in minority groups and special categories. Other examples include the government's raising the age of mandatory retirement and its encouragement of hiring disabled employees and veterans (see Chapter 3).

The types of people employed and the tasks they perform also determine the kind of planning necessary. An organization may not need to plan very far in advance for unskilled jobs, since there will usually be an abundant supply of readily available workers for these jobs. Certain high-skill jobs, on the other hand, may require planning activities that project a year or two into the future. When an organization plans for executive-level replacements, such as a new CEO, the planning process may have to anticipate the company's needs 10 or more years into the future.

Strategic and Human Resource Planning

Exhibit 5-1 models the HR planning process. As the model indicates, HR planning goes hand in hand with an organization's strategic planning. **Strategic planning** refers to an organization's decision about what it wants to accomplish (its mission) and how it wants to go about accomplishing it.[3] Although HR planning is important for developing a strategic plan, it is perhaps even more critical to the implementation of that plan. Thus, once the strategy is set, the HRM function must do its part to ensure the strategy's success, thereby helping the organization to achieve its objectives.[4]

The acknowledgment that HR policies and practices have critical linkages with an organization's overall strategy is generally termed **strategic human resource management (SHRM).** A central premise of the strategic perspective of HR is that human resource policies will have direct effects on an organization's profitability. As such, HR must "fit"

EXHIBIT 5-1
The Human Resource Planning Process

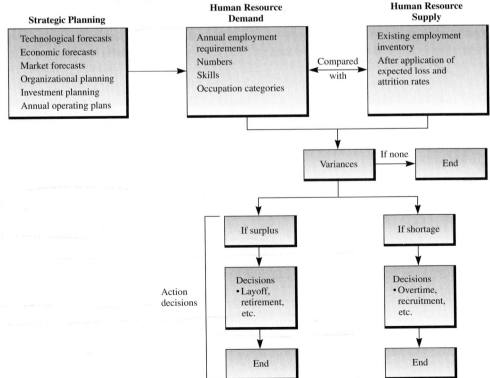

strategically with the mission of the organization. For example, an organization in a stable environment whose goal is to maintain steady rates of growth may need an entirely different recruitment and selection perspective than an organization whose goal is rapid expansion into uncertain markets. While there is not yet a wealth of research supporting this premise, there is growing theoretical and practitioner evidence supporting the linkages.[5]

The HR Planning Process

All effective HR planning shares certain features. It is generally agreed that HR planning involves four distinct phases or stages.[6]

1. Situation analysis or environmental scanning.
2. Forecasting demand for human resources.
3. Analysis of the supply of human resources.
4. Development of plans for action.

Situation Analysis and Environmental Scanning

The first stage of HR planning is the point at which HRM and strategic planning initially interact. The strategic plan must adapt to environmental circumstances, and HRM is one of the primary mechanisms that an organization can use during the adaptation process.[7] For example, rapid technological changes in the environment can force an organization to quickly identify and hire employees with new skills that previously weren't needed by the organization. Without an effective HR plan to support the recruitment and selection functions in the organization, it would be impossible to move fast enough to stay competitive. Following the merger between Kmart and Sears (valued at $12.3 billion) in 2005, the new company is in the process of revamping its human resources strategy to fit the new direction and strategic goals of the organization.[8]

The problems associated with changing environments are greater today than ever before because success now depends on an ability to be a "global scanner." Global scanning is, in fact, considered one of the essential strategic skills for modern management.[9]

Forecasting Demand for Employees

The next phase of an effective HR planning process is estimating not only how many but also what kinds of employees will be needed. Forecasting yields advance estimates or calculations of the organization's staffing requirements. Although many quantitative tools can help with forecasting, it involves a great deal of human judgment. In addition, many successful HR planners rely heavily on their "gut instincts" about future conditions. For example, planners at Unilever attribute much of their global success to such instincts.[10]

It should be obvious that the demand for employees is closely tied to the strategic direction that the organization has chosen. Are we in a growth mode? Or are we engaged in reengineering that will shrink our workforce in the coming years? Trying to estimate how many and what kind of workers will be needed in the future is clearly an incredibly difficult task, especially for organizations that confront rapidly changing environments such as those found in the computer industry. Nonetheless, a number of techniques available to organizations help reduce this kind of uncertainty. Four of these techniques will be briefly described in the following sections. These include expert estimates, trend projections, statistical modeling, and unit-demand forecasting. As will be seen, three of these strategies utilize a "top-down" perspective while the latter attacks forecasting from the "bottom up." In all cases, it is extremely important to understand that virtually all planning activities in modern organizations require close collaboration between the HR department and line management.

HR Journal — *Aging Baby Boomers: A Solution to Pending Labor Shortages?*

The baby boomers, or those born between 1946 and 1964, represent a large share of the U.S. labor market. Over the next decade or so, many of these individuals are expected to retire, leaving large gaps to fill in the U.S. workforce. Given the fact that the United States has progressively moved toward a knowledge-based economy, many of these vacated jobs will require trained individuals with postsecondary education. Unfortunately, projections indicate that the United States could face shortages as high as 14 million postsecondary workers.

One solution? Entice these experienced, older workers to continue working. There is evidence to support that many older individuals are willing to keep working well into their "golden years." Between 2002 and 2012, the annual growth rate of the number of employees who are 55 years old and older is projected to be 4 times that of the overall labor force. By 2012, these older employees will represent nearly 20 percent of the U.S. workforce. In addition, the number of workers who will be 65 years old and older is expected to reach 17.5 million by 2012.

Given that the traditional retirement age in the United States is 65 years old, why are so many baby boomers projected to keep working? Possible explanations for this trend are that some older employees have insufficient savings, pension plans, and investment portfolios that won't allow them to retire; some individuals define themselves by their work and don't want to lose this part of themselves; some are able to reduce their work hours in order to balance work with other family and personal interests; and many older workers are healthier and enjoy the social contact and personal rewards from working.

Tips for managing these valuable and experienced older workers include:

1. *Identify and utilize these workers' knowledge, skills, and abilities* For example, an employee with 35 years of experience may be an excellent mentor and/or trainer of entry-level and less experienced employees.

2. *Provide these employees with flextime or other work-life balance options* Many older workers are more likely to be retained if they are allowed to balance their work schedule with family and personal interests, or other activities often pursued during retirement.

3. *Be prepared to provide alternative forms of training for older employees* For example, individuals have different learning styles and often need to learn at their own pace. Training programs should be adopted to these older individuals in order to keep their skills current.

Sources: Symposium on Older Workers (February 9, 2005), Co-sponsored by the AARP Global Aging Program, the Wharton School's Center for Human Resources, and Boettner Center for Pensions and Retirement Research; Tony Carnevale (January 2005), "The Coming Labor and Skills Shortage," *Training and Development*, Vol. 59, Iss. 1, pp. 36–41; Mitra Toossi (February 2004), "Labor Force Projections to 2012: The Graying of the U.S. Workforce," *Monthly Labor Review*, U.S. Bureau of Labor Statistics.

One of the most important keys to effective planning is accurately and freely sharing all available information. This can only occur when everyone is involved in the process.

The Expert Estimate

The least mathematically sophisticated approach to employment forecasting is for an "expert" or group of experts to provide the organization with demand estimates based on experience, guesses, intuition, and subjective assessments of available economic and labor force indicators.

Concerns over a single individual's ability to provide accurate estimates of such complex issues led to the development of the **Delphi technique.** Originally developed by the Rand Corporation,[11] the Delphi technique elicits expert estimates from a number of individuals in an iterative manner—estimates are revised by each individual based on knowledge of the other individuals' estimates.

Another group-based judgment forecasting method is called the **nominal group technique (NGT).** Individual generation of estimates is followed by group brainstorming

EXHIBIT 5-2
Sample Trend
Projection
Employment Forecast
for Rugby Sporting
Goods Company

Year Actual Data	Sales	Employees Census	Employees Forecast Adjusted for Annual Productivity Rate Increase of 3 Percent
2003	$100,000,000	5,000	5,000
2004	120,000,000	6,000	5,825
2005	140,000,000	7,000	6,598
2006	160,000,000	8,000	7,321
Forecast	Sales Forecast	Employee Forecast	
2007	$180,000,000	9,000	7,996
2008	200,000,000	10,000	8,626

sessions in the hope of generating one group decision that is preferred over any of the individual decisions.[12] NGT can be an effective forecasting tool for environments and problems more complex than an individual can master.[13] It can also help to offset domination by a single person in group decision making by creating a situation where everyone has an equal opportunity to provide opinions.[14]

Trend Projection

The second top-down technique develops a forecast based on a past relationship between a factor related to employment and employment itself. For example, in many businesses, sales levels are related to employment needs. The planner can develop a table or graph showing past relationships between sales and employment. Exhibit 5-2 gives an example of a trend-projection forecast for a hypothetical company, Rugby Sporting Goods Company. Note that as Rugby's sales increased, so did the firm's employment needs. But the increases were not linear. Suppose that in late 2003 Rugby instituted a productivity plan that led to a 3 percent increase in productivity per year. As Rugby forecasted employee needs, it adjusted them for expected productivity gains for 2007 and 2008.

Modeling and Multiple-Predictive Techniques

The third top-down approach to prediction of demand uses the most sophisticated forecasting and modeling techniques. Trend projections relate a single factor (such as sales) to employment. The more advanced approaches relate many factors to employment such as sales, gross national product, and discretionary income. Or they mathematically model the organization and use simulations with methods such as Markov models and analytical formulations such as regression analysis.

The use of the *Markov chain analysis* involves developing a matrix to show the probability of an employee's moving from one position to another or leaving the organization. A full treatment of HRM applications of Markov analysis is found in management science or operations management literature.[15]

Markov analysis begins with an analysis of staffing levels from one period to another. Suppose that professional nursing employees have shifted from hospitals I, II, and III in the Houston Medical Center complex. That is, they quit working in one hospital and went to work for another in the medical center. An HR specialist in hospital I is interested in analyzing the human resource shifts that are occurring between her hospital and hospitals II and III. Exhibit 5-3 illustrates the movement of nurses.

The HR specialists could calculate transition probabilities for all three hospitals. That is, the probability that a hospital will retain its nurses can be calculated. Exhibit 5-4 illustrates the transition probabilities for the retention of professional nurses.

EXHIBIT 5-3
Movement of Nurses
during 2005–2006

Hospital	2006 Level of Nurses	Gain	Loss	2005 Level of Nurses
I	200	60	40	220
II	500	40	50	490
III	300	35	45	290

The data in Exhibit 5-4 indicate that hospital I has a probability of .80 of retaining its nurses, while hospital II has a probability of .90 and hospital III has a probability of .85. Both hospitals II and III have a higher probability of retaining their nursing staff. Therefore, the HR specialist in hospital I needs to study further the issue of why her hospital has a lower probability of retention. Is it because of some particular HRM program? Markov analysis can help identify the probability of lower retention, but it does not suggest any particular solution to the potential problem.

Regression analysis is a mathematical procedure that predicts the *dependent variable* on the basis of knowledge of factors known as *independent variables.* When only one dependent and one independent variable are studied, the process is known as *simple linear regression.* When there is more than one independent variable being considered, the technique is referred to as *multiple regression.*[16]

Most uses of multiple regression emphasize prediction from two or more independent variables. As computer processing speed and capacity have increased, the number of variables used to predict the relevant outcome is virtually limitless. Thus, the HR planning specialist can quickly and easily determine the relationship between a large number of predictors and the dependent variable of interest using any one of a number of commercially available statistical packages such as SPSS or SAS.

Unit-Demand Forecasting

The unit (which can be an entire department, a project team, or some other group of employees) forecast is a bottom-up approach to forecasting demand. Headquarters sums these unit forecasts, and the result becomes the employment forecast. The unit manager analyzes the person-by-person, job-by-job needs in the present as well as the future. By analyzing present and future requirements of the job and the skills of the incumbents, this method focuses on quality of workers.

In larger organizations, an HR executive at headquarters who is responsible for the employment demand forecast will improve the estimates by checking with the managers in the field. If the units forecast their own needs, the HR executive would sum their estimates to arrive at the forecast.

What happens if both bottom-up and top-down approaches are used, and the forecasts conflict? In all probability, the manager reconciles the two totals by averaging them or examining more closely the major variances between the two. The Delphi technique could be used to do this. NGT could also be useful in resolving any discrepancies between different experts' opinions. Thus, one or several of the previously mentioned forecast techniques can be used together to produce a single employment forecast.

It should be apparent that HR planning requires the cooperation of many people in the organization. A strategic plan must be communicated to operational managers and HR

HRMEMO

The Worker Adjustment and Retraining Notification Act (WARN) became effective on February 4, 1989. It requires organizations with more than 100 employees to provide 60 days' advance notice of plant closings and certain mass layoffs. For more information on WARN, visit www.doleta.gov/programs/factsht/warn.htm.

EXHIBIT 5-4
Probabilities of
Transition

Hospital	2006	Nurses Lost	Nurses Retained	Probability of Retention
I	200	40	160	160/200 = .80
II	500	50	450	450/500 = .90
III	300	45	255	255/300 = .85

professionals, who must in turn provide higher levels of management with data about their human resource needs. The planners are major sources of data and information for development of strategy.[17] Thus, the HR planning function plays a critical role in making sure that strategy implementation is effective throughout the organization.

Analyzing the Current Supply of Employees

The third phase of HR planning is designed to answer the question, "How many and what kinds of employees do I currently have in terms of the skills and training necessary for the future?" It should be obvious that this phase of HR planning involves much more than simply counting the number of current employees in the organization.

The Skills Inventory

The major tool used to assess the current supply of employees is the **skills inventory.** In some organizations, there will also be a separate inventory just for managers called a *management inventory.* Both of these serve the same purpose: to note what kinds of skills, abilities, experiences, and training the employees currently have. By keeping track of these, the organization can quickly determine whether a particular skill is available when it is needed. Skills inventories are also useful in career planning, management development, and related activities. A *skills inventory* in its simplest form is a list of names, characteristics, and skills of the people working for the organization. It provides a way to acquire these data and makes them available where needed in an efficient manner.

For a small organization, it is relatively easy to know how many employees there are, what they do, and what they can do. A mom-and-pop grocery store may employ only the owners and may have only two part-time helpers to plan for. When they see that one part-time employee is going to graduate in June, they know they need to replace him or her. Sources of supply could include the owners' children, their other part-time helper (who could be converted into a full-time assistant), and the local school's employment office.

It is quite a different situation with, say, a school system employing hundreds of people at numerous locations, or such mammoth organizations as Procter & Gamble and IBM. These kinds of organizations must know how many full-time and peripheral employees they have working for them, and where. They must know what skills prospective employees would need to replace people who have quit, retired, or been fired or what skills current employees need in order to be relocated for new functions or more work.

Skills inventories vary greatly in their sophistication. Some are as simple as a file drawer containing index cards with relevant information typed on them. Others are tied into extremely expensive and complex computer databases.

Contents of the Skills Inventory

Once the decision has been made to create a skills inventory, the HR manager must determine what information will be contained in the system. The only data available to the organization for later use will be whatever has been designed into the system.

The list of data that might be coded into skills inventories is almost endless, and it must be tailored to the needs of each organization. Some of the more common items include name, employee number, present location, date of birth, date of employment, job classification, specific skills and knowledge, education, field of education (formal education and courses taken since leaving school), knowledge of a foreign language, professional qualifications, publications, licenses, patents, hobbies, a supervisory evaluation of the employee's capabilities, and salary range. Items often omitted, but becoming increasingly important, are the employee's own stated career goals and objectives, including geographical preferences and intended retirement date.

The components of a skills inventory are shown in Exhibit 5-5. Note the main category headings: (I) data summarizing the employee's past, (II) data summarizing the status of present skills, (III) data that focus on the future.

EXHIBIT 5-5   **Components of the Skills Inventory**

Source: By permission of *Personnel Journal* (March 1987), p. 130.

I. Data summarizing the employee's past.

  A. Titles and brief job description highlights from positions held in the last two to five years.
   1. This organization.
   2. Previous organization(s).

  B. Critical skills needed or developed while in these positions.
   1. Manual.
   2. Cognitive.
   3. Creative.

  C. Educational achievements.
   1. High school: job-relevant classes.
   2. College.
    a. Major.
    b. Minor.
    c. Job-relevant courses.

  D. Significant special projects accomplished during the last three years.
   1. This organization.
   2. Previous organization(s).

II. Data summarizing status of present skills.

  A. Skill-related highlights: last three performance appraisals.

  B. Employee's perception of what is done well on present job, e.g., skill competencies, perceptions of how skills could be improved or augmented.

  C. Same data as II.B, from the employee's superior.

III. Data that focus on the future.

  A. Personal career goals.
   1. One year.
   2. Three years.
   3. Identify specific positions and aspirations. Avoid global generalities, i.e., "higher up."

  B. Views of the individual's present superior(s) as to what he or she could be prepared to become. List specific positions.

  C. Specific training and development efforts the individual is motivated to undertake.
   1. On-the-job.
   2. Off-the-job.
   3. Classroom.
   4. Experiential.

The modern, sophisticated skills inventory is, however, much more than a simple listing of employees' current skill levels. For example, AMP, Inc., which manufactures electronic connection devices and currently employs about 16,000 workers, has a skills inventory cataloging 94 different job classifications across 13 labor grades. The company's Manufacturing Skills Inventory System (MSIS) helps it respond to a variety of complex issues:[18]

Do workers have the skills necessary for developing and producing new and innovative products?

Which skills must be mastered before someone is hired?

Which skills will be learned after being hired?

What skills are necessary for a worker to receive a certain promotion?

Who is available to serve as a mentor for other workers?

How effective are the people who have been targeted to be mentors?

Maintaining the Skills Inventory

While designing the system is the most difficult part of developing a skills inventory, planning for the gathering, maintaining, handling, and updating of data is also important. The two principal methods for gathering data are the interview and the questionnaire. The questionnaire is faster and less expensive when many employees are involved, but inaccuracies often prevail. People often do not spend enough time on a questionnaire. Therefore, some experts contend that a trained interviewer can complete the reports more quickly and accurately, a procedure which in the long run more than offsets the costs of the interviewer.

A procedure for keeping the files updated must also be planned. For some organizations, an annual update is adequate. In others, where changes are made often and use is frequent, shorter update periods may be necessary. Some organizations update changeable data monthly and less changeable data annually.

Finally, a decision whether to store the data manually or on the computer must be made. This decision is based on the cost of the computer and frequency of use of the data. The computer also provides the possibility of using comparative analyses of employment over a period of time.

Skills inventories are useful only if management uses the data in making significant decisions. Top-management support is necessary here. Before a manager uses the skills inventory as an aid in selection decisions, he or she must be trained to avoid abuse of the system. Examples of abuse are:

- Making requests simply on the basis that "it would be nice to know."
- Making requests for searches that are not backed up by bona fide requisitions that have been budgeted.
- Specifying too many characteristics for a desired employee so that no one fits all the characteristics.

Action Decisions in Human Resource Planning

After the HR planning system has analyzed both the supply of and the demand for future workers, these two forecasts are compared to determine what, if any, action should be taken. Whenever there is a discrepancy between these two estimates, the organization needs to choose a course of action to eliminate the gap.

Action Decisions with a Shortage of Employees

When employment specialists comparing demand with supply find that the supply of workers is less than the demand, several possibilities are open to the organization. If the shortage is small and employees are willing to work overtime, it can be filled with present employees. If there is a shortage of highly skilled employees, training and promotions of present employees, together with the recruitment of less-skilled employees, are possibilities. This decision can also include recalling employees who were previously laid off.

Intense global competition, rapid technological change, and fears caused by recent workforce reductions have also led many organizations to increase their use of part-time workers, subcontractors, and independent professionals in response to changing demands. And, while the number of these "contingent workers" in the United States has declined slightly, they still constitute a sizable portion of the workforce. There are at least 5.4 million people in the United States who can be considered contingent workers.[19]

Using contingent workers gives many organizations more flexibility in dealing with temporary shortages of labor than does maintaining more traditional full-time employees. On any given day, 2 million temporary workers are on the job somewhere in the United States,[20] with no guarantee of employment beyond today.

Action Decisions in Surplus Conditions

When comparison of demand for and supply of employees indicates a surplus, the alternative solutions include attrition, early retirements, demotions, layoffs, and terminations. Decisions in surplus conditions are some of the most difficult that managers must make, because the employees who are considered surplus are seldom responsible for the conditions leading to the surplus. A shortage of a raw material such as fuel or a poorly designed or poorly marketed product can cause an organization to have a surplus of employees.

HRMEMO

Within the next few years, the U.S. federal government will be facing an extreme shortage of qualified employees; 51 percent of the nation's 1.8 million federal employees will be eligible to take full or early retirement by 2005. The Department of Defense is facing similar potential shortages of civilian information technology (IT) workers. And in the beginning of 2004, the U.S. Army reported that it was 30 percent below its goal of signing up new recruits for full-time status and 45 percent below for reservists.

Sources: Christopher Cooper and Greg Jaffe (October 20, 2004), "Army's Recruiters Miss Target for Enlistees in Latest Month; Reserves Fall 45% Short," *The Wall Street Journal,* p. A4; Gary Anthes (March 2002), "Uncle Sam's Brain Drain," *Computerworld,* pp. 36–38; Melynda Wilcox (September 2001), "Oh, No, Please Don't Go," *Kiplinger's Personal Finance,* pp. 20–22; Jennifer Reingold and Diane Brady (September 20, 1999), "Brain Drain," *BusinessWeek,* pp. 113–126.

HR Journal

HR Business Process Outsourcing: A Fast Growing Trend in the Industry

Renewed focus on strategic goals, acceleration of regulatory and legal changes, pressure to increase efficiency and productivity, and continuous effort to reduce costs have forced many organizations to outsource part or all of their HR processes. Defined as contracting with a service provider to manage people (e.g., recruiting), processes (e.g., payroll), and technologies (e.g., HRISs) related to a company's HR functions, HR business process outsourcing (HRBP) is fast becoming a viable option for many firms. As an indication of its growing popularity, approximately 85 percent of companies are believed to outsource at least one component of their HR function, and total spending on HR business process outsourcing in the United States is expected to reach $14 billion by 2009.

There are several examples of companies that are already outsourcing several aspects of their HR functions. Prudential Financial Inc. has decided to outsource its human resources information systems and administrative functions at a cost of $700 million over 10 years. Hewitt Associates, a leading vendor of outsourced human resources services, landed the contract and will manage all U.S.-based payroll, the HR call center, HR information systems and support, employee data, and records management for Prudential's 47,000 employees. PepsiCo has recently entered into a 10-year agreement with HR outsourcing firm Hewitt Associates to delegate its employee benefits administration, payroll, and call center services. The 10-year deal has been said to be valued at $200 million.

Similarly, International Paper Co. has entered into a 10-year, $600 million arrangement to outsource its human resources functions. As with Prudential, Hewitt Associates will manage International Paper's payroll process, benefits administration, relocation and outplacement services, and human resources information services for 70,000 employees and 80,000 retirees. According to Paul Kerre, vice president of human resources, International Paper hired Hewitt because of its guaranteed cost savings, reductions in business IT spending, and experience in managing third party vendors. Other organizations that have outsourced large portions of their human resource departments include Bank of America Corp. and Canadian Imperial Bank of Commerce.

Is your organization a candidate for HR outsourcing? To find out, please ask yourself the following questions:

Question 1 Do you want your HR department to focus on core business outcomes?

Question 2 Have you experienced rapid growth that has left your organization with a variety of complex processes?

Question 3 Is your HR budget too constrained to support major technological upgrades or complete system overhauls?

If you answer "yes" to any of the questions above, then it may make sense to contact some consulting firms and/or HRBPOs to learn more about the HR outsourcing option.

www.prudential.com

www.hewitt.com

www.internationalpaper.com

Sources: Gary McWilliams (April 13, 2005), "Business Processes Decline as Share of Outsourcing," *The Wall Street Journal*, p. D13; Pamela Babcock (August 2004), "Hewitt and Exult Create Outsourcing Powerhouse," *HRMagazine*, Vol. 49, Iss. 8, pp. 29–31; Denise Pelham (April 2002), "Is It Time to Outsource HR?" *Training*, pp. 50–52; Tischelle George (January 2002), "Prudential Outsources HR Systems to Exult," *Informationweek.com*; Elisabeth Goodridge (October 2001), "Paper Vendor Outsources HR," *Informationweek.com*; Louis Finan, James Konieczny, and Bill Zadell (2000), "For Better or for Worse: Questions for HR Professionals to Ask a Prospective Outsourcing Partner," *Benefits Quarterly*, pp. 7–13; Nancy Mobley (October 2000), "What You Need to Know about Outsourcing HR Functions," *HR Focus*, pp. 7–10.

As a first approach to dealing with a surplus, most organizations avoid layoffs by relying on attrition, early retirement, and creation of work, and the like. Many organizations can reduce their workforce simply by not replacing those who retire or quit (attrition). Sometimes this approach is accelerated by encouraging employees close to retirement to leave early, but there are drawbacks to this approach if the early retirement program is not carefully planned. First, statistics indicate that workers over 50 tend to be healthier, have fewer work-related injuries, and are less likely to change jobs than their younger counterparts.[21] Also, large amounts of retirements are expected to lead to acute skills shortages that will negatively affect companies' ability to compete in the global marketplace. Thus, without proper planning and retention strategies, organizations run the risk of losing their best employees.[22] Second, by the year 2010 the median age of the U.S. workforce will be 40.6 years, which means more than half of all U.S. workers will be legally protected by the Age Discrimination in Employment Act. This act permits workers who are 40 years or older to bring lawsuits against their employers for age-based discrimination. Thus, organizations will need to be very careful in terms to how they design, encourage, and implement early retirement programs in the future.[23] Third, care must be taken not to offer promises that won't be kept. Once certain benefits are promised, it may be illegal to change them without approval of the early retirees.[24]

If voluntary reductions in force such as early retirement programs aren't successful in eliminating the gap between forecasted supplies of and demand for human resources, an organization might have to contemplate temporary or permanent layoffs. Statistics indicate the unemployment rate as of April 2005 is 5.2 percent.[25] In the first half of 2004, U.S. employers announced over 408,000 job cuts.[26]

Some experts believe that in recent years, American corporations have too frequently and quickly turned to layoffs and have failed to fully plan for and evaluate the consequences of their actions. A recent survey of 500 HR executives found, in fact, that one-third of the respondents believed that the company had let go too many workers.[27] In addition, data suggest that layoffs do not lead to better financial performance in the long run[28] and poorly planned reductions in the workforce can have disastrous effects on morale.[29]

Human Resource Information Systems

It should be obvious by now that the key to successful HR planning is information. All of the activities discussed in this chapter assume that the organization is able to collect, store, and evaluate large amounts of information about the internal and external environments. For many organizations, mechanical techniques for dealing with these large amounts of information are no longer adequate. Fortunately, there now exist very sophisticated computerized systems that allow organizations to cope with these information demands.

A **human resource information system (HRIS)** is much more than a computerized skills inventory. An HRIS is an integrated approach to acquiring, storing, analyzing, and controlling the flow of information throughout an organization.[30] Highly developed HRISs can be useful in nearly all HRM functions and can greatly increase efficiency and response times of various traditionally labor- and time-intensive human resource activities.[31] The system might contain a program for tracking applicants, a skills inventory, a career planning program, and employee service programs such as an electronic bulletin board. Its applications are, therefore, almost endless.

One of the most common uses of an HRIS is in recruitment and tracking of applicants. By using its applicant tracking program, along with supply and demand analysis, Bell Helicopter Company applied its HRIS to help secure a multi-billion-dollar government contract. The presence of an integrated HRIS convinced a Navy review team that Bell could acquire the necessary technical staff for meeting contract due dates by avoiding a supply-and-demand gap.[32] This capacity was viewed as critical for the Navy's project.

Many other organizations have developed highly sophisticated tracking programs, and most of these have proved cost-effective. For example, Merck & Company, Inc., determined that a typical applicant had to fill in his or her social security number on at least 22 different occasions during the application process. Eliminating this kind of unnecessary redundancy saved the company considerable money.[33] MCI Telecommunications uses SmartSearch™," an automated resume tracking system, to identify qualified applicants quickly and accurately.[34] The University of Michigan uses an HRIS to manage the pay, benefits, and pensions of current and former faculty and administrators.[35] Each of these companies is convinced that its HR planning has improved with the use of such systems.

In contrast to these relatively specialized HRISs, computer technology has also made it possible for organizations to integrate multiple HR needs into a single system. Apple Computer's system allows employees to enroll in benefit programs directly from their personal computers. Line managers can process traditional employee transactions such as pay increases, and they can use learning modules that instruct them in skill improvement programs such as conducting legal performance analysis.[36] Chevron has also moved toward general systems. The company had over 200 different HR systems, most of which couldn't communicate with one another. Now there is one system with data on all Chevron employees worldwide. The company estimates that it has saved nearly $2,000 per employee by removing these redundancies. And with over 50,000 employees, the savings have been substantial.[37]

In contrast either to Apple Computer's HRIS, which is designed to be used by every employee in the company, or to systems that serve a single function, a third kind of HRIS has been developed specifically for use by upper-level executives. Systems of this third kind are sometimes referred to as **executive information systems (EISs)**.[38] For example, after a corporate restructuring eliminated several layers of management, Phillips Petroleum installed an EIS in order to support its managers and increase their span of control. The company estimates that its system was able to save over $100 million by decentralizing decision making and delivering needed information directly to the managers.

The introduction of computerized HRISs has allowed organizations to broaden their view of replacement planning. **Succession planning** has become more than simply charting expected replacements for a given position. Many experts now suggest that specifying one particular replacement for a specific job is pointless, given the changing nature of business. Rather, succession planning is now considered an integral part of a comprehensive career planning program, which can be greatly assisted by a computerized HRIS.[39]

Several factors are making succession planning for executive level positions more important than ever before.[40] There are large numbers of aging executives at a point in their career where retirement is a distinct possibility. Of the 500 companies in the Standard and Poor's Index, 17 percent have CEOs age 63 and older. And early retirement appears to be an increasingly popular choice among middle-level managers (those who might be expected to ascend to the executive ranks). When AT&T offered its recent voluntary retirement packages as a staff reduction strategy, 50 percent more middle-level managers accepted the buyout than the company had anticipated. It is, therefore, not surprising that the average Fortune 500 company anticipates 33 percent turnover among its executives over the next five years.[41]

These statistics are especially sobering when one also considers that recent surveys indicate that a majority of HR executives do not believe that their organizations are adequately prepared for executive turnover because of an absence of effective succession planning.[42]

Clearly, succession planning must assume a higher priority in many corporations. In addition, however, many progressive companies now realize that a critical part of any successful succession plan is a comprehensive retention plan. One way to minimize the need for replacing senior executives is to strategically plan ways to entice them to delay retirement or to alter their work arrangements with the company. For example, corporations such as Chevron, Prudential Insurance, and Monsanto systematically offer consulting and part-time assignments to executives who might otherwise leave the organization.[43] These companies see this type of HR flexibility as an essential part of their future success.

Succession planning is not only a means for dealing with anticipated transition in executive leadership, but also a way of coping with unanticipated departures, either from losses to competitors or to death, which is a reality of an aging executive workforce. This need for better succession planning could not be more immediate when one considers the results of a recent study by Drake Beam Morin (an outplacement and career development consulting group) that approximately half of the CEOs of 450 of the world's largest corporations held their jobs for less than three years. This, combined with the fact that 20 percent of the largest corporations in the United States replaced their CEOs in 2000, underscores how important it is to develop tomorrow's leaders.[44]

Employees' Privacy, Identity Theft, and HRIS

There is no question that HRISs have dramatically increased the effectiveness of HR planning. However, the introduction of these computer systems has not been without problems. One of the major concerns is that an HRIS makes it easier for someone from within (or outside of) the organization to invade the privacy of employees. The friendlier the system, the easier it can be for unauthorized access to personnel files to occur.[45]

Unlawful access to employees' personnel records can lead to their identity being used by thieves for fraudulent reasons. This illegal activity, known as *identity theft,* occurs when someone uses another person's name, address, social security number, or other identifying information without the person's knowledge with the intent to commit fraud or other crimes.[46] Identity thieves often turn to unsuspecting organizations, for this represents one-stop shopping for electronically stored personnel files, payroll and tax records, and benefits information.[47] The thieves use the employee's personal information to engage in one or more of the following fraudulent acts: going on spending sprees with the employee's debit/credit cards, opening new credit card accounts in the employee's name and then using all of the available credit to make big ticket purchases, taking out auto loans in the employee's name, and opening a bank account in the employee's name, and writing bad checks on that account.[48]

Identity theft is fast becoming a major national problem. According to the Federal Trade Commission (FTC), which monitors the issue, the number of complaints from victims of identify theft in the United States has increased from 1,380 in 1999 to a projected 210,000 in 2003.[49] Even though identity theft is a felony under the federal Identity Theft and Assumption Deterrence Act of 1998, over 3,000 complaints are being received each week at the FTC's Identity Theft Clearinghouse, a help desk, databank, and law enforcement aid.[50] Projections indicate that complaints about identity theft will continue to escalate.

The costs of identity theft to the employee are numerous: it is estimated that a victim of identity theft will need to spend on average 175 hours researching and tracking the crime, 23 months correcting credit reports, and $800 in out-of-pocket expenses to restore their financial health and standing.[51]

Although it is impossible for an organization to guarantee that information about employees will not be seen or used inappropriately by unauthorized persons, several safeguards can help to minimize the risks to privacy in an HRIS. Exhibit 5-6 summarizes the steps that organizations should take to ensure that their HRIS is relatively secure and is used only for its intended purposes.

EXHIBIT 5-6
Safegaurding Privacy in an HRIS

Source: Adapted from: Robert Stambaugh (February 1990), "Protecting Employee Data Privacy," *Computers in HR Management,* pp. 12–20.

- Review information-gathering practices to determine best way to collect data.
- Limit the information you collect to what's relevant to a specific business decision.
- Inform employees about the types of information kept on file and how that information is used.
- Let employees inspect and, if necessary, correct the information maintained on them.
- Keep sensitive information separate from other records.
- Limit the internal use of personal information to those activities where it is necessary.
- Disclose personal information about an employee to outsiders only after the employee consents.

After reading this chapter, talking to friends from other firms, and examining some literature, Ted Sloane was not at all confused about HRISs. He called his vice president of human resource management, Anne Wilson, and said, "Annie, I want to thank you for calling my attention to how we could use and benefit from an HRIS. Without good forward planning, we are going to be in trouble with the law. Let's move ahead and set up an HRIS. By the way, are you familiar with the IBM HRIS system? It's a dandy."

Employees' rights should also be carefully guarded when an organization develops an HRIS. By their very nature, HRISs create the potential for significant amounts of private information about employees being disseminated. Because there is potential for abuse, organizations should carefully evaluate their policies regarding access to HRIS data. An organization must also determine how much information, legally and ethically, it wishes to disclose to the employee in question. Currently, there is no federal legislation guaranteeing employees the right to inspect and amend data in an HRIS. Many states have passed such legislation, however. Finally, an organization should determine how much control its employees should have over the release of personal information. Research has found that the release of information from an HRIS is perceived to be the greatest threat to privacy when employees don't retain the right to authorize the release.[52] Thus, the organization must attempt to strike a balance between employees' privacy and having a user-friendly, easily accessible HRIS.

Summary

As with nearly all of the HRM activities discussed in this book, there is no one best method for conducting HR planning. How much planning is needed, which forecasting techniques will work best, and how far into the future these estimates should extend all differ from organization to organization.

Surveys indicate, however, that many companies probably do not devote enough time and energy to the HR planning process. Others are not aware that many solutions exist to any gap that might develop between the supply and demand of labor.[53] Finally, organizations must begin to realize that an effective HR plan should work in partnership with a strategic plan. For this to happen, organizational goals must be clearly understood and effectively communicated to employees.[54] Organizations throughout the United States now understand how critical HR planning is to this process. Companies around the world, such as Fiat, Pirelli, and Benetton of Italy, attribute much of their recent success to HR planning and its related policies and programs.[55]

To summarize the major points covered in this chapter:

1. The major reasons for formal employment planning are to achieve
   a. More effective and efficient use of human resources.
   b. More satisfied and better-developed employees.
   c. More effective equal opportunity planning.

2. The human resource planning process is a joint responsibility of HR and operating managers, with each performing specific functions in the process.

3. Four forecasting techniques used to determine workforce needs described in the chapter are expert estimates, trend projection, modeling, and unit forecasting.

4. An important step in the planning process is to determine the availability of those presently employed by the organization who can fill projected vacancies. The skills inventory can serve this purpose.

5. Action decisions where there is a shortage of employees depend on the magnitude of the shortage and include overtime, retraining of less-skilled employees, hiring additional employees, and subcontracting some of the work.

6. A growing number of firms are now using computerized human resource information systems to help in the planning process. HRISs perform a number of functions, including applicant tracking, succession planning, skills inventories, and employee services.

7. Action decisions where there is a surplus of employees include attrition, early retirement, demotions, layoffs, and terminations.

8. Organizations need to analyze the supply of and demand for employees in advance so they can take necessary steps to reschedule, recruit, or lay off employees. The organization should analyze workforce composition to determine whether it meets legal constraints.

Human resource planning can be an integral part of the HRM program. It is directly related to recruitment, selection, training, and promotion. By matching supply and demand, the organization can know how many people of what type it needs to fill positions from within (by promotion or training) and how many it must acquire from outside (by recruitment and selection).

Chapters 7 and 8 are devoted to recruitment and selection, in which employment needs are filled from outside the organization when personnel and employment planning decisions show this need.

Key Terms

Delphi technique, *p. 132*
executive information system (EIS), *p. 140*
human resource information system (HRIS), *p. 139*

human resource planning, *p. 129*
nominal group technique (NGT), *p. 132*
skills inventory, *p. 135*

strategic human resource management, *p. 130*
strategic planning, *p. 130*
succession planning, *p. 140*

Questions for Review and Discussion

1. What is human resource planning? How does it relate to other human resource management activities?

2. What is an HRIS? How can an organization use it to increase the efficiency and decrease the costs within the HR department?

3. Describe the pros and cons associated with outsourcing most of your organization's HR functions to an independent vendor for a contract period of 10 years.

4. What factors would affect your choice of an HR planning system? What factors would influence your choice of forecasting methods?

5. Considering the huge number of pending retirements in the United States, what should your organization do to prepare for this phenomenon? How will you ensure that your organization has the necessary human resources it needs for the next 20 years?

6. Describe the contents of a skills inventory. How is this information used in HR planning?

7. What are some of the costs associated with identity theft? If one of your employees was a victim of identity theft, how might that influence their productivity at work during the weeks or months following the crime?

8. What kinds of action decisions are available to an organization when there is a surplus of labor? A labor shortage?

9. What is succession planning? How have HRISs helped companies to integrate career planning with effective succession planning?

10. In your opinion, will HR planning become more or less important as we near the time in which the baby boom generation will begin to retire? Explain.

HRM Legal Advisor

Based on *Gatch* v. *Milacron, Inc.,* 02-3186 (U.S. Court of Appeals for the Sixth Circuit, 111 Fed. Appx. 785; 2004 U.S. App. Lexis 19105).

The Facts

The plaintiff in this case, Robert M. Gatch, was employed as a supervisor of tool services at the plastics injection machinery business (PIMB) unit at Milacron, Inc. Based in Afton, Ohio, the Milacron plant manufactures metal cutting and plastics technology. The case was an appeal by Milacron, Inc., to overturn an earlier U.S. District Court decision that ruled in Gatch's favor. Since 1973, Gatch has been continuously employed by the company (except for one 10-month layoff in the 1970s). Since that time, he has held a variety of positions and received a master's degree in business administration. From the late 1970s until 1999, he held the same supervisor of tool services position. However, in 1999, as part of a workforce reduction, the position of supervisor of tool services was eliminated, and Gatch was demoted to an hourly position as an assembler at a decreased level of pay. Although 38 positions were affected at the facility, the 60-year-old Gatch was the only supervisor affected by the reduction. Milacron argued that the reduction was a result of a drop in sales and profitability by the PIMB unit from the last quarter of 1998 to the first quarter in 1999. The workforce reductions saved the company approximately $1 million.

Later in 1999, the company offered a voluntary retirement package to workers aged 55 and over who had 15 years of seniority. Gatch's direct supervisor recommended that Gatch take the offer of early retirement. Gatch testified that he was subjected to comments about his age and prompted to take early retirement on multiple occasions when co-workers said such derogatory statements as "Hey old man, when are you going to take early retirement?"

Initial Filing

On December 12, 1999, Gatch filed an action against his employer, Milacron, Inc., alleging age discrimination in violation of the Age Discrimination in Employment Act (ADEA). A jury sided with Gatch by finding that Milacron, Inc., had violated the ADEA and awarded Gatch a total of $336,379 for back pay and other compensatory damages.

Appeal

Milacron, Inc., filed an appeal of the lower court decision on August 31, 2004, with the U.S. Court of Appeals for the Sixth Court. Milacron hoped that the appeal would overturn the lower court's ruling, which favored Gatch, the plaintiff. The judge from the U.S. Court of Appeals upheld the plaintiff's claim that Milacron, Inc., violated the ADEA, but decided that the awarded damages were excessive. As a result, the judge remanded the damages issue to the district court for closer scrutiny and judgment. It is possible that the amount of the damages will be reduced.

Human Resource Implications

Effective HR planning sometimes calls for a reduction in the workforce. It is important that such reductions are based on carefully drafted personnel policies and procedures that avoid unlawful criteria such as age (as in this case), race, national origin, gender, religion, disability, and other characteristics that are protected by the law (see Chapter 3). Workforce reduction policies should outline reduction procedures without limiting terminations, transfers, and demotions to economic layoff situations.

Notes

1. Bill Macaleer and Jones Shannon (January 2003), "Does HR Planning Improve Business Performance?" *Industrial Management,* Vol. 45, Iss.1, pp. 14–21; Ronald C. Page and David M. Van De Voort (1989), "Job Analysis and HR Planning," in Wayne F. Cascio (ed.), *Human Resource Planning Employment & Placement* (Washington, DC: Bureau of National Affairs), pp. 34–72.

2. U.S. Department of Labor (May 2003), "The Changing Workforce and Workplace," Strategic Plan for Fiscal Years 2003–2008 (www.dol.gov/_sec/stratplan/main.htm).

3. Steven Manderscheid and Mitchell Kusy (2005), "How to Design Strategy with No Dust—Just Results!" *Organizational Development Journal,* Vol. 23, Iss. 2, pp. 92–71; Alan Scharf (January–February 1991), "Secrets of Strategic Planning: Responding to the Opportunities of Tomorrow," *Industrial Management,* pp. 9–10.

4. Bob Kane and Ian Palmer (1995), "Strategic HRM or Managing the Employment Relationship," *International Journal of Manpower,* pp. 6–21.

5. Kurt Fischer (2003), "Transforming HR Globally: The Center of Excellence Approach," *Human Resource Planning,* Vol. 26, Iss. 2, pp. 9–11; Patrick M. Wright (1998), "Strategy—HR Fit: Does It Really Matter," *Human Resource Planning,* pp. 56–57.

6. Wayne F. Cascio (2003), *Managing Human Resources,* 6th ed. (Boston: McGraw-Hill), p. 177; Page and Van De Voort, op. cit., p. 62.

7. Simon Lam and John Schaubroeck (1998), "Integrating HR Planning and Organizational Strategy," *Human Resource Management Journal,* pp. 5–19.

8. Patricia Sellers (May 2005), "Fast Eddie Roughs Up Sears' Staff," *Fortune,* Vol. 151, Iss. 9, p. 20.

9. Christian Zeller (2004), "North Atlantic Innovation Relations of Swiss Pharmaceuticals and the Proximities with Regional Biotech Arenas," *Economic Geography,* Vol. 80, Iss. 1, pp. 83–112; Sanjay Singh, Hugh Watson, and Richard Watson (May 2002), "EIS Support for the Strategic Management Process," *Decision Support Systems,* pp. 71–85; William H. Davidson (Winter 1991), "The Role of Global Scanning in Business Planning," *Organization Dynamics,* pp. 4–16.

10. F. A. Maljers (April 1990), "Strategic Planning and Intuition in Unilever," *Long Range Planning,* pp. 63–68.

11. N. Dalkey (1969), *The Delphi Method: An Experimental Study of Group Opinion* (Santa Monica, CA: Rand).

12. Joseph Conlin (September 1989), "Brainstorming: It's Not as Easy as You Think," *Successful Meetings,* pp. 30–34.

13. Ken Blanchard (October 1992), "Meetings Can Be Effective," *Supervisory Management,* pp. 5–6.

14. Michael Finley (March 1992), "Belling the Bully," *HRMagazine,* pp. 82–86.

15. Michael Ransom and Ronald L. Oaxaca (January 2005), "Intrafirm Mobility and Sex Differences in Pay," *Industrial & Labor Relations Review,* Vol. 58, Iss. 2, pp. 219–237; Sally McClean (March 27, 1991), "Manpower Planning Models and Their Estimation," *European Journal of Operations Research,* pp. 179–187; B. G. Raghavendra (July 1991), "A Bivariate Model for Markov Manpower Planning Systems," *Journal of the Operational Research Society,* pp. 565–570.

16. Patricia Cohen, Jacob Cohen, Stephen G. West, and Leona S. Aiken (August 2002), *Applied Multiple Regression/Correlation Analysis for the Behavioral Sciences,* 3rd Ed. (Mahwah, NJ: Lawrence Erlbaum Associates); Neal W. Schmitt and Richard J. Klimoski (1991), *Research Methods in Human Resources Management* (Cincinnati, OH: South-Western Publishing), pp. 59–79.

17. Henry Mintzberg (January–February 1994), "The Fall and Rise of Strategic Planning," *Harvard Business Review,* pp. 107–114.

18. Dennis Guessford, Albert Boynton, Jr., Robert Laudeman, and Joseph Giusti (June 1993), "Tracking Job Skills Improves Performance," *Personnel Journal,* pp. 109–114.

19. Bureau of Labor Statistics (May 2001), "Contingent and Alternative Employment Arrangements, February 2001" (http://stats.bls.gov/news.release/conemp.nr0.htm).

20. Donna Albrecht (April 1998), "Reaching New Heights," *Workforce,* pp. 42–48.

21. Alison Wellner (March 2002), "Tapping a Silver Mine," *HRMagazine,* pp. 26–32; Anne Fisher (September 30, 1996), "Wanted: Aging Baby-Boomers," *Fortune,* p. 204.

22. Roberta Fusaro (July–August 2001), "Needed: Experienced Workers," *Harvard Business Review,* pp. 20–21.

23. Robert J. Grossman (August 2003), "Are You Ignoring Older Workers," *HRMagazine,* Vol. 48, Iss. 8, pp. 40–46; Michael Barrier (March 2002), "An Age-Old Problem," *HRMagazine,* pp. 34–37.

24. Jeff D. Opdyke (September 15, 2004), "With Thousands of Pensions Closing, How Safe Is Yours?" *The Wall Street Journal*, D1; Betty Southard Murphy, Wayne E. Barlow, and Diane D. Hatch (May 1994), "GM Unlawfully Cuts Retiree Health Benefits," *Personnel Journal*, pp. 37–38.

25. http://www.bls.gov/eag/eag.us.htm

26. "Job Cut Plans Rise" (June 1, 2004), CnnMoney Online (http://money.cnn.com/2004/06/01/news/economy/challenger).

27. Sherry Kuczynski (June 1999), "Help! I Shrunk the Company!" *HRMagazine*, pp. 40–45.

28. Victor B. Wayhan and Steve Werner (2000), "The Impact of Workforce Reductions on Financial Performance: A Longitudinal Perspective," *Journal of Management*, Vol. 26, Iss. 2, pp. 341–363; Alan Downs (October 1995), "The Truth about Layoffs," *Management Review*, pp. 57–61.

29. Sherry Kuczynski, op. cit., pp. 40–45.

30. Alfred J. Walker (May 2001), *Web-Based Human Resources* (New York: McGraw-Hill/Irwin); Michael J. Kavanagh, Hal G. Gueutal, and Scott I. Tannenbaum (1990), *Human Resource Information Systems: Development and Application* (Boston: PWS-Kent), p. 29.

31. Bill Copeland (April 2004), "Making HR Your Business," *CA Magazine*, Vol. 137, Iss. 3, pp. 45–47; Andrew Targowski and Satish Deshpande (2001), "The Utility and Selection of an HRIS," *Advances in Competitiveness Research*, pp. 42–56.

32. Jac Fitz-Enz (March 1990), "HR Forecasts That Will Benefit Your Bottom Line," *Computers in HR Management*, pp. 24–33.

33. Charlene Solomon (June 1993), "Working Smarter: How HR Can Help," *Personnel Journal*, pp. 54–64.

34. Larry Stevens (April 1993), "Resume Scanning Simplifies Tracking," *Personnel Journal*, pp. 77–79.

35. Dan Caterinicchia (February 2005), "University HR's Self-Service Solution," *HRMagazine*, Vol. 50, Iss. 2, pp. 105–110.

36. Erik Sherman (May 2005), "Use Technology to Stay in SOX Compliance," *HRMagazine*, Vol. 50, Iss. 5, pp. 95–100; Jim Witschger (March 2005), "Praise for People-Trak," *T + D*, Vol. 59, Iss. 3, pp. 55–57; Jennifer Laabs (November 1993), "Electronic Campus Captures Apple's Corporate Memory," *Personnel Journal*, pp. 104–110; Kirk Anderson (March 1990), "Apple's HRIS Changes How HR Works," *Computers in HR Management*, pp. 14–23.

37. Christine Ellis (July 2001), "Sharing Best Practices Globally," *Training*, Vol. 38, Iss. 7, pp. 32–39; Jay F. Stright Jr. (September 1993), "Strategic Goals Guide HRMS Development," *Personnel Journal*, pp. 68–78.

38. Doug Bartholomew (October 2004), "Manufacturers Get Smart," *Industry Week*, Vol. 253, Iss. 10, pp. 27–30; Jeretta Horn Nord and G. Daryl Nord (August 1995), "Executive Information Systems: A Study and Comparative Analysis," *Information Management*, pp. 95–106.

39. Steve Bates (April 2002), "Succession Planning Lags, APQC Survey Discovers," *HRMagazine*, pp. 12–14.

40. Zhiang Lin and Dan Li (February 2004), "The Performance Consequences of Top Management Successions," *Group & Organization Management*, Vol. 29, Iss. 1, pp. 32–66; William Rothwell (May–June 2002), "Putting Success into Your Succession Planning," *The Journal of Business Strategy*, pp. 32–37.

41. Robert Grossman (February 1999), "Heirs Unapparent," *HRMagazine*, pp. 36–44.

42. Sheila Anne Feeney (August 2003), "Irreplaceable You," *Workforce Management*, Vol. 82, Iss. 8, pp. 36–41; Eve Golden (June 1998), "Nothing Succeeds Like Succession," *Across the Board*, pp. 36–40.

43. Jennifer Reingold and Diane Brady (September 20, 1999), "Brain Drain," *BusinessWeek*, pp. 112–126.

44. Bill Leonard (May 2001), "Turnover at the Top," *HRMagazine*, pp. 46–52.

45. Jessica Marquez (May 2005), "Small Lapses Can Lead to Identity Theft," *Workforce Management*, Vol. 84, Iss. 5, pp. 22–23; Robert Stambaugh (February 1990), "Protecting Employee Data Privacy," *Computers in HR Management*, pp. 12–20.

46. See www.ftc.gov.

47. Susan J. Wells (December 2002), "Stolen Identity," *HRMagazine,* Vol. 47, Iss. 12, pp. 30–38.

48. See www.ftc.gov.

49. See www.ftc.gov.

50. Wells, op cit., p. 30.

51. Wells, Ibid.

52. Erik Eddy, Dianna Stone, and Eugene Stone-Romero (Summer 1999), "The Effects of Information Management Policies on Reactions to Human Resource Information Systems: An Integration of Privacy and Procedural Justice Perspectives," *Personnel Psychology,* pp. 335–358.

53. David M. Reid (April 1990), "Where Planning Fails in Practice," *Long Range Planning,* pp. 85–93.

54. Toyohiro Kono (August 1990), "Corporate Culture and Long Range Planning," *Long Range Planning,* pp. 9–19.

55. Arnaldo Camuffo and Giovanni Costa (Winter 1993), "Strategic Human Resource Management—Italian Style," *Sloan Management Review,* pp. 59–67.

Application Case 5-1

Human Resource Planning and Virtual Human Resource Management

Just a few years ago, computer technology offered a revolutionary change in human resource management. Organizations experimented with computerized skills inventories, pay and benefits administration, and applicant tracking systems. Today, the revolution continues but is undergoing fundamental changes as computer technology and the Internet grow at unprecedented rates. Human resource management is moving away from a mainframe technology to the world of virtual reality, with the Internet at its core. Although many forces drive this change, one of the most important is the globalization of business. As organizations spread their operations and personnel worldwide, the need for a truly global, integrated human resource information system has reached critical levels. The most obvious answer—virtual human resource management on the World Wide Web.

Surveys indicate that in the past year alone, the percentage of U.S. companies using the Web for its HR system has almost doubled. As recently as 1997, approximately 27 percent of surveyed organizations reported such use. Now that number has reached 50 percent, and almost 75 percent of organizations indicate they plan to integrate their HR activities with the Web sometime during the next two years.

The most common uses of the Internet in human resource planning are in corporate communications, applicant and resume tracking, and benefits and retirement planning. In the area of recruiting, Humana Inc. has created one of the most advanced applicant identification and tracking systems in the world. Humana is an HMO with approximately 20,000 employees and 6 million subscribers. Their human resource recruiters can rapidly identify, contact, and track qualified applicants for virtually any job opening in their organization. Their success revolves around a specialized software application, Softshoe Select, provided by and linked to Hotjobs.com. This software automatically searches millions of individual Web pages looking for resumes that meet any need that Humana may have. While setup costs are relatively large (a one-time fee of $50,000 for licensing and configuration in addition to a $2,000 per month lease), organizations such as Humana find that the costs are well worth the efforts. Humana, for example, estimates that it previously spent an average of $128 in advertising to find a single qualified applicant's resume. Today, they estimate that the cost is approximately $.06. For Humana, that translates into an annual savings of $8.3 million.

The Internet is also helping revolutionize a number of other human resource planning activities for many organizations. Citibank, for example, has a single global HRIS that maintains a detailed skills inventory, compensation database, and HR practices for 98 countries and 10,000 managerial personnel worldwide. Numerous other global employers have created employee self-service compensation and benefits systems that allow employees from around the globe to manage many of their own HR activities. For example, employees at Shell Oil Company manage their retirement plans, maintain and/or change health care coverage, and track other personally relevant information all through an automated, self-service system.

Use of the Internet in these kinds of human resource planning activities is not, however, without danger. The ease of access to so much information always has the potential to create both legal and ethical abuse, both by employees and by external "hackers," or unauthorized users of the system. Organizations must take all necessary precautions to safeguard the privacy and integrity of these virtual human resource systems. The challenges are immense, but the organizational consequences can be invaluable.

Source: Prepared by James Phillips using information from Samuel Greengard (August 1998), "Humana Takes Online Recruiting to a Hire Level," *Workforce,* p. 75; Scott Hays (March 1999), "Reach Out to Expats via the Web," *Workforce,* pp. 46–47; Gary Meyer (April 1999), "Softshoe Select: An Engine for Internet-Based Recruiting," *HRMagazine,* pp. 112–116; Steven McCormick (October 1998), "The Virtual HR Organization," *Management Accounting,* pp. 48–51; and Linda Stroh, Sven Grasshoff, Andre Rude, and Nancy Carter (April 1998), "Integrated HR Systems Help Develop Global Leaders," *HRMagazine,* pp. 14–17.

Discussion Questions

1. How has the emergence of the Internet changed the way that organizations plan and manage their human resource needs?

2. What kinds of future human resource activities might we see developed over the next several years?

3. What are the legal and ethical issues surrounding the use of the Internet by individual employees for human resource activities? Are you concerned about violations of your own privacy because of these kinds of Web applications?

4. What specialized skills will the future HRIS professional need in order to effectively manage an organization's virtual human resource function?

Chapter

Job Analysis and Design

Learning Objectives

After studying this chapter, you should be able to:

1. **Define** the terms *job analysis, job description,* and *job specification.*

2. **Illustrate** the uses that job analysis information can have in an organization's HRM.

3. **Describe** four methods used to collect job analysis information.

4. **Interpret** job codes and information found in the *Dictionary of Occupational Titles.*

5. **List** the five core job dimensions used in job enrichment programs.

6. **Compare** the strengths and weaknesses of the mechanistic and motivational approaches to job design.

7. **Describe** briefly how job descriptions are changing as the nature of jobs has changed.

Internet/Web Resources

General Sites
www.doleta.gov/programs/onet
www.opm.gov/
www.paq2.com
www.pstc.com
www.knowledgepoint.com

Company Sites
www.toyota.com
www.onetcenter.org
www.chrysler.com
www.att.com
www.hp.com
www.pfizer.com
www.chevron.com
www.coca-cola.com
www.fedex.com
www.ge.com
www.gm.com
www.motorola.com
www.pg.com
www.xerox.com
www.monster.com
www.careerbuilder.com
www.hotjobs.com
www.indeed.com
www.simplyhired.com
www.workzoo.com

Jean Davis is the new director of human resources of Sprowl Manufacturing, a division of the MBTI Corporation. Jean wanted to start a job analysis program immediately. Six weeks after she took over, job analysis questionnaires (six pages each) were given to employees. The results were puzzling. Responses from the operating employees (machinists, lift operators, technicians, draftspeople, and mechanics) were quite different from responses from their supervisors about these jobs.

The fact that supervisors viewed the jobs differently from those doing the work fueled Jean's desire to do a job analysis. She wanted to study and specifically define the jobs so that misunderstandings, arguments, and false expectations could be kept to a minimum.

The supervisors listed job duties as simple and routine. The operating employees disagreed and claimed that their jobs were complicated and constrained by limited resources. They complained that work areas were hot, stuffy, and uncomfortable. These disagreements soon became the basis for some open hostility between supervisors and workers. Finally, Nick Mannis, a machinist, confronted a supervisor, Rog Wilkes, and threatened to punch him over the "lies" Rog and other supervisors had concocted in the job analysis.

Jean was worried that the job analysis program was getting totally out of hand. She had to do something about it. Everyone was getting up in arms over a program Jean felt was necessary.

Should a manager like Jean, who knows a lot about HRM, but who was not trained in the specifics of job analysis, undertake this kind of program?

Organizations have evolved because the overall mission and objectives of most institutions are too large for any single person to accomplish. Consequently, the organization must have a systematic way to determine which employees are expected to perform a particular function or task that must be accomplished. The cornerstone of the organization is, therefore, the set of jobs performed by its employees. These jobs, in turn, provide the mechanism for coordinating and linking the various activities of the organization that are necessary for success. As a result, studying and understanding jobs through the process known as *job analysis* is a vital part of any HRM program.

Job analysis provides answers to questions such as these:[1]

How much time is taken to complete important tasks?

Which tasks are grouped together and considered a job?

How can a job be designed or structured so that the employees' performance can be enhanced?

What kinds of behaviors are needed to perform the job?

What kind of person (in terms of traits and experience) is best suited for the job?

How can the information acquired by a job analysis be used in the development of HRM programs?

This chapter clarifies the contributions made by job analysis to an organization's HRM program and specific activities. Furthermore, the careful planning needed and the various techniques of a job analysis program are highlighted. Finally, the importance of job analysis in the design of jobs is discussed. The chapter shows that job analysis is a necessary part of HRM and in many respects is the foundation upon which all other HRM activities must be constructed. The nature of the work to be performed is one of the fundamental inputs into all major HRM functions. This is another way of saying that how workers' responsibilities and duties are segmented helps to shape and determine virtually all other facets of organizational functioning. As such, understanding exactly what constitutes any particular job is critical to developing HRM activities that support the organization's mission.

The Vocabulary of Job Analysis

Before considering the process and techniques involved in job analysis, one should learn the language of job analysis. Although many of these terms are often used interchangeably by people who are unfamiliar with job analysis, the expert will use them more precisely in order to avoid confusion and misinterpretation. Precision in the use of these terms is, in fact, required by federal and state legislation. It is therefore important for the HR manager to use each of them in a way that is consistent with such legislation.

The following definitions are consistent with those provided by the U.S. Employment Service and the U.S. Office of Personnel Management:[2]

- **Job analysis**   A purposeful, systematic process for collecting information on the important work-related aspects of a job.[3]
- **Job description**   The principal product of a job analysis. It represents a written summary of the job as an identifiable organizational unit. *daily Duties*
- **Job specification**   A written explanation of the knowledge, skills, abilities, traits, and other characteristics (KSAOs) necessary for effective performance on a given job.
- **Tasks**   Coordinated and aggregated series of work elements used to produce an output (e.g., a unit of production or service to a client).
- **Position**   Consists of the responsibilities and duties performed by an individual. There are as many positions in an organization as there are employees.
- **Job**   Group of positions that are similar in their duties, such as computer programmer or compensation specialist.
- **Job family**   Group of two or more jobs that have similar duties.

The Steps in Job Analysis

The job analysis process involves a number of steps, which are outlined in Exhibit 6-1.[4] As it appears in the exhibit, the process assumes that the job analysis is being conducted in an ongoing organization, in other words, an organization that is already in operation as opposed to a new venture.

EXHIBIT 6-1   **Steps in the Job Analysis Process (1–6) and Its Relationship to HRM and Job Design**

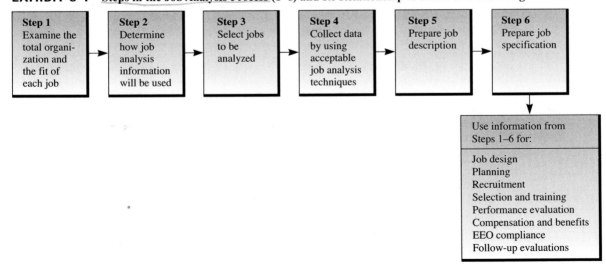

| Step 1 Examine the total organization and the fit of each job | Step 2 Determine how job analysis information will be used | Step 3 Select jobs to be analyzed | Step 4 Collect data by using acceptable job analysis techniques | Step 5 Prepare job description | Step 6 Prepare job specification |

Use information from Steps 1–6 for:

Job design
Planning
Recruitment
Selection and training
Performance evaluation
Compensation and benefits
EEO compliance
Follow-up evaluations

Step 1 provides a broad view of how each job fits into the total fabric of the organization. Organization charts and process charts (discussed later) are used to complete step 1. Step 2 encourages those involved to determine how the job analysis and job design information will be used. This step is further explained in the next section. Since it is usually too costly and time-consuming to analyze every job, a representative sample of jobs needs to be selected. In step 3, jobs that are to be analyzed are selected.

Step 4 involves the use of acceptable job analysis techniques. The techniques are used to collect data on the characteristics of the job, the required behaviors, and the characteristics an employee needs to perform the job. The information collected in step 4 is then used in step 5 to develop a job description. Next, in step 6, a job specification is prepared.

The knowledge and data collected in steps 1 through 6 are used as the foundation for virtually every other HRM activity. As shown in Exhibit 6-1, these include activities such as recruitment, selection, training, performance evaluation, and compensation. The information gathered during job analysis is essential to each of these.

As is also shown in the exhibit, the information gathered is used in job design and redesign, which are discussed in detail later in this chapter. Job analysis provides information necessary for organizing work in ways that allow employees to be both productive and satisfied. Finally, information from job analysis can be used in an organization's follow-up evaluations of its job design. At this step, it is important for an organization to evaluate its efforts and determine whether the goals of productivity and satisfaction are in fact being achieved.

The Uses of Job Analysis

HR managers, specialists, and managers in general know that job analysis has many uses. Some of these individuals now believe that there is no longer even a choice about whether job analysis should be conducted. Administrative guidelines accompanying various civil rights and EEO laws and judicial recommendations are clear. The question has become how to conduct a legally defensible job analysis rather than whether to conduct such an analysis at all.[5] In terms of staffing and selection activities, job analysis plays an important role in the *Uniform Guidelines on Employee Selection Procedures* (1978), a set of policies designed to minimize or prevent workplace discrimination practices. The UGESP emphasizes that job analysis should be used when validating or assessing the accuracy of organizational selection procedures.[6] In addition, job analysis is critical to assessments of discrimination under most employment-related laws, including the Civil Rights Act of 1991 and the Americans with Disabilities Act of 1990. Job analysis is linked with these discrimination laws through rulings from numerous Supreme Court decisions. The quality of job analysis conducted by an organization is frequently a primary determinant of whether it has acted properly.

On the basis of these court decisions, a good job analysis must provide the following if it is to be viewed favorably:[7]

1. It should yield a thorough, clear job description.
2. The frequency and importance of task behaviors should be assessed.
3. It must allow for an accurate assessment of the knowledge, skills, abilities, and other characteristics (KSAOs) required by the job.
4. It must yield information about the relationship between job duties and these KSAOs. That is, it must clearly determine which KSAOs are important for each job duty.

In addition to helping organizations satisfy their legal requirements, job analysis is closely tied to HRM programs and activities. It is used extensively in each of the following areas:

1. *Recruitment and selection* Job analysis information helps recruiters seek and find the right persons for the organization. And, to hire the right person, selection testing must

HRMemo

Before asking employees and supervisors for their assistance in conducting several job analyses, HR managers need to communicate to these individuals why job analyses are important and how the information will be used. If not, the HR manager may encounter resistance from busy employees and managers.

assess the most critical skills and abilities needed to perform a job. This information comes from job analysis.

2. *Training and career development* Knowing the skills necessary for jobs is essential to building effective training programs. Moreover, helping people to move efficiently from one career stage to another can only be accomplished with information from job analysis.

3. *Compensation* Compensation is usually tied to the duties and responsibilities of a job. Thus, proper compensation demands accurate assessments of what various jobs entail.

4. *Strategic planning* More and more, managers are beginning to realize that job analysis is another important tool in an organization's overall strategic planning efforts. Effective job analysis can help organizations to change, eliminate, or otherwise restructure work and work flow processes to meet the changing demands of uncertain environments.

It should be obvious from this list that the potential uses of job analysis cover the entire domain of HRM activities. It is, in fact, difficult to imagine how an organization could effectively hire, train, appraise, compensate, or utilize its human resources without the kinds of information derived from job analysis. But the value of job analysis doesn't end with HRM. Managers involved in virtually all aspects of planning, organizing, controlling, and directing in the organization also benefit from job analysis information.

Who Should Conduct the Job Analysis?

The steps spelled out in Exhibit 6-1 suggest that care and planning are important features of any job analysis. Part of that planning should involve carefully choosing the people who will conduct the analysis. If an organization has only an occasional need for job analysis information, it may hire a temporary job analyst from outside. Other organizations will have job analysis experts employed full-time. Still other organizations will use supervisors, job incumbents, or some combination of these to collect job analysis information.

Each of these choices has strengths and weaknesses. For example, job incumbents are a good source of information about what work is actually being done rather than what work is supposed to be done. In addition, involving incumbents in the job analysis process might increase their acceptance of any work changes stemming from the results of the analysis.[8] On the other hand, job analysis should describe the work activities of a job independent of any personal attributes of a given job incumbent. Because incumbents tend to exaggerate the responsibilities and importance of their work, this objectivity might be difficult to achieve when incumbents conduct the job analysis. Thus, the choice of who should analyze a job depends on many factors, including the location and complexity of the jobs to be analyzed, how receptive incumbents might be to an external analyst, and the ultimate intended purpose of the results of the analysis.[9]

Regardless of who collects the information, the individuals should thoroughly understand people, jobs, and the total organizational system. They should also have considerable knowledge about how work is expected to flow within the organization.

The Use of Charts

The job analyst has to select the best methods and procedures available to conduct the analysis. However, even before this selection is made, an overview of the organization and its jobs is required. An overview provides the job analyst with an informed picture of the total arrangement of departments, units, and jobs. Additionally, this overview will provide the job analyst with a better understanding of the flow of work through the organization.

HR Journal   *Reengineering: The Strategic Job Analysis Challenge*

A 1990 *Harvard Business Review* article entitled "Reengineering Work: Don't Automate, Obliterate" introduced managers to the concept of reengineering. According to its author, Michael Hammer, the heart of reengineering is the need for organizations to break away from their traditional rules about work and from the assumptions that underlie how that work is efficiently accomplished. This requires a complete redesign of existing work into jobs that previously didn't exist. Specifically, reengineering designs jobs around outcomes rather than tasks. This means that a single individual will be responsible for performing all aspects of a process rather than a limited subset of tasks.

Mutual Benefit Life Insurance implemented a complete reengineering program several years ago. Their job analyses indicated that the application process included 30 separate steps that spanned five different departments. Typical turnaround time was between 5 and 25 days, with most of the time spent passing the application between departments. In response to this inefficiency, the company created a new job titled case manager. A case manager became responsible for the entire application process for any given individual. The reengineering doubled the volume of work that was being completed; at the same time, the company was able to eliminate 100 unnecessary field office positions.

Similar efforts to streamline operations and make bureaucracy more efficient and less cumbersome are being enacted by Toyota Motor Corporation, the world's fourth largest automobile manufacturer with 2003 sales of U.S.\$146 billion, 51 manufacturing companies in 26 countries/locations, 264,000 employees worldwide, and markets for vehicles in more than 140 countries. Toyota is creating an integrated, flexible global manufacturing system that will encourage process redesign, ultimately cutting billions of dollars in expenses. The initiative focuses on creating and implementing a new global standard for manufacturing which will attempt to realize new synergies between the company's IT and production systems. The project will be aimed at Toyota's North American parts supply network that includes 1,500 Lexus and Toyota dealers and its 450 suppliers. In order to make this project a reality, the company will need to redesign several existing jobs to support these new initiatives. Job analysis is likely to play an important role in this change process.

Sources: Michael Hammer (November–December 2001), "The New Business Agenda," *Strategy & Leadership,* pp. 42–43; Brian Bremner, Chester Dawson, Kathleen Kerwin, Christopher Palmeri, and Paul Magnusson (November 17, 2003), "Can Anything Stop Toyota? An Insider Look at How It's Reinventing the Auto Industry," *BusinessWeek,* Iss. 3858, pp. 114–121; www.toyota.co.jp/en/about_toyota/overview/index.html; John Teresko (January 2001), "Toyota's New Challenge," *Industry Week,* pp. 71–74; Michael Hammer (July–August 1990), "Reengineering Work: Don't Automate, Obliterate," *Harvard Business Review,* pp. 104–112; John Thackray (June 1993), "Fads, Fixes, and Fiction," *Management Today,* pp. 40–42; David Warner (October 1993), "Bureaucracy, Heal Thyself," *Nation's Business,* pp. 66–68.

To gain these useful insights about the structure and process of the organization, two types of charts are especially helpful. An **organization chart** presents the relationships among departments and units of the firm. The line functions (the individuals performing the work duties) and staff functions (the advisers) are also spelled out. A typical organizational chart will yield information about the number of vertical levels in the organization, the number of different functional departments, and the formal reporting relationships that exist.

A second type of chart, the **process chart,** shows how a specific set of jobs are related to each other.[10] Thus, rather than simply showing the structural relationships among job titles (as in a typical organizational chart), the process chart shows the flow of activities and work necessary to produce a desired product or service.

Methods of Data Collection

There are four basic methods, which can be used separately or in combination, of collecting job analysis data—observation, interview, questionnaires, and job incumbent diaries or logs. In each of these methods, the information about the job is collected and then the job is studied in terms of tasks completed by the job incumbent (person presently working on the job). This type of job analysis is referred to as *job-oriented*. On the other hand, a job can be analyzed in terms of behaviors or what the job incumbent does to perform the job (such as computing, coordinating, or negotiating). This is referred to as *work-oriented* job analysis.[11] Both of these orientations are acceptable under the *Uniform Guidelines on Employee Selection Procedures* as long as they identify job duties and behaviors that are critical to performing the job.

The four methods—or any combination of them—must focus on critical information. Since time and cost are considerations, managers need to collect comparable, valid data. Consequently, some form of core information is needed no matter what data collection method is used.[12] A professional job analyst typically conducts extensive interviews with incumbents and supervisors, collects records about the job, and, if feasible, directly observes the job incumbents performing the job.[13]

A questionnaire called the **job analysis information format (JAIF)** can provide the basic core information for use with any job analysis method—observation, interview, questionnaire, or incumbent diary or log. It permits the job analyst to collect information that provides a thorough picture of the job, job duties, and requirements.

Job incumbents are asked to complete the JAIF. These answers (of course, some questions may not be answered or can't be answered because the job incumbent doesn't know the answer) are then used to specifically structure the data collection technique that will eventually be implemented. Exhibit 6-2 presents a portion of one type of JAIF.

Differences among job incumbents should be considered during the analysis of JAIF information, in addition to the actual job analysis. The job analyst should not assume that all incumbents or their supervisors will view a job in the same way. A safeguard against developing a distorted picture of a job is for the job analyst to collect information from a variety of incumbents. The job analyst should probably try to get information from males and females, older and younger workers, and high- and low-performing incumbents (the research is mixed about whether there will be differences between them in terms of their view of the job).[14] Finally, the job analyst should not assume that all incumbents and supervisors have the same amount of knowledge about a job. This is important because research indicates that too little knowledge about a job can lead to inaccurate job descriptions.[15]

Observation

Direct observation is used for jobs that require manual, standardized, and short-job-cycle activities. Jobs performed by an automobile assembly-line worker, an insurance company filing clerk, and an inventory stockroom employee are examples of these. The job analyst must observe a representative sample of individuals performing these jobs. Observation is usually not appropriate where the job involves significant mental activity, such as the work of a research scientist, a lawyer, or a mathematician.

The observation technique requires that the job analyst be trained to observe *relevant* job behaviors. In conducting an observation, the job analyst must remain as unobtrusive as possible. He or she must stay out of the way so that the work can be performed.

Interviews

Interviewing job incumbents is often done in combination with observation. Interviews are probably the technique used most widely in collecting data for job analysis. They permit the job analyst to talk face to face with job incumbents. The job incumbent can ask questions of the job analyst, and this interview serves as an opportunity for the analyst to explain how the knowledge and information gained from the job analysis will be used.

Interviews can be conducted with a single job incumbent, with a group of individuals, or with a supervisor who is knowledgeable about the job. Usually a structured set of questions will be used in interviews so that answers from individuals or groups can be compared.

EXHIBIT 6-2

JOB ANALYSIS INFORMATION FORMAT

Your Job Title _____   *Code* _____ *Date* _____

Class Title _____   *Department* _____

Your Name _____   *Facility* _____

Supervisor's Title _____   *Prepared by* _____

Superior's Name _____   *Hours Worked* _____ AM/PM _____ *to* AM/PM _____

1. What is the general purpose of your job?

2. What was your last job? If it was in another organization, please name it.

3. To what job would you normally expect to be promoted?

4. If you regularly supervise others, list them by name and job title.

5. If you supervise others, please check those activities that are part of your supervisory duties:

   __ Hiring   __ Developing   __ Directing   __ Disciplining

   __ Orienting   __ Coaching   __ Measuring performance   __ Terminating

   __ Training   __ Counseling   __ Promoting   __ Other _____

   __ Scheduling   __ Budgeting   __ Compensating

6. How would you describe the successful completion and results of your work?

7. *Job Duties*—Please briefly describe what you do and, if possible, how you do it. Indicate those duties you consider to be most important and/or most difficult.

   a. Daily duties—

   b. Periodic duties (please indicate whether weekly, monthly, quarterly, etc.)—

   c. Duties performed at irregular intervals—

   d. How long have you been performing these duties?

   e. Are you now performing unnecessary duties? If yes, please describe.

   f. Should you be performing duties not now included in your job? If yes, please describe.

(continued)

EXHIBIT 6-2 *(concluded)*

8. *Education.* Please check the blank that indicates the educational requirements for the job, not your *own* educational background.

   a. _____ No formal education required.

   b. _____ Less than high school diploma.

   c. _____ High school diploma or equivalent.

   d. _____ 2-year college certificate or equivalent.

   e. _____ 4-year college degree.

   f. _____ Education beyond undergraduate degree and/or professional license.

   List advanced degrees or specific professional license or certificate required.

   Please indicate the education you had when you were placed on this job.

9. *Experience.* Please check the amount needed to perform your job.

   a. _____ None.

   b. _____ Less than one month.

   c. _____ One month to less than six months.

   d. _____ Six months to one year.

   e. _____ One to three years.

   f. _____ Three to five years.

   g. _____ Five to 10 years.

   h. _____ Over 10 years.

   Please indicate the experience you had when you were placed on this job.

10. *Skills.* Please list any skills required in the performance of your job. (For example, degree of accuracy, alertness, precision in working with described tools, methods, systems, etc.)

    Please list skills you possessed when you were placed on this job.

11. *Equipment.* Does your work require the use of any equipment? Yes _____ No _____ If yes, please list the equipment and check whether you use it rarely, occasionally, or frequently.

Equipment	Rarely	Occasionally	Frequently
a. _____	_____	_____	_____
b. _____	_____	_____	_____
c. _____	_____	_____	_____
d. _____	_____	_____	_____

Although interviews can yield useful job analysis information, an awareness of their potential limitations is also needed. Interviews are difficult to standardize—different interviewers may ask different questions and the same interviewer might unintentionally ask different questions of different respondents. There is also a real possibility that the information provided by the respondent will be unintentionally distorted by the interviewer. Finally, the costs of interviewing can be very high, especially if group interviews are not practical.[16]

Questionnaires

The use of questionnaires is usually the least costly method for collecting information. It is an effective way to collect a large amount of information in a short period of time. The JAIF in Exhibit 6-2 is a structured questionnaire. It includes specific questions about the job, job requirements, working conditions, and equipment. A less structured, more open-ended approach would be to ask job incumbents to describe their job in their own terms. This open-ended format would permit job incumbents to use their own words and ideas to describe the job.

The format and degree of structure that a questionnaire should have are debatable issues. Job analysts have their own personal preferences on this matter. There really is no best format for a questionnaire. However, here are a few hints that will make the questionnaire easier to use:

- Keep it as *short as possible*—people do not generally like to complete forms.
- *Explain* what the questionnaire is being used for—people want to know why it must be completed. Jean Davis (in this chapter's Career Challenge) failed to explain her job analysis questionnaire. Employees wanted to know why the questions were being asked and how their responses would be used.
- Keep it *simple*—do not try to impress people with technical language. Use the simplest language to make a point or ask a question.
- *Test* the questionnaire before using it—in order to improve the questionnaire, ask some job incumbents to complete it and to comment on its features. This test will permit the analyst to modify the format before using the questionnaire in final form.

Job Incumbent Diary or Log

The diary or log is a recording by job incumbents of job duties, frequency of the duties, and when the duties are accomplished. This technique requires the job incumbent to keep a diary or log. Unfortunately, most individuals are not disciplined enough to keep such a diary or log. If a diary or log is kept up to date, it can provide good information about the job. Comparisons on a daily, weekly, or monthly basis can be made. This permits an examination of the routineness or nonroutineness of job duties. The diary or log is useful when attempting to analyze jobs that are difficult to observe, such as those performed by engineers, scientists, and senior executives.

Which Method to Use?

Although any of these four basic methods can be used either alone or in combination, there is no general agreement about which methods of job analysis yield the best information. Many experts agree that, at the very least, interviews should not be relied on as the sole data collection method.[17] In addition, the various methods may not be interchangeable; certain methods seem to be better suited to a given situation than others.[18]

In the absence of a strong theoretical reason why one method should be superior to another, most organizations base their choice on their current needs.[19] In other words, the choice of a method is determined by circumstances such as the purpose of the analysis and time and budget constraints.

Since these four basic methods seem to have different strengths and weaknesses, many organizations are turning to a **multimethod job analysis approach.**[20] In this approach, the job analyst first conducts interviews with incumbents and supervisors in conjunction with on-site observation. Next, a task survey based on expert judgments is constructed and administered. Finally, a statistical analysis of the responses to the task survey is conducted in order to assess their consistency and to identify any systematic variation in them. There might, for example, be variation in the descriptions provided by incumbents and supervisors, by incumbents at different geographic locations, or by members of different departments. Regardless, differences in how the job has been described need to be resolved so there is general agreement about its true nature.

Using a comprehensive process such as the multimethod job analysis approach will, of course, be relatively expensive and time-consuming. However, it does offer one distinct advantage over any of the basic methods used alone: the quality of information derived from a more comprehensive approach is strongly endorsed by the courts in cases that rely on job analysis information.[21]

Specific Quantitative Techniques

The four methods of data collection for job analysis just described were presented in general terms. They form the basis for construction of specific techniques that have gained popularity across many types of organizations. When they are used properly, these specific techniques can provide systematic and quantitative procedures that yield information about what job duties are being accomplished and what knowledge, skills, abilities, and other human characteristics (KSAOs) are needed to perform the job. Three of the more popular quantitative techniques are functional job analysis, the position analysis questionnaire, and the management position description questionnaire.

Functional Job Analysis

Physically
Mentally
dealing w/ customer

Functional job analysis (FJA) is the cumulative result of approximately 60 years of research on analyzing and describing jobs. It was originally conceived in the late 1940s and was developed as a mechanism for improving the classification of jobs contained in the *Dictionary of Occupational Titles* (DOT),[22] which was the primary source used by the U.S. Employment Service for descriptive information about jobs.

When someone is interested in a general description of a job, the DOT serves as a good starting point. DOT descriptions help a job analyst to begin learning what is involved in a particular job. FJA is then used to elaborate and more thoroughly describe the content of a job. The main focus of FJA is to create a common language for accurately describing a large number of jobs in ways that can be reliably reproduced by other experts. Following is a brief summary of FJA. A thorough description of FJA procedures can be found in works by Fine and associates.[23]

FJA assumes that jobs can be described in terms of three basic relationships that the incumbent has with his or her work. In order to complete the tasks involved in a job, the worker must physically relate to "things," use mental resources to process "data," and interact with "people." The extent to which a job involves each of these three components forms the basis for a job description prepared with FJA. Using behavioral terms, each of these relationships with work can be organized along a continuum of complexity (lowest to highest). Exhibit 6-3 provides one scale and examples for each of the scale items.

One advantage of the FJA is that each job has a quantitative score. Thus, jobs can be arranged for compensation or other HRM purposes because jobs with similar ratings are assumed to be similar. For example, all jobs with 5, 6, 2 or 2, 0, 1 scores could be grouped together and treated in much the same way.[24]

EXHIBIT 6-3 **Worker Function Scale and Examples from Functional Job Analysis (FJA)**

Source: Adapted from Sidney A. Fine and Steven Cronshaw (1999), *Functional Job Analysis* (Mahwah, NJ: Erlbaum), pp. 207–208.

People Functions Scale	Entry-Level Salesperson	Company Trainer
	Organizational Examples	
1A: Taking instructions—helping	Stays within assigned territory.	Delivers requested programs.
1B: Serving	Sends product samples to customers.	Answers trainees' questions.
2: Exchanging information	Asks questions to assess needs of customers.	Asks trainees for feedback.
3A: Sourcing information	Refers customer to production manager.	Directs trainees to additional resources.
3B: Persuading	Convinces customer to purchase product.	Persuades trainees of importance of topic.
3C: Coaching	Gives encouragement to new assistant salesperson.	Checks on and helps trainees postprogram.
3D: Directing	Lightens mood with customer when appropriate.	Creates entertaining class environment.
4A: Consulting	Informs customer about product specifications.	Defines and clarifies key concepts.
4B: Instructing	Demonstrates how product works.	Teaches trainees new computer software.
4C: Treating	n/a	n/a
5: Supervising	Structures job of assistant salesperson.	Evaluates learning of trainees.
6: Negotiating	Bargains over price with customer.	Asks for larger budget from vice president of human resource department.
7: Mentoring	Counsels assistant salesperson on career issues.	Advises new trainer on how to deliver a training program.
8: Leading	Models behavior for new salespeople.	Sets a vision as to why development is important.

In the 1990s, the U.S. Department of Labor Employment and Training Administration undertook a major job analysis initiative known as the **Occupational Information Network (O*NET).** The O*NET, which is replacing the DOT, is a comprehensive and flexible Internet accessible database that describes occupations, worker KSAOs, and workplace requirements.[25]

Encompassing over 60 years of occupational information, the O*NET allows individuals to describe work accurately and efficiently. It is a much more user-friendly source for occupational data (compared to the DOT) because of the ease and flexibility associated with Web access and the fact that 12,000 different occupations of the DOT were reduced to just over 1,000 in the O*NET. As illustrated in Exhibit 6-4, the data contained in the O*NET are categorized into six separate groups referred to as the O*NET Content Model.

Who are the typical users of the O*NET? A wide variety of individuals can use these occupational data, for example[26]:

- Human resources professionals can use it to develop job descriptions and specifications, develop employee training programs, and structure compensation and reward systems.
- Career counselors can use the information to advise students and clients about the requirements of different occupations.
- Recruiters can use the data to identify candidates who are more likely to fit well with their organization.
- Trainers and educators use this information to match training objectives with job tasks or requirements.

EXHIBIT 6-4
The O*NET Content Model

Source: www.onetcenter.org/content.html.

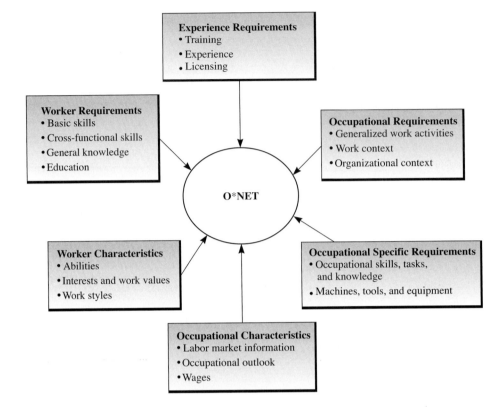

Position Analysis Questionnaire

A structured questionnaire for quantitatively assessing jobs was developed by researchers at Purdue University. It is called the **position analysis questionnaire (PAQ)**.[27] The PAQ contains 195 items (11 of these are shown in Exhibit 6-5). Because the questionnaire requires considerable experience and a high level of reading comprehension to complete properly, it is often filled out by a trained job analyst. The job analyst must decide whether each item applies to a particular job. For example, measuring devices (item 6) play a very substantial role (5) for the job being analyzed in Exhibit 6-5.

The 195 items contained on the PAQ are placed in six major sections:

1. *Information input* Where and how does the job incumbent get job information?
2. *Mental processes* What reasoning, decision-making, and planning processes are used to perform the job?
3. *Work output* What physical activities and tools are used to perform the job?
4. *Relationship with other people* What relationships with others are required to perform the job?
5. *Job context* In what physical and social context is the job performed?
6. *Other job characteristics* What activities, conditions, or characteristics other than those described in sections 1 through 5 are relevant?

Computerized programs are available for scoring PAQ ratings on the basis of seven dimensions—(1) decision making, (2) communication, (3) social responsibilities, (4) performing skilled activities, (5) being physically active, (6) operating vehicles or equipment, and (7) processing information. These scores permit the development of profiles for jobs analyzed and the comparison of jobs.

EXHIBIT 6-5   Portions of a Completed Page from the Position analysis Questionnaire

Source: Position Analysis Questionnaire, Occupational Research Center, Department of Psychological Sciences, Purdue University. Position Analysis Questionnaire, copyright 1979 by Purdue Research Foundation, West Lafayette, IN 47807, Reprinted by permission.

INFORMATION INPUT

1.   INFORMATION INPUT

1.1 Sources of Job Information

Rate each of the following items in terms of the extent to which it is used by the worker as a source of information in performing his or her job.

	Extent of Use (U)
NA	Does not apply
1	Normal/very infrequent
2	Occasional
3	Moderate
4	Considerable
5	Very substantial

1.1.1 Visual Sources of Job Information

1 | 4 Written materials (books, reports, office notes, articles, job instructions, signs, etc.)

2 | 2 Quantitative materials (materials which deal with quantities or amounts, such as graphs, accounts, specifications, tables of numbers, etc.)

3 | 1 Pictorial materials (pictures or picturelike materials used as *sources* of information, for example, drawings, blueprints, diagrams, maps, tracings, photographic films, x-ray films, TV pictures, etc.)

4 | 1 Patterns/related devices (templates, stencils, patterns, etc., used as *sources* of information when observed during use; do not include here materials described in item 3 above)

5 | 2 Visual displays (dials, gauges, signal lights, radarscopes, speedometers, clocks, etc.)

6 | 5 Measuring devices (rulers, calipers, tire pressure gauges, scales, thickness gauges, pipettes, thermometers, protractors, etc., used to obtain visual information about physical measurements; do *not* include here devices described in item 5 above)

7 | 4 Mechanical devices (tools, equipment, machinery, and other mechanical devices which are *sources* of information when observed during use or operation)

8 | 3 Materials in process (parts, materials, objects, etc., which are *sources* of information when being modified, worked on, or otherwise processed, such as bread dough being mixed, workpiece being turned in a lathe, fabric being cut, shoe being resoled, etc.)

9 | 4 Materials *not* in process (parts, materials, objects, etc., not in the process of being changed or modified, which are *sources* of information when being inspected, handled, packaged, distributed, or selected, etc., such as items or materials in inventory, storage, or distribution channels, items being inspected, etc.)

10 | 3 Features of nature (landscapes, fields, geological samples, vegetation, cloud formations, and other features of nature which are *observed* or *inspected* to provide information)

11 | 2 Man-made features of environment (structures, buildings, dams, highways, bridges, docks, railroads, and other "man-made" or altered aspects of the indoor and outdoor environment which are observed or inspected to provide job information; do not consider equipment, machines, etc., that an individual uses in his or her work, as covered by item 7)

Note: This shows 11 of the "information input" questions or elements. Other PAQ pages contain questions regarding mental processes, work output, relationships with others, job context, and other job characteristics.

Like other job analysis techniques, the PAQ has advantages and disadvantages. One of its biggest advantages is that it has been widely used and researched. The available evidence indicates that it can be an effective technique for a variety of intended purposes.[28] It is reliable in that there is little variance among job analysts' ratings of the same jobs. It seems to be an effective way of establishing differences in abilities required for jobs.[29] It also seems valid in that jobs rated higher with the PAQ prove to be those that are compensated at higher rates.

A major problem with the PAQ is its length. It requires time and patience to complete. In addition, since no specific work activities are described, behavioral activities performed in jobs may distort actual task differences in the jobs. For example, the profiles for a typist, belly dancer, and male ballet dancer may be quite similar, since all involve fine motor movements.[30] Some research suggests that the PAQ is capable only of measuring job stereotypes.[31] If this is true, then the PAQ may be providing little more than common knowledge about a job. That is, ratings on the PAQ might represent information that makes up the job analyst's stereotype about the work in question rather than actual differences among jobs.

Management Position Description Questionnaire

Conducting a job analysis for managerial jobs offers a significant challenge to the analyst because of the disparity across positions, levels in the hierarchy, and type of industry (for example, industrial, medical, government). An attempt to systematically analyze managerial jobs was conducted at Control Data Corporation. The result of the work is the **management position description questionnaire (MPDQ)**.[32]

The MPDQ is a checklist of 208 items related to the concerns and responsibilities of managers. It is designed to be a comprehensive description of managerial work, and it is intended for use across most industrial settings. The latest version of the MPDQ is classified into 15 sections. Items were grouped into sections in order to reduce the time it requires to complete the questionnaire, and to help with the interpretation of responses:[33]

1. General information.
2. Decision making.
3. Planning and organizing.
4. Administering.
5. Controlling.
6. Supervising.
7. Consulting and innovating.
8. Contacts (section 8 appears in Exhibit 6-6).
9. Coordinating.
10. Representing.
11. Monitoring business indicators.
12. Overall ratings.
13. Knowledge, skills, and abilities.
12. Organization chart.
15. Comments and reactions.

Although the FJA, PAQ, and MPDQ are all intended for use across a large range of jobs, many other methods of quantitative job analysis are also receiving attention. The **common metric questionnaire (CMQ)**,[34] which is completed by an incumbent, is a job analysis instrument with several potential advantages over existing measures. The items are at a reading level more appropriate for many jobs; they are more behaviorally concrete, thereby making it easier for incumbents to rate their jobs; and the CMQ is applicable to both exempt and nonexempt positions, which may increase the number of intrajob skill-based comparisons that may be made.

Considerable research on job analysis is currently being conducted in Europe, focusing on alternative quantitative methods. In Germany, for example, several techniques have the common goal of analyzing and describing work at the task level, independent of any particular incumbent's perceptions. Thus, these approaches are expected to be well suited to situations where job content or manufacturing technology is changing.[35]

Job Descriptions and Specifications

As previously mentioned, the job description (see Exhibit 6-1) is one of the primary outputs provided by a systematic job analysis. Simply stated, a job description is a written description of what the job entails. It is, however, difficult to overemphasize how important thorough, accurate, and current job descriptions are to an organization. Many changes occurring in recent years have increased the need for such job descriptions. These changes include (1) the incredible number of organizational restructurings that have occurred (e.g., downsizing); (2) the need to implement new and creative ways to motivate and reward employees; (3) the accelerated rate at which technology is changing work environments; and (4) new, more stringent federal regulation of employment practices through legislation like the Americans with Disabilities Act and the Civil Rights Act of 1991.[36] Though some HR managers feel that technology and rapidly changing jobs will eventually decrease the need for job descriptions,[37] it still seems unlikely that there are any relevant aspects of human resources that do not depend on accurate job descriptions.

While there is no standard format for a job description, almost all well-written, useful descriptions will include information on:[38]

- *Job title*—title of the job and other identifying information such as its wage and benefits classification.
- *Summary*—brief one- or two-sentence statement describing the purpose of the job and what outputs are expected from job incumbents.
- *Equipment*—clear statement of the tools, equipment, and information required for effectively performing the job.
- *Environment*—description of the working conditions of the job, the location of the job, and other relevant characteristics of the immediate work environment such as hazards and noise levels.
- *Activities*—includes a description of the job duties, responsibilities, and behaviors performed on the job. Also describes the social interactions associated with the work (for example, size of work group, amount of dependency in the work).

The job specification evolves from the job description. It addresses the question "What personal traits and experience are needed to perform the job effectively?" The job specification is especially useful in offering guidance for recruitment and selection. For example, suppose that you were looking for an HR professional to fill the position described in Exhibit 6-7. From the job specification, you would know that the successful applicant would have a college education and would already have at least six years of experience in HRM.

Determining what skills, knowledge, or abilities are required for performing a particular job must be done systematically. R. J. Harvey offers the following guidelines for arriving at the characteristics that should be included on a job specification:[39]

1. All job tasks must be identified and rated in terms of importance using sound job analysis techniques.

2. A panel of experts, incumbents, or supervisors should specify the necessary skills for performing each of the job tasks identified.

3. The importance of each skill must be rated.

HRMEMO

A fast way to find job descriptions for a particular job is to use the large job search Internet Web sites like www.monster.com, www.careerbuilder.com, and www.hotjobs.com. Smaller but more specialized job search Web sites can also be useful sources of job descriptions, including www.indeed.com, www.simplyhired.com, and www.workzoo.com.

EXHIBIT 6-6   **Rating Internal and External Contacts Using the Management Position Description Questionnaire (MPDQ)**

To achieve organizational goals, managers and consultants may be required to communicate with employees at many levels within the corporation and with influential people outside the corporation.

The purposes of these contacts may include such functions as:

- Informing
- Receiving information
- Influencing
- Promoting
- Selling
- Directing
- Coordinating
- Integrating
- Negotiating

DIRECTIONS:

Describe the nature of your contacts by completing the charts on the opposite page as follows:

STEP 1

Mark an "X" in the box to the left of the kinds of individuals that represent your major contacts internal and external to Control Data Corporation.

STEP 2

For each contact checked, print a number between 0 and 4 in each column to indicate how significant a part of your position that PURPOSE is. (Remember to consider both its *importance* in light of all other position activities and its *frequency* of occurrence.)

0-**Definitely not** a part of the position.
1-A **minor** part of the position.
2-A **moderate** part of the position.
3-A **substantial** part of the position.
4-A **crucial** and **most significant** part of the position.

STEP 3

If you have any other contacts please elaborate on their nature and purpose below.

226 _____

_____

_____

_____

_____

_____

_____

_____

_____

_____

_____

EXHIBIT 6-6 *(continued)*

STEP 1   STEP 2

CONTACTS	PURPOSE

INTERNAL	Share information regarding past, present, or anticipated activities or decisions	Influence others to act or decide in a manner consistent with my objectives	Direct and/or integrate the plans, activities, or decisions of others
Executive or senior vice president and above 159	167	175	183
Vice president 160	168	176	184
General/regional manager, director, or executive consultant 161	169	177	185
Department/district manager, or senior consultant 162	170	178	186
Section/branch manager or consultant 163	171	179	187
Unit manager 164	172	180	188
Exempt employees 165	173	181	189
Nonexempt employees 166	174	182	190

EXTERNAL	Provide, obtain, or exchange information or advice	Promote the organization or its products/ services	Sell products/ services	Negotiate contracts, settlements, etc.
Customers at a level equivalent to or above a Control Data general/ regional manager 191	198	205	212	219
Customers at a level lower than a Control Data general/ regional manager 192	199	206	213	220
Representatives of major suppliers, for example, joint ventures, subcontractors for major contracts 193	200	207	214	221
Employees of suppliers who provide Control Data with parts or services 194	201	208	215	222
Representatives of influential community organizations 195	202	209	216	223
Individuals such as applicants, stockholders 196	203	210	217	224
Representatives of federal or state governments such as defense contract auditors, government inspectors, etc. 197	204	211	218	225

EXHIBIT 6-7 Job Description of a Human Resource Manager

Job Title: Human Resource Manager	Department: HRM Date: Jan. 2, 2006

General description of the job

Performs responsible administrative work managing personnel activities of a large state agency or institution. Work involves responsibility for the planning and administration of an HRM program that includes recruitment, examination, selection, evaluation, appointment, promotion, transfer, and recommended change of status of agency employees, and a system of communication for disseminating necessary information to workers. Works under general supervision, exercising initiative and independent judgment in the performance of assigned tasks.

Job activities

Participates in overall planning and policy making to provide effective and uniform personnel services.

Communicates policy through organization levels by bulletins, meetings, and personal contact.

Interviews applicants, evaluates qualifications, classifies applications.

Recruits and screens applicants to fill vacancies and reviews applications of qualified persons.

Confers with supervisors on personnel matters, including placement problems, retention or release of probationary employees, transfers, demotions, and dismissals of permanent employees.

Supervises administration of tests.

Initiates personnel training activities and coordinates these activities with work of officials and supervisors.

Establishes effective service rating system; trains unit supervisors in making employee evaluations.

Maintains employee personnel files.

Supervises a group of employees directly and through subordinates.

Performs related work as assigned.

General qualification requirements

Experience and training

Should have considerable experience in area of HRM administration. Six-year minimum.

Education

Graduation from a four-year college or university, with major work in human resources, business administration, or industrial psychology.

Knowledge, skills, and abilities

Considerable knowledge of principles and practices of HRM selection and assignment of personnel; job evaluation.

Responsibility

Supervises a department of three HRM professionals, one clerk, and one secretary.

4. Any other characteristics necessary for performing the job should be identified. These include things such as physical requirements and professional certification.

5. Each skill that has been identified needs to be specifically linked to each job task.

Any trait or skill that is stated on the job specification should actually be required for performance of the job. The Americans with Disabilities Act makes the job analyst's responsibilities even greater in this area. Job specifications need to differentiate clearly between *essential* and *nonessential* skills.[40] Essential skills are those for which alternative ways of accomplishing the job are not possible. Nonessential skills can be accommodated by changing the structure or work methods of the job. If disabled people could accomplish the job successfully after such accommodation, then it should be done.

Job Analysis and Strategic Human Resource Management

The HR Journal appearing earlier in this chapter suggests that process and work reengineering will be the strategic HR challenge for the coming years. There are many signs that the fundamental nature of work may be changing. Functional areas are not as important as they once were for defining a person's job. Instead, interdisciplinary or cross-functional teams consisting of persons with extremely diverse backgrounds are becoming increasingly common. Not surprisingly, therefore, one of the major complaints about reengineering is that once an organization's processes have been reconstructed, new job responsibilities may be poorly defined for the new environment.[41]

Despite these potential difficulties, organizations will have to continually adapt to rapidly changing business environments. Thus, reengineering of one kind or another is likely in a majority of organizations. This inevitability creates a new problem for the job analyst. While the job analyst has traditionally been charged with creating descriptions of jobs as they exist in an organization, the new job analyst will also have to describe jobs that will exist in the *future* organization. As mentioned elsewhere in this text, there is a growing acknowledgment of the need to match human resource activities with an organization's strategic planning.[42] An important part of this task will be an ability for job analysts to write job specifications that accurately detail the knowledge and skills that will complement the future strategic initiatives of the organization.[43] In the future, job descriptions will no longer be snapshots of a static entity called a "job." To the contrary, **strategic job analysis** will have to be capable of capturing both the present and the future.[44]

Compounding the potential problems that reengineering can introduce, many work environments will also offer employees much greater flexibility in when and how they work. Organizations such as AT&T, Hewlett-Packard, and Pfizer have all implemented flexible working environments to meet the needs of an increasingly diverse workforce. These programs include variations on traditional work such as compressed work schedules, telecommuting, job sharing, and flexible hours.[45] Although it is currently unclear whether these new work arrangements will lend themselves to accurate description through the quantitative methods covered in this chapter, it is safe to assume that effective organizational functioning will require some type of job analysis to be competently conducted.[46]

Job Analysis and Employee Competencies

Over the past decade, some HR departments have increasingly analyzed jobs in a way that is consistent with the changing nature of business and management practices. Much more general than traditional knowledge, skills, and abilities needed to perform one specific job, *competencies* are general attributes employees need to do well across multiple jobs or within the organization as a whole. For example, competencies might include anything from "teamwork" to "leadership potential." As jobs are reengineered, TQM programs are implemented, and the value of teamwork is emphasized, many organizations are identifying, communicating, and rewarding a variety of broad-based competencies that successful employees should possess. Also termed "competency modeling," such usage of competencies in HR practices reflects an organization's desire to achieve the following:

- Communicate job requirements in ways that extend beyond the specific job itself;
- Describe and measure the organization's workforce in more general, competency terms; and
- Design and implement staffing programs focused around competencies (rather than specific jobs) as a way of increasing staffing flexibility in job assignments.[47]

Job Design

Once a thorough job analysis has been conducted and there are high-quality job descriptions and job specifications available, an organization can use this information for designing or redesigning jobs. This information is very useful for structuring job elements, duties, and tasks in a manner that will help to achieve optimal performance and satisfaction.

There is, however, no one best way to design a job. Different situations call for different arrangements of job characteristics. In addition, approaches to job design place different emphasis on performance and satisfaction as desired outcomes. In other words, certain methods of job design are primarily interested in improving performance; others are more concerned with satisfaction. Thus, it is unlikely that any one approach will fully satisfy all of the goals of a manager. This means that the choice of job design will involve making trade-offs based on the more critical needs of the organization.[48]

Perspectives on the design of work can be classified into four major categories: (1) the perceptual-motor approach, (2) the biological approach, (3) the mechanistic approach, and (4) the motivational approach.[49] Both the perceptual-motor approach and the biological approach have their roots in human factors engineering. Their major focus is on the integration of human and machine systems. Thus, they emphasize equipment design and the proper match between machines and operators.

The two remaining approaches more clearly highlight the potential trade-offs that must frequently be made by organizations with regard to job design. They are also the two that have received the most attention in the management literature. The mechanistic approach is best exemplified by Taylor's scientific management and the motivational approach by job enrichment.

Scientific Management and the Mechanistic Approach

get paid off your production.

Job design was a central issue in F. W. Taylor's model of scientific management. His use of job design is an excellent example of the rational approach and shows how certain perspectives focus more heavily on productivity than on satisfaction. In 1911, he stated:

> Perhaps the most prominent single element in modern scientific management is the task idea. The work of every workman is fully planned out by the management at least one day in advance, and each man receives in most cases complete written instructions, describing in detail the task which he is to accomplish. . . . This task specifies not only what is to be done but how it is to be done and the exact time allowed for doing it.[50]

The work of Taylor and the principles of scientific management initiated a great deal of interest in systematically studying the structure of jobs. The emphasis was clearly on structuring jobs so that they were broken down into simple, repetitive tasks. Once learned, these tasks could be done quickly and efficiently.

Although the principles of scientific management were formally introduced in the early 1900s and many current methods of job design criticize the use of the repetitive-task structure, many of the principles are still relevant today. Among these are recommendations stemming from Taylor's scientific management, such as the following:

- Work should be studied scientifically. (This is what job analysis attempts to do.)
- Work should be arranged so that workers can be efficient.
- Employees selected for work should be matched to the demands of the job. (Job descriptions and job specifications used in recruitment and selection should achieve this.)
- Employees should be trained to perform the job.
- Monetary compensation should be tied directly to performance and should be used to reward the performance of employees.

Many managers find the scientific management approach to job design appealing because these kinds of recommendations point toward improving organizational performance. It is assumed that the specialization and routine nature of jobs designed according to scientific management principles will lead to higher levels of output and require minimal training before employees are able to master the work. Despite the appeal of these potential advantages, research has found that repetitive, highly specialized work can lead to dissatisfaction among employees.[51] Thus, the gains in efficiency that scientific management may offer can be offset by losses in satisfaction and higher levels of absenteeism and turnover.

Early strategies for overcoming some of the problems associated with jobs designed according to scientific management focused on job enlargement.[52] **Job enlargement** attempts to increase satisfaction by giving employees a greater variety of things to do. The expansion of the work is, however, considered horizontal, since the employees are not given more responsibility or authority in decision making. Rather, they are merely allowed to do a greater number of tasks. Thus, an enlarged job is not as specialized or routine as a job designed according to scientific management, but it may not be any more meaningful.

Job Enrichment: A Motivational Approach

In the past two decades, much work has been directed at changing jobs in more meaningful ways than job enlargement was able to do. Rather than simply increasing the variety of tasks performed by an employee, **job enrichment** tries to design jobs in ways that help incumbents satisfy their needs for growth, recognition, and responsibility. Thus, enrichment differs from enlargement because the job is expanded vertically; employees are given responsibility that might have previously been part of a supervisor's job.[53]

The notion of satisfying employees' needs as a way of designing jobs comes from Frederic Herzberg's two-factor theory of work motivation. His basic idea is that employees will be motivated by jobs that enhance their feelings of self-worth.[54]

Although there are many different approaches to job enrichment, the **job characteristics model** is one of the most widely publicized.[55] This model is depicted in Exhibit 6-8. It shows that for a job to lead to desired outcomes it must possess certain "core job dimensions." These include

- *Skill variety*—degree to which the job requires a variety of different activities in carrying out the work, which involves the use of a number of an individual's skills and talents.

- *Task identity*—degree to which the job requires completion of a "whole" and identifiable piece of work—that is, doing a job from beginning to end with a visible outcome.

EXHIBIT 6-8 The Job Characteristics Model of Work Motivation

Source: Adapted from J. Richard Hackman and R. G. Oldham (August 1976), "Motivation through the Design of Work: Test of a Theory," *Organizational Behavior and Human Performance*, p. 256.

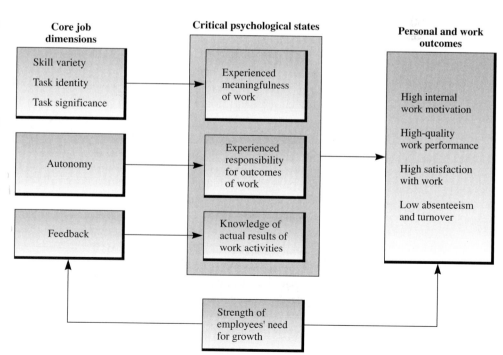

- *Task significance*—degree to which the job has a substantial impact on the lives or work of other people, whether in the immediate organization or in the external environment.
- *Autonomy*—degree to which the job provides substantial freedom, independence, and discretion to the individual in scheduling the work and in determining the procedures to be used in carrying it out.
- *Feedback*—degree to which carrying out the activities required by the job results in the individual's obtaining direct and clear information about the effectiveness of his or her performance.

If these core dimensions are present in a job, they are expected to create three critical psychological states in job incumbents.[56] The key psychological states that are necessary for motivation and satisfaction are:

1. *Experienced meaningfulness*—degree to which the job incumbent experiences work as important, valuable, and worthwhile.
2. *Experienced responsibility*—extent to which the job incumbent feels personally responsible and accountable for the results of the work performed.
3. *Knowledge of results*—understanding that a job incumbent receives about how effectively he or she is performing the job.

The more these three states are experienced, the more internal work motivation the job incumbent will feel. To the extent that these three states are important to the job incumbent, he or she will then be motivated to perform well and will be satisfied with the job.

As presented in Exhibit 6-8, three job dimensions—**skill variety, task identity,** and **task significance**—all contribute to a sense of meaningfulness. **Autonomy** is directly related to feelings of responsibility. The more control job incumbents feel they have over their jobs, the more they will feel responsible. **Feedback** is related to knowledge of results. For job incumbents to be internally motivated, they must have a sense of the quality of their performance. This sense comes from feedback.

The job characteristics model describes the relationships that are predicted to exist among four sets of factors—(1) core job dimensions, (2) psychological states, (3) personal and work-related outcomes, and (4) strength of needs. Since different people have different capabilities and needs, it is important to be aware of the potential for individual differences to moderate the linkages shown in Exhibit 6-8. If, for example, a person does not have a strong need for personal growth, then job enrichment will probably have less effect than it would for a person who values personal growth.

Many job enrichment programs have been implemented in the United States and in other countries around the world. After 20 years of research, however, there are no clear answers about the effectiveness of enrichment. Generally, studies support the expectation that jobs perceived to possess the core dimensions of the job characteristics model are more satisfying.[57] On the other hand, the relationships between the critical psychological states and employees' reactions to enrichment are not yet fully understood.[58] Research also suggests that increasing the scope of a job beyond certain levels can have detrimental effects on workers.[59]

Work-Family Balance and Job Design

Organizations are directing more attention and resources toward helping employees balance their work and family demands. Driving this work-family tension are a number of variables related to the changing demographics of the workforce. For example, the number of women and single parents entering the workforce is expected to continue increasing. Often viewed as primary caregivers, these individuals will experience stress as they attempt to balance career and family priorities. Another example of demographic changes includes the increase in dual-career couples. In some cases, caregiving responsibilities may be shared, leading both working spouses to require flexible work arrangements to meet family life and career cycle needs. The aging population will be another factor that requires a response from working-age caregivers. As the baby boom generation reaches retirement age, this issue will grow in importance.

How are organizations responding to these challenges? Although not as dramatic as originally anticipated, a trend is emerging in which some organizations are trying to accommodate diverse employees' needs by offering flexible work arrangements. Examples of flexible work arrangements include job sharing, flextime, and telecommuting. It is believed that by allowing employees more control over their work lives, they will be better able to balance their work-home demands. Many have argued that companies that offer and encourage participation in such family-friendly work arrangements will reap one or more of the following benefits: higher recruitment and retention rates, improved morale, lower absenteeism and tardiness, and higher levels of employee productivity.

Job sharing is a work arrangement in which two or more employees divide a job's responsibilities, hours, and benefits among themselves.[60] Several steps are critical to the success of such job-sharing programs, including identifying those jobs that can be shared, understanding employees' individual sharing style, and matching "partners" who have complementary scheduling needs and skills.[61] Companies such as CoreStates Financial, Bank of America, AT&T, Kraft, and Household International all have job-sharing options available for their employees.

Flextime is another type of flexible work arrangement in which employees can choose when to be at the office.[62] For example, employees may decide that instead of working 5 days a week for 8 hours a day, they may prefer to work a 4-day/10-hour per day work schedule. With this schedule, the employees do not have to be at the office on Friday. To avoid peak rush hour, other employees might use their flextime to arrive at and leave from work one hour later Monday through Friday. For example, Eli Lilly reports that 5,600 of the company's 22,600 U.S. employees, or 25 percent of its workforce, work some type of flexible schedule.[63] One research study concluded that flexible workweek schedules had a positive influence on employee performance, job satisfaction, and absenteeism.[64] These authors also reported that flextime programs should not be too unstructured and that they lose some of their effectiveness over time. Companies that offer flextime options include Hewlett-Packard, Merrill Lynch, and Cigna.

Telecommuting refers to the work arrangement that allows employees to work in their homes part- or full-time, maintaining their connection and communication with the office through phone, fax, and computer.[65] Though oftentimes resisted by managers who fear loss of control and subordinate accessibility, one company has taken a methodical approach to implementing a telecommuting program. Pfizer Inc., a large health care company, took the following steps to establish their program:

1. Chose a small division to pilot the telecommuting initiative.
2. Limited the number of days to work at home to two per week.
3. Opened the program to all employees of the division.
4. Required interested employees to satisfy a formal proposal and performance standards.
5. Required demonstration that the work could be accomplished off-site and that the employee could sustain and/or enhance performance.

Although organizations like Pfizer and the other family-friendly firms are moving forward to attract, motivate, and retain employees with diverse nonwork needs, organizations need to consider three important issues when developing and implementing such flexible work arrangement options. First, every attempt should be made to open these programs to all employees. The risk here is that if only certain groups are offered these options, then

What do you now think about Jean Davis's job analysis process? Do you see why some type of training in job analysis is required? Jean really lacked sufficient training, and this lack was clearly revealed as the process got out of hand.

Using questionnaires requires preparation and careful initial steps. A trained job analyst knows that distribution of questionnaires without an explanation is bound to set off negative feelings. Jean failed to plan thoroughly what she wanted to do. She was a new boss, and this alone was threatening to many people. A new person has to establish rapport with employees before changing things.

In the case of Sprowl Manufacturing, Jean's haste and lack of preparation have now caused the situation to reach a boiling point. She needs to backtrack and slow down. Perhaps distributing memos, holding open discussions with informal leaders, and using the expertise of trained job analysts can improve the atmosphere at Sprowl.

What would you advise Jean to do about job analysis at this point?

excluded groups may feel discriminated against. Managers need to be aware that excluded employees can create a backlash against work-family programs.[66] Second, having the CEO of an organization announce these programs is not enough to effect change. Many career-minded employees do not take advantage of job sharing, flextime, or telecommuting for fear of being derailed from their career progression.[67] In order to make these programs an accepted part of the organization, managers need to be trained and rewarded for encouraging their subordinates to use them without fear of derailing their good standing within the firm. Third, organizations need to be mindful of the laws that may impact how these flexible work arrangement policies are developed and managed. Some applicable laws include the Fair Labor Standards Act, workers' compensation, and the Occupational Safety and Health Act.[68]

Job Design: The Next Challenge

In the late 1980s and early 1990s, European and Asian competitors of American corporations were revolutionizing job design by turning away from the basic elements of scientific management and embracing the quality management movement. More recently, self-directed teams have become important ingredients in the success of manufacturers worldwide.[69] And now, because of the competitive pressures that foreign business has placed on them, American corporations—including Chevron, Coca-Cola, Federal Express, General Electric, General Motors, Motorola, Procter & Gamble, and Xerox, to name a few—are also implementing self-directed work teams.[70] Countless others are reengineering their work processes, hoping to regain their competitive advantage.

Regardless of the specific nature of redesign, many organizations have learned the hard way that reengineering cannot succeed unless careful attention is also paid to the effects on how employees use their skills. The appropriate response to these changes is exemplified by Coopers & Lybrand's **competency alignment process (CAP)**. CAP involves the systematic study, analysis, and assessment of jobs and the skills needed to perform them in the reengineered organization. To accomplish this goal, CAP determines current skill levels of employees in order to identify skill gaps. When a skill deficiency exists for the reengineered organization, it can then be eliminated through a variety of programs including training, redeployment, and outsourcing.[71] Without these or similarly intense efforts, the reengineering will probably not succeed. Thus, job analysts and other HR professionals are a crucial link in the reengineering processes upon which so many corporations are staking their competitive future.

Summary

This chapter has emphasized the major role that job analysis plays in HRM activities and programs. Each part of the diagnostic HRM model is in some way affected by job analysis. The job is the major building block of an organization. Therefore, it is essential that each characteristic of each job in an organization be clearly understood.

To summarize the major points covered in this chapter:

1. There are six sequential steps in job analysis, starting with examining the total organization and the fit of jobs and concluding with the preparation of a job specification (see Exhibit 6-1).

2. The uses of job analysis information seem endless. Strategic planning, recruitment, selection, training, compensation, and job design all benefit immensely from job analysis information.

3. Conducting job analysis is not for amateurs. Training is required.

4. Before conducting a job analysis, organization and process charts should be consulted to acquire an overview of the organization.

5. Four general job analysis techniques can be used separately or in combination: observation, interviews, questionnaires, and job incumbent diaries or logs.

6. The multimethod approach to job analysis uses a combination of these four general methods. It is a comprehensive approach and is currently viewed very favorably from a legal perspective.

7. Functional job analysis (FJA) is used to describe the nature of jobs, prepare job descriptions, and provide details on job specifications. The job is described in terms of data, people, and things.

8. The *Dictionary of Occupational Titles* is a listing of over 20,000 jobs on the basis of occupational code, title, industry.

9. The position analysis questionnaire (PAQ) is a 195-item structured instrument used to quantitatively assess jobs on the basis of decision making, communication and social responsibilities, performing skilled activities, being physically active, operating vehicles or equipment, and processing information.

10. The management position description questionnaire (MPDQ) is a checklist of 208 items that assesses the concerns and responsibilities of managers.

11. Job design involves structuring job elements, duties, and tasks to achieve optimal performance and satisfaction.

12. Job design was a concern of F. W. Taylor, the famous industrial engineer and father of what is called *scientific management*.

13. Job enrichment involves designing jobs so that employees' needs for growth, recognition, and responsibility are satisfied.

14. Reengineering is more than job redesign. It is taking a new look at the entire flow of work through an organization. Without adaptable job descriptions, however, it cannot succeed.

Key Terms

autonomy, *p. 172*
common metric questionnaire (CMQ), *p. 164*
competency alignment process (CAP), *p. 174*
feedback, *p. 172*
functional job analysis (FJA), *p. 160*
job, *p. 152*
job analysis, *p. 152*
job analysis information format (JAIF), *p. 156*

job characteristics model, *p. 171*
job description, *p. 152*
job enlargement, *p. 171*
job enrichment, *p. 171*
job family, *p. 152*
job specification, *p. 152*
management position description questionnaire (MPDQ), *p. 164*
multimethod job analysis approach, *p. 160*

Occupational Information Network (O*NET), *p. 161*
organization chart, *p. 155*
position, *p. 152*
position analysis questionnaire (PAQ), *p. 162*
process chart, *p. 155*
skill variety, *p. 172*
strategic job analysis, *p. 169*
task, *p. 152*
task identity, *p. 172*
task significance, *p. 172*

Questions for Review and Discussion

1. Job analysis is used to provide answers to several questions. Please identify five of those questions.
2. Job analysis often serves as a "cornerstone" of HRM. Please describe three HRM functions or activities that use job analysis in some way.
3. How might job analysis be helpful to an organization that is being sued for sex discrimination in promotion?
4. As a current (or future) manager, how will you communicate the requirements of an entry-level customer service representative to a candidate who just arrived at your office for an interview? Will you describe the job in terms of competencies? Knowledge, skills, and abilities? Both? Explain your answer.
5. What core information should be included in most job descriptions and job specifications?
6. What is the difference between an essential and a nonessential skill? How are these related to the Americans with Disabilities Act?
7. Describe the mechanistic and motivational models of job design. What is the emphasis of each?
8. Assume that you're a manager who needs to design three new jobs for your department in a company. Will you apply the job characteristics model of job enrichment to these new jobs? Why or why not?
9. What is the O*NET? How and when would a job analyst use the O*NET?
10. What challenges does the concept of reengineering pose for job analysis and human resources?

HRM Legal Advisor

Based on *Worthington* v. *City of New Haven,* 1999 U.S. Dist. LEXIS 16104.

The Facts

Patricia Worthington was hired by the City of New Haven on December 23, 1991, as an Account Clerk I in its Tax Office. According to the City's job description, the Account Clerk I position required bookkeeping, maintaining accounts, preparing payrolls and financial reports, checking receipts and vouchers, receiving payments, and various other clerical duties. On February 3, 1992, Ms. Worthington, who had preexisting back, neck, and knee injuries, fell at work. As a result of the fall, she suffered neck and lower back pain when sitting for extended times. Following the accident, Ms. Worthington requested three accommodations from the City: (1) an ergonomic chair with neck and back support, (2) replacement of overhead shelves with waist level shelves, and (3) modification of her job duties so that she avoided standing for long periods of time. Despite recommendations from her doctor for the ergonomic chair and letters from the Connecticut Bureau of Rehabilitative Services suggesting a worksite evaluation, the City repeatedly denied Ms. Worthington's requests for accommodations based on a lack of funds. On May 24, 1993, she filed a grievance with the City. After an investigation, the City agreed to provide Ms. Worthington with a more comfortable chair. On July 13, 1993, she filed a grievance with the union, complaining that she was still required to stand for long periods of time. On April 13, 1994, Ms. Worthington filed a disability discrimination suit under the Americans with Disabilities Act in U.S. District Court for the District of Connecticut. Later in that same month, the City provided Ms. Worthington with an ergonomic chair. Following surgery for spinal problems aggravated by her fall at work, Ms. Worthington ceased working on March 25, 1995, due to her disability.

The Court's Decision

To recover under the ADA, a plaintiff must prove that he or she is a "qualified individual with a disability who can perform the essential functions of their job, with or without accommodations." According to the ADA, a disability is (1) a physical or mental impairment that substantially limits one or more major life activities, (2) a record of such impairment, or (3) being regarded as having such an impairment. The court found that Ms. Worthington had a physical impairment of her musculoskeletal system that substantially limited her ability to walk and stand for long periods of time. Thus, Ms. Worthington had a disability under the ADA. Further, the court found that Ms. Worthington did indeed possess the required education, experience, and skills for the Account Clerk I position. The court examined the City's job description for Account Clerk I to determine if Ms. Worthington could perform the essential functions of the job either with or without accommodations. The court found that the essential functions of Account Clerk I involved preparation of payrolls and financial reports, maintenance of accounts and parking tag books, and checking receipts and vouchers, which could all be performed with only occasional standing. The City claimed that filling in for an employee who collected parking fines which involved standing for long periods of time was also an essential function of Ms. Worthington's job. However, the court disagreed and awarded Ms. Worthington $150,000 in compensatory damages, holding that she was a qualified individual with a disability who could perform the essential functions of the Account Clerk I position with reasonable accommodations.

Human Resource Implications

Organizations must carefully define essential and nonessential job functions in their job descriptions and be prepared to provide reasonable accommodations requested by employees. According to the ADA, essential functions are the fundamental but not marginal duties of a job. A job duty is essential if (1) the position exists to perform the function, (2) there are a limited number of employees who are available to perform the function, and (3) the employee was hired for an expertise or ability to perform a particular function. In differentiating between essential and nonessential job functions in job descriptions, employers should also consider how much time an employee spends performing a job duty and the consequences of not requiring an employee to perform the duty.

Notes

1. Michael T. Brannick and Edward L. Levine (2002), *Job Analysis: Methods, Research, and Applications for Human Resource Management in the New Millennium* (Thousand Oaks, CA: Sage Publications), pp. 4–6; Ivan Robertson and Mike Smith (November 2001), "Personnel Selection," *Journal of Occupational and Organizational Psychology,* pp. 441–472; Edward T. Cornelius (1988), "Practical Findings from Job Analysis Research," in Sidney Gael (ed.), *The Job Analysis Handbook for Business, Industry, and Government,* Vol. 1 (New York: Wiley), pp. 48–68.

2. Bureau of Intergovernmental Personnel Programs (1973), "Job Analysis: Developing and Documenting Data" (Washington, DC: U.S. Government Printing Office).

3. Herbert Heneman, Timothy Judge, and Robert Heneman (2002), *Staffing Organizations,* 4th ed. (Burr Ridge, IL: McGraw-Hill/Irwin), pp. 198–199.

4. Jai Ghorpade and Thomas J. Atchison (Summer 1980), "The Concept of Job Analysis: A Review and Some Suggestions," *Public Personnel Management Journal,* pp. 134–144; and Ronald A. Ash and Edward L. Levine (November–December 1980), "A Framework for Evaluating Job Analysis Methods," *Personnel,* pp. 53–59.

5. Eric J. Felsberg (2004), "Conducting Job Analyses and Drafting Lawful Job Descriptions under the Americans with Disabilities Act," *Employment Relations Today,* Vol. 31, Iss. 3, pp. 91–94; Gerard P. Panaro (1990), *Employment Law Manual* (Boston: Warren, Gorham & Lamont), pp. 3.27–3.33.

6. Heneman, Judge, and Heneman, op. cit., pp. 198–199.

7. Panaro, op. cit., pp. 3.27–3.33.

8. Robert J. Harvey (1991), "Job Analysis," in Marvin D. Dunnette and Leaetta M. Hough (eds.), *Handbook of Industrial and Organizational Psychology,* 2nd ed., Vol. 2 (Palo Alto, CA: Consulting Psychologists Press), pp. 71–163.

9. Harvey, op. cit., p. 312.

10. William J. Latzko (2004), "Enhancing Management Reports: The Contribution of Process," *ASQ Annual Quality Congress Proceedings,* Vol. 58, pp. 9–17; Richard I. Henderson (1989), *Compensation Management: Rewarding Performance,* 5th ed. (Englewood Cliffs, NJ: Prentice-Hall), p. 100.

11. John G. Veres III, Toni S. Locklear, and Ronald R. Sims (1990), "Job Analysis in Practice: A Brief Review of the Role of Job Analysis in Human Resources Management," in Gerald R. Ferris, Kendrith M. Rowland, and M. Ronald Buckley (eds.), *Human Resource Management: Perspectives and Issues,* 2nd ed. (Boston: Allyn and Bacon), pp. 86–89.

12. Henderson, op. cit., pp. 138–139.

13. Helen Palmer and Will Valet (2001), "Job Analysis: Targeting Needed Skills," *Employment Relations Today,* Vol. 28, Iss. 3, pp. 85–92; L. Friedman and Robert J. Harvey (Winter 1986), "Can Recruiters with Reduced Job Description Information Provide Accurate Position Analysis Questionnaire (PAQ) Ratings?" *Personnel Psychology,* pp. 779–789.

14. Patrick R. Conley and Paul R. Sackett (August 1987), "Effects of Using High- versus Low-Performing Job Incumbents as Sources of Job Analysis Information," *Journal of Applied Psychology,* pp. 434–437; and Patrick M. Wright, Chris Anderson, Kari Tolzman, and Tom Helton (August 1990), "An Examination of the Relationship between Employee Performance and Job Analysis Ratings," in Lawrence Jauch and Jerry Wall (eds.), *Academy of Management Best Papers Proceedings* (Academy of Management), pp. 229–303.

15. Siu-Ki Henty To and Brian H. Kleiner (2000), "How to Hire Employees Effectively," *Management Research News,* Vol. 23, Iss. 7/8, pp. 84–89; Robert J. Harvey and Susana R. Lozada-Larsen (August 1988), "Influence of Amount of Job Descriptive Information on Job Analysis Rating Accuracy," *Journal of Applied Psychology,* pp. 457–461.

16. Harvey, op. cit., p. 333.

17. Ibid.

18. Erich P. Prien, Kristin O. Prien, and Louis G. Gamble (March 2004), "Perspectives on Nonconventional Job Analysis Methodologies," *Journal of Business Psychology,* Vol. 18, No. 3, pp. 337–48; Edward L. Levine, Ronald A. Ash, Hardy Hall, and Frank Sistrunk (June 1983), "Evaluation of Job Analysis Methods by Experienced Job Analysts," *Academy of Management Journal,* pp. 339–348.

19. Michael Brannick and Edward Levine (2002), *Job Analysis: Methods, Research, and Applications for Human Resource Management in the New Millennium* (Thousand Oaks, CA: Corwin Press); Edward L. Levine, James N. Thomas, and Frank Sistrunk (1988), "Selecting a Job Analysis Approach," in Sidney Gael (ed.), *The Job Analysis Handbook for Business, Industry, and Government,* Vol. 1 (New York: Wiley), pp. 339–352.

20. Benjamin Schneider and A. M. Konz (Spring 1989), "Strategic Job Analysis," *Human Resource Management,* pp. 53–54.

21. Veres, Locklear, and Sims, op. cit., p. 92.

22. U.S. Department of Labor (1991), *Dictionary of Occupational Titles,* 4th ed. (Washington, DC: U.S. Government Printing Office); U.S. Department of Labor (1977), *Dictionary of Occupational Titles,* 4th ed. (Washington, DC: U.S. Government Printing Office).

23. Sidney Fine and Steven Cronshaw (1999), *Functional Job Analysis* (Mahwah, NJ: Lawrence Erlbaum Associates); Sidney A. Fine and Maury Getkate (1995), *Benchmark Tasks for Job Analysis: Guide for Functional Job Analysis* (FJA) *Scales* (Mahwah, NJ: Lawrence Erlbaum Associates).

24. Sidney A. Fine (1988), "Functional Job Analysis," in Sidney Gael (ed.), *The Job Analysis Handbook for Business, Industry, and Government,* Vol. 2 (New York: Wiley), p. 1029.

25. Patrick D. Converse, Frederick L. Oswald, Michael A. Gillespie, Kevin A. Field, and Elizabeth B. Bizot (2004), "Matching Individuals to Occupations Using Abilities and the O*NET: Issues and an Application in Career Guidance," *Personnel Psychology,* Vol. 57, pp. 451–487; Norman Peterson, Michael Mumford, Walter Borman, Richard Jeanneret, and Edwin Fleishman (Summer 2001), "Understanding Work Using the Occupational Informational Network (O*NET): Implications for Practice and Research," *Personnel Psychology,* pp. 451–492. O*NET can be found on the Web at http://www.onetcenter.org/.

26. www.onetcenter.org/overview.html.

27. Ernest J. McCormick, Paul R. Jeanneret, and Robert C. Mecham (August 1972), "A Study of Job Characteristics and Job Dimensions as Based on the Position Analysis Questionnaire

(PAQ)," *Journal of Applied Psychology,* pp. 347–368; and Ernest J. McCormick, Paul R. Jeanneret, and Robert C. Mecham (1978), *User's Manual for the Position Analysis Questionnaire System II* (West Lafayette, IN: Purdue University Press).

28. Erich C. Dierdorff and Mark A. Wilson (2003), "A Meta-Analysis of Job Analysis Reliability," *Journal of Applied Psychology,* Vol. 88, No. 4, pp. 635–646; Ernest J. McCormick, Angelo S. DeNisi, and James B. Shaw (February 1979), "Use of the Position Analysis Questionnaire for Establishing the Job Component Validity of Tests," *Journal of Applied Psychology,* pp. 51–56.

29. Robert C. Carter and Robert J. Biersner (1987), "Job Requirements Derived from the Position Analysis Questionnaire and Validated Using Military Aptitude Test Scores," *Journal of Occupational Psychology,* pp. 311–321.

30. Wayne F. Cascio (1989), *Managing Human Resources: Productivity, Quality of Work Life, Profits,* 2nd ed. (New York: McGraw-Hill), p. 129.

31. Angelo S. DeNisi, Edwin T. Cornelius III, and Allyn G. Blencoe (May 1987), "Further Investigation of Common Knowledge Effects on Job Analysis Ratings," *Journal of Applied Psychology,* pp. 262–268; and Robert J. Harvey and Theodore L. Hayes (Summer 1986), "Monte Carlo Baselines for Interrater Reliability Correlations Using the Position Analysis Questionnaire," *Personnel Psychology,* pp. 345–357.

32. Walter W. Tornow and Patrick R. Pinto (August 1976), "The Development of a Managerial Job Taxonomy: A System for Describing, Classifying, and Evaluating Executive Positions," *Journal of Applied Psychology,* pp. 410–418.

33. Ronald C. Page (1988), "Management Position Description Questionnaire," in Sidney Gael (ed.), *The Job Analysis Handbook for Business, Industry, and Government,* Vol. 2 (New York: Wiley), pp. 860–879.

34. Robert J. Harvey (1993), "The Development of the Common-Metric Questionnaire," Research Monograph, Personnel Systems and Technologies Corporation and Virginia Polytechnic Institute State University.

35. Harmut Wachter, Brita Modrow-Thiel, and Giselind Rossmann (1994), "Work Design and Computer-Controlled Systems: Job Analysis under Automation—ATAA," *Logistics Information Management,* pp. 44–52.

36. Carla Joinson (January 2001), "Refocusing Job Descriptions," *HRMagazine,* Vol. 46, Iss. 1, pp. 66–72; Robert J. Sahl (Fall 1992), "Pressing Reasons for Accurate Job Descriptions," *Human Resource Professional,* pp. 18–20.

37. Sharon Leonard (August 2000), "The Demise of Job Descriptions," *HRMagazine,* pp. 184–185.

38. Jai Ghorpade (1988), *Job Analysis: A Handbook for the Human Resource Director* (Englewood Cliffs, NJ: Prentice-Hall), pp. 93–134.

39. Harvey, op. cit., p. 383.

40. Eric J. Felsberg (2004), "Conducting Job Analyses and Drafting Lawful Job Descriptions under the Americans with Disabilities Act," *Employment Relations Today,* Vol. 31, Iss. 3, pp. 91–94; Nancy Asquith and Daniel E. Feld (1994), *Employment Testing Manual: 1994 Cumulative Supplement* (Boston: Warren, Gorham, Lamont), pp. 3–6/3–7.

41. Danny G. Langdon and Kathleen S. Whiteside (May 1996), "Redefining Jobs and Work in Changing Organizations," *HRMagazine,* pp. 97–101.

42. Susan Jackson and Randall Schuler (2003), *Managing Human Resources through Strategic Partnerships,* 8th ed. (Mason, OH: South-Western), pp. 4–5; John E. Butler, Gerald R. Ferris, and Nancy K. Napier (1991), *Strategy and Human Resources Management* (Cincinnati, OH: South-Western).

43. Timothy P. Summers and Suzanne B. Summers (1997), "Strategic Skills Analysis for Selection and Development," *Human Resource Planning,* pp. 14–19.

44. Schneider and Konz, op. cit., pp. 51–63.

45. Cynthia R. Cunningham and Shelley S. Murray (February 2005), "Two Executives, One Career," *Harvard Business Review,* Vol. 83, Iss. 2, pp. 125–32; Tom Duffy (July 2001), "Alternative Work Arrangements," *Network World,* pp. 39–40; Karen A. Edelman (October 1996), "Workplace Flexibility Boosts Profits," *Across the Board,* pp. 56–57; and

Miriam Basch Scott (September 1996), "Flexibility Improves Workplace at Owens Corning, Dun & Bradstreet Information Systems," *Employee Benefit Plan Review,* pp. 30–31.

46. Karen E. May (April 1996), "Work in the 21st Century: Implications for Job Analysis," www.siop.org/tip.backissues/tipapr96/may.htm.

47. Filip Lievens, Juan I. Sanchez, and Wilfred De Corte (2004), "Easing the Inferential Leap in Competency Modeling: The Effects of Task-Related Information and Subject Matter Expertise," *Personnel Psychology,* Vol. 57, Iss. 4, pp. 881–905; Jergen Sandberg (March 2001), "Understanding Competence at Work," *Harvard Business Review,* pp. 24–28; Heneman, Judge, and Heneman, op. cit., pp. 184–186; Jeffery Shippmann, Ronald Ash, Linda Carr, and Beryl Hesketh (2000), "The Practice of Competency Modeling," *Personnel Psychology,* pp. 703–740.

48. Michael A. Campion and Carol L. McClelland (June 1993), "Follow-Up and Extension of the Interdisciplinary Costs and Benefits of Enlarged Jobs," *Journal of Applied Psychology,* pp. 339–351.

49. Michael A. Campion and Gina J. Medsker (1991), "Job Design," in G. Salvendy (ed.), *Handbook of Industrial Engineering,* 2nd ed. (New York, Wiley), pp. 845–881.

50. Frederick W. Taylor (1911), *The Principles of Scientific Management* (New York: Harper & Row), p. 21.

51. David A. Nadler, J. Richard Hackman, and Edward E. Lawler III (1979), *Managing Organizational Behavior* (Boston: Little, Brown), p. 79.

52. Ricky W. Griffin (1982), *Task Design: An Integrative Approach* (Glenview, IL: Scott, Foresman), p. 21.

53. Griffin, op. cit., pp. 31–34.

54. Frederick Herzberg, B. Mausner, and B. Snyderman (1959), *The Motivation to Work* (New York: Wiley).

55. J. Richard Hackman and Greg R. Oldham (August 1976), "Motivation through the Design of Work: Test of a Theory," *Organizational Behavior and Human Performance,* pp. 250–279; and J. Richard Hackman, Greg R. Oldham, R. Janson, and K. Purdy (Summer 1975), "A New Strategy for Job Enrichment," *California Management Review,* pp. 57–71.

56. Hackman and Oldham, op. cit., pp. 250–279.

57. Mrugank V. Thakor and Ashwin W. Joshi (May 2005), "Motivating Salesperson Customer Orientation: Insights from the Job Characteristics Model," *Journal of Business Research,* Vol. 58, Iss. 5, pp. 584–602; Nancy G. Dodd and Daniel C. Ganster (July 1996), "The Interactive Effects of Variety, Autonomy, and Feedback on Attitudes and Performance," *Journal of Organizational Behavior,* pp. 329–347.

58. Robert W. Renn and Robert J. Vandenberg (Summer 1995), "The Critical Psychological States: An Underrepresented Component in Job Characteristics Model Research," *Journal of Management,* pp. 279–303.

59. A. S. Evangelista and Lisa A. Burke (2003), "Work Redesign and Performance Management in Times of Downsizing," *Business Horizon*, Vol. 46, Iss. 2, pp. 71–76; Jia Lin Xie and Gary Johns (October 1995), "Job Scope and Stress: Can Job Scope Be Too High?" *Academy of Management Journal,* pp. 1288–1309.

60. Mohamed Branine (2003), "Part-Time Work and Job Sharing in Health Care: Is the NHS a Family-Friendly Employer?" *Journal of Health Organization and Management,* Vol. 17, Iss. 1, pp. 53–69; Luis R. Gomez-Mejia, David B. Balkin, and Robert L. Cardy (2000), *Managing Human Resources,* 3rd ed. (Upper Saddle River, NJ: Prentice Hall).

61. Cunningham and Murray, op cit., p. 125; Charlene Solomon (September 1994), "Job Sharing: One Job, Double Headache?" *Personnel Journal,* pp. 88–93.

62. Gomez-Mejia et al., *Managing Human Resources.*

63. Charlotte Huff (May 2005), "With Flextime, Less Can Be More," *Workforce Management,* Vol. 84, Iss. 5, pp. 65–69.

64. Boris B. Baltes, Thomas E. Briggs, Joseph W. Huff, Julie A. Wright, and George A. Neuman (August 1999), "Flexible and Compressed Workweek Schedules: A Meta-Analysis of Their Effects on Work-Related Criteria," *Journal of Applied Psychology,* pp. 496–513.

65. Timothy D. Golden and John F. Veiga (2005), "The Impact and Extent of Telecommuting on Job Satisfaction: Resolving Inconsistent Findings," *Journal of Management,* Vol. 31, Iss. 2, pp. 301–318.

66. Janet Wiscombe (October 2002), "Tearing Down the 'Maternal Wall,' *Workforce,* Vol. 81, Iss. 10, p. 15; Sharon Leonard (July 2000), "The Baby Gap," *HRMagazine,* pp. 368–370.

67. Keith Hammonds, Roy Furchgott, Steve Hamm, and Paul Judge (September 1997), "Work and Family," *BusinessWeek,* pp. 96–101.

68. Gillian Flynn and Sarah F. Gale (October 2001), "The Legalities of Flextime," *Workforce,* pp. 62–66.

69. Jane Gibson and Dana Tesone (November 2001), "Management Fads: Emergence, Evolution, and Implications for Managers," *The Academy of Management Executive,* pp. 122–133.

70. Michael W. Piczak and Reuben Z. Hauser (May 1996), "Self-Directed Work Teams: A Guide to Implementation," *Quality Progress,* pp. 81–87.

71. Nicholas F. Horney and Richard Koonce (December 1995), "The Missing Piece in Reengineering," *Training and Development,* pp. 37–43.

Application Case 6-1

Job Analysis: Assistant Store Managers at Today's Fashion

Mary Watson was recently promoted to the position of regional sales manager for Today's Fashion, a national chain of specialty clothing stores with 200 outlets across the country. Mary is the regional manager for the Pacific Coast, which is one of Today's Fashion's largest markets. She manages 35 outlets in California and Oregon; each of these outlets has a store manager who reports directly to Mary.

Each outlet has between three and five assistant store managers, depending on the number of specialty departments. Each assistant manager is responsible for one particular specialty department. These departments vary considerably in size and in the number of sales clerks reporting to the assistant manager. Because the chain's success lies in being receptive to local customers' tastes and buying habits, each store has a different collection of merchandise, and several different combinations of departments can be found in Mary's region. The departments include casual wear, formal wear, shoes, cosmetics, and jewelry.

EXHIBIT 6A-1
Today's Fashion
Job Description/
Job Specification

Job Title: Assistant Store Manager
Reports to: Store Manager

General Description of the Job

Manages the daily functions of a specialty department in the retail operations. The assistant store manager has responsibility for customer service, supervision of salesclerks, training of new employees, merchandising, and maintenance of inventory.

Principal Duties and Responsibilities

1. Assists customers in merchandise selections, returns, and layaway as needed.
2. Clarifies any questions or problems that a salesclerk encounters.
3. Trains, coordinates, directs, and supervises department salesclerks daily.
4. Maintains inventory records.
5. Prepares the department for opening at the beginning of each day.
6. Ensures that the department remains professionally organized and orderly.

General Qualification Requirements

Education:
1. Minimum: Four-year college degree in marketing or related discipline from an
             accredited program.

Experience:
1. Minimum: Six months to one year in a retail environment.
2. Preferred: One to three years as a salesclerk for Today's Fashion.

Knowledge, skills, abilities:
1. Basic math
2. Effective interpersonal skills
3. Good judgment and independent thought
4. Self-starter/highly motivated
5. High integrity
6. Good typing and computer skills

Physical requirements:
1. Standing and walking required for more than 90 percent of work time.
2. Ability to lift and carry boxes weighing approximately 15 pounds or less.

Prior to being appointed to the regional sales manager position, Mary had been both a store manager and an assistant manager in a casual-wear department. While she was an assistant manager, Mary had often thought that she was responsible for many aspects of store management that other assistant managers were not held responsible for. In addition, she never really felt comfortable that her store manager had clearly defined her areas of responsibility. Thus, despite the chain's success, Mary felt that there was considerable room for improvement in how Today's Fashion was managed. As a result, one of the first things Mary did after being appointed to the regional sales position was to initiate a job analysis for the job of assistant store manager.

Mary had earned a BBA degree with a marketing emphasis from the University of Wyoming. Although she had no formal training in job analysis, she was confident that she could construct an accurate and useful job description and specification for the assistant manager job, primarily because of her personal experience with that position. However, rather than simply writing from her own experience, Mary interviewed three current assistant store managers from the outlet closest to her regional office in Sacramento. On the basis of these interviews and her own experience, Mary constructed the job description and job specification shown in Exhibit 6A-1. She hopes that these documents will form the basis of a new selection program that she wants to implement for her region. She believes that the best way to improve store management is to hire assistant store managers who are qualified to perform successfully.

Discussion Questions

1. Critically evaluate the job analysis that Mary conducted for the position of assistant store manager. Has she used appropriate methods? What are the strengths and weaknesses of her efforts?

2. What kinds of factors about Today's Fashion and its operations should Mary have examined more seriously in order to improve her job analysis?

3. Carefully read the job description and job specification that Mary prepared. Do they appear to be thorough? Do you think that they are adequate to serve as a basis for a new selection system? How well do you think these documents will work if Mary is sued for discrimination in her hiring practices? Why?

Application Case 6-2

Job Analysis and Maternity Leave: Calming the Boss's and Co-workers' Nerves

Maternity leave occurs when a female employee, upon giving birth to a child, takes time off to care for the child. This leave can be either paid or unpaid and is usually limited to six weeks. However, the new mother may decide to take up to six months away from work, though this is almost always without pay. *Are there any negative repercussions associated with taking time off to care for an infant?* Apparently, the answer is "yes." Female employees who participate in maternity leave sometimes feel that their co-workers and supervisors question their commitment to the organization and to their own career progression due to their decision to stop working for a short period of time. Also, co-workers and supervisors sometimes feel overwhelmed with having to deal with the extra work that has to be absorbed from the individual who is taking maternity leave. In extreme cases, these individuals may feel "put upon" or "betrayed" by the once committed individual who is now taking "time off." Of course, anyone who has dedicated themselves to caring for an infant understands very well that such a responsibility is a 24 hour a day, 7 days a week endeavor.

So, what can an individual who is planning to take maternity leave do to ease the tension and misperceptions among her colleagues and supervisor? It is suggested that the pregnant individual create a detailed job analysis that includes which tasks/projects need to be accomplished before she leaves on maternity leave, which tasks/projects can be delegated to which co-workers, and which tasks/projects can wait until she returns from maternity leave. Though there are many other steps that can be taken to ease the transition between work and maternity leave, the job analysis will help break down and possibly prevent the "maternal wall" from being a barrier to the long-term retention and utilization of a valued employee.

Discussion Questions

1. Assume that you (male or female) were going to take a 6-week leave of absence from your job 5 months from now. How do you think your supervisor and co-workers would react to the news? Explain.

2. Do a brief job analysis of your current (or a past job), including a job description and job specification/qualifications. Which tasks, duties, or responsibilities could you finish before your leave of absence? Which could you delegate to your co-workers? Which would have to wait until you return from the leave of absence?

3. Assume that you received a lot of negative comments from your supervisor and co-workers when you "announced" that you'd be taking a 6-week leave of absence. How would that make you feel? Would it have any impact on your commitment to the organization?

Sources: Joan C. Williams (October 2004), "The Maternal Wall," *Harvard Business Review*, Vol. 82, Iss. 10, p. 26; Meina Liu and Patrice M. Buzzanell (2004), "Negotiating Maternity Leave Expectations: Perceived Tensions between Ethics of Justice and Caring," *The Journal of Business Communication*, Vol. 41, Iss. 4, pp. 323–50; Sue Shellenbarger (May 20, 2004), "Baby Blues: The Dangers of the Trend toward Shorter Maternity Leaves," *The Wall Street Journal*, p. D1.

Chapter

Recruitment

Learning Objectives

After studying this chapter, you should be able to:

1. **Discuss** how to develop an effective recruiting program for an organization.
2. **Describe** the recruiting process: who does it, how recruiters do it, and where they find recruits.
3. **Define** what is meant by a realistic job preview.
4. **Identify** typical flaws that college students find in recruiters.
5. **Discuss** different strategies that organizations might use to recruit blue-collar, white-collar, managerial, technical, and professional applicants.

Internet/Web Resources

General Sites
www.hireright.com
www.sireport.com
www.jobweb.org
www.verizon.com/about/careers
www.naceweb.org
www.eeoc.gov
www.bls.gov
www.conference-board.org

Company Sites
www.pearsonps.com
www.forrester.com
www.ge.com
www.iflyswa.com
www.hp.com
www.schwab.com
www.national.com
www.amoco.com
www.accenture.com

Career Challenge

Clark Kirby was just entering the office of the vice president of human resource management, Lois Yates. Clark had worked for Gunther Manufacturing for 10 years in Los Angeles. After a short management training program, Clark spent almost two years as operating supervisor in a plant. After that, a position opened up in the HR department. Clark had majored in personnel at California State University at Los Angeles and wanted to try HRM work. He moved up in the department headquarters during the next seven years.

Gunther was a growing firm. For a medium-sized operation, it had one of the fastest growth records in the industry. Now Gunther was opening a new plant in the quickly expanding Tampa market.

Lois had selected Clark to be the human resource manager for the Tampa plant. This was what Clark had been waiting for: a chance to be on his own and to show what he could do for Lois, who had been very supportive of his career, and for Gunther. He was very excited as he entered Lois's office.

Lois greeted him with, "Well, Clark, I hope you realize how much we are counting on you in Tampa. Shortly you'll be meeting your new plant manager, Ed Humphrey. You'll be working for him but responsible to me to see that Gunther's HRM policies are carried out.

"The plant will be staffed initially with the following employees. These are, in effect, your recruiting quotas:

Managers	38
Professional and technical	10
Clerical	44
Skilled employees	104
Semiskilled employees	400

You'll receive a budget for maximum initial pay for this group shortly.

"You and Ed should work out the details. You can recruit some employees from the home office and other plants, but excessive raiding is not allowed. Remember, too, that Gunther has an equal employment opportunity problem. Wherever possible, try to hire qualified minorities and women to help us meet our internal goals.

"Your own HR office consists of yourself, one HR specialist to help you run the employment office, and one clerical employee. Good luck!"

Clark quickly arranged for a meeting with Ed, his new boss. Ed, about 50 years old, was a high school graduate who had started with Gunther as a blue-collar employee when he was 18 years old. After 10 years in various blue-collar positions, Ed became a foreman. Eight years later he was selected as an assistant to the plant manager. After several years in this position, he was made one of three assistant plant managers at a Gunther plant in Chicago. He held that position until being given this new position of plant manager at the Tampa plant.

After introductions, Clark and Ed talked.

Clark Here are the figures for employees that Lois gave me. She also said we could recruit some people from Gunther, but not to raid beyond company policy. Also, Lois said we needed to do an exceptional job recruiting minorities and women because we have an EEO problem.

Ed Let's get something straight right off. You work for me now, not Lois. Here's a list of 20 managers I want to take with me. It's your job to persuade them to come to Tampa with me. In cases where my help might persuade some to come along, call on me. But I'm very stressed now trying to get machinery ordered, the plant laid out, financing arranged, and so on. Call on me only when you must, *understand?*

Oh, one more thing. That EEO *#/OX—you can forget that. The Tampa plant is going to be the most efficient in the company, or else! And if that means hiring the best workers and they all turn out to be white men, that's tough, you get me? Keep me posted on what's happening. Good to have you on board.

After some thought, Clark decided to use job posting as a method of attracting professional-technical and managerial employees at the Los Angeles office to the new plant in Tampa. He also made the personal contacts Ed asked for in recruiting managerial employees, and the skills inventory was used to come up with more applicants. Clark contacted these also. He did not use job posting or the skills inventory for clerical, skilled, or semi-skilled employees. He knew that for Gunther, as with most organizations, these categories of employees rarely wish to move to another location. Most companies don't want to pay relocation costs for these categories of employment, either.

Clark went to Tampa and set up the employment office at the new location. He ran an ad in Tampa's afternoon paper and placed a job listing with a private employment agency for the HR specialist and clerk-typist for his office. Then he hired these two employees and set up the office to receive walk-ins. He provided application blanks and policy guidelines on when selection would proceed.

Clark listed the available positions with the U.S. Employment Service. He also contacted private agencies. He selected the private agencies after calling a number of HR managers in the Tampa area in similar businesses who were also members of the Society of Human Resource Management. The HR specialist notified all the vocational-technical schools, junior colleges, and colleges in the Tampa area. Also, all high school guidance counseling departments were notified. Clark wondered what other media he ought to use to publicize the positions.

Clark found out quickly, as you will find in this chapter, that recruitment is a little more complicated than he originally thought.

Before an organization can fill a job vacancy, it must find people who not only are qualified for the position but also want the job. This chapter describes the recruiting process as one of the ways that an organization can deal with shortages in its human resources needs. **Recruitment** refers to organizational activities that influence the number and types of applicants who apply for a job and whether the applicants accept jobs that are offered.[1] Thus, recruitment is directly related to both human resource planning and selection. In addition, recruiting often represents the first contact between organizations and prospective employees. As such, care should be taken to create a positive first impression with these job applications.

Although recruitment can be quite expensive, organizations have not always treated it as systematically as other HR functions, such as selection. During the coming years, however, the importance of recruitment will probably increase for many organizations. Even with a modest rise in recession-based unemployment at the beginning of the 21st century, fears of a looming tight labor market in the United States continue to plague organizations of all sizes.[2] Driven by the inevitable retirements of baby boomers and fewer numbers of young people entering into the workforce,[3] the labor shortage has caused many companies to develop retention strategies to hold onto their valued employees. For example, Hewlett-Packard Co. and Charles Schwab Corp. have preferred freezes or cut pay to avoid layoffs.[4] Despite the fact that organizational layoffs reached a 10-year high at the end of the 1990s, experts anticipate a growing number of labor shortages in high-skills areas.[5]

The recruiting process begins with an attempt to find employees with the abilities and attitudes desired by the organization and to match them with the tasks to be performed. Whether potential employees will respond to the recruiting effort depends on the attitudes they have developed toward those tasks and the organization on the basis of their past social and working experiences. Their perception of the task will also be affected by the work climate in the organization.

187

How difficult the recruiting job is depends on a number of factors: external influences such as government and union restrictions and the labor market, plus the employer's requirements and candidates' preferences. External factors are discussed first, and the important interaction of the organization as a recruiter and the employee as a recruit is examined in the next section.

External Influences

Government and Union Restrictions

Government regulations prohibiting discrimination in hiring and employment have a direct impact on recruiting practices. As described in detail in Chapter 3, government agencies can and do review the following information about recruiting to see if an organization has violated the law:

- List of recruitment sources (such as job search Web sites, employment agencies, civic organizations, schools) for each job category.
- Recruiting advertising.
- Estimates of the firm's employment needs for the coming year.
- Statistics on the number of applicants processed by demographic category (sex, race, and so on) and by job category or level.
- Checklists to show what evidence was used to verify the legal right to work.

Although there is no guaranteed way to avoid legal entanglements associated with recruiting, Exhibit 7-1 provides some basic principles of sound recruiting practices.

The **Immigration Reform and Control Act (IRCA) of 1986** has placed a major responsibility on employers for stopping the flow of illegal immigration to the United States. The employer—not the government—is the chief enforcer of the prohibition against the unauthorized recruitment and employment of foreign-born individuals.[6] Under the law's "employer sanctions" arrangement, all employers are required to screen every applicant's eligibility for lawful employment and maintain records demonstrating employment authorization.

The IRCA is a complex piece of legislation, but its basic features fit into four broad categories:

1. Employer's duty not to recruit, hire, or continue to employ "unauthorized aliens."
2. Employer's duty to verify the identity and work authorization of every new employee.
3. Employer's duty not to discriminate on the basis of citizenship or national origin.
4. Amnesty rights of certain illegal aliens who are eligible to achieve temporary or permanent resident status in the country.

Despite the difficulty that organizations have determining whether a worker is legally employable, the government is currently planning to step up its enforcement of the IRCA.

EXHIBIT 7-1
Guidelines for Legal Recruitment

Source: Jonathan A. Segal (2001), "An Offer They Couldn't Refuse," *HRMagazine,* Vol. 46, Iss. 4, pp. 131–139.

1. Establish general guidelines for recruiters.
2. Make sure applicants complete, sign, and date an application for employment, including certain legal certifications.
3. Use outcome-oriented job descriptions.
4. Utilize an offer letter that outlines the commitments the organization is prepared to keep.
5. State that employment is "at-will."
6. List salary, frequency of pay increases, and benefits.
7. State conditions upon which employment may be subject.

HR Journal   *Internet Talent Auctions: "What Is My Bid for This Highly Skilled Employee?"*

As mentioned earlier in this chapter, unemployment in the United States has recently hit record low levels and, despite massive layoffs in some industries, experts are predicting no end to critical shortages of skilled labor. These shortages are expected to be especially acute in high-tech industries such as computers and wireless communications. To remain competitive, organizations in these industries must find new and innovative ways to identify, attract, and hire people with the skills needed. Clearly, the Internet is one of the tools being used more and more frequently to satisfy these difficult recruiting goals.

Recently, there has been another twist to Internet use in organizational recruitment and selection. The talent auction has arrived. The largest job posting site in the world, www.monster.com, has added another capability to its Internet services. Contract and temporary workers can now register at the Web site, and organizations are given the opportunity to bid against one another for a given worker. Though little research has been conducted to assess the success of these recruiting innovations, there appears to be a considerable organizational interest in the concept.

It should be kept in mind that in spite of the meteoric rise in the use of the Internet for recruitment and job search activities, Web postings still only represent approximately 2 percent of all job listings. In addition, the unwary user should not be lulled into believing that the Internet can easily replace other forms of recruiting. For example, it is difficult if not impossible for an organization to capture the degree of fit between an applicant's personality and the organization's culture from an electronic resume alone. At the same time, organizations that do not begin to capitalize on the Internet might soon find themselves at a competitive disadvantage. In addition, new developments occur almost daily that make the Internet more effective. One way to stay current regarding **online recruiting** is to enroll in Internet-based courses that teach the latest in advanced online recruiting techniques. Such courses are available from a variety of vendors, including Recruiting-Online.com (http://www.recruiting-online.com/home.html). Course content at Recruiting-Online includes the following "how-tos": build a candidate database, manage contact with thousands of passive job-seeker candidates, take advantage of newsgroups and listservs, find resumes of people with any skill set or in any location in the world, and obtain e-mail addresses of employees at companies that are merging or downsizing. Chances are, virtual recruiting is here to stay.

Additional money will be spent on hiring more investigators, attorneys, and support staff, but some money will also be devoted to ensuring that legal applicants are not discriminated against because of the stepped-up enforcement activities.

Labor Market Conditions

Another external environmental factor affecting recruiting is labor market conditions (these were described in some detail in Chapter 2). If there is a surplus of labor at recruiting time, even informal attempts at recruiting will probably attract more than enough applicants. However, when full employment is nearly reached in an area, skillful and prolonged recruiting may be necessary to attract any applicants who fulfill the expectations of the organization. Obviously, how many applicants are available also depends on whether the economy is growing. When companies are not creating new jobs, there is often an oversupply of qualified labor.

An employer can find out about the current employment picture in several ways. The federal Department of Labor issues employment reports, and state divisions of employment security and labor usually can provide information about specific types of employees. There are also sources of information on local employment conditions as they affect their members. Current college recruiting efforts are analyzed by the Conference Board, A. C. Nielsen, and the Endicott Report, which appears in the *Journal of College Placement*. Various personnel journals, the *Monthly Labor Review*, and *The Wall Street Journal* also regularly report on employment conditions.

Composition of Labor Force and Location of Organization

The influence of HRM law on activities was noted in Chapter 3. As the number of legal requirements has increased, it has become important for an organization to analyze the composition of its workforce. Such an analysis is done to determine whether the firm's employment practices are discriminatory.

The location of the organization and the relevant labor market will play a major role in the composition of the workforce. That is, the number of African American, Hispanic, Asian or Pacific Islander, Native American, or Alaskan native employees in the workforce depends largely on the availability of these minority employees in the relevant labor market.

Regardless of the location of the organization, an aggressive diversity management program will be essential for organizations entering the 21st century. Due in part to skills shortages, progressive organizations now understand that effective diversity management is an integral strategic tool for enhancing competitiveness. For diversity management to work, however, it must be valued by the organization.[7] But for those organizations such as Allstate Insurance with the foresight to embrace diversity, the benefits can be tremendous in terms of outcomes ranging from higher productivity to increased customer satisfaction.[8]

Interactions of the Recruit and the Organization

After considering how external factors such as government, unions, labor market conditions, composition of the workforce, and location of the organization restrict recruiting options, the next step in understanding the recruiting process is to consider the interaction between the applicants and the organization in recruiting.

In Exhibit 7-1, the nature of the organization and the goals of the managers are highlighted, as is the nature of the task. The techniques used and sources of recruits vary with the job. As far as the applicants are concerned, their abilities and past work experience affect how they go about seeking a job.

The Organization's View of Recruiting

Several aspects affect recruiting from the organization's viewpoint: the recruiting requirements set, organizational policies and procedures, and the organization's image.

Recruiting Requirements

The recruiting process necessarily begins with a detailed job description and job specification.[9] Without these, it is impossible for recruiters to determine how well any particular applicant fits the job. It should be made clear to the recruiter which requirements are absolutely essential and which are merely desirable. This can help the organization avoid unrealistic expectations for potential employees: An employer might expect applicants who stand first in their class, are presidents of extracurricular activities, have worked their way through school, are good-looking, have 10 years' experience (at age 21), and are willing to work long hours for almost no money. Contrasting with this unrealistic approach, the effective organization examines the specifications that are absolutely necessary for the job. Then it uses these as its beginning expectations for recruits (see the sections on job analysis, job description, and job specifications in Chapter 6).

Organizational Policies and Practices

In some organizations, HRM policies and practices affect recruiting and who is recruited. One of the most significant of these is promotion from within. For all practical purposes, this policy means that many organizations recruit from outside the organization only at the initial hiring level. Most employees favor this approach. They feel this is fair to present loyal employees and assures them of a secure future and a fair chance at promotion. Some employers also feel this practice helps protect trade secrets. The techniques used for internal recruiting will be discussed later in this chapter.

Is promotion from within a good policy? Not always. An organization may become so stable that it is set in its ways. The business does not compete effectively, or the government bureau will not adjust to legislative requirements. In such cases, promotion from within may be detrimental, and new employees from outside might be helpful.

Other policies can also affect recruiting. Certain organizations have always hired more than their fair share of the disabled, veterans, or ex-convicts, for example, and they may look to these sources first. Others may be involved in nepotism and favor relatives. All these policies affect who is recruited.

Organizational Image

The image of the employer generally held by the public can also affect recruitment. All else being equal, it should be easier for an organization with a positive corporate image to attract and retain employees than an organization with a negative image.[10] Thus, for those organizations that reach the top of *Fortune* magazine's "most admired" list, such as Dell, General Electric, and Starbucks,[11] the time and effort needed to recruit high-quality workers may be less than for competitors who rank poorly. Recruitment should also be somewhat easier for companies that exude a strong community presence or positive name recognition.[12]

In sum, the ideal job specifications preferred by an organization may have to be adjusted to meet the realities of the labor market, government, or union restrictions; the limitations of its policies and practices; and its image. If an inadequate number of high-quality people apply, the organization may have to adjust the job to fit the best applicant or increase its recruiting efforts.

The Potential Employee's View of Recruiting

Exhibit 7-1 highlighted several factors relevant to how a recruit looks for a job. The applicant has abilities, attitudes, and preferences based on past work experiences and influences of parents, teachers, and others. These factors affect recruits in two ways: how they set their job preferences, and how they go about seeking a job. Understanding these is vital to effective recruiting.

Preferences of Recruits for Organizations and Jobs

Just as organizations have ideal specifications for recruits, so do recruits have a set of preferences for jobs. A student leaving college generally expects to obtain a job that actually requires college-level education and skills. The graduate might also have strong geographic preferences and expectations about salary and may anticipate that advancement will occur rapidly. However, such a recruit is not necessarily going to find her or his ideal job. Although the Bureau of Labor Statistics predicts that the total number of college-level job openings between now and 2008 will nearly equal the number of college-educated entrants to the labor force, there will still be approximately 6 million college graduates either unemployed or underemployed (i.e., working in positions that do not require a bachelor's degree). For example, significant numbers of college graduates will likely be working as retail sales employees, food preparers and servers, motor vehicle operators, and in administrative support roles.[13] Recruits also face barriers to finding their ideal job, barriers created by economic conditions, government and union restrictions, and the limits of organizational policies and practices. The recruit must anticipate compromises, just as the organization must.

From the individual's point of view, choosing an organization involves at least two major steps. First, the individual chooses an occupation—perhaps in high school or early in college. Then she or he chooses the organization to work for within that broader occupation.

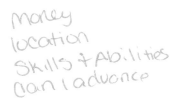

What factors affect the choice of occupation and organization? Obviously, there are many, many factors that influence these decisions. But a survey conducted by the National Association of Colleges and Employers found that occupational choice is most heavily influenced by parents, followed by teachers, career counselors, friends, and relatives.[14] As previously mentioned, choice of an organization might be influenced by corporate image. Additionally, many recruits prefer larger, well-established firms over smaller organizations.[15] Research also suggests that satisfaction with the communication process in recruitment is critical to attracting applicants.[16] In reality, however, this decision isn't always purely rational; it is also affected by unconscious processes, chance, and luck.

Job Search and Finding a Job: The Recruit

People who are successful at finding the "right job" tend to follow similar research processes. It is not always enough to simply be in the right place at the right time. The effective job searcher creates opportunities in a systematic way. An effective **job search** involves several steps including self-assessment, information gathering, networking, targeting specific jobs, and successful self-presentation.[17]

The job search is a process that begins with self-assessment. The purpose of self-assessments is for job searchers to recognize their career goals and their strengths and weaknesses, interests and values, and preferred lifestyles. This information is used later in the search to help the applicant assess whether there is a fit with a particular job offer. The assessment is similar to what organizational recruiters will be doing, but from the perspective of the applicant.

Information gathering and networking are methods for generating lists of potential employers and jobs. Sources of information include newspapers, trade publications, college recruitment offices, and organizational "insiders."

Many questions about possible employers must be answered before a list of alternatives can be generated.

1. Do I have a size preference: small, medium, or large, or no particular size?
2. Do I have sector preference (private, not for profit, or public sector)?
3. What kinds of industries interest me? This question is usually based on interests in products or services. Do I prefer working with mechanical objects or counseling people? This is a crucial question.
4. Have I checked to make sure that the sector, product, or service has a good future and will lead to growth and opportunity?

Once these kinds of questions have been answered, the job seeker can generate a list of prospective employers using a wide variety of sources including newspapers, personal contacts, and the Internet. When the job seeker has decided where he or she will send a resume, self-presentation becomes critical. Research suggests that recruiters want to see a resume and cover letter that is tailored to the position and is truthful.[18] The cover letter and resume should include these items, in order of importance:

1. Position you seek.
2. Your specific job objectives.
3. Your career objectives.
4. Reason you seek employment.
5. An indication that you know something about the organization.

Unfortunately for the organizational recruiter, not all job seekers provide truthful resumes.[19] A survey conducted by Reid Psychological Systems (part of Pearson Performance Solutions) found that as many as 95 percent of college students are willing to be less than

HRMEMO

Finding someone within the company to "walk" your resume into the recruiter or hiring manager's hands can substantially increase the applicant's chances of being interviewed and hired. Social networking leads to jobs!

Source: Jessica Mintz (March 1, 2005), "Large Firms Increasingly Rely on Employees for Job Referrals," *The Wall Street Journal*, p. B4.

Handwritten margin notes: Money / location / Skills + Abilities / can I advance

truthful about themselves when they are searching for a job.[20] And with the use of resume databases constantly increasing as an initial screening tool,[21] the temptation to embellish one's own qualifications might be difficult to ignore. But job seekers need to understand that in the long run little can be gained from such practices, especially since falsification of an application is typically grounds for dismissal.

Successful job seekers also prepare carefully for job interviews. They do their "homework" and learn as much about the company as possible. In addition, they use "impression management" tactics to their advantage.[22] Although it is not a good idea to present an unrealistic picture of one's qualifications, interviewers are strongly influenced by an applicant's interpersonal and communication styles during the interview. In fact, characteristics such as these are primary determinants of recruiters' firm-specific judgments about an applicant's suitability.[23]

Methods of Recruiting

Once an organization has decided it needs additional or replacement employees, it is faced with the decision of how to generate the necessary applications. The organization can look to sources internal to the company and, if necessary, to sources external to the company. Most organizations have to use both internal and external sources to generate a sufficient number of applicants. Whenever there is an inadequate supply of labor and skills inside the organization, it must effectively "get its message across" to external candidates. It is here that the organization's choice of a particular method of recruitment can make all the difference in the success of the recruiting efforts.

Internal Recruiting

Job Posting

Organizations can make effective use of skills inventories for identifying internal applicants for job vacancies. It is difficult, however, for HR managers to be aware of all current employees who might be interested in the vacancy. To help with this problem, they use an approach called job posting and bidding.

In the past, job posting was little more than the use of bulletin boards and company publications for advertising job openings. Today, however, job posting has become one of the more innovative recruiting techniques being used by organizations. Many companies now see job posting as an integrated component of an effective career management system.

A model job posting program was implemented at National Semiconductor. Postings are computerized and easily accessible to employees via the company's intranet. Computer software allows the employees to match an available job with their skills and experience. It then highlights where gaps exist so the employees know what is necessary if they wish to be competitive for a given job.[24] Amoco's career management system includes a similar type of job posting program. Openings in this organization are posted on a worldwide electronic system. If an employee applies for a transfer to a posted position and is turned down, then the person who posted the job is required to send the "applicant" specific feedback about why he or she was not selected.[25]

Inside Moonlighting and Employees' Friends

If there is a short-term shortage, or if no great amount of additional work is necessary, the organization can use inside moonlighting. It could offer to pay bonuses of various types to people not on a time payroll to entice workers into wanting to take on a "second" job. Nationally, it is estimated that approximately 6 percent of all employed people have held more than one job at the same time.[26] Moonlighting is so common at some organizations that HR departments consider issuing "moonlighting policies" that include the communication of performance expectations, prevention of conflict of interest, and protection of proprietary information.[27] Thus, some persons will clearly be motivated to accept the additional work if they are fairly compensated.

Before going outside to recruit, many organizations ask present employees to encourage friends or relatives to apply. Some organizations even offer "finders fees" in the form of monetary incentives for a successful referral. When used wisely, referrals of this kind can be a powerful recruiting technique. Organizations must be careful, however, not to accidentally violate equal employment laws while they are using employee referrals. For example, in *EEOC* v. *Detroit Edison* (1975),[28] the U.S. Court of Appeals, Sixth Circuit, found a history of racial discrimination that was related to recruitment. The court stated:

> The practice of relying on referrals by a predominantly white workforce rather than seeking new employees in the marketplace for jobs was found to be discriminating.

This case suggests that employee referrals should be used cautiously, especially if the workforce is already racially or culturally imbalanced. It also suggests that it might not be wise to rely exclusively on referrals but rather to use them as supplements to other kinds of recruiting activities.

External Recruiting

When an organization has exhausted its internal supply of applicants, it must turn to external sources to supplement its workforce. Research indicates that walk-ins provide an important external source of applicants. As labor shortages increase, however, organizations are becoming more proactive in their recruitment efforts.

A number of methods are available for external recruiting. Media advertising, e-recruiting, employment agencies, executive search firms, special-events recruiting, and summer internships are discussed here. There is also a separate section on college recruitment of potential managers and professionals.

Media Advertisements

HRMEMO

Several new job Web sites have been created to help stay-at-home mothers who want to return to the workforce: jobsandmoms.com, jobsformoms.com, womenforhire.com, womenatworknetwork. com, and en-parent.com.

Source: Hilary Stout and Anne Marie Chaker (May 6, 2004), "Mom for Hire: Industry Springs Up around Mothers Returning to Work," *The Wall Street Journal,* p. D1.

Organizations advertise to acquire recruits. Various media are used, the most common being help-wanted ads in daily newspapers. Organizations also advertise for people in trade and professional publications. Other media used are billboards, subway and bus cards, radio, telephone, and television. Some job seekers do a reverse twist; they advertise for a situation wanted and reward anyone who tips them off about a job.

In developing a recruitment advertisement, a good place to begin is with the corporate image. General Mills used its Trix cereal logo to create instant recognition among MBA graduates. The ad featured the Trix rabbit with the headline, "It's Not Kid Stuff Anymore." The copy continued, "Now you're an MBA who's looking for a dynamic growth-directed career environment . . . Look to General Mills. Because it's not kid stuff anymore. It's your future."[29]

Simply using a corporate logo is not enough, however. Effective recruiting advertising is consistent with the overall corporate image; that is, the advertisement is seen as an extension of the company. Therefore, it must be representative of the values that the corporation is seeking in its employees. Booz-Allen Hamilton's advertising campaign has successfully achieved this congruence by conveying in its ads the importance of employee work-life balance: "We believe business should always have a human side."[30]

An innovative way to attract nurses was used in an ad campaign for Children's Hospital Medical Center in Cincinnati. The ad appealed to nurses' sense of pride in themselves and their profession. The ad ran in the *Cincinnati Enquirer* newspaper. The headlines— "Nurses are smart and they know how to make you feel better," "Nurses are there to make sure you don't get real scared," "Nurses are kind and they don't laugh when you cry"— were written in a child's handwriting and combined with pictures of nurses and children in the style of a child's drawing.

EXHIBIT 7-2
A Questionable Want Ad

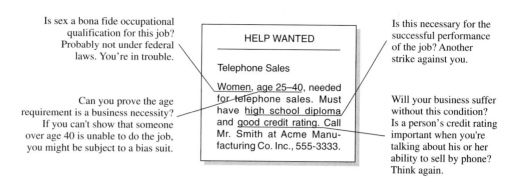

Is sex a bona fide occupational qualification for this job? Probably not under federal laws. You're in trouble.

Can you prove the age requirement is a business necessity? If you can't show that someone over age 40 is unable to do the job, you might be subject to a bias suit.

Is this necessary for the successful performance of the job? Another strike against you.

Will your business suffer without this condition? Is a person's credit rating important when you're talking about his or her ability to sell by phone? Think again.

Another innovative way to attract prospective employees with particular skills is the use of recorded want ads. Want ad recordings were used by 40 companies recruiting engineers and scientists at a New York City convention. At a special recruiting center, job hunters were able to pick up a telephone and hear a three-minute taped recruiting message that included a job description and details about how to contact the company.

Help-wanted ads must be carefully prepared. Media must be chosen, coded for study, and analyzed for impact afterward. If the organization's name is not used and a box number is substituted, the impact may not be as great, but if the name is used, too many applicants may appear, and screening procedures for too many people can be costly. This is a difficult decision to make in preparing recruitment advertisements.

In addition, ads need to comply with EEO requirements and not violate the law. For example, HR recruiters find that including diversity in recruitment ads helps to attract more employees from diverse populations.[31] Ads need to be written to avoid indicating preferences for a particular race, religion, or gender or a particular place of national origin. The advertisement shown in Exhibit 7-2 is the type that will create trouble for a firm. Look at the questions that could be raised by this ad.

E-Recruiting

Perhaps no method has ever had as revolutionary an effect on organizational recruitment practices as the Internet.[32] According to Forrester Research of Cambridge, Massachusetts, there are approximately 30,000 different Web sites devoted in some manner to job posting activities;[33] and approximately 71 percent of all job listings occur on just a handful of the "big boards" such as Monster (monster.com), CareerBuilder (careerbuilder.com), HotJobs (hotjobs.com), and America's Job Bank (jobsearch.org). Some of these large job-placement Web sites have reported huge increases in the number of resumes posted and visitors received in the first month of 2005. For example, Monster.com received 3.3 million new and updated resumes while CareerBuilders.com reported 21 million visitors to its Web site.[34]

Overall, the e-recruiting market in the United States is expected to grow from just $500 million in 2000 to over $5.0 billion in 2008.[35] Quite obviously, the Internet has become one of the most prominent of all worldwide recruiting methods. It has become such an important source of job search information that GTE Corporation (Verizon) now receives between 20,000 and 30,000 e-mail resumes each year.[36] Current estimates are that over 95 percent of all U.S. companies now utilize the Internet for some or all of their recruitment-related activities.[37]

There are many reasons for the popularity of the Internet as a method of recruitment. From the organization's perspective, it is a relatively inexpensive way to attract qualified applicants. For example, using an executive search firm might cost an organization as much as one-third of a position's first-year salary as a commission. A large, multicolored advertisement in a professional journal can easily cost $10,000 or more. Compare these figures with the cost of using the "post a job express" option at **Monster.com** (http://www.monster.com) in which a job is posted for 60 days in a single geographic location at a cost of about $300. This e-recruiting option provides almost immediate access to thousands of prospective applicants.

From the job seeker's perspective, the Internet allows for searches over a broader array of geographic and company postings than was ever before possible. To assist them, job searchers can use any number of the following Internet-based job searching Web sites (for more information, see http://jobsearch.about.com/):

- *www.HotJobs.com* Search by career field, location, and company.
- *www.CareerBuilder.com* Search by location, job title, keyword, and salary.
- *www.Dice.com* Leading technology job board with permanent and contract jobs.
- *www.FlipDog.com* Search thousands of employment opportunities gathered directly from organizations' Web sites.
- *www.Jobs.com* Search for jobs, post your resume, and review career resources.
- *www.NationJob.com* Job listings will be identified and sent to personal e-mail addresses.
- *www.jobcentral.com* Search job listings by keyword, state, metro area linked directly to the Web sites of large employers.

There are other online services, such as **CareerPath.com** (http://www.career-path.com), which catalogs more than 100,000 traditional newspaper recruiting ads from large newspapers across the United States in one easily searchable database. Finally, there are many other, more specialized online sites that focus on jobs in particular areas such as health care, higher education, and federal employment.[38]

Organizations are also beginning to see that having their own human resources Web page on the Internet can be an effective addition to their overall recruitment strategy. A typical organizational home page will provide background information about the company, its products and services, and employment opportunities and application procedures. Many also include online resume templates that can be completed and sent via the Internet.[39]

As such job search Web sites proliferate on the Web, recruiters need to be aware of some of the legal risks of using e-recruiting at their companies. The HR Journal reviews four of the potential risks that need to be considered.

Employment Agencies and Executive Search Firms

Although similar in purpose, employment agencies and executive search firms differ in many important ways. Executive search firms tend to concentrate their efforts on higher-level managerial positions with salaries in excess of $50,000, while agencies deal primarily with middle-level management or below. Most executive search firms are on retainer, which means that the organization pays them a fee whether or not their efforts are successful. In contrast, agencies are usually paid only when they have actually provided a new hire. Finally, executive search firms usually charge higher fees for their services. One of the reasons that organizations are willing to pay these higher fees is that executive search firms frequently engage in their recruiting efforts while maintaining the confidentiality of both the recruiting organization and the person being recruited.[40]

Special-Events Recruiting

When the supply of employees available is not large or when the organization is new or not well known, some organizations have successfully used special events to attract potential employees. They may stage open houses, schedule visits to headquarters, provide literature, and advertise these events in appropriate media. To attract professionals, organizations may

HR Journal   *Job Seekers Can Use E-Resources to Land That Great Job!*

The large job search Web sites like Monster and Careerbuilder offer job seekers a wide variety of useful and free online resources that can help with all aspects of their careers, from preparing for interviews to learning how to negotiate for higher starting salaries. Here are some of the resources available on Monster's Career Advice Web page:

1. *Interview Center* Job seekers can complete virtual interviews that ask random questions; also, they can receive expert advice and learn several tips about etiquette. For example, job seekers can take the "virtual campus interview" where they answer questions online (and get immediate feedback) that are typically asked during on-campus interviews.

2. *Job Profiles* From accountant to CIA agent, job seekers can get the scoop on 120 real-world professions by reading realistic job descriptions.

3. *Resume Center* Learn how to write a persuasive, targeted resume and cover letter.

4. *Salary Center* Job seekers can key in a job category (e.g., bank teller) that they're interested in and the zip code where they live; the salary calculator produces real salary information of the job category in that zip code area.

5. *Self-Assessment Center* These tests and quizzes can help job seekers improve their interview skills and learn more about which careers fit with their personalities.

Similarly, the Careerbuilder Web site offers advice about resume writing and interviewing, but this Web site also includes information on starting your own business, working from home, training opportunities, and continuing education. Most of these online services are free and available to job seekers who have an Internet connection.

Sources: David Brown (April 5, 2004), "Unwanted Online Jobseekers Swamp HR Staff," *Canadian HR Reporter*, Vol. 17, Iss. 7, pp. 1–3; http://content.monster.com/basics/; and http://www.careerbuilder.com (click on "Advice and Resources").

have hospitality suites at professional meetings. Executives also make speeches at association meetings or schools to get the organization's image across. Ford Motor Company has conducted symposia on college campuses and sponsored cultural events to attract attention to its qualifications as a good employer.

One of the most interesting approaches is to provide job fairs. A group of firms sponsors a meeting or exhibition at which each has a booth to publicize jobs available. Though sometimes challenging to manage in times of higher unemployment,[41] some experts claim recruiting costs have been reduced by 80 percent using these methods. They may be scheduled on holidays to reach college students who are home at that time or to give people who are already employed a chance to look around. This technique is especially useful for smaller, less well-known employers. It appeals to job seekers who wish to locate in a particular area and those wanting to minimize travel and interview time. For example, a recent job fair held in Denver was able to generate 8,300 job candidates in one day.[42] And, yes, there is an Internet site to help the recruit. The Web site www.jobweb.com/search/cfairs provides current listings of when and where job fairs will be held in the United States.

Summer Internships

Another approach to recruiting and getting specialized work done that has been tried by organizations is to hire students as interns during the summer or part time during the school year. The list of organizations using internships is extensive; it includes AT&T, General Motors, most major accounting firms, the life insurance industry, and so forth. The use of internships is, in fact, dramatically increasing. Some estimates suggest that nearly one out of every three students at four-year universities will have one or more internship experiences before graduation.[43] Internship programs have a number of purposes. They allow organizations to get specific projects done, expose themselves to talented potential employees who may become their "recruiters" at school, and provide trial-run employment to determine if they want to hire particular people full time.[44]

The realities of the job market of the 1990s have also introduced two new reasons for internship programs. First, many organizations now see them as a way to attract the best people in areas where there are labor shortages. To do so, companies such as Accenture and BAT Industries (a tobacco firm) actually begin identifying talented students in their senior year in high school, help them with college expenses, and provide paid work experiences. Their hope is to develop a lasting relationship with these talented young people.[45]

A second new reason that organizations are using more internships is to improve the diversity of their recruitment efforts. Many companies claim that they want to be more aggressive in recruiting minorities but say that the competition for talented people is severe. To help, Inroads Inc. of Saint Louis locates and places high-performing minority students in internship programs. Inroads has working relationships with organizations in 33 different states. Its major supporters include NationsBank, GE Capital Services, and AT&T.[46]

From the student's point of view, the summer internship means a job with pay; NCR, for example, provides students with approximately 600 paid internships each year.[47] An internship can also mean real work experience for the student, a possible future job, a chance to use one's talents in a realistic environment, and in some cases earning course credit hours. In a way, it is a short form of some co-op college work and study programs.

There are costs to these programs, of course. Sometimes the interns take up a lot of supervisory time, and their work is not always the best. But the major problem some organizations have encountered concerns the expectations of students. Some students expect everything to be perfect at work. When it is not, they get negative impressions about the organization they have worked for, assuming that it is less well organized than others in the field. Such disillusioned students become reverse recruiters.

College Recruiting

There is a growing gap between the skills that organizations will need over the next several years and those currently possessed by potential employees. College recruiting can be extremely difficult, time-consuming, and expensive for the organization. Nonetheless, recruiters generally believe that college recruiting is one of the most effective ways of identifying talented employees.[48] All this suggests that college recruiting will continue to play an important role in organizations' overall recruitment strategies, but that organizations will be careful about controlling expenses.

The college recruiting process is similar in some ways to other recruiting. However, in college recruiting, the organization sends an employee, usually called a *recruiter,* to a campus to interview candidates and describe the organization to them. Coinciding with the visit, brochures and other literature about the organization are often distributed. The organization may also run ads to attract students or may conduct seminars at which company executives talk about various facets of the organization.

In the typical procedure, those seeking employment register at the college placement service. This placement service is a labor market exchange providing opportunities for students and employers to meet and discuss potential hiring. During the recruiting season (from about mid-October to mid-March), candidates are advised of scheduled visits through student newspapers, mailings, bulletin boards, and so forth. At the placement service, they reserve preliminary interviews with employers they want to see and are given brochures and other literature about the firms. After the preliminary interviews and before leaving the campus, the recruiter invites the chosen candidates to make a site visit at a later date. Those lower on the list are told they are being considered and are called upon if students chosen first decide not to accept employment with the firm.

Students who are invited to the site are given more job information and meet appropriate potential supervisors and other executives. They are entertained and may be given a series of tests as well. The organization bears all expenses. If the organization wants to hire an individual, he or she is given an offer before leaving the site or shortly thereafter by mail or phone.[49] Some bargaining may take place on salary and benefits, depending on the current labor market. The candidate then decides whether to accept or reject the offer.

As with other forms of recruiting, organizations are becoming more creative in their use of colleges and universities. Many of the changes are designed to reduce overall recruiting costs while maintaining a strong flow of applicants into the organization. The trend seems to be for an organization to develop a stronger, ongoing relationship with a relatively select number of schools. For example, Monsanto recently cut the size of its university recruiting list by 50 percent, and it may reduce the size of that list even further—down to as few as 10 or 12 schools—for its recruiting activities in engineering. This reduction is, in part, made possible by Monsanto's increased activity in internship programs.[50]

The Effective College Recruiter

Various people influence the applicant during the process of choosing a job: peers, family, spouse, friends, and professors. One of the most important influences remains, however, the recruiter. The recruiter is the filter and the matcher, the one who is actually seen by the applicants and is viewed as an extension of the organization. The recruiter is seen a primary example of the kind of person the organization values and wants to attract in the future.

For these reasons, recruiters must be carefully chosen by the organization. Good recruiters convey an image and appearance that reflect favorably on the organization. They must be outgoing, self-motivated, and obviously good salespeople. In addition, however, good recruiters also possess well-developed interpersonal skills because part of their responsibility should be to determine why job offers are accepted or rejected by candidates. Finally, recruiters should be very familiar with the company they represent, for at least two reasons. First, applicants want to discuss opportunities with someone they perceive to be knowledgeable about the company. Second, the recruiters need to be able to determine whether the applicant will fit into the value system of the organization.

Students prefer recruiters who have work experience in their specialties and have some personal knowledge of the university they are visiting. Students also have preferences for specific behavior during the recruiting interview. Characteristics they want most in the recruiter are friendliness, knowledge, personal interest in the applicant, and truthfulness. Some applicants prefer enthusiastic and knowledgeable communicators.[51]

Major flaws students have found in typical recruiters include the following:

Lack of interest in the applicant Students infer indifference if the recruiter's presentation is mechanical, bureaucratic, and programmed. One student reported, "The company might just as well have sent a tape recorder."

Lack of enthusiasm If the recruiter seems bored, students infer that he or she represents a dull and uninteresting company.

Interviews that are stressful or too personal Students resent too many personal questions about their social class, their parents, and so forth. They want to be evaluated for their own accomplishments. They, like most people, also unanimously reject stressful or sarcastic interviewing styles.

Time allocation by recruiters The final criticism of recruiters has to do with how much time they talk and how much they let applicants talk or ask questions. From the point of view of the applicant, much of the recruiter's time is wasted if it includes a long, canned history of the company, number of employees, branches, products, assets, pension plans, and so forth. Many of the questions the recruiter asks applicants are answered on the application blank anyway.

Good recruiters are not going to guarantee success in filling positions, however. Although they can and do make a difference, applicants' decisions are affected more by characteristics of the job and the organization than they are by particular characteristics of recruiters. Other research also suggests that recruiters may have very little positive influence on an applicant's choice. Recruiters do make a difference when they do not present themselves well. In this case, they can have a negative effect on applicants even when the job and the organization are both appealing.[52]

Realistic Job Previews

It is important for recruiters to provide realistic expectations about the job. When they do so, there is significantly lower turnover of new employees, and the same number of people apply. Researchers have found that most recruiters give general, glowing descriptions of the company rather than a balanced or truthful presentation.

Research suggests that recruitment can be made more effective through the use of **realistic job previews (RJPs)**.[53] A realistic job preview provides the prospective employee with pertinent information about the job without distortion or exaggeration. In traditional job previews, the job is presented as attractive, interesting, and stimulating. Some jobs are all of these things. However, most jobs have some unattractive features.[54] The RJP presents the full picture, warts and all, as suggested in Exhibit 7-3.

Exhibit 7-3 presents the typical consequences of traditional previews versus realistic previews. In practice, realistic job previews can be used in a variety of ways. For example, some pharmaceutical companies like Pfizer have been known to encourage job candidates to accompany (or "shadow") one of the firm's sales representatives to experience firsthand what the job is like. Although typically reserved for the final two or three candidates for the sales position, this provides candidates with a realistic picture of what a pharmaceutical sales representative does each day: whether it's calling on doctors, restocking samples, completing company paperwork, digging for competitive information, and the like. In other companies, a realistic job preview may only consist of the interviewer discussing the positive and negative aspects of the job in question. Studies conducted at Southern New England Telephone, Prudential Insurance Co., Texas Instruments, and the U.S. Military Academy have used and reported on the RJP.[55] The results indicated that:

Newly hired employees who received RJPs have a higher rate of job survival than those hired using traditional previews.

EXHIBIT 7-3

Typical Consequences of Job Preview Procedures

Source: Adapted from John P. Wanous (1992), *Organizational Entry: Recruitment, Orientation, and Socialization of Newcomers* (Boston: Addison-Wesley), pp. 53–86; John P. Wanous (July–August 1975), "Tell It Like It Is at Realistic Job Preview," *Personnel*, p. 54.

TRADITIONAL PREVIEW	REALISTIC PREVIEW
Sets initial job expectations too high.	Sets job expectations realistically.
↓	↓
Job is typically viewed as attractive, stimulating, and challenging.	Job may or may not be attractive, depending on individual's needs.
↓	↓
High rate of acceptance of job offers.	Some accept, some reject job offer.
↓	↓
Work experience disconfirms expectations.	Work experience confirms expectations.
↓	↓
Dissatisfaction and realization that job is not matched to needs.	Satisfaction; needs matched to job.
↓	↓
Low job survival, dissatisfaction, frequent thoughts of quitting.	High job survival, satisfaction, infrequent thoughts of quitting.

Employees hired after RJPs indicate higher satisfaction.

RJPs can set the job expectations of new employees at realistic levels.

RJPs do not reduce the flow of highly capable applicants.

These findings suggest that RJPs can be used as an inoculation against disappointment with the realities of a job. At this stage of development, however, there is no conclusive evidence supporting the effectiveness of realistic job previews.[56] Although it seems clear that RJPs can have beneficial effects, at present there is still uncertainty as to why RJPs have the effects they do and in what contexts they are likely to be the most effective.

Alternatives to Recruitment

An organization's human resource plan may suggest that additional or replacement employees are needed. However, because of the cost and permanence of recruiting individuals, an alternative to recruitment may be used.

Overtime

When a firm faces pressures to meet a production goal, it may mean that employees need to work overtime. By having employees work overtime, organizations avoid the costs of recruiting and having additional employees. Overtime can also provide employees with additional income. However, there are potential problems: fatigue, increased accidents, and increased absenteeism.

On a limited, short-term basis, having some employees work overtime may be an alternative to recruitment. Continuous overtime, though, has often resulted in higher labor costs and reduced productivity.

Outsourcing

Outsourcing, sometimes called "staff sourcing," involves paying a fee to a leasing company or professional employer organization (PEO) that handles payroll, employee benefits, and routine human resource management functions for the client company.[57] Leasing is especially attractive to small and midsize firms that might not otherwise be able to afford a full-service human resources department. But while small businesses can expect to save from 15 to 30 percent of benefit costs such as health insurance premiums by using leased employees, care must be exercised in choosing a leasing company. In recent years, at least six leasing companies have gone bankrupt, leaving approximately 36,000 workers and hundreds of small businesses liable for millions of dollars associated with health care and other workers' compensation claims.[58]

Temporary Employment

One of the most noticeable effects of the downsizing epidemic and the labor shortages of the past two decades has been a dramatic rise in the use of temporary employees. Historically, temporary employment agencies were seen only as sources of semiskilled clerical help during peak work periods. Today, "just-in-time" employees can be found staffing all types of jobs in organizations, including professional, technical, and higher executive positions.[59] There are, in fact, nearly 7,000 temporary employment agencies across the United States that have been in business for more than one year.[60]

The major advantages of temporary employees include relatively low labor costs, an easily accessible source of experienced labor, and flexibility in responding to future changes in the demand for workers.[61] The cost advantage of using temporary help stems from the fact that the organization does not have to provide fringe benefits, training, or a compensation and career plan. The temporary worker can move in and out of the firm when the workload requires such movement. A disadvantage of hiring temporary help is

Clark Kirby got prices of ads from all the Tampa papers, including suburban and ethnic papers. He also discussed the impact and readership of the papers with the human resource managers he'd befriended. On this basis, he chose the major Tampa afternoon paper, the leading black newspaper, the leading Hispanic paper, and a suburban paper in an area near the plant.

He also investigated the leading radio stations and selected the one that had the highest rating of the top three and the lowest commercial cost. He chose commuter times to run the radio ads. The advertising approach was innovative.

The pay and working conditions offered at the Tampa plant were competitive. After Clark's recruiting campaign, he had the following numbers of applicants:

Managerial positions	68
Professional-technical	10
Clerical	78
Skilled employees	110
Semiskilled employees	720

Clark notified Ed of the results. The job was now to select the best applicants. Clark knew that would be no easy job.

Effective selection and hiring are the subjects of Chapter 8.

that these individuals do not know the culture or work flow of the firm. This unfamiliarity detracts from their commitment to organizational and departmental goals.

Cost-Benefit Analysis of Recruiting

Many aspects of recruitment, such as the effectiveness of recruiters, can be evaluated. Organizations assign goals to recruiting by types of employees. For example, a goal for a recruiter might be to hire 350 unskilled and semiskilled employees, or 100 technicians, or 100 machinists, or 100 managerial employees per year. Then the organization can decide who are the best recruiters. They may be those who meet or exceed quotas and those whose recruits stay with the organization and are evaluated well by their superiors.

Sources of recruits can also be evaluated. In college recruiting, the organization can divide the number of job acceptances by the number of campus interviews to compute the cost per hire at each college. Then it drops from the list those campuses that are not productive.

The methods of recruiting that are used by a company can be evaluated along various dimensions. In addition, the organization can calculate the cost of each method (such as advertising) and divide it by the benefits it yields (acceptances of offers). The organization can also examine how much accurate job information was provided during the recruitment process.

Another aspect of recruiting that can be evaluated is what is referred to as the *quality of hire*. This measure can provide management with an assessment of the quality of new employees being recruited and hired.[62] The quality-of-hire measure is calculated as follows:

$$QH = (PR + HP + HR)/N$$

where

QH = quality of recruits hired

PR = average job performance ratings (20 items on scale) of new hirees
(e.g., 4 on a 5-point scale or 20 items $\times$ 4)

HP = percent of new hires promoted within one year (such as 35 percent)

HR = percent of hires retained after one year (e.g., 85 percent)

N = number of indicators used

Therefore,

$$QH = (80 + 35 + 85)/3$$
$$= 200/3$$
$$= 66.6\%$$

The 66 percent quality-of-hire rate is a relative value. It will be up to management to determine whether this represents an excellent, good, fair, or poor level.

Some caution must be exercised with the quality-of-hire measure when evaluating the recruitment strategy. Performance ratings and promotion rates are all beyond the control of a recruiter. A good new employee can be driven away by a lack of opportunities for promotion, inequitable performance ratings, or job market conditions that have nothing to do with the effectiveness of the recruiter. Nevertheless, the quality-of-hire measure can provide some insight into the recruiter's ability to attract employees.

Summary

This chapter has demonstrated the process whereby organizations recruit additional employees; suggested the importance of recruiting; and shown who recruits, where, and how.

To summarize the major points covered in this chapter:

1. Recruiting is the set of activities an organization uses to attract job candidates who have the abilities and attitudes needed to help the organization achieve its objectives.

2. External factors that affect the recruiting process include influences such as government and union restrictions, the state of the labor market, the composition of the labor force, and the location of the organization. The passage of the Immigration Reform and Control Act of 1986 has placed a major responsibility on employers to stop the flow of illegal immigration to the United States.

3. Three factors affect recruiting from the organization's viewpoint: recruiting requirements, organizational policies and procedures, and the organization's image.

4. Applicants' abilities, attitudes, and preferences—based on past work experiences and influences by parents, teachers, and others—affect them in two ways: how they set job preferences, and how they go about seeking a job.

5. In larger organizations, the HR department does the recruiting; in smaller organizations, multipurpose HR people or operating managers recruit and interview applicants.

6. Two sources of recruits could be used to fill needs for additional employees: present employees (internal) or those not presently affiliated with the organization (external).
   a. Internal sources can be tapped through the use of job posting and bidding; moonlighting by present employees; and seeking recommendations from present employees regarding friends who might fill vacancies.
   b. External sources include walk-ins, referrals from schools, and state employment offices.

7. Alternatives to recruiting personnel when work must be completed include overtime, temporary employees, and employee leasing.

8. Advertising, personal recruiting, computerized matching services, special-event recruiting, and summer internships are among the methods that can be used to recruit external applicants.

9. The criteria that characterize a successful college recruiter include
   a. Showing a genuine interest in the applicant.
   b. Being enthusiastic.
   c. Employing a style that is neither too personal nor too stressful.
   d. Allotting enough time for applicants' comments and questions.

10. A better job of recruiting and matching employees to jobs will mean lower employee turnover and greater employee satisfaction and organizational effectiveness.

11. The Internet is revolutionizing organizational recruitment and may become the primary job search tool in the coming years.

Key Terms

CareerPath.com, *p. 196*
e-recruiting, *p. 194*
employment
agencies, *p. 196*
executive search
firms, *p. 196*

Immigration Reform and
Control Act (IRCA)
of 1986, *p. 188*
job posting, *p. 193*
job search, *p. 192*
Monster.com, *p. 196*

online recruiting, *p. 189*
outsourcing, *p. 201*
realistic job previews
(RJPs), *p. 200*
recruitment, *p. 187*

Questions for Review and Discussion

1. What guidelines should be followed to make sure that recruitment advertising does not violate equal employment laws?

2. How can an organization's image help its recruiting efforts? In what ways can it hurt those efforts?

3. What role do job descriptions and job specifications play in an effective recruitment program?

4. Considering that there are millions of resumes posted on the Web, what steps should recruiters follow to screen out unqualified candidates in a fair and nondiscriminatory manner? Explain your answer.

5. What has led to an increased use of temporary employees in organizations? What are the major advantages of using temporary employees?

6. Discuss how such Web sites as Monster.com, Hotjobs.com, and Careerbuilder.com have changed how companies recruit potential job applicants and how individual applicants look for jobs.

7. What are the advantages and disadvantages of recruiters providing a realistic job preview to job applicants? What are some instances when realistic job previews should not be used?

8. Visit three different job search Web sites. Search for a job in a particular region of the United States. Which of the three Web sites is most useful to job seekers? Explain your answer.

9. What are the characteristics of an effective and an ineffective college recruiter?

10. What are the relative strengths and weaknesses of promotion from within as a recruitment technique?

HRM Legal Advisor

Based on *U.S.* v. *The City of Warren, Michigan,* 138 F.3d 1083 (U.S. App. Sixth Cir. 1998).

The Facts

The city of Warren, Michigan, is located in Macomb County, adjacent to Detroit. Census reports in 1980 indicated that Warren's labor force was comprised of 0.2 percent African Americans. The African American labor force in the remainder of Macomb County was 1.3 percent, while Detroit's labor force was 59.7 percent African American. In recruiting employees, Warren placed advertisements in three newspapers that were circulated primarily in Macomb County and placed job postings in municipal buildings. Warren did not advertise municipal jobs in Detroit newspapers. Additionally, Warren required applicants for all jobs except police and firefighters to be residents of Warren. As a result, the city's municipal workforce was approximately 1 percent African American. In February of 1986, the U.S. Department of Justice notified the City of Warren that it planned to initiate an investigation of Warren's recruiting practices, alleging that they potentially discriminated against African

Americans on the basis of race. After its investigation indicating that Warren's residency requirement and recruiting media had an adverse impact against African Americans, the United States filed a suit in district court alleging race discrimination under Title VII of the 1964 Civil Rights Act. The City of Warren argued that disparate impact analysis was not applicable to recruiting practices.

The Court's Decision

The U.S. Court of Appeals for the Sixth Circuit ruled that the disparate impact theory of discrimination was applicable to any "facially neutral policy with a discriminatory effect to Title VII." Further, the court held that "Warren's limitation of its applicant pool to the residents of the overwhelmingly white city, combined with its refusal to publicize jobs outside the racially homogeneous county, produced a de facto barrier between employment opportunities and members of a protected class."

Human Resource Implications

A basic assumption of this case is that the City of Warren should have been recruiting employees from the greater Detroit area. The U.S. Supreme Court has indicated that a company's proper geographic recruiting area should include locations from which applicants or employees are likely to commute. Companies should consider general commuting patterns as well as public transportation availability in determining where to recruit employees. Employers may avoid discrimination problems related to recruiting by ensuring that its internal and external recruiting tools are unbiased and sufficiently reach the company's qualified labor market.

Notes

1. James A. Breaugh (1992), *Recruitment: Science and Practice* (Boston: Kent), p. 4.
2. Steve Tarter (June 7, 2005), "Skilled Labor Shortage Looms," *Knight Ridder Tribune Business News*, p. 1; Aaron Bernstein (May 2002), "Too Many Workers? Not for Long," *BusinessWeek*, pp. 126–130.
3. Diane Arthur (2001), *The Employee Recruitment and Retention Handbook* (New York: American Management Association), p. 3; Glenn McEvoy and Mary Jo Blahna (September–October 2001), "Engagement or Disengagement? Older Workers and the Looming Labor Shortage," *Business Horizons*, pp. 46–52.
4. Dean Foust (December 2001), "A Smarter Squeeze," *BusinessWeek*, pp. 42–44.
5. Roger E. Herman (2004), "Strategic Planning for the Impending Labor Shortage," *Employment Relations Today*, Vol. 31, Iss. 1, pp. 19–25; Peter Francese (November 2001), "Looming Labor Shortages," *American Demographics*, pp. 34–35; Shari Caudron (September 1999), "The Looming Leadership Crisis," *Workforce*, pp. 72–79.
6. Sherrie A. Kossoudji and Deborah A. Cobb-Clark (2002), "Coming Out of the Shadows: Learning about Legal Status and Wages from the Legalized Population," *Journal of Labor Economics*, Vol. 20, Iss. 3, pp. 598–629; Gillian Flynn (September 1995), "The Immigration Reform and Control Act Demands a Closer Look," *Personnel Journal*, pp. 151, 153; Wayne E. Barlow, Diane D. Hatch, and Betty Southard Murphy (April 1996), "Recent Legal Decisions Affect You," *Personnel Journal*, p. 142.
7. Orlando C. Richard, Tim Barnett, Sean Dwyer, & Ken Chadwick (2004), "Cultural Diversity in Management, Firm Performance, and the Moderating Role of Entrepreneurial Orientation Dimensions," *Academy of Management Journal*, Vol. 47, Iss. 2, pp. 255–67; John Ivancevich and Jacqueline Gilbert (Spring 2000), "Diversity Management: Time for a New Approach," *Public Personnel Management*, pp. 75–92; Jacqueline A. Gilbert, Bette Ann Stead, and John M. Ivancevich (August 1999), "Diversity Management: A New Organizational Paradigm," *Journal of Business Ethics*, pp. 61–76.
8. Louisa Wah (July–August 1999), "Diversity at Allstate: A Competitive Weapon," *Management Review*, pp. 24–30.

9. J. Scott Lord (1989), "External and Internal Recruitment," in Wayne F. Cascio (ed.), *Human Resource Planning, Employment, & Placement* (Washington, DC: Bureau of National Affairs), pp. 73–102.

10. Anita Varghese (November 19, 2003), "It's How You Are Seen That Counts," *Businessline,* p. 1; Alexandra Harkavy (July–August 2000), "Do I Really Want to Work for This Company?" *Across the Board,* pp. 14–19; Robert D. Gatewood, Mary A. Gowan, and Gary J. Lautenschlager (April 1993), "Corporate Image, Recruitment Image, and Initial Job Choice Decisions," *Academy of Management Journal,* pp. 414–427.

11. Jerry Useem (March 7, 2005), "America's Most Admired Companies," *Fortune,* Vol. 151, Iss. 5, pp. 67–70.

12. Joanne Cleaver (May 2003), "Lust for Lists," *Workforce,* Vol. 82, Iss. 5, pp. 44–48; Gillian Flynn (August 1995), "Pop Quiz: How Do You Recruit the Best College Grads?" *Personnel Journal,* pp. 12–18.

13. Chad Fleetwood and Kristina Shelley (Fall 2000), "The Outlook for College Graduates, 1998–2008: A Balancing Act," *Occupational Outlook Quarterly,* pp. 2–9.

14. Matthew Mariani (Spring 1996), "Students Offer Views on Career Choices," *Occupational Outlook Quarterly,* p. 44.

15. Edward D. Bewayo (May 1990), "What College Recruits Expect of Employers," *Personnel,* pp. 30–34.

16. Susan Strauss, Jeffrey Miles, and Laurie Levesque (2001), "The Effects of Videoconference, Telephone, and Face-to-Face Media on Interviewer and Applicant Judgments in Employment Interviews," *Journal of Management,* pp. 363–381; Steven M. Ralston and Robert Brady (January 1994), "The Relative Influence of Interview Communication Satisfaction on Applicants' Recruitment Interview Decisions," *Journal of Business Communication,* pp. 61–77.

17. Lisa Munniksma (2005), "Career Matchmakers," *HRMagazine,* Vol. 50, Iss. 2, pp. 93–97; David Bowman and R. Kweskin (1990), *Q: How Do I Find the Right Job* (New York: Wiley).

18. Anne Fisher (June 28, 2004), "How to Ruin an Online Job Hunt," *Fortune,* Vol. 149, Iss. 13, p. 43; Hubert Field and William Holley (March 1976), "Resume Preparation: An Empirical Study of Personnel Managers' Perceptions," *Vocational Guidance Journal,* pp. 229–237.

19. Joey George and Kent Marett (2004), "The Truth about Lies," *HRMagazine,* Vol. 49, Iss. 5, pp. 87–92; Jeffrey Kluger (June 2002), "Pumping Up Your Past," *Time,* pp. 45–47.

20. Elaine McShulskis (August 1997), "Beware College Grads Willing to Lie for a Job," *HRMagazine,* pp. 22–24.

21. Tischelle George (August 12, 2002), "Monster Offers More Options," *InformationWeek,* Iss. 901, p. 51; Bill Leonard (April 1993), "Resume Databases to Dominate Field," *HRMagazine,* pp. 59–60.

22. Wei-Chi Tsai, Chien-Cheng Chen, and Su-Fen Chiu (2004), "Exploring Boundaries of the Effects of Applicant Impression Management Tactics on Job Interviews," *Journal of Management,* Vol. 31, Iss. 1, pp. 108–125; Sandy Wayne and Robert Liden (February 1995), "Effects of Impression Management on Performance Ratings," *Academy of Management Journal,* pp. 232–252.

23. Sara Rynes and Barry Gerhart (Spring 1990), "Interviewer Assessments of Applicant 'Fit': An Exploratory Investigation," *Personnel Psychology,* pp. 13–36.

24. Milan Moravec (September 1990), "Effective Job Posting Fills Dual Needs," *HRMagazine,* pp. 76–80.

25. Marc Hequet (April 1995), "The Amoco Plan," *Training,* p. 31.

26. Sandra E. Martin (2004), "Is Moonlighting Right for You?" *MoneySense,* Vol. 6, Iss. 1, pp. 9–11; Bill Leonard (July 1997), "Rate of Moonlighting among Workers Holds a Steady Pace," *HRMagazine,* p. 10.

27. Carolyn Hirschman (October 2000), "Do You Need a Moonlighting Policy?" *HRMagazine,* pp. 46–54.

28. *EEOC v. Detroit Edison Company* (1975), U.S. Court of Appeals, Sixth Circuit (Cincinnati), 515F. 2d. 301.

29. Margaret Magnus (August 1986), "Recruitment Ad Vantages," *Personnel Journal,* pp. 58–79.

30. Michelle Neely Martinez (2000), "Winning Ways to Recruit," *HRMagazine,* Vol. 45, Iss. 6, pp. 56–65.

31. Ruth Thaler-Carter (June 2001), "Diversify Your Recruitment Advertising," *HRMagazine,* pp. 92–100.

32. Tim Elkington (2005), "Bright Future for Online Recruitment," *Personnel Today,* p. 9; Marlene Piturro (January 2000), "The Power of E-cruiting," *Management Review,* pp. 33–37.

33. Bob Tedeschi (March 28, 2005), "So Far, There's a Truce between the Big Job Search Boards and New Employment Sites That Scan the Big Boards' Listings," *The New York Times,* p. C5; AP Online (December 3, 1999), "Employers Use Web to Recruit," www.investing.lycos.com.

34. Diane Stafford (February 15, 2005), "Kansas City Star Workplace Column," *Knight Ridder Tribune Business News,* p. 1.

35. "How Four Companies Final Common e-Recruiting Challenges," Human Resource Department Management Report, April 2005, pp. 6–7.

36. AP Online, op. cit. (December 3, 1999).

37. Jon Swartz (February 19, 2001), "E-Recruiters Swim through a Sea of Resumes," *USA Today,* p. 3B.

38. Shirley Duglin Kennedy (July–August 1996), "Need a New Job? Get to Work on the Web," *Information Today,* pp. 38–39.

39. Samuel Greengard (March 1996), "10 Tips for Getting Net Results," *Personnel Journal,* p. 28.

40. Perri Capell (May 3, 2005), "Executive-Search Firms to Find Changed Playing Field," *The Wall Street Journal,* p. B6; J. Scott Lord (1989), "External and Internal Recruitment," in Wayne F. Cascio (ed.), *Human Resource Planning, Employment, and Placement* (Washington, DC: Bureau of National Affairs), pp. 73–102.

41. Martha Frase-Blunt (April 2002), "Job Fair Challenges for HR," *HRMagazine,* pp. 62–66.

42. Marsha Austin (January 14, 2003), "Denver Job Fair Draws Record 8,300 Job Seekers," *Knight Ridder Tribune Business News,* p. 1.

43. Bibi S. Watson (June 1995), "The Intern Turnaround," *Management Review,* pp. 9–12.

44. Steve Quinn (May 31, 2005), "Great Expectations for Interns," *Knight Ridder Tribune Business News,* p. 1; Steart Deck (March 2000), "6 Degrees of Hire Learning," *CIO,* pp. 132–140.

45. Michelle Halpern (November 22, 2004), "Students for Hire," *Marketing,* Vol. 109, Iss. 38, p. 32; Jilly Welch (September 12, 1996), "Employers in Rush to Capture Young Talent," *Personnel Management,* p. 9.

46. Michelle Neely Martinez (March 1996), "Looking for Young Talent? Inroads Helps Diversify Efforts," *HRMagazine,* pp. 73–76.

47. Dawn Gunsch (September 1993), "Comprehensive College Strategy Strengthens NCR's Recruitment," *Personnel Journal,* pp. 58–62.

48. Michelle V. Rafter (2004), "CNA Brings Recruiting In-House and Saves Millions," *Workforce Management,* Vol. 83, Iss. 8, pp. 61–63; David E. Terpstra (May 1996), "The Search for Effective Methods," *HR Focus,* pp. 16–17.

49. Thomas J. Bergman and M. Susan Taylor (May–June 1984), "College Recruitment: What Attracts Students to Organizations," *Personnel,* pp. 34–36.

50. Watson, op. cit., pp. 9–12.

51. John Boudreau and Sara Rynes (March 1987), "Giving It the Old College Try," *Personnel Administrator,* pp. 78–85.

52. Gene J. Koprowski (2004), "Rude Awakening," *HRMagazine,* Vol. 49, Iss. 9, pp. 50–56; Andrea Poe (May 2000), "Face Value," *HRMagazine,* pp. 60–68; Therese Hoff Macan and Robert L. Dipboye (Winter 1990), "The Relationship of Interviewers' Preinterview Impressions to Selection and Recruitment Outcomes," *Personnel Psychology,* pp. 745–768.

53. Jean M. Phillips (December 1998), "Effects of Realistic Job Previews on Multiple Organizational Outcomes: A Meta-Analysis," *Academy of Management Journal,* pp. 673–690.

54. Larry Reibstein (June 10, 1987), "Crushed Hopes: When a New Job Proves to Be Something Different," *The Wall Street Journal,* p. 25.

55. P. Popovich and John P. Wanous (October 1982), "The Realistic Job Preview as a Persuasive Communication," *Academy of Management Review,* pp. 570–578.

56. Steven L. Premack and John P. Wanous (December 1985), "A Meta-Analysis of Realistic Job Preview Experiments," *Journal of Applied Psychology,* pp. 706–719; and James A. Breaugh (October 1983), "Realistic Job Previews: A Critical Appraisal and Future Research Directions," *Academy of Management Review,* pp. 612–619.

57. Linda K. Stroh (2003), "Outsourcing HR Functions: When and When Not to Go Outside," *Journal of Leadership & Organizational Studies,* Vol. 10, Iss. 1, pp. 19–32; Brian Klass, John McClendon, and Thomas Gainey (Spring 2002), "Trust and the Role of Professional Employer Organizations: Managing HR in Small and Medium Enterprises," *Journal of Managerial Issues,* pp. 31–48; John Polson (Spring 2002), "The PEO Phenomenon: Co-Employment at Work," *Employee Relations Law Journal,* pp. 7–25; T. Joe Willey (Winter 1993), "Employee Leasing Comes of Age," *Human Resources Professional,* pp. 18–20.

58. Rosalind Resnick (November 1992), "Leasing Workers," *Nation's Business,* pp. 20–28.

59. Brenda Paik Sunoo (April 1996), "From Santa to CEO—Temps Play All Roles," *Personnel Journal,* pp. 34–44.

60. Brenda Paik Sunoo (April 1999), "Temp Firms Turn Up the Heat on Hiring," *Workforce,* pp. 50–54.

61. Bas Koene and Maarten van Riemsdijk (2005), "Managing Temporary Workers: Work Identity, Diversity and Operational HR Choices," *Human Resource Management Journal,* Vol. 15, Iss. 1, pp. 76–92; George S. Odiorne (July 1990), "Beating the 1990s' Labor Shortage," *Training,* pp. 32–35.

62. Ann Macaulay, Joyce Grant, and Uyen Vu (2005), "Gauging HR's Contribution," *Canadian HR Reporter,* Vol. 18, Iss. 10, pp. 5–8; This measure was developed by Jac Fitz-Enz (1984) in *How to Measure Human Resource Management* (New York: McGraw-Hill), pp. 86–87.

EXERCISE 7-1

Netiquette: Effectively Communicating with E-Mail

PURPOSE

Whether it's submitting an electronic resume and cover letter or sending out an invitation to come in for an interview, job seekers and recruiters often need to communicate with one another via e-mail. The purpose of this exercise is to research and understand best practices regarding the sending of e-mail.

GROUP SIZE

To be performed individually.

TIME REQUIRED

Approximately 45 minutes.

OTHER

Internet connection and search engine needed.

EXERCISE

How many times have you wished, right after pressing the "send" button of your e-mail program, that you could take back and soften the message you just launched into global cyberspace? What kind of emotion was behind your e-mail? Maybe none, but will the recipient perceive it that way?

Several articles and Web sites can be found on the Internet to help improve effectiveness with e-mail communication.

Using your favorite search engine (e.g., www.google.com, www.yahoo.com, etc.), search and identify 10 sources that provide tips and advice on how to use e-mail in an effective manner. Summarize the best practices and be prepared to present or write a brief overview of your findings. Be sure to include which tips are particularly important to help you improve your own e-mail use.

Source: Adapted from Robert Konopaske and John M. Ivancevich (2004), *Global Management and Organizational Behavior* (New York: McGraw-Hill/Irwin), p. 416.

Application Case 7-1

So Long to the Sunday Classifieds

In a time when many companies are cutting costs across their operations, a growing number of HR departments are changing the ways they recruit. Their goal: to boost recruiting efficiency (reducing recruiting costs per hire). Their means: innovative recruiting approaches that bring imagination and aggressiveness to a company's overall recruiting function. Innovations are occurring in several elements of the recruiting process. Here is a look at innovations in several areas.

Recruitment Advertising

An increasing number of companies are supplementing and even replacing the traditional classified ad with creative, clever, eye-catching ads. These ads are essentially a company's resume and cover letter, designed to send a unique and memorable message about the company to sought-after prospective applicants. Recently, *Personnel Journal* reviewed several hundred ads submitted by subscribers and reported some trends in this type of advertising. They include:

1. **Use of Employees in Ads** Instead of the traditional testimonials, more company ads are spotlighting employees, talking about their skills, jobs, and accomplishments. For example, General Dynamics has run a series of ads that, by comparisons with great inventors, compliments profiled employees and their colleagues. For example, one ad headline in the series proclaims, "We're looking for another Newton . . . And another Newman" (Howard Newman, one of General Dynamics' senior project engineers). The ad's text showcases Mr. Newman's accomplishments and long tenure with the company and then urges those interested and qualified to "join Howard in the pursuit of technology excellence and discovery; apply for a position with us. . . . Who knows? You might become the next Newman." In some other ads in the series, General Dynamics has declared, "We're looking for another Edison . . . And another Hardison" (electrical engineer Corrine Hardison). Like many employee-spotlight ads developed by other companies, this series portrays the corporation as a place where very talented and dedicated people work and reach their potential.

2. **Promotion of Intangible Benefits** In cases where a job is highly attractive and thus doesn't need promoting, employers have turned to emphasizing certain intangible benefits of the company such as opportunities for advancement, employment security, creative freedom, and entrepreneurial opportunities. Lockheed Missile & Space Company has run a series of sports-related ads that promote company benefits. One such ad is entitled "Net Gain." Featuring a tennis racket and tennis balls in a partly closed briefcase, the text says, "Along with a diverse and challenging project list, Lockheed Missile & Space Company makes a point of providing employees with truly comprehensive recreational programs and facilities." The Saint Paul Medical Center has developed a series of one-word headline ads that promote certain themes such as "Commitment" (describing the center's commitment to patients' care and employees' career development) and "Balance" ("Between caring professionals . . . between tradition and technology . . . between performance and opportunity"). Washington University in Saint Louis uses creative advertising to promote its flexible work schedules, and in one ad entitled "Even you-know-who rested on the seventh day," the company published its nursing salaries.

3. **Point-of-Purchase Recruitment** A growing number of service companies with high turnover in low-skill jobs are recruiting using point-of-purchase ads. For example, Pizza Hut places recruiting coupons on its carry-out boxes. Featuring a drawing of a large lead pencil, the ad suggests, "If you want a good job, get the lead out." The coupon provides a mini-resume form for

Source: Written by Kim Stewart and adapted from Bob Martin (August 1987), "Recruitment Ad Ventures," *Personnel Journal,* pp. 46–54; J. Scott Lord (November 1987), "Contract Recruiting Comes of Age," *Personnel Administrator,* pp. 49–53; Maury Hanigan (November 1987), "Campus Recruiters Upgrade Their Pitch," *Personnel Administrator,* pp. 55–58; and Margaret Magnus (February 1987), "Is Your Recruitment All It Can Be?" *Personnel Journal,* pp. 54–63.

prospective applicants who don't have resumes. The Quik Wok Chinese food take-out chain uses bag-stuffers that picture a broken fortune cookie and proclaim "Not everyone will have the good fortune to work at Quik Wok." The stuffer describes job opportunities. The success of point-of-purchase ads has eliminated Quik Wok's use of classified ads. Other users have found the strategy to be a low-cost, highly efficient, and flexible form of recruiting; when a new position needs to be filled, they simply distribute the bag stuffers.

Contract Recruiting

Companies in fast-growing industries are seeking the expertise of a relatively new type of external specialist: the contract recruiter. This specialist is contracted on a temporary basis to perform recruiting functions for different job openings. The recruiter screens resumes, conducts telephone and in-person interviews, coordinates campus recruiting, prepares and executes formal offers, and performs any number of contractual recruiting responsibilities. He or she is not affiliated with an employment agency and does not receive a commission or a percentage of the hiree's salary. Rather, the recruiter is self-employed and is paid at an hourly rate negotiated with the client company.

These self-employed specialists are becoming popular because they can provide several benefits to client companies. When a company is undergoing exceptionally fast growth with immediate hiring needs, a recruiter can be quickly brought in to handle the suddenly burdensome task. The recruiting is performed without hiring permanent (and later unnecessary) staff. For example, when GTE in Needham, Massachusetts, suddenly found itself with a Department of Defense contract requiring 1,200 professional employees to be hired in 16 months, GTE turned to 12 contract recruiters who became an instant employment department. They set up the system, completed the task, and then trained their replacements before departing 16 months later. The cosmetics manufacturer Helene Curtis, Inc., regularly calls on contract recruiters to help the company handle its 15 to 20 percent yearly growth. Recruiters can also serve as external, objective advisers to the company's human resource function.

Some contract recruiters develop expertise in certain employment fields (such as electrical engineering or computer software design). Companies with hiring needs in these areas benefit from the specialists' contacts and highly focused capabilities. Some companies hire the same recruiters time and again, finding that the subsequent knowledge of the company's recruiting needs and functions that the recruiter acquires helps to further reduce per-hire costs.

Campus Recruiting

With declining college enrollments and growing demand for recruits with college degrees, companies are finding that recruiting on college campuses has become very competitive. As a result, many are launching strategies to both boost their offer-acceptance rates and lower their recruiting costs.

Rather than select recruits from the placement office's resume file, some companies are identifying a number of students in their junior year and focusing efforts on these select recruits. More firms are establishing programs that educate professors more fully on the company's career opportunities for graduates. For example, Macy's brings professors to a showcase store where the educators spend a day observing trainees and meeting with managers. Other companies, such as Citibank, hire professors to lecture in the company's training programs. Organizations such as Texas Instruments also provide executives as guest lecturers at several universities. These actions are designed to enhance the professors' knowledge of the company, which it is hoped will be communicated to students, and to develop executives' relationships with certain schools.

Some companies are also refining their recruitment brochures. Rather than providing the traditional, very general brochure on the company, firms are now developing smaller, more individualized publications that provide information on particular jobs and departments and information on the community where a prospective applicant would work (for instance, information on cost of living and community recreation facilities). Invitation letters to a campus interview are personalized, often explaining why the company is interested in that particular student. More companies are producing recruiting videos for show on campus. Companies are also paying more attention to the quality of their on-campus interviewers, providing their recruiters with training in communications skills.

And many firms are replacing the form rejection letter with one that is more tactful and considerate. Firms are mindful of the impact that a word-of-mouth reputation created by an inconsiderate, uninterested recruiter can have on a company's campus recruiting efforts.

Computer Databases

Computer databases are being developed as job and resume data banks. For example, Job Stores, Inc., has developed a franchise chain of "stop and shop" employment centers located in high-traffic shopping malls. At any center, a job hunter can tap the Job Stores Network computer database by obtaining a computer printout on job openings in the local area and nationwide. The fee: $75 for 90 days' access to the network. Any company can list its job openings on the network at no charge. In seeking participation from businesses, Job Stores' franchises focus on job openings that companies usually don't fill via employment agencies.

JobNet, another computer database network, allows job hunters to place their resumes in the network at no charge. Companies pay a fee for access to the database, which has over 1 million resumes of technical professionals online. A company can search the database by specifying any of a number of criteria, such as how recent the resume is. Career Technologies runs the network and obtains resumes via job fairs, advertising, and exclusive contracts with over 20 professional associations and societies.

Some college placement centers are also establishing computer databases to link students with prospective jobs. For example, the Career Connection Company of State College, Pennsylvania, has established Job Search, a computer database of job information. The network provides job listings (up to 20 lines each provided by companies) and is available for all students.

Employee Referrals

Lastly, companies are adding pizzazz to the widely used employee referral and bounty system. A growing number of companies are aggressively promoting referral campaigns with special themes and prizes. Referral bonuses run the gamut from money and trips to time off and credit used to "buy" items from a special catalog. Many referral programs are periodically given a boost with new bonuses and new themes.

Discussion Questions

1. Assess the effectiveness of a recruitment advertising strategy that relies on imaginative, highly visual, eye-catching ads. What are the potential strengths and drawbacks of this approach to recruitment advertising?
2. What type of company (in what kind of industry) would benefit most from contract recruiters? What type would benefit least?
3. Suppose you are faced with the task of developing a college recruiting strategy for obtaining talented business school graduates with degrees in management information systems (developing and managing a company computer information network). Demand for these individuals is currently very high; supply is limited. Develop a recruiting strategy that addresses innovations discussed in the case and includes your own ideas.

Application Case 7-2

Are New Recruits Looking for Work-Life Balance?

Anyone who has tried to balance his or her time between a busy job and a fulfilling personal life knows how challenging this can be. An indisputable fact is that work and personal lives are interconnected. Companies know this. Potential recruits also know this. It's become more of an issue in recent years due to some important demographic changes that are affecting many workers. For example, companies are experiencing rising demand for the expansion of child care and elder care programs. This is not surprising given the aging of the U.S. population and that Gen Xers are starting to have families. Thus, many recruits who are members of the "sandwich generation" (i.e., they are sandwiched between elderly parents and young children and therefore have to provide care for both sets of family members) consider as part of their employment decisions the number and type of work-life balance programs that potential employers offer. Other demographic changes that are contributing to this rise in the demand for work-life balance programs include the increase of single parents entering the workforce and an increase of dual-career couples. In both cases, parents who shoulder caregiving responsibilities often seek flexible work arrangements and more flexible career cycles. Flexible career cycles allow individuals to leave their career tracks temporarily to raise a child, care for a sick parent, and so on. These individuals are welcomed back to work and placed back into career-oriented positions.

Are companies using work-life balance programs to attract top candidates to join their firms? The answer is yes. Whirlpool attempts to attract recruits with the company's family friendly culture. To illustrate, the company arranged for housing for an intern and his family for the entire summer.

At Xerox, two executives successfully share one job so that they can have more time at home with their young children. After 10 years, the job sharing arrangement is working whereby both executives report high levels of satisfaction with the arrangement, and the company has been able to retain two productive and experienced employees.

Flextime programs that allow employees limited control over which days and hours they have to be working at the office are becoming popular at many companies. For example, an employee may prefer to work a 4-day/10-hour-a-day week instead of a traditional 5-day/8-hour-a-day week. The shorter workweek may allow the employee to attend children's sporting events, provide weekend care for an elderly parent, or engage in other important activities. Companies such as Hewlett-Packard, Merrill Lynch, Deloitte Touche, and Cigna have implemented flextime programs.

Related to flextime is telecommuting, which allows employees to work in their home part or full time while being connected to the office via the Internet, phone lines, and the like. Although some managers and supervisors fear a loss of control from this type of work-family arrangement, companies like Pfizer have been careful to create an effective telecommuting policy. For example, in order to qualify for this program, Pfizer employees are required to demonstrate that the work can be accomplished off-site, to submit a formal proposal outlining performance standards, and to limit the number of days worked off-site to no more than two per week.

Work-life balance programs such as job sharing, flextime, and telecommuting are designed for both retaining current employees and attracting potential employees to the firm. As new college graduates increasingly find themselves providing care to both their aging parents and young children, the value of these programs will only increase. Undoubtedly, this will make work-life friendly companies more attractive in the marketplace.

Discussion Questions

1. Why is there a need for companies to offer work-family balance programs such as flextime, telecommuting, and job sharing?
2. Of the three programs discussed above, which would be the most important program for you personally when deciding whether or not to join an employer? Why?
3. Some organizations do not believe in offering any of these work-life balance programs. What do you think their reasoning is? Explain.

Sources: Nancy R. Baldiga (2005), "Opportunity and Balance: Is Your Organization Ready to Provide Both?" *Journal of Accountancy*, Vol. 199, Iss. 5, pp. 39–45; Amanda Beeler (2003), "It Takes Two," *Sales and Marketing Management* 155, No. 8, pp. 3–8; Sue Shellenbarger (November 21, 2001), "Job Candidates Prepare to Sacrifice Frills and Balance—For Now," *The Wall Street Journal*, p. B1.

Chapter 8

Selection

Learning Objectives

After studying this chapter, you should be able to:

1. **Define** the steps in the selection process.
2. **List** what selection criteria are available and how they can be used to make selection more effective.
3. **Describe** how to use selection tools such as interviews and biodata more effectively.
4. **Compare** the different types of validity—content, construct, and criteria-related.
5. **Discuss** the value of controversial selection methods such as drug testing and integrity testing in light of current organizational and social environments.

Internet / Web Resources

General Sites

www.issid.org/issid.html

www.drugfreeworkplace.org

www.unl.edu/buros

www.psychologicalscience.org

www.polygraph.org

www.eeoc.gov

www.dol.gov

Company Sites

www.gmat.org

www.amanet.org

www.att.com

www.disney.com

www.bechtel.com

www.wonderlic.com

Career Challenge

Clark Kirby and his assistants had recruited 986 applicants for the 596 positions Gunther would have at its Tampa plant. But before getting too satisfied, he realized that there was a big job ahead of him. Which 596 of the 986 should be hired? And who should do the hiring?

The HR specialist had done some preliminary screening, and most of the applicants had completed an application blank. But where should he go from there?

Clark called Ed Humphrey, the plant manager, and asked if he wanted to be involved in the hiring. Ed said that he had time to choose only his top management team. The rest was up to Clark. Ed reminded Clark that the company didn't want them to raid other plants—that was simply against company policy. Clark said he knew that and would abide by company policy.

Clark was faced with making 596 selection decisions. As this chapter shows, selection involves making many decisions. Selection is a vital and continuous process in an organization. Employee selection is important because the goals of the organization can be accomplished only if the right match is made between the person and the job.

Selection is the process by which an organization chooses from a list of applicants the person or persons who best meet the selection criteria for the position available, considering current environmental conditions. Although this definition emphasizes the effectiveness of selection, decisions about whom to hire must also be made efficiently and within the boundaries set forth in equal employment opportunity legislation. Thus, there are actually multiple goals associated with an organization's selection process.

At a basic level, all selection programs attempt to identify the applicants who have the highest chance of meeting or exceeding the organization's standards of performance. In this case, however, *performance* does not refer simply to quantity of output. It can also involve other objectives, such as quality of output, absenteeism, theft, employees' satisfaction, and career development. Compounding the problem of developing an effective selection system is the fact that the goal isn't always to find applicants who have the most of a given quality. Rather, selection is the search for an optimal match between the job and the amount of any particular characteristic that an applicant may possess. For example, depending on the job, more intelligence isn't always better than less. Or, it is possible for an applicant to be too socially skilled if the job doesn't require high levels of such skills.[1] This situation can easily lead to the selection of overqualified candidates.[2] Thus, it is highly unlikely that a selection system can effectively cope with all possible objectives. As a result, one of the initial tasks involved in developing and implementing an effective selection process is for the organization to identify which objective is most important for its circumstances.

Influences on the Selection Process

As Clark Kirby sets out to hire 596 employees, he will follow a selection process influenced by many factors. We'll begin by examining the factors in the internal and external environments.

Environmental Circumstances Influencing Selection

Internal Environment

A number of characteristics of the organization can influence the amount and type of selection processes it uses to hire needed employees. Size, complexity, and technological volatility are a few of these. Since the development and implementation of large-scale selection efforts can be very costly, complex selection systems are most often found in larger organizations with the economic resources necessary to pay for such systems. Size alone, however, doesn't determine how selection is approached. For an organization to recover the costs of developing an expensive selection system, there must be a sufficient number of jobs that need to be filled. In structurally complex organizations with many job titles but very few occupants, the number of years needed to get back the money invested in such a selection system may be too great to justify its initial expense.

Another characteristic of the organization that is an important determinant of the kind of selection system it develops is its attitude about hiring from within. Many organizations have elaborate internal job posting programs (as was discussed in Chapter 7) designed to help fill as many job vacancies as possible from within. Other organizations look more quickly to external personnel pools of new employees. While these two models of filling job vacancies will have some overlapping selection processes, each will also focus to some extent on different criteria and different techniques.

External Environment

The external environment is an equally important determinant of the kind of selection system that an organization utilizes. Not only are most organizations subject to federal employment laws and regulations, but there are many state-specific regulations that also affect what an organization can and cannot do in its selection system. Some states, for example, have imposed much tighter limits than others on an organization's ability to test applicants for drug use. Similarly, a number of states provide past employers with more protection against being sued by a former employee because of information that may have been divulged during checking of references. Any or all of these state-specific issues can affect the selection system that is ultimately used.

One of the most significant environmental influences on selection is the size, composition, and availability of local labor markets. These, in turn, are affected by economic, social, and political pressures on a community. At a basic level, when unemployment rates are low, it may be difficult for an organization to identify, attract, and hire the number of people it needs. On the other hand, when there is an oversupply of qualified applicants, selection strategies can be very different.

Those who work in human resource management evaluate the effects of the labor market on selection decisions by using a selection ratio:

$$\text{Selection ratio} = \frac{\text{number of applicants hired}}{\text{total number of applicants}}$$

Consider Clark Kirby's problem at Gunther. The selection ratios are as follows: managers 38/68, or about 1:2; professional/technical, 10/10, or 1:1; clerical, 44/78, or about 1:2; skilled, 104/110, or about 1:1; semiskilled, 400/720, or almost 1:2. When the selection ratio gets close to 1:1, it is called a *high selection ratio.* Under these circumstances, the selection process is short and unsophisticated, although it may not be effective. As the number of applicants increases relative to the number who are hired, the selection ratio is said to be low. With a lower selection ratio, for example 1:2, the process becomes more detailed. A ratio of 1:2 also means that the organization can be more selective in its choice than when the ratio is 1:1. It is, therefore, more likely that employees who fit the organization's criteria for success will be hired. It is also likely, however, that the organization will have to invest more time and money in the selection decision when the ratio is 1:2.

Selection Criteria

At the core of any effective selection system is an understanding of what characteristics are essential for high performance. This is where the critical role of job analysis in selection becomes most apparent, because that list of characteristics should have been identified during the process of job analysis and should now be accurately reflected in the job specification. Thus, from a performance perspective, the goal of any selection system is to accurately determine which applicants possess the knowledge, skills, abilities, and other characteristics (KSAOs) dictated by the job. Additionally, the selection system must be capable of distinguishing between characteristics that are needed at the time of hiring, those that are systematically acquired during training, and those that are routinely developed after a person has been placed on the job. Different selection criteria may, indeed, be needed to assess these qualitatively different KSAOs.

Categories of Criteria

With these potential differences in mind, the criteria typically used by organizations for making selection decisions can be summarized in several broad categories: education, experience, physical characteristics, and other personal characteristics.

Formal Education

An employer selecting from a pool of job applicants wants to find the person who has the right abilities and attitudes to be successful. A large number of cognitive, motor, physical, and interpersonal attributes are present because of genetic predispositions and because they were learned at home, at school, on the job, and so on. One of the more common cost-effective ways to screen for many of these abilities is by using educational accomplishment as a surrogate for or summary of the measures of those abilities. For example, although this is unfortunately not always true, it usually is safe to assume that anyone who has successfully completed high school or its equivalent has basic reading, writing, arithmetic, and interpersonal skills.

For certain jobs, the employer may stipulate that the education (especially for college-level requirements) is in a particular area of expertise, such as accounting or management. The employer might also prefer that the degree be from certain institutions, that the grade point average be higher than some minimum, and that certain honors have been achieved. To be legal, educational standards such as these must be related to successful performance of the job. Care must be exercised not to set standards that are higher than actually required by the job.

Experience and Past Performance

Another useful criterion for selecting employees is experience and past performance. Many selection specialists believe that past performance on a similar job might be one of the best indicators of future performance. In addition, employers often consider experience to be a good indicator of ability and work-related attitudes. Their reasoning is that a prospective employee who has performed the job before and is applying for a similar job must like the work and must be able to do the job well. Research supports these assumptions. Over a large number of studies, experience is related to job performance.[3] But the organization must have a rational basis for defining what it means by "relevant experience." Not all previous experiences are equally good predictors of performance on a given job. For example, should two applicants applying for a job as an internal auditor be given the same credit for previous work experience if both have five years in the accounting profession but one has been an auditor for another organization and the other a tax specialist for the IRS?

Physical Characteristics

In the past, many employers consciously or unconsciously used physical characteristics (including how an applicant looked) as a criterion. Studies found that employers were more likely to hire and pay better wages to taller men, and airlines chose flight attendants and companies hired receptionists on the basis of beauty (or their definition of it). Many times, such practices discriminated against ethnic groups, women, and handicapped people. For this reason, they are now illegal unless it can be shown that a physical characteristic is directly related to effectiveness at work. For example, visual acuity (eyesight) would be a physical characteristic that could be used to hire commercial airline pilots. It might not, however, be legally used for hiring a telephone reservations agent for an airline.

In a similar way, candidates for a job cannot be screened out by arbitrary height, weight, or similar requirements. These can be used as selection criteria only when the job involves tasks that require them.

Personal Characteristics and Personality Type

The final criterion category is a catchall that includes *personal characteristics* and *personality types.* Personal characteristics include marital status, sex, age, and so on. Some employers have, for example, preferred "stable" married employees over single people because they have assumed that married people have a lower turnover rate. On the other hand, other employers might seek out single people for some jobs, since a single person might be more likely to accept a transfer or a lengthy overseas assignment.

Age, too, has sometimes been used as a criterion. While it is illegal to discriminate against people who are over the age of 40, there is no federal law that specifically addresses this issue for younger people. However, minimum and maximum age restrictions for jobs can be used only if they are clearly job-related. Thus, age should be used as a selection criterion only after very careful thought and consideration. This issue will certainly become more important by the year 2010; this is when the median age in the United States will be 40.6 years. By that time, more than half of all American workers will be legally protected by the Age Discrimination in Employment Act (ADEA).[4]

Specific aptitudes and skills can also be considered part of this category of criteria. Although education and past experience are often used as measures of ability, many organizations also try to assess whether applicants possess certain aptitudes. For example, a successful applicant for pilot training in the military does not need actual flying experience. Rather, the military uses spatial-relations aptitude as one criterion.

Many employers also prefer to hire people with certain personality types. Some jobs, such as being a lifeguard, may require essentially no consideration of an applicant's personality. Many jobs fall between these extremes. For example, one particular aspect of personality—such as being outgoing—may be useful for salespeople, caseworkers, or others who work extensively with the public.

Although once viewed in an unfavorable light due to perceptions of low predictive validity, recent findings on personality tests have been much more positive regarding the link between personality and job performance.[5] Much of this change can be attributed to the development and validation of the Big Five personality factors. Known as emotional stability, extroversion, openness to experience, agreeableness, and conscientiousness, the Big Five describe behavioral traits that may explain up to 75 percent of an individual's personality.[6] Of the five dimensions, conscientiousness and emotional stability have been shown to predict performance across most occupational groupings.[7]

As with other personal characteristics, selection using any aspect of personality should always be based on whether it is really necessary for high performance. Many personality measures run an even greater risk of being legally challenged as an invasion of privacy than other kinds of selection tools. Thus, the organization wishing to use personality as a criterion

HR Journal   *Is "Self-Efficacy" Part of Your Personality?*

Self-efficacy is the belief that one can perform well in a given situation. For example, a person with high levels of self-efficacy will tend to believe that she can do well in an interview situation, pass a difficult exam at school, or make a successful presentation to a new client.

Research on self-efficacy has led to several consistent findings. They indicated that self-efficacy is associated with work-related performance, career choice, learning and achievement, and adaptability to new technology; and noted that certain training methods could enhance self-efficacy in individual trainees. A related large-scale research study found that individuals high in self-efficacy tended to perform at a higher level. Also supporting these conclusions is the research by Bandura and Locke who found that, when combined with goal setting, individuals with high levels of self-efficacy tend to display higher levels of motivation and performance.

Thus, feelings of self-efficacy have a number of managerial and organizational implications:

- *Selection decisions:* Organizations should select individuals who have a strong sense of self-efficacy. These individuals will be motivated to engage in the behaviors that will help them perform well. A measure of self-efficacy can be administered during the hiring/promotion process.

- *Training programs:* Organizations should consider employee levels of self-efficacy when determining who is chosen for training programs. If the training budget is limited, then more return (i.e., performance) on training investment can be realized by sending only those employees high in self-efficacy. These individuals will tend to learn more from the training, ultimately transferring that learning to enhance their job performance.

- *Goal setting and performance:* Organizations can encourage higher performance goals from employees who have high levels of self-efficacy. This will lead to higher levels of performance from employees, a critical outcome for many organizations in this era of hypercompetition.

Source: John M. Ivancevich, Robert Konopaske, and Michael T. Matteson (2005), *Organizational Behavior and Management* (New York: McGraw-Hill/Irwin); Albert Bandura and Edwin Locke (February 2003), "Negative Self-Efficacy and Goal Effects Revisited," *Journal of Applied Psychology*, 88, 1, pp. 87–99; Marilyn E. Gist and Terence R. Mitchell (1992), "Self-Efficacy: A Theoretical Analysis of Its Determinants and Malleability," *Academy of Management Review*, 17, 2, pp. 183–201; Alexander D. Stajkovic and Fred Luthans (1998), "Self-Efficacy and Work-Related Performance: A Meta-Analysis," *Psychological Bulletin*, 124, 2, pp. 240–262.

must be certain that successful and unsuccessful employees can be distinguished in terms of their personalities. It is probably unwise to use personality as a general criterion for screening out "undesirable" applicants, since the same personality characteristic that leads to failure in one job might lead to success in another.[8] In part, because of this fact, there is still considerable debate whether general, broad personality measures or more specific ones are the best to use in selection.[9]

Reliability and Validity of Selection Criteria

Once an organization has decided upon a set of selection criteria, a technique for assessing each of these must be chosen. The alternatives are numerous: application blanks and biodata forms, interviews, psychological tests of aptitude and personality, work sample tests of present skills, physical and medical testing, and checks of previous experience through references. Regardless of the method chosen for collecting information about applicants, the organization must be certain that the information is both *reliable* and *valid*.

Reliability

The main goal of selection is to make accurate predictions about people. The organization wants to make its best guess about who will be a successful employee. In this way, the organization can avoid hiring the wrong person for a job. In other words, the main purpose of selection is to make decisions about people. If these decisions are going to be correct, the techniques used for making them must yield reliable information.

Reliability refers to how stable or repeatable a measurement is over a variety of testing conditions.[10] As a simple example, imagine that you tried to use a tape measure to determine how tall an applicant for a job as a firefighter was, because there are both minimum and maximum height restrictions for the job. If you measured a given applicant three successive times and obtained values of 6 feet, 6 feet $\frac{1}{2}$ inch, and 5 feet $11\frac{1}{2}$ inches, you may not know the applicant's exact height, but you would have a fairly good idea. On the other hand, imagine that your three attempts yielded values of 6 feet, 6 feet 6 inches, and 5 feet 4 inches. In this latter case, you would have virtually no idea how tall the applicant actually was. The point is that although reliability is rarely perfect, a measuring tool can still be useful if it is only somewhat unreliable. Once the measurements become too inconsistent, however, they become meaningless.

The reliability of a selection tool can be judged in a variety of ways. In practice, one common way to assess reliability is to correlate the scores of applicants given the same test on two different occasions. This is called *test-retest reliability. Alternative-form reliability* is determined by correlating scores from two alternate forms of the same test. Most standardized academic achievement tests like the SAT and the GMAT have numerous forms, all of which are assumed to be reliable. An applicant's score should not vary much according to which form of the test he or she happens to take. When a measuring tool relies on the judgments of people (such as in an employment interview), reliability is often determined by using *interrater reliability.* This refers to the extent to which two or more interviewers' assessments are consistent with each other.

Validity

For a selection tool to be useful, it is not sufficient for it to be repeatable or stable. Both legally and organizationally, the measures that it yields must also be valid. There are many ways of assessing validity, but all of them focus on two issues. **Validity** addresses the questions of what a test measures and how well it has measured it.[11] In selection, the primary concern is whether the assessment technique results in accurate predictions about the future success or failure of an applicant.

To illustrate these two issues and the relationship between validity and reliability, let's return to our example of measuring the firefighter applicant's height. As noted previously, if the measurement is too unreliable, then it will be impossible to determine his or her correct height. Even if the tape gives the same measurements (high reliability), it might still have very little accuracy (validity). For example, the tape measure may not have been calibrated properly at the factory where it was made (the manufacturer may have thought it was marking in feet and inches when it was actually using centimeters). If so, it will be almost impossible to accurately determine the applicant's height. Finally, this tape measure might be perfectly reliable and an accurate way to measure height, but if you try to weigh applicants with it, it will yield totally useless information.

To summarize, for a measuring tool to be useful, it must be reliable, valid, and put to the use for which it was actually intended.

A detailed explanation of the various strategies for determining the validity of a selection tool can be found in the *Principles for the Validation and Use of Personnel Selection Procedures,* a set of professional standards developed by a committee of members from the Society for Industrial and Organizational Psychology (SIOP).[12] The following, however, are brief descriptions of three types of validity that the HR specialist should be familiar with: (1) content, (2) construct, and (3) criterion-related.

Content Validity   The degree to which a test, interview, or performance evaluation measures the skill, knowledge, or ability to perform the job is called **content validity.**

An example of a content-valid test is a typing test for a secretarial position. Such a test can roughly replicate conditions on the job. The applicant can be given a typical sample of typing work under "normal" working conditions. Thus, the applicant would be asked to type a typical piece of work (letter, internal memo, tabular data) using the same kind of typewriter or word processor that would be encountered on the actual job. If the content of the typing test is actually representative of the work that is done on the job, then the test is said to be content-valid.

Content validity is not appropriate for more abstract job behaviors, such as leadership potential, leadership style, or work ethic. When selection procedures involve the use of tests to measure leadership characteristics or personality, construct validity rather than content validity is appropriate.

Construct Validity A construct is a trait that is not typically observable. For example, we cannot see leadership; we can only assume that it exists from the behavior someone displays. A test therefore has **construct validity** when it actually measures the unobservable trait that it claims to measure. Because traits cannot be directly observed, however, construct validity cannot be established in a single study but can be assumed to exist only on the basis of a large body of empirical work yielding consistent results.[13]

The *Uniform Guidelines on Employee Selection Procedures* have established three stringent requirements for demonstrating the construct validity of a selection technique.[14]

1. A job analysis must systematically define both the work behaviors involved in the job and the constructs that are believed to be important to job performance.
2. The test must measure one of those constructs. In selecting a project manager, for instance, there must be evidence that the test validly measures leadership. For example, scores on the test might correlate with leadership ratings given to other employees in other organizations upon previous administration of the test.
3. The construct must be related to the performance of critical work behavior. For example, it must be shown that leadership ability is correlated with job performance for the position of project manager. That is, it is necessary to conduct a criterion validity study between leadership and job performance, or to use such data collected by another test to support the claim of construct validity.

Criterion-Related Validity The extent to which a selection technique can accurately predict one or more important elements of job behavior is referred to as **criterion-related validity.** Scores on a test or performance in some simulated exercise are correlated with measures of actual on-the-job performance. The test is called a *predictor;* the performance score is referred to as a *criterion.* Criteria relevant to personnel selection include measures such as quality or quantity of output, supervisory ratings, absenteeism, accidents, sales, or whatever the organization deems most relevant. However, the choice of a criterion is at the very heart of determining whether a selection system is legal.[15] The organization must exercise care in choosing a measure that best reflects the actual contributions of employees to its effectiveness. Not all criteria can be predicted equally well from any particular type of selection tool.[16]

Two popularly used types of criterion-related validity are predictive and concurrent. *Predictive validity* is determined by using the scores obtained from a sample of applicants for a job. The steps in a predictive-validity study for a given test are:

1. Administer the test to a large sample of applicants.
2. Select individuals for the job. It is actually preferable if the test whose validity is being measured is not used in the hiring decisions.
3. Wait an appropriate amount of time and then collect measures of job performance.
4. Assess the strength of the predictor-criterion relationship (typically by calculating a correlation coefficient).

Predictive validity is an important form of criterion-related validity, but it does have drawbacks. The employer first must wait until it has hired a large number of people for whom it has predictor scores and then until it can obtain meaningful measures of job performance for the people who were hired. For some jobs, the time it takes to determine who is a good employee can be long.

Concurrent validity is also used to determine whether a selection test can predict job performance. In concurrent validation, the first step is to administer the tests to present employees performing the job. At approximately the same time, performance measures for these employees are also collected. The test scores are then correlated with the performance measures. If the test is significantly related to performance, it would be a candidate for future use with applicants in the selection process.

The biggest advantage of concurrent validation is that it can be conducted relatively quickly. Therefore, it is usually less expensive than predictive validation. However, there are several potential problems associated with the use of concurrent validation. First, this method uses experienced employees. If experience is important in job performance, such validation will be biased in favor of applicants with experience. Second, present employees often balk at completing tests. They are puzzled by the request to take a battery of tests and often will not provide honest answers or their best answers. Third, there is a self-selection bias that can restrict the range of test scores. Among present employees, there is likely to be a restriction because the least skilled and least able workers have been terminated, demoted, or transferred, and the most skilled and most able have been placed in more responsible jobs.

Despite these potential problems, concurrent validation can be an effective method for assessing the validity of certain kinds of selection tests.[17] However, it should not automatically be used as an alternative to predictive validation simply because it can be done more quickly. The organization should carefully analyze its circumstances before choosing which of the methods to use.

The Selection Process

In the past, selection was often thought to be an easy decision. Decisions were based on the subjective likes or dislikes of the boss. Selection tools were designed to aid this gut reaction. Today, selection is viewed as much more than simply relying on intuition.

The selection decision is usually perceived as a series of steps through which applicants pass. At each step, more applicants are screened out by the organization, or more applicants accept other job offers and drop from the list of applicants. Exhibit 8-1 illustrates a typical series of steps for the selection process.

This series is not universal. For example, government employers test at step 2 instead of step 3, as do some private- and third-sector employers. It is important to note that few organizations use all steps, for they can be time-consuming and expensive; and some steps, such as 3 and 4, may be performed concurrently or at about the same time. Generally speaking, the more important the job, the more each step is likely to be used formally.

Step 1: Preliminary Screening

The most common first step in any selection process usually involves asking an applicant to complete an application form. *Application blanks,* as these are typically referred to, vary in length and sophistication. Nearly all application blanks ask for enough information to determine whether the individual is minimally qualified for the position. For example, application blanks can be a useful initial screening tool for jobs that require some type of professional certification (e.g., a teaching certificate). In this way, the application blank can eliminate the need for subsequent interviews to gather this information. This makes the

EXHIBIT 8-1
Typical Selection
Decision Process

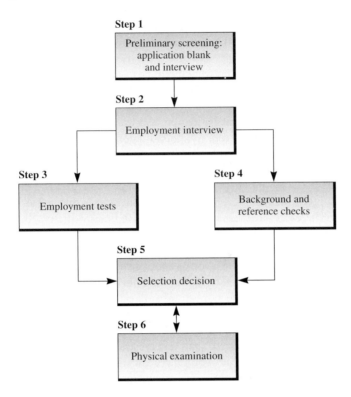

selection process far more efficient, first, by reducing the number of applicants that need to be interviewed and, second, by allowing interviewers to focus on other kinds of information (e.g., personality, communication skills) that are perhaps more difficult to obtain.

Although application blanks can be very useful selection tools, organizations must never forget that they are subject to the same legal standards as any other selection method. Thus, care must be taken that the application blank does not directly or indirectly violate federal or state laws related to employment discrimination.[18] The same guidelines hold true for Web-based or online applications.[19] The application blank should not be designed in a way that forces applicants to reveal irrelevant information about themselves, especially information related to sex, race, religion, color, natural origin, age, or disabilities. Care should be taken to ask only for information that will help the organization make a better job-related assessment of the applicant. For example, asking applicants for the year in which they graduated from high school can narrow down their age to within one or two years. Is it important to know in what year someone graduated, or simply that he or she graduated?

Currently accepted application blanks also generally limit questions that imply something about the applicant's physical health. Since a physical exam should be given only after a conditional offer of employment, the application blank is not an appropriate place to gather most information of this kind.

With a dramatic increase in the number of lawsuits being filed against organizations for "wrongful termination" and with an erosion of organizations' right to hire and fire whomever they wish, many organizations are now adding very important clauses at the beginning or end of their application blanks. Some terms of these clauses appear in employee handbooks as well. The purpose of the clauses, regardless of where they appear, is twofold. First, they help protect the organization against unjustified lawsuits; and second, they help ensure that applicants and employees understand the terms of their employment relationship with the organization.

EXHIBIT 8-2   **The Not-So-Fine Print of Modern Application Blanks**

Statement on Affirmative Action-Equal Employment Opportunity

It is the policy of this company to afford all applicants the right to equal employment opportunities. In accordance with this policy, all vacancies will be filled by qualified candidates without regard to race, color, religion, sex, age, national origin, or disability status except where there is a bona fide occupational qualification. If you are disabled and need reasonable forms of accommodation in order to complete this application blank or any other component of the application process, they will be provided.

Statement on Employment at Will

If you are offered and accept employment with this company, your employment will be considered "at will." It can therefore be terminated at any time and for any reason not expressly prohibited by state or federal law at the discretion of the company. The company retains the right to change, modify, suspend, or cancel any policy or practice that pertains to your employment without advance notice, without having to give cause or justification to any employee. Recognition of these rights is a condition of employment for anyone accepting a job offer from this company. Any written or oral statements by an agent of this company that contradict these policies are invalid and should not be relied on; only the president of this company can amend this policy.

Mandatory Arbitration Clause

By signing this application blank, you agree that any controversy or claim arising out of or relating to your application and/or if you are offered and accept employment with this company, your employment contract or breach thereof shall be settled by arbitration administered by the American Arbitration Association in accordance with its applicable rules. You further agree that should you submit any controversy or claim to arbitration under this policy, you agree to abide by and perform any award rendered by the arbitrator(s).

Three of the more common clauses that now appear on application blanks and in employee handbooks cover (1) applicant's rights as they relate to the organization's hiring practices, (2) the scope of an employment contract, and (3) (one of the newest) grievances: a statement indicating that the applicant, the employee, or both agree to resolve all grievances against the organization through arbitration and mediation rather than through a lawsuit. The legal subtleties of these clauses are too complex to cover in detail at this time, but examples of the wording currently being used by organizations appear in Exhibit 8-2.

A potentially useful supplement to the traditional application blank is the **biographical information blank (BIB).** A BIB usually contains many more items than a typical application blank and asks for information related to a much wider array of attitudes and experiences. BIB items are based on an assumption that these prior behaviors and experiences will be strongly related to an applicant's future behavior.[20] For example, a common BIB item asks applicants to list their favorite subjects in high school. Use of the responses to an item such as this assumes that people who preferred English will perform differently on a given job from people who preferred science or math. Whether such an item should be included on a BIB, however, depends on its ability to differentiate the performance of good and poor workers on the job in question. Recent research indicates that BIBs can help to predict job performance in certain instances. For example, a recent research study found that BIB items can account for incremental predictability of key performance variables beyond that accounted for by incumbent experience on the job, relevant Big Five personality constructs, and general mental ability.[21]

Another variation to the traditional application blank is the **weighted application blank,** an application form that is designed to be scored more systematically and is more like the BIB. To develop the scoring system for a weighted application blank, high and low performers who currently work for the company are compared on a variety of characteristics (e.g., education, years of experience, and so on) that were known at the time they applied for a job. Weights are assigned to the degree of difference on each characteristic. A zero may be assigned for "no difference," ± 1 for a small difference, and ± 2 for a large difference. The weights are then totaled for each applicant, and the one with the highest score is the preferred choice.

Applicants who are judged as minimally qualified on the basis of the application blank will then proceed to the next phase of the selection process. The next step will often be one or more interviews and/or additional employment testing.

Step 2: Employment Interview

Other than application blanks, the interview is definitely the selection technique most often encountered by persons applying for a job in the United States.[22] Not surprisingly, the topic of interviews has generated hundreds of research studies over the past 20 years, covering such topics as verbal-nonverbal behavior, personality characteristics, impression management, interviewer-interviewee similarity, and preinterview impressions (for a complete review, see Posthuma, Morgenson, and Campion, 2002).[23] Because interviews are so widely used to select new employees, they must maximize their potential for identifying qualified persons. Two strategies for making the most out of an interview are (1) structuring the interview to be reliable and valid, and (2) training managers to use the best available interviewing techniques.

Types of Interviews

Employment interviews vary along at least two important dimensions: how structured the interview is and whether it focuses on historical information about the applicant or attempts to place the applicant in hypothetical situations to assess how she or he might respond in the future.

An *unstructured interview* has no predetermined script or protocol. Questions are not prepared in advance; there is no attempt to guarantee that applicants are asked the same questions. Typically, the interviewer does not have a scoring protocol either.

When used by some highly skilled interviewers, the unstructured interview may lead to useful insights about an applicant. However, substantial research over the past 30 years indicates that **structured interviews,** regardless of their specific format, will generally be more reliable and valid than unstructured interviews.[24] During the structured interview, the interviewer has a standardized list of questions to ask of all applicants. These questions should have been generated with the aid of a thorough job analysis in order to identify specific types of information sought during the interview. In addition, a scoring form similar to the one shown in Exhibit 8-3 will be used by the interviewer for recording applicants' responses.

The importance of structure in the interview is further underscored by the fact that standardization should lower the possibility that intentional or unintentional biases held by the interviewer will affect the outcomes of the process. This, in turn, should lead to less differential impact on women and minorities[25] and a better chance for the organization to successfully defend itself if it happens to be sued.[26]

The second dimension along which interviews can vary is whether they focus on past experience and behavior or on hypothetical future behavior. In recent years, two types of structured interviews have emerged and gained popularity in the United States.[27] The first, the *behavioral description interview* (BDI), asks applicants to relate actual incidents from their past relevant work experience to the job for which they are applying. BDIs are based on the assumption that the past is the best predictor of the future.[28] An example of this type of interview question would be "Thinking back to your last job, tell me about a time when you resolved a conflict with a customer?" Follow-up questions would include "What was the outcome?" and "How did you control your frustration?"

The *situational interview* (SI) also seeks to identify whether an applicant possesses relevant job knowledge and motivation, but it achieves this goal in a different manner. SI questions encourage applicants to respond to hypothetical situations they might encounter on the job for which they applied.[29] For example, an applicant for a pharmaceutical sales position might be asked "If one of the physicians in your sales territory asked you to

EXHIBIT 8-3   Structured Employment Interview Form—Executive Position

Date _____ 19 ___

Rating [1] [2] [3] [4]   Comments: _____

SUMMARY

In making final rating, be sure to consider not only what the applicant can do but also his/her stability, industry, perseverance, loyalty, ability to get along with others, self-reliance, leadership, maturity, and motivation.

_____
_____
_____
_____

Interviewer: _____ Job considered for: _____

Name _____ Date of birth _____ Phone no. _____
The Age Discrimination in Employment Act and relevant FEP Acts prohibit discrimination with respect to individuals who are at least 40 but less than 65 years of age.

Present address _____ City _____ State _____ How long there? _____

Were you in the Armed Forces of the U.S.? Yes, branch _____ Date _____ 19 ___ to _____ 19 ___
(Not to be asked in New Jersey)
_____ 19 ___ to _____ 19 ___

If not, why not? _____

Were you hospitalized in the service? _____

Are you drawing compensation? Yes____ No____

Are you employed now?   Yes ☐   No ☐ (If yes) How soon available? _____
What are relationships with present employer?

Why are you applying for this position? _____
Is his/her underlying reason a desire for prestige, security, or earnings?

WORK EXPERIENCE. Cover all positions. This information is very important. Interviewer should record last position first. Every month since leaving school should be accounted for. Experience in Armed Forces should be covered as a job (in New Jersey exclude military questions).

LAST OR PRESENT POSITION _____

Company _____ _____ From _____ 19 _____ to _____ 19 _____

How was job obtained? _____ Whom did you know there? _____
Has applicant shown self-reliance in getting jobs?

Nature of work at start _____ Starting salary _____
Will applicant's previous experience be helpful on this job?

In what way did the job change? _____
Has applicant made good work progress?

Nature of work at leaving _____ Salary at leaving _____
How much responsibility has applicant had?   Any indication of ambition?

Superior _____ Title _____ What is he/she like? _____
Did applicant get along with superior?

How closely does (or did) he/she supervise you? _____ What authority do (or did) you have? _____

Number of people you supervised _____ What did they do? _____
Is applicant a leader?

Responsibility for policy formulation _____
Has applicant had management responsibility?

To what extent could you use initiative and judgment? _____
Did applicant actively seek responsibility?

provide supporting research and other documentation regarding the efficacy of a new drug, how would you go about finding that information?" Responses to this and other hypothetical questions are then scored according to their appropriateness for the job.

Overall, the research findings on situational interviews indicate that questions about past experience have higher validity than the future-oriented hypothetical questions.[30] However, future-oriented questions can also be useful if used properly.[31]

HR Journal — *Winning the Interview Game*

Job seekers know that the interview is a critical part of the job hunt process. If performed well, then job offers will come. If not done properly, then polite "thanks, but no thanks" letters rejecting the job seeker will be sent from the company in the days following the interview. So, how can a job seeker improve his or her chances of having a good interview and, thus, ultimately receiving a job offer? Several experts at monster.com, careerbuilders.com, and hotjobs.com suggest the following tips:

I. PRIOR TO THE INTERVIEW—PREPARE
Research and Practice
Start by knowing your own background and work experience inside and out. Job seekers should be able to discuss several different examples from their own work and/or school experiences; these examples should be used to reinforce answers to tough interview questions. For example, when asked about previous presentation experience, the job seeker should be able to quickly provide real examples of successful client presentations at a previous job and/or group presentations while in school.

Second, job seekers need to also prepare for the interview by doing extensive research on the company. Doing some Web-based research is a good way to start, but it shouldn't end there. Interviewers are impressed when a job seeker shows that he or she has done a lot of information gathering about the company. Good sources for this information include packets from the HR department, conversations with current/former employees, conversations with the investor relations/public relations department, annual reports, company press releases, and the like. From this research, prepare three excellent questions to ask the interviewer.

A third area of preparation is rehearsing and practicing every aspect of the interview. Practicing with a "straight-faced" friend or family member, dress up in your interviewing clothes and practice shaking hands, greeting the "interviewer," introducing yourself, maintaining eye contact and body posture, answering common interview questions, and asking for the job. The more you practice, the better you'll be in the actual interview.

Dress
First impressions, which are often formed in the first minute or two of an interview, can make a huge difference as to whether or not you receive a job offer. So, it's important to dress in a manner that is appropriate and which creates a favorable impression.

There are hundreds of guides for "dressing for success" for interviews on the Web and in bookstores. But one way to learn is by asking the advice of a sales associate at a reputable retail store that sells business suits and clothing. These individuals usually have several tips and can show the job seeker several outfits that are appropriate.

II. DURING THE INTERVIEW—CONFIDENCE AND ENTHUSIASM
By being prepared (see Part I above), your confidence will increase. Even so, expect some stress and nervousness as natural. One way to manage these "nerves" is by, before the interview, doing something that helps to calm you such as exercise, yoga, meditation, and the like. Also, consider the following tips from the experts:

1. Arrive 10 to 15 minutes before your scheduled interview time (never be late to an interview).
2. Use a firm handshake, make good eye contact with the interviewer, and maintain good body posture while sitting in the chair.
3. Convey that you are very interested in the job and exhibit enthusiasm.
4. Bring an extra copy of your resume in case the interviewer needs it.
5. Listen and observe carefully; try to get an idea of what the interviewer is looking for in a candidate.
6. Communicate your experience and skills.
7. Act professionally, politely, and be honest.
8. Focus on what you offer the interviewer to help solve his or her problems.
9. Ask a few questions that show that you did extensive research on the company. (Do not ask about salary, vacation time, benefits, etc.—wait until the interviewer mentions these topics.)
10. Ask when the hiring decision will be made and if you can follow up with the interviewer a week later.

In addition, successful job seekers are very familiar with how to answer the most common interview questions. Here are some questions that you are likely to be asked:

"Tell me about yourself."

"Why did you leave your last job?"

"What's your biggest weakness?"

"Do you have any questions for me?"

HR Journal   *Winning the Interview Game (concluded)*

For answering strategies to these and other common interview questions, see the Web-based sources below.

III. AFTER THE INTERVIEW—STAY CONNECTED AND FOLLOW UP

Within one day of the interview, a thank-you note should be sent by both e-mail and traditional mail. Make sure you thank the interviewer for his or her time and indicate that you are very interested in the job and will be following up. One week later, send a follow-up e-mail or try to reach the interviewer by telephone. Leave messages. Be polite and indicate that you are still interested in the job and would like to know the status of the hiring process. Remember, persistence is an important part of landing the great job!

Sources: Valerie Lipow, "Interviewing 101" (http://hourlyandskilled.monster.com/retail/articles/retailinterviewing/); Carole Martin, "Nonverbal Communications: Escape the Pitfalls" (http://interview.monster.com/articles/actions) accessed June 8, 2005; "Dressing for the Job Interview" (http://www.careerbuilder.com/jobseeker/careerbytes/0403dressing.htm) accessed June 12, 2005; Kate Lorenz, "Hiring Manager Secrets: The 5 Smartest Interview Moves" (http://www.careerbuilder.com/jobseeker/careerbytes/0604topinterviewmoves.htm) accessed June 12, 2005; Todd Anten, "How to Answer the Four Most Common Interview Questions" (http://hotjobs.yahoo.com/interview/How_to_Answer_the_Four_Most_Common_Interview_Questions_20021018-1721.html?subtopic=Interview+Preparation) accessed July 1, 2005.

Training for Interviewing

Despite recent optimism about the validity of employment interviews, many questions about their effectiveness remain unanswered. For years, there have been significant concerns that interviewers may differ considerably in their accuracy, and the potential for bias always exists, since the interview relies so heavily on personal judgments. Exhibit 8-4 summarizes many of the problems that might limit the accuracy of a typical interview. Errors such as these have been the focus of many training programs for interviewers. Generally speaking, however, properly designed training programs do seem capable of reducing many of the errors found in traditional unstructured interviews. This appears to

EXHIBIT 8-4
Errors That Can Occur in the Employment Interview

Source: Robert D. Gatewood and Hubert S. Feild (1998), *Human Resource Selection,* 4th ed. (Fort Worth, TX: Dryden), pp. 494–495. Copyright © 1998 by The Dryden Press; reprinted by permission of the publisher.

1. Excessive talking by the interviewer that limits the amount of job-related information obtained from interviewees.
2. Inconsistency in the questions used with applicants, which results in different types of information being gathered from each applicant.
3. Asking questions that are either unrelated or only slightly related to performance on the job.
4. Inability to put the interviewee at ease during the interview, making it difficult to gather spontaneous or follow-up information.
5. Overconfidence in the interviewer's ability to evaluate applicants, which results in hasty decisions.
6. Stereotyping applicants and allowing personal bias to influence evaluations.
7. Being influenced by the nonverbal behavior of applicants.
8. Rating many applicants the same in evaluations, such as superior (leniency error), average (central tendency error), or poor (stringency error).
9. Allowing one or two either good or bad characteristics of an applicant to influence the evaluation of all other characteristics (halo effect).
10. Allowing the quality of the applicants who preceded the present applicant to influence the ratings of the present applicant (contrast effect).
11. Making an evaluation of the applicant within the first minutes of the interview (first impression error).
12. Favorably evaluating an applicant because he or she is similar to the interviewer in some way (similar-to-me error).

be especially true when the training is used in conjunction with a structured interview format.[32] Training can provide managers with a better understanding of how to ask questions, how to properly record applicants' responses, and to some extent how to be aware of potential biases. Moreover, recent evidence suggests that when a trained interviewer takes behaviorally oriented notes during the interview, validity can be enhanced.[33] For over two decades, the University of Houston's psychology department has sponsored the *Interviewing Institute* (Personnel Psychology Services Center), which offers public workshops in all aspects of employment interviewing. For more information, address e-mail to PsychService@uh.edu.

Step 3: Employment Tests

A technique that some organizations use to aid their selection decisions is the employment test. An employment test is a mechanism (either a paper-and-pencil test or a simulation exercise) that attempts to measure certain characteristics of individuals. These characteristics range from aptitudes, such as manual dexterity, to intelligence to personality.

It can be very expensive to develop a test to measure these kinds of characteristics. For this reason alone, many employers purchase existing tests from a variety of sources. There are literally hundreds of published tests from which to choose, and some of the more useful tests cost as little as $1 per applicant. Anyone interested in selecting a test for use in personnel selection can begin with the *Mental Measurements Yearbook,*[34] which summarizes many of the tests and includes a brief evaluation of their effectiveness.

Regardless of whether an organization develops its own test or purchases an existing one, additional costs are associated with using tests in selection. Any of these devices should be validated before it is actually used to make hiring decisions. However, validation studies are expensive if they are conducted properly. The validation process becomes even more expensive if questions of discrimination arise. In such instances, the organization is expected to validate its selection devices separately for members of majority and minority groups.

Despite the potentially staggering costs associated with employment tests, many more than pay for themselves through increased efficiency in selection. In addition, research suggests that contrary to a perception that applicants avoid applying for jobs that involve extensive testing, applicant withdrawal from any given selection system is unrelated to the presence of testing.[35]

Various kinds of tests can be used for selecting employees. The type of test that is ultimately used will depend on a number of factors, including the budgetary constraints of the organization, the complexity and difficulty of the job, the size and quality of applicant populations, and of course the knowledge, skills, abilities, and other characteristics required by the job. In the following sections, several of the more common categories of selection tests will be described.

Job Sample Performance Tests

A job sample performance test requires the applicant to actually do a sample of the work that the job involves in a controlled situation. Examples of performance tests include:

- Programming test for computer programmers.
- Standard driving course for delivery persons.
- Standardized typing, word processing, or spreadsheet applications problems for secretarial and clerical help.
- Auditions used by a symphony orchestra or ballet company.
- Simulated "in basket" tests for managers. A standardized set of memos, requests, and so on, is given to the applicant, who must dispense with them as she or he would if the work were real.

Variations of these job sample performance tests are used in many organizations. Applicants are frequently asked to run the machines they would run if they got the job. Then the quantity and quality of their work are systematically graded and compared with the work of other applicants.

Over a large number of selection situations, job sample performance tests have demonstrated some of the highest validities of all selection tests. The presumed superiority of these tests over other types of selection tools lies in their direct and obvious relationship with performance on the job. However, for this relationship to actually exist, the content of the job must be well documented through job analyses. Care must be taken not to confuse face validity with actual validity. Face validity is how good a test looks for a given situation. Many tests that are valid also look valid, but that is not always the case. Sometimes a test that appears to have no logical relationship to a particular job may prove to be a valid predictor of performance on that job. Nonetheless, job sample tests are a proven method of selection in many organizations.

Cognitive Ability Tests

Over the years, researchers have identified a large number of specific mental abilities for which selection tests are now available. Perhaps the two best known cognitive abilities are math and verbal. These form the basis for tests such as the Scholastic Aptitude Test (SAT) and the Graduate Record Examination (GRE), to name two. Verbal and math abilities are also measured by a variety of tests developed specifically for use in human resource selection. Still other tests that measure these abilities were developed for use in other areas of psychology but now have been successfully adapted to selection.

Wechsler Adult Intelligence Scale   The Wechsler is a comprehensive paper-and-pencil test of 14 sections grouped into two scores. The verbal score includes general information, arithmetic, similarities, vocabulary, and other items. The performance score includes picture completion, picture arrangement, object assembly, and similar items.

Wonderlic Personnel Test   The Wonderlic uses a variety of perceptual, verbal, and arithmetical items that provide a total score. (Other well-known tests include the Differential Aptitude Test, the SRA Primary Mental Abilities Test, and multiple aptitude tests.)

California Test of Mental Maturity (Adult Level)   This is a test of mental ability administered to groups and scored by machine. Scores are developed from a series of short tests on spatial relationships, verbal concepts, logic and reasoning, numerical reasoning, memory, and others. The scores are converted to IQ equivalents, and profiles are developed for analyzing performance.

Other Cognitive Tests   There are numerous other examples of cognitive tests that have been used successfully in selection but may not be as well known as measures of verbal and math ability or general intellectual ability. For example, Exhibit 8-5 shows an excerpt from a test called the *Minnesota Paper Form Board Test* (MPFB), which is a measure of spatial relations. *Spatial relations* refers to an ability to visualize things on paper as they might appear in actual three-dimensional space. An architect or draftsperson must be able to look at a set of blueprints and clearly know what the actual object (building, house, bridge, etc.) will look like. Similarly, pilots must be able to quickly orient themselves even when they are flying other than straight and level with the ground. Tests of spatial relations have proved effective for these and certain other jobs.

Clerical aptitude is still another cognitive ability that has proved useful in selecting people for a wide array of jobs. Exhibit 8-6 is the first page of the Minnesota Clerical Test, one of the more popular measures of clerical aptitude. This test requires applicants to rapidly check numbers and names for accuracy. The ability to rapidly compare entries such as these is a good predictor of many types of job performance, especially in secretarial and clerical jobs.

EXHIBIT 8-5
Excerpt from Revised Minnesota Paper Form Board Test

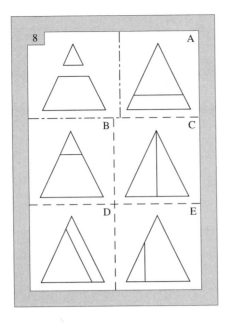

Psychomotor Ability Simulations

There are a number of tests that measure an applicant's psychomotor abilities, although these are not as popular as they once were. They include choice reaction time, speed of limb movement, and finger dexterity. One of these is the O'Connor Finger and Tweezer Dexterity Test (see Exhibit 8-7). The person being tested picks up pins with the tweezer and row by row inserts them in the holes across the board with the hand normally used. These tests are used for positions with high manual requirements, such as assembling radio or TV components and watches.

EXHIBIT 8-6

MINNESOTA CLERICAL TEST
(formerly the Minnesota Vocational Test for Clerical Workers)
by Dorothy M. Andrews, Donald G. Patterson, and Howard P. Longstaff

Name _____   Name _____
TEST 1-Number Comparison   TEST 2-Name Comparison
Number Right_____   Number Right_____
Number Wrong _____   Number Wrong _____
Score = R − W_____   Score = R − W_____
Percentile Rating _____   Percentile Rating _____
Norms Used _____   Norms Used _____

INSTRUCTIONS

On the inside pages there are two tests. One of the tests consists of pairs of names and the other of pairs of numbers. If the two names or the two numbers of a pair are exactly the same make a check mark ( ) on the line between them: if they are different, make no mark on that line. When the examiner says "Stop!" draw a line under the last pair at which you have looked.

Samples done correctly of pairs of Numbers
79542 _____ 79524
1234567 _√_ 1234567

Samples done correctly of pairs of Names
John C. Linder _____ John C. Lender
Investors Syndicate _√_ Investors Syndicate

This is a test for speed and accuracy. Work as fast as you can without making mistakes. Do not turn this page until you are told to begin.

EXHIBIT 8-7
O'Connor Finger and Tweezer Dexterity Test Equipment

Personality Inventories and Temperament Tests

Potentially, the least reliable of the employment tests are instruments that attempt to measure a person's personality or temperament. The most frequently used inventory is the Minnesota Multiphasic Personality Inventory. Other paper-and-pencil inventories are the California Psychological Inventory, the Minnesota Counseling Inventory, the Manifest Anxiety Scale, and the Edwards Personal Preference Schedule.

A more optimistic picture of the value of personality inventories comes from efforts to specifically construct a measure for a particular job. That is, some of the disappointing results previously obtained with personality inventories in selection could be attributed to a mismatch between the test and the situation in which it was being used.[36] When personality tests are constructed to measure work-related characteristics such as achievement and dependability, they can show good validities.[37]

A different approach, not as direct as the self-reporting inventory, utilizes projective techniques to present vague stimuli. The reactions provide data on which psychologists base their assessment and interpretation of a personality. The stimuli are purposely vague to reach unconscious aspects of the personality. Many techniques are used. The most common are the Rorschach Inkblot Test and the Thematic Apperception Test.

The Rorschach Inkblot Test was first described in 1921. The test involves 10 cards, on each of which is printed a bilateral symmetrical inkblot similar to that illustrated in Exhibit 8-8.[38] The person responding is asked to tell what he or she sees in the inkblot. The examiner keeps a verbatim record of the responses, the time taken to make the responses, emotional expressions, and other incidental behavior. Then a trained interpreter analyzes the data and reaches conclusions about the personality patterns of the person being examined.

Polygraph and Honesty Tests

Another method currently used by some employers to test employees is the polygraph, sometimes erroneously called a *lie detector.* The polygraph is an instrument that records

EXHIBIT 8-8
Inkblot of the Type Employed in the Rorschach Technique

HRMEMO

The Myers-Briggs Type Indicator is a very popular test that measures four qualities of an individual's personality: introversion/ extroversion, sensing/ intuition, thinking/ feeling, judging/ perceiving. Scores are used in a variety of ways, including matching people with careers, team building, organizational change, and leader- ship development.

Sources: Ariana Eunjung Cha (March 27, 2005), "Employers Relying on Personality Tests to Screen Applicants," *The Washington Post,* p. A01; Karin Garrety, Richard Badham, Viviane Morrigan, Will Rifkin, and Michael Zanko (2003), "The Use of Personality Typing in Organization Change: Discourse, Emotions and the Reflexive Subject," *Human Relations,* Vol. 56, Iss. 2, pp. 211–35.

changes in breathing, blood pressure, pulse, and skin response associated with sweating of palms, and then plots these reactions on paper. The person being tested with a polygraph attached is asked a series of questions. Some are neutral, to achieve a normal response; others are stressful, to indicate a response made under pressure. Thus, the applicant may be asked, "Is your name Smith?" Then, "Have you ever stolen from an employer?"

Although originally developed for police work, the polygraph had become an extremely popular selection tool by the mid-1980s. It has been estimated that, prior to 1988, nearly 2 million polygraph tests had been administered each year by private employers in the United States.[39] This popularity was understandable because on-the-job crime had increased tremendously; it was estimated that dishonest employees cost employers about $65 billion per year in theft and other acts of dishonesty.[40] Since a polygraph will cost only about $25, it seems like a small investment to help reduce dishonesty in the workplace.

In recent years, objections have been raised to the use of the polygraph in personnel selection. There are concerns that it is an invasion of an applicant's privacy and that its use can lead to self-incrimination, which would be a violation of the Fifth Amendment to the Constitution. However, the most serious question concerning the polygraph was whether it was, in fact, a reliable and valid method for predicting on-the-job dishonesty. In a recent quantitative review of polygraph tests, it was reported that electrodermal measures correctly identified 76 percent of participants with concealed knowledge, indicating that 24 percent of subjects were able to conceal information without detection.[41]

These concerns became serious enough that the federal government passed the **Employee Polygraph Protection Act** of 1988. This legislation has made it illegal for most private organizations to use the polygraph as a selection device. Government agen- cies and certain contractors for the Department of Defense and the Department of Energy are exempt from the act. In addition, private employers whose business involves security and controlled substances are also allowed to continue using the polygraph. Finally, it is still legal to use the polygraph as a part of an ongoing investigation of dishonesty as long as the individual employee's rights are safe-guarded.[42]

Organizations searching for an alternative to the polygraph are increasingly turning to paper-and-pencil tests of honesty. Estimates are that 5,000 to 6,000 firms in the United States now use these during screening.[43] The two most common types of preem- ployment honesty tests are overt integrity tests and personality-based integrity tests.[44] Overt integrity tests ask more direct questions to assess dishonest behavior, as well as gather a history of theft and other illegal activities. In comparison, personality-based integrity tests attempt to assess an individual's predisposition toward deviant and dis- ruptive behavior.[45] Although some critics believe that preemployment honesty tests gen- erate an unacceptable level of false positive results (i.e., a job candidate is incorrectly classified as a potential thief when, in fact, he or she is not),[46] several researchers have provided evidence that certain honesty tests have acceptable levels of validity and reli- ability. For example, a comprehensive meta-analysis on over a half million subjects reported that honesty tests are valid for predicting counterproductive behaviors on the job such as theft, disciplinary problems, and absenteeism. In addition, this study reported that job candidate scores on honesty tests could also be used to predict future supervisory ratings of job performance.[47]

Step 4: Reference Checks and Recommendations

If you have ever applied for a job, you were probably asked to provide a list of people whom the organization could contact to get information about you. These references might have been work-related (such as a former supervisor or co-worker), or they might have been personal (such as friends, clergy, or family members). In either case, to the extent that you could, you provided the organization with a list of people who you believed would generally speak favorably about you. Rarely, when given the opportunity, does someone knowingly include the name of a reference who will give a negative impression to the new organization.

This built-in bias in favor of the applicant is precisely the reason that general references have often been criticized as sources of useful information. Many argue that they will seldom provide an organization with meaningful information about applicants. Equally important, however, are genuine concerns over the legality of asking for and providing such information. Giving out confidential information about a former employee could be construed as a violation of the employee's right to privacy, and giving a negative recommendation opens the reference up to a defamation lawsuit.[48] Most reasonable people would agree that managers should not be allowed to lie about a former employee or to be malicious while providing reference information. On the other hand, not all references can be positive, and managers should not have to fear being sued simply for being honest about a former employee.

In any event, fears of being sued have led many managers to refuse to provide references for former employees. The trend in this direction has also caused organizations to include explicit statements in their employee handbooks about corporate policies on checking references. Rather than risk a lawsuit, managers are instructed to give out only verifiable kinds of information such as dates of employment and job title. Under these circumstances, it is almost certain that references will be of little or no value to the hiring organization except as a check on the accuracy of information contained on the application blank.

Organizations must also be wary of any policy which suggests that all references should be neutral in nature. Employment attorneys are cautioning organizations to be aware of a new problem which they are labeling "negligent referrals." If an organization is aware of important negative information about a former employee and fails to reveal this information during an inquiry by a prospective employer, it might find itself in "legal hot water."[49] At the present time, the legal status surrounding reference-checking and providing recommendations is just not clear at all.

Perhaps because references have become such dangerous business, at least 32 states have passed laws that give managers some immunity from being sued for providing good-faith, job-related information about their employees.[50] Most of these laws are, however, too new to determine whether they will be effective.

Step 5: Physical Examinations

Careful adherence to the Americans with Disabilities Act indicates that physical examinations can be used to screen out unqualified individuals but generally should be required only after a conditional offer of employment has been made. However, if an organization is going to use such examinations, all individuals who are conditionally offered employment should be required to have one. These requirements do not mean that an organization must hire an individual with a disability if that person cannot perform the essential functions of the job. They do, however, help to protect the rights of individuals with disabilities who are qualified.[51]

A Note on Drug Testing

Perhaps no other selection practice elicits a more emotional reaction than an organizational **drug-testing program.** A recent survey by the American Management Association indicates, however, that approximately 62 percent of American corporations are now using drug tests.[52] Moreover, the Department of Transportation mandates both drug and alcohol testing for virtually all employers who have truck and delivery drivers with commercial licenses.[53]

Why is there such a strong emphasis on alcohol and substance abuse in the workplace? Consider the following statistics compiled from a number of sources by the U.S.

HRMEMO

In a recent Gallup poll commissioned by the Institute for a Drug-Free Workplace, a significant majority of Americans supported drug testing as a condition of employment for all surveyed occupations. The greatest need was perceived for occupations entrusted with the safety of others such as airline pilot, doctor, and school bus driver.

Source: www. drugfreeworkplace.org/ survey.htm.

Department of Labor. It is estimated that there are 14.8 million illicit drug users in the United States and three-quarters of these persons are employed either full- or part-time. More than 14 percent of employed Americans report being heavy drinkers. More than one in three workers between the ages of 18 and 25 are binge drinkers (i.e., five or more drinks on one occasion). Alcohol abuse costs U.S. corporations 500 million lost work days each year.[54] Coupled with estimated losses of $120 billion annually attributable to drug abuse,[55] the costs to business are staggering.

The reliability of drug tests is, however, a major concern, for at least two reasons. First, even when a particular drug test is deemed very accurate if typical employment test standards are applied, there is a potential for the test to yield a questionably high number of false positives—the test indicates that the applicant is using illegal drugs when in reality he or she is not.[56] Second, the personal consequences of being falsely labeled as a drug user are more severe than those of a false positive on other types of selection tests—a math test, for example. In the former case, the implication is that the applicant has broken the law; in the latter case, the implication is simply that the applicant has more math ability than he or she has in reality.

Also, the legality of drug-testing programs has not been universally established, although many organizational programs have withstood challenges in court. Thus, it is not possible to determine whether any particular drug-testing program that doesn't fall under a federal mandate will, in fact, be legal. However, the best guess is that most good-faith drug testing programs will be legally acceptable if the organization has taken steps to:

- Inform all job applicants of the organization's drug-testing screening program.
- Establish a high-quality control testing procedure with a reliable testing laboratory.
- Perform any drug tests in a professional, nonthreatening manner.
- Keep all results confidential.

Selection of Managers

The particular types of employment tests that are used in an organization vary with the type of employee being hired. Many of the techniques that have been discussed in this chapter (the interview, for example) are common to most occupations. Others, such as cognitive ability testing, are used with a wide assortment of jobs and occupations ranging from blue-collar to managerial positions. However, because of the costs associated with a bad decision and the complexities of managerial work, organizations frequently expend more time, effort, and money hiring middle- to upper-level executives than they spend hiring for positions lower on the organizational chart. One of the best-known multiple selection methods used for these purposes is the **assessment center.** The assessment center was first used by the German military in World War II. The Office of Strategic Services (OSS) in the United States began to use it in the mid-1940s. American Telephone and Telegraph Company (AT&T) introduced the assessment center to the world of business in the 1950s. Since 1956, AT&T has used assessment centers to evaluate more than 200,000 prospective and current employees.[57]

An assessment center uses a wide array of methods, including several interviews, work samples and simulations, and many kinds of paper-and-pencil tests of abilities and attitudes.[58] Exhibit 8-9 presents briefly a typical $2\frac{1}{2}$ day assessment center schedule.

Most assessment centers are similar in a number of areas:

1. Groups of approximately 12 individuals are evaluated. Individual and group activities are observed and evaluated.
2. Multiple methods of assessment are used—interviewing, objective testing, projective testing, games, role-playing, and other methods.

EXHIBIT 8-9
Assessment Center Schedule (2½ Days)

Day 1	Day 2	Day 3
A. Orientation of approximately 12 ratees.	A. Individual decision-making exercise—Ratees are asked to make a decision about some problem that must be solved. (Raters observe fact-finding skills, understanding of problem-solving procedures, and propensity for taking risks.)	A. Individual case analysis and presentation. (Raters observe problem-solving ability, method of preparation, ability to handle questions, and communication skills.)
B. Break up into groups of four or six to play management simulation game. (Raters observe planning ability, problem-solving skill, interaction skills, communication ability.)	B. In-basket exercise. (Raters observe decision making under stress, organizing ability, memory, and ability to delegate.)	B. Evaluation of other ratees. (Peer evaluations.)
C. Psychological testing—Measure verbal and numerical skills.	C. Role-playing of performance evaluation interview. (Raters observe empathy, ability to react, counseling skills, and how information is used.)	
D. Interview with raters. (Ratees discuss goals, motivation, and career plans.)	D. Group problem solving. (Raters observe leadership ability and ability to work in a group.)	
E. Small-group discussion of case incidents. (Raters observe confidence, persuasiveness, decision-making flexibility.)		

3. Assessors are usually a panel of line managers from the organization. They can, however, be consultants or outsiders trained to conduct assessments.

4. Assessment centers are relevant to the job, and thus have high appeal because of this relevance.

As a result of assessees participating as part of a group and as individuals—completing exercises, interviews, and tests—the assessors have a large volume of data on each individual. Individuals are then evaluated on a number of dimensions, such as organizational and planning ability, decisiveness, flexibility, resistance to stress, poise, and personal styles.

The raters' judgments are consolidated and developed into a final report. Each assessee's performance in the center can be described if the organization wants this type of report. Portions of the individual reports are fed back to each assessee, usually by one or more members of the assessment team.

Because it is an integrated attempt to measure a variety of characteristics of managers, the assessment center report permits the organization to make a number of determinations about human resources:

- Qualifications of individuals for particular positions.
- Promotability of individuals.
- How individuals function in a group.
- Type of training and development needed to improve behaviors of individuals.
- How good assessors are in observing, evaluating, and reporting on the performance of others (assessees).

Overall, the results of research on assessment centers have indicated that they are a valid way to select managers[59]—but they are not without disadvantages. Generally speaking, well-designed assessment centers are a relatively expensive way to hire managers. As such, they are not a reasonable alternative for many smaller organizations. Moreover, there are circumstances in which less costly and less administratively complicated techniques

What did Clark Kirby do? He didn't have the resources or time to hire all 596. Besides, he believed that operating managers should participate in decisions. So his strategy was to hire the managers first. Then he had the managers help screen and hire the clerical and semiskilled employees.

As far as selection objectives were concerned, Clark accepted the home office's objectives: to hire the employees who were most likely to be effective and satisfied. He accepted the job specifications for the most similar positions he could find in the Chicago plant. These specifications listed minimal requirements in education and experience for managers and professional and technical employees. For clerical employees, the emphasis was on minimal experience plus scores on performance simulation tests. For skilled and semiskilled employees, the job specifications also included minimal experience and test scores on performance simulation tests.

Clark decided that because of time pressures and the nature of the different jobs, he would use the following selection process.

- Managers: screening interview, application blank, interview, reference check.
- Professional and technical: screening interview, application blank, interview, reference check.
- Clerical: screening interview, application blank, interview, tests.
- Skilled: screening interview, application blank, tests, and interviews for marginal applicants.
- Semiskilled: screening interview, application blank, tests, and interviews for marginal applicants.

Clark and Ed hired the managers. Clark himself hired the professionals. While these groups were being hired, an HR specialist administered the tests to the clerical employees and supervised the reference checks for the managers and professionals. The HR specialist hired the clerical employees with help from the managers and professionals for the clerical personnel who were to be under their direct supervision.

Then Clark and the HR specialist administered the tests to skilled and semiskilled employees. Clark hired the clearly well-qualified semiskilled employees, except in marginal cases. Candidates received a review and were interviewed by the managers to whom they would report. A similar process was used to hire the semiskilled employees. Since there were few choices among professional-technical and skilled employees, it was more efficient not to involve the new managers.

Several problems developed. Clark and Ed had no trouble agreeing on 20 managerial candidates. But in 18 additional cases, Clark felt he had found better candidates, whereas Ed wanted more Chicago people that he knew. Among Clark's choices were many more qualified minority and female managerial candidates than Ed wanted to accept. In the end, they compromised. Ed gave up half his choices to Clark, and Clark did likewise.

There were also problems in the skilled professional categories. These people generally wanted more pay than the budget called for. And the last 20 percent hired were somewhat below minimal specifications. Clark appealed for a bigger budget, given these conditions. The home office gave him half of what he needed. He had to generate the other half by paying less for the bottom 20 percent of the semiskilled and clerical employees. Clark alerted Ed to the probable competence problem, promising that he'd begin developing a list of qualified applicants in these categories in case they were needed.

In sum, Clark hired the people needed within the adjusted budget, on time, and generally with the required specifications. He was able to make a contribution to equal employment opportunity objectives by hiring somewhat more minorities and women than the total population, less than he could have and less than Lois wanted, but more than Ed wanted. All were qualified. No reverse discrimination took place.

are just as effective in managerial selection.[60] Therefore, they are frequently not the technique of choice even for organizations that have the resources to utilize them.

Cost-Benefit Analysis for the Selection Decision

Once an organization has made a commitment to investigate what types of selection devices it will use, it must attempt to evaluate whether its efforts will be worthwhile. Ultimately, a large part of the answer to this question involves the utility of the selection process. **Utility** refers to the degree to which using a selection system improves the quality of the individuals being selected by the organization.[61]

Utility has two related components. *Statistical utility* is the extent to which a selection technique allows an organization to better predict who will be successful. *Organizational utility,* which is dependent, in part, on statistical utility, is a matter of costs and benefits. In other words, answering the question whether the selection system should be developed and used is ultimately an issue of whether it saves the organization more money than it costs.

Generally speaking, an analysis of the costs versus the benefits of selection requires estimates of the direct and indirect costs associated with the selection system. Direct costs include such things as the price of the tests, the salary paid to an interviewer, and the equipment used in a work sample test. Indirect costs include changes in public image associated with implementing procedures such as drug testing.

The organization must also estimate how much money it will save by hiring more qualified employees using the selection system. These savings can come from improved outcomes such as higher levels of quality or quantity of output, reduced absenteeism, lower accident rates, and less turnover.

Sometimes, when an organization's managers see how costly systematic selection can be, they wonder whether it will ever have benefits. The answer to this basic question depends on many factors. But valid selection procedures can yield enormous benefits, especially in situations where the direct and indirect costs of hiring a poor performer are high. Imagine the costs associated with a single wrong hiring decision when airlines are selecting pilots. Pilot errors can cost the company millions of dollars in destroyed or damaged equipment, and no amount of money can offset the potential loss of human life that may be involved.

One final note about selection and a cost-benefit analysis of it—the way that an organization hires employees is directly tied to other human resource programs. Perhaps the most important linkage is with training. Many trade-off decisions must be made between selection and training. At the very least, the organization should realize that putting more money into selection can significantly reduce the amount of money it must spend on training, especially if the increased commitment to selection allows the organization to hire a more capable workforce.

Summary

This chapter has explained what is involved in making effective selection decisions. The basic objective of selection is to obtain the employees who are most likely to meet the organization's standards of performance and who will be satisfied and developed on the job.

To summarize the major points covered in this chapter:

1. Selection is influenced by environmental characteristics: whether the organization is public or private, labor market conditions and the selection ratio, union requirements, and legal restrictions on selection.

2. Reasonable criteria for the choice must be set prior to selection. The best way to identify these criteria is through thorough job analysis.

3. The typical selection process can include up to five steps:
   a. Preliminary screening with an application blank and a brief interview.
   b. Employment interviews.
   c. Employment tests.
   d. Reference checks and letters of recommendation.
   e. Physical examination as a part of a conditional job offer.

4. For more important positions (measured by higher pay and responsibility), the selection decision is more likely to be formalized and to use more selection techniques.

5. Many organizations prefer to select people already in the organization instead of outside candidates.

6. The accuracy of selection decisions can often be increased if both HR professionals and operating managers are involved in hiring.

7. Using a greater number of accepted methods to gather data for selection decisions increases the number of successful candidates selected.

8. Larger organizations are more likely to use sophisticated selection techniques.

9. For more measurable jobs or for those lower in the hierarchy, tests can be used more effectively in the selection decisions.

10. A selection system will make some mistakes; and even if the most able applicant is chosen, there is no guarantee of successful performance on the job.

11. Accurate selection tests are a major tool in helping organizations avoid the costs of poor performance; they also help to ensure that an organization is hiring people in legally acceptable ways.

Key Terms

assessment center, p. 234
biographical information blank (BIB), p. 223
construct validity, p. 220
content validity, p. 219
criterion-related validity, p. 220

drug-testing program, p. 233
Employee Polygraph Protection Act, p. 232
reliability, p. 219
selection, p. 214

structured employment interview, p. 224
utility, p. 237
validity, p. 219
weighted application blank, p. 223

Questions for Review and Discussion

1. What are the goals of selection? What factors influence an organization's choice of selection methods?

2. Why should a selection method be both valid and reliable? What could happen legally if a company uses a selection method that lacks these characteristics?

3. What are the major types of employment interviews? What are the characteristics of each type?

4. What are some errors that an interviewer may commit? Describe them and any potential legal implications of committing these errors.

5. Describe the two types of paper-and-pencil honesty tests. Should your organization make job applicants complete one? Why or why not?

6. Why do you think that conscientiousness, one of the Big Five personality dimensions, is such a good predictor of successful job performance across most occupations? Explain your answer.

7. What activities do companies typically engage in during the "preliminary screening" stage of the selection process?

8. What is the current status of drug testing in American organizations? Do you think drug testing is justifiable? Why?

9. What is the Employee Polygraph Protection Act? What alternatives to polygraphs are organizations using? Are these alternatives effective?

10. What are the implications of the Americans with Disabilities Act for selection?

HRM Legal Advisor

Based on *Equal Employment Opportunity Commission* v. *The Chrysler Corporation,* 917 F. Supp. 1164 (U.S. Dist. Court for the Eastern Dist. of Michigan, Southern Division 1996).

The Facts

On July 20, 1993, David Darling applied for a job as an electrician with the Chrysler Corporation. His application was sent to Chrysler's Sterling Heights Stamping plant, which had an opening for an electrician. Sterling's facilities manager, James Allen, interviewed Mr. Darling and was favorably impressed with his experience teaching electrical and welding classes. No other applicants had experience training other electricians. At Mr. Allen's request, the head of human resources at the Sterling facility made a conditional job offer to Mr. Darling requiring satisfactory results on drug and medical tests. When the drug test indicated that Mr. Darling's blood sugar level was elevated, he met with a private physician, Dr. Bradley C. Berger. Dr. Berger diagnosed Mr. Darling with a Type II diabetes mellitus and recommended a diet for his condition; no medication was prescribed. Dr. Berger also indicated in a letter that Mr. Darling could "work without restrictions." Approximately one month later, Sterling's plant physician, Dr. Onder, administered further blood tests, which also indicated elevated blood sugar levels. As a result, Dr. Onder would not authorize Mr. Darling for employment and placed restrictions on climbing and the operation of moving machinery. Further tests conducted by Dr. Berger the following month indicated a decrease in Mr. Darling's blood sugar level to within a normal range. Dr. Berger again stated in a letter that Mr. Darling could work without restrictions. Approximately one week later, Chrysler withdrew the conditional job offer citing Mr. Darling's high blood sugar as the reason. Mr. Darling filed a claim of disability discrimination with the EEOC, which initiated a suit against Chrysler on Mr. Darling's behalf seeking back pay, benefits, and compensatory damages. Because Mr. Darling was hired by Chrysler as an electrician in its Highland Park facility approximately one year later, his potential damages were limited to back pay and benefits for one year.

To make a valid claim of disability discrimination under the Americans with Disabilities Act (ADA), a plaintiff must prove that (1) he or she is disabled, (2) he or she is qualified, and (3) adverse employment action was taken because of the disability. Does Mr. Darling have a valid claim?

The Court's Decision

The U.S. District Court for the Eastern District of Michigan found that Mr. Darling was disabled under the ADA because "Chrysler regarded Darling as having an impairment which significantly restricted his ability to perform either a class of jobs or a broad range of jobs in various classes." The court further found that Mr. Darling was qualified for the job of electrician, rejecting Chrysler's argument that diabetes rendered him unqualified. The court also rejected Chrysler's defense that Mr. Darling's elevated blood sugar posed a "direct threat" stating that there was no evidence of a "high probability of substantial harm to the health and safety of others." Finally, the court concluded that Chrysler's blanket exclusion of individuals with blood sugar levels over 140 mg/dl violated the ADA, proving that the company failed to make individual assessments of applicants' qualifications for specific positions. The court issued an injunction that prohibited Chrysler from further application of its blanket exclusionary policy.

Human Resource Implications

This case highlights the importance of ensuring that selection criteria are tailored for the specific requirements of a job. With respect to the ADA, companies must determine whether medical requirements are job related. This means that companies must perform individualized assessments of the medical standards required for each job to assess whether job-specific risks exist. Blanket exclusionary policies such as Chrysler's will be highly scrutinized by courts.

Notes

1. Adrian Furnham (February 1999), "The Dark Side of Talent," *Across the Board,* pp. 9–10.

2. Susan J. Wells (October 2004), "Too Good to Hire," *HRMagazine,* Vol. 49, Iss. 10, pp. 48–55; Joann Lubin (March 2001), "When You Really Want to Take a Job That Is Beneath You," *The Wall Street Journal,* p. B1.

3. Jennifer P. Bott, Daniel J. Svyantec, Scott A. Goodman, and David S. Bernal (2003), "Expanding the Performance Domain: Who Says Nice Guys Finish Last?" *International Journal of Organizational Analysis,* Vol. 11, Iss. 2, pp. 137–53; Miguel A. Quinones, Kevin J. Ford, and Mark S. Teachout (Winter 1995), "The Relationship between Work Experience and Job Performance: A Conceptual and Meta-Analytic Review," *Personnel Psychology,* pp. 887–910.

4. Michael Barrier (March 2002), "An Age-Old Problem," *HRMagazine,* pp. 34–37.

5. Herbert Heneman, Timothy Judge, and Robert Heneman (2000), *Staffing Organizations,* 3rd ed. (New York: Irwin McGraw-Hill), pp. 427–432.

6. Ibid.

7. Jesus F. Salgado (September 2003), "Predicting Job Performance Using FFM and Non-FFM Personality Measures," *Journal of Occupational and Organizational Psychology,* Vol. 76, Part 3, pp. 323–46; Gregory Hurtz and John Donovan (December 2000), "Personality and Job Performance: The Big Five Revisited," *Journal of Applied Psychology,* pp. 869–879; Timothy Judge and J. E. Bono (1998), "Relationship of Core Self-Evaluation to Job Satisfaction and Job Performance: A Meta-Analysis," Working paper, University of Iowa; Murray Barrick and Michael Mount (1991), "The Big Five Personality Dimensions and Job Performance: A Meta-Analysis," *Personnel Psychology,* 44, pp. 1–26.

8. John Bourbeau (1996 Cumulative Supplement), *Employment Testing Manual* (Boston: Warren, Gorham, & Lamont), p. 9.08.

9. Robert B. Tett, Jacquelyn R. Steele, and Russell S. Beauregard (May 2003), "Broad and Narrow Measures on Both Sides of the Personality–Job Performance Relationship," *Journal of Organizational Behavior,* Vol. 24, Iss. 3, pp. 335–56; Sampo V. Paunonen, Mitchell G. Rothstein, and Douglas N. Jackson (May 1999), "Narrow Reasoning about the Use of Broad Personality Measures for Personnel Selection," *Journal of Organizational Behavior,* pp. 389–405.

10. Jum C. Nunnally (1978), *Psychometric Theory,* 2nd ed. (New York: McGraw-Hill), p. 191.

11. Jum Nunnally and Ira Bernstein (1994), *Psychometric Theory,* 3rd ed. (New York: Irwin/McGraw-Hill), p. 83; Wayne F. Cascio (1991), *Applied Psychology in Personnel Management,* 4th ed. (Englewood Cliffs, NJ: Prentice Hall), p. 151.

12. Society for Industrial and Organizational Psychology (1987), *Principles for the Validation and Use of Personnel Selection Procedures,* 3rd ed. (College Park, MD: Society).

13. Ibid.

14. T. G. Abram (August 1979), "Overview of Uniform Selection Guidelines: Pitfalls for the Unwary Employer," *Labor Law Journal,* pp. 495–502.

15. Bourbeau, *Employment Testing Manual,* p. 3.06.

16. Barry Nathan and Ralph A. Alexander (Autumn 1988), "A Comparison of Criteria for Test Validation: A Meta-Analytic Investigation," *Personnel Psychology,* pp. 517–535.

17. Gerald V. Barrett, James S. Phillips, and Ralph A. Alexander (February 1981), "Concurrent and Predictive Validity Designs: A Critical Reanalysis," *Journal of Applied Psychology,* pp. 1–6.

18. J. Craig Wallace and Stephen J. Vodanovich (2004), "Personnel Application Blanks: Persistence and Knowledge of Legally Inadvisable Application Blank Items," *Public Personnel Management,* Vol. 33, Iss. 3, pp. 331–50; Timothy S. Bland & Sue S. Stalcup (March 1999), "Build a Legal Employment Application," *HRMagazine,* pp. 129–133.

19. Craig Wallace, Mary Tye, and Stephen Vodanovich (Winter 2000), "Applying for Jobs Online: Examining the Legality of Internet-Based Application Forms," *Public Personnel Management,* pp. 497–504.

20. Frederick L. Oswald, Neal Schmitt, Brian H. Kim, Lauren J. Ramsay, and Michael A. Gillespie (April 2004), "Developing a Biodata Measure and Situational Judgment Inventory as Predictors of College Student Performance," *Journal of Applied Psychology,* Vol. 89, Iss. 2, pp. 187–207; Bernard J. Nickels (1994), "The Nature of Biodata," in Garnett S. Stokes, Michael D. Mumford, and William A. Owens (eds.), *Biodata Handbook* (Palo Alto, CA: CPP Books).

21. Michael Mount, L. W. Witt, and Murray Barrick (Summer 2000), "Incremental Validity of Empirically Keyed Biodata Scales over GMA and the Five Factor Personality Constructs," *Personnel Psychology,* pp. 299–323.

22. American Society for Personnel Administration (1983), "Employment Selection Procedures," *ASPA-BNA Survey No. 45* (Washington, DC: Bureau of National Affairs).

23. Richard Posthuma, Frederick Morgenson, Michael Campion (Spring 2002), "Beyond Employment Interview Validity: A Comprehensive Narrative Review of Recent Research and Trend over Time," *Personnel Psychology,* pp. 1–81.

24. Filip Lievens and Anneleen De Paepe (2004), "An Empirical Investigation of Interviewer-Related Factors That Discourage the Use of High Structure Interviews," *Journal of Organizational Behavior,* Vol. 25, Iss. 1, pp. 29–46; Frank L. Schmidt and Mark Rader (Summer 1999), "Exploring the Boundary Conditions for Interview Validity: Meta-Analytic Validity Findings for a New Interview Type," *Personnel Psychology,* pp. 445–464.

25. Allen I. Huffcutt and Philip L. Roth (April 1998), "Racial Group Differences in Employment Interview Evaluations," *Journal of Applied Psychology,* pp. 179–189.

26. Laura Gollub Williamson, James E. Campion, Stanley B. Malos, Mark V. Roehling, and Michael A. Campion (December 1997), "Employment Interview on Trial: Linking Interview Structure with Litigation Outcomes," *Journal of Applied Psychology,* pp. 900–912.

27. Ute-Christine Klehe and Gary P. Latham (June 2005), "The Predictive and Incremental Validity of the Situational and Patterned Behavior Description Interviews for Team Playing Behavior," *International Journal of Selection and Assessment,* Vol. 13, Iss. 2, pp. 108–124; Allen Huffcutt, Jeff Weekley, Willi Wiesner, Tim DeGroot, and Casey Jones (Autumn 2001), "Comparison of Situational and Behavior Descriptive Interview Questions for Higher-Level Positions," *Personnel Psychology,* pp. 619–644.

28. "Using Behavioral Interviewing to Help You Hire the Best of the Best" (August 2004), *HR Focus,* Vol. 81, Iss. 8, pp. 5–8; T. Janz (1989), "The Patterned Behavior Description Interview: The Best Prophet of the Future Is the Past," In R. W. Eder and G. R. Ferris (Eds.), *The Employment Interview: Theory, Research, and Practice* (Newbury Park, CA: Sage), pp. 158–168; T. Janz (1982), "Initial Comparisons of Patterned Behavior Description Interviews versus Unstructured Interviews," *Journal of Applied Psychology,* pp. 577–580.

29. Posthuma et al., op. cit., p. 619; Gary P. Latham, Lise M. Saari, Elliot D. Pursell, and Michael A. Campion (August 1980), "The Situational Interview," *Journal of Applied Psychology,* pp. 422–427.

30. Elaine D. Pulakos and Neal Schmitt (Summer 1995), "Experience-Based and Situational Interview Questions: Studies of Validity," *Personnel Psychology,* pp. 289–308.

31. Sue-Chan Christina and Gary P. Latham (2004), "The Situational Interview as a Predictor of Academic and Team Performance: A Study of the Mediating Effects of Cognitive Ability and Emotional Intelligence," *International Journal of Selection and Assessment,* Vol. 12, Iss. 4, pp. 312–20; Michael A. Campion, James E. Campion, and Peter J. Hudson, Jr. (December 1994), "Structured Interviewing: A Note on Incremental Validity and Alternative Question Types," *Journal of Applied Psychology,* pp. 998–1002.

32. Elaine D. Pulakos, Neal Schmitt, David Whitney, and Matthew Smith (Spring 1996), "Individual Differences in Interviewer Ratings: The Impact of Standardization, Consensus Discussion, and Sampling Error on the Validity of a Structured Interview," *Personnel Psychology,* pp. 85–102.

33. Jennifer R. Burnett, Chenche Fan, Stephan J. Motowidlo, and Tim Degroot (Summer 1998), "Interview Notes and Validity," *Personnel Psychology,* pp. 375–396.

34. Buros Institute of Mental Measurements (2003), *The Fifteenth Mental Measurements Yearbook.*

35. Mark J. Schmit and Ann Marie Ryan (Winter 1997), "Applicant Withdrawal: The Role of Test-Taking Attitudes and Racial Differences," *Personnel Psychology,* pp. 855–876.

36. John R. Hollenbeck and Ellen M. Whitener (March 1988), "Reclaiming Personality Traits for Personnel Selection: Self-Esteem as an Illustrative Case," *Journal of Management,* pp. 81–92.

37. Margaret Jenkins and Richard Griffith (2004), "Using Personality Constructs to Predict Performance: Narrow or Broad Bandwidth," *Journal of Business and Psychology,* Vol. 19, Iss. 2, pp. 255–69; L. M. Hough, N. K. Eaton, M. D. Dunnette, J. D. Kamp, and R. A. McCloy (October 1990), "Criterion Related Validities of Personality Constructs and the Effect of Response Distortion on Those Validities," *Journal of Applied Psychology,* pp. 581–595.

38. H. Rorschach (1942), *Psychodiagnostics: A Diagnostic Test Based on Perception* (Berne, Switzerland: Huber).

39. James A. Douglas, Daniel E. Feld and Nancy Asquith (1989), *Employment Testing Manual* (Boston: Warren, Gorham, and Lamont), p. 13:4.

40. S. L. Jacobs (March 11, 1985), "Owners Who Ignore Security Make Worker Dishonesty Easy," *The Wall Street Journal.*

41. Vance MacLaren (August 2001), "A Quantitative Review of the Guilt Knowledge Test," *Journal of Applied Psychology,* pp. 674–683.

42. Lawrence Peikes and Meghan D. Burns (July 2005), "Court Report: Polygraph Test Request Unlawful," *HRMagazine,* Vol. 50, Iss. 7, p. 110; Douglas, Feld, and Asquith, op. cit., p. 13:11.

43. Congress of the United States, Office of Technology Assessment (September 1990), "The Use of Integrity Tests for Pre-Employment Screening" (Washington, DC: U.S. Government Printing Office), OTA-SET-442.

44. James E. Wanek, Paul R. Sackett, and Deniz S. Ones (2003), "Towards an Understanding of Integrity Test Similarities and Differences: An Item-Level Analysis of Seven Tests," *Personnel Psychology,* Vol. 56, Iss. 4, pp. 873–94; Paul Sackett, Laura Burris, C. Callahan (1989), "Integrity Testing for Personnel Selection: An Update," *Personnel Psychology,* pp. 491–528; Paul Sacket and M. Harris (1984), "Honesty Testing for Personnel Selection: A Review and Critique," *Personnel Psychology,* pp. 221–245.

45. Joyce Hogan and Kimberly Brinkmeyer (Autumn 1997), "Bridging the Gap between Overt and Personality-Based Integrity Tests," *Personnel Psychology,* pp. 587–599.

46. Dan Dalton and Michael Metzger (February 1993), "Integrity Testing for Personnel Selection: An Unsparing Perspective," *Journal of Business Ethics,* pp. 147–161.

47. Deniz Ones, Chockalingam Viswesvaran, and Frank Schmidt (August 1993), "Comprehensive Meta-Analysis of Integrity Test Validities: Findings and Implications for Personnel Selection and Theories of Job Performance," *Journal of Applied Psychology,* pp. 679–703.

48. Diane Cadrain (November 2004), "HR Professionals Stymied by Vanishing Job References," *HRMagazine,* Vol. 49, Iss. 11, pp. 31–32; Joan M. Clay and Elvis C. Stephens (April 1996), "The Defamation Trap in Employee References," *Cornell Hotel and Restaurant Administration Quarterly,* pp. 18–24.

49. Phillip M. Perry (May 1995), "Cut Your Risk When Giving References," *HR Focus,* pp. 15–16.

50. Jane Bahls (January 1999), "Available upon Request," *HRMagazine,* pp. 2–6; Bill Leonard (December 1995), "Reference-Checking Laws: Now What?" *HRMagazine,* pp. 57–62.

51. *Analysis of the Americans with Disabilities Act and Implementing EEOC Regulations* (1991) (New York: The Research Institute of America), pp. 31–33.

52. "AMA 2004 Workplace Testing Survey: Medical Testing," American Management Association (http://www.amanet.org/research/pdfs/Medical_testing_04.pdf).

53. Mireille Jacobson (April 2003), "Drug Testing in the Truck Industry: The Effect on Highway Safety," *Journal of Law and Economics,* Vol. 46, Iss. 1, pp. 131–57; Julie Candler (January 1996), "A Sobering Law for Truckers," *Nations Business,* pp. 26–28.

54. U.S. Department of Labor, http://www.dol.gov/asp/programs/drugs/workingpartners/Screen15.htm; U.S. Department of Labor, www.dol.gov/dol/asp/public/programs/drugs/facts.htm.

55. Don Rhodes (October 1998), "Drugs in the Workplace," *Occupational Health & Safety,* pp. 136–138.

56. Kris Maher (April 13, 2004), "The Jungle," *The Wall Street Journal,* p. B4; Darold T. Barnum and John M. Gleason (July 1994), "The Credibility of Drug Tests: A Multi-Stage Bayesian Analysis," *Industrial and Labor Relations Review,* pp. 610–621.

57. "Assessment Centers" (June 1987), *Small Business Report,* pp. 22–24.

58. Task Force on Assessment Center Guidelines (Winter 1989), "Guidelines and Ethical Considerations for Assessment Center Operations," *Public Personnel Management,* pp. 457–470.

59. Paul W. B. Atkins and Robert E. Wood (2002), "Self versus Others' Ratings as Predictors of Assessment Center Ratings: Validation Evidence for 360-Degree Feedback Programs," *Personnel Psychology,* Vol. 55, Iss. 4, pp. 871–904; Barbara B. Gaugler, Douglas B. Rosenthal, George C. Thornton III, and C. Cynthia Bentson (August 1987), "Meta-Analysis of Assessment Center Validity," *Journal of Applied Psychology,* pp. 493–511.

60. Zipora Shechtman (June 1992), "A Group Assessment Procedure as a Predictor of On-the-Job Performance of Teachers," *Journal of Applied Psychology,* pp. 383–387.

61. Robert D. Gatewood and Hubert S. Feild (1994), *Human Resource Selection* (Fort Worth, TX: Dryden), pp. 241–245.

EXERCISE 8-1

Posting Your Resume Online

PURPOSE

As Application Case 8-2 discusses, many organizations are using online resume screening software to sift through thousands of resumes to determine which candidates can move on to the next step in the selection process. Ultimately, job candidates have to get over this first hurdle before they can get hired. So, the better a job seeker's online resume, the better the chances of getting hired.

GROUP SIZE

To be performed individually.

TIME REQUIRED

Approximately 1 hour.

OTHER

Internet connection and search engine needed.

EXERCISE PART I

Using your favorite search engine, visit three to four online job search Web sites (e.g., www.monster.com, www.careerbuilder.com, www.hotjobs.com) and search for information and instructions regarding how to post a resume online.

PART II

Using the information you learned from Part I, create or edit your resume so that it can be posted onto one of the online job search sites above (or, use another online job search Web site).

PART III

Visit one of the online Web sites and post your resume. Be sure to print a copy of the listing to show your instructor.

Source: Konopaske and Ivancevich (copyright 2005).

Application Case 8-1

Bechtel Power Corporation's Use of Objective Welding Tests

Charles Ligons, an African American, was a welder at the Iowa Electric Light and Power Duane Arnold Energy Center construction site at Palo, Iowa. He worked at the site for Bechtel Power Corporation. Bechtel required that its welders be qualified in accordance with standards of the American Society of Mechanical Engineers Code. That code prescribes objective criteria for testing welders on various types of welding work and for placing them in two categories: (1) A-LH, under which a welder qualifies to perform general welding jobs, and (2) AT-LH, involving more difficult welding procedures.

Prior to his arrival at the Palo site, Ligons passed a test that qualified him under AT-LH to perform heliarc welding. During his first week of employment, however, Ligons was required to report to the test shop for training and testing as a result of observations made by a welding engineer of a weld that Ligons had improperly prepared. Following a one-week training period, Ligons passed a simple plate welding test but failed the same heliarc welding test he had passed before coming to Palo. Ligons spent several weeks on at least three separate occasions training to improve his competence in heliarc welding.

On February 9, approximately 18 months after coming to the Palo site, Ligons was laid off with 58 other welders, all of whom were white. Ligons was informed that he was eligible for rehire when more welders were needed. The layoff was a result of a general reduction of the Palo workforce.

Ligons was rehired in September. He required further training and testing for recertification. After about one month of training, he passed only the test qualifying him for the least difficult type of welding. About four months after being rehired, he was again laid off with five other welders.

Ligons believed that race was a motivating factor in the decision to lay him off. Bechtel claimed, however, that its testing procedures for upgrading a welder's qualifications had a relationship to the jobs for which they were used. It stated that the welding tests were based on objective welding standards set by the American Society of Mechanical Engineers. Bechtel was contractually bound to ensure that its welders were qualified and that all welding performed on the job complied with the American Society of Mechanical Engineers Code.

Discussion Questions

1. Do you believe that welding tests are necessary for the type of job Charles Ligons worked on?
2. Was the first layoff of Ligons legitimate?
3. Did the company attempt to help Ligons maintain and upgrade his welding competence?

Application Case 8-2

Are Traditional Resumes Gone Forever?

The answer to this question is most likely "no, not yet." However, the trend at many organizations is toward using computer software to match candidates' qualifications to current job openings. How does it work? Instead of mailing an 8 ½ by 11 inch paper resume to a hiring manager or human resource representative, job seekers are now asked to visit the company Web site to type in their resume online. After that, the resume is screened and evaluated by a computer program on such factors as relevant keywords, past experience, and education. Resumes are even screened for other reasons. For example, estimates indicate that up to 20 percent of online resumes are knocked out of consideration due to excessive job hopping and/or the resume contains typos and grammatical errors.

What types of companies are using these resume screening software programs? Companies like Home Depot, BellSouth, Walgreens, United Parcel Service, Blockbuster, and Target all claim that online resume technology saves their hiring managers a lot of time and money; and the promising resumes are instantly available to company personnel. This makes the hiring process much more efficient.

Another benefit of the online resume posting process has to do with the geographic reach the company can have with regard to candidates. At General Electric, every job opening is posted on the internal career Web site. If the hiring unit decides that it wants to advertise the ad outside of the company, then the job opening is posted on the company Web site and can attract applicants from around the world. Currently, GE receives approximately 15,000 resumes monthly, roughly half of which are submitted via the online company Web site. GE managers believe that some candidates, even though they do not live in the immediate location of the hiring unit, would be willing to relocate if they found the right job at GE.

Some organizations, in addition to screening resumes on their own company Web sites, pay to post jobs on popular online recruiting Web sites. The largest online recruiting Web sites include monster.com, careerbuilders.com, and hotjobs.com.

What does all of this mean for job seekers? The rules of the resume submission process are changing. Job seekers need to modify their resumes so that they contain relevant keywords that are more likely to be identified by these online resume screening software programs. Now more than ever, resumes have to be typo-free and written with excellent grammar. Also, job seekers need to practice submitting their resumes online. Perhaps they should start off by submitting their resumes to a smaller online recruiting Web site. After that, they can submit their resume to the large boards (monster.com, etc.) and to specific company Web sites.

Discussion Questions

1. Why are so many companies shifting to online resume screening programs to sift through applicants' resumes?

2. Can you think of any disadvantages associated with the use of online resume screening? From the company's perspective? The candidate's perspective?

3. What can job seekers do to improve their chances of making it through the online resume screening process and getting an interview?

Sources: Joe Walker (May 22, 2005), "Computers for Recruiters," *Knight Ridder Tribune Business News*, p. 1; Igor Kotlyar and Kim Ades (May 2002), "Don't Overlook Recruiting Tools," *HRMagazine*, Vol. 47, Iss. 5, pp. 97–101; Rachel Emma Silverman (February 1, 2000), "Your Career Matters: Resumes Become Multimedia Productions," *The Wall Street Journal*, p. B16; Sarah Fister (May 1999), "Online Recruiting: Good, Fast and Cheap?" *Training*, Vol. 36, Iss. 5, pp. 26–28.

Video Case

Creative Staffing Solutions: A Pipeline of Human Assets

Finding the talent, competence, and expertise needed to operate a business, run a project, or grow a company is always a challenging job. In the recent labor market, even with an economic downturn, firms have had difficulty finding enough employees who are skilled in specific areas such as management information technology, software programming, and technical sales.

There are also firms interested in attracting people willing to work part-time or on a temporary basis to develop and complete a particular project. A temporary work basis differs from "traditional" temporary assignments, which often last a week or two while a permanent employee is ill or on vacation. Instead, some companies want people who can stay on the job for six months or a year.

Creative Staffing Solutions (CSS), a temporary and alternative staffing firm, provides workers to companies. "Temping," as it used to be called, is a $40 billion industry as more and more companies turn to staffing agencies for help. Companies are willing to pay for these employees. "For high-tech workers, this is an employee's market," notes Marc Brailov of the American Electronics Association. "It is very important for Internet companies to create and offer incentives to attract and retain employees." That's where Creative Staffing Solutions (CSS) comes in.

CSS, a minority-owned firm founded by Mel Rhone, now has clients ranging from small companies to large organizations such as AT&T, Hershey's, and Lockheed Martin. CSS specializes in finding IT professionals, engineers, computer programmers, and other high-tech workers for its clients. On one side of the process, a CSS manager meets with and interviews the HR manager at the client firm to determine the firm's needs. On the other side, CSS managers screen, interview, and test prospective job candidates' work history, grammar, spelling, math, computer skills, and so forth. CSS makes it possible for job hunters to post their resumes on the CSS Web site, where staffing managers can review them. In addition, CSS's staffing managers peruse Internet job sites in search of potential matches.

According to CSS managers, the alternative staffing solution meets the needs of both the company and the worker. Firms obtain screened, highly skilled, and motivated workers for a designated period. Currently, many high-tech firms prefer to hire temporary workers. They like to hire people to complete a specific project, such as development of a new computer system. Workers also benefit. "You get to make your own schedule," remarks CSS staffing manager Joy Thomas. Because CSS tests and trains candidates, people who want to improve their job skills can find plenty of opportunity through the company. Some workers are looking to change careers but are afraid to make a total commitment without knowing whether they will like the new field. Filling a temporary position can give them a good taste for what the field will be like. Occasionally CSS sends a worker to fill one temporary position at a company, and the person moves on to a completely different job at the firm. The arrangement gives both parties convenience and flexibility.

Rhone foresees a future in which temporary and alternative staffing will be routine in American industry, and he wants his company to be ready to grab every opportunity that comes its way. A study by the National Association of Temporary and Staffing Services found that 90 percent of companies surveyed employ temporary help. "Companies are incorporating temp workers in long-term plans, whereas 15 years ago they used temps just to fill occasional holes," remarks Richard Wahlquist, executive vice president of the association. The same holds true for today's workers. "The way Americans seek work has fundamentally shifted—so many young

Sources: John M. Ivancevich and Thomas N. Duening (2002), *Managing Einsteins: Leading High-Tech Workers in the Digital Age* (New York: McGraw-Hill); J. Lyman (April 30, 2001), "Uncle Sam May Help Train IT Geeks," *E-Commerce Times*, www.ecommercetimes.com; J. Kuriantcizk (March 19, 2001), "A Temporary Boom in the Job Market," *U.S. News & World Report*, www.usnews.com; P. Key (January 19, 2001), "Author/Innovator Gives Penn Large Gift," *Philadelphia Business Journal*, http://philadelphia.bcentral.com; R. Naraine (January 10, 2001), "Tech Worker Shortage Remains Despite Layoffs," *Internet.com News*, www.atnewyork.com.

adults look to temp agencies first, to get a taste of different fields, that we are a central part of the job search process," says Wahlquist. Creative Staffing Solutions intends to remain part of the process as well.

Discussion Questions

1. How can Creative Staffing Solutions create a learning environment for job candidates before they accept a position or while they are between positions?

2. What type of job candidates would use the temporary job support and services provided by a firm like CSS?

3. What difficulties might Creative Staffing Solutions have to deal with in using electronic job and resume posting?

Rewarding Human Resources

Part 3

Part Three discusses an extremely important part of a firm's overall HRM program: performance evaluation and compensation.

Chapter 9, "Performance Evaluation and Management," introduces the job of evaluating performance of employees. This extremely difficult job requires care in the development of measures to assess performance.

The subject of compensation and pay is introduced in Chapter 10, "Compensation: An Overview." It discusses the potential impact of pay on employees as well as determination of pay level, pay structure, and individual pay. Chapter 11, "Compensation: Methods and Policies," completes this discussion by focusing on incentives and pay programs, managerial compensation, and several significant policy issues regarding compensation.

Chapter 12, "Employee Benefits and Services," covers benefits, services, and pensions. The potential effects of benefits and services that employers provide for employees are discussed.

Performance Evaluation and Management

Learning Objectives

After studying this chapter you should be able to:

1. **Define** the terms *performance management* and *performance evaluation*.

2. **Discuss** various types of rating errors that can occur in performance evaluation programs.

3. **Compare** the advantages of various performance evaluation techniques.

4. **Discuss** the 360-degree feedback system's potential strengths and problems.

5. **Describe** the process of feedback review and the skills required for it.

Internet/Web Resources

General Sites

www.performance-appraisal.com/intro.htm

Company Sites

www.metlife.com

www.weyerhaeuser.com

www.bridgestone-firestone.com

Career Challenge

Ed went to work in the maintenance department of Partridge Enterprises, a medium-sized firm, about a year ago. He enjoys working in maintenance because he has always liked to work with his hands. His supervisor, Hector, is a good maintenance man who helps Ed when he doesn't understand a probblem. But Ed has often wished he knew what Hector thinks of him on the job. Hector never tells Ed how he is doing. It seems that Hector chews him out about once a month. Ed wonders, Doesn't he think I am trying to do a good job? Doesn't he think I am a good maintenance man?

Knowing answers to these questions is important to Ed, because someday he'd like to move up. He hears that Joe is going to retire next year. Joe's job is better and pays more. Ed wonders if he has a chance to get the job. He also has heard that business at some branches is not good right now. People have been laid off. If the crunch hits the New York branch where Ed works, he might get laid off. He knows seniority is a factor in layoffs, but so is performance. He wishes he knew how he was doing so that he could improve himself, move up, and avoid getting laid off. Ed wants some kind of feedback from his boss.

The setting: Office of the executive vice president of Partridge Enterprises. Present are the executive vice president and the vice presidents of the corporation.

Tom (executive vice president) As you know, we're here to make a recommendation to John [the president] on what if anything to do about Mary's suggestion. Mary, why don't you review the issue?

Mary (vice president, human resource management) You all received a copy of my memo to J. B. As you know, when I came here three years ago, I felt one of our top priorities in HRM would be to get an evaluation system running. We need this because performance evaluation is an outstanding motivation technique. After much thought and planning, the results are in my memo. I recommend we institute management by objectives evaluation systems for vice presidents through section heads and a graphic rating scale for levels below that. The MBO would be done quarterly and the rating scale semiannually, and we'd tie rewards such as raises and promotions to the results of the evaluations.

The details are in the memo. We're too big and geographically dispersed now to continue using our informal system.

Tom Sounds good to me.

Dave (vice president, marketing) Me too.

Fred (vice president, manufacturing) Well, it doesn't to me. We had one of these paper-mill forms systems here 10 years ago, and it was a waste of time. It just meant more paperwork for us down on the firing line. You staff people sit up here dreaming up more for us to do. We're overburdened now. Besides, I called a few buddies in big firms who have P.E. They say it involves a lot of training of evaluators, and it makes half the employees mad when they don't get 100 percent scores on the "grade report." It gets down to a lot of politics when it's all said and done.

If you recommend this, I'll send J.B. a counterproposal.

This chapter focuses on *performance management and evaluation*—the HRM activity designed to satisfy Ed's needs for performance feedback.

Performance management is the process by which executives, managers, and supervisors work to align employee performance with the firm's goals. An effective performance management process has a precise definition of excellent performance, uses measurements of performance, and provides feedback to employees about their performance.[1] Thus, it defines, measures, monitors, and gives feedback. Performance evaluation is a crucial part of a firm's performance management process. The HR

HR Journal   *Some Insight into Making Performance Management Work*

Although HRM professionals have long been convinced of the benefits that can accrue from performance management (PM) plans—incentive pay, bonuses, pay-for-performance, and so on—they must still persuade top executives, managers, and employees.

Who's using PM plans? More than 40 percent of the 500-plus HRM professionals who responded to the Setting & Managing 2005 Compensation Survey said they are using incentives, bonuses, or pay-for-performance plans. These plans are especially popular in the finance/banking and health care sectors.

Despite the enthusiasm of HRMs, performance management programs have been getting a bad rap from workers. Only three out of 10 employees surveyed by Watson Wyatt last year said their companies' PM programs helped them to improve job performance. In fact, only 19 percent of the surveyed workers thought their employers' PM systems helped any poor performers to improve. This doesn't mean that performance management is a failure. It means that organizations must change how workers perceive these efforts if they are to deliver fully on their promise.

"Unfortunately, too many organizations view their PM programs as 'organizational wallpaper.' They exist in the background and aren't expected to add value," commented Scott Cohen, performance management specialist and national director for talent management at Watson Wyatt.

Suggestions from Watson Wyatt on how to improve the "image" and effects of PM include:

- Eliminate "HR-speak" in the performance management process. Use business language instead.

- Set appropriate goals. Allow employees at all levels to focus on and achieve organizational goals.

- Make the difficult decisions. PM won't work if you don't recognize excellent performance metrics and consistently apply them.

- Develop a performance culture. This includes improving managers' coaching skills, raising the bar on expectations, and helping workers get to that next level.

- Before managers attempt to implement a PM program two myths should be carefully considered:

Myth: Performance management is an HRM application.

Reality: Although HRM owns the PM "process," PM is important throughout the business. View it as a "management process" instead of an HRM one.

Myth: Performance management needn't be implemented until the end of the annual review cycle.

Reality: PM should be an ongoing process—not a once-a-year event. Take the time to design the solution right the first time, and develop a broader PM plan that communicates your goals and expectations.

What's measured and rewarded in an organization's PM system should tie into the current business strategy. Goals should cascade down from the top. (In some companies, the CEO's goals, as well as those of each employee, are posted on the company intranet, making alignment easier to accomplish.) But goals should also mirror and reinforce a company's desired behaviors and guiding principles—i.e., its culture.

HRMs understand both the connection between the organization's culture and successful PM programs and the alignment between corporate goals and performance that represents ideal performance—something that continues to elude many organizations. A report from the Aberdeen Group (Boston; www.aberdeen.com), Business at Risk: Is Employee Performance Management the Antidote?, considers issues that can help improve the prognosis for true alignment.

A survey that Aberdeen conducted along with Brainbench (www.brainbench.com) and Synygy Performance Management (www.synygy.com) identified the culprit that creates the lack of alignment: Employees and enterprise performance management still are not linked in many organizations. It's not the fault of the organization, though, the report concludes: Most do not know how to make this all-important connection.

What can be done? Research suggests these tactics:

- Train managers. Overall employee performance management can only be as good as the hiring manager's ability to set objectives clearly; articulate goals and their relative value; define the levels of performance expected and required; and explain how the employee is to achieve those levels.

- Address employee expectations. Employees may be negative about PM programs because their expectations are unrealistic, the Aberdeen survey suggests.

Source: "Making Performance Management Work" (May 2005), *HR Focus*, pp. 1–4.

Journal box on performance management points out some guidelines for improving an organization's performance management program.

From a strategic and competitive advantage perspective it is important to integrate employee performance with organizational performance goals. A group of employees who perform in a manner that does not help the firm accomplish its goals is incongruent with short- or long-term survival. Most experts believe that a firm's strategy must be aligned with employees' competencies and performance if profitability, growth, effectiveness, and valuation are to be achieved.[2]

Managers have a responsibility to develop, implement, monitor, and modify measures of performance. Unfortunately, not all measures are easy to develop. The measurement of tangible outcomes such as computers, automobiles, or television sets can be done with precision. However, the measurement of services or intangible outcomes produced by a teacher, accountant, or lawyer is difficult to provide. Although striving for precision when defining, measuring, monitoring, and modifying performance is certainly a worthy goal, it is easier to explain and seek than to accomplish, especially with many professionals, service employees, and "knowledge workers" (e.g., research and development technicians or engineers).[3] Knowledge workers provide intangible intellectual capital which contributes to the accomplishment of performance goals.

Performance evaluation is the activity used to determine the extent to which an employee performs work effectively. Other terms for performance evaluation include *performance review, personnel rating, merit rating, performance appraisal, employee appraisal,* and *employee evaluation.*

In many organizations, two evaluation systems exist side by side: the formal and the informal. Managers often think about how well employees are doing; this is the informal system. Political and interpersonal processes influence it, so those employees who are liked better than others have an edge. By contrast, a formal performance evaluation is a system set up by the organization to regularly and systematically evaluate employees' performance. This chapter focuses only on formal performance evaluation systems.

The Case for Using Formal Evaluation

Purposes of Evaluation

Should Ed be evaluated by his supervisor? In order to answer that question, think about Ed's situation in the Career Challenge. Then consider the following potential purposes that can be served by a well-designed formal evaluation system:

- *Development* It can determine which employees need more training, and it can help evaluate the results of training programs. It helps the subordinate–supervisor counseling relationship, and it encourages supervisors to observe subordinates' behavior to help employees.

- *Motivation* It can encourage initiative, develop a sense of responsibility, and stimulate efforts to perform better.

- *Human resource and employment planning* It can serve as a valuable input to skills inventories and human resource planning.

- *Communications* It can serve as a basis for an ongoing discussion between superior and subordinate about job-related matters. Through interaction and an effective feedback process, the parties get to know each other better.

- *Legal compliance* It can serve as a legally defensible reason for promotions, transfers, rewards, and discharges.

- *HRM research* It can be used to validate selection tools such as a testing program.

HR Journal   *Pause and Take Notice*

Not everyone is standing in line cheering about using performance appraisal to accomplish a host of worthy goals. The quality expert W. Edwards Deming believed that performance appraisal systems and formats were flawed and inaccurate—a farce based on false assumptions and too much subjectivity. He used to say that performance appraisal was one of the seven deadly sins afflicting management.

Deming listed a number of reasons why performance appraisals were flawed:

- They nourish short-term performance and deflect attention from long-term planning.

- They leave ratees bitter, desolate, and feeling inferior and unfit for work because they are afraid to present a divergent point of view.

- They are detrimental to teamwork because they foster rivalry, politics, and fear. Employees are rewarded for promoting themselves for their own good.

- They focus on the end product, not leadership to help people.

- The measures used to evaluate performance are not meaningful, because supervisors and subordinates are pressured to use numbers and count something.

- The measures discourage quality. People will concentrate on meeting numbers: they won't take time to improve a design if their goals involve quantity or deadlines.

If all of Deming's charges are true, they are a serious indictment of performance appraisal. Each of his charges raises valid points and suggests that improvements can be made. But despite Deming's criticisms, performance appraisals will continue to be widely used and adapted to fit a particular situation. Research indicates that goal setting, when built into an appraisal system, can be effective. Quality-related goals should be infused into appraisals that deal with short- and long-term individual and team accomplishments.

Although Deming, rightfully so, points out many areas for improvement, performance appraisal can be a valuable practice. Rewarding, developing, and motivating will undoubtedly continue to use performance appraisal information. As you read this chapter, think about Deming's insightful criticisms and how each of the formats and methods portrayed can be improved.

Source: Adapted from Sidney P. Rubenstein (September 1993), "Democracy and Quality as an Integrated System," *Quality Progress,* pp. 51–56; Jim M. Graber, Roger E. Breisch, and Walter E. Breisch (June 1992), "Performance Appraisals and Deming: A Misunderstanding?" *Quality Progress,* pp. 59–62; and Peter R. Scholtes (Spring 1992), "Performance Appraisal: The Case against a Traditional Tool," *Maryland Workplace,* pp. 2–3, 10.

Of all the relationships between performance evaluation and other HRM activities, none has been more crucial to understand than the one between evaluations and equal employment opportunity, especially as it applies to promotions and terminations. Unless evaluations are considered fair and decisions made using them treat everyone with dignity, there will likely be intense conflict. A worthy goal of an evaluation is that employees consider it meaningful, helpful, fair, and honest. Unfortunately, this goal is difficult to attain because of a number of factors including unfairness, negative practices, and a short-term focus.

Critics of performance evaluation systems offer some meaningful insights. The HR Journal provides some points raised by the quality expert W. Edwards Deming. His critique should be considered as you learn more about performance evaluation approaches.

Performance Evaluation and the Law

The *Uniform Guidelines on Employment Selection Procedures* were issued by the Equal Employment Opportunity Commission in 1978 to provide organizations with information about how to comply with federal employment legislation. These guidelines were intended to apply to all human resource decisions. However, more attention was devoted to selection than to performance evaluation, and the requirements for appraisal systems are therefore less clearly defined. Thus, it is actually more difficult to determine what makes a performance evaluation system legal than a selection system.[4]

Most performance evaluation procedures rely to some extent on supervisors' judgments about an employee's behavior. These judgments are usually summarized by using one of several paper-and-pencil methods, each of which is designed to provide an accurate picture of the employee. Once employees' work-related behavior has been judged, the supervisors' ratings are used as input in making human resource decisions such as promotions, pay, transfers, and other matters.

Because supervisors' judgments have been used during the evaluation process, bias can exist in these decisions, whether it is intentional or not. Many of the more common sources of bias in performance evaluations will be discussed later in this chapter.

A number of court rulings have focused on the responsibility of management to develop and use a performance evaluation system in a legally defensible way. One of the most important early cases was *Brito* v. *Zia Company* (1973),[5] in which the company was found to be in violation of the law. The court ruled that the company had not shown that its performance evaluation instrument was valid in the sense that it related to important elements in the jobs for which the employees were being evaluated. For example, some raters had little daily contact with the ratees.

Since the decision in *Brito* v. *Zia Company,* there have been many other lawsuits concerned with the adequacy of performance evaluations. These have dealt with issues of sex, race, and age discrimination in terminations, promotions, and layoffs. As mentioned previously, however, the courts' interpretations of what constitutes a legal performance evaluation system are not as straightforward as they are for selection systems. An analysis of court rulings has concluded that when a performance evaluation system is challenged, its actual validity is a less explicit issue than when a selection system has been challenged.[6]

While an organization should be concerned about the validity of its performance evaluations, the way the system was developed and whether it is applied consistently currently seem more important from a legal perspective. In age discrimination cases, it also appears that the type of decision being challenged is important for determining how much proof a company will be required to produce.[7]

Despite this lack of clear guidelines, several important recommendations should be followed before developing and using a performance evaluation system. These have been summarized in Exhibit 9-1.

EXHIBIT 9-1
Suggestions to Follow for Developing and Implementing Legally Defensible Appraisal Systems

Source: Adapted from H. J. Bernardin and W. Cascio (1987), "Performance Appraisal and the Law," in R. S. Schuler, S. A. Youngblood, and V. Huber (Eds.), *Readings in Personnel and Human Resource Management,* 3d ed. (St. Paul, MN: West).

1. Procedures for human resource decisions must not differ as a function of the race, sex, national origin, religion, or age of those affected by such decisions.
2. Objective, nonrated, and uncontaminated data should be used whenever available.
3. A formal system of review or appeal should be available for disagreement over appraisals.
4. More than one independent evaluator of performance should be used.
5. A formal, standardized system for evaluation should be used.
6. Ratings on traits such as dependability, drive, aptitude, and attitude should be avoided.
7. Performance evaluation data should be empirically validated.
8. Specific performance standards should be communicated to employees.
9. Raters should be provided with written instructions on how to complete the performance evaluations.
10. Employees should be evaluated on specific work dimensions rather than a single overall or global measure.
11. Behavioral documentation should be required for extreme ratings (e.g., critical incidents).
12. Employees should be provided with an opportunity to review their appraisals.

Format of Evaluation

To provide information that can serve the organization's goals and that complies with the law, a performance evaluation system must provide accurate and reliable data. The ability to generate accurate and reliable data is enhanced if a systematic process is followed. The following six steps can provide the basis for such a systematic process:

1. Establish performance standards for each position and the criteria for evaluation.
2. Establish performance evaluation policies on when to rate, how often to rate, and who should rate.
3. Have raters gather data on employees' performance.
4. Have raters (and employees in some systems) evaluate employees' performance.
5. Discuss the evaluation with the employee.
6. Make decisions and file the evaluation.

Step 1 of this process is completed when an organization conducts a job analysis. Recall from Chapter 6 that one of the primary reasons for conducting job analyses is to write job descriptions, and an important part of a job description is a clear statement of the performance dimensions and standards expected from incumbents. In addition, the job analysis should have determined how these dimensions and standards are going to be measured.

Establish Criteria

The dimensions of performance upon which an employee is evaluated are called the *criteria of evaluation.* Examples include quality of work, quantity of work, and cost of work. One of the major problems with many performance evaluations is that they require supervisors to make person evaluations rather than performance evaluations. That is, the evaluation criterion in some systems is the personality of the incumbents rather than their levels of performance.

An effective criterion should possess the following characteristics:[8]

- *Reliability* A measure of performance must be consistent. Perhaps the most important type of consistency for a performance measure is **interrater reliability.** If different raters view the same worker, they should arrive at similar conclusions about the quality of that worker's output.
- *Relevance* A measure of performance must be related to the actual output of an incumbent as logically as possible.
- *Sensitivity* Any criterion must be able to reflect the difference between high and low performers. That is, high and low performers must receive criterion scores that accurately represent the difference in their performance.
- *Practicality* The criterion must be measurable, and data collection cannot be inefficient or too disruptive.

Most studies indicate that multiple criteria are necessary to measure performance completely. The multiple criteria are added together statistically or combined into a single multifaceted measure. The choice of criteria is not an easy process. One must be careful to evaluate both activities (for example, number of calls a salesperson makes) and results (for example, dollars of sales). A combination of criteria using results and activities is desirable.

How do you weigh the importance of multiple criteria? For example, if a salesperson is being evaluated on number of calls as well as sales dollars and is high on one and low on the other, what is the person's overall rating? Management must weigh these criteria.

Set Policies on Who Evaluates, When, and How Often

When should evaluation be done? In the United States a majority of organizations continue to evaluate performance on an annual basis. A small proportion (15.6 percent) evaluate performance twice a year, and an even smaller proportion (3.6 percent) have implemented quarterly evaluations.[9] For those organizations that continue to rely on annual evaluations, there are two choices for when to actually conduct the evaluations. In many organizations, performance evaluations are scheduled for arbitrary dates, such as the date the person was hired (anniversary date). Alternatively, all employees may be evaluated on or near a single calendar date. Although the single-day approach is convenient administratively, it probably is not a good idea. It requires raters to spend a lot of time conducting evaluation interviews and completing forms at one time, which may lead them to want to "get it over with" quickly. In addition, it may not be related to the normal task cycle of the employee; this factor can make it difficult for the manager to evaluate performance effectively.

It makes more sense to schedule the evaluation at the completion of a task cycle. For example, tax accountants see their year as April 16 to April 15. For most professors and teachers, the year starts at the beginning of the fall term and terminates after the spring term. For others without a clear task cycle based on dates, one way to set the date is by setting goals. Goals can be established in such a way that the manager and employee agree on the task cycle, which terminates with an evaluation of the employee's performance during that cycle.

Who Should Evaluate the Employee?

As Exhibit 9-2 shows, performance evaluation is another HRM activity that involves cooperation between the line operating managers and the HR specialists. The operating manager (immediate supervisor) is, however, the person responsible for conducting the actual appraisal in a vast majority of cases. But there are other possibilities that organizations should consider as well.

Rating by a Committee of Several Supervisors The supervisors chosen are those most likely to come into contact with the employee. This approach has the advantages of offsetting bias on the part of one superior and adding additional information to the evaluation, especially if it follows a group meeting format.

Rating by the Employee's Peers (Co-workers) In the peer evaluation system, the co-workers must know the level of performance of the employee being evaluated. For this system to work, it is preferable for the evaluating peers to trust one another and not to be in compe-

EXHIBIT 9-2
Involvement of Human Resource and Operating Managers in Performance Evaluation Management

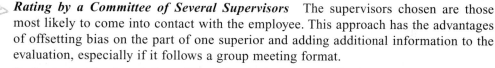

Performance Evaluation Function	Operating Manager (OM)	Human Resource Manager
Establish performance standards	Approves the standards	Calculated by HRM and engineers
Set policy on when performance evaluation takes place	Approves the policy	Recommends the policy
Set policy on who evaluates	Approves the policy	Recommends the policy
Choose the evaluation system	Approves the policy	Recommends the policy
Train the raters	Done by HRM	
Review employees' performance	Done by OM	
Discuss the evaluation with the employees	Done by OM	
File the performance evaluation		Done by HRM

tition for raises and promotions. This approach may be useful when the tasks of the work unit require frequent working contact among peers.[10]

Rating by the Employee's Subordinates Exxon has used this system, and it is used in some universities (students evaluate the faculty's teaching effectiveness). It is used more for the developmental aspects of performance evaluation than are some of the other methods. Managers are less likely to accept being rated by subordinates if the information is going to be used for administrative purposes (for example, raises and promotions) than if it is used for development. This source of rating information is also more acceptable if the managers believe that their subordinates are familiar with the job. Also, subordinates' evaluations should probably be restricted to "people oriented" issues such as leadership and delegation, rather than organizing, planning, and other less easily observed aspects of the manager's performance.[11]

Rating by Someone outside the Immediate Work Situation Known as the field review technique, this method uses a specialized appraiser from outside the job setting, such as a human resource specialist, to rate the employee. This approach is often costly, so it is generally used only for exceptionally important jobs. It might be used for the entire workforce if accusations of prejudice must be countered. A crucial consideration is that the outside evaluator is not likely to have as much data as evaluators in any of the other four approaches. The use of an outside evaluator represents a somewhat atypical approach to appraising performance.

Self-Evaluation In this case, the employee evaluates herself or himself with the techniques used by other evaluators. This approach seems to be used more often for developmental (as opposed to evaluative) aspects of performance evaluation. It is also used to evaluate an employee who works in physical isolation.

Self-evaluations have often been met with skepticism by organizations because the self-interests of the employee could outweigh an objective evaluation.[12] However, research has demonstrated that self-evaluations can correlate reasonably well with supervisors' ratings; especially if the employees have information about their co-workers' performance, employees can provide accurate appraisals of their own performances.[13]

Rating by a Combination of Approaches A survey of Fortune 500 companies showed that only about 10 percent of employees were satisfied with their organization's performance evaluation methods.[14] It is not surprising, therefore, that organizations are experimenting with alternatives to the traditional "supervisor only" downward appraisal. One system of appraising performance that appears to be growing in popularity is the **360-degree feedback** system. As the name implies, this method uses multiple appraisers, including supervisors, subordinates, and peers of the target person. In some cases, it also includes self-appraisals. The appraisal is 360 degrees in that information is collected and feedback is provided in full circular fashion—top to bottom and back to the top.

Many organizations now utilize some form of 360-degree programs. The program at British Aerospace is typical.[15] The upward portion of the feedback program involves an anonymous system whereby team members provide information about their supervisors, using a questionnaire. Then, these results are collated so that a report can be prepared for the manager. Anonymity is generally considered important, except in an environment where there is an exceptionally high degree of trust.

Research suggests that including upward and peer feedback in an appraisal can have positive effects on managers' behavior. In addition, these effects seem to be sustainable over time.[16] Thus, there appears to be a future for 360-degree programs. And, while these programs were originally believed to be useful primarily to develop feedback, according to one recent survey 90 percent of companies using 360-degree programs used the information to help with personnel decisions such as merit pay increases and promotions.[17]

HR Journal
360-Degree Feedback Provides the Power of Listening

Like a compass, 360-degree feedback systems act to help managers gain a panoramic view of the impact they are having in the work landscape. While the 360-degree method has gained popularity over the past decade among corporate leaders for employee developmental purposes, the feedback system can also serve as a listening device for managers to provide information about how well they are communicating. What's more, when employees are allowed to give input about how their manager's style is being perceived, empowering results take place.

For performance evaluations, the traditional supervisor–subordinate appraisal still is the most widely used system. But the 360-degree method serves to help managers gain insights into how they are being perceived by others. One of the keys to this tool is anonymity, since some people would share insights they would not otherwise reveal when facing the receiver directly.

"Raters" are people who routinely interact with the person receiving input, and they are recruited from among superiors, peers, subordinates, suppliers, among other internal and external customers. The number of responses is not so important as the relevance of the feedback. The most effective application of the device provides input on behaviors employees can readily see. Additional insight can be gained, as recipients of the process compare their own perceptions of effectiveness with that of others.

In short, the 360-degree feedback system provides several advantages. First, much time can be saved, as ineffective managerial methods are exposed directly, rather than potentially causing a revolving door effect in a department. Second, the tool helps a team, as a whole, learn more effectively.

As employees give feedback about their manager's performance, they feel their ideas make a difference and they are more willing to respond to future direction. Third, managers become aware of personal developmental needs that can contribute to the morale and goals of the entire organization.

Another helpful side effect is that the manger can receive valuable personal feedback about how internal and external customers value his or her products or services. A final benefit is that since many people give the feedback, discrimination and personal insults can be avoided because the focus is not on one or two impressions.

There are some precautions to observe, however, when using 360-degree feedback methods. Perhaps the greatest drawback occurs when the procedure is not carried out in conjunction with organizational goals in mind. Sometimes, managers who receive 360-degree feedback are left to figure out how to deal with results on their own, without clear guidance about how to make things better. For instance, is customer service a primary goal of the organization? Then make sure to ask how internal and external customers are being served. For this reason, a group of people who actually have to live with the results of the feedback should be chosen to develop input procedures.

The 360-degree process can be misapplied, if raters in the process do not receive adequate training as to how to provide feedback. In addition, there is the danger that input can leak over into performance evaluations, so proper guidelines are essential, while emphasizing the context of this method.

Another potential negative side effect of 360-degree feedback comes from the fact that it is usually anonymous. While some researchers believe raters give more honest feedback under anonymity, some feedback providers take this as an opportunity to vent their frustrations, or they give glowing responses.

If a manager wants clarification or further understanding, it is difficult to solicit information when the feedback is anonymous. This is where well-trained administrators can step in to monitor the process and keep feedback on track. To cure this pitfall, a good administrator of the process could act as a discreet liaison to probe for more specific insights. Or, when a manager has good rapport with employees and they do not fear reprisal for giving honest feedback, a facilitator could create a one-on-one environment for feedback.

There are many good resources available to help organizations embark on the 360-degree feedback loop. You can even go to an online company for help at www.360-degreefeedback.com.

The manager who listens well will quickly discover that the roles of facilitator, energizer, and resource person are vastly more effective than the roles of lecturer or commander in achieving company goals. Best of all, the listening approach to increase motivation and productivity comes at no additional cost to the company.

The bottom line is that employees at all levels want to know their insights and efforts matter to their managers and company. When workers feel excluded, they become secluded. Simply listening to your employees affords the motivational results money can't buy.

Source: Adapted from Alan Bailey (March 15, 2005), "How to Square the Circle on 360-Degree Feedback," *Personnel Today,* p. 17; and Bryan R. Fisher (August 2004), "Listen to What's Really Going On," *Supervision,* pp. 9–11.

EXHIBIT 9-3
Some Positive and
Negative Features of
360-Degree Appraisal
System

Positive	Negative
Multiple perspectives of a person's performance.	Feedback from all sources can be overwhelming.
Ratings can evaluate person based on actual contact and observation.	Rater can hide in a group of raters and provide harsh evaluations.
Feedback is provided from multiple directions—above, below, peer.	Conflicting ratings can be confusing and frustrating.
Anonymous, upward feedback which results in full participation.	Providing feedback that is constructive requires a plan and well-trained raters. This is not typically found in organizations.
Learning about weaknesses and strengths is motivational.	

However, improper attempts to introduce 360-degree systems into cultures not prepared for them (e.g., where there is a low level of trust or too much competition) can have predictably disastrous effects.[18]

Exhibit 9-3 lists a number of positive and negative features associated with 360-degree feedback systems. These types of issues need to be considered before adopting a 360-degree feedback system.

The 360-degree feedback approach can be viewed as a method for managers to acquire information about their style, methods, and approach. There is a listening advantage provided by the 360-degree feedback approach. The HR Journal spells out the power and impact of listening for managers.

Selected Evaluation Techniques

There are many ways to evaluate employees; some of the most common will be described here. Generally speaking, these methods can be divided into two broad categories. One category consists of methods that evaluate employees individually. In other words, the supervisor evaluates each employee without explicit, direct comparisons with other employees; plus the standards of performance are defined without reference to other employees.

The second category depends on multiple-person evaluations. Multiple-person evaluations require the supervisor to directly and intentionally compare the performance of one employee with that of other employees. Thus, the standards of performance are relative: an employee's performance is defined as good or bad on the basis of comparison with other employees' performance.

Individual Evaluation Methods

Graphic Rating Scale

Several individual evaluation methods are used in business today, but the oldest and perhaps the most common one is the graphic rating scale. Using this technique, the rater is presented with a set of traits such as those shown in Exhibit 9-4 and is asked to rate employees on each of the characteristics listed. The number of characteristics rated varies from a few to several dozen.

The ratings can be in a series of boxes (as in the exhibit), or they can be on a continuous scale (0–9 or the like). In the latter case, the rater places a check above descriptive words ranging from none to maximum. Typically, these ratings are then assigned points. For example, in Exhibit 9-4 *outstanding* may be assigned a score of 4 and *unsatisfactory* a score of 0. Total scores are then computed. In some plans, greater weight may be given to traits that are regarded as more important. Raters are often asked to explain each rating with a sentence or two.

EXHIBIT 9-4
Typical Graphic Rating Scale

Name _____ Department _____ Date _____

	Outstanding	Good	Satisfactory	Fair	Unsatisfactory
Quantity of work	☐	☐	☐	☐	☐
Quality of work	☐	☐	☐	☐	☐
Knowledge of job	☐	☐	☐	☐	☐
Personal qualities	☐	☐	☐	☐	☐
Cooperation	☐	☐	☐	☐	☐
Dependability	☐	☐	☐	☐	☐
Initiative	☐	☐	☐	☐	☐

Quantity of work — Volume of acceptable work under normal conditions
Comments:

Quality of work — Thoroughness, neatness, and accuracy of work
Comments:

Knowledge of job — Clear understanding of the facts or factors pertinent to the job
Comments:

Personal qualities — Personality, appearance, sociability, leadership, integrity
Comments:

Cooperation — Ability and willingness to work with associates, supervisors, and subordinates toward common goals
Comments:

Dependability — Conscientious, thorough, accurate, reliable with respect to attendance, lunch periods, reliefs, etc.
Comments:

Initiative — Earnestness in seeking increased responsibilities, self-starting, unafraid to proceed alone
Comments:

To make the scale more effective, two modifications have been designed. One is the *mixed standard scale.* Instead of just rating a trait such as initiative, the rater is given three statements to describe the trait; for example:

She is a real self-starter. She always takes the initiative, and her superior never has to stimulate her. (Best description.)

While generally she shows initiative, occasionally her superior has to prod her to get her work done.

She has a tendency to sit around and wait for directions. (Poorest description.)

After each description, the rater places a check mark (the employee fits the description), a plus sign (the employee is better than the statement), or a minus sign (the employee is poorer than the statement). The resulting 7-point scale is purported to be better than the graphic rating scale.

EXHIBIT 9-5
Forced-Choice Items

Instructions: Rank from 1 to 4 the following sets of statements according to how they describe the manner in which_____

(name of employee)

performs the job. A rank of 1 should be used for the most descriptive statement, and a rank of 4 should be given for the least descriptive. No ties are allowed.

_____ Does not anticipate difficulties
_____ Grasps explanations quickly
_____ Rarely wastes time
_____ Easy to talk to
_____ A leader in group activities
_____ Wastes time on unimportant things
_____ Cool and calm at all times
_____ Hard worker

The second modification is to add operational and benchmark statements to describe different levels of performance. For example, if the employee is evaluated on job knowledge, the form gives a specific example: "What has the employee done to actually demonstrate depth, currency, or breadth of job knowledge in the performance of duties? Consider both quality and quantity of work." The performance descriptions are designed to guide the rater by giving examples of people who deserve a particular rating (see Exhibit 9-5).

Forced Choice

Several potential problems with graphic rating scales led to the development of alternative rating methods. Graphic rating scales were thought to lead to many different errors of evaluation (to be discussed in a later section). Forced-choice methods were developed because graphic rating scales allowed supervisors to rate everyone high. As a result, there was no way to distinguish between good and poor performers. Recall that sensitivity is a necessary characteristic of a good criterion.

In a **forced-choice format,** the rater must choose from a set of descriptive statements about an employee. Typical sets of these statements are shown in Exhibit 9-5. Forced-choice items are usually prepared by an HR specialist, and then supervisors or others familiar with the ratees' performance evaluate how applicable each statement is. That is, they determine which statements describe effective or ineffective behavior.

Neutral statements are also sometimes included in forced-choice items. When the supervisors evaluate their employees, they check the statements that describe the employee or, if the items are like the ones shown in Exhibit 9-5, they rank the statements from most to least descriptive. The HR department then adds up the number of statements in each category (for example, effective behavior), and they are summed into an effectiveness index. Forced choice can be used by superiors, peers, subordinates, or a combination of these in evaluating employees.

Essay Evaluation

In the essay technique of evaluation, the rater may be asked to describe the strong and weak aspects of the employee's behavior. In some organizations, the essay technique is the only one used; in others, the essay is combined with another form such as a graphic rating scale. In this case, the essay summarizes the scale, elaborates on some of the ratings, or discusses additional dimensions that are not on the scale. In both these approaches, the essay can be open-ended, but in most cases there are guidelines on the topics to be covered, the purpose of the essay, and so on. The essay method can be used by raters who are superiors, peers,

EXHIBIT 9-6
Sample Essay
Statement

Marge has been absolutely dynamic in perking up the San Antonio region's sales. She has increased sales an average of 8 percent for the past 11 months, while cutting costs of acquiring a sale by $198 per sale. Letter after letter is received in headquarters complimenting us for having Marge as a salesperson. The customers respect her work and style. She has also trained three new sales trainees in the use of the new spreadsheet inventory control system. Her enthusiasm is contagious, and she has been one of the bright lights in showing others how to sell with a smile and high energy.

On two occasions, Marge blew up when asked to report in detail on two important service calls. She claimed that she lost her composure because the pressure was unbearable. Although she apologized to Chris, the sales district manager, Marge will have to learn that we operate on a closely controlled system. If she can control her quick-trigger temper, the sky is the limit for this outstanding sales star.

or subordinates of the employee to be evaluated. A sample of an essay evaluation for a salesperson is presented in Exhibit 9-6.

There is criticism about the accuracy and relevance of essay evaluations.[19] However, they do offer flexibility, and in an organization that emphasizes customer satisfaction, an evaluator can specifically address the ratee's achievements in this area. This flexibility to discuss what the organization is attempting to accomplish is one strength of essays. On the other hand, comparing essays written by the same or different raters is difficult. Skilled writers can paint a better picture of an employee than can unskilled writers.

Critical Incident Technique

Simply stated, this technique requires raters to maintain a log of behavioral incidents that represent either effective or ineffective performance for each employee being rated. These incidents are **critical incidents.** Because these incidents might not be directly comparable for different ratees, lists of standardized incidents can be prepared by an HR specialist in consultation with the operating managers. The rating task then becomes one of logging each time a subordinate engages in one of these behaviors.

An example of a good critical incident for a salesclerk is the following:

May 1—Dan listened patiently to the customer's complaint, answered the woman's questions, and then took back the merchandise, giving the customer full credit for the returned product. He was polite, prompt, and interested in her problem.

On the other hand, a bad critical incident might read as follows:

August 12—Dan stayed eight minutes over on his break during the busiest part of the day. He failed to answer three store managers' calls on the intercom to report to cash register 4 immediately.

Two factors make the critical incident technique successful. First, the supervisor has to be given enough time to observe each subordinate during the evaluation period. This is necessary so enough incidents are observed. Second, it is unreasonable to expect a supervisor to remember all of the incidents that were observed. Therefore, the supervisor must be willing to take the time to record the incidents that are seen in the log for each employee. Otherwise, many of the incidents might be forgotten. Keeping a diary in the form of a log should be a valuable aid in formulating an accurate appraisal of employees' strengths and weaknesses, since there is evidence that the more accurately a supervisor remembers behaviors, the more accurately she or he can evaluate them.[20]

If such logs are used, the critical incidents that are recorded are valuable for performance evaluation interviews. If done properly, the logs can help to avoid many common rating errors and help facilitate discussions about how an employee's performance can be improved.

EXHIBIT 9-7
Weighted Checklist
for a Lead Technician
Position

Check all of those statements that are accurate descriptions of the behavior and activities of _____ for the period from _____ to _____	
(name) (date) (date)	
Check as many or as few as apply.	**Weights**
_____ Is a decisive decision maker	10.0
_____ Seems to be focused in addressing pressing problems	8.7
_____ Is concerned about the quality of the work completed	10.0
_____ Reviews carefully the work of technicians who report to him/her	7.4
_____ Tactfully corrects poor-quality work of technicians	6.5
_____ Is able to delegate a job to subordinate technicians	6.3
_____ Is easy to work with	8.2
_____ Is able to clearly communicate guidelines for improving work	8.0
_____ Is sensitive to the needs of fellow workers	7.9
_____ Gives credit freely to those who deserve recognition	6.1
_____ Works well with people outside the work team	6.9

Note: Weights are not included on the actual weighted checklist to be completed. The items checked are added together to derive an overall score. A higher score indicates better performance.

Checklists and Weighted Checklists

Another type of individual evaluation method is the checklist. In its simplest form, the checklist is a set of objectives or descriptive statements. If the rater believes that the employee possesses a trait listed, the rater checks the item; if not, the rater leaves it blank. A rating score from the checklist equals the number of checks.

A variation of the checklist is the *weighted checklist.* Supervisors and HR specialists familiar with the jobs to be evaluated prepare a long list of descriptive statements about effective and ineffective behavior on jobs; this process is similar to the critical incident process. Judges who have observed behavior on the job sort the statements into piles describing behavior that is scaled from excellent to poor. When there is reasonable agreement on an item (for example, when the standard deviation is small), it is included in the weighted checklist. The weight is the average score of the raters prior to use of the checklist.

An example of a weighted checklist is presented in Exhibit 9-7. The supervisors or other raters receive the checklist without the scores and check the items that apply, as with an unweighted checklist. The employee's evaluation is the sum of the scores (weights) on the items checked. Checklists and weighted checklists can be used by evaluators who are superiors, peers, or subordinates.

Behaviorally Anchored Rating Scales

Smith and Kendall developed what is referred to as the **behaviorally anchored rating scale (BARS)** or the *behavioral expectation scale* (BES).[21] The BARS approach relies on the use of critical incidents to serve as anchor statements on a scale. A BARS rating form usually contains 6 to 10 specifically defined performance dimensions, each with five or six critical incident "anchors." Exhibit 9-8 presents one performance dimension for police patrol competence. The anchor statement for a rating of 9 is "This patrol officer applies a full range of procedural skills and can be expected to perform all assignments in an excellent manner." The rater would read the anchors and place an X at some point on the scale for the ratee.

A BARS usually contains the following features:

1. Six to ten performance dimensions are identified and defined by raters and ratees (a group is selected to construct the form).
2. The dimensions are anchored with positive and negative critical incidents.

EXHIBIT 9-8
A Behaviorally Anchored Rating Scale for Police Patrol Officer

Source: Example provided by Jacob Joseph, University of Alaska, Fairbanks. Used by permission.

Job Knowledge: Awareness of precedures, laws, and court rulings and changes in them.

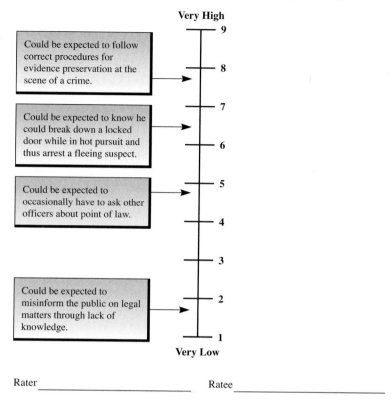

3. Each ratee is then rated on the dimensions.
4. Ratings are fed back using the terms displayed on the form.

The exact construction of a BARS is too complex for presentation here. However, it should be noted that usually two to four days are needed to develop a BARS. The result of the developmental work is a jargon-free rating scale that is closely related to the requirements of a given job.

Behavioral Observation Scales

Latham and associates developed the **behavioral observation scale (BOS)** as an approach to performance evaluation.[22] Like BARS, the BOS uses the critical incident technique to identify a series of behaviors covering the domain of the job. A major difference between BARS and BOS is that instead of identifying those behaviors exhibited by the ratee during a rating period, the rater indicates on a scale how often the ratee was actually observed engaging in the specific behaviors identified in the BOS.

Exhibit 9-9 presents four behavioral items that are used to appraise the performance of a first-line supervisor in a manufacturing plant. In this BOS appraisal form, 25 behavioral items are identified. The maximum score is 125 (25×5), and the minimum score is 25. Supervisors with scores above 115 are considered excellent performers, while a score in the 25 to 34 range is considered extremely poor. Each firm using a BOS must determine the meaning and importance of the total score for its ratees.

BARS and BOS were developed in the hope that they would yield more objective ratings than other rating scale formats (most notably, graphic rating scales) because they were behaviorally based. Unfortunately, years of research have suggested that this hope was

EXHIBIT 9-9
Sample BOS Items
for Supervisor

For each behavior listed use the following:

5   represents 95—100% of the time
4   represents 85—94% of the time
3   represents 75—84% of the time
2   represents 50—74% of the time
1   represents 0—49% of the time

Is accurate in preparing cost reports for Johnson project crew.
Almost never   1   2   3   4   5   Almost always

Practices sound energy conservation in supervising project crews.
Almost never   1   2   3   4   5   Almost always

Is available for technical consultation when needed.
Almost never   1   2   3   4   5   Almost always

Develops fair and equitable work schedule.
Almost never   1   2   3   4   5   Almost always

unwarranted. Most researchers interested in performance appraisal now agree with Landy and Farr, who concluded over 20 years ago that the format of a rating scale has minimal effects on the quality of a performance appraisal system.[23]

If behavior-oriented approaches have any advantage over other formats, it is in the development process that is typically used. Because supervisors and subordinates are involved in the development of the scales, these scales are generally better received, both by the persons who must complete them and by the persons whose performance is being assessed.[24]

A second possible benefit of the behavioral approach is that it helps focus managers' attention on important critical incidents for effective job performance. The incidents allow the supervisor to discuss specific types of good and bad performance with the subordinate, and this may make the feedback more acceptable than if the supervisor talks in vague generalities.[25]

Multiple-Person Evaluation Methods

By design, the methods of performance evaluation described so far are supposed to be used for evaluating employees one at a time—with no direct comparisons between employees. In this section, three techniques that compare one employee's performance with that of one or more others will be discussed. While they differ in some ways, all three of these techniques yield a similar kind of information: a list of employees ranked from best to worst.

Ranking

In their simplest form, rankings ask a supervisor to generate a list of subordinates in order on some overall criterion. This can be very difficult to do if the supervisor is asked to rank a large number of subordinates—over 20, say. Also, it is much easier for the supervisor to rank the best and worst employees in a reliable way than it is to rank the average ones. Because of this difficulty, a variation of simple rankings is alternative rankings. In this approach, the evaluators pick the top employee first, then the bottom employee next. Then the second best is chosen, followed by the second worst. This process is followed until all persons have been ranked.

Paired Comparison

This approach was designed to make the ranking process easier for the supervisor and perhaps more reliable, especially when there are many people to rank. Rather than asking the supervisor to rank everyone at once (which theoretically means that she or he must be

EXHIBIT 9-10   **Paired Comparison Ranking for Employees in a Marketing Research Unit**

Employees to be ranked:

Leslie Moore

Eddie Dorsey

Tina Little

Art Willis

RATING CARDS FILLED OUT BY SUPERVISOR

✓ Leslie Moore ___ Eddie Dorsey	___ Leslie Moore ✓ Tina Little	___ Leslie Moore ✓ Art Willis
✓ Tina Little ___ Eddie Dorsey	✓ Art Willis ___ Eddie Dorsey	✓ Leslie Moore ___ Art Willis

Final ranking:

1. Tina Little

2. Art Willis

3. Leslie Moore

4. Eddie Dorsey

thinking about the strengths and weaknesses of everyone at the same time), the **paired comparison** method presents the supervisor with a series of cards, each of which contains only two subordinates' names. The supervisor is then asked to choose which of these two persons is the higher performer. Thus, only the performance of these two individuals is being considered. For the technique to work properly, every possible pair of subordinates must be presented to the supervisor. In this way, she or he must rank each person one at a time, against all other persons to be ranked. The final ranking is then determined by counting how many times a given employee was chosen as the better performer across all of the comparisons.

Exhibit 9-10 shows the results of a paired comparison for a small work group of four persons. As shown, Tina Little would be the highest-ranked employee and Eddie Dorsey would be the lowest.

A major potential limitation of paired comparisons is the number of comparisons that must be made, especially in larger work groups. For all pairs to be represented, there must be $n(n - 1)/2$ pairs, where n equals the number of people to be ranked. Thus, with only 10 subordinates, a supervisor will have to go through $10(10 - 1)/2$ or 45 pairs of names. With large numbers of subordinates, this can be a tedious assignment for the supervisor.

Forced Distribution

The **forced distribution** system is similar to grading on a curve. The rater is asked to rate employees on the basis of some organizationally determined, preexisting distribution

HR Journal   *Quota Rating System at Ford Motor Co.*

After years of use, Ford Motor Co. eliminated its grading on a curve performance evaluation system. A number of current and former Ford executives filed lawsuits claiming the system is discriminating. Ford used a procedure in which executives were graded as A, B, and C. Ten percent of the managers being evaluated had to receive a "C" or unsatisfactory performance grade. Managers who received a C were required to receive coaching and counseling.

One of the "C" rated managers had always received "A" ratings until he clashed with senior managers about a safety device. Since he made the complaints, his ratings have gone from "As" to "Cs." The employee believes he is being retaliated against.

The feeling among many managers at Ford is that a quota system that forces evaluators to rate at least 10 percent of those being rated as unsatisfactory is causing morale problems. The Ford appraisal system was copied from General Electric (GE), which had to deal with its own morale problems. GE revised its system, which has a 1 (unsatisfactory) to 5 (excellent) rating scale. At GE almost everyone except the top 10 percent felt demoralized. GE streamlined its system to three grades, assigning 70 percent, or the vast majority, the middle grade and rewarding some of them with stock options. At Ford, when a manager receives a "C," there is no bonus.

Although the president of Ford defended the A, B, C quota system, the pressure to change it became so great that the quota requirement was eventually dropped. Managers are still evaluated as A, B, or C, but there is no requirement that 10 percent must be rated unsatisfactory.

Soon after President Nasser changed the rating system, he left Ford. A number of lawsuits were filed, and in some cases Ford settled with plaintiffs.

Source: Norishko Shirouzu and Joseph B. White (July 9, 2001), "Ford May Change White-Collar Job Rating System," *The Wall Street Journal,* pp. A3 and A4; and Norishko Shirouzu (July 16, 2001), "Ford Stops Using Letter Rankings to Rate Workers," *The Wall Street Journal,* pp. B1 and B4.

of categories. For example, a professor may decide ahead of time that the top 10 percent of scores on the next test will receive an A, the next 20 percent will receive a B, the middle 40 percent will get a C, and so on until the bottom 10 percent receive an F.

The key to this system is that the predetermined distribution must be followed by a rater, regardless of how well the students (in the case of a test) or the employees performed. So if a class of students did extremely well on our hypothetical professor's test, many of the students might still be very disappointed, since 10 percent will still receive an F, even if they got a large number of questions correct. On the other hand, if the class as a whole did very poorly on the test, 10 percent would nonetheless receive an A, as long as they did better than everyone else. That is, a student's grade is determined by how well he or she did relative to the other students and to the predetermined grade distribution that the professor desired. The same would be true in an organization where a supervisor is told by the company to use a particular distribution. A supervisor with all exceptional subordinates will necessarily have to rate some poorly; a supervisor with mediocre subordinates will have to rate some highly.

A variation of forced distribution is the point allocation technique (PAT). In PAT, each rater is given a number of points per employee in the group to be evaluated, and the total points for all employees evaluated cannot exceed the number of points per employee times the number of employees evaluated. The points are allocated on a criterion basis. Forced distribution and PAT are most likely to be used by superiors but could be used by peers or subordinates.

Ford Motor Company has used a forced distribution grading system that resulted in many complaints. The above HR Journal discusses the Ford informal system.

Management by Objectives

In most of the traditional performance evaluation systems, the raters judge past performance and attempt to report their judgments using one of the techniques described above.

Because performance evaluation is used for making important decisions that affect employees, the rater is placed in a difficult and somewhat antagonistic role.

McGregor believed that, instead of creating antagonisms because of judgments, the superior should work with subordinates to set goals. This would enable subordinates to exercise self-control and manage their job performance. From the early beliefs of McGregor, Drucker, and Odiorne has emerged the **management by objectives (MBO)** approach.[26]

MBO is more than just an evaluation program and process. It is viewed as a philosophy of managerial practice, a method by which managers and subordinates plan, organize, control, communicate, and debate. By setting objectives through participation or by assignment from a superior, the subordinate is provided with a course to follow and a target to shoot for while performing the job. Usually, an MBO program follows a systematic process, such as the following:

1. The superior and subordinate conduct meetings to define key tasks of the subordinate and to set a limited number of objectives (goals).
2. The participants set objectives that are realistic, challenging, clear, and comprehensive.
3. The superior, after consulting with the subordinate, establishes the criteria for assessing the accomplishment of the objectives.
4. Dates for reviewing intermediate progress are agreed upon and used.
5. The superior and subordinate make any required modifications in the original objectives.
6. A final evaluation by the superior is made and a meeting is held with the subordinate in a counseling, encouraging session.
7. Objectives for the next cycle are set by the subordinate after consulting with the superior, keeping in mind the previous cycle and future expectations.

MBO-type programs have been used in organizations throughout the world.[27] Various types of objectives have been set in these programs. A sample of objectives taken from actual MBO evaluation forms is presented in Exhibit 9-11. Most of these objectives are

EXHIBIT 9-11
Examples of MBO Evaluation Objectives

Occupation in Organization	Type of Organization	Objective Statement
Sales representative	Medium: Petrochemical firm	Contact six new clients in West AVA region and sell to at least two of these new clients within the next semiannual cycle.
Product manager	Large: Food processing plant	Increase market share of creamy peanut butter by at least 3.5 percent before next objective meeting (nine months from today) without increasing costs by more than 2 percent.
Skilled machinist	Small: Job shop	Reduce flange rejects by 8 percent by August 15.
Accountant	Small: CPA firm	Attend two auditing seminars to improve and update audit knowledge by the end of summer (September 15).
Plant manager	Medium: Assembly-line plant	Decrease absenteeism of operating employees from 18.9 percent to under 10 percent by January 1.
Engineer	Large: Construction company	Complete power plant tower project within 30 days of government-specified target date (November 10).

stated in the language of the job or occupation. Some of them are routine, others are innovative, and some are personal, such as the accountant's objectives.

For MBO and other performance management programs to be effective, both the manager and the subordinate must be actively involved in the objective formulation process, and they must also agree on the nature of performance assessment—what measures will be used to evaluate success and failure.[28]

Historically, one of the central features of MBO was that discussions about subordinates' performance centered on results. This was, in fact, presumed to be one of MBO's greatest advantages over other evaluation systems. Interestingly, many current perspectives on improving quality in American manufacturing find that some MBO programs are too results-oriented and insufficiently process-oriented. For example, W. Edwards Deming has for many years argued that a focus on numerical goals, managing by results, and taking immediate action on any error (such as a complaint or delay) has led to a dysfunctional management style in American corporations. His major complaint is that MBO places too much emphasis on detecting problems and too little emphasis on preventing those difficulties before they occur. In contrast to traditional MBO, he argues that the focus must be on the process underlying the system of production. The manager and employee should work cooperatively to improve this underlying basis for productivity. To do so, managers must be coaches and counselors, not judges.[29]

Does this mean that MBO and the total quality management are incompatible? Not necessarily, but any organization that tries to implement such a system must be aware of the critical implications. Some observers have suggested that the most important implication is an acknowledgment that any employee's performance is affected both by his or her ability and motivation and by the production system that is in place. With this acknowledgment, an organization can begin to understand how best to establish objectives and facilitate employees' productivity. So too, it must at least consider a system of appraisal in which someone's merit is not tied exclusively to whether objectives and goals were met. Rather, the MBO should be viewed also as an impetus for changing the system—not merely as an appraisal process.[30]

A number of other pitfalls and problems with MBO have been identified. These include the following:

- Too much paperwork is involved.
- Too many objectives are set, and confusion occurs. (It appears to be more efficient to work with only four, five, or six objectives.)
- MBO is forced into jobs where establishing objectives is extremely difficult.
- There may be a failure to tie in MBO results with rewards. The question "Why are we doing this?" is often asked.
- There is too much emphasis on the short term.
- Superiors are not trained in the MBO process and the mechanics involved.
- Original objectives are never modified.
- MBO is used as a rigid control device that intimidates rather than motivates.

These and other problems need to be minimized or overcome if MBO is to have any chance of success.[31] In some situations, MBO is very effective; in other cases, it is costly and disruptive. Just as with the other evaluation techniques available, managers need to examine purposes, costs, benefits, and their own preferences before selecting or discarding an MBO program.

Which Technique to Use

Perhaps you now feel overwhelmed by the large number of evaluation techniques. You should know that not all of them are used very often. The graphic rating scale is the

EXHIBIT 9-12
Some Advantages and
Disadvantages of
Various Performance
Evaluation
Techniques

Individual Methods	Comments
Rating Scales	Easy to use, easy to complete, relatively low cost; focuses too much on person instead of performance.
Forced Choice	Selectively low cost, easy to use, difficult to explain to those evaluated.
Essay	Good in providing specific feedback if evaluator is a good writer, difficult in making comparisons across those being evaluated.
Critical Incidents	Time-consuming, must be disciplined to log in incidents, reveals critical behaviors that can be fed back easily.
Behavior Scales	Difficult to develop, time-consuming, great for providing specific feedback to aid in improving performance.
Multiple Methods	**Comments**
Ranking and Paired Comparisons	Hard to use for providing feedback, good for making comparisons among employees.
MBO	Focuses on results that are important, sometimes too short-term oriented, does not engage in comparisons among employees.

most widely used technique. Studies indicate that the essay method is also widely used, usually as part of a graphic rating scale form. Checklists are common, too. Studies show that other methods—such as forced choice, critical incident, BARS, BOS, field review, and MBO—combined are used by only about 5 percent of firms. Ranking and paired comparison are used by 10 to 13 percent of employers. MBO is most likely to be used for managerial, professional, and technical employees, not production and office personnel.[32]

Which techniques should be used in a specific instance? The literature on the shortcomings, strengths, reliabilities, and validities of each of the techniques is vast. In essence, studies show that each technique is sometimes good and sometimes poor. The major problems are not with the techniques themselves but with how they are used and by whom. Untrained raters or raters who have little talent or motivation to evaluate well can destroy or hamper any evaluation technique. The rater is more critical than the technique in developing effective evaluation systems.

Exhibit 9-12 presents a summary of some of the strengths and weaknesses of the various performance evaluation techniques.

Potential Problems in Performance Evaluations

Regardless of which technique or system is chosen, there are going to be many problems encountered in its use. None of the techniques is perfect; they all have limitations. Some of these limitations are common to all of the techniques, while others are more frequently encountered with certain ones.

Opposition to Evaluation

Most employees are wary of performance evaluation. Perhaps the most common fear is of subjectivity on the part of the rater. Subjective bias and favoritism are real problems that create opposition to most performance evaluation systems. These fears are hidden, however, and other, more general arguments are provided. For example, those who oppose the use of formal performance evaluation systems argue that

- They focus too much attention on alleviating symptoms of poor performance rather than identifying the underlying causes.

HR Journal   *A Performance System–Reward Disconnect*

A Japanese company and a California company decided to have a canoe race on the Columbia River. Both teams practiced hard and long to reach their peak performance before the race.

On the big day, the Japanese won by a mile.

Afterward, the California team became very discouraged and depressed. The management of the California company decided that they had to find a reason for the crushing defeat. A "Measurement Team" made up of senior management was formed to investigate and recommend appropriate action.

Their conclusion was that the Japanese company had 8 people rowing and 1 person steering.

So the management of the California company hired a consulting company and paid them incredible amounts of money. They advised that too many people were steering the boat and not enough people were rowing.

To prevent losing to the Japanese again the next year, the rowing team's management structure was totally reorganized to 4 steering supervisors, 3 area steering superintendents, and 1 assistant superintendent steering manager.

They also implemented a new performance system that would give the 1 person rowing the boat greater incentive to work harder. It was called the "Rowing Team Quality First Program," with meetings, dinners, and free pens for the rower, "We must give the rower empowerment and enrichment throughout this quality program."

The next year the Japanese won by 2 miles. Humiliated, the management of the California company laid off the rower for poor performance, halted development of a new canoe, sold the paddles, and canceled all capital investments for new equipment. Then they used the money saved by giving a High Performance Award to the steering managers and distributed the rest of the money as bonuses to the senior executives.

Source: Anonymous—found at www.zigonperf.com/humor/canoe_race.html, accessed June 2005.

- Managers and employees dislike the evaluation process. Raters especially have problems with reaching decisions about the performance levels of employees.
- Employees who are not evaluated in the top performance category experience a reverse motivation effect: They slow down (employee problems).

System Design and Operating Problems

Performance evaluation systems break down because they are poorly designed. The design can be blamed if the criteria for evaluation are poor, the technique used is cumbersome, or the system is more form than substance. If the criteria used focus solely on activities rather than output (results), or on personality traits rather than performance, the evaluation may not be well received. Some evaluation techniques take a long time to carry out or require extensive written analysis, both of which many managers resist. If this is the problem, another technique can be chosen. Finally, some systems are not online and running. Some supervisors use the system, but others just haphazardly fill out the paperwork. Top management's support for performance evaluation can remedy this problem of ritualism.

The HR Journal box uses some humor to illustrate how organizations can become inaccurate in developing a system that uses measurement that is inappropriate. In some instances there is a disconnect between the performance system and the firm's reward program. Does the hypothetical canoe racing humor in the HR Journal sound familiar?

Rater Problems

Even if the system is well designed, problems can arise if the raters (usually supervisors) are not cooperative and well trained. Supervisors may not be comfortable with the process of evaluation, or what Douglas McGregor called "playing God."[33] This is often because they have not been adequately trained or have not participated in the design of the program.

EXHIBIT 9-13
**Rating Scale with
Unclear Standards:
Graphic Rating Scale
for Laboratory
Scientists**

Performance Dimension	Scale: Place an X for Rating of _____				
	Outstanding	Good	Fair	Below Accepted	Poor
Quality of technical reports					
Quantity of technical reports					
Creativeness					
Social interaction ability					

Inadequate training of raters can lead to a series of problems in completing performance evaluations, including:

- Problems with standards of evaluation.
- Halo effect.
- Leniency or harshness.
- Central tendency error.
- "Recency of events" error.
- Contrast effects.
- Personal bias (stereotyping; "similar to me").

Standards of Evaluation

Problems with evaluation standards arise because of perceptual differences in the meaning of the words used to evaluate employees. Thus, *good, adequate, satisfactory,* and *excellent* may mean different things to different evaluators. Some teachers are "easy A's," while others almost never give an A. They differ in their interpretation of excellent. If only one rater is used, the evaluation can be distorted. This difficulty arises most often in graphic rating scales but may also appear with essays, critical incidents, and checklists.

For example, Exhibit 9-13 presents a rating scale with unclear standards for four performance dimensions that are difficult to rate. What does "good" performance for quality of work mean? How does it differ from a "fair" rating? How would you interpret the quality or quantity of performance? This rating scale is ambiguous. Perhaps defining the meaning of each dimension and training raters to apply the five ratings consistently could reduce the potential rating problem.

The Halo Effect

At one time, it was believed that halo errors in ratings were the major problem in performance evaluation. **Halo error** occurs when a rater assigns ratings for several dimensions of performance on the basis of an overall general impression of the ratee.

Halo error can be either positive or negative, meaning that the initial impression can cause the ratings to be either too low or too high. Suppose that an information systems manager thought that one particular computer programmer was the best in the department at developing new software. If, solely on the basis of this impression, the programmer is given high ratings on decision making, getting along with peers, and leadership potential, then a halo error has occurred.

A problem with understanding and dealing with halo error is that the ratings represent an error only if they are not justified. That is, imagine that our computer programmer deserved high ratings on the three dimensions of performance other than programming. Even though the manager was basing the ratings on a general impression, they could represent an accurate evaluation. In other words, it is important to realize that there is a difference between *halo errors* and *true halo,* which occurs when uniformly high or low ratings across different aspects of performance are actually justified by the ratee's performance.

Interestingly, halo errors are not as common as was once believed.[34] Raters do seem to be able to distinguish halo errors from true halo in many situations. When halo errors do occur, however, they can be very difficult to eliminate.[35] One procedure to reduce this type of error is to have the rater evaluate all subordinates on one dimension before proceeding to another dimension. The theory underlying this practice is that thinking of one dimension at a time forces the rater to think in specific instead of overall terms when evaluating subordinates.

Leniency or Harshness Error

Performance evaluations require the rater to objectively reach a conclusion about performance. Being objective is difficult for everyone. Raters have their own rose-colored glasses with which they "objectively" view subordinates. Consequently, **leniency** or **harshness rating error** may occur in raters' evaluations of their subordinates. Some raters see everything as good—these are lenient raters. Other raters see everything as bad—these are harsh raters.

Raters can assess their own tendencies toward harsh and lenient rating by examining their ratings. This self-assessment is sometimes startling. Another method used to reduce harsh and lenient rating is to ask raters to distribute ratings—forcing a normal distribution (for example, 10 percent of the subordinates will be rated as excellent, 20 percent rated as good, 40 percent rated as fair, 20 percent rated below fair, and 10 percent rated as poor).

Central Tendency Error

A **central tendency error** occurs when a rater avoids using high or low ratings and assigns average ratings. The rater resorts to a philosophy that everyone is about average and rates subordinates around a 4 on a 1 to 7 scale or a 3 on a 1 to 5 scale. This type of "average" rating is almost useless—it fails to discriminate between subordinates. Thus, it offers little information for making HRM decisions regarding compensation, promotion, training, or what should be fed back to ratees. Raters must be made aware of the importance of discriminating across ratees and the use of evaluations. This sometimes stimulates raters to use less central (average) ratings.

"Recency of Events" Error

One difficulty with many of the evaluation systems is the time frame of the behavior being evaluated. Raters forget more about past behavior than current behavior. Thus, many persons are evaluated more on the results of the past several weeks than on six months' average behavior. This is called a **"recency of events" rating error.**

Some employees are well aware of this difficulty. If they know the date of the evaluation, they make it their business to be visible and noticed in many positive ways for several weeks in advance. Many evaluation systems suffer from this difficulty. It can be mitigated by using a technique such as critical incident or management by objectives (MBO) or by irregularly scheduled evaluations.

Contrast Effects

Recall that with the individual performance evaluation techniques each employee is supposed to be rated without regard to other employees' performance. Some evidence, however, suggests that supervisors have a very difficult time doing this. If a supervisor lets another employee's performance influence the ratings that are given to someone else, then a **contrast effect** has occurred.[36] For example, when the performance of an average employee is evaluated immediately after the performance of an outstanding employee, the supervisor might end up rating the average person as "below average" or "poor."

Contrast effects can also occur when a supervisor unknowingly compares employees' present performance with their past performance and this comparison affects ratings.

Those who have been poor performers in the past could get rated "above average" if they improve their performance, even if the improvement actually only brings their performance up to "average."

Contrast effects are another rating problem that is difficult to eliminate. Fortunately, this type of error seems to dissipate over time, as more information about employees' performance is gathered.[37]

Personal Bias Error

A **personal bias rating error** is (as the term implies) an error related to a personal bias held by a supervisor. There are several kinds of personal bias errors. Some can be conscious, such as blatant discrimination against someone because of sex or race. Or some supervisors might try to "play favorites" and rate people they like higher than people they don't like.[38]

Other personal bias errors are more subtle, and the supervisor might be totally unaware of them. For example, an error sometimes occurs when a rater gives a higher rating because the ratee has qualities or characteristics similar to the rater's.

Personal bias errors have been detected in many studies of performance evaluation. Research indicates that personal liking can affect the attributions a manager makes about a subordinate's level of performance as well as the kind of feedback that he or she will give.[39] However, "trait" ratings seem to be more strongly affected than "outcome" ratings by personal biases such as liking.[40] Moreover, errors associated with ratees' sex and race do occur. The effect of these errors is generally small when supervisors have adequate performance-related information upon which to base ratings,[41] but even small effects for characteristics such as sex, age, and race are cause for concern. Thus, organizations should attempt to eliminate even small effects for these characteristics.

Eliminating Rater Errors

As mentioned earlier, behavior-based rating scales were originally designed to help eliminate the kinds of rating errors just described. But when such scales didn't demonstrate any consistent superiority over other rating formats, researchers began to concentrate more on the rating *process*.[42] In other words, more recent efforts to improve performance evaluations in organizations have centered on helping raters to more accurately observe, recall, and report behavior.

Rater Training

One popular way to improve managers' ability to conduct effective performance appraisals is through rater training programs. Many types of programs exist, differing in focus, cost, and duration. The two most popular types are training programs designed to eliminate common rating errors such as halo error and training programs designed to improve the supervisor's observation and recording skills.

Programs dealing with errors do seem to eliminate many of these from ratings. In addition, even short, relatively inexpensive programs are effective at accomplishing this goal. However, there is much less evidence that this kind of training actually increases the accuracy of appraisals. Programs focused on observation and recording skills may offer greater improvements in accuracy than those that simply focus on errors.[43]

In either case, training alone will probably not solve all the problems of performance appraisal. Unless raters are motivated to use the system effectively and unless they are given the opportunity to observe their subordinates' performance, errors such as those discussed are likely to continue.

Avoiding Problems with Employees

For the evaluation system to work well, the employees must understand it and feel that it is a fair way to evaluate performance. In addition, they must believe that the system is

Let's get back to Ed and his supervisor, Hector. Now that the vice presidents have had their meeting about performance evaluation, the tentative decision to start up Mary's plan has been passed on to the department heads.

Bob (department head)   I'm just reviewing your suggested pay and promotion recommendations for your unit, Hector. You know I try to delegate as much as I can. But I know some of the people you have recommended for big raises and promotions, and I notice some surprising omissions. Since I'm responsible for the whole department, I'd like to review this with you. Understand, I'm not trying to undercut you, Hector.

Hector (supervisor)   Oh, I understand, Bob. No problem! Where do you want to start?

Bob   Let me just make suggestions. I note that Mo, who's always been in our high-reward group, isn't here, nor is Ed, a good worker. And you do have Joe in your high-reward group. In the past, he never appeared there. How did you make these recommendations?

Hector   I looked my people over and used my best judgment.

Bob   Well, Hector, what facts did you use—did you look at the quarterly output printout, their personnel files, or what? How about performance evaluations? Partridge is thinking about a formal system to evaluate employees and help to decide who should be promoted and get raises.

Hector   I believe I know my people best. I don't need to go through a lot of paperwork and files to come up with my recommendations.

used correctly for making decisions concerning pay increases and promotions. Thus, for a performance evaluation system to work well, it should be as simple as possible— unnecessary complexity in rating forms or other evaluation procedures can lead to dissatisfaction among employees.[44] The system should also be implemented in a way that fully informs employees about how it is going to be used.[45]

One way to help foster understanding about the system is to allow employees to participate in its development. It can also be helpful if they are trained in performance evaluation methods so they can better understand how difficult the process can be. Self-evaluation can be a useful addition to an evaluation system, especially for purposes of facilitating performance evaluation discussions with a supervisor.

With regard to fairness, performance evaluation is in some ways like grading systems in schools. If you have received grades that you thought were unfair, inequitable, incorrectly computed, or based on the "wrong things" (for example, always agreeing with the instructor), you know what your reactions were! Students will say "I got an A" for a course in which they worked hard and were fairly rewarded. They will say "*He* (or *she*) gave me a D" if they feel it was unfair. Their reaction sometimes is to give up or to get angry. Similar responses can come from employees as well. If raters are incompetent or unfair, the employees may resist, sabotage, or ignore the rating program.

The Feedback Interview

An effective performance evaluation system involves two-way communication. That is, there must be active communication between the supervisor and the subordinate about performance. Evaluation should not be viewed simply as a once-a-year completion of rating forms. On the contrary, it is a continuing process.

EXHIBIT 9-14
Suggestions for Effective Evaluation Interviews: Steps and Skills

1. Raters and ratees should **prepare** for the meeting and be ready to discuss the employee's past performance against the objectives for the period.

2. The rater should put the employee **at ease** and stress that the interview is not a disciplinary session, but a time to review past work in order to improve the employee's future performance, satisfaction, and personal development.

3. The rater should **budget the time** so that the employee has approximately half the time to discuss the evaluation and his or her future behavior.

4. The rater should use **facts**, not opinions. Evidence must be available to document the claims and counterclaims.

5. The rater should structure the interview as follows:

   • First, open with **specific positive remarks:** For example, if the employee's quantity of work is good, the superior might say, "John, your work output is excellent. You processed 10 percent more claims than were budgeted."

   • Second, sandwich performance shortcomings between two discussions of positive results, and orient the discussion to **performance, not personal criticisms.** Stress that the purpose of bringing the specific issues up is to alleviate problems in the future, not to criticize the past. Probably no more than one or two important negative points should be brought up at one evaluation. It is difficult for many people to work toward improving more than two points. The handling of negative comments is crucial. They should be phrased specifically and be related to performance, and it should be apparent to the employee that their purpose is not to criticize but to improve future performance. Many people become very defensive when criticized. Of course, the interviews should be private, between the employee and the evaluator.

   • Third, conclude with **positive comments** and overall evaluation results.

6. The rater should **guard against overwhelming** the ratee with information. Too much information can be confusing, although too little can be frustrating. The rater must balance the amount of information that is provided.

7. The rater should **encourage the ratee's involvement** and self-review and evaluation. Ask the ratee to do his or her own evaluation on a periodic basis.

8. The final aspect of the interview should **focus on future** objectives and how the superior can help the employee achieve organizational and personal goals. Properly done, the interview contributes importantly to the purposes of performance evaluation.

To help with this communication, the supervisor should hold an evaluation interview with each subordinate in order to discuss his or her appraisal and to set objectives for the upcoming appraisal period. In addition, experts advise that actions concerning the employee's development or salary should not be discussed during this interview.[46] Thus, although most organizations with formal evaluation systems give employees feedback, many are not doing it in the best way possible. Exhibit 9-14 provides eight specific interview suggestions that can help make the feedback session productive, educational, and informative.

Metropolitan Property and Casualty Insurance Company incorporates the feedback interview, which has led to an entirely new focus in appraisal. After the company became dissatisfied with its traditional approach, it implemented a program, called "Focus on Achievement."[47] Rather than emphasizing evaluations of past performance, this new perspective attempts to focus attention on future improvements in performance. The program is based on several key assumptions, all of which stress that the employee is responsible for his or her performance and that the supervisor's role in appraisal is primarily one of helping subordinates to achieve their own personal goals. A similar program was developed at Weyerhaeuser.[48] Both programs begin with the basic assumption that employees want to perform well and that appraisals should not be used as a way of controlling behavior, but rather as an important link in the feedback chain. Two-way communication is critical to these and other similar programs.

Hector was not very happy about having to take time out from his supervisory duties to attend a required training session about the new evaluation system for all managers. But he'd had some problems with his boss, Bob, over pay and promotions.

The session began with some short lectures. But most of the session involved practice on how to complete the rating forms for several kinds of employees. The supervisors were encouraged to review their employees' files and to jot down notes about employees' good and bad performances. They also practiced the evaluation interviews on each other. Given the ratings, they completed interviews on a very good, an average, and a poor employee. Other policies were also covered. They learned about the new MBO system and how it was going to work. Still, Hector was a bit skeptical.

Hector thought he'd better start the evaluations, since Bob had asked him how they were going. Hector decided to do Ed first. He still was a little worried about how it would go. Ed had been trained in what to expect. "Hope they haven't built him up too high," Hector thought. In reviewing the files, his notes, and his observations, Hector realized he had overlooked how well Ed had come along. He had done an excellent job, so Hector rated him highly.

Hector called Ed in for the interview. Hector referred to his notes and started and ended the interview on a positive note. He talked just a little about the shortcomings he'd noticed and offered to help Ed improve. At the beginning of the interview, Ed had been nervous. But he beamed at the end.

Hector finished the interview by saying he was recommending Ed for a good raise at the earliest chance. Over the next few days, Ed seemed to be especially happy. Maybe it was Hector's imagination, but he seemed to be working a bit harder, too, although he was already a good worker.

The training, formal system, and well-prepared feedback interview seemed to pay off.

Following these suggestions is not always easy. There are obviously times when the supervisor must be a judge and not just a counselor. With appropriate interviewing skills, however, many of the problems with communicating performance to subordinates can be overcome. These skills include the ability to speak clearly, listen carefully, gather and analyze information thoroughly, and negotiate the amount of and the use of resources. A poor feedback interview occurs because of poor preparation, error and miscalculation about the purpose of the sessions, and failure of the rater and the ratee to achieve some accuracy in understanding each other. A rater should always realize that a ratee's belief in the fairness of an appraisal will be a major determinant of her or his reaction to the system.[49] When subordinates trust the supervisor to conduct fair and unbiased appraisals, their satisfaction with the system increases dramatically.[50]

None of this suggests that a manager should never be a judge or should never criticize poor performance. Sometimes there is no choice but to give negative feedback to an employee. Under these circumstances, it can be very helpful to let the negative information flow naturally from the conversation in the appraisal interview.[51] In other words, rather than emphasizing the negative, it is easier for subordinates to accept criticism if discussions of shortcomings are seen as part of the larger topic of discussion: ways of improving future performance. By focusing on job-related problems, involving the ratee in setting realistic performance goals, and providing useful information in a nonthreatening manner, a rater can effectively use the interview. The feedback interview is designed to accomplish goals such as (1) recognizing and encouraging superior performance so that it will continue, (2) sustaining acceptable behaviors, and (3) changing the behavior of ratees whose performance is not meeting organizational standards.

Performance feedback reviews are designed to prevent situations such as Ed's confusion and Hector's failure to give him positive feedback. If the evaluation has been properly done, the employee knows where he or she stands and has received positive feedback on accomplishments and help on shortcomings. This is the developmental aspect of performance evaluation. The reward aspect can include pay raises (see Chapters 10 and 11).

Summary

Formal performance evaluation of employees is the HRM process by which the organization determines how effectively the employee is performing the job. It takes place primarily for white-collar, professional-technical, and managerial employees. It rarely is done for part-time employees, and only for about half of all blue-collar employees. Although the data are not entirely clear and criticisms in some cases are warranted, it appears that, if properly done, performance evaluations and feedback can be useful for most organizations and most employees.

To summarize the major points covered in this chapter:

1. Performance management is the process and actions taken to align employee performance and organizational goals. A tool in performance management is performance evaluation.

2. The purposes that a formal performance evaluation can serve include
   a. Development.
   b. Reward.
   c. Human resource planning.
   d. Validation.

3. For a formal performance evaluation to be effective, six steps must be taken:
   a. Establish performance standards for each position.
   b. Establish performance evaluation policies on when and how often to evaluate, who should evaluate, the criteria for evaluation, and the evaluation tools to be used.
   c. Have raters gather data on employees' performance.
   d. Evaluate employees' performance.
   e. Discuss the evaluation with the employee.
   f. Make decisions and file the evaluation.

4. Performance evaluation systems have problems because of
   a. Systems design and operating difficulties.
   b. Problems with the rater:
      1. Problems with standards of evaluation.
      2. Halo effect.
      3. Leniency or harshness rating error.
      4. Central tendency error.
      5. "Recency of events" rating error.
      6. Contrast effect.
      7. Personal biases.
   c. Employees' problems with performance evaluation:
      1. Employees don't understand the system or its purpose.
      2. Employees are not work-oriented.
      3. Evaluation may be below the employee's expectations.

5. Performance evaluation interviews that involve feeding back evaluation information can be effective if the evaluation information is meaningful, clear, and helpful. On the other hand, feeding back information can be quite stressful if the evaluation is considered unfair, inaccurate, and poorly designed. Selecting the best evaluation approach for the employees and managers to use is an important decision.

6. Properly performed, performance evaluation can contribute to organizational objectives and employees' development and satisfaction. These are goals of performance management.

Key Terms

behaviorally anchored rating scale (BARS), *p. 264*
behavioral observation scale (BOS), *p. 265*
central tendency error, *p. 274*
contrast effect, *p. 274*
criteria relevance, *p. 256*
criteria sensitivity, *p. 256*

critical incident, *p. 263*
forced-choice format, *p. 262*
forced distribution, *p. 267*
halo error, *p. 273*
interrater reliability, *p. 256*
leniency or harshness rating error, *p. 274*
management by objectives (MBO), *p. 269*

paired comparison, *p. 267*
performance evaluation, *p. 253*
performance management, *p. 251*
personal bias rating error, *p. 275*
"recency of events" rating error, *p. 274*
360-degree feedback, *p. 258*

Questions for Review and Discussion

1. What is "360-degree feedback"? What advantages might it have over more traditional performance appraisal systems that use only downward feedback? What are some of the potential problems that could occur in using a 360-degree feedback system?

2. Why would training in conducting performance evaluations be an important issue for organizations to consider?

3. Review three of the evaluation approaches discussed in this chapter by applying W. Edwards Deming's criticisms. How does each approach fare?

4. How often should formal performance evaluations take place? Informal ones? How often do they take place?

5. Who usually evaluates employees in organizations? Who should do so? Under what circumstances? What criteria should be used to evaluate employees? Which ones are used?

6. Explain why performance management is important in accomplishing organizational goals.

7. What are the characteristics of an effective appraisal interview? How should new and experienced employees be treated differently during the interview?

8. What should an organization do in order to help make sure that its performance evaluation system is legal? What is the role of job analysis in this process?

9. What is MBO? What advantages does it have over traditional performance evaluation methods? What are its weaknesses?

10. What are the major reasons for employee complaints about performance appraisal systems?

HRM Legal Advisor

Based on *Bals* v. *Verduzco,* 600 N.E.2d 1353 (Supreme Court of Indiana 1992).

The Facts

Daniel Bals was hired by Inland Steel Company in January 1982 as an associate engineer and was promoted to turn foreman after seven months. His direct supervisor, Albert Verduzco, was responsible for evaluating Mr. Bals' performance. As a result of repeated negative performance evaluations, Inland Steel terminated Mr. Bals in March 1994. Mr. Bals subsequently filed a lawsuit against his supervisor for defamation. To prove a valid claim of defamation, a plaintiff must show that false information is communicated or "published" to a third person and results in damage to the plaintiff's reputation in the eyes of the third person. Courts have protected good faith performance evaluations from defamation claims with a qualified privilege. However, the privilege may be lost if the communicator abuses it. Abuse of the qualified privilege occurs when the communication was motivated by ill will, when there is excessive publication of the information, or if the communicator had reason to believe that the information was false.

The Court's Decision

After rulings in favor of Mr. Verduzco by the trial court and appeals court, the case was appealed to the Supreme Court of Indiana. The Supreme Court considered two primary issues: (1) whether performance evaluation information communicated within a company can be considered "published" and (2) whether Mr. Verduzco abused the qualified privilege given to employee performance evaluations. Citing other jurisdictions that consider "damage to one's reputation within a corporate community to be just as devastating as that effected by defamation spread to the outside," the Supreme Court of Indiana held that intracompany communication of performance evaluation information meets the required "publication" element of a defamation claim. Further, the court held that Mr. Bals' evidence regarding the evaluations' factual accuracy did not prove that Mr. Verduzco knew or had reason to know that the information in the performance evaluations was not true. The lower courts' decisions were affirmed.

Human Resource Implications

Because courts have protected performance evaluations with the qualified privilege, supervisors should not be afraid of negative evaluations leading to defamation claims. However, supervisors must ensure that performance evaluations are conducted in good faith. To avoid an excessive publication abuse, supervisors should make performance evaluations available only to management or human resource personnel with a valid need for the information. Abuse of the privilege may also be avoided by documenting evaluations with performance-related data. Keeping an ongoing log of employees' performance and behaviors may be helpful in this regard.

Notes

1. Herman Aquinis (2005), *Performance Management* (Prentice-Hall, Upper Saddle River, NJ).
2. Thomas A. Davenport (2005), *Thinking for a Living: How to Get Better Performance and Results from Knowledge Workers* (Boston: Harvard University Press).
3. Ibid.
4. Gerald V. Barrett and Mary C. Kernan (Autumn 1987), "Performance Appraisal and Terminations: A Review of Court Decisions since *Brito* v. *Zia* with Implications for Personnel Practices," *Personnel Psychology,* pp. 489–504.
5. *Brito* v. *Zia Co.,* 478 F. 2d 1200 (Tenth Cir., 1973).
6. Charles H. Fleischer (2005), *HR for Small Business* (New York: Sourcebook).
7. Ibid.
8. Wayne F. Casio (1991), *Applied Psychology in Personnel Management,* 4th ed. (Englewood Cliffs, NJ: Prentice-Hall), pp. 64–65.
9. Brien N. Smith, Jeffrey S. Hornsby, and Roslyn Shirmeyer (Summer 1996), "Current Trends in Performance Appraisal: An Examination of Managerial Practice," *SAM Advanced Management Journal,* pp. 10–15.
10. Sherrie Gong (2002), *Hiring the Best and the Brightest* (New York: AMACOM).
11. Glen Shepard (2005), *How to Make Performance Evaluations Really Work* (New York: John Wiley).
12. Meshack M. Sagini (2001), *Organizational Behavior: The Challenges of the New Millennium* (New York: University Press).

13. Ibid.

14. Mary N. Vinson (April 1996), "The Pros and Cons of 360-Degree Feedback: Making It Work," *Training and Development,* pp. 11–12.

15. See *Leadership Quarterly,* Vol. 9 (1998), special issue on 360-degree feedback in leadership research.

16. Richard R. Reilly, James W. Smither, and Nicholas L. Vasilopoulos (Autumn 1996), "A Longitudinal Study of Upward Feedback," *Personnel Psychology,* pp. 599–612.

17. Don L. Bohl (September–October 1996), "Minisurvey: 360-Degree Appraisals Yield Superior Results, Survey Shows," *Compensation and Benefits Review,* pp. 16–19.

18. Michael J. Gibbs, Kenneth A. Merchant, Wim A. Van der Stede, and Mark E. Vargus, "The Benefits of Evaluating Performance Subjectively," *Performance Improvement,* May–June 2005, pp. 26–32.

19. Judy Cameron and W. David Pierce (2002), *Rewards and Intrinsic Motivation* (Westport, CT: Quorum).

20. Juan L. Sanchez and Phillip De La Torre (February 1996), "A Second Look at the Relationship between Rating and Behavioral Accuracy in Performance Appraisal," *Journal of Applied Psychology,* pp. 3–10.

21. Patricia C. Smith and L. M. Kendall (April 1963), "Retranslation of Expectations: An Approach to the Construction of Unambiguous Anchors for Rating Scales," *Journal of Applied Psychology,* pp. 149–155.

22. Gary P. Latham, Charles H. Fay, and Lise M. Saari (Summer 1979), "The Development of Behavioral Observation Scales for Appraising the Performance of Foremen," *Personnel Psychology,* pp. 290–311.

23. Frank L. Landy and J. L. Farr (1980), "Performance Rating," *Psychological Bulletin,* pp. 72–107.

24. Amy Del Pro (2005), *The Performance Appraisal Handbook* (Berkeley, CA: Nolo).

25. Tom W. Good (2002), *Information Literacy and Workplace Performance* (Westport, CT: Quorum).

26. Douglas M. McGregor (1960), *The Human Side of Enterprise* (New York: McGraw-Hill); Peter F. Drucker (1954), *The Practice of Management* (New York: Harper and Row); and George S. Odiorne (1965), *Management by Objectives* (New York: Pitman).

27. Brenda Pack Sunoo (March 1999), "Creating Worker Competency Roadmaps," *Workforce,* pp. 72–75.

28. Robert B. Campbell and Lynne Moses Garfinkel (June 1996), "Strategies for Success in Measuring Performance," *HR Magazine,* pp. 98–104.

29. Jurgen Kluge, Wolfram Stein, and Thomas Licht (2001), *Knowledge Unplugging* (New York: Palgrave).

30. A. D. Amar (2002), *Managing Knowledge Workers: Unleashing Innovation and Productivity* (Westport, CT: Quorum).

31. Nadia Nedjah and Luiza de Macedo Mourelle (Eds.) (2005), *Real-World Multi-Objective System Engineering* (New York: Nova Science Publishers).

32. Robert L. Cardy and Gregory H. Dobbins (1994), *Performance Appraisal—Alternative Perspectives* (Cincinnati, OH: South-Western), pp. 25–61.

33. Douglas McGregor (May 1957), "An Uneasy Look at Performance Appraisal," *Harvard Business Review.*

34. Kevin R. Murphy and Rebecca L. Anhalt (August 1992), "Is Halo Error a Property of the Rater, Ratees, or the Specific Behavior Observed?" *Journal of Applied Psychology,* pp. 494–500; Kevin R. Murphy and Douglas H. Reynolds (May 1988), "Does True Halo Affect Observed Halo?" *Journal of Applied Psychology,* pp. 235–238.

35. Elaine Pulakos, Neal Schmitt, and C. Ostroff (February 1986), "A Warning about the Use of a Standard Deviation across Dimensions within Rates to Measure Halo," *Journal of Applied Psychology,* pp. 29–32.

36. Todd J. Maurer and Ralph A. Alexander (February 1991), "Contrast Effects in Behavioral Measurement: An Investigation of Alternative Process Explanations," *Journal of Applied Psychology,* pp. 3–10.

37. Grote, op. cit.

38. Landy and Farr, op. cit.

39. Heike Bruch and Sumantra Ghoshal (2004), *A Bias for Action* (Boston: Harvard Business School Press).

40. Arup Varma, Angelo S. DeNisi, and Lawrence H. Pete (Summer 1996), "Interpersonal Affect and Performance Appraisal: A Field Study," *Personnel Psychology,* pp. 341–360.

41. Chockalingham Visavesavaran, Frank C. Schmidt, and Denez S. Orea (April 2002), "The Moderating Influence of Job Performance Dimensions on Convergency of Supervisory and Peer Ratings of Job Performance: Unconfounding Constraint-Level Convergency and Rating Difficulty," *Journal of Applied Psychology,* pp. 345–354.

42. Ibid.

43. Ibid.

44. Abraham Tesser, Diederik A. Stapel, and Joanne V. Wood (2002), *Self and Motivation,* Washington, DC: American Psychological Association.

45. Jack J. Phillips (2005), *Investing in Your Company's Human Capital: Strategies to Avoid Spending Too Little or Too Much* (New York: AMACOM).

46. Manuel London (2003), *Job Feedback* (Mahwah, NJ: Lawrence Earlbaum).

47. Joseph P. McCarthy (February 1991), "A New Focus on Achievement," *Personnel Journal,* pp. 74–715.

48. Leslie E Sorensen (July 1990), "Appraisal at Weyerhaeuser: Improving Staff Performance," *Management Accounting,* pp. 42–47.

49. M. Susan Taylor, Kay B. Tracy, Monika K. Renard, J. Kline Harrison, and Stephen J. Carroll (September 1995), "Due Process in Performance Appraisal: A Quasi-Experiment in Procedural Justice," *Administrative Science Quarterly,* pp. 495–523.

50. Matthew Gilbert (2005), *The Workplace Revolution: Restoring Trust in Business and Bringing Meaning to Our Work* (New York: Conan Press).

51. Kees van der Heyden (2005), *Scenarios: The Art of Strategic Conversation* (New York: John Wiley).

EXERCISE 9-1	**OBJECTIVE**
Selecting and Appraising Administrative Assistants at Row Engineering	The exercise is designed to have the student use knowledge about selection and performance appraisal to design an appraisal system.

INTRODUCTION

Row Engineering (name disguised) is a major engineering contractor, supplying aerospace firms, NASA, and the military with sophisticated equipment designs. Because of their rapidly expanding business, Row executives have decided that a formal management information system (MIS) is needed. The MIS may be used to monitor progress on projects, limit employees' access to classified information, reduce unnecessary duplication across similar projects, and generally increase efficiency by ensuring that the proper managers and engineers receive timely and relevant information for decision making.

Row has four major design facilities scattered throughout the southern and eastern United States in areas where approximately 50 percent of all high school graduates are black. Engineers at the different facilities typically work on different projects. Thus, Row executives have decided that one MIS department should be established for each of the

Source: This exercise was developed by Dr. William H. Ross, Jr., University of Wisconsin, La Crosse.

four facilities. While these will be linked by computer, each MIS department will have a great deal of autonomy.

Each MIS department will be made up of one administrator, seven administrative assistants, numerous technical personnel (for example, computer programmers), and clerical staff (for example, data entry personnel). The 28 administrative assistant positions will be key entry-level managerial positions. The administrative assistants will be responsible for securing and maintaining information for their assigned MIS area. Also, some may eventually be promoted to middle management positions in the future. Typical duties of an administrative assistant will include

A. Determining appropriate information needs from various projects for the MIS database. To do so requires cooperation with project engineers and managers as well as personnel from other departments.

B. Working with other MIS administrative assistants to develop standardized information reporting procedures. Such procedures facilitate the aggregation and comparison of specific types of information from different projects.

C. Creating and distributing instruction manuals outlining correct procedures for acquiring and reporting information for various departments. Sometimes administrative assistants will provide orientation sessions for company personnel.

D. Ensuring that necessary and timely information is supplied by each project or department, using standardized reporting procedures.

E. Supervising technical and clerical staff who are responsible for data input and retrieval.

F. Supervising technical staff who develop and purchase information software.

G. Maintaining project security by documenting computer analyses, ensuring that only authorized personnel receive relevant information, supervising clerical staff, and preventing unauthorized photocopying of specific types of information.

H. Supplying information, as requested, to project managers, specific departments, and contract monitors.

I. Documenting and supplying information to the fiscal services department regarding monthly time and computer-use expenditures for various projects. Fiscal services uses this information when comparing actual and estimated (budgeted) expenditures for projects and departments. Determining the MIS department's own budget needs.

About one year ago, the HR department conducted a formal job analysis of all existing administrative assistant positions throughout the corporation. From this analysis, a common job description was derived. This job description is reproduced as on page 285.

DESIGNING THE PERFORMANCE APPRAISAL SYSTEM

Currently, all Row Engineering employees, including administrative assistants, are evaluated using a one-item 10-point global rating scale. Ratings of either Unsatisfactory (1) or Superior (10) must be accompanied with written documentation. (See page 286.) In addition to the rating supervisor, the department head and the evaluated employee must sign the form, indicating that they have read the evaluation.

Recently, the HR manager has become concerned about the use of this type of rating scale. He has hired your human resource consulting firm to design a better performance appraisal system for the administrative assistant position with all the MIS departments.

Assignment: Write a three- to six-page report of this company describing and explaining your appraisal system. Your report should incorporate the following points;

A. Tactful explanation of the limitations of the present performance appraisal system.

B. Identification of the relevant dimensions (criteria) that should be measured in the new performance appraisal system. That is, how will the company distinguish the superior

---

 ROW ENGINEERING

HOURLY JOB DESCRIPTION

Job Title: Administrative Assistant   4–11–1193

I.   Function

To provide administrative support to a company organization.

II. Controls

Works under the direct supervision of a higher level administrator or technical manager but must exercise considerable judgment in the performance of assignments.

III. Major Duties

A. Utilizes a thorough knowledge of functions, activities, personnel, and organizations to perform various administrative duties.

B. Prepares charts and reports to reflect performance and overall efficiency of operations. Prepares, analyzes, and evaluates data pertaining to cost and maintains systems for effective cost control.

C. Confers with operating managers to determine requirements for space, equipment, supplies, and other facilities. Provides coordination with purchasing, plant services, and other company service organizations in meeting these requirements.

D. Conducts introductory nontechnical interviews with job applicants, briefing them on general functions of the company element and obtaining pertinent information for use in subsequent technical interviews. Keeps management informed of interviews, schedules, job offers extended, rejections, acceptances, and anticipated starting dates.

E. Coordinates the introduction and indoctrination of new employees to the company element. Compiles materials for use in indoctrination lectures, welcomes new employees, and arranges for tours of facilities. Ensures that all required paperwork is completed.

IV. Requirements

Requires a high school education, with college-level courses highly desirable, and approximately five (5) years of administrative experience or a B.S. degree in Business Administration.

ROW FORM NO. 06206 ORIG.

---

administrative assistants from those whose performance is merely adequate (or even inadequate)? Assume that the provided job description is correct.

C. How will each dimension be measured?

D. If you use some type of overall measure of performance, tell how you will measure it on a 100-point scale (100 = best). If you have several performance measures, tell how they will be combined into a composite criterion score. This composite score should be measured on a 100-point scale.

E. What weaknesses (if any) exist in your system? How will these be overcome?

A LEARNING NOTE

This exercise encourages the student to consider the uses, strengths, and weaknesses of a performance appraisal system.

◤ ROW ENGINEERING			**ROW ENGINEERING**
EMPLOYEE NAME	EMPLOYEE NO.	COST CENTER	DATE
RATING-SUPERVISOR-APPROVAL	DEPARTMENT HEAD-APPROVAL		EMPLOYEE

CIRCLE APPROPRIATE RATING

UNSATISFACTORY   1   2   3   4   5   6   7   8   9   10   SUPERIOR

(WRITTEN DOCUMENTATION REQUIRED FOR RATINGS OF SUPERIOR OR UNSATISFACTORY AND FOR CLASSIFICATION CHANGES)

Application Case 9-1

Evaluating Store Managers at Bridgestone/ Firestone Tire & Rubber

Bridgestone/Firestone is the second-largest tire company in the United States, with about 18 percent of the market. Bridgestone/Firestone manufactures and sells tires and related products for cars, trucks, buses, tractors, and airplanes. The tires are sold to automakers and consumers through 2,100 stores and many independent dealers. The stores are the vital link to the consumer.

Description of Store Manager Responsibilities

Summary of Duties

Has responsibility for securing maximum sales volume and maximum net profits. Supervises all phases of store operation—selling, merchandise display, service, pricing, inventories, credits and collections, operation, and maintenance. Responsible for the control of all store assets and prevention of merchandise shortages.

Interviews, selects, trains, and supervises all employees; follows their progress and development. Conducts employee meetings and follows closely for satisfactory productivity.

Sets sales quotas for employees and follows for accomplishment. Works with salespeople and personally calls on commercial and dealer accounts.

Interprets and explains store operating policies and procedures to subordinates and follows for adherence. Investigates complaints and makes adjustments. Maintains store cleanliness.

A. *Human resource administration*—30 percent
   1. Directly supervises pivotal employees and, through them, the other employees; directs activities, schedules duties and hours of work, and follows for productivity and sales results. Instructs or directs the instruction of new and present employees in work procedure, results expected, sales quota program, product and price information, and so on, and follows for adherence to instructions. (Daily)
   2. Interviews applicants, obtains formal applications, determines qualifications (using employment questionnaires), and selects best people for open jobs or files applications for future consideration. (Weekly)
   3. Determines number of employees needed for profitable store operations, considering individual sales productivity, salary expense, anticipated human resource requirements, and so on. (Monthly)
   4. Prepares, plans for, and conducts employee meetings, instructing about new products and policies, developing sales enthusiasm, explaining incentive programs, holding sales demonstrations, and so on. (Semimonthly)
   5. Trains and directs the training of new employees, following established training programs for effective utilization, conducting on-the-job training, and supervising training activities for own employees and those being trained for other assignments. (Weekly)

B. *Selling and sales promotion*—30 percent
   1. Breaks down store's sales into individual daily amounts for each employee, follows progress of employee in meeting quotas, and determines and takes action necessary to help him or her reach the objective. (Daily)
   2. Works with salesperson in setting up sales objectives and reviewing accomplishments, using call and sales record sheets, and following to secure maximum sales effort and effective use of time. Makes calls with salespeople to determine effectiveness of contacts, reasons for lack of progress, and so on, giving help in closing sales and securing additional business. (Daily)

EXHIBIT 9-1A **Setting Standards and Recording Results**

Instructions: This worksheet is to be used during the year for the purpose of providing supporting information for the annual employee assessment. First list the six most important job duties of the employee in decreasing order of importance. Establish standards for each major job duty. Record the employee's performance against the standard established (1, 2, 3, or 4). Refer to the employee's work results in the performance feedback or post assessment interview.

Major Job Duties (Taken from Job Description)	Standard of Performance (Measure of Criterion of Success)	Emplyee's Performance (Percentage of Time Standard Is Met)			
		Less than 50%	50% to 75%	76% to 89%	90% or More
1.					
2.					
3.					
4.					
5.					
6.					

3. Contacts personally and by telephone inactive accounts and prospective customers, promoting and soliciting sale of merchandise and services, and following to close the sales. Review prospect cards, assigns them to employees, and follows to secure sales from each. (Daily)

4. Contacts selected commercial and dealer accounts for special sales promotion and solicitation, determining sales possibilities and requirements, selling merchandise and services, and so on. (Daily)

5. Prepares advertising copy, following merchandising program suggestions, and arranges for insertion of advertisements in local newspaper. Makes sure employees are alerted and store has merchandise to back up advertising. (Weekly)

6. Maintains a firm retail, commercial, and wholesale pricing program according to established policies.

C. *Inventory sales and expense control*—15 percent

1. Reviews stock turnover records for overstock conditions, determines necessary corrective steps, and takes the appropriate action. Establishes stock levels and orders according to sales results recorded in the stock ledgers for new tires and retreads. (Also major appliances monthly).

2. Prepares sales and expense budget covering projected sales and expenses for the period. (Monthly)

3. Reviews expense control sheet, comparing actual expenses with budget figures; determines and takes action necessary to keep within the approved budget. (Daily)

EXHIBIT 9-1B **Work Review Comments**

Instructions: Review the employee's performance against the standards established. Analyze the employee's performance in terms of quality (how good), quantity (how much), and work methods (how the employee went about getting work results). What job duties are being handled particulaly well by the employee? What job standards are not being met? Complete this section before conducting the interview with the employee.

PERFORMANCE STRENGTHS ABOVE JOB STANDARDS: _____

_____

_____

_____

PERFORMANCE AREAS BELOW JOB STANDARDS: _____

_____

_____

_____

III. INTERVIEW RESULTS AND DEVELOPMENT PLAN

Instructions: The work counseling interview is an important part of any work results program. Section III should be completed after holding the interview. Comment on the employee's reaction to performance feedback and the plan you and the employee have developed for improving work results. Be specific in your description of the results of the interview and the developmental steps you and the employee have agreed upon.

EMPLOYEE'S REACTION TO PERFORMANCE FEEDBACK: _____

_____

_____

_____

PLAN FOR IMPROVING WORK RESULTS: _____

_____

_____

_____

_____

_____

Employee's Signature

RATER TO PROCEED TO SECTION IV

4. Is responsible for the completeness and accuracy of all inventories, accounting inventories, markup, markdown inventories, and so on.

D. *Checking*—10 percent

1. Checks stock, automotive equipment, service floor, and so on, continually observing store activities and determining that equipment is maintained in good operating condition. Makes inspection trips through all parts of the store, checking observance of safety and fire precautions, protection of company assets, and so on. Checks credit information secured for

commercial and dealer accounts, and works with office and credit manager in setting up credit limits. (Weekly)

2. Is responsible for and investigates all cash shortages, open tickets, and missing tickets.

3. Investigates customer complaints, making adjustment or taking appropriate action for customer satisfaction. (Daily)

E. *Miscellaneous functions*—15 percent

1. Reads and signs Store Operating Policy and Office Procedure Letters; analyzes and puts into operation new policies and procedures as received. (Weekly)

2. Prepares letter to district manager covering progress of the store, store plans, results secured, market and special conditions, and so on. (Monthly)

3. Inspects tires and other merchandise in for adjustment, determines appropriate settlement, prepares claim forms, and issues credit, replaces, and so on. Makes all policy adjustments. (Daily)

4. Attends district sales and civic organizations meetings and takes part in civic affairs, community drives, and so on. (Weekly)

Discussion Questions

1. Do you consider the description of the Firestone store manager's responsibilities important information that the raters of managers need to be knowledgeable about?

2. Does the portion of the performance evaluation form used at Bridgestone/Firestone require any subjective judgements or considerations on the part of the rater?

3. Suppose that a Bridgestone/Firestone manager received an outstanding performance evaluation. Does this mean that he or she is promotable? Why?

Application Case 9-2
The Politics of Performance Appraisal

Every Friday, Max Steadman, Jim Cobun, Lynne Sims, and Tom Hamilton meet at Charley's Food Place after work for refreshments. The four friends work as managers at Eckel Industries, a manufacturer of arc welding equipment in Minneapolis. The one-plant company employs about 2,000 people. The four managers work in the manufacturing division. Max, 35, manages the company's 25 quality control inspectors. Lynne, 33, works as a supervisor in inventory management. Jim, 34, is a first-line supervisor in the metal coating department. Tom, 28, supervises a team of assemblers. The four managers' tenures at Eckel Industries range from one year (Tom) to 12 years (Max).

The group is close-knit: Lynne, Jim, and Max's friendship stems from their years as undergraduate business students at the University of Minnesota. Tom, the newcomer, joined the group after meeting the three at an Eckel management seminar last year. Weekly get-togethers at Charley's have become a comfortable habit for the group and provide an opportunity to relax, exchange the latest gossip heard around the plant, and give and receive advice about problems encountered on the job.

This week's topic of discussion: performance appraisal, specifically the company's annual review process, which the plant's management conducted in the last week. Each of the four managers completed evaluation forms (graphic rating scale format) on each of his or her subordinates and met with each subordinate to discuss the appraisal.

Tom This was the first time I've appraised my people, and I dreaded it. For me, it's been the worst week of the year. Evaluating is difficult; it's highly subjective and inexact. Your emotions creep into the process. I got angry at one of my assembly workers last week, and I still felt the anger when I was filling out the evaluation forms. Don't tell me that my frustration with the guy didn't bias my appraisal. I think it did. And I think the technique is flawed. Tell me—what's the difference between a five and a six on "cooperation"?

Jim   The scales are a problem. So is memory. Remember our course in human resource management in college? Phillips said that, according to research, when we sit down to evaluate someone's performance in the past year, we will be able to actively recall and use only 15 percent of the performance we observed.

Lynne   I think political considerations are always a part of the process. I know I consider many other factors besides a person's actual performance when I appraise him.

Tom   Like what?

Lynne   Like the appraisal will become part of the permanent written record that affects his career. Like the person I evaluate today, I have to work with tomorrow. Given that, the difference between a five and a six on cooperation isn't that relevant, because frankly, if a five makes him mad, and he's happy with a six. . . .

Max   Then you give him the six. Accuracy is important, but I'll admit it—accuracy isn't my primary objective when I evaluate my workers. My objective is to motivate and reward them so they'll perform better. I use the review process to do what's best for my people and my department. If that means fine-tuning the evaluations to do that, I will.

Tom   What's an example of fine-tuning?

Max   Jim, do you remember three years ago when the company lowered the ceiling on merit raises? The top merit increase that any employee could get was 4 percent. I boosted the ratings of my folks to get the best merit increases for them. The year before that, the ceiling was 8 percent. The best they could get was less than what most of them received the year before. I felt they deserved the 4 percent, so I gave the marks that got them what I felt they deserved.

Lynne   I've inflated ratings to encourage someone who is having personal problems but is normally a good employee. A couple of years ago, one of my better people was going through a painful divorce, and it was showing in her work. I don't think it's fair to kick people when they're down.

Tom   Or make her complacent.

Lynne   No, I don't think so. I felt she realized her work was suffering. I wanted to give her encouragement; it was my way of telling her she had some support and that she wasn't in danger of losing her job.

Jim   There's another situation where I think fine-tuning is merited—when someone's work has been mediocre or even poor for most of the year, but it improves substantially in the last two, three months or so. If I think the guy is really trying and is doing much better, I'd give him a rating that's higher than his work over the whole year deserves. It encourages him to keep improving. If I give him a mediocre rating, what does that tell him?

Tom   What if he's really working hard, but not doing so great?

Jim   If I think he has what it takes, I'd boost the rating to motivate him to keep trying until he gets there.

Max   I know of one or two managers who've inflated ratings to get rid of a pain in the neck, some young guy who's transferred in and thinks he'll be there a short time. He's not good, but thinks he is, and creates all sorts of problems. Or his performance is okay, but he just doesn't fit in with the rest of the department. A year or two of good ratings is a sure trick for getting rid of him.

Tom   Yes, but you're passing the problem on to someone else.

Max   True, but it's no longer my problem.

Tom   All the examples you've talked about involve inflating evaluations. What about deflating them, giving someone less than you really think he deserves? Is that justified?

Lynne   I'd hesitate to do that because it can create problems. It can backfire.

Max   But it does happen. You can lower a guy's ratings to shock him, to jolt him into performing better. Sometimes, you can work with people, coach them, try to help them improve, and it just doesn't work. A basement-level rating can tell someone you mean business. You can say that isn't fair, and for the time being, it isn't. But what if you feel that if the guy doesn't shape up, he faces being fired in a year or two, and putting him in the cellar, ratings-wise, will solve

<table>
<tr><td></td><td>his problem? It's fair in the long run if the effect is that he improves his work and keeps his job.</td></tr>
<tr><td>**Jim**</td><td>Sometimes, you get someone who's a real rebel, who always questions you, sometimes even oversteps his bounds. I think deflating his evaluation is merited just to remind him who's the boss.</td></tr>
<tr><td>**Lynne**</td><td>I'd consider lowering the true rating if someone had a long record of rather questionable performance, and I think the best alternative for the person is to consider another job with another company. A low appraisal sends him a message to consider quitting and start looking for another job.</td></tr>
<tr><td>**Max**</td><td>What if you believe the situation is hopeless, and you've made up your mind that you're going to fire the guy as soon as you've found a suitable replacement? The courts have chipped away at management's right to fire. Today, when you fire someone, you must have a strong case. I think once a manager decides to fire, appraisals become very negative. Anything good that you say about the subordinate can be used later against you. Deflating the ratings protects you from being sued and sometimes speeds up the termination process.</td></tr>
<tr><td>**Tom**</td><td>I understand your point, but I still believe that accuracy is the top priority in performance appraisal. Let me play devil's advocate for a minute. First, Jim, you complained about our memory limitations introducing a bias into appraisal. Doesn't introducing politics into the process further distort the truth by introducing yet another bias? Even more important, most would agree that one key to motivating people is providing true feedback—the facts about how they're doing so they know where they stand. Then you talk with them about how to improve their performance. When you distort an evaluation—however slightly— are you providing this kind of feedback?</td></tr>
<tr><td>**Max**</td><td>I think you're overstating the degree of fine-tuning.</td></tr>
<tr><td>**Tom**</td><td>Distortion, you mean.</td></tr>
<tr><td>**Max**</td><td>No, fine-tuning. I'm not talking about giving a guy a seven when he deserves a two or vice versa. It's not that extreme. I'm talking about making slight changes in the ratings when you think that the change can make a big difference in terms of achieving what you think is best for the person and for your department.</td></tr>
<tr><td>**Tom**</td><td>But when you fine-tune, you're manipulating your people. Why not give them the most accurate evaluation, and let the chips fall where they may? Give them the facts, and let them decide.</td></tr>
<tr><td>**Max**</td><td>Because most of good managing is psychology—understanding people, their strengths and shortcomings; knowing how to motivate, reward, and act to do what's in their and your department's best interest. And sometimes total accuracy is not the best path.</td></tr>
<tr><td>**Jim**</td><td>All this discussion raises a question. What's the difference between fine-tuning and significant distortion? Where do you draw the line?</td></tr>
<tr><td>**Lynne**</td><td>That's about as easy a question as what's the difference between a five and six. On the form, I mean.</td></tr>
</table>

Discussion Questions

1. In your opinion, and from an HRM perspective, what are the objectives of employee performance evaluation?

2. On the basis of these objectives, evaluate the perspectives about performance appraisal presented by the managers.

3. Assume you are the vice president of HRM at Eckel Industries and that you are aware that fine-tuning evaluations is a prevalent practice among Eckel managers. If you disagree with this perspective, what steps would you take to reduce the practice?

Source: Written by Kim Stewart. Several of the perspectives presented here were drawn from an insightful study reported to Clinton O. Longenecker, Henry P. Sims, Jr., and Dennis A. Gioia (August 1987), "Behind the Mask: The Politics of Employee Appraisal," *Academy of Management Executive*, pp. 183–191.

Chapter 10

Compensation: An Overview

Learning Objectives

After studying this chapter you should be able to:

1. **Define** compensation and differentiate among direct financial compensation, indirect financial compensation, and nonfinancial rewards.

2. **Describe** the strategic importance of human resource management (HRM) activities performed in organizations.

3. **Explain** how compensation systems relate to employees' motivation, productivity, and satisfaction.

4. **Explain** how external factors (labor markets, the economy, the government, and unions) and internal factors (size and age of the organization, labor budget, and who is involved in pay decisions) relate to a firm's compensation policy.

5. **Discuss** how pay surveys help managers create efficient and equitable pay systems.

6. **Describe** the job evaluation process.

Internet/Web Resources

General Sites
www.futurestep.com
www.compdatasurvey.com
www.berkshire-aap.com

Company Sites
www.burgerking.com
www.whirlpoolcorp.com

Career Challenge

Decker Manufacturing is a large company that was founded in 1945 by Gary Decker. Decker is located in the suburbs of Philadelphia and employs 1,500 people ranging from janitors to the corporate executive team. Most of the workforce is made up of semiskilled labor, such as crane operators, press operators, and shipping clerks. Decker's product line consists of pharmaceutical stoppers made of various polymers and rubber. The plant manufactures and assembles various laboratory items such as blood collection tubes and stoppers. Its customers are large pharmaceutical firms that supply various products to hospitals and labs. Its market is worldwide, with many of the best customers in Europe and Asia. Brad Decker replaced his father as CEO five years ago.

The senior Decker, an entrepreneur with a high school education, had been a traditional manager who tried to keep his hands on every phase of the operation. Gary Decker took pride in Decker Manufacturing's reputation for fair pay and satisfied employees. Even as the firm expanded from its initial size of 100 employees to the present 1,500, Gary had been involved in all aspects of the compensation plan; he had the final word on pay rates for all employees. He based pay on experience, potential, and how much each employee needed to support his or her family. As a result, Decker Manufacturing had low absenteeism and turnover.

After Brad took over, several environmental factors began to challenge the company founder's approach to compensation. Several new competitors had entered the marketplace, paying lower wages than Decker, so they were more profitable. Key business had been lost because Decker had to charge more for its products in order to maintain the compensation system's above-average pay strategy. At the same time, turnover had increased because employees at Decker felt they were not compensated fairly.

Cheryl Sussen, human resource manager, made a point of this distressing trend at a staff meeting.

Cheryl   Brad, I think you're aware that our compensation policy is seriously out of date. We're paying the highest wages in the industry, but we're steadily losing employees because they don't think they are being paid fairly.

Brad   I know. Pop always emphasized that workers would be loyal if we treated them as individuals. He based his pay decisions on how big a family an employee was trying to support. Maybe we ended up with too many exceptions to our pay policy.

Cheryl   The reality is that most of our competitors are opening plants in third world countries so they can keep labor costs down. In order to compete we have to bring our labor costs into line with those of our competition. To do that we need to reevaluate the whole pay system. At the same time, we need to find out why our employees think their pay is unfair. I've asked Jerry Wallace, our compensation director, to review our job evaluation system so that we can develop pay that is perceived as equitable and is still competitive within the industry.

Compensation is the human resource management function that deals with every type of reward individuals receive in exchange for performing organizational tasks. It is the major cost of doing business for many organizations at the start of the 21st century.[1] It is the chief reason why most individuals seek employment. It is an exchange relationship. Employees trade labor and loyalty for financial and nonfinancial compensation (pay, benefits, services, recognition, etc.). Employers in the United States (private industry and state and local government) paid an average of $22.22 per hour worked in 2004. Of this amount, about 73 percent, $15.62, was paid in straight-time wages and salaries. Benefits accounted for the remaining 27 percent, an average of $6.60 per hour.[2]

Financial compensation is either direct or indirect. **Direct financial compensation** consists of the pay an employee receives in the form of wages, salaries, bonuses, or commissions. **Indirect financial compensation,** or benefits, consists of all financial rewards that are not included in direct financial compensation. Typical benefits include vacation, various kinds of insurance, services like child care or elder care, and so forth. Chapters 10 and 11 cover direct financial compensation; Chapter 12 will deal with benefits.

Nonfinancial rewards like praise, self-esteem, and recognition, although not discussed in this text, affect employees' motivation, productivity, and satisfaction. A more comprehensive study of compensation would include a special section on nonfinancial rewards.

From the employee's point of view, pay is a necessity of life. It is one of the chief reasons people seek employment. Pay is the means by which they provide for their own and their families' needs. Compensation does more than provide for the physiological needs of employees, however. What a person is paid indicates his or her worth to an organization. For the employer, compensation is one of the most important HRM functions. In today's service-based economy, pay often equals 50 percent or more of the cash flow of an organization. It is one of the major methods used to attract employees and motivate them for more effective performance. Compensation is also a significant component of the economy: for the past 30 years, salaries and wages have equaled about 60 percent of the gross national product of the United States and Canada.[3]

Objective of Compensation

The objective of the compensation function is to create a system of rewards that is equitable to the employer and employee alike. The desired outcome is an employee who is attracted to the work and motivated to do a good job for the employer. Patton suggests that in compensation policy there are seven criteria for effectiveness.[4] Compensation should be:

1. *Adequate*   Minimal governmental, union, and managerial levels should be met.
2. *Equitable*   Each person should be paid fairly, in line with his or her effort, abilities, and training.
3. *Balanced*   Pay, benefits, and other rewards should provide a reasonable total reward package.
4. *Cost-effective*   Pay should not be excessive, considering what the organization can afford to pay.
5. *Secure*   Pay should be enough to help an employee feel secure and aid him or her in satisfying basic needs.
6. *Incentive-providing*   Pay should motivate effective and productive work.
7. *Acceptable to the employee*   The employee should understand the pay system and feel it is a reasonable system for the enterprise and himself or herself.

External Influences on Compensation

Among the factors that influence pay and compensation policies are those outside the organization: the labor market, the economy, the government, and unions.

The Labor Market and Compensation

Although many feel that human labor should not be regulated by forces such as supply and demand, it does in fact happen. In times of full employment, wages and salaries may have to be higher to attract and retain enough qualified employees; in depressions, pay can be lower. Pay may also be higher if few skilled employees are available in the job market.

This situation may occur because unions or accrediting associations limit the numbers certified to do the job. In certain locations, because of higher birthrates or a recent loss of a major employer, more people may be seeking work. These factors lead to what is called *differential pay levels.* At any one time in a particular locale, rates for unskilled labor seek a single level, and rates for minimally skilled clerical work seek another. Research evidence in labor economics provides adequate support for the impact of labor market conditions on compensation. Besides differences in pay levels by occupations in a locale, there are also differences between government and private employees and exempt and nonexempt employees, as well as international differences.

Traditional styles of management, along with traditional styles of rewarding employees, have already been changing in response to the diversity in the labor market. *Workforce diversity* means more than simply listing the demographic characteristics of existing and new entrants. It means differing value systems (such as liberal versus conservative and traditional versus futurist), lifestyles, body types—the list goes on and on. Diversity isn't limited to multiracial, multicultural, and multiethnic impacts on the workplace. It refers to any mixture of items characterized by differences and similarities.

Perhaps the easiest relationship to imagine between rewards and diversity has to do with benefits. Rapidly changing demographics will require employers to offer more, and more varied, benefits to motivate, satisfy, and retain employees.[5] For example, in order to attract experienced retirees back to work, Dana Corporation began offering a prorated benefits package to get employees to work part-time and a flexible contract so that they could work only part of the year to remain eligible for Social Security.[6]

Yet another dimension of labor market diversity having an impact on reward systems is the increasing level of formal education. In 2005, over 50 percent of all adult Americans have some college education, 50 percent of all college students are over 25, and more than half of all college graduates are women. This increasingly educated population will not hesitate to ask for changes in pay and benefits to fit the needs of their changing lifestyles.

Let's look at a few more diverse groups. Generation X has the highest percentage of members who have finished high school and college. This generation values financial security as a top goal and would like to attain power and status. However, the members of generation X don't always bring applicable job skills to the organization. Designing a reward system that would motivate them is in conflict with the value that they actually bring. Two other types of employees that are increasingly filling jobs are technological experts—sometimes called "nerds"—and temporary or contingent workers. Both present challenges with regard to compensation.[7] Besides having more technology to play with, what motivates nerds? Temps in the 21st century are a permanent fixture, not just people who fill in for secretaries on vacation but workers ranging from the top to the bottom of organizations.

The HR Journal box points out the value of a college education in terms of earnings and also what HRM surveys suggest are what organizations should be doing to keep generation X and others satisfied and motivated.

Compensation and an International Labor Force

Employers have been transporting cheap labor to work "on site" since the building of the pyramids.[8] Chinese railway builders were transported to the American West at the turn of the 19th century, and workers were flown into Britain's Gatwick Airport from Ireland to work on the Channel Tunnel. Compensation specialists must base their plans on a competitive global marketplace. Issues that affect the compensation strategies of organizations competing in a global marketplace include the followings:[9]

- *Global wage differentials verging on the extreme* For example, computer consultants in the United States earn over $100 an hour; in India, consultants work for the same firm for $10 an hour!

HR Journal   *A Few Points to Ponder about Earnings and Organizational Attractiveness*

EARNINGS AND EDUCATION

The average yearly salary of workers:

Advanced degree	$74,602
Bachelor's degree	51,206
High school diploma	27,915
No high school diploma	18,734

Over a 40-year career the differences in earnings between these four categories can be significant.

SURVEYS OF MOST ADMIRED COMPANY STRATEGIES TO RETAIN AND MOTIVATE EMPLOYEES (SEVEN TOP ITEMS):

1. Honest, ethical management.
2. Excellent pay and benefits.
3. Profit sharing, employee stock options.
4. Respect for employees.
5. Meetings to communicate what company faces.
6. Extra-generous vacations and sabbaticals.
7. Strong career development, coaching, and mentoring.

The top seven slots shift slightly each year, but these categories are consistently in the top 15 lists.

Source: Adapted from "Earnings Soar with Education" (March 15, 2005), *USA Today,* p. A1; and www.funfacts.com/world.htm, accessed June 20, 2005.

- *Moving American employees to foreign locations* Keeping employees and families at foreign sites costs three to five times the annual base pay at home. Costs vary tremendously from country to country—for example, Mexico City versus Tokyo. Compensation problems involve appropriate salary allowances, tax laws, travel and relocation funds, education for dependents, and emergency leaves.

- *Employing local (foreign) managers and workers* A survey of Forbes 500 top managers said that compensation of foreign nationals is a "hodgepodge" or a "nightmare." Providing pay packages is much harder for foreign nationals than for Americans abroad. Few foreign field offices have a compensation expert on staff. The result is low overhead at home and high frustration and inefficiency abroad.

- *Moving foreign workers to the United States for training or work assignments* Inpatriates are company employees from foreign sites who come to the United States on assignment or for training. Since the assignment is usually of limited duration, compensation specialists must decide how they will be paid: Should they receive the same as American employees, the same as they get at home, or a third sum which allows them to maintain their usual lifestyle in the United States, which in most cases is more expensive?

- *Offshoring the outsourcing of jobs, projects, and work to foreign countries* Organizations are attempting to cut labor costs by shifting work overseas where labor costs are significantly lower.[10] It is estimated that worldwide spending on job relocation to foreign countries was about $3.7 trillion in 2001 and is expected to be over $5.0 trillion in 2005.

Economic consideration and the growth of technology have contributed to the offshore explosion among U.S. organizations. The low cost of living in developing countries allows management to pay workers less than American workers. A computer analyst in the United States earns an average of $63,000 a year. In India, the same worker earns less than $6,000.

A countermovement is beginning: a backlash against offshoring. For example, some companies have learned that their customers can get frustrated with overseas help. Apparently, not having a close connection between the customer/client and the organization's employees is considered to be distracting or impersonal.

Economic Conditions and Compensation

Also affecting compensation as an external factor are the economic conditions of the industry, especially the *degree of competitiveness,* which affects the organization's ability to pay high wages. The more competitive the situation, the less able the organization is to pay higher wages. Ability to pay is also a consequence of the relative productivity of the organization, industry, or sector. If a firm is very productive, it can pay higher wages. Productivity can be increased by advanced technology, more efficient operating methods, a harder-working and more talented workforce, or a combination of these factors.

One productivity index used by many organizations as a criterion in determining a general level of wages is the Bureau of Labor Statistics' "output per man-hour in manufacturing." This productivity index is published in each issue of the *Monthly Labor Review.* For about 70 years, productivity increased at an average annual rate of approximately 3 percent. The percentage increase in average weekly earnings in the United States is very closely related to the percentage change in productivity plus the percentage change in the consumer price index. More recently, the productivity index has improved, to 2.9.[11]

Government Influences and Compensation

The government directly affects compensation through wage controls and guidelines, which prohibit an increase in compensation for certain workers at certain times, and laws that establish minimum wage rates and wage and hour regulations and prevent discrimination.

Wage Controls and Guidelines

Several times in the past the United States had established wage freezes and guidelines. President Harry Truman imposed a wage and price freeze from 1951 to 1953, and President Richard Nixon imposed freezes from 1971 to 1974. *Wage freezes* are government orders that forbid wage increases. *Wage controls* limit the size of wage increases. *Wage guidelines* are similar to wage controls, but they are voluntary rather than mandatory.

Three acts have been passed since 1942 aimed at stabilizing the economy:

- *Wage Stabilization Act (1942)* A wage freeze imposed to slow inflation during World War II, which set "going rates" of pay for key occupations.
- *Defense Production Act (1950)* A similar wage freeze imposed during the Korean War.
- *Economic Stabilization Act (1970)* This granted the president of the United States the authority to impose wage and price controls in times of national necessity.

The use of wage freezes, controls, and guidelines is very controversial. Advocates believe that such restrictions dramatically reduce inflation. Critics argue that the benefit is more than overcome by the disruption of resource allocation and the market process.

Wage and Hour Regulations

The **Fair Labor Standards Act (FLSA)** of 1938 is the basic pay regulation act in the United States.[12] It was passed to try to counteract the abuses encountered by production (line) workers in the manufacturing sector of the economy, who were working long hours for low pay.

In the act, there are four provisions: minimum wage, overtime, child labor, and the Equal Pay Act of 1963.[13] FLSA is comprehensive, covering businesses with two or more employees engaged in interstate commerce, in the production of goods for interstate

HR Journal   *On-Call Pay*

A computer system crashes. An emergency room doctor calls in sick. A snowstorm blocks a main highway, and three specialists can't make it to work. Employees on call respond to this kind of emergency everyday. How should they be compensated for being on call? No two firms have the same policy.

In the old days, workers waited for a telephone call to call them to work. Today, pagers, cell phones, and laptops allow the on-call worker to pursue other activities. The Fair Labor Standards Act of 1938 is vague about on-call pay. Nonexempt workers (nonmanagers) must remain close to an employer's premises, so they can be immediately reached. A nurse wearing a beeper can go out to dinner, sleep, or carry on a normal life, which means she will not receive on-call pay. If an hourly worker is called to work, he or she must be paid for a minimum number of hours (typically at least two hours).

Employers that pay exempt (managerial, technical professional) workers for being on call may risk violating federal labor laws unless they have an appropriate compensation system. If exempt workers receive extra pay by the hour for being on call, employers could be seen as treating them like nonexempt (nonmanagerial hourly) employees. This could be interpreted as a violation of the Fair Labor Standards Act.

The Taylor Group, a software firm in New Hampshire, pays a flat rate to employees (five) who are on call to answer client questions. They receive $100 per weekday and $170 for 24 hour/7 days duty. They usually respond to calls from their homes. Since these workers must wear a beeper and respond, the firm believes that it is only fair to pay them for being on call.

In a nutshell, exempt workers who are paid for being on call should not receive hourly pay. Experts recommend that employers like the Taylor Group are doing the right thing by paying a flat rate for on-call duties. Proceeding with caution when paying for on-call work means that exempt and nonexempt status makes a big difference.

Source: Carolyn Huschman (August 1999), "Paying for Waiting," *HR Magazine,* pp. 98–105.

commerce, or in handling, selling, or working on goods or materials that have been moved in or produced for interstate commerce. About 92 percent of nonsupervisory farm and nonfarm wage earners are covered. It is administered by the Department of Labor, which also acts as the enforcement agency through the Wage and Hour Division of the Employment Standards Administration (ESA).[14]

Minimum Wage   The **minimum wage** provision of FLSA establishes an income floor for low-paying jobs.[15] As you can see in Exhibit 10-1, the provision has been amended several times since 1938, when the minimum wage was set at 25 cents per hour. The latest change was a two-tiered raise from $4.25 per hour to $4.75 in October 1996 and then to $5.15 per

EXHIBIT 10-1
Historical Progression of the Minimum Wage

Source: Department of Labor (June 2005).

Year	Rate per Hour
1938	$0.25
1939	0.30
1945	0.40
1956	1.00
1968	1.60
1974	2.00
1979	2.90
1981	3.35
1993	4.25
1996	4.75
1997–2005	5.15

hour in September 1997. The typical minimum-wage worker is female, over age 25, and employed part-time. In fact, 3 in 5 of these workers are women, often the family's main or only wage earner. One-third of the total are teenagers on their first job.[16]

Employees under 20 years of age may be paid an "opportunity wage" of $\frac{1}{3}$ of the total per hour during the first 90 consecutive days of employment. Certain full-time students, student learners, apprentices, and disabled employees may be paid less than minimum wage under special certificates issued by the Department of Labor. Employers of workers who get tips (like waitresses and waiters) must pay a cash wage of at least $2.13 per hour.

The minimum wage is one of the most controversial provisions. Basic disagreement about its effects centers on the view of classical economists, who contend that any rise in the minimum wage will soon be offset by an immediate rise in the level of unemployment.[17] However, not all economists agree that the minimum wage is detrimental; some hold that the minimum wage does not raise the level of unemployment in the long run—rather, it harmlessly raises the wages of the lowest-paid workers. The impact on the change in the minimum wage on small businesses (50 or fewer employees) will be a 5.3 percent increase in wage costs for employees currently earning less than the new minimum. Businesses most likely to be affected are retailing, food, and lodging.

Overtime Pay   Virtually all hourly (nonexempt) employees must receive overtime compensation for working more than 40 hours in a given week or 8 hours on a given day. The law requires "time and a half": $1\frac{1}{2}$ times the base wage for hours in excess of 40 per week or 8 per day.[18] Salaried (exempt) employees do not receive overtime pay. A more precise definition of a salaried employee is one who regularly receives a predetermined amount constituting all or part of his or her compensation.

Making a distinction between **exempt** and **nonexempt** workers is not always easy. See Exhibit 10-2 for guidelines. Exempt individuals are those in managerial, administrative, or professional positions who are paid on a salaried basis. But an employee classified as

EXHIBIT 10-2
FLSA Exemption Guidelines

Source: Department of Labor (December 1996).

The following are examples of employees exempt from both the minimum wage and overtime:

- Executive, administrative, and professional employees (including teachers and academic administrative personnel in elementary and secondary schools, and certain skilled computer professionals as provided in P. L. 101-583, November 15, 1990), and outside salespersons.
- Employees of seasonal amusement or recreational establishments.
- Employees of certain small newspapers and switchboard operators of small telephone companies.
- Seamen employed on foreign vessels.
- Employees engaged in fishing operations.
- Farm workers employed on small farms (i.e., those that used less than 500 "man-days" of farm labor in any calendar quarter of the preceding calendar year).
- Casual baby-sitters and persons employed as companions to the elderly or infirm.

The following are examples of employees exempt from the act's overtime pay requirements only:

- Certain commissioned employees of retail or service establishments.
- Auto, truck, trailer, farm implement, boat or aircraft salesworkers, or parts clerks and mechanics servicing autos, trucks, or farm implements who are employed by nonmanufacturing establishments primarily engaged in selling these items to ultimate purchasers.
- Railroad and air carrier employees, taxi drivers, certain employees of motor carriers, seamen on American vessels, and local delivery employees paid on approved trip rate plans.
- Announcers, news editors, and chief engineers of certain nonmetropolitan broadcasting stations.
- Domestic service workers who reside in their employer's residence.
- Employees of motion picture theaters.
- Farm workers.

manager, technical, or professional who is paid on an hourly basis is nonexempt. If federal and state law conflict, the one that is most generous to the employee applies. Violation of the overtime provision can result in a requirement to pay for uncompensated overtime, civil penalties, and liquidated damages.

Child Labor   Child labor is any economic activity performed by an individual under the age of 15. It is employment that prevents children under 15 from attending school or requires them to work under conditions that are hazardous to their physical and mental health. This provision forbids employing minors under 14 in nonagricultural jobs, restricts hours of work, and limits occupations for 14- and 15-year-olds. It also forbids 16- and 17-year-olds to be employed in hazardous occupations.

Burger King faced a highly publicized lawsuit based on repeated violation of the child labor provision.[19] The company agreed to pay more than $500,000 in fines for allegedly allowing 14- and 15-year-olds to work past federally imposed deadlines at over 800 company-owned stores. Violations have also been quite frequent in the textile and garment industries. The Child Labor Coalition, a lobbying group made up of 35 organizations devoted to reforming child labor laws, has drafted a model law calling for stricter enforcement and stronger penalties for violations. Proposed penalties include publishing the names, addresses, and number of violations for repeat offenders.

Equal Pay Act of 1963 (EPA)   The Equal Pay Act of 1963 (EPA) is an amendment to the FLSA. Its purpose is to guarantee that women holding essentially the same jobs as men will be treated with respect and fairly compensated regarding all rewards of work: wages, salaries, commissions, overtime pay, bonuses, premium pay, and benefits.[20] Comparisons cannot be made between individuals holding the same job at different companies. Employers may pay workers of one gender more than another on the basis of merit, seniority, quality or quantity of production, or any factor other than sex. The gender gap in pay in 2001 averaged 26 percent; the average woman made 74 percent of the earnings of the average white male.[21]

Four elements are used to establish the equality of positions: skill, effort, responsibility, and working conditions. The difference in wages includes not just the money earned as base pay but also any type of compensation such as vacations, holiday pay, leave of absence, overtime pay, lodging, food, and reimbursement for clothing or other expenses. When filing a claim under EPA, all the plaintiff has to do is prove that one man or one woman is making more for doing the same job. In one recent court case, the judge found that two positions with the same job title (office manager) were not equal because the man had less supervision than the woman; therefore, it was legal for the man to make 20 percent more. In an effort to close the remaining earnings gap, there has been a growing movement in the last few years to have the widely accepted concept of **equal pay** for equal jobs expanded to include equal pay for comparable jobs.

The doctrine of **comparable worth** (sometimes called *pay equity*) is not the concept that women and men should be paid equally for performing equal jobs. Rather, comparable worth attempts to prove that employers systematically discriminate by paying women less than their work is *intrinsically worth,* versus what they pay men who work in comparable (equally valuable) positions—and to remedy this situation.

The term *comparable worth* means different things to different people. First, comparable worth relates to jobs that are dissimilar in their content (e.g., nurse and plumber) but of equal value to the organization and society. Second, women appear to be concentrated in lower-paying, predominantly female jobs. Yet when men take "women's work," they tend to be at the top of the pay scale there too. Advocates of comparable worth therefore contend that individuals who perform jobs that require similar skills, effort, and responsibility under similar work conditions should be compensated equally regardless of gender.[22]

The notion of *value* is extremely important in examining differentials between men and women. Most people would agree that water is more valuable than diamonds, but diamonds are much more expensive than water. This differential arises because the supply of water is abundant relative to demand. When secretaries, librarians, and cashiers are in short supply, what employers have to pay them will rise.

To close the gap between women's and men's pay regardless of the issue (equal pay or comparable worth), women's real wages have to rise faster than men's. Men's do not have to fall. You can see that the gap has been closing. However, it is important to note that this isn't just because women's wages rose but also because the real earnings of men fell during the same period. If men's annual earnings had remained at 1979 levels, the earnings ratio would have risen to only 63 percent rather than 71.4 percent. This means that nearly three-quarters of the reduction in the gender wage gap has been due to falling earnings for men, not increasing earnings for women.[23]

Other Pay Legislation

The Walsh-Healy Act of 1936 requires organizations doing business with the federal government to pay wages at least equal to the industry minimum. It parallels the Fair Labor Standards Act on child labor and requires time-and-a-half pay for any work performed after eight hours a day. It exempts some industries, however—again, like FLSA. The Davis-Bacon Act of 1931 requires the payment of minimum prevailing wages of the locality to workers engaged in federally sponsored public works. The McNamara-O'Hara Service Contract Act requires employers who have contracts with the federal government of $2,500 per year or more, or who provide services to federal agencies as contractors or subcontractors, to pay prevailing wages and fringe benefits to their employees.

The Civil Rights Act of 1964 and the Age Discrimination Act of 1967 are designed to ensure that all people of similar ability, seniority, and background receive the same pay for the same work. The Equal Employment Opportunity Commission enforces the Civil Rights Act, while the Wage and Hour Division enforces the Equal Pay Act and the Age Discrimination Act.

The Federal Wage Garnishment Act (1970) is designed to limit the amount deducted from a person's pay to reduce debts. It also prohibits an employer from firing an employee if the employee goes into debt only once and has pay garnished. The employer may deduct as much from the paycheck as required by court orders for alimony or child support, debts due for taxes, or bankruptcy court rulings.

Other Government Influences

The government directly affects the amount of pay the employee takes home by requiring employers to deduct funds from employees' wages. Deductions include federal income taxes, Social Security taxes, and possibly state and local income taxes. The federal government also has other laws governing pay deductions.

In addition to the laws and regulations just discussed, the government influences compensation in many other ways. If the government is the employer, it can legislate pay levels by setting statutory rates. For example, at the county level the pay scale for teachers can be set by law or by edict of the school board, and pay depends on revenues from the current tax base. If taxes decline relative to organizations' revenue streams, the organization cannot pay higher wages, no matter how much it may wish to.

The government affects compensation through its employment-level policy too. One of the goals of the federal government is full employment of all citizens seeking work. The government may even create jobs for certain categories of workers, thus reducing the supply of workers available and affecting pay rates.

Union Influences and Compensation

Another important external influence on an employer's compensation program is labor unionization. Unionized workers work longer hours and make more than nonunionized workers.

Unions have an effect whether or not the organization's employees are unionized. Unions have tended to be pacesetters in demands for pay, benefits, and improved working conditions. There is reasonable evidence that unions tend to increase pay levels, although this is more likely where an industry has been organized by strong unions. If the organization stays in an area where unions are strong, its compensation policies will be affected.

There is a supportive interaction between unions and government influences on compensation. Several federal laws apply. For example, the Davis-Bacon Act and similar laws require employers with government contracts to pay prevailing wages. Prevailing wages for any locale are determined by the Department of Labor. In most instances, the prevailing wage is the union wage in that region. So unions help determine wages even for nonunionized employees.

When a union is trying to organize employees at a particular place of employment, the organizing campaign places constraints on the compensation manager. The Wagner Act makes it illegal to change wage rates during the organizing campaign, so wages are effectively frozen for the duration. Refusal to bargain over wages is prohibited by this act. This means that the compensation manager is bound by the results of the collective bargaining process in setting wages.

The union is more likely to increase the compensation of its members when the organization is financially and competitively strong, the union is financially strong enough to support a strike, the union has the support of other unions, and general economic and labor market conditions are such that unemployment is low and the economy is strong. Unions also bargain over working conditions and other policies that affect compensation. Unions tend to prefer fixed pay for each job category or rate ranges that are administered primarily to reflect seniority rather than merit increases. This is true in the private sector and other sectors. Unions press for time pay rather than merit pay when the amount of performance expected is tied to technology (such as the assembly line). Although union membership in the United States has continued to decline, the influence of unions on wages cannot be counted out.

Internal Influences on Compensation

In addition to the external influences on compensation already discussed, several internal factors affect pay: the size, age, and labor budget of the organization and who is involved in making pay decisions for the organization. Little is known about the relationship between organization size and pay. Generally speaking, it appears that larger organizations tend to have higher pay. Nor is much known about the relationship between age and pay, although some researchers contend that newer enterprises tend to pay more than old ones. Thus only the labor budget and who makes the decisions will be discussed below.

The Labor Budget

The labor budget normally identifies the amount of money available for annual employee compensation. Every unit of the organization is influenced by the size of the labor budget. A firm's budget does not normally state the exact amount of money allocated to each employee; rather, it states how much is available for the unit or division. Discretion in allocating pay is then left to the department heads and supervisors. Theoretically, the close contact between supervisors and employees should allow for accurate performance appraisals and proper allocation of labor dollars.

Who Makes Compensation Decisions

More is known about who makes compensation decisions than about some other factors, but this is still not a simple matter. Decisions on how much to pay, what system to use, what benefits to offer, and so forth, are influenced from the top to the bottom of the organization. In large, publicly held organizations, the stockholders and the board have a great deal of say about pay, especially at the top of the organization. Top management makes decisions that determine the total amount of the firm's budget to be earmarked for pay, the form of pay to be used (e.g., time-based versus incentive pay), and other pay policies. As the firm grows in size, compensation specialists, general managers, and job incumbents may also have input.

Large organizations are now involving more individuals in determining pay. For example, until recently Whirlpool Corporation allowed only corporate executives to make major reward decisions.[24] Pressures from international competition have changed its approach. Today, top managers and compensation specialists jointly establish overall financial and operating goals for the corporation. Then each level of management establishes its own plan to support corporate compensation objectives. The new system rests on performance appraisals directly linked to overall strategic goals for the firm. All employees, even the CEO, participate in the performance appraisal process, from which all changes in pay flow. Even smaller firms are giving employees a say in determining pay. For instance, Com-Com Industries, a small metal-stamping shop in Cleveland, Ohio, allows workers to set compensation rates, through a volunteer committee of 10 to 15 members.[25] They determine wage rates for jobs ranging from floor sweeper to president, using market pricing. The committee even completes its own pay survey of the local competition.

Compensation and Motivation

Does a well-designed pay system motivate employees to perform better, or does it create greater satisfaction? The answer to this question has varied from the "yes" of Aristotle in ancient Greece and of scientific management in the early 1900s to the "no" of human relations theorists in the 1930s. Although most compensation experts believe that pay affects the motivation of employees, the controversy still rages. It is not possible to settle this age-old dispute here, but the various positions will be presented briefly.

Pay and Motivation

Motivation is the set of attitudes and values that predisposes a person to act in a specific, goal-directed manner.[26] It is an invisible inner state that energizes human goal-directed behavior, which can be divided into two components: (1) the direction of behavior (working to reach a goal) and (2) the strength of the behavior (how hard or strongly the individual will work).[27] In motivating employees, historically the focus has been on money. From Aristotle through Frederick W. Taylor, the "father of scientific management theory," philosophers, scientists, industrial engineers, and managers believed that money was the only thing that motivates. Beginning with the 1930s, sociologists, psychologists, and other human relations theorists theorized that various cognitive and acognitive processes also affect the relationships between pay and motivation.

Needs theorists including Maslow (who developed a well-known hierarchy of needs) and McGregor, Alderfer, and McClelland (who modified that hierarchy) say that all human behavior stems from needs or drives, which are innately biological in origin.[28] Maslow's hierarchy of needs takes the form of a pyramid. In ascending order, the needs are physiological, safety, social, esteem, and self-actualization. Lower-order needs (physiological and safety) motivate employees toward earning direct financial compensation to buy shelter and do things like provide for retirement.

Herzberg's two-factor theory of motivation tries to find out what people want from work.[29] According to this theory, two sets of factors influence work behavior: dissatisfiers (hygiene factors) and satisfiers (motivators). Hygiene factors relate to the context of jobs and include pay, working conditions, supervision, and so on. They do not motivate. Motivators include factors like achievement, recognition, responsibility, advancement, growth, and the work itself. Motivators become operational only when dissatisfiers are removed. Herzberg concludes that changing pay will not motivate. But if pay is inadequate, or of the wrong type, or mismatched to employees' needs in any way, dissatisfaction results.

Social comparison theories suggest that **motivation** is greatly influenced by how fairly an employee feels or thinks he or she is being paid. These theories are very important tools for developing compensation systems. According to Homan's distributive justice or **exchange theory** and Adams's **equity theory,** a major determinant of an employee's productivity and satisfaction arises from the degree of fairness (equity) or unfairness (inequity) that an employee perceives in the workplace, in comparison with others.[30] The degree of equity is defined as a ratio of an employee's inputs (effort, attendance, etc.) to outcomes (pay, benefits, services, etc.), compared with a similar ratio for a *significant other*. The significant other is usually a fellow employee holding the same job in the same organization. The key to understanding social comparison theories is the idea of *perceived fairness:* Does the employee *think* he or she is being paid fairly? These theories help explain how two people with the same experience, job title, job responsibilities, and pay may have different perceptions of fairness. One employee may be entirely satisfied with the pay, and the other may feel cheated and act accordingly. To reduce these feelings, the dissatisfied employee would change the quality or quantity of his or her input. The result could be increased absenteeism, lower quality, lower quantity, or even quitting the job.

Expectancy (valence-instrumentality-expectancy) theory also helps managers to understand the relationship between motivation and pay. According to Tolman and Vroom's expectancy theory, motivation depends on the expectation that effort will produce performances.[31] Humans form a mental picture about the likelihood that a given level of effort will result in a desired outcome. Various outcomes have different levels of desirability or valence. A direct application of expectancy theory to compensation is the idea of earning days of vacation or sick leave. Workers can look in the employees' handbook and see that if they remain with the company 5 years, 10 vacation days per year will be earned; staying 10 years results in an additional 5 vacation days a year, and so forth. At the same time, they will become senior employees, earning other desired outcomes, like annual raises—a concept called the *instrumentality of goal-directed behavior.*

Finally, according to **reinforcement, behavior modification,** and other **social-behaviorist theories** developed by Pavlov, Watson, Thorndike, and Skinner, motivation results from the direct interaction of the individual with the external environment, not from innate or internal processes like needs or perceptions.[32] Behavior is contingent upon presentation of rewards, delivery of punishment, or withholding of rewards. In other words, human behavior is motivated by the extent to which it has been rewarded or punished, on the basis of an automatic stimulus-response. If pay, benefits, and services are rewards received after performing certain tasks—like getting to work on time, remaining with the company, meeting production goals, and the like—then the desired behavior will be repeated. When managers reward, punish, or withhold rewards like raises, the desired behavior should result.

It would be nice to tell you that linking pay and motivation is a simple task. However, since different things motivate different individuals and theorists don't agree on what will motivate, this is actually a complicated and difficult, if not impossible, task. What is of most interest to most managers, compensation specialists, and employees is the relationship between compensation and motivation in two special contexts: employees' satisfaction and productivity.

Pay and Employees' Satisfaction

Satisfaction is an evaluative term that describes an attitude of liking or disliking. Pay satisfaction, therefore, refers to an employee's liking for or dislike of the employer's compensation package, including pay and benefits.[33] Even though at least 3,500 scholarly articles have been written about pay satisfaction, research on it is not very definitive.[34] It has failed to find convincing evidence that workers' satisfaction leads to increases in productivity. And although it seems logical to assume that employees derive satisfaction from being paid well or getting desired benefits or services, this is a very subjective conclusion. In fact, the sheer complexity of reward systems made up of numerous components like base pay, bonuses, benefits, and services makes it even more difficult to research employees' satisfaction. The clearest indication of satisfaction may be patterns of absenteeism and turnover.

Edward Lawler developed a model based on equity theory to help explain dissatisfaction and satisfaction with pay. The distinction between the amount employees receive and the amount they think others are receiving is the immediate cause. If they believe the two amounts are equal, pay satisfaction results. The feedback loop between the employee's perception and fairness and subsequent work behavior leads to fluctuations in output.[35] Expectancy theory can also be used to get employees to motivate themselves, on the basis of their views of what they want and how they can get it. Research conducted by Simons found which components of the pay system will lead to satisfaction differed by type of workers: Industrial workers preferred interesting jobs more than high pay; hotel workers preferred high wages above everything else.[36]

Other research studies found that important predictors of pay satisfaction include pay desired versus pay earned, feelings of being entitled or deserving, and relative deprivation theory.[37] Relative deprivation theory suggests that pay dissatisfaction is a function of six important judgments: (1) a discrepancy between what employees want and what they receive, (2) a discrepancy between a comparison outcome and what they get, (3) past expectations of receiving more rewards, (4) low expectations for the future, (5) a feeling of deserving or being entitled to more than they are getting, and (6) a feeling that they are not personally responsible for poor results.

Herzberg's hygiene theory (discussed earlier) adds another twist.[38] He proposed that the opposite of job satisfaction is not dissatisfaction but just the absence of satisfaction. Nor is the absence of dissatisfaction necessarily positive satisfaction. When applying his theory to pay, he reached the conclusion that pay simply prevents workers from being demotivated.

Pay and Employees' Productivity

Increasing payroll costs and competition in the global marketplace have caused managers throughout the United States to search for ways to increase productivity by linking compensation to employees' performance.[39] High performance requires much more than motivation. Ability, adequate equipment, good physical working conditions, effective leadership and management, health, safety, and other conditions all help raise performance levels. But employees' motivation to work harder and better is obviously an important factor. A number of studies indicate that if pay is tied to performance, the employee produces a higher quality and quantity of work.[40] The following HR Journal discusses pay for performance at MetLife.

Early evidence linking pay and performance is found in the Code of Hammurabi, written in the 18th century B.C., which documents the use of a minimum wage, a fixed wage, and incentive rewards.[41] Traveling merchants were paid on the basis of a strong performance incentive—unless investors received double profits, these merchants weren't paid. However, during the Middle Ages it was "common knowledge" that workers would be productive only as long as they needed to be, perhaps working three days a week and

HR Journal   *MetLife's Pay for Performance System*

A survey by Hewitt Associates LLC found that nearly 8 of 10 companies have some kind of variable pay system, up from fewer than 5 in 10 in 1990. MetLife reports that change to a pay-for-performance approach has been difficult. MetLife placed all employees on a rating scale that is subject to change based on the performance of specific goals and core behaviors. Since the shift, the company's return on equity has jumped from 7 percent in 1999 to over 10.5 percent in 2001.

At MetLife and other firms, pay for performance means a variable pay approach that is anchored to a measurement of performance. It yields a variable compensation that must be re-earned each year and doesn't permanently increase base salary.

MetLife measures employees and managers by comparing each person to others who are on the same level. Employees are measured on a 1 to 5 scale. The company then calculates which employees are at the top, in the middle, and at the bottom. Employees who rate a 3 receive about 65 percent more in bonuses than those who earn a 2. A person rated 3 might receive a bonus of $6,900, whereas one who received a rating of 2 would get $4,200.

MetLife is concentrating a great deal on the most senior 250 of the firm's over 46,000 employees. They are evaluated on their individual performance results and on answers to such questions as, Are they team players? Are they dedicated to learning? Do they develop others? Are they showing partnership? At MetLife, the focus is on the individual, but you must be a team player. A person must rate high on teamwork and partnership to do well in the pay-for-performance system.

Source: Janet Wiscombe (August 26, 2002), "Can Pay for Performance Work?" *Workforce Online,* http://www.workforce.com/archive/feature/23/06/78/index.php.

spending the other four celebrating. The dawn of industrialism found capitalists seeking a way to use rewards to encourage productivity: the incentive wage.

Incentive wages were supported by early economists on the basis of the "hungry man" theory. Since a hungry worker would want to earn money to buy food, wages should be kept at the subsistence level so that workers would be motivated to be highly productive. Adam Smith (1776) modified this to develop the "economic man" theory.[42] Instead of physiological needs, money became the motivator for work. The more money each individual made, the harder he or she would work; output would increase as wages rose. Thus the basis of the modern wage incentive plan was set.

Frederick W. Taylor built on Smith's theory, urging managers to learn to design jobs properly and then link pay directly to measurable productivity.[43] Under his plan, workers who met production standards were paid 125 percent of base pay while those who failed to meet standards were paid a very low wage. Variations of Taylor's incentive pay are still in widespread use. Incentive pay will be discussed in depth in Chapter 11.

Not everyone agrees with this—some researchers argue that if you tie pay to performance, you will destroy the intrinsic rewards a person gets from doing the job well.[44] Intrinsic rewards are powerful motivators too, but research on them has been limited to only a few studies. The importance of money to employees varies among individuals.

If the organization claims to have an incentive pay system, and in fact pays for seniority, the motivation effects of pay will be lost. The key to making compensation systems more effective is to be sure that they are directly connected to expected behaviors.[45]

Research on the relationship between pay and employees' satisfaction and between pay and productivity continues, but with contradictory results.[46] It still can be concluded, however, that pay is an important outcome to employees.[47] Studying pay, performance, productivity, and job satisfaction is especially important because of their link to employees' subsequent behaviors, including absenteeism and turnover, union organizing, and assumption of responsibility.

Compensation Decisions

Pay for a particular position is set relative to three groups:

- Employees working on similar jobs in other organizations (group A).
- Employees working on different jobs within the organization (group B).
- Employees working on the same job within the organization (group C).

The decision to examine pay relative to group A, that is, the pay level, is called the *pay-level decision*. The objective of the pay-level decision is to keep the organization competitive in the labor market. The major tool used in this decision is the pay survey. The pay decision relative to group B is called the *pay-structure decision*. The pay structure involves setting a value on each job within the organization relative to all other jobs. This uses an approach called job evaluation. The decision involving pay relative to group C is called *individual pay determination.*

The Pay-Level Decision

The **pay level** is decided by managers who compare the pay of people working inside the organization with those outside it. This decision is affected by multiple interacting factors that affect pay levels upward, downward, or laterally. When factors such as managerial attitudes, the labor market, and competition change, the pressures on pay levels shift.[48]

The pay-level strategy is a major strategic choice managers must make.[49] Essentially, three pay-level strategies—high, low, or comparable—can be chosen.

Test question

High-Pay Strategy

In this strategy, managers choose to pay at higher-than-average levels. The assumption behind this strategy is that you get what you pay for. These managers believe that paying higher wages and salaries will attract and hold the best employees, and that this is the most effective long-range policy. Organizations using this strategy are sometimes called *pacesetters*. The strategy may be influenced by pay criteria such as paying a living wage or paying on the basis of productivity.

Low-Pay Strategy

At the opposite extreme is the low-pay strategy. In this case, the manager pays at the minimum level needed to hire enough employees. This strategy may be used because this is all the organization can pay—the ability to pay is restricted by other internal or external factors such as a limited labor budget or a forecasted decline in sales and profits.

Comparable-Pay Strategy

The most frequently used strategy is to set the pay level at the going wage level. The wage criteria are comparable wages, perhaps modified by cost-of-living or purchasing power adjustments. For example, the Federal Pay Comparability Act of 1970 limits federal government compensation to the comparable wage paid in the private sector at the time. This going wage is determined from pay surveys. Thus, the policy of a manager following this strategy is to pay the current market rate in the community or industry, ±5 percent or so.

Choice of a Strategy

These three strategies are usually set for the total organization, although the strategy might have to be modified for a few hard-to-fill jobs from time to time. The choice of strategy partially reflects the motivation and attitudes held by the manager. If the manager has a high need for recognition, the high-pay strategy might be chosen; otherwise, the low-paying strategy might be chosen. Another factor is the ethical and moral attitude of the manager. If the manager is ethically oriented, then a low-pay strategy is not likely to be chosen willingly.

Two other factors affect the choice of pay-level strategy: the degree to which an organization can attract and retain personnel and the organization's ability to pay. Factors affecting the attraction and retention of human resources include the availability of qualified labor, job security, and level of benefits. A few factors affecting the ability to pay include the cost of labor, the firm's profit margins, and the stage of the firm (new or established). For these factors to be salient, they must vary across the relevant labor market. If, for example, all firms have high labor costs, they will all tend to pay below-average wages.

But remember: The many external factors affecting the process, such as government and unions, are compounded by employees' job preferences, which include pay and non-pay aspects. And many employees do not have a sophisticated or comprehensive knowledge of all these factors. So you can see that the organization has a great deal of room for maneuvering in the pay-level decision. To help make the decision, managers use a tool called a *pay* or *wage survey, market pricing,* or *benchmarking.*

Pay Surveys

Pay surveys are techniques and instruments used to collect data about compensation paid to employees by all employers in a geographic area, an industry, or an occupational group.[50] They must be carefully designed, because their results are quoted and used in making compensation decisions. Surveys help managers gauge the exact market rates for various positions.[51] Obtaining valid, reliable information about pay is critical to creating a compensation system that supports corporate goals.[52]

Who Conducts Pay Surveys?

Pay surveys are conducted by professional and consulting enterprises, trade associations, the government, unions, and competitors. Some examples of where to find surveys are listed in Exhibit 10-3. Additionally, an annual report published by Personnel Systems

EXHIBIT 10-3
Sources of Pay Surveys

Government Sources

Bureau of Labor Statistics
Federal Reserve Banks
Monthly Labor Review

Professional and Trade Organizations

Administrative Management Society
American Association of Management
Society for Human Resource Management

Surveys Conducted by Other Organizations

Bureau of National Affairs
Consulting Firms
Hay Associates
Management Compensation Services
Pay Data Service

Surveys by Journals

BusinessWeek
Compensation and Benefits Review
Dun's
Forbes
Fortune
Hospital Administration
Nation's Business

Associates, "Survey Sources for U.S. and International Pay and Benefits Surveys," lists over 750 surveys conducted by commercial, private, and government organizations. Many large organizations design and administer their own pay surveys.

There are a number of ways an organization can acquire competitive salary information: (1) purchasing an existing survey, (2) joining an existing survey, (3) conducting a survey, (4) doing a telephone survey of competitors, and (5) collecting information from proxy statements.[53]

Usefulness of Surveys

A number of critical issues determine the usefulness of surveys: First is the jobs covered. Other employers cannot be expected to complete endless data requests for all the organization's jobs. However, a minimum of 30 percent of the jobs should be matched with market data to ensure an equitable evaluation of the firm's compensation system.[54] If the point method of job evaluation is used (as described later in this chapter), the key jobs might be selected for surveying, since they cover all pay ranges. The jobs that most employees hold should also be on the list (data-entry clerks and underwriters for an insurance company, for example).

The second issue concerns *who will be surveyed*. Most organizations tend to compare themselves with similar competitors in their industry. American Airlines might compare its pay rates with those of United Airlines, for example. However, it has been shown that employees might not compare their pay with that offered by competitors at all. Their basis of comparison might be friends' employers or employers that they worked with previously. If the survey is to be useful, employees should be involved in choosing the organizations to be surveyed. The employers surveyed should include the most dominant ones in the area and a small sample of those suggested by employees.

Third is *the method used*. One method is the personal interview, which develops the most accurate responses but is also expensive. Mailed questionnaires are probably the most frequently used method and are one of the cheapest. The only criterion for participation in a mass mailing pay survey is paying a fee to receive a copy of the summary report. This fact makes it difficult to determine if the survey is at all representative of anything.[55] The jobs being surveyed by mail must be clearly defined, or the data may not be reliable. Telephone inquiries, as a follow-up to the mail questionnaires, are used to gather data. This procedure is quick, but it is also difficult to get detailed data over the phone.

The fourth issue determining the usefulness of pay surveys is *the information gathered*. The best surveys do the following:

1. Use clear, concise job descriptions.
2. Give clearly written instructions for participants to follow.
3. Include a good sample of organizations, with names identified.
4. Have a consistent sample of participants for each iteration.
5. Provide data on base pay, bonuses, and total compensation.
6. Provide 25th, 50th, and 75th percentile data for both base and total compensation.
7. Include information on benefits.
8. List numbers of incumbents for each job surveyed.
9. Are completed by human resource professionals.
10. Are reviewed by experienced compensation professionals.[56]

It is important to remember that no matter what the source, pay surveys are just one piece of the puzzle necessary to make the pay-level decision. The firm's size, financial performance, and strategic initiatives are also important considerations.

Jerry Wallace responded to Cheryl's request with a report showing that some employees were paid on the basis of seniority: the annual raise system was based on years of service. However, entry-level pay, especially for plant jobs, was based more on family need than on job experience and skill. As a result, people doing the same job at about the same performance level received different paychecks. Without a pay secrecy policy, it was easy for employees to find out how much other people were paid. Some employees who had just started on the line made more than those who had been at Decker for years.

Even though Decker's average wage was 15 percent above average for the industry, job satisfaction was low, and turnover continued to increase. Jerry pointed out that the labor market was favorable because other firms were downsizing, so replacements could be found easily. The problem, he said, was that Decker couldn't afford to pay high wages, but previous pay policy had created the expectation of an above-average wage.

The Pay Structure Decision

The next step is to construct an internal pay hierarchy or **pay structure.** The traditional way to develop the pay structure was to make a systematic comparison between the worth of one job and the worth of another, using job evaluation. The job evaluation process described below is based on the job-worth model for determining pay. More techniques of determining pay (skill-base, knowledge-base, competency, feedback, and the total compensation approach) will be introduced in Chapter 11.

Job Evaluation

Job evaluation is a formal process by which the relative worth of various jobs in the organization is determined for pay purposes. A systematic comparison of the worth of one job with that of another job eventually results in the creation of a wage or salary hierarchy unique to the organization. Essentially, job evaluation relates the amount of pay for each job to the extent to which that job contributes to organizational effectiveness. It is not always easy to determine the worth of all jobs in an organization. Job evaluation involves making judgments that are subject to errors on the part of job evaluators. It may be obvious that the effective physician will contribute more to the goals of patient care in the hospital than the nurse's aide. The point at issue is *how much* the differential is worth, and this means that a judgment must be made.

Since computing exactly how much a particular job contributes to organizational effectiveness is difficult, proxies for effectiveness are used. These proxies include skills required to do the job, amount and significance of responsibility involved, effort required, and working conditions. Compensation must vary with the differing demands of various jobs if employees are to be satisfied and if the organization is to be able to attract the personnel it wants.

Once an organization decides to use job evaluation, a series of decisions must be made to ensure its effectiveness. Part of the decision to use job evaluation, or the first step in using it effectively, is for management to involve employees (and, where appropriate, the union) in the system and its implementation. Employees should be allowed to express their perceptions of the relative merits of their jobs. This participation affords an opportunity to explain the fairly complicated process of job evaluation to those most directly affected by it, and it will usually lead to better communications and improved understanding among employees.

After the program is off to a cooperative start, usually a committee of about five members evaluates the jobs. Ideally, the committee includes employees, managers, and HR specialists. All members should be familiar with the jobs to be evaluated.

EXHIBIT 10-4
Comparison of Job
Evaluation Systems

Comparison Basis	Nonquantitative Comparison (Job as Whole)	Quantitative Comparison (Parts of Factors of Jobs)
Job versus job	Job ranking	Factor comparison
Job versus scale	Job grading or classification	Point system

Job evaluation is usually performed by analyzing job descriptions and, occasionally, job specifications. It is usually suggested that job descriptions be split into several series, such as managerial, professional-technical, clerical, and operative. It makes sense in writing job descriptions to use words that are keyed to the job evaluation factors.

Another essential step in effective job evaluation is to select and weigh the criteria (compensable factors) used to evaluate the job. Although research is sparse in this area, it appears that the results are the same whether all factors or just a few factors are considered, especially if the job evaluation is carefully designed and scaled. Typical of the factors most frequently used for job evaluation are education, experience, amount of responsibility, job knowledge, work hazards, and working conditions. It is important that the factors used be accepted as valid for the job by those being evaluated.

Four frequently used methods of job evaluation are

1. Job ranking
2. Classification
3. Point system
4. Factor comparison

Job evaluation systems can be classified as shown in Exhibit 10-4.

Ranking of Jobs

The system used primarily in smaller, simpler organizations is the **ranking of jobs.** Instead of analyzing the full complexity of jobs by evaluating parts of jobs, the job-ranking method has the evaluator rank-order whole jobs, from the simplest to the most challenging.

There is no assurance that the ranking thus provided is composed of equal-interval ranks. The differential between the highest job and the next highest job may not be exactly the same as that between the lowest and next lowest. If the system is used in an organization with many jobs, it is clumsy to use, and the reliability of the ratings is not good. Because of these problems, ranking is probably the least frequently used method of job evaluation.

Classification or Grading System

The **classification or grading system** groups a set of jobs together into a grade or classification. Then these sets of jobs are ranked by levels of difficulty or sophistication. It is a job-to-standard comparison, which solves many of the problems of simple job ranking.

First, the job evaluator decides how many categories or classifications the job structure has to be broken into. Typically, there are around 8, with the number varying from 5 to 15.[57] The most publicized example of a classification system is the United States Office of Personnel Management General Schedule. It has 18 grades with 10 pay steps within the pay grades. This classification system is used in making compensation decisions for over 3 million federal employees.

The second step is to write definitions of each class. The definitions provide the production standards upon which the compensation system will be built. Exhibit 10-5 shows

EXHIBIT 10-5
Computer Analyst Classification System

Class I	Computer work, no managerial responsibility
Class II	Computer work, no managerial responsibility, team involvement
Class III	Computer work of medium complexity, no managerial responsibility, team responsibilities
Class IV	Computer work of medium complexity, managerial responsibility, team authority
Class V	Complex computer work, managerial responsibility, team leadership

a five-level classification system with definitions for computer analysts. Once the classes are defined, jobs to be evaluated are compared with the definitions and put into the appropriate classification.

This method of job evaluation provides specific standards for compensation and accommodates any changes in the value of individual jobs. A job classification system can be constructed quickly, simply, and cheaply. It is easy to understand and easy to communicate to employees. Classification does have drawbacks, however. It is more detailed than job ranking, and it assumes a rigid relationship between job factors and value. As a result, especially in large firms, jobs are forced to fit into categories that are not entirely appropriate. Feelings of inequity can result. Deciding how many classifications there should be is also a problem. If there are too few classes, it will be difficult to differentiate job value and resulting wage levels. Too many classes make writing definitions almost impossible.

Point System The greatest number of job evaluation plans use the **point system**.[58] It is the most frequently used because it is more sophisticated than ranking and classification systems and it is relatively easy to use.

Essentially, the point system requires evaluators to quantify the value of the elements of a job. On the basis of the job description or interviews with job occupants, points are assigned to the degree of various compensable factors required to do the job. For example, points are assigned on the basis of skill required, physical and mental effort needed, degree of dangerous or unpleasant working conditions involved, and amount of responsibility involved in the job. When these are summed, the job has been evaluated.

As shown in Exhibit 10-6, factor 1, education, has five degrees, as do factors 2 and 3. On the other hand, factor 4 has three degrees, while factor 5 has four degrees. The maximum number of points is calculated by multiplying the points in the system by the assigned weights. For education, the maximum points would be 250 (50 percent weight multiplied by 500 maximum points).

An advantage of the point system is that it can be easily interpreted and explained to employees. On the other hand, it is time-consuming to develop a point system.

Factor Comparison The **factor comparison method** was originated by Eugene Benge. Like the point system, it permits the job evaluation process to be done factor by factor. It differs from the point method in that jobs are evaluated or compared against a "benchmark" of

EXHIBIT 10-6
Evaluation Points for Insurance Clerical Job (500-Point System)

Factor	Weight	Degrees				
		1st	2nd	3rd	4th	5th
1. Education	50%	50	100	150	200	250
2. Experience	25	12	12	24	36	48
3. Complexity of job	12	12	24	36	48	60
4. Relationships with others	8	8	24	40		
5. Working conditions	5	10	15	20	25	

key points. A factor comparison scale, instead of a point scale, is used to compare five universal job factors:

1. *Responsibilities* Money, human resource, records, and supervisor responsibilities of the job.
2. *Skill* Facility in muscular coordination and training in the interpretation of sensory requirements.
3. *Physical effort* Sitting, standing, walking, lifting, moving, and so on.
4. *Mental effort* Intelligence, problem solving, reasoning, and imagination.
5. *Working conditions* Environmental factors such as noise, ventilation, hours, heat, hazards, fumes, and cleanliness.

The factor comparison method has some advantages and disadvantages. One advantage is that it is a step-by-step formal method of evaluation. Furthermore, it shows how the differences in factor rankings translate into dollars and cents. Probably the most negative aspect of the factor comparison method is its complexity. Although the method is easy to explain to subordinates, it is difficult to show them how such a system is developed. There is also the issue of subjectivity. Despite the systematic nature of the factor comparison method, it still relies on the subjective judgments of a committee or a group of evaluators. Of course, subjectivity is also a problem with each of the other job evaluation methods. Furthermore, as more jobs change and new jobs emerge, job evaluation is being supplemented by performance-based pay as individual and team contributions to productivity become more prominent indicators of success and value added.

Pay Classes, Rate Changes, and Classifications

After completion of the job evaluation, the pay-structure process is completed by establishing pay curves, pay classes, rate ranges, and job classifications. At intervals of, say, 50 points, a new pay class is marked off.

The **pay curve** illustrated in Exhibit 10-7 is based on information obtained from wage and salary surveys and modified as necessary to reflect Zacha Electronics' (mid-size firm in the Northeast) policy to pay at, above, or below prevailing rates. This exhibit shows a single-rate pay system rather than a rate-range system in that all jobs within a given labor class will receive the same rate of pay. In this example, pay classes are determined by the point value that is in turn determined through a point system method of job evaluation.

EXHIBIT 10-7
Pay Classes and
Pay Curve

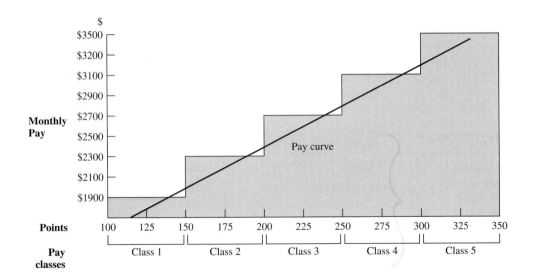

EXHIBIT 10-8
Pay Class Graph with
Range of Pay

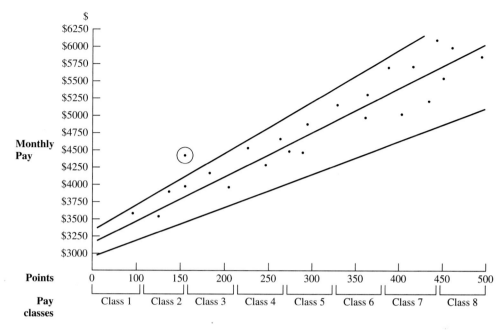

A **pay class** (also called a **pay grade**) is a grouping of a variety of jobs that are similar in terms of difficulty and responsibility. If an organization uses the factor comparison or point system of job evaluation, this is accomplished by use of pay-class graphs or point conversion tables. An example of a pay-class graph used by Zacha Electronics is given in Exhibit 10-7.

Exhibit 10-8, another pay-class graph, demonstrates how data from a wage and salary survey are combined with job evaluation information to determine the pay structure for an organization. A compensation trend line is derived by first establishing the general pay pattern, plotting the surveyed rates of key jobs against the point value of these jobs. The trend line can then be determined by a variety of methods, ranging from a simple eyeball estimate of the pay trend to a formalized statistical formulation of a regression line based on the "sum of the least squares" method. The appropriate pay rate for any job can then be ascertained by calculating the point value of the job and observing the pay level for that value as shown by the trend line. By taking a set percentage (for example, 15 percent) above and below the trend line, minimum and maximum limit lines can be established. These limit lines can be used to help set the minimum and maximum rates if a pay range is used instead of a single rate for each job. The limit lines can also be used in place of the trend line for organizations that wish to establish pay levels above market—the pay leaders— or those that want to pay slightly under the prevailing rate.

Although it is possible for a pay class to have a single pay rate (as in Exhibit 10-8), the more likely condition is a **pay range.** These ranges can have the same spread, or the spread can increase as the pay rate increases. An example of a pay structure with increasing rate ranges is given in Exhibit 10-8. The ranges are usually divided into a series of steps. Thus, within class 4 (215–265 points), there might be four steps:

Pay Range ($ Monthly)

Step 1	$5,000–5,400
Step 2	$5,401–5,600
Step 3	$5,601–5,850
Step 4	$5,851–6,100

These steps in effect are money raises within a pay range to help take care of the needs of individual pay determination (to be discussed in Chapter 11). Similar ranges would ordinarily be determined for all other classes to illustrate the pay structure for all jobs in the pay plan. Within-grade increases are typically based upon seniority, merit, or a combination of both (as described in Chapter 11).

The entire pay structure should be evaluated periodically and adjusted to reflect changes in labor market conditions, level of inflation, and other factors affecting pay. Although the typical structure is shown as linear, generally a more fair structure is curvilinear, with rates increasing exponentially as pay increases.

Delayering and Broadbanding

In an attempt to improve the efficiency and to reduce the complexities of job-based pay structures some organizations are using delayering or broadbanding approaches.[59]

Delayering

This process involves a reduction of the total number of job levels resulting in a flatter job structure. **Delayering** can increase flexibility by allowing employees to move among a wider range of job tasks without having to adjust pay with each move. Pratt and Whitney delayered by reducing 11 pay grades and 3,000 job descriptions for entry-level through middle-management positions to 6 pay grades and a few hundred job descriptions.[60]

Broadbanding

The concept of broadbanding is one in which the number of salary ranges is significantly reduced,[61] creating a smaller number of broad salary ranges and placing more emphasis on basing salary increases on individual performance. **Broadbanding** involves collapsing multiple salary grades and ranges into a few wide levels known as bands.[62] Using the broadbanding approach, entry-level employees with minimal qualifications start at the range minimum. Instead of annual increases, movement through these ranges depends on performance. All raises become merit raises, which are determined individually. With fewer, broader salary ranges, organizations deemphasize traditional job evaluation and organizational hierarchy. Broadbanding gives managers more flexibility in moving employees through the pay structures.[63] Broadbanding also supports corporate strategies of more flexible career development, building cross-functional skills, and more effective pay administration. Organizations can thus be more flexible in rewarding top performers while saving money on mediocre employees.

Although flexibility is a positive side of broadbanding, there may be drawbacks. When shifting the ability to make pay decisions to managers, the firm must be aware of the possible abuse of power. Favoritism can result in unfair use of broadbands. However, the use of broadbanding can increase flexibility if managers implement it fairly and treat every employee fairly.[64]

The Individual Pay Decision

This chapter has begun the discussion of compensation by stating the objectives of compensation and explaining the multiple meanings of pay at work, external and internal factors influencing compensation, pay levels, pay surveys, and pay structures and their determination. At this point, the compensation analyst and operating managers have information on comparable pay levels of competitors and the surrounding area and a system for evaluating jobs so that differentials between job descriptions can be established.

Another decision must be made before the organization can complete the job of building an effective, efficient pay system. How does the organization determine what two people doing the same job—for example, computer programmer—should make? Should all

Brad reviewed Jerry's report and then called him and Cheryl into the office.

Brad The handwriting is on the wall. We have to overhaul our compensation policy quickly. Where do we start?

Jerry Let's adopt what's called the broadbanding approach. We can set up a committee of supervisors and job incumbents and look at our existing system of pay ranges and classes. We can begin to identify basic inequities that were caused by our old philosophy and start to communicate the constraints on pay that have been created by the new global competition. I recommend taking our present system and reducing the number of ranges to five or six. All entry-level employees will get minimum wage and move through the ranges on the basis of a combination of seniority and individual performance. What do you think?

Cheryl I think it sounds intriguing; but basically what you are suggesting is a more variable, less fixed compensation policy. Is Decker ready for that?

Brad We have to be!

computer programmers be paid the same? If not, on what basis should the differential in compensation rest? The decision is called *individual pay determination.*[65] These questions will be answered in Chapter 11.

Summary

To summarize the major points covered in this chapter:

1. Compensation is the HRM function that deals with every type of reward that individuals receive in exchange for performing organizational tasks—wages, salaries, bonuses, commissions, benefits, and nonfinancial rewards like praise.

2. The objective of the compensation function is to create a system of rewards that is equitable to the employer and employee alike.

3. Compensation should be adequate, equitable, cost-effective, secure, incentive-providing, and acceptable to the employee.

4. Motivation theories like the "economic man" theory, Maslow's hierarchy of needs, equity theory, exchange theory, and behavior modification suggest a relationship between pay and motivation.

5. *Pay satisfaction* refers to an employee's liking for or dislike of the employer's compensation package, including pay and benefits. Much research has been conducted about the relationship, but it has not been clarified.

6. There is early evidence linking pay and productivity from the time of the Code of Hammurabi in the 18th century B.C. However, high performance requires more than understanding the relationship among pay, motivation, satisfaction, and productivity.

7. The pay-structure decision involves comparing jobs within the organization to determine their relative worth.

8. Determining the worth of a job is difficult because it involves measurement and subjective decisions. Using systematic job evaluation procedures is one way to determine net worth.

9. The four most widely used methods of job evaluation are job ranking, classification, the point system, and factor comparison.

10. The wave curve (or line) illustrates the average target wage for each pay class.

11. Most managers group similar jobs into pay classes or rate ranges.

12. Broadbanding is a new system for condensing rate ranges into broader classifications. It allows an employer to create a more flexible compensation program based on individual contributions.

13. The wave curve (or line) illustrates the average target wage for each pay class.

14.   Most managers group similar jobs into pay classes or rate ranges.

15.   Broadbanding is a new system for condensing rate ranges into broader classifications. It allows an employer to create a more flexible compensation program based on individual contributions.

Key Terms

broadbanding, *p. 316*
classification or grading system, *p. 312*
comparable worth, *p. 301*
compensation, *p. 294*
delayering, *p. 316*
direct financial compensation, *p. 295*
equal pay, *p. 301*
equity theory, *p. 305*
exchange theory, *p. 305*
exempt employee, *p. 300*

factor comparison method, *p. 313*
Fair Labor Standards Act (FLSA), *p. 298*
indirect financial compensation, *p. 295*
job evaluation, *p. 311*
minimum wage, *p. 299*
motivation, *p. 305*
nonexempt employee, *p. 300*
pay class or pay grade, *p. 315*

pay curve, *p. 314*
pay level, *p. 308*
pay range, *p. 315*
pay satisfaction, *p. 306*
pay structure, *p. 311*
pay surveys, *p. 309*
point system, *p. 313*
ranking of jobs, *p. 312*
reinforcement, behavior modification, social-behaviorist theories, *p. 305*

Questions for Review and Discussion

1.   What is the difference between direct and indirect financial compensation?

2.   Pay for each individual in the United States is set relative to three groups. Name them and explain why each is important.

3.   What is pay satisfaction? Why is it so difficult to measure and to relate it to a compensation system?

4.   Linking pay and productivity has been around since the days of the Babylonians. How much do we really know about the relationship?

5.   What is the difference between equal pay and comparable worth? Why are these concepts so important?

6.   In locating a new office that would employ about 300 employees, how would compensation play a role in making the decision for where the new office should be located?

7.   How would you go about deciding if a pay survey you want to buy had the necessary characteristics to be useful to your organization?

8.   Define the pay-structure decision. What is job evaluation, and how does it help managers build a pay structure?

9.   Do you believe that outsourcing is here to stay or is it a passing fad? Explain.

10.   Define the term *broadbanding*. How does it relate to traditional job evaluation outcomes like pay ranges and classes?

HRM Legal Advisor

Based on *Reich* v. *John Alden Life Insurance Co.,* 940 F. Supp. 418 (1996, Mass. U.S. District Court).

The Facts

John Alden Life Insurance Company designs and sells health, dental, disability, and life insurance through marketing representatives. The primary function of marketing representatives is to contact independent insurance agents through cold calls or follow-up calls and provide them with information and customer assistance for John Alden's products. The independent agents then make recommendations and facilitate the sale of insurance products to end-purchasers; John Alden's marketing representatives typically do not interact with end-purchasers. The marketing representatives hired by John Alden are generally college graduates with two to six years of experience in marketing; they earn an average annual income of $50,000. This income consists of a base salary, incentive compensation based upon number of products sold, and a bonus related to the performance of products sold. The marketing representatives typically work from 7:30 A.M. to 5:30 P.M. with a one-hour lunch break and are not compensated for working overtime. The Secretary of the U.S. Department of Labor brought an action against John Alden for violating the Fair Labor Standards Act (FLSA), which requires covered employers to pay employees one-and-a-half times their normal rate of pay for working hours exceeding 40 hours per week. John Alden claims that its marketing representatives fall under the FLSA's administrative exemption from overtime pay.

The FLSA provides the following "short test" for an administrative exemption from overtime pay: (1) employees earn more than $250 per week, (2) employees' primary duties consist of "the performance of office or nonmanual work directly related to management policies or general business operations of the employer or the employer's customers," and (3) these duties require employees to exercise discretion and independent judgment. Do you think that John Alden's marketing representatives should be considered as administrative employees under the FLSA? Should marketing representatives receive overtime compensation?

The Court's Decision

Both the Secretary of Labor and John Alden stipulated that marketing representatives make more than $250 per week and that their primary duties are "to contact and deal with licensed independent insurance agents, and related activities, in order to increase purchases of John Alden insurance products by end-purchasers who are in contact with the agents." The U.S. District Court for the District of Massachusetts held that these primary duties are indeed related to the management of John Alden's policies or general business operation, and that the marketing representatives exercise substantial discretion in interactions with independent agents. Thus, John Alden's marketing representatives may be considered administrative employees under the FLSA and are exempt from overtime compensation.

Human Resource Implications

The FLSA provides overtime pay exemptions for administrative, executive, and professional employees. However, employers should avoid simply labeling employees as salaried and exempt. The FLSA contains specific criteria to be considered when classifying employees into exempt categories. In determining whether exemptions apply, the Department of Labor and courts will carefully examine the specific nature of employees' jobs. Thus, to avoid FLSA violations, human resource professions should focus on primary tasks and duties outlined in job descriptions when classifying exempt employees.

Notes

1. George A. Milkovich and Jerry A. Newman (2005), *Compensation* (Burr Ridge, IL: McGraw-Hill).
2. Bureau of Labor Statistics (June 2005), *Employer Costs for Employee,* www.bls.gov.
3. Ibid.
4. Thomas Patton (1977), *Pay* (New York: Free Press).
5. Joseph J. Martocchio (2006), *Employee Benefits* (Burr Ridge, IL: McGraw-Hill/Irwin).
6. See *Generation X: American Generations Series* (2004), (New York: New Strategist Publications).
7. Bruce R. Ellig (2002), *The Complete Guide to Executive Compensation* (New York: McGraw-Hill).
8. Ibid.
9. Marina N. Whitman (1999), *New World, New Rules: The Changing Role of the American Corporation* (Boston: Harvard University Press).
10. Michelle V. Rafter (June 2005), "Adventures in Outsourcing," *Workforce Management,* pp. 51–55.

11. Ed Michaels, Helen Handfield-Jones, and Beth Axelrod (2001), *The War for Talent* (Boston: Harvard Business School Press).

12. Joseph J. Martocchio (2000), *Strategic Compensation: A Human Resource Management Approach* (Saddle River, NJ: Prentice-Hall).

13. Edward E. Potter and Judith A. Youngman (1995), *Keeping America Competitive: Employment Policy for the Twenty-First Century* (Lakewood, CO: Glenbridge).

14. Fay Hansen (1996), "FLSA Compliance and Enforcement," *Compensation and Benefits Review,* pp. 8–13.

15. Milkovich and Newman, op. cit.

16. Calvin Woodward (1996), "Many Living on Minimum Wage Just Get By," *Corpus Christi Caller-Times,* p. B-1.

17. J. P. Formby, J. A. Bishop, and H. Kim (2005), *Minimum Wages and Poverty: An Evaluation of Policy Alternatives* (Greenwich, CN: JAI Press).

18. Tracie L. Washington (1996), "Misclassifying Executives as 'Exempt' Can Lead to Costly Penalties," *Texas Banking,* Vol. 85, Iss. 2, p. 8.

19. Jill Kanin-Lovers (1990), "Revisiting the Fair Labor Standards Act," *Journal of Compensation and Benefits,* Vol. 6, Iss. 3, pp. 48–50.

20. John H. Davis (January–February 1997), "The Future of Salary Surveys When Jobs Disappear," *Compensation and Benefits Review,* p. 18.

21. Roy D. Adler (November 2001), "Women in the Executive Suite Correlate to High Profits," *Harvard Business Review,* p. 30.

22. Ibid.

23. Institute for Women's Policy Research (1996), "The Wage Gap: Women's and Men's Earnings," http://iwpr.org/wagegap.htm.

24. Hewitt Associates (1995), "Case Studies: Whirlpool, NIKE, Salmon and PSEG," *Compensation and Benefits Review,* pp. 71–74.

25. Ibid.

26. Donna Dee Prose (2003), *Smart Things to Know about Motivation* (San Francisco: Jossey-Bass).

27. Salvatore R. Maddi and Deborah M. Khoshaba (2005), *Resilience at Work: How to Succeed No Matter What Life Throws at You* (New York: American Management Association).

28. John M. Reeve (2000), *Understanding Motivation and Emotion* (San Francisco: Jossey-Bass).

29. Frederick Herzberg (1959), *The Motivation to Work* (New York: Wiley); and Herzberg (1968), "One More Time: How Do You Motivate Employees?" *Harvard Business Review.*

30. Thomas M. Malone (2004), *The Future of Work* (Boston, MA: Harvard University Press).

31. Sheila M. Rious and Louis A. Penner (December 2001), "The Causes of Organizational Citizenship Behavior: A Motivational Analysis," *Journal of Applied Psychology,* pp. 1306–1314.

32. Joseph Pear and Garry L. Martin (2002), *Behavior Modification: What It Is and How to Do It* (Saddle River, NJ: Prentice-Hall).

33. Kenneth Mericle and Dong-One Kim (2002), *Determinants of Skill Acquisition under Pay-for-Performance System* (Berkeley: University of California Working Paper).

34. Timothy A. Judge, Daniel Heller, and Michael K. Mount (June 2002), "Five Factor Model of Personality and Job Satisfaction: A Meta-Analysis," *Journal of Applied Psychology,* pp. 530–541.

35. E. E. Lawler (1981), *Pay and Development* (Reading, MA: Addison-Wesley).

36. Tony Simons (1995), "Motivating Hotel Employees," *Cornell Hotel and Restaurant Administration Quarterly,* Vol. 36, Iss. 7, pp. 20–27.

37. Timothy Lee Doré (2005), *The Relationship between Job Characteristics, Job Satisfaction, and Turnover Intention among Software Developers* (Ann Arbor, MI: Dissertation.com).

38. Bob Filipczak (1996), "Can't Buy Me Love," *Training,* pp. 29–34.

39. Duncan Brown and Michael Armstrong (2000), *Paying for Contributions: Performance Related Pay Strategies* (New York: Kogan Page).

40. Edward E. Lawler, III (2000), *Rewarding Excellence: Pay Strategies for the New Economy* (San Francisco: Jossey-Bass).

41. E. Brian Peach and Daniel A. Wren (1992), "Historical Context," in B. L. Hopkins and Thomas C. Mawhinney (Eds.), *Pay for Performance: History Controversy, and Evidence* (New York: Haworth), pp. 1–26.

42. Adams Smith (1776), *Wealth of Nations.*

43. F. W. Taylor (1903), *Shop Management* (New York: Harper and Row).

44. Steve Bates (May 2002), "Piecing Together Executive Compensation," *HR Magazine,* pp. 60–69.

45. Terry Gillen (2001), *The Performance Management Activity Pack* (New York: AMACOM).

46. Barry M. Staw and Yochi Cohen-Charash (February 2005), "The Dispositional Approach to Job Satisfaction: More Than a Mirage, But Not Yet an Oasis," *Journal of Organizational Behavior,* pp. 59–78.

47. Gay Blau (1994), "Testing the Level and Importance of Pay Referent on Pay Level Satisfaction," *Human Relations,* Vol. 47, Iss. 10, pp. 1251ff.

48. Bates, op. cit.

49. Ellig, op. cit.

50. Bill Leonard (March 2002), "GM Drives HR to the Next Level," *HR Magazine,* pp. 46–51.

51. Ibid.

52. Frank Jossi (June 2002), "Take a Peek Inside," *HR Magazine,* pp. 46–53.

53. Christine Galea (2005), "The 2005 Compensation Survey," *Sales & Marketing Management,* pp. 24–29.

54. Ibid.

55. Emily Pavlovic (1994), "Choosing the Best Salary Surveys," *HR Magazine,* Vol. 39, Iss. 4, pp. 44–48.

56. Marc J. Wallace Jr. and Charles H. Fay (1988), *Compensation Theory and Practice,* 2nd ed. (Boston: PWS-Kent).

57. Robert L. Heneman (2002), *Strategic Reward Management: Design, Implementation, and Evaluation* (New York: Information Age Publishing).

58. Howard Risher (1999), *Aligning Pay and Results* (New York: AMACOM).

59. Reinventing Human Resource Management (1999), HRM02: Reform the General Schedule Classification and Basic Pay System.

60. www.iqpc.com (conference on broadbanding), Brigette W. Schay (1998), Broadcasting, Center for Personnel Research (Aleranlian, VA).

61. Kenan S. Abosch and Janice S. Hand (1994), *Broadbanding Models* (Scottsdale, AZ: American Compensation Assoc.).

62. Ibid.

63. Kenan S. Abosch and Beverly L Hmurovic (Summer 1998), "A Traveler's Guide to Global Broadbanding," *ACA Journal,* pp. 38–47.

64. Ibid.

65. William W. Holley Jr. and Kenneth M. Jennings (1997), *The Labor Relations Process,* 6th ed. (Forth Worth: Dryden).

Application Case 10-1

The Comparable Worth Debate

Twin Oaks Hospital is a privately owned facility that serves Lexington, Colorado (population approximately 250,000). The 100-bed hospital has a staff of 350 employees, including over 200 nurses and 40 clerical and secretarial employees (an almost exclusively female group). In the last month, discontent concerning pay levels has been mounting among the hospital's nurses and secretarial-clerical employees. Discontent was spurred by recent developments at the Lexington Memorial Hospital, a public facility. There, the hospital administration agreed to demands by nurses and secretarial-clerical workers for a 5 percent pay increase. The administration further agreed to launch a job evaluation program that would evaluate the nursing and secretarial-clerical jobs on the basis of comparable worth. The administrators pledged that the study's findings would be used as the basis for any further pay adjustments.

The administration's moves came after demonstrations by nurses and clerical-secretarial workers and by a clear threat of unionization by the Union of American Nurses and the United Office Workers. Union organizers had held discussions with the nurses and office employees and had circulated the results of a comparable worth study (shown in Exhibit 10-1A) to illustrate the extent of pay inequities.

David Hardy, director of personnel at Twin Oaks, was acutely aware of the troubles brewing at his hospital. He knew that union organizers were meeting with employees and distributing the study flier. Overall, Twin Oaks' pay levels for its nurses and office staff were very similar to the levels at Lexington Memorial before the 5 percent increase. However, the levels were not competitive with compensation available in Denver, which is located about 100 miles north of Lexington. In the last week, Hardy had met with representatives of the two employee groups at their request. There, the spokeswomen made three requests: an immediate 5 percent pay increase, the establishment of a job evaluation program based on the concept of comparable worth, and a pledge to base wage adjustments on the findings of the study.

Hardy informed James Bledsoe, the hospital director, of the employees' requests: Bledsoe asked for a recommendation for action within three days. Before developing an action plan Hardy met with his two top aides (Janet Sawyer and Charles Cooper) for an initial, informal discussion of the situation. In Hardy's view, the key question focused on whether to evaluate the jobs on the basis of comparable worth.

"I favor launching the job evaluation program," said Janet Sawyer. "Nationwide, there is a disturbingly large gap between the pay levels of predominantly male and female jobs. Consider that there's no difference in the median education levels of men and women—about 12.6 years. Yet with the same median amount of education, women on the average earn 40.8 percent of a man's median pay. If we take a close look at our compensation levels across jobs from the perspective of comparable worth, we'll probably find some pretty disturbing gaps of our own.

"There's a growing precedent for comparable worth–based pay adjustments," she continued. "Over 30 states have comparable worth bills pending or commissions that are studying the issue. Minnesota has had comparable worth–based pay policies for its employees since 1983, and several city governments have implemented the concept."

"That's precedent in the public sector, not private industry," said Charles Cooper. "I would favor a pay increase, perhaps 5 percent, to keep us competitive with Lexington Memorial. However, agreeing to a job evaluation based on comparable worth is opening the door to a very questionable and costly concept.

"I'm troubled by the concept of comparable worth for three reasons," he continued. "First, if you implement comparable worth, you destroy our free market system. The market does discriminate, but on the basis of supply and demand, which accurately reflects a job's worth. The market is blind to gender."

"I'm not so sure about its visual shortcomings in that regard," Janet said.

"I agree with Janet that a sizable wage gap does exist," Charles continued. "But according to some studies, much of that gap is not due to gender. For example, I've just reviewed a study by the U.S. Labor Department that found that over 50 percent of the gap between men's and women's pay

EXHIBIT 10-1A   **Findings from One Comparable Worth Study**

	Head Nurse	Electrician	Clerk/Typist	Truck Driver
Knowledge and Skills	244 RN license; good judgment; people skills	122 Apprenticeship; technical know-how	106 High school diploma; word processing—60 wpm	61 Chauffeur's license
Mental Demands	106 Life-and-death decisions; administer doctors' orders; emotional stability	30 Troubleshooting; public safety	26 Always told what to do; pressure to get work done; monotony	10 Heavy traffic; speed limits
Responsibility	122 Supervise patient care; manage ward staff	30 Order supplies; safe wiring	35 Neat documents; manage small tasks	13 Truck maintenance; on-time deliveries
Working Conditions	11 Always on feet; constant demands; rotating shifts	15 Cramped quarters; strenuous assignments; fairly dangerous	0 Padded seat; constant interruptions; regular hours	13 Erratic schedule; tight space, long hours
Total Points	483	197	167	97
Monthly Salary	$2,950	$2,350	$1,820	$2,055

is due to vocational training, the industries that women choose, and geographical location. The remaining gap could be due to sex discrimination, but frankly I'm not willing to destroy the free market system to find out.

"Second, there's the issue of implementation," Charles said. "Here, comparable worth floats in a sea of subjectivity. If we conduct the evaluation, we must evaluate all jobs in the hospital, not just the nurses, secretaries, and clerical workers. Doing so requires one evaluation system with one set of job factors. Which factors do we use? How do we weigh the factors in calculating a job's worth? Few objective guidelines exist for us to use.

"And suppose we did implement comparable worth," he continued. "We might create internal pay equity across our jobs but it would not address our need to be externally competitive. For example, suppose we determine that two jobs are very similar in worth, almost identical. Using comparable worth as a basis, we provide the same pay for both jobs. However, marketwise we're paying far too much for one job and far too little for another. How do we attract people for the underpaid position? We end up with too many applicants for jobs already filled and not enough for jobs that go unfilled.

"Third, there's our primary concern—costs. We won't know how much comparable worth will cost us until we're into the evaluation program. However, given adjustments made in clerical and secretarial pay by government offices that have implemented comparable worth, the cost should be hefty. Look at the estimated price tag for implementing comparable worth nationwide—over $150 billion. Business and society would pay the bill via inflation and lowered productivity."

"We could conduct an effective job evaluation program—other companies have done it," Janet countered. "General Electric has overhauled its job evaluation methods to reflect concerns about comparable worth. BankAmerica has also made some changes; it's incorporated job factors into predominantly female jobs that weren't there before, such as physical demands for computer VDT operators and bank tellers. We could also talk with Lexington Memorial about how they plan to conduct their job evaluation program.

"I'd suggest that we develop a job evaluation plan that's tailor-made for our hospital," Janet continued. "We could form a committee composed of 6 to 10 members with representatives from all functional areas. The committee would be charged with identifying the elements that should be considered in evaluating all jobs in the hospital. It would also determine the weights for all factors. For some factors, such as knowledge and experience, accountability and judgment would be more difficult. But we could do it; others have done it."

"What about costs?" David Hardy asked.

"Charles is right," Janet replied. "We won't really know until the evaluation task is complete. But as a very rough estimate, I'd say we would be raising the nursing and office workers' pay by at least 10 percent, probably more. However, we can phase in the increase over a number of years, a bit at a time'"

"What happens if the evaluation determines that some male-dominated jobs are overpaid?" asked Charles. "Do we reduce our pay while boosting the women's? Threat of unionization is a factor in regard to the nurses and clerical staff. What about the possibility of male employees unionizing because of pay cuts?"

"We'd have to address that question," Janet replied. "But given that most of our staff are women, overall our employees would benefit from comparable worth."

"You know, I've heard a lot about women benefiting from comparable worth," said David Hardy. "But over the long term, I'm not sure. It seems to me that if the concept is implemented nationwide, companies will have a higher wage bill with no increase in productivity. So they may pay the bill by reducing the number of jobs with the highest wage increases—jobs that women hold. Many women may find themselves out of work."

"That might be," Janet said. "However, that hasn't happened in countries like Australia and Great Britain that have actively closed much of the gender-based wage gap in recent years."

"Any other thoughts?" asked David.

"We should take a good look at a pay increase, and perhaps even more than the 5 percent requested," Charles said. "But stay away from comparable worth. For private business, it's uncharted and dangerous territory."

"This whole situation has raised questions in my mind about the fairness and validity of our pay structure," Janet said. "We may have problems. Let's look at it, and let's consider comparable worth. We may not be able to go the full 90 yards. How about a first step?"

Discussion Questions

1. In your view, is comparable worth a legitimate strategy for determining job compensation?
2. As the director of Twin Oaks' HR department, what recommendations would you make to James Bledsoe?
3. From an HRM perspective, what are the challenges of implementing comparable worth?

Source: Originally written by Kim Stewart. Modified slightly through various editions, most recently for the 2007 edition. The situation, names, and characters are fictitious. Facts and some perspectives are drawn from Peter B. Olney Jr. (March–April 1987), "Meeting the Challenge of Comparable Worth: Part I," *Compensation and Benefits Review,* pp. 34–44; Barbara R. Bergmann (May–June 1987), "Pay Equity—Surprising Answers to Hard Questions," *Challenge,* pp. 45–51; and Daniel Seligman (May 14, 1984), "Pay Equity Is a Bad Idea," *Fortune,* p. 133.

11

Compensation: Methods and Policies

Learning Objectives

After studying this chapter you should be able to:

1. **Understand** how individual pay is determined.
2. **Define** variable pay and discuss the various incentive programs that can be used in such a system.
3. **Explain** why merit pay may cause employees to compete rather than cooperate.
4. **Compare** the various gainsharing systems (Lincoln Electric plan, Scanlon plan, Rucker plan, ImproShare, business plan, gainsharing, winsharing, and spot gainsharing).
5. **Recognize** the significant changes in and learn to differentiate among these innovations: skill-based, knowledge-based, credential-based, feedback, and competency-based pay.
6. **Describe** such pay issues as secrecy, security, and compression.

Internet/Web Resources

General Sites
www.nceo.org
www.fed.org/leading_companies
www.acaonline.com
www.benefitslink.com
www.towers.com/towers
www.mercerhr.com
www.qualitydigest.com/jul/gainshre. html#anchor90368

Company Sites
www.lincolnelectric.com
www.broan.com
www.aa.com
www.lmco.com
www.polaroid.com
www.generalmills.com
www.xerox.com
www.fritolay.com

Career Challenge

Joe Paderewski sat in his big office in the rear of the Cardeson National Bank. Guido Panelli, his executive vice president, came in to drop off Mary Renfro's report on compensation and to discuss other problems CNB was having with people and pay.

"CNB pays the going rate for salaries," Joe declared. "And there's our bonus system—when profits allow it. But turnover is still high."

"Some of those leaving said their new employers would have performance share programs," Guido said.

At Branch 1, Tom Nichols, the manager, was having a meeting with the tellers' supervisors to discuss pay. He hadn't wanted to attend the meeting; he didn't like meetings, and he knew this one would be bad. The tellers were never satisfied with their pay. Back in school, Torn had learned that pay was one thing that was never easily settled; people were always griping about it.

The meeting went like this:

Chet Tom, we're here because the troops are unhappy.

Tom The troops are always unhappy.

Chet Sure, but this time it's serious. My people are tired of punching time clocks and getting paid by the hour. Everyone else here at the bank gets salaries—52 weeks a year. Why don't my tellers?

Tom Well, you know, it's always been done that way. Besides . . .

Chet Don't give me that "it's always been done that way" stuff. You can do something about it. Talk to Joe. My people want the security of a regular paycheck and the dignity of no time clock. You know the union's been around. What are we going to do about it?

The other supervisors shook their heads, and Tom didn't know what to say.

Branch 2 was having its own problems. One day there was an incident involving two tellers and a supervisor. It all started when the following dialogue took place:

Martha Did you hear that Joanne makes $1.50 more an hour than me? I've been here longer than she has.

Sandra Why not go to June about it? She's the boss.

Martha (to June) How come Joanne makes $1.50 per hour more than me? I've been here longer.

June How do you know that's true? We don't reveal salaries around here, and it's against company policy to discuss other people's pay.

Martha Never mind how I found out. And let's cut the company policy stuff. Why is Joanne paid more than I am?

It is now raise time again, and Joe is getting flak from all sides. He believes he can afford about 3.5 percent for raises. But who should get them?

After Guido left his office, Joe went over the situation in his mind. "Some deserve no raise, really," he thought. "Others deserve something; a few deserve a lot.

But how should I divide the money? Should I really give no raise at all to some? And how much should the average employee get? The cost of living has gone up 3 percent. If I give them much more than that, there won't be enough to give big raises to the people who really deserve them, like Mary and Guido. And that says nothing about the people who deserve raises because, as Mary keeps saying, their base pay is too low. And what about the people who are being promoted? How am I going to allocate this raise money?"

Joe decided to talk to Mary about the problems and get her to fill him in on the latest research on pay.

Joe Mary, I'm having problems with pay again. Will you give me a rundown on what's new? Especially things like pay secrecy, incentive pay, and how we can use pay to get our employees to increase productivity. What about skill-based pay?

Mary Let me fill you in on some new trends in compensation. I think some of these may help us here at the bank.

Mary briefed Joe on pay secrecy, pay compression, variable pay, and other incentive plans, while emphasizing why she thought moving to a skill-based pay system might help solve both the turnover and the lack of productivity.

As you will recall from Chapter 10, Patten developed seven criteria for judging an organization's compensation plan. If a compensation plan meets all of these criteria, it will accomplish the objective of providing a system of rewards equitable to both the employer and the employee. Chapter 10 focused on the first three of these criteria: a compensation system should be adequate and equitable and provide incentives. The remaining four criteria will be discussed primarily in this chapter; a compensation system should be:

- *Secure* This refers to the extent to which the employee's pay seems adequate to satisfy basic needs.
- *Balanced* This refers to the extent to which pay is a reasonable part of the total reward package, which includes benefits, promotions, and so on. (Chapter 12 discusses benefits.)
- *Cost-effective* This refers to cost-effectiveness for the organization.
- *Acceptable to the employee* This has to do with whether employees think the pay system makes sense. Three aspects of acceptability will be discussed: whether pay should be secret, communication to achieve acceptability, and employees' participation in pay decision making.

Determination of Individual Pay

To the individual employee, the most important compensation decision is how much he or she will earn. This chapter presents various approaches to answering the question of individual pay.

To determine individual pay, two issues need to be addressed. First, management must answer these questions: How should one employee be paid relative to another when they both hold the same job in the organization? Should we pay all employees doing the same work at the same level the same? Second, if not, on what basis should we make the distinction—seniority or merit or some other basis?

Most employers do pay different rates to employees performing the same job.[1] Pay differentials are based on:

1. Individual differences in experience, skills, and performance.
2. Expectations that seniority, higher performance, or both deserve higher pay.

Reasons for choosing to pay employees at different rates for the same job include the following:[2]

- Pay differentials allow firms to recognize that different employees performing the same job make substantially different contributions to meeting organizational goals.
- Differentials allow employers to communicate a changed emphasis on important job roles, skills, knowledge, etc.

- Differentials provide organizations with an important tool for emphasizing norms of enterprise without having employees change jobs, that is, promotion.
- Without differentials, the pay system violates the internal equity norms of most employees, reducing satisfaction with pay and making attraction and retention of employees more difficult.
- Pay differentials allow firms to recognize market changes between jobs in the same grade without requiring a major overhaul of the whole compensation system.

Methods of Payment

Employees can be paid for the time they work, the output they produce, skills, knowledge, and competencies or a combination of these factors.

Flat Rates

In the unionized firm where wages are established by collective bargaining, single flat rates rather than different rates are often paid. For example, all "Administrative Assistants" might make $11.00 per hour, regardless of seniority or performance. Flat rates correspond to some midpoint on a market survey for a given job. Using a flat rate does not mean that seniority and experience do not differ. It means that employers and the union choose not to recognize these variations when setting wage rates. Unions insist on ignoring performance differentials for many reasons. They contend that performance measures are inequitable. Jobs need cooperative effort that could be destroyed by wage differentials. Sales organizations, for example, pay a flat rate for a job and add a bonus or incentive to recognize individual differences. Choosing to pay a flat rate versus different rates for the same job depends on the objectives established by the compensation analyst. Recognizing individual differences assumes that employees are not interchangeable or equally productive. By using pay differentials to recognize these differences, managers are trying to encourage an experienced, efficient, and satisfied workforce.

Payment for Time Worked

The majority of employees are paid for time worked in the form of wages or salaries, defined as follows:

→ **Wage** Pay calculated at an hourly rate. Nonexempt employees who are covered by overtime and reporting provisions of the Fair Labor Standards Act are paid wages.

→ **Salary** Pay calculated at an annual or monthly rate rather than hourly. Those who are exempt from regulations of the Fair Labor Standards Act and do not receive overtime pay receive salaries.[3]

Pay ranges, pay classifications, and similar tools are developed for individual pay determination, the final step in a time-based pay system.

The wages and salaries of employees are typically adjusted at some point during the year. Historically, the adjustments have resulted in pay increases. Most employees expect to get at least one raise annually. However, when the general economy isn't healthy or in the case of increased foreign competition in some industries, employees have actually accepted decreases in pay.

Pay is usually adjusted upward through four types of increases: (1) a general, across-the-board increase for all employees; (2) merit increases paid to some employees, based on some indicator of job performance; (3) a cost-of-living adjustment (COLA) based on the consumer price index (CPI); and (4) seniority. Typically, hourly employees in unionized firms are likely to receive general increases whereas exempt salaried employees are more likely to receive merit pay increases.

EXHIBIT 11-1

Source: Adapted from American Compensation Association (1996), *Report on the 1996–1997 ACA Salary Budget Survey* (Scottsdale, AZ: Management Compensation Services), p. 9.

Employees in United States (by Region) and Canada Receiving Variable Pay, Percent						
Employees	National	Eastern	Central	Southern	Western	Canadian
Hourly nonunion	60.0	50.4	62.3	67.1	61.8	76.5
Nonexempt	64.3	59.8	66.1	67.5	65.2	72.4
Exempt	66.1	63.9	67.1	66.0	67.8	76.0

Variable Pay: Incentive Compensation

International competition and global economic restructuring are requiring businesses to become measurably more productive. Pay strategies and pay systems used for years are outdated, and continued reliance on outdated pay systems is one reason why American business organizations cannot successfully compete internationally.[4] An article in *HRMagazine* reported this growing realization that traditional pay systems do not effectively link pay to performance or productivity.[5] As a result, managers have increasingly turned to variable pay plans. Variable pay can be defined as

> Any compensation plan that emphasizes a shared focus on organizational success, broadens opportunities for incentives to nontraditional groups (such as nonexecutives or nonmanagers), and operates outside the base pay increase system.[6]

It is estimated that over 60 percent of medium to large firms in the United States have some type of variable pay program for nonexecutives.[7] Sixty-six percent of respondents have variable pay programs for executives. Included in the ACA calculations as variable pay are individual incentive awards, special individual recognition awards, group and team awards, and scheduled lump-sum awards. As you will see from Exhibit 11-1, which shows percent of employees receiving variable pay in three categories (hourly nonunion, nonexempt, and exempt), a higher percentage of Canadian employees of all three types receive variable pay adjustments.

In order to implement successful variable pay systems, companies must be sure their plans are based on clear goals, unambiguous measurements, and visible linkage to employees' efforts. Key design factors include:

1. *Support by management* Executives and line managers must demonstrate commitment.
2. *Acceptance by employees* Employees must accept the plan as equitable.
3. *Supportive organizational culture* The organization's culture must be based on teamwork, trust, and involvement of employees at all levels when setting performance goals.
4. *Timing* The plan must be launched when there is minimal risk of economic downturns that would affect the size of the awards.[8]

Hewlett-Packard (HP) Systems has for many years been an example of innovation and trendsetting human resources policies, including introducing new types of variable pay. HP acquired Colorado Memory Systems, a small manufacturer of computer components and wanted to have a smooth acquisition. At the time of the acquisition, Colorado Memory was about to go public, and loyal employees were eager to become owners of the business. HP wanted to keep Colorado's employees loyal and enthusiastic, so it designed a variable pay system that would help retain employees and assimilate them into HP at the same time. Building on an existing profit-sharing plan, HP created a new system for Colorado. First, base pay for all employees was raised to 90 percent of comparable pay at HP. The remaining 10 percent was dedicated to a gainsharing scheme called "success sharing."

EXHIBIT 11-2
Rialto
Manufacturing's
Salary Classifications

Employee's Performance	Bottom Third	Middle Third	Top Third
Outstanding	12–15%	9–11%	6–8%
Good	8–11	6–8	4–5
Average	4–7	4–5	2–3
Marginally satisfactory	1–3	3	1
Unsatisfactory	No increase	No increase	No increase

At the end of the first quarter, Colorado employees exceeded their goals by 20 percent and took home a matching 20 percent quarterly bonus![9]

With variable pay, a percentage of an employee's paycheck is put at risk. The result is that if business goals aren't met, the pay rate will not rise above the lower base salary. Annual raises are not guaranteed. For example, base pay might be set at $30,000 with a variable award or end-of-year bonus of up to $6,000. The individual could earn all or part of the bonus by meeting objectives: lowering costs, raising productivity, raising quality, or increasing customer satisfaction. Base pay the next year would return to $30,000, and the employee would again be eligible to compete for the additional variable reward.

Flexibility is essential and can be built into the variable compensation plan by taking a **total compensation approach.**[10] Total compensation includes three elements:

1. Base pay is matched closely to competition, according to the organization's ability to pay and attract quality talent. Base pay serves as a platform for variable pay.

2. **Variable pay** is the centerpiece of the total compensation approach. Methods include gainsharing, winsharing, lump-sum bonuses, individual variable pay, and so forth. It is flexible and links the future of the firm and the employee in a positive manner.

3. Indirect pay adds cost-effective benefits keyed to supporting the goals of the organization and sharing costs. (Benefits will be discussed in Chapter 12.)

Variable pay helps manage labor costs. However, it does not guarantee equitable treatment of employees. Financial insecurity is built into the system. Economic downturn, new competition, or some other force beyond the employee's control may lead to lower profits and lower or nonexistent bonuses. As a result productivity may actually decline. The following sections discuss different types of variable pay.

Methods for paying employees on the basis of output are usually referred to as *incentive* forms of compensation. Incentive compensation can be paid individually, to the work group, or on an enterprisewide basis. Incentive compensation assumes it is possible and useful to tie performance directly to pay, an issue discussed in detail in Chapter 10.

Merit Incentives

The most widely used plan for managing individual performance is merit pay. Heneman defines **merit pay** as "individual pay increases based on the rated performance of individual employees in a previous time period," or a reward based on how well an employee has done the job.[11] Traditionally, merit pay results in a higher base salary after the annual performance evaluation. Merit increases are usually spread evenly throughout the subsequent year. Exhibit 11-2 illustrates how a merit pay raise is related to performance rating at Rialto Manufacturing Company, a medium-sized firm in Florida.

Although between 80 and 90 percent of private sector firms offer merit raises, little research has directly examined merit pay or its effect on performances.[12] One study, however, is quite interesting.[13] It investigated what size merit increase is necessary to get the desired results in terms of motivation. The findings showed that anything less than 6 to 7 percent was not motivating, and that merit increases above that level could actually be demotivating.

Advocates of merit pay call it the most valid type of pay increase. They argue that it is directly tied to performance because awards are linked to the performance appraisal system.[14] Rewarding the best performers with the largest pay is claimed to be a powerful motivator. However, this premise has two flawed assumptions: (1) that competence and incompetence are distributed in roughly the same percentages in a work group; and (2) that every supervisor is a competent evaluator. Researchers have questioned whether merit pay as currently implemented has anything to do with performance or, rather, whether it tolerates, rewards, and even encourages mediocrity.[15]

In practice, many merit pay systems fail to reward superior performance because of three problems:[16]

1. Employees fail to make the connection between pay and performance.
2. The secrecy of the reward is perceived by other employees as inequity.
3. The size of the merit award has little effect on performance.

Merit plans can work in circumstances where the job is well designed and the performance criteria are both well delineated and assessable.[17] However, because most current merit pay focuses only on the individual, it is more likely to cause employees to compete with each other for resources than to collaborate or share resources.

The merit pay system depends on the reward to produce an effect rather than planning and designing the effect at the outset. Merit pay should promise an increased salary to an employee in exchange for the employee's promise to perform satisfactory future work of a specified and mutually agreed upon complexity.[18] The truth is that many existing merit plans are not clearly linked to an individual's performance, and merit increases are not always viewed as meaningful.

Individual Incentives

Perhaps the oldest form of compensation is the individual incentive plan, in which the employee is paid for units produced. Today, the individual incentive plan takes several forms: piecework, production bonuses, and commissions. These methods seek to achieve the incentive goal of compensation.[19]

Straight piecework is an individual incentive plan where pay determination fluctuates based on units of production per time period (usually pieces per hour).[20] An example of an organization that uses straight piecework is a sewing mill that has set an hourly standard for machine operators of sewing 25 shirts per hour. Wages are calculated by multiplying the number of shirts completed by the piece rate for one shirt. Employees who exceed the standard of 25 shirts per hour make higher wages based on the additional piece rate per unit completed. This is probably the most frequently used piecework incentive plan. Work standards are set through work measurement studies as modified by collective bargaining. The actual piece rates may emerge from data collected by pay surveys. This incentive system is easy for employees to understand, but setting the work standards is extremely difficult.

The **standard-hour plan** bases wages on completion of a job or task in some expected period of time.[21] You have probably encountered the standard-hour plan when you took your car to a garage to be fixed. The labor costs on your bill are based on an estimate of how long it should take to do any given task like change spark plugs or replace brakes. For example, the average time to replace brakes may be two hours. If the mechanic is extremely efficient, the job may be finished in an hour and a half, but your bill will reflect the charge for two hours of labor, and the mechanic will be paid accordingly. Standard-hour plans are ideal pay plans for long cycle operations and highly skilled, nonrepetitive jobs.[22]

Another variation of the straight piecework rate is the **differential piece rate** or **Taylor plan.** Originally developed by Frederick W. Taylor, the originator of scientific management theory, the differential piece rate uses two separate piecework rates: one for those who produce below or up to standard and another for those who produce above standard.[23] Using the example of the sewing factory, the employees who made up to 25 shirts per hour might receive a piece rate of 50 cents per shirt. Those who made more than 25 shirts per hour would be paid at a higher rate, perhaps 60 cents per shirt. This system was designed to reward the highly efficient worker and penalize the less efficient.

Production bonus systems pay an employee an hourly rate plus a bonus when the employee exceeds the standard. The bonus usually equals approximately 50 percent of labor savings. This system is not widely used in the United States. In Japan, all employees receive semiannual production bonuses in December and June. The bonus is related to basic pay and is expressed as a multiple of the monthly salary.[24]

Commissions paid to sales employees are another type of individual incentive. A **commission** is compensation based on a percentage of sales in units or dollars. *Straight commission* is the equivalent of straight piecework. The commission paid is typically a percentage of the price of the item. For example, real estate salespeople are paid a percentage of the price of any property they sell, typically between 7 and 9 percent. A sales variation of the production bonus system pays the salesperson a small salary and a commission or bonus when he or she exceeds the budgeted sales goal.

Individual incentives are used more frequently in some industries (clothing, steel, textiles) than others (lumber, beverage, bakery), and more in some jobs (sales, production) than others (maintenance, clerical). Individual incentives are possible only in situations where performance can be specified in terms of output (sales dollars generated, number of items completed). In addition, employees must work independently of each other so that individual incentives can be applied equitably.

Are individual incentives effective? The theory predicts that piece rates encourage workers to earn more, and empirically they do.[25] But firms with piece rate systems frequently find significant organizational problems resulting from their compensation plans.[26] Case studies of two small companies—Acme Industrial Parts and Gotham Furniture—concluded that piece rate systems rendered the companies noncompetitive and unprofitable. If an employer tries to change work standards or pay rates, workers often oppose these changes because they fear that new methods or standards may reduce their piece rates more than they reduce the effort per piece.[27] Most studies indicate that individual incentives increase output. But while production increases, other performance criteria may suffer. For example, in sales, straight commission can lead to less attention being paid to servicing accounts. Hard-to-sell clients may be ignored for the quick, easy sale. Some jobs that are paid at piece rate probably should not be—for example, paying lab technicians individual incentives for the number of tests completed per hour. Patients waiting for lab results on illnesses such as AIDS or cervical cancer certainly would prefer that the technicians who examined their tests took their time rather than rushing to build up paychecks.

For incentive plans to work, they must be well designed and administered. It appears that an individual incentive plan is likely to be more effective under certain circumstances.[28]

- The task is liked.
- The task is not boring.
- The supervisor reinforces and supports the system.
- The plan is acceptable to employees and managers and probably includes them in the plan's design.
- The incentive is financially sufficient to induce increased output.
- Quality of work is not especially important.
- Most delays in work are under the employees' control.

Team Incentives

Piecework, production bonuses, commissions, and other individual incentives can be paid to teams of individuals. This might be done when it is difficult to measure individual output, when cooperation is needed to complete a task or project, and when management feels this is a more appropriate measure on which to base incentives. Team incentive plans also reduce administrative costs. Most compensation professionals report that companies are increasingly interested in new group reward strategies, particularly small-group incentives.[29] Small-group incentive plans are one of the newest and fastest-growing reward strategies.

There are a number of logical reasons why a team incentive plan is chosen. In some situations, jobs and work output are so interrelated that it is impossible to specifically pinpoint individual performance. In such a situation, a team incentive could be used. The Japanese have used team incentives to help foster group cohesiveness and reduce jealousy. They assume that rewarding only one individual or a few workers will discourage a sense of teamwork.[30] In the United States, however, individual spirit and individual self-confidence are not fully supported by a teamwork approach. Thus, in the United States, there may be a clash between societal norms and group incentive systems. For small-group incentives to be effective, management must define its objectives carefully and then analyze the situation to select the most appropriate group incentive.

Several aspects of team-based incentive pay need further research: When should team pay be introduced—before, with, or after creation of work teams? How can an organization avoid making mistakes when switching to team incentives?[31]

In individual and group incentive systems, competition can result in withholding information or resources, political gamesmanship, not helping others, and even sabotaging the work of others. These behaviors can be costly to an organization. In an attempt to minimize these problems of interindividual and intergroup competition, some organizations have elected to use organizationwide incentive plans.

Organizationwide Incentives

Payments shared by all members of the organization are a much more common incentive reward than individual or group incentives. These organizationwide payments are usually based on one of two performance concepts: a sharing of profits generated by the efforts of all employees altogether and a sharing of money saved as a result of employees' efforts to reduce costs.[32] Three approaches to incentive plans are used at the organizationwide level: suggestion systems, company group incentive plans (gainsharing), and profit sharing.

Suggestion Systems   Suggestion systems, one of the oldest management tools, are pervasive in both public and private organizations. A **suggestion system** is a formal method of obtaining employees' advice about improvements in organizational effectiveness; it includes some kind of reward based on the successful application of the idea. The key to successful suggestion systems is employees' involvements.[33] Implementation of these programs has proved quite cost-effective. For example, American Airlines's IdeAAs in Action program has provided total savings of nearly $250 million as employees' participation has grown from 6 to 20 percent.[34]

Suggestion systems can improve employee relations, foster high-quality products, reduce costs, and increase revenue.[35] They are frequently administered by the human resource department. In Japan, suggestion systems are one of the main practical forms of worker participation schemes.[36]

Effective administration of the suggestion program is essential to its success. At Broan Manufacturing Company in Hartford, Wisconsin, employees get little furry stick-on bears or ducks for every suggestion they submit to the company's suggestion system. The program, called Broan's Fresh Ideas, named for the company's 11 "air freshener" products, has generated more than $1.4 million worth of ideas in the last four years. For any idea that saves up to $200, employees receive one chance in a prize drawing. Ideas that result in greater savings receive additional chances. Every year at a banquet for successful suggesters, drawings are held for a variety of prizes including money and extra vacation days. The program is successful because it involves employees on all levels, has the support of management, and uses in-house publicity.[37]

Essential elements for a successful suggestion system include:

- Management commitment.
- Clear goals.
- Designated administrator.
- Structured award system.
- Regular publicity.
- Immediate response to each suggestion.[38]

The National Association of Suggestion Systems suggests that a firm should investigate what competitors are doing and talk to employees to find out what will motivate them.[39] In the past decade, many companies dropped cash awards and moved toward recognition and other awards, such as company stock. There is also movement away from individually based suggestion systems to a team approach such as the one adopted at Hallmark.[40]

Gainsharing Incentive Plans   **Gainsharing plans** are companywide group incentive plans that, through a financial formula for distributing organizationwide gains, unite diverse organizational elements in the common pursuit of improved organizational effectiveness.[41] These systems share the benefits of improved productivity, reduced costs, or improved quality in the form of cash bonuses.[42] Common elements of these programs—hours worked, dollars spent on labor, and dollars spent on waste—serve as reliable standards of performance; programs are built on a standard of how many hours are required to produce a given

EXHIBIT 11-3
Characteristics Associated with Successful Gainsharing Plans

Source: Charles P. Gowen III (1991), "Gainsharing Programs: An Overview of History and Research," *Journal of Organizational Behavior Management,* Vol. II, Iss. 2, p. 86.

1. Organizational unit of less than 500 employees.
2. Stable productivity and costs for a few years.
3. Simple financial measures of productivity and costs.
4. Growing or expandable market for the firm's products or services.
5. Product costs affected by employees' behavior.
6. Organizational climate characterized by openness and high level of trust.
7. Participative style of management.
8. No union or a union favorable to cooperative efforts.
9. Limited or no use of overtime.
10. Seasonal stability of sales or production.
11. High to moderate interdependence among employees' tasks.
12. Low capital investment changes for the past few years and next few years.
13. Few product changes in near past and near future.
14. Corporate financial staff trusted by employees and able to communicate financial information about productivity and costs.
15. Willingness on the part of management to disclose corporate financial results to employees.
16. Trusted plant manager able to communicate production goals and results.
17. Management able to work with critical suggestions for change.
18. Supportive attitude by the parent corporation toward the organizational unit's change and development.
19. Employees who are technically knowledgeable and motivated by participation and greater financial incentives. Maintenance and engineering staff competent and willing to respond to new challenges.

HR Journal   *Lincoln's Time Line Offers a Concise Picture*

110 YEARS OF EXCELLENCE

Lincoln's tradition of innovative solutions, technological leadership, and commitment to customers, employees, and shareholders stems from the vision of its founder, John C. Lincoln, and his brother, James F. Lincoln.

1895—John C. Lincoln founded The Lincoln Electric Company with a capital investment of $200.00. The product: electric motors of his own design.

1900–1919—John C.'s younger brother, James F. Lincoln, joined the company as a salesman in 1907. Meanwhile, the product line had been expanded to include battery chargers for electric automobiles. A welding set is first made by the Lincoln brothers in 1909. In 1911, Lincoln Electric introduced the first variable voltage, single operator, portable welding machine in the world.

1920–1939—Lincoln's production of welders surpassed that of motors for the first time in 1922, making welding the company's primary business. In 1927, Lincoln introduced the Fleetweld 5 coated electrode which produced welds with 20 to 50 percent higher tensile strength and 100 percent greater ductility than those made with bare electrodes.

Lincoln Electric employees earned paid vacations, among the first in the nation, in 1923. The first Lincoln employee stock ownership plan, one of the first in the country, was initiated in 1925. An employee suggestion program was implemented in 1929. Lincoln employees received their first annual Incentive Bonus in 1934. While the average Lincoln worker's pay more than doubled during the decade of the Great Depression, electrodes which had sold for $0.16/lb in 1929 were selling for less than $0.06/lb by 1942.

1940–1949—World War II brought a dramatic expansion of Lincoln Electric's business, with welded ship hulls creating an enormous new market for arc welding products. After many Lincoln workers were drafted, the company hired large numbers of women and minority factory workers for the first time. Motor production was suspended to focus resources on supporting the wartime welding product demand.

1950–1969—James F. Lincoln continued to enhance Incentive Management, adding a cost of living multiplier, formal merit rating, and guaranteed continuous employment. In 1959, John C. Lincoln passed away.

1990–1995—In, 1992, Mr. Donald Hastings became chairman and Frederick W. Mackenbach was promoted to president. In 1991, an expanded world headquarters facility opened with expanded and renovated Weld Technology and training center operations. Foreign operations were consolidated and reorganized.

In 1993, during the global reorganization, Don Hastings and Fred Mackenbach urged the company's U.S. employees to pursue record levels of production and sales. In true Lincoln spirit, they responded by voluntarily postponing 614 weeks of vacation in order to meet customer demand for product. Sales records were set every quarter since mid-1993.

1998—In 1998, Lincoln also distributed its 65th consecutive bonus to employees and achieved the fifth consecutive year of record financial performance. In investor news, shareholders approved the formation of a holding company, Lincoln Electric Holdings, Inc. With this transition came a conversion from dual class stock (voting and nonvoting) to a single-class, all voting stock. This action doubled the number of outstanding shares.

Source: www.lincolnelectric.com/corporate/about/history.asp, accessed July 5, 2005.

---

level of output. Gainsharing incentive systems have proved exceptionally effective in enhancing organizationwide teamwork in thousands of manufacturing and service organizations. Exhibit 11-3 lists characteristics associated with successful gainsharing plans. The gainsharing system is intended to improve overall organizational performance by allowing employees who contribute to performance results to share in the proceeds.

There are four commonly used organizationwide gainsharing plans: Lincoln Electric, Scanlon, Rucker, and ImproShare, along with variations of each. Plans differ according to the degree of employees' involvement and the types of financial incentives.[43]

Lincoln Electric Plan   The most successful gainsharing or productivity sharing plan at a single company is the Lincoln Electric plan. Lincoln is a Cleveland-based manufacturer of welding machines and motors. Its gainsharing plan was developed by James F. Lincoln in 1907. James, son of the founder, John C. Lincoln, had begun work at Lincoln for $50 a month and a 2 percent sales commission. He immediately saw a need for employees' commitment to helping the company develop new technology, so he created an advisory committee elected by the workers, with one member for every 100 employees.[44] The plan he began in 1907 expanded and was still thriving in 1999.

Under the Lincoln plan, employees are paid only for what they individually produce. There are no paid holidays, no sick leaves, and no unions. Promotions are based on merit, job reassignments must be accepted, and overtime is mandatory. The basic compensation system at Lincoln rests on the following principles: (1) All compensation is based on piecework. (2) There are no perquisites for managers. (3) After two years of employment, the worker cannot be laid off. (4) There is no mandatory retirement.

An advisory board consisting of several executives and about 30 employees reviews and makes suggestions for improvements. The firm has a stock purchase plan in which about two-thirds of the employees participate; they now own about one-third of the total stock. The stock is privately traded and not sold on any exchange. Employees hire the replacements for vacancies in their work group. The company basically subcontracts the work to the work group, using past performance and time studies as standards of performance. When these standards are beaten, the employees share generously. This bonus is not used as a substitute for adequate wages and benefits. In 1993, production workers received bonuses averaging between $18,000 and $22,000, equal to approximately half their salaries. The average Lincoln employee earned $45,000 that year.[45] Some individuals bid to go to work for Lincoln Electric.

Between 1986 and 1991, Lincoln added plants in Brazil and Mexico, established joint ventures with Venezuela, built a factory in Japan, and formed a strategic alliance with a Norwegian company. The global recession of the early 1990s caused the company to downsize at some of these international locations. But in the United States, the Lincoln Electric incentive plan has gone 40 years without a single layoff. The company has also gone more than 57 years without losing any money in its domestic business.

Three other gainsharing plans—the Scanlon plan, the Rucker plan, and ImproShare—are compared on 11 dimensions in Exhibit 11-4. Each of these plans will be discussed briefly.

Scanlon Plan The Scanlon plan is a combination suggestion, group incentive, and employee participation scheme that has been adopted by many small and medium-sized manufacturing firms.[46] In the late 1930s, Joe Scanlon, an unemployed steel worker, created a system of labor–management relations that has now been adopted by over 2,000 companies of all sizes, union and nonunion, in many industries. To involve all employees in the problem-solving process and to improve overall productivity, Scanlon organized employees into productivity teams responsible for exploring any idea that would improve quality and output, eliminate waste, and save time. Scanlon realized that both white- and blue-collar employees must cooperate to make productivity improvements, so the next step in the Scanlon plan is to organize a steering committee to (1) evaluate suggestions, (2) get budget approval, (3) establish priorities, and (4) report back to the employee teams. Gainsharing was used so that all employees would benefit financially from productivity improvements resulting from the suggestion system. The actual gainsharing formula is designed to suit the needs of the individual firm.[47]

Rucker Plan The philosophy of Rucker plans falls between the humanistic orientation of Scanlon plans and the ideal of an economically driven and rewarded employee of ImproShare. The Rucker plan has almost the same participatory elements as the Scanlon plan, but in smaller degrees.[48] However, the Rucker plan is less an employee-participation scheme than a practical realization that line workers have information that can help managers improve their skills. Rucker plans are based on employees' involvement and suggestions. Some have two committees, production and screening, while others have

EXHIBIT 11-4   Comparative Analysis of Three Gainsharing Plans

Source: Adapted from Christopher S. Miller and Michael H. Schuster (Summer 1987), "Gainsharing Plans: A Comparative Analysis," *Organizational Dynamics* 16 (1), p. 48.

Program Dimension	Scanlon	Rucker	ImproShare
1. Philosophy; theory	Original single unit; share improvements; people capable of and willing to make suggestions, want to make ideas	Primarily economic incentive; some reliance on employees' participation	Economic incentives increase performance
2. Primary goal	Productivity improvement	Improved productivity	Improved productivity
3. Subsidiary goals	Attitudes, communication, work behaviors, quality, cost reduction	Attitudes, communication, work behaviors, quality, cost reduction	Attitudes, work
4. Workers' participation	Two levels of committees: screening (one) and production (many)	Screening committee and production committee (sometimes)	Bonus committee tion
5. Suggestion making	Formal system	Formal system	None
6. Role of supervisor	Chair of production committee	None	None
7. Role of managers	Direct participation in bonus committee assignments	Idea coordinators: Evaluate suggestions, committee assignments	None None
8. Bonus formula	$\dfrac{\text{Sales}}{\text{Payroll}}$	$\dfrac{\text{Bargaining-unit payroll}}{\text{Production value}}$	Engineering standard $\times$ BPF*
9. Frequency of payout	Monthly	Monthly	Weekly
10. Role of union	Negotiated provisions; membership on screening committee	Negotiated provisions; screening committee membership	Negotiated provisions
11. Impact on management style	Substantial	Slight	None

*BPF = Base productivity factor.

only a screening committee. If there are two committees, the production committee has 10 to 15 hourly employees and an assortment of managers as members. It meets monthly to review suggestions and discuss production problems. The screening committee is composed of hourly employees, the union leadership, and key management personnel. Its primary purpose is to administer the bonus program; there is less emphasis on immediate issues of productivity or quality. It also may discuss production problems and long-range economic goals. One manager, the *idea coordinator*, directs suggestions to the appropriate managers for review and follows the ideas through investigation to provide feedback to employees. Rucker plans, like Scanlon plans, relate bonus earnings to financial performance.

ImproShare   ImproShare was developed by Mitchell Fein. It supports consultative management practices.[49] It typically does not have any shop-floor participation. The basic underlying principle is raising the employees' motivation to work. ImproShare ties economic rewards to performance without any attempt at meaningful participation by employees. Some firms do have a bonus committee to review the previous month's bonus calculations, however. Bonuses are calculated using a base productivity factor (BPF) involving engineered time standards, absorption of indirect hours, and actual hours worked.

Both Rucker and ImproShare plans are copyrighted programs. However, the plans can be duplicated without the aid of consultants. Various companies and unions have adapted the plans successfully to fit their own particular circumstances.

Recently, new gainsharing schemes like business plan gainsharing and winsharing began to be developed.[50] *Business plan gainsharing* follows the variable pay model and uses a broader range of business goals as the basis for funding the plan and determining awards. Future-oriented goals determine performance standards. For example, a chemical manufacturing company that needed to improve cost management in order to stay in business implemented business plan gainsharing, enabling employees to share half of the cost savings of performance below a budgeted cost per pound produced. New performance standards set for the system were actually developed to communicate the company's financial, safety, environmental, and strategic goals. Fifty percent of the award was tied to meeting financial goals, 25 percent to improving safety, and 25 percent to reducing environmental releases.

Winsharing grants awards funded by work teams' contributions to profitability.[51] All employees in the group "win" or share equally when productivity, profit, quality, and customer service targets are met. The plan differs from profit sharing in that winsharing has group measures that determine funding in addition to profit. To grant awards the company must actually profit from the results of the team's efforts. For example, a major electronics firm wanted to improve profit performance and become a world-class manufacturing organization. The company set a winsharing goal of increasing organizational profit to an appropriate level. Half the financial rewards were shared with employees and half with the organization. The plan paid all employees in the organization based on the overall bottom line, modified by quality improvements and cost savings.

Traditional gainsharing plans like the Scanlon plan are not designed to address many of the complex issues facing companies today. They fall short in three areas:[52] (1) they have a tendency to become institutionalized and thus fail to continue to vary pay with performance; (2) they are not flexible enough to reward "star performers"; and (3) service-sector firms are unable to isolate or measure gains in productivity. (In particular, quality of service is almost impossible to measure.) Therefore, a new form of gainsharing, spot gainsharing, has been born.

Spot gainsharing focuses on a specific problem in a specific department rather than on performance improvements for the whole organization. Its goal is to produce peak performance from participants during a specified time period. It is generally short and focused on a specific solution to a specific production problem. For example, perhaps a company would like to eliminate a backlog of work. Savings associated with the solution of the problem, less the administrative costs of the spot gainsharing plan, are split between the company and its participating employees. When the problem is solved, the plan is terminated. Because employees know the plan will end once the problem is solved, bonuses are perceived as a reward for the extra effort, not an extension of the wage structure as in the Scanlon, Rucker, and ImproShare plans.

For spot gainsharing to be successful, the firm must identify a clear business need unrelated to any specific failure on the part of management or employees in the unit, to be sure employees are not creating issues to trigger incentives. To identify real problems, managers should investigate the source of the problem, looking for conditions beyond the employees' control such as increased volume, high turnover, and reorganization.

The most critical factor in the success of any gainsharing plan is employees' involvement.[53] Workers must be motivated to assume new and expanded roles because any plan will fail without employees' enthusiasm, support, and trust. Surveys of employees can obtain information to predict how the workforce will respond to the gainsharing scheme. The firm will also have to dedicate cost-accounting support resources sufficient to ensure accurate and challenging productivity targets.

Not all gainsharing plans are successful, of course. Unsuccessful plans are characterized by poorly designed bonus formulas, extended periods of poor financial performance where low or no bonuses are paid, lack of management support for employees' participation, increasing cost factors that undermine the bonus formula, poor communication, lack of trust, administration costs that exceed the benefits of the plan, and apathy on the part of employees.[54]

Profit-Sharing Plans   **Profit-sharing plans** distribute a fixed percentage of total organizational profit to employees in the form of cash bonuses or deferred bonus amounts. The first profit-sharing plan was developed at a glassworks in New Geneva, Pennsylvania, in 1794 by Albert Gallatin, secretary of the treasury under presidents Jefferson and Madison. Gallatin believed democratic principles should be applied to industrial operations.[55] Little research has been done on profit sharing, however, and the practice of profit sharing is not dominant in other industrialized countries.[56]

These plans are typically found in three combinations:

1. Cash or current distribution plans provide full payment to participants soon after profits have been determined; this is usually quarterly or annually.
2. Deferred plans credit a portion of current profits to employees' accounts with cash payments made at the time of retirement, disability, severance, or death.
3. A combination of both incorporates aspects of current and deferred options.

Eighty percent of the companies with some form of profit sharing use the deferred option. Almost 19 percent use the combination option. Only 1 percent of the plans feature cash payouts.[57] It is important to note that the incentive value of profit-sharing plans *declines* as the time between performance and payoff increases and as the size of the payoff declines relative to previous years. Therefore, the incentive value of working to increase the company's current profits when rewards are distributed much later is, at best, minimal.

Profit-sharing plans do offer two distinct advantages. They do not need elaborate cost-accounting systems to calculate rewards, and they are easily implemented by companies of any size. Smaller companies usually use the current distribution method, while larger organizations usually use the deferred option. American Velvet Company, a small manufacturing plant in Stonington, Massachusetts, began profit sharing with a deferred plan in 1939. In the 1970s, employees voted to change the plan to a cash payout. Annual profit sharing is paid to employees on the basis of their pay. Currently, awards average 10 percent of pay. The firm's chief financial officer, Charles Cardente, reports that profit sharing has helped Velvet's employees to recognize their common interests with the company. As a result, union workers recently contributed from their profit sharing to enable the company to purchase new equipment.[58]

Ownership

Employee ownership plans are similar to profit sharing and are intended to increase worker commitment and performance. Under an employee stock ownership plan (ESOP), employees receive stock in the company. An ESOP is a qualified, defined contribution employee benefit plan that invests primarily in the stock of the employer company. ESOPs are *qualified* (i.e., tax-qualified) in that in return for meeting certain rules designed to protect the interests of plan participants, ESOP sponsors receive various tax benefits. ESOPs are *defined contribution plans* in that the employer makes yearly contributions that accumulate to produce a benefit that is not defined in advance. (In contrast, many pension plans are defined benefit plans; employees are guaranteed a specified benefit, which the company funds by making the necessary contributions.)

Technically, an ESOP is a kind of stock bonus plan, or a combination of a stock bonus plan and a money purchase pension plan. Stock bonus plans were used originally in the 1920s. They are in reality employee benefit plans designed to pay their benefits out in the form of company stock. Money purchase pension plans are retirement-oriented plans that commit the company to a minimum annual contribution. An ESOP is simply a variation of a stock bonus or stock bonus/money purchase plan that is designed to invest primarily in employer stock.[59] If the value of the stock increases, the stock owners (employees) could, by selling their stock, receive a good return.

People-Based Pay

Compensation design has been changing to meet the environmental challenges of the 21st century.[60] The bureaucratic *job-based* approach used in determining pay is no longer the only game in town, nor will it be the major format used to design pay systems in the future. Instead, the new designs will be *people-based.* One of the factors driving this change is the fact that the major "growth engines" in our economy are not manufacturing but the service and knowledge sectors. Jobs in these sectors range from burger flipping to highly technical research and development to business-to-business e-commerce. There are several different variants of people-based pay: skill-based, knowledge-based, credential-based, feedback, and competency-based.

Skill-based pay can be defined as an alternative to job-based pay. It sets pay levels on the basis of how many skills employees have or how many jobs they can do.[61] Although most firms are not using skill-based pay organizationwide, an increasing number of firms are using it for some number of their employees.[62] Polaroid Corporation has adopted it for the whole company. Procter & Gamble has implemented it in 30 plants. Expected positive outcomes of changing to the new model include increased quality, higher productivity, a more flexible workforce, improved morale, and decreased absenteeism and turnover.

Here's how it works. When a new skill is added to an existing job, the employee can earn a pay increase by mastering the new skill. Several methods for defining individual skills exist: direct observation of incumbents, testing, and measurable results. Instead of a detailed job description, "person" and "skill block" descriptions are developed. Skill block descriptions are priced much as in job evaluation. To date most skill-based pay systems focus on nonexempt manufacturing workers and others who engage in routine high-volume jobs. The more a job involves skills that are relatively easy to identify in terms of desired performance outcomes, the better the fit of the pay model.[63]

Skill-based pay, in reality, is difficult to design, does not fit all situations, and involves a time-consuming process of constructing skill blocks, mapping pay progressions, and assigning dollar values to each skill.[64] It works best when built on a broad base of skills in stable but expanding work environments.[65] Its major advantage for employers is that it can be used to replace annual raises. Under the skill-based system, no one gets a raise, even when promoted, until he or she has demonstrated proficiency with new skills. Think about it. You could in theory get a promotion but use the same skills you already used on your other job. In that case, no raise would be forthcoming. Variations on the skill-based approach are used according to the type of skills required.

Knowledge-based pay is defined as a variation that rewards employees for acquiring additional knowledge both within the current job category and in new job categories. This innovation is most aptly illustrated by trying to stretch the skill-based model to professionals, managers, and some technical personnel.[66] A study compared two manufacturing plants in the same corporation. One used the traditional job-centered pay design; the other used a knowledge-based design. After 10 months, the facility using pay for knowledge had significantly higher quality and significantly lower absenteeism and accidents. However, the traditional plant had higher productivity.

Credential-based pay rests on the fact that the individual must have a diploma or license or must pass one or more examinations from a third party professional or regulatory agency. For example, a lawyer must be a member of the state bar association, and a medical doctor must have passed state licensing exams. Credential-based pay is much more cut-and-dried than skill-based or knowledge-based pay.

Feedback pay is based on aligning pay with strategic business objectives and then establishing a direct connection between the jobholder and his or her part in accomplishing these goals. This design must conform to four principles: (1) it flows directly from the organization's strategic business goals, (2) it directly links employees' actions to these goals, (3) it provides sufficient opportunity for rewards to hold employees' attention, and (4) it is timely.[67] Many major companies like General Electric, Xerox, General Mills, Hewlett-Packard, Honeywell, and Frito-Lay use skill- and knowledge-based designs to link pay to strategy. This model replaces job descriptions with mission statements as a means of directing employees.[68]

Competency-based pay is actually a combination of skill-based pay, knowledge-based pay, and credential-based pay. In fact, the term is often applied to skill-based pay designs used with highly educated "knowledge workers."[69] In addition to skills, knowledge, and credentials, competency-based pay includes cognitive or subjective measures not usually considered in evaluating a job. Characteristics like an individual's values, motives, personality traits, self-image, and even social role are included. Because the definition is so inclusive, it is very difficult for compensation specialists and managers to put a dollar value on this model. It is important to note that competencies are independent of the job and can be taken from job to job by the individual.

Executive Pay

The Enron scandals of 2001 brought increased attention to CEO compensation and stock option programs. Some question whether any CEO is worth the pay packages that for some total over $500 million annually.

When it comes to executive-level pay, the mantra is to "pay for performance." Data on executive pay are annually provided by *BusinessWeek*'s Executive Pay Scorecard, *The Wall Street Journal*/Mercer Human Resources CEO Compensation survey, a Pearl Meyer & Partners analysis for *The New York Times,* CEO Pay Survey, and a *USA Today* analysis. These sources have put a bright spotlight on executive-level pay.[70]

The 2004 *BusinessWeek* data indicated that CEO compensation averaged $9.6 million—a 15 percent increase from $8.3 million in 2003. *The New York Times* analysis conducted by Pearl Meyer & Partners found that CEOs at the 179 companies it studied are paid on average $9.8 million, an increase of 12 percent from 2003. In spite of these fairly large annual increases there is some evidence that executive pay is being tied more closely to performance than it was in pre-Enron scandal years.

CEO compensation in 50 top-performing manufacturing firms, which included base salary, bonus, and long-term incentives, shows a stronger relationship with pay and performance. Exhibit 11-5 illustrates the pay–performance connection more clearly.

As these manufacturing CEOs know firsthand, boards of directors and investors are demanding a stronger pay–performance relationship than a few years ago. At General Electric Co. the board tied the equity portion of Jeffrey Immelt's (chairperson and CEO)[71] compensation to the company's cash generation performance and to total shareholder return meeting or beating the Standard & Poor's 500. At the same time, grants to managers below GE's senior executive level, previously 100 percent stock options, became a combination of 60 percent stock options and 40 percent restricted stock.

Mercer Human Resource Consulting's study of 350 of the largest U.S. publicly held firms also shows across industry sectors that the popularity of stock options is waning.[72] Exhibit 11-6 presents CEO compensation by business sector. The Mercer survey found that CEOs receiving stock options fell, from $295 million in 2002 to $278 million in 2003 to $273 million in 2004. More and more boards of directors want to carefully review the portfolio of long-term incentives awarded to senior executives.

In a specific attack on the flaws that still exist in setting executive-level compensation, Bebchuk and Fried contend that managers still use their power over boards of directors to obtain higher compensation. That is, they decouple pay from performance.

EXHIBIT 11-5
Pay–Performance Connection in Manufacturing

Source: DolmatConnell and Partners Inc.

Base Salary	
2004	$834,000
2003	$775,000
Change	+7.6%
Bonus	
2004	$1,410,000
2003	$1,131,000
Change	+24.7%
Long-Term Incentives	
2004	$5,461,000
2003	$3,589,000
Change	+52.2%

Company Financial Results	
Revenue Growth	
2004	+14%
2003	+13%
Net Income Growth	
2004	+17%
2003	+19%
Total Shareholder Return	
2004	+20%
2003	$3,589,000

Executive compensation has been growing dramatically for the past two decades. Certainly it has grown much faster than that of the average worker. In 2003 the average company CEO made 500 times what the average worker made.[73] In 1991 this gap was about 140 times.

Lead Hollywood actors routinely earn over $10 million per film. The National Basketball Association's players' average salary is over $4 million per year. These types of salaries

EXHIBIT 11-6
CEO Compensation by Business Sectors

Source: Mercer Human Resource Consulting. Sample is the 350 largest U.S. publicly traded firms. Total direct compensation includes base salary, annual bonus, and long-term incentive grant values (including the binomial value of stock options, restricted stock, and other long-term initiatives).

			% Change from 2003		
Sector	Salary & Bonus (S&B)	Total Direct Comp (TDC)	S&B	TDC	Company
Basic Materials	$2,200,000	$5,529,600	58.2%	21.7%	64.8%
Consumer Goods	$3,425,000	$9,575,500	25.0%	33.1%	18.8%
Consumer Services	$1,698,100	$5,075,200	8.7%	1.7%	10.2%
Financial	$3,129,600	$8,471,400	5.2%	2.2%	17.6%
Health Care	$2,202,500	$10,343,600	4.8%	7.4%	13.7%
Industrials	$2,183,300	$5,766,600	24.9%	28.6%	40.8%
Oil & Gas	$3,900,000	$10,594,600	15.3%	29.9%	78.0%
Technology	$2,181,900	$8,766,000	11.5%	15.2%	82.1%
Telecommunications	$3,228,900	$16,382,500	0.5%	−3.6%	0.3%
Utilities	$1,899,000	$4,984,400	8.1%	10.4%	16.4%

involve negotiation at arm's length with their employees. Executives, on the other hand, can and do in many cases establish their own compensation.

Executive compensation in many cases had been excessive for a number of reasons.[74] First, many boards of directors are passive and do not play an active or questioning role in setting executive compensation. Second, executive pay is higher than would be obtained under thorough and intense arm's-length bargaining. Thus, the pay is less sensitive to actual performance. Third, the compensation portion is in many cases a less significant amount of the total pay amount. Finally, salary and nonperformance compensation packets lack incentives that align managers and shareholder interests.[75]

Bebchuk and Fried's theory and explanation of "too much pay for nonperformance" suggests a number of steps to improve the link between pay and performance. A stock option is a right granted by a corporation to an individual to purchase a specific number of shares of stock at the firm at a predetermined price during a specified period of time. For example, a CEO or an employee could receive a grant of options, with an exercise equal to the market price on the date of the grant, with a period of time (e.g., 10 years) in which to exercise the option or purchase the stock.

Theoretically, stock options allow employees to share in the future growth of the value of a company without risking their money until they exercise the options to buy the shares. In many cases, the gain on a stock option is substantially greater than a person's annual compensation. Stock options are not taxed at the time they are available; rather a person pays taxes only when the option is exercised and/or the stock is sold.

Issues in Compensation Administration

Managers must make policy decisions on three issues in compensation administration. These issues involve the extent to which (1) compensation will be secret, (2) compensation will be secure, and (3) pay is compressed.

Pay Secrecy or Openness

A debatable compensation issue is the extent to which the pay of employees is known by others in the enterprise. How would you feel if your co-workers could find out what you make? Would you care? As with other issues, opinions differ.

There are degrees of secretiveness and openness on pay. In many institutions and organizations, pay ranges and even an individual's pay are open to the public and fellow employees. Examples are the public sector (federal, state, and local governments), some universities, and unionized wage employees. This is called the **open system.**

The opposite is the **secret system,** in which pay is regarded as privileged information known only to the employee, her or his superior, and staff employees such as HRM and payroll. In the most secrecy-oriented organizations, employees are told they cannot discuss pay matters and, specifically, their own pay. The National Labor Relations Board has ruled that this is not a legitimate policy. Corporate presidents differ in their preferences for full disclosure of employee compensation. For example, Robert Howell, TeleCheck Services, believes that an open pay system is a means of improving productivity, whereas Kenneth Porter of Can-Am Groups thinks open pay schemes just increase employees' dissatisfaction.[76]

There is increasing recognition that some employees want a more open pay system. Opening up a system and providing more information to employees certainly have costs and benefits. However, if an organization wishes to reduce the manipulative aura surrounding pay, actual or perceived, it must share additional information about pay with employees. As firms post job openings to make employees aware of opportunities, information on pay becomes a critical decision.

As a step in deciding how much secrecy or how much openness is needed, managers first must clearly determine through observation (listening, talking, discussion in groups) what their employees want to know about pay. Then managers must decide if providing that information will harm or benefit the firm. Finally, the conditions cited above concerning the objective measuring of performance, degree of interdependence, and causal relationships to performance must be carefully weighed.

Pay Security

Current compensation can motivate performance. So can the belief that there will be future security in compensation. Various plans for providing this security have been developed: a guaranteed annual wage, supplementary unemployment benefits, cost-of-living allowances (COLAs), severance pay, seniority rules, and employment contracts.

A few companies provide a **guaranteed annual wage (GAW)** to employees who meet certain characteristics. For this type of plan to work, general employee–management relations must be good, and the demand for the product or service must be steady. The best known such plans are those of Procter & Gamble, Hormel Meats, and the Nunn-Bush Shoe Company. In one plan, the employer guarantees the employee a certain number of weeks of work at a certain wage after the worker has passed a probation period (say, two years). Morton Salt Company guarantees 80 percent of full-time work to all employees after one year of standard employment. Procter & Gamble has invoked its emergency clause only once since 1923—in 1933, for a brief period at three plants. In the Hormel and Spiegel plans and others, a minimum income is guaranteed.[77]

In the **supplementary unemployment benefits (SUB)** approach, the employer adds to unemployment compensation payments to help the employee achieve income security, if not job security (as in the GAW). The automobile, steel, rubber, garment, and glass industries, among others, contribute to a fund from which laid-off employees are paid. During the recession of 1973–1974, many of these funds in the auto industry went bankrupt. They provide less income security than was thought. But studies of plans in which unemployment was less severe show that the system has helped.

Cost-of-living adjustments (COLAS) are wage increases or decreases pegged to the rise or fall in the cost of living.[78] In a COLA plan, data from the Bureau of Labor Statistics are used to make wage and salary adjustments. The consumer price index (CPI), which measures changes in the price of a hypothetical "basket" of goods and services, is used as a cost-of-living index. The adjustment is not based on performance of the firm. The COLA was created by unions to protect members from erosion of real wages when inflation rates were high. Union contracts were negotiated to contain an escalator clause that permitted an annual review of wages and a pay raise if the increase in the cost of living warranted it. Nonunion firms also adopted the COLA. Many firms have used the COLA to compensate employees who are relocated to a high-cost location. These COLAs are usually phased out over a specified time, in the belief that annual raises and promotions will meet the increased living costs of the area.[79] The Bureau of Labor Statistics and the American Compensation Association report that the difference between salary increases and the CPI has been between 0 and 1.4 percent in the last five years. Employees have begun to feel entitled to COLAS, so this negligible difference between base pay and true merit is not enough to motivate higher performances.[80]

In many organizations, the employer provides an income bridge from employment to unemployment and back to employment. This is **severance pay.** Typically, it amounts to one week's pay for each year of service. About 25 percent of union contracts require such severance pay. It doesn't guarantee a job, but it helps the employee when a job is lost.

A week after Mary and Joe discussed her suggestions for the compensation plan, Guido and Mary found Joe in his office. He'd spent much of the time since their last meeting at the branch offices—very unusual behavior for him.

Guido   Boss, are you free?

Joe   I'm glad to see you and Mary. I was just thinking about how we could make our compensation system here at the bank more equitable. Maybe some of your suggestions will help us deal with high turnover and low productivity.

Mary   Great! What things do you think we should change?

Joe   I've already appointed John Bolts to investigate who is letting out the salary information around here. I think that we should try to maintain pay secrecy. I'm very interested in that new variable pay plan you mentioned. I think skill-based pay is the way to go instead of our old annual raise system. The most important thing is to get all of our employees involved in contributing to the bottom line. So I'd like you to design a suggestion system too. Let's get this bank ready for the 21st century.

Guido and Mary   Right, boss.

In times of layoff, the basic security for most employees is their seniority. If an organization is unionized, the contract normally specifies how seniority is to be computed. Seniority guarantees jobs (and thus compensation) to employees with the longest continuous employment in the organization or work unit. Even in nonunionized situations, a strong seniority norm prevails, which gives some security to senior employees.

Pay Compression

Pay compression occurs when employees perceive too narrow a difference between their own pay and that of their colleagues.[81] Many companies in the United States face a narrowing of a gap between senior and junior employees and between supervisors and subordinates.[82] Differentials of 10 percent or less are not unusual, and in some instances junior employees are brought in at salaries greater than those of their superiors. The resulting low morale can lead to decreasing productivity and higher absenteeism and turnover. One way to identify pay compression is to examine the relationship between salaries and incumbents' years of experience with the company.

Solutions for the problem of pay compression include the following: (1) reexamining how many entry-level people are needed; (2) reassessing recruitment itself; (3) focusing on the job evaluation process, emphasizing performance instead of salary-grade assignment; (4) basing all salaries on longevity; (5) giving first-line supervisors and other managers the authority to recommend equity adjustments for incumbents who have been unfairly victimized by pay compression; and (6) limiting the hiring of new employees seeking excessive salaries.[83]

Summary

Chapter 11 has continued the discussion of compensation by presenting some important issues: individual pay determination, methods of payment, variable pay, incentive forms of pay, new pay innovations, executive pay, and compensation administration issues. Chapter 12 will complete the discussion of the compensation system by covering all forms of indirect compensation (both mandatory and voluntary benefits).

To summarize the main points covered in this chapter:

1. Determining individual pay involved asking the question, "How should one employee be paid relative to another doing the same job?"

2. Methods of payment include

    a. Flat rates

    b. Pay for time worked (wages and salaries)

3. There is a growing realization that traditional pay systems do not effectively link pay to performance. The trend is toward a total compensation approach made up of base pay, variable pay, and indirect pay or benefits.

4. Flexibility is an essential ingredient in any compensation plan and can be built using a variable pay approach.

5. Methods for paying employees on the basis of output are usually referred to as incentive forms of pay. These include merit pay, individual incentives, team incentives, and organizationwide incentives.

6. The most widely used plan for managing individual performance is merit pay.

7. Individual incentives pay the employee on the basis of units produced or dollar value of sales. Methods include straight piecework, standard-hour plan, differential piece rate (Taylor plan), commission, and production bonus systems.

8. Team incentives are used to build a team culture, with rewards provided on a group basis.

9. Organizationwide incentives, where rewards are based on shared profits generated through employees' efforts or on money saved as a result of employees' efforts to reduce costs, are the most common incentive pay systems.

10. Suggestion systems can improve employee relations, foster high-quality products, reduce costs, and increase revenue.

11. Gainsharing incentive plans, including the Lincoln Electric plan, Scanlon plan, Rucker plan, ImproShare, business plan gainsharing, and winsharing, are companywide group incentive plans that unite employees to improve organizational effectiveness through a financial formula for distributing organizationwide gains.

12. Spot gainsharing plans focus on a specific problem in a specific department rather than on improving performance throughout the whole organization.

13. The most critical factor in the success of any gainsharing plan is employees' involvement.

14. Profit-sharing plans distribute a fixed percentage of total organizational profit to employees in the form of cash or deferred bonuses.

15. Person-based pay designs like skilled-based, knowledge-based, credential-based, feedback, and competency-based pay are alternatives to job-based pay that set pay levels on the basis of how many skills an employee has, how much knowledge an employee acquires, and the like.

16. CEO pay is a very important consideration in designing comparative-performance reward packages that are fair to all employees.

17. Managers make policy decisions on three compensation administration issues: pay secrecy, pay security, and pay compression.

Key Terms

commission, *p. 332*
competency-based pay, *p. 341*
cost-of-living adjustment (COLA), *p. 344*
credential-based pay, *p. 340*
differential piece rate (Taylor plan), *p. 331*
feedback pay, *p. 341*
gainsharing plans, *p. 335*
guaranteed annual wage (GAW), *p. 344*

knowledge-based pay, *p. 340*
merit pay, *p. 330*
open system, *p. 343*
pay compression, *p. 345*
production bonus system, *p. 332*
profit-sharing plans, *p. 339*
salary, *p. 328*
secret system, *p. 343*
severance pay, *p. 344*

skill-based pay, *p. 340*
spot gainsharing, *p. 338*
standard-hour plan, *p. 331*
straight piecework, *p. 331*
suggestion system, *p. 333*
supplementary unemployment benefits (SUB), *p. 344*
total compensation approach, *p. 330*
variable pay, *p. 330*
wage, *p. 328*

Questions for Discussion and Review

1. Should the federal government regulate and control executive compensation? Why?
2. What are some of the advantages and the disadvantages of a merit-based compensation system?
3. Is pay compression a potential problem in terms of employee morale? Why?
4. Why are more firms not using the Lincoln Electric compensation-type plan?
5. What gainsharing system do you believe is the most effective? Why?
6. Explain why executive stock option plans became very popular in the 1990s? Should stock option plans be used as a part of executive compensation packages? Why?
7. How can a person's acquisition of knowledge be determined so that his or her pay can be changed? Explain.
8. Explain the meaning and intent of a feedback pay system.
9. Explain the concept of a variable pay system.
10. Outline a plan to develop a fair and equitable compensation system.

HRM legal Advisor

Based on *Scaling Equipment Products Co., Inc.* v. *Al Velarde,* 644 So. 2d 904 (Supreme Court of Alabama 1994).

The Facts

On April 20, 1989, Al Velarde received an offer letter from Sealing Equipment Products Co., Inc. (SEPCO), a manufacturer and distributor of fluid sealing products. The letter offered Mr. Velarde a position as an international sales representative for Latin America and South America, and indicated that "commissions would be paid on all sales shipped to these markets" and that monthly sales reports would be sent to Mr. Velarde for his review. Mr. Velarde began work for SEPCO on May 1, 1989. On July 21, 1989, Mr. Velarde met with the president of SEPCO who orally promised that Mr. Velarde would serve as SEPCO's exclusive sales representative in the Latin American and South American markets.

Later that same day, this promise was restated in a letter sent to Mr. Velarde indicating that his "commission rate will be 7 percent of all sales in your territory exceeding a 30 percent gross profit," and that SEPCO would "pay the sales commission of shipments (less credits and freight) two weeks after month end on all sales." Despite repeated requests for the promised monthly sales reports, Mr. Velarde did not receive any such reports until May 1990. Additionally, Mr. Velarde learned that SEPCO had sold some of its products to a New Jersey company, but sent them to a New Jersey packing and forwarding company that shipped the products to a company in Venezuela. When Mr. Velarde requested a commission on the sale, he was informed by SEPCO that the sale was to a domestic account which did not fall into his international territory. Upon SEPCO's refusal to pay the commission, Mr. Velarde resigned in July 1990 and filed a branch of contract and fraud suit against the company in October 1990. Was there a valid contract between SEPCO and Mr. Velarde regarding sales commissions? Should Mr. Velarde receive the sales commission?

The Court's Decision

A jury decided in favor of Mr. Velarde and awarded him $191,552.25 in compensatory and punitive damages. SEPCO appealed the verdict and the case went to the Supreme Court of Alabama. The court upheld the jury's breach of contract verdict, ruling that a contract with ambiguous terms existed, which warranted a jury examination of the facts surrounding the contract. Further, the court found that because SEPCO knew that the products were being shipped to Venezuela, there was sufficient evidence to support the fraud claim.

Human Resource Implications

In drafting compensation contracts, companies should make the language as specific as possible and adhere to it. Mr. Velarde's offer letter stated that SEPCO would pay him commissions on all sales shipped to Latin America or South America. Because the letter's language could reasonably have had more than one meaning, a jury was charged with determining the appropriate interpretation. The result was a costly verdict for SEPCO.

Notes

1. George Milkovich and Jerry M. Newman (2005), *Compensation* (Burr Ridge, IL: McGraw-Hill/Irwin).
2. Fay Hansen (May–June 2002), "Currents in Compensation and Benefits," *Compensation and Benefits Review,* pp. 7–14.
3. Ibid.
4. Mark Poerio and Eric Keller (June 2005), "Executive Compensation 2005: Many Forces, One Direction," *Compensation & Benefits Review,* pp. 41–45.
5. Lynn Summers (January–February 2005), "Integrated Pay for Performance: The High-Tech Marriage of Compensation Management and Performance Management," *Compensation Benefits News,* pp. 18–25.
6. Steven E. Gross and Jeffrey P. Bacher (January–February 1993), "The New Variable Pay Programs: How Some Succeed, Why Some Don't," *Compensation and Benefits Review,* Vol. 25, Iss. 1, p. 51.
7. Patricia K. Zingheim (July–August 2002), "Pay Changes Going Forward," *Compensation and Benefits Review,* pp. 48–53.
8. Lawrence A. Juebbers (September 1999), "Laying the Foundation for Global Compensation," *Workforce,* pp. 1–4.
9. David Kilpatrick (April 15, 2002), "After the Accolades, Now What?" *Fortune,* p. 50.
10. *The 2002–2003 Total Salary Increase Budget Survey* (2002), (New York: World at Work).
11. IOMA (March 2000), "Four Studies Reveal How Alternative Pay Is Being Put to Work," *IOMAs Pay for Performance Report.*
12. Milkovich and Newman, op. cit.
13. Shirley Fung (June 1999), "A Raise by Any Other Name," *Across the Board,* p. 63.
14. David E. Terpstra and Andre Honoree (January–February 2005), "Employees' Responses to Merit Pay Inequity," *Compensation & Benefits Review,* pp. 51–58.
15. "Merit Pay Increase Projections for 2004 Lowered to 34%" (March 2004), *Report on Salary Surveys,* pp. 6–7.
16. Milkovich, op. cit.
17. Lucian A. Bebchuk and Jesse M. Fried (2003), "Executive Compensation as an Agency Problem," *Journal of Economic Perspective,* pp. 71–92.
18. Ibid.
19. Sarah W Peck (June 2004), "The Carrot versus the Stick: The Role of Incentive Compensation and Debt Obligations in the Success of LBOs," *American Business Review,* pp. 1–11.
20. Milkovich and Newman, op. cit.
21. Ibid., p. 341.
22. J. Pfeffer (May–June 1998), "Six Dangerous Myths about Pay," *Harvard Business Review,* pp. 109–119.
23. "The Value of Pay Data on the Web" (September 2000), *Workspan,* pp. 25–28.
24. "How Companies Are Preparing to Modify Compensation Plans" (March 2005), *Report on Salary Survey,* pp. 1–6.

25. Jerry Ledford, Paul Mulvey, and Peter Leblanc (2000), *The Rewards of Work: What Employees Value* (Scottsdale, AZ: World at Work).

26. T. R. Mitchell and A. E. Mickey (July 1999), "The Meaning of Money: An Individual Differences Perspective," *Academy of Management Review,* pp. 568–578.

27. Milkovich and Newman, op. cit.

28. Douglas P. O'Bannon and Craig L. Pearce (Fall 1999), "An Exploratory Examination of Gainsharing in Service Organizations: Implication for Citizenship and Behavior and Pay Satisfaction," *Journal of Managerial Issues,* pp. 363–378.

29. Andrea R. Drake, Susan F. Haka, and Sue P. Ravenscroft (July 1999), "Cost System and Incentive Structure Effects on Innovation, Efficiency, and Profitability in Teams," *Accounting Review,* pp. 323–345.

30. Vincent Alonzo, Kenneth Hein, Ari Zeyer, Jeannie Casison (April 1999), "1999 Motivator of the Year," *Incentive,* pp. 39–46.

31. H. Heinemann and T. Judge (2000), "Pay and Employee Satisfaction," *Compensation in Organizations: Current Research & Practice,* S. L. Rynes and B. Gerhart (Eds.) (San Francisco: Jossey-Bass).

32. David J. Teece (2002), *Managing Intellectual Capital* (New York: Oxford).

33. Michael J. Polzin (Spring 1998), "Employee Suggestion Systems: Boosting Productivity and Profits," *Human Resource Planning,* pp. 49–50.

34. Paul E. Tesluk, Robert J. Vance, and John E. Mathieu (September 1999), "Examining Employee Involvement in the Context of Participative Work Environment," *Group & Organization Management,* pp. 271–299.

35. David Levine, D. Belman, G. Charness, E. Groshen, and K. C. O'Shaughnessy (2001), *The New Employment Contract: Evidence from How Little Wage Structures Have Changed* (Kalamazoo: Upjohn Institute).

36. Lloyd Geoffrey (August 1999), "Stuff the Suggestions Box," *Total Quality Management,* pp. 869–875.

37. Doreen Mangen (February 1992), "It's Just a Suggestion," *Small Business Reports,* 17, 2, pp. 30–40.

38. S. L. Rynes and B. Gerhart (Eds.) (2000), *Compensation in Organizations: Current Research & Practice* (San Francisco: Jossey-Bass).

39. Ibid.

40. Michael E. Trunko (February 1993), "Open to Suggestions," *HR Magazine,* Vol. 38, Iss. 2, pp. 88–89.

41. Peter T. Chingos (Ed) (2004), *Responsible Executive Compensation for a New Era of Accountability* (San Francisco: Jossey-Bass).

42. Jim McDermott (April 2000), "Employee Incentives That Work," *Cabinet Maker,* pp. 42–44.

43. Ibid.

44. Milkovich and Newman, op. cit.

45. www.lincolnelectric.com/corporate/about/history.asp accessed on July 5, 2005.

46. P. Zingheim and J. R. Schuster (2000), *Pay People Right* (San Francisco: Jossey-Bass).

47. Ibid.

48. Ibid.

49. Ibid.

50. Ibid.

51. Ibid.

52. Ibid.

53. Thomas M. Welbourne and Luis R. Gomez Mejia (1995), "Gainsharing: A Critical Review and a Future Research Agenda," *Journal of Management* 21, 3, pp. 559–609.

54. Barry W. Thomas and Madeline Hess Olson (1988), "Gainsharing: The Design Guarantees Success," *Personnel Journal* 67, 5, pp. 73–79.

55. B. J. Hall (March–April 2000), "What You Need to Know about Stock Options," *Harvard Business Review,* pp. 121–129.

56. D. Kruse and J. Blasi (April 2000), "Employee Ownership, Employee Attributes and Firm Performance," *Journal of Employee Ownership, Law, and Finance,* pp. 37–48.

57. Ibid.

58. Sheldon H. Smith (September 1999), "In Vogue Compensation Plans," *Trusts & Estates,* pp. 20–30.

59. An Introduction to ESOPs (1999), NCEO (National Center of Employee Ownership), http://www.nceo.org/nceo/intro.htm.

60. Milkovich and Newman, op. cit.

61. Chingos, op. cit.

62. Ibid.

63. Bebchuk and Fried, op. cit.

64. Hugh Bucknell Mercer (2005), *Magic Numbers for Human Resource Management* (San Francisco: Jossey-Bass).

65. Ibid.

66. Ibid.

67. Theodore R. Buyinski (1995), "Feedback Pay: Compensation as a Business Management Tool," *Compensation and Benefits Review,* Vol. 27, Iss. 3, pp. 62–70.

68. Ibid.

69. Howard Risher (Ed.) (1999), *Aligning Pay and Results* (New York: American Management Association).

70. John S. McClenahen (July 2005), "The New Rules," *Industry Week,* pp. 40–48.

71. Ibid.

72. Ibid.

73. Cambridge Law Article on Executive Compensation (December 11, 2004), "CEOs and Their Indian Rope Trick," *Economist,* p. 61.

74. Stephen M. Bainbridge (May 2005), "Executive Compensation: Who Decides?" *Texas Law Review,* pp. 1605–1662.

75. Ibid.

76. "How to Avoid 'Fallout' from Pay Compression" (November 2004), *HR Focus,* pp. 3–4.

77. Scott Seegart and Brian H. Kleiner (May–June 1993), "The Future of Labor Management Relations," *Industrial Management* 35, 3, pp. 15–16.

78. Mike Losey, Sue Meisinger, and Dave Ulrich (Eds) (2005), *The Future of Human Resource Management: 64 Thought Leaders Explore the Critical HR Issues of Today and Tomorrow* (San Francisco: Jossey-Bass).

79. Mary Koskoski (November 2000), "Alternate CPI Aggregations: Two Approaches," *Monthly Labor Review,* pp. 31–39.

80. Ibid.

81. Ibid.

82. Todd Manes and Dennis M. Graham, *Creating a Total Rewards Strategy: A Tool Kit for Designing Business Based Plans,* New York: American Management Association, 2003.

83. Ibid.

Application Case 11-1

Customizing Bonus Pay Plans

Navigant Consulting Inc., a Chicago-based management consultancy, is the product of more than 25 acquisitions over six years. No wonder that, until recently, its short-term incentive-pay system was seriously flawed. There was no consistent method of rewarding performance.

"It was difficult to manage so many disparate incentive tools," says Julie Howard, vice president and human-capital officer. "It was a mess." Even companies with only one system are struggling to make it more effective.

So last summer Navigant redesigned the system. Its short-term cash bonus plan now consists of two basic elements: Incentive pay for Navigant's 400 senior professionals is based largely on the company's performance, while its 800 consulting and administrative staff are rewarded primarily according to individual performance.

It's too soon to tell fully what effect the change has had, though already the company is seeing reduced attrition. The hope is that the incentive plan will help the nearly $600 million (in sales) company recover from years of losses. So far, "people are very excited about it," says Howard, who has been touring the country to explain the program to employees. "Clarity is a big thing."

Navigant is one of an increasing number of companies that now offer incentive pay to many non-management personnel, linking pay more closely to performance, as it shifts from fixed to more-variable annual compensation. In a survey of 2,400 companies last year, consulting firm William M. Mercer found that 56 percent provided incentive pay to employees below the executive level (65 percent when nonprofit health care companies were excluded).

But companies clearly are struggling to design their incentive programs in an effective way. The soul-searching is aimed at motivating employees up and down the line to help companies meet their overall goals. Of course, plan specifics vary with a company's culture, size, industry, and competitive position. But any winning formula must address the following question: To what degree should payouts be linked to the performance of the corporation as a whole; to that of an employee's division, plant, team, or project; to the achievement of individual goals; or to some combination of all of these?

Consultants say incentive programs on the leading edge are combining goals and custom-fitting the combination to the rank of employees, much the way Navigant has done. At stake is nothing less than a company's ability to compete, and that challenge will only grow as the economy slows. No surprise then that CFOs are getting more deeply involved in design efforts. As the overseers of human resources, they view payroll expense increasingly as an investment in human capital, and incentive compensation as something that can improve the returns on that investment.

Unfortunately, theory does not translate easily into practice: In one survey of 771 companies, management and HR consulting firm Towers Perrin found that less than a third of companies with incentive programs of any kind see a significant impact on results. Navigant nonetheless has high hopes for its new plan. If the revised incentive system is as effective as the company expects, says CFO Ben Perks, who helped align the new plan with the company's goals, "it's a win/win/win—for the employees, the company, and the shareholders."

Navigant isn't alone. Ever since the end of the recession of the early 1990s, companies have been struggling to attract, motivate, and retain employees without greatly increasing fixed costs. Merit raises alone, however, have been insufficient to achieve those goals; the measly 4.2 percent on average that U.S. companies have budgeted in recent years for annual raises does not allow for significant differentiation among employees, according to Mercer. Long-term incentives such as stock options and restricted stock, meanwhile, may be more effective as a retention tool than as a goad to performance, and may be ineffectual in any case unless the market rebounds.

Incentive pay added to raises fills the gap, enabling companies to hand out greater rewards to deserving employees while minimizing costs, since the incentive shrinks in bad times. For greater cost savings, some employers are going so far as to replace raises with incentives over a phase-in period of a few years. Others have even reduced base pay for new workers while dressing up incentives.

Consultants believe that as the economy slows, the trend toward more variable pay will continue. Global competition remains strong, and in a downturn, there will be a need to improve productivity.

Indeed, companies may begin taking advantage of workers' growing job insecurity to implement new incentive plans that reduce base pay in return for greater potential incentive rewards. Already, says Steve Gross, who heads the U.S. compensation consulting practice at Mercer, more troubled companies "are saying, 'If you don't accept these plans, we're going to move the work offshore.'" For others, employee retention will remain a driving factor. " 'It took so much energy to hire these folks, we don't want to make them unhappy,'" he adds.

So far, according to the latest data available, incentive systems typically pay bonuses to all eligible employees based on the overall profitability of the company, at least among large companies. The Towers Perrin report found that 44 percent of the companies surveyed—the largest segment for any incentive plan type—used organizationwide incentive plans in which payouts were linked to a companywide measure, and distributions were made from a pool in proportion to salary. This approach is not only straightforward, it also sends a clear message that "we're all in this together."

To be sure, many companies have been raising the bar in this area. Instead of paying out bonuses whenever a company achieves profitability, programs increasingly hold out until the company reaches a specified profit level. At that threshold, the company either begins paying a preset ratio of profits earned beyond that point or a predetermined bonus pool.

Consider a plan started by The Boeing Co., which has been under growing competitive pressure. Boeing's program, its first broad-based incentive scheme for 88,000 nonexecutive, nonunion employees, is based entirely on the achievement of a predetermined level of annual corporate performance—net profit minus a certain charge (which the company would not specify). In the first year employees could earn an extra 5 days of pay—on top of annual raises and rewards for some employees involved in certain projects—if the company met the target, and up to 10 days' pay if the company exceeded it. In the end, employees earned 7.85 extra days of pay.

"The intent was to offer the opportunity for all nonunion Boeing employees to share in the success of the company and get employees to think more like owners of the company," says Bruce Hanson, Boeing's manager of compensation and benefits. The program's message, he says, is "a shared-destiny message, as a company to move Boeing toward its overall profit target. We want you to be engaged, ask questions, offer suggestions to the organization" to help reach that profit. The message was reinforced by the company's decision to use the same performance metric in figuring executives' incentive pay—an amount that is then modified by an executive's individual performance against his or her preset goals. Another reinforcement: for this year, the board doubled the potential incentive reward.

But tying bonuses to corporate-level results has a potential downside. While the top officers and even division managers spend their days on activities that directly affect a company's sales and profits, lower-level employees have little influence on overall results. The goal, therefore, is not within what consultants like to call their "line of sight." Furthermore, this kind of incentive system—as well as those based purely on the performance of the employee's plant or division— can breed resentment from those who believe they work harder than others who receive the same rewards.

Yet fewer companies link bonuses to each individual's performance on one or more specific activities. Among those that do is a retailer that pays sales clerks double time for any sick days they don't use. "You pay out if behavior milestones are achieved, regardless of profits, which is pretty direct and understandable," says Carl Weinberg, a principal at Unifi Network, the HR consulting subsidiary of PricewaterhouseCoopers.

One obvious drawback: Companies may find themselves paying out bonuses at a time when the company has no profits and cannot afford extra payments. What's more, Weinberg says, "there's the risk that people will ignore other behaviors that you're not rewarding."

Yet companies such as Boeing recognize that they need to do more to motivate lower-level employees than tie incentive pay to corporatewide goals. Plant managers, Hanson says, are encouraged to translate the overall corporate economic profit target into goals specific to their factories, such as cost savings and additional revenue. "We're continuously trying to do a better job at that," he says.

Other companies are going a step further by adding team and individual targets that must also be met to reap the full reward. And the resulting incentive brew is increasingly the norm. The Towers Perrin survey indicates that 62 percent of companies with organizationwide incentive plans include an "individual performance modifier," in which an employee is measured against preestablished personal goals for the year. By providing rewards for such specific goals, these employers are trying to directly influence an employee's behavior.

In these multitarget programs, the higher the rank of the employee, the more the bonus is linked to broader financial goals; the lower the rank, the more the bonus is linked to team or individual measures of operational performance as well as financial measures. Usually no bonuses are paid out to anyone unless the company makes a profit or reaches a threshold profit level, and then the size of an employee's bonus is based on that individual's performance against his or her personal goals. The link to corporate profits allows everyone a broader perspective and the ability to make decisions in light of the company's overall objectives.

Typically, each employee receives a scorecard listing a few goals for the coming year, against which the employee's manager measures progress during the year. The challenge is to set the goals correctly. First, the scorecard shouldn't have too many—consultants advise three to five at most. Then, of course, the goals have to be the right ones for the company.

Consider the case of kitchen-cabinet maker American Woodmark Corp., which implemented an incentive pay system for its 3,500 employees. Previously, the Winchester, Virginia–based company had given employees just one annual priority. But it found that because workers were so focused on meeting that goal, they were neglecting other important concerns. For instance, the company found that when it instructed its managers to design incentives that would improve quality, productivity declined.

SoAmerican Woodmark adopted the scorecard approach, in which each employee's scorecard states goals for the company as a whole as well as goals specific to the employee's plant. "The scorecard allows us to get all of the key priorities defined," says William Brandt, chairman of the $400 million (in sales) company.

Companywide goals are divided into the areas of cost, quality, delivery, and safety. Lower-level goals are set to support those, so that if each of the 11 plants meets its targets, the result will be the achievement of the companywide targets. And if each team at a plant meets its targets, they will add up to that plant's targets, and so on down to the individual level.

According to consultants, the biggest potential problem with multitarget plans is their complexity. With so many different targets—qualitative as well as quantitative—they are tough to manage. But the hardest part is setting them up in the first place. "The biggest hurdle for companies to clear is to set goals, to determine job by job and person by person what the right goals are," says Laury Sejen, a compensation consultant at Watson Wyatt Worldwide.

That, indeed, is what Navigant's financial and HR executives faced last year when redesigning its compensation system.

Success is hardly guaranteed. In its survey, Towers Perrin found that only 20 percent of companies with individual incentives and 31 percent with team incentives reported that their pay-for-performance plans had a significant impact on business results. But results were even worse for companies with organizationwide incentive goals: only 17 percent reported such improvement.

Still, some prominent management theorists believe that no variable-pay plan can work well. W. Edwards Deming, the famed management guru, believed that variable pay forced companies to rank workers against each other, setting up a competitive environment that could lead employees to work against each other.

However, communication may make a big difference. For starters, employees must know at the beginning of the year exactly what their bonus will be tied to. In fact, says Sejen, "our recommendation for best practice is for the manager and the employee to have a conversation" about appropriate individual goals. "The concept of employee buy-in is important."

During the year, "feedback has to be frequent," says William Abernathy, an incentive pay consultant who runs his own firm, Abernathy & Associates, in Memphis. "Annual is useless."

At American Woodmark, a team's performance relative to certain goals is posted daily or sometimes even hourly, Brandt says. Boeing delivers quarterly reports to employees on how well the company is performing against its target, and what that might mean in terms of potential extra days' pay at year-end.

In the end, says Abernathy, a good plan requires lots of planning, and with that comes complexity. "You can make it easy," he says, "but it won't work."

Discussion Questions

1. Why is it important to include operating employees (nonmanagers) in the development and use of an incentive program?
2. What is the individual performance modifier that the Towers Perrin survey identified? Explain it in managerial terms.
3. American Woodmark's scorecard approach can be most effectively used with what type of organizations? Employees?

Source: Adapted from Richard D. Landsberg (May 2005), "Executive Bonus: Carve Up or Carve Out? Make the Rules Work for You!" *Journal of Financial Service Professionals,* p. 12-1; Hilary Rosenberg, (June 2001), "Building a Better Carrot," *CFO Magazine,* pp. 8–14; and Michael K. Ozanian and Elizabeth MacDonald (May 9, 2000), "Paychecks on Steroids," *Forbes,* p. 134.

Employee Benefits and Services

Learning Objectives

After studying this chapter you should be able to:

1. **Define** indirect financial compensation.
2. **Explain** why organizations provide benefits and services to employees.
3. **Differentiate** between mandated and voluntary benefits.
4. **Describe** the various types of benefits and services offered by most American companies.
5. **Explain** how to manage an effective benefits program.

Internet/Web Resources

General Sites

www.abr.com

www.the401k.com

www.troweprice.com

www.ifebp.org/jobs

Company Sites

www.arco.com

www.alcoa.com

Career Challenge

Carl Reems was the president of Coy Manufacturing of Whiting, Indiana. It was Carl's intention to keep his workforce as satisfied and productive as possible. A number of problems concerning the Coy employee benefits and services package had come to a head over the past few months. Carl listened to a presentation that Pete Lakich, Coy's director of human resources, made to the firm's executive committee. In the presentation, Pete used some figures that seemed wrong to Carl. Pete claimed that in manufacturing firms in the Whiting area (located just southeast of Chicago), the average cost of benefits and services per worker totaled $7,400. In fact, Pete gave a specific item-by-item breakdown of these costs to the committee.

After the meeting, Carl had this talk with Pete:

Carl   Pete, where did you get those benefit figures? They seem wrong.

Pete   Carl, these are facts based on my program of monitoring costs.

Carl   We must be paying the highest benefits in the entire area!

Pete   As a matter of fact, we're on the low end of the scale. Among similar firms in our area we are in the bottom third in benefit costs.

Carl   Do you think this is one of the reasons we're not able to recruit and hold skilled employees?

Pete   I'm not certain, but there's probably some connection. You know how employees exchange and compare information about wages, benefits, and services.

Carl   Let's look at the entire range of our benefits and services and see what's needed to become more competitive. We could probably even improve production and morale by improving benefits and services.

Pete   We do need to take a look, but we can't be so certain that more and better benefits and services can make productivity and morale jump up. Most of our employees don't even know what benefits cost.

Carl   Pete, you're just too conservative about the power of money. The carrot and the stick can always do the job, even in Whiting, Indiana.

Pete   Don't jump to conclusions.

Do you agree with Carl or Pete about the motivational power of benefits and services?

Indirect financial compensation is called benefits and services. It can be defined as all employer-provided rewards and services, other than wages or salaries, arising from the following categories: legally required social insurance payments, private insurance, and retirement plans; payment for time not worked; extra cash payments other than bonuses based on performance; and costs of services like subsidized cafeterias, clothing allowances, and so on.[1] Unlike pay for performance and other incentive plans, most benefits and services are available to workers as long as they are employed by an organization regardless of seniority or performance.

This definition of benefits and services can be applied to thousands of programs. There is a lack of agreement on what is included, purposes served, responsibility for programs, costs and values of the various elements, units in which the costs and values are measured, and criteria for decision making. Decisions about indirect compensation are more complex than those concerned with wages and salaries. Significant changes have occurred in employees' attitudes, corporate philosophies, and business necessities since the inception of most benefits programs in the 1950s. Currently, employers face rising benefits costs resulting from increased legislation, insurers' insolvency, the cost of advanced medical

EXHIBIT 12-1
Changes in Benefits Programs

Then	Now
Nuclear families of working male with female and 2.3 children at home	Double-income families with and without children, and single-head families
Employment for large part of career	Multiple career industry, and job moves
White male–dominated workforce	Multicultural workforce
Cradle-to-grave expectations	Portability issues
Paternalistic employer	Shared responsibility
Entitlement perception of benefits	Benefits as part of total compensation
Low cost of benefits	Benefits costs escalating faster than consumer price index and an employer's ability to pay
Protection for illness	Promotion of wellness
Single set of benefits	Cafeteria and customized benefits programs

technologies, the aging workforce, new immigration, more women in the workforce, and global competitions.[2] Exhibit 12-1 shows some of the changes that have affected benefits programs.

Background

Why Do Employers Offer Benefits and Services?

The programs offered in work organizations today are the product of efforts in this area for the past 60 years. Before World War II, employers offered a few benefits and services because they had the employees' welfare at heart or because they wanted to keep a union out. But most benefit programs began in earnest during the war, when wages were strictly regulated.

The unions pushed for nonwage compensation increases, and they got them. Court cases in the late 1940s confirmed the right of unions to bargain for benefits: *Inland Steel* v. *National Labor Relations Board* (1948) over pensions, and *W. W. Cross* v. *National Labor Relations Board* over insurance. The growth of these programs indicates the extent to which unions have used this right. In 1929, benefits cost the employer 3 percent of total wages and salaries; by 1949, the cost was up to 16 percent; and in the 1970s, it was nearly 30 percent. By 2004, the benefits and services slice of labor costs ranged from 20 to 60 percent of payroll. This figure can be broken down as follows: 8.7 percent of payroll went for legally required social insurance payments, 5.1 percent for private pension plans, 10.3 percent to insurance plans, and the remaining 14 percent for all other types of benefits.[3]

Some employers provide these programs for labor market reasons, that is, to keep the organization competitive in recruiting and retaining employees. Others provide them to keep a union out or because the union has won them during negotiations. Another reason often given for providing benefits and services is that they increase employees' performance. Is this reasoning valid? In a study of benefits, it was found that none of these reasons explained the degree to which benefits and services were provided.[4]

Who Makes Decisions about Benefits?

HR executives often seek professional advice from specialists such as members of the Society of Professional Benefit Administrators. These are independent consultants who are employed by benefit carriers like insurance companies. In very large organizations, the compensation department may have a specialist in benefits, usually called a *manager*

EXHIBIT 12-2
The Role of
Operating and HR
Managers in Benefits
and Services

Benefits and Services Function	Operating Manager (OM)	HR Manager (HRM)
Benefits and services budget	Preliminary budget approved or adjusted by top management	Preliminary budget developed by HRM
Voluntary benefits and services	Programs approved by OM (top management)	Programs recommended by HRM
Communication of benefits and services	OM cooperates with HRM	Primary duty of HRM
Evaluation of benefits and services		Done by HRM
Administration of benefits and services programs		Done by HRM

or *director of employee benefits.* Exhibit 12-2 shows who is involved in decisions about benefits and services within an organization. How these decisions are made is discussed later in the chapter. Many authorities argue that all organizations should have benefits and services, but there is little concrete evidence that they affect employees' productivity or satisfaction.

In the 1940s and 1950s, a major thrust of union bargaining was for increased or innovative benefits. Union pressure for additional holidays was followed by demands for such benefits as group automobile insurance, dental care, and prepaid legal fees. Union leaders have varied the strategy and tactics they use to get "more." The long-range goal is getting employers to perceive benefits not as compensation but as part of their own social responsibility. Today unions are trying desperately to hold all the gains that were made in previous decades and to stop the pervasive erosion of such benefits as pensions and health care.

For over 50 years, public policy has played a role in determining what benefits an employee receives.[5] First, the government mandates (legally requires) certain benefits: old age and survivors' insurance (social security), disability insurance, Medicare, unemployment insurance, and workers' compensation. In addition, through preferential tax treatment, the government encourages businesses to provide other benefits. Current policy allows firms to deduct benefit expenses, and the value of benefits is not counted as current income for employees. Passage of the Welfare Fund Disclosure Act requires descriptions and reports of benefits plans. The National Labor Relations Board and the courts have stringent rules on eligibility for benefits and employers' ability to change an established benefits plan.

Economic and labor market conditions influence decisions about benefits because in tight labor markets organizations seeking the best employees compete by offering better benefits and services, which are nontaxable income. In addition, the composition of the labor market has had an increasing impact on the type of benefits and services offered. For example, the increased number of women in the workforce has resulted in increasing pressure for longer maternity leaves, family leave benefits, child care services, and elder care services. The aging of the workforce means that such services and benefits as preretirement planning, health insurance, and pensions are increasingly demanded.

The amount of money an employer spends on benefits is related directly to the financial health of the employer and the industry. Healthy, profitable companies tend to expand benefits during good times. But when the economy weakens or profits fall, the cost of the benefit programs intensifies financial problems. Benefit costs must be passed on to someone. For example, health care costs alone add over $1,000 to the price of every American-made car.[6] The portion of hourly wages devoted to legally required benefits—including social security, workers' compensation, and unemployment insurance—averages about 8.6 percent of total employee compensation.[7]

Mandated Benefits Programs

Three benefits programs offered by private and not-for-profit employers are mandated by federal and state governments. An employer has no choice about offering **mandated benefits programs** and cannot change them in any way without getting involved in the political process to change the existing laws. The three mandated programs are unemployment insurance, social security, and workers' compensation.

Unemployment Insurance

In the 1930s, when unemployment was very high, the government was pressured to create programs to take care of people who were out of work through no fault of their own. **Unemployment insurance** (UI) was set up in the United States as part of the Social Security Act of 1935. In July 2005, the average unemployment rate for the United States was approximately 5.0 percent.[8]

Unemployment insurance was designed with several objectives:

1. To provide periodic cash income to workers during short periods of involuntary unemployment.
2. To help the unemployed find jobs.
3. To encourage employers to stabilize employment.
4. To stabilize the labor supply by providing benefits so that skilled and experienced workers are not forced to seek other jobs during short-term unemployment.[9]

Unemployment insurance and allied systems for railroad, federal government, and military employees cover 95 percent of the labor force. Major groups excluded from UI are self-employed workers, employees of small firms with less than four employees, domestics, farm employees, state and local government employees, and nonprofit employers such as hospitals.

To be eligible for compensation, the employee must have worked a minimum number of weeks, be without a job, and be willing to accept a suitable position offered through a state Unemployment Compensation Commission. A Supreme Court decision granted unemployment insurance benefits to strikers after an eight-week strike period. The Court ruled that neither the Social Security Act nor the National Labor Relations Act specifically forbids paying benefits to strikers. Each state decides whether to permit or prohibit such payments.[10]

Federal unemployment tax for employers in all states accounts for 0.8 percent of payroll. The tax pays for administrative costs associated with unemployment compensation, provides a percentage of benefits paid under extended benefits programs during periods of high unemployment, and maintains a loan fund for use when a state lacks funds to pay benefits due for any month. Unemployment tax rates, eligibility requirements, weekly benefits, and duration of regular benefits vary from state to state.[11]

Before benefits are paid, the reason for being unemployed must be assessed.[12] An applicant can be disqualified for voluntarily quitting a job. On the other hand, a negotiated quit, that is, quitting to avoid discharge, is a legitimate reason for collecting unemployment benefits. Some states penalize employers who report such quits as voluntary. Discharge for work-related misconduct usually means the applicant is disqualified. Proper documentation is an employer's best protection in unemployment hearings.

The employee receives compensation for a limited period, typically a maximum of 26 weeks. In most states the weekly benefit amount is equal to 1/26 of the worker's average earnings, yielding a total benefit of 50 percent of earnings. Minimum and maximum benefit amounts are set by the federal government. Minimum benefits usually range from $5 (New Jersey) to $102 (Rhode Island) per week, maximum benefits from $133 (Puerto Rico) to $646 (Massachusetts), and the average benefit from $90 to $175.

Unemployment compensation in both Canada and Europe differs from that provided in the United States.[13] For example, in Europe, employees who are placed on reduced work schedules (fewer hours per week) receive short-term unemployment compensation. Research has shown that the American practice of paying unemployment only to those working zero hours can encourage the overuse of temporary layoffs. Canada, which has a much more liberal unemployment benefits program that includes both wider eligibility and faster delivery of benefits, has a much higher unemployment rate than the United States.

Social Security

In 1935, the pension portion of the **social security** system was established under the Old-Age, Survivors, and Disability Insurance (OASDI) program. The goal of the pension portion was to provide income to retired people to supplement savings, private pensions, and part-time work. It was created at a time when the wealthy continued to live alone, the average person moved in with relatives, and the poor with no one to help them were put in a "poorhouse," or government-supported retirement home.

The basic concept was that the employee and employer were to pay taxes that would cover the retirement payments each employee would later receive in a self-funding insurance program. Initially, two goals were sought: adequate payments for all, and individual equity, which means that each employee was to receive what he or she and the employer had put into the fund. In the past 20 years, however, individual equity has lost out.

Social security taxes are paid by employers and employees. Both pay a percentage of the employee's pay to the government. The percentage rose to 7.65 for both employee and employer in 1990. How much is paid by employee and employer is calculated on the average monthly wage (weighted toward the later years). Social security payments make up about one-third of total federal outlays in the United States.[14] Those receiving social security pensions can work part-time, up to a maximum amount that is increased each year to reflect inflation. Just about all employees except civilian federal government employees are eligible for social security coverage. Self-employed people must join the system.

In 2005 the government collected more payroll taxes than it paid out in benefits. Recall that social security is a pay-as-you-go system. In 1950 there were about 16 covered workers for each social security beneficiary. Today there are about 3.3 workers paying taxes for each beneficiary. Most people, especially politicians, agree that something must be done to fix social security. In the summer of 2005 there were numerous alternatives being debated to offset paying out more in benefits than what is being collected in payroll taxes. The estimate is that by 2018 changes in the social security system will have to be implemented.

Employees born in 1937 or earlier become eligible to receive full benefits at age 65 or reduced benefits at age 62. An employee born in 1960 or later will not be able to retire with full benefits until age 67. If an employee dies, a family with children under 18 receives survivor benefits, regardless of the employee's age. An employee who is totally disabled before age 65 becomes eligible to receive insurance benefits. Under Medicare provisions of the social security system, eligible individuals aged 65 and older receive payments for doctor and hospital bills, as well as other related benefits and services.

Retirement benefits used to be tax-free, but in 1984 some benefits became taxable.[15] For single people, up to 85 percent of social security benefits are taxable if they earn provisional income of $34,000 or more. Married couples filing jointly must pay taxes on provisional income of $44,000 or more. ("Provisional income" means adjusted gross income plus any tax-exempt interest from municipal bonds plus half of social security.) It is possible to avoid these taxes by switching income to other types of assets.

The growth of international business has created another problem for companies dealing with social security payments.[16] The United States has international social security agreements with several countries. If such an agreement does not exist, social security law requires contributions to be paid on earnings of United States citizens or residents working for American employers *anywhere in the world*. As a result, United States citizens may have to make double contributions—once to the American plan and once to the country in which they are employed. No contributions are necessary for United States citizens employed by a foreign company, however.

Because of the increasing numbers of Americans who spend at least part of their careers in more than one country, the United States has established agreements with other governments to coordinate social security benefits. The principal objectives of these agreements are to ensure equality of treatment, prevent duplicate contributions or gaps, provide that contributions are paid in the location where the worker is employed, and guarantee benefits to the employee's family when they have not accompanied the employee to the foreign assignments.[17] Total benefits may not exceed the highest pension that the employee would have been paid if his or her entire career had been spent in a single country. Benefits are administered by the state where the retired employee resides; a pensioner may have to wait two or three years to know what income he or she will receive.

Social security systems in many countries around the globe are in crisis, exacting a heavy financial burden while providing inadequate benefits.[18] Employers worldwide must assume more responsibility for employee benefits as governments try to cut the cost of social security and national health insurance programs.[19] Steps taken by foreign governments to meet this challenge include (1) reducing the level of future benefits and (2) increasing social security taxes. There are also a growing number of countries that allow voluntary private retirement accounts.

The HR Journal box provides a quick view of social security around the world.1 As an increasing number of workers reach retirement age, the ratio of active workers to social security recipients will decline alarmingly.[20] Demographic projections in many countries show a consistent trend in the ratio of pensioners to social security contributors from the current 20 to 30 percent to nearer 40 to 50 percent over the next 40 years. The same demographic trends threaten the long-term financial security of Americans. These trends include longer life expectancy, an increasing risk of suffering long-term disability in old age, evolving work patterns, and new family norms. As a consequence, the seniors of the 21st century will need more money than previous generations did to maintain their standard of living.[21] In addition, less than half of all employees work for a company that provides a private pension, so many retirees will rely solely on social security benefits.[22]

The social security retirement benefit is free from state income tax provisions in about 24 states and is entirely free from federal tax. There is, however, a taxation test that must be met to keep the benefit free from taxation. Beneficiaries under age 65 are allowed to make only $9,120 annually or less; those between 65 and 69 are allowed to make $14,500 annually or less. If these benefit limits are exceeded, the social security benefit is reduced $1 for every $2 in excess of the limit for those under age 65 and $1 for every $3 for those 65 to 69. A person who is 70 years old or older is not penalized for excess earnings.

Employers and employees must pay a payroll tax to fund social security benefits. Each party pays a tax of 6.2 percent (12.4 percent total) on the first $90,000 of the employee's earnings. Of the 12.4 percent, 4.75 percent funds the Old Age, Survivors, Disability, and Health Insurance (OASDHI) program and 1.45 percent funds Medicare (Part A). An additional tax of 1.45 percent is assessed on all earnings for Medicare.

HR Journal

Besides the United States, how many countries have social security programs?

  a. About 10
  b. Around 70
  c. Less than 90
  d. More than 170

What is your answer? The correct answer is d. More than 170 countries have social security programs. The United States established its social security system in 1935. Germany initiated the first social security system in the 1880s. Another 25 countries had social insurance in place before the United States.

The political debate about what to do with the U.S. social security program continues. There are some lessons to be learned from other countries. The issue of allowing individuals to have private accounts is perhaps the most controversial. Here are few examples of what other countries are doing in terms of private accounts:

CHILE

A system of mandatory private accounts was started in 1981. The traditional social insurance system is being phased out. Workers contribute 10 percent of their earnings into personal accounts. Assets in the private accounts amount to $54 billion, nearly two-thirds of national output.

Large fees of about 20 percent of the total deposited have eaten some of the glitter from the privatization system. Only about 60 percent of workers contribute to the personal account system.

BRITAIN

Since 1978 workers have been permitted to stop paying into one of the state pension systems if they redirect part of their payroll tax to an approved private pension plan.

British retirees receive modest payouts from the traditional state pension system. In 1988, worried that the baby boomer retirement might eventually bankrupt the state system, the government allowed individuals to opt out of the supplementary state plan and set up private accounts. It also allowed employees to opt out of company pensions and use part of their payroll taxes to fund their new "personal pensions."

Since the bursting of the high-flying stock market in 2000, fewer people have wanted the private accounts. The support for privatization is now lukewarm.

MEXICO

Since 1991, employees are required to contribute 20 percent of each worker's earnings into a private savings account, and workers are given the option to make additional tax-free contributions.

SWEDEN

The system is pay-as-you-go, but there is a small tier of compulsory private savings. About 2.5 percent of average earnings are credited to personal accounts. The overall system is funded by payroll taxes of 18.5 percent (in the United States, payroll tax is 12.4 percent). The individual uses 2.5 percent of the total to fund "premium/personal accounts," which taxpayers manage themselves. From about 660 mutual funds registered to do business in Sweden, individuals can choose a maximum of five.

There is no perfect or best system as can be seen from the few examples and descriptions.

Source: Adapted from Matt Moffett (February 3, 2005), "From Nations That Have Tried Similar Pensions, Some Lessons," *The Wall Street Journal;* "Social Security around the World," www.washingtonpost.com, accessed July 9, 2005; and John Voss (April 7, 2004), "Social Security Programs Can Be Found around the World," *Columbus Federal Voice.*

A number of changes in the social security system are being considered in an attempt to control future costs and benefits.[23] Probable changes include (1) higher taxes on social security benefits; (2) participation of all state, local, and federal civil servants in the social security program; (3) beginning in the next three or four decades, longer work and later retirement; (4) dramatic changes in the social security, Medicare, and overall health care systems; and (5) reduction in benefits.

Workers' Compensation

Employees who incur expenses as a result of job-related illnesses or accidents receive a degree of financial protection from **workers' compensation** benefits.[24] The workers'

HR Journal
A Major Workers' Compensation Challenge in California

After winning authority to borrow to keep California afloat, a test for Governor Arnold Schwarzenegger is workers' compensation. He will have to work hard to fix California's workers' compensation system, the program that provides cash benefits and medical services to millions of workers injured on the job.

"I call on the Legislature to deliver real workers' comp reform to my desk by March 1," Governor Schwarzenegger said in his state of the state address in January 2004. "Modest reform is not enough."

That deadline has come and gone. With the Legislature still deliberating and the governor drafting a ballot initiative, it is unclear what will happen next—but it is clear that the state workers' compensation system needs surgery. The predicament highlights what can go wrong in workers' compensation, a program that generally works well in most states.

Workers' compensation was the nation's first social insurance program. Most states passed laws in the 1910s and 1920s that made companies liable for workplace injuries on a no-fault basis, but limited the amount they had to pay. Workers gave up the right to sue their employer. The conventional wisdom is that workers and employers gained because the prevailing court system had been unpredictable and inefficient. Workers had typically received little from filing a negligence suit, and legal costs were high.

After California passed workers' compensation legislation in 1911, legal disputes were all but eliminated: fewer than 2 percent of claims for permanent injuries were contested in 1924–25. The central problem in California now is that the costs paid by employers are the highest in the country, while the benefits received by workers are about average—in part because many cases are disputed, which wastes resources.

Total costs for California employers increased to $29 billion in 2003—eight times the gross domestic product of Haiti—from $11 billion in 1998. By one estimate, the average employer in California pays 5.2 percent of payroll for workers' compensation insurance, more than twice the average of other states. Rates are much higher in hazardous occupations: 43 percent for loggers, 33 percent for roofers, 22 percent for carpenters, and 18 percent for truck drivers.

The governor maintains that these high costs are the main reason jobs are leaving the state. But this confuses who writes the check (employers) with who bears the burden of the program (employees). Research has found that most workers' compensation costs are shifted to workers in the form of lower wages over time, so the effect on jobs is probably minimal.

Nonetheless, reducing inefficiency and administrative costs is to everyone's benefit. The main problems with California's system are that 30 percent of claimants who miss more than a week of work hire a lawyer—much higher than in the other states—according to Robert Reville, director of the Rand Institute for Civil Justice. Lawyers are involved in three-quarters of permanent disability cases, and their legal fees averaged $8,352 in 2002, or 20 percent of combined medical and cash benefits. For a system intended to reduce litigation, these figures represent failure.

Professor John Burton of the Rutgers School of Management and Labor Relations, widely considered the nation's leading workers' compensation scholar, traced many of California's problems to its complex system for rating permanent injuries that are only partly disabling. Such injuries account for almost 90 percent of benefit costs in California and 70 percent nationwide. Because the system gives much discretion, litigation is common for hard-to-measure medical conditions like back sprains. Furthermore, some injuries, like those to the shoulder, receive particularly low benefits compared with the wage loss workers experience.

The adversarial relationship that develops between workers and employers in contested claims causes California to have one of the lowest return-to-work rates of all states.

Medical costs are high, almost as high as the cash benefits that are meant to replace lost wages. Because workers' compensation insurance pays all the bills, doctors and patients have little incentive to restrain costs. Increasingly, in California and elsewhere, health care providers are shifting medical costs to workers' compensation by prescribing more services or charging more per service.

Medical costs are also high because workers and employers often hire dueling doctors to bolster their cases. Doctors selected by workers tend to rate a given injury as 34 percent more severe than doctors selected by employers or insurers; independent doctors tend to be between, but closer to employers' doctors. With this much difference of opinion, it is no wonder that so many cases are disputed.

While there is much agreement about the source of the problems, there is considerable disagreement about the solutions.

continued

HR Journal   *A Major Workers' Compensation Challenge in California (concluded)*

Professor Burton proposes using the American Medical Association's guidelines for rating the severity of disabilities. The guidelines are used in most states and provide a more objective and more clear basis for decisions, although he acknowledges that they are imperfect and should be adjusted to reflect earnings losses associated with various injuries.

He also proposes basing claimants' lawyers' fees on the difference between the amount employers offer and the award workers receive—the lawyers' value added—rather than the full amount of the award. And to foster cooperation, he suggests giving lawyers a bonus if workers return to work for a specified length of time.

A draft ballot initiative by Governor Schwarzenegger would raise the burden of proof for workers to receive benefits; require physicians to use objective, observable medical evidence to assess injuries; restrict an employee's choice of doctor to those agreed to by his or her employer; deny compensation for impairments that

result from cumulative activities, like back sprains, unless they are proved to be "predominantly caused by actual activities of employment"; and deny compensation for other impairments unless a single work-related incident caused at least 10 percent of the disability.

Although restricting choice of doctor is controversial in California, Professor Burton notes that other states have limited the access to doctors for years.

He warns, however, that not compensating employees for injuries that arise from work but cannot be pinpointed to a particular event could have a major unintended consequence: employers could possibly be sued for large damages outside the workers' compensation system.

Source: A. B. Kreuger, "Schwarzenegger's Next Big Challenge," *The New York Times Online,* http://www.nytimes.com, accessed July 9, 2005; and Tom Abate (March 29, 2004), "Politics: Workers' Compensation," *San Francisco Chronicle.*

compensation programs are administered individually by the various states. Employers pay the entire cost of workers' compensation insurance. The cost of premiums is tied directly to each employer's past experience with job-related accidents and illnesses.

All states plus the District of Columbia have workers' compensation laws, but only one state, Texas, does not require participation. Eligibility for benefits varies from state to state. A percentage of the disabled employee's weekly wage is provided for up to 26 weeks. Benefits range from 60 to 75 percent of the average weekly wage.[25] Workers' compensation claims have become increasingly expensive over the past 10 years, and these costs will escalate in the years ahead.

Workers' compensation costs are growing faster than health care insurance expenses because of several factors: escalating fraudulent claims, the expansion of "compensable injuries," and fewer restrictions to eligibility for benefits than in health care plans.[26] Therefore, many states are modifying their existing legislation. A growing number of states are providing workers' compensation through alternative sources (a combination of life, disability, accident, and health or other insurance). A number of states added deductibles to their plans: Kentucky, Minnesota, Mississippi, Missouri, and Colorado.[27]

The crisis in workers' compensation is a major concern of California. The HR Journal box shows how significant the California problem has become.

Voluntary Benefits

In addition to the benefits required by law, many employers also provide other kinds of benefits voluntarily: compensation for time not worked, insurance protection, and retirement plans. There are many differences in employers' practices regarding these benefits. Exhibit 12-3 lists typical voluntary benefits by category.

EXHIBIT 12-3   Typical Voluntary Benefits

Employee Benefit Program			Services
Paid leave	**Medical care**	Long-term disability	Education programs
Holidays	Employee coverage:	Wholly employer-financed	Tuition reimbursement
Vacations	Wholly employer-financed	Partly employer-financed	Preretirement programs
Sick leave	Partly employer-financed	**Retirement**	Child care
Rest time	Family coverage:	Defined benefit pension	Elder care
Jury duty leave	Wholly employer-financed	Wholly employer-financed	Financial services
Funeral leave	Partly employer-financed	Partly employer-financed	Relocation services
Military leave	**Dental care**	Defined contribution	Social and recreational programs
Personal leave	Employee coverage:	Savings and thrift	
Lunch time	Wholly employer-financed	Deferred profit sharing	
Maternity leave	Partly employer-financed	Employee stock ownership	
Paternity leave	Family coverage:	Money purchase pension	
Unpaid leave	Wholly employer-financed	**Miscellaneous**	
Maternity leave	Partly employer-financed	Reimbursement accounts	
Paternity leave	**Other insurance**	Flexible benefits plans	
Life insurance	Sickness and accident		
Wholly employer-financed	Wholly employer-financed		
Partly employer-financed	Partly employer-financed		

Compensation for Time Off

Can you imagine going to work 6 days a week, 12 hours a day, 52 weeks a year—for life? That's what life used to be like, although it has been shown that employees did not always work hard all that time. The concept of a paid holiday or vacation with pay did not exist. Now, most employers compensate for time that employees have not worked: break time, get-ready time, washup time, clothes-changing time, paid lunch and rest periods, coffee breaks, and so on. Employers also pay employees when they are not actually at work—holidays, vacations, sick leave, funeral leave, jury duty, and other personal leaves, such as to fulfill military obligations. The Bureau of Labor Statistics has reported that the availability and details of time-off benefits vary widely by size of the establishment. The smaller the business, the fewer the provisions for time off with pay.[28] Firms employing fewer than 100 workers provide time off only for holidays or base time off on individual performance, while medium and large firms offer a full range of leave.

Vacations are generally a highly preferred benefit. Preferences for holidays vary, and lower-paid and female employees have stronger preferences for sick leave. Unions have negotiated hard for added time off to give their members more leisure and to create jobs. The sections below take a closer took at the time off offered by employers.

Paid Holidays

Probably the most frequently offered of these times off with pay are paid holidays. The typical number of paid holidays has been increasing. Currently, 10 or more paid holidays are provided to full-time employees. The most typical holidays are New Year's Day, Memorial Day, July 4, Labor Day, Thanksgiving Day, and Christmas. The new minivacation dates created by Congress through the federal Monday-holiday law allow for three-day weekends in February for President's Day, in May for Memorial Day, in October for Columbus Day, and in November for Veterans' Day.

HR Journal *Managing Workers' Compensation Claims*

Disability costs are like an iceberg to corporate America. The direct costs are like the snow-white cap employers can see; the indirect costs are like the bulky mass that hides under the waves waiting to sink the ship. Direct costs of managing workers' disability claims include medical leave, short-term disability premiums, long-term disability premiums, disability pensions, workers' compensation, the disability component of social security, and other miscellaneous accident insurance costs. Hidden costs include replacement wages, including costs of temporary help, lower productivity from replacement workers, overtime pay, higher potential for accident and illness claims from inexperienced workers, hiring costs, and training costs. Management or administration costs include claims administration, safety and health training, safety support personnel, and vocational rehabilitation.

To reduce overall workers' compensation claims and control the costs listed above, progressive companies are integrating workers' compensation programs with safety, health, and health care programs. They are also devoting special attention to getting occupationally injured workers back to work as soon as possible. In fact, some benchmark programs actually move these workers to low-impact jobs and combine that with physical therapy so that little or no work time is lost. Since total disability costs are running between 8 and 10 percent of payroll, switching to this approach—called "managed disability"—is very attractive.

An example of a company that has been extremely successful in controlling workers' compensation claims and getting people back to work is Disney, Inc. First, the corporation self-insures and self-administers its workers' compensation program. Common injuries at Disney's theme parks are back, wrist, and knee sprains. Injured employees ("cast members") are treated like customers. First aid centers are strategically located throughout the parks; pamphlets explaining workers' compensation rights are passed out routinely to all employees; a company nurse visits or calls all injured workers and provides a detailed explanation of what the employee can and cannot do; and, if possible, individuals are transferred to a limited job program (like making pizza boxes) while they recuperate, so that minimal job time is lost. As a result, Disney has become a model in managing workers' compensation claims for such corporate giants as IBM, Xerox, and GTE.

Source: Adapted from Joseph McCafferty (1996), "Adding Insight to Injury," *CFO* 12, 6, pp. 55–62; *Chief Executive* (1994), *The Disability Imperative* (brief supp.), pp. 2–5; John S. Tortarolo and Phillip L. Polakoff (1995), "The Future of Disability Management Is Integration," *Benefits Quarterly* 11, 3, pp. 49–55.

Paid Vacations

Another example of voluntary compensation offered for time not worked is paid vacations. The United States is the only major country that does not mandate paid vacations. In China workers receive three weeks. European Union countries average six weeks. Paid vacations are the *most expensive benefit* for American employers. Most organizations offer vacations with pay after a certain minimum period of service. The theory behind vacations is that they provide an opportunity for employees to rest and refresh themselves; when they return, it is hoped that they will be more effective. Employees have pressed for more leisure to enjoy the fruit of their labors.

Government and military employees traditionally have been given 30 days' vacation per year. The typical vacation in the private sector is one week of paid vacation for an employee of less than a year's service and two weeks for 1 to 10 years' service. Three-week vacations are offered annually to veterans of 10 to 20 years, and four weeks to the over-20-year employees. In some firms, if employees don't take their vacations by the end of the year or a specified date, they forfeit the vacation days. Also, in some firms, if an employee is sick during a vacation, rescheduling the vacation is permitted.

International Vacation Benefits

American employees earn higher real wages and have greater personal wealth than many foreign workers, but they receive substantially less paid vacation than their international

EXHIBIT 12-4
Global Vacation Time

Number of days

Sweden	30
France	30
Austria	30
Germany	30
Great Britain	25
Australia	20
New Zealand	15
Japan	10
Canada	10
United States	24

■ 30-year service   □ 10-year service   ▨ 5-year service

▨ Employer-sponsored   ▨ Legally required

counterparts, especially those in Western Europe. For example, workers in Western Europe get a guaranteed four or five weeks regardless of length of service.[29] In Japan, workers receive vacation leave comparable to that in the United States, but employees must often be forced to take time off. Research on vacation patterns in Europe has shown that unions were an important factor in achieving longer vacations for all employees. If unions in the United States were allowed to be as politically active as they are in Europe, vacation schemes here would be more comparable to the rest of the industrialized world. Exhibit 12-4 compares vacation allowances globally.

Personal Time Off

Many employers give employees paid time off for funerals, medical and dental appointments, sickness in the family, religious observances, marriage, personal-choice holidays, and birthdays. If an organization uses flextime scheduling, the need for time off is minimized. A BNA survey found that 9 out of 10 medium and large firms provide paid jury duty; 9 out of 10 provide paid leave for funerals of close relatives; and 7 out of 10 provide paid leave for military duty. Typically, in this last case, the pay is the difference between normal pay and military pay. Many policies apply to leaves for personal reasons, such as sickness in the family or marriage.

Sick Leave

Most employees of medium and large firms are protected from loss of income during short-term disability due to non-work-related sickness or injury.[30] In most situations, organizations allow and pay for 1 sick day per month or 12 per year. The employee would receive full pay for this time period. This benefit usually accrues over time, but upon termination most organizations do not pay for any sick leave not taken. An exception to this policy is state and federal employees, who can accrue sick leave and get paid for the balance of unused leave upon termination. Sick leave is always funded entirely by the employer. Benefits may vary by length of service; and some companies will pay reduced sick leave benefits for a specified length of time when the employee exceeds those guaranteed at full pay. More white-collar employees than blue-collar employees are covered by sick leave provisions. Accident and sickness insurance plans are more common with blue-collar employees.[31] A physician's written excuse is often necessary in order to be eligible for pay and to return to work if the illness is longer than three days.[32]

EXHIBIT 12-5
Family Leave*
Policies around the
World

Source: Karen Matthes
(March 1992), "Is Family
Leave Legislation Necessary?"
HR Focus, p. 3.

Country	Duration of Leave (Weeks)	Number of Paid Weeks and Percent of Normal Pay (Paid By Government and/or Employer)
Canada	17–41	15 weeks/60%
France	18	16 weeks/90%
Germany	14–26	14–19 weeks/100%
Japan	12	12 weeks/60%
Sweden	12–52	38 weeks/90%

* As debate over federal family leave legislation continues in the United States, other industrialized nations have established policies.

A liberal sick-leave policy can cause *excessive* absenteeism. It may communicate that the company does not value good attendance. Some firms use *sick-leave banks* to cut down on sick leave. Employees deposit a set portion of their earned sick-leave days into a company pool. Should an employee use all of his or her compensated sick leave, an application for withdrawal from the sick-leave bank can be made. However, these requests are carefully screened by a committee. The sick-leave bank has psychological benefits. Members become conservative in using banked days, using only what they need so that co-workers will have what they need in case of long-term illness or accidents.

Family Leave

The typical nuclear American family—husband, wife, and two children—made up 40 percent of all households in the mid-1970s. In 2005, this model fit less than 10 percent of all families. The number of families headed by a single provider doubled between 1970 and 1983, and the trend continues. Females heading families with children under the age of 18 doubled between 1980 and 1990, from 2.9 million to 5.9 million. Approximately 8 percent of all adults will never marry and more than 20 million young adults have had to move back home because they could not afford to live on their own.[33] With most industrialized nations providing generous family leave for employees (see Exhibit 12-5) the United States passed the Family and Medical Leave Act **(FMLA)** into law in February 1993.

Generally, FMLA stipulates that most employers with 50 or more employees must provide up to 12 weeks of unpaid leave to eligible employees during any 12-month period.[34] The stated purpose of this act is to allow employees to balance the demands of the workplace with the needs of family members. The birth of a child, adoption or placement of a foster child, and the serious illness, injury, or mental condition of a family member are events that qualify for FMLA.[35] Employees must have been employed for a full 12 months to be eligible, and the employer must continue group health insurance during the leave.[36] The employee must be allowed to return to the same job or an equivalent job. FMLA authorizes the Department of Labor to investigate and resolve any complaints by employees. Requirements are especially significant for small to medium-sized firms, which may not be able to meet all of the act's requirements.

Maternity and Parental Leave

The demands faced by expectant employees and working parents have created pressures to further accommodate childbirth, adoption, and child-rearing responsibilities for both women and men. The Pregnancy Discrimination Act of 1978, an amendment to Title VII of the Civil Rights Act, requires that pregnancy be treated just like any other temporary disability. Before the act, temporary disability benefits for pregnancy were paid in the form of either sick leave or disability insurance, if at all. Maternity leave and benefits are usually limited to six weeks, with or without pay. In addition to maternity leave, a few organizations provide paternity leave. For example, Bell Telephone gives fathers and mothers the option to take a six-month unpaid leave without losing benefits when a child is born. Mothers and fathers on Bell's plan are guaranteed the same job, or a similar one, at the same pay when they return to work.

Increased foreign competition and the growth of international business will also have an impact.[37] Parental leave policies are already established in Western Europe. For example, Germany has a complex set of special benefits including health and financial protection for pregnant women and young parents. Sweden has the most comprehensive and best-funded parental leave policy. The experience with family leave policies in Europe offers several lessons: A limited program of leave entitlements has a positive effect on productivity and creates few problems for employers; basic coverage should be established by law, giving employers the option to extend or embellish it; and basic parental leave benefits should carry some form of financial payment.

Employer-Purchased Insurance

The many risks encountered throughout life—illness (including drug dependency and AIDS), accident, permanent disability, and death, among others—can be offset by buying insurance. Midsized and large employers can buy insurance more cheaply than can individual employees, so employer-sponsored insurance is a preferred benefit. Historically, insurance premiums were paid in full by the employer, but in the turbulent business environment of the 2000s the employee is being forced to pay an increasing share of the expense. Three major forms of insurance are involved: health, life, and disability income replacement.

Health Insurance

Rising health care costs have reached crisis proportions in the United States.[38] Approximately 82 percent of full-time employees of midsized to large private firms participated in employer-provided health care plans in 1993, down from 90 percent in 1990.[39] This decline is due to the increasing number of plans that require contributions from employees. Small firms with fewer than 100 employees provided some kind of health coverage for about 66 percent of their employees. But only one-tenth of all part-time employees received medical benefits.[40] In 2004, approximately 40 million Americans had no health insurance.[41]

Less than 10 years ago, only 6 percent of payroll went to health care benefits. In 2004, the figure exceeds 19 percent of payroll cost.[42] Several factors help to continue this inflationary path: increasing health care labor costs, more sophisticated technology and costly tests, rising malpractice insurance premiums, oversupply of hospital beds, overutilization of fee-for-service medicine, and consumers' belief that health coverage is an entitlement.

Studies indicate that employees prefer health insurance over most other benefits. Typically, health insurance includes hospitalization (room, board, and hospital service charges), surgical fees (actual surgical fees or maximum limits), and major medical fees, (maximum benefits typically $5,000 to $10,000 beyond hospitalization and surgical payments). Most employees get basic coverage. Plans for salaried employees typically are of the major medical variety and provide "last-dollar coverage." This means that the employee must pay the first $200 of the cost or a similar deductible each year. Benefits may be based on either a specific cash allowance for various procedures or a service benefit that pays the full amount of all reasonable charges.

Negotiated plans for unionized workers generally have expanded coverage that provides specific benefits rather than comprehensive major medical coverage. This approach is preferred by union leaders because they assume individual benefits that can be clearly labeled will impress union members, and these benefits can be obtained with no deductible payments by employees. Some of the more rapidly expanding benefits of the negotiated plans are prescription drugs, vision care, mental health services, and dental care. For example, typical dental coverage ranges from $1,000 to $2,000 yearly.

EXHIBIT 12-6   **Health Care Costs and Outcomes in Selected Countries**

Source: Organization for Economic Cooperation and Development (1998), OECD Health Data 98 (Paris).

	Life Expectancy	Infant Mortality*	Healths Expenditures†	Health Expenditure as a Percentage	Doctors per 1,000	Average Days Inpatient
Japan	77/83	.38	$1,673	7.2%	1.8	45
Korea	70/76	.90	543	4.0	1.1	13
Canada	75/81	.60	2,065	9.6	2.1	12
United Kingdom	74/79	.62	1,297	6.9	1.6	10
France	74/82	.49	1,989	9.7	2.9	11
Germany	74/80	.50	2,233	10.5	3.4	14
Mexico	60/77	1.70	358	4.6	2.6	8
United States	73/79	.80	3,898	14.0	1.6	4

* Per 1,000 live births.

† Adjusted for purchasing power, U.S. dollars.

The specific types of health care coverage vary from organization to organization. Traditional membership programs like Blue Cross/Blue Shield pay for both physician and hospital expenses as these costs are incurred. However, this approach is not preventive and does nothing to encourage lifestyle changes that might lead to fewer claims. To comply with the Health Maintenance Act of 1973, it became necessary for businesses to provide alternative health care plans.[43] As claims and costs escalated and more expenses were shared with employees, two new alternative approaches were offered: health maintenance organizations (HMOs) and preferred provider organizations (PPOs). These, and similar schemes, are known as managed care. Exhibit 12-6 illustrates how the United States compares to other countries on health care costs and other health care–related factors.

Health Maintenance Organizations

A health maintenance organization is distinctly different from the traditional health care plan. An **HMO** is a medical organization consisting of medical and health specialists offering both outpatient and hospital coverage for a fixed monthly fee. All HMOs have one common element: prepayment for comprehensive health care that promotes preventive, healthy lifestyles. To operate efficiently, HMOs contain costs. Although increasingly popular, especially with employers, the fact that an enrollee may have to leave his or her family doctor for one who works with the plan has caused resistance among employees.

Preferred Provider Organizations

A **PPO** is a health care plan based on agreements between doctors, hospitals, and other related medical service facilities with an employer or an insurance company. They provide services for a fixed fee. A precise definition of PPOs is difficult to give, but most include a select panel of providers, an emphasis on cost efficiency, marketing to purchasers rather than users, and some flexibility in choice of providers, together with financial incentives to use selected providers. PPOs, like HMOs, must provide cost-efficient health care and emphasize cost containment in order to compete. Cost controls include obtaining discounts from providers, using payment schemes to pass some risk back to providers, and using utilization controls.

Consolidated Omnibus Budget Reconciliation Act of 1985

Section 162 (k) of the Consolidated Omnibus Budget Reconciliation Act of 1985 **(COBRA)** stipulates that employers with more than 20 employees are required to offer continuation of health care coverage for 18 to 36 months after termination of an employee. COBRA has been amended three times since 1985.[44] The act requires most employers to offer employees who leave the company the option of remaining members of the company's group health plans. Usually, employees who leave the company may extend coverage, at their own expense, for up to 18 months after terminations. For employees who were disabled when they left the company or who were working reduced hours, coverage can be extended to 29 months. COBRA explicitly states that spouses and children of covered employees can continue their coverage even if the employee dies or becomes eligible for Medicare. Disabled qualified beneficiaries can be charged up to 150 percent of the plan's applicable premiums since the passage of the Omnibus Budget Reconciliation Act of 1989 (OBRA).

If an employer fails to comply with COBRA and OBRA regulations, the employer will not be allowed to deduct contributions made to that or any other group health plan.

Long-Term-Care Legislation

The number of Americans older than 65 will double over the next 25 to 30 years.[45] Many private firms have already begun to provide long-term-care insurance. Originally long-term health care covered nursing home stays only; but plans have become increasingly innovative, offering more flexible benefits including home care delivered by professionals or family members. The largest group of employees with comprehensive long-term coverage are members of the United Auto Workers union working for General Motors, Ford, and Chrysler Corporation.[46] Long-term plans are funded by employees' contributions.

Life Insurance

Group life insurance is one of the oldest and most widely available employee benefits. Almost all full-time employees of medium and large private firms are covered, and close to two-thirds of full-time employees of small firms also receive coverage.[47] Life insurance benefits are the traditional means of providing financial support for survivors following an employee's death. This insurance usually provides a lump-sum benefit to the designated beneficiary. Most plans include coverage for retirees and dependents of employees. Many also allow employees to increase the value of the policy at attractive group rates. In the majority of plans, the employer pays the whole premium for the employee; approximately 12 percent of all employers require employees to assist in financing the plan. In a typical program for a large company, the amount of insurance provided by the plan increases as salary increases, the typical amount being twice the salary.

Disability Income Replacement Insurance

What happens to employees who have accidents at work that leave them unable to work, temporarily or permanently? Workers' compensation pays a very small part of these costs, since it was designed primarily to take care of short-term disability. Employer-funded long-term disability insurance is designed to cover these cases, with payments supplementing benefits from workers' compensation, social security, and other agencies.

Approximately one-third of the plans provide survivors' benefits equal to the employee's monthly benefit for a limited time. The duration of short-term disability benefits averages 26 weeks. Long-term disability income replacement plans are designed to kick in after six months of short-term benefits along with other permanent disability benefits such as pension payments and social security. The goal of long-term benefits is to provide employees with at least half pay until pension time.

The majority of employees covered by income replacement insurance are blue-collar workers receiving lump-sum payments. For other employees, coverage is tied to salary level. Some disability payments are very large. A roofer in Georgia who fell at work and was permanently disabled received over $5 million.

Income in Retirement

Most elderly Americans believe that security in the later years rests on a three-legged stool consisting of social security, savings, and private pensions. By the year 2010, social security and private pensions combined will provide no more than 40 percent of retirement income. More and more retirees will have to finance retirement by going back to work or remaining in the workplace longer. When these factors are combined with increasing longevity and inflation, the retiree of the early 2000s will find it more and more difficult to maintain the same standard of living.

All of the legs of the stool are wobbling. Personal savings are no longer considered a secure nest egg. Americans are noted for their anemic savings rates. Real estate investments no longer have a guaranteed payoff for the retiree with a paid-off home. The health of social security is still at risk because of deficit spending, and many private pensions have been defunded. Therefore, it is important to examine employees' savings patterns, including individual retirement accounts (IRAs), simplified employee pension IRAs (SEP-IRAs), and private pensions.

Retirement Income from Savings and Work

Personal savings are an increasingly important source of retirement income. Studies find that people save more if their incomes are high. Employees covered by private pensions are more likely to save money for retirement than those without them. After social security was mandated, there was little change in personal savings rates until the mid-1970s. As people were forced to pay escalating social security taxes, their personal savings for retirement tended to decline. Thanks to medical science and improved lifestyles, people are living longer and so need to save more for retirement. More retirees may have to return to work to supplement social security payments in order to maintain the standard of living they desire. However, social security does not allow much work after retirement, so the law and the needs of retirees are in conflict.

Individual Retirement Accounts (IRAs)

Any employee can make annual tax-free contributions of up to $3,000 to an individual retirement account **(IRA)** even if he or she is already enrolled in a company pension plan. These funds are tax-deferred until the employee retires, shifting the tax burden to later years when lower personal income would equate to lower taxable income.

SEP (Simplified Employee Pension) IRAs

Only 12 percent of small firms with fewer than 10 people are covered by a pension, compared with 82 percent where payroll is 250 employees or more.[48] Small companies can implement simplified employee pension IRAs (SEP-IRAs) for each of their employees, however. What the company actually does is finance an individual retirement account for each employee. Maximum annual contribution to each account is $40,000 or up to 25 percent of compensation, whichever is less. Business contributions to the accounts are tax-deductible and are not subject to social security or unemployment taxes. Funds are taxable when withdrawn upon retirement.[49]

401(k) Plans

Internal Revenue Code Section **401(k)** allows employees to save on a tax-deferred basis by entering into salary deferral agreements with their employer. The 1981 law permitted maximum salary deferral of $30,000 annually. The 1986 Tax Reform Act, however, reduced the salary deferral to $7,000, subject to slight increases as the cost of living increases. In 2005 the dollar limit on the amount a person could defer was $14,000. Deferrals to a 401(k) plan must be coordinated with other salary deferrals if the individual

HR Journal   *The Web-Centric 401(k)*

A few decades ago, the 401(k) was an innovative but obscure new retirement benefit. Today there are over 45 million participants and $1.75 trillion in 401(k) assets. The 401(k) is the most popular retirement plan and, in many cases, represents an individual's most substantial financial assets.

Managing a 401(k) plan is time-consuming and a paper-intensive process. Web technology is beginning to play a major role in helping participants make decisions about their 401(k) balances and plans. Today over 50 percent of existing 401(k) plans provide online access.

Several factors are fueling the online trend. Companies are asking leaner HRM staffs to do more with less and to leverage corporate investments in international intranet technology to control costs.

Respondents to company surveys indicate that Web technology enables them to control the costs of supporting investment changes, loans, deferral changes, investment education, and plan enrollment.

Participant inquiries on the Web are estimated to cost one-tenth as much as those by telephone.

A Web-centric 401(k) is able to streamline and automate traditionally tedious procedures such as loan approvals, can enable sponsors to eliminate waste and paper, and can help employees obtain quick answers to commonly asked questions. Employees can execute transactions with one click, view real-time account data, have their accounts automatically rebalanced, and be prompted by automated e-mail alerts when action or review is needed.

The Web-centric 401(k) plans are a combination of high-tech and high-touch. More and more employees like the access to their balances so that they can track what is happening on a real-time basis. Employee retirement planning is made easier when the Web-centric system for 401(k)s is available.

Source: Adapted from: Gur Huberman and Wei Jiang, "Offering a Choice in 401(k) Plans," accessed at www.columbia.edu/~wj2006/One_Over_N.pdfan/. J. Spencer Williams (December 2001), "The Web-Centric 401(k)," *Employee Benefits Journal*, pp. 38–39.

participates in other plans. The 401(k) plan helps employees save for retirement and encourages saving.[50] In some plans, employers match employees' contributions. Most employees prefer 401(k)s to IRAs, and the number of firms offering such plans has risen dramatically in the last 10 years.

Some firms are using Web-centric 401(k) systems and finding that employees enjoy the access and freedom to review their balances. The above HR Journal discusses the value provided by Web-centric 401(k) plans.

Private Pensions

Private pensions are a relatively new benefit. Globally there are nearly 100 million private pension participants in Australia, Canada, France, Germany, Japan, the Netherlands, Switzerland, the United Kingdom, and the United States.[51] Virtually no other country has private pension coverage. Prior to 1950, less than one-sixth of the nonagricultural workforce was covered. In the 1950s, coverage was doubled; and by 1960, about 15 million workers were covered. After the era of merger mania in the 1980s, many private pension plans were defunded. In the United States, private pension participation is at an all-time low of only 43 percent of the labor force. Only 21 percent of self-employed workers are covered.[52]

Government Regulation of Private Pensions

The law regulating private pensions is the Employment Retirement Income Security Act **(ERISA)** of 1974 and its subsequent amendments. ERISA was designed to cover practically all employee benefit plans of private employers, including multiemployer plans. Basically, the legislation was developed to ensure that employees covered under pension plans would receive the benefits promised. Existing regulations were tightened in ERISA, but the major impact of the law is in the minimum standards established, which all private pension plans

EXHIBIT 12-7
Major Provisions of
ERISA

Eligibility Requirements

Organizations are prohibited from establishing requirements of more than one year of service, or an age greater than 25, whichever is later.

Benefits Formula

A benefits formula expresses the relationship between wages and salaries earned while employed and pension paid. Most benefits formulas are based on the average of the final several years of employment. The actual pension benefits are determined by multiplying the average earnings times the number of years of service times the stipulated percentage, generally between 1 and 3 percent.

Vesting

Vesting is the right to participate in a pension plan. It is based on the length of time a worker must be employed before he or she has a right to a pension or a portion of it should the employee quit.

Portability

Portability is the right to transfer pension credits accrued from one employer to another. It becomes possible when several employers pool their pensions through reciprocal agreements.

Fiduciaries

Fiduciaries are people responsible for pension trust funds. The "prudent man" rule is established as the standard for handling and investing pension plan funds. Fiduciaries may not (1) deal with the fund for their own accounts, (2) receive personal consideration from any party dealing with the fund, (3) make loans between the fund and a party-in-interest, or (4) invest more than 10 percent of the assets of the pension plan in securities of the employer.

Reporting/Disclosure

The law requires the employer to provide employees with a comprehensive booklet describing major plan provisions and to report detailed financial information on the plan annually to the secretary of labor.

are required to meet. ERISA does not require an employer to have a private pension plan. In fact, many existing private pension plans were terminated so employers would not have to meet ERISA's requirements. The major provisions of the law are summarized in Exhibit 12-7.

Pension Benefits

A **defined benefit pension plan** specifies the benefit workers will get at retirement. The amount typically is a fixed monthly income for life or a variation of the lump-sum cash payment. The employer is responsible for annually contributing an amount into a trust fund so that the money will be sufficient to pay the promised benefit. Contributions are calculated actuarially and are based on variables like how long the participants are expected to live, their lifetime earnings, and how much return the trust portfolio will receive annually. Pension payout formulas vary widely. For example, the University of Houston pays an employee with 30 years' service and an average annual salary of $50,000 a pension of $22,700 per year.

A **defined contribution pension plan** usually specifies the employer's contribution but cannot predetermine the employee's actual pension benefit. The plan establishes rules for contributions; the money is invested and projections are offered as to probable retirement income levels. Defined contribution plans include savings and thrift accounts, profit-sharing plans, money purchase pensions, and stock ownership plans. Recently, many of these plans are being funded with employees' contributions to tax-deferred vehicles like 401(k) plans.

Both types of plans specify age or length of service (or both) needed to receive full retirement benefits. For example, the plan may make full benefits available if any one of the following requirements is met: (1) age 65 with five years of service, (2) age 60 with 20 years of service, or (3) age 55 with 30 years of service.

Employee Services

Employee services is something of a catchall category of voluntary benefits, including all other benefits or services provided by employers. These are such varied programs as cafeterias; saunas and gyms; free parking lots; commuter vans; infirmaries; ability to purchase company products at a discount; and death, personal, and financial counseling. Several of the services more frequently provided will be discussed here.

Stock Ownership Plans

Many companies encourage employees to purchase company stock (often at advantageous prices) to increase their incentive to work, their satisfaction, the quality of their work, and to reduce absenteeism and turnover. Purchase plans often allow for payroll deductions or company financing of the stock. Sometimes, the company will agree to buy the stock back at a guaranteed rate if it appears that the employee would take a significant loss. Companies use these plans for the same reasons as they do profit-sharing plans: When employees become partners in the business, they work harder.

Education Programs

Many organizations support off-the-job general education for their employees. Employees can receive up to $5,250 annually in tax-free educational assistance benefits from their employers under Section 127 of the Internal Revenue Code.[53] Reimbursements for graduate-level courses are taxable for employees. The nontaxable status of other tuition reimbursement plans is uncertain. Despite this uncertainty, employers still offer a broad range of educational benefits. The typical user of the program earns between $10,000 and $40,000 annually. About 71 percent of all reimbursements are for undergraduate courses. Eighty-five percent of employees who are eligible to participate do so. The two categories of employees who are most likely to participate are salaried full-time and nonunion hourly personnel.

Preretirement Programs

Because of the continued trend toward early retirement, companies are increasingly offering employees a preretirement planning program. Preretirement programs may include seminars, booklets, other informational materials, and even retirement rehearsals or phased-retirement plans. More than 75 large corporations like Merck, Atlantic Richfield, and Alcoa have adopted the National Council on the Aging's retirement planning program. Basic topics in most preretirement programs include health, money management, legal issues, and housing. The ideal program is presented over time, each session dealing in depth with one particular issue.[54]

Child Care

Each day at least 5,000 parents fail to come to work or to find employment because they cannot find adequate and affordable child care. An increasing number of employers, both large and small, are responding with company-sponsored child care programs. Alternatives include flexible work hours, establishing workstations at home, offering lists of available child care facilities, and providing on-site programs. Follow-up studies of companies offering these programs have consistently revealed that absenteeism and turnover fall while job satisfaction, productivity, and loyalty soar.[55]

Elder Care

People 65 or older will make up 23 percent of the population of the United States by 2050. The 65 or older U.S. population numbered 35.9 million in 2003. There are over 50,000 persons ages 100 or more. The ratio of the elderly to those of working age was approximately

20 per 100 in 1990 and will be 22 per 100 by 2010.[56] Research shows that at least 20 percent of all employees already provide assistance to one or more elderly relatives or friends. On average, these employees spend from 6 to 35 hours per week providing this care. At least 50 percent of these employees also have children at home. The burden falls more heavily on the working women, who traditionally took care of elderly relatives and did not work outside the home. The employee who is also a caregiver to seniors experiences the following problems: missed work (58 percent), loss of pay (47 percent), and less energy to work well (15 percent). The employer of these individuals experiences problems as well: extensive telephone calls, tardiness, excessive absenteeism, unscheduled time off, and loss of concentration because of concern for the dependent person's (or persons') welfare. The result is reduced productivity.

Elder care, including providing disability insurance for employees that covers nursing-home care for elderly relatives, is an emerging employee benefit. Employee services provided include referrals for day care for seniors, nursing home referrals, and training programs that deal with caregiving.

Financial Services

Some organizations help and encourage their employees to save funds through employee savings plans, credit unions, and thrift plans. Essentially, savings plans encourage thrift by matching all or part of an employee's contribution, up to about 5 percent of the wage or salary. Credit unions help employees by providing loans at reasonable and market-competitive rates of interest.

In thrift plans, most funds are often invested for distribution at retirement. When companies have thrift plans, about 85 percent of employees participate.

Financial planning services are also offered, especially to executives and professional personnel.[57]

Social and Recreational Programs

Today, more than 50,000 organizations provide recreation facilities for employees, on or off the job.[58] Some experts foresee a growing trend to release employees from work time to participate in company-sponsored sports activities. These activities are intended to keep employees physically fit and tie them to their employers.

There are no available studies of the value, if any, of such benefits to the employer. These plans could be extensions of the paternalistic antiunion activities of some employers in the 1920s and later. Studies of employees' preferences indicate that recreational services are the least preferred of all benefits and services offered by organizations.

Flexible Benefits Plans and Reimbursement Accounts

It is apparent from the preceding discussion that employers have traditionally offered their workers benefit plans in a number of areas such as health care, life insurance, and retirement. Typically, the only choice the employee has is between one plan and another in any given area—for example, between a commercial health insurance plan and a health maintenance organization. With the continued escalation in the cost of benefits and the diversity of the labor force, two new approaches to offering benefits have attracted considerable attention—flexible benefits and reimbursement accounts.

A **flexible (cafeteria) benefits plan** allows employees to choose between two or more types of benefits. Common choices include health care, life insurance, disability insurance, and the option of receiving cash to spend on coverage in the open market. **Reimbursement accounts** or **flexible spending accounts** provide funds from which employees pay for expenses not covered by the regular benefits package. The accounts

EXHIBIT 12-8 **Administering the Benefits Program**

Source: Lynn Gaughan and Jorg Kasparek (NCR Corp.) and John Hagens and Jeff Young (September 2000), "Employee a Customer," *Workspan*, pp. 31–37.

A Costs: Please modify this "base" benefit package into another which you would most prefer, bearing in mind that selecting different levels will impact your cash pay (see box to right).

Base Benefit Package	$11,460
Chosen Benefit Package	$11,460
Change in Cash Pay	$0

FEATURE   ALTERNATIVE LEVELS

Feature					
Medical Plan	Opt Out −$4,800	Traditional-Basic Current A Base	HMO −$800	Traditional-Enhanced +$1,000	PPO +$1,300
Long-Term Disability Plan	Opt Out −$840	50% of Your Salary Current A Base	60% of Your Salary +240	70% of Your Salary +480	
Life Insurance	None A Base	1 Times Your Salary +$240	2 Times Your Salary Current +$480	3 Times Your Salary +$720	4 Times Your Salary +$960
401(K) Plan	None −$1,800	3% Match 5-Year Vesting +$1,200	6% Match 5-Year Vesting Current A Base	6% Match 5-Year Vesting $900	10% Match No Vesting $2,400
Paid Parental/ Family Leave	None Current −$180	3-Day Leave A Base	12-Week Leave 1/2 Salary +$540	12-Week Leave Full Salary +$1,800	

are usually pretax deductions so that the employee saves on federal taxes. Funds can be allocated for unreimbursed health care, child care, and care for elderly or disabled relatives.

Flexible benefits and reimbursement accounts can increase employees' satisfaction and save employers from spending money on coverage that the employees don't want.[59] These plans provide for benefit trade-offs and cost sharing. However, sufficient coverage must be provided in key areas like health care, life insurance, and disability regardless of the choices made by the individual employee. Flexible plans that can easily self-adjust to changing circumstances and costs should also be designed.

NCR has adopted what is called a "customer oriented benefits plan." This plan allows employees to exchange some of their base salary for greater coverage of specific and preferred benefits. The NCR plan is illustrated in Exhibit 12-8.

Managing an Effective Benefits Program

When top managers make decisions about benefits and services, they must consider the following facts:[60]

- Mandated programs must be funded.
- There is little evidence that benefits and services really motivate performance. Nor do they necessarily increase satisfaction.

After talking to other presidents and reading some literature that Pete gave him, Carl better understood Pete's conservatism about benefits and services. Carl reviewed what researchers have found and became convinced that pouring money into benefits and services doesn't mean that absenteeism will decrease, production will increase, or loyalty will improve. "Employees have simply come to expect employers to provide competitive benefits and services," Carl thought. "I'm sure glad Pete brought this to my attention."

- Most employees view benefits and services as entitlements.
- Unions, competitors, and industry trends continue to pressure managers to provide or increase voluntary benefits.
- Costs of benefits and services continue to escalate dramatically.

To manage a benefits program effectively, certain steps are necessary. Four of these are discussed next.

Step 1: Set Objectives and Strategy for Benefits

There are three strategies for benefits:

1. *Pacesetter strategy*   Be first with the newest benefits employees desire.
2. *Comparable benefits strategy*   Match the benefits programs similar organizations offer.
3. *Minimum benefits strategy*   Offer the mandatory benefits and those that are most desired and least costly.

The decision about which strategy to use is made on the basis of management's goals. The third strategy may be chosen because of inability to pay more benefits or because management believes the employees want more pay and fewer benefits. Before costly benefits and services are offered, management must set objectives that fit its benefits strategy.

Step 2: Involve Participants and Unions

Whatever strategy is chosen, it makes sense to find out what those involved desire in benefits and services. Yet, in most organizations, top managers alone judge which benefits the employees prefer. Without getting some input on employees' preferences, it is impossible to make these decisions intelligently. This is similar to a marketing manager trying to decide on consumers' preferences with no market research.

Therefore, it is wise to permit (and encourage) employees' participation in decision making on benefits and services. When employees share in these decisions, they show more interest in them. One way to let employees participate in the decisions is to poll them with attitude surveys. Another is to set up employee benefits advisory committees.

When the organization is unionized, it is vital that the union leadership be involved. Many times, the leadership knows what employees want in benefits. Sometimes, however, the leadership tries to maximize benefits without having determined what employees want. It is useful to involve the union leadership in preference studies so that all parties are seeking benefits desired by the employees.

Step 3: Communicate Benefits

Another method for improving the effectiveness of benefits and services is to develop an effective communication program. How can benefits and services affect the satisfaction and performance of employees if they do not know about or understand the benefits?

Yet most studies of employees and executives indicate they are unaware of the benefits or significantly undervalue their cost and usefulness.

It has always been desirable to improve communications, for this reason. But now there is also another reason. For pensions, ERISA requires employers to communicate with employees by sending them an annual report on the pension plan and basic information on their pensions in language they can understand. Many communication media can be used: employee handbooks, company newspapers, magazines, or newsletters; booklets; bulletin boards; annual reports; payroll stuffers; and reports to employees.

Step 4: Monitor Costs Closely

In addition to considering costs involved in the choice of benefits, it is vital that managers make sure the programs are administered correctly. Review of insurance claims is especially important. More efficient administration procedures using computerized methods also can lead to greater savings and more satisfied employees.

Together, these four steps will make any benefits program more effective.

Cost-Benefit Analysis of Benefits

Conrad Fiorello tells a story about a gunman who suddenly appeared at the paymaster's window at a large plant and demanded, "Never mind the payroll, bud. Just hand over the welfare and pension funds, the group insurance premiums, and the withholding taxes." When benefits costs increase, the price of products and services increases. Then companies are less competitive, especially with countries where the government pays for benefits. Higher benefits also can reduce permanent employment, since it is cheaper to pay overtime or to hire part-time employees than to pay full-time wages and benefits. It may also reduce employees' mobility, but most evidence thus far shows that it does not affect turnover at all.

It is rational for employees to want additional benefits, since benefits constitute tax-free income. The costs of such benefits, however, have been rising substantially, and many organizations cannot afford to offer benefits and high wages as well.

The costs of benefits can be calculated fairly easily:

1. Total cost of benefits annually for all employees.
2. Cost per employee per year—basis 1 divided by number of employee hours worked.
3. Percentage of payroll—basis 1 divided by annual payroll.
4. Cost per employee per hour—basis 2 divided by employee hours worked.

The benefits side of the equation is another issue, however. There has been little significant empirical research on the effects of benefits on productivity.

Summary

Chapter 12 has described benefits and services as part of the rewards that reinforce loyal service to the employer. The chapter described mandated and voluntary employee benefits and some critical decisions regarding benefits, such as communication, administration, flexible benefit plans, and employees' participation.

To summarize the main points covered in this chapter:

1. Indirect financial compensation can be defined as all employer-provided rewards and services, other than wages or salaries, arising from the following categories: legally required social insurance payments, private insurance, retirement plans, payment for time not worked, extra cash payments other than bonuses based on performance, and costs of services like subsidized cafeterias, clothing allowances, and so forth.

2. Employers provide benefits and services (1) because some, like social security, are mandated by the federal government; (2) to keep compensation competitive with other employers; (3) as a result of negotiations with unions; and (4) to increase employees' productivity.

3. Mandated benefit programs in the private and nonprofit sectors include unemployment insurance, social security, and workers' compensation.

4. Two kinds of benefits many employers provide voluntarily are:
   a. Compensation for time not worked (break time, coffee breaks, clothes-changing time, holidays, sick leave, vacations, and so on).
   b. Insurance protection (health, disability and accident, and life).

5. Retirement income is received from three principal sources:
   a. Social security payments.
   b. Private pension plans.
   c. Private savings, investments, and postretirement employment.

6. The employee Retirement Income Security Act (ERISA) of 1974 is the law regulating private pensions.

7. Employee services are voluntary benefits provided by employers, including stock ownership plans (ESOPs), preretirement planning and other educational programs, child care, elder care, financial services, and help with housing and relocation.

8. To manage the benefit program effectively, follow these steps:
   a. Develop objectives and a benefit strategy.
   b. Involve participants and unions in benefit decisions.
   c. Communicate the benefits effectively.
   d. Monitor costs closely.

9. To avoid administrative nightmares, employers should concentrate on fewer benefit plans and if possible implement those preferred by most employees.

Key Terms

COBRA, *p. 370*
defined contribution pension plan, *p. 374*
defined benefit pension plan, *p. 374*
ERISA, *p. 373*
flexible (cafeteria) benefits plan, *p. 376*
flexible spending account, *p. 376*

FMLA, *p. 368*
401(k), *p. 372*
HMO, *p. 370*
indirect financial compensation, *p. 356*
IRA, *p. 372*
mandated benefits programs, *p. 359*
PPO, *p. 370*

reimbursement account, *p. 376*
social security, *p. 360*
unemployment insurance, *p. 359*
workers' compensation, *p. 362*

Questions for Review and Discussion

1. Differentiate between indirect financial compensation from wages and salaries. Why are decisions about indirect compensation more complex than decisions about other forms of compensation?

2. Can employers pay out the pension benefits they have promised? If they can't, what should be done for retirees that are left without their pension benefits?

3. What is meant by the term **mandated benefit**? Describe government-mandated benefits. What are the advantages and disadvantages of each?

4. What three general types of benefits do most medium-sized and large firms provide voluntarily? Describe each briefly.

5. What is meant when it is said that many employees view benefits and services as entitlements? How can employers make employees realize that benefits and services must be earned?

6. Discuss the implications of the Family and Medical Leave Act for a small firm and for a family.

7. What factors make health insurance such an expensive benefit to provide?

8. What services do you think are most important to today's increasingly diverse workforce? Why?
9. What are the cornerstones of retirement income? How stable is each one?
10. Outline some proactive steps managers should take in managing a benefits program. Why is each step important?

HRM Legal Advisor

Based on *Mark Duckworth* v. *Pratt & Whitney, Inc.,* 152 F.3d 1 (U.S. App. First Cir. 1998).

The Facts

Mark Duckworth began working for Pratt & Whitney in its North Berwick, Maine, manufacturing plant in 1980. In December 1994, Mr. Duckworth was laid off. His "Employment Termination Record" completed by his supervisor in January 1995 indicated in the "Rehire Status" section that Mr. Duckworth had poor attendance, missing 52 days of work in 1994 resulting from a serious health condition. Mr. Duckworth's medical problems resulted from an accident in which he suffered a punctured lung and broken ribs. The 52 days were taken as medical leave under the Family and Medical Leave ACT (FMLA). In October 1996, Mr. Duckworth applied with Pratt & Whitney and was not rehired. Mr. Duckworth filed a suit against Pratt & Whitney in August 1997, alleging that the company discriminated against him because he had exercised his FMLA right of medical leave in 1994. Regarding discrimination, the FMLA states that it is "unlawful for any employer to interfere with, restrain, or deny the exercise of or the attempt to exercise, any right provided under this subchapter." The act further states that a discrimination action ". . . may be maintained against any employer . . . by any one or more employees for and in behalf of—(a) the employees; or (b) the employees and other employees similarly situated." Pratt & Whitney argued that Mr. Duckworth was not an employee of the company at the time he applied for rehire and thus was not eligible for FMLA protection against discrimination. Should Mr. Duckworth be protected by the FMLA? Does the FMLA prohibit the consideration of medical leave data in making rehire decisions?

The Court's Decision

The U.S. Department of Labor (DOL) is the federal agency that enforces the FMLA. In interpreting the language and intent of the FMLA, the DOL issued a regulation stating:

"An employer is prohibited from discriminating against employees or prospective employees who have used FMLA leave. . . . Employers cannot use the taking of FMLA leave as a negative factor in employment actions, such as hiring, promotions, or disciplinary actions. . . ." The U.S. District Court for the District of Maine rejected the DOL's interpretation of the FMLA stating that the act unambiguously specifies "employees" and does not include prospective employees such as Mr. Duckworth at the time he applied for rehire. The U.S. Court of Appeals for the First Circuit, however, found that the term "employee" in the FMLA was ambiguous and did not necessarily exclude prospective employees from protection. The appeals court gave deference to the DOL's statutory interpretation based on FMLA provisions giving the agency a wide range of authority to "prescribe such regulations as are necessary to carry out the Act."

Human Resource Implications

Although the DOL's regulations are subject to judicial review, courts such as the First Circuit are willing to defer to well-reasoned interpretations made pursuant to statutory authority. The FMLA specifically gives interpretive authority to the DOL. Thus, employers should carefully consider the agency's regulations in implementing the FMLA. This case clearly supports the DOL's position prohibiting employers from discriminating against job applicants on the basis of past FMLA leave.

Notes

1. Burton T. Beam Jr. and John J. McFadden (2004), *Employee Benefits* (Chicago: Dearborn Real Estate Education).
2. Ibid.
3. Reports, charts, tables at www.bls.gov, accessed throughout April–July 2005.
4. Shawn A. Smith and Rebecca A. Mazin (2004), *HR Answer Book* (New York: AMACOM).
5. *SHRM 2004–2005 Workplace Forecast: A Strategic Outlook* (2005) (Alexandria, VA: Society for Human Resource Management).
6. Steven G. Vernon (1993), *Employee Benefits: Valuation, Analysis, and Strategies* (New York: Wiley).
7. See www.bls.gov/ncs/ect/home.htm as of January 2005.
8. Announced on July 7, 2005, www.cnn.com.
9. Philip K. Robins and Robert G. Spiegelman (Eds.) (2001), *Reemployment* (Kalamazoo, MI: W. E. Upjohn Institute).
10. *Harvard Business Review on Compensation* (2001) (Cambridge, MA: Harvard Business School Press).
11. Ibid.
12. Ibid.
13. Mark A. Huselid, Brian E. Becker, and Richard W. Beatty (2005), *The Workforce Scorecard: Managing Human Capital to Execute Strategy* (Boston: Harvard University Press).
14. Ibid.
15. Ethan Pope, *Social Security: What's in It for You* (2005) (New York: Moody Press).
16. Ibid.
17. Lita Epstein (2002), *The Complete Idiot's Guide to Social Security* (New York: Alpha Books).
18. J. Robert Treanor, Robert J. Myers, and Dale R. Detlefs (2002), *Mercer Guide to Social Security and Medicine* (New York: Mercer).
19. Ibid.
20. Pope, op. cit.
21. Ibid.
22. Twila Slesnick and John C. Suttle (2002), *IRAs, 401(k)s, and Other Retirement Plans* (Berkeley, CA: Nolo).
23. Debate continues each year. See Congressional Record for Discussions in U.S. Congress.
24. Edward J. Priz (2005), *Ultimate Guide to Workers' Compensation Insurance* (Irvine, CA: Entrepreneur Press).
25. Ibid.
26. William O. Cleverley and Andrew E. Cameron (2002), *Essentials of Health Care Finance* (Aspen, CO: Aspen).
27. Ibid.
28. Joseph J. Martocchio (2006), *Employee Benefits: A Primer for Human Resource Professionals* (Burr Ridge, IL: Irwin/McGraw-Hill).
29. Ibid.
30. Ibid.
31. Gary Dessler (2005), *Human Resource Management* (Saddle River, NJ: Prentice-Hall).
32. Martocchio, op. cit.
33. Kurt H. Decker (2000), *Family and Medical Leave in a Nutshell* (Cincinnati, OH: West Group).
34. Ibid.
35. Ibid.
36. Steven K. Wisensale (2001), *Family Leave Policy* (New York: Sharp).

37. W. Chan Kim and Renee Mauborgne (2005), *Blue Ocean Strategy: How to Create Uncontested Market Space and Make Competition Irrelevant* (Boston: Harvard Business School Press).

38. Cleverley and Cameron, op. cit.

39. Dee Marella (2005), *Who Cares: A Loving Guide for My Future Caregivers* (Bradenton, FL: DC Press).

40. Ibid.

41. Rhoda D. Orin (2001), *Making Them Pay* (New York: St. Martins).

42. *Coverage Matters* (2001) (New York: National Academy Press).

43. Ibid.

44. Frank J. Bitzer (2005), *2005 Benefit Facts* (New York: National Underwriter Co.).

45. Ibid.

46. Ibid.

47. Ibid.

48. Neil Downing (2002), *The New IRAs* (New York: Kaplan).

49. R. Evan Inglis and Steven G. Vernon (August 1999), "A Better Retirement Plan," *HR Magazine,* pp. 91–96.

50. Bitzer, op. cit.

51. Everett Allen Jr., Dennis F. Mahoney, Jerry S. Rosenbloom, and Joseph Melone (2002), *Pension Planning* (New York: McGraw-Hill).

52. Ibid.

53. Stefan Remaekers (May 2005), "Educational Support, Empowerment, and Its Risks: The Correct Voice of Support," *Educational Theory,* pp. 150–163.

54. "Popularity of 'Phased Retirement' Programs Increases" (December 1999), *HR Magazine,* p. 32.

55. Linda S. Nelson and Alan E. Nelson (2000), *Child Care Administration* (New York: Goodheart-Wilcox).

56. Ann Cason (2005), *Circles of Care: How to Set Up Quality Care for Our Elders in the Comfort of Their Homes* (Boston: Shambhala).

57. James E. Stowers and Jack Jonathan (2005), *Yes I Can . . . Achieve Financial Independence: A New Diet for Financial Independence* (St. Catharines, ON: Andrews McMeel Publishing).

58. William G. Emener, William S. Hutchison, and Michael A. Richard (Eds.) (2005), *Employee Assistance Programs: Wellness/Enrichment Programming* (Springfield, IL: C. C. Thomas).

59. Martocchio, op. cit.

60. Robert J. Grossman (January 2000), "Measuring Up," *HR Magazine,* pp. 28–35.

Application Case 12-1

Benefits Are Vanishing

Ray Brice expected to retire from United Airlines (UAL) and receive a $1,200-a-month pension. Suddenly hope ran out for Ray Brice and 35,000 other UAL retirees. The government Pension Benefit Guaranty Corp (PBGC) announced it would not guarantee the bankrupt airline's loans—virtually ensuring that if the airline's parent company is to remain in business, it will have to chop away at expensive pension and retiree medical benefits. The numbers are daunting. UAL owes $598 million in pension payments in the next six months and a total of $4.1 billion by the end of 2008, plus an additional $1 billion for retiree health care benefits, obligations the ailing airline can't begin to meet. And if United finds a way to get out of its promises, competitors American Airlines (AMR), Delta Air Lines (DAL), and Northwest Airlines (NWAC) are sure to try to as well.

UAL workers are about to find out what other airline employees already know: The cost of broken retirement promises can be steep. Of the airline's many crises, the biggest was the pilots' pension plan, a sinkhole of unfunded liabilities.

Why are retirees being left out in the cold? An unsavory brew of factors has come together to put stress on the retirement system like never before. First, there's the simple fact that Americans are living longer in retirement, and that costs more. Next come internal corporate issues, including soaring health care costs and long-term underfunding of pension promises. Perhaps most important, in the global economy, long-established U.S. companies are competing against younger rivals here and abroad that pay little or nothing toward their workers' retirement, giving the older companies a huge incentive to dump their plans. "The house isn't burning now, but we will have a crisis soon if some of these issues aren't fixed," says Steven A. Kandarian, who ended a two-year stint as the executive director of the Pension Benefit Guaranty Corp (the little known federal agency that insures private pensions) in February. Kandarian is not optimistic about how that crisis might play out, either. "By that time it will be too late to save the system. Then you just play triage."

As industry after industry and company after company strive to limit, or eliminate, their so-called legacy costs, a historic shift is taking place. No one voted on it and Congress never debated the issue, but with little fanfare we have entered into a vast reorganization of our retirement system, from employer funded to employee and government funded, a sort of stealth nationalization of retirement. As the burden moves from companies to individuals—who have traditionally been notoriously poor planners—it becomes near certain that in the end, a bigger portion will fall on the shoulders of taxpayers. "Where the vacuum develops, the government is forced to step in," says Sylvester J. Schieber, a vice president at benefit-consulting firm Watson Wyatt Worldwide (WW). "If we think we can walk away from these obligations scot-free, that's just a dream."

Evidence of the shift is everywhere. Traditional pensions—so-called defined-benefit plans—and retiree health insurance were once all but universal at large companies. Today experts can think of no major company that has instituted guaranteed pensions in the past decade. None of the companies that have become household names in recent times have them: not Microsoft (MSFT), not Wal-Mart Stores (WMT), not Southwest Airlines (LUV). In 1999, IBM, which has old-style benefits and contributed almost $4 billion to shore up its pension plans in 2002, did a study of its competitors and found 75 percent did not offer a pension plan and fewer still paid for retiree health care.

Instead, companies are much more likely to offer defined-contribution plans, such as 401(k)s, to which they contribute a set amount. In 1977, there were 14.6 million people with defined-contribution benefits; today there are an estimated 62.5 million. Part of their appeal has been that a more mobile workforce can take their benefits with them as they hop from job to job. But just as important, they cost less for employers. Donald E. Fuerst, a retirement actuary at Mercer Human Resource Consulting LLC, notes that while even a well-matched 401(k) often costs no more than 3 percent of payroll, a typical defined-benefit plan can cost 5 percent to 6 percent of payroll.

Despite the stampede to defined-contribution plans, there are still 44 million Americans covered by old-fashioned pensions that promise a set payout at retirement. All told, they're owed more than $1 trillion by 30,000 different companies. Many of those employers have also promised tens of billions of dollars more in health care coverage for retirees. Even transferring a small part of the burden to individuals or the government can have a profound impact on the corporate bottom line. The decision by Congress to have Medicare cover the cost of prescription drugs, for example, will lighten corporate retiree health care obligations by billions of dollars. Equipment maker Deere & Co. (DE) estimates that the move will shave $300 million to $400 million off its future health care liabilities starting this year.

The U.S. Treasury, on the other hand, pays and pays dearly. That drug benefit, which takes effect in 2006, is expected to cost the government the equivalent of 1 percent of gross domestic product by 2010, and other potentially big taxpayer costs are looming, too. In mid-April, over the objections of the PBGC, Congress granted a two-year reprieve from catch-up pension contributions for two of the most troubled industries: airlines and steel. Congress also lowered the interest rate all companies use to calculate long-term obligations, lowering pension liabilities. While these moves lighten the corporate burden, they increase the chances taxpayers will have to step in. "The less funding required, the more risk that's shifting to the government," says Peter R. Orszag, a pension expert and senior fellow in economic studies at the Brookings Institution. "The question is: How comfortable are we with the risk of failure?"

Company-sponsored health care, which generally covers retirees not yet eligible for Medicare and supplements what Medicare will pay, is likely to disappear even faster than company pensions. Subject to fewer federal regulations, those benefits are easier to rescind and companies are fast doing so. It's much harder to renege on pension promises. So instead, many profitable companies are simply freezing plans and denying the benefits to new employees. Last fall, Aon Consulting (AON) found that 150 of the 1,000 companies they surveyed had frozen their pension plans in the previous two years, a dramatic increase from earlier years. Another 60 companies said they were actively considering following suit.

The government bailout fund is $9.7 billion in the red, and social security and personal savings are hardly going to be enough

The cost of honoring PBGC's commitments could be higher than anyone is expecting. The government bailout fund has relied on having enough healthy companies to pony up premiums to cover plans that fail. But in a scenario of rising plan terminations, healthy companies with strong plans still in the PBGC system would be asked to pay more. For corporations already fretting that pensions have become a competitive liability and a turnoff to investors, this could be the tipping point. Faced with higher insurance costs, they could opt out, rapidly accelerating the system's decline as the remaining healthy participants become overwhelmed by the needy. In the end, the problem would land with Congress, which could be forced to undertake a savings-and-loan-type bailout. It's almost too painful to think about, and so no one does. But when the bill comes due, it will almost certainly be addressed to taxpayers.

Most worrisome is the record number of pension plans in danger of going under. According to the PBGC, as of September 2003, there was at least $86 billion in pension obligations promised by companies deemed financially weak. That's up from $35 billion the year before. And it's on top of a record number of companies that managed to dump their troubled pension plans on the PBGC last year: 152. In 2003, a record 206,000 people became PBGC pensioners, including 95,000 from its biggest takeover ever, Bethlehem Steel Corp.

Companies are racing to cut or drop retiree medical benefits to give a quick boost to their bottom lines.

Retiree health care coverage, which is easier to eliminate than pensions, is disappearing even faster. Unlike pensions, which are accrued and funded over time, retiree health care is paid for out of current cash accounts, so any cuts immediately bolster the bottom line. Estimates are that as many as half of the companies offering retiree health care 10 years ago have now dropped the benefit entirely. Many of those that have not yet slammed the door are requiring their former workers to bear more of the cost. Some 22 percent of the retirees who still get such benefits are now required to pay the insurance premiums themselves, according to a study by Hewitt Associates Inc. (HEW). Some 20 percent of employers told Hewitt that they might make retirees pay within the next three years. This hits hardest those who retire before 65 and are not yet eligible for Medicare. But even older retirees suffer when they lose supplemental health benefits like prescription coverage.

It's not just struggling companies, either. IBM, which is already fighting with retirees in court over changes made to its pension plan in the 1990s, is now getting an earful from angry retirees about health care costs. In 1999, IBM capped how much retiree health care it would pay per year at $7,500 of each employee's annual medical-insurance costs. Although IBM is certainly in no financial distress—the company earned $7.6 billion on $89 billion in sales last year—Big Blue says its medical costs have been rising faster than revenue. Last year the company says it spent $335 million on retiree health care.

This year, for the first time, many IBM retirees are beginning to hit the $7,500 limit. Sandy Anderson, who worked as a manager at IBM's semiconductor business for 32 years and today is the acting president of a group of 2,000 retirees called Benefits Restoration Inc., saw his own insurance bill triple this year. He suspects that the company is trying to make the perk so expensive that retirees drop it, a cumulative savings calculated by the group at $100,000 per dropout.

But more than that, Anderson is angry that as a manager, IBM encouraged him to talk to his staff about retirement benefits as part of their overall compensation. The job market was tight, and IBM's message was our salaries aren't the highest, but we will take care of you when you stop working, he says. Now he feels the company is reneging. "I feel I've misled a lot of people, that I've lied to people," says Anderson. "It does not sit well with me at all." IBM says its opt-out levels are low and that it often sees retirees return to the plan after opting out for a period of time. The company also argues that it has not changed its approach to retiree medical benefits for more than a decade and that the rising cost of health care is the real issue.

Discussion Questions

1. Is it ethical for a company to promise benefits and then years later walk away from the promise? Discuss.
2. Should the government pay for all pension guarantees?
3. Why is retiree health care coverage easier to eliminate than pension benefits?

Source: N. Byrnes and D. Welch, "The Benefits Trap," *BusinessWeek Online,* accessed July 9, 2005; and Sue Kirchhoff (May 15, 2005), "Pension Funding Problems Grow," *USA Today.*

Video Case

Budget Rent-a-Car and International Compensation

In the corporate offices of Budget Rent-a-Car in Lisle, Illinois, Jack McEnery, the corporate vice president of training and compensation, and Sylvia McGeachie, vice president of human resources for Europe, the Middle East, and Africa, were discussing the implementation of the new incentive plan. The plan appeared to be developing smoothly, and both were pleased by the progress they had made in resolving various administrative issues. It was, however, clear from the discussion that neither previous practice nor theory was available to guide their actions. Most organizations have only recently begun to cope with the ambiguous issues that were being discussed by McEnery and McGeachie.

Suddenly, McGeachie became quiet and thoughtful and then said, "You know, Jack, France mandated compulsory profit sharing in 1967 for companies operating within France. This is going to impact our incentive plan. Are we going to factor in this required compensation before the incentives are determined? We certainly don't want to pay for both. That would mean, in effect, a double bonus for managers."

In France, the Law of 1967 enacted mandatory, private profit sharing. Any employer with more than 100 employees must establish a profit-sharing plan within a prescribed framework. The total employees' share in profits is determined at the end of each year. The minimum requirement is that the profit-sharing formula applies to the excess, if any, of the after-tax profit minus 5 percent of invested capital. Allocation is made on the basis of salary. Typically, the profit sharing is distributed in the form of company shares, with a restriction that employees cannot cash these shares for five years.

Budget's incentive plan was designed to support a global strategy that would reward salaried employees for achieving corporate goals. If 70 percent of the corporate goals regarding profitability are reached, there is a payout to all exempt employees. The amount is based both on profit and on the salary grade of the exempt employee. No base pay is at risk; however, considerable additional compensation may be possible when profit goals are achieved. For example, a manager may receive 25 percent of his or her salary immediately and 25 percent after three years. A vice president may receive 40 percent of his or her salary via an immediate payout and an equivalent amount in three years. Twenty percent of the payout relates to the level of total corporate profitability, another 20 percent relates to regional profitability, and 60 percent depends on the achievement of local goals (in this case, France).

Budget's intention was to align pay practices with business strategy and also compensate employees internationally in a fair, comparable manner. The philosophy was that of "think globally, but act locally." Since France had mandated profit sharing, however, several issues occurred to McEnery and McGeachie as they discussed the incentive plan.

Budget's History

Budget was founded in 1958 by Morris Mirkin and Jules Lederer in a Los Angeles storefront. They began renting Chevys at $4 a day and $.04 a mile. In the mid-1960s, Budget began international operations when it opened operations in Canada and Puerto Rico. Expansion into Great Britain occurred a few years later.

As of 1993, Budget Rent-a-Car is the third largest company in the car rental industry. There are approximately 3,200 locations worldwide (about half are owned by licensees). Sales in 1992 were $2.4 billion, with half of the sales accounted for by licensees. There are 160,000 vehicles available for rent worldwide.

Issues in Compensation

During a continuation of their discussion, McEnery asked McGeachie, "Do you think that with the mandated profit-sharing process in France we can create a sufficiently motivating environment with Budget's incentive plan? I think it is important that we avoid underpayment since that will be frustrating and may be perceived as unfair by employees. On the other hand, overpayment is both inappropriate for Budget and possibly demotivating. Why, after all, if you already get a high reward for moderate effort make an extraordinary effort?"

"I agree," McGeachie responded, "but I think that if we ensure that the rewards are high enough beyond the legal requirements, motivation will be strong. We must try to ensure in France that approximately the same level of pay related to profit is at risk as in other countries. It is my perception after working a great deal with the French that although historically the government has had a socialistic orientation, there would be few differences among the French managers in how they would react to incentives as compared with other Europeans. French managers have become cosmopolitan in understanding the trends of business across Europe, and incentive compensation is a very important issue right now. We must discuss the issue with our people in France, but I think in this area, at least, we will see similar reactions and motivation."

After some consideration, McEnery suggested, "So we have to consider the factors that might interfere with the level of the reward." "That's right," said McGeachie, "and one critical issue to consider is the income tax rate of the French. Although the income tax also funds health care coverage and pensions, it is very high. There is a rapidly sliding scale based on income, with no deductions allowed except for dependents. For instance, the income tax rate is 50 percent at the American equivalent of approximately $52,000. The same incentive amount will equate to less reward in France as compared with the United States because of taxes."

"Let me play devil's advocate," said McEnery, "and suggest that while pay is a concern of the company and employee, the income tax rate is the concern of the citizen and the government of a country." (Some compensation specialists believe that the analysis should be pretax; otherwise, every time a government changes the tax structure, the compensation structure of organizations would need revision.)

The discussion was continued later with the marketing manager in France, Bertrand Guidard. Guidard stated, "Employee reactions to incentives will depend, in France, on the level of the employee. Higher-level employees are very concerned about profitability in France since they recognize this relates to the future of Budget in France as well as to their bonus. The incentive plan is very motivating for managers, although I don't believe that lower level employees are motivated by the idea of possible incentives. We need an incentive plan, although it has to be possible to reach."

Conclusions

In international compensation, there are two forces that must be considered simultaneously. First, there must be a global vision that allows an organization to formulate a business strategy that crosses national borders. Many argue that a single marketplace has been created by competitiveness of global operations. Particularly in a service organization, the ability to attract and retain customers is critical. The emphasis on quality in service has become a monumental concern. Poor service may send more customers to the global competition than price or quality.

The second consideration is the impact of local conditions. Culture, and even operations of an international organization, will vary across borders. Therefore, an international compensation decision involves the reinforcement of global strategy but also must recognize and reward differences in cultural approaches. Communication is critical about both basic compensation philosophy and the way goals are set, measured, and rewarded.

The management of human resources may be the key to global success. Compensation strategies therefore need to reinforce the concept of service delivery. The incentive plan described for Budget was designed to maintain the motivation and satisfaction of management employees, as well as to ensure the company's competitive ability to attract and retain the best employees.

Discussion Questions

1. What do you think Budget should do about the incentive plan in France?
2. Do you think that compensation decisions should be made pre- or post-tax? Defend your position.

3. What should "think globally, act locally" mean when implementing an incentive plan such as Budget's?

4. Put yourself in the position of a manager for Budget. How do you reconcile the issue of government-mandated profit sharing versus additional incentives designed by Budget? Would compensation be likely to affect your behavior or other managers' behavior in different ways?

Sources: "The Quality Imperative—What It Takes to Win in the Global Economy" (October 25, 1991), *BusinessWeek* (whole issue); D. J. Carey and P. D. Howes (1992), "Developing a Global Pay Program," *Journal of International Compensation and Benefits* 1, 1, pp. 30–34; F. K. Hahn (November–December, 1991), "Shaping Compensation Packages in Global Companies," *Journal of Compensation and Benefits*, pp. 11–16; J. S. Hyman and R. G. Kantor (1992), "The Globalization of Compensation," *Journal of International Compensation and Benefits*, 1, 1, pp. 25–29; M. J. Marquardt and D. W. Engel (1993), *Global Human Resource Development* (Englewood Cliffs, NJ: Prentice-Hall).

Part 4

Developing Human Resources

Part Four covers the training and development of employees. Chapter 13, "Training and Development," focuses on improving employees' abilities and skills. Chapter 14, "Career Planning and Development," looks at an area of growing importance in organizations.

13

Training and Development

Learning Objectives

After studying this chapter you should be able to:

1. **Define** training and learning.
2. **Describe** the characteristics of an orientation program.
3. **Explain** the role a performance analysis can play in identifying employees' needs for training.
4. **Discuss** the differences among development programs targeted for individuals, for groups, and for the total organization.
5. **Explain** the importance of evaluation training and development and how it can be done in an organization.
6. **Compare** the distinct characteristics of goal setting, behavior modification, and team building.

Internet/Web Resources

General Sites
www.breakthebarriers.com

www.unext.com

www.traininghouse.com

http://www.netg.com/interactnow/

http://www.mindleaders.com/

www.trainlink.com

www.astd.org

Company Sites
www.national.com

www.ppg.com

www.dnb.com

http://www.ge.com/en/

www.mobil.com

www.ralston.com

www.jcpenney.com

Harold Matthews was unhappy. He'd just had an unpleasant visit with his boss, Bill Custer. Harold is vice president of operations of Young Enterprises, a firm employing about 1,600 persons in the Los Angeles area. The firm manufactures parts for a large aircraft firm nearby.

Since Young Enterprises serves primarily one customer, costs are a major factor in their negotiations. Bill Custer told Harold that the new contract was not as good as the last one. Costs needed to be cut. Since labor costs are a high percentage of the total, Harold must begin to work on these. At the same time, purchasing was working on reducing materials costs and finance was trying to find ways to reduce the cost of capital.

Harold has decided to consult two groups about the cost cutting: HRM managers and his managers. First, he called a meeting of the department heads and key supervisors and prepared his figures. The facts are:

- Young Enterprises's labor costs are rising faster than their competitors' are and faster than the cost of living.
- These costs are higher any way you measure them: number of employees per unit of output, cost per unit of output, and so on. What's more, the trend is worsening.

At the meeting, Harold explained the facts. Then he asked the managers for suggestions. He encouraged them to manage each employee closely to make sure that the firm gets a fair day's work for a fair day's pay. Harold took notes of the comments his managers made.

Sally Feldman (supervisor)   One of my problems is that the people HRM sends me are not producing at the productivity levels of the people I've lost through quits and retirement.

Art Jones (department head)   Let's face it, when you look at the records, our recent output isn't up to what we expected when we installed the new machines.

Sam Jacobs (supervisor)   The problem is our current crop of employees. They ain't what they used to be!

Harold wondered if they were just passing the buck—or if there was some truth to the complaints. He invited Gwen Meridith, the HRM vice president, in for help.

Harold   Gwen, production costs are up and labor efficiency is down. The managers are blaming it on the employees. We installed new technology to get production up. It's up, but not to what it should be, given our investment. What do you think is going on?

Gwen   I suspect that part of what they say has some truth to it. Lately, the job market is tight. Last week, I had 20 jobs to fill and only 20 applicants. About half really were somewhat marginal. And let's fact it, we installed new technology with little preparation of the employees.

Harold   What can we do? We have a serious cost problem.

Gwen   The job market is still tight. I don't see any improvement in the near future. Sounds as if we ought to gear up that training program I've been talking about.

Harold   You prepare something for Bill. Then you and I will go to see him about it.

Training and development are processes that attempt to provide an employee with information, skills, and an understanding of the organization and its goals. In addition, training and development are designed to help a person continue to make positive contributions in the form of good performance. Orientation is designed to start the employee in a direction that is compatible with the firm's mission, goals, and culture. Before training or development occurs in some firms an employee proceeds through an orientation to learn what the organization stands for and the type of work he or she is expected to perform.

Orientation introduces new employees to the organization and to his or her new tasks, managers, and work groups. Walking into a new job is often a lonely and confusing event. The newcomer doesn't usually know what to say or whom to say it to, or even where he or she is supposed to be. Getting started is difficult for any new employee simply because being new means not knowing what to expect, having to cope with a major life change (the job), and feeling unsure about the future. These ingredients suggest that "newness anxiety" will naturally be significant. It takes time to learn the ropes, but a good orientation program can help make this time a positive experience. The first few days on the job are crucial in helping the employee get started in the right direction with a positive attitude and feeling.

Different degrees of orientation are needed, depending on the experience, career path, and age of the new employee. A 50-year-old manager who is transferring to another department in the same company at the same job level may need only minimal orientation. However, a 22-year-old technician who is starting her first full-time job after attending a trade school may need a full-blown orientation. Any orientation is designed to make the person more comfortable, knowledgeable, and ready to work within the firm's culture, structures, and employee mix. Thus, examining the background of the employee is important in designing the proper type of orientation program.

This chapter will address orientation, training, and development in sequence. Each is important to the success of the firm and each must be used to optimize desired end results.

Orientation orients, directs, and guides employees to understand the work, firm, colleagues, and mission.

Training helps employees do their current work better.

Development prepares individuals for the future. It focuses on learning and personal development.

Introduction to Orientation

Effectively done, orientation serves a number of purposes. In general, the orientation process is similar to what sociologists call *socialization*. Socialization occurs when a new employee learns the norms, values, work procedures, and patterns of behavior and dress that are expected in the organization. Some of the principal purposes of orientation are discussed in the next few sections.

Organizational socialization consists of social processes through which organizations transmit to members the expectations associated with their roles.[1] In practice, members of the established group (company, unit, culture) communicate to newcomers systematic sets of expectations for how they should behave. People undergoing socialization respond both cognitively and emotionally.[2] First, they receive and attempt to understand the cultural messages being sent to them by the agents of socialization (co-workers, superiors, subordinates, customers). Second, to various degrees they agree with and emotionally accept those messages. If messages sent are not understood or accepted, people being socialized must invent their own behaviors.

Goals of Orientation

An orientation program is an attempt to send clear messages and provide accurate information about the company culture, the job, and expectations. Unfortunately, what is clear to one person may be muddled to another. Clear messages that are understood and accepted can achieve a number of orientation goals, such as the following.

To Reduce Anxiety

Anxiety in this case means fear of failure on the job. It is a normal fear of the unknown, focused on the ability to do the job. This anxiety can be made worse if current employees ignore the new employee.

To Reduce Turnover

If employees perceive themselves as ineffective, unwanted, or unneeded, they may react to these feelings by quitting. Turnover is high during the break-in period, and effective orientation can reduce this costly reaction.

To Save Time

Improperly oriented employees must still get the job done, and to do so they need help. The most likely people to provide this help are co-workers and supervisors, who will have to spend time breaking in new employees. Good orientation programs save everyone time.

To Develop Realistic Expectations

In what sociologists call the *older professions* (law, medicine) or *total institutions* (the church, prison, the army), job expectations are clear because they have been developed over long years of training and education. Society has built up a set of attitudes and behaviors that are considered proper for these jobs. For most of the world of work, however, this does not hold true. New employees must learn realistically what the organization expects of them, and their own expectations of the job must be neither too low nor too high.[3] Each worker must incorporate the job and its work values into his or her self-image. Orientation helps this process.

Who Orients New Employees?

In smaller organizations, the operating manager usually does all the orienting. In some unionized organizations, union officials are involved. HRM also helps train the operating manager for more effective orientation.

National Semiconductor Corp. became involved in a benchmark project to improve its orientation of employees. The firm had concluded that its existing orientation was not the best, and it began to revamp the program. It used Walt Disney—a firm that has a reputation for an outstanding orientation program—as a model.[4]

National Semiconductor also used a "college hire assimilation program" (CHAP). Most new hires out of college are general trainees. The goals of CHAP are to ease the transition from school to work, accelerate productivity, encourage teamwork, build a personal and professional network, and install corporate values. CHAP consists of 40 hours of activity and instruction during the first three months of employment. The new hires work on rotating assignments in different departments. At the end of the three months, they have career planning sessions with an in-house career counselor to help them decide in which area they wish to work.

How Orientation Works

Orientation programs for new employees vary from quite informal, primarily oral efforts, to formal schedules that supplement spoken presentations with written handouts. Formal orientations often include a tour of the facilities or slides, charts, and pictures of them. Usually, the latter are used when a larger number of employees must be oriented.

Instead of a quick and information-overloaded orientation program, a more systematic and guided procedure is appropriate. Following are a few guidelines for such a program:

1. Orientation should begin with the most relevant and immediate kinds of information and then proceed to more general policies of the organization. It should occur at a pace that the new employee is comfortable with.

HR Journal   *Making New Hires Feel Welcome*

According the experts, it takes about six months for a mid-level manager to learn the "ropes" and the system of a new employee. During this time of observing and learning, co-workers are picking up the slack and their morale is sagging. Becoming acclimated is time-consuming, but a very crucial part of becoming a committed employee.

For any new employee, the first day of work is always nerve-wracking. New people, new rules, new expectations—it's all very unsettling. And when the dust finally clears and new hires settle into their daily routines, many of them—more than 50 percent in some sectors—will choose to quit within a year. The money spent training these new employees will have been wasted, and in companies that have come to expect this sort of attrition, even more money will be thrown away training their replacements, half of whom will also quit.

And so the cycle goes.

High turnover rates may seem like a chronic illness, but they are really more like a disease—they have a cause, and they can be treated. Indeed, many companies are discovering (or, in some cases, re-discovering) that one of the keys to developing and retaining quality employees is a multifaceted approach to new-hire orientation that goes well beyond those first few hectic days. In fact, the most ambitious programs treat the first few weeks and months as a transition period in which a company's culture, passion, pride, and procedures are communicated using a creative variety of tools and techniques designed to develop and nurture those delicate threads of trust and faith that bind good companies and their employees together over the long haul.

Of course, such programs cost considerably more than a how-are-you and a handshake, but this cost must be weighed against the cost of re-training new people for the same positions over and over again. If good first impressions aren't reinforced in the first few hours and days of a new person's tenure, the chances that a new hire will start immediately developing his or her exit strategy rise dramatically.

Karen Lawson, author of *New Employee Orientation Training*, says many companies are beginning to recognize the payoff from investing in new-hire programs that go beyond a welcome letter and a copy of the employee handbook. The return comes in two primary forms: (1) Improved retention means fewer hires that have to be trained from scratch, and (2) more loyal, dedicated employees are also more experienced, knowledgeable workers who contribute that much more to the collective overall competence of an organization. And it all starts on that crucial first day.

"The impression an employee gets that first day is critical in terms of their understanding and feeling welcome in that organization's culture," says Lawson. "If it's done well, a new-hire orientation should convey the company's philosophy, purpose and values." It should also lay a solid foundation for the employee's success. A good orientation program, says Lawson, should confirm for the new hire that they are a valued addition to the team, and that the hire and the company are a good match.

"There is more questioning now," she says of today's workers. "New employees are asking, 'How do I fit in here? Did I make the right choice?'" According to Lawson, younger people are especially sensitive to such issues as whether a company embraces diversity in its workforce and treats people like valuable individuals rather than a means to a profitable end.

A vital step toward preventing chronic turnover, says Lawson, is developing an orientation program that blends online instruction, classroom interaction, and interpersonal dialogue to deliver a consistent, well-constructed, and thought-out program that immerses new employees in a company's culture and clearly defines their role in the organization's overall success. In most cases, says Lawson, the payoff in employee longevity and loyalty is well worth the up-front investment.

Randstad North America is a staffing company based in Atlanta that trains up to 800 agents per year and faces about a 40 percent turnover rate in those positions. Randstad's employee-orientation program used to include sending new hires a welcome letter, a company video, and a bag of popcorn. Since then, however, the company has completely revamped its entire orientation process in order to improve retention and, ultimately, feed the bottom line.

"We now have a 16-week program that's monitored and evaluated, and fully supported by the top leadership in the company," says Vince Eugenio, Randstad's chief learning officer and global e-learning head. Now, a direct manager personally calls a new employee before his or her first day at work and offers a welcome. During the first two days of employment, district managers provide what Eugenio calls a "deep dive into the culture of the company." Regional directors, another step up the chain, conduct one-on-one pulse-taking calls several times during the first few weeks to make sure new hires are on track. Randstad also uses online learning to supplement classroom and

HR Journal   *Making New Hires Feel Welcome*   (continued)

on-the-job training, and employs a learning management system to help managers track the progress of their hires, whose performance is checked by a variety of assessments, including tests, checklists, and other evaluations.

Alison McIsaac, Randstad's national manager of curriculum development, plays a key role in Randstad's onboarding process. "We wanted it to be more than corporate rah-rah," she explains. The idea is to build stronger manager–employee bonds right from the start. To make sure managers have a vested interest in the success of their newbies, they too are assessed on a monthly basis, and incentives are linked to the performance of their charges. Skills are built incrementally over a four-month period, and overall progress is monitored and evaluated almost every step of the way.

"It's a very defined process," says McIsaac. "It's not just about what new hires have to learn and do, but also about what managers have to do."

Randstad isn't the only company overhauling its new-employee education program to meet the challenges of a more fickle workforce. A month or two into their jobs, new employees at electric utility PacifiCorp—who receive a standard one-day initiation—also began taking a three-part Connections curriculum designed to help them better understand their role in working at the regulated electric utility.

"The Connections program connects the dots between an employee's contribution to the company and the different parts of the company and how they work together," says Janna Sondenaa, PacifiCorp's learning manager.

The three-step Connections process begins as participants arrive at one location, often the company headquarters in Portland, Oregon, and spend a day learning a core curriculum that has been identified as essential by human resource and training professionals and by company executives. The first half of the day is spent with an instructor and the second half is designed as a lab environment. "They can actually get in and do learning that same day," Sondenaa says. For the second step, employees return to their work environment in any one of six states, incorporating online learning into their job schedules. Then employees return for the third step: one more day of classroom training.

Sondenaa says PacifiCorp blended online and instructor-led learning over a period of two months because of the nature of the material and the logistical difficulties of pulling new hires off the job for an extended period of time. "We had to come up with a cost-effective and efficient way of letting newer employees get the training and yet be respectful of the job they have to do," she explains.

Understanding the product—electricity—and what it means to sell it to the customer is central to the training. PacifiCorp is an investor-owned utility that serves 1.5 million customers with electricity needs. Its 6,000-plus employees do everything from mining coal and climbing utility poles to supporting field operations and managing educational programs about energy conservation.

But not everyone understands electricity or the electric industry, so training helps remind new hires why electricity is so important to daily life—and hence why their jobs are so important—as well as why following established procedures is so vital to maintaining the electrical infrastructure.

Applied Materials, a supplier of semiconductor equipment based in Santa Clara, California greets new hires with a one-day "Welcome to Applied" series. This series—taught in two U.S. locations, or globally through videoconferencing or an Internet meeting site—begins with a three-hour core seminar about the company's vision, values, and mission, as well as IT resources, tools, human resources, benefits, and quality control. "Immediately, new hires get a fundamental understanding of Applied's vision, mission, and values," says Diana Hayden, managing director of Applied Global University. "The program gives everybody we hire the same message."

"Everybody" includes temporary workers and contract employees as well. The company's perspective is that it is just as important for temporary employees to do a good job, get results, and feel connected with other areas of the company, Hayden says.

The second part of the one-day training is location-specific information focusing on such things as records, payroll, benefits, and security. During their first six months, employees enroll in programs—delivered live and online—that focus on human resources, confidential and proprietary information, affirmative action, doing business with integrity, intellectual property, and safety. Furthermore, employees undergo another one-day program, within 45 days, that dives deeper into the strategies and objectives of the corporation, and further clarifies employees' understanding of their role and contribution to the company as a whole. The agenda includes discussions about business acumen,

(continued)

HR Journal · *Making New Hires Feel Welcome* (concluded)

organizational structure, products, performance management, self-performance management, meetings, and developing leadership at all levels.

For organizations considering an overhaul of their new-hire orientation program, those who have done it say there are a couple of key elements to remember. The first, says PacifiCorp learning manager Janna Sondenaa, is getting buy-in from top executives—which, in most cases, means being able to translate the up-front investment in new-employee training to bottom-line savings and other tangible benefits to the company.

Once the top management is convinced, Applied Materials' Diana Hayden offers this advice: Don't do too much too soon, and give employees a sense of

what they've joined. Communicating how every employee's job serves the overall mission of the company is key. "It is critically important for people to have an understanding of what the company does, what the company stands for, how to be successful, how to fit in, and how to navigate the company's culture," Hayden explains. The first thing a new hire wants to know is that the company they are working for values their skills, she says. No matter what business you're in, that fundamental fact never seems to change.

Source: Kristen Gustafson (June 2005), "A Better Welcome Mat," *Training*, pp. 34–39; and Derek Moscato (April 2005), "Using Technology to Get Employees on Board," *HR Magazine*, pp. 107–109.

2. The most significant part of orientation is the human side: giving new employees knowledge of what supervisors and co-workers are like, telling them how long it should take to reach standards of effective work, and encouraging them to seek help and advice when needed.

3. New employees should be "sponsored" or directed in the immediate environment by an experienced worker or supervisor who can respond to questions and keep in close touch during the early induction period.

4. New employees should be gradually introduced to the people with whom they will work, rather than given a superficial introduction to all of them on the first day. The object should be to help them know their co-workers and supervisors.

5. New employees should be allowed sufficient time to get their feet on the ground before job demands on them are increased.

The accompanying HR Journal presents some orientation programs offered by Randstad and Applied Materials. The two firms believe that orienting new employees is important in making them glad that they came to work for them.

Orientation Follow-Up

The final phase of a well-designed and systematic orientation program is the assignment of the new employee to the job. At this point, the supervisor is supposed to take over and continue the orientation program. One way to ensure adequate orientation is to design a feedback system to control the program or use management by objectives. A form could be used to communicate this feedback from the trainee. The new employee could be instructed, "Complete this checklist as well as you can. Then take it to your supervisor, who will go over it with you and give you any additional information you may need." The job information form is signed by employee and supervisor. An appointment set up with the orientation group in the first month on the job provides a follow-up opportunity to determine how well the employee is adjusting and permits evaluation of the orientation program. The form is designed not to test knowledge but to help improve the process of orientation. Even in organizations with superb orientation programs, the time inevitably arrives when training and/or development is needed.

Introduction to Training

Training is important for new or present employees. Training is, in short, an attempt to improve current or future performance. The following specific points are important to know about training:

- Training is the systematic process of altering the behavior of employees in a direction that will achieve organization goals. Training is related to present job skills and abilities. It has a current orientation and helps employees master specific skills and abilities needed to be successful.[5]
- A formal training program is an effort by the employer to provide opportunities for the employee to acquire job-related skills, attitudes, and knowledge.
- **Learning** is the act by which the individual acquires skills, knowledge, and abilities that result in a relatively permanent change in his or her behavior.
- Any behavior that has been learned is a skill. Therefore, improvement of skills is what training will accomplish. Motor skills, cognitive skills, and interpersonal skills are targets of training programs.

One way to display the meaning and comprehensiveness of training and development is to use a visual model of how it unfolds in an organization. The needs assessment phase serves as the formulation for decisions that must be made at later phases. It is important for the needs assessment to be complete, timely, and accurate.

Needs assessment is a process that is used to determine if and what type of training is necessary. It usually involves an organizational, person, and task analysis. *Organizational analysis* involves examining a firm's mission, resources, and goals to determine if training can be used to improve the firm's success, growth, and strategy. *Person analysis* involves the determination of who needs training and their readiness for training. *Task analysis* involves the identification of the tasks, knowledge, skill, and behaviors that should be included in a training program.

Interviews, surveys, reviews of records, observation, and discussions with management and subject matter experts (SMEs) are methods used to conduct a needs assessment. These data and information gathering techniques provide a profile of *what* type of training is needed, *who* should be trained, *when* training should be conducted, and *whether* training is the preferred approach.

After a needs assessment is completed, *instructional objectives* lead to the selection and design of specific and customized instructional programs. If assessment and the selection and design of programs are done carefully, the training and development can be *monitored* and *evaluated*.

Goals of Training

As Exhibit 13-1 indicates, evaluation can provide information about when various training goals have been accomplished. Some important goals are:

- *Training validity* Did the trainees learn skills or acquire knowledge or abilities during the training?
- *Transfer validity* Did the knowledge, skills, or abilities learned in training lead to improved performance on the job?

EXHIBIT 13-1   **A General Systems Model of Training and Development**

Source: From I. L. Goldstein (1993), *Training in Organizations: Needs Assessment, Development, and Evaluation,* 2nd ed. (Monterey, CA: Brooks/Cole), p. 21. Reprinted by permission of the publisher.

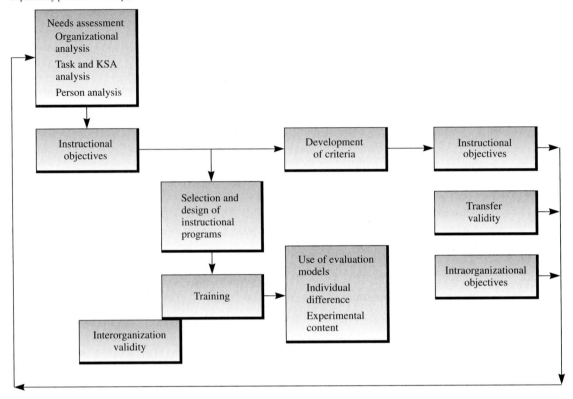

- *Intraorganizational validity* Is the job performance of a new group of trainees in the same organization that developed the program comparable to the job performance of the original training group(s)?
- *Interorganizational validity* Can a training program that has been validated in one organization be used successfully in another firm?

These questions (goals) result in different evaluation procedures to examine what, if anything, training and development have accomplished.[6]

Learning Theory and Training

Since training is a form of education, some of the findings regarding learning theory logically apply to training. These principles can be important in the design of both formal and informal training programs. The following is a brief summary of the way learning principles can be applied to job training.[7]

The Trainee Must Be Motivated to Learn

In order to learn, a person must want to learn. In the context of training, motivation influences a person's enthusiasm for training, keeps attention focused on the training activities, and reinforces what is learned. Motivation is influenced by the beliefs and perceptions of the trainee. If a trainee is not motivated, little can be accomplished in a training program.

The Trainee Must Be Able to Learn

To learn complex things, a person must have certain aptitudes. Do you think that thousands of repetitions and hours of training would enable any person to hit a major league pitcher's curveball out of a baseball park? The ability to learn plays a role in whether what is taught in a training program can be understood and applied back at work.

The Learning Must Be Reinforced

Behavioral psychologists have demonstrated that people learn best with fairly immediate reinforcement of appropriate behavior. The learner must be rewarded for new behavior in ways that satisfy needs, such as pay, recognition, and promotion. Standards of performance should be set for the learner. Benchmarks for learning provide goals and give a feeling of accomplishment when reached. These standards provide a measure for meaningful feedback.

The Training Must Provide for Practice of the Material

Time is required to assimilate what has been learned, to accept it, to internalize it, and to build confidence in it. This requires practice and repetition of the material.

The Material Presented Must Be Meaningful

Appropriate materials for sequential learning (cases, problems, discussion outlines, reading lists) must be provided. The trainer acts as an aid in an efficient learning process.

The learning methods used should be as varied as possible. It is boredom that destroys learning, not fatigue. Any method—whether an old-fashioned lecture or programmed learning or a challenging computer game—will begin to bore some learners if overused.

The Material Must Be Communicated Effectively

Communication must be done in a unified way and over enough time to allow absorption.

The Material Taught Must Transfer to the Job

The trainer must do her or his best to make the training as close to the reality of the job as possible. Thus, when the trainee returns to the job, the training can be applied immediately.

"Learning Organizations"

Peter Senge popularized the concept of **learning organizations** in his book *The Fifth Discipline.* He described them as places "where people continually expand their capacity to create the results they truly desire, where new and expansive patterns of thinking are nurtured, where collective aspiration is set free, and where people are continually learning how to learn together."[8]

Learning organizations appear to be proficient in a number of activities: systematic problem solving, experimentation with new approaches, learning from their own experience and history, learning from the experiences and best practices of others, and transferring knowledge quickly and efficiently throughout the organization.[9] Learning in firms such as Xerox, General Electric, and Pittsburgh Plate Glass (PPG) has been traced using a learning perspective involving three stages: (1) cognitive—members are exposed to new ideas, expand their knowledge, and begin to think differently; (2) behavioral—employees begin to alter their behavior; and (3) improvement of performance—changes in behavior lead to measurable improvements in results.[10]

In an organization dedicated to creating a learning environment, training is a top priority. Learning organizations do not simply appear. They are fostered by devoting time, energy, and resources on a continuous basis to the training and development of employees (managerial and nonmanagerial). Taking steps to encourage learning through training and development activities and forums is essential if improved understanding, performance, and effectiveness are goals.

Training Activities

Training magazine produces an annual training industry report. The report focuses primarily on firms with 100 or more employees; according to Dun & Bradstreet, there are

EXHIBIT 13-2 **Instructional Methods: Frequency of Use**

Source: "Training Magazine Annual Report of Training," (October 2004), *Training,* p. 32.

Methods	everused	Seldom used	Often used	Always used
Case Studies	17%	40%	39%	4%
Classroom w/instructor, traditional	3	13	67	18
Classroom w/instructor, virtual	40	41	17	2
Computer-based games	50	41	9	1
Non-computer-based games	35	44	19	2
Experiential programs	34	46	18	25
Performance support	20	40	38	2
Public seminars	8	40	48	4
Role playing	19	47	31	3
Self-study, Web-based	16	42	37	6
Self-study, non-computer	29	48	20	3
Virtual reality programs	81	16	2	0

146,961 such organizations in the United States. The 2001 industry report indicated the following:

- Total dollars budgeted for formal training of organizations with 100 or more employees—$51.4 billion.
- A large segment of the training budget, 38 percent, is used for salaries of trainers and other support personnel.[11]

Instructor-led training continues to be the preferred and dominant method of delivering training. Exhibit 13-2 presents the frequency of use of various methods for delivering training.

Exhibit 13-3 presents the instructional media used in delivering training. The Internet/intranet/extranet have continued to be used more each year for the past five years.

The blend of e-learning and traditional methods of delivering training is illustrated in Exhibit 13-4. As presented, training in computer systems/applications, computer systems/programming, technological skills/knowledge, and management skills/development each rely heavily on e-learning and traditional classroom methods.

Managers realize how important and how large the commitment to training is for the future of their organizations. The consensus accounting model reported by the American Society for

EXHIBIT 13-3
Training Budget Breakdowns 1999–2001

Source: Tammy Galvin (October 2001), *2001 Industry Report, Training,* p. 46.

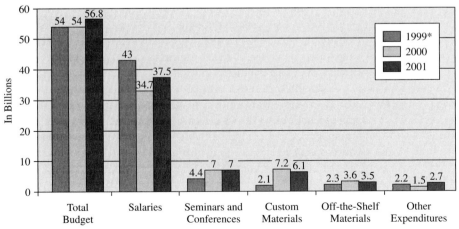

* Does not include $4.5 billion in facilities/overhead; $4.1 billion in hardware.

EXHIBIT 13-4
**Methods by Which
Types of Training Are
Provided**

Source: "Training Magazine
Annual Report of Training"
(October 2004), *Training,* p. 36.

Method	E-Learning	Traditional	Both	Do Not Provide
Communication skills	4%	62%	25%	10%
Computer systems/application	8	33	57	2
Computer systems/programming	7	20	45	28
Customer service	2	54	25	18
Executive development	1	51	25	23
Personal growth	5	39	31	25
Sales	18	32	23	44
Supervisory skills	3	59	30	9
Technological skills/knowledge	4	42	45	9

Training and Development (www.astd.org) helps firms assess the costs and benefits of their training and development program.[12] The consensus model consists of four steps:

1. Establish an organization-specific definition of training.
2. Determine all training cost categories.
3. Calculate training costs.
4. Code costs.

The economic costs of training (e.g., salaries of trainers, lost time away from work, materials, travel, accommodations) need to be continually reviewed, and a training program must be evaluated to determine if it has made a specific contribution (e.g., performance improvement, morale enhancement, increased self-confidence) to the organization's goals.

Managing the Training Program

Determining Needs and Objectives

The first step in managing training is to determine training needs and set objectives for these needs. In effect, the trainers are preparing a training forecast (this is the assessment phase in Exhibit 13-1).

The needs assessment involves analyzing the organization's needs; the knowledge, skill, and ability needed to perform the job; and the person or jobholder's needs. The organizational needs assessment requires an examination of the long- and short-term objectives of the firm. The organization's financial, social, human resource, growth, and market objectives need to be matched with the firm's human talent, structure, climate, and efficiency. Where is the organization going, and does it have the capability to get there? These are the important questions that need to be assessed. Typically, objectives, ratios, organization charts, historical records on absenteeism, quality of production, efficiency, and performance appraisals will be carefully reviewed.

The knowledge, skills, and abilities (K, S, A) needed to perform the job are carefully considered. What are the tasks? What skills are needed to perform well? What does performing well mean? Data from current employees, supervisors, and experts must be collected to complete this part of a needs assessment.

The employee's needs also must be considered. Asking people what their needs are on the job and asking them to perform tasks can provide information and data. Examining the employee's performance against a standard or compared with that of co-workers can help identify strengths, weaknesses, and needs. Determining if a person can do the job is an important step in improving the firm's ability to match the person with the best job for him or her.

Each of these assessment categories is important. However, focusing on the person's needs is especially important. It is at the individual or group level that training is conducted.

EXHIBIT 13-5
Performance Analysis: Analyzing Training Needs

Source: Adapted from Donald Michalak and Edwin Yager (1979), *Making the Training Process Work* (New York: Harper and Row).

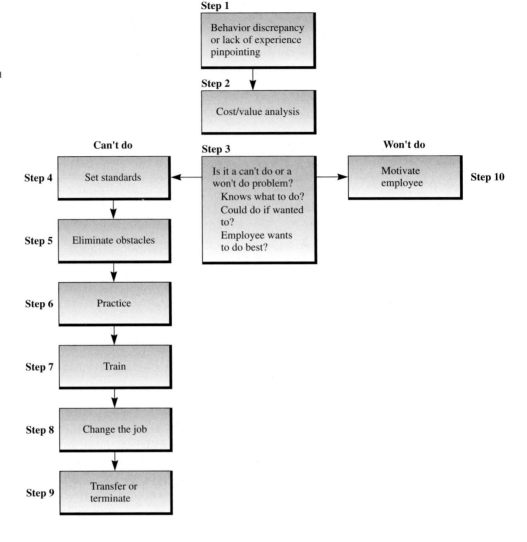

Step 1

Behavior discrepancy or lack of experience pinpointing

Step 2

Cost/value analysis

Can't do

Step 3

Is it a can't do or a won't do problem?
   Knows what to do?
   Could do if wanted to?
   Employee wants to do best?

Won't do

Step 10 — Motivate employee

Step 4 — Set standards

Step 5 — Eliminate obstacles

Step 6 — Practice

Step 7 — Train

Step 8 — Change the job

Step 9 — Transfer or terminate

There are four ways to determine employees' needs for training:[13]

1. Observe employees.
2. Listen to employees.
3. Ask supervisors about employees' needs.
4. Examine the problems employees have.

In essence, any gaps between expected and actual results suggest a need for training.[14] Active solicitation of suggestions from employees, supervisors, managers, and training committees can also provide ideas.

By observing, asking, and listening, a manager or HR specialist is actually conducting a **performance analysis.**[15] There are a number of specific steps in using a performance analysis to determine training needs. Exhibit 13-5 outlines these steps.

Step 1: Behavioral Discrepancy

The first step is to appraise employees' performance. How are the employees doing now, and how should they be doing? If a secretary is using a Dell word processor to prepare budgets and takes an average of 7.5 hours to complete the work, this record of

HR Journal   *Why Organizations Still Aren't Learning*

It is a lot easier to talk about a "learning organization" than to create one. Peter M. Senge knew that even when he introduced the concept to the business world in his landmark book, *The Fifth Discipline: The Art and Practice of the Learning Organization* (Doubleday/Currency).

Throughout the 1990s and into the 2000s, the learning organization has been a particular *cause celebre* for trainers and organization development specialists, and not just because "learning" is in the name. Trainers are attracted to Senge's championship of human values in the workplace, to his viewpoint that teams are the core performance units in organizations, and to his insistence that leadership occurs at many levels in an organization, not just in the executive suite. Indeed he argues that line managers and even nonmanagers must function as leaders in order for any lasting organizational change to occur.

Listed below are a few opinions and viewpoints held and promoted by Senge regarding the Five Disciplines:

1. **Systems Thinking.** This is the "fifth discipline" of the book's title, singled out because it underlies the other four. It is a learnable, habitual thinking process that allows one to look at events in an organization—or life—and see patterns of complex interrelationships. With conceptual themes stretching from environmentalism to Zen philosophy, systems thinking takes the doctrine of the interconnectedness of everything and brings it to bear on organizational life.

2. **Personal Mastery.** This is the discipline of continually clarifying and deepening one's personal vision of what could or should be, and remaining clear about how that vision differs from reality. The disparity should cause a "creative tension" that motivates us to change.

3. **Mental Models.** Mental models are deeply ingrained assumptions, generalizations, or images that influence how we understand the world and how we choose to respond to various situations we face. We all have mental models. The "discipline" is to understand and clarify them, and to distinguish between those we espouse and those we actually use to guide our actions—our "theories-in-practice."

4. **Shared Vision.** Better understood as a group competency than an individual skill, this is the practice of developing a vision for a team or an organization. It has to do with discovering a shared picture of the future that will foster genuine commitment and enrollment rather than just compliance.

5. **Team Learning.** The key to this discipline is a phenomenon called "dialogue," in which members of a team suspend their assumptions and take up a "think together" mode that embraces the collective good and eschews individual self-interest.

Source: Joel Schettler (April 2002), "Learning by Doing," *Training*, pp. 38–43; and Ron Zemke (September 1999), "Why Organizations Still Aren't Learning," *Training*, pp. 40–49.

performance can be used to assess his or her performance. If performance is 2 hours over what is expected, there is a behavioral discrepancy—a difference between actual and expected.

Step 2: Cost-Value Analysis

Next, the manager must determine the cost and value of correcting the identity behavioral discrepancy. Is it worth the cost, time, and expense to have the secretary prepare the budgets in less than 7.5 hours?

Step 3: Is It a "Can't Do" or "Won't Do" Situation?

It is important to determine if the employee could do the expected job if he or she wanted to. Three questions need to be answered: (1) Does the person know what to do in terms of performance? (2) Could the person do the job if he or she wanted to? and (3) Does the person want to do the job? Answering these questions requires skillful observation, listening, and asking on the part of the person conducting the performance analysis.

Young Enterprises did not have a separate training department. So Gwen, with the assistance of Bob McGarrah, the director of training and development, began to think about a training program to help Harold Matthews reach his goal. The program might not have been needed if the job market weren't so tight. But since applicants were so scarce, the training program was very important at this point.

Gwen Bob, what we need to determine is what training programs we should have right now. What do you suggest we do?

Bob The typical approach is to use organizational analysis, operational analysis, and person analysis. Besides, we need to do some sort of cost-benefit analysis to see if the training is worth the effort. This will give us a set of training objectives for a program or set of programs. Then we design the program content and methods around these. After the program is run, we evaluate it.

Gwen At this point, let's set the objectives and design the program. Then we'll go back to Harold to see if he has any additional suggestions.

Step 4: Set Standards

An administrative assistant who doesn't know what the standard is may underperform. Establishing a standard and clearly communicating it can improve performance.

Step 5: Remove Obstacles

Not being able to complete budgets on time may be caused by frequent breakdowns of equipment (the Dell system) or by not receiving a job on time. Time, equipment, and people can be obstacles that result in behavioral discrepancies.

Step 6: Practice

Practice, practice, practice may be one avenue to performing a job better. Does the manager permit the employee the needed practice time?

Step 7: Training

If the performance analysis indicates that behaviors need to be altered, training becomes a viable consideration. Any training approaches available should be weighed and considered to find the one best suited to correct the behavior discrepancy.

Step 8: Change the Job

Redesigning the job through job enrichment, job simplification, or job enlargement may be the best solution.

Step 9: Transfer or Terminate

If all else has failed, the employee may have to be transferred or terminated.

Step 10: Create a Motivational Climate

In some cases, there may be a problem with motivation: A skilled and able employee may not want to perform the job as required. A manager may then have to use a motivational approach that converts this undermotivated person into a motivated high performer. Rewards, punishment, discipline, or some combination may be needed to create a positive climate that results in the employee's utilizing his or her skills optimally.

A performance analysis is a sound procedure that can provide insight into training needs and objectives. Such an analysis may reveal that training is not the best solution to the behavioral discrepancies identified. If this is the case, other solutions will surface as the performance analysis is conducted.[16]

If, however, the performance analysis identifies a need for training, then it is necessary to establish specific, measurable training objectives. Training objectives should be expressed in behavioral terms, if at all possible. For example, the behavioral training objectives of a leadership training program at Pritex are:

- To develop a cadre of leaders who will assume positions of accountability in the next three years.
- To demonstrate listening and feedback skills that result in improved employee response to the firm's personal development program.
- To increase employee satisfaction with managerial practices as displayed in the firm's annual climate survey.

By using behaviorally based objectives, the intent of the training program is identified. In some cases, it is difficult to specify behavioral objectives. For example, a new job may not have objectives, because the manager is still attempting to clarify what behaviors are required. However, if behaviors can't be identified, one might be inclined to ask what the reason for the training is. A vague, ambiguous answer might suggest that the training purpose is not particularly important.

Choosing Trainers and Trainees

Great care must be exercised in choosing effective instructors or trainers. To some extent, the success of the training program depends on proper selection of the person who performs the training task.[17] Personal characteristics (such as the ability to speak well, to write convincingly, to organize the work of others, to be inventive, and to inspire others to greater achievements) are important factors in the selection of trainers. The process of analyzing needs and developing a training program can be accomplished by company trainers. HR specialists or hired outside consultants who report to the HR manager or other top managers are also used to perform a needs analysis and to conduct the training.[18]

Although much formal training is performed by professional trainers, often managers may be the best trainers technically, especially if a qualified trainer helps them prepare the material. Using managers as trainers overcomes the frequent criticism that "training is OK in the classroom, but it won't work on the shop floor or back on the job." The presence of trained trainers is a major factor in whether the training program is successful. It will help if these principles of learning are followed:

- Provide time for practice of the material.
- Require practice and repetition of the material.
- Communicate the material effectively.

Unfortunately, identifying and using the best qualified trainers is not a perfect process. Some companies assume the most technologically competent individuals would be an ideal or the best trainer. Selecting a trainer that has no understanding of learning, training delivery, individual motivation, and training techniques is doomed to fail. As a cautionary suggestion, a review of the trainer's understanding of theory, methods, and delivery should precede placing anyone in a trainer position.

Another planning factor is the selection of trainees who will participate in the programs. In some cases, this is obvious; the program may have been designed to train particular new employees in certain skills. In some cases, the training program is designed to help with EEO goals; in others, it is to help employees find better jobs elsewhere when layoffs are necessary, or to retrain older employees. Techniques similar to hiring procedures may be used to select trainees, especially when those who attend the program may be promoted or receive higher wages or salaries as a result.

Training and Development Instructional Methods

After needs and objectives have been determined and trainees and trainers have been selected, the program is run. This is the second phase shown in Exhibit 13-1. This phase includes selection of content and methods to be used and the actual training and/or development method. In many situations a combination of instructional methods are used.

On-the-Job Training

Probably the most widely used method of training (formal and informal) is on-the-job training. It is estimated that more than 60 percent of training occurs on the job. The employee is placed into the real work situation and shown the job and the tricks of the trade by an experienced employee or the supervisor.

Although this program is apparently simple and relatively less costly, if it is not handled properly the costs can be high—damaged machinery, unsatisfied customers, misfiled forms, and poorly taught workers. To prevent these problems, trainers must be carefully selected and trained. The trainee should be placed with a trainer who is similar in background and personality. The trainer should be motivated for training and rewarded for doing it well. The trainer should use effective techniques in instructing the trainee. One approach to systematic on-the-job training is the job instruction training (JIT) system developed during World War II.[19]

In this system, the trainers first train the supervisors, who in turn train the employees. Exhibit 13-6 describes the steps of JIT training as given in the War Manpower Commission's

EXHIBIT 13-6
Job Instruction Training (JIT) Methods

Here's what you must do to get ready to teach a job:

1. Decide what the learner must be taught in order to do the job efficiently, safely, economically, and intelligently.
2. Have the right tools, equipment, supplies, and material ready.
3. Have the workplace properly arranged, just as the worker will be expected to keep it.

Then, you should instruct the learner by the following four basic steps:

Step I—Preparation (of the Learner)

1. Put the learner at ease.
2. Find out what he or she already knows about the job.
3. Get the learner interested and desirous of learning the job.

Step II—Presentation (of the Operations and Knowledge)

1. Tell, show, illustrate, and question in order to put over the new knowledge and operations.
2. Instruct slowly, clearly, completely, and patiently, one point at a time.
3. Check, question, and repeat.
4. Make sure the learner really knows.

Step III—Performance Tryout

1. Test the learner by having him or her perform the job.
2. Ask questions beginning with why, how, when, or where.
3. Observe performance, correct errors, and repeat instructions if necessary.
4. Continue until you know that the learner knows.

Step IV—Follow-Up

1. Put the employee on his or her own.
2. Check frequently to be sure the learner follows instructions.
3. Taper off extra supervision and close follow-up until the person is qualified to work with normal supervision.

Remember—if the learner hasn't learned, the teacher hasn't taught.

bulletin "Training within Industry Series" in 1945. The instructions given to supervisors on how to train new or present employees are given in Exhibit 13-6.

Toll-free hotlines can help improve a firm's customer service. Toll-free numbers give customers an easy way to complain or ask questions. Training individuals to handle complaints and questions is done on the job in a number of firms. General Electric (GE), for example, trains customer service operators on the job so that the realism of listening, thinking, and responding on the spot hits home.[20] GE's answer center in Louisville, Kentucky, is open 24 hours a day. It employs 180 telephone representatives, 150 customer service reps, and 30 technicians. It handles 2 million calls from customers each year. Each rep is trained and is able to handle about 100 calls a day, each one lasting about 3.5 minutes. After learning about the firm's products, the rep is trained on the telephone. Communication and telephone skills are observed and critiqued. Other firms that use 800 numbers and on-the-job training include Armstrong Floors and Ceiling Building Products Division, JC Penney, and Ralston-Purina.

ExxonMobil Oil uses an on-the-job training approach to achieve excellence among engineers in the exploration and producing division.[21] The objective at Mobil Oil is based on the premise that the most significant development of an engineer takes place on the job. Thus, competence and mastery of tasks are accomplished through

- Challenging assignments.
- Good role models.
- Timely and comprehensive coaching.

These features are built into ExxonMobil's Leadership Development Program (LDP), which trained over 2,000 employees in 2004.

Case Method

One widespread technique is the **case method,** which uses a written description of a real decision-making situation in the organization or a situation that occurred in another organization. Managers are asked to study the case to identify the problems, analyze the problems for their significance, propose solutions, choose the best solution, and implement it. More learning takes place if there is interaction between the managers and the instructor. The instructor's role is that of a catalyst and facilitator. A good instructor is able to get everyone involved in solving the problem.

The case method lends itself more to some kinds of material. For example, with analysis of business policies, case studies work better than more rigidly structured approaches. It is easier to listen to a lecture and be given a formula than to tease the formula out of a case, for instance. With good instructors and good cases, the case method is a very effective device for improving and clarifying rational decision making.[22]

The trainer using the case method must guard against (1) dominating the discussion, (2) permitting a few people to dominate the discussion, or (3) leading the discussion toward his or her preferred solution. As a catalyst, the instructor should encourage divergent viewpoints, initiate discussion on points the managers are missing, and be thoroughly prepared.[23]

One variation of the case method is the incident method. In the *incident method,* just the bare outlines of a problem are given initially, and the students are assigned a role in which to view the incident. Additional data are available if the students ask the right questions. Each student "solves" the case, and groups based on similarity of solutions are formed. Each group then formulates a strong statement of position, and the groups debate or role-play their solutions. The instructor may describe what actually happened in the case and the consequences, and then the groups compare their solutions with the results. The final step is for participants to try to apply this knowledge to their own job situations.

Role Playing

Role playing is a cross between the case method and an attitude development program. Each person is assigned a role in a situation (such as a case) and asked to play the role and to react to other players' role playing. The player is asked to pretend to be a focal person in the situation and to react to the stimuli as that person would. The players are provided with background information on the situation and the players. Usually, a brief script is provided for the participants. Sometimes, the role playing is videotaped and reanalyzed as part of the development situation. Often, role playing is done in small groups of a dozen or so. The success of this method depends on the ability of the players to play the assigned roles believably. If done well, role playing can help a manager become more aware of and more sensitive to the feelings of others.

Although role playing is a cross between the two, comparison of the general forms of role playing and the case method suggests a few differences between them:[24]

Case Study	Role Play
1. Presents a problem for analysis and discussion.	1. Places the problem in a real-life situation.
2. Uses problems that have already occurred in the company or elsewhere.	2. Uses problems that are now current or are happening on the job.
3. Deals with problems involving others.	3. Deals with problems in which participants themselves are involved.
4. Deals with emotional and attitudinal aspects in an intellectual frame of reference.	4. Deals with emotional and attitudinal aspects in an experiential frame of reference.
5. Emphasizes using facts and making assumptions.	5. Emphasizes feelings.
6. Trains in the exercise of judgments.	6. Trains in emotional control.
7. Provides practice in analysis of problems.	7. Provides practice in interpersonal skills.

In-Basket Technique

Another method used to develop managerial decision-making abilities is the **in-basket technique.** The participant is given materials (typically memos or descriptions of things to do) that include typical items from a specific manager's mail, e-mail, and a telephone list. Important and pressing matters, such as out-of-stock positions, complaints by customers, and a demand for a report from a superior, are mixed in with routine business matters, such as a request to speak at a dinner or a decision on the date of the company picnic four weeks hence. The trainee is analyzed and critiqued on the number of decisions made in the time allotted, the quality of the decisions, and the priorities chosen for making them. In order to generate interest, the in-basket materials must be realistic, job-related, and not impossible to make decisions on.

Management Games

Essentially, **management games** describe the operating characteristics of a company, industry, or enterprise. These descriptions take the form of equations that are manipulated after decisions have been made. Management games emphasize development of problem-solving skills.

In a typical computerized management game procedure, teams of players are asked to make a series of operating (or top-management) decisions. In one game, for example, the players are asked to decide on such matters as the price of the product, purchase of materials, production scheduling, funds borrowing, marketing, and R&D expenditures. When each player on the team has made a decision, the interactions of these decisions are computed (manually or by computer) in accordance with the model. For example, if price is linearly related to volume, a decrease in price of *x* percent will affect the volume, subject to general price levels. Players on the team reconcile their individual decisions with those of the other team members before making a final decision. Then each team's decision is compared with those of the other teams. The result of that team's profit, market share, and so forth is compared, and a winner or best team performance is determined.

Looking Glass is a management game that permits individuals to participate as managers in the simulation of a hypothetical glass manufacturing company with 4,000 employees and $200 million in annual sales.[25] Executives from IBM, AT&T, Monsanto, and Union Carbide have used Looking Glass to provide a picture to participants of their management style. Looking Glass was developed at the Center for Creative Leadership, a nonprofit think tank in Greensboro, North Carolina.

Another management game used to develop managers is Simmons Simulator, Inc., a fictional high-technology multinational firm with $3 billion in annual sales. It is used to train top managers at IBM in the company's corporate planning process.

Financial Services Industry is a third game; it simulates a business day in which managers grapple with planning decisions that are influenced by technological change and government deregulation of the financial industry.

Hard evidence is scarce on whether Looking Glass, Simmons Simulator, or Financial Services accomplishes the desired outcomes. A major concern is to rigorously assess whether participation in management games means that the manager is a better performer back on the job.

Advantages of games include the integration of several interacting decisions, the ability to experiment with decisions, the provision of feedback on decisions, and the requirement that decisions be made with inadequate data, which usually simulates reality. The main criticisms of most games concern their limitation of novelty or reactivity in decision making, the cost of development and administration, the unreality of some of the models, and the disturbing tendency of many participants to look for the key to winning the game instead of concentrating on making good decisions. Many participants seem to feel that the games are rigged—that a few factors or even a single factor may be the key to winning.

Behavior Modeling

A development approach for improving interpersonal skills is **behavior modeling,** which is also called *interaction management* or *imitating models.*[26] The key to behavior modeling is learning through observation or imagination. Thus, modeling is a "vicarious process" that emphasizes observation.

One behavior modeling approach begins by identifying 19 interpersonal problems that employees, especially managers, face. Typical problems are gaining acceptance as a new supervisor, handling discrimination complaints, delegating responsibility, improving attendance, disciplining effectively, overcoming resistance to change, setting performance goals, motivating average performance, handling emotional situations, reducing tardiness, and taking corrective action.[27]

There are four steps in the process:

1. Modeling of effective behavior—often by use of films.
2. Role playing.
3. Social reinforcement—trainees and trainers praise effective role playing.
4. Transfer of training to the job.

Behavior modeling has been introduced into such organizations as AT&T, General Electric, IBM, RCA, Boise Cascade, Kaiser Corporation, Olin, and BF Goodrich. The research evidence is generally positive. In a series of studies, groups trained in behavior modeling have outperformed groups who received no training or traditional management development training.[28]

Behavior modeling offers a number of promising possibilities in organizations.[29] One especially important need in organizations is to develop effective leaders. Modeling appears to offer some promise for developing leadership skills, if used in conjunction with videotape methods.[30] The participants can view their styles, behaviors, strengths, and weaknesses and learn from this personal firsthand view. People who see themselves in action have a vivid reminder that they can benefit from practice.

Outdoor-Oriented Programs

Cases, games, modeling, and role playing are still popular, but an increasingly popular form of development is outdoor or real-life, action-oriented programs. Leadership, teamwork, and risk taking are top-priority items in the **outdoor-oriented programs.** The programs, conducted in remote areas, combine outdoor skills with classroom seminars.[31] Most of the programs have taken their cues from Outward Bound programs, originated in the early 1960s. River rafting, mountain climbing, night searching, team competition, boat races, rope climbing, and problem-solving exercises are popular types of outdoor training.

One example of an action-oriented exercise is the "zip line" cable. A cable stretches from a cliff high above a river and ends in a field on the other side. The individual grabs a handle, jumps off the cliff, and rockets down the cable to the field, usually twisting, yelling, and holding on for dear life.

Teamwork and trust are objectives that outdoor programs attempt to achieve. Do these outdoor programs work? When a participant returns to the office, is he or she more team-oriented? To date, there is little carefully designed research available indicating that these programs are effective.[32] The popularity of these programs is based on the opinion that they appear to be action packed, participants like them, and they involve healthy exercise. However, some critics question whether an organization has a right to send or encourage a person to participate in a program that requires some athletic ability, enjoyment of the outdoors, or risk.

Which Training and/or Development Approach Should Be Used?

Deciding on an approach or a combination of approaches must be done by weighing various criteria. The choice can be made on the basis of number of managers to be developed, relative costs per manager for each method, availability of development materials in various forms (including the instructor's capabilities), and employees' relative efficiency in learning. In general, the more active the manager, the greater the motivation to learn—and thus the higher the probability of success. If there are only a few instructors, individualized programmed instruction may be considered. If none of the managers is capable of giving certain instructions, outside instructors may be contacted, or movies or videotapes might be used. Finally, the method used should reflect the degree of active participation desired for the program.

Inevitably, the effectiveness of each form of development or training must be evaluated. There are studies to support the effectiveness of most methods; if a method is appropriate for the particular program in question, it should be used.

The classic debate continues about which development approach or technique is best. Some favor a combination of approaches, while others prefer an array of humanist or behaviorist techniques.[33] The techniques of behaviorism include behavioral modeling, role playing, positive reinforcement, and simulations. The preferred techniques of the humanist approach to development (associated with Carl Rogers) include self-assessment, visualization, and guided reflection. There are also advocates of cognitive approaches who believe that lectures, discussion, readings, and debates are the best approach to use.

EXHIBIT 13-7
Objectives of Three Approaches to Learning

Objective	Techniques		
	Humanist	**Cognitivist**	**Behaviorist**
Knowledge			
Transmit information	Inductive discussion Inductive game Debrief experience Relevance discussion Active elaboration	Lecture/film Graphic illustration Panel/interview SME Class presentation Reading Question and answer Review	Multiple-choice Memorization Association
Verify information	Confirmatory discussion	Test	Question with answer
Skill			
Induce response	Discuss action Visualize action Inductive case study	List steps Demonstration Success stories	Behavioral model Behavioral samples Prompting/cueing
Strengthen response (practice)	Mental rehearsal Project	Case study	Worksheets Skill drill (game) Simulation Role playing
Apply the skill	Action plan Planning guide Elaboration (skit) Contract	Coaching/feedback	Realistic practice Job aid prompts On-job reinforcement
Attitude			
	Self-assessment Encounter experience Discussion of beliefs Reverse role playing Guided reflection Group decision	Authority statement Vicarious experience Debate Testimony	Assessment Pleasant experience Reinforcement

Exhibit 13-7 presents the learning objectives offered by the three approaches to learning. The objectives can involve knowledge, skill, or attitude. To accomplish these objectives, an array of humanist, cognitivist, and behaviorist techniques are available. On the basis of theory and research, it appears that simpler tasks, like word processing or filing, are learned efficiently by behaviorist techniques. On the other hand, more complex tasks, such as learning how to be an effective leader of employees, often require cognitive and humanistic approaches. Also, the ability of the learner needs to be considered. More sophisticated learners usually require more cognitive approaches and a chance to discuss their viewpoints.

On-the-Job Training for Managers

On-the-job management training is the preferred type from many points of view, especially because of its relevance and immediate transferability to the job. There are three widely used approaches to training managers on the job. These programs are not mutually exclusive; often they are run simultaneously.

Coaching and Counseling   One of the best and most frequently used methods of training new managers is for effective managers to teach them.[34] The coach-superior sets a good example of what a manager does. He or she also answers questions and explains why things are done the way they are. It is the coach-superior's obligation to see that the manager-trainee makes the proper contacts so that the job can be learned easily and performed adequately. In some ways, the relationship between the coach-superior and the manager-trainee resembles the buddy system in employee training.

One technique the superior may use is to have decision-making meetings with the trainee. During these meetings, procedures are agreed upon. If the trainee is to learn, the superior must give him or her enough authority to make decisions and perhaps even make mistakes. This approach not only provides opportunities to learn but also requires effective delegation, which develops a feeling of mutual confidence. Appropriately chosen committee assignments can be used as a form of coaching and counseling.

Although most organizations use coaching and counseling as either a formal or an informal management development technique, it is not without its problems. Coaching and counseling fail when inadequate time is set aside for them, when the subordinate is allowed to make no mistakes, if rivalry develops, or if the dependency needs of the subordinate are not recognized or accepted by the superior. In sum, many experts contend that coaching and counseling, when coupled with planned rotation through jobs and functions, are effective techniques. They can fit the manager's background and utilize the principle of learning by doing what has proven effective. Finally, the method involves the supervisors, which is essential to successful management development.

Transitory Anticipatory Experiences Another approach to management training is to provide transitory experiences. Once it has been determined that a person will be promoted to a specific job, provision is made for a short period before the promotion in which she or he learns the new job, performing some new duties while still performing most of the old ones. This intermediate arrangement is labeled differently in various organizations: assistant understudy, multiple management, or management **apprenticeship.**

The main characteristic of this type of program is that it gives partial prior experience to a person likely to hold a position in the future.[35] In some approaches, the trainee performs a part of the actual job; thus, an assistant does some parts of the job for the incumbent. In multiple management, several decision-making bodies make decisions about the same problem and compare them. Decisions made by a junior board or group are compared with those of senior management groups. Another variation is to provide trainees with a series of assignments that are part of the new job in order to train them and broaden their experiences.

To the extent that transitory experiences simulate the future job and are challenging, they seem to provide an eminently reasonable approach to management development. Little systematic study has been made of the effectiveness of this approach, however, and it appears to be used less often than coaching or counseling.

Transfers and Rotation In another on-the-job approach, trainees are rotated through a series of jobs to broaden their managerial experience. Organizations often have developed programmed career plans that include a mix of functional and geographic transfers.

Advocates of rotation and transfer contend that this approach broadens the manager's background, accelerates the promotion of highly competent individuals, introduces more new ideas into the organization, and increases the effectiveness of the organization. But some research evidence questions these conclusions.[36] Individual differences affect whether the results will be positive, and generalists may not be the most effective managers in many specialized positions.

Geographic transfers are desirable when fundamentally different job situations exist at various places. They allow new ideas to be tried instead of meeting each situation with the comment, "We always do it that way here." As in many other types of development, trained supervisors can make this technique more effective.

In general, because of the perceived relevance of on-the-job experience, it should be provided in management development programs. Because of individual differences in development and rewards by organizations, however, off-the-job development programs should supplement it where expertise is not readily available inside the organization. Exclusively on-the-job programs lead to a narrow perspective and the inhibition of new ideas.

Off-the-Job Training

Organizations with the biggest training programs often use off-the-job training. A survey of training directors in Fortune 500 companies examined their views of which off-the-job training techniques were the most effective for specific objectives. The training directors indicated that if knowledge was the objective, it would be best to use programmed instruction. On the other hand, if the training was intended to improve problem-solving skills, then it would be better to use the case method of training (for example, having participants analyze job-related cases). Research suggests that the most popular methods of instruction for off-the-job training are lecture-discussion, programmed instruction, and computer-assisted instruction (CAI).[37]

Lecture-Discussion Approach   The most frequently used training method is for a trainer to give a lecture and involve the trainee in a discussion of the material to be learned. Effective classroom presentation supplements lecture with audiovisual aids such as blackboards, slides, and mock-ups. Frequently, these lectures are videotaped or audiotaped. The method allows the trainers' message to be given in many locations and to be repeated as often as needed for the benefit of the trainees. Videotape recording also allows for self-confrontation, which is especially useful in such programs as sales training and interpersonal relations. The trainee's presentation can be taped and played back for analysis.

Computers   Each day more firms are using **computer-assisted instruction** (CAI), widely used to train employees. The advantages for training include allowing trainees to learn at their own pace, enabling trainees to study areas that need improvement, and—depending on availability of personal computers—flexibility. The computer has changed the way people at work learn. Learning is more self-initiated and individualized. A number of computer training methods are becoming more widely used.[38]

The **Internet** offers ways to increase learning, link resources, and share valuable knowledge inside and outside an organization. People can use the Internet to deliver training in the following ways, either individually or in combination with other instruction methods:

- E-mail for accessing course material and sharing information.
- Bulletin boards, forums, and newsgroups for posting comments and questions.
- Interactive tutorials and courses that let trainees take courses online.
- Real-time conferencing that places all participants in the same virtual classroom. Trainees can download documents, tutorials, and software.

Intranets are internal, proprietary electronic networks, similar to the Internet. Typically, an intranet delivers programs that have been developed or customized for an organization's particular learning needs. Listserve discussion groups and virtual-learning campuses are just a few ways organizations are using intranets to share information among employees.

Some intranets can also support the delivery of CD-ROM-based training. As CD-ROM programs continue to become more sophisticated, trainers can learn more about them through the use of "authoring" software, which ranges in difficulty from straightforward, template-based programs to more complex applications requiring expert programming skills.

HRM practitioners and trainers should also have a working knowledge of multimedia technology. It enhances learning in individual and group settings with audio, animation, graphics, and interactive video delivered via computer. Those capabilities let trainees retrieve information when they want it and in the way that makes the most sense to them.

HR Journal · *The View from the Middle*

For some managers, online learning is the wave of a future, to be joyously embraced—inevitable, irresistible, and unquestionable. For others, it's a scary step into the unknown. Still others wonder whether it's the latest iteration of a long, much-ballyhooed succession of teaching technologies that for years have been supposed to transform the way trainers train and learners learn.

Any of the visions may turn out to be right. Perhaps all of them. Nonetheless, it's clear that some organizations are already deeply committed to online delivery of training. They've built new courseware, transformed existing programs, bought off-the-shelf or customized applications, uploaded the results to Web sites, or set up server space on internal intranets. They've started charting who's using these courses and at what cost and with what results.

For example, DuPont uses e-learning to teach legal compliance and ethics to 55,000 employees working in 70 countries. The company wants everyone to take the issues of ethics and compliance seriously.

At the same time, due to a variety of circumstances, other organizations are waiting, even resisting, a technological sea change that has the potential to disorient trainers and learners alike while busting budgets and creating new issues—from constant fighting for bandwidth to extending the training charter beyond the traditional borders of the business.

For now, the first steps most organizations are taking into online learning are tentative. They're neither in the fast lane nor on the shoulder of the information superhighway, but moving at a pace dictated by conditions around them.

Judging from initial review, online learning is still a small slice of the overall training pie. Estimates of the amount of training that has moved online to date range from minuscule fractions up to a third; well under 10 percent is typical.

But regardless of where the needle points now, it seems destined to move significantly in the next few years. "We currently have only one course online using our intranet, a mandatory ethics course. But we have plans to add many more this year," says Elaine Voci, training manager for USA Group, a student loan company with headquarters in Indianapolis.

"NEO, our new-employee orientation, is online," offers Kathryn Perkins, program manager for Kindred Communications of Bellevue, Washington. "We have sent 15 employees through so far, with positive feedback."

At ARINC Inc., an Annapolis, Maryland–based company that develops and operates communications and information-processing systems for the aviation and travel industries, all ISO training is now accomplished online via an intranet. According to Tom Nickel, manager of training and development, the measurement for success is simple: Each business unit involved has been certified to ISO standards on its first attempt.

"Getting training online has given us the ability to manage time most effectively," he states. "People enrolled in the course are usually proceeding at a rate that is comfortable to them, while doing the course work at a time that is convenient to their schedule. We also find that once a new concept or skill is learned via online training, the time gap from acquiring to implementation is much shorter. I believe that this is a direct result of the online training being designed to present compact blocks of information students can use much faster than those acquired through the traditional learning environment."

Not every foray into online courseware has been glitch-free, however. At Liberty Bank in Middletown, Connecticut, so many participants failed to finish initial self-paced PC training programs that an outside supplier is now under contract to provide conventional instructor-led training. "Although the courses were part of certification," says Judy Dockery, manager of training and organization development, "no one used the lab to complete these pieces"

Nonetheless, Dockery says the bank soon will put some of its mandatory compliance training online. The intent, she explains, is "to touch more of the population. By working through our intranet, the program will be much easier for them to access."

Regardless of their experience to date, when trainers get out their crystal balls and look to the next few years, what they invariably see is increasing levels of online training. "Online could represent up to 70 percent or even 80 percent of what we do in-house," says Sue Dence, a training officer with the Naval Undersea Warfare Center Division in Newport, Rhode Island, a Department of Defense naval research and development lab with some 3,000 employees. A significant slice of that will be mandatory training, she notes: diversity training, sexual harassment training, government ethics, and new-employee orientation. Currently, almost 20 percent of the center's training is available online.

Source: Susan Schott Karr (November 2004), "Sarbanes-Oxley Training Gets Web Enabled," *Financial Executive*, pp. 24–26; Patti Shank (May 2002), "No More Yawns," *Online Learning*, pp. 22–23; Mike Flanigan (May 2002), "Good Science," *Online Learning*, p. 32.

Training and OmniTech Consulting Group Inc. of Chicago assessed the use of **multimedia-based training (MBT)** in 146 of the Fortune 1000 Firms. MBT was defined as an interactive learning experience incorporating the use of either CD-ROM or World Wide Web technology (via Internet or intranet).[39]

Virtual reality (VR) is a step beyond multimedia. VR is a computer-based technology that enables users to learn in a three-dimensional environment. The trainer can, by using a simulated situation, interact in real time with its components by viewing a virtual model on a computer screen or through a head-mounted display.

Motorola is an example of a company adapting VR for training purposes. Through its Motorola University, the company is testing PC-based VR technology by reproducing an assembly-line setting in which employees will be trained. Traditionally, employees were sent to one of three training centers around the world for a three-day, hands-on training class. The cost of transporting and lodging trainees was high, and the demand for training outstripped the availability. Motorola had previously attempted to set up additional sites that physically re-created the assembly line, but found that installing them was difficult and that getting the necessary machinery was expensive.[40]

The Virtual Reality Institute was established in the United States to offer training and consulting services to corporate clients. Northern Telecom, a developer of communications products, and Superscape, a leading builder of VR tools for desktop computers, announced the release of new virtual reality training software for telephone console attendants. On a service call, an appliance technician is asked to fix a broken refrigerator but discovers that he hasn't worked on that particular model before. No problem—he pulls out his laptop computer, accesses a phone line, and within moments downloads schematics and technical data on the appliance. The technician can also reach immediate interactive technical assistance that literally talks him through repair procedures.[41]

The type of training the repairman received is generally called **distance training** or **distance learning**—some experts have taken to using the term "just-in-time training." Whatever you choose to call it, the nature of corporate training is changing. The trainer is quickly evolving into someone who facilitates, guides, and acts as a mentor for employers and employees, helping them find and use the best and most timely training available. The goal of the corporate trainer should now be to find, interpret, and assess a wide range of information and technologically sophisticated products.

"Intersector directors" is the term used by Karen Mantyla, president of Quiet Power Inc.—a professional development consulting firm based in Washington, D.C.—to describe the new training role. "Trainers must redirect their thinking in how to provide skill development training to seize opportunities and maintain their status as a viable competitor within their industry," she says.

Stetord, a Norwegian oil company, uses virtual reality to initiate remote controlled oil rigs. Trained engineers control all aspects of drilling in oil fields and in the Norwegian Sea.[42]

By virtue of their industry and size, some organizations have already seized opportunities that have placed them on the leading edge of integrating technology into workforce training programs. These companies include AT&T, Ford Motor Co., Intel Corp., and Aetna Life & Casualty. The United States government is also considered a trendsetter when it comes to using high-tech training techniques.

The government's development of local- and wide-area computer networks and electronic mail capabilities has given many federal agencies a distinct technological advantage over the private sector. A Department of Defense initiative was the origin of the Internet.

Since the government has used technology for many years to share information, federal agencies have naturally gravitated to distance learning. The distance-learning programs that the agencies have created are cost-efficient and effective because the various agencies

After Bob and Gwen performed the training needs analysis, they isolated the skills training necessary. The supervisors and employees said the key need was improved training in the use of the new equipment. They also identified other work-related skills that appeared to decrease employees' efficiency.

Then Bob prepared a proposed training program. The training needs analysis had identified the employees who needed the training the most. For trainers, he decided to propose that the manufacturer of the new equipment should provide a trainer. This person would train Bob and several supervisors who appeared to have the greatest potential to run employee training programs. He also proposed that the manufacturer provide mock-ups of the machines to use in the training (if any were available). Lacking that, slides would be used. Then the firm would use several machines for training alone—a semi-**vestibule** approach. The cost would be minimal. The manufacturer would provide the training free.

Harold approved the plan, and the training sessions were conducted. Two months after the training was completed, however, there was little change in results. Gwen realized that they had not done as good a job in the cost feasibility study as they should have. No formal evaluation of the training had been planned or done.

Gwen and Bob went back to the supervisors to interview them on what had happened.

Sandy Feldman (supervisor)   I told you people the problem was who you hired. Training clowns like the ones I've got won't help.

Sam Jacobs (supervisor)   I thought that training would help. It did a little, for a while. But my problem has become discipline. They know how to do the job—they just don't seem to want to do it.

Harry Samson (supervisor)   Maybe the problem was how the training was done—I don't know. I see few real results so far.

Bob and Gwen decided to do a formal evaluation of the next training program. As for what to do now, performance evaluation time was coming up. Maybe rewards for better employees would help. Maybe the labor market had opened up and some terminations and rehirings would be the answer. They'd just have to keep working on it until they could really help Harold and the company.

---

don't have to reinvent the wheel; agencies share resources and review analyses and studies through the Government Alliance for Training and Education (GATE). The developed coursework, material, and programming are then made available to government agencies through the Government Education and Training Network (GETN).

A good example of how GETN works is an ethics training course that was offered to all government agencies via distance learning at the time of this writing. All federal employees are required to have ethics training, and agencies can have the course downlinked to their office sites. The ethics training course was developed as a collaborative effort through GATE. The IRS donated instructional designers to create the course curriculum, while another agency provided the studio and office space for the course's original site.[43]

Management Development: An Overview

What Is Management Development?

Organizations and their environments are dynamic and constantly changing. New technologies are developed, competitors enter and leave markets, inflation increases, and productivity fluctuates. These are the kinds of changes that managers face. The development of managers and nonmanagers is a continuous process in the most successful firms. It is an area of study directed toward using behavioral science knowledge to deal with problems of change.[44]

EXHIBIT 13-8
Diagnostic Steps in Development Programs

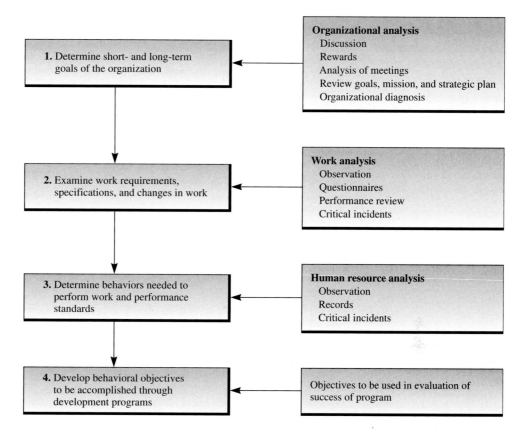

Management development should be planned, since it requires systematic diagnosis, development of a program, and the mobilization of resources (trainers, participants, teaching aids). It involves either the entire system or an entire unit. It must have top-management commitment if it is to be a success.

Exhibit 13-8 lists a variety of development approaches that are available to managers. There is no one best approach. The crucial point to consider is what the diagnosis shows.

Development: Individual Techniques

One way to classify development techniques is on the basis of the target area they are intended to affect. There are three major target areas: (1) individual, (2) group, and (3) organizational. Goal setting is designed to improve an individual's ability to set and achieve goals. Behavioral modification is the use of individual learning through reinforcement. Team building focuses on the group and total quality management (TQM) targets the organization as a whole.

Goal Setting

A *goal* is the object of an action; it is what a person attempts to accomplish. For example, attempts to sell more products, to improve customers' satisfaction with service, and to decrease absenteeism in a department by 5 percent are goals. Since 1968, when E. A. Locke presented what is now considered a classic paper, there has been considerable and growing interest in applying goal setting to organizational problems and issues.[45]

Locke proposed that goal setting is a cognitive process of some practical utility. His view is that an individual's conscious goals and intentions are the primary determinants of behavior. That is, "one of the commonly observed characteristics of intentional behavior is that it tends to keep going until it reaches completion."[46] Once a person starts something (e.g., a job, a new project), he or she pushes on until a goal is achieved. Intent plays a prominent role in goal-setting theory. Also, the theory places specific emphasis on the importance of conscious goals in explaining motivated behavior. Locke has used the notion of intentions and conscious goals to propose and provide research support for the thesis that harder conscious goals result in higher levels of performance if these goals are accepted by the individual.

The Goal-Setting Process

Goal setting seems simple, and most people assume that they have inherent skills to set and use goals. However, it has been found that training in specific goal-setting skills can be very effective.

Locke describes the attributes of the mental (cognitive) processes of goal setting. The attributes of goals that he highlights are specificity, difficulty, and intensity. *Specificity* is the degree of quantitative precision (clarity) of the goal. *Difficulty* is the degree of proficiency or the level of performance sought. *Intensity* pertains to the process of setting the goal or of determining how to reach it.[47] To date, intensity has not been widely studied, although a related concept, commitment, has been considered in some studies. Commitment is the amount of effort used to achieve a goal.

The key steps in goal setting are (1) diagnosis; (2) preparing the employees for goal setting by increased interpersonal interaction, communication, training, and action plans; (3) emphasizing the attributes of goals that should be understood by a manager and subordinates; (4) conducting intermediate reviews to make necessary adjustments in established goals; and (5) performing a final review to check the goals set, modified, and accomplished. Each of these steps needs to be carefully planned and implemented if goal setting is to be an effective motivational technique. In too many applications of goal setting, training and development are ignored, with the excuse that no training is needed.

Research on Goal Setting

Locke's original paper contributed to a considerable increase in laboratory and field research on goal setting. Another force behind the increased interest and research was the demand of managers for practical and specific techniques that they could apply in their organizations. Goal setting offered such a technique for some managers.[48] The degree of support for goal setting as a viable motivational technique is captured best by the authors of a meta-analytic study of the effects of goal setting on task performance:

> If there is ever to be a viable candidate from the organizational sciences for elevation to the lofty status of a scientific law of nature, then the relationships between goal difficulty, specificity, commitment, and task performance are most worthy of serious consideration.[49]

Research has shown that specific goals lead to higher output than vague goals such as "Do your best."[50] Field experiments using clerical workers, maintenance technicians, marketing personnel, truckers, engineers, typists, and manufacturing employees have compared specific goals versus do-your-best goals.[51] The vast majority of these studies support, partly or in total, the hypothesis that specific goals lead to better performance than do value goals. In fact, in 99 out of 100 studies reviewed by Locke and his associates, specific goals produced better results.[52]

> The setting of a goal that is both specific and challenging leads to an increase in performance because it makes it clearer to the individual what he is supposed to do. This in turn may provide the worker with a sense of achievement, recognition, and commitment in that he can compare how well he is doing now versus how well he has done in the past and, in some instances, how well he is doing in comparison to others.

Individual Differences and Goal Setting

Scattered throughout the goal-setting literature are studies that examine the effects of individual differences on goal setting. Most of these studies have examined the effects of education, race, and job tenure on the goal-setting process. A study involving electronics technicians found that goal difficulty (challenge) was significantly related to performance only for those technicians with 12 or more years of education. For technicians with less education, goal clarity (i.e., having a clear understanding of the goal) and goal feedback (i.e., receiving feedback on how results matched the goal) were significantly related to performance.[53]

In a field experiment, loggers working under assigned, participative, and do-your-best conditions were compared. Researchers found that participative goal setting affected the performance of the less educated loggers but not of the more educated loggers.[54]

One study of white-collar employees examined three explanations of why participation in goal setting may lead to improved job performance: a social factor, group discussion; a motivational factor, being involved in the goal-setting process; and a cognitive factor, sharing information.[55] Results of this study indicated that the social and motivational factors increased quantity of performance, learning the task, goal acceptance, group commitment, and satisfaction.

Another study examined race as a variable in goal setting. It found that goal clarity and goal feedback were related to performance for African Americans only.[56] In contrast, goal difficulty (challenge) was found to be related to performance for whites only. The researchers proposed that clarity and feedback may have affected the African American goal setters because they had a higher need for security. Goal clarity and accurate feedback are ways of increasing security.

Criticisms of Goal Setting

There are some arguments against goal setting or against becoming too enthusiastic about it. Some managers and researchers have found the following:

- Goal setting is rather complex and difficult to sustain.
- Goal setting works well for simple jobs—clerks, typists, loggers, and technicians—but not for complex jobs. Goal setting with jobs in which goals are not easily measured (e.g., teaching, nursing, engineering, accounting) has posed some problems.
- Goal setting encourages game playing. Setting low goals in order to look good later is one game played by subordinates who do not want to be caught short. Managers play the game of setting an initial goal that is generally not achievable and then finding out how subordinates react.
- Goal setting is used as another check on employees. It is a control device to monitor performance.
- Accomplishment of goals can become an obsession. In some situations, goal setters have become so obsessed with achieving their goals that they neglect other important areas of their jobs.

Still, under the right conditions, goal setting can be a very powerful technique for motivating employees. When used correctly, carefully monitored, and actively supported by managers, it can improve performance. (Goal difficulty and goal acceptance are two attributes that need to be considered by management.) The clear implication for managers is that getting employees to set and strive to attain specific, relatively hard goals can generate a strong motivational force.

Behavior Modification

The basic assumption of operant conditioning is that behavior is influenced by its consequences. B. E. Skinner's work with animals led to the use of the term *operant conditioning.*

However, the term more often used when principles of operant conditioning are applied to individuals is behavior modification (also called B-mod and behavior mod). Thus, **behavior modification** is individual learning through reinforcement.

Organizational behavior modification (also called *OB mod* or *OBM*) is a more general term that designates "the systematic reinforcement of desirable organizational behavior and the nonreinforcement or punishment of unwanted organizational behavior."[57] OB mod is an operant approach to organizational behavior; "organizational" has been added to indicate that the operant approach is being used in work settings. In this discussion, however, the terms *behavior modification* and *organizational behavior modification* are used interchangeably.

Principles of Operant Conditioning

Several principles of operant conditioning can aid managers attempting to influence behavior. Reinforcement is an extremely important principle of learning. In a general sense, motivation is an internal cause of behavior, while reinforcement is an external cause. **Positive reinforcement** is anything that both increases the strength of response and induces repetition of the behavior that preceded the reinforcements.[58] Without reinforcement, no measurable modification of behavior takes place.

Managers often use positive reinforcement to modify behavior. In some cases, positive reinforcers work as predicted; in other cases, however, they do not modify behavior in the desired direction, because of competing reinforcement contingencies. When reinforcers are not made contingent on the behavior desired by the manager, desired behaviors do not occur. Also, giving reinforcers long after the occurrence of the desired behaviors decreases the probability of their recurrence.

Negative reinforcement refers to an increase in the frequency of a response following removal of a negative reinforcer immediately after the response. An event is a *negative reinforcer* if its removal after a response increases the performance of that response. A familiar example of negative reinforcement in the summer months in, say, Phoenix and Houston is turning on the automobile air conditioner on a stiflingly hot day. Turning on the air conditioner (the behavior) usually minimizes or terminates an aversive condition, namely being hot (negative reinforcer). This increases the probability of having an operating air-conditioning system in the summer months. Similarly, exerting a high degree of effort to complete a job may be negatively reinforced by not having to listen to a nagging boss. By working hard, the employee is able to keep the boss away. The unpleasant boss is removed because the employee works hard.

Punishment is an uncomfortable consequence of a particular behavioral response.[59] A professor who takes off 10 points for each day a paper is late is using punishment. A mechanic who doesn't hand in his report and is suspended for one day with a loss of pay is being punished. Punishment, when applied, sends a message not to do something. It is certainly a controversial method of behavior modification. Some people believe that punishment is the opposite of reward and is just as effective in changing behavior. Others consider punishment a poor approach to learning, for reasons such as the following:

- Results of punishment are not as predictable as those of reward.
- Effects of punishment are less permanent than those of reward.
- Punishment is frequently accompanied by negative attitudes toward the administrator of the punishment as well as toward the activity that led to the punishment.

Despite the potential costs of using punishment, it has been and will continue to be used as a method of altering behavior. In situations where the costs of not punishing outweigh the advantages, punishment may be an appropriate method. For example, punishing a worker who deliberately and overtly slows down the flow of work may be an economically necessary way of altering behavior. (However, there might be ways of dealing with the problem other than punishment.) The point is that punishment and its use depend on the situation and on the manager's style of altering behavior.

Extinction reduces undesired behavior through nonreinforcement. When positive reinforcement for a learned response is withheld, individuals continue to practice that behavior for some period of time. If this nonreinforcement continues, however, the behavior decreases and eventually disappears.

An important base for these four important principles—positive reinforcement, negative reinforcement, punishment, and extinction—is Thorndike's classic *law of effect:*

> Of several responses to the same situation, those that are accompanied or closely followed by satisfaction (reinforcement) . . . will be more likely to recur; those which are accompanied or closely followed by discomfort (punishment) . . . will be less likely to occur.[60]

The idea that the consequences of behavior—rewards or punishments—are critical in determining future behavior remains an important foundation for the use of operant conditioning in organizational settings. Recall that positive reinforcement occurs when a positively valued consequence (e.g., a promotion) follows a response to a stimulus. Negative reinforcement occurs when a behavior causes an undesirable factor to be taken away (e.g., a nagging boss). Punishment occurs when an undesired behavior is followed by an unpleasant consequence (e.g., loss of pay). In punishment, the behavior is weakened by withdrawing something positive.

Behavior Modification: A Managerial Perspective

Behavior modification is based on the assumption that behavior is more important than its "psychological causes," such as the needs, motives, and values held by individuals.[61] Thus, a behaviorist such as B. F. Skinner focuses on specific behaviors and not on such intangibles as "esteem" or "personality structure." For example, a behaviorist, told that an employee is not performing well, would probably ask, "What specific behaviors led to this conclusion?" Discrete and distinguishable behaviors are important in developing any behavior modification plan to correct a performance problem.

In addition, there is an emphasis on the consequences of behavior. For example, suppose that all new management trainees are given a two-day training program on preparing budget reports. Shortly after the training sessions, managers notice that few reports are prepared correctly. One explanation may be that the training program was ineffective. However, behaviorists might approach the problem from a different direction. First, they could determine whether the trainees understand the importance of correct reports. They might then find out which trainees are turning in correct reports and what consequences, if any, are being received by these trainees. It could be that turning in correct reports results in no observable consequences. Similarly, submitting an incorrect report may also result in no positive or negative consequences. The behaviorists might recommend developing a program of positive and negative consequences to improve the trainees' reports (e.g., recognition, praise, a meeting with the boss to go over mistakes). Behaviorists believe that people tend to repeat behaviors that lead to positive consequences.

The proposed application of behavior modification in organizations follows a five-step problem-solving process similar to that shown in Exhibit 13-9:[62]

1. Managers must identify and define the specific behavior. A behavior is pinpointed when it can be accurately observed and reliably recorded. For a behavior to be pinpointed as important, there must be positive answers to two questions: (1) Can it be seen? (2) Can it be measured?

2. Managers must measure or count the occurrences of the pinpointed behavior. This count provides managers with a clear perspective of the strength of the behavior under the present, or before-change, situation.

EXHIBIT 13-9
**Applied Behavior
Modification: A
Manager's Step-by-
Step Procedure**

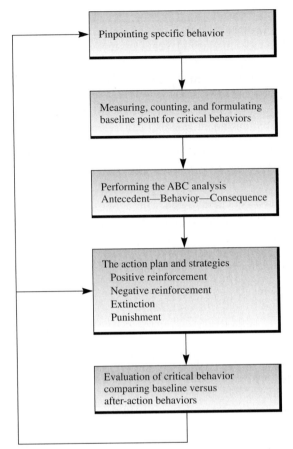

Feedback to make changes

3. Managers conduct an analysis of the ABCs of the behavior—a process also called functionally analyzing the behavior.[63] Thomas Connellan has developed a set of performance analysis questions to get at the source of a problem. These are presented in Exhibit 13-10.[64] In analyzing below average performance, for example, managers

EXHIBIT 13-10
**Questions for
Performance Analysis**

Source: Thomas K. Connellan
(1978), *How to Improve Human
Performance: Behaviorism in
Business* (New York: Harper &
Row), p. 51 Copyright © 1978
by Thomas K. Connellan,
Trustee. Reprinted by permis-
sion of Harper Collins
Publishers, Inc.

Antecedent

Does the employee know what is expected?
Are the standards clear?
Have they been communicated?
Are they realistic?

Behavior

Can the behavior be performed?
Could the employee do it if his or her life depended on it?
Does something prevent its occurrence?

Consequence

Are the consequences weighted in favor of performance?
Are improvements being reinforced?
Do we note improvement even though the improvement may
   still leave the employee below company standards?
Is reinforcement specific?

EXHIBIT 13-11
Using the ABC Analysis for Below Average Performance

A Antecedents	B Behaviors	C Consequences

Skill set:
    Strengths & deficiencies
Personal health
Poor communication
    of performance
    expectations
Poor job review
Poor job orientation
Lack of training
	Not helping colleagues
	Apathetic
	Argumentative
	Tardy
	Daydreaming
	Not communicating regularly
	More frequent absences
		Meeting with manager
		Review of performance over last
		four quarters on analysis of this
		manager
		Note placed in personnel file
		Reprimand
		Suspension without pay
		Termination

using a question format and the type of framework shown in Exhibit 13-11 are systematically viewing the problem of below average performance in terms of antecedents, behaviors, and consequences.

4. The first three steps in an applied behavior modification program set the stage for the actual modification.
5. The fifth step involves evaluation.

Criticisms of Behavior Modification

Critics have attacked behavior modification on a number of grounds. A frequent concern with the use of reinforcers is that there is no real change underlying behavior; the person is just being bribed to perform. However, bribery refers to illicit use of rewards to corrupt someone's conduct. In reinforcement, outcomes are delivered for behaviors designed to benefit the person and the organization. Thus, the criticism, although logical, really does not apply to the reinforcers typically used in organizations.

Locke believes that it is a mistake to view reinforcements as modifying responses automatically, independent of a person's beliefs, values, or mental processes. He says that this theory is simple and appealing but that the facts do not support it. Locke claims that people can learn by seeing others get reinforcement and by imitating those who are reinforced. There is also self-reinforcement, which operant conditioning theorists ignore.[65]

Another criticism focuses on the point that individuals can become too dependent on extrinsic reinforcers (e.g., pay). Thus, behavior may become dependent on the reinforcer and may never be performed without the promise of the reinforcer. The point is also made that when reinforcement is no longer provided, the behavior eventually becomes extinct. However, some studies show that extinction does not always occur when reinforcers are terminated—but these studies involve mostly children and mental patients. Whether the same results can be expected of normal adults has not been adequately tested.

Development: Team Building

Numerous development techniques improve the effectiveness of groups, such as process consultation, survey feedback, and team building. In order to more fully understand these types of techniques, team building is presented here.

Team building is a development process that helps or prepares organization members to work more efficiently or effectively in groups. It is designed to enhance individual team members' problem-solving skills, communication, and sensitivity to others.[66]

Any organization depends on the cooperation of a number of people if it is to be successful. Consequently, teams of people have to work on a temporary or permanent basis in harmony.[67] Task forces, committees, project teams, and interdepartmental groups are the kinds of teams that are frequently brought together.

In one organization, team building followed this pattern.[68]

1. *Team skills workshop* Production teams in the firm went through a 2 1/2-day workshop that included various experiential exercises.

2. *Data collection* Attitude and job data were collected from all teams (individual members).

3. *Data confrontation* Consultants presented data to teams. It was discussed, and problem areas were sorted out. Priorities were also established by each team.

4. *Action planning* Teams developed their own tentative plans to solve problems.

5. *Team building* The teams finalized plans to solve all the problems identified in step 4 and considered barriers to overcome.

6. *Intergroup team building* The groups that were interdependent met for two days to establish a mutually acceptable plan.

When team building is successful, participation is encouraged and sustained. There also can be improved communication and problem solving within and between teams. Team building has proved to be most successful when the technique is tailored to fit the needs and problems of the groups involved.[69]

How far can organizations go with team building? Some observers believe that "teams," or what some refer to as high-performance teams, are the wave of the future. At Corning, management recognizes 3,000 teams that are empowered to complete their tasks as they determine how best to do the job.[70] The teams typically consist of 3 to 30 workers, sometimes blue-collar, sometimes white-collar, and sometimes both.

A number of firms that have encouraged and rewarded teams are receiving a lot of attention.

- At a General Mills cereal plant in Lodi, California, teams schedule, operate, and maintain machinery so efficiently that the factory runs with no managers present during the night shift.

- A team of Chaparral steel mill workers traveled around the world to observe and evaluate production machinery. The team selected and installed the plant's machinery.

- After organizing its home office operations into teams, Aetna Life & Casualty reduced the ratio of middle managers to workers from 1 to 7 to 1 to 30 while at the same time improving customer service.[71]

Federal Express has been particularly successful using teams in its back-office operations in Memphis. As part of a companywide push to convert to teams, Fedex organized its 1,000 clerical workers into superteams of 5 to 10 people. Efficiency and accuracy have improved significantly.

Development: An Organizationwide Technique

By *organizationwide,* experts mean that a total system is involved or that a clearly identifiable unit, department, or plan is the target. The independence of the identifiable system or subsystem is extremely important when using an organizationwide technique.

Total Quality Management (TQM)

Total quality management (TQM) is a philosophy, a process, and a set of principles that provide an organization with what is needed to continuously improve its effectiveness.

TQM involves everyone in the firm in developing and fine-tuning processes that are customer-oriented, flexible, and responsive to improving the quality of every activity and function of the organization.[72] To achieve change and to convert to TQM, there must be changes in attitudes, communication, employee involvement, and commitment. This is a large undertaking in any organization. Because of attitudes' effect on productivity and quality, clearly they must be addressed in any TQM program.

Bringing about TQM is difficult but can be made easier by understanding resistance to change and how to overcome resistance. Too often managers are aware of resistance but don't address its causes, such as fear, inertia, and self-interest.

The Chief Executive Officer

The power to make change happen is often largely vested in management. Management must show the way, articulate the vision, and show by example that total quality is mandatory. Improved communications initiated by management must be a top priority. Merely inundating workers with information about quality isn't the best approach. Communication must be a two-way process. Everyone must have an opportunity for input into the TQM strategy and the changes brought about by TQM.

The chief executive officer must communicate that he or she is making a commitment to achieve total quality in everything that's done in the organization. The CEO must be committed to establishing a companywide communications program that involves managers and workers. The communication must include the following:

- What's meant by *total quality management.*
- Why it's important.
- How it will be accomplished.
- Why the CEO is involved and committed.
- What benefits will be achieved.

Management must be prepared for resistance to change in any normal pattern or set of procedures. "Business as usual" is changed when a TQM program is initiated. TQM represents a change in culture, and it may take a number of years to become effective and ingrained. Even though TQM can be initiated by a CEO, it must be practiced by a staff lower in the hierarchy.

Evaluation of Training and Development

At the outset of this chapter, the problem Gwen Meridith and Harold Matthews face is deciding whether the training offered was effective. They had not designed a formal evaluation of the training program. This section focuses on such evaluation.

The evaluation step is the final phase of the training and development program. Cost-benefit analysis generally is more feasible for training and development than for many other HRM functions. Costs are relatively easy to compute: They equal direct costs of training (trainer, materials, and lost productivity, if training is done on company time) plus indirect costs (a fair share of the administrative overhead of the HR department).[73]

Essentially, the evaluation should be made by comparing the results (the benefits) with the objectives of the training and development program that were set in the assessment phase. It is easier to evaluate the results of some programs (for example, typing) than others (for example, Outward Bound training and leadership).[74] The criteria used to evaluate training and development depend on the objectives of the program and who sets the criteria: management, the trainers, or the trainees. For example, one study found that trainees who were asked to develop their own evaluative criteria chose standards that varied from knowledge of the subject to the amount of socializing allowed during training sessions.[75]

HR Journal   *Strategic Measurement: A Top Priority*

For years, measurement and evaluation have been treated as afterthoughts in the workplace learning and performance training community. The focus has been on measuring basic needs, but most of the subsequent activity focused on ensuring a good implementation. If the subject of evaluation came up, it was discussed as a method for selling the program, ensuring future funding, or trying to make a link to the business. There were intuitive beliefs that training influenced the bottom line, but, because there was no control strategy, attempting to document results was a daunting and sometimes risky task.

Today, the profession has made significant advances in redefining the role of training, most notably with American Society of Training Directors's (ASTD) 2004 competency study, "Mapping the Future: Shaping New Workplace Learning and Performance Competencies." Training is becoming more strategic and is defining clear value propositions for organizational success. The roles of learning strategist and business partner are supplementing the important roles of professional specialist and project manager. The effects of those changes are felt everywhere, including the area of measurement and evaluation. ASTD's new model requires professionals in most areas of expertise to conduct needs analyses, monitor progress, evaluate outcomes, and provide feedback for change.

Training professionals have learned new methods for measurement and evaluation and are applying them in different contexts. Examples detailing how a project manager or professional specialist can tactically apply measurement methods are plentiful. But what about strategic approaches to measurement?

Measurement is far more than a set of methods. It's an integrated part of how trainers partner with stakeholders and implement their strategies. Without the strategic perspective, measurement tools tend to define rather than facilitate our solutions.

Most organizations use some form of an employee satisfaction or culture survey to gather valuable feedback for change and serve as an indicator of the training program's influence. Recent studies have refocused many of those surveys on the concept of employee engagement, which is a proven driver of employee loyalty and discretionary effort. Those outcomes lead to higher performance and retention. Engagement surveys, in their current form, represent the next generation of macro-level measures of training success. Through proven statistical relationships to outcomes such as turnover, productivity, and profitability engagement,

surveys are an obvious lead measure of organizational outcomes. While it might be difficult to link training programs directly to an organizational outcome, it's much easier to link them to the level of employee engagement.

The content of most employee engagement surveys addresses issues such as goal alignment, collaboration, support and recognition, and development. All of those work environment qualities are direct correlates and outcomes of most training programs. In effect, measures of employee engagement serve as proxy measures for organizational success that have a direct link to training programs. Most traditional measures of employee satisfaction or culture don't include that value proposition link to the bottom line.

At CompUSA, the goal was to focus its HR strategy by aligning it with companywide strategies for improving the business. Organizational leaders determined that one way to promote growth was through building engagement in its team members. Director of Training and Development Tom Labadie knew that employee engagement was significantly related to increased customer satisfaction. Another benefit was long-term retention of team members, who gain experience and build stronger relationships with customers. Labadie's philosophy was that engagement drives customer satisfaction, and the tool that CompUSA used allowed them to track progress and target action plans for training programs.

After field-testing an employee engagement survey with a small group of stores, CompUSA administered the survey nationwide to more than 200 stores. That measure, Development Dimension International's E3 survey, provided a baseline for engagement and gave managers and employees a common reference point. Essentially, the engagement survey built a sense of sharing accountability in the workforce and made obvious links to potential training solutions.

At the HR level, trainers used the engagement results to build a strategic training plan. The training function met internally to review the numbers and determine priorities relative to engagement scores and other issues. Regional HR managers also set goals concerning the changes they would pursue. Regional HR directors then partnered with regional managers to set improvement goals for engagement. The hope was that improvements would affect team success and that scores would improve.

Managers took feedback from the survey and developed action plans at the individual level. The engagement

HR Journal   *Strategic Measurement: A Top Priority (continued)*

scores were examined during performance reviews. To avoid a "rank and spank" mentality associated with store performance in some retail organizations, managers were prompted to talk with their supervisors about why their engagement scores were high or low and address any outstanding issues. Divisional HR managers met with regional managers to discuss activities that would further engage team members and build a winning culture, and created action plans. In a year, CompUSA plans to re-administer the engagement measure to track its progress.

Everyone at CompUSA, from the president and CEO down, is linked to the idea of creating a winning culture. Labadie describes how, when you walk into stores with high engagement scores, you can sense the positive tone. Employees whistle and smile, they approach customers, and the store gives off that elusive approachable feeling that customers appreciate.

From a measurement standpoint, Labadie feels that the engagement measure is an excellent way of tracking the influence of training programs. Engagement links to company strategies (developing a "winning culture" and growth), tracks progress over time, and has a direct link to training programs. In addition, the common reference point builds accountability for managers and offers a universally valued measure of progress.

Author Dan Tobin writes, "If you start and end all of your learning efforts by focusing on your organization's goals, you will never be asked to do an ROI analysis to justify your budget."

The topic of return on investment is popular, and there are many books, articles, and resources that give specific step-by-step instructions on how to administer the appropriate analyses. While ROI has its place, some would argue that ROI studies for specific programs aren't necessary if the program being evaluated is appropriately selected, positioned, and implemented. Intangible benefits can be quantified, but is such a calculation necessary if the program plays a clear role in the realization of a company strategy? Has ROI become a hammer in search of a nail?

Most organizations conduct ROI studies to demonstrate the value of a program to internal customers or to choose between two or more potential paths of action. However little research has been conducted to demonstrate that ROI results create compelling cases or shift opinions. In fact, one controlled laboratory study conducted by University of Toronto professors Gary Latham and Glen Whyte found that ROI studies, or

utility analyses, actually reduce the support of a manager for implementing a valid selection procedure.

Those findings don't mean that we shouldn't conduct ROI studies. Rather, we should be more careful about how we use them and understand the situation warrants such an approach. Training professionals need to work with internal customers, such as management and senior leaders, to create measurement contracts that clearly outline program expectations or objectives and how they'll be tracked. Program success should be evaluated in terms of the agreed-upon expectations and how well the program accomplished those objectives. That return-on-expectations, or ROE, approach is a more appropriate and broadly applied method than ROI.

During the past few years, Wyeth (WLP) evolved from being a holding company (American Home Products) into an integrated health care company that's focused on original research and development. The organization developed a new mission, vision, and values, and created a focus on the people, not just the numbers. For Wyeth Consumer Healthcare (WCH), a division of Wyeth, attracting, developing, and retaining talent has been a "top 5" priority for the past 10 years. Today, senior leaders buy into the idea of human capital and focus explicitly on driving a talent management strategy. Recent changes include a direct reporting relationship between the HR executive and the president. HR is building strong relationships with strategic leadership and moving away from a transactional role.

This year, WCH's competency development and interviewing training team won an internal Global Excellence Award for their work evaluating changes in the interviewing process. That award is given to up to 10 teams each year that take action to produce a significant business impact. The project didn't include an ROI study, but it did an excellent job of managing customer expectations and providing measurement outcomes in line with program expectations.

The selection process at WCH had been working well, but the team recognized an opportunity to improve the system. They used Development Dimension International's Target selection system to help interviewers become better prepared to conduct valid candidate interviews. The team worked to establish expectations for changing the system and held meetings with senior leaders to provide examples of successful interviewing processes at other organizations to gain their buy-in (influencing stakeholders). They also made links between the overall talent management

(continued)

HR Journal   *Strategic Measurement: A Top Priority   (concluded)*

strategy and showed how better preparing interviewers would promote the strategy (thinking strategically).

Fortunately, the organization had already created the business case for the value of a competency-based HR system. Senior HR leaders were receptive and saw competency-based interviewing as a natural step in the process. The team wasn't pressured to document ROI or link to outcomes (such as turnover) because it was clear that the program supported the business strategy. Their agreement for measurement was approved in advance and included achievable and realistic goals. Outcomes of the study included documented improvements in interviewing skills, confidence, and quality of the interview process.

The measurement process at WCH included the application of both strategic and tactical measurement tools. Rather than assuming that ROI or other analyses would be appropriate for the situation, WCH took the time to manage stakeholder expectations and identify links to the corporate strategy. In that way, the individuals involved create realistic and valid measures that accurately reflect the desired outcomes of the program.

Operating nearly 200 hospitals and a range of surgery and ambulatory care centers in 24 states, as well as the United Kingdom and Switzerland, Hospital Corporation of America is a large and dispersed organization. It's important for the company to coordinate training professionals at individual locations and unify their efforts toward a common set of metrics. HCA has been using an HR scorecard, or "dashboard," for the past four years, after it was initiated in response to a recruitment and retention task force.

The scorecard has been through several iterations over the years. Currently, the scorecard focuses on a mix of lead and lag measures, such as labor costs productivity, employee survey scores, and labor supply. Eventually, it will be enhanced to include more detailed measures of financials, customer satisfaction, quality, and operations.

Donna Yurdin, assistant vice president of organizational effectiveness, points out that the HR scorecard has been instrumental in increasing the visibility of HR and its impact on the business. Most important, the scorecard helps to focus the organization on opportunities for improvement and prioritizing the levers for change. In the health care industry, market changes and governmental regulations are always affecting business priorities. The scorecard keeps HCA focused on what's important for supporting human capital effectiveness. Yurdin's work with the HCA scorecard illustrates how training professionals can focus on driving results and applying business acumen when creating a value proposition for HR.

For example, the organization was experiencing higher levels of turnover in the 6- to 12-month new-hire period. HCA added a tenure-based breakout of turnover to the scorecard and introduced improvements in selection and onboarding to address the need. The dashboard served as a lag measure for onboarding. In the future, HCA could evaluate the implementation of selection and onboarding changes to predict future changes in short-term turnover.

Although HCA hopes to improve and expand its scorecard, Yurdin has a lot of advice for organizations considering their own HR scorecard: "There needs to be a collaborative effort between HR, business operations, and department heads to find external measures allowing you to gauge your progress. It all comes down to the scorecard needing to speak to the organization. You can't just take an example from another organization and make it work. Your scorecard needs to be reflective of the business culture and serve as a living document that changes over time as your business changes."

Source: Paul Bernthal (May 2005), "Measurement Gets Strategic," *Training & Development*, pp. 53–58.

Criteria for Evaluation

There are three types of criteria for evaluating training: internal, external, and participants' reaction. Internal criteria are directly associated with the content of the program—for example, whether the employee learned the facts or guidelines covered in the program. External criteria are related more to the ultimate purpose of the program—for example, improving the effectiveness of the employee. Possible external criteria include job performance rating, the degree of learning transferred from training and development sessions to on-the-job situations, and increases in sales volume or decreases in turnover. Participants' reaction, or how the subjects feel about the benefits of a specific training or development experience, is commonly used as an internal criterion.

Most experts argue that it is more effective to use multiple criteria to evaluate training.[76] Others contend that a single criterion, such as the extent of transfer of training to on-the-job performance or other aspects of performance, is a satisfactory approach to evaluation.

One view of a multiple-criterion evaluation system was developed by Kirkpatrick.[77] He suggests measuring the following:

- *Participants' reaction* Whether subjects like or dislike the program. The participant indicates his or her satisfaction with the program.
- *Learning* The extent to which the subjects have assimilated the knowledge offered and skills practiced in the training program. Does the participant score higher on tests after the training or development than before?
- *Behavior* An external measure of changes or lack of changes in job behavior; the ratings a participant received in performance appraisal (comparison of "before" and "after" ratings).
- *Results* The effect of the program on organizational dimensions such as employee turnover, productivity, volume of sales, or error-free letters typed.

At present, many firms assess reactions, but very few measure behavioral results.

The HR Journal box just presented discusses strategic measurement at a number of companies and what they have determined.

A Matrix Guide for Evaluation

One useful device for addressing the issue of evaluation is a systematic evaluation matrix. A matrix, because of its organization, can help those involved with training and development programs to systematically review relevant issues or questions. Exhibit 13-12 presents such a matrix, which could be used as a guideline for evaluating any of the programs and techniques covered in this chapter.

EXHIBIT 13-12   **An Evaluation Matrix: Issues to Consider**

Relevant Issues to Evaluate	What to Measure	What to Examine for Answers	How to Collect Data
1. Are the participants learning, changing attitudes, or improving skills?	Participants' attitudes or skills before and after (even during) training or development sessions	Comments Method of participation Co-workers Superiors	Interviews Questionnaires Records Observations
2 Are the training or development materials used on the job?	Participant's on-the-job performance, behavior, and style	Subordinates' performance, attitudes, and style	Records Interviews Questionnaires Critical incidents Observations
3. What are the costs of training and development programs and techniques?	Fixed and variable costs of conducting training or development	Cost of trainers Participant's time Travel expenses Consultants' fees Training aids Rent Utilities	Budget records
4. How long does the training or development have an effect on participants?	Participant's on-the-job performance, behavior, and style over an extended period of time	Subordinates' performance, attitudes, and style	Records Interviews Questionnaires Critical incidents Observations (collected a number of times)

After absorbing the material Bob brought her, Gwen approached Lester Young, Young Enterprises's president, on an informal basis.

Gwen You know, Les, our last attitude survey indicated major dissatisfaction with our development program at Young. We've been doing some research in our shop about development programs, I'm sure I couldn't work it into this year's budget, but we're only six weeks away from the new budget. I feel the program is very important at this time. As you know, we were not completely satisfied with the training program on the new machinery. In addition, one or two of our supervisors have come in to complain about the lack of any organization development program for them. How would you like us to proceed?

Lester I heard some talk about OD at a recent American Manufacturers Association meeting. I hear it's quite costly. We may have some problems in this area, but we're in no position to make a major investment in development at the present time in view of our earnings situation. Why not work up a modest program for presentation to the budget and goals meeting six weeks from now—no more than 5 percent of your current budget as an increment.

Gwen Will do, Les.

Gwen and Bob put together a proposal that they viewed as phase I. They proposed a supervisory development program with some help from the HR department for one-half of 1 percent of current budget.

After investigating the potential costs of an OD consultant, they felt they should begin to move in the development area. They proposed some beginning funds for planning an OD program, the first phase of which would involve initial diagnosis and collection of a small sample of data. They proposed to set up an experiment using a behavior-modeling program in one unit for supervisory style, with a control group. Evaluation procedures were to be formal. They specified desired outputs: better readings from the attitude survey, some improvements in turnover and absenteeism, and some results in the productivity problem.

Lester and the budget and goals committee accepted the proposal. Phase I began, and it was successful. Little by little, the company accepted a development program.

The relevant issues—improvement in skills, training and development materials, costs, and long-term effects—are crucial questions that can be answered by use of evaluation. But the issues and questions provide only the direction that evaluation can take. The actual design and data collection require following the scientific method used by behavioral scientists. Simply asking participants if they liked the program after they have attended a sensitivity group or a behavioral modeling session is not very scientific. What would you expect to be the answer? Certainly, most of us like new experiences, new ideas. However, this does not mean that a program is good or beneficial for improving performance or increasing interpersonal skills on the job. Perhaps the most pressing question is whether what is learned in training transfers to the job. Another crucial issue is what strategies management can use to facilitate transfer of learning to the job.[78]

Someone in authority (usually someone above the HR specialist involved in the training or development, such as a director of human resources or vice president of operations) must hold those who train and develop employees accountable. The efficient use of people, dollars, and facilities must be clearly shown. This can be done only if the evaluation phase is completed and sound research designs are used. Evaluation is certainly not easy, but it is a necessary and often glossed-over part of training and developments.[79]

In sum, formal training and development have been shown to be more effective than informal or no training and development. However, for most training and development programs the results tend to be assumed rather than evaluated.

Summary

To summarize the major points covered in this chapter:

1. The principal purposes of orientation are:
   a. To reduce start-up costs of a new employee.
   b. To reduce the fear and anxiety of the new employee.
   c. To reduce turnover.
   d. To save time for supervisors and co-workers.
   e. To develop realistic job expectations, positive attitudes toward the employer, and job satisfaction.

2. Training is a form of education to which the following learning principles can be applied:
   a. Trainee must be motivated to learn.
   b. Trainee must be able to learn.
   c. Learning must be reinforced.
   d. Training must provide for practice of the material.
   e. Material presented must be meaningful.
   f. Material taught must transfer to the job.

3. Purposes of training and development include:
   a. To improve the quantity of output.
   b. To improve the quality of output.
   c. To lower the costs of waste and equipment maintenance.
   d. To lower the number and costs of accidents.
   e. To lower turnover and absenteeism and increase employees' job satisfaction.
   f. To prevent employee obsolescence.

4. When employee turnover is great, it is more important for the organization to provide formal technical training for employees.

5. Effective organizations design their training programs only after assessing the organization's and individual's training needs and setting training objectives.

6. Training approaches for employees include:
   a. On-the-job training (for managers, these include coaching and counseling; transitory experiences; and transfers and rotation).
   b. Off-the-job training (discussion, programmed instruction, and computer-assisted technologies including virtual reality, multimedia-based training, distance learning, and interactive video training).

7. Management development is the process by which managers gain the experience, skills, and attitudes to become or remain successful leaders in their organization.

8. Management and professional development is designed to reduce obsolescence and to increase employees' satisfaction and productivity.

9. The final phase of any training and development program should be evaluation. However, this phase is often bypassed by organizations. Also, there are some cases where rigorous evaluation may not illustrate qualitative improvements.

Key Terms

apprentice training, *p. 414*
behavior modeling, *p. 411*
behavior modification, *p. 422*
case method, *p. 409*
computer-assisted instruction (CAI), *p. 415*
development, *p. 394*
distance learning (distance training), *p. 417*
extinction, *p. 423*
goal setting, *p. 420*
in-basket technique, *p. 410*

Internet, *p. 415*
intranet, *p. 415*
learning, *p. 399*
learning organizations, *p. 401*
management games, *p. 410*
multimedia-based training (MBT), *p. 417*
negative reinforcement, *p. 422*
orientation, *p. 394*
outdoor action-oriented programs, *p. 412*
performance analysis, *p. 404*

positive reinforcement, *p. 422*
punishment, *p. 422*
role playing, *p. 410*
team building, *p. 425*
total quality management (TQM) training, *p. 426*
training, *p. 394*
vestibule training, *p. 418*
virtual reality (VR), *p. 417*

1. Why is training an important requirement for organizations to undertake?
2. Do you believe that acceptance of training programs would be better in organizations classified as learning organizations? Why?
3. What are the main purposes of orientation programs? What aspects of orientation seem to be the most neglected?
4. Why is the evaluation and assessment of training and development programs so difficult?
5. Will e-learning or online training replace classroom training? Why?
6. What should training in goal setting involve, and who should participate in such training?
7. How could a person's expectations about training influence what he or she learns in a formal training program?
8. What barriers exist that hamper the transfer of learning from the training classroom to back on the job?
9. Why is a needs assessment a requirement for determining what training should be provided? Unfortunately, too many organizations bypass the needs assessment. Why?
10. Describe why a performance analysis may indicate that training is now needed to solve a particular problem.

HRM Legal Advisor

Based on *Shaner* v. *Synthes,* 1998 U.S. Dist. LEXIS 20009.

The Facts

Robert Shaner was hired as a programmer analyst in September 1991 by Synthes, a manufacturer of orthopedic implant instruments. Mr. Shaner was diagnosed with multiple sclerosis in August 1992 and notified his employer of his condition in November 1994. In April 1994, he filed a disability discrimination claim with the EEOC against Synthes for denial of training requests. Mr. Shaner claimed that he repeatedly requested Excel training from Synthes both before and after disclosing his medical condition and was denied each time. He also alleges that other programmers in the company received the training and that he was the only programmer in his group who had been denied Excel training. Synthes rebutted by stating that Mr. Shaner's requests for training were denied even before the company learned of his condition, thus the denial was not based on disability discrimination. Additionally, Synthes indicated that at the time Mr. Shaner requested Excel training, it was not being offered to anyone in his group. Further, after January 1994, Excel was not needed to effectively perform the job of programmer.

The Americans with Disabilities Act states that companies are prohibited from discriminating against "a qualified individual with a disability because of the disability of such individual in regard to job application procedures, the hiring, advancement, or discharge of employees, compensation, job training, and other terms and conditions of employment." To prove a valid claim for disability discrimination in denial of job training, a plaintiff must show that he or she is qualified, has a disability, and was denied training because of the disability. A company can defend its denial by asserting a legitimate nondiscriminatory reason for its actions. Was Mr. Shaner denied training because of his disability? Did Synthes meet its burden of proof?

The Court's Decision

The U.S. District Court for the Eastern District of Pennsylvania held that Mr. Shaner did establish a prima facie case of disability discrimination under the ADA. Having been hired by Synthes, he was considered qualified for his position. Additionally, multiple sclerosis is considered a physical impairment that substantially limits one or more major life activities under the ADA. The court further found that there was some evidence of disability discrimination given the denials of training following Mr. Shaner's disclosure of his condition.

However, the court found Synthes's reasons for the denial to be nondiscriminatory. The court was particularly persuaded by the company's statements that no employees received the training or needed the training after January 1994 and that they knew nothing of the plaintiff's condition until November 1994.

Human Resource Implications

This case highlights the importance of consistency and fairness in offering training opportunities to employees. The Americans with Disabilities Act as well as other EEO laws prohibit discriminating against employees in training as well as other terms and conditions of employment. Synthes prevailed in this case because they were able to document dates and job-related reasons for training and denials of training. Employers should ensure that employee training and development opportunities are related to specific job needs, performance, or merit rather than subjective criteria that may be construed as discrimination.

Notes

1. Ellen Ek, Ulla Sovio, and Jouko Remes (June 2005), "Social Predictions of Unsuccessful Entrance into the Labor Market—A Socialization Process Perspective," *Journal of Vocational Behavior,* pp. 471–486.
2. Clifton Scott and Karen Kroman Myers (February 2005), "The Socialization of Emotion: Learning Emotion Management at the Fire Station," *Journal of Applied Communication Research,* pp. 67–92.
3. Doris M. Sims (2001), *Creative New Orientation Programs* (New York: McGraw-Hill).
4. Kimi Yoshino and Dave McKibben (July 17, 2005), "Disneyland: Fifty Years of Magic," *Los Angeles Times.*
5. Clifton O. Longnecker and Laurence S. Fink (January 2005), *Management Training: Benefits and Lost Opportunities, Industrial & Commercial Training,* pp. 25–30.
6. Donald Kirkpatrick (January 1996), "Great Ideas Revisited," *Training & Development,* pp. 54–59.
7. Salley B. Sawyer and Daniel V. Eastmond (Spring 2005), "Learning Theories and the Design of E-Learning Environments," *Quarterly Review of Distance Education,* pp. 77–80.
8. Peter M. Senge (1990), *The Fifth Discipline* (New York: Doubleday), p. 3.
9. David A. Garvin (July–August 1993), "Building a Learning Organization," *Harvard Business Review,* pp. 78–92.
10. Donald Waters (1999), *101 Ways to Improve Business Performance* (London: Kogen Page Ltd.).
11. "2001 Industry Report" (October 2002), *Training,* pp. 30–48.
12. Donna Goldwasser (January 2001), "Beyond ROI," *Training,* pp. 82–90.
13. Kirkpatrick, op. cit., pp. 54–59.
14. Ibid.
15. Donald Michalak and Edwin Yager (1979), *Making the Training Process Work* (New York: Harper & Row). A pioneer in developing the use of behavioral objectives for performance analysis is Robert Mazer. See Robert F. Mazer (1962), *Preparing Instructional Objectives* (Palo Alto: Fearon); and Robert F. Mazer (1989), *Preparing Instructional Objectives* (Belmont, CA: Putnam, Learning).
16. Allison Possett and Kendra Sheldon (2001), *Beyond the Podium: Delivering Training and Performance to a Digital World* (New York: John Wiley).
17. Paul G. Whitmore (2002), *How to Make Smart Decisions about Training* (Atlanta: CEP Press).
18. Roger Schwartz (2002), *The Skilled Facilitator* (New York: John Wiley).
19. J. David Viale (1997), *JIT Forecasting and Master Scheduling* (New York: Crisp).
20. Chris Lee (August 1990), "1-800-Training," *Training,* pp. 39–45.

21. Jeremy Cobb and John Bibbs (Fall 1990). "New Competency-Based On-the-Job Program for Developing Professional Excellence in Engineering," *The Journal of Management Development,* pp. 60–72.

22. Andrew B. Bartmess (March–April 1994), "HRB Case Study: The Plant Location Puzzle," *Harvard Business Review,* pp. 20–37.

23. Glenn Parker (2002), *Team Depot* (San Francisco: Jossey-Bass).

24. Jim Adams and Andre LaMothe (Eds.) (2002), *Programming Roles Play Games with Direct X* (New York: Premier Press).

25. Jane M. Howell (November 1991), "Through the Looking Glass," *Journal of Management Education,* pp. 412–427.

26. Thomas C. Mawhinney (2000), "OBM Today and Tomorrow: Then and Now," *Journal of Organizational Behavior Management,* Vol. 20, pp. 73–137.

27. Don M. Ricks (November 1999), "The Proximity Principle," *Training,* p. 148.

28. Henry P. Sims Jr. and Peter Lorenzi (1992), *The New Leadership Paradigm: Social Learning and Cognition in Organizations* (Newbury Park, CA: Sage).

29. Dianne H. B. Welsh, Fred Luthans, and Steven M. Sommer (1992), "Organizational Behavior Modification Goes to Russia: Replicating an Experimental Analysis across Cultures and Tasks," *Journal of Organizational Behavior Management,* 13, 2, pp. 15–36.

30. Albert Bandura (1999), "Social Cognitive Theory: An Agentic Perspective," *Asian Journal of Social Psychology,* Vol. 2, 21–41.

31. Arun Maira and Peter Scott-Morgan (1997), *Accelerating Organization* (New York: McGraw-Hill), pp. 60–61.

32. Elizabeth Weldon (2000), "The Development of Product and Process Involvements in Work Groups," *Group and Organizational Management,* Vol. 25, pp. 244–268.

33. Stephen Proctor and David Buchanan (2000), "Teamworking in Its Contexts: Antecedents, Nature, and Dimension," *Human Relations,* Vol. 53, pp. 1387–1424.

34. Ronald A. Heifetz and Marty Linsky (June 2002), "A Survival Guide for Leaders," *Harvard Business Review,* pp. 65–75.

35. Douglas T. Hall (November 1996), "Protean Careers of the 21st Century," *Academy of Management Executive,* pp. 8–16.

36. Liz Simpson (June 2002), "What's Going On in Your Company?" *Training,* pp. 30–34.

37. Devendra Agochiya (2002), *Every Trainer's Handbook* (San Francisco: Jossey-Bass).

38. Kristine Ellis (September 2002), "Hot Values of Hot Air?" *Training,* pp. 60–64.

39. "Multimedia Training in the Fortune 1000" (September 1996), *Training,* pp. 53–60.

40. Maureen Minehan (August 1996), "Virtual Reality: The Next Step in Training," *HRMagazine,* p. 144.

41. Bill Leonard (April 1996), "Distance Learning: Work & Training Overlap," *HRMagazine,* pp. 41–47.

42. Norwegian Oil Co.

43. Constance Redley Smith (May 1996), "Taking the Distance Out of Distance Learning," *Training & Development,* pp. 87–89.

44. Jerry Hedge and Elaine Pulakos (2002), *Implementing Organizational Interventions* (San Francisco: Jossey-Bass).

45. Edwin A. Locke and Gary P. Latham (September 2002), "Building a Practically Useful Theory of Goal Setting and Task Motivation," *American Psychologist,* pp. 705–717.

46. Thomas A. Ryan (1970), *Intentional Behavior* (New York: Ronald Press), p. 95.

47. Locke and Latham, op. cit.

48. D. Vande Walle, D. Cron, and J. Slocum (2001), "The Role of Goal Orientation Following Performance Feedback," *Journal of Applied Psychology,* 86, pp. 621–640.

49. Anthony J. Mento, Robert P. Steel, and Ronald J. Karren (February 1987), "A Meta-Analytic Study of the Effects of Goal Setting on Task Performance: 1966–1984," *Organizational Behavior and Human Decision Processes,* p. 53.

50. Locke and Latham, op. cit.

51. Ibid.

52. Edwin A. Locke, K. N. Shaw, Lisa M. Saari, and Gary P. Latham (July 1984), "Goal Setting and Task Performances: 1969–1980," *Psychological Bulletin,* p. 129.

53. John M. Ivancevich and J. Timothy McMahon (August 1977), "Education as Moderator of Goal-Setting Effectiveness," *Journal of Vocational Behavior,* pp. 83–94.

54. Gary P. Latham and Gary A. Yukl (June 1975), "Assigned versus Participative Goal Setting with Educated and Uneducated Wood Workers," *Journal of Applied Psychology,* pp. 299–302.

55. Miriam Erez and R. Arad (August 1986), "Participative Goal Setting: Social, Motivational, and Cognitive Factors," *Journal of Applied Psychology,* pp. 591–597.

56. John M. Ivancevich and J. Timothy McMahon (December 1977), "Black-White Differences in a Goal Setting Program," *Organizational Behavior and Human Performance,* pp. 287–300.

57. Joseph N. Riccardi (May 2005), "Achieving Human Service Outcomes through Competency-Based Training: A Guide for Managers," *Behavior Modification,* pp. 488–507.

58. Matt J. Gray and Brett T. Litz (January 2005), "Behavioral Interventions for Recent Trauma: Empirically Informed Practice Guidelines," *Behavior Modification,* pp. 189–215.

59. Yoav Vardi and Eli Weitz (2003), *Misbehavior in Organizations* (Mahwah, NJ: Erlbaum).

60. Edward L. Thorndike (1911), *Animal Intelligence* (New York: MacMillan), p. 244.

61. *The Journal of Organizational Behavior* covers behavior modification theory, research, and application.

62. Fred Luthans (2005), *Organizational Behavior* (New York: McGraw-Hill).

63. Thomas K. Connellan (1978), *How to Improve Human Performance: Behaviorism in Business and Industry* (New York: Harper & Row), pp. 48–75.

64. Ibid.

65. Edwin A. Locke (October 1977), "The Myths of Behavior Mod in Organizations," *Academy of Management Review,* pp. 543–553.

66. Frank La Fasto and Carl Larson (2002), W*hen Teams Work Best* (Thousand Oaks, CA: Sage).

67. Laura Beth Jones (2002), *Teach Your Team to Fish* (New York: Crown Books).

68. Bob Stewart and Sarah Powel (2004), "Team Building and Team Working," *Team Performance Management,* pp. 35–38.

69. J. Richard Hackman (2002), *Leading Teams* (Boston, MA: Harvard Business School Press).

70. Manfred F. R. deVries Kets (February 2005), "Leadership Group Coaching in Action: The Zen of Creating High Performance Teams," *Academy of Management Executive,* pp. 61–76.

71. Thomas F. O'Boyle (June 4, 1990), "From Pyramid to Pancake," *The Wall Street Journal,* pp. B37–38.

72. Edward E. Lawler, Susan Albers Mohrman, George Benson, and Susan Albers (2001), *Organizing for High Performance* (New York: John Wiley).

73. 2004 Industry Report, op. cit.

74. Jack Phillips, Timothy Bothell, and Lynne Sneed (2002), *The Project Management Scorecard* (Woburn, MA: Butterworth Heinemann).

75. C. H. Hale (2002), *Performance Based Evaluation* (New York: John Wiley).

76. Ibid.

77. Donald Kirkpatrick (1998), *Evaluating Training Programs* (New York: Berrett-Koehler).

78. Michael Dulworth and Frank Bordonaro (2005), *Corporate Learning: Proven and Practical Guidelines for Building a Sustainable Learning Strategy* (New York: Pfeffer).

79. Ibid.

EXERCISE 13-1

Assessing Training Needs

OBJECTIVE

This exercise illustrates how to properly assess training needs.

SET UP THE EXERCISE

1. Select a job to analyze. Choose a job that you have some familiarity with or have actually held.
2. Prepare or obtain a job description for it. What are the major duties and responsibilities? Also, what activities must be done to complete the job?
3. In specific terms, what are the observable behaviors that a jobholder must perform?
4. After completing steps 1 though 3, outline what type of training would be beneficial to improve performance in this job. What training methods seem to be best suited for this job?

A NOTE ON LEARNING

This exercise emphasizes the type of careful analysis that must be conducted in determining specific needs for training.

Application Case 13-1

Dunkin' Donuts and Domino's Pizza: Training for Quality and Hustle

Dunkin' Donuts and Domino's Pizza share the same requirement for success: Provide a high-quality product at impressive speed. Domino's guarantees a hot, tasty pizza delivered to your doorstep as soon as possible. Dunkin' Donuts promises fresh doughnuts every four hours and fresh coffee every 18 minutes.

To meet this requirement, both fast-food companies face the same training challenge: Train a very young (typically aged 18 to 21) and inexperienced workforce to meet rigorous performance standards. Both companies must train in an industry where turnover averages 300 to 400 percent yearly and where company locations are widely dispersed. Domino's operates 3,800 stores throughout the United States and seven foreign countries: Dunkin' Donuts has 1,400 shops spanning the United States and 12 foreign countries.

The two companies approach this training challenge with a highly decentralized training function. At Domino's Pizza, 85 percent of a nonsupervisory employee's training occurs on the job and is provided by the store manager or franchise owner. Each employee is usually trained to fill most of the shop's five hourly jobs (order taker, pizza maker, oven tender, router, and driver), which helps during rush hours when a crew member doesn't appear for work. Performance standards are demanding; the order taker must answer a call within three rings and take the order within 45 seconds. The pizza maker must make the pizza and place it in the oven within one minute. The oven tender must take one pizza out while putting another one in within five seconds and cut and box the pizza by the count of 15. Domino's encourages dedication to speed by keeping tabs on the fastest service and delivery times reported by its stores and publishing them as "box scores" in The Pepperoni Press, the company newspaper.

Although the bulk of training is on the job far away from corporate headquarters, Domino's corporate training staff maintains some control over training by providing a variety of training aids. The staff makes available to shop management 14 videotapes (with instructor's manuals) on such tasks as delivery, dough management, image, and pizza making. Each shop is equipped with a VCR. The videos are upbeat, fast-moving, and musical (MTV-style) with a heavy dose of comedy geared to its high school and college-aged audience. Young Domino's employees play the roles in the videos.

Each shop also displays corporate-produced training posters with job hints and reminders throughout the work area. Above the production line, for example, are large color pictures of how a pizza should look at each step of the production process. Two popular posters are a glossy color picture of "The Perfect Pepperoni" pizza and a picture of a pizza cursed with the 10 common flaws (for example, scorched vegetables, air bubbles). The training materials communicate many key points with Domino's-styled lingo, "Dominese."

Store managers (aged 21 to 25) are trained by a six-course, typically six-month MIT program that includes coursework in pizza dough management, people management, cost management, and how to conduct on-the-job training of hourly employees. Manager trainees progress through five levels of training with higher performance requirements and more responsibilities added at each level. On-the-job training is an important part of the training program.

Many franchise owners (and all company-owned stores) send management trainees to the regional training center for classes taught by corporate trainers; however, management training often is decentralized, with franchise owners conducting the MIT courses themselves. Franchise owners must be certified to conduct the formal courses for their manager trainees. The certification process requires that the owner complete a "Training Dynamics" course on how to teach manager trainees; observe certified teachers training the MIT series of courses; and then co-teach the series with a regional trainer, who must approve the franchisee's performance. The quality of training provided by franchise owners is enhanced by the owners' substantial in-store management experience. Only Domino's store managers may apply for franchise ownership.

Domino's corporate training staff is also involved in developing franchise owners by means of a rigorous training program for all prospective owners. The training includes a series of courses on contracts, site selection, store construction, and marketing, with an early, heavy emphasis on the nitty-gritty aspects of ownership to discourage those who are less than totally committed.

Like Domino's Pizza, Dunkin' Donuts's corporate training staff conducts a demanding training program for its franchise owners. Prospective franchisees undergo six weeks of training at Dunkin' Donuts University in Braintree, Massachusetts. There, they spend four weeks in production training, learning how to make doughnuts, coffee, soup, and other products, and how to operate and maintain the production equipment. Performance standards are rigorous; the final production test requires that a trainee make 140 doughnuts per hour (enough to fill a shop's doughnut case). Each batch of doughnuts is weighed and measured for length and height. If a batch of six cake doughnuts is one ounce too light or too heavy, for example, the batch fails the test.

Franchisees spend the last two weeks focusing on financial aspects of the business and on developing employee management skills (for example, supervising, performance appraisal, and interpersonal communication). The 12-member training staff conducting the program are all former store managers or district sales managers with about 10 years' experience with the company.

Training of hourly employees is totally decentralized. Franchise owners serve as trainers and receive how-to instruction for this task. Like Domino's Pizza, Dunkin' Donuts's corporate training staff also provides training video cassettes for owners to use. Quarterly clinics on quality control are also conducted by the company's district managers and technical advisers.

Dunkin' Donuts uses a different and decentralized approach to training its store managers who are not franchise owners. Rather than have franchise owners conduct the training, the company selects experienced store managers and trains them as store manager trainers. Their trainers train new managers using a program and materials developed by the corporate staff. This decentralized approach is relatively new for Dunkin' Donuts and was adopted after the company dropped its 12-week training program conducted totally at corporate headquarters. With the centralized approach, turnover among new managers was 50 percent during training. Under the new decentralized, on-site approach, turnover during training is about 0.5 percent, and annual training costs have decreased from $418,000 to $172,000.

People-related management skills are emphasized in training both franchise owners and store managers. Dunkin' Donuts credits this emphasis as a major reason why its annual turnover rate for hourly workers (80 percent) is considerably less than the industry average.

Discussion Questions

1. What are the strengths and shortcomings of a decentralized approach to training managers and hourly employees? Discuss.
2. Develop a plan for determining the training needs of the hourly paid staff of a Domino's Pizza franchise.
3. In your opinion, why was the turnover rate among management trainees in Dunkin' Donuts's centralized program so high?

14

Career Planning and Development

Learning Objectives

After studying this chapter you should be able to:

1. **Define** the term *career.*
2. **Describe** the potential organizational benefits that can result from mentoring relationships.
3. **Explain** why organizations need to be concerned about dual-career couples.
4. **Discuss** how career "pathing" can be used within an organization.
5. **State** how career planning is done in organizations.

Internet/Web Resources

General Sites

www.nceo.org

www.www.careerbuilder.com

www.monster.com

www.joboptions.com

www.hotjobs.com

www.monstertrak.com

Company Sites

www.att.com

www.lehman.com

www.pg.com

www.coors.com

www.campbellsoup.com

www.benjerry.com

Career Challenge

Jim Lucio was a 50-year-old executive with Neal Engineering Construction Company in Mesa, Arizona, a suburb of Phoenix. Despite his professional engineering training and his good position with the company, Jim had an identity problem. This conversation between Jim and Norbert Wislinski, his boss, indicates a midcareer concern.

Norb   Jim, you're really moving on the Salt River Project. Costs are under control and you've been able to control Tony (the chief engineer).

Jim   To be honest, Norb, I'm sick of the project, Tony, and everything about the job. I can't sleep, eat, or relax.

Norb   I'm sorry to hear that. Do you need some time off?

Jim   No. I need to rethink my whole career. I've just lost my intensity. It hasn't been sudden. It's been growing over the last year.

Norb   You know I'll do anything I can to help you. You're what made this company a success.

Jim   Thanks. But I really have to do some soul-searching. I've always wanted to own my own business, be my own boss. I just haven't been brave enough to take the plunge.

Norb   Jim, you know I'm selfish. I need you here at Neal, but if you make the break, I'll help you any way I can.

Jim   Thanks again, Norb. I have to think more about this. It's a whole career change. Serious business for a 50-year-old engineer.

Jim Lucio has changed, and now he is trying to cope with his thoughts and feelings. This is a difficult time in Jim's life. He seems to have it all, but something is missing. He is not satisfied. Norb is an understanding manager who also seems to realize that Jim Lucio is at a midcareer point in life and wants to make a change.

Global competition and changes in economic conditions are causing many organizations of all sizes to restructure. Experts tend to agree that self-management by all employees in an organization is the new human resources reality for the coming years. These changes mean that organizations today must be more aware than ever before of how best to utilize the talents of employees at all levels of the company. Capable people must be available to fill the new, bigger, and technologically more sophisticated jobs of the modern organization. Moreover, the contemporary concern for developing the full potential of all employees through job opportunities that provide responsibility, advancement, and challenging work reinforces such efforts. Even organizations facing a stable or a contracting future recognize that a key to performance is the development of human resources.

As organizations change, so do their employees. For example, a recently hired manager has different needs and aspirations from a midcareer or preretirement manager. All of us move through a fairly uniform pattern of phases during our careers. The different phases produce different opportunities and stresses that affect job performance. Effective managers comprehend these implications and facilitate the efforts of employees who wish to confront and deal with their career and life needs.

Managers and employees should be involved with their own career development. Yet individual employees often lack the ability and the information needed to systematically develop their own career plans in ways that can work to their benefit and to the benefit of the organization—although there is a growing interest in providing individuals with this kind of information.

This chapter reviews a number of programs that organizations and employees can use to plan and develop careers. Most of these programs have focused on managers, but more

EXHIBIT 14-1 **Career Development System: Linking Organizational Needs with Individual Needs**

Source: T. G. Gutteridge, Z. B. Leibowitz, and J. E. Shore (1993), *Organizational Career Development: Benchmarks for Building a World-Class Workforce* (San Francisco: Jossey-Bass).

ORGANIZATIONAL NEEDS	ISSUE:	INDIVIDUAL NEEDS
What are the organization's major strategic issues over the next two to three years? • What are the most critical needs and challenges that the organization will face over the next two to three years? • What critical skills, knowledge, and experience will be needed to meet these challenges? • What staffing levels will be required? • Does the organization have the strength necessary to meet the critical challenges?	Are employees developing themselves in a way that links personal effectiveness and satisfaction with the achievement of the organization's strategic objectives?	How do I find career opportunities within the organization that will do the following? • Use my strengths • Address my developmental needs • Provide challenges • Match my interests • Match my values • Match my personal style

and more organizations are beginning to recognize that nonmanagers at all levels need career planning.

Careers do not just happen in isolation from environmental and personal factors. Every person's career goes through a series of stages. Each of these stages may or may not be influenced by attitudes, motivation, the nature of the task, economic conditions, and so forth. Every employee must be sensitive to the "career cycle" and the role that different influences can play at different points.

An adequate matching of individual needs, abilities, preferences, motivation, and organizational opportunities will not just happen. Individuals, organizations, and experts in areas such as HRM all must take responsibility for things they can control. Employees must have a clear picture of the opportunities available now and anticipated in the future. Organizations should not guess at or assume some set of career needs. Likewise, employees should not have to guess how career development occurs in the organization. A sharing of information, an understanding of "career stages," and concern about the forces that influence careers must be established as part of ongoing career planning and development. Anything less will probably result in the inefficient use of human resources.

Exhibit 14-1 shows in everyday terms how organizational needs and individual needs are linked so that the individuals' satisfaction with their careers can be accomplished through strategic organizational objectives.[1] The individual must be involved in his or her own diagnosis, prescription, implementation, and evaluation.

The Concept of Career

The concept of **career** has many meanings. The popular meaning is probably reflected in the idea of moving upward in one's chosen line of work—making more money; having more responsibility; and acquiring more status, prestige, and power. Although typically restricted to lines of work that involve gainful employment, the concept of career can apply to other life pursuits. For example, we can think of homemakers, parents, and volunteer workers as having careers; they too advance in the sense that their talents and abilities to handle larger responsibilities grow with time and experience. A parent of teenagers plays a far different role from the one he or she played when the children were preschoolers.

A concise definition of a career that emphasizes its importance is offered by Greenhaus:

A career is the pattern of work-related experiences (e.g., job positions, job duties, decisions, and subjective interpretations about work-related events) and activities over the span of the person's work life.[2]

HR Journal   *Generational Difference*

A typical workplace includes four separate generations of employees, each with its own unique style and mind-set. Teaching managers and workers about their differences is becoming a top priority across industries, jobs, and organizations.

The approximately 46 million generation Xers (born 1962 to 1975) tend to view careers and make career choices differently than their parents. The baby boomer generation, about 76 million strong (parents born 1946 to 1961), attempted to balance work and family life. Gen Xers (20s to mid-30s) are not so impressed with balance or cradle-to-grave job security.

Gen Xers have witnessed downsizing, restructuring, and early retirement as the main issues faced by their parents. Thus, Gen Xers want flexibility, training and education, more money and benefits, and more opportunities. They are inclined to move from company to company and are not focused on loyalty. Gen Xers want to do the work and move to the next challenge. As far as loyalty is concerned, Xers will stay as long as the employer offers something that they value.

Mentoring and coaching are means of meeting Gen Xers' high demand for learning and personal development. Helping Xers feel as though they are growing, learning, and developing is what employers need to be concerned about.

Another key attraction point for Gen Xers is flexible working hours. They want the flexibility to complete work requirements on a schedule that they have some control over. Rigid work schedules, top-down hierarchy, and complete job security don't make good sense to the Xers. Freedom, taking risks, self-actualization, and continuous personal growth mean more.

If employers want to motivate and retain Gen Xers, they will have to provide flexibility, independence, growth, and training opportunities.

Generation Y, about 72 million members born between 1976 and 1995, is entering the workforce in growing numbers now. They have strong opinions about the ideal career path. There is a lack of interest in climbing the corporate ladder. They also are entering their careers with different expectations than baby boomers and generation Xers. They want to negotiate higher starting salaries, attempting to use multiple job offers to receive signing bonuses. Generation Xers also assume that they will be changing jobs frequently This results in taking a short-term career outlook without having goals to develop within their company.

Although generation Ys bring exceptional technical skills, are entrepreneurial, and have a deep social consciousness, they will be surprised at what they have to learn in the "real" organizational world. There is going to be a high need for supporting the next generation, which will be the next big challenge for their managers and the HRM function.

Source: Adapted from Paul Harris (May 2005), "Boomer vs. Echo Boomer: The Work War," *Training & Development Journal,* pp. 44–49; Julie Wallace (April 2001) "After X Comes Y," *HRMagazine,* p. 192; Shelly Reese (June 1999), "The New Wave of Gen X Workers," *Business & Health,* pp. 19–23; and Harry S. Dent, Jr. (1998), *The Roaring 2000s* (New York: Simon & Schuster).

This definition emphasizes that the term *career* does not imply success or failure except in the judgment of the individual, that a career consists of both attitudes and behavior, and that it is an ongoing sequence of work-related activities. Yet, even though the concept of career is clearly work-related, it must be understood that a person's nonwork life and roles play a significant part in a career. For example, the attitudes of a 50-year-old midcareer manager (midcareer means at or above the midpoint of a person's working tenure) about a job advancement involving greater responsibilities can be quite different from those of a manager nearing retirement. A single person's reaction to a promotion involving relocation is likely to be different from that of a father or mother of school-age children.

The values of society change over time and, consequently, how a person reacts to a career may be modified. Today, a growing number of people who are in managerial and professional careers seem less obsessed with advancement, continual success, and a continually

EXHIBIT 14-2
Career Stages and
Important Needs

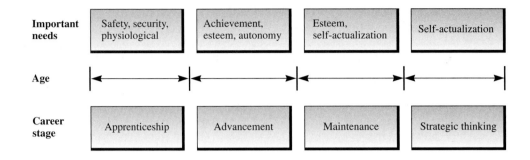

increasing salary. Family needs and spending time off the job with loved ones are becoming topics that individuals are discussing and considering more completely.[3]

Career Stages

Most working people prepare for their occupation by undergoing some form of organized education in high school, trade school, vocational school, or college. They then take a first job, but the chances are that they will move to other jobs in the same organization or in other organizations. Eventually, over the course of their career, they settle into a position in which they remain until retirement. The duration of each stage varies among individuals, but most working people go through all of these stages.

Studies of **career stages** have found that needs and expectations change as the individual moves through the stages.[4] Exhibit 14-2 summarizes the relationship between career stages and individuals' needs.

Managers at American Telephone and Telegraph (AT&T), for example, expressed considerable concern for safety needs during the initial years on their jobs. This phase, termed the *establishment phase,* ordinarily lasted during the first five years of employment.

Following the establishment phase is the *advancement phase,* which lasts approximately from age 30 to age 45. During this period, the AT&T managers expressed considerably less concern for safety and more concern for achievement, esteem, and autonomy.

The *maintenance phase* follows the advancement phase. This period is marked by efforts to stabilize the gains of the past. Although no new gains may be made, the maintenance phase can be a period of creativity, since the individual has satisfied many of the psychological and financial needs associated with earlier phases. Although each individual and each career will be different, it is reasonable to assume that esteem and self-actualization would be the most important needs in the maintenance phase. But, as we will see, many people experience what is called a *midcareer crisis* during the maintenance phase. Such people are not achieving satisfaction from their work, and consequently they may experience psychological discomfort.

The maintenance phase is followed by the *retirement phase.* The individual has, in effect, completed one career, and he or she may move on to another one. During this phase, the individual may have opportunities to experience self-actualization through activities that it was impossible to pursue while working. Painting, gardening, volunteer service, and quiet reflection are some of the many positive avenues that have been followed by retirees. But the individual's financial and health status may make it necessary to spend the retirement years worrying about satisfying needs. Preretirement planning programs are becoming more common in organizations today as one way of allowing retirees to focus on other, more fulfilling needs.[5]

The fact that individuals pass through different stages during their careers is evident. It is also understandable that individual needs and motives are different from one stage to the next. But managing careers requires a more complete description of what happens to individuals during these stages. One group of individuals whose careers are of special significance to the performance of modern organizations are the *professionals*. "Knowledge workers"—such as professional accountants, information systems specialists, scientists, and engineers—are one of the fastest-growing segments of the workforce. This segment constitutes 32 percent of the workforce at present (blue-collar workers make up 33 percent).[6]

Stage I

Young professionals enter an organization with technical knowledge but often without an understanding of the organization's demands and expectations. Consequently, they must work fairly closely with more experienced people. The relationship that develops between the young professionals and their supervisors is an *apprenticeship*. The central activities in which apprentices are expected to show competence include learning and following directions. To move successfully and effectively through stage I, one must be able to accept the psychological state of dependence. Some professionals cannot cope with being placed in a situation similar to that which they experienced in school. They find that they are still being directed by an authority figure, just as they were in school, whereas they had anticipated that their first job would provide considerably more freedom.

Stage II

Once through the dependent relationship of stage I, the professional employee moves into stage II, which calls for working independently. Passage to this stage depends on the employee's having demonstrated competence in some specific technical area. The technical expertise may be in a content area, such as taxation, product testing, or quality assurance, or it may be in a skill area, such as computer applications. The professional's primary activity in stage II is to be an *independent contributor* of ideas in the chosen area. The professional is expected to rely much less on direction from others. The psychological state of independence may pose some problems because it is in such stark contrast to the state of dependence required in stage I. Stage II is extremely important for the professional's future career growth. Those who fail at this stage typically do so because they do not have the necessary self-confidence.

In the Career Challenge at the beginning of this chapter, there is an indication that Jim Lucio is at stage II in his career development. Jim values his independence. He wants to be his own boss and run his own business. Independence is a high priority for him, as it is for most professionals at stage II.

Stage III

Professionals who enter stage III are expected to become the mentors of those in stage I. They also tend to broaden their interests and to deal more and more with people outside the organization. Thus, the central activities of professionals at this stage are *training* and *interaction* with others. Stage III professionals assume responsibility for the work of others, and this characteristic of the stage can cause considerable psychological stress. In previous stages, the professional was responsible only for his or her own work. But now it is the work of others that is of primary concern. Individuals who cannot cope with this new requirement may decide to shift back to stage II. Individuals who derive satisfaction from seeing other people move on to bigger and better jobs will be content to remain in stage III until retirement.

A **mentoring relationship** has been defined as the relationship between an experienced employee and a junior employee, in which the experienced person helps the junior person with effective socialization by sharing information gained through experience with the organization. This kind of relationship is expected to contribute to the junior employee's instruction, job performance, and retention.[7]

HR Journal   *Helping Employees Find Their Career Bearings*

We live in an uncertain world. New technologies, global trade, widespread relocation of manufacturing and services, and the rapid growth of electronic commerce all suggest uncertainty is here to say. What implications does that pose for our careers and how can we better understand those implications?

First, ours is a knowledge-driven economy. New knowledge is persistently creating and interacting with new technology, leaving behind long-established ways of working and inviting a major shift in the way we see the economic world. Much of the uneasiness we experience revolves around questions of what knowledge is being generated, and where.

Second, the subjective career reigns supreme. In an unpredictable world, our subjective careers—our passions, motivations, identities, and attachment to others—provide continuity of meaning and purpose. The subjective career takes precedence over any objective career, that is, any preordained sequence of occupational or organizational seniority that we relied on in more stable times.

Many professionals, however, haven't realized the implications of the knowledge-driven economy for themselves, their clients, or their organizations. How can we better navigate our careers in the years ahead?

THE INTELLIGENT ORGANIZATION

If you look inside the "intelligent enterprise" (the ideal knowledge-driven organization), you'll find three key attributes:

Culture
The organization's culture reflects its vision, mission, and shared values. It shapes how people inside and outside the organization work together.

Capabilities
The organization delivers goods or services through its overall skills and knowledge.

Connections
The organization engages its host industry through its internal (employees) and external (suppliers, customers, and partners) connections.

Those three attributes are interdependent. For example, an organizational culture that emphasizes customer orientation will affect people's motivation to develop new customer-focused capabilities. Those new capabilities will, in turn, influence the organization's connections with its suppliers and customers. The changed connections will make new demands that will either reinforce or challenge the organization's existing culture, which again will require developing new capabilities. Organizations that are aware of those interconnections can actively monitor the three attributes to anticipate impending economic changes.

The idea of the intelligent career picks up where the intelligent organization leaves off. The intelligent career framework involves three "ways of knowing," which are concerned with

- Why we work—our motivation, values, and identity.
- How we work—our application of skills and knowledge.
- With whom we work—our relationships, reputations, and career supports.

The three ways of knowing correspond to and interact with the culture, capabilities, and connections of employer organizations. However the correspondence is general rather than specific. There's an invitation for each of us to engage in a deeper, inherently subjective interpretation of our own career situations and to consider how our careers might unfold in a variety of possible employment situations.

The three ways of knowing are also interdependent. For example, a love of traveling might lead you to study languages: knowing-why to knowing-how. Once you start learning a language, you might want to meet with people from another culture who speak that language: knowing-how to knowing-whom. Meeting people from another culture might lead you to explore new career possibilities that you wouldn't have anticipated before: knowing-whom to knowing-why.

Individuals who are aware of those connections are better prepared to both seek out and benefit from potential career opportunities.

Consider your own career through the lens of the three ways of knowing. What's going on with your career right now? What can you say about your investments so far in each of the ways of knowing? What can you say about the links between them? How can you get your career bearings?

One approach is to reflect on statements relevant to each of the ways of knowing perhaps in collaboration with a career consultant or coach. Typically, the same statement will mean different things to different people. For example, "I like to gain a sense of achievement from my work," may involve climbing the organizational ladder for one person while for another

HR Journal   *Helping Employees Find Their Career Bearings (concluded)*

person it may involve being respected by one's peers. The different meanings are components of the different subjective careers of the people involved.

Consider a global information technology company with a majority of young engineers among its employees. Like other companies in the same business, the organization had become accustomed to high growth rates, an expanding workforce, and almost automatic promotions and salary increases for several years. Suddenly, the market changed and, without continuing company growth, further career opportunities dwindled. The young engineers who were used to the company taking care of their career success became frustrated. The company needed to create a new culture and, within it, a new understanding about careers to avoid losing key employees.

The company decided to run internal workshops to help all employees find their career bearings and to explain that they, as individuals, needed to take charge of their future careers.

The workshops were designed around the concept of intelligent careers, and they helped the employees

- Find new identification with their profession and the technical challenges that it faced (knowing-why).
- Determine their individual learning agendas (knowing-how).

- Value the colleagueship associated with working together on new projects (knowing-whom).

It wasn't easy for every employee to accept that change in perspective. There was, and is, some resistance to this new thinking. However, the word is spreading, and the organization anticipates seeing improved results in the key indicators of higher job satisfaction and lower turnover among its most valuable employees.

The emergent and knowledge-driven economy insists on constant change in the way organizations function and in the career opportunities that arise. It is imperative that organizations and individuals are aware of—and able to succeed in—the economic circumstance of our time.

The concept of intelligent careers provides a way for individuals to find their bearings and personally navigate their careers. At the same time, it allows organizations to gain a better understanding of the diversity of their employees—their different dreams, talents, and attachments—and to provide for career coaching that benefits both parties.

Source: Adapted from Kristen M. Poulsen and Michael B. Arthur (May 2005), "Intelligent Career Navigation," *Training & Development Journal,* pp. 77–80; Nancy Gibbs (May 16, 2005), "Midlife Crisis? Bring It On!" *Time,* pp. 52–61.

In a successful mentoring relationship, the junior person's career is enhanced by a range of activities (coaching, exposure and visibility, and protection) that the senior person facilitates. Also, the mentoring relationship provides the junior person with support that helps him or her acquire a sense of personal identity. The person in stage III serving as a mentor can derive tremendous satisfaction from the growth, development, and advancement of a protégé.[8]

In the past, it has been difficult for women and minorities to establish mentoring relationships.[9]

Research has suggested that some men hesitate to act as mentor for a female protégé because of the sexual innuendoes that often accompany such relationships. In addition, some research indicates that senior women are also somewhat reluctant to mentor junior women because they perceive significant organizational risks in doing so.[10] As the number of women and minorities reaching senior levels of management increases, however, it is hoped that the opportunity for them to mentor junior colleagues will also increase.

Stage IV

Some professional employees remain in stage III; for these professionals, stage III is the career maintenance phase. Other professionals progress to yet another stage. Not all professionals experience stage IV, because its fundamental characteristic involves *shaping the direction of the organization itself.* Although we usually think of such activity as being undertaken by only one individual in an organization—its chief executive—in fact, it may be undertaken by many others. For example, key personnel in product development, process manufacturing, or technological research may be in stage IV. As a consequence of their performance in stage III of their careers, stage IV professionals direct their attention to long-range strategic planning. In doing so, they play the roles of manager, entrepreneur, and idea generator. Their primary job relationships are to identify and sponsor the careers of their successors and to interact with key people outside the organization. The most significant shift for a person in stage IV is to accept the decisions of subordinates without second-guessing them. Stage IV professionals must learn to influence—that is, practice leadership through such indirect means as idea planting, personnel selection, and organizational design. These shifts can be difficult for an individual who has relied on direct supervision in the past.

The concept of career stages is fundamental for understanding and managing career development. It is necessary to comprehend *life stages* as well. Individuals go through career stages as they go through life stages, but the interaction between career stages and life stages is not easy to understand.

Career Choices

Perhaps the most important decision a person makes is what career he or she should pursue. At some point, you will probably make a career decision and ask yourself questions such as, What do I want to be when I grow up? What are my strengths and weaknesses? Why can't I sell more products?

The following HR Journal discusses how making career choices is an individual responsibility.

Career Choice and Personality

John L. Holland, a career counseling expert, has proposed and researched a theory of career (vocational) choice.[11] Holland suggests that the choice of a career is an expression of personality and not a random event, though chance can play a role. He also believes that what a person accomplishes and derives from a career depends on the congruence between his or her personality and the job environment.

Holland contends that each individual to some extent resembles one of six personality types.

1. *Realistic* This individual prefers activities involving the manipulation of machinery or tools. Example: a machinist.
2. *Investigative* This individual prefers to be analytical, curious, methodical, and precise. Example: a research scientist.
3. *Artistic* This person is expressive, nonconforming, original, and introspective. Example: an interior decorator.
4. *Social* This person enjoys working with and helping others and purposefully avoids systematic activities involving tools and machinery. Example: a school counselor.
5. *Enterprising* This person enjoys activities that permit him or her to influence others to accomplish goals. Example: a lawyer.
6. *Conventional* This individual enjoys the systematic manipulation of data, filing records, or reproducing materials. Example: an accountant.

The more one resembles any given type, the more likely one is to display some of the behaviors and traits associated with that type.

Holland suggests that, whereas one personality type predominates, individuals use a wide range of strategies for coping with their environment, and that many strategies fall within the

EXHIBIT 14-3
Choosing an Occupational Orientation (Holland's Hexagon)

Source: Richard Bolles and Mark Emery Bolles (2005), *The 2005 What Color Is Your Parachute?* (Berkeley, CA: Ten Speed, 2005), p. 80.

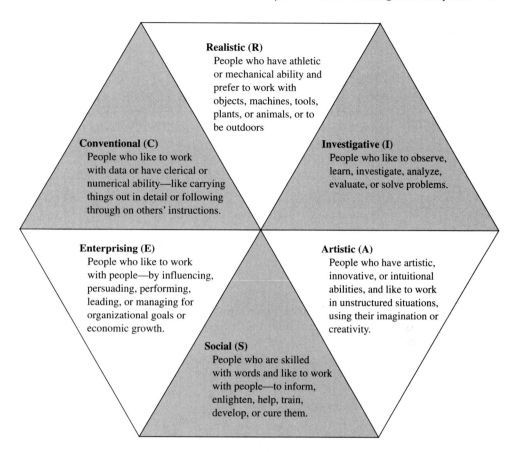

Realistic (R)
People who have athletic or mechanical ability and prefer to work with objects, machines, tools, plants, or animals, or to be outdoors

Investigative (I)
People who like to observe, learn, investigate, analyze, evaluate, or solve problems.

Conventional (C)
People who like to work with data or have clerical or numerical ability—like carrying things out in detail or following through on others' instructions.

Enterprising (E)
People who like to work with people—by influencing, persuading, performing, leading, or managing for organizational goals or economic growth.

Artistic (A)
People who have artistic, innovative, or intuitional abilities, and like to work in unstructured situations, using their imagination or creativity.

Social (S)
People who are skilled with words and like to work with people—to inform, enlighten, help, train, develop, or cure them.

boundaries of two or more types. Holland uses a hexagon to illustrate the closeness and distance between the six personality types; see Exhibit 14-3. He has determined by research that the closer two orientations are in the hexagon arrangement, the more similar are the personality types. Therefore, he claims that the adjacent types (for example, realistic-investigative and social-enterprising) are similar, while nonadjacent types (for example, realistic-social and artistic-conventional) are dissimilar.[12] Using Holland's analysis and logic, one would conclude that if a person's predominant and secondary orientations are similar, he or she will have a relatively easy time selecting a career. On the other hand, dissimilar predominant and secondary orientations may result in difficulty choosing a career.

Various quantitative instruments have been used to assess a person's resemblance to the six personality types.[13] The Vocational Preference Inventory asks a person to indicate the vocations that appeal to him or her, from a list of 84 occupational titles (14 titles for each of the six scales). The person's responses are scored and profiled. The higher a person's score on a scale, the greater the resemblance to the type that scale represents.

Examining Your Skills

Determining what skills one has is extremely important in making career choices. Holland's work on career choice suggests that simply preferring one career or occupation over another is not enough. A person must have or be able to develop the skills required to perform the job. A person may have an investigative orientation, but whether he or she has the skills to be a research scientist, physician, or biologist will play a significant part in which specific occupation is selected. The *Dictionary of Occupational Titles (DOT)*, published by the U.S. Government Printing Office, provides information on the skills required for more than 20,000 jobs.

EXHIBIT 14-4

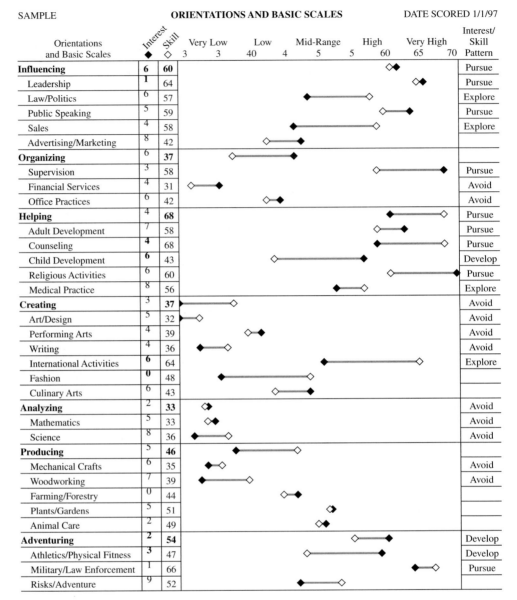

Another way to measure both interests and skills is the Campbell Interest and Skill Survey (CISS). This inventory has been used to help employees review their career paths and to assist organizations in utilizing employees effectively. A six-part response scale is used for assessment of 200 items about interests and 120 items about skills. The scores are translated into seven orientations: (1) influencing, (2) organizing, (3) helping, (4) creating, (5) analyzing, (6) producing, and (7) adventuring.[14] The seven orientations are further subdivided into 29 areas such as leadership, writing, and science. A person's interest is displayed as a solid diamond (♦); a *skill* is an open diamond (◊). The interest score designates a person's liking or preference for an activity; the skill score reveals how confident a person is about performing the activity. Exhibit 14-4 shows a profile for one person on the seven orientations, ranging from 30 to 70.

If a person scores high on interests and skills, it is recommended that he or she seriously consider the orientation or activity. A person who scores high in interest but low in skill is encouraged to develop his or her skills. A low interest score combined with a high skill score suggests that exploration is needed. Finally, a low interest score and a low skill score suggest avoidance of an orientation or activity. In Exhibit 14-4, the respondent is not oriented toward analyzing, but influencing may be an area to pursue, especially in such occupations as law and politics and public speaking.

Career Development: A Commitment

When an organization understands the importance of career development, it can offer numerous opportunities to employees.[15] These opportunities can involve simply a tuition reimbursement program or a detailed counseling service for developing individual career path plans. An example of the type of career development programs available in various organizations and industries is presented in Exhibit 14-5.

The programs presented in Exhibit 14-5 are most valuable when they are (1) offered regularly, (2) open to all employees, and (3) modified when evaluation indicates that change is necessary. The overall objective of these programs is to match employees' needs and goals with current or future career opportunities in the organization. Thus, a well-designed career development effort will assist employees in determining their own career needs, develop and publicize available career opportunities in the organization, and match employees' needs and goals with the organization. This commitment to career development can delay the obsolescence of human resources that is so costly to an organization.

At Owens-Illinois, Inc., for example, a formal career opportunity program is used. It is the firm's policy to promote from within the company whenever possible. The career opportunity program provides several services to employees:

It makes available a broad range of information about available jobs and the qualifications needed to fill them.

It provides a system through which qualified employees may apply for these positions.

It helps employees establish career goals.

It encourages a meaningful dialogue between employees and supervisors about the employees' career goals.

The supervisor who makes a hiring decision explains it in writing. No matter who is selected for the job, the explanation is returned to each employee who applied.

Although career planning is important during all phases of a career, three points in a typical career seem to be particularly crucial. The *recent hiree* begins a career with a particular job, and experiences in this first assignment have an important effect on shaping the rest of his or her career.[16] The *midcareer* person is subject to pressures and responsibilities different from those of the recent hiree, but he or she is also at a turning point: a point where stagnation is a serious concern. Finally, the *preretirement* person is facing an uncertain future from an economic, social, and interpersonal standpoint. The following sections describe some problems with career development—and some solutions—for people at these three critical points.

Career Development for Recent Hirees

Recently hired employees face many anxious moments. They have selected their positions on the basis of expectations regarding the demands that the organization will make of them and what they will receive in exchange for meeting those demands.[17] Young managers, particularly those with college training, expect opportunities to utilize their training in ways that lead to recognition and advancement. In too many instances, recently hired managers are soon disappointed with their initial career decisions.

EXHIBIT 14-5
Career Development Programs

Source: Reprinted by permission of the publisher, M. A. Morgan (March–April 1979), from "Career Development Strategies in Industry: Where Are We and Where Should We Be?" *Personnel*, p. 16 © 1979 by AMACON, a division of American Management Associations. All rights reserved.

Career Counseling

Career counseling during the employment interview

Career counseling during the performance appraisal session

Psychological assessment and career alternative planning

Career counseling as part of the day-to-day supervisor/subordinate relationship

Special career counseling for high-potential employees

Counseling for downward transfers

Career Pathing

Planned job progression for new employees

Career pathing to help managers acquire the necessary experience for future jobs

Committee performs an annual review of management personnel's strengths and weaknesses and then develops a five-year career plan for each

Plan job moves for high-potential employees to place them in a particular target job

Rotate first-level supervisors through various departments to prepare them for upper-management positions

Human Resources

Computerized inventory of backgrounds and skills to help identify replacements

Succession planning or replacement charts at all levels of management

Career Information Systems

Job posting for all nonofficer positions; individual can bid to be considered

Job posting for hourly employees and career counseling for salaried employees

Management or Supervisory Development

Special program for those moving from hourly employment to management

Responsibility of the department head to develop managers

Management development committee to look after the career development of management

In-house advanced management program

Training

In-house supervisory training

Technical skills training for lower levels

Outside management seminars

Formalized job rotation programs

Intern programs

Responsibility of manager for one-the-job training

Tuition reimbursement program

Special Groups

Outplacement programs

Minority indoctrination training program

Career management seminars for women

Preretirement counseling

Career counseling and job rotation for women and minorities

Refresher courses for midcareer managers

Presupervisory training program for women and minorities

Causes of Early Career Difficulties

Although the specific causes of early career disappointments vary from person to person, some general causes have been identified. Studies of the early career problems of young managers typically find that those who experience frustration are victims of "reality shock." These young managers perceive a mismatch between what they thought the organization was and what it actually is. Several factors contribute to reality shock, and it is important for young managers and their managers to be aware of them.

Initial Job Challenge

The first jobs of young managers often demand far less of them than they are capable of delivering. Consequently, young managers believe that they are unable to demonstrate their full capabilities and that, in a sense, they are being stifled. This particular cause is especially damaging if the recruiter has been overly enthusiastic in "selling" the organization.

Some young managers are able to create challenging jobs even when their assignments are fairly routine. They do this by thinking of ways to do their jobs differently and better. They may also be able to persuade their managers to give them more leeway and more to do. Unfortunately, many young managers are unable to create challenge. Their previous experiences in school were typically experiences in which challenges had been given to them by their teachers. The challenge had been created for them, not by them.

Initial Job Satisfaction

Recently hired managers with college training often believe they can perform at levels beyond those of their initial assignments. After all, they have been exposed to the latest managerial theories and techniques, and in their minds, at least, they are ready to run the company. Disappointment and dissatisfaction are the sure outcomes when they discover that their self-evaluations are not shared by others in the organization. The consequences of unrealistic aspirations and routine initial assignments are low job satisfaction, in particular, and low satisfaction of growth and self-actualization needs, in general.

Initial Job Performance Evaluation

Feedback on performance is an important managerial responsibility. Yet many managers are inadequately trained to meet this responsibility. They simply do not know how to evaluate the performance of their subordinates. This management deficiency is especially damaging to new managers. They have not been in the organization long enough to be socialized by their peers and other employees. They are not yet sure of what they are expected to believe, what values to hold, or what behaviors are expected of them. They naturally look to their own managers to guide them through this early phase. But when their managers fail to evaluate their performance accurately, they remain ignorant and confused as to whether they are achieving what the organization expects of them.

Not all young managers experience problems associated with their initial assignments. But those who do and who leave the organization as a consequence of their frustrations represent a waste of talent and money. While turnover and job change can be healthy and a good decision, the loss of potentially successful employees will frequently cost far more than a well-designed career management program capable of helping new hires avoid such problems.

How to Counteract Early Career Problems

Research has indicated that the retention and development of young, talented employees can be increased by a number of different organizational practices. While most of these early career interventions have focused on developing managers, there is no reason to believe that other employees can't also benefit from similar programs. It is now being recognized that blue-collar workers are valuable assets and need career development in much the same way that managers do. Workers at any level of the organization accumulate skills through their experiences and therefore must also have access to systematic career development.[18]

Realistic Job Previews

One way to counteract the unrealistic expectations of new recruits is to provide realistic information during the recruiting process. As discussed in Chapter 7, this practice is based on the idea that a recruit should know both the bad and the good things to expect from a job and the organization. Through realistic job previews (RJPs), recruits are given opportunities to learn not only the benefits they may expect, but also the drawbacks. Studies have shown that the recruitment rate is the same for those who receive RJPs as for those who do not.[19] More important, those who receive RJPs are more likely to remain on the job and to be satisfied with it than are those who have been selected without using RJPs. The practice of "telling it like it is" is used by a number of organizations, including the Prudential Insurance Company, Texas Instruments, and the United States Military Academy.

Challenging Initial Assignments

Managers of newly hired people should be encouraged to slot them into the most demanding of the available jobs. Successful implementation of this policy requires managers to take some risks, because managers are accountable for the performance of their subordinates. If the assignments are too far beyond the ability of the subordinates, the managers and the subordinates share the cost of failure. Thus, most managers prefer to bring their subordinates along slowly by giving them progressively more difficult and challenging jobs, but only after the subordinates have demonstrated their ability. Newly hired managers have potential for performance but have not demonstrated performance. Thus, it is risky to assign an individual to a task for which there is a high probability of failure. But studies have indicated that managers who experienced initial job challenge were more effective in their later years.[20]

Enriched Initial Assignments

Job enrichment is an established practice for motivating employees with strong needs for growth and achievement. If the nature of the job to be assigned is not intrinsically challenging, the newly hired manager's superior can enrich the assignment. The usual ways to enrich a job include giving the new manager more authority and responsibility, permitting the new manager to interact directly with customers and clients, and enabling the new manager to implement his or her own ideas (rather than merely recommending them to the boss).

Demanding Bosses

A practice that seems to have considerable promise for increasing the retention rate of young managers is to assign them initially to demanding supervisors. In this context, demanding should not be interpreted as "autocratic." Rather, the type of boss most likely to get new hires off in the right direction is one who has high but achievable expectations for their performance. Such a boss instills in the young managers the understanding that high performance is expected and rewarded and, equally important, that the boss is always ready to assist them through coaching and counseling.

The benefits of challenging, enriched early experiences are not limited to the early phase of a career. Individuals who successfully meet these early challenges are obviously better prepared to contribute to the organization in their middle and late careers as well. Moreover, setting the stage for successfully managing a career can help to avoid many problems of stagnation and dissatisfaction.

Career Development during Midcareer

Managers and other employees who reach the midcareer stage of development are typically key people in their organizations. Logically, they now occupy key positions in the organization and are often quite successful economically. Despite these indicators of success, rather serious crises are frequently associated with midcareer. These can include higher levels of stress that come with success, personal and family problems associated with midlife crisis and transition, and dealing with the notion that one's most productive years may already be past. Attempting to deal with all of these pressures can lead to job withdrawal, substance abuse, and depression. At the same time, midcareer can be rewarding if effective career management programs are in place.

One important approach used to develop midcareer managers is training.[21] Making training available to improve skills, improve knowledge, and help employees grow intellectually sends a signal to the trainees that they are valued. The mere fact that the company shows an interest introduces the Hawthorne effect. It is a signal that the trainees are needed, valued, and still attractive to the firm. It is especially important at midcareer to receive such signals from the organization.

The Midcareer Plateau

Managers face the **midcareer plateau** during the adult stage of life and the maintenance phase of careers. At this point, the likelihood of additional upward promotion is usually quite low. Two reasons account for the plateau. First, there are simply fewer jobs at the top of organizations, and even though the manager has the ability to perform at that level, no opening exists. Second, openings may exist, but the manager may lack the ability, the skills, or the desire to fill them.[22]

Managers who find themselves stifled in their present jobs tend to cope with the problems in fairly consistent ways. They suffer from depression, poor health, and fear of and hostility toward their subordinates. Eventually, they "retire" on the job or leave the organization physically and permanently. Any one of these ways of coping results in lowered job performance and, of course, lowered organizational performances.[23]

The midcareer, middle-age crisis has been depicted in novels, movies, dramas, and psychological studies. Although each individual's story is different and unique, the scenarios have many features in common. Each story, and the research, indicates that the midcareer crisis is real and has psychological and often physical effects that can become dangerous if not properly handled. Jim Lucio, for example, has insomnia, has lost his appetite, and is on edge because of his midcareer crisis.

Of course, not all managers respond to their situations in the same ways. Some, perhaps most, cope constructively. Following are a few examples of some individuals who coped effectively:

- John W. Culligan, 70, became chairperson of the executive committee at American Home Products; he was 64 when he was promoted and had been a fixture in the company for 42 years.
- Thomas S. Derek retired from a 30-year career as a life insurance agent and decided to start the Ugly Duckling Rent-A-Car agency in Tucson.
- Joyce Fox got her first job at 41 and became a senior vice president in charge of international loans at American Express Bank.

But there are also many stories of individuals who just play along and seem to be at a plateau or are never recognized.[24] Usually, some event or person is needed to trigger a series of changes and opportunities. John Culligan waited patiently after reaching a plateau; Thomas Derek changed careers; Joyce Fox decided that her age was not a detriment and entered the labor force exuding confidence, wisdom, and maturity. Each of these individuals used their own tailor-made career plateau coping strategy. In the following HR Journal, a burnout expert describes the kind of workplace environment that can combat career burnout.

How to Counteract Midcareer Problems

Counteracting the problems that managers face at midcareer involves providing counseling and alternatives.

HR Journal   *An Expert Talks about Burnout*

Christina Maslach is one of the world's leading experts on job burnout, a pioneering researcher and the author of the Maslach Burnout Inventory (MBI)—the most widely used research measure in its field. She has been selected a Fellow of the American Association for the Advancement of Science, which cites her for ground-breaking work on the application of social psychology to contemporary problems.

Professor Maslach talks with James Nelson about how companies can handle job burnout and its high costs to both the employee and the organization. She suggests a road map for effective intervention strategies that turns the syndromes of exhaustion, cynicism, and ineffectiveness into energy, involvement, and achievement.

JOB BURNOUT IS OFTEN UNDERSTOOD IN CONNECTION WITH FATIGUE. COULD YOU EXPLAIN WHAT BURNOUT IS?

The point you're raising is part of the problem because everyone has their own idea of what burnout means. It's a very evocative term. Burnout was initially a very slippery concept with no standard definition, so there was not always a basis for constructive communication about either the problem or its solutions.

We have found three interrelated dimensions, which together comprise this psychological syndrome. The first is what we call "exhaustion," which is when people feel drained and lack the mental or physical energy to get on with whatever they need to do. I should add that if exhaustion were the only symptom we observe, there would be no reason to call it any other name than exhaustion. So there's something more going on there.

We talk about the second dimension primarily in terms of "cynicism." This is a negative evaluation and reaction to the job, the work one needs to do and the people one works with. It often begins as a response to the work overload leading to the exhaustion, so people will back off and do less. People begin to think very negatively about the workplace and their colleagues. One hallmark is when people develop a strong negative, hostile, cynical, dehumanized response to their job, the workplace in general, and everyone who's part of it. Having this set of feelings about the workplace means the way people do their job is different. They start doing the very minimum instead of their very best. This has important implications for the quality of work performed and both the individual and the organization suffer.

The third dimension is essentially a negative self-evaluation, which we talk about as a decline in people's sense of their own professional effectiveness. Rather than being negative about the job and their colleagues, people develop a negative sense of who they are and what they're doing. In essence they don't like the person they've become.

DO ALL THREE DIMENSIONS ALWAYS OCCUR TOGETHER, OR MIGHT THE PERSON ONLY SUFFER FROM EXHAUSTION WITHOUT ANY SIGN OF CYNICISM OR LOW SELF-EVALUATION?

People can range from high to low across a continuum on all three dimensions. It's important to understand what happens over time. Normally, it's hard for someone to remain high on exhaustion and low on cynicism for a long time. Over time, either the exhaustion will fade or the cynicism will rise.

CAN BURNOUT BECOME A SERIOUS MENTAL HEALTH PROBLEM?

Let me give you an example. One of the questions has been, isn't job burnout simple depression? Our research suggests no, it's not depression but burnout could be an important precursor to people becoming depressed. It is basically a response to mismatches between the workplace and the individual, and the strains it puts on them. If an individual is not able to cope effectively and get back to a more engaged involvement with their work, they could become very depressed—not only about their job but also about themselves and their entire life.

IS BURNOUT MORE PREVALENT IN EITHER MEN OR WOMEN?

Men and women are much more similar in this than they are different. There is a consistent but very small tendency for men to score higher on the cynicism dimension than women. You've got to be careful in looking at this. People often assume there must be substantial differences between men and women. The data just don't support that view.

FROM THE RESEARCH YOU'VE DONE, DOES BURNOUT SOMETIMES TEND TO OCCUR IN CLUSTERS?

There's not a lot of good research on this but there is some suggestive evidence that this can happen. It's a clue there might be something particular going on within a specific unit which is different from the rest of the organization. This would need a closer look, especially at the unit's supervisory staff.

IS THERE ANY EVIDENCE TO SUGGEST THAT BURNOUT IS MORE PREVALENT IN SOME COUNTRIES AND CULTURES THAN IN OTHERS?

None whatsoever. Research has been done in many different countries and quite a few of the leading researchers are in Europe. So the major indicators and dimensions have been studied across borders and cultures. The same insights and findings keep emerging in whatever country is being studied, while there are, of course, always some cultural nuances.

WHAT ABOUT A HIGH PREVALENCE AMONG HIGH-RESPONSIBILITY MANAGERIAL AND KNOWLEDGE WORKER STAFF AS OPPOSED TO MANUAL LABOR WORKERS?

The answer to that is counterintuitive because you might expect to see higher stress levels among senior level managers who shoulder the responsibility of running the organization. In fact, the research does not indicate any increased vulnerability for certain occupational groups, be they white- or blue-collar employees.

The bottom line is that job burnout is all about mismatches—a mismatch between the individual and their job, or between the individual and their workplace environment. So any good prevention strategy has got to aim to reduce these.

WHAT PREVENTATIVE MEASURES CAN ORGANIZATIONS TAKE TO AVOID THESE MISMATCHES?

Companies should look at the key dimensions of their workplace and how they affect their employees' engagement with their jobs. We've identified six such dimensions. When there is a good match between the employees and these six dimensions—whatever their job—you'll find a greater engagement with work and less burnout. As you'd expect, burnout lifts when the mismatches between employees and these six dimensions increase.

WOULD YOU ELABORATE ON WHAT THESE SIX DIMENSIONS ARE?

The first one is "workload." Essentially, we are talking about whether employees are in a situation where they can manage the work they have to do. And whether the resources are there for them to sustain the workload. If you have an overload situation where there is continually too much work to do, with too little time and too few resources, at some point employees are going to feel overwhelmed. You will then see higher burnout—particularly in the exhaustion dimension.

The second dimension deals with "control," which also has to do with autonomy. When people feel they have a reasonable amount of control over their work, you will see higher positive engagement. But if people feel they're not really calling the shots, or they're dealing with a chaotic situation where it's not clear who's making the decision and who's accountable for what, again you'll see high stress levels.

Mismatches in control most often indicate the employees have insufficient control over the resources needed to do the work or have insufficient authority to pursue the work in a way they feel is most effective. It's distressing for people to feel responsible for results while lacking the capacity to deliver.

The third one is "reward and recognition." This is the extent to which the employee receives feedback—positive when they're doing something well or negative when they're not. This allows them to have a good sense of their job progress. An example of a mismatch could be insufficient financial rewards and benefits equal to the work being done. But equally important is the lack of social rewards as when the employee's work is ignored and not appreciated by others. This lack of recognition devalues both the work and the worker, and the lack of reward is associated with feelings of ineffectiveness.

The fourth area we call the workplace "community." This includes colleagues, supervisory staff, the people one supervises—really anyone with whom the employee has ongoing work relationships. When these relationships are going well with mutual trust and support, it's like money in the bank in terms of engagement and feeling positive about the job. This kind of social support reaffirms a person's membership in a group with a shared sense of values. Chronic and unresolved conflict with others on the job will destroy a sense of community. This produces constant negative feelings of frustration and hostility and reduces the likelihood of social support, hence higher stress and burnout levels.

The fifth dimension deals with "fairness." Whatever the rules of the organization, all research points to people

(continued)

HR Journal — *An Expert Talks about Burnout (concluded)*

expecting to be treated fairly and with respect. Mutual respect is central to a shared sense of community. Unfairness can occur when there is inequality of workloads or pay, or when promotions are handled unjustly. This can engender a huge amount of anger and hostility, which fuels a deep sense of cynicism about the workplace as well as being emotionally upsetting and exhausting. A sense of being treated unfairly can also lead to acts of getting even.

The sixth area of mismatch occurs when there is a conflict between "values." In some cases employees may feel constrained to do things they perceive as unethical and not in accord with their personal core values—such as having to tell a customer less than the full truth in order to make a sale. This sort of moral erosion is too much for some people. People can also be caught between conflicting values of the organization—as when the lofty mission statement is tested against actual practices. If people are working in a situation where there is value conflict, it can sometimes be enough to lead to job burnout even if the other five dimensions are working well.

Source: James Nelson (April 2005), "Christina Maslach—How to Prevent Burnout," *New Zealand Management*, p. 43; and Mary Cheryl Dona-Paras (October 15, 2002), "Cure for Career Burnout," JobStreet.com (www.jobstreet.com).

Midcareer Counseling

Organizations such as Du Pont, Alcoa, and Western Electric employ full-time staff psychiatrists to assist employees in dealing with career, health, and family problems.[25] In the context of such counseling, midcareer managers are provided with professional help in dealing with the depression and stress they may experience. Since midcareer managers are usually well-educated and articulate, they often only need someone to talk to, someone skilled in the art of listening. The process of verbalizing their problems to an objective listener is often enough to enable midcareer managers to recognize their problems and to cope with them constructively.

Midcareer Alternatives

Effective resolution of the problems of midcareer crises requires the existence of acceptable alternatives. The organization cannot be expected to go beyond counseling for personal and family problems. But when the crisis is precipitated primarily by career-related factors, the organization can be an important source of alternatives. In many instances, the organization simply needs to accept career moves that are usually viewed as unacceptable. Three career moves that have potential for counteracting the problems of midcareer managers are lateral transfers, downward transfers, and fallback positions.[26]

Lateral transfers involve moves at the same organizational level from one department to another. A manager who has plateaued in production could be transferred to a similar level in sales, engineering, or some other area. The move would require the manager to learn the technical demands of the new position quickly, and there would be a period of reduced performance as this learning occurred. But, once qualified, the manager would bring the perspectives of both areas to bear on decisions.

Downward transfers are equated with failure in our society; an effective manager simply does not consider a move downward to be a respectable alternative. Yet downward transfers are, in many instances, not only respectable but entirely acceptable alternatives, particularly when one or more of the following conditions exist:

- The manager values the quality of life afforded by a specific geographic area and may desire a downward transfer in order to stay in or move to that area.
- The manager views the downward transfer as a way to establish a base for future promotions.

- The manager is faced with two alternatives: dismissal or a downward move.
- The manager wants to pursue autonomy and self-actualization in nonjob activities—such as religious, civic, or political activities—and for that reason may welcome the reduced responsibility (and demands) of a lower-level position.

The use of *fallback positions* is another way to reduce the risk of lateral and downward transfers. The practice involves identifying in advance a position to which the transferred manager can return if the new position does not work out. By identifying the fallback position in advance, the organization informs everyone who is affected that some risk is involved but that the organization is willing to accept some of the responsibility for it and that returning to the fallback job will not be viewed as "failure." Companies such as Heublein, Procter & Gamble, Continental Can, and Lehman Brothers have used fallback positions to remove some of the risk of lateral and upward moves. The practice appears to have considerable promise for protecting the careers of highly specialized technicians and professionals who are making their first moves into general management positions.

The suggestion that organizations initiate practices and programs to assist managers through midcareer crises does not excuse managers from taking responsibility for themselves. Individuals who deal honestly and constructively with their lives and careers will early on take steps to minimize the risk of becoming obsolete or redundant. At the outset of their management careers, they can begin to formulate their career plans and paths. Often, they will be assisted in this process by the organization that employs them.

Preretirement Problems

Although people are living longer and federal laws protect older workers against discrimination on the basis of age, many organizations are ill-prepared to help retirees develop a truly secure retirement. There are still serious concerns about how well workers in this country are prepared for the dramatic changes that retirement brings. The problem is becoming increasingly important as workers retire at earlier ages while at the same time many organizations are cutting retirement benefits to reduce costs.[27]

How to Minimize Retirement Adjustment Problems

To deal effectively with retirement issues, organizations need to consider questions such as the following:

- When do employees plan to retire?
- Who is attracted to early retirement?
- What do employees plan to do during retirement? Can the organization help them prepare for these activities?
- Do retirees plan a second career? Can the organization assist in this preparation?
- Which retirees can still be consulted by the organization to help new employees?

These and similar questions can be addressed through counseling and education programs for preretirees. Retirement is feared by some and anticipated by others. Counseling and education programs can make the transition from employment to retirement much smoother.

In most cases, the retired person must learn to accept a reduced role, to manage a less structured life, and to make new accommodations to family and community. Educational workshops and seminars and counseling sessions are an invaluable way to help the preretirement person make the transition from work to retirement. These activities can be initiated by HR departments.

IBM is one organization that has attempted to aid in this transition by offering tuition rebates for courses on any topic within three years of retirement. Many IBM preretirees have taken advantage of this program to prepare for second careers (learning new skills, professions, and small-business management).[28]

Adolph Coors Co. has a different approach. It has implemented a retirement planning program designed to help employees make better financial decisions about their retirement. The program includes financial planning computer software available to everyone, promotion of individual retirement programs, and a comprehensive educational program to make people more aware of the realities of retirement.[29]

By the year 2016, the annual number of retirees will be approximately 4 million. In the wake of downsizing, companies are discovering that many of their best employees took early retirement packages. A growing number of companies have found that they need retirees to come back to work. Retiree-work programs are appearing across industries. Instead of the retirees having problems with adjustment, the organization is having major problems.[30] Travelers Insurance uses a bank of retirees to fill temporary work needs. The firm believes that it saves more than $1 million a year with the program. The human resource director at Travelers, Florence Johnson, states, "There is no learning curve. These people know the environment. They know the system; they know the culture." The skills gap between new incoming employees and organizational needs is likely to encourage more firms to attempt calling retirees back to work and rehiring them.

Career Planning and Pathing

The practice of organizational **career planning** involves matching an individual's career aspirations with the opportunities available in an organization. **Career pathing** is the sequencing of the specific jobs that are associated with those opportunities. The career planning and career pathing processes are shown in Exhibit 14-6.

If career management is to be successful, the individual and the organization must assume an equal share of the responsibility for it. The individual must identify his or her aspirations and abilities and, through counseling, recognize what training and development are required for a particular career path. The organization must identify its needs and opportunities and, through workforce planning, provide the necessary career information and training to its employees.

EXHIBIT 14-6
A Career Planning Process

Source: Based on John C. Alpin and Darlene K. Gerster (March–April 1978), "Career Development: An Integration of Individual and Organizational Needs," *Personnel*, p. 25.

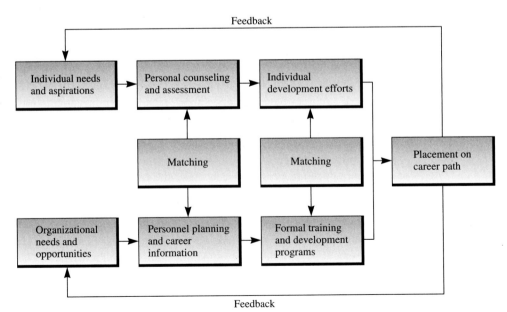

Such companies as Weyerhaeuser, Nabisco, Gulf Oil, ExxonMobil, and Eaton use career development programs to identify a broad pool of talent available for promotion and transfer opportunities. Companies often restrict career counseling to managerial and professional staff, but IBM, GE, and TRW provide career counseling for both blue-collar and managerial personnel.

Career Planning

Individual and organizational needs and opportunities can be matched in a variety of ways. According to a survey by the American Management Association (AMA), the most widely used approaches are counseling by the personnel staff and career counseling by supervisors. These approaches are often quite informal. Somewhat more formal and less widely, although increasingly, used practices involve workshops, seminars, and self-assessment centers.

Informal Counseling

The HR staffs of organizations often include counseling services for employees who wish to assess their abilities and interests. The counseling process can also move into personal concerns; this is proper because, as we have already seen, life concerns are important factors in determining career aspirations. In this context, career counseling is viewed by the organization as a service to its employees, though not as a primary service.

Career counseling by supervisors is usually included in performance evaluations. The question of where the employee is going in the organization arises quite naturally in this setting. In fact, the inclusion of career information in performance appraisal has created the current interest in career planning. A characteristic of effective performance evaluation is to let the employee know not only how well he or she has done, but also what the future holds. Thus, supervisors must be able to counsel the employee in terms of organizational needs and opportunities not only within the specific department, but throughout the organization. Since supervisors usually have limited information about the total organization, it is often necessary to adopt more formal and systematic counseling approaches.

Formal Counseling

Workshops, assessment centers, and career development centers are being used increasingly in organizations. Typically, such formal practices are designed to serve specific groups of employees. Management trainees and "high potential" or "fast track" management candidates have received most of the attention to date. However, women and minority employees have been given increased attention. Career development programs for women and minority employees are viewed as indications of an organization's commitment to affirmative action.

One example of a formal organizational career planning system is Syntex Corporation's Career Development Center. The center was the result of the realization that the managers in Syntex were too caught up in their own jobs to counsel their subordinates. The center's staff first identifies the individual's strengths and weaknesses in eight skill areas that Syntex believes to be related to effective management:

1. Problem analysis.
2. Communication.
3. Goal setting.
4. Making decisions and handling conflicts.
5. Selecting, training, and motivating employees.
6. Controlling employees.
7. Interpersonal competence.
8. Use of time.

On the basis of scores in the eight areas, each manager sets career and personal goals. The center's staff assists the manager to set realistic goals that reflect his or her strengths and weaknesses in the eight areas.

The high point of each manager's career planning effort is attendance at a weeklong seminar. Usually attended by 24 managers at a time, the seminar places each participant in simulated management situations that require applications of the eight skill areas. Subsequently, each candidate reviews his or her own career plan, a plan that includes career goals, timetables, and required personal development. The purpose of the seminar is to encourage realistic self-appraisal. Following the seminar, participants meet with their immediate supervisors to set up their career development plans.

Organizations can use a variety of practices to facilitate their employees' career plans. One of the oldest and most widely used practices is some form of *tuition aid program.* Employees can take advantage of educational and training opportunities available at nearby schools, and the organization pays some or all of the tuition. J. I. Case, a Tenneco company with corporate offices in Racine, Wisconsin, is but one of many organizations that provide in-house courses and seminars as well as tuition reimbursement for courses related to the individual's job.

Another practice is *job posting;* that is, the organization publicizes job openings as they occur. The employees are thus made aware of the opportunities. Effective job posting requires more than simply placing a notice on the company bulletin board. At a minimum, job posting should meet the following conditions:

- It should include promotions and transfers as well as permanent vacancies.
- Available jobs should be posted at least three to six weeks prior to external recruiting.
- Eligibility rules should be explicit and straightforward.
- Standards for selection and bidding instructions should be stated clearly.
- Vacationing employees should be given the opportunity to apply ahead of time.
- Employees who apply but are rejected should be notified of the reason in writing, and a record of the reason should be placed in their personnel files.

Human resource information system (HRIS) technology has been one of the most significant career management tools introduced in recent years. An HRIS has special potential because it not only enhances an individual's career planning activities but also saves money for the organization.

Many corporations are relying more heavily than ever before on filling job vacancies from within. The key to success in filling these vacancies is information flow. That is, the organization must make sure that any potentially qualified applicants know about the job opening and its requirements. Likewise, the organization must know which current employees possess the necessary skills for the vacancy. An effective HRIS and job posting program does both.

For example, 3M Company has implemented a "job information system," which is an electronic job posting system that lists 98 percent of all jobs companywide. Everyone in the company has access to this information and can electronically apply for a posted opening.[31] One interesting aspect of this system, from the perspective of career development, has been the large number of lateral moves that people have applied for and been offered. This has allowed many employees who might have otherwise stagnated or left the organization to make a fresh start in their careers.

The World Wide Web is becoming a valuable resource for people who want to help their careers. Thousands of private, public, and nonprofit organizations utilize their Web sites to recruit and inform employees. The employment or job link located in the site map and the directory or home page can be used to learn about positions the firm wants to fill.[32] Links to many of these sites can be found in such directories as America's Employers or Hoover's Top Employees.

Career Pathing

The result of career planning is the placement of an individual in a job that is the first of a sequential series of jobs. From the perspective of the organization, career paths are important in workforce planning. An organization's future workforce depends on the projected passage of individuals through the ranks. From the perspective of the individual, a career path is the sequence of jobs that he or she desires to undertake in order to achieve personal and career goals. Although it is virtually impossible to completely integrate organizational and individual needs in the design of career paths, systematic career planning has the potential for closing the gap between the needs of the individual and the needs of the organization.[33]

Traditional career paths have emphasized upward mobility in a single occupation or functional area. When recruiting personnel, the organization's representative will speak of engineers', accountants', or salespersons' career paths. In these contexts, the recruiter will describe the different jobs that typical individuals will hold as they work progressively upward in an organization. Each job, or "rung" of the career ladder, is reached when the individual has accumulated the necessary experience and ability and has demonstrated that he or she is ready for promotion. Implicit in such career paths is the attitude that failure has occurred whenever an individual does not move up after a certain amount of time has elapsed. Such attitudes make it difficult to use lateral and downward transfers as alternatives for managers who no longer wish to pay the price of upward promotion.

An alternative to traditional career pathing is to base career paths on real-world experiences and individualized preferences. Paths of this kind would have several characteristics:

1. They would include lateral and downward possibilities, as well as upward possibilities, and they would not be tied to "normal" rates of progress.
2. They would be tentative and responsive to changes in organizational needs.
3. They would be flexible enough to take into account the qualities of individuals.
4. Each job along the paths would be specified in terms of acquirable skills, knowledge, and other specific attributes, not merely in terms of educational credentials, age, or work experience.[34]

Realistic career paths, rather than traditional ones, are necessary for effective employee counseling. In the absence of such information, the employee can only guess at what is available.

An example of a career path for general management in a telephone company is shown in Exhibit 14-7. According to the path, the average duration of a manager's assignment in first-level management is four years—$2\frac{1}{2}$ years as a staff assistant in the home office and $1\frac{1}{2}$ years as the manager of a district office in a small city. By the 14th year, the average manager should have reached the fourth level of management. The assignment at this level might be that of manager of the commercial sales and operations division. Obviously, not all managers reach the fifth level, much less the seventh (president). As one nears the top of the organization, the number of openings declines and the number of candidates increases.

Career Development Programs: Problems and Issues

Organizations that undertake career development programs are certain to encounter some difficult issues along the way.[35] The following problems are based on the actual experiences of some organizations.

EXHIBIT 14-7
**Career Path for
General Management
in a Telephone
Company**

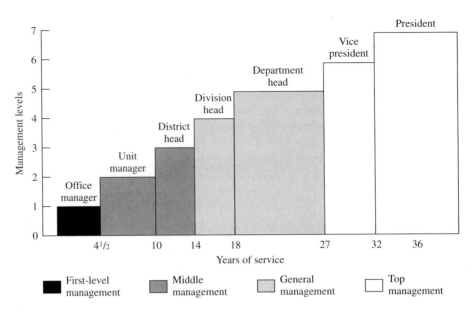

Integrating Career Development and Workforce Planning

The relationship between career development and workforce planning is obvious. Career development provides a supply of talents and abilities; workforce planning projects the demand for talents and abilities. It would seem that organizations undertaking one of these activities would undertake the other. Surely it makes little sense to develop people and then have no place to put them; or to project needs for people, but have no program to supply them. In fact, though, some organizations do have one or the other but not both.

Even companies that make use of both career development programs and workforce planning have difficulty integrating them. One reason is that each is done by different specialists. Career development is often done by psychologists, but workforce planning is the job of economists and systems analysts. Practitioners of these two disciplines sometimes have trouble communicating with each other because their training and backgrounds create barriers to effective communication.

A second reason for failure to integrate the efforts of career development and workforce planning is related to the organizational structure. Career development is usually the function of personnel departments. Workforce planning is the function of planning staffs. The two activities are carried out in two organizationally distinct units. The manager who is responsible for both units may be the chief executive officer or a group executive.

Managing Dual Careers

As more and more women enter the working world and pursue careers, organizations will increasingly confront the problems of **dual careers.** In the past, many companies would not employ both a husband and wife. Now there are so many dual-career couples in the workplace that organizations are actively seeking ways to accommodate the unique pressures that exist when both adult members of a household are employed.

One very obvious source of difficulty arises when one member of a dual-career couple is offered a promotion that involves relocation. This places the individual in a difficult situation because promotions offer considerable success for many managers. However, since many talented people can be lost if the organization is too inflexible, many organizations are now implementing special career planning programs for dual-career couples. Spouse career relocation counseling is, in fact, an important part of many of these programs.[36]

The issue of paternity leaves also has overtones for dual-career couples. Cray Research, Inc., offers family leave for fathers who want to take time off after their new babies are born.[37] Many of these eligible males have wives who work. However, how many of the 4,000 eligible Cray employees have taken paternity leave in the past year? No more than four. Taking six months off is assumed to be fatal to a person's career. Peer pressure helps perpetuate the belief that paternity leaves unfairly burdened co-workers with extra assignments.

At the headquarters of Campbell Soup Co. in Camden, New Jersey, not a single employee has taken paternity leave in the three years since the firm began offering a three-month unpaid benefit. Dow Jones & Co. has offered a six-month unpaid leave for three years, but only 10 men have taken the leave. Some couples have adopted a compromise on paternity leave by having the husband work at home while the wife recovers. Again, a compromise, or not taking the leave at all, is the rule because of assumed consequences for the man's career.

At present, more than 53 million employed men and women are two-career couples. There is no reason to believe that the number will decrease with time; in fact, the reasonable assumption is that both the number and the proportion of dual-career couples will increase. Data compiled by the Department of Labor indicate that 29 percent of working wives—10.2 million women—make more than their husbands. This figure has grown by nearly 35 percent since 1988.[38] Among upper-income women, the numbers are much higher. Why is this happening when women, on average, make only 70 percent of their male counterparts? A few reasons are that women are better educated than they used to be, more women are working full-time, and equal opportunity laws have removed or lowered some barriers that had previously held women back at work.

Following are a few hints for organizations dealing with dual-career couples:

- An organization should conduct a survey of employees that gathers statistics and information regarding the incidence of dual careers in its present and projected workforce. The survey should determine (a) how many employees are at present part of a two-career situation, (b) how many people interviewed for positions are part of a dual-career situation, (c) where and at what level in the organization the dual-career employees are, (d) what conflicts these employees now have, and (e) whether dual-career employees perceive company policy and practices to be helpful to their careers and to the careers of their spouses.

- Recruiters should devise methods that present realistic previews of what the company offers dual-career couples. Orientation sessions conducted by HR departments should include information that helps such couples identify potential problems.

- Policies regarding career development and transfers must be revised. Since the usual policies are based on the traditional one-career family, they are inapplicable to dual-career situations. The key is to provide more flexibility.

- The company should consider providing dual-career couples with special assistance in career management. Couples are typically ill-prepared to cope with the problems posed by two careers. When wives earn more than their husbands, marriages often face strain and a need for adjustment.

- The organization can establish cooperative arrangements with other organizations. When an organization wants to relocate a dual-career partner, cooperative organizations can be sources of employment for the other partner.

- The most important immediate step is to establish flexible working hours. Allowing couples the privilege of arranging their work schedules so that these will be compatible with family demands is an effective way to meet some of the problems of managing dual-career marriages.[39]

It would be a mistake to believe that dual-career problems exist only for managerial and professional personnel. Nonmanagerial personnel are also members of dual-career families. Managers will confront problems in scheduling overtime for these people and in transferring them to different shifts.

An especially difficult dual-career situation arises when one spouse is relocated abroad. Such factors as visits home, extended vacation benefits, family culture training, and electronic connections via e-mail must then be considered. When both parties in a marriage take their career seriously, it is important to address the problem of separation before the assignment begins.[40] Unless both partners are being relocated overseas at the same time and to the same location, the issues of adjustment, stress, and distance should be seriously addressed. Dealing creatively with dual-career expatriates is necessary before the assignment is made.

Career Planning and Equal Employment Opportunity

Although the Civil Rights Act of 1964 is now over 40 years old and tremendous strides have been made in providing women and minorities with equal employment opportunity, one area in which the results of affirmative action have been somewhat disappointing is career development to upper levels of organizations.

Researchers suggest that a **glass ceiling** blocking upward career advancement is still a reality.[41] They hold that there are still people who believe that women and minorities do not have the abilities, style, or background to be effective managers. This reluctance to admit that some women and minorities do have managerial abilities is discouraging. In many cases, women and minorities feeling such resistance decide to leave the corporate workforce, resulting in a drain of needed corporate and managerial talent.

The HR Journal on the opposite page discusses a few steps that can possibly shatter the glass ceiling.

After 25 years of affirmative action, participation by minorities in the largest, most powerful companies in the United States at the top or senior levels is still minimal. According to the Bureau of Labor, white males make up 90 percent of officers in the largest corporations.[42] There are companies that illustrate that equal opportunity is a part of their culture. For example, California has over 140,000 employees, of which over 48,000 are ethnic minorities. About 19,000 African Americans work for Citigroup. At Federal Express about half of their employees (approximately 50,000) are ethnic minorities.[43]

In the midst of EEO and affirmative action, and despite the lack of data supporting the claim that affirmative action has permitted whites to be replaced, white males are concerned about government orders, government directives, and governmental involvement in equal opportunity. Of course, above-average white males still appear to progress; and below-average performers will always lag behind. The threat is most keenly felt when the economy slows down and what few promotions are available go to women and minorities. White males are not much comforted to be told that such practices are temporary and are intended to correct past injuries. So what can managers do to help?

No company practice can guarantee that average-performing white male employees will go along with affirmative action programs. But some practices offer promise. The company should provide open and complete information about promotions. Instead of being secretive about promotions (in the hope that if white males aren't told they are being passed over for promotion, they won't notice it), the organization should provide information that permits white males to see precisely where they stand. If given such information, they will be less likely to overestimate their relative disadvantage and will be able to assess their position in the organization more accurately.

Downsizing and Job Loss

Although an increasing number of companies consider their employees to be an important asset, downsizing continues in many organizations. On the surface, downsizing makes

HR Journal   *Breaking through a Glass Ceiling Requires Action*

We have come a long way toward achieving gender equality in society and in the workplace. But we still have a long way to go, particularly when it comes to finding women at the highest levels of management. Women account for 45 percent of the workforce, for example, yet women represent fewer than 15 percent of Fortune 500 officers.

In most organizations, there is still a glass ceiling—that invisible but often impenetrable barrier that makes it more difficult for talented women to rise as high as men of equal (or sometimes lesser) talent.

Fortunately, employers increasingly recognize the business benefits of gender diversity independent of legal mandate. For example, shattering the glass ceiling is in an employer's economic self-interest relative to recruiting top-notch talent and expanding the employer's customer base. But glass ceiling initiatives on behalf of women are themselves fraught with the risk of unlawfully discriminating against men.

To obtain the benefits of gender diversity, some employers consider gender favorably in hiring and promotion decisions. Title VII of the Civil Rights Act of 1964 protects women (among others) from employment discrimination, but it also restricts employers' freedom to consider gender to women's advantage.

On the one hand, it is established that Title VII prohibits an employer from imposing gender quotas. On the other hand, the U.S. Supreme Court has made it clear, in *Johnson* v. *Transportation Agency,* 480 U.S. 616 (1987), that an employer may consider gender as one factor in an affirmative action plan that has the remedial purpose of correcting the employers' past discrimination or where there is a "manifest imbalance" in traditionally segregated job categories.

But the high court has yet to rule definitively on whether an employer can consider gender as a "plus" in the absence of a remedial purpose (i.e., to remedy prior discrimination or a manifest imbalance).

Employers cannot reserve positions for women. However, they can and should increase the diversity of the applicant pool. Ordinarily, this means not limiting recruiting to word-of-mouth—an approach that may perpetuate the EEO profile of upper management. Most white male executives probably will be acquainted with more white men than, for example, women of color whom they could refer for available senior positions.

Generally, employers should post positions internally and supplement their internal posting with diversified external recruiting. This should include targeted recruiting through associations, publications, Web Sites, and so on, that are geared toward women.

But what if the ultimate decision maker would like to hire a known, qualified white male candidate? The known candidate comes into the process with a very strong presumption in his favor, not directly because of his gender, but because he is a known quantity. In these circumstances, increasing the diversity of the applicant pool may do nothing more than increase the legal risk because there is a greater likelihood that a woman who makes it to the finals will challenge the decision. Individuals who are not interviewed and do not have their expectations raised are unlikely to challenge the decision.

Accordingly, when the ultimate decision maker has a candidate in mind, it is legally dicey for HR to insist on following a process that will not change the end result. Process just for the sake of process not only increases the employer's ultimate legal risk but also wastes the time and efforts of qualified applicants who don't have a prayer.

While women and men alike struggle with work-life balance, in our society the burden of family still falls more heavily on women. According to a U.S. Census Bureau Report, 26 percent of married women with children under 15 who stayed out of the labor force through 2003 did so to care for home and family. Only 0.7 percent of out-of-work married men remained unemployed for that reason. Reports are commonplace that professional women are more likely than their male counterparts to abandon existing or potential employment opportunities because of competing pressures at home.

Aware of this reality, many organizations appropriately have become more flexible. This flexibility includes allowing meaningful part-time work and telecommuting. While flexibility is a good thing, so is consistency. And this is where another legal minefield lies.

Many organizations are adopting increasingly flexible policies to attract and retain women, but they must allow men the same flexibility. It is unlawful—and unfair—for employers to deprive fathers of the same accommodations that they provide to mothers.

Accordingly managers need training on how to reconcile two values that sometimes compete: flexibility and consistency. Managers need to be consistently flexible.

(continued)

Sometimes managers become so concerned about work-life balance that they make decisions for their subordinates based on their own calculus of the balance. Stated otherwise, some managers do not offer women with children (particularly young children) assignments that involve substantial travel or exceedingly long hours.

Even if well intended, this kind of paternalism is not only inappropriate but also unlawful. Women don't need men (or other women) to decide what's good for them. Organizations should communicate that fact as part of management training.

When assessing retention problems, organizations often focus heavily on why employees leave. But the reasons why employees stay are just as important. For all employees, mentoring is important in terms of both career development and emotional bonding with the organization. However, mentoring is particularly important for women, who are more likely than men to face overt and covert gender bias.

Where an organization does not have a formal mentoring program, the de facto mentoring that exists tends to exclude women. We often informally mentor people who remind us of ourselves; most men don't see themselves when they look in a woman's face.

For this reason, many organizations have instituted formal mentoring programs that in some cases are limited to or geared primarily toward women. Such a limitation creates potential legal problems. The employer is offering something that a court would likely find to be a tangible employment benefit that has been unlawfully restricted on the basis of protected group status.

Accordingly, eligibility for participation in mentoring programs should be defined in gender-neutral ways. Within the context of these programs, employers can focus on issues unique to women, people of color—and even white men. Formal mentoring programs also should avoid matching partners based on gender. Where men hold disproportionate power in an organization, gender-based matches give men of promise greater access to the inner circle than women of equal promise.

Matching based on gender also has major business flaw. It deprives men in power of the opportunity to learn from the experiences and perceptions of promising women. With this knowledge, men become better managers.

Most employers provide training not only on harassment but also on discrimination as applied to tangible employment actions. The absence of such training exposes an employer not only to a greater risk of liability but also to punitive damages if liability is found.

But sometimes the training is too successful. Managers become so risk averse that they avoid managing and socializing with those who might pose a greater legal risk—in other words, those who are different from them.

The sad reality is that the fear of sex discrimination and harassment claims has increased gender-based avoidance, which itself constitutes discrimination. For many professional women, covert marginalization is a greater obstacle to advancement than overt bias or hostile behavior.

Training on legal issues needs to address this marginalizaton, lest the training shore up the glass ceiling. Specifically, managers need to understand that discrimination often arises out of what they don't do, as much as what they do. If a woman is struggling, for example, her manager should respond as directly as he would to a floundering male employee. If he doesn't, she probably won't improve like the male comparator who is managed more aggressively. When away on business, male managers should not avoid women. Nor should they participate in activities that are likely to make women uncomfortable, such as going to strip clubs.

Women often are marginalized within the margins of tangible employment decisions. Employers need to address these margins in their training, policies, and practices.

No matter how stellar an employer's training, policies, and practices, so long as decision makers have discretion, there is potential for gender bias. Accordingly, employers need to audit the results.

- Are a disproportionate number of women being rejected because they are perceived as either not strong enough or too strong? Is a collaborative style perceived as weak and an assertive style perceived as too aggressive?

- Do women in the organization make 79 cents on the dollar of what men in comparable positions make? In other words, do your pay practices resemble the national average?

- Does the formal assignment system exist on paper only? Does overt or covert customer preference along gender lines affect who gets the plum projects?

HR Journal *Breaking through a Glass Ceiling Requires Action (concluded)*

While employers need the answers to these and other questions, the problem is that the data the employer uncovers may be discoverable in litigation and then could be used against the employer. Engaging an attorney to conduct the audit independent of actual or threatened litigation does not eliminate the risk. While the advice given may be privileged, the underlying data may not be.

Some employers assume there is a privilege for self-analysis independent of the attorney-client privilege. Courts have not routinely adopted such a privilege, even though public policy in favor of eradicating discrimination would clearly favor it. That self-audits are not without legal risk does not mean that employers should not do them. There is a legal risk in not taking the legal risk. Waiting until a plaintiff discovers the problem is not a viable answer from either a business or legal perspective.

Source: Adapted from Jonathan A. Segal (April 2005), "Shatter the Glass Ceiling: Dodge the Shards," *HR Magazine*, pp. 121–126; and Rebecca Winters (January 31, 2005), "Harvard's Crimson Face," *Time*, p. 52.

sense when it eliminates unneeded positions and reduces bureaucracy.[44] Some experts, however, believe that downsizing is a negative factor since it eliminates an organization's memory and sense of values. Recognizing that downsizing doesn't always add value, some firms are exploring more humane options. Among these options are retraining, laterally transferring employees, and temporary work.

Rhino Foods did not want to downsize and instead used retiring and transfers. Some Rhino workers were outplaced to its biggest customer Ben & Jerry's Ice Cream. They learned new skills, earned the same or higher pay, and kept their Rhino benefits and seniority. They rejoined Rhino when business improved.

A **job layoff** exists when three conditions occur: (1) there is no work available at the time and the employee is sent home, (2) management expects the no-work situation to be temporary, and (3) management intends to recall the employee. **Job loss,** on the other hand, means that the employee has permanently lost his or her job.[45] In layoff and job loss situations, there is obviously a halt to any career development and progress.[46] No company is immune to eliminating jobs. Some of the pillars of the business world—such as General Motors, Hewlett-Packard, AT&T, Monsanto, American Airlines, Inc., Sears Roebuck & Co., and ITT—have laid people off.[47]

Effects of Job Loss

Research has shown that job loss produces dangerous increases in personal stress. For instance, the work of the sociologist Harvey Brenner provides convincing evidence of the effects of job loss. He shows that higher levels of job loss (unemployment) have been associated with higher levels of social disorders, first admissions to mental hospitals, and suicide.[48] Such associations raise a number of important questions. Who is most vulnerable to the stress caused by job loss, and why? Do short-term layoffs have different effects from permanent job loss? How important are such factors as support from family and friends in mitigating the impact of job loss?

Cobb and Kasl conducted a $2\frac{1}{2}$-year study of the effects of job loss on 100 employees before and after losing their jobs.[49] They found that

- Job loss is stressful and requires several months for a person to adjust.
- Job loss is associated with depression, anomie, and suspicion.
- Self-reports of illness and drug use were high during the anticipation phase, dropped at termination, and rose again at six months.
- Those who were unemployed longer and had less social support experienced more stress.

Although Cobb and Kasl's study was well designed, it had a number of limitations. The sample size was only 100. Also, the sample was predominantly composed of white middle-aged males. Still, this research and other, similar studies have resulted in a number of tentative conclusions:[50]

- Denial or disbelief is a typical initial response to rumors of job loss.
- As rumors circulate and as some individuals lose their jobs, there is a high level of anxiety among the remaining employees.
- Several weeks after job loss, there is a period of relaxation and relief, of optimism, and vigorous efforts to find a new job.
- Friends and family can play a major supporting role.
- Four or more months after job loss, those workers still unemployed go through a period of doubt—in which some people experience panic, rage, and erratic behavior.

The likelihood that a person will experience all of these stages depends on the duration of unemployment (how long his or her career is halted). Differences of personality and circumstances (such as age and degree of financial security) influence the timing and the intensity of effects.

Managerial Responses to Layoffs and Job Loss

Consistently strong performance is one effective way to guard against the need for job layoffs or job loss.[51] An efficient performance appraisal system can help management pinpoint poor performance and initiate corrective steps. Even when managers use performance appraisal systems, there may be other uncontrollable events such as a cutback in market demand, reduced availability of resources, and competitive forces that require some form of cutback.

The best time to prepare for job layoff and job loss is when business is good. Establishment of *layoff criteria* is an important step. Seniority is the criterion most commonly used in determining who will be laid off. However, if a valued and reliable performance appraisal system is in place, it could be used to make decisions. Some firms use a panel of managers from outside the work unit being cut back to decide who will be laid off and who will stay.

The creation of an *outplacement services* unit within the HRM unit or hiring an outplacement consultant is another valuable step in preparing for possible job layoffs and job loss.[52] **Outplacement** consists of a variety of job placement services that an organization offers to people who are being asked to leave.[53] These services may include help with resumes, including a laid off person's spouse in discussions and any training, use of company telephones for calling potential employers, letters of introduction, reference letters, payment of placement fees, and career counseling. In some cases, a company may pay for retraining as a person learns the skills necessary to begin a career again elsewhere or to enter a new career.[54] Outplaced employees sometimes form support groups so that they can exchange information about job openings and feelings.

First Union Corporation, a bank in Charlotte, North Carolina, used a variety of outplacement services when it acquired Core States Financial Corporation.[55] A total of 1,300 jobs were cut and severance payments totaled $209 million. First Union provided funding for college classes, temporary job assignments, testing services, counseling, workshops, and skills analysis support for all laid-off employees. In the first few months after being laid off about 85 percent of the workers were placed.

In addition to outplacement services, organizations can provide payments so that individuals have some financial resources to draw upon during the transition between jobs. The most common is *severance pay,* based on the employees' years of service.

Since job layoffs and job loss are expected to continue into the foreseeable future, management must continue to study the problems and experiment with solutions.[56] There are

After thinking about his goals, his present position, and the future he saw at Neal, Jim Lucio made the decision to leave the company. It wasn't easy, and he had some fears. But Jim really felt that a second career was best for him. He didn't make a hasty decision; he knew the meaning of a midcareer crisis. A few of his close friends had made hasty career decisions and had regretted them only a few months afterward.

Jim decided to go after something he had always wanted: his own business. He considered his needs, where he was going at Neal, and what skills he had acquired and developed over the years. He now is a partner in a database management system company in Hamilton, Ohio. He has felt good, slept well, and jumped into his second career with enthusiasm. Norb and everyone at Neal wished him well. His co-workers even had a party for Jim to show him that they cared and wanted him to be happy in his new career as a business owner.

still many gaps in our understanding of what happens to people when their careers are halted temporarily or permanently. We need more information on:

- Women's and minority workers' reactions to job layoffs and loss.
- Long-range effects of job loss.
- How personality predisposes reactions to job loss.
- Effectiveness of outplacement services.

Much work needs to be done and managerial action needs to be taken on the effects of career halt. As stated by Harry Maurer,

> Work, if the longing of the unemployed is any indication, remains a fundamental need—even in the crushing form it has increasingly assumed in the modern world. It provides not simply a livelihood, but an essential passage into the human community. It makes us less alone.[57]

Summary

This chapter has discussed the importance of career planning and development.

To summarize the major points covered in this chapter:

1. A career is an ongoing sequence of work-related activities. It is work-related—not something that occurs in isolation.
2. Individuals go through four career stages—apprenticeship, advancement, maintenance, and strategic thinking.
3. Mentoring can be extremely important to a junior employee in terms of career development.
4. In selecting a career, individuals are expressing a part of their personality.
5. Three points in careers are of particular importance for career development—when a person is just hired, at midcareer, and at preretirement.
6. Programs to combat problems of the new hiree include realistic job previews, challenging initial assignments, and demanding bosses.
7. Programs to combat midcareer problems include counseling to illustrate and develop midcareer alternatives (transfers, retraining).
8. Programs to combat preretirement problems include counseling, workshops, and seminars on what to expect, alternative careers, and coping with change.
9. Career pathing can inform people about the sequence of job opportunities in the organization.
10. Career planning involves matching a person's aspirations with opportunities. Some common practices involve counseling, seminars, and self-assessment centers.

11. An issue of growing importance is the dual-career couple. Organizations need to become more active in finding ways to minimize problems of dual-career couples.

12. Career progress and development can halt because of a temporary cutback or a permanent reduction in the workforce. A layoff or job loss can create psychological and behavioral problems for individuals and families that are affected.

Key Terms

career, *p. 442*
career pathing, *p. 460*
career planning, *p. 460*
career stages, *p. 444*

dual careers, *p. 464*
glass ceilings, *p. 466*
job layoff, *p. 469*
job loss, *p. 469*

mentoring
relationship, *p. 445*
midcareer plateau, *p. 455*
outplacement, *p. 470*

Questions for Review and Discussion

1. Do you believe that it is possible to ask people to serve as mentors or become mentees? Why?

2. Why do recently retired people need to be prepared for the differences between work and retirement?

3. Certainly not all Gen Xers, baby boomers, or generation Ys want the same things from a career. What generation are you in, and what do you want in terms of a career?

4. What defines *career success* to you?

5. Why are some people satisfied with what is identified as a midcareer plateau while others at the same point experience career burnout?

6. Should organizations be concerned about dual-career issues such as career conflict, downsizing of a spouse, relocation, and differences in salary? Why?

7. Have you made a career choice? What is it, and do you have the skills and personality for the particular career? How did you determine this?

8. In John Holland's system, skills are divided into six clusters or families. Which cluster best describes you? Does your skill cluster match up well with the kind of career you will pursue?

9. Women and minorities often face what is called a glass ceiling. Why would some individuals hinder or block the advancement of people up the management ladder?

10. How should the manager evaluate the effectiveness of outplacement services?

HRM Legal Advisor

Based on *Jorge Vega and Eusebio Leon* v. *Kodak Caribbean, Ltd.,* 3 F.3d 476 (U.S. Court of Appeals for the First Circuit 1993).

The Facts

In September 1989, the defendant, Kodak Caribbean, made a decision to downsize its Puerto Rico operations and met with its employees to explain its voluntary separation program (VSP). Employees also received literature outlining the program's implementation including a description of benefits and severance pay calculations. Plaintiffs Vega and Leon, both over 40 years of age, decided to retire under Kodak's VSP and signed election forms in October 1989. Mr. Vega received $52,671.00 and Mr. Leon received $28,163.16 in severance pay. In 1990 both Mr. Vega and Mr. Leon filed age discrimination suites against Kodak alleging that the VSP violated the Age Discrimination in Employment Act (ADEA).

To establish an ADEA claim in a reduction-in-force (RIF) situation, a plaintiff must first prove that he/she (1) is within the protected age group, (2) meets the employer's performance expectations,

(3) was actually or constructively discharged, and (4) the employer did not treat age neutrally in reducing its workforce. Do you think that the plaintiffs were constructively discharged? Did the VSP's implementation discriminate against employees 40 or older?

The Court's Decision

The U.S. Court of Appeals for the First Circuit found that "mere offers for early retirement, even those that include attractive incentives designed to induce employees who might otherwise stay on the job to separate from the employer's service, do not transgress the ADEA," To prove an ADEA violation, plaintiffs must show that the early retirement offer was a vehicle for ridding the company of older employees. Finding no evidence to this effect, the appeals court affirmed the district court's ruling in favor of the defendant.

Human Resource Implications

The appeals court's opinion in this case indicates that employers should take some precautions when making early retirement offers to employees as part of a RIF. Taking the following advice may help to minimize ADEA claims:

- Do not offer employees a "take it or leave it" choice between early retirement with benefits and discharge without benefits. This may be construed as constructive discharge.
- Let employees know that if a sufficient number of employees take voluntary early retirement, layoffs may not be necessary.
- When offering early retirement, do not indicate which specific employees would be laid off if voluntary separation failed to sufficiently reduce the workforce.
- Never make threats or warnings that involuntarily separated employees would be treated less favorably than those who choose early retirement.

Notes

1. Michael Farr (2005), *Overnight Career Choice: Discover Your Ideal Job in Just a Few Hours* (New York: JIST Works).
2. Jeffrey H. Greenhaus (1987), *Career Management* (Hinsdale, IL: Dryden), pp. 6–7.
3. James S. Boles, Howard W. Gay, Heather Howard Domafrio (Fall 2001), "An Investigation into the Inter-Relationship of Family-Work Conflict and Work Satisfaction," *Journal of Managerial Issues,* pp. 376–390.
4. Richard N. Bolles (2005), *The 2005 What Color Is Your Parachute?* (Berkeley, CA: Ten Speed Press).
5. Free retirement guide at www.americanexpress.com/getadvice, accessed on July 23, 2005.
6. James T. Shutta (2005), *Business Performance: Through Lean Six Sigma: Linking the Knowledge Worker, the Twelve Pillars, and Baldridge* (New York: ASQ Quality Press).
7. Louis J. Zachary (2005), *Creating a Mentoring Culture: The Organization's Guide* (San Francisco: Jossey-Bass).
8. Ibid.
9. Maureen T. Grene and Mary Puetzer (October 2002), "The Value of Mentoring: A Strategic Approach to Retention and Recruitment," *Journal of Nursing Care Quality,* pp. 67–74.
10. Betty Huizenga (2002), *Gifts of Gold: Gathering, Training, and Encouraging Mentors* (Elgin, IL: David C. Cook).
11. John L. Holland (April 1996), "Exploring Careers with a Typology," *American Psychologist,* pp. 397–406.
12. Ibid.
13. John H. Holland (1994), *The Self-Directed Search* (Odessa, Florida, Psychological Assessment Resources).

14. Campbell Interest and Skill Survey (1992) is developed and distributed by NCS Assessments, P.O. Box 1416, Minneapolis, MN 55440.

15. Ellis Weiner (September 2, 2002), "My Goals," *New Yorker,* p. 48.

16. Marcus Buckingham and Donald O. Clifton (2001), *Now, Discover Your Strengths* (New York: Free Press).

17. Alan M. Saks and Blake E. Ashford (August 2002), "Is Job Search Related to Employment Quality? It All Depends on Fit," *Journal of Applied Psychology,* pp. 646–654.

18. Spencer G. Niles and JoAnn Harris-Bowlsbey (2001), *Career Development Interventions in the 21st Century* (Upper Saddle River, NJ: Prentice-Hall).

19. Peter W. Horn, Rodger W. Griffith, Leslie E. Palich, and Jeffrey S. Bracker (Spring 1999), "Revisiting Met Expectations as a Reason Why Realistic Job Previews Work," *Personnel Psychology,* pp. 97–112.

20. Suresh Radhakrishnan and Joshua Rowen (May 1999), "Job Challenge in a Principal-Agent Setting," *Journal of Operational Research,* pp. 138–157.

21. Joel Summers (June 1999), "How to Broaden Your Career Program," *HR Focus,* p. 6.

22. Hermenia Ibarra (2002), *Working Identity: Unconventional Strategies for Reinventing Your Career* (Cambridge, MA: Harvard Business Review).

23. Linda M. Buell (2001), *Simplify Your Life: A Journal of Personal Discovery* (Poway, CA: Simplify Life).

24. Robert Simons (July–August 2005), "Displaying High Performance Jobs," *Harvard Business Review,* pp. 54–62.

25. "Fortune's 2005 Top Employers Full List," www.fortune.com, accessed July 25, 2005.

26. Angela Karr (June 2002), "4 Questions about Career Pathing," *Customer Interface,* pp. 38–41.

27. www.americanexpress, op. cit.

28. Ibarra, op. cit.

29. Arleen Jacobires (May 1999), "Retirement Programs Cover 70% of Employees," *Pensions & Investment Age,* p. 25.

30. Lydia Bronte (March–April 2002), "Is Retirement Dangerous to Your Health," *Across the Board,* pp. 52–55.

31. Ibid.

32. See www.websearch.com/websrch.tab.main/search.web/career/, accessed July 24, 2005.

33. Damien Gainshaw, Huh Beynon, Jill Rubery, and Kevin Ward (February 2002), "The Restructuring of Career Paths in Large Service Sector Organizations: Delayering, Upskilling and Polarization," *Sociological Review,* pp. 89–110.

34. Carey Jackson (August 1999), "Career Path," *Hospital & Health Networks,* p. 20.

35. P. Surlcarrajan (March 2002), "How to Retain Your Job," *Siliconindia,* pp. 58–62.

36. Hans-Peter Blossfeld and Sonja Drobnic (Eds.) (2002), *Careers of Couples in Contemporary Societies: From Male Breadwinner to Dual Earner Families* (New York: Oxford Press).

37. Suzanne Alexander (August 24, 1990), "Fears for Careers Curb Paternity Leaves," *The Wall Street Journal,* pp. B1, B8.

38. See www.dol.gov for continuously changing data.

39. Lonnie Golden (March 2001), "Flexible Work Time: Correlates and Consequences of Work Scheduling," *American Behavioral Scientist,* pp. 1157–1178.

40. Sue Schellenbarger (June 3, 2004), "The Juggling Act Revisited," *The Wall Street Journal,* p. D1.

41. Ann M. Morrison and Mary Ann Von Glinow (February 1990), "Women and Minorities in Management," *American Psychologist,* pp. 200–208.

42. Sonia Alleyne, Alfred A. Edmond, Jr., Sarina P. Spruell, and Carolyn M. Brown (July 2005), "The 30 Best Companies for Diversity," *Black Enterprise,* pp. 112–125.

43. Annual Report of Federal Express, 2004.

44. "Report: Most U.S. Layoffs in Years" (August 15, 2002), *Career Network,* http://careers.usatoday.com/service/usa/national/content/news/layoffs/2001-12-27-layoff-record.

45. John M. Ivancevich and Michael T. Matteson (2005), *Organizational Behavior and Management* (Burr Ridge, IL: McGraw–Hill), p. 291.

46. Ibid.

47. Carol Herberger and A. Senia (February 1999), "A Tale of Two Cities," *Utility Business*, pp. 36–40.

48. Susan Holm and Jane Hovland (December 1999), "Waiting for the Other Shoe to Drop: Help for the Job Insecure Employee," *Journal of Employment*, pp. 156–166.

49. S. Cobb and S. V. Kasl (1977), *Termination: The Consequences of Job Loss* (Cincinnati: Department of Health, Education, and Welfare).

50. R. Catalano and C. D. Dooley (March 1983), "Health Effects of Economic Instability: A Test of Economic Stress Hypothesis," *Journal of Health and Social Behavior*, pp. 46–60.

51. Lori G. Kletzer (2005), *Workers at Risk: Job Loss from Apparel Textiles, Footwear, and Furniture* (New York: Institute for International Economics).

52. Carrie R. Leana and Daniel C. Feldman (1992), *Coping with Job Loss* (New York: Lexington Books), pp. 166–174.

53. Mary A. Gowan and Sylvia C. Nassar-McMillan, "Examination of Differences in Participation in Outplacement Programs after a Job Loss," *Journal of Employment Counseling*, pp. 185–196.

54. See www.fiveoclockclub.com/about/_index.hshtml discusses SHTML.

55. Carolyn Huschman (August 1998), "Time for Change," *HRMagazine*, pp. 80–87.

56. Marc Cooper (October 2001), "Labor Sifts the Ashes," *Nation*, pp. 18–21.

57. Gene Koretz (April 12, 1999), "Loss Anxiety about Job Loss," *BusinessWeek*, p. 26.

EXERCISE 14-1
My Career Audit

OBJECTIVE

Reaching dilemmas or plateaus in a career is quite common. Feeling "stuck" can be very emotional, as well as motivational. Even if you are not stuck it is healthy to examine, firsthand, your career. The purpose of the career audit is to carefully review where you are today and where you would like to be in the future.

STEPS IN THE AUDIT

The following steps are intended to help you acquire an up-to-date picture of your career.

1. Recall the objective you had for your first (or most recent job). Use this job to take each of the next steps.

2. Identify three projects that you worked on that made you feel good. Why did you feel good?

3. What unique attributes do you offer an employer? Come up with at least six distinct attributes.

4. What weaknesses do you have? Identify at least three weaknesses and be specific. How do you plan to minimize or eliminate these weaknesses? Develop a plan, schedule, and monitoring system.

5. Establish five specific career goals for the next five-year period. Write the goals out and have a good friend critique and rate them on clarity, challenge, specificity, motivational value, realism, and importance. What is your grade? Try again until you receive five "A+" grades.

6. Prepare your work portfolio, which includes the positive contributions you can offer an employer. A portfolio is a record of specific contributions and PROOF that you can and have made these value-added contributions.

7. Compare your audit with that of a friend in the class. Are you in excellent shape or do you need some rework? Honesty will help you survive in the career marketplace.

Application Case 14-1

The Dual-Career Couple

America's workforce has in the past been largely made up of the heads of traditional families—husbands who work as breadwinners while wives remain home to raise the children. However, today the "traditional family" represents less than 10 percent of all households. Increasingly, both spouses are launching careers and earning incomes. Dual-career couples now account for 40 percent of the workforce (more than 53 million employees), and their numbers will substantially increase. The situation of two spouses with careers that are both considered important has become something managers can't ignore. As more women enter the workforce, dual-career couples will become a consideration in decisions about hiring, promotion, relocation, and job commitment.

The advent of the dual-career couple poses challenges for the working spouses and for business. According to one survey of more than 800 dual-career couples by Catalyst, couples experience a myriad of problems, most notably difficulties with allocating time (the top-ranked complaint), finances, poor communication, and conflicts over housework. For couples with children, meeting the demands of career and family usually becomes the top concern. Studies indicate that dual-career families need (1) benefit plans that enable couples to have children without jeopardizing their careers, (2) more flexible work arrangements to help balance the demands of family and career, (3) freedom from anxieties about child care while at work, and (4) assistance from the employer in finding employment for the spouse when an employee relocates (this is a need for both parents and childless couples).

For businesses, the challenge lies in helping to ease the problems of dual-career couples, especially those with children. According to a study commissioned by *Fortune* magazine, organizations are losing productivity and employees because of the demands of family life. The study found that among the 400 working parents surveyed, problems with child care were the most significant predictors of absenteeism and low productivity.

For example, 41 percent of those surveyed had taken at least one day off in the three months preceding the survey to handle family matters; 10 percent had taken from three to five days. (On a national scale, these figures amount to hundreds of millions of dollars in lost productivity.) About 60 percent of the parents polled expressed concerns about time and attention given to their children, and these anxieties were linked to lower productivity. Overall, many experts advise that companies that ignore the problems of dual-career couples and working parents stand to lose output and even valued employees. Companies are beginning to respond to these needs in a number of ways.

Hiring Spouses of Employees or Helping Them Find Jobs

Studies indicate that more employees are refusing relocation assignments if their working spouses cannot find acceptable jobs. In response, many companies have recently begun to offer services for "trailing spouses." These services include arranging interviews with prospective employers, providing instruction in resume writing, interviewing, and contract negotiation, and even paying plane fares for job-hunting trips. Some companies (General Mills, 3M, American Express) use outside placement services to find jobs for trailing spouses. More than 150 companies in northern New Jersey created and use a job bank that provides leads for job-hunting spouses.

A small but growing number of companies (including Chase Manhattan Bank and O'Melveny & Myers, one of the nation's largest law firms) are breaking tradition and hiring two-career couples. Martin Marietta maintains an affirmative hire-a-couple policy and hires about 100 couples a year at its Denver division. Proponents assert that couples who work for the same company share the same goals, are often more committed to the company, and are more willing to work longer hours. Hiring couples help attract and keep top employees, and relocations are also easier for the couple and the company.

Providing Day-Care Assistance

More than 10,000 companies now provide day-care services and financial assistance or referral services for child care. For example, American Savings and Loan Association established the Little Mavericks School of Learning in 1983 for 150 children of employees on a site within walking distance of several of its satellite branch locations. This center was established as a nonprofit subsidiary with a staff of 35, and its services include regular day care, holiday care, sick-child care, Boy Scout and Girl Scout programs, a kindergarten program, and after-school classes. Fees range from $135 to $235 a month, depending on the type of service, and parents pay through payroll deductions. Company officials report that the center has substantially reduced absenteeism and personal phone calls and that it has been a substantial boon to recruitment and retention. However, as many couples have found, limited openings mean that not all parent employees can be served; and some employees get preferential treatment—sometimes even those who can afford external day-care services.

Many companies contract outside day-care services run by professional groups, thus relieving the company of the headaches of running a center. For example, IBM contracted the Work/Family Directions child-care consulting group to establish 16,000 home-based family centers and to open 3,000 day-care centers for IBM employees and other families throughout the United States. About 80 companies have created programs to help parents of sick children. If a child of an employee of First Bank System (Minneapolis) becomes ill, the company will pay 75 percent of the bill for the child's stay at Chicken Soup, a sick-child day-care center. The policy enables parents to keep working and saves the company money. A growing number of companies arrange to send trained nurses to the sick child's home.

Other companies provide partial reimbursement for child care services. Zayre Corporation pays up to $20 a week for day-care services for employees who work at corporate headquarters. A growing number of cafeteria fringe benefits programs enable employees to allocate a portion of fringe benefits to pay for day-care services. Chemical Bank pays these benefits quarterly in pretax dollars.

Providing Flexible Time Off

A number of companies combine vacation and sick leave to increase the amount of time off for family life. At Hewlett-Packard, for example, employees receive their regular vacation days plus five additional days of unused sick leave. Employees can take the time off in any increments at any time. Employees can carry a number of unused days over to the next year (the number is determined by tenure), and employees who leave the company receive cash value for their unused days (at their current salary level).

Providing Job Sharing

This program enables two people to share a job on a part-time basis and is a major boon to spouses who want to continue their careers while raising children. The program was first established by Steelcase, Inc., in Grand Rapids, Michigan, where company officials say that the program has reduced turnover and absenteeism, boosted morale, and helped achieve affirmative action objectives. However, job sharing can be difficult to implement; the program requires that a job be divided into two related but separate assignments, that the job sharers are compatible, and that the supervisor can provide task continuity between them.

Discussion Questions

1. What are the advantages and potential liabilities of hiring two-career couples, beyond those noted in the case?

2. Many of the services for dual-career couples and parent employees are provided by large corporations that have far greater financial resources than smaller companies. Identify and discuss

potential ways in which a small company's HRM function can alleviate the challenges facing employees who are parents and employees with working spouses.

3. Suppose that a dual-career couple involves spouses who are at different career stages. Does this situation pose problems for the couple? For the organization or organizations employing them? Discuss.

Originally written by Kim Stewart and adapted from Kimberly Garts Crum (May 2005), "A Mother's Place," *Today's Woman*, p. 40; Rachel Connelly, Deborah DeGriff, and Rachel Willis (2004), *Kids at Work* (New York: W. E. Upjohn Institute for Employment Research); Patricia Sellers (August 5, 1996), "Women, Sex, and Power," *Fortune*, pp. 42–56; Kim Clark (August 5, 1996), "Women, Men, and Money," *Fortune*, pp. 60–61; Veronica J. Schmidt and Norman A. Scott (August 1987), "Work and Family Life: A Delicate Balance," *Personnel Administrator*, pp. 40–46; Fern Schumer Chapman (February 16, 1987), "Executive Guilt: Who's Taking Care of the Children?" *Fortune*, pp. 30–37; Anostasic Toufexis (November 16, 1987), "Dual Careers, Doleful Dilemmas," *Time*, p. 90; Irene Pave (December 16, 1985), "Move Me, Move My Spouse," *BusinessWeek*, pp. 57, 60; Ronald F. Ribark (August 1987), "Mission Possible: Meeting Family Demands," *Personnel Administrator*, pp. 70–79; and Lawrence Rout (May 28, 1980), "Pleasures and Problems Face Married Couples Hired by Some Firms," *The Wall Street Journal*, pp. 1, 28.

Video Case

Hotjobs.com

Making a career choice is something college students should pay attention to throughout their college years. There is no right choice. There are, however, what should be called best choices. Best choices for each individual. This video case presents some examples of successful individuals and their thinking about careers. It also offers a few pointers that are well worth some careful thought.

Research suggests that each college student will in his or her life have about six to eight different jobs. There is also research that points out that individuals also are likely to change or shift careers a few times. What do you like to do? Can you find a job that will allow you to do what you like doing?

As the individual examples in the video suggest, there is some thinking and planning that goes into making a job choice and a career plan. The words of Matt Hoffman of Hoffman Sports Association suggest that it is important to take an inventory of your skills. Garrett Boone, co-founder of Container Store, recommends that a student should, "find your passion". Scott Ross suggests that students "become entrepreneurial when you are young". These are each sound suggestions that can help college students sharpen their thinking about and planning for a professional career.

Learning to think, behave, and perform like a professional involves using a systematic and carefully thought out approach. Some of the "be a professional" advice that stands out in the video case is the following:

1. Nurture your passion.
2. Intake course that are inspiring and interesting.
3. Learn as much as you can about implementing professional strategies.
4. Develop a system to learn about industries.
5. Prepare an excellent, accurate, and current resume.
6. Network.
7. Be prepared to change careers.

Career success is associated with passion, fun and a sense of personal development. Elizabeth Bryant of Southwest Airlines proposes that even when you are enjoying your job and career progress, the path you are taking will likely change. Thinking and acting like a confident professional will help you can make the needed modifications when things actually change.

In closing the video case cites the wisdom of Chinese philosopher Confucius who stated, "Choose a job you can love, you will never have to work another day in your life." Wouldn't' this the be most gratifying situation—loving your job so much that you have so much fun and fulfillment that the word "work" never applies to your situation?

Discussion Questions

1. Compare your thoughts about a career with one of the individuals in the video case that is most congruent and one of the individuals that is least congruent with your logic and thinking.
2. Why is making a favorable first impression such an important professional career strategy?
3. Is your current resume professional? Explain.
4. What job or career are you passionate about? What are you doing to secure the job or start the ideal career?

Part 5

Labor–Management Relations and Promoting Safety and Health

Three chapters make up Part Five. Chapter 15, "Labor Relations and Collective Bargaining," focuses on labor unions, their history, influence, structure, and techniques used in bargaining with management. In Chapter 16, "Managing Employee Discipline," positive discipline and punishment are examined in terms of where, when, and why each may be appropriate. Chapter 17, "Promoting Safety and Health," discusses safety, security, and health issues that managers need to be knowledgeable about. A safe, secure, and healthy workforce is an important asset of any organization.

Chapter 15

Labor Relations and Collective Bargaining

Learning Objectives

After studying this chapter you should be able to:

1. **Define** *labor relations, labor union,* and *collective bargaining.*
2. **Outline** the history of unions in both the private and public sectors.
3. **Explain** the role of the legal system in creating the labor relations climate in the United States.
4. **Discuss** the union organization and collective bargaining processes.
5. **Explain** how a grievance system is part of administering and interpreting a labor agreement.
6. **Identify** current trends in unionization in the United States.

Internet/Web Resources

General Sites
www.aflcio.org
www.ilr.cornell.edu/library/default.html
www.afscme.org
www.flra.gov
www.nlrb.gov
www.nrtw.org

Company Sites
www.aestaley.com
www.sag.com
www.washgas.com

Career Challenge

Hardisty Manufacturing Company (HMC) is a 40-year-old firm located in the Boston area. It manufactures consumer goods and has a volatile technology that has been changing rapidly, especially since the 1990s. At present it employs 1,000 people, mostly semiskilled and unskilled plant production workers. The president and founder of the company is Tom Hardisty. He used to work for the largest firm in the industry until he had a fight with his boss, quit, and went into competition with his former employer.

Like all other companies in the industry, HMC is unionized. About 750 of the employees belong to Local 201, which is affiliated with the AFL-CIO. Tom Hardisty himself was a union member until he became a supervisor while working for a competitor. Until recently HMC has enjoyed fairly cordial relationships with union officials and members of the local. Sure, there is the usual flurry of union activity and posturing as contract negotiations come up every three years, but for the most part union leadership and the rank-and-file members seem satisfied. HMC pays above-average wages to all of its production workers and has never laid off anyone in the plant.

The business climate around Boston and in the industry as a whole has undergone quite a few dramatic changes since the 1990s, however. Recessionary economic conditions and heated foreign competition have eaten into HMC's orders and profits. Escalating health care costs have made the generous benefits package that Local 201 negotiated with Hardisty increasingly expensive. Many of HMC's older employees are nearing retirement age, and they are looking forward to a secure retirement with the nice pension checks the union has also arranged.

Tom is worried. Unemployment in the Boston area has been high for years, and he would like to take advantage of this by hiring some nonunion labor, which would be much less expensive. However, he knows that this won't help much at present because Local 201 has negotiated for a union shop. Tom thinks the survival of HMC rides on cutting labor expenses, especially the higher-than-average wages and expensive benefits for retirees. He would also like to get more flexible work rules: The new high-tech production equipment he purchased should allow him to switch orders in hours, but with the existing union contract, it takes days. Tom is even considering moving the plant to Mexico since the successful ratification of the North American Free Trade Agreement. With these challenges in mind, he calls in Samantha Masters, his labor relations director, to discuss how to handle the subject with the union. Samantha immediately begins to recite labor law. She warns Tom that the union is still powerful in their industry and that he must proceed with caution.

Chapter 15 introduces a powerful political and economic force in American society—the labor union. A **labor union** can be defined as an organization of employees that uses collective action to advance its members' interests in regard to wages and working conditions. Many employees of private and public firms have joined unions. Regardless of the sector of the economy in which these individuals are employed, their philosophy is the same: strength can be found in joining together. In general, there are two types of unions: industrial and craft. Members of an *industrial union* are all employees in a company or industry, regardless of occupation. Members of a *craft union* belong to one craft or to a closely related group of occupations.

Labor unions are discussed in the context of **labor relations**—the continuous relationship between a defined group of employees and management. The relationship includes the negotiation of a written contract concerning pay, hours, and other terms and conditions of employment as well as the interpretation and administration of this contract over its period of coverage.

The primary function of this chapter is to outline the history of the labor relations movement in the United States, introduce relevant labor laws that legitimize the relationship between labor and management, describe the structure of unions in the United States, and

HR Journal   *Can CAFTA Be a NAFTA Success?*

It is over 11 years since NAFTA was initiated between the United States, Canada, and Mexico. The initial period of NAFTA's existence was made difficult by the implosion of the Mexican economy during the first year of the treaty.

Today, while there are several problems in Mexico, the economy has experienced remarkable growth. There are very few organizations similar to NAFTA in size and scope. The only organization that could compare to NAFTA would be the European Union.

NAFTA and the EU currently represent almost 60 percent of the world's GDP. NAFTA went into effect on January 1, 1994. Since then, the economies of Canada, Mexico, and the United States have experienced significant economic growth. NAFTA experienced an increase of almost 42 percent from 1994 to 2000 with the United States at 43.4 percent, Canada with 28.2 percent, and Mexico at 34.5 percent. The EU grew less than 3 percent from 1994 to 2000. While Ireland and Great Britain grew significantly during this time, France, Germany, and Italy actually declined. These countries are three of the four largest economies in the EU and are well over half of the total GDP. Austria and Belgium declined during this period, while Finland, Greece, Luxembourg, and Portugal experienced double-digit growth in GDP, but less than 15 percent each from 1994 to 2000.

If the EU is the standard by which the success of NAFTA must be measured, then NAFTA is a success, especially compared to the EU. Trade unions are established to increase the wealth and standard of living of the citizens of the member countries, providing the citizens of those countries with more goods and services than they would otherwise be able to achieve. NAFTA has accomplished this for its members.

On the other hand, the success of the EU is questionable. If the objective is to raise the standard of living, then the EU's success is in doubt. From 1994 to 2000, the GDP of the EU increased by less than 3 percent. In three of the four largest economies, the GDP declined, making the per capita GDP lower than it was at the beginning of 1994. Five of the fifteen countries in the EU, three of the largest, experienced a decline in their GDP.

If Britain is removed from the EU, then the GDP for the trade organization would actually decline by about 2 percent instead of increasing by 3 percent. The GDP for the UK increased more than the GDP for the entire European Union, even when Britain is included.

It is coming to Congress soon for an up or down vote: the Central American Free Trade Agreement, better known as CAFTA. A decade since the passage of NAFTA—the controversial North American Free Trade Agreement—there is sure to be a lively debate over the passage of the new Central American trade pact. But if the economic performance of NAFTA is any guide, CAFTA should be approved.

CAFTA will unite the United States and six Central American trade partners—the Dominican Republic, Costa Rica, El Salvador, Guatemala, Honduras, and Nicaragua—to create the second-largest free-trade zone in Latin America for U.S. exports, which currently boasts about $32 billion a year in two-way trade.

The new trade agreement will eliminate 80 percent of tariffs on most goods and services immediately and phase out most remaining tariffs over 10 years. The best part of the deal is that the United States is finally going to get the same access to the markets of our Central American neighbors that they have enjoyed to U.S. markets since the 1980s under a previous trade agreement (the Caribbean Basin Initiative). Under that agreement, 80 percent of Central American imports already enter the United States duty-free.

If CAFTA is passed by Congress, more than half of U.S. farm exports to Central America will become duty-free immediately, including beef, cotton, wheat, soybeans, fruits and vegetables, processed food products, and wine, with remaining tariffs phased out over the next 15 to 20 years. Tariffs on autos and auto parts will be phased out over five years. Textiles and apparel will be duty-free and quota-free immediately under the agreement.

Who will the big winner be under CAFTA? The consumer. Lower tariffs mean lower prices and a greater variety of goods and services.

Will there be a big loser? U.S. labor unions are already gearing up to knock CAFTA down, fearing another "giant sucking sound" of jobs moving south, as predicted would happen under NAFTA—the 1993 trade pact between the United States, Canada, and Mexico. But according to a recent Carnegie Endowment report by Sandra Polaski, "NAFTA's Promise and Reality," the net impact of NAFTA on U.S. employment has been virtually job neutral. "The best models to date suggest that NAFTA has caused either no net change in (U.S.) employment or a very small net gain of jobs," Polaski finds.

HR Journal   *Can CAFTA Be a NAFTA Success? (concluded)*

Not exactly the big job-creator that the Clinton administration promised when it pushed for NAFTA's passage in 1993, but hardly the job killer that the unions predicted.

It is hard to argue with NAFTA's many benefits, too. Total trade among NAFTA partners more than doubled from $302 billion in 1993 to $652 billion in 2003—over a third of total U.S. exports. During the same period, U.S. auto exports alone to Mexico jumped from $95 million to $3.2 billion.

Relaxed investment restrictions under NAFTA boosted U.S. direct investment in Mexico by more than 240 percent from 1994 to 2002, helping Mexican consumers buy all those American cars. Meanwhile, Mexico's investment in the United States increased 280 percent over the same period, helping our economy, too.

In the information technology sector, NAFTA partners account for about 30 percent of total U.S. IT exports and are our largest export markets for information and communication technology. American IT exports to Mexico increased by about 240 percent from 1992 to 2002.

More important, before NAFTA, U.S. firms often were forced to locate production in Mexico as a condition of exporting to the Mexican market. After NAFTA, many of those firms relocated some of their Mexican production back to U.S. plants.

How did all this play out for the NAFTA economies? Since the North American Free Trade Agreement went into effect, the United States and Canadian economies each grew by about 40 percent while the Mexican economy grew by almost a third. Per capita income rose 22 percent in the United States, 28 percent in Canada, and 12 percent in Mexico. Not bad.

Of course, there were many other factors that helped our economies flourish since the trade pact went into effect, but it appears that it substantially contributed to economic growth throughout the region with a net impact on U.S. employment.

Source: Adapted from Robert Batterson (March 10, 2005), "NAFTA Spells Success for CAFTA," *San Diego Union Tribune;* Jim Abrams (July 25, 2005), "Supporters Gain Some Votes," *Washington Post;* and Fred Maidment (October 1, 2003), "Is NAFTA a Success?," *World Trade Magazine.*

discuss the organizing and collective bargaining processes. All of this is presented in the context of the effects of labor relations on the HRM function.[1] A company's HRM policies and practices may affect employees' interest in unionizing. Thus, managers need to be concerned with unions; they may negotiate with union representatives at the bargaining table or face employees who want to form a union.

The union is the key organization in effective collective bargaining relationships. Union officials and management interact daily and at contract time. Union and managerial attitudes toward each other affect the degree of peace and effectiveness that can exist in labor–management relations.

Two other environmental factors influence the nature of collective bargaining: labor market conditions and government. *Labor market conditions* influence both management and the unions in their relationships. If the labor market has a surplus and the demand for goods is soft, management has an advantage. The company can sustain a strike and perhaps even benefit economically from one. Under those conditions, union members are less likely to vote for a strike. When the labor market is tight and the demand for goods strong, the union has the advantage. The other factor is *government,* which creates the legal environment in which labor relations take place. Government boards rule on legal differences in the system, and government mediators and conciliators often help settle disputes. As discussed in this chapter's HR Journal, governments may also enter into agreements such as NAFTA, which can affect other external environmental factors including economic conditions, composition of the labor force, and organizational locations.

Early Collective Action and Union Formation

Collective action on the part of skilled workers was not unheard of even during the formative years of our republic. Employers, however, successfully resisted the earliest efforts to organize unions. In 1794, the Philadelphia Federal Society of journeyman Cordwainers (shoemakers) organized a strike to protest wage cuts. Striking journeymen were found to have engaged in criminal conspiracy and each was fined $8.20.[2] This doctrine remained a key management weapon until 1842 when the Massachusetts Supreme Court in *Commonwealth* v. *Hunt* decided that criminal conspiracy did not exist if unions did not use illegal tactics to achieve legitimate goals.[3]

Rapid industrial expansion began during the Civil War. By the time the war was over, huge industrial monopolies controlled major sectors of the American economy. Employment conditions included long work hours, unsafe working conditions, low wages, and high unemployment. The turbulent period following the war brought growing recognition of the labor union approach to solving workers' social and economic problems.[4] The first union to achieve significant size and influence was the **Knights of Labor,** formed around 1869. This group attracted employees and local unions from all crafts and occupational areas. The Knights had two objectives: (1) to establish one large union for all employees regardless of trade; and (2) to replace the American political and economic system of capitalism with socialism. The strength of the Knights of Labor was diluted because it failed to integrate the industrial and craft needs and interests of skilled and unskilled members.

A group of craft unions left the Knights of Labor around 1886 to form the **American Federation of Labor (AFL).** They elected Samuel Gompers of the Cigar Maker's Union as president. Initially, the AFL restricted membership to skilled tradespeople such as machinists, bricklayers, and carpenters. Growth in the union movement was slow from 1886 to 1935. In 1935, the Congress of Industrial Organizations (CIO) was formed by John L. Lewis, president of the United Mine Workers, in cooperation with a number of presidents expelled from the AFL. The CIO grew quickly, using the industrial union structures to organize employees in mass production jobs. Craft, semiskilled, the unskilled employees within an industry—such as assembly-line workers, machinists, and assemblers—could be members of the same CIO-affiliated union. Soon, the AFL began to offer membership to unskilled workers as well. Competition for new union members led to bitter conflicts between the AFL and CIO until they merged in 1955, forming the AFL-CIO, which will be discussed later in the chapter.

Labor Legislation Overview

The union–management pattern of interaction is governed by state and federal laws.[5] The earliest federal legislation affecting unions and management was narrowly focused on the railroad industry. Congress passed the **Arbitration Act of 1888** to encourage the voluntary settlement of labor disputes in this industry through arbitration. In 1926, Congress passed the **Railway Labor Act** giving railroad employees the right to organize and bargain collectively with management. This act also prohibited the use of **yellow-dog contracts** in which employees promised not to join labor unions in exchange for employment.

In the 1930s, the federal government became involved in labor disputes outside the railroad industry. The **Norris-LaGuardia Act,** also called the *Anti-Injunction Act,* was passed in 1932. The act limited the use of injunctions by federal courts to stop union picketing, boycotts, and strikes. Additionally, the act extended the prohibition of yellow-dog contracts beyond the railroad industry.

Labor law today is still linked to three significant federal statutes:

1. National Labor Relations Act (1935 Wagner Act).
2. Labor Management Relations Act (1947 Taft-Hartley Act).
3. Labor–Management Reporting and Disclosure Act (1959 Landrum-Griffin Act).

National Labor Relations Act (Wagner Act)

The National Labor Relations Act, better known as the **Wagner Act,** was passed in 1935 to encourage the growth of trade unions and restrain management from interfering with this growth. As originally drafted, it included seven topics:

1. Recognition of employees' rights to bargain collectively.
2. Limitation on collective bargaining.
3. Representation.
4. Certification and **decertification elections.**
5. Terms of collective bargaining agreements.
6. Problem of company unions.
7. Right to strike.[6]

This act made the government take an active role in union–management relationships by restricting the activities of management. Unfair practices by employers specified in the Wagner Act are summarized in Exhibit 15-1.

Justification of the Wagner Act was based upon the notion that an individual employee has unequal bargaining power when compared with the position of the employer.[7] Employers strongly objected and fought to have the act declared unconstitutional. In a 5–4 decision, however, the U.S. Supreme Court upheld the Wagner Act in *National Labor Relations Board* v. *Jones and Laughlin Steel,*[8] ruling that Congress did not exceed its power to regulate interstate commerce.

The power to implement the Wagner Act was given to a five-person **National Labor Relations Board (NLRB)** and a staff of lawyers and other personnel responsible to the board. The board sets up elections to determine if a given group of workers wishes to have a union as a bargaining representative. The board also investigates complaints of unfair labor practices. If a charge of unfair labor practices is filed with the NLRB and an investigation is initiated, the NLRB has an array of alternatives.

EXHIBIT 15-1
Unfair Labor Practices by Employers

- *Interfering with, restraining, or coercing employees in the exercise of their rights to organize* (threatening employees with loss of job if they vote for a union, granting wage increases deliberately timed to discourage employees from joining a union).
- *Dominating or interfering with the affairs of a union* (taking an active part in the affairs of a union, such as a supervisor actively participating in a union; showing favoritism to one union over another in an organization attempt).
- *Discriminating in regard to hiring, tenure, or any employment condition for the purpose of encouraging or discouraging membership in any union organization* (discharging an employee if he or she urges others to join a union, demoting an employee for union activity).
- *Discriminating against or discharging an employee because he or she has filed charges or given testimony under the Wagner Act* (discriminating against, firing, or demoting an employee because he or she gave testimony to NLRB officials or filed charges against the employer with the NLRB).
- *Refusal to bargain collectively with representatives of the employees; that is, bargain in good faith* (refusal to provide financial data, if requested by the union, when the organization pleads losses; refusal to bargain about a mandatory subject, such as hours and wages; refusal to meet with union representatives duly appointed by a certified bargaining unit).

EXHIBIT 15-2
Unfair Labor Practices

- *Restraining or coercing employees in the exercise of their right to join or not to join a union, except when an agreement is made by the employer and union that a condition of employment will be joining the union—a union security clause authorizing a union shop* (picketing as a mass and physically barring other employees from entering a company facility, acting violently toward nonunion employees, threatening employees for not supporting union activities).
- *Causing an employer to discriminate against an employee other than for nonpayment of dues or initiation fees* (causing an employer to discriminate against an employee for antiunion activity, forcing the employer to hire only workers satisfactory to the union).
- *Refusal to bargain with an employer in good faith* (insistence on negotiating illegal provisions such as the administration's prerogative to appoint supervisors, refusing to meet with the employer's representative, termination of an existing contract or strike without the appropriate notice).
- *Inducing, encouraging, threatening, or coercing any individual to engage in strikes, refuse to work, or boycott where the objective is to:*

    Force or require any employer or self-employed person to recognize or join any labor organization or employer organization.

    Force or require an employer or self-employed person to cease using the products of or doing business with another person, or force any other employer to recognize or bargain with the union unless it has been certified by the NLRB.

    Force an employer to apply pressure to another employer to recognize a union. Examples are picketing a hospital so that it will apply pressure on a subcontractor (food service, maintenance, emergency department) to recognize a union; or forcing an employer to do business only with others, such as suppliers, who have a union; or picketing by another union for recognition when a different one is already certified.

- *Charging excessive or discriminatory membership fees* (charging a higher initiation fee to employees who did not join the union until after a union-security agreement is in force).
- *Causing an employer to give payment for services not performed (featherbedding)* (forcing an employer to add people to the payroll when they are not needed, forcing payment to employees who provide no services).

Labor Management Relations Act (Taft-Hartley Act)

In 1947, Congress passed the Labor Management Relations Act, also known as the **Taft-Hartley Act,** which amended and supplemented the Wagner Act. The Taft-Hartley Act guaranteed employees' bargaining rights and specifically forbade the five unfair labor practices by employers first established in the Wagner Act. The Taft-Hartley Act also specified unfair labor practices by a union. Unions were restrained from such practices as those shown in Exhibit 15-2.

Labor–Management Reporting and Disclosure Act (Landrum-Griffin Act)

In the 1950s, congressional investigations uncovered a number of illegal practices on the part of unions. At this time, Congress assumed that individual union members were still not protected enough by the labor laws in existence. In 1959, Congress passed the Labor–Management Reporting and Disclosure Act, also known as the **Landrum-Griffin Act,** to regulate the internal affairs of unions.

This act gives every union member the right to (1) nominate candidates for union office, (2) vote in union elections, and (3) attend union meetings. Union members also have the right to examine union accounts and records. In addition, the union is required to submit an annual financial report to the secretary of labor. Employers must report any payments or loans made to unions, the officers, or members. This portion of the act was designed to eliminate what are called sweetheart contracts, under which union leaders and management agree to terms that work to their mutual benefit, but maintain poor working conditions for other employees.

Structure and Management of Unions

Union structure in the United States consists of four levels: (1) the federation of unions (AFL-CIO), (2) intermediate, (3) national, and (4) local. Each will be discussed briefly.

Federation of Unions

Today, over 68 national and international labor unions representing over 13 million employees belong to the *American Federation of Labor-Congress of Industrial Organizations* **(AFL-CIO),** a voluntary federation that was formed in 1955 when the American Federation of Labor merged with the Congress of Industrial Organization.[9] The stated mission of the AFL-CIO is as follows: "Strengthening working families by enabling more workers to join together in unions, building a stronger political voice for working families, providing a new voice for workers in the global economy and creating a more effective voice for working families in our communities."[10] National headquarters provides many services to affiliated unions including training for regional and local union leaders, organizing assistance, strike funds, and data for use in contract negotiations.

The chief governing body of the AFL-CIO is the biennial convention, which sets policy. Between conventions, the executive officers, assisted by a 51-member executive council and the general board, run the organization. Executive officers include the president, executive vice president, and the secretary-treasurer. The general board consists of the 51 executive council members, a chief officer representing each affiliated union, representatives of the AFL-CIO's trade and industrial departments, and four representatives of the state federations.[11]

Intermediate Union Bodies

Intermediate organizing bodies interface with the AFL-CIO and with national and local units.[12] Intermediate units include regional or district offices, trade conferences, conference boards, and joint councils. They are usually affiliated with a national union and provide services to a given geographic area. The purpose of these intermediate bodies is to help coordinate union membership, organize discussions of issues pertaining to the relationships between labor and management, and join together local unions with similar goals. They may provide office space and other facilities for local unions.

National Unions

The constitution of a national union establishes the rules, policies, and procedures under which local unions may be chartered and become members. Each national union exercises some control over the local unions. These controls usually deal with collecting dues, admitting new members to the local, and using union funds. The national also provides the local unions with support for organizing campaigns and administrating contracts. There are approximately 100 national union organizations ranging in size from over 1.4 million members such as the International Brotherhood of Teamsters[13] to just 18 members.

Local Unions

The grass roots of labor organizations in the United States are the local craft or industrial unions totaling over 60,000. Local unions have a direct influence over membership. Through the local, members exercise their complaints and pay the dues that support the national union.

The activities of locals are conducted by officials elected by the members. The elected officials include a president, vice president, secretary-treasurer, business representative, and committee chairperson. Elected officials of local unions often have full-time jobs in addition to their regular union duties. In many local unions, the *business representative* is the dominant person. The major responsibilities of the business representative are to negotiate and administer the labor agreement and to settle problems that may arise in connection with the contract. The business representative also collects dues, recruits new members, coordinates social activities, and arranges union meetings.

The **union steward** represents the interests of the local union members in their relations with managers on the job. In the automobile industry, the steward devotes full time to solving disputes that arise in connection with the union–management labor contract. Stewards are the union's direct link to management. They are the front-line representatives who must work for the workers they represent and strive to keep the lines of communication, trust, and respect open between union members and management.

The Union Organizing Campaign

Employees generally join unions to satisfy needs that are important to them.[14] Although needs and their importance differ among individuals, some of the more prevalent needs include the following:

- Job security.
- Socialization and group membership.
- Safe and healthy working conditions.
- Communication link to management.
- Fair compensation.

Consistent with these needs, the conditions in the workplace that are most likely to trigger union organizing are lack of job security, low wages, the use of subcontracting, hostile supervisory practices, and inadequate health care or other benefits. The AFL-CIO describes union organizing as "the labor movement's lifeblood and the most critical element in the pursuit of our historic goal of helping working people secure justice, dignity, and a voice in the workplace and throughout society."[15] This section will outline the organizing process and discuss the roles of employees, the union, management, and the NLRB in that process. Exhibit 15-3 portrays a model summarizing the organizing process in sectors in which the NLRB has jurisdiction.

Authorization Card Campaign and Union Certification

An **authorization card** is a document indicating that an employee wants to be represented by a union in collective bargaining.[16] When signed by an employee, the card authorizes the union to represent that employee during negotiations. At least 30 percent of the employees must sign before the NLRB can be petitioned to hold a representation election. However, if over 50 percent of the employees sign up, the union can ask the company directly that it be named representative without a certification election.

There are three other ways that a union can be certified. If the union can demonstrate that it represents a majority of the firm's employees, management can recognize the union as the exclusive bargaining representative voluntarily. Most unions achieve recognition through petitioning the National Labor Relations Board for a **certification election** after the authorization cards demonstrate employees' interest.[17] The NLRB will conduct a secret-ballot election which is usually held within 45 days of the initial request. If the union receives a simple majority (50 percent plus one vote), the NLRB certifies the union as the exclusive bargaining representative, and collective bargaining begins. If the union fails to receive a majority of the votes cast, it cannot represent the employees and a new representation election cannot be held for that **bargaining unit** for one year. The third way that a union can be recognized is for the NLRB to direct the employer to recognize the

EXHIBIT 15-3
Sequence of
Organizing Events

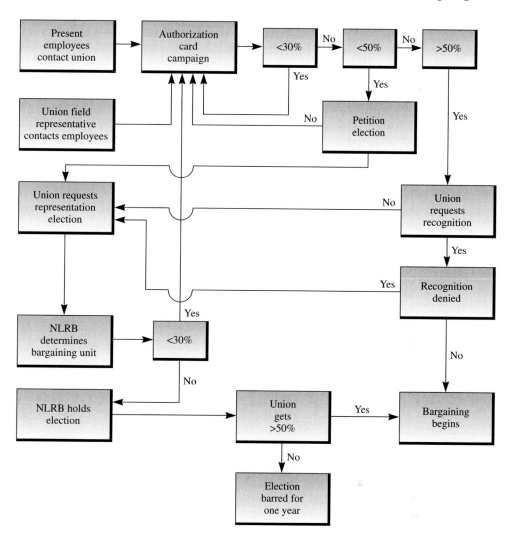

union without an election.[18] This occurs when the employer engages in serious unfair labor practices during the union organizing campaign.

Union Security

Once a union is elected as the organization's legitimate bargaining agent, a primary concern becomes union security or preservation of membership. Unions want to increase their security by requiring all employees to join the union, particularly if it was voted in by a slim margin. In such cases, some employees obviously don't want to join the union. Different types of union "shops" have developed as a result.[19]

Levels of Union Security

An **open shop** is one in which there is neither a union present nor an effort by management to keep the union out. The employees have total freedom to decide whether or not they want a union. This type of shop is a prime target for union organizing efforts.

When management tries to keep a union out without violating any labor laws, a **restricted shop** exists. A restricted shop is an attitude rather than a formal arrangement.

Management may try to provide wages and fringe benefits that make the union and what it can offer unattractive. This is a legal effort to make the union's organizing ineffective.[20] It is illegal to create a restricted shop by dismissing employees who want to unionize, by trying to influence employees who are thinking about starting a union, or by promising rewards if the union is voted down.

In an **agency shop,** all nonmanagerial employees must pay union dues whether or not they are members of the union. This means that no employee is a "free rider," someone who does not belong to a union or pay dues but enjoys union benefits. Everyone pays for the services of an organized union even though some employees are not members. Unions in the public sector are increasingly seeking agency shop agreements.

In a **preferential shop,** the union is recognized, and union members are given preference in some areas. For example, union members may be given preference over nonunion members in staffing decisions. If there is an excessive amount of preferential treatment, a closed shop may exist, which is prohibited by the Taft-Hartley Act.

A **closed shop** requires that a new employee be a union member when hired. The union itself provides labor to the organization. Although this type of acting shop is illegal, modified closed shops are found in the construction, printing, and maritime industries. For example, an ironworkers' union hall sends out union members to construction sites on request. A nonunion member has little chance to be sent from the union hall to a job because the union's business agent makes the assignments. Union members elect the business agent, while the nonunion members have no vote.

A **union shop** requires the employee to join a union after being hired. An employer may hire any person, but within a certain period of time that employee must become a union member or lose the job. Under the Taft-Hartley Act, this period cannot be shorter than 30 days. However, under the Landrum-Griffin Act, this period can be shortened to seven days in the construction industry only. The U.S. Supreme Court has ruled that an employee can satisfy the membership requirement by simply paying union initiation fees and dues[21] so long as such payments do not support activities unrelated to collective bargaining, grievance resolution, or contract administration.[22] The issue of compulsory union membership was further

EXHIBIT 15-4

Source: National Right to Work Legal Defense Foundation Inc. (2002), Right to Work States, http://www.nrtw.org/rtws.htm.

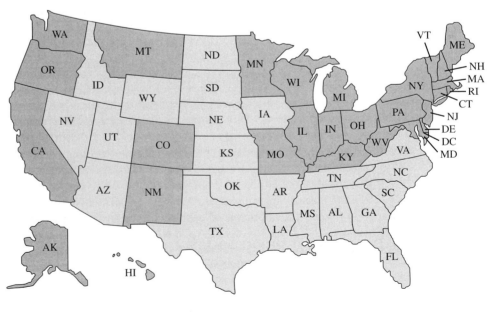

☐ States with right-to-work laws and Guam   ☐ States without right-to-work laws

addressed by a recent Supreme Court decision. In *Marquez* v. *Screen Actors Guild (SAG)* (1998), the court ruled that a collective bargaining agreement's compulsory unionism clause need not explain alternatives to formal union membership. However, the union must inform employees that the membership requirement may be met by paying union fees and dues.[23]

Right-to-Work Requirements

One of the most important elements of the Taft-Hartley Act is section 14B, involving right-to-work requirements. This section provides that should any state wish to pass legislation more restrictive of union security than the union shop, the state is free to do so. This means that states may prohibit labor contracts that make union membership a condition of retaining employment. Exhibit 15-4 on the opposite page indicates the 22 states that have enacted **right-to-work laws** to date. These 22 states ban any form of compulsory union membership.

In right-to-work states, employees are permitted to resign from union membership at any time. Employees who choose to resign may be prohibited from participating in internal union activities such as union elections and meetings. However, resignation does not affect employee benefits provided by the employer under a collective bargaining agreement.[24]

Public Employee Associations

Background

An increasingly important factor in American labor relations is the growth of employees' associations in the public sector.[25] Public employees first organized during the early 1800s in federal shipyards. In 1836, a strike at a naval shipyard in Washington, D.C., involved a direct confrontation with President Andrew Jackson. Jackson personally granted the strikers a 10-hour workday, beginning the history of direct presidential involvement with federal employee associations. The postal workers organized the first nationally prominent employee association beginning in 1863. By 1890, the National Association of Letter Carriers was created, with rural letter carriers joining their urban colleagues. Other groups of federal employees began to organize nationally by 1896. In 1912, customs inspectors were successful in their efforts to organize, and the National Federation of Government Employees was formed as an umbrella organization covering all federal civilian employees except postal workers and a few others affiliated with the AFL. Finally, two larger general-purpose federal organizations were formed: the American Federation of Government Employees (AFGE) in 1932 and the National Association of Government Employees (NAGE) in 1934.

State and local government associations were not very evident until the 1960s, although these unions also began to form in the 1800s. For example, local employees like teachers, firefighters, and police officers tended to form associations along craft lines affiliating with the AFL as follows: the National Teachers Association (NTA) in 1857, the International Association of Fire Fighters (IAFF) in 1916, and the Fraternal Order of the Police in 1897. The National Education Association, created in 1870 when the NTA and two other teachers' associations merged, is the oldest nationally affiliated state or local union. The American Federation of State, County, and Municipal Employees (AFSCME) started originally as the Wisconsin State Employees' Association in 1932.

Today, AFSCME is the largest state and local union and the second largest member of the AFL-CIO with over 1.3 million members.[26] According to the Bureau of Labor Statistics, union membership among public employees has steadily increased since 1983 with 36 percent of all public employees belonging to unions in 2004.[27]

Public Sector Labor Legislation

Collective bargaining in the public sector is relatively new in the United States and has not been fully developed. There is more clarity for federal employees than others. In 1962,

President John Kennedy issued Executive Order 10988, which began the process of creating a federal collective bargaining system which would parallel private sector bargaining. However, it included a strong management rights clause and banned strikes and the union shop. In 1969, President Richard Nixon issued Executive Order 11491, which updated 10988. This new order gave the secretary of labor the authority to determine bargaining units, supervise union recognition, and examine unfair labor practices. Additionally, it established the Federal Labor Relations Council (FLRC). In 1975, President Gerald Ford issued Executive Order 11823, which requires federal agencies to bargain with their employees on all issues unless the agency can show a compelling need not to negotiate and provides for an FLRC-appointed final arbitrator. The Civil Service Reform Act was passed in 1978, abolishing the Civil Service Commission. The act placed federal employees' labor rights under the Federal Labor Relations Authority (FLRA),[28] a three-member bipartisan group that administers the labor relations program. It also created the Office of Labor–Management Relations to provide technical advice to agencies on labor policies, leadership, and contract administration.

Collective Bargaining

Collective bargaining is a process by which the representatives of the organization meet and attempt to work out a contract with the employees' representative—the union. Collective means that together representatives attempt to negotiate an agreement. Bargaining is the process of cajoling, debating, discussing, and threatening in order to bring about a favorable agreement for those represented.

The collective bargaining process and the final agreement reached are influenced by many variables. Exhibit 15-5 graphically identifies some of the variables influencing the union and management representatives. For example, the state of the economy affects collective bargaining. In a tight economy, a union's push for higher wages is less likely to succeed, because it would be inflationary. The firm's representative must also consider whether the company can pay an increased wage, given current and expected economic conditions.

There are three basic types of collective bargaining: distributive bargaining, integrative bargaining, and concession bargaining.[29] **Distributive bargaining** occurs when labor and management are in conflict on an issue and when the outcome is a win-lose situation. For example, if the union wins an increase of 40 cents per hour, management has lost some of its profit. **Integrative bargaining** occurs when the two sides face a

EXHIBIT 15-5
Forces Influencing the Bargaining Process

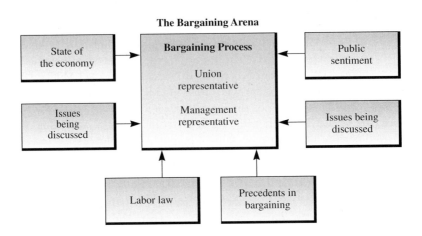

common problem, for example, high absenteeism among employees. Both parties can attack the problem and seek a solution that provides for a win-win outcome. Integrative bargaining can result in accommodation of both sides' needs without cost or through a simultaneous gain. **Concession bargaining** exists when something of importance is given back to management. Concessions can consist of wage cuts, wage freezes of previously negotiated increases, benefits, reductions, changes in work rules that result in increased flexibility for management, and other similar actions.

The actual process of negotiating a collective bargaining agreement involves a number of steps: (1) prenegotiation, (2) selecting negotiators, (3) developing a bargaining strategy, (4) using the best tactics, (5) reaching a formal contractual agreement, and (6) ratifying the contract.

Prenegotiation

In collective bargaining, both sides attempt to receive concessions that will help them achieve their objectives. As soon as a contract is signed by union and management, both parties begin preparing for the next collective bargaining sessions. Even with no union, that is useful. Thus, the importance of careful prenegotiation preparation cannot be overemphasized.

Data of all types are maintained by both unions and management. Exhibit 15-6 presents examples of data that are useful to both management and unions. In addition to the internal and external data, it is also important to check the background of the union negotiators. This will allow management to interpret the style and personalities of these negotiators.

Selecting the Negotiators

Members of the bargaining team on both sides are called **negotiators** and usually represent areas of particular interest in the contract or have expertise in specific negotiated areas. Each side is led by a person designated the chief negotiator. On the management side, the chief negotiator is usually the top HRM or labor relations executive of the organization. Management will also include at least one line manager, usually the plant manager. This person can answer questions related to the day-to-day administration of the contract

EXHIBIT 15-6
Bargaining Data for Negotiators

Internal to the Firm	External to the Firm
Number of workers in each job classification	Comparative industry wage rates
Compensation per worker	Comparative occupational wage rates
Minimum and maximum pay in each job classification	Comparative fringe benefits
Overtime pay per hour and number of annual overtime hours worked by job classification	Consumer price index
Number of employees, by categories, who work on each shift	Patterns of relevant bargaining settlements
Cost of shift differential premiums	
History of recent negotiations	
Cost of fringe benefits	
Cost-of-living increases	
Vacation costs by years of service of employees	
Demographic data on the bargaining unit—members by sex, age, and seniority	
Cost and duration of lunch breaks and rest periods	
Outline of incentive, progression, evaluation, training, safety, and promotion plans	
Grievance and arbitration awards	

and to negotiating issues. The team of negotiators typically consists of an HR expert, a lawyer, a manager or vice president with knowledge of the entire business organization, and various experts (for example, an employee benefits manager).

The union also uses the team approach. The union team generally consists of business agents, shop stewards, the local union president (chief negotiator), and—when the negotiation is very important—representatives from the national union headquarters. The union team is often elected by the union members, and the chief negotiator may have little input into the selection process.[30] One or more rank-and-file members will be on the team. They come from various operating departments to be sure that concerns of different departments are equally represented.

The negotiating teams (union and management) meet independently before the actual bargaining sessions and plan the best strategy to use. This preparation identifies the chief spokesperson and the roles of each member of the team. Specific roles that are performed include:

- *Leader* (chief negotiator), usually the senior team member.
- *Summarizer,* the person who summarizes the negotiations to date.
- *Recorder,* the person who both keeps notes on various agreements and observes the opposition team.[31]

Developing a Bargaining Strategy

Because the labor agreement must be used for a long time, it is important to develop a winning strategy and tactics. The *strategy* is the plan and policies that will be pursued at the bargaining table. **Tactics** are the specific actions taken in the bargaining sessions. It is important to spell out the strategy and tactics because bargaining is a give-and-take process with characteristics of a poker game, a political campaign, or a heated debate.[32]

An important issue in mapping out a strategy involves the maximum concessions that will be granted. By shifting a position during bargaining, the other side may build up expectations that are difficult to change. By granting too much, one side may be viewed as weak. How far management or the union will go before it risks a work stoppage or *lockout* is considered before the sessions begin and is part of the strategic plan.

Another part of management's strategic plan is to develop the total cost profile of the maximum concession package—what these concessions will cost the company today and in the future. Will HRM policies or production procedures have to be changed if these concessions are granted? This form of planning helps management determine how willing it is to take a strike. Planning for a strike is certainly difficult, but the issue should be included in strategy planning.

Most negotiations are conducted today in the same manner as they have been done since collective bargaining became legal. The two sides sit face to face across a table and orally try to reach an agreement. However, the rooms in which these agreements are hammered out now have an added element: a computer terminal. In fact, many bargaining rooms have become electronic meeting rooms.[33] A room filled with computers can help the negotiators in many ways: by reducing ambiguity, reducing misunderstandings and mistrusts, tracking progress, saving time between sessions, and preparing the final agreement. Bargaining tools available on personal computers include a contract log, an electronic bargaining book (EBB), an article checklist, and a proposal editor.

Using the Best Tactics

Tactics are calculated actions used by both parties. Occasionally, tactics are used to mislead the other party. But they are also used to secure an agreement that is favorable to either management or the union. A number of popular tactics have been used by both unions and management to secure a favorable agreement, including:[34]

1. *Conflict-based* Each party is uncompromising, takes a hard line, and resists any overtures for compromise or agreement. Typically, what happens is that one party mirrors the other party's actions.

2. *Armed truce* Each party views the other as an adversary. Although they are adversaries, it is recognized that an agreement must be worked out under the guidelines specified by the law. In fact, the law is followed to the letter to reach agreement.

3. *Power bargaining* Each party accepts the other party with the knowledge that a balance of power exists. It would be nonproductive to pursue a strategy of trying to eliminate the other party in the relationship.

4. *Accommodation* Both parties adjust to each other. Positive compromises, flexibility, and tolerance are used, rather than emotion and raw power. It is claimed that most managers and union leaders have engaged in accommodation for the bulk of union–management bargaining issues.

5. *Cooperation* Each side accepts the other as a full partner. This means that management and the union work together not only on everyday matters but in such difficult areas as technological change, improvements in quality of work life, and business decision making.

If either party in a negotiation does not bargain in good faith, unfair labor practices can be charged. The costs, publicity, and hostility associated with not bargaining in good faith are usually too significant to disregard. Lack of good faith may be demonstrated by the following:

- Unwillingness to make counterproposals.
- Constantly changing positions.
- Use of delaying tactics.
- Withdrawing concessions after they have been made.
- Refusal to provide necessary data for negotiations.

Reaching a Formal Contractual Agreement

The union–management contract designates the formal terms of agreement. The average contract is designed to last for two or three years. Contracts range in size from a few word-processed pages to more than 100 pages, depending on the issues covered, the size of the organization, and the union. The typical labor contract is divided into sections and appendixes. The standard sections that are covered in many labor agreements are shown in Exhibit 15-7. The exhibit shows that a major part of the contract is concerned with such employment issues as wages, hours, fringe benefits, and overtime.

EXHIBIT 15-7
Content of a Labor Agreement

Source: Adapted from USX Corporation and the United Steelworkers Union, "Labor Agreement."

Purpose and intent of the parties	Vacations
Scope of the agreement	Seniority
Management	Safety and health
Responsibilities of the parties	Military service
Union membership and checkoff	Severance allowance
Adjustment of grievance	Savings and vacation plan
Arbitration	Supplemental unemployment benefits program
Suspension and discharge cases	S.U.B. and insurance grievances
Rates of pay	Prior agreements
Hours of work	Termination date
Overtime and holidays	

In general, the contract spells out the authority and responsibilities of both union and management. Management rights appear in one of two forms. The first involves a statement that the control and operation of the business are the right of management except in cases specified in the contract. The second is a list of all management activities that are not subject to sharing with the union. Included are such topics as planning and scheduling production, purchasing equipment, and making final hiring decisions.

The union's rights spelled out in the contract involve such issues as the role the union will play in laying off members or in such areas as promotion and transfer. The union stresses seniority as a means of reducing the tendency for discrimination and favoritism in HRM decision making.

Contract Ratification

After resolving their differences and agreeing on contract language with management, the union negotiators must submit the tentative agreement to the members for *ratification.* Ratification usually requires a simple majority vote. This vote is not actually a legal requirement for reaching agreement, but it has become a practice for union leadership to affirm their compact with the membership. Although not all members may be totally satisfied with the final agreement, a vote for ratification means that they can at least live with it. About 10 percent of tentative agreements are rejected.

Failure to Reach Agreement

When labor and management are unable to reach settlement on a mandatory bargaining issue (wages, hours, or other terms and conditions of employment), or when the membership refuses to ratify a tentative agreement, a bargaining impasse has occurred. Impasses can occur for a number of reasons:

- The settlement ranges of the negotiating parties do not overlap.
- One or both sides may have failed to communicate enough information to reach settlement.
- The union membership may feel that its leadership did not bargain in good faith.

Possible outcomes of a labor impasse include work stoppages by either the union (strike) or management (lockout) and seeking the help of a neutral third party to reach agreement. Another possible outcome is permanent replacements.

Strikes

A strike is an effort by employees to withhold work so that the employer will make greater concessions at the bargaining table. The strike, or a potential strike, is a major bargaining weapon used by the union. But before a union strikes, it needs to consider the legality of striking, the members' willingness to endure the hardships of a long strike, and the employer's ability to operate the organization without union members. The greater the employer's ability to operate the organization, the less chance the union will have of gaining its demands. There are a number of different types of strikes, including the following:

- **Economic strike**—based on a demand for higher wages or better fringe benefits than the employer wants to provide.
- **Jurisdictional strike**—exists when two unions argue over who has the right to perform a job. For example, bricklayers and ironworkers may both want to install steel rods in doorways, since the rods are made a part of the brickwork and are needed to hold up heavy steel doors. If either group strikes to force the employer to grant the work to its members, that is a jurisdictional strike. This type of strike is illegal under the Taft-Hartley Act.

- **Wildcat strike**—unapproved strike that occurs suddenly because one union subgroup has not been satisfied by a grievance decision or by some managerial action. The union leaders do not sanction this type of strike.
- **Sitdown strike**—employees strike but remain in the plant. Such strikes are illegal in the United States because they are an invasion of private property.

Less than 10 percent of contract negotiations end in a strike. According to the Bureau of Labor Statistics, the number of union walkouts involving at least 1,000 employees dropped from a high of 424 in 1974 to only 17 in 2004, resulting in 170,700 idled workers with 3.3 million workdays of idleness.[35] If and when a union mounts a strike, it usually resorts to **picketing,** placing members at plant entrances to advertise the dispute and discourage people from entering or leaving the company's premises. This practice is designed to shut the company down during the strike. Peaceful persuasion through the formation of a picket line is legal, but violence is not. Picketing may also take place, without a strike, to publicize a union's viewpoints about an employer.

Another type of union pressure is the **boycott,** refusing to buy a company's products or services. In a primary boycott, union members do not patronize the boycotted firm. This type of boycott is legal. A secondary boycott occurs when a supplier of a boycotted firm is threatened with a union strike unless it stops business with the boycotted company. This type of boycott is generally illegal under the Taft-Hartley Act. A special type of boycott is the *hot cargo agreement.* Under this agreement, the employer permits union members to avoid working with materials that come from employers who have been struck by a union. This type of boycott is illegal according to the Labor–Management Disclosure Act, except in the construction and clothing industries.

Lockouts

Management's response to union pressures may be to continue operation with a skeleton crew of managerial personnel, to shut down the plant, or to lock the employees out. The **lockout** is an effort to force the union to stop harassing the employer or to accept the conditions set by management. Lockouts are also used to prevent union work slowdowns, damage to property, or violence related to a labor dispute. Many states allow locked-out employees to draw unemployment benefits, thereby weakening the lockout. In practice, the lockout is more of a threat than a weapon actually used by management.

An example of a lockout was what occurred on the West Coast between the International Longshore and Warehouse Union (ILWU) and the Pacific Maritime Association. The lockout of over 10,000 dock workers at all 29 West Coast ports had a ripple effect throughout the United States and around the world. Railroads, trucking companies, and airlines were each impacted, as well as the U.S. economy, which some claim lost over $1 billion a day because of the lockout.[36]

For 15 weeks Washington Gas Light Company locked out 1,100 service workers, engineers, technicians, and field personnel who belonged to the independent International Union of Gas Workers. Union members had refused the company's final contract offer as unacceptable because the company demanded inflexible work schedules and hours; replacement of full-time employees with part-time and temporary employees; transfer of employees between departments without notice; unilateral changes in health care, pension, 401(k), and long-term disability plans; and the right to discontinue any department at any time without bargaining over an issue. Before the union could call a strike, the company locked the employees out. Union members capitulated and returned to work under the company's unilaterally imposed terms.

When employees at A. E. Staley's corn processing plant failed to strike following the company's imposition of a 12-hour rotating work schedule, they were locked out. They remained locked out for over 18 months.[37] In 1996, when an Indonesian-owned company,

Trailmobile of Charleston, Illinois, offered a three-year wage freeze on the heels of a four-year wage freeze, the 1,200 union members elected to keep working during continued negotiations, but the company locked them out.[38] Imposition of a lockout can work against the company's interests, though, since workers who are locked out—unlike those who strike—cannot be permanently replaced, and hiring **permanent replacements** is one of management's most potent antilabor tools today.

Permanent Replacements

It has long been a tactic used by companies facing loss of production during a protracted strike to replace missing workers. When a settlement was reached, however, replacements were terminated as union members returned to their jobs. Although the National Labor Relations Act protects the right of workers to organize, engage in collective bargaining, and strike, it does not forbid companies to hire replacement workers, nor is there a prohibition against making these replacements permanent. In fact, as mentioned earlier, since the bitter copper mining strike it has become more likely that strikers will be replaced permanently. The attempts described above by Staley and Trailmobile to force a strike were actually ploys; their ultimate aim was to hire permanent replacements. These attempts failed because locked-out workers cannot be permanently replaced.

Third Party Intervention

In the case of an impasse, three major types of third party interventions are possible: mediation, fact-finding, and interest arbitration. Both parties have to agree to use any of these solutions. Each one is progressively more constraining on the freedom of the parties.

Mediation and Fact-Finding

Mediation is the process in which a neutral third party helps labor and management reach agreements. It is an inexpensive alternative to strikes when an impasse is reached during negotiations. The Federal Mediation and Conciliation Service (FMCS)[39] was created as an independent agency by the Taft-Hartley Act in 1947 and employs approximately 300 mediators who mediate about 15,000 labor disagreements per year without charge to participants. In the rail and air transport industries, mediation services are provided by the National Mediation Board,[40] an independent agency created by the Railway Labor Act.

Mediation is actually a continuum of possible techniques (short of imposing a resolution) that can be used to persuade the parties to resume negotiations. **Conciliation,** the first step in this continuum, attempts to persuade disputing parties to meet and discuss their problems. Its purpose is to get the parties meeting and talking again.[41] When the duty to bargain in good faith was imposed on both labor and management in 1947, the role of conciliation in the mediation process was largely annulled.

A **mediator** is a reviewer of facts, a creative facilitator, and a professional listener.[42] He or she relies on the power of persuasion to get both parties to settle a dispute. A successful mediator possesses the following characteristics: impartiality, sincerity, communication skills, persistence, self-control, expertise, creativity, and general acceptability as a neutral party.[43] These attributes are essential in order to have management and labor reconcile their differences. Mediators make suggestions that may be accepted or rejected by both parties or either party.[44]

In **fact-finding,** a neutral third party studies the issues in a dispute and recommends a reasonable settlement. Both mediation and fact-finding assist the union and management in reaching their own agreement.

Interest Arbitration

Interest arbitration is the final technique for resolving an impasse. In arbitration, a neutral third party imposes a settlement on the disputing parties. As defined by the Supreme

Court, *interest arbitration* occurs when no agreement exists or a change is sought and when the parties have an interest in the outcome because the contract will specify future rights. Interest arbitration is often used to solve impasses in the public sector.[45]

Administering the Contract

Day-to-day compliance with the provisions of the contract is an important responsibility of the supervisor or first-line manager. This individual is the management representative who works most closely with union members. As the representative of management, the supervisor must discipline workers, handle grievances, and prepare for such actions as strikes.

Discipline

Most contracts agree that management in a unionized firm has a right to discipline workers, provided that all discipline follows legal due process.[46] If an employee challenges a disciplinary action, the burden of proof rests with the company. It is important that when an employee breaks rules or performs below standard, the supervisor acts immediately by calling a meeting with the employee. A formal discipline interview should be scheduled. Discipline should not be used if the supervisor has failed to make workplace rules clear or to warn the employee in advance.

Many union–management contracts specify the types of discipline and the offenses for which corrective action will be taken. Some of the infractions that are typically spelled out are:

- *Incompetence*—failure to perform the assigned job.
- *Misconduct*—insubordination, dishonesty, or violating a rule, such as smoking in a restricted area.
- *Violations of the contract*—initiating a strike when there is a no-strike clause, for example.

Grievances

A **grievance** is a complaint, whether valid or not, about an organizational policy, procedure, or managerial practice that creates dissatisfaction or discomforts. The complaint may be made by an individual or by the union. Grievance procedures are usually followed in unionized companies, but they are also important channels of communication in nonunionized organizations. In a unionized organization, the contract contains a clause covering the steps to be followed and how the grievance will be handled. The number of steps varies from contract to contract. But a labor union is not essential for establishing a procedure. Exhibit 15-8 illustrates a four-step grievance procedure used in a unionized company:

1. The employee meets with the supervisor and the union steward and presents the grievance. Most grievances are settled at this point.
2. If the grievance is not settled at step 1, there is a conference between middle management and union officials (a business agent or union committee).
3. At this point, a representative of top management and top union officials (for example, the union president) attempt to settle the grievance.
4. Both parties (union and management) turn the grievance over to an arbitrator, who makes a decision. Arbitration is usually handled by a mutually agreed upon single individual or a panel with an odd number of members.[47]

Although most grievances are handled at step 1, there are a number of important principles for managers to follow. They should (1) take every grievance seriously;

EXHIBIT 15-8
A Grievance
Procedure: A
Unionized Situation

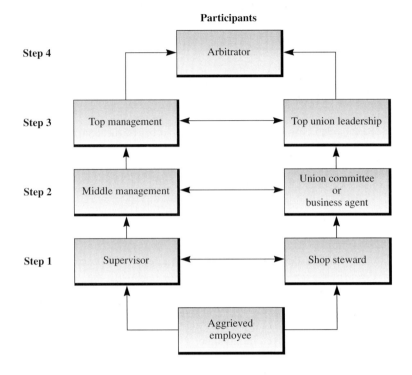

Participants

Step 4 — Arbitrator

Step 3 — Top management ↔ Top union leadership

Step 2 — Middle management ↔ Union committee or business agent

Step 1 — Supervisor ↔ Shop steward

Aggrieved employee

(2) work with the union representative; (3) gather all information available on the grievance; (4) after weighing all the facts, provide an answer to the employee voicing the grievance; and (5) after the grievance is settled, attempt to move on to other matters.

In a unionized setting, an important determinant of the outcome of any grievance is the climate of labor relations.[48] Grievances are more likely to be settled favorably when the climate is positive. When the climate is cooperative and harmonious, the chance that grievances will be granted or partially granted at lower levels in the process is increased tremendously. However, when the relationship is distant or hostile, more grievances are denied or withdrawn.

Arbitration

The grievance procedure does not always result in an acceptable solution. When a deadlock occurs, most contracts (about 96 percent) call for arbitration. **Arbitration** is a quasi-judicial process in which the parties agree to submit an unresolvable dispute to a neutral third party for binding settlement. Both parties submit their positions, and the arbitrator makes a decision.

The arbitration clause of a collective bargaining agreement typically specifies how a dispute goes to arbitration. Recently, the U.S. Supreme Court addressed the issue of whether a general arbitration clause prohibits employees from filing a discrimination lawsuit prior to arbitration. In *Wright* v. *Universal Maritime Serv. Corp.,*[49] the court ruled that employees may file discrimination suits unless prior arbitration is specifically required in the arbitration clause. Upon reaching arbitration, a dispute would normally have gone through the first three steps in the grievance procedure. At the last step, for instance, if management denies the grievance or fails to modify its position sufficiently to satisfy the union, the union can request arbitration.

Procedures for selection of an arbitrator are usually written into the contract. The most typical arrangement is to use a single impartial arbitrator who hears the evidence and renders

Tom and Samantha had lunch and continued their discussion of the constraints the union placed on HMC. Both concluded that the next step was to get prepared for the contract negotiation coming up next year. They would try to build on the history of good relations between management and Local 201 to make progress at the bargaining table that would keep both the union and its members happy and allow HMC to continue to survive in the turbulent new century.

an award, or to have a tripartite board consisting of a management representative, a union representative, and an impartial chairperson.

Arbitrators generally come from three major sources. The first group consists of attorneys who are full-time arbitrators. The second group is made up of academics who are experts in labor law, human resources management, and labor economics. The third group includes respected members of the community, such as teachers and the clergy.

The *award* is the decision reached by the arbitrator. It conveys the decision, a summary of the evidence, and the rationale for the decision. In preparing the award, the arbitrator must examine three issues:

1. Can the dispute be arbitrated?
2. Did the grievance allege an actual violation of the contract?
3. Were the grievance procedures followed in a timely manner?

The arbitrator works hard to ensure that the award draws from the framework and intent of the contract. Most contracts prohibit arbitrators from adding to or subtracting from the intent of the contract. The arbitrator must clearly show how the award fits the meaning of the contract.

The fees charged by arbitrators are a major expense. The normal daily fee is between $400 and $500, plus travel and study time. Both sides usually engage an attorney, and this too is quite expensive. Also, employees involved in the complaint from both the labor and the management side must be paid their regular wages during the arbitration process. Costs are divided equally between management and the union and may cause problems for some unions. A financially unstable union is sometimes reluctant to become involved in arbitration at all. This reluctance can undermine union members' respect for and image of the union.

The Changing Climate of Unionization in the United States

Union membership increased significantly from 1933 to 1947. In 1933, there were only 3 million union members, accounting for approximately 7 percent of the total labor force; by 1947, there were 15 million union members. Labor unionism in the United States reached its peak membership of 40 percent of the civilian labor force in 1955 when most union members were in the manufacturing segment of the private sector. Since the 1960s, union membership has steadily decreased.

A famous management theorist, Peter Drucker, predicted years ago that by the year 2010 industrial workers will make up only 5 to 10 percent of the workforce in developed noncommunist countries.[50] This means that the early base of unionism will be almost completely eroded. According to the Bureau of Labor Statistics' Current Population Survey, union membership in the United States has steadily declined from 20.1 percent of all nonagricultural employees in 1983 to 12 percent of the workforce in 2004.[51] Hawaii had the highest membership with 26.5 percent and North Carolina had the lowest with only 4.2 percent of employees in unions.[52]

At least five factors are important in the erosion of unions' power:

1. Increased competition in a global market.[53]
2. Shift in the workforce from manufacturing to an economy based on service, knowledge, and information.[54]
3. New waves of immigration, both legal and illegal, from Mexico, Central America, South America, and Asia.[55]
4. Slowing or decreasing demand by nonunionized employees for union representation.
5. Growing size of the contingent labor force.[56]

Union Membership Trends

In the 21st century, union organizers are devising new organizing tactics[57] and are becoming more effective in organizing different types of workers.[58] For example, the Teamsters have aggressively recruited new members and have thus stopped their drastic decline in membership. In fact, they won union certification at some companies—like Overnite Transportation—that had been able to fend off unions for decades.

According to the AFL-CIO, many unions have begun to reclaim lost ground.[59] Research reported by the AFL-CIO indicates that general attitudes toward unions are improving. From 1993 to 1999, there was a decline in negative attitudes toward unions from 34 percent to 23 percent.[60] This trend was particularly evident in young adults from 18 to 34 years of age. Moreover, a majority of employees surveyed indicated that unionized employees were better off than nonunionized employees and that increased union representation would be good for the United States.

In 2004, union membership was higher for African Americans (17 percent) than for either whites (13.5 percent) or Hispanics (11 percent). African American men have the highest rate of union membership. And older employees, those between 35 and 64, were more likely to be members. It is interesting to note that today over 1.7 million wage and salary workers are represented by a union in their workplace, although they are not union members themselves. Median wages for union members were $781 per week compared with a median of $612 for nonunion employees.[61]

The scope of the organizing campaign is also changing.[62] Unions are now trying to organize new bargaining units outside their traditional industries. In the past, a union focused on organizing a single industry or specific types of jobs. With the decline of heavy industry, this kind of union organizing is no longer productive. Today, it is not unusual for unions to recruit new members from industries other than those defined as their primary jurisdictions. In 2004, approximately 7.9 percent of union members worked in private industry, while about 37.5 percent of the remainder were government employees.[63] Protective services such as police officers and firefighters had the highest proportion of union members (41.3 percent). Other industries included transportation (24.9 percent), construction (14.7 percent), and manufacturing (12.9 percent). Union membership was lowest in finance, insurance, and real estate (2 percent).

The HR Journal on the opposite page illustrates differing viewpoints on how to increase the clout of union members.

Global Unionization

The International Confederation of Free Trade Unions (ICFTU) claims 157 million members in 148 countries. The ICFTU has three regional organizations representing Asia and the Pacific, Africa, and the Americas. It also is closely linked to the European Trade Union Confederation.

The United States, with over 16 million union members in 2005, has more unionized workers than any country except for China, Russia, and the Ukraine. However, the largest

HR Journal   *Labor Unions Disagree on Tactics*

In addition to management versus labor disagreements and conflict, there are also labor versus labor hassles. The most united labor group has been the AFL-CIO (56 unions) until the Teamsters, Service Employees International Union, and United Brotherhood of Carpenters decided to break away from the umbrella organization.

The Teamsters, United Brotherhood of Carpenters, and the Service Employees International Union, the largest AFL-CIO affiliate with 1.8 million members, left the federation after failing to reform it. "In our view, we must have more union members in order to change the political climate that is undermining workers' rights in this country," said Teamsters President James P. Hoffa. "The AFL-CIO has chosen the opposite approach." Hoffa added that his group's proposals to stop the bleeding of membership from unions were ignored. "We proposed that the AFL-CIO embark on a new course of action that would not only protect our existing Teamsters members and their families but lead to thousands of new working men and women to have the opportunity to organize into a strong union that would give them the chance to achieve the American dream to own their own home, send their kids to college, and plan a strong retirement," he said.

AFL-CIO President John Sweeney said the unions' bolting from the parent organization would be a "grievous insult" to working people and their unions.

"At a time when our corporate and conservative adversaries have created the most powerful antiworker political machine in the history of our country, a divided movement hurts the hopes of working families for a better life," said Sweeney, who once led SEIU, during his keynote address to the AFL-CIO 50th anniversary convention.

Seven labor groups have formed a separate umbrella group—the Change to Win Coalition—with the goal of reversing declines in union membership. The AFL-CIO has been accused of sacrificing labor union membership for building political clout in Washington, D.C.

At the convention on Monday, Sweeney, who is running unopposed for a third term as president of the AFL-CIO, said he was "very angry" at Hoffa and SEIU President Andy Stern, who was a protégé of Sweeney's when the AFL-CIO chief led the SEIU.

The Change to Win Coalition argues that the AFL-CIO is beyond repair since Sweeney refuses to step down and the group spends too much money on political donations rather than focusing on outreach to workers who need help organizing and adapting to the changes in society and the economy, including automation, globalization, and transition from a manufacturing and industrial-based economy to a service-oriented one. Critics say the changes have lowered leverage of Sweeney, who is stuck thinking in terms of the industrial base rather than considering new approaches. SEIU is one of the few unions where membership has increased over recent years.

"Our world has changed, our economy has changed, employers have changed," said Stern, who said the decision to bolt was neither happy nor easy. "But the AFL-CIO is not willing to make fundamental changes as well. By contrast, SEIU has changed."

It's the biggest rift in organized labor since 1938, when the CIO split from the AFL. The organizations reunited in the mid-1950s. At that time, one in three private-sector workers belonged to a labor group. Now, less than 10 percent of private-sector workers are unionized.

Source: "Carpenter's Union Joins Breakaway Labor Group" (June 27, 2005), *Associated Press;* and "Teamsters, SEIU Bolt the AFL-CIO" (July 25, 2005), *Fox News,* accessed at www.foxnews.com on July 25, 2005.

union memberships as a percentage of the workforce are found in Sweden (79 percent), Finland (71 percent), and Germany (31 percent). The United States union membership as a percentage of the workforce is about 12 percent.

China has over 134 million union members. The unions in China are associated with local issues and concerns. Wal-Mart has learned firsthand about the power of China's unions as presented in the HR Journal that follows.

In Europe it is common to have union contracts cover even nonunion workers. For example, in Germany the 9.5 million union members represent about 31 percent of the employed workers. However, union contracts in Germany cover about 26 million workers.

HR Journal   *Wal-Mart in China*

The All-China Federation of Trade Unions (ACFTU) is an umbrella organization for China's trade unions. It was founded in 1934 and now has a membership of 134 million in more than 1.7 million unions.

The primary functions of Chinese trade unions are to

1. Protect the legitimate interests and democratic rights of workers.
2. Mobilize workers and staff members to take part in the construction and reform of economic and social development.
3. Represent and organize the workers and staff members.
4. Educate the workers and staff members to improve their ideological and moral qualities and raise their scientific and cultural levels.

The world's largest retailer Wal-Mart has come under pressure from the ACFTU to allow Chinese workers to join a trade union.

China's state-run labor union has threatened legal action against foreign businesses over the right to organize workers at their Chinese operations. Wal-Mart has been required to establish a union branch if employees request one. Experts said the decision had more to do with the state exerting political influence than seeking to provide greater rights to employees.

Independent trade unions are illegal in China, with all workers belonging to the Communist party–controlled umbrella body, All China Federation of Trade Unions (ACFTU). Workers who go on strike over pay and workplace abuses are dismissed while organizers of labor protests face imprisonment.

The All-China Federation of Trade Unions has been pressing the world's largest retailer to establish branches in its stores. Wal-Mart had previously said that it would not allow unions to operate, saying that it preferred to deal with its 20,000 Chinese employees directly.

"Currently there are no unions in Wal-Mart China because associates have not requested that one be formed," the company said in a statement. "Should associates request formation of a union, Wal-Mart China would respect their wishes and honor its obligation under China's Trade Union Law."

Experts such as Li Qiang of the New York–based China Labor Watch say the ACFTU has had a poor record in improving labor rights. "Efforts to set up ACFTU unions in foreign enterprises have been going on for some time," Agence France Presse quoted Mr. Li as saying. "It is still unclear if they will work to protect workers' rights or help local governments accommodate more foreign companies."

China's national legislature conducted an investigation into how companies were complying with the country's labor laws. It found that several leading multinational firms, including Wal-Mart, were resisting efforts to set up union branches. Wal-Mart in 2004 opened its 40th store on the Chinese mainland.

Source: Adapted from "All-China Federation of Trade Unions," www.acftu.org, access July 26, 2005; and "Wal-Mart Approves Unions in China" (November 24, 2004), *BBC News*, accessed at http://newsvote.bbc.co.uk on July 26, 2005.

This means that the influence of unions is much greater than would be suggested by the total union membership in countries such as Germany, France, and Argentina.

Unions around the world are strong and becoming more powerful in terms of wages, working conditions, and community employer relationships. In comparison to the United States, unions in many countries in Latin America, Europe, and Asia are involved heavily in national politics and issues. For example, in Great Britain the labor party is a major political entity consisting of various unions, socialist societies, and constituent labor units. It is the principal central-left political party in Great Britain. In addition to the labor party there is the conservative party and the liberal democrats.

Union Organizing Trends

In an effort to stop downward membership trends, unions are investing heavily in the organizing function. For example, the AFL-CIO is spending one-third of its annual budget on organizing, coordinating, and helping member unions restructure.[64] Unions are also utilizing innovative strategies to attract employees. They are providing members access to credit cards, prepaid legal expenses, term life insurance, and travel clubs. Increasingly, unions are also using e-mail and the Internet to disseminate their messages. The use of this technology as union organizing tools, however, raises legal issues yet to be addressed by the NLRB or the courts.

According to the NLRB and court decisions, unions are permitted to orally solicit employees during nonwork hours in both work and nonwork areas. However, employers may prohibit the dissemination of union literature in work areas.[65] Although the question of how to handle union organizing activities conducted via e-mail has not been answered, the NLRB has ruled that an employer is prohibited from banning union literature while allowing other non-work-related information exchanges.[66] Thus legal scholars have made the following suggestions for employers wishing to implement e-mail policies:

- Prohibit all personal, nonwork communications on the company e-mail system.
- Communicate to employees that the e-mail system and e-mail messages are company property.
- Notify employees that all communication through the company e-mail system may be monitored by the company.
- Require all employees to read the policy and sign an acknowledgment of receipt and agreement to adhere to its rules.[67]

The future of American unions and whether or not they will remain an important part of our economy will depend on the following critical factors:

1. Quality of union leadership.
2. Willingness to experiment with innovative organizing techniques.
3. Frequent involvement with the rank-and-file employee.
4. Ability to appeal to better-educated professional, service, and knowledge workers.
5. Genuine cooperation with management.[68]

Summary

To summarize the major points in this chapter:

1. A *labor union* (employee association) is an organization of employees formed to advance, through collective action, its members' interests in regard to wages and working conditions.

2. *Labor relations* are the continuous relationship between a defined group of employees (represented by a union or association) and management (one or more employers). This relationship includes the negotiation of a written contract concerning pay, hours, and other terms and conditions of employment, as well as interpretation and administration of this contract over its period of coverage.

3. Unions have existed in the United States since the colonial era. A brief history of labor organizations would mention the Knights of Labor (1869), the American Federation of Labor (1886), and the Congress of Industrial Organizations (1935). The AFL and the CIO merged to form the AFL-CIO in 1955.

4. Three major laws affecting labor–management relations in the United States are the Wagner Act (1935), the Taft-Hartley Act (1947), and the Landrum-Griffin Act (1959). The Wagner Act created the National Labor Relations Board, which protects the employee's right to organize, investigates unfair management or labor practices, and supervises organizing campaigns.

5. The union structure in the United States consists of four levels: the federation of unions, intermediate, national, and local.

6. Unions appeal to workers for various reasons: job security, the need to socialize, protection against unsafe or unhealthy working conditions, a communication link to management, and fair

wages. Conditions in the workplace most likely to trigger organizing are lack of job security, low wages, hostile supervisory practices, and inadequate benefits.

7. *Organizing* is the process of forming a bargaining unit and petitioning the NLRB for recognition. The bargaining unit is two or more employees who share common employment interests and may reasonably be grouped together.

8. The organizing process includes the authorization card campaign, the certification election, and negotiation of the initial labor agreement.

9. Unions want union security in order to preserve membership. Different types of shops (restricted, open, agency, preferential, union, and closed) represent various degrees of union security.

10. Public sector unions first organized during the 1800s at the federal level. State and local government associations were not very evident until the 1960s. Thirty-six percent of all government workers belong to unions.

11. *Collective bargaining* is the process by which unions and management establish the terms and conditions of employment.

12. The steps in the collective bargaining process include prenegotiation, selecting negotiators, developing the bargaining strategy, using the best bargaining tactics, reaching a formal contractual agreement, and ratifying the contract.

13. A *strike* is an effort by workers to withhold services so the employer will make greater concessions at the bargaining table.

14. A *lockout* is the managerial equivalent of a strike. Management can continue operating with a skeleton crew of managers, shut down the plant, or lock employees out.

15. Third party techniques that can help create an agreement range from mediation and fact-finding to interest arbitration. *Mediation* is a continuum of possible techniques that can be used to persuade the parties to resume negotiations. *Interest arbitration* resolves an impasse by having a neutral third party impose a settlement on the disputing parties.

16. A *grievance* is a complaint about an organizational policy, procedure, or managerial practice that creates dissatisfaction or discomfort.

17. *Arbitration* is a quasi-judicial process in which the parties agree to submit an unresolvable dispute to a neutral party for binding settlement.

18. Union membership peaked in the United States in 1955, when 40 percent of the workforce were members. By 2004, membership had fallen to 12 percent.

19. Unions have a major political influence in many countries around the world.

Key Terms

AFL-CIO, *p. 489*
agency shop, *p. 492*
American Federation of Labor (AFL), *p. 486*
arbitration, *p. 502*
Arbitration Act of 1888, *p. 486*
authorization card, *p. 490*
bargaining unit, *p. 490*
boycott, *p. 499*
certification election, *p. 490*
closed shop, *p. 492*
collective bargaining, *p. 494*
concession bargaining, *p. 495*
conciliation, *p. 500*
decertification election, *p. 487*
distributive bargaining, *p. 494*

economic strike, *p. 498*
fact-finding, *p. 500*
grievance, *p. 501*
integrative bargaining, *p. 494*
interest arbitration, *p. 500*
jurisdictional strike, *p. 498*
Knights of Labor, *p. 486*
labor relations, *p. 483*
labor union, *p. 483*
Landrum-Griffin Act, *p. 488*
lockout, *p. 499*
mediation, *p. 500*
mediator, *p. 500*
National Labor Relations Board (NLRB), *p. 487*
negotiator, *p. 495*

Norris-LaGuardia Act, *p. 486*
open shop, *p. 491*
permanent replacement, *p. 500*
picketing, *p. 499*
preferential shop, *p. 492*
Railway Labor Act, *p. 486*
restricted shop, *p. 491*
right-to-work laws, *p. 492*
sitdown strike, *p. 499*
tactics, *p. 496*
Taft-Hartley Act, *p. 488*
union shop, *p. 492*
union steward, *p. 490*
Wagner Act, *p. 486*
wildcat strike, *p. 499*
yellow-dog contract, *p. 486*

Questions for Review and Discussion

1. What is a labor union? Define the term *labor relations.*
2. Identify and describe the key labor organizations that helped establish labor relations in the United States.
3. Explain the impact of the Railway Labor Act and the Wagner Act on the growth of trade unions.
4. The union structure in the United States consists of four levels. Identify and describe each.
5. What conditions in the workplace are most likely to trigger a union organizing campaign?
6. Describe the representation campaign from authorization cards through certification of the union. How can unions be decertified?
7. Compare and contrast labor organizations in the public sector to those in the private sector.
8. What is collective bargaining? What major functions does this process perform in organizations?
9. What is a bargaining unit? How does the NLRB determine if it is appropriate?
10. Describe current trends in union membership and union organizing.

HRM Legal Advisor

Based on *Exxel/Atmos, Inc.* v. *NLRB,* 147 F.3d 972 (D.C. Cir. 1998)

The Facts

Exxel/Atmos, Inc., is a small New Jersey company that manufactures nongas aerosol delivery systems. In September 1990, the United Steelworkers of America were recognized as the exclusive bargaining representative of the company's production and maintenance employees. However, in May 1991, Exxel/Atmos refused a request by the union to bargain. The National Labor Relations Board (NLRB) ordered the company "to recognize, meet, and bargain collectively in good faith," ruling that refusal to bargain violated the National Labor Relations Act.

On December 7, 1994, the president of Exxel/Atmos held a meeting with the production and maintenance employees in which he indicated that the company was required to bargain with the union unless the union was decertified and explained the procedures for decertification. During the week of December 23rd, the employees each received a $100 Christmas bonus. On January 10, the company canceled all scheduled bargaining sessions with the union, and on January 26, the employees filed a decertification petition. Exxel/Atmos continued to refuse to bargain with the union pending the decertification election. The NLRB found that the meeting, $100 bonus, and refusal to bargain were violations of the NLRB and again ordered the company to bargain with the union. Exxel/Atmos then petitioned the U.S. Court of Appeals for the District of Columbia Circuit to review the NLRB's order. The NLRB cross-petitioned the court to enforce its bargaining order.

The Court's Decision

The court of appeals ruled that simply assisting employees in filing a decertification petition is not a violation of the NLRA. Employers' conduct violates section 8(a)(1) if the conduct "interferes with, restrains, or coerces employees" in their union decertification decision. However, section 158(c) indicates that simply "expressing any views, argument, or opinion, or the dissemination thereof, whether in written, printed, graphic, or visual form, shall not constitute or be evidence of an unfair labor practice . . . if such expression contains no threat of reprisal or force of promise of benefit." The court concluded that in meeting with employees, the president communicated accurate information while not making any threats or promises of benefits. Further, the court ruled that the NLRB was incorrect in its assessment that the $100 Christmas bonus constituted an unfair labor practice as part of "a concerted strategy to weaken and discredit the union in the eyes of the employees."

Implications for Managers

Managers and human resource professionals must exercise caution in communicating with employees regarding union issues such as decertification. It is particularly important to avoid any appearance of threats or inappropriate promises. The company president in this case provided basic decertification information and referred interested employees to contact the NLRB for further information. He also expressed to the employees that the decertification decision was completely up to them and that the company would take no adverse actions against employees based upon their decision. In its decision, the appeals court indicated "the company could not have been more careful about not interfering with the employees' free choice and yet still informed them of the availability of the decertification procedure."

Notes

1. John W. Budd and James G. Scoville (2005), *The Ethics of Human Resources and Industrial Relations* (Ithaca, NY: IL Press).

2. P. Taft (1964), *Organized Labor in American History* (New York: Harper and Row), pp. 563–578.

3. *Commonwealth v. Hunt,* 45 Mass. 111 (Supreme Court of Massachusetts 1842).

4. Patrick J. Cihon and James Castagenra (2001), *Employment and Labor Law* (Cincinnati, OH: South-Western Learning).

5. Archibald S. S. Cox, Derick Bols, Matthew W. Finkin, and Robert Gorman (2001), *Labor Law* (New York: Foundation Press).

6. Kenneth Casebeer (1989), "Drafts on the Wagner Act," *Industrial Relations Law Journal,* Vol. 11, Iss. 1, pp. 73–131.

7. Ibid.

8. *National Labor Relations Board v. Jones and Laughlin Steel,* 331 U.S. 416 (1947).

9. American Federation of Labor-Congress of Industrial Organizations (AFL-CIO), http://www.aflcio.org/aboutus/faq/.

10. Ibid.

11. Budd and Scoville, op. cit.

12. Larry K. Goodwin (Summer 1993), "Win-Win Negotiations: A Model for Cooperative Labor Relations," *Public Manager,* Vol. 22, Iss. 2, pp. 18–21.

13. International Brotherhood of Teamsters, http://www.teamster.org, accessed July 1, 2005.

14. Cihon and Castagenra, op. cit.

15. Ibid.

16. Linda Markowitz (1999), *Worker Activism after Successful Union Organizing* (New York: M. E. Sharpe).

17. Ibid.

18. Ibid.

19. Thomas A. Kochin (2005), *Restoring the American Dream: A Working Family's Agenda for America* (Boston: MIT Press).

20. Markowitz, op. cit.

21. NLRB *v. General Motors Corp.,* 373 U.S. 734, 742-743 (1963).

22. *Communications Workers v. Beck,* 487 U.S. 735, 745, 762-763 (1988).

23. *Marquez v. Screen Actors Guild (SAG),* 119 S.Ct. 292 (1998).

24. National Right to Work Legal Defense Foundation, Inc., http://nrtw.org/rtws.htm.

25. Amy Sterling Casil (2005), *The Department of Labor* (New York: Rosen Central).

26. The American Federation of State, County, and Municipal Employees, http://www.afscme.org/about.

27. Ibid.

28. Ibid.

29. Michael R. Carel and Christina Heavrin (2000), *Labor Relations and Collective Bargaining* (New York: Pearson).

30. Susan Eren (2002), *Labor Pains: Inside America's New Union Movement* (New York: Monthly Review Press).

31. John A. Fossum (2006), *Labor Relations: Development, Structure, Processes* (Burr Ridge, IL: McGraw-Hill).

32. Alice K. Flanagan (2005), *The Lowell Mill Girls* (New York: Compass Point Books).

33. Hal C. Gueutal and Dianna L. Stone (2005), *The Brave New World of eHR* (San Francisco: Jossey-Bass).

34. Fossum, op. cit.

35. Bureau of Labor Statistics Work Stoppages in 2004, www.bls.gov/opub/ted/2005.

36. Simon Avery, "Port Lockout Hurts Businesses," www.delawareonline.com. Retrieved October 2, 2002.

37. Thomas Frank and David Mulcahey (1995), "Decatur Lockout-Hunger Striking in the Corn Belt," *Nation,* Vol. 261, Iss. 15, pp. 540–542.

38. Leah Samuel (1996), "Trailmobile Workers Win," *The Progressive,* Vol. 69, Iss. 8, p. 15.

39. The Federal Mediation and Conciliation Service (FMCS), http://fmcs.gov.

40. National Mediation Board, http://nmb.gov.

41. Peter Lovenheim (2002), *Becoming a Mediator* (New York: John Wiley & Sons).

42. Robert A. Baruch Bush and Joseph P. Folger (2004), *The Promise of Mediation: The Transformative Approach to Conflict* (San Francisco: Jossey-Bass).

43. Ibid.

44. John Winslade and Gerald Monk (2000), *Narrative Mediation: A New Approach to Conflict Resolution* (New York: John Wiley & Sons).

45. Andreas F. Lowenfeld (2002), *Lowenfeld's International Litigation* (Cincinnati, OH: West Group).

46. Ibid.

47. Lowenfeld, op. cit.

48. N. Humphreys (2005), *Trade Union and Collective Employment* (Jordan Publishing).

49. *Wright* v. *Universal Maritime Serv.* Corp., 525 U.S. 70 (1998).

50. Peter F. Drucker (March 20, 1990), "Peter Drucker Asks: Will Unions Ever Be Useful Organs of Society?" *Industry Week,* Vol. 238, Iss. 6, pp. 16–22.

51. Bureau of Labor Statistics, Current Population Survey, http://bls.census.gov/cps/cpsmain.htm.

52. Union Member Summary, http://www.bls.gov/news.release/union2.nr0.htm. Retrieved July 6, 2005.

53. Folger, op. cit.

54. Humphreys, op. cit.

55. Ibid.

56. Ibid.

57. Humphreys, op. cit.

58. P. J. Dowling and D. E. Welch (2005), *International Human Resource Management* (Cincinnati, OH: Thomson South-Western).

59. David Whitford (September 28, 1998), "Labor's Lost Chance," *Fortune,* Vol. 138, Iss. 6, pp. 177–182.

60. AFL-CIO, Labor Day 1999, America's Attitudes toward Unions, http:www.aflcio.org/labor99/am_attitude.htm.

61. www.aflcio.org, accessed July 25, 2005.

62. Enrem, op. cit.

63. Ibid.

64. Markowitz, op. cit.

65. Humphreys, op. cit.

66. *E.I. du Ponte de Nemours and Co.*, 311 NLRB 893 (1993).

67. William F. Kershner (March 1999), Union Organizing in the New Millennium, http://www.pepperlaw.com/pepper/publications.cfm.

68. Fossum, op. cit.

EXERCISE 15-1

Reporting on Labor Unions

OBJECTIVE

To enable students to collect, evaluate, and present information about labor unions.

SET UP THE EXERCISE

1. Assign individuals or small teams of students to research American and international unions so that an up-to-date comparison can be made among labor organizations.

2. Have each team make a brief presentation of their findings to the class. Characteristics to be researched include membership demographics, size, affiliation with national or other labor organizations or confederations, recent organizing campaigns, and strikes and lockouts.

3. Have the students begin their research using the following Internet site: http://aflcio.org/unionand/internat.htm.

EXERCISE 15-2

Union–Management Contract Negotiations

OBJECTIVE

To permit individuals to become involved in labor–management contract negotiations in a role-playing session.

SET UP THE EXERCISE

1. Form an even number of groups of four to eight people. Half of the groups will be union teams and the other half will be management teams.

2. Read the description of the Dana Lou Corporation of Hamilton, Ohio.

3. Review and discuss in groups the four bargaining issues and the data collected on competitors (15 minutes).

4. The instructor will provide the union teams with the union negotiator's instructions and the management teams with the management negotiator's instructions.

5. Groups face off against each other (one management team versus one union team). The negotiator represents the team's position.

6. Individuals should answer the exercise questions after step 2 of the negotiations.

DANA LOU CORPORATION

Dana Lou Corporation is a medium-sized company with about 1,100 employees in Hamilton, Ohio, a suburb of Cincinnati. It competes in the electronic repair parts industry and is slightly larger than most of its main competitors. The firm's success (profitability and growth) has been attributed to a dedicated workforce that takes great pride in its work.

In 1964, the Communications Workers of America (CWA) organized the plant. Since then, labor–management relations have been good, and there were only two days lost to a strike, in 1972. Labor and management both feel that the cooperation between them is much better than that found in other firms of the same size in the area.

The current labor–management contract expires in three weeks. Representatives from the union and management have been negotiating a number of bargaining issues for the last three days, but there seems to be little agreement.

BARGAINING ISSUES

1. Republic National Medical and Dental Insurance Protection
   a. Present contract: Dana Lou pays 50 percent of premiumes for all full-time employees.
   b. New contract issues: CWA wants Dana Lou to pay the full premium; management wants to hold the line.

In terms of costs, the data look like this:

Percent of Premium Paid	Dana Lou Contribution
0	-0-
25	$ 55,000
50	110,000
75	165,000
100	220,000

2. Preventive health director, staff and participation
   a. Present contract: Dana Lou has two part-time physicians and two full-time nurses (cost is $66,000 per year).
   b. New contract issues: CWA wants a full-time fitness director, a full-time physician, counselors for alcohol and drug abuse problems, and partial payment of employees' use of YMCA and YWCA exercise facilities (estimated increase over present arrangement, $108,000).

3. Vacation benefits
   a. Present contract: One week with full pay for the first year; two weeks for employees with 2 to 10 years of service, and three weeks for employees with over 10 years.
   b. New contract issues: CWA wants all employees with 15 or more years of service to have four weeks of full paid vacation. Management wants no change in the present program.

4. Wage increases for skilled quality inspectors
   a. Present contract: Inspectors' rate is $10.05 per hour; the rate for inspector apprentices is $6.40.
   b. New contract issues: CWA wants an increase of $0.50 per hour for the plant's 95 inspectors and a $0.40 per hour increase for the plant's 25 inspector apprentices. Management wants to hold the line on salary increases because it believes that layoffs will have to occur. The union's proposal would cost Dana Lou 95 times $0.50 = $47.50 and 25 times $0.40 + $10.00 or $57.50 total per hour.

NEGOTIATIONS

1. One member from each of the two groups facing each other will negotiate the four issues. The rest of the group must remain quiet during the negotiations. The negotiators should role-play for exactly 20 minutes. At the end of this time, they should record the agreement points reached.

FINAL AGREEMENTS
Medical and dental protection

_____
_____
_____
_____
_____

Competitor Data (Hamilton, Ohio, Survey)

	Blue Fox Corp.	Wintex, Inc.	Lafley Mfg.
Company contribution to medical and dental insurance	100%	50%	50%
Preventive health director	No	No	No
Payment of physical fitness fees for employees	Yes	No	Yes
Vacation benefits	1 week in first year; 3 weeks all employees after 1 year	2 weeks all employees until 10 years of service and then 3 weeks	2 weeks all employees for first 5 years and then 3 weeks
Wage rate inspectors	$9.80	$8.97	$9.95
Inspector apprentices	$7.90	$6.95	$7.40

Preventive health director/Staff and participation

_____
_____
_____

Vacation benefits

_____
_____
_____

Wage increases

_____
_____
_____

2. Each individual is to analyze the negotiations:
How successful were the negotiators?

_____
_____
_____

Would you have negotiated differently? How?

_____
_____
_____

Were the negotiators prepared?

_____
_____
_____

A LEARNING NOTE
This exercise will illustrate how difficult discussing issues can be when people have a fixed attitude or position.

Application Case 15-1

The Union's Demand for Recognition and Bargaining Rights

Background

The employer owned and managed an apartment building and townhouse complex, where it employed a number of janitorial workers. On December 5, the union held an organizing meeting with these workers and obtained signed authorization cards from 6 of the employees in a proposed unit of 11 employees. One other employee in the unit was already a member of the union. On December 8, Orval Schimmel,* a union organizer, advised Thomas Hall, the employer's property manager, that the union represented recognition and bargaining rights. Hall responded that he had nothing to do with union matters and that the appropriate person with whom to speak was vice president Carl Alton.

On December 8, after the union had first requested recognition, a maintenance supervisor, Larry Melton, telephoned an employee, George Thompson, at his home and asked if any union people had contacted him. Thompson replied that none had. The next morning Melton entered the maintenance office, where the janitorial employees reported for work, and asked another employee, Alice Coleman, "What has the union done to you?" Coleman did not reply. Melton then entered his own office and called in a third employee, Theo Ewing. Melton told Ewing that he knew that the employees had brought in an organizer and wanted to organize a union. He then asked Ewing whether he had attended the meeting and whether he knew who sent for the organizer. When Ewing denied attending the meeting and any knowledge about who sent for the organizer, Melton repeated the questions and told Ewing not to sign anything or talk to any organizer and to keep him informed of any such activities. On the evening of December 9, Melton again telephoned George Thompson and asked whether he had spoken to any union people. Thompson admitted that he had but refused to offer any further information. Melton continued to question him about why he was doing this and who attended the meeting. After several unsuccessful attempts to elicit additional information, Melton said to Thompson, "You are either on my side of the fence or your side of the fence. . . . You always had it good. I have given you . . . you got a nice job, you got an apartment. . . . This is your last chance." Thompson still refused to answer.

That same evening, December 9, Melton telephoned Gloria Greer, another employee, and asked why she had not told him about the union meeting. Greer denied knowledge of the meeting. Melton then telephoned Ewing and asked who brought in the organizer. He repeatedly attempted to elicit this information, but Ewing said he did not know. Melton ended the conversation by telling Ewing to keep his ears and eyes open and to let him know if he heard anything. He also told him not to sign anything.

On December 24, Larry Melton was terminated by the company, and he was replaced by Leo Nord. At about this same time, the company announced that it was improving its sickness and health benefits program for employees, including a new benefit to cover maternity medical expenses for employees and their spouses.

On January 30, the morning of the representational election, Leo Nord told Cecil Snow that if the union won the election, the employer would take the rent-free apartments away from the janitors' helpers and charge the head janitors for the second bedroom in their apartments.

On January 30, the union lost the representation election 6 to 4. The union filed numerous charges of unfair labor practices, claiming that these violations had dissipated the union's majority status as established by the authorization cards. These violations, in the union's view, were so serious and widespread that they made a fair rerun election unlikely. The union requested that the company be ordered to recognize the union and bargain with the union on the basis of the prounion majority previously established by the signed authorization cards, which it had secured in early December.

*The names of all individuals have been disguised.

Position of the Union

The union filed charges of unfair labor practices against the company, claiming that the company had violated Section 8(a) (1) of the LMRA by:

a. Repeatedly interrogating employees concerning their union activities.
b. Threatening employees with deprivation of benefits if the union should be elected to represent them.
c. Threatening an employee for refusing to reveal the identities of employees who attended a union meeting.
d. Informing an employee that it knew (or heard) the employee had joined the union.
e. Promising to pay and paying employees for certain medical benefits to discourage them from supporting the union.

The union urged that the company should be found in violation of the act accordingly and ordered to cease and desist from these practices. Further, because the company's violations were so severe and pervasive, a valid union majority status had been dissipated, and it would be impossible to have a fair rerun election in the climate created by the company's actions. The union requested that the company should be ordered by the NLRB to recognize the union's majority status as of December 8, and to bargain with the union as the authorized representative of a bargaining unit of janitorial employees.

Position of the Company

The company presented a number of contentions in urging that the union's charges be dismissed.

First of all, company management claimed that it was unaware of the telephone calls and other questioning of employees conducted by its former supervisor Larry Melton. Regardless, most of Melton's statements and questions to employees were not coercive, but they were legitimate inquiries necessary to determine whether the union had the majority status that it claimed. Melton never specifically threatened the employee George Thompson on December 9; his statement to Thompson was very vague and inconclusive.

Concerning the granting of improved sickness and health benefits in late December, the company contended that the improved benefits were part of the company's annual review of its benefit program. The company announced the change in benefits to coincide with the Christmas season, and this had nothing to do with the union's representational campaign.

The company pointed out that Larry Melton was terminated by the company on December 24, and the election was not held until January 30. Thus Melton's influence on the election, if any, had "totally evaporated" and was no longer a factor. The statement of the new supervisor, Leo Nord, to the employee Cecil Snow on that day did not constitute a threat, but it was a legitimate prediction and Nord's own personal opinion concerning what unionization logically would bring to the company. This was "free speech" protected by Section 8(c) of the act.

Finally the company claimed that even if the Board held that the company had violated the act in any way, such violations were minor and did not influence the outcome of the representational election, which the union lost. The union's claim to a majority status in December, based on signed authorization cards, was never accepted by the company or verified by the NLRB. The union was promulgating charges against the company in an effort to gain representational rights after losing an NLRB election. The election was a true determination of the majority of the employees' feelings, and the Board should allow the results of the election to stand.

Discussion Questions

1. Evaluate the various claims made by the union and counterclaims made by the company regarding the charges of unfair labor practices. Which of the arguments are most persuasive?
2. Was the statement by Nord to Snow on the date of the representational election a threat or a legitimate prediction and personal opinion protected by the free speech provisions of the act?

3. Was the company obligated to accept the union's majority status claim on the basis of the authorization cards submitted by the union?

4. If the company is found to have violated the act, what would be the appropriate remedy, a bargaining order or a new election?

Source: Adapted from USX Corporation and the United Steelworkers Union, "Labor Agreement"; Sterling H. Schoen and Raymond L. Hilgert (1989), *Cases in Collective Bargaining and Industrial Relations,* 6th ed. (Burr Ridge, IL: Irwin), pp. 94–97.

16

Managing Employee Discipline

Learning Objectives

After studying this chapter you should be able to:

1. **Describe** steps that can be taken to prevent theft by employees.
2. **Discuss** the elements of a disciplinary system.
3. **Define** *employment at will.*
4. **Explain** why some employees are opposed to drug testing.
5. **Describe** why it is important to carefully and thoroughly document each discipline step taken in an organization.

Internet/Web Resources

General Sites

http://www.drugfreeworkplace.org

http://eap-sap.com

http://www.fmcsa.dot.gov/safetyprogs/drugs/engtesting.htm

http://www.findlaw.com/adr/prg

www.nida.nih.gov

Company Sites

www.gsk.com/index.htm

www.boeing.com

www.ncr.com

www.sees.com

www.mcgraw-hill.com

www.daimlerchrysler.com

Career Challenge

Managers supervise many types of employees as part of their work. Most employees perform effectively most of the time. But any management development session eventually comes around to a discussion of employees like Al, Susan, Joyce, or Tom. These four employees are employed by a small conglomerate in the Boston area, Judge Incorporated. Judge owns manufacturing and retailing units.

- Al is the salesperson who had the largest sales increase of any of the sales force just after he was hired. Later, his sales dropped off. When his supervisor checked, Al was found to be making just enough sales calls to reach his quota.

- Susan is a good worker. However, there are a few days when all the forms she prepares have serious errors on them. These apparently are the days when Susan is drinking.

- Joyce seems to do good work. She is courteous to the customers. She puts the stock up quickly and marks the prices accurately. But Joyce takes more than her paycheck home every week.

- Tom is a pretty good employee. But John, his supervisor, is driven up the wall by him. Tom just can't seem to follow the company rules. And when John tries to talk to him about it, Tom gives him a hard time. Sometimes Tom even seems to threaten John if he tries to do anything about the problem.

At present, Judge Incorporated has no well-organized system for handling any of these situations and behavior.

These examples illustrate a time-consuming and worrisome aspect of the HRM job: dealing fairly with the difficult or misbehaving employee. The seriousness of the problem is reinforced by the fact that most cases going to arbitration involve disciplinary matters. Moreover, the tasks of assessing credibility, quelling emotions, and determining the seriousness of behaviors heighten the complexity of resolving discipline and termination cases.[1]

A few examples of misbehavior that may require managerial attention and action are presented in Exhibit 16-1.

An employee's attitude toward work is a crucial factor in productivity or performance, and discipline may play an important part in this attitude. The kind of discipline system used is normally related to the organization. It will be more formal in larger organizations, especially those that are unionized. It is quite informal in small organizations.

Generally, an employee's manager is the person primarily involved in disciplining employees. HR specialists may become involved as advisers if they are asked to do so

EXHIBIT 16-1
Employee Misbehavior: May Require Disciplinary Action

Arson	Intimidation
Blackmail	Kickbacks
Bribery	Lying
Bullying	Misinformation
Cheating	Neglecting responsibility
Discrimination	Privacy violation
Dishonesty	Revenge
Disruptive behavior	Sabotage
Drug and substance abuse	Theft
Espionage	Threats
Fraud	Violence
Incivility	Withholding information

by the manager. Sometimes the HR manager serves as a second step in investigation and appeal of a disciplinary case. Or, when the union is involved, the HR manager may advise the operating manager on interpretation of the contract for a specific case.

Discipline is one of the most challenging areas in the HRM function. In dealing with difficult employees, HR managers must diagnose both internal and external environmental factors in discipline situations, prescribe and implement appropriate remedial actions, and evaluate the effectiveness of their decisions. Throughout this process, it is critical to recognize that employees have rights protected by federal and state laws. For example, as discussed in Chapter 3, an employee may not be disciplined or terminated in a manner that violates discrimination laws. Managers must also be aware of their state's position on employment-at-will. Some states allow employers to terminate employees for almost any reason that does not violate federal or state statutes, while others require just cause. The next section will discuss four categories of difficult employees as well as applicable legal considerations.

Categories of Difficult Employees

Employees whose behavior can be described as difficult can be classified into one of four categories:

1. Those whose quality or quantity of work is unsatisfactory, owing to lack of abilities, training, or motivation. (Al is an example.)
2. Those whose personal problems off the job begin to affect their productivity on the job. These problems can include alcoholism, drugs, or family relationships. (Susan is an example.)
3. Those who violate laws while on the job by such behavior as stealing from the organization or its employees or physical abuse of employees or property. (Joyce is an example.)
4. Those who consistently break company rules and do not respond to supervisory reactions. (Tom is an example.)

The difficulty of determining the causes of any human behavior pattern was noted in Chapter 2. It is especially difficult to assess the causes of undesired behavior, but Miner has devised a useful approach for analyzing deficient behavior; he provides a checklist of possible causes:[2]

- Problems of intelligence and job knowledge.
- Emotional problems.
- Motivational problems.
- Physical problems.
- Family problems.
- Problems caused by work groups.
- Problems originating in company policies.
- Problems stemming from society and its values.
- Problems from the work context (for example, economic forces) and the work itself.

Many of these causes can influence deficient behavior, which can result from behavior of the employee alone, behavior of the employer alone, or interaction of the employee and employer. Al's behavior (category 1), which is directly related to the work situation, could be caused by emotional, motivational, or organizational problems. If Susan is drinking (category 2) because of family problems, then the primary cause of her behavior is outside the control of the employer. Frequently, difficult behavior is caused by personal and employment conditions that feed one another. Joyce's behavior—theft—and other illegal activities (category 3) are normally dealt with by security departments and usually result in termination and possibly prosecution of the employee. Tom's behavior (category 4) is often caused by motivational, job, or emotional problems.

Category 1: Ineffective Employees

Employees whose performance is due to factors directly related to work are theoretically the easiest to work with and to adjust. Chapter 13 introduced a systematic approach for investigating discrepancies between performance and needs. This approach is applicable not only for training but also for coping with ineffective, poorly performing employees. Recall that managers must consider some key issues. For example, the employee is not performing well; the manager thinks there is a problem with training. There are three general questions a manager might use to analyze the problem:

1. *What is the discrepancy?* Why do I think there is a training problem? What is the difference between what is being done and what is supposed to be done? What is the event that causes me to say that things aren't right? Why am I dissatisfied?

2. *Is it important?* Why is the discrepancy important? What would happen if I left the discrepancy alone? Could doing something to resolve the discrepancy have any worthwhile result?

3. *Is it a deficiency in skills?* Could the employee do it if he or she really had to, or if it were a matter of life and death? Are the employee's present skills adequate for the desired performance?

If there is a deficiency in skills, then it must be corrected. On the other hand, if the problem does not have to do with skills, then it must be addressed in terms of removing obstacles, creating a more positive motivational climate, or bringing about some type of job change.

In summary, ineffective performance may be the result of various factors: skills, the job, or the motivational climate. Each of these factors must be carefully weighed in considering Al's declining sales described in the opening Career Challenge.

Category 2: Alcoholic and Substance-Abusing Employees

Prevalence and Cost

Substance abuse is believed to affect 12 percent of the workforce, costing organizations over $200 billion per year in lost productivity and related expenses.[3] Additionally, studies have indicated that substance abuse is one of the leading causes of recent increases in workplace violence.[4] Compared to employees who are not alcohol abusers, problem drinkers take two and one-half times more absences of eight days or more, and receive three times as much sick leave and accident benefits.[5] Studies have indicated that drug abusers are one-third less productive, have three and a half times more workplace accidents, and make five times as many workers' compensation claims as non–drug abusers.[6]

Alcohol Testing

Organizational alcohol abuse programs that include alcohol testing are increasing in popularity. About 75 percent of the full-time workforce does not consider a drug test an invasion of privacy. According to two surveys supported by the National Institute on Drug Abuse, about 28.4 percent of U.S. workplaces test employees for alcohol abuse; of these workplaces, 31.7 percent are required by federal law to conduct alcohol tests.[7] For example, the Omnibus Transportation Employee Testing Act of 1991[8] mandates alcohol and drug testing for safety-sensitive employees in the aviation, motor carrier, railroad, and mass transit industries. The Federal Highway Administration (FHWA) and Department of

HR Journal   *An Alternative to Workplace Drug Testing*

A number of HR professionals suggest that impairment testing is a better method to use than drug testing in the workplace. Also called fitness-for-duty or performance-based testing, impairment testing measures whether or not an employee is alert enough for work. From early tests that required participants to keep a cursor on track during a video game–like simulation, the industry has evolved toward a focus on evaluation through assessing eye movements. An employee looks into a dark viewpoint, then follows a light. The light mimes a sobriety test for probability cause.

The impairment testing of eye movements then analyzes a person's response in comparison to his or her normal baseline eye response, compiled from an average of three previous tests taken of the employee. Once the baseline is established and stored, employees might be asked to complete a test. In 90 seconds the employer would know if a person is fit to fly a plane, operate heavy equipment, fight a fire, or drive a school bus.

Impairment tests can catch employees who are impaired because of problems that a drug test can't identify: fatigue, sleep deprivation, stress, and alcohol use. The use of impairment tests are also less invasive than the typical drug test that involves processing urine samples.

Research on impairment testing shows that 82 percent of employers found impairment testing improved safety, 90 percent of employees accepted impairment testing, and 87 percent of employers found impairment testing superior to urine testing.

Unfortunately, to date most organizations have not heard of or used impairment testing. There is also a cost consideration. Purchasing eye movement test equipment could mean buying a $25,000 piece of equipment. However, consider the legal costs of having a performance impaired employee cause an accident. One accident and legal costs would certainly exceed $25,000.

Source: "Impairment Testing—Does It Work?" National Workrights Institute, pp. 1–6, www.workrights.org, accessed on July 28, 2005; Evelyn Beck (February 2001), "Is the Time Right for Impairment Testing?" *Workforce*, pp. 69–71.

Transportation (DOT) have issued rules for implementing testing programs pursuant to this statute.[9] Alcohol testing is considered a medical test under the Americans with Disabilities Act (ADA), thus precluding employers from giving alcohol tests in the selection process prior to making a conditional job offer.[10] However, the ADA does not preempt conflicting FHWA and DOT regulations requiring testing.

Drug Testing

Drug testing is conducted in over 65 percent of the largest workplaces and is used to screen applicants as well as employees who may be tested for cause, randomly, or following rehabilitation.[11] Over 53 million drug tests are conducted annually. About 90 percent of the drug tests use urine samples. Statistics released by SmithKline Beecham Corp., a leading drug testing company, suggest that organizations' drug testing programs may reduce employee drug use. Their results indicate that positive drug tests decreased from 18.1 percent in 1987 to only 5 percent of employees tested in 1997.[12]

The ADA does not include current illegal drug users in its definition of a "qualified individual with a disability" and does not consider tests for illegal drugs as medical tests, thus allowing employers to test both applicants and employees.[13] However, organizations must consider other federal as well as state laws that may regulate employee drug testing. For example, California's constitutional privacy protection has limited the use of random drug testing by California employers.[14] Employers could face negligence and defamation claims for false positive drug test results. Choosing reputable drug testing labs and releasing test results only to immediate supervisors and others with a legitimate need to know can help avoid these types of claims.[15] For public sector employees, the Fourth Amendment to the U.S. Constitution, which prohibits unreasonable searches and seizures, provides some additional privacy protection. In applying the Fourth Amendment to drug testing by government employers, the Supreme Court has generally held that drug testing may be conducted for reasonable cause (e.g., after accidents) and to ensure public safety.[16]

An alternative to drug testing is called **impairment testing.** The HR Journal on the opposite page introduces this form of testing alternative.

Employee Assistance Programs (EAPs)

Employee assistance programs began appearing in the United States around 1950, when substance abuse was first addressed as a major problem in organizations. Under these programs, "constructive confrontation" became the standard procedure.[17] The employee was given an ultimatum: correct the problem or leave.

Today, EAPs are available to over half of the U.S. workforce and take a broader, more comprehensive approach.[18] The new philosophy is that the firm has no right to interfere with the private lives of its workers, but it does have a right to impose standards of behavior and performance at work. EAPs are not confined to substance abuse and can include coverage for emotional problems, financial difficulties, AIDS, elder care, and other problems that may impair performances.[19] Most EAPs share the following characteristics:

• Employees needing assistance are identified and referred to the program.
• The employee is introduced into the program, and his or her problem is evaluated. The employee receives counseling and may be given a referral for treatment.
• Employees receive professional diagnosis and treatment. These are usually provided by outside agencies.

Although the effectiveness of EAPs is still debated, organizations have had favorable results. For example, Boeing reported a savings of $2 million in decreased employee medical claims and a 29 percent reduction in absenteeism, while Southern Pacific Railroad reported a 71 percent decrease in injuries.[20] Four years after implementing an EAP, McDonnell Douglas reported a $6 million savings.[21]

At most organizations with EAPs, managers are trained to follow specific procedures when they become aware that an employee's performance is declining. Managers should serve only to identify the performance or behavioral decline and should not diagnose problems or provide rehabilitative counseling. Referring employees to EAPs and indicating that the referral is based upon suspicions of alcoholism may risk "perceived disability" claims under the ADA.[22]

Large and small employers have found positive benefits created by having EAPs. The HR Journal on the next page points out the popularity of EAPs.

Category 3: Participants in Theft, Fraud, and Other Illegal Acts

Employers often have to deal with employees who engage in various illegal acts including employee theft, misuse of company facilities or property, disclosure of trade secrets, embezzlement, sabotage of products, or use of company telephones and credit cards for personal use. A survey of security directors at Fortune 1000 companies identified employee theft as the greatest security threat to organizations today.[23] It has been estimated that employee theft costs organizations over $600 billion annually.[24]

The HR Journal on page 526 encourages companies to be proactive when facing theft and fraud.

Human resource managers utilize discipline, termination, as well as rehabilitation to address employee dishonesty problems. Increasingly, proactive approaches emphasizing problem recognition and conflict confrontation have been adopted.[25] Responsibility for

HR Journal   *EAPs*

Do you know where employees turn when they have legal, financial, mental health, or other personal problems? If they share their problems with an untrained co-worker or a friend or a bartender, they probably don't have access to an employee assistance program (EAP), a confidential counseling and referral service provided as an employee benefit by many employers. And their employer's agent or broker probably hasn't done a good job of communicating how this benefit supports productivity, wellness, and managerial efficiency as well as mental health and, in addition, has become affordable to employers of all sizes.

EAPs have been around for decades and have slowly become an employee benefits staple. According to the 2004 Mercer National Survey of Employer-Sponsored Health Plans, about 74 percent of large employers provide EAP benefits to employees, up from 71 percent the previous year.

Some employers, about 18 percent, contract the services from the same vendors that administer mental health and substance abuse services, but most contract with a separate EAP vendor. Typical EAP programs, about 85 percent, provide an average of six or more short-term, face-to-face counseling sessions. About 15 percent provide telephone-only counseling, the survey says.

Small employers, however, are less likely to provide EAPs, industry sources say; and when they do, they provide fewer counseling sessions and less integration with other benefits. However, EAP providers, most of whom contract directly with health plans or other employee benefit insurers, are working hard to justify their value to small and medium-sized employers and provide more affordable options.

For example, In May (2005), Assurant Employee Benefits in Kansas City, Missouri, announced a new set of EAP services designed to meet the needs and budgets of small employers. The new plans are provided by New Directions Behavioral Health, in Overland Park, Kansas—Assurant's own corporate EAP provider—and can be packaged with any of the insurer's group life or disability programs. The EAP services range in cost from about 45 cents per employee per month for phone assessment and referral only to about $2.50 per employee per month for a traditional EAP with six counseling sessions and training and support services to management as well as employee counseling.

"We have been providing EAP services packaged with life and disability insurance and other benefits since 1991," explains Melonie Jones, second vice president of life and disability marketing. "But, generally, we have

been providing a high level of benefit that has been out of the price range for many smaller employers."

However, a growing recognition of the significant impact EAPs can have on productivity, absenteeism, and job performance has spurred changes designed to make the services available to bigger market segments, she says.

The least expensive of the new set of services, EssentialAssist, allows employers to purchase a toll-free, 24-hour-a-day telephone assessment and referral service supported by Internet-based resources with or without up to six face-to-face private counseling sessions.

The insurer also offers a second tier of services, EssentialAssist Plus, which includes the telephone service, up to six counseling sessions, and services for management including quarterly utilization reports and training services.

Stacey Kreps, New Directions's director of communications, says the basic level of service with telephone-only assessment and referral is not just a token benefit with little practical value. While private counseling sessions provide employees with opportunities to make appointments with off-site counselors and extended conversations about their problems, telephone counseling can provide immediate access to assistance that can accelerate an employee's search for help.

"Whenever employees face some sort of personal or family problem, their pursuit of advice or resources is going to take a toll on their job attention and productivity," she explains. "Any access to assessment and referral services can only reduce their time spent on the next step in their search for assistance and improve productivity."

Web-based resources can also provide timely and useful answers to referral questions about legal and financial issues and work-life needs such as child care and elder care, she adds.

EAP providers also claim to be able to document quantitative return on investment (ROI) for EAP services. For example, Kreps says New Directions is completing a study which indicates that access to EAP services can help reduce pharmacy costs for mental health and other treatments payable under health plans. Other recent EAP research supports the argument that the benefits can reduce employer costs for a wide range of health and productivity issues—key sales points for agents and brokers, providers say.

In January (2005) Managed Health Network, a division of HealthNet, Inc., in Port Richmond, California, announced the results of an ROI study leading to a way to measure EAP value. Deidre Hiatt, Ph.D., vice president of quality management at MHN and co-author of the study, says, "Decisions on purchasing EAP services

HR Journal   *EAPs (concluded)*

have traditionally been made by analyzing satisfaction and utilization data, but increasingly EAP programs are being asked to show financial return on investment. We cannot do this."

The study examined treatment outcome data on more than 10,000 employees with depression to determine the likely value associated with effective treatment through an EAP. Hiatt says the provider chose depression because it is the most common mental health problem in the workplace with the greatest overall impact on job performance. She says studies indicate that one of every 20 employees shows symptoms of depression and predict that by 2020, the disorder will be the second most prevalent cause of disability.

"Our outcome research showed that two-thirds of employees (who contacted the EAP) reported at least moderate symptoms of depression at the time they accessed the service, and approximately half of the treated employees showed no symptoms after treatment," she says. MHN measured the impact of this treatment result with earlier research on lost time associated with depression to generate an "ROI calculator" employers can use to measure the impact of the EAP on their own depression problem.

Steve Kessler, MHN director of business development, suggests that agents and brokers use this sort of research to communicate to managers the job-related value of EAPs as well as the personal value. "The ROI calculator helps employers make the leap from intuitive value to truly quantitative value, making is much easier for benefits vice presidents and chief financial officers to see the impact of the EAP program," he says.

"EAPs should really be Employer Assistance Programs or Workplace Assistance Programs," says Edward Trieber, Ph.D., managing director of Harris Rothenberg, Inc., a New York–based EAP provider and training company. "While employees benefit from EAP counseling and referral, it is the employer and the workplace that benefits most from improved productivity and a better work/life balance."

Source: Adapted from Len Strazewski (July 2005), "Investing in EAPs–Employee Assistance Programs," *Rough Notes*, pp. 52–53; and Donald Smeltzer (January 2005), "More Bang for Your EAP Buck," *Employee Benefit Plan Review*, pp. 14–15.

crime prevention is also given to human resource departments. A variety of tools such as security programs and preemployment screening mechanisms are used to prevent employee theft and other illegal acts. Most companies engage in at least minimal security operations such as identification or "badge" systems, special safeguards for or destruction of sensitive documents, and escort services for visitors. Exhibit 16-2 provides a list of additional security steps to minimize employee theft.

EXHIBIT 16-2
Ways to Minimize Theft by Employees

1. Normal good housekeeping practices—no piles of rubbish or rejects or boxes, no unused machines with tarpaulins on them, and no unlocked, empty drawers—will help ensure that there are no places where stolen goods can be hidden. The first act of the thief is to divert merchandise from the normal traffic flow.

2. Paperwork must be carefully examined and checked at all stages so invoices cannot be stolen or altered.

3. Employees' cars should not be parked close to their places of work. There should be no usable cover between the plant doors and the cars.

4. Do not allow employees to make sales to themselves, their friends, or their family members.

5. Whether the plant or office is open or closed at night, bright lights should blaze all around the perimeter, so no one can enter or leave without being seen.

6. There should be adequate measures to control issuance of keys. There have been cases where a manager or supervisor would come back at night for a tryst with a girlfriend or a boyfriend and give the friend an armload of merchandise to take home. Key control is very important.

7. As far as possible, everyone entering or leaving should have an identification card.

8. Unused doors should be kept locked. If only two must be open to handle the normal flow of traffic, the rest should include alarms.

9. Everything of value that thieves could possibly remove, not just obvious items, must be safeguarded.

HR Journal   *The Deep Bite of Theft and Fraud*

Owners and managers want to believe that their employees are honest, hard-working, and have only the company's best interests at heart. And most employees do fit that description. There are some, however, who feel that they are entitled to an occasional box of pens or unlimited copies run off from the company machine. These sorts of unintentional perks may go unnoticed by management, but they do add up. And the reality is that few companies recognized the deep bite that employee theft—big or small—can take out of a company's profit margin. That is, until a major incident makes headlines or cuts into their own bottom line.

Take a nationally known beverage retailer, for example. This Pacific Northwest business found success with premium coffee and expanded rapidly—so rapidly that it perhaps outgrew its internal controls. Managers no doubt kept an eye on employees to make sure they did not pass out free beverages to their friends. But despite these internal controls, in 2001 an employee created a fictitious consulting firm, submitted invoices to the beverage retailer, and arranged for the retailer to send payments to a special post office box. In less than a year, this employee embezzled $3.7 million, using the money to buy a collection of automobiles, motorcycles, a yacht, real estate, three grand pianos, and a variety of other luxury goods.

That same year, a leading boat manufacturer filed suit against it former CFO, accusing him of embezzling $14 million in company funds over 16 years to finance his own stock purchases, run three businesses, and pay personal credit card expenses. In another case, an employee of a subsidiary of a well-known computer company falsely billed the company for more than $500,000.

Fast forward to 2005. A national office supply retailer begins the year by firing four employees who are believed to have fabricated documentation for $3.3 million in invoices to the company. This fraud was only uncovered when a vendor complained that kickbacks were being demanded and bills were being falsified.

Are these isolated incidents? Not according to the Association of Certified Fraud Examiners (ACFE). In their "2004 Report to the Nation on Occupational Fraud and Abuse," the ACFE reported that the typical U.S. company loses 6 percent of its annual revenues to employee fraud. Nationally, that translates to about $660 billion in corporate losses per year.

The report notes that fraud can happen at any level of a company, from the mailroom employee to the account executive to the senior executive. While fraud is more frequent at lower levels, the damage is usually more substantial when high-level executives are involved. The AOFE found that the median loss when executives are involved ($900,000) was more than six times the median loss caused by managers ($140,000) and more than 14 times that involving low-level employees ($62,000).

Despite the examples cited at the beginning of this article. Losses are not limited to major corporations. Small businesses are often the hardest hit by employee fraud. Almost half of the fraud cases studied by the ACFE involved small businesses, with the median loss pegged at almost $100,000. That is a difficult amount for any company to lose, let alone a small business with limited resources.

The AOFE's report also looked at recovery of losses and found disheartening news. The median recovery in all cases was only about 20 percent of the loss amount and in almost 40 percent of the cases, nothing was recovered at all. The report's conclusion: "The most cost-effective way to deal with fraud is to prevent it. Once fraud occurs, it is expensive and time-consuming to try to recover what was stolen, and often those efforts prove futile."

Experts say that any company can fall victim to employee fraud. But companies are not helpless. There are five red flags that signal an increased opportunity for fraud. Companies should watch for these situations and take extra precautions.

Fast growth

Mergers

Outside vendors

High-value inventory

Expense accounts

The aforementioned red flags tell a company when to be concerned. At the same time, they point to the solution because they all share the same issue: lack of control across the span of a company's assets and activities. Strong internal controls, explicitly implemented and rigidly adhered to, provide a company with the best defense against employee fraud.

Those internal controls should address payroll falsification (phantom employees), collections by outside employees, fraudulent refunds, kickbacks, cash-register theft, bank account reconciliation, and fictitious vendors.

HR Journal — *The Deep Bite of Theft and Fraud (concluded)*

There are a wide variety of effective controls, but a common theme is to have a separation of duties whenever employees handle money. For instance, if one employee reviews invoices and authorizes payment, then someone else should write and send the check, and yet another employee should reconcile the bank statements.

In addition to a separation of duties, redundancy is also a powerful tool. This means having more than one person looking at the same transaction. For example, checks should be co-signed rather than authorized by only one person, and multiple employees should have responsibility for overseeing specific bank accounts. This prevents one employee from "lapping" or moving funds from account to account ahead of any audit so that no irregularities are detected.

Centralized processes also allow tighter control. When procurement is centralized, employees in satellite offices are not able to buy more than needed and then resell or return items for cash. When inventory is centralized, employees know that the company's assets are tracked and monitored.

Internal controls should also be used to detect fictitious vendors. In addition, processes should be in place to verify that vendors exist, that they are performing their duties for the company, and that payment is in line with the services provided.

While internal controls are vital, they are not the only solution to detecting and discouraging employee fraud. In fact, today more fraud is found by accident than through the strength of internal controls. However, neither internal controls nor accidents top the list of how fraud is detected. The ACFE found that almost 40 percent of fraud is discovered through company tips. The majority of the tips come from employees, but customers, vendors, and anonymous callers are also common sources.

Federal policymakers believe that employee fraud tips have such value that they incorporated them into the Sarbanes-Oxley Act. As a result, publicly held companies must now create a mechanism for receiving information about questionable accounting and auditing matters.

Encouraging tips requires that companies create a channel for people to use, establish trust and rapport with employees or others, and have a responsive, investigative capability to follow up on tips. A number of companies have established ethics hotline phone numbers. This confidential service allows employees to report corporate financial irregularities, as well as embezzlement, falsification of contracts, and other fraud. Employees who might be reluctant to report what they see or hear for fear of retaliation can use this type of service in an anonymous fashion.

Another mechanism for controlling employee fraud is to institute careful hiring practices, although this approach is less effective than strong internal controls or a forum for tips. Unicru, a company that specializes in helping other companies recruit and hire employees, has found that 70 percent of "internal shrinkage," or theft by employees, is carried out by people who are on the job for less than 30 days. Eliminating job candidates who have a track record of holding prior jobs for fewer than 90 days is one way to limit exposure to shrinkage.

Checking job applicants for criminal backgrounds makes good business sense. However, the Association of Certified Fraud Examiners found that only 12 percent of the fraud-committing employees had a previous conviction. In addition, employment screening processes may vary from country to country, which can be challenging for large multinational firms. That means weeding out bad apples is important but not nearly as important as setting up internal systems to discourage fraud before it begins.

Source: Adapted from Cary Meiners (April 2005), "Detecting and Eliminating the Unintentional Perk," *Risk Management,* pp. 50–53; and "Embezzlement/Employee Theft" (February 2005), www.mw3c.org.

As discussed in Chapter 8, the Employee Polygraph Protection Act of 1988[26] prohibits the use of polygraph tests to gauge the honesty of current and prospective employees in most situations. Since this act was passed, many organizations have begun using written "integrity tests" to prescreen applicants for honesty.[27] Results of research examining the validity of integrity tests indicate that they predict dysfunctional employee behaviors including theft moderately well.[28] Moreover, studies suggest that integrity tests do not have an adverse impact on groups protected by EEO laws.[29]

HR Journal *When Abuse Affects Performance*

The problem of alcoholism among executive employees (managers) has by no means disappeared. What does seem to be on the decline, however, is companies' ability to ignore the problem. Indeed, the awareness that alcoholism is a disease has been codified in law. The Americans with Disabilities Act of 1991 (ADA) officially recognized alcoholism as a disability and stipulates that individuals may not be fired because they are alcoholic. It sounds promising, but will ADA really make much change in how companies deal with alcohol problems? Alcoholism causes over 500 million lost workdays each year.

"It should help," says Harold Swift, former president of the Minnesota-based Hazelden Foundation, a nationally known treatment organization. Jim Cline, a psychologist and consultant with the Employee Advisory Resources (EAR) division at Ceridian Corporation, adds that companies today generally are more enlightened on the subject of chemical abuse but many have a long way to go. "I have heard employers say things like, 'We've got a way to deal with troubled employees here—we get rid of them.'" ADA may offer some protection against such attitudes, he continues. "But we all know reality is different," he says, because discrimination can take very subtle forms.

Perhaps the most difficult aspect of dealing with employees' substance abuse is the first step: acknowledging that it exists. One CFO from a company in Cleveland, after consulting with the company's attorney, refused to talk even when promised anonymity.

"They say it's lonely at the top, and there is some truth to that," says Swift. "Executives would be very reluctant to admit they need help in today's environment," he adds, noting that co-workers often direct much anger and moralizing at them. Executives also worry about future job prospects if they admit they need treatment. But companies, too, are reluctant to raise the issue, fearing their reputations will be tarnished if it's known that any executive is recovering from addiction to alcohol or drugs.

One person who has helped many corporations deal with this difficult issue is Ken Majcen, president of Majcen & Associates, which is based in Cleveland but has set up employee and executive assistance programs (EAPs) nationwide. Majcen himself once lost a job as a sales representative because of his alcoholism, and he became a chemical dependency counselor.

Before he will get involved in a particular case, he insists that the company document specific instances when an individual's job performance has been impaired because of alcohol, illegal drugs, or stress. It's not enough, in other words, for the person to be a substance abuser. The abuse must be affecting work performance. "What we want to do is talk about facts and their consequences," Majcen says. "It eliminates the potential of discriminating against an individual."

When performance problems are identified, Majcen will meet with other co-workers, friends, and family (though he usually avoids involving children) to talk about the issues. If he feels there is a dependency problem, he arranges an "intervention": confronting the executive about his or her problem, usually with co-workers, family, and friends present to reinforce the message. Usually the individual is then taken directly to a treatment center. Majcen follows up with case management for as long as a year, assisting the company in drafting a return-to-work agreement. Many such agreements include random drug testing or mandatory attendance at AA meetings.

Does it work? Majcen's success rate is about 60 percent. "To bat .600 is pretty good," he says. "You're going to lose some people. A lot of people would rather die from substance abuse than live without it."

What can be done by a co-worker who spots chemical abuse in an executive? When Cline at Ceridian is approached in such a case, he advises co-workers to approach the person one-to-one, perhaps at lunch. He even suggests to some that they threaten to quit unless the executive seeks help. But he adds, "It's a very difficult thing to do anything about, especially when they're dealing with the kind of executive who might blow up unexpectedly." If all else fails, he says, he will resort to an intervention.

Source: "How Does Substance Abuse Impact the Workplace?" U.S. Department of Labor, www.dol.gov/elaws/asp/drugfree/benefits.htm, accessed on July 26, 2005; Mark Engebretson (January–February 1993), "When to Say When," *Business Ethics*, p. 15. This article (slightly adapted) is reprinted with permission from *Business Ethics Magazine,* 52 S. 10th Street, Suite 110, Minneapolis, MN 55403-2001, 1-800-769-9852 (612-962-4700 in Minnesota).

Category 4: Rule Violators

Difficult employees in the fourth category consistently violate company rules, such as those prohibiting sleeping on the job, having weapons at work, fighting at work, coming in late, or abusing the supervisor. A particularly difficult issue is that of workplace violence. According to research conducted by the Bureau of Labor Statistics, homicide is one of the leading causes of death of U.S. employees.[30] Other research has indicated that each year about 2 million employees are physically attacked, more than 6 million receive threats, and 16 million are the target of some form of harassment.[31] Over an 18-month period, the U.S. Post Office recorded 500 cases of violence by employees toward supervisors and 200 cases of violence by supervisors toward employees. Chapter 17 will discuss in detail workplace violence.

The Post Office was determined to improve employees' safety and developed a six-strategy program to prevent violence:

1. *Selection* The goal of the Postal Service is to hire selectively, ensuring that it gets the right people in the jobs in the first place. Its prescreening process includes administering competency tests and contracting with an outside firm to do thorough background checks.

2. *Security* "To protect people from homicide and other violence, a certain amount of security is necessary," says Ann Wright, manager for safety and health, who managed the program until the agency brought in a full-time coordinator. What that amount is varies from location to location. The Postal Service has 47,000 facilities that range from one-person post offices to 24-hour plants employing 4,000 people. Some facilities rely on awareness programs and training on such issues as how to report incidents. Others employ security guards, set up surveillance cameras on the premises, or require access badges. Management at each location assesses the measures that should be taken with the Postal Inspection Service—the law-enforcement arm of the Postal Service.

3. *Policy* "We're trying to promote a clean, direct, absolute, and well-known policy related to violence," Wright says. That includes a prohibition on any kind of weapon on Postal Service property, including parking lots; a no-tolerance philosophy toward threats of any kind; and a protocol to intervene early. "There's no minor incident of violence," says Wright. "We want to take action even if there's just pushing, yelling, or cussing on the floor so that we can preclude those incidents from escalating into something bigger." For this reason, the policy also includes reporting all incidents.

4. *Climate* A healthy workplace is a safe workplace, so the Postal Service has an intense initiative to improve the agency's environment. It's putting managers and supervisors through a series of training sessions that deal with such issues as empowerment of employees, resolution of conflicts, and positive reinforcement. It's also working with its unions to improve the grievance process. Some post offices are testing intervention teams, consisting of cross-functional groups of employees and managers, that intervene when their facility's climate isn't conducive to a good work environment. And the agency has instituted an opinion survey that measures employees' satisfaction and promotes better interaction between managers and employees.

5. *Employee support* The Postal Service has beefed up its employee assistance program (EAP) and conducts training with supervisors and managers on how best to use the EAP and how to educate employees on how to use it. The agency also has implemented an orientation program for all the employees, explaining its EAP. And in addition to the EAP, the Postal Service has installed a 24-hour, toll-free hotline that employees can call to report threats or concerns. "We are trying to catch problems that individuals might have early enough so that we can deal with them before they get to the point at which somebody loses control," Wright says. "We're also trying to make the point with our managers and supervisors that firing people doesn't necessarily solve the problem.

Quite a few of our most violent incidents have been by terminated employees who come back and shoot people. So that's part of the support system that we're trying to build."

6. *Separation* Because termination does become necessary at times, the agency currently is creating policies and procedures for terminating employees in the most effective way. It's also evaluating methods for assessing whether people being dismissed may be dangerous. Because this is a recent initiative, no specific strategies have been developed yet.

Certainly violence in the workplace is a problem, but there is a lot of confusion among researchers and others attempting to measure it and develop corrective steps. Some of the confusion is caused by factors such as the following:

- Not all violence is reported by the victims. The Department of Justice found that more than 50 percent of employees who were victimized did not report the incident.

- Statistics do not usually include off-duty employees or nonemployees (customers) who are victimized in a work setting (such as at a quick-stop grocery store). For example, the homicide of a customer shot during a store robbery is not counted.

- In about 90 percent of homicides and 68 percent of assaults in the workplace, customers or strangers are the perpetrators. This is especially important because improved counseling programs or selection methods may improve workplace safety, but these steps will not eliminate violence.

- Identifying violence-prone people may be beyond the skill of even the best trained managers.

Organizations are now beginning to implement a variety of programs designed to combat increased occurrences of workplace violence. Specifically, human resource departments are developing zero-tolerance policies, creating crisis management teams, designing preselection screening tools, and providing employee assistance programs.[32] Exhibit 16-3

EXHIBIT 16-3
Warning Signs of Employee Violence

Source: Mark Braverman, Dennis L. Johnson, John G. Kurutz, and John B. Kiehlbauch (February 1995), "Scenario for Supervisors," *HRMagazine,* pp. 63–67.

1. Has difficulty accepting authority/criticism.
2. Holds grudges—especially against supervisors.
3. Sabotages company property and/or equipment.
4. Expresses desire to harass co-workers or management.
5. Unwanted romantic interest/sexual harassment.
6. Physical/verbal intimidation (e.g., stalking, phone calls).
7. Progressive misconduct.
8. Argumentative/uncooperative.
9. History of interpersonal conflict.
10. Has been fired or laid off, or perceives he or she soon will be.
11. Unstable/dysfunctional family.
12. Decreased social connectedness/support.
13. Extremist opinions and attitudes (e.g., religious, political).
14. Intrigued by previous workplace violence incidents.
15. Needed help in past but did not receive it.
16. Exhibits paranoid behavior and/or depression.
17. Has difficulty controlling temper.
18. Sense of entitlement.
19. Emotionally injured.
20. Has a preoccupation with weapons or brings weapon(s) to work.
21. Substance abuse.
22. Obsession with a particular person.

provides a list of warning signs of violence that have been used by crisis management teams to assess potential threats.

Failing to take reasonable steps to prevent violence in the workplace can create legal liability for companies. Preventable workplace violence could result in Occupational Safety and Health Act (OSHA) violations or state workers' compensation claims. Some states also recognize "negligent hiring and retention" causes of action. For example, in New York, employers may be liable for employees' violent acts if the employer knew or should have known about employees' violent or harmful tendencies.[33] Companies may face a legal dilemma when an employee with a psychiatric disorder poses a risk of violence; they must comply with the ADA while also maintaining a safe workplace. Under the ADA, an employer cannot discriminate against such employees unless they pose a "direct threat" to someone's health or safety and the problem cannot be solved with a reasonable accommodation. However, negligence claims may arise when organizations fail to dismiss employees because the actual or threatened misconduct does not amount to a direct threat.[34]

The Discipline Process

Exhibit 16-4 is a model of the discipline process. The employer establishes goals and rules and communicates them to employees. Employees' behavior is then assessed, and modification may be found desirable. This process is an attempt to prevent difficulties and is positive in nature. It is designed to help employees succeed.

The first element in the process is the establishment of rules for work and behavior. Work goals and standards were discussed as part of performance evaluation (Chapter 9). Through whatever method is used (time and motion study, examination of past performance or performance by others, management by objectives), a set of minimally acceptable work goals is established. Behavior rules cover many facets of on-the-job behavior. They can be categorized as concerning behavior that is directly or indirectly related to productivity. Both types are often negatively described as prohibited behavior. Exhibit 16-5 lists some examples of rules for employees' behavior.

The second important element in the disciplinary process is the *communication* of the rules to all employees. Unless employees are aware of the rules, they can hardly be expected to follow them. Closely related to this element are employees' willingness to accept the rules, and the enforceability of the rules. If employees or their representatives participate in the formation of the rules, their cooperation is more likely. Employees must be convinced that the rule is fair and related to effectiveness on the job.

It is useful for management to seek employees' advice on periodic revision of rules. The objective is to reduce the number of rules to the minimum and enforce those that are

EXHIBIT 16-4   **Elements in a Disciplinary System**

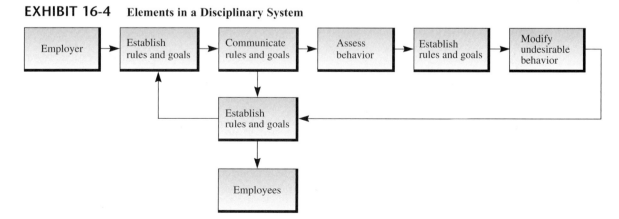

EXHIBIT 16-5
Examples of Rules for Employees' Behavior

I. Rules directly related to productivity
   A. Time
      1. Starting and late times
      2. Quitting time
      3. Maximum break and lunch times
      4. Maximum absenteeism
   B. Prohibited behavior
      1. No sleeping on the job
      2. No leaving workplace without permission
      3. No drinking on the job
      4. No drug taking on the job
      5. Limited nonemployer activities during work hours
   C. Insubordination
      1. Penalties for refusal to obey supervisors
      2. Rules against slowdowns and sit-downs
   D. Illegal behavior
      1. Theft
      2. Falsification
   E. Safety
      1. No smoking
      2. Safety regulations
      3. Sanitation requirements
      4. No fighting
      5. No dangerous weapons

II. Rules indirectly related to productivity
   A. Prevention of moonlighting
   B. Prohibition of gambling
   C. Prohibition of selling or soliciting at work
   D. Regulations for clothing and uniform
   E. Rules about fraternization with other employees at work or off the job

important. Customs and conditions change. Rules, like laws, need regular updating to achieve the respect and acceptance necessary for order in the workplace.

The third element of the disciplinary process is a mechanism for assessment. In most organizations, performance evaluation is the mechanism for assessing deficiencies in behavior at work. Behavior that involves breaking rules usually comes to the attention of management when it is observed or when difficulties arise and investigation reveals certain behavior as the cause.

Finally, the disciplinary process concludes with a system of *administering punishment* or *motivating change.* This varies from supervisory administration of discipline to formal systems somewhat like courts or grievance procedures.

Approaches to Discipline

Discipline for each of the categories of behavior just discussed can be applied in various ways. A negative approach is to emphasize the punitive effects on undesirable behavior. A more positive approach emphasizes what can be done to prevent the undesirable behavior from recurring.

The Hot Stove Rule

One view of discipline is referred to as the **hot stove rule.**[35] This approach to discipline is discussed in terms of what happens when a person touches a hot stove. The consequences are:

1. *Warning system* Before any behavior has occurred, a good manager has communicated what the consequences of the undesirable behavior are.

2. *Immediate burn* If discipline is required, it must occur immediately after the undesirable act is observed. The person must see the connection between the act and the discipline.

3. *Consistency* There are no favorites—stoves burn everyone alike. Any employee who performs the same undesirable act will be disciplined similarly.

4. *Impersonality* Disciplinary action is not pointed toward a person; it is meant to eliminate undesirable behaviors.

As noted, the hot stove rule assumes that the discipline applied will be impersonal. However, a serious question arises: whether every employee is equal. Is a newly hired employee with only a few weeks on the job and unfamiliar with company rules and programs the same as an employee with 20 years of job tenure? People, situations, and undesirable behaviors differ, and the hot stove rule, if followed to the letter, fails to recognize individual and situational differences.

Progressive Discipline

The **progressive pattern of discipline** is an approach in which a sequence of penalties is administered, each one slightly more severe than the previous one. In other words, the goal is to build a discipline program that progresses from less severe to more severe punishment. The objective of any progressive discipline program is to create and maintain a productive, responsive workforce.[36]

One example of a progressive discipline approach applied to unexcused absences is the program used at Hudson Manufacturing. The progressive steps are outlined in Exhibit 16-6. Hudson's progressive approach becomes especially harsh after three unexcused absences. It is important in any disciplinary system to formally record what the policy is and when and what action was taken. The Hudson approach does this. The courts are especially sensitive to the quality of records kept by management in using a progressive discipline approach. The following steps have been recommended to document progressive disciplinary actions and managers' good faith attempts to rehabilitate employees:

1. Identify the problem and explain how the employee's behavior detrimentally affected the organization.

EXHIBIT 16-6
Hudson Manufacturing's Progressive Discipline for Unexcused Absences

An unexcused absence is defined in the labor–management agreement Sec. 7, paragraph 12, pp. 9–181 as any absence not approved by the immediate manager of the employee. Hudson permits absence for personal illness, jury duty, vacation, and death in the family according to Sec. 7, paragraph 15, pp. 9–184 specifications. In each case the supervisor must be consulted. Other absences must be approved before they occur. Failure to comply with the unexcused absence guidelines will be subject to the following:

- First violation will result in an oral warning within 48 hours of return to work and a written record of the act being placed in the employee's file.
- Second violation will result in a written warning being placed in the employee's file within 48 hours of return to work.
- Third violation will result in a two-week layoff without pay and a statement of the layoff being placed in the employee's file.
- Fourth violation will result in a two-week layoff without pay and a statement of the layoff being placed in the employee's file.
- Fifth violation will result in the immediate and permanent dismissal of the employee.
- The record of unexcused absence will begin anew after three years. All unexcused absences on the record will be eliminated and a new file will begin every three years.

As suggested, it is important to document everything. Make sure that dates, times, participants in discussions, and process steps are documented. Every incident, communication, and application of discipline must be documented and the employee should be notified of exactly what has been documented. The employer must document, document, document. Too much documentation is much better than skimpy or no documentation.

2. Provide a clear warning and explain the consequences of failing to make the necessary behavioral changes.

3. Document progressive disciplinary actions taken to prove the employee's failure to make behavioral changes.

4. Demonstrate that disciplinary actions were consistently applied to others under similar circumstances.[37]

Positive Discipline

There are at least two basic problems with hot stove rules and progressive discipline: they focus on past behavior, and there is also a possibility that employees who are disciplined in a punitive way will not build commitment into their jobs or feel better about the job or the company. In contrast to those punitive approaches, there is another approach: **positive discipline.** Advocates of the positive approach view it as future-oriented, as working with employees to solve problems so that problems do not occur again.

General Electric (GE) Meter Business Department in Somersworth, New Hampshire, uses a positive approach to discipline.[38] In General Electric's system, there are written reminders about behaviors and no warnings. A "decision-making leave" is the final disciplinary step, instead of suspension or termination. If the employee, after the leave, fails to commit to the rules and policies of the firm, he or she is then discharged.

A cross section of supervisors and line managers implemented GE's positive discipline. The team developed a 12-phase communication program that included meetings, slide and tape presentations, brochures, and training to explain the program and its features to employees. In the first two years of the program, the number of formal disciplinary steps taken was significantly reduced compared with the previous period, when punitive discipline was used. In the second year of the program, 3,295 counseling sessions were conducted by supervisors to discuss a specific need for improvement and to gain the employees' agreement to make necessary corrections. The effectiveness of these meetings is demonstrated by the fact that only 65 oral reminders were issued. Seven employees were placed on decision-making leave; all seven returned without any need to discharge them.

Some of the employees' comments on GE's positive discipline program are:

- "I think whenever a company will treat us like adults, as individuals, it's a good thing."
- "It certainly is an improvement. . . . Now when you do something wrong . . . they talk with you rather than talk down to you. You feel like an adult."
- "The decision-making leave with pay makes you feel guilty. I'd feel like a heel!"

In a survey regarding the effectiveness of positive discipline programs, human resource managers provided favorable reviews.[39] Participants indicated that positive discipline was fairly successful in obtaining either behavioral compliance or voluntary separation. They also reported that providing paid decision-making leave was ineffective in dealing with poor attendance problems; programs were modified to provide unpaid leave in those situations.

The positive discipline approach recognizes that people make mistakes. It deemphasizes punitive action by management; yet it still uses the most punishing consequence of all, being discharged.

The Disciplinary Interview: A Constructive Approach

As previously mentioned, managers in some cases must tell an employee in clear terms that his or her behavior or job performance is below par. Suppose that this is accomplished through a discussion of poor performance, which is in essence a disciplinary interview.[40]

Several guidelines can help the manager accomplish a constructive discussion with the ineffective performer.

1. Root out the causes. The manager needs to determine which problems are playing a role in the poor performance. This can be done by listening to the employee and to his or her co-workers and by observation of the employee on the job.
2. Analyze the reasons for poor performance. Examine such factors as
   a. Lack of skill and training to do the job.
   b. Low effort.
   c. Situational circumstances beyond the employee's control.
3. Prepare for the disciplinary interview. After analyzing possible causes and reasons for poor performance, prepare for the interview. Check the employee's previous record and talk to previous supervisors about the employee.
4. Conduct the interview with care and professionalism.
   a. Keep it private—public criticism is too stark and often negative.
   b. Criticize selectively—emphasize job-related causes. Tell the employee what you think and try to avoid being aggressive. Stay calm and be polite at all times.
   c. Let the employee speak—be a good listener; don't rush the meeting. Allow the employee to give his or her side of the story. A good rule is to show you are listening by asking questions that indicate that you are receiving the message being delivered.
   d. Take one point at a time—don't confuse points. Focus on one problem at a time.
   e. Attack the problem and not the person—in focusing on each point, remember to attack the act and not the self-concept.
5. Issuing the discipline. Don't make a joke of having to discipline the employee. There really is nothing funny about being disciplined for poor performance or inappropriate behavior. Prescribe the disciplinary steps to be taken in specific terms and with a specific timetable. Do not end the disciplinary interview until you are certain that the employee understands the discipline and what is expected. Also, assure the employee that his or her future performance will be judged without considering past problems, such as ineffective performance.
6. Don't expect to win a popularity contest. A person who administers discipline in an equitable and firm manner will not win popularity contests. However, this person will be respected, and a manager who is respected is invaluable to an organization. The disciplinary interview is a serious part of the management job that unfortunately must be conducted regularly.

These few guidelines are designed to correct a problem or modify ineffective behaviors and are not intended to embarrass or publicly ridicule an employee. A constructive disciplinary interview can play an instrumental role in converting an ineffective performer into a productive member of the organization.

Legal Challenges to Discipline and Termination

As previously discussed, termination is the ultimate step for employers utilizing the hot stove rule, progressive discipline, or positive discipline. Each year, U.S. employers in the private sector fire about 3 million employees for noneconomic reasons.[41] Termination has many costs, both direct and indirect. One of the greatest costs is incurred through legal challenges. Research has indicated that the average jury award for wrongful discharge cases is $602,000 and that the average defense attorney's fees exceed $125,000 per case.[42] The following section addresses legal bases for wrongful discharge cases as well as alternative dispute resolution methods for avoiding litigation.

Employment at Will

The doctrine of **employment at will** originated in the 19th century and is based on the view that an employment contract is a private matter between free agents, an employee and an employer. In an employment-at-will situation, an employee is hired for an indefinite duration in the absence of a written contract, and either the employer or the employee may end the employment relationship for any reason at any time. Over time, however, federal and state laws have narrowed the employment-at-will concept and have created several exceptions. For example, as discussed in Chapter 3, EEO statutes prohibit organizations from terminating employees for discriminatory reasons. Three nonstatutory exceptions have been established by state courts: (1) the existence of an implied contract, (2) covenant of good faith and fair dealing, and (3) violation of public policy.[43]

Public Policy

This exception argues that an employer cannot fire an employee for reasons that violate public policy. States adopting a broad public policy exception recognize violations when an individual is discharged for asserting a statutory right, refusing to commit an illegal act, or refusing to violate professional codes of ethics.[44] California was among the first states recognizing a public policy exception. In *Peterman* v. *Teamsters* (1959), the California Court of Appeals ruled that it was against public policy for the Teamsters' Union to fire a business agent for refusing to give false testimony before a legislative committee.[45] In some states, such as Texas, refusing to commit an illegal act for which there are criminal sanctions is the only public policy exception recognized. In *Sabine Pilot Service, Inc.* v. *Hauck* (1985), the Supreme Court of Texas held that "public policy, as expressed in the laws of this state and the United States which carry criminal penalties, requires a very narrow exception to the employment-at-will doctrine."[46]

Implied Contract

States recognizing implied contract actions do so to uphold promises made by employers to employees. Courts interpreting this exception broadly have found implied promises of job tenure for employees with satisfactory performance records in employee handbooks, in personnel manuals, and in oral statements that an employee would not be discharged without just cause. For example, in *Pugh* v. *See Candies, Inc.* (1981), the California Court of Appeals found an implied contract based upon the 32-year duration of the plaintiff's employment, his promotions and commendations, assurances he received, and the employer's personnel policies.[47] Other states such as Alabama only recognize implied contracts based upon written statements including those made in employee handbooks.[48]

Good Faith and Fair Dealing

A small group of states have held that employers must deal with employees fairly and in good faith. When applied broadly, states such as Alaska apply the covenant of good faith and fair dealing to noncontractual at-will employment relationships and allow plaintiffs to sue in tort as well as in contract. More often, however, states have restricted this exception to contractual situations in which employees allege denial of earned benefits. For example, in *Fortune* v. *National Cash Register* (1977), the Massachusetts Appellate Court held that an implied covenant of good faith and fair dealing existed in a written contract that reserved to the employer the right to fire an employee for any reason.[49] The employee in this case, a 61-year-old salesperson with 40 years of service, was able to prove that the employer fired him to avoid paying sales commissions on a multi-million-dollar order.

HR Journal   *Signing Off on At-Will Employment*

A straightforward statement that can be altered slightly to fit (1) a job application form, (2) a handbook sample, or (3) a job offer can be useful in displaying the intent of employers.

AT-WILL JOB OFFER LANGUAGE:

I (NAME—employee) acknowledge that by accepting this job offer I will be an employee of (NAME—employer). I will be subject to dismissal or discipline without notice of cause. I understand that no representative of (company name), other than the president, has the authority and right to change the terms of at-will employment and that any change that occurs must be accomplished in a formal, written employment contract.

_____   _____

Signature   Date

An employer's best protection regarding at will is to include in the job application form, employee handbook, and job offer letters a statement regarding at will. The above HR Journal includes such a statement.

Alternative Dispute Resolution

Alternative dispute resolution (ADR) refers to using methods other than formal court litigation to resolve a dispute. ADR became formally institutionalized in the United States in 1922 and has since been used most extensively in the labor–management arena; most unionized contracts contain some form of binding dispute resolutions.[50]

Advantages and Methods

Overall, ADR is less time-consuming, less expensive, and more confidential than traditional litigation. Additionally, the nonadversarial nature of ADR makes it easier for the disputants to work together in the future. The four most common ADR methods used today include:

1. *Mediation* An impartial third party is engaged by the disputants to assist them in negotiating their own solution.
2. *Arbitration* The parties submit their dispute to a neutral third party, who will rule on it. Arbitrators are chosen by the disputing parties on the basis of expertise.
3. *Summary jury trial* Lawyers for the parties present a brief synopsis of their case to a jury that, after deliberations, makes a nonbinding advisory decision.
4. *Minitrial* After both parties briefly present their case, a panel of senior executives from the firm, who are not involved and who usually have the help of an outside neutral person, negotiate a resolution.

The American Arbitration Association handles over 230,000 cases each year.[51] Of these cases, most are resolved through using mediation or arbitration, although other methods such as minitrials are gaining in popularity.

ADR Programs in Organizations

McGraw-Hill has implemented an ADR program called Fast and Impartial Resolution (FAIR) for its more than 15,000 publishing, financial services, magazine, and broadcasting divisions in 35 locations.[52] The three-step FAIR program is voluntary and begins with bringing in a supervisor or human resources representative to resolve employment disputes. If this initial step is unsuccessful, the parties then attempt mediation. If mediation fails, the dispute is then resolved through arbitration.

Jeremy Schultz, the HR vice president at Judge Incorporated, is reflecting on the results of his interviews with four supervisors this week. These supervisors are responsible for Al, Susan, Joyce, and Tom.

Because of these four and many similar employees, Jeremy decides to set up a formal disciplinary system. In consultation with the supervisors and selected employees, he sets up in written form the rules of working at Judge. The performance evaluation system is strengthened to make the goals clearer.

Jeremy runs some training sessions and communicates the new system to the employees. The new discipline system sets up a step-by-step process and a set of "costs":

- *First violation or problem: Counseling by supervisor.*
- *Second violation or problem: Counseling by supervisor and recording in personnel file.*
- *Third violation or problem: Disciplinary layoff.*
- *Fourth violation or problem: Discharge.*

For alcohol or drug problems, counseling at counseling centers is required, or discharge will result. Violations of the law result in discharge and prosecution.

In all cases of disciplinary layoff, the employee will receive counseling from HRM. If there appear to be problems between supervisor and employee, Jeremy will serve as an ombudsman or alternative dispute resolution (ADR) will be used.

With regard to Al, Susan, Joyce, and Tom, Jeremy recommends the following actions:

Al   Transfer him to a new supervisor. There appears to be a personality conflict between Al and his supervisor. (The transfer did not help. Eventually, Al received a disciplinary layoff and later was terminated, in spite of counseling.)

Susan   Ask her to join Alcoholics Anonymous. (She did and got her drinking problem under control.)

Joyce   Watch for evidence that she is stealing. (When this evidence was clear, she was terminated and prosecuted. The judge gave her a suspended sentence.)

Tom   Give him counseling about his behavior. (The supervisor later reported that Tom had become a better employee.)

As the number of wrongful discharge cases filed and the amounts of jury awards have risen, companies are increasingly turning to *mandatory* binding arbitration to resolve employee disputes. Those companies adopting such programs include JCPenney, LensCrafters, Philip Morris, and Chrysler Corporation.[53] The legality of compulsory arbitration when applied to statutory claims, however, is an unsettled issue.

The Supreme Court first addressed mandatory arbitration agreements in *Alexander* v. *Gardner-Denver Co.* (1974).[54] In this case, the court held that a union could not waive an employee's statutory right by including an agreement to arbitrate Title VII claims in its collective bargaining agreement. However, in *Gilmer* v. *Interstate/Johnson Lane Corp.* (1991), the Supreme Court upheld mandatory predispute agreements to arbitrate age discrimination claims under the Age Discrimination in Employment Act.[55] The court emphasized that fraudulently induced and unfair agreements would be set aside.

Lower courts have subsequently addressed the issue of defining "fair" agreements. For example, in *Shankle* v. *B-G Maintenance Management of Colorado, Inc.,* the Tenth Circuit ruled that a mandatory arbitration agreement containing a fee-splitting provision was unenforceable.[56] The arbitration agreement at issue in this case contained the following provision: "I will be responsible for one half of the arbitrator's fees, and the company is responsible for the remaining half. If I am unable to pay my share, the company will advance the entirety of the arbitrator's fees; however, I will remain liable for my one-half." The court held that this provision served as a disincentive to arbitrate and rendered ADR ineffective and inaccessible due to the cost imposed on employees. The plaintiff in this case would have been responsible for $1,875 to $5,000 in arbitration fees. Courts have also found that mandatory arbitration is unfair when employers controlled lists of available arbitrators and failed to provide employees with arbitration rules and procedures.[57]

The following guidelines have been suggested by labor and employment attorneys as minimum fairness requirements for mandatory arbitration agreements:

- Use arbitrators with labor/employment expertise.
- Make fair discovery methods available for employees.
- Employers should be responsible for costs.
- Employees should have a right to legal representation during arbitration proceedings.
- Written opinions must be provided by arbitrators.
- Arbitrators' decisions should be subject to judicial review.

Summary

Some of the most difficult human resource management problems involve handling difficult or ineffective employees. Guidelines for assessing the causes and how to deal with these situations follow:

1. Most deviant or difficult employees' problems probably have multiple causes. Some of these are:
   a. Problems of intelligence and job knowledge.
   b. Emotional problems.
   c. Motivational problems.
   d. Physical problems.
   e. Family problems.
   f. Problems caused by the work group.
   g. Problems originating in company policies.
   h. Problems stemming from society and its values.
   i. Problems from the work context (for example, economic forces) and the work itself.

2. Categories of employees that cause discipline problems include:
   a. Ineffective employees.
   b. Alcoholic and drug-abusing employees.
   c. Participants in theft, crime, and illegal acts.
   d. Rule violators.

3. The discipline process involves the following:
   a. The employer establishes rules and goals.
   b. These rules and goals are communicated to employees.
   c. Employees' behavior is assessed.
   d. Undesirable behavior is modified, punished, and so on.
   e. Depending on the behavior, its severity, and the number of offenses, an employee may be terminated.

4. For such problems as alcoholism and drug addiction, employers should concentrate on trying to modify the effects and advise rehabilitation and counseling.

5. For discipline systems to be effective, the disciplinary review must take place as soon after the action as possible. It must be applied consistently and impersonally.

Discipline is an area in which help is needed from many areas: supervisors, HRM, the work group, arbitrators, and top management. Each has a crucial role to play if the discipline system is to be effective.

Key Terms	alternative dispute resolution (ADR), *p. 537*	employee drug testing, *p. 522*	impairment testing, *p. 523*
	employee assistance program (EAP), *p. 523*	employment at will, *p. 536*	positive discipline, *p. 534*
		hot stove rule, *p. 532*	progressive pattern of discipline, *p. 533*

Questions for Review and Discussion

1. In developing an EAP, what role should managers play?
2. Can violence in the workplace be eliminated? Why?
3. What are the limitations of applying the hot stove rule to all employees?
4. How serious a problem is the substance abusing employee at work? How should the substance abusing employee be handled?
5. Discuss the legal implications of conducting drug tests on employees. Are impairment tests treated differently by the law than drug tests?
6. Why is employment at will treated differently in various states?
7. How serious is the problem of an employee who violates criminal laws? How should the employee be dealt with?
8. Describe the key elements in the discipline process.
9. What actions can an organization initiate to better control employee theft and fraud?
10. Can employers require applicants/employees to sign mandatory arbitration agreements as a condition of employment?

HRM Legal Advisor

Based on *Holihan* v. *Lucky Stores, Inc.,* 87 F.3d 362 (Ninth Cir. 1996).

The Problem: Complaints against the Plaintiff

Richard Holihan was hired by Lucky Stores in 1966 and was promoted to store manager in 1976. He successfully managed eight different stores in the Lucky chain until 1992 and was commended by the company for being its all-time profit producer. However, in April 1992, other employees began complaining that Mr. Holihan was hostile and abusive toward them. On July 30, 1992, Lucky's district manager, Mark Church, and the grocery supervisor, Gary Donne, met with Mr. Holihan to discuss the complaints. At this meeting, Mr. Church asked Mr. Holihan if he was having any "problems" that the company could help with. Mr. Holihan denied that he had behaved abusively and stated that he was not having any problems. The company transferred Mr. Holihan to another location, but received 51 complaints from 13 different employees within the first three months. The employees alleged that Mr. Holihan "threw food off shelves and ordered employees to clean it up, repeatedly threatened to fire the entire staff for no valid reason, and violated money handling and other office procedures."

The Company's Response and the Plaintiff's Subsequent Lawsuit

On October 22, 1992, Mr. Church again met with Mr. Holihan, who denied most of the new allegations. Mr. Church then offered him two alternatives: (1) suspension pending investigation of the complaints, or (2) a leave of absence contingent on EAP counseling. Mr. Holihan sought counseling from the EAP and began his leave on October 26, 1992. The EAP-referred psychologist diagnosed Mr. Holihan as "experiencing stress-related problems precipitated by work" and recommended a 3-month medical leave. Mr. Holihan requested four leave extensions, and was granted three. Lucky Stores denied his last request and fired him in May 1993 upon learning that, while on leave, Mr. Holihan had worked up to 80 hours per week selling real estate and preparing to open a sign making company. In September 1993, Mr. Holihan reapplied and was offered a job as a clerk due to a lack of open management jobs. He turned down the job and in May 1994 filed a disability discrimination claim against Lucky Stores.

The Courts' Decisions

The district court held that Mr. Holihan was not disabled under the ADA. On appeal, the Ninth Circuit found that although Mr. Holihan did not have a mental or physical impairment that substantially limited a major life activity as evidenced by his pursuit of real estate and sign making businesses, Lucky could have "regarded" Mr. Holihan as disabled. The court cited Mr. Church's question about whether he was having any "problems" and encouragement to seek EAP counseling as evidence of the perceived disability. In 1997, Lucky appealed to the U.S. Supreme Court, which refused to hear the case, thus letting the Ninth Circuit ruling stand. A settlement has subsequently been reached between Mr. Holihan and Lucky Stores.

Employer Implications

Managers must exercise caution when making EAP referrals. When meeting with employees, managers should neither ask about personal problems that may exist nor conclude that counseling is warranted. This behavior could create a "perceived disability" problem. Managers should base their referral and/or disciplinary action on work-related factors such as decreased productivity or excessive absenteeism.

Notes

1. Yoav Vardi and Ely Weitz (2004), *Misbehavior in Organizations* (Mahwah, NJ: Laurence Erlbaum).
2. John Miner (1975), *The Challenge of Managing* (Philadelphia: Saunders).
3. Workplace Substance Abuse (2005) (Washington, DC, U.S. Department of Labor).
4. Giovinella Gonthier and Kevin Morrissey (2002), *Rude Awakening* (New York: Kaplan).
5. *Workplace Substance Abuse,* op. cit.
6. Tyler Hartwell, Paul Steele, and Nathaniel F. Rodman (June 1998), "Workplace Alcohol-Testing Programs: Prevalence and Trends," *Monthly Labor Review,* pp. 27–34.
7. Drug and Alcohol Testing Rules: An Overview, http://www.ecoc.gov/docs/prempt.text.
8. Tyler D. Hartwell, Paul D. Steele, Michael T. French, and Nathaniel E. Rodman (November 1996), "Prevalence of Drug Testing in the Workplace," *Monthly Labor Review,* pp. 35–40.
9. Pete Sanders and Steve Myers (2005), *Drinking Alcohol (Choices and Decisions)* (New York: Stargazer).
10. Americans with Disabilities Act, http://www.eeoc.gov/laws/ada.html.
11. Tracey J. Jarvis, Jenny Tebbutt, Richard P. Mattick, Fiona Shand, and Hick Heather (2005), *Treatment Approaches for Alcohol and Drug Dependence: An Introductory Guide* (New York: John Wiley & Sons).
12. Jane Easter Bahis (March 1998), "Dealing with Drugs: Keep It Legal," *HRMagazine,* pp. 104–116.
13. Ibid.
14. Ibid.
15. Jarvis, et. al., op. cit.
16. Sandy Smith (August 2004), "What Every Employer Should Know about Drug Testing in the Workplace," *Occupational Hazards,* pp. 45–47.
17. Nan Van Den Bergh (2000), *Emerging Trends for EAPs in the 21st Century* (New York: Haworth).
18. Michael Prime (September 2002), "EAP Use Surges after 9/11," *Business Insurance,* pp. 1–2.

19. Employee Assistance Programs: North America, *Occupational Health and Safety,* June 2002, pp. 1–8.

20. Don Rhodes (October 1998), "Drugs in the Workplace," *Occupational Health and Safety,* pp. 136–138.

21. Gary L. Wirt (November 1998), "The ABCs of EAPs," *HRFocus,* p. 12.

22. Donald Smeltzer (January 2005), "More Bang for Your EAP Buck," *Employee Benefit Plan Review,* pp. 14–15.

23. Philip H. Purpa (2002), *Security and Loss Prevention* (New York: Butterworth Heinemann).

24. Gerald Mars (Ed.) (2001), *Occupational Crime* (New York: Ashgate Publishing).

25. Robert McGarvey (January 2000), "Lords of Discipline," *Entrepreneur,* pp. 127–130.

26. Wayne J. Camara and Dianne L. Schneider (February 1994), "Integrity Tests," *American Psychologist,* pp. 112–119.

27. Nathan Luther (Fall 2000), "Integrity Testing and Job Performance within High Performance Work Teams," *Journal of Business Psychology,* pp. 19–25.

28. Deniz Ones and Viswesvaran Chockalingam (February 1998), "Gender, Age, and Race Differences on Overt Integrity Tests: Results across Four Large-Scale Job Applicant Data Sets," *Journal of Applied Psychology,* pp. 35–42.

29. Ibid.

30. "OSHA Prepares to Turn the Spotlight on Workplace Homicides" (January 2005), *Security Directors Report,* pp. 2–4.

31. Kathy Gurchiek (July 2005), "Workplace Violence on the Upswing," *HR Magazine,* pp. 27–28.

32. Janet Wiscombe (October 2002), "Vigilance Stops Violence," *Workforce,* pp 38–42.

33. "How to Predict and Prevent Workplace Violence" (April 2005), *HR Focus,* pp. 10–11.

34. Marion M. LeBlanc and Kevin E. Kelloware (June 2002), "Predictors and Outcomes of Workplace Violence and Aggression," *Journal of Applied Psychology,* pp. 444–453.

35. S. Ackroyd and P. Thompson (2004), *Organizational Misbehavior* (London: Sage).

36. Sonia Hunter and Brian H. Kleiner (2004), "Effective Grievance Handling Procedures," *Management Research News,* Vol. 27, pp. 85–94.

37. "You Be the Judge: Termination" (March 2002), *HRBriefing,* pp. 4–6.

38. McGarvey, op. cit.

39. Ibid.

40. Adam Agard (May 2005), "Using Objectivity," *Supervision,* pp. 11–14.

41. Paul Over and Scott Schaefer (June 2002), "Litigation Costs and Returns to Experience," *American Economic Review,* pp. 683–705.

42. Ibid.

43. Amy Delpo and Lisa Guerin (2001), *Dealing with Problem Employees* (Berkeley, CA: Nolo).

44. David J. Walsh and Joshua L. Schwartz (Summer 1996), "State Common Law Wrongful Discharge Doctrines: Up-Date, Refinement, and Rationales," *American Business Law Journal,* pp. 645–689.

45. *Sabine Pilot Service, Inc. v. Hauck,* 687 S.W.2d 733, 735 (Tex. 1985).

46. *Pugh v. See Candies, Inc.,* 116 Cal. App. 3d 311, 171 Cal. Rept. 917 (1981).

47. *Hoffman-LaRocbe, Inc. v. Campbell,* 512 So.2d 725 (Ala. 1985).

48. *Fortune v. National Cash Register,* 373 Mass. 96, 364 N.E.2d 1251 (1977).

49. Wyatt McDowell and Lyle Sussman (May–June 1996), "Overcoming the Pathology of Litigation. An ADR Primer for Executives," *Business Horizons,* pp. 23–29.

50. Phillip M. Armstrong (May–July 2005), "Georgia-Pacific's ADR Program: A Critical Review after 10 Years," *Dispute Resolution Journal,* pp. 18–22.

51. See www.adr.org, accessed "Overview Section" on July 26, 2005.

52. Evan J. Spelfogel (May 1999), "Mandatory Arbitration vs. Employment Litigation," *Dispute Resolution Journal,* pp. 78–81.

53. Jean R. Sternlight (October 2000), "As Mandatory Binding Arbitration Meets the Class Action, Will the Class Action Survive?" *William and Mary Law Review,* pp. 1–125.

54. *Gilmer v. Interstate/Johnson Lane Corp* (1991*)* 500 U.S. 20.

55. *Shankle v. B-G Maintenance Management of Colorado, Inc.* (1999), 163 E3d 1230 (Tenth Cir.)

56. Susan Long (August 1999), "Unfair Arbitration Agreement Not Enforceable," *HR Focus*, p. 3.

57. Spelfogel, op. cit., p. 80.

EXERCISE 16-1

Making Difficult Decisions

OBJECTIVE

The primary objective of this exercise is to permit individuals to decide whether actions taken by management are legally defensible under the employment-at-will concept. The exercise illustrates the importance of considering state laws when making termination decisions.

SET UP THE EXERCISE

1. Form groups of six to eight students to analyze and discuss each of the following situations.

2. Groups should first identify employment-at-will exceptions recognized by courts in the state in which their college or university is located or in a state assigned by the instructor. To do this, students can use Web sites such as FindLaw, http://www.findlaw.com, which contain state law information.

3. Each group should then determine whether the terminations described in the situations below are legally justified in their state. Then each group should prepare a brief statement explaining its decision and discussing any applicable employment-at-will exceptions.

4. Review each of the group decisions with the entire class.

MR. TOROSYAN

Mr. Torosyan was hired as a chemist in a pharmaceutical company. At the time he was hired, the company's employee handbook clearly stated that employees would not be fired without just cause. The handbook further detailed a process for appealing adverse employment decisions. The company later modified its manual to include a statement that employees were terminable at-will. Mr. Torosyan was sent to a training seminar out of state and upon returning, he submitted an expense report that contained some undocumented items that the company suspected were personal. He was subsequently fired for falsifying his expense report and was denied the option to appeal the termination decision as outlined in the employee handbook.

MS. PRESSMAN

Ms. Pressman worked as a medical imaging technologist for a chemical company for four years. During her employment, Ms. Pressman learned that her supervisor was involved with a competing company's medical imaging business on his own time. Because Ms. Pressman felt that this created a conflict of interest, she confronted her supervisor about it. Her supervisor became angry, gave her negative performance evaluations over the next year, and she was subsequently terminated for poor performance. During the previous three years, Ms. Pressman's evaluations had consistently indicated that her performance exceeded the company's expectations.

MR. MANSFIELD

Mr. Mansfield was a technician in the machine shop of Millfield Corporation. During his employment, he met at lunchtime, during breaks, and after work with employees, attempting to persuade them to start and support a union. After six months of meetings, Mr. Mansfield was informed by his supervisor that he was fired. He was told that he had violated union organization procedures and was using the company premises without permission to organize a union. Therefore, because he had violated the rules about union organizing, he was terminated.

Application Case 16-1

The Case for and against Drug Testing

Experts agree that over 70 percent of all illicit drug users in the United States are employed. A Gallup survey of employees found that 37 percent of all respondents said that workplace drug use problems had increased in the last five years. A majority supported drug screening tests.

In two short months, top management at Castulon Corporation realized that the company had employees who might have a problem with drug abuse. In October, an electronics engineer was found at his desk clearly stoned. ("He literally fell off his chair," the engineer's supervisor said.) In November a security guard discovered two employees in the company parking lot during the lunch hour, snorting cocaine in a car. All three employees were fired. Bob McRary, CEO of Castulon Corp., was particularly disturbed by these incidents. Castulon manufactures electronic systems that monitor and control the levels of hazardous chemicals at industrial plants. Any mistakes made by drug-dependent employees in the design or production of a system could provide disastrous results for users.

McRary assigned Michael O'Brien, vice president of human resources, the task of writing a proposal for a drug-testing program for job applicants and for Castulon's 600 employees. The proposal would recommend procedures for establishing a program and propose the program's content. The proposal would also present a comprehensive coverage of the pros and cons of establishing drug testing at Castulon. Undecided, McRary wanted to review all sides of the question before making a decision.

Michael O'Brien sought the help of Norman Sterling, director of employee relations, and Beverly Shaver, director of employee recruitment and selection, in preparing the proposal. As he often did when handling difficult issues, O'Brien asked each director to assume one position—either for or against mandatory drug testing—and to prepare a 10-page position paper presenting his or her views, based on research and a thorough consideration of the issues at hand. O'Brien would use the papers as input for the final proposal.

Today, Norman Sterling (who chose the advocate's position) and Beverly Shaver (who selected the opponent's view) submitted their papers to O'Brien. Now, in O'Brien's office and at his request, the two managers are discussing their positions.

"I accepted this assignment initially supporting a drug-testing program, and after considering the issues, I'm even more convinced that we need one, for three primary reasons" Norman Sterling asserted.

"First, we have a responsibility for providing a safe workplace for our employees, and any drug use on the job compromises safety," he continued. "There's no question that drug use results in more accidents on the job. One study that compared employees who use drugs with nonusers found that an employee who uses drugs is almost four times more likely to be involved in a job-related accident.

"If you want more evidence, look at the transportation industry," Sterling continued, thumbing through his report to read a passage. "In the train industry alone, numerous accidents have been attributed to mistakes made by drug- or alcohol-impaired employees. Those accidents cost lives, injured people, and destroyed millions in property. In our company, we should be very concerned because our manufacturing people work with heavy equipment. A drug user may not only hurt himself but injure other workers.

"We can solve the problem of inaccuracy by performing second and even third tests when an initial positive finding is obtained," Sterling countered. "We could use a different and more thorough procedure and a different laboratory to reduce the chances that a sample will be mishandled."

"We could, but costs are a big factor," Shaver replied. "The EMIT costs about $40 per test. We can expect a lot of false positives, from what I've read. Given the high false-positive rates, I wouldn't trust a second or even third follow-up EMIT test. We could use the most reliable test—the gas chromatography–mass spectroscopy test. It costs $80 per test. With 600 employees and a few hundred applicants each year, costs could get out of hand."

"What are the issues?" O'Brien asked.

"There's the issue of individual rights," Shaver asserted. "Mandatory drug testing essentially involves searching the contents of an individual's most valued possession—his or her body—and searching without probable cause. Doesn't the 14th Amendment to the Constitution guarantee an individual's right to be secure against unreasonable searches without probable cause?"

"The 14th Amendment doesn't apply to most dealings between a private company and its employees, including drug testing," Sterling asserted. "We're on sure footing with a drug-testing program as long as it is fairly and consistently administered and thoroughly documented, and as long as we don't reveal test results to a third party."

"Technically, the 14th Amendment doesn't apply, but the spirit of the amendment should," Shaver said. "Here's my most serious concern. When we implement mandatory drug testing, we are presuming that our employees are guilty, not innocent. That's what we're communicating to them. It's an act of distrust, and it violates the spirit of mutual trust we've maintained with our employees.

"We have the best employees in the industry," she continued. "They're highly committed to Castulon; they often go the extra mile on their own without being asked. I think that's the case because we've stayed out of their private lives but have been supportive. There's a deep, mutual trust here. Mandatory drug testing violates the trust, and I think it will undermine our relationship with employees."

"Yes, we could make our people feel like criminals if the program is badly handled," Sterling responded. "But it wouldn't be. No trust is violated if we explain the potential costs of drug use and make employees feel as if they're cooperating to resolve a troublesome problem, not as if they're potential criminals."

"Norman, I'll quote Lewis Maltby, vice president of Drexel Engineering, who's written widely on why his company will not implement drug testing," Shaver said. "When you say to an employee, 'You're doing a great job, but just the same, I want you to pee in this jar and I'm sending someone to watch you' you've undermined that trust."

"Folks, I feel like I'm moderating a debate," O'Brien said. "So, any closing remarks? Beverly?"

"Again, I'm disturbed about the effect that a drug testing program will have on our employees. And the issue of privacy. I wonder if we have the right to information that test results would give us—information about whether an employee is being treated for asthma, heart disease, diabetes, depression, or a host of other illnesses. But essentially, I feel that if we do have a drug problem, we can deal with it more effectively in other ways. As a preventive strategy, we can be very selective in our hiring by thoroughly evaluating job candidates, especially their past work record. We can train managers to identify employees who are possibly drug-dependent. There are other strategies that don't have the potentially explosive results a testing program will have."

"If the employees are approached carefully, I don't think they will be offended by the program," Sterling said. "As for more selective hiring, we are already very selective, and as far as drug use is concerned, our careful selection procedure has failed in at least three cases. We need a program that definitely works, and drug testing fits the bill."

Michael O'Brien rose from his desk. "Thank you both for your input," he said. "I'll send you a copy of the proposal once I submit it to Bob later this week. He says he'll make a decision soon after reviewing the proposal. I'll let you know."

Discussion Questions

1. Should Castulon Corporation establish a drug-testing program? If so, recommend a specific policy for the program that includes disciplinary procedures for dealing with employees who test positive for drug use.

2. What are the most difficult challenges facing an organization in establishing a drug-testing program? Discuss.

3. Some observers assert that, since alcohol abuse is more prevalent in the workplace and its effects are just as costly, companies should also test for alcohol use. Do you agree? Explain.

Source: Written by Kim Stewart and changes have been made with each edition. Facts and several perspectives were drawn from Janice Castro (March 17, 1981), "Bottling the Enemy Within," *Time*, p. 52ff; Lewis L. Moltby (June 1987), "Why Drug Testing Is a Bad Idea," *Inc.*, pp. 152–153; Ian A. Miners, Nick Nykodym, and Diane M. Somerdyke-Traband (August 1987), "Put Drug Detection to the Test" *Personnel Journal*, pp. 90–97; and Anne Marie O'Keefe (June 1987), "The Case against Drug Testing," *Psychology Today*, pp. 34–36, 38.

17

Promoting Safety and Health

Learning Objectives

After studying this chapter, you should be able to:

1. **Define** *safety* and *health hazards.*
2. **Discuss** the causes of work-related accidents and illnesses: the task to be done, the working conditions, and the nature of the employee.
3. **Explain** the legal environment of occupational health and safety regulations, including OSHA and its proposed amendments.
4. **Discuss** the impact of stress, violence, IEQ, AIDS, and repetitive motion injuries on the workplace.
5. **Calculate** the costs and benefits of an organizational health and safety program.

Internet/Web Resources

General Sites

www.osha.gov

www.nsc.org

www.cdc.org

www.niehs.nih.gov

www.nlm.nih.gov

www.asse.org

Company Sites

www.jnj.com

www.bankamerica.com

www.northwesternmutual.com

www.dixiechemical.com

www.coors.com

www.prudential.com

www.levistrauss.com

Career Challenge

Ted Spengler was on cloud nine. Ever since he graduated from Kendall State University with a degree in business administration five years ago, he had been waiting for a chance to transfer to the human resource department. He had paid his dues and spent three years on a job rotation program to learn the business. He had spent the next two years as a supervisor in the plant. He felt ready for the next step in his career plan—to eventually become a human resource director.

Ted worked for Fort Technical Systems, a growing firm that manufactured computer boards. The technology included minute craftsmanship and the use of caustic chemicals as cleaning agents for the computer chips. Two hundred employees worked in the plant as skilled technicians and assemblers. Another hundred support staff people included shippers, clerks, secretaries, salespeople, and so forth. The company had a reputation as a good place to work.

In order to comply with the federal Occupational Safety and Health Act and state safety regulations, the human resource department had created a slot called safety director. That's the job that Ted had landed. He remembered studying about the importance of occupational safety and health in his introductory human resource class at Kendall, but he hadn't had any other special courses. He had read over the job description for his new position, however, and realized that he would have his hands full.

First, he was in charge of compiling all statistics on workplace accidents and fatalities. He had to correlate statistics on absenteeism with medical claims under Kendall's disability insurance plan. Reports were to be shared monthly with the human resource director, Fred Wayne, and the plant manager, Zhao Wen, at the Safety Committee meetings. It looked as though tons of forms had to be filed with OSHA and a couple of state agencies. Ted also was assigned the tasks of developing a new safety training program for the technicians who handled dangerous chemicals, finding a new supplier for the special protective gloves worn for cleaning chips, drafting an AIDS policy for Fort, and revising the cost-benefit analysis of its new wellness program. Ted rolled up his sleeves and thought, "What should I do first?"

This chapter covers the important topics of workplace safety and health. Historically, the manufacturer's workplace, the factory, was filled with risks like dangerous machinery and poor lighting and in mines, for example, not only was every miner subjected to high risk of death by floods, cave-ins, and poison gas, but all were susceptible to a form of emphysema called "black lung" disease. Many workers were locked into their factories in unsanitary and unsafe conditions. Fire claimed the lives of hundreds of workers near the turn of the century in the United States. The modern service industry's workplace is just as hazardous, with high levels of stress and repetitive motion disorders such as carpal tunnel syndrome. And the risks present in manufacturing have been matched by accidents like the fire in a poultry plant in North Carolina—a disaster which killed workers who were trying to escape through locked fire exits.

Background

It is important to differentiate between occupational safety hazards and health hazards. **Safety hazards** are aspects of the work environment that have the potential of causing immediate and sometimes violent harm or even death. Examples of safety hazards include poorly maintained equipment, unsafe machinery, exposure to hazardous chemicals, and so on. Potential injuries include loss of hearing, eyesight, or body parts; cuts, sprains, burns, bruises, and broken bones; and electric shock. **Health hazards** are aspects of the work environment that slowly and cumulatively (often irreversibly) lead to deterioration of health. The person may develop a chronic or life-threatening illness or become permanently disabled. Typical causes are physical and biological hazards, toxic and carcinogenic dusts and chemicals, and stressful working conditions; these can cause cancer, heavy-metal and other poisoning, respiratory disease, and psychological disorders like depression.

Safety and health hazards in the workplace can harm others as well as employees. In December 1984 the worst industrial accident in history occurred: Poisonous methyl isocyanate gas leaked from a storage tank at a Union Carbide (purchased by Dow Chemical in 2001) plant in Bhopal, India, killing 3,000 people (both employees and people living near the plant). Another 300,000 were injured.[1] The accident was the result of operating errors, design flaws, maintenance failures, and training deficiencies.

Union Carbide was sued for billions of dollars; compensation settlements totaled $1 billion. In many of the lawsuits, Union Carbide's own 1982 safety report on the plant has been used because it noted "a higher potential for a serious accident or more serious consequences if an accident should occur." Also:

> That report "strongly" recommended, among other things, the installation of a larger system that would supplement or replace one of the plant's main safety devices, a water spray designed to contain a chemical leak. That change was never made, plant employees said, and [when the leak happened] that spray was not high enough to reach the escaping gas.[2]

Another example of safety and health hazards at the workplace can be traced to Manville Corporation's manufacture of products with a toxic substance known as asbestos. The substance is a mineral that was once widely used in piping and insulation products.[3] Thousands of people claimed to have contracted respiratory diseases as a result of contact with the substance; for many, the diseases did not manifest symptoms until many years after exposure.[4] The complicated aspect of this case was that early reports indicated that asbestos dust was harmful to humans and yet the products continued to be manufactured and sold.[5] These decisions not only affected the thousands of victims and their families, but also led to product liability judgments that forced Manville to reorganize under Chapter 11 of the Federal Bankruptcy Code in August 1982 and to turn over approximately 80 percent of common stock, $1.6 billion in accounts receivable, and approximately $1 billion in cash.[6] To this day, lawsuits continue to be filed against this company on behalf of those individuals affected by the mineral fiber.

Job hazards span all levels of the economy. "Trench cave-ins, toxic chemicals, infectious diseases, video display terminals, and job design problems put millions of U.S. workers at risk of injuries and illnesses."[7] Statistics on workplace safety and health hazards are open to debate. For example, although the Bureau of Labor Statistics started compiling statistics on injury and fatality rates in the iron and steel industry in 1912, it was not until the passage of the Occupational Safety and Health Act (OSHA) in 1970 that recording and reporting of occupational safety and health statistics became mandatory. Since 1972, the Bureau has conducted an annual survey of 280,000 private sector organizations, which is used to compile reports on injuries, illnesses, and fatalities. In 2003, there were 4.4 million nonfatal injuries and illnesses in the private sector alone, with approximately 1.3 million involving lost work time.[8] Injury rates are higher for medium-size firms (50 to 249 workers) than for smaller or larger firms. Exhibit 17-1 documents nonfatal occupational injuries per 100 full-time workers for industries with 100,000 or more injuries in one year.

About 1.6 million of the injuries, or nearly 28 percent, were in only nine industries: (1) eating and drinking places, (2) hospitals, (3) nursing and personal care facilities, (4) trucking and courier services, (5) grocery stores, (6) department stores, (7) motor vehicles and equipment, (8) hotels and motels, and (9) air transportation.

More than three-fifths of all cases (about 500,000 total cases) were in the manufacturing sector of the economy. Disorders associated with repeated trauma, like carpal tunnel syndrome, accounted for about 60 percent of illnesses reported. At a time of record

EXHIBIT 17-1
Nonfatal
Occupational
Injuries and Illnesses
(Number of Cases
and Incidence Rates
by Private Industry,
2003)

Source: Bureau of Labor
Statistics (December 2004),
U.S. Department of Labor.

Industry*	NAICS Code†	Incidence Rate‡ 2003	Total Cases (in thousands) 2003
Light truck and utility vehicle manufacturing	336112	18.0	14.3
Bottled water manufacturing	312112	16.7	2.9
Soft drink manufacturing	312111	13.8	11.4
Refrigerated warehousing and storage	49312	13.1	5.4
Couriers	4921	12.8	49.8
Amusement parks and arcades	7131	12.2	12.1
Framing contractors	23813	12.0	13.6

*Industries with high incidence rates of total nonfatal occupational injury and illness cases, private industry, 2003.
†North American Industry Classification System—United States, 2002.
‡The incidence rates represent the number of injuries and illnesses per 100 full-time workers and were calculated as: (N/EH) × 200,000.

participation in the labor force, the incidence of occupational injury and illness has been decreasing. Two factors that account for the decrease are (1) enhanced job safety training over the past 20 years and (2) greater compliance with safety and health standards by both employers and employees.

About 15 workers are killed in American workplaces each day. Fatal injuries at work can often be traced to hazardous or unsafe work conditions and practices. It is impossible to fully assess the scope of these events. But to narrow this information gap, the Bureau of Labor Statistics has designed a Census of Fatal Occupational Injuries (CFOI) to generate verified counts of fatal work injuries along with information on how the injuries occurred.[9] The first CFOI was conducted in 1991, with participation from only 31 of the 50 states. To control discrepancies in reporting, multiple sources were used to compile the information: death certificates, state workers' compensation reports, state coroners' reports, OSHA reports, news media, toxicology reports, autopsy reports, follow-up questionnaires, state motor vehicle reports, and other federal reports.

In 2002, 5,534 people died as a result of work-related injuries in all sectors of the economy. This represented a small decline (about 2 percent) from 2001. It was reported that this decline in fatal injuries was due to a decrease in the number of job-related deaths from highway incidents. Although lower than the previous year, highway fatalities continued to be the leading cause of on-the-job deaths in 2002. The second most common cause of death comes from falls experienced on the job, including when workers fall from one level to a lower level (e.g., off a ladder). The third leading cause of work-related fatalities was homicide. From 1992 to 2002, the total number of homicides has decreased from 1,044 to 609, which represents a 42 percent decrease.[10] Exhibit 17-2 shows data on workplace homicides for selected industries from 1998 to 2002.

EXHIBIT 17-2
Workplace
Homicides: Selected
Industries

Source: U.S. Department of
Labor (2003), Bureau of Labor
Statistics, Census of Fatal
Occupational Injuries.

Industry	1998	1999	2000	2001	2002	Average
Trucking (except local)	328	362	345	329	352	343
Grocery stores	120	97	128	111	89	109
Automotive repair shops	80	82	81	66	78	77
Detective and armored car services	36	39	35	40	43	39
Public order and safety	34	35	31	33	24	31
Hotels and motels	30	29	32	33	28	30
Real estate agents and managers	16	14	21	15	16	16
Total homicides	644	658	673	627	630	

Victims of those workplace homicides were most likely to be store personnel, gas station attendants, or taxicab drivers. About 10 percent were police officers or security guards killed in the line of duty. Homicide is the number 1 cause of workplace fatalities for self-employed people and for several minority groups (African Americans, Hispanics, Asian and Pacific Islanders) because they are more likely to be employed in high-risk occupations.

Accidents, illnesses, and fatalities are not evenly distributed among occupations in the United States. Employees facing serious dangers to their health and safety include police, firefighters, miners, construction and transportation workers, meatpackers, sheet metal workers, manufacturers of recreational vehicles, lumber workers and woodworkers, and others employed in manufacturing and agriculture.

Regardless of type, all of these events are tragic for the employees and their families, co-workers, and employers. There is pain at the time of the accident, and there can be psychological problems later for the families of both survivors and victims who die. In addition to pain, suffering, and death, there are also directly measurable costs to both employee and employer. In 2003, a total of 1.3 million injuries and illnesses in private industry forced workers to be away from work; while injuries and illnesses forced another 980,000 workers to be either transferred or placed on restricted work activity.[11] Occupational health and safety issues are responsible for the direct costs of workers' compensation and indirect costs of lost productivity for enterprises. In 1999, workers' compensation benefits and costs amounted to over $1.2 trillion when the cost of replacement wages was included in the calculation.[12] Other indirect costs not included in the calculation include damage to plant and equipment, costs of replacement employees, and time costs for supervisors and human resource staff members investigating and reporting the accident or illness. Because of both the humanitarian desire of management to reduce suffering and the huge direct and indirect costs of occupational accidents, deaths, and illnesses, the effective enterprise tries hard to create safe and healthy conditions at work.

Until recently, the typical response to concern about health and safety was to compensate the victims of job-related accidents with workers' compensation and similar insurance payments. This chapter will discuss various compensation approaches and organizational programs designed to prevent accidents, health hazards, and deaths at work.

Causes of Work-Related Accidents and Illnesses

Work-related accidents and illnesses have many causes. The major causes of occupational accidents are

- Tasks.
- Working conditions.
- Nature of the employees.

Examples of causes related to the task and working conditions include poorly designed or inadequately repaired machines, lack of protective equipment, and the presence of dangerous chemicals or gases. Other working conditions that contribute to accidents include excessive work hours, leading to fatigue; noise; lack of proper lighting; boredom; and horseplay and fighting. The National Institute for Occupational Safety and Health (NIOSH) is charged with finding out more about the causes of accidents and occupational health hazards. Exhibit 17-3 lists selected examples of job and safety hazards and their possible outcomes.

EXHIBIT 17-3   **Examples of Job and Safety Hazards**

Occupation	Potential Hazard	Possible Outcome
Textile workers	Cotton dust	Brown lung or byssinosis (a debilitating lung disease)
	Noise	Temporary or permanent hearing loss
	Chemical exposures	
	Aniline-based dyes	Bladder cancer and liver damage
	Formaldehyde	Dermatitis, allergic lung disease, possibly cancer
	Furfuraldehyde	Dermatitis, respiratory irritation, fatigue, headache, tremors, numbness of the tongue
	Moving machine parts without barriers	Loss of fingers or hands
Hospital workers	Infectious diseases	
	Hepatitis	Liver damage
	Herpes simplex virus	Painful skin lesions
	Chemical exposure	
	Anesthetic gases	Spontaneous abortions
	Metallic mercury	Poisoning of nervous system and kidneys
	Inorganic acids and alkalis	Irritation to respiratory tract and skin
	Physical hazards	
	Ionizing radiation	Burns, birth defects, cancer
	Microwave radiation	Sterility, harm to eyes, possible increased risk of cataracts
	UV light	Burning or sensitization of skin, skin cancer, cataracts
	Safety hazards	
	Lifting or carrying	Back pain or permanent back injury
	Puncture wounds from syringes	Infections
Welders	Infrared and visible light radiation	Burns, headaches, fatigue, eye damage
	UV radiation	Burns, skin tumors, eye damage
	Chemical exposure	
	Carbon monoxide	Cardiovascular disease
	Acetylene	Asphyxiation, fire, explosion
	Metallic oxides	Contact dermatitis, eye irritation, respiratory irritation, metal fume fever (symptoms similar to flu), possible kidney damage.
	Phosphine	Lethal at even low doses: irritating to eyes, nose, skin; acts as anesthetic
Clerical workers	Improperly designed chairs and workstations; lack of movement	Backache; aggravation of hemorrhoids, varicose veins, and other blood-circulation conditions; eyestrain
	Noise	Hearing impairment, stress reaction
	Exposure to chemicals	
	Ozone from copy machines	Irritation of eyes, nose, throat; respiratory damage
	Benzene and toluene in rubber cement and "cleaners"	Benzene is associated with several blood diseases (including leukemia), and toluene may cause intoxication
	Methanol and ammonia in duplicating machine solvents	Irritation to eyes, nose and throat

There are data to indicate that some employees have more accidents than the average. Such a person is said to be an **accident repeater.** Employees who (1) are under 30 years of age, (2) lack psychomotor and perceptual skills, (3) are impulsive, and (4) are easily bored are more likely than others to have accidents.[13] Although some believe accident-proneness can be measured by a set of attitude or motivational instruments, most experts who have examined the data carefully do not believe that attitudinal and motivational "causes" of accidents significantly influence accident rates. We need to know much more about accident-proneness before such serious actions as attempting to screen out the accident-prone person are implemented.

Who Is Involved with Safety and Health?

As with other HRM functions, the success of a safety and health program requires the support and cooperation of managers. But it is more complicated than that. In some organizations, safety is a separate function, though both managers and staff still have their parts to play to protect employees.

Top management must support safety and health with an adequate budget. Managers must give it their personal support by talking about safety and health with everyone in the firm. Acting on reports about safety is another way top managers can be involved in these efforts. Without this support, the effort to ensure safety and health is hampered. Some organizations have responded to the environmental problems that can increase accidents, deaths, and disabilities by placing the responsibility for employees' health and safety with the chief executive officer of the organization: the hospital administrator, the agency administrator, the company president. This is the approach taken by most smaller organizations that are concerned about health and safety. Operating managers are also responsible, since accidents and injuries will take place and health hazards will exist in the work unit. They must be aware of health and safety considerations and cooperate with the specialists who can help them reduce accidents and occupational illnesses. In larger and some medium-sized organizations, there is a safety unit in the HR department. This chapter will illustrate what a safety and health specialist does.

The success of the safety program rests primarily on how well employees and managers follow and comply with safety rules and regulations. Often, this relationship is formalized in the creation of a safety committee consisting of the safety specialist, representative employees, and managers. Usually there are two levels of safety committees. At the policy level is the committee made up of major division heads; this committee sets policy and rules, investigates major hazards, and has responsibility for the budget. At the departmental level, both supervisors and employees are members. Safety committees are concerned with the organization's entire safety program: inspection, design, record keeping, training, and motivation. The more people who can be involved through the committees, the more likely that the program will be successful.

Finally, the government inspector plays a role in keeping the organization on its toes regarding the safety of the employees.

A number of environmental factors are important for the health and safety of employees. Probably the most crucial factor is the **nature of the task,** especially as it is affected by the technology and working conditions of the organizational environment. For instance, health and safety problems are a lot more serious for coal miners—whose working conditions require them to breathe coal dust in the air—than for an office employee. An X-ray technician has a much greater chance of getting cancer as a result of working conditions than does an elementary school teacher.

A second vital factor is **employees' attitudes** toward health and safety. Attitudes can vary from concern for safety and cooperation regarding safety programs to apathy. If employees are apathetic, the best employer or safety program and the most stringent safety inspection by the government or the safety specialists in the HR department will not improve conditions.

The third factor affecting health and safety programs is economic conditions. We would accept the worst possible assumptions about human nature if we believed that any employer *knowingly* would choose to provide dangerous working conditions or would refuse to provide reasonable safeguards for employees. But there is a lack of knowledge about the consequences of some dangerous working conditions, and even when there is such knowledge, economic conditions can prevent employers from doing all they might wish. The risks of being a uranium miner are well known: 10 to 11 percent will die of cancer within 10 years. As long as there are no alternative extraction methods and as long as there is a need for uranium, some employees will be risking shorter lives in these jobs. Engineers and scientists are constantly at work to determine dangers and to prevent or mitigate consequences. But the costs of some of the prevention programs are such that the enterprise may find them prohibitive.

A fourth factor is the *unions*. Many unions have been very concerned about the safety and health of their members and have pressured employers in collective bargaining for better programs. Some unions have taken extraordinary steps to protect their members' health and safety. For example, the Teamsters' Union hired a nationally known occupational health expert to investigate unexplained illnesses at the Robert Shaw Controls Company plant in Ohio. The United Rubber Workers' contract calls for a study of effects of benzene on people exposed to it. The Oil, Chemical, and Atomic Workers' Unions have been subsidizing medical interns and residents to study occupational health conditions in plants where their members work. Unions also have used their political power to get legislation passed to improve the safety and health of members.

A fifth factor is *management's goals*. Some socially responsible managers and owners had active safety programs long before the laws required them. They made safety and health an important strategic goal and implemented it with significant safety considerations designed into the enterprise's layout. The safety programs included statistics, contests, and training sessions. Other managers, not so safety-conscious, did little other than what was required by law. Thus, managerial attitudes play a large part in the significance of the enterprise's health and safety program.

A sixth factor affecting health and safety on the job is *government*. For years federal and state governments have attempted to legislate to improve occupational safety and health. The government has tried to take a leading role in holding an organization responsible for prevention of accidents, disabilities, occupational illnesses, and deaths related to hazards in the workplace.

Governmental Responses to Safety and Health Problems

Before 1970, there was a widespread feeling across all sectors of American society that private organizations were not doing enough to ensure safe and healthy working conditions. The federal law in effect, the Walsh-Healy Act, was thought to be too weak or inadequately enforced, and state programs were incomplete, diverse, and lacking in authority. In 1936 alone 35,000 workplace deaths were reported. Lobbying by unions and employees led to the passage of several federal laws related to specific occupations, like the Coal Mine Health and Safety Act of 1969. This movement toward federal supervision of health and safety programs culminated in the passage of the **Occupational Safety and Health Act** (OSHA) in 1970. The basic requirements of OSHA are presented in Exhibit 17-4. In the year that OSHA became law, an estimated 14,200 workers died, 2.2 million suffered disabilities, and another 300,000 to 500,000 suffered from occupationally induced illnesses.[14]

The act, administered by the **Occupational Safety and Health Administration (OSHA)** of the Department of Labor, also created the National Institute of Occupational Safety and Health (NIOSH) to conduct research and develop safety and health standards for the workplace. The law was the product of three years of intensive legislative lobbying designed to remedy safety problems on the job and provide employment "free from recognized hazards." OSHA provisions originally applied to 4.1 million businesses and 57 million employees in almost every organization engaged in interstate commerce.[15]

OSHA has been enforced by federal inspectors or in partnership with state safety and health agencies. It encourages the states to assume responsibility for developing

EXHIBIT 17-4
Job Safety and Health Protection Requirements per OSHA

Source: *OSHA Bulletin.*

The Occupational Safety and Health Act of 1970 provides job safety and health protection for workers through the promotion of safe and healthful working conditions throughout the nation. The Occupational Safety and Health Administration (OSHA) of the Department of Labor has the primary responsibility for administering the Act. OSHA issues occupational safety and health standards, and its Compliance Safety and Health Officers conduct jobsite inspection to ensure compliance with the Act. Requirements of the act include the following:

Employers:

Each employer must furnish to each employee employment and a place of employment free from recognized hazards that are causing or are likely to cause death or serious harm to employees; and shall comply with occupational safety and health standards issued under the Act.

Employees:

Each employee shall comply with all occupational safety and health standards, rules, regulations, and orders issued under the Act that apply to his or her own actions and conduct on the job.

Inspection:

The Act requires that a representative of the employer and a representative authorized by the employees be given an opportunity to accompany the OSHA inspector for the purpose of aiding the inspection.

Complaint:

Employees or their representatives have the right to file a complaint with the nearest OSHA office requesting an inspection if they believe unsafe or unhealthful conditions exist in their workplace. The Act provides that employees may not be discharged or discriminated against in any way for filing safety and health complaints or otherwise exercising their rights under the Act.

Citation:

If upon inspection OSHA believes an employer has violated the Act, a citation alleging such violations will be issued to the employer. Each citation will specify a time period within which the alleged violation must be corrected.

Proposed Penalty:

The Act provides for mandatory penalties against employers of up to $1,000 for each nonserious violation. Penalties of up to $1,000 per day may be proposed for failure to correct violations within the proposed time period. Also, any employer who willfully or repeatedly violates the Act may be assessed penalties of up to $70,000 for each violation. Criminal penalties are also provided in the Act.

Voluntary Activity:

While providing penalties for violations, the Act also encourages efforts by labor and management, before an OSHA inspection, to reduce injuries and illnesses arising out of employment. Such cooperative action would initially focus on the identification and elimination of hazards that could cause death, injury, or illness to employees and supervisors.

and administering occupational safety and health laws and carrying out their own statistical programs. Before being granted full authority for its programs, a state must go through three steps. First, the state plan must have the preliminary approval of OSHA. Second, the state promises to take "developmental steps" to do certain things at certain times, such as adjusting legislation, hiring inspectors, and providing for an industrial hygiene laboratory. OSHA monitors the state plan for three years, and if the state fulfills these obligations, the third step is a trial period at full enforcement levels for at least a year. At the end of this intensive evaluation period, a final decision is made by OSHA on the qualifications of the state program.

If OSHA and the employer fail to provide safe working conditions, employees as individuals or through their unions can seek injunctions against the employer to force it to do so or submit to an inspection of the workplace. The employer cannot discriminate against an employee who takes these actions. OSHA has many requirements, but the three that most directly affect most employers are

- Meeting safety standards set by OSHA.
- Submitting to OSHA inspections.
- Keeping records and reporting accidents and illnesses.

OSHA Safety Standards

OSHA has established safety standards, defined as "practices, means, operations, or processes, reasonably necessary to provide safe . . . employment." The standards can affect any aspect of the workplace; new standards were established or proposed, for example, for such factors as lead, mercury, silica, benzene, talc dust, cotton dust, asbestos, and general health hazards. The standards may be industrywide or may apply only to a specific enterprise.

The assistant secretary of labor revises, modifies, or revokes existing standards or creates new ones on his or her own initiative or on the basis of petitions from interested parties (employees or unions). The National Institute of Occupational Safety and Health in the Department of Health and Human Services (HHS) is responsible for doing research from which standards are developed and for training those involved to implement them. Federal or national standards (such as those of the National Fire Protection Association) have also become OSHA standards. And temporary emergency standards can be created for imminent danger. Employers may be granted temporary variances by showing inability to comply with a standard within the time allowed if they have a plan to protect employees against the hazard.

The employer is responsible for knowing what these standards are and abiding by them. This is not easy. The *initial* standards were published in *The Federal Register* and interpretations of the standards are issued yearly *by volume*. The responsible manager is subject to thousands of pages of such standards. If they are not met, an organization can be shut down, and the responsible manager can be fined or jailed for not meeting OSHA's standards.

OSHA Inspections

To make sure the law is obeyed, OSHA inspectors visit places of employment, on their own schedules or on invitation of an employer, union, or employee. An employee who requests an inspection need not be identified to the employer. If the employer is found guilty of a violation, the penalty can reach up to $70,000 (for each violation). If the violation is not corrected in the time period granted, a penalty of $7,000 per day is issued. A willful first violation involving the death of a worker can result in a penalty of $70,000 and six months in jail. A second conviction involving the death of a worker can mean a $140,000 fine and one year in jail.

OSHA inspectors examine the premises for compliance and the records for accuracy. They categorize a violation as *imminent danger* (in which case they can close the business), *serious* (which calls for a major fine), *nonserious* (fine of up to $1,000), or *minimum* (small—notification is given, but no fine). The employer has the right to appeal fines or citations within OSHA (up to the level of the OSHA Review Commission) or in the courts.

OSHA inspections are not necessarily limited to the traditional workplace. According to the Bureau of Labor Statistics, nearly 20 million people in the United States performed some part of their primary job at home in 2001.[16] With so many home-based workers, does this mean that OSHA should treat these home offices just like they do other work sites? At the very least, this would mean that OSHA would reserve the right to conduct inspections of those parts of workers' homes dedicated to work activity. So far, public opinion is opposed to this potential intrusion into private lives. But, contrary to the perception that homes are much safer than work environments, some data are starting to emerge that indicate an increase in the number of home office injuries. The American Society of Safety

EXHIBIT 17-5   **Guide for Reporting and Recording Accidents, Illnesses, and Deaths**

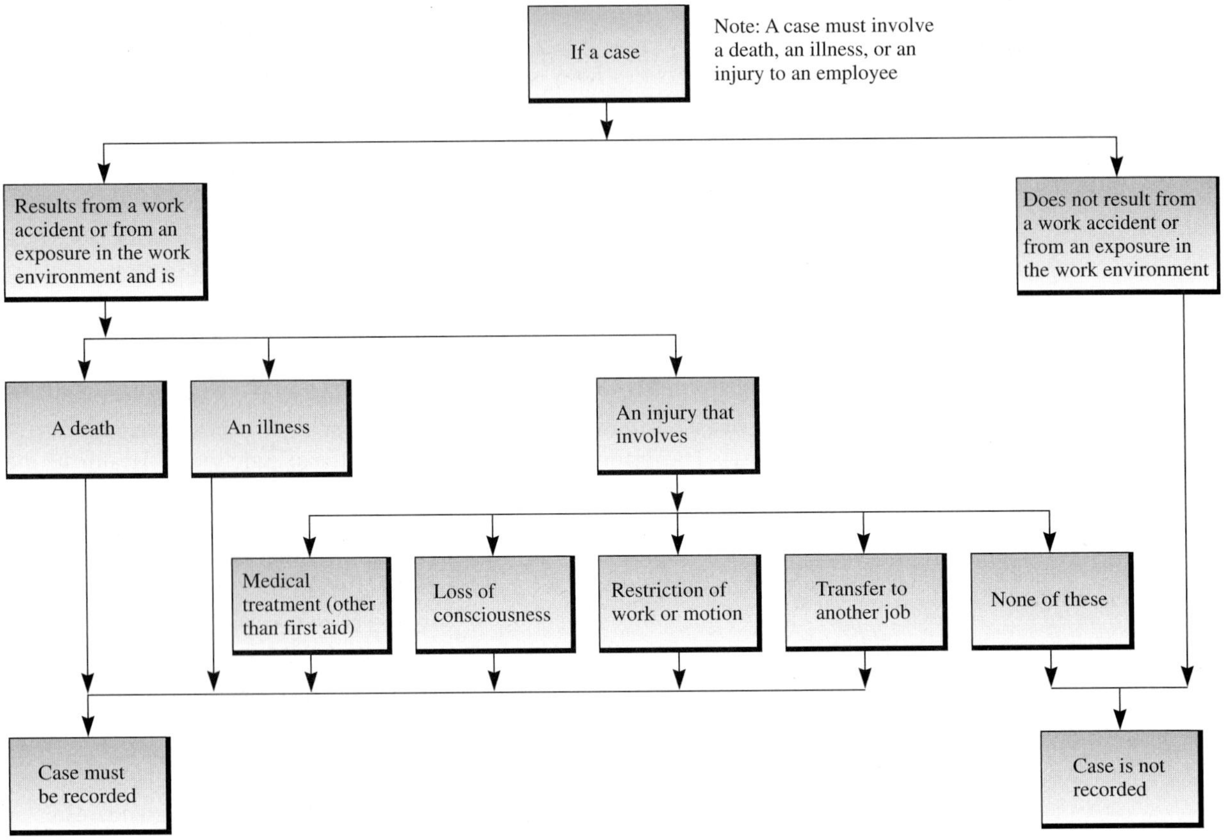

Engineers (ASSE) reports that injuries often occur in homes due to falls, improper wiring, poor air quality, eyestrain, and fire.

OSHA Record Keeping and Reporting

The third major OSHA requirement is that the employer keep standardized records of illnesses and injuries and calculate accident ratios. These are shown to OSHA compliance officers who ask to see them. Accidents and illnesses that must be reported are those that result in deaths, disabilities that cause the employee to miss work, and injuries that require treatment by a physician. An OSHA guide to when to report and record an illness, injury, or death is shown in Exhibit 17-5. Injuries or illnesses that require only first aid and involve no loss of work time need not be reported. To avoid reporting incidents, employers go to great lengths to categorize them as "minor injuries," trying to treat them through first aid and keeping the employee on the job (even a make-work job). Reporting might lead to an OSHA inspection or raise their workers' compensation insurance rates. The employer must also report accident frequency and severity rates. The firm must post OSHA Form 102—a summary of the report of injuries and illnesses—in a prominent place at work.

During the years when Ronald Reagan was president, OSHA's budget was cut by 25 percent and enforcement of its principles was nearly nonexistent.[17] Under Presidents George Bush (Senior) and Bill Clinton, the agency put health and safety issues on the front burner. A tougher OSHA did the following:

- Wrote a proposal that would require workers to wear seat belts if they drive as part of their jobs.
- Set guidelines to prevent repetitive-motion disorders.

HR Journal   *OSHA Modifies Record-Keeping Regulations*

Effective on January 1, 2002, OSHA issued a revised rule to improve the system employers use to track and record workplace injuries and illnesses. Estimated to affect some 1.3 million work sites in the United States, the introduction of Form 300 and Form 300A is part of a larger agency effort to help streamline and modernize OSHA reporting requirements. Like the previous rule (set in 1986), organizations with 10 or fewer employees as well as employers in those industries that fall into the low-hazard category (e.g., retail, service, and finance) are exempt from most of the requirements of the new rule.

Employers that fail to comply with or properly maintain OSHA's new Form 300 reporting requirements may face penalties of $1,000 per year. The agency has also indicated that a separate penalty of $1,000 may be levied against employers for each OSHA 301 Form (up to a maximum of $7,000) that was not completed annually. OSHA's Recordkeeping Policies and Procedures Manual CPL 2–0.131 (see www.osha.gov) provides additional information as to how the agency is enforcing this new rule.

The new rule updates the following three record-keeping forms:

- *OSHA Form 300* (log of work-related injuries and illnesses): simplified and printed on smaller legal size paper.
- *OSHA Form 301* (injury and illness report): includes more data about how the injury or illness occurred.
- *OSHA Form 300A* (summary of work-related injuries and illnesses): a separate form updated to make it easier to calculate incidence rates).

Other highlights from the newly revised rule on recording illnesses and injuries in the workplace include the following:

- Takes steps to protect employee privacy concerns.
- Includes new definitions of medical treatment, first aid, and restricted work to simplify recording decisions.
- Records needlestick injuries involving contamination by another's blood or bodily fluids.
- Clarifies definition of "restricted work."
- Simplifies recording of musculoskeletal disorders (MSDs).
- Eliminates term "lost workdays" and focuses on "days away" or "days restricted."
- Requires employers to allow employees to report injuries and illnesses.
- Requires the annual summary of injuries and illnesses to be posted for three months (from February to April), instead of one (February).

Some believe the most impactful change has to do with the fact that the new rule requires the owner or most senior manager or corporate officer at a location to sign and certify that the information has been reviewed and is correct.

Even though this new rule is in place, employers are required to keep (but not add to or further update) Form 200s and 101s from previous years.

Source: Jerry Laws (January 2004), "The New Form 300," *Occupational Health & Safety*, Vol. 73, Iss. 1, p. 84; Bob Whitmore (July 2002), Bureau of National Affairs, BNA Daily Report: Penalties for Recordkeeping Violations Detailed in OSHA Enforcement Instruction; Harry Smith (January 2002), "What Do the New Form 300 Regulations Mean to You?" *Occupational Health & Safety,* pp. 58–60; Bill Wright (January 2001), "OSHA Revises Recordkeeping Regulations," *Occupational Health & Safety Administration,* U.S. Department of Labor.

- Enacted a new rule to protect health care workers from exposure to HIV and hepatitis B.
- Used large fines to punish companies for breaking OSHA guidelines.

After initially decreasing OSHA's budget by $5.9 million in 2003 (compared with the funding received in 2002), President George W. Bush has proposed a budget of $468 million for the agency in 2005.[18]

OSHA: A Report Card[19]

Due to OSHA more employees are likely to exercise their rights concerning business hazards:

- Right to request an OSHA inspection.
- Right to be present during the inspection.

- Right to protection from reprisal for reporting the company to OSHA.
- Right to access his or her company medical records.
- Right to refuse to work if there is a real danger of death or serious injury or illness from job hazards.

What can a manager or HRM specialist do to help keep the enterprise in compliance with OSHA? The HR specialist should know the standards that apply to the organization and check to see that they are being met. HRM is also responsible for keeping OSHA records up to date and filing them on time. The operating manager must know the standards that apply to his or her unit or department and see that the unit meets the standards. As citizens, all managers should see to it that OSHA is effective at the organization. But they can also write their congressional representatives to improve it so that:

Standards are understandable and focus on important items.

Advisory inspections are permitted.

Records and reports are minimized, efficient, and correct.

Organizational Responses to Safety and Health Issues

The safety department or unit and the safety committee can take a number of approaches to improving the safety of working conditions:

1. Prevention and design.
2. Inspection and research.
3. Training and motivation.

Safety Design and Preventive Approaches

Numerous preventive measures have been adopted by organizations in attempts to improve their safety records. One is to design more safety into the workplace through safety engineering. Engineers have helped through the study of human factors engineering, which seeks to make jobs more comfortable, less confusing, and less fatiguing. This can keep employees more alert and less vulnerable to accidents.

For example, safety engineers can design safety into the workplace using an analytical design approach. This total design approach analyzes all factors involved in the job, including such factors as speed of an assembly line, stresses in the work, and job design. On the basis of this analysis, steps are taken to improve safety precautions. Protective guards are designed for machinery and equipment. Color coding warns of dangerous areas. Standard safety colors, which should be taught in safety class, include gray for machinery and red where an area presents danger of fire. Other dangers may be highlighted by bright orange paint.

Inspection, Reporting, and Accident Research

A second activity of safety departments or specialists is to inspect the workplace with the goal of reducing accidents and illnesses. The safety specialist is looking for a number of things, including answers to these questions:

Are safety rules being observed? How many near misses have occurred?

Are safety guards, protective equipment, and so on being used?

Are there potential hazards in the workplace that safety redesign could improve?

Are there potential occupational health hazards?

At regular intervals during the work year, safety and personnel specialists carry out accident research, that is, systematic evaluation of the evidence concerning accidents and health hazards. Data for this research should be gathered from both external and internal sources. Safety and health journals point out recent findings that should stimulate the safety specialist to look for hazardous conditions at the workplace. Reports from the National Institute of Occupational Safety and Health (NIOSH), the research organization created by the OSHA legislation, also provides important data for research. Data developed at the workplace included accident reports, inspection reports by the government and the organization's safety specialists, and recommendations of the safety committees.

Accident research often involves computation of organizational accident rates. These are compared with industry and national figures to determine the organization's relative safety performance. Several statistics are computed. Accident frequency rate is computed per million hours of work, as follows:

$$\text{Frequency rate} = \frac{\text{number of accidents} \times 1{,}000{,}000}{\text{number of work hours in the period}}$$

The accidents used in this computation are those causing the worker to lose work time. The accident severity rate is computed as follows:

$$\text{Accident severity rate} = \frac{\text{number of accidents} \times 1{,}000{,}000}{\text{number of work hours in the period}}$$

OSHA suggests reporting accidents as number of injuries per 100 full-time employees per year as a simpler approach. The formula is:

$$\frac{\text{Number of illnesses and injuries}}{\text{Total hours worked by all employees for the year}} \times 200{,}000$$

The base equals the number of workers employed (100 full-time equivalent) working full-time (for example, 40 hours per week and for 50 weeks if vacation is 2 weeks). The organization's statistics should be compared with the industry's statistics and government statistics (from the Department of Labor and OSHA). Most studies find that although effective accident research should be very complex, in reality it is unsophisticated and unscientific.

Safety Training and Motivation Programs

The third approach organizations take to safety is training and motivation programs. Safety training usually is part of the orientation program. It also takes place at different points during the employee's career. This training is usually voluntary, but some is required by government agencies. Studies of the effectiveness of such training are mixed. Some studies indicate that some methods, such as job instruction training (JIT) and accident simulations, are more effective than others. Others contend that successes are accounted for by the employee's perception that management really believes in safety training.[20] A few studies find that the programs make employees more aware of safety, but not necessarily safer in their behavior. Nevertheless, effectively developed safety training programs can help provide a safer environment for all employees.

Preventive Health Programs: A Wellness Approach

One way of defining *health* is to say that it is the *absence of disease.* You will remember from the beginning of this chapter that health hazards like physical and biological hazards, toxic and cancer-causing dusts and chemicals, and stressful working conditions put

addition to the other health risks that the average employee meets in his or her daily life outside the workplace. A more informative definition of **health** is "a state of physical, mental, and social well-being."[21] This definition points to the relationships among body, mind, and social patterns. An employee's health can be harmed through disease, accident, or stress.[22] Managers now realize that they must be concerned about the general health of employees, including their psychological well-being. An otherwise competent employee who is depressed and has low self-esteem is as nonproductive as one who is injured and hospitalized.

A number of factors are contributing to the sharp rise in the cost of health benefits.[23] These include:

1. Aging of the workforce. Older employees have more chronic illnesses.
2. Competition among health insurance carriers that raises instead of lowers the cost of care.
3. Shifting of cost from the government to the private sector.
4. Inefficiency of health care providers.
5. Increasing malpractice litigation.
6. Failure of employers to respond to these changing patterns.

As a result, more and more companies are switching from the traditional health care scheme of insuring against health crises as they occur to a preventive or wellness approach to health care management.

The **preventive** or **wellness approach** encourages employees to make lifestyle changes now through better nutrition, regular exercise programs, abstinence from smoking and alcohol, stress counseling, and annual physical examinations.[24]

One large company that has adopted the preventive approach to health care successfully is the Adolph Coors Company in Golden, Colorado.[25] Over the 10 years since the program was first instituted, Coors estimated a savings of approximately $1.99 million annually from decreasing medical claims, decreased absenteeism, and increased productivity. Each $1 spent on the wellness program provided a $6.15 payback. During the same 10-year period, comparably sized organizations saw health care costs rise 18 percent while Coors's rose only 5 percent.

Chairman William Coors said that wellness had become part of the corporate culture. The first step in the program was the opening of a 25,000-square-foot wellness facility, a completely equipped gym that all Coors employees were encouraged to use. Various new programs were also instituted, including stress management, weight loss, smoking cessation, nutritional counseling, risk assessment, and orthopedic rehabilitation. Both employees and their spouses were encouraged to take advantage of free mammography and blood pressure screenings, employee and family counseling, and pre- and postnatal education offered on site.

The Coors wellness program was based on a six-step model of behavioral change: awareness, education, incentives, programs, self-action, and follow-up and support. Each employee was made aware through a health hazard appraisal (HHA), a statistical evaluation of that person's individual health risks. The HHA included suggestions for lowering risk and changing behavior to live a longer, healthier life. Incentives included refunding the cost of weight-loss programs if the loss was maintained for a full 12 months. Various programs like the gym and nutritional counseling were offered on-site as support.

Coors identified what it considered 12 key elements of a successful wellness program:

1. Support and direction by the CEO.
2. Wellness as a stated priority in the company's policy statement.
3. Inclusion of family members as well as the employee.

4. Accessibility of the program to the whole family.
5. Employees' input into programs offered, times, and so on.
6. Needs assessment before each phase of the program was instituted.
7. Periodic in-house evaluation to be sure objectives were being met.
8. Ongoing communication of the program's goals and components.
9. HRM monitoring of related issues like AIDS, cancer, and so on.
10. Community involvement.
11. Staffing with qualified health care specialists.
12. Establishment of a separate budget for the wellness program.

Many other companies employing thousands of employees have reported exceptional paybacks from adopting the wellness approach. The Prudential Insurance Company reported that its Houston office reduced disability days by 20 percent and obtained $1.93 savings for every dollar invested in its in-house exercise programs. Its major medical costs dropped from $574 to $302 per employee in just two years.[26] A fitness program including regular exercise and various health education and lifestyle improvement classes was started at the Canadian Life Assurance Company, resulting in a 22 percent drop in absenteeism. Johnson & Johnson took a wellness approach called "Live for Life," including nutrition, stress management, smoking cessation, and fitness. It compared 5,000 employees who enrolled in the program with 3,000 who did not and found that hospital costs per person were 34 percent lower for participants than for nonparticipants! Nonparticipants averaged 76 hours of absence each year while participants averaged 56 hours (20 hours less). Quaker Oats has been offering its 6,000 U.S.-based employees a number of promotion programs for the past 20 years. Employees and their spouses can earn up to $600 in credits for benefits by participating in the company's voluntary health risk appraisal (a confidential lifestyle questionnaire administered by a third party) and health screening (blood, cholesterol, and weight). Also, additional credits can be earned by pledging not to misuse/abuse alcohol, drugs or prescription medications; not to use tobacco products; and to exercise. Results of the overall program are promising. The number and severity of medical claims have decreased and several employees in the program have moved from the high-risk category to moderate- or low-risk category—saving Quaker Oats about $2 million per annum.[27]

Midsized and small employers can offer scaled-down versions of the corporate giants' wellness programs while still reaping the same benefits. It is important that the same 12 steps detailed by Coors be followed regardless of the company's size, however. The wellness approach can also be successfully integrated with a health benefits plan for retirees.[28] An ongoing research program in California is monitoring the impact of Senior Healthtrac, a program designed to improve retirees' health and lower medical costs. The plan has been offered to 250,000 older Americans, many of whom were employees of BankAmerica and Blue Shield of California. After just a year, about $133 per year in direct savings in medical costs for each participant was recorded.

The wellness or preventive approach is not foolproof, particularly if it is adopted without fully understanding the necessity of commitment by management and manager–employee communication.[29] Almost 80 percent of corporations offering a wellness program continue without any quantifiable proof that the program is saving them money or increasing productivity. Promised reductions in health care premiums from insurers are not always delivered and are minimal at best. Employees who need help most may not participate. Note, therefore, that the immediate benefits of a preventive approach to health care are minimal and that the ultimate payback is in the long term. Another possible snag is that some wellness programs that contain financial incentives for employees to meet certain criteria may conflict with the Americans with Disabilities Act.[30]

Nevertheless it remains true that health promotion programs that can help employees develop healthier lifestyles, reduce their risk factors, and use health services more appropriately are effective strategies to help management control the cost of health and disability benefits.[31]

Safety and Health Issues

HRMEMO

Frequent business travelers, or road warriors, often experience what is known as travel stress. Defined as the perceptual, emotional, behavioral, and physical responses made by an individual during one or more of the phases of travel, travel stress can occur before, during, or after trips. If left unchecked, travel stress can eventually lead to absenteeism, burnout, productivity fluctuations, and turnover.

Source: Adapted from J. M. Ivancevich, R. Konopaske, and R. S. DeFrank (2003), "Business Travel Stress: A Model, Propositions and Managerial Implications," *Work & Stress*, Vol. 17, pp. 138–157; Richard DeFrank, Robert Konopaske, and John Ivancevich (May 2000), "Executive Travel Stress: Perils of the Road Warrior," *Academy of Management Executive*, pp. 58–71.

There is increasing evidence that there may be just as many safety and health hazards in the modern workplace as there were during the rise of the factory system. Some of them are actually the same—for example, the dangerous work environment in construction trades. Others seem to be a result of changing technology, demographics, and lifestyle factors. It would be impossible to address all the safety and health issues facing managers in the workplace of the early 21st century, so we have chosen some of the most interesting and pervasive to examine in a bit more depth: stress, violence, indoor environmental quality, HIV-AIDS, and cumulative trauma disorders (CTDs) (such as carpal tunnel syndrome). Each issue presents the same problem: how to balance the rights of the individual against the rights of the rest of the workforce and the economic imperatives of the firm.

Stress Management

Stress is a common experience that is part of everyone's life. It can be good for a person. Good stress, called *eustress,* is what helps a person complete a report on time or generate a good, quick problem-solving procedure. Unfortunately, stress can also be a major negative aspect of the workplace. The American Institute of Stress estimates that stress costs U.S. employers between $200 billion and $300 billion a year in increased workers' compensation claims, lost productivity, higher health care costs, and turnover.[32]

The concept of stress is very difficult to pin down in specific terms. There are experts who think of stress as the pressures in the world that produce emotional discomfort. Others feel that emotional discomfort is the stress that is caused by pressures or conditions called *stressors.* Still others view stress in terms of physiological or body reactions: blood pressure, heart rate, or hormone levels.[33] We will define stress as a person's physical, chemical, and mental reactions to stressors or stimuli in the environment. Stress occurs whenever environmental forces (stimuli) throw bodily and mental functions out of equilibrium.

Stress and Disease

Job-related stress has been associated with a vast array of diseases, such as coronary heart disease, hypertension, peptic ulcers, colitis, and various psychological problems including anxiety and depression. Research has shown that stress directly affects the endocrine system, the cardiovascular system, the muscular system, and the emotions.[34] It also has a general arousal influence on the entire body.

"Person-Environment Fit"

Changes in the work and personal environment are inevitable. Too often, managers underestimate how changes can throw a person off kilter. A person who does not feel comfortable with his or her work environment is in what psychologists refer to as a *state of disequilibrium.* The person's skills, abilities, and goals do not fit with the work environment (boss, co-workers, compensation system). Lack of fit between the person and the environment can have results on several levels: subjective (feeling fatigued), behavioral (accident-proneness), cognitive (a mental block), physiological (elevated blood pressure), and organizational (higher absence rate).[35]

Research studies point out that these levels of stress caused by disequilibrium or lack of fit are costly. The costs to an organization are found in premature deaths of employees, higher rates of accidents, performance inefficiencies, increased turnover, increased disability payments, and many other areas.[36]

Stressors

One way to attack the cost of stress is to identify the stressors that contribute to it. Following are two examples: workload and role conflict.

Workload A person's workload can cause stress. Workload can relate to the quantity of the work or the quality of the activity to be completed (for instance, mental requirements). Underload as well as overload can create problems. Overload can cause a person to work long hours to stay even, which can result in fatigue and more accidents. On the other hand, boredom can set in if a person is underloaded. A bored worker often avoids work by staying at home more frequently. The worker who is bored and stays at home often mopes around, which results in a lack of adequate exercise to maintain a healthy body.[37] It is a vicious circle.

Role Conflict How a person behaves in a given job depends on many factors. A combination of the expectations and demands an employee places upon him- or herself and those of co-workers results in a set of forces called **role pressures.** When a situation arises in which two or more role pressures are at odds, role conflict exists. Role conflict exists whenever compliance with one set of pressures makes compliance with another set difficult, objectionable, or impossible.

Researchers have found that conflict is associated with job dissatisfaction and anxiety.[38] It has also been linked to heart disease, elevated blood pressure, and excessive eating. Role conflict seems to undermine a peaceful work state and leads to physiological and psychological changes.

Coping with Stress

Stress is inevitable. However, when it hurts the individual, co-workers, or the organization, it must be addressed. There are two ways to cope with stress. The first is to eliminate the stressor by changing policies, the structure, the work requirements, or whatever is necessary. The second approach is to deal with stress individually.

Programs for coping with stress at the individual level include meditation, biofeedback, exercise, and diet. These programs help some people relax, feel better, and regenerate energy.

There are also organizational programs. Experts in organizations can use their knowledge about stress and health to develop and implement organization-sponsored workshops and seminars for coping with stress. In addition, these experts can recommend structural, job, and policy changes that can eventually improve the well-being of employees.

Levi Strauss & Co. has an ongoing stress management program in which 1,500 employees have participated in an all-day seminar. Relaxation techniques and self-motivation procedures are taught; and examination of life goals, identification of harmful personality traits, and behavior modification techniques are part of the program.

The HR department has a role to play in programs for coping with stress. It can provide specialists, facilities, monitoring or evaluation, and other important resources. Organizations such as IBM, Tenneco, Control Data, Shell, and Prudential already have HR employees performing such duties as setting up exercise classes, initiating fitness programs, and providing diet counseling. More and more organizations have become concerned about and involved in stress management in the early part of the 21st century. Stress management programs are even being developed in Japan, where white-collar employees are paying a high price for success: alcoholism, mental breakdowns, and suicide. The Japanese name for the phenomenon is "karoushi," defined as death from overwork. It is also called "stress death," resulting from the cumulative long-range effects of working in a situation where one feels trapped and powerless to effect any change for the better.[39]

During the past 20 years, stress management programs have met with variable success. It is not enough to inform employees about the risks of stress. Even pointing out behaviors that cause or increase stress does not mean that the employee will change his or her negative behavior. The desire to change behavior may not be enough. Therefore, guidelines to follow when instituting a stress management program must include knowledgeable presenters and programs that are relevant and specific to each individual and to each work environment.

Violence in the Workplace[40]

Earlier in this chapter, homicide in the workplace was discussed. But the statistics presented there did not include deaths of bystanders and nonemployees, which could number in the thousands. In fact, a report by the Justice Department said that over 1.7 million violent crimes occur in American workplaces each year. A single case of violence in the workplace can cost an employer more than $250,000 in lost work time and legal expenses.

Twenty-five percent of all workers claim that they have been harassed, threatened, or attacked on their jobs each year, according to a survey by Northwestern Mutual Life Insurance. Of that number, 15 percent claimed to have been physically attacked at some time in their working lives. Attacks are most often perpetrated by customers or clients (44 percent); however, the ones we hear about most are often the work of disgruntled current or former employees. Included in the statistics are homicides, physical attacks, rapes, aggravated and other assaults, threats, intimidation, coercion, all forms of harassment, and any other act that creates a hostile work environment.

A recent report by the Centers for Disease Control and Prevention began with the following description of one week of violence in workplaces:

> During one week, an owner of a pawn shop, a convenience store clerk, a psychologist, two sanitation managers, a tavern owner, a fisherman, a cook, two cab drivers, a co-owner of a furniture store, a restaurant manager, a maintenance supervisor, a video store owner, and a postal carrier were all victims of workplace homicide. . . . Guns were by far the most frequently used weapon in these crimes, accounting for 75% of workplace homicide deaths. Knives and other types of cutting and piercing instruments were used in only 14% of all homicides.

OSHA does not have a specific standard for workplace violence. However, several states have developed standards or recommendations. Washington state adopted crime prevention guidelines for late-night retail establishments. The New Jersey Public Employees Occupational Safety and Health Program published guidelines to assist public employees in health care facilities to help protect themselves from violent and aggressive behavior. California is helping its employers establish, implement, and maintain an effective Injury and Illness Prevention Program, which will address the hazards associated with workplace violence.

In determining liability, violent behavior is divided into three categories:

1. *Violence by an employee directed at a third party independent of the workplace* For example, in one incident a bus driver molested several young passengers. Employers can be held liable under the theories of negligent hire or negligent retention. In the case of the bus driver, the church that had hired him was held responsible because he had a previous history of child molestation.

2. *Violence by an employee directed at another employee* The employer can be held liable by OSHA, state workers' compensation regulations, or common-law principles of negligence with regard to workers.

3. *Violence by a nonemployee (third party) directed at an employee in the workplace* The employer's liability is the same as in case 2.

Preventing workplace violence is a complicated process. Human resource policies, employee assistance counseling, and security measures are all part of a comprehensive approach. The first step that needs to be taken is to develop preemployment screening. This is quite difficult to implement, however, because the employer must be sure not to violate any of the applicant's civil rights, especially those relating to Title VII of the Civil Rights Act and the Americans with Disabilities Act.

Postemployment measures include these:

1. Create a culture of mutual respect, including open communication, empowerment, and recognition.
2. Develop supervisory training classes in negotiation, communication, listening, team building, and conflict resolution.
3. Refer troubled employees to employee assistance programs (EAPs) to help deal with work, family, marital, financial, and other personal problems.
4. Provide emotional support and outplacement programs for laid-off employees.
5. Conduct exit interviews that will identify potentially violent responses to termination.
6. Implement a clear, well-communicated, easily accessible grievance procedure and encourage employees to use it.
7. Develop a confidential reporting system that allows employees to report threats or inappropriate behavior, which may indicate a potential for violence.
8. Strictly control access to the workplace with an up-to-date security system, consistently enforced.
9. Train supervisors to recognize the signs of drug and alcohol abuse, depression, and other emotional disorders.
10. Develop and implement a crisis plan to deal with violent incidents, including escape routes, how to report the incident, and how to avoid further trouble.

Indoor Environmental Quality (IEQ)[41]

Over the last 10 years, more and more employees have expressed concerns over the quality of the indoor office environment. Two terms you should be familiar with in this context are **indoor environmental quality (IEQ)** and **sick-building syndrome.** IEQ refers to the quality of the air in a business environment. Sick-building syndrome covers a wide range of symptoms employees believe can be caused by the building itself. For example, one office building near Washington, D.C., had to be evacuated several times because of a noxious odor that was making employees violently ill. The reason that employees zero in on IEQ is that symptoms are often alleviated by leaving the building.

The National Institute for Occupational Safety and Health (NIOSH) evaluates potential health hazards in the workplace through its Health Hazard Evaluation (HHE) Program. Any employer, employee, employee representative, state or local government agency, or federal agency can ask NIOSH investigators to conduct an evaluation.

Besides air quality, other factors that contribute to indoor environmental quality and sick-building syndrome include discomfort, noise, poor lighting, ergonomic stressors like poorly designed equipment or jobs, and job-related psychological stressors. Typically, a wide spectrum of symptoms are reported: headaches, unusual fatigue, itching or burning of eyes and skin, nasal congestion, dry throat, and nausea.

There are many reasons why IEQ problems may be increasing. Ventilation requirements were changed in the 1970s to help preserve fossil fuels, and new buildings became virtually airtight. Computers and other new technologies forced changes in the way work was accomplished, creating ergonomic and organizational stress. A World Health Organizational Committee survey conducted in the 1980s found that approximately

30 percent of new and remodeled buildings worldwide may be the subject of complaints related to air quality.

Sick-building syndrome has been linked to several factors. These include inadequate ventilation and chemical contaminants from indoor sources like adhesives, carpeting, upholstery, copy machines, pesticides, and cleaning agents. The author recently developed a recurrence of asthma owing to a solvent used to remove old carpet and glue used to lay the new carpet. Other factors are chemical contaminants from outdoor sources (motor vehicle exhaust fumes, etc.); biological contaminants (bacteria, molds, pollen, and viruses); inadequate temperature; and high levels of humidity. Pollutants that are most frequently in the news include secondhand smoke, asbestos, and radon. Workers' compensation claims based on IEQs have become increasingly frequent.

Solutions to problems with IEQ and sick-building syndrome usually include combinations of the following: removal of the pollutant; modification of ventilation (that is, increasing rates and air distribution); cleaning the air; installing particle control devices; and banning smoking. Education and communication are also important elements of both remedial and preventive IEQ control.

An increasing number of employers are recognizing the fact that smokers have more health problems than nonsmokers do. According to reports, health care expenditures in the United States directly related to smoking total $72 billion per year. In a study conducted by the National Cancer Institute, nearly 70 percent of the 80,661 employees responding said they worked in places where smoking was banned in either the office or other common areas. This compares to 47 percent in 1993.[42] In the mid-1980s, only 3 percent were banned from smoking in the workplace.

Some employers have gone so far as to not hire anyone who smokes. Smokers' rights groups challenge the legality of this policy. Some claim that addiction to tobacco is a disability under either the Americans with Disabilities Act or specific state laws. There is no specific set of rulings available, but it appears that lawsuits about smoking in the workplace and as a hiring decision factor are going to become more prevalent in the next decade.

HIV-AIDS in the Workplace[43]

Human immunodeficiency virus (HIV) and acquired immune deficiency syndrome (AIDS) were first reported in the United States in the late 1970s. Each of the letters in AIDS stands for a word:

Acquired: The disease is passed from one person to another.

Immune: It attacks the body's immune system—the system that protects the body from disease.

Deficiency: The defense system is not working.

Syndrome: It leads to a group of symptoms or illnesses, occurring together, that indicate a particular disease or condition.

HIV-AIDS is transmitted by blood, body products, or sexual activity; it is a disease caused by the HIV retrovirus. It is not spread through casual contact, but exposure to infected blood or body products can lead to infection if the individual exposed has an open wound.

At the beginning of the 21st century the World Health Organization (WHO) has estimated that over 33 million people were infected with HIV. More than 500,000 Americans have contracted AIDS since the late 1970s, and approximately 97 percent of those are of working age. Seventy-five percent are between the ages of 25 to 44, the prime working cohort. Between ages 25 and 44, AIDS is the second leading cause of death, right behind cancer. As many as 1 million Americans may be infected with HIV-AIDS but have not as yet developed symptoms. While it was once thought that there was a dormancy period between initial infection and the development of full-blown AIDS, several medical researchers have recently reported evidence that the deadly virus begins spreading within just a few days of the initial contact.

Individuals infected with HIV-AIDS are protected under the Americans with Disabilities Act, but the disease is quite different from most other disabilities. Because of the complex nature of the infection and the multiplicity of AIDS-related illnesses, greater understanding is required of the general medical symptoms and of how the legislation should be applied. HR managers and other managers may have a hard job determining just how to comply with the law. Be that as it may, the doctrine of "reasonable accommodation" applies.[44]

According to the Centers for Disease Control, every employer in the United States will eventually have at least one employee with AIDS. It has even been reported that AIDS may become the number 1 American business problem as the 21st century progresses. Significant productivity has already been lost from illness, disability, and premature death. Fear of the disease by co-workers has also contributed significantly to lost productivity. A case of AIDS at work is a serious issue for both the employee and that person's fellow employees. Disclosure raises a potential for retaliation from peers, supervisors, and other employees in general. At New England Telephone & Telegraph Company, for instance, an employee named Paul told his supervisor that he had AIDS. The supervisor allegedly passed the information along to co-workers. Some of them began to threaten Paul, and he was fired. He sued his employer, charging disability discrimination, breach of privacy, and other violations of state law (the state involved was Massachusetts). The case was settled out of court, and Paul was reemployed. When he returned to work, his co-workers walked out. Medical experts had to be called in to discuss HIV-AIDS and how it was transmitted before the other employees would return to work.

OSHA passed its Bloodborne Pathogen Standards in July 1992. These apply to all workplaces with employees who could reasonably be expected to come into contact with blood or body fluids. Employers must develop, implement, and adhere to the following guidelines: develop an exposure control plan; take universal precautions to avoid contamination; develop cleaning protocols; have workers wear personal protective equipment; communicate the presence of hazards; and inform, train, and keep records of all possible incidents. It must be noted, however, that few jobs exist where having HIV-AIDS prohibits an employee from performing essential job functions. Should such a situation arise, the employer is expected to provide reasonable accommodations, which might include changes in equipment or work assignments. The primary job of any manager who knows that an employee has HIV-AIDS is to *preserve the individual's privacy.*

A company can choose one of three approaches when dealing with AIDS:

1. Categorizing AIDS under a comprehensive life-threatening illness policy.
2. Forming an AIDS-specific policy.
3. No policy.

BankAmerica uses the first approach, identifying all resources available through the company's HR department for any employees facing a life-threatening illness. The policy also includes 10 guidelines for managers of stricken employees. Morrison and Foerster, a law firm, has a six-point AIDS-specific policy. If the no-policy approach is chosen, the workforce must be kept informed about AIDS and told that people with AIDS are *entitled* to remain employed.

Hotlines, job flexibility, part-time work, flexible hours, and working at home are other approaches to keep the worker gainfully employed. In addition, the federal government is suggesting that employers establish guidelines on accidents involving the handling of blood or other body fluids, to control the spread of the infection.

AIDS-HIV is a syndrome that remains almost 100 percent fatal. Its treatment will cost American businesses and individual citizens billions of dollars each year. The AIDS

HRMEMO

HIV and AIDS are not only a global humanity problem, but also a global business problem. In some regions of the world, it is expected that the death toll due to AIDS will have a major impact on availability and productivity of working-age populations. For example, in sub-Saharan Africa, more than 25 million people are infected with HIV (in addition to the 11.5 million individuals who have already died from AIDS). Global businesses must join forces with local governments and international health agencies to help identify and implement immediate workable solutions.

Sources: Emily Oster (May 2005), "Sexually Transmitted Infections, Sexual Behavior, and the HIV/AIDS Epidemic," *The Quarterly Journal of Economics*, Vol. 120, Iss. 2, pp. 467–515; Naomi Junghae (September 2001), "Impact of HIV and AIDS on Businesses: Risk Management Approaches," *Benefits & Compensation International,* pp. 15–19; John Carey (February 2001), "One Step Forward, Two Back?" *BusinessWeek*, pp. 69–71.

epidemic has pointed out the weaknesses in our health care system: lack of preventive medicine, a shortage of hospitals ready to deal with the chronically ill, and no universal access to health insurance.

Cumulative Trauma Disorders (CTDs)[45]

Repetitive stress injuries (RSIs) and **cumulative trauma disorders (CTDs)** have reached epidemic proportions, according to the Centers for Disease Control and Prevention. These disorders are being reported at an alarming rate in all types of workplaces: meatpacking and chicken processing plants, grocery stores, and offices filled with personal computers. According to data from the Bureau of Labor Statistics, approximately 67 percent of newly reported occupational illnesses in private industry in 2000 were disorders related to RSI and CTDs. Of the 242,000 cases, many of these were classified as carpal tunnel syndrome or noise-induced hearing loss. The sectors most affected by RSIs and CTDs include manufacturing (164,000 cases), services (29,000 cases), and wholesale and retail trade (21,000 cases). In terms of trends, the number of RSIs and CTDs increased from approximately 20,000 in 1981 to 332,000 cases in 1994. Fortunately, the period between 1995 and 2000 has seen a decline in the number of reported cases to a total of 242,000 cases in 2000.

Cumulative trauma disorder and repetitive stress injury (RSI) are not specific medical conditions. CTD usually refers to conditions that arise from obvious trauma or injury that occurs more than once. For example, if a woman injures her back lifting a box at work and then injures it later, she could claim to be suffering from CTD. RSI refers to a repetitive activity which is not in itself harmful or injurious but which is alleged to become harmful owing to the sheer number of repetitions. Common examples in the workplace include dragging a mouse to move the computer's cursor and sliding products across the automatic price sensor of a cash register in a grocery store. Carpal tunnel syndrome is the most frequently reported CTD.

Carpal tunnel syndrome (CTS) refers to the eight bones in the wrist, called carpals, which form a tunnel-like structure filled with flexor tendons. The tendons control finger movements, and the median nerve pathway to the sensory nerves in the hand runs through the tunnel as well. Repetitive flexing and extension of the wrist can cause thickening of the protective sheaths that surround the tendons. As a result, carpal tunnel syndrome can arise. It includes painful tingling in one or both hands at night, a feeling of uselessness in the fingers, and tingling during the day, followed by decreased ability and strength to squeeze things. In advanced cases, muscles atrophy and hand strength is lost.

Research by NIOSH has linked carpal tunnel syndrome to many occupations, especially those in the manufacturing sector. Jobs involving cutting, assembling small parts, finishing, sewing, and cleaning seem to be especially associated with CTS. No nationwide statistics on the incidence or the cost of CTS are currently available. The Bureau of National Affairs has estimated, however, that a single case of CTS can cost as much as $30,000 to treat. Treatment can involve surgery, physical therapy, and anti-inflammatory medication. Prevention of CTS focuses on ways to relieve awkward wrist positions and forceful arm and hand movements on the job. Other solutions involve modifying workstations, rotating jobs, and providing frequent rest breaks.

Ergonomics, the study of workplace design to minimize repetitive motion disorders and stress, is the way that OSHA has chosen to implement preventive policies. Although OSHA's attempts to pass an ergonomic "one size fits all" standard were defeated,[46] many companies see the common sense of designing computer workstations, assembly-line tasks, and other jobs that require repetitive motion in a way that the risks of repetitive motion disorders are minimized. By taking a proactive stance and implementing ergonomically oriented changes, many organizations have realized substantial savings and higher levels of worker productivity. In the 1990s, the U.S. Postal Service estimated that carpal

HRMemo

Break reminders can be delivered from a new breed of ergonomic software programs such as RSIGuard and ErgoSentry. Functioning much like an egg timer, these programs can be downloaded (usually as freeware or shareware) from the Web and used to help prevent repetitive motion injuries such as carpal tunnel syndrome. Measuring both the amount of time and the intensity with which the employee is using a keyboard and mouse, the software makes suggestions about when to take breaks.

Source: Adapted from Sally McGrne (March 2001), "Ergonomic Programs That Pester Users to Take Those Breaks," *New York Times,* p. G10.

Ted thought back over this first year in the job of safety director. It had been busy and challenging, but he felt that his biggest challenge lay ahead of him. Fred Wayne had just stopped by and dropped another task on his desk. There was a rumor around the plant that Lorrie Mills was returning from a long leave of absence, and her co-workers were saying that if she came back, they would quit. Lorrie, only 30, had developed cancer about two years previously. Ted and other personnel in the HR department were aware of her diagnosis and that she had successfully undergone a long course of radiation therapy. Over the past six months she had contacted Fort regarding her progress. She was, indeed, ready to come back, and Zaho Wen in the plant was happy about that. She had been one of the best team supervisors Fort had. However, he too had alerted Ted about the rumors and fear that some of her subordinates were expressing. They just didn't feel comfortable around anyone who had been that sick. Some of them even believed that cancer was contagious! Given the new Americans with Disabilities Act and the nondiscrimination policies in California, Ted needed to do some damage control. He had to smooth Lorrie's way back to work and deal with the problem of possible turnover by the frightened employees. His AIDS training program had been very effective in defusing a similar situation. Ted felt the best thing to do was offer a plantwide training program on cancer and also on Fort's nondiscrimination policy. The safety director's job was a real challenge!

tunnel syndrome alone had cost the organization between $18 million and $30 million in lost productivity and health care costs. An ergonomic program was implemented in their automated mail sorting sites that saved the organization approximately $10 million. After implementing its own ergonomic program, the insurance company ITT Hartford Group experienced a 69 percent reduction of reported injuries (9.6 to 3 for every 1,000 employees) and the number of workdays lost due to repetitive injuries dropped from 33 to 7.[47]

Although repetitive motion injuries are not a new issue in the workplace, awareness of the problem has grown tremendously over the last 25 years. The number of ergonomics-related injuries and illnesses being reported continues to escalate, and the workdays lost as a result are becoming very significant. Employers must contend with lost productivity, increased absenteeism, threats of lawsuits under OSHA, and fines. One solution is to implement your own ergonomics policy. The safety and health manager of Dixie Chemical Company, Mark Hansen, confirms that the basic elements of a good ergonomics program include commitment by senior management, involvement by employees, ongoing review and evaluation, training and education, coordination of companywide scheduling, data collection, surveillance, detailed job design, and medical management. A key first step is determining which employees and jobs are at the most risk. Once the ergonomics program is in place, periodic review is required to be sure that it can cope with changes in staff, management, technology, and the facility. For more information, visit The Ergonomics Center of North Carolina State University (www.theergonomicscenter.com).

Evaluation of Safety and Health Programs

Health and (especially) safety programs have begun to receive more attention in recent years. The consequences of inadequate programs are measurable: increased workers' compensation payments, increased lawsuits, larger insurance costs, fines from OSHA, and pressures from unions. A safety management program requires these steps:

1. Establishment of indicator systems (for example, accident statistics).
2. Development of effective reporting systems.

3. Development of rules and procedures.

4. Rewarding supervisors for effective management of the safety function.

Support from top management is needed, and the proper design of jobs and interactions of workers and machines is necessary, but probably the key is participation by employees.

A health and safety program can be evaluated fairly directly in a cost-benefit sense. The costs of safety specialists, new safety devices, and other measures can be calculated. Reductions in accidents, lowered insurance costs, and lowered fines can be weighed against these costs. Programs can be judged by other measurable criteria, such as improvements in job performance, decreases in sick leave, and reductions in disciplinary actions and grievances.[48] Records of claims and referrals must also be kept. At the same time, managers must realize that cause-and-effect relationships may be complex, and benefits of a health and safety program are both tangible and intangible. The most cost-effective safety programs need not be the most expensive. Programs that combine a number of approaches—safety criteria like improvements in job performance and decreases in sick leave, off-the-job safety, safety training, safety meetings, medical facilities, and strong participation by top management—work when the emphasis is on the engineering aspects of safety. Cost-benefit studies of health and safety programs can be very helpful in analyzing and improving them.

Summary

To summarize the major points covered in this chapter:

1. *Safety hazards* are aspects of the work environment that have the potential of causing immediate and sometimes violent harm or even death to an employee.

2. *Health hazards* are aspects of the work environment that slowly and cumulatively (often irreversibly) lead to deterioration of an employee's health. The person may develop a chronic or life-threatening illness or become permanently disabled.

3. Safety and health hazards in the workplace can affect others as well as employees: the gas leak from a storage tank at a Union Carbide plant in Bhopal, India, claimed over 3,000 lives.

4. The major causes of work-related accidents and illnesses are the task to be done, the working conditions, and the nature of the employees.

5. The Occupational Safety and Health Act is the culmination of the movement for federal supervision of health safety programs. It has requirements, such as these:
   a. Meeting safety standards set by OSHA.
   b. Submitting to OSHA inspections.
   c. Keeping records and reporting accidents and illnesses.

6. Organizational responses to safety and health can take three approaches:
   a. Prevention and design
   b. Inspection and research
   c. Training and motivation

7. The preventive or wellness approach to health care encourages employees to make lifestyle changes through better nutrition, regular exercise, abstinence from smoking and alcohol, stress counseling, and annual physical examinations.

8. Stress can play a major role in the health of employees. Thus, more firms are now concerned about understanding and managing stress. Individual- and organization-based stress management programs are being used.

9. Violence in the workplace has become a major risk. Twenty-five percent of all workers claim that they have been harassed, threatened, or attacked on the job each year.

10. Indoor environmental quality (IEQ) has become a major concern. IEQ refers to the quality of the air in a business environment. Sick-building syndrome covers a wide range of symptoms employees believe can be caused by the building itself.

11. AIDS is a devastating disease that has become a problem that managers must address. Some firms are attempting to educate the workforce so that misconceptions and fear do not create a nonproductive work environment.

12. Cumulative trauma disorders, including repetitive motion or stress injuries, are being reported more frequently each day. CTDs are conditions that arise from obvious trauma or injury that occurs more than once. Repetitive motion or stress injuries refer to a repetitive activity which is not of itself harmful but which is alleged to become harmful owing to the sheer number of repetitions.

13. A health and safety program should be periodically evaluated to be sure it is providing both service to employees and payback to the company's bottom line.

Key Terms

accident repeater, *p. 551*
carpal tunnel syndrome (CTS), *p. 568*
cumulative trauma disorder (CTD), *p. 568*
employees' attitudes, *p. 552*
health, *p. 560*
health hazards, *p. 547*
HIV-AIDS, *p. 566*

indoor environmental quality (IEQ), *p. 565*
nature of task, *p. 552*
Occupational Safety and Health Act (1970), *p. 553*
Occupational Safety and Health Administration (OSHA), *p. 553*

preventive (wellness) programs, *p. 560*
repetitive stress injury (RSI), *p. 568*
role pressures, *p. 563*
safety hazards, *p. 547*
sick-building syndrome, *p. 565*
stress, *p. 562*

Questions for Review and Discussion

1. If you were a plant manager and just received news that there is a safety hazard and health hazard in the assembly area of the plant, which would you attend to first? Why?

2. Should whether a person smokes or not be used in hiring decisions? How about whether the person qualifies for promotion? Explain.

3. Some people believe that there are few (if any) risks associated with working in nonmanufacturing work environments—like in a restaurant, hospital, or counseling center. What would you tell these people to convince them of the potential safety and health hazards in these work sites?

4. Why should organizations be concerned about the consequences of occupational stress? What steps should be taken to educate employees on this issue?

5. What legal requirements must an organization meet regarding health and safety?

6. You have been named safety director of your company. Outline the steps you would follow in developing an effective safety management program.

7. Assume you are in charge of safety for a retail store in the mall. What steps can you take to decrease the risk of a violent act being committed at your store?

8. Explain how the quality of an organization's indoor environment can relate to the number of sick days its employees take.

9. Develop a working definition of *ergonomics* as it applies to sitting in a classroom lecture room or studying for an exam. How would you go about making those situations less stressful?

10. A good safety management program requires several steps. What are they? Write a short management training program that would get this message across.

Notes

1. "Asia: Bhopal's Deadly Legacy in India" (November 27, 2004), *The Economist*, Vol. 373, Iss. 8403, p. 76; Ian Mitroff, Paul Shrivastava, and Firdaus E. Udivactra (November 1987), *Effective Crisis Management*, pp. 283–291.

2. "Bhopal" (January 28, 1985), *New York Times*, p. 24.

3. Susan Warren (January 27, 2003), "Asbestos Quagmire-Plaintiffs Target Companies Whose Premises Contained Any Form of Deadly Material," *The Wall Street Journal*, p. B1; Cynthia Mitchell (June 1986), "Trustees Named for Manville's Asbestos Fund-Action Puts Concern Closer to Leaving Chapter 11," *The Wall Street Journal*, p. 1.

4. Ibid.

5. Thomas Stephens (January 1988), "Manville-Asbestos Ethical Issues Shaping Business Practices," *Financier*, pp. 33–37.

6. George Dillon (July–August 1991), "Does It Pay to Do the Right Thing?" *Across the Board*, pp. 15–19.

7. Bureau of Labor Statistics (1999), *Workplace Injuries and Illnesses in 1997*, http://www.stats.bls.gov/news.release/osh.nws.htm.

8. Bureau of Labor Statistics (August 2003), U.S. Department of Labor.

9. Guy Tuscano and Janice Windau (September 1992), "Fatal Work Injuries: Census for 31 States," *Monthly Labor Review* 115, 9, pp. 3–8.

10. Bureau of Labor Statistics (August 2003), U.S. Department of Labor, Census of Fatal Occupational Injuries.

11. Bureau of Labor Statistics (March 2005), U.S. Department of Labor, "Lost-Worktime Injuries and Illnesses: Characteristics and Resulting Days Away from Work, 2003."

12. Bureau of Labor Statistics (August 2003), U.S. Department of Labor.

13. James Campbell Quick, Debra L. Nelson, and Jonathan D. Quick (1990), *Stress and Challenge at the Top: The Paradox of the Successful Executive* (Chichester: Wiley), p. 29.

14. D. S. Thelam, D. Ledgerwood, and C. F. Walters (October 1985), "Health and Safety in the Workplace: A New Challenge for Business Schools," *Personnel Administrator*, pp. 37–38.

15. Helen L. Richardson (June 1990), "De-Stress," *Transportation and Distribution* 31, 6, pp. 22–25.

16. Bureau of Labor Statistics (March 2002), U.S. Department of Labor, *Work at Home in 2001*; Stephen Nickson (November 2000), "Home Work," *Risk Management*, pp. 8–12.

17. "A New Chief Has OSHA Growling Again" (August 20, 1990), *BusinessWeek*, p. 57.

18. U.S. Department of Labor, Occupational Safety and Health Administration, "OSHA Facts— December 2004" (www.osha.gov/as/opa/oshafacts.html); Occupational Safety and Health Administration (February 2002), U.S. Department of Labor, *OSHA Trade News Release*.

19. This section is based on R. Henry Moore (June 1990), "OSHA: What's Ahead for the 1990s," *Personnel*, pp. 66–69.

20. Linda F. Johnson (August 1999), "Benchmarks for Successful Training," *Occupational Health & Safety*, pp. 104–106.

21. Gloria C. Gordon and Mary Sue Henifin (1981), "Health and Safety, Job Stress, and Shift Work," in H. Metzer and Walter R. Nord (Eds.), *Making Organizations Human and Productive* (New York: Wiley), p. 322.

22. David Ryan and Roger Watson (July 2004), "A Healthier Future," *Occupational Health*, Vol. 56, Iss. 7, pp. 20–25; Shelly Reese (August 1999), "Setting the Pace," *Business & Health*, pp. 17–18.

23. "Health Costs Add to U.S. Ills" (October 6, 2003), *Employee Benefits*, p. 22; Mark Campbell (Summer 2002), "How Health Plan Sponsors Can Cope with Spiraling Drug Costs," *Compensation & Benefits Management*, pp. 5–8; William J. Heisler, W. David Jones, and Philip O. Benham, Jr. (1988), *Managing Human Resources Issues: Confronting Challenges and Choosing Options* (San Francisco: Jossey-Bass), pp. 55–60.

24. Susan R. Madsen (2003), "Wellness in the Workplace: Preparing Employees for Change," *Organization Development Journal*, Vol. 21, Iss. 1, pp. 46–54; Don R. Powell (September 1999), "Characteristics of Successful Wellness Programs," *Employee Benefits Journal*, pp. 15–21.

25. Shari Caudron and Michael Rozek (July 1990), "The Wellness Payoff," *Personnel Journal* 69, 7, pp. 54–62.

26. Dennis Thompson (March 1990), "Wellness Programs Work for Small Employers Too," *Personnel,* pp. 26–28.

27. William Atkinson (May 2001), "Is Wellness Incentive Money Well Spent?" *Business and Health,* pp. 23–27.

28. Lauren Paetsch (May 2002), "Wellness Program Helps Company Reduce Health Care Costs, Increase Productivity," *Employee Benefit Plan Review,* pp. 30–31; Harry Harrington and Nancy Richardson (August 1990), "Retiree Wellness Plan Cuts Health Costs," *Personnel Journal,* pp. 60, 62.

29. Anna-Liisa Elo and Anneli Leppenen (April 1999), "Efforts of Health Promotion Teams to Improve the Psychological Work Environment," *Journal of Occupational Health Psychology,* pp. 87–91.

30. William E. Lissy and Marlene Morgenstern (July–August 1993), "Wellness Incentives May Be Discriminatory," *Compensation and Benefits Review* 25, 4, pp. 12–13.

31. Stephanie Pronk (2005), "Population Health Improvement: The Next Era of the Health Care Management Evolution," *Benefits Quarterly,* Vol. 21, Iss. 3, pp. 12–17; Susan M. Seidler (July–August 1993), "The Health Project: Using Model Program Data to Design Effective Health Promotion Programs," *Compensation and Benefits Review* 25, 4, pp. 30–37.

32. William Atkinson (December 2000), "When Stress Won't Go Away," *HRMagazine,* pp. 104–110.

33. Daniel C. Ganster (2005), "Executive Job Demands: Suggestions from a Stress and Decision Making Perspective," *Academy of Management Review,* Vol. 30, Iss. 3, pp. 492–502; Terry A. Beehr (1995), *Psychological Stress in the Workplace* (New York: Routledge).

34. Lennart Levi, Steven L. Sauter, and Teruichi Shimomitsu (October 1999), "Work-Related Stress—It's Time to Act," *Journal of Occupational Health Psychology,* pp. 394–396.

35. D. Bunce and M. A. West (March 1996), "Stress Management and Innovation Interventions at Work," *Human Relations,* pp. 209–232.

36. Ronald J. Burke (January 2000), "Workaholism in Organizations: Psychological and Physical Well-Being Consequences," *Stress Medicine,* pp. 11–16.

37. "Underworked Employees Are Least Happy—Balance Is Preferred" (February 2005), *Workspan,* Vol. 48, Iss. 2, p. 14; Jacquelyn Lynn (May–June 1999), "Making Stress Work for You," *Commercial Law Bulletin,* pp. 32–33.

38. Peter Hom and Angelo Kinicki (October 2001), "Toward a Greater Understanding of How Dissatisfaction Drives Employee Turnover," *Academy of Management Journal,* pp. 975–987; "Workplace Stress" (August 1991), *HRMagazine* 36, 8, pp. 75–76.

39. Walter Tubbs (November 1993), "Karoushi: Stress-Death and the Meaning of Work," *Journal of Business Ethics* 12, 11, pp. 869–877.

40. Vaughan Bowie, Bonnie Fisher, and Cary Cooper (Eds.) (August 1, 2005), *Workplace Violence: Issues, Trends, and Strategies* (Devon, UK: Willan Publishing); Mark Braverman (1999), *Preventing Workplace Violence* (Thousand Oaks, CA: Sage).

41. Adapted from United States Environmental Protection Agency (1997), *Indoor Air Facts 4: Sick Building Syndrome,* http://www.epa.gov; Centers for Disease Control (1997), *Indoor Environmental Quality,* ftp://ftp.edc.gov; IURS Employment Review (1996), *Workplace Smoking Policies I: Content and Motives* 602, pp. 10–16; White House (1997), *Vice President Gore Sends Message to Businesses,* http://www.oshadata.com/fxvpgore.htm.

42. Risk Factor Monitoring & Methods Branch (2002), Division of Cancer Control & Population Sciences—National Cancer Institute; Lin Grensing-Pophal (May 1999), "Smokin' in the Workplace," *HRMagazine,* pp. 58–66.

43. Sally Roberts (April 19, 1999), "Employers Advised to Educate Workplace on HIV/AIDS Issues," *Business Insurance,* p. 17.

44. Diane Cadrain (February 2005), "Advocates for the Disabled Seek Overhaul of ADA," *HRMagazine,* Vol. 50, Iss. 2, pp. 27–30; Jeffery Mello (May 1999), "Ethics in Employment

Law: The Americans with Disabilities Act and the Employee with HIV," *Journal of Business Ethics,* pp. 67–83.

45. "Musculoskeletal and Repetitive Motion Injuries—Is There a Solution?" (1966), *Risk Management,* 43, 6, p. 46; Valerie Frazee (1996), "Repetitive Motion Injuries Decline," *Personnel Journal* 75, 8, pp. 24–25; James A. Morrissey (1996), "Washington Outlook," *Textile World* 146, 2, p. 18; "Cost of Risk Decreases" (1996), *IIE Solutions* 28, 7, p. 8; "Repetitive Motion Injuries Drop by Two Percent" (1996), *Facilities Design and Management* 15, 7, p. 11; Gregg LaBar (1996), "Ergonomics: Are Auto Makers on the Right Track?" *Occupational Hazards* 58, 10, pp. 96–104; Brooke E. Smith (1997), "The Bogus Epidemic," *Magazine of HAL-PC User Group,* http://www.hal-pc.org/journal; Centers for Disease Control (1997), *Carpal Tunnel Syndrome,* ftp://ftp.cdc.gov/pub/General_information/niosh/carpalts.txt.

46. James L. Nash (May 2005), "Report: Repetitive Motion Injuries Are Still No. 1," *Occupational Hazards,* Vol. 67, Iss. 5, p. 13; Mary Aichlmayr (March 2002), "Ergonomics' 15 Minutes," *Transportation & Distribution,* pp. 46–50; Laura Sullivan (November 2001), "Ergonomic Filibuster," *Risk Management,* pp. 61–63.

47. Dominic Bencivenga (August 1996), "Finding the Right Fit: The Economics of Ergonomics," *HRMagazine,* pp. 1–9.

48. William Atkinson and Steven Van Yoder (September 1999), "On-the-Job Safety Starts at the Top," *Business and Health,* pp. 33–37.

EXERCISE 17-1

Preparing for an OSHA Inspection

PURPOSE

Many organizations need to be prepared for the possibility of an inspection by the Occupational Safety and Health Administration (OSHA). The purpose of this exercise is to increase understanding of the OSHA inspection process and the many resources available on the Web to assist in preparing for such an inspection.

GROUP SIZE

To be performed individually.

TIME REQUIRED

Approximately 45 minutes.

OTHER

Internet connection and search engine required.

EXERCISE

Part I—Using a search engine, visit the OSHA Web site (www.osha.gov) and research how OSHA performs inspections at companies. Be prepared to describe a typical OSHA inspection. (*Hint:* Type in the keyword "inspection" in the Web site search box.)

Part II—Surf the Web to identify five consulting companies that specialize in helping client companies to prepare for OSHA inspections.

Summarize your findings from Parts I and II on a 1- to 2-page report and be prepared to discuss it in class.

Source: Robert Konopaske and John M. Ivancevich (Copyright 2005).

Application Case 17-1

Campus Food Systems

As part of a master's program in food services management, Cindy Breen has just begun her internship with Campus Food Systems (CFS). CFS is a self-operated university food service department at Cindy's alma mater, Gulfport State College. As a department, CFS reports directly to the vice president of administration, the office generally responsible for nonacademic matters co-funded by the school. Self-operated food service programs try to minimize loss rather than maximize profit. They are operated by employees of the institution, as opposed to contract operations run by professional management companies like Marriott Corporation and ARA Services, profit-making enterprises.

CFS employs about 60 full-time employees. In addition, the staff is supplemented by almost 100 students who provide part-time labor. Thus approximately 160 employees, largely part-time, are responsible for providing three distinct dining services to the Gulfport campus: Watkins Dining Hall (traditional cafeteria service for residents); Sea Breeze Cafe (fast-food service for students, faculty, staff, and guests); and Catering (a full range of catering services offered both on and off campus). A fourth function, Stores, orders, receives, inventories, and disburses food and nonfood supplies to the other three operations.

Cindy knows that most self-operated food service programs are located at much larger universities. A small operation like CFS is always vulnerable to a takeover threat from large contractors like Marriott. Smaller schools are easy targets. Also, turnover in the administration makes the threat of a takeover stronger—and Gulfport has just changed presidents. President Sheila Dawes comes from a large university that used ARA to administer dining-room operations. Cindy's supervisor, Jake Platt, has told her that she must help him assure the new college president that CFS should remain self-operated.

Cindy has been working at CFS for only two weeks, and Jake has just assigned her to manage the student help. Her responsibilities include interviewing, selecting, training, scheduling, and disciplining about 100 part-time employees. She also has been charged with preparing a report, Work Accidents in the Food Service Areas, for the previous calendar year. This report will be sent to President Dawes and the Human Resource Department and forwarded to both state and OSHA agencies to comply with state and federal safety and health legislation. Jake has told her to minimize the severity of the reported occupational illness and accidents. He says that CFS can't afford to "inflate" these statistics. They might attract President Dawes's attention. Jake also hinted to Cindy that both her grade in the internship and a favorable job recommendation rest on how she handles the accident report. Some of the accidents Jake has asked her to minimize include the following:

- Bill Black, part-time employee, fractured and cut his right hand when a spring-loaded piston on a food cart snapped back and caught his hand between the cart and a heavy loading cart door. Cindy has learned that Bill's injury has resulted in a permanent partial disability of two fingers.
- Leslie Campbell, Ophrah Moses, Cici Potts, Winnie Chung, and George Wilson all cut their hands on the same meat slicer at different times. Each accident was caused when another employee failed to replace the knife guard after cleaning it.
- Winston Knapp received burns on his face, chest, legs, and stomach when hot water splashed out of the steamer into which he had lowered a tray of hot food.

Jake has also asked Cindy to omit any accidents for which reports were not made to Human Resources at the time of the incident. So far, Cindy has documented 46 such incidents, ranging from a box falling on a student's head to severe cuts from broken glass and knives. But Jake has said not to worry: They were all student employees who used their parents' health insurance to cover medical expenses.

Cindy is distressed by the number of accidents that have occurred during the previous calendar year at CFS. She has just reviewed data from the Bureau of Labor Statistics for 1995 in her Restaurant Management class. Cindy knows that working in food service can be quite dangerous, but the number of accidents at CFS during the last year is about 20 percent more than in other, comparable small food service operations. In addition, she has found that many accidents were never reported to the state.

Another problem with the incident reports Jake has supplied Cindy to compile her report is the fact that they fail to mention Rick James, a student employee who contracted a severe case of salmonella poisoning from handling diseased seafood. Rick has just returned from a three-month hospital stay. He had been so ill that he had become paralyzed and at first was not expected to live. He missed almost a whole semester of school. Since Rick's illness, CFS has forbidden student employees to handle raw seafood, but that rule has been frequently violated, owing to high absenteeism and turnover of full-time personnel.

Cindy sits contemplating what her sense of values tells her to do next. She has jotted down her alternatives:

1. Prepare the report as Jake has asked, with omissions.
2. Prepare the report, but include the incident reports.
3. Prepare the report including all incident reports, previously unreported accidents, and Rick's serious illness.
4. Go to Fred White, CFS director and Jake's supervisor, and give him a complete report.
5. Send the complete report directly to President Dawes.
6. Call OSHA and ask for someone to inspect CFS.
7. Leak the story to the student newspaper and the local press.

Discussion Question

What should Cindy do and why? Frame your answer in terms of a safe and healthy workplace.

Source: Written by Jean M. Hanebury, associate professor of management, Texas A&M University–Corpus Christi.

Video Case

OSHA and Unions versus Manufacturers: Is Workplace Ergonomics a Problem?

During the Industrial Revolution a century ago, workplace injuries were so commonplace that they were simply considered one of the hazards of having a job. Children and adults were often maimed or disfigured in factory accidents. Today strict regulations cover safety in the workplace, guided by the U.S. Department of Labor's Occupational Safety and Health Administration (OSHA).

During the past couple of decades, as industry itself has changed, a different type of injury has emerged: musculoskeletal disorders (MSDs). MSDs are injuries resulting from overexertion and repetitive motion, such as constantly lifting heavy loads or grabbing and twisting a piece of machinery. People who sit at computer workstations all day are susceptible to MSDs as well, particularly carpal tunnel syndrome, which affects the nerves of the hand, wrist, and arm. According to OSHA, about one third of repetitive stress injuries, or 600,000, are serious enough to require time off the job, which means that businesses pay for these injuries not only in medical costs but in lost productivity. They can also contribute to high employee turnover. No one disputes that these injuries occur. But various experts, industry leaders, and politicians argue about how severe the injuries are, who should pay for them, what should be done about them, and who takes ultimate responsibility for the safety of workers.

One aspect of the whole issue of workplace injuries is ergonomics: "The applied science of equipment design, intended to reduce operator fatigue and discomfort, or as OSHA puts it, the science of fitting the job to the worker." Ergonomics involves everything from developing new equipment, including desk chairs that support the back properly and flexible splints to support the wrist while typing, to designing better ways to use the equipment, such as the proper way to hold a computer mouse.

OSHA has proposed new guidelines for better ergonomic standards, targeting jobs where workers perform repetitive tasks, whether they are in processing poultry or delivering packages. The proposal required employers that received reports from workers who were suffering from MSDs to respond promptly with an evaluation and follow-up health care. Workers who needed time off could receive 90 percent of their pay and 100 percent of their benefits. Not surprisingly, arguments for and against the proposal broke out. OSHA spokesperson Charles Jeffers claimed that the guidelines "will save employers $9 billion every year from what they've currently been spending on these problems." Peg Seminario of the AFL-CIO noted that the guidelines did not go far enough because they did not cover "workers in construction, agriculture, or maritime, who have very serious problems." Pat Cleary of the National Association of Manufacturers argued that "there's a central flaw here and that is that there is no . . . consensus in the scientific or medical community about the causes of ergonomics injuries." Debates over the proposed rules' merit were further clouded by the Small Business Administration's prediction that implementing the standards would cost industries $18 billion. OSHA had forecast a mere $4.2 billion.

Just before he left office, President Bill Clinton signed the bill into law which was overturned by incoming President George Bush and the new Congress. Calling the workplace safety regulations "unduly burdensome and overly broad," Bush signed a measure to roll back the new rules.

Where do these actions leave workers and businesses in regard to workplace injuries? Legally, businesses are not required to redesign work systems or continue full pay and benefits for an extended period after work-related injury. But if the goal of a company is to find and keep the best employees, perhaps developing good ergonomic practices makes good business sense. The high cost of treatment and turnover, not to mention lowered productivity, points toward prevention as a competitive strategy. "Good ergonomics in the office should not be a big burden in a company and may be a way to retain good employees."

Discussion Questions

1. Do you agree or disagree that ergonomics in the workplace should be covered by federal regulations? Explain your answers.

2. Choose a job with which you are familiar and discuss the possibilities for repetitive stress injuries that could occur on this job and ways they could be prevented.

3. Imagine that you are the human resources manager for a company that hires workers for the job selected in question 2. What steps might you encourage company officials to take to identify and prevent potential MSDs?

Sources: "Ergonomics Rules" (June 19, 2001), *Workforce,* www.workforce.com; J. Jones (March 22, 2001), "Bush Expected to Rescind OSHA Rules," *InfoWorld,* www.cnn.com; M. Allen (March 21, 2001), "Bush Signs Repeal of Ergonomics Rules," *Washington Post,* www.washingtonpost.com; J. Kuhnhenn, "House Joins Senate in Repeal of Workplace Ergonomics Rules," *San Jose Mercury News,* www.siliconvalley.com; K. Kiely (March 7, 2001), "House Votes to Repeal Ergonomics Rule," *USA Today,* www.usatoday.com; D. Espo (March 6, 2001), "Senate Votes to Repeal Ergonomics Rules," ABCNews.com, www.abcnews.com; P. Thibodeau (November 13, 2000), "OSHA Releases Final Version of Workplace Ergonomics Rules," *ComputerWorld,* www.computerworld.com; video transcript, "Working Better" (November 22, 1999), *Online NewsHour,* www.pbs.org.

Appendix  B

Measuring Human Resource Activities

Traditionally, the HR department has been evaluated in vague, subjective terms. This has occurred for two basic reasons: the wrong questions were being asked, and management bought the claim that it was not possible to apply quantitative methods to a function that was viewed principally from a qualitative standpoint.

The staff and management of what is called the *human resources department* allowed that misperception to perpetuate itself. From the inception of the first HR department until modern times, few people seemed to be concerned about the performance of the department. There was no formal career path into or through HRM, and the few institutions of higher learning that taught HRM did not bother to teach measurement techniques. As a result, people did not know how to evaluate their work objectively. For some, the application of cold numbers to a function whose apparent mission was to "help employees with their problems" and to "improve morale" seemed to be a conflict of values. Others did not want to take on the extra work of collecting data and performing the calculations because they saw no use for it. Senior management had not asked for it. In time, a hidden fear developed. The department was often maligned by others within the larger organization. Many HR people developed the attitude that their job was not too important, and that if they were to go to the trouble of quantitatively measuring and reporting their work, the numbers would confirm the perception that they were not doing well. This attitude still exists in the minds of many today.

Every manager must understand why a company is in business. The purpose of business is to earn a profit. This is the harsh reality of the real world. Being nice to people is fine. Supporting the development of people is a worthy endeavor. Helping workers improve their skills and confidence is an excellent undertaking. But the core of businesses is to make money. If a firm doesn't make money, how can it survive? Who will subsidize the firm? Do you think that a not-for-profit firm can survive without making money? If the human resource department is to be considered an essential unit, it must measure its value and its contributions to the firm.

As a result of not proving its value to the organization in objective terms, the human resources department is not considered part of the mainstream of organizational management. It is viewed as a cost center and a reactive maintenance activity. In order to turn that outmoded attitude around, it is necessary for human resources management to learn to

Originally prepared by Jac Fitz-Enz, president of Saratoga Institute. Adapted and updated in each edition by author of this text.

speak the language of business, which is numbers. A mathematical methodology needs to be applied: a system that serves both as a day-to-day monitoring instrument and as a model for cost justification and cost-benefit analysis of specific projects or programs.

Two of the foremost management authorities, Peter Drucker and W. Edwards Deming, have come out strongly for the development of measurement skill as an essential capability of a manager.

Basic Principles

The application of quantitative methods to human resources management has generated a set of basic principles that are critical to the success of the measurement system. These are based on the experience of managers in many types and sizes of organizations.

1. *The productivity and effectiveness of any function can be measured by some combination of cost, time, quantity, or quality indexes.* In some cases, psychological measures of attitude and morale are also useful and possible.

2. *A measurement system promotes productivity by focusing attention on the important issues, tasks, and objectives.* A quantitative system helps to clarify not only what is to be accomplished, but also how well it should be done.

3. *Professional and knowledge workers are best measured as a group.* In order to be optimally effective, a professional group needs to work together. Measuring the work of individuals relative to each other promotes divisiveness and counterproductive competition.

4. *Managers can be measured by the efficiency and effectiveness of the units they manage.* The nature of managerial work is to get things done through other people. Therefore, it follows that the output of the group is an indication of the skill of the manager. There are obvious exceptions to this, but the rule applies nevertheless.

5. *The ultimate measurement is not efficiency, but effectiveness.* The objective of an organization is not only to create the most output with the least input. More important is to create the most appropriate outcome at any given point in time.

Building Blocks of a Measurement System

The first problems that people face when they set out to build a measurement system are the apparent multitude of activities that are taking place and the seemingly impossible task of differentiating, isolating, and labeling quantifiable variables. It is somewhat analogous to looking at a 1,000-pound steer and wondering how you can get a hamburger out of it. The solution is relatively simple.

Only four classes of variables can be subjected to a quantitative system. They are

1. *People* (as described by their organizational roles, such as receptionist, clerk, recruiter, trainer, compensation analyst, or manager).

2. *Things* (physical objects such as equipment, files, application forms, facilities, and supplies).

3. *Processes* (people doing something with a thing or with another person such as interviewing, filing, training, scheduling, and counseling).

4. *Results* (the outcomes of the interactions of people, things, and processes).

Everything within the department or related to the department's activity, whether it be inside the larger organization or outside it (such as a job applicant), can be classified into one of these four categories.

The next step is to list all the variables within each category that one might want to measure in some way. Then, the variables can be compared one at a time with each other until a relationship that can be expressed in terms of cost, time, quantity (volume or frequency), or quality becomes evident. This outcome is the *dependent variable.*

Examples of some typical dependent variables, often called *measures* by human resource managers, are interviews per hire, absenteeism rate, hours per trainee, average hire cost, counseling hours per topic, records processed per clerk, and ratio of benefit costs to payroll cost.

Once the dependent variables are chosen for inclusion in the measurement system, an equation must be created to complete the measure. Equations are often self-evident. Examples are:

$$\text{Average hire cost} = \frac{\text{selection cost}}{\text{number hired}}$$

$$\text{Absenteeism rate} = \frac{\text{number of days absent}}{\text{number of workdays available}}$$

$$\text{Average health care cost} = \frac{\text{total cost of health benefits}}{\text{total number of employees}}$$

$$\text{Cost per trainee hour} = \frac{\text{total cost of training}}{\text{number trained} \times \text{hours trained}}$$

How to Quantify Quality

One refuge that opponents of measurement have sought is the issue of quality. They argue that the work of the human resources function is highly qualitative and therefore inherently not susceptible to quantification. The issue of quality is not the sole province of the human resource department. Products must be manufactured to quality specifications. Salespeople must sell only to accounts that pay their bills. Although it is clear that quality is everyone's criterion, that does not solve the problem of how to quantify it.

The solution lies in the creation of a composite measure. For example, if the issue is recruiters' effectiveness, one must first decide what constitutes effectiveness. Clearly, it is a function of more than one measure. If effectiveness could be defined by one objective term, it would not be subjective. A recruiter's effectiveness may be defined as a combination of how fast hires are accomplished, how cheaply they are achieved, how many are completed, and the quality of the people hired. And therein lies another potential problem. "Hire quality" is a subjective issue itself. In order to use it in the effectiveness measure, it must first be quantified. So a composite of hire quality needs to be constructed, the quality objectified, and that quantitative value plugged into the formula for recruiters' effectiveness. The end result might look like this:

$$\text{Recruiter's effectiveness} = \frac{\text{CH} + \text{TFJ} + \text{QH} + (\text{other chosen indexes})}{\text{number of indexes used}}$$

where

Cost of hire (CH) = $450 (average)

Time to fill jobs (TFJ) = 15 days (on average)

Quality of hires (QH) = 90 percent (per quality measure)

EXHIBIT B-1
HRM Audit: An Illustration (an Interview with the Operating Manager)

Source: Reprinted by permission and adopted to 1997 terminology from "Auditing PAIR" by Walter R. Mahler in D. Yoder and H. Henemon, Eds., *ASPA Handbook of Personnel and Industrial Relations*, pp. 2–103. Copyright © 1979 by The Bureau of National Affairs, Inc., Washington, DC 20037.

1. What would you say are the objectives of your plant?
2. As you see it, what are the major responsibilities of managers?
3. Have there been any important changes in these over the last few years in the plant?
4. Are there any HRM responsibilities on which you think many managers need to do a better job?
5. What are some of the good things about employee relations in this plant?
6. Do you feel there are any important problems or difficulties in the plant? Causes? How widespread? Corrective measures?
7. Do you have any HRM goals for the year?
8. Overall, how well do you feel the HRM department does its job? Changes the department should make?

Community Relations

9. What are managers expected to do about community relations? Is there plant pressure? Reaction to pressures?
10. What have you done about community relations? Do you encourage subordinates to participate in them? What are your personal activities?

Safety and Medical

11. Who is responsible for safety in your area? Role of group leaders?
12. What do you do about safety? Regular actions? Results achieved?
13. Do you have any important safety problems in your operation? Causes? Cures? How widespread?
14. What does the specialist do? How helpful are his or her activities? Other things he or she should do?
15. Are there any other comments or suggestions about safety you would like to make?
16. Have you any comments about the dispensary? Employees' time involved? Types of service offered? Courtesy?

Communication

17. How do you keep your people informed? What are your regular communication activities? Particular problems?
18. How do you go about finding out information from employees? Channels and methods? How regularly are such channels used? How much information is passed on to employee superiors? How much interest do supervisors show? Does the HRM department provide information?
19. Has the HRM department helped improve communication in the plant? What assistance is needed? Nature of assistance provided?
20. Has the HRM department helped you with your own communication activities?

Communication Channels Available

21. What improvement is needed in these?
22. Are there any other comments about communication you'd like to make? Any changes or improvements you'd especially like to see?

HRM Planning

23. What kind of plans do you have for meeting the future HRM needs of your own component? Indicate plans for hourly and nonexempt workers. How far do plans extend into the future?
24. What does your manager do about planning for future HRM needs? How is this planning related to your own planning?
25. What part does the personnel department play in planning for the future HRM needs of your component? Of the plant as a whole?

Human Resource Development

26. How is the training of employees handled in your group? (if response is on-the-job training: Who does it? Procedures followed?)
27. What changes or improvements do you think should be made in the on-the-job training of employees? Why?

EXHIBIT B-1
(continued)

28. What changes or improvements do you feel are needed in the amount or kind of classroom training given here? Why?

29. Have you worked with your subordinates on improving their current job performance? Inside or outside regular appraisal? Procedure? Employees' reaction? Results? Improvements needed?

30. Have you worked with subordinates on plans for preparing for future job responsibilities? Inside or outside regular appraisal? Procedure? Employees' reaction? Results? Improvements needed?

31. What does HRM do to help you with your training and development problems?

32. Do you have any other comments on HRM development or training?

HRM Practices

33. How are employees added to your work group? New employees, for example. (*Probe:* Specify exempt, nonexempt, hourly. Procedure followed? How are decisions made? Contribution of HRM? Changes needed and reasons? Transfers?)

34. How is bumping or downgrading handled? (*Probe:* Specify nonexempt or hourly. Procedure followed? How are decisions made? Contribution of HRM? Changes needed and reasons?)

35. How are promotions into or out of your group handled? (*Probe:* Specify exempt, nonexempt, hourly. Procedure followed? How are decisions made? Contribution of HRM? Changes needed and reasons?)

36. Do you have any problems with layoffs? (*Probe:* Nature of problems? Possible solutions? Contribution of HRM?)

37. How do you handle probationary periods? (*Probe:* Specify hourly, nonexempt, exempt. Length of period? Union's attitude? How handled?)

38. How are inefficient people handled? (*Probe:* Specify hourly, nonexempt, exempt. How do you handle? How do other supervisors handle? Frequency?)

Salary Administration–Exempt

39. What is your responsibility for salary administration for exempt employees? (*Probe:* Position evaluation? Determining increases? Degree of authority?)

40. How do you go about deciding on salary increases? (*Probe:* Procedure? Weight given to merit? Informing employees? Timing?)

41. What are your major problems in salary administration? (*Probe:* Employee-centered? Self-centered? Plan-centered?)

42. Has the HRM department assisted you with your salary administration problems? How? (*Probe:* Administrator's role? Nature of assistance? Additional assistance needed and reasons?)

Salary Administration–Nonexempt

43. What is your responsibility for salary administration for nonexempt employees? (*Probe:* Nature of plan? Position evaluation? Changes needed and reasons?)

44. How has the HRM department helped in nonexempt salary administration? (*Probe:* Specify HRM or other salary administrators. Nature of assistance? Additional assistance needed and reasons?)

Plus others . . .

Dollars, days, and percent can be normalized by comparing them with a preset goal and calculating percent of goal achievement for each. Each issue can also be weighted by importance. A simple illustration (omitting "other" undefined variables) is

Goal Achievement Percent X Weighting

Measure	Result	Goal	Factors
Cost of hire	$450	$500	11% × 4 = 444
Time to fill	15	12	80% × 3 = 240
Quality	90%	85%	106% × 5 = 530
			1,214
	1,214 ÷ 12 = 101%		

Exhibit. B-1 presents the building blocks of an HRM audit around which measures can be developed.

Summary

In order for the human resources function to take its place as an integral part of the organization, it must learn to use the language of business, which is numbers. This applies whether the organization is profit or not-for-profit. A number of personal, departmental, and organizational values can be derived from maintaining a quantitative performance measurement system. Personally, the people in the department are able to see how well they are doing. They are able to identify problems in early stages and find the source and the solution. They have data to build cost justification proposals that will help them obtain needed resources. They will be able to prove their contribution to the productivity and profitability of the larger organization. As a result of all this, they will gain the respect and position they desire.

Sources of Information about Human Resource Management: Where to Find Facts and Figures

This appendix is divided into three main parts: *periodicals, publishers,* and *organizations* speciallizing in providing information in a variety of areas of HRM. While the listings are not intended to be exhaustive, they do provide a good cross section of major sources of facts and figures.

The listings contain the names of national organizations. You might consult your local chamber of commerce, college or university, and human resource management association chapter for information and resources as well.

I. PERIODICALS

A. General business journals that often contain HRM material:

Academy of Management Executive

Advanced Management Journal

Business Horizons

California Management Review

Harvard Business Review

MIT Sloan Management Review

Organizational Dynamics

B. Specialized journals. HRM specialists can advance their knowledge of the field by reading specialized journals. These include

Administrative Management

American Federationist

Source: Originally Paul N. Keaton, University of Wisconsin, LaCrosse, with author updates made for every new edition.

Arbitration Journal

BNAC Communication (quarterly)

Bulletin on Training (monthly)

Compensation and Benefits Review (quarterly)

Employment Benefit Plan Review

Employee Relations Law Journal

HR Focus

HR Managing

Human Resource Management

Human Resource Planning

Industrial Relations (triannual)

Industrial Relations News (weekly)

Labor Law Journal (monthly)

Monthly Labor Review (monthly)

National Productivity

Personnel (bimonthly)

Personnel Management (monthly)

Personnel Management Abstracts (quarterly)

Public Personnel Management (bimonthly)

Training (monthly)

Training and Development Journal (monthly)

Workforce (monthly)

C. Scholarly journals. The following is a list of publications written primarily for scholars and executives interested in HR management. Reading these requires more technical training than is required for the journals listed above.

Academy of Management Journal

Academy of Management Review

Human Organization

Human Relations

Human Resource Management

Industrial and Labor Relations Review

Industrial Relations

Journal of Applied Behavioral Science

Journal of Applied Psychology

Journal of Human Resources

Journal of Labor Research

Journal of Vocational Behavior

Organizational Behavior and Human Decision Processes

Personnel Psychology

Training: Journal of Human Resource Development

II. ORGANIZATIONS*

A. Private

American Arbitration Association (AAA)
355 Madison Avenue, Floor 10
New York, NY 10017
(212) 716-5800

American Association for Counseling and Development (AACD)
[formerly American Personnel and Guidance Association (APGA)]
5999 Stevenson Avenue
Alexandria, VA, 22304
(703) 823-9800

American Compensation Association (ACA)
P.O. Box 29312
Phoenix, AZ 85038-9312
(602) 951-9191

American Management Association (AMA)
1601 Broadway
New York: NY 10019
(212) 586-8100

American Psychological Association (APA)
750 1st Street, NE
Washington, DC 20002
(202) 336-5500

American Society for Hospital Personnel Administration (ASHPA)
840 North Lake Shore Drive
Chicago, IL 60611
(312) 280-6358

American Society for Training and Development (ASTD)
1640 King Street
Alexandria, VA 22313-8100

Association of Private Pension and Welfare Plans (APPWP)
1725 K Street, NW, Suite 801
Washington, DC 20006
(202) 659-8274

College and University Personnel Association (CUPA)
11 DuPont Circle, Suite 120
Washington, DC 20036
(202) 462-1038

Human Resource Planning Society
317 Madison Ave, Suite 1509
New York, NY 10017
(212) 490-6387

*Deborah M. Burek, Ed. (1991), *Encyclopedia of Associations*, 25th ed. (Detroit Gale Research Company).

Industrial Relations Research Association
7226 Social Science Building
University of Wisconsin
Madison, WI 53760
(608) 262-2762

International Association for Personnel Women (IAPW)
5820 Wilshire Boulevard, Suite 500
Los Angeles, CA 90036
(213) 937-9000

International Association of Pupil Personnel Workers (IAPPW)
% William E. Myer
P. O. Box 36
Barnesville, MD 20838
(301) 340-7501

National Association of Educational Office Personnel (NAEOP)
1902 Association Drive
Reston, VA 22091
(703) 860-2888

National Association of Manufacturers (NAM)
1331 Pennsylvania Ave., NW
Washington, DC 20004
(202) 637-3182

National Association of Para-Legals Personnel (NAPLP)
% Howard W. Ross
9431 North Leamington
Skokie, IL 60077
(312) 676-9263

National Association of Personnel Consultants (NAPC)
3133 Mount Vernon Avenue
Alexandria, VA 22305
(703) 684-0180

National Association of Pupil Personnel Administrators (NAPPA)
225 North Washington Street
Alexandria, VA 22314
(703) 549-9117

National Association of Student Personnel Administrators (NASPA)
160 Rightmire Hall
1060 Cermacek Road
Columbus, OH 43210
(614) 422-4445

National Labor-Management Foundation (NLMF)
1901 L Street, NW, Suite 711
Washington, DC 20036
(202) 296-8577

Newspaper Personnel Relations Association (NPRA)
11600 Sunrise Valley Drive
Reston, VA 22091
(703) 648-1000

Prentice-Hall Personnel Service, Prentice-Hall, Inc.
Sylvan Avenue
Englewood Cliffs, NJ 07632

Society for Human Resource Management (SHRM)
1800 Duke Street
Alexandria, VA 22314
(703) 548-3440

Special Interest Group for Computer Personnel Research (SIGCPR)
5776 Stoneridge Mail Road
Atrium, Suite 350
Pleasanton, CA 94566
(415) 463-2800

U.S. Chamber of Commerce
1615 H Street, NW
Washington, DC 20062

World At Work
14040 N. Northsight Blvd.
Scottsdale, AZ 85260
(480) 483-8352

B. Federal government

Bureau of Labor Statistics (BLS), Department of Labor
3rd Street and Constitution Avenue, NW
Washington, DC 20210

Equal Employment Opportunity Commission (EEOC)
2401 E Street, NW
Washington, DC 20506

Federal Mediation and Conciliation Service
Washington, DC 20427

Occupational Safety and Health Administration (OSHA)
200 Constitution Avenue, NW
Washington, DC 20210

Office of Federal Contract Compliance (OFCC)
200 Constitution Avenue, NW
Washington, DC 20210

C. Addresses of a sample of labor unions in the United States, listed alphabetically
by trade with membership figures and national affiliation

AFL-CIO
815 16th Street, NW
Washington, DC 20006
(202) 637-5000
13,000,000

Airline Pilots Association, International (ALPA)
1625 Massachusetts Avenue, NW
Washington, DC 20036
(703) 689-2210
44,000

Amalgamated Clothing and Textile Workers Union (ACTWU)
15 Union Square
New York, NY 10003
272,669   AFL-CIO, CLC

Communications Workers of America (CWA)
501 3rd Street, NW
Washington, DC 20001
(202) 434-1100
650,000   AFL-CIO

United Food and Commercial Workers International Union (UFCWIU)
Suffridge Building
1775 K Street, NW
Washington, DC 20006
1,300,000   AFL-CIO

American Federation of State, County, and Municipal Employees (AFSCME)
162S L Street, NW
Washington, DC 20036
1,200,000   AFL-CIO

International Association of Machinists and Aerospace Workers (IAM)
1300 Connecticut Avenue
Washington, DC 20036
800,000   AFL-CIO

International Union, United Mine Workers of America (UMWA)
900 15th Street, NW
Washington, DC 20005
240,000

International Union, United Automobile,
Aerospace and Agricultural Implement Workers of America (UAW)
8000 West Jefferson
Detroit, MI 48214
1,197,000   AFL-CIO

United Brotherhood of Carpenters and Joiners of America (UBC)
101 Constitution Avenue, NW
Washington, DC 20001
700,000   AFL-CIO

Oil, Chemical, and Atomic Workers International Union (OCAW)
P. O. Box 2812
Denver, CO 80201
120,000   AFL-CIO

American Postal Workers Union (APVTU)
1300 L Street, NW
Washington, DC 20005
320,000   AFL-CIO

United Steel Workers of America (USWA)
Five Gateway Center
Pittsburgh, PA 15222
750,000   AFL-CIO

American Federation of Teachers (AFT)
555 New Jersey Avenue, NW
Washington, DC 20001
1,000,000   AFL-CIO

National Education Association (NEA)
1201 16th Street, NW
Washington, DC 20036
2,700,000

International Brotherhood of Teamsters, Chauffeurs, Warehousemen,
and Helpers of America (IBT)
25 Louisiana Avenue, NW
Washington, DC 20001
1,400,000

Appendix D

Career Planning

Career planning is an individualized process. Each of us has a unique set of values, interests, and work and personal experiences. Understanding how this unique set of factors blends is an important part of career planning. But it is also necessary to understand the requirements of various jobs so that your own personality and intellectual abilities can be matched with the job. Your career decisions will shape your lifestyle.

College students eventually have to find out how they fit into the spectrum of career choices available. The purpose of this appendix is to provide

1. A few career basics and hints on self-assessment.
2. Information on the mechanics of getting a job.

Career Basics and Self-Analysis

First, before thinking about specific career areas, sit back and spend more time mulling over those things that you want from a career. Here are a few questions to consider:

- Do you want a job or a career? Do you want it to be personally satisfying, or are the financial rewards enough? How important is career advancement?
- Are the status and prestige associated with a career important to you?
- What about financial rewards?
- Do you have geographical preferences? What about living in a large versus a small city?
- What size employer would you prefer? Might this preference change later on?

Now, think about yourself for a minute.

- What education, experience, and skills do you have to offer?
- Are you quantitatively ("thing") oriented or qualitatively ("people") oriented, or do you enjoy both? Organizations have places for both types.
- What are your weak and strong points? How will they relate to your performance on the job?
- What kind of work is interesting to you?
- What kind of work do you like?
- What kind of work will make you feel worthwhile?

A personal evaluation of these and similar questions is a worthwhile exercise. These questions may help you develop a job or career identity.

Professional Help for Self-Assessment

Professional counselors can help you decide which career path to take. Most high schools and colleges provide free counseling services, in which trained professionals help students perform a realistic self-assessment.

Vocational tests are often used to verify one's self-analysis and to reveal any hidden personal characteristics. This information is then explained and interpreted by professional counselors. No one test or battery of tests can make a career choice for you. But tests can supplement the information you are reviewing as you mull over career opportunities and personal characteristics. Your college placement office has counselors who can recommend which tests are most appropriate.

In addition, the counselor can help you with your self-assessment by providing publications discussing career opportunities. Some widely publicized and frequently used publications include

- *College Placement Annual,* College Placement Council, Inc., 62 Highland Avenue, Bethlehem, PA 18017 (215) 868-1421.
  Published annually. Provides information on current job openings in companies, as well as suggestions on preparing resumes and interviewing for jobs.
- *Occupational Outlook Handbook,* U.S. Department of Labor, Government Printing Office, Washington, DC (202) 783-3238.
  Published annually. Lists all major companies, with a brief description of job requirements, opportunities available, and future job prospects.

Self-assessment, help from a professional counselor, and career publications can provide the background information necessary to properly plan your career. But in the final analysis, you alone must make the career decision and seek appropriate job opportunities. A counselor, parent, or friend cannot make a career decision for you.

The Job Search: A Plan

In school, you prepare for examinations by organizing your notes and planning. In searching for a job, you also need to organize and plan. The first job after college can affect your entire career, so a plan is a must. Without a plan, you will lose valuable time and experience unnecessary frustration. There is no single best job-search plan, but there are some basic principles. Because your time is limited, you should use a systematic procedure to narrow the number of job possibilities.

When evaluating any particular career, you should consider some specific issues. As you think over the broad career options available, examine them with the following areas in mind:

- What are the qualifications for the job? Will you need more education or more experience?
- What is the financial situation? Is the salary reasonable? How good are the benefits? What salary is likely in three to five years? Is there going to be a conflict between the value you place on money and your returns from this job?
- What are the opportunities for advancement? Do these appear to agree with your aspirations?
- What is the present supply and demand for this field and what might it be in the future?
- Will the job involve much travel? Is that desirable or undesirable? How mobile are you?

- What is the atmosphere associated with the job? Is it pressure-filled and demanding? Cooperative? Tranquil? Creative?
- Is this job something that you will be proud of? Does it fit your self-image?
- Is it work that you will enjoy? Is it in line with your goals and ethics? Will you be happy?

Within any given career choice, one faces a number of prospective employers. Each company offers different conditions, opportunities, and rewards to its employees. Here are some important questions to ask about the firms you are considering:

- Does the company have opportunities for a person with my skills, aptitudes, and goals?
- What are the promotion opportunities in the company?
- Does the company usually promote from within?
- What type of professional development is available for new employees?
- What kind of working environment exists within the company?
- What is the future growth potential for the company and the industry?

Answers to these kinds of questions will enable you to narrow the available job opportunities. Answers can be found in such sources as company annual reports, *Standard and Poor's Corporation Records,* and *Dun and Bradstreet's Reference Book of Manufacturers.* Another source is the company's employees. If you know some employees, ask them for firsthand information.

Most companies furnish brochures on career opportunities. These sources are impressive, but they often give a totally positive picture of the company. Consult your school's placement officer to learn more about each company and to determine the accuracy of the brochures.

There are two other sources you should consult—newspapers and professional magazines. The classified ads, especially in the Sunday or weekend editions, provide a lot of job information. These advertisements usually provide information about job vacancies, the type of people the company is looking for, and the person or post office box to contact if you are interested. An outstanding listing of job opportunities appears in *The Wall Street Journal.* It lists jobs at the highest level as well as openings at the supervisory level.

Professional magazines, such as *HR Managing, Training and Industry, Human Resource Management,* and *Nation's Business,* often list vacancies. These advertisements are for recent graduates or people with work experience. If you are interested in a particular occupation, consulting the professional magazines in that functional area can be helpful. Specialized trade journals are also good sources for job leads. Even the yellow pages in phone directories are a helpful guide to companies operating in a particular area. Talk to family, friends, faculty members, and others who may know of job leads or people with pertinent information.

Utilizing the Web

A large number of business, government, and nonprofit organizations are utilizing the Web to recruit employees. In addition, information about pursuing a career and searching for employment can be found on the Web.

Employer Sites

Are you interested in obtaining a position with a particular employer? Thousands of private, public, and nonprofit organizations utilize a portion of their Web sites to recruit employees. The "career," "employment," or "job" links located in the firm's site map and the director or home page of an organization's Web site can be used to learn about positions that the employer wants to fill.

In addition to providing the titles and brief descriptions of positions that they want to fill, the Web sites of employers can be an important resource in other ways. Such sites usually contain information about an organization's products or services, human resource policies, benefit programs, and recruitment contacts. Much of this information can be of help in determining whether you would want to apply for a position with an organization.

Job Listings

You don't have to limit your search to the sites of individual employers to find job openings on the Web. A great many business, government, and nonprofit organizations list positions that they want to fill on one or more of the many compilations of employment opportunities that are on the Web. America's Job Bank identifies about one million openings posted with state employment agencies. More than a quarter million job openings can be found on Careerpath and the Job Factory.

Management Recruiters

Many executive search firms have established Web sites. Some provide information about the managerial and professional positions that they are attempting to fill and/or solicit resumes from experienced executives. Futurestep.com and LAIcompass.com are among the subsidiaries that management recruiters have established for the purpose of recruiting on the Web. You can obtain information about, as well as links to, executive search firms on such sites as the Recruiters Online Network and SearchBase.

Resume Postings

You can make your qualifications known to a great many organizations by posting your resume on Web sites such as Career Mart and JobOptions. Employers and recruiters are able to search electronically through such extensive compilations of resumes for "key words" that indicate that the qualifications of an individual may match the requirements for a position.

E-Mail Communications

E-mail can be used to inquire about employment opportunities, submit cover letters with resume attachments, and conduct follow-up correspondence with prospective employers. You also can use e-mail to supplement telephoning, meetings, and letter writing as means of establishing and maintaining networking contacts.

Search Assistance

A wealth of information and practical advice about searching for employment can be obtained on sites such as The Riley Guide and *The Wall Street Journal.* This can include suggestions about finding job openings, networking techniques, preparing paper and electronic resumes, corresponding with employers, answering interview questions, and negotiating job offers.

Career Advice

Several Web sites furnish an extensive amount of career advice. This can include information about assessing personal aptitudes and interests, prerequisites for various careers, and the employment outlook and salary ranges for many occupations. Sites such as the Career Resource Center, MSU Career Resources on the Web, and What Color Is Your Parachute also furnish suggestions about searching for employment as well as links to other career and employment-related Web sites.

Personalizing Through a Resume

After personal and professional self-assessments and a job search via newspapers, professional magazines, and employment agencies, the next step is to personalize your campaign. You must communicate to others who you are. The basic devices used to communicate are the resume, letters, the telephone, and personal interviews.

A *resume* is a written summary of who you are. It is a concise picture of you and your credentials for a job. A resume should highlight your qualifications, achievements, and career objectives. It should be designed to present you as an attractive candidate for a job.

There is no generally accepted format for a resume. Its purpose is to introduce you to the employer and to get you an interview. Few, if any, employers hire college graduates solely on the contents of a resume. In most cases, you can attract attention with a one-page resume. Longer resumes are for people who have had extensive professional experience.

Employers like resumes that read well and look attractive. Resumes read well if they are concise, grammatically correct, and easy to follow. Resumes look more inviting if they are reproduced on a laser printer on high-quality paper. Some companies prepare professional resumes for a fee; the yellow pages in the telephone directory can provide names of firms that sell this service.

Other elements found in good resumes are job objectives, educational background, college activities, work experiences, and references. The arrangement of these elements is a personal decision. But keep the resume uncluttered and neatly blocked to create an attractive and informative resume with eye appeal. Exhibit D-1 presents an example of an effective resume.

It may be necessary to prepare a different resume for each employer so that your credentials can be slanted for the job openings. Whether you think a different resume for each company can do the job is a decision that only you can make.

Just as important as the points to include are some points to avoid in preparing your resume.

- Don't state what salary you want.
- Don't send a resume with false information.
- Don't send a resume that is sloppy and contains typographical or grammatical errors.
- Don't clutter your resume with unnecessary information.
- Don't inform employers that you will accept only a certain kind of position.
- Don't use fancy colors or gimmicks to sell yourself.

A cover letter should accompany the resume. The objective of the cover letter is to introduce you. It can also encourage the employer to read your resume and meet with you. The cover letter should not duplicate the more detailed resume. Instead, it should add to what is presented in the resume and show that you are really interested in working for the company. The cover letter also reveals how well you can communicate. This clue is often used

EXHIBIT D-1
Sample Resume

JILL M. MURPHY
4896 CRELING DRIVE
NEW YORK, NY 10011
(212) 555-0019

OBJECTIVE   A challenging executive-level position in marketing, utilizing analytical and problem-solving skills.

EDUCATION

May 1990	New York University
Sept. 1985	School of Business Administration
	Major: Marketing and Finance
	G.P.A. 3.9; Dean's List; NYU tuition scholarship
	School of Social Sciences
	G.P.A. 3.9; Dean's List; concentration in mathematics and psychology.
June 1985	Notre Dame High School
Sept. 1982	G.P.A. 3.9
	Class Honors; Phi Beta Kappa; National Honor Society; State Champion, Women's Extemporaneous Speaking, 1979; Major Delegation Award at National Model United Nations in Washington, DC, 1978, 1979.

EXPERIENCE

January 1999– **Vice President**—Europe, PepsiCo.
Present   Responsible for European markets and sales.
               Responsible for all planning, real estate, and recruitment.

May 1990–   **Assistant Marketing Manager**, PepsiCo.
January 1999   Responsibilities included the coordination of planning, implementing, and evaluating the Pepsi Challenge Program in New York City. This required close liaison with PepsiCo's marketing and sales activities as well as its advertising agency and the media. Achieved increase of over 100% in program participants, totaling over 60,000 people.

               Planned and implemented Mountain Dew sampling program.

               On own initiative, developed a Coordinators' Handbook, which PepsiCo plans to distribute nationwide.

Sept. 1987   **Vice President**, Alpha Kappa Gamma Sorority
May 1988   Responsible for housing policies, human resource planning, and discipline.

Sept. 1986   **Assistant Treasurer**, Alpha Kappa Gamma Sorority
Sept. 1987   Responsible for funds to finance all sorority events. Included collection, recording, and billing for sixty-five individual accounts.

Summer 1986   **Salesperson**, Revlon, Inc.

Summer 1985   **Information Manager**, Summer Concert Series at New York University.

ACTIVITIES   Project Director, Marketing Club at New York University; Seminar for Republican Campaign Coordinators, Washington, D.C.; New York University Campus Orchestra; NYC Symphony Youth Orchestra.

REFERENCES   Available on request

by employers to put prospective employees into one of two categories: a good communicator or a poor communicator.

Employers receive cover letters and resumes from many more job applicants than they could ever hire or even interview. Therefore, they screen whatever letters and resumes they receive. Screening is often accomplished rather quickly, so it is better to present your story and objectives concisely and neatly.

The number of letters and resumes you send depends on your strategy. Some people narrow down their list of organizations to the ones they really would like to work for and prepare a personal cover letter to accompany the resume. Other candidates use a "shotgun" approach. They mail numerous letters and resumes to any company with an opening in a particular area of interest. Newspapers, professional magazines, listings in the placement office, telephone directories, directories of organizations, and tips from friends are used to develop a potential list. Then perhaps as many as 200 letters and resumes are sent out.

The Interview Strategy

An outstanding cover letter, resume, and job-search strategy are not enough to get you the job you want. You must also perform well at the interview. The interview is an oral presentation with a representative of a company. A good recruiter is interested in how a job candidate expresses himself or herself. The interviewer is both an information source and an information prober. As an information source, the interviewer provides you with knowledge about careers in the organization and the company in general. As a prober, the interviewer wants to determine what makes you tick and what kind of person you are.

An Interview Plan

In searching for job openings, it is necessary to have a plan. This is also true of a successful interview. In order to do a good job at the interview, you must be thoroughly prepared. Of course, you must know yourself and what type of career you want. The interviewer will probe into the areas you covered in your self-assessment and in developing your career objective. During the interview, you must make it clear why a person with your strengths and objectives should be hired by the company.

The preparation for answering the question "Why you?" involves some homework. You should gather facts about the employer. Annual reports, opinions from employees of the firm, brochures, up-to-date financial data from *The Wall Street Journal,* and recent newspaper articles can be used. Exhibit D-2 identifies some of the information that can be used to prepare for the interview. Whether the initial interview is on campus or in the office of the president of the company, preparation will impress the interviewer. This preparedness will allow you to explore other important areas about the company that you don't know about. It will also allow the interviewer to probe into such areas as your grades, motivation, maturity, ability to communicate, and work experience. This information is important for the company in deciding whether to have you visit for a second, more in-depth interview.

EXHIBIT D-2
Homework Information for the Interview

Location of headquarters, offices, plants
Officers of the organization
Future growth plans of the company
Product lines
Sales, profit, and dividend picture
Price of stock (if available)
Competitors of the company
Organizational structure
Kind of entry-level positions available
Career paths followed by graduates
Union situation
Type of programs available for employees (stock option, medical, educational)

EXHIBIT D-3
**Some Questions
Frequently Asked by
Interviewers**

Why do you want to work for our company?

What kind of career do you have planned?

What have you learned in school to prepare for a career?

What are some of the things you are looking for in a company?

How has your previous job experience prepared you for a career?

What are your strengths? Weaknesses?

Why did you attend this school?

What do you consider to be a worthwhile achievement of yours?

Are you a leader? Explain.

How do you plan to continue developing yourself?

Why did you select your major?

What can I tell you about my company?

Preparation for the interview also involves your personal appearance and motivational state. There isn't enough space here to focus extensively on dress, hair, and value codes. The next best advice is to be yourself and to come prepared to meet with a representative of the organization. If you are to work as an accountant for some firm, then you must comply with standards of performance as well as dress and appearance codes. Use your own judgment, but be realistic: Employers don't like shoulder-length hair on a male salesperson or barefooted production supervisors. These biases will not be corrected in an interview, so don't be a crusader for a cause. The interview is not the best place to project a personal distaste for or discomfort with dress or hair-length standards.

Interviewing makes most people slightly nervous. But if you are well prepared and really motivated to talk to the representative, the interview will probably go well. Consider the interview as a challenge you can meet because you are interested in succeeding. An alert candidate with modest confidence has a good chance of impressing the interviewer.

The Actual Interview

The interview has been called a conversation with a purpose. During the interview, the company representative and the candidate both attempt to determine if a match exists. Are you the right person for the job? The attempt to match person and job follows a question-and-answer routine. The ability to answer questions quickly, honestly, and intelligently is important. The best way to provide a good set of answers is to be prepared.

Exhibit D-3 provides a list of some commonly asked questions. The way you answer these and similar questions is what the interviewer evaluates. Remember that the interviewer is trying to get to know you better by watching and listening.

One effective way to prepare for the interview session is to practice answering the questions in Exhibit D-3 before attending the actual interview. This does not mean developing "pat" or formal answers, but it does mean being ready to respond intelligently. The sincerity of the response and the intelligent organization of an answer must come through in the interview.

Most interviewers eventually get around to asking about your career plans. The purpose of asking these kinds of questions is to determine your reasonableness, maturity, motivation, and goals. The important point is to illustrate by your response that you have given serious thought to your career plans. An unrealistic, disorganized, or unprepared career plan is one way to fail in the interview. Interviewers consider a candidate immature if he or she seems to be still searching and basically confused.

At various points in the interview, it may be appropriate to ask questions. These questions should be important and should not be asked just to appear intelligent. If something is important in evaluating the company, ask the question. It is also valuable if you can ask a question that displays meaningfulness. But don't ask so many questions that the interviewer is answering one after the other. Some frequently asked questions are summarized in Exhibit D-4.

EXHIBIT D-4
Some Questions Frequently Asked by Job Candidates

How is performance evaluated?
How much transfer from one location to another is there?
What is the company's promotion policy?
Does the company have development programs?
How much responsibility is a new employer given? Can you provide me with some examples?
What preferences are given to applicants with graduate degrees?
What type of image does the company have in the community?
What schools provide the bulk of managerial talent in the company?
What are the company's policies for paying for graduate study?
What social obligations would I have?
What community service obligations would I have?

The majority of interviews last between 20 and 30 minutes. It is best to close on a positive and concise note. Summarize your interests, and express whether you are still interested in the company. The interviewers will close by stating that you will hear from the company. You may want to ask if he or she can give you an approximate idea of how long it will be before you hear from the company. Typically, an organization will contact a candidate within four or five weeks after the interview.

One valuable practice to follow after the actual interview is to write down some of the points covered. List the interviewer's name, when the company will contact you, and your overall impression of the company. These notes can be useful if you are called for a later interview. Any person talking to 10 or more companies usually has some trouble recalling the conversation if no notes are available.

One issue that may or may not come up during the interview is salary. Most companies pay a competitive starting wage. Therefore, it is really not that important to ask what your starting salary will be. Individuals with similar education, experience, and background are normally paid the same. Instead of asking about salary in the initial interview, do some checking in the placement office at your school or with friends working in similar jobs.

Should you send a thank-you letter after the interview? This seems to be a good way to refresh the interviewer's memory. The follow-up letter should be short. Expressing your appreciation for the interview shows sincerity. It also provides an opportunity to state that you are still interested in the company.

Interviewers are important processors of information for the company, so it is important to impress them. Unfortunately, not every candidate can win (winning means that the candidate will be asked to visit the company or to undergo further interviewing). "Why was I rejected?" is a question everyone has to ask at some point. Exhibit D-5 lists some of the reasons why candidates are not successful in an interview.

EXHIBIT D-5
Some Reasons for Not Winning

Disorganized and not prepared
Sloppy appearance
Abrasive and overbearing
Unrealistic goals or image of oneself
Inability to communicate effectively
No interest shown in the type of company interviewed
Not alert
Poor grades
Interested only in money
Provided contradictory answers to questions

Visiting the Company and the Job Offer

If you are fortunate enough to be invited for a company visit, consider yourself successful. The letter of invitation or telephone message will specify some available dates. If you are still interested in the company, you must send a formal acceptance. Even if you are not interested in visiting, a short note thanking the company demonstrates your courtesy.

In some cases, your visit will be coordinated by the interviewer you already met. However, it may be the personnel department or management development officer who handles the details. The important point is not who will be coordinating but that you must again prepare for a series of interviews. During this series, you should be asking specific questions about job duties, performance expectations, salary, fringe benefits, and career paths. It is at this phase of the career and employment decision process that you need this kind of information.

One of the main reasons for inviting candidates to visit the company is to introduce them to managers and the organization. These introductions will be brief, but they are important. It is reasonable to expect to meet five or more individuals during the company visit. In some cases, you will be given a tour of the plant, office, or laboratory. A wide array of people will be asked to comment on your employability after you leave. So consider every interview important, and remember to act alert, organized, and interested. You may be bored because many questions are repeated by different managers, but remember that sincerity and interest are variables that these managers will each be asked to comment on.

During the company visit, you will probably not be given a job offer. In most situations, a week to two weeks may pass before the company contacts you.

If you are successful, you will receive a formal job offer. After receiving the offer, make an immediate acknowledgment. Thank the employer and indicate an approximate date when you will give your decision.

A Concluding Note

This appendix has focused on planning. Self-assessment, seeking professional help, the job search, personalizing your job campaign, interviewing, and visiting companies all involve planning. The person who plans his or her campaign to find a worthwhile and satisfying job will be more successful than the disorganized person. Thus, the most important principle in finding the best job for you is to work hard at planning each stage. Good luck!

Excellent Reference Updated Annually on Careers

Richard N. Bolles (2005), *What Color Is Your Parachute?* (Berkeley, CA: Ten Speed Press).

Glossary

A

absenteeism The failure of employees to report to work when they are scheduled to do so.

accident repeater A person who has had more than one accident.

accident research The systematic evaluation of the evidence concerning accidents and health hazards.

adverse impact A situation in which a significantly higher percentage of members of a protected group (women, African Americans, Hispanics) in the available population are rejected for employment, placement, or promotion.

affirmative action Preferential treatment in hiring, recruitment, promotion, and development for groups that have been discriminated against.

AFL-CIO A group of union members that merged membership in 1955 from the American Federation of Labor and the Congress of Industrial Organizations.

Age Discrimination Employment Act of 1967 (amended 1978 and 1986) Protects workers between the ages of 40 and 70 against job discrimination.

agency shop A situation in which all employees pay union dues whether or not they are union members.

alternative dispute resolution (ADR) A method for solving conflict or disputes that does not use the process and remedies of the legal system.

American Federation of Labor (AFL) A union group devoted to improving economic and working conditions for craft employees.

Americans with Disabilities Act of 1990 A comprehensive antidiscrimination law aimed at integrating the disabled into the workplace. It prohibits all employers from discriminating against disabled employees or job applicants when making employment decisions.

applicant tracking system Computer programs that generate job requisition information and cross-reference applicants' qualifications with job openings.

apprentice training A combination of on-the-job and off-the-job training. The apprentice, while learning the job, is paid less than the master worker. Some of the jobs in which one serves as an apprentice include electrician, barber, tool and die maker, and plumber.

arbitration A quasi-judicial process in which the parties agree to submit the unresolvable dispute to a neutral third party for binding settlement.

Arbitration Act of 1888 The first federal statute dealing with national strikes. Two means were provided for the adjustment of labor disputes–voluntary arbitration and investigation.

assessment center A selection technique that uses simulations, tests, interviews, and observations to obtain information about candidates.

attitude (or opinion) survey A set of written instruments completed by employees expressing their reactions to the employer's policies and practices.

authorization card A document indicating by a simple yes or no vote whether an employee wants to be represented by a union or employee association.

autonomy The degree to which the job provides substantial freedom, independence, and discretion to the individual in scheduling the work and in determining the procedures to be used in carrying it out.

B

balance sheet approach Form of compensation for expatriates that attempts to maintain the employees' standard of living during the international assignment, so that the expatriate does not gain or lose as a result of the international relocation.

bargaining impasse Failure to reach an agreement on a mandatory bargaining issue during contract negotiations or failure of the rank-and-file membership to ratify the new contract.

bargaining unit Two or more employees who share common employment interests and conditions and may reasonably be grouped together.

behavior modeling Learning by observing a role model's behavior. The fundamental characteristic of modeling is that learning takes place by observation or imagination of another individual's experience.

behavior modification Individual learning through reinforcement.

behavioral observation scale (BOS) A method similar to the BARS that uses the critical incident technique to identify a series of behaviors that describe the job. A 1 (almost never) to 5 (almost always) format is used to rate the behaviors.

behaviorally anchored rating scale (BARS) A rating scale that uses critical incidents as anchor statements placed along a scale. Typically, 6 to 10 performance dimensions, each with 5 to 6 critical incident anchors, are rated per employee.

biographical information blank (BIB) A more detailed form used to supplement an application blank. Asks for information related to a much wider array of attitudes and experiences.

bona fide occupational qualification (BFOQ)   A defense against discrimination only where age, sex, religion, or national origin is an actual qualification to perform the job.

Boulwarism   An unfair management practice in which management works out a final offer and presents it to the union at the bargaining table.

boycott   In a primary boycott, union members do not patronize the boycotted firm. In a secondary boycott, a supplier of a boycotted firm is threatened with a union strike unless it stops doing business with the firm. This latter type of boycott is illegal under the Taft-Hartley Act.

broadbanding   A system for condensing compensation rate ranges into broader classifications.

burnout   Severe state of stress that shows as exhaustion, depersonalization, and low accomplishment.

C

career   Individually perceived sequences of attitudes and behaviors associated with work-related experiences and activities over the span of an individual's work life.

career path   A sequence of positions through which an organization moves an employee.

career pathing   A graphical/cognitive plotting of positions through which a person moves in his/her career.

career planning   Charting out a number of positions and jobs that will be needed to progress in an organization or a profession.

career stages   The distinct stages that individuals go through in their careers, typically including establishment, advancement, maintenance, and retirement.

carpal tunnel syndrome   Occurs when the median nerve, which runs from the forearm into the hand, becomes pressed or squeezed at the wrist.

case method   A training technique in which a description (a case) of a real situation is analyzed by participants. The interaction of the participants and trainer is valuable in improving the degree of learning that occurs.

CD-ROM   Compact disk used to hold text, graphics, and stereo sound.

central tendency error   A rating tendency to give ratees an average rating on each criteria. That is, on a 1 to 7 scale, circling all 4s; or on a 1 to 5 scale, selecting all 3s.

certification election   Once employees demonstrate an interest in joining a union, the National Labor Relations Board requires that within a period of time (often set at 45 days) a certification election must occur. If the union was 50 percent plus one vote, it becomes the exclusive bargaining unit.

Civil Rights Act of 1964: Title VII   An important law that prohibits employers, unions, employment agencies, and joint labor–management committees controlling apprenticeship or training programs from discriminating on the basis of race, color, religion, sex, or national origin.

Civil Rights Act of 1991   Allows for compensatory and punitive damages in intentional discrimination cases; allows for jury trials when damages are sought.

classification or grading system   A job evaluation method that groups jobs together into a grade or classification.

closed shop   A situation in which a new employee must be a union member when hired. Popular in the construction, maritime, and printing industries.

COBRA   The Consolidated Omnibus Budget Reconciliation Act of 1985 requires that employers with more than 20 employees must offer continuation of health care coverage for 18 to 36 months after an employee quits, dies, or is terminated.

codetermination   The concept of workers playing a direct, major role in corporate decision making.

collective bargaining   The process by which representatives of the organization meet and attempt to work out a contract with representatives of the union.

commission   A commission is compensation based on a percentage of sales in units or dollars.

common metric questionnaire (CMQ)   An instrument that includes survey questions on background contacts with people, decision making, physical and mechanical attributes, and work setting.

Commonwealth v. Hunt   The Massachusetts Supreme Court decision that decided that criminal conspiracy did not exist if unions did not use illegal tactics to achieve goals.

comparable worth   An issue that has been raised by women and the courts in recent years. It means that the concept of equal pay for equal jobs should be expanded to the notion of equal pay for comparable jobs. If a job is comparable to other jobs as determined by job content analysis, that job's pay should be comparable.

compensation   Compensation is the HRM function that deals with every type of reward that individuals receive in return for performing organizational tasks.

competency alignment process (CAP)   A process in which the competencies in a job description match the competencies in the performance review.

competency based pay   A combination of skill-based, knowledge-based, and credential-based pay system.

concession bargaining   Bargaining in which something of importance is given back to management by the union.

conciliation   The first step in the mediation continuum, which involves an attempt to persuade disputing parties to meet and discuss their problems.

Congress of Industrial Organizations (CIO)   A union formed by John L. Lewis, president of the United Mine Workers, to organize industrial and mass-production workers; it was devoted to improving economic and working conditions.

construct validity A demonstrated relationship between underlying traits inferred from behavior and a set of test measures related to those traits.

content validity The degree to which a test, interview, or performance evaluation measures skills, knowledge, or ability to perform.

contingent workers These include temporaries, part-timers, contract, leased (outsourced), and other workers who are hired to handle extra job tasks or workloads.

contrast effect A rating error that occurs when a rater allows an individual's prior performance or other recently evaluated individuals to affect the ratings given to an employee.

cost-of-living adjustment (COLA) Wage increase or decrease pegged to the rise and fall in the cost-of-living index.

craft union A group of individuals who belong to one craft or closely related group of occupations (e.g., carpenters, bricklayers).

credential-based pay Pay based on the number and type of credentials (i.e. CPA, CFA) a person has earned.

criteria relevance A good measure of performance must be reliable, valid, and closely related to an employee's actual level of productivity.

criteria sensitivity A good measure of performance should reflect actual differences between high and low performers.

criterion-related validity The extent to which a selection technique is predictive of or correlated with important elements of job behavior.

critical incident rating The system of selecting very effective and ineffective examples of job behavior and rating whether an employee displays the type of behaviors specified in the critical incidents.

culture shock The feelings of frustration and confusion that result from being constantly subjected to strange and unfamiliar cues about what to do and how to get it done when trying to live in a new culture.

cumulative trauma disorder (CTD) A response to so many demands on a body. This is a group of symptoms such as pain, tingling, or weakness and other disorders.

D

decertification election An election in which employees who are represented by a union vote to drop the union.

defined benefit pension plan A pension plan that specifies the benefit workers will get at retirement.

defined contribution pension plan A pension plan that usually specifies the employer's contribution but cannot predetermine the employee's actual pension benefit.

delayering Allowing workers to move among a wider range of tasks without having to adjust pay with each move.

Delphi technique A technique to elect information and judgments from participants to facilitate problem solving, and decision making. Usually participants are not together and they are not connected via e-mail, mail, or fax.

differential piece rate (Taylor plan) A piecework plan that pays on the basis of two separate piecework rates: one for those who produce below or up to standard and another for those who produce above standard.

direct financial compensation Consists of the pay a person receives in the form of wages, salaries, bonuses, or commissions.

disparate treatment The view that discrimination occurs due to different treatment given to a person because of race, sex, national origin, age, or disability factors.

distributive bargaining Occurs when labor and management are in conflict on an issue and when the outcome is a win-lose situation.

distributive justice theory A theory of motivation that argues that a major determinant of an employee's productivity and satisfaction arises from the degree of equity in the workplace, defined in terms of a ratio of an employee's inputs (effort, attendance, and so on) to outcomes (pay, benefits, and so on) as compared with a similar ratio for a relevant other.

diversity (1) The condition that describes the variety of people who make up the contemporary workforce (i.e., African Americans, Hispanics, Asians, Caucasians, and so on). (2) Any mixture of themes characterized by differences and similarities.

downshifters People who want to slow down at work so that they can enjoy nonwork time and leisure.

downsizing A reduction in a company's workforce.

drug-testing program A program that uses screening techniques to determine if drugs exist in a person's system.

dual-career couple A situation in which a husband and wife both have careers.

E

early retirement Retirement before the usual age of 65.

e-commerce Electronic or Internet transactions that result in the exchange of goods and services.

e-recruiting The use of an online system to recruit job candidates.

economic man theory A theory of motivation that holds that people work only for money.

economic strike A strike caused by disagreement over primarily economic issues.

elder care Care provided to an elderly relative by a full or part-time employee.

employee assistance program (EAP) A program designed to help employees with personal, family, and work problems. Although these programs are voluntary, managers are instructed on how to confront the problems when they occur.

employee drug testing   A drug testing program focused on screening employees for drugs.

employee leasing   Paying a leasing firm to provide the organization with a ready-made pool of human resources.

Employee Polygraph Protection Act   Legislation that makes it illegal for most private organizations to use the polygraph as a selection technique.

employees' attitudes   Employees' beliefs and feelings about situations, people, programs, or events.

employment at will   A condition under which an employer is free to terminate the employment relationship for some specific reason or even for no reason at all. In a growing number of courts, the employer's right to terminate at will is being challenged.

Equal Employment Opportunity Commission (EEOC)   The Civil Rights Act, Title VII, 1964, gave the EEOC limited powers to resolve charges of discrimination and interpret the meaning of Title VII. In 1972, Congress gave the EEOC the power to sue employers in the federal courts.

equal employment opportunity programs (EEO)   Programs implemented by employers to prevent employment discrimination in the workplace or to take remedial action to offset past employment discrimination.

equal pay   Equal pay for equal work for men and women. Equal work is defined as work requiring equal skills, effort, and responsibility under similar working conditions.

Equal Pay Act   The Equal Pay Act requires equal pay for equal work performed by men and women.

equity theory   A motivation theory that argues that a major determinant of employees' productivity and satisfaction arises from the degree of fairness or unfairness that they perceive in the workplace.

ERISA   Employment Retirement Income Security Act of 1974; covers practically all employee benefit plans of private employees, including multiemployer plans.

ESOP   An employee stock ownership plan authorized by Congress and funded through the mechanism of an employee stock ownership trust (ESOT).

ethnocentric HRM perspective   A view of HRM whereby an organization thinks that the way of doing things in the parent country is the best way, no matter where business is done.

exchange theory   See *distributive justice theory.*

executive information system (EIS)   A specialized information system used by top executives in HR planning.

executive search firm   A "head hunting" firm that specializes in upper-level executive recruitment. Executive search firms are usually on retainer and charge higher fees than regular employment agencies.

exempt employee   A person working in a job that is not subject to the provisions of the Fair Labor Standards Act (1938) with respect to minimum wage and overtime pay. Most professionals, executives, administrators, and outside salespeople are classified as exempt.

expatriate manager   A manager who is on assignment in a country other than the parent country of the organization. This person is also called a parent country national (PCN).

external environmental influences   The environmental forces outside the organization, such as unions, government, and economic conditions.

extinction   A decline in the rate of a response brought about by nonreinforcement.

F

fact-finding   An impasse resolution technique involving a neutral third party who studies the issues in a dispute and recommends a reasonable settlement.

factor comparison method   A job evaluation method that uses a factor-by-factor comparison. A factor comparison scale, instead of a point scale, is used. Five universal job factors used to compare jobs are responsibility, skills, physical effort, mental effort, and working conditions.

Fair Labor Standards Act (FLSA)   A 1938 law that set specific minimum wage and overtime pay rates.

Family and Medical Leave Act (FMLA)   Social legislation that stipulates that most employers with 50 or more employees must provide up to 12 weeks of unpaid leave to eligible employees during any 12-month period. The purpose is to allow employees to balance the demands of the workplace with the needs of family members.

Family Medical Leave Act of 1993   Allows employees to take off any amount of time as a result of a disability from pregnancy or serious illness of the employee, spouse, child, or parent with a guarantee of reinstatement to their old jobs or similar jobs when they return.

FASS 106   An accounting procedure that requires companies to begin accruing the projected cost of postretirement benefits during the employee's working career.

feedback   The degree to which carrying out the work activities required by the job results in the individual's obtaining direct and clear information about the effectiveness of his or her performance.

feedback pay   Based on aligning pay with strategic objections and then establishing a direct connection between the employee and his or her contribution to goal accomplishments.

financial core   Members of a union who pay union dues but choose not to engage in any other union-related activity.

flexible (cafeteria) benefits plan   A benefits plan that allows employees to choose between two or more types of benefits.

flexible spending account   An employee sets aside or saves money to pay for items such as health insurance co-pays, child care, or prescription medication.

forced-choice format   A type of individually oriented rating format whereby the rater must choose which of several statements about work behavior is most descriptive of an employee.

forced distribution   A method of ranking similar to grading on a curve. Only certain percentages of employees can be ranked high, average, or low.

Foreign Corrupt Practices Act of 1977 (FCPA)   A law that makes it illegal for an American organization to pay bribes to foreign officials for the purpose of getting a competitive advantage in doing business.

401(k)   The section of the Internal Revenue Code that allows employees to save on a tax-deferred basis by entering into salary deferral agreements with an employer.

403(b)   The section of the Internal Revenue Code that allows employees of educational and other nonprofit organizations to make tax-deferred contributions toward retirement. The salary deferral agreements with employers are similar to those for the 401(k).

four-fifths rule   Discrimination is likely to occur if the selection rate for a protected group is less than 4/5 of the selection rate for a majority group.

functional job analysis (FJA)   A job analysis method that attempts to identify what a worker does in performing a job in terms of data, people, and things.

G

gainsharing plans   Companywide group incentive plans that, through a financial formula for distributing organizationwide gains, unite diverse organizational elements in the common pursuit of improved organizational effectiveness.

genetic testing   The use of blood and urine samples to determine whether a job applicant carries genetic traits that could predispose him or her to adverse health effects when exposed to certain chemicals or job-related toxins.

geocentric HRM perspective   A view of HRM whereby nationality is ignored and managers are hired on the basis of qualifications.

glass ceiling   A hypothetical barrier that seems to face minorities and women in advancing up the management hierarchy.

global corporation   A corporation with a geocentric HRM perspective. National boundaries are ignored and HRM is viewed as a way of integrating operations all over the world.

global HRM   The policies and practices related to managing people in an internationally oriented business.

goal setting   A process that appears to motivate individuals to attempt to accomplish specific goals.

grid OD   A program that involves six phases designed to improve organizational performance. The phases include determining the participants' leadership styles, team building, intergroup development, and evaluation.

grievance   A complaint about a job that creates dissatisfaction or discomfort for the worker.

guaranteed annual wage (GAW)   A plan in which the employer guarantees the employee a certain number of weeks of work at a certain wage after the worker has passed a probation period.

H

halo error   A rating error that occurs when a rater assigns ratings on the basis of an overall impression (positive or negative) of the person being rated.

harshness rating error   The tendency to rate everyone low on the criteria being evaluated.

health   The state of physical, mental, and social well-being.

health hazards   Aspects of the work environment that slowly and cumulatively (and often irreversibly) lead to deterioration of an employee's health.

HIV-AIDS   Human immuno-deficiency virus (HIV) and acquired immune deficiency syndrome (AIDS) is a disease transmitted by blood, body products, or sexual activity.

HMO   Health maintenance organization; a medical organization consisting of medical and health specialists; it stresses preventive medicine.

host country national   An employee of an international organization who is from the local workforce rather than being from the parent country of the organization.

hot cargo agreement   The employer permits union members to avoid working with materials that come from employers who have been struck by a union. This type of boycott is illegal.

hot stove rule   A discipline program that is described in terms of touching a hot stove. It involves an immediate burn, a warning system, consistency, and impersonal application of discipline.

HRM objectives   The ends an HRM department attempts to accomplish. Some of the specific HRM objectives are (1) to provide the organization with well-trained and well-motivated employees, (2) to communicate HRM policies to all employees, and (3) to employ the skills and abilities of the workforce efficiently.

HRM policy   A general guide to decision making in important decision areas.

HRM procedure   A specific direction to action. It tells a person how to do a particular activity.

HRM strategy   The plan that integrates HRM objectives, policies, and procedures.

human resource information system (HRIS)   The method used by an organization to collect, store, analyze, report, and evaluate information and data on people, jobs, and costs.

human resource management (HRM)   A function performed in organizations that facilitates the most effective use of people (employees) to achieve organizational and individual goals. Terms used interchangeably with HRM include *personnel, human resource management,* and *employee development.*

human resource planning   The process that helps to provide adequate human resources to achieve future organizational objectives. It includes forecasting future needs for employees of various types, comparing these needs with the present workforce, and determining the numbers or types of employees to be recruited into or phased out of the organization's employment group.

I

identity theft This is the act of using another person's name, address, social security number, or other identifying information without the person's knowledge with the intent to commit fraud or other crimes.

Immigration Reform and Control Act (IRCA) of 1986 All employers are required to screen every job applicant's eligibility for lawful employment. Thus, the employer has a major responsibility for not permitting illegal immigrants to be or remain employed.

impairment testing Testing to judge whether one can carry out job duties or is impaired. Also called fitness-for-duty testing.

indirect financial compensation All financial rewards (benefits and services) that are not included in direct financial compensation.

indoor environment quality (IEQ) This refers to the quality of air in a building or work unit.

industrial union Union in which all members are employees in a company or an industry.

injunction A court decree to stop an activity.

inpatriate An international manager from another country who is transferred to the parent country market (i.e., where the firm's headquarters is located) on a semipermanent or permanent assignment.

integrative bargaining Occurs when the two sides face a common problem and when the outcome of bargaining is a win-win situation.

interest arbitration An impasse resolution technique in which a neutral third party imposes a settlement on the disputing parties.

internal environmental influences The organization's internal environmental forces, such as goals, organizational style, tasks, work group, and the leader's style of influencing.

Internet A system of over 30 million computers all connected together and communicating with each other.

interrater reliability The extent that two or more raters give consistent/similar scores on ratings.

intranet A firm's internal electronic networks, similar to the Internet.

IRA An individual retirement account.

J

job A group of positions that are similar in their duties, such as computer programmer or compensation specialist.

job analysis The process of gathering, analyzing, and synthesizing information about jobs.

job analysis information format (JAIF) A questionnaire that provides core information about a job, job duties, and job requirements.

job characteristics model A mode of job design based on the view that three psychological states toward a job affect a person's motivation and satisfaction. These states are experienced meaningfulness, experienced responsibility, and knowledge of results. A job's skill variety, identity, and task significance contribute to meaningfulness; autonomy is related to responsibility; and feedback is related to knowledge of results.

job description The job analysis provides information about the job that results in a description of what the job entails.

job enlargement A method of designing jobs that increases the number of tasks performed by a job incumbent without increasing the level of responsibility. It is sometimes called horizontal job change.

job enrichment A method of designing a job so that employees can satisfy needs for growth, recognition, and responsibility while performing the job. The job characteristics model is used in establishing a job enrichment strategy.

job evaluation The formal process by which the relative worth of various jobs in the organization is determined for pay purposes.

job family A group of two or more jobs that have similar duties.

job layoff A condition that exists when no work is available and the employee is sent home, management views the situation as temporary, and management intends to recall the employee.

job loss A condition in which there is no work and the individual is sent home permanently.

job posting A listing of job openings that includes job specifications, appearing on a bulletin board or in company publications.

job search The set of activities a person (job candidate) initiates to seek and find a position that will be comfortable and rewarding.

job security The guarantee that, at least during the life of any union contract, an employee's job will continue to exist.

job security agreement A pact between GM and the UAW that guaranteed employees eliminated in one department jobs in another department at the same wage.

job specification A second product of job analysis. It is a written explanation of the knowledge, skills, abilities, traits, and other characteristics necessary for effective job performance.

jurisdictional strike A strike that occurs when two unions argue and disagree over who has the right to perform a job.

K

Knights of Labor Founded in 1869, this was the first union to achieve significant size and influence in the United States.

knowledge-based pay   Knowledge-based pay rewards employees for acquiring additional knowledge both within the current job and in new job categories.

L

labor relations   The continuous relationship between a defined group of employees (e.g., a union or association) and an employer.

labor union (employee association)   An organization of employees that uses collective action to advance its members' interests in wages and working conditions.

Landrum-Griffin Act   A labor law passed in 1959 that is referred to as the bill of rights of union members. It was designed to regulate and audit the internal affairs of unions.

learning   The act by which a person acquires skills, knowledge, and abilities that result in a relatively permanent change in his or her behavior.

leniency rating error   The tendency to rate everyone high or excellent on all criteria.

life events   Changes in a person's life that can contribute to stress.

lockout   A management response to union pressures in which a skeleton crew of managerial personnel is used to maintain a workplace; the plant is closed to employees.

M

management by objectives (MBO)   A managerial practice where managers and subordinates jointly plan, organize, control, communicate, and debate the subordinate's job and performance. As a performance evaluation technique, it focuses on establishing and measuring specific objectives.

management development   The process by which managers gain the experience, skills, and attitudes to become or remain successful leaders in their organizations.

management position description questionnaire (MPDQ)   A checklist of 208 items related to concerns and responsibilities of managers.

managing diversity   Taking into consideration the differences in people and respecting these differences while working to optimize job and team performance.

mandated benefits programs   Three types of benefits that an employer must provide employees because of state and federal regulations: unemployment insurance, social security, and workers' compensation.

mandatory bargaining issue   Wages, hours, and other terms and conditions of employment.

maquiladora plants   Foreign-owned manufacturing and assembly plants along the northern Mexican border. The majority of these plants are owned by U.S. companies and most of the plants' output is exported to the United States.

mediation   A process in which a neutral third party helps through persuasion to bring together labor and management. The dispute is settled because of the skills and suggestions of a mediator.

mediator   A neutral third party who uses persuasion to settle disputes between labor and management.

mentoring relationship   A relationship between a junior and senior colleague that is considered by the junior person to be helpful in his or her career development.

merit pay   Individual pay increases based on the rated performance of the individual employee in a previous time period.

midcareer plateau   A point reached during the adult stage of life where a person feels stifled and is not progressing as he or she had planned or would like.

minimum wage   The Fair Labor Standards Act of 1938, as amended, states that all employers covered by the law must pay an employee at least a minimum wage. In June 2000, the minimum was $5.15 per hour.

Monster.com   A one-stop career management resource for job seekers and employers.

motivation   The attitudes that predispose a person to act in a specific goal-directed way. It is an internal state that directs a person's behavior.

multimedia-based training   An interactive learning experience that incorporates the use of either CD-ROM or World Wide Web technology.

multimethod job analysis approach   Job analysis that combines interviews, on-site observation, task surveys, and statistical analysis of the survey responses.

multinational corporation   An international organization with operations that are defined by national boundaries to a greater extent than in a global corporation.

N

National Labor Relations Board (NLRB)   A government regulatory body that administers labor laws and regulations in the private and nonprofit sectors.

nature of task   The characteristics or attributes of the task being worked on.

negative reinforcement   An increase in the frequency of a response following removal of a negative reinforcer immediately after the response.

negotiation   A give-and-take debate, discussion, and bargaining used to reach agreements.

nominal group technique (NGT)   A process in which ideas are generated about a problem and which are displayed, discussed, and modified to reach the most optimal solution.

nonexempt employee   A person working in a job that is subject to the minimum wage and overtime pay provisions of the Fair Labor Standards Act. Blue-collar and clerical workers are two major groups of nonexempt employees.

Norris-LaGuardia Act   Also called the anti-injunction act, limited the use of injunctions by federal courts, boycotts, and strikes.

O

OBRA The Omnibus Budget Reconciliation Act of 1989 modifies coverage under COBRA.

Occupational Information Network (O*NET) A database that serves as a replacement for the Dictionary of Occupational Titles (DOT).

Occupational Safety and Health Act (1970) An act designed to protect the safety and health of employees. According to this act, employers are responsible for providing workplaces free from hazards to safety and health.

Occupational Safety and Health Administration (OSHA) The government agency responsible for carrying out and administrating the Occupational Safety and Health Act.

online recruitment The use of the Internet to provide information to prospective job applicants.

open shop A work situation in which a union is not present and there is no management effort to keep the union out.

open system A pay system where pay ranges and even an individual's pay are open to the public and fellow employees.

organization chart A chart that presents the relationship among departments and units of the firm.

orientation The HRM activity that introduces new employees to the organization and to the employees' new tasks, superiors, and work groups.

outplacement Service provided by some firms to individuals who are asked to leave permanently. The services may include resume preparation, counseling, and training.

outsourcing The practice of hiring another firm to complete work that is important and must be done efficiently.

P

paired comparison A method of ranking whereby subordinates are placed in all possible pairs and the supervisor must choose which of the two in each pair is the better performer.

parent country national An employee from the corporation's home country who is on assignment in another country. Usually called an expatriate.

pay class A convenient grouping of a variety of jobs that are similar in difficulty and responsibility.

pay compression A situation in which employees perceive too narrow a difference between their own pay and that of their colleagues.

pay curve A graphical portrayal of pay information based on survey data collected.

pay level Pay set relative to employees working on similar jobs in other organizations.

pay range A set of data that indicates pay differences between pay classes.

pay satisfaction The degree of satisfaction an employee has regarding his or her compensation and its fairness.

pay structure Pay set relative to employees working on different jobs within the organization.

pay surveys Surveys of the compensation paid to employees by all employers in a geographic area, an industry, or an occupational group.

Pension Benefit Guaranty Corporation Set up by ERISA to pay pensions to employees of firms whose pension plans become bankrupt; funded by taxpayers.

performance analysis A systematic procedure that is used to determine if training is needed to correct behavior deficiencies.

performance evaluation The HRM activity that is used to determine the extent to which an employee is performing the job effectively.

performance management Includes activities to ensure that goals are consistently being met in an effective and efficient manner.

permanent replacement Attempting to replace union workers with permanent replacements. In a strike situation, management can replace union workers. However, unions would bargain long and hard to prevent the permanent replacement strategy.

personal bias rating error The bias a rater has about individual characteristics, attitudes, backgrounds, and so on, that influence a rating more than performance.

personality The characteristic way a person thinks and behaves in adjusting to his or her environment. It includes the person's traits, values, motives, genetic blueprint, attitudes, abilities, and behavior patterns.

picketing Placing union members at the plant entrances to advertise the dispute and discourage people from entering or leaving the company's premises during a strike.

point system The most widely used job evaluation method. It requires evaluators to quantify the value of the elements of a job. On the basis of the job description or interviews with job occupants, points are assigned to the degree of various factors required to do the job.

position The responsibilities and duties performed by an individual. There are as many positions as there are employees.

position analysis questionnaire (PAQ) A structured questionnaire of 194 items used to quantitatively assess jobs. It assesses information input, mental processes, work output, relationships, job contacts, and various other characteristics.

positive discipline A fair discipline approach that attempts to educate employees about what behavior and performance are expected.

positive reinforcement Anything that both increases the strength of response and induces repetition of the behavior that preceded the reinforcement.

PPO A managed health care plan based on agreements between doctors, hospitals, and other related medical service facilities with an employer or insurance company; it provides services for a fixed fee.

preferential shop The union is recognized and union members are given preference in some areas. These preferences violate the Taft-Hartley Act.

Pregnancy Discrimination Act of 1978 This law makes it illegal to discriminate on the basis of pregnancy, childbirth, or related medical conditions in employment decisions.

preventive (wellness) program A program instituted within an organization to achieve a high level of wellness among employees and to decrease costs of impaired health. Programs typically involve health screening exams, stress testing, and physicians' recommendations.

process chart A chart that displays how jobs are linked or related to each other.

production bonus system An individual incentive system that pays an employee an hourly rate plus a bonus when the employee exceeds the standard.

productivity The output of goods and services per unit of input of resources used in a production process.

profit-sharing plans Profit-sharing plans distribute a fixed percentage of total organizational profit to employees in the form of cash-deferred bonus amounts.

progressive pattern of discipline A discipline program that proceeds from less severe disciplinary actions (a discussion) to very severe action (being discharged). Each step in the progression becomes more severe.

punishment An uncomfortable consequence of a particular behavior.

Q

quid pro quo harassment Form of harassment that occurs when submission to or rejection of sexual behavior is used as a basis for making a job-related decision.

R

Railway Labor Act A labor law passed in 1926 that provides railroad (and later airline) employees with the right to organize and bargain collectively with management.

ranking of jobs A job evaluation method often used in smaller organizations, in which the evaluator ranks jobs from the simplest to the most challenging—for example, clerk to research scientist.

realistic job preview A briefing that provides a job candidate with accurate and clear information about the attractive and unattractive features of a job. Being realistic so that expectations are accurate is the objective of a realistic job preview.

"recency of events" rating error A tendency to use the most recent events to evaluate performance instead of using a longer, more complete time frame.

recruitment The set of activities an organization uses to attract job candidates who have the abilities and attitudes needed to help the organization achieve its objectives.

red circle rates A pay rate above a wage or salary level that is considered maximum for the job class. This means that the job is overpaid and overrated.

Rehabilitation Act of 1973 An act that is enforced by the Office of Federal Contract Compliance Programs (OFCCP). It requires that all employers with government contracts of $2,500 or more set up affirmative action programs for the disabled.

reimbursement account An account into which employees can place tax-deferred funds that can be used to pay for expenses not covered by the regular benefits package.

reinforcement Based on the notion that people do things because they know other things (e.g. rewards) may follow. Consequences which give rewards increase a behavior.

reliability Refers to a selection technique's freedom from systematic errors of measurement or its consistency under different conditions.

repatriation The process of being reintegrated back into domestic operations after being on an international assignment outside of the organization's parent country.

repetitive stress injury An injury caused by repetitive movements such as using a computer mouse over and over.

replacement chart A display or chart usually of technical, professional, and managerial employees. It includes name, title, age, length of service, and other relevant information on present employees.

representation election A vote to determine if a particular group will represent the workers in collective bargaining.

restricted shop A practice initiated by management to keep a union out without violating labor laws. A restricted shop is an attitude rather than a formal arrangement.

restructuring Redesigning a work unit, job, or project by establishing a new structure in terms of hierarchy, reporting lines, span of control, decision making latitude, etc.

reverse culture shock Similar in nature to culture shock (see term), reverse culture shock occurs when an individual returns to the home country after living in another culture.

right-to-work laws Laws that specify that two people doing the same job must be paid the same wages, whether or not they are union members. Nineteen states have right-to-work laws.

role playing The acting out of a role by participants as others in the training session observe.

role pressures The pressure created by performing a role or doing a set of tasks. For example, performing the role of an air traffic controller is one in which role pressure is usually high.

S

safety hazards   Aspects of the work environment that have the potential of immediate and sometimes violent harm to an employee.

salary   Pay calculated at an annual or monthly rate rather than hourly.

secret system   A compensation system where pay is regarded as privileged information known only to the employee, the supervisor, and staff employees such as HRM and payroll.

selection   The process by which an organization chooses from a list of applicants the person or people who best meet the selection criteria for the position available, considering current environmental conditions.

SEP-IRA   Simplified employee pension IRAs; these can be implemented by small employers to help employees finance their retirement.

severance pay   An income bridge from employment to unemployment and back to employment, provided by some employers.

sexual harassment   Unwelcome sexual attention that causes the recipient distress and results in an inability on the part of the recipient to effectively perform the job.

sick-building syndrome   A situation in which occupants of a building are experiencing acute health problems that appear to be associated with the time spent in the building.

sitdown strike   Employees are on strike, but remain on the physical site such as their office or plant location.

skills gap   The mismatch between the high-skill demands of jobs and the lack of qualifications of job applicants.

skills inventory   A list of the names, personal characteristics, and skills of the people working for the organization. It provides a way to acquire these data and makes them available where needed in an efficient manner.

skill variety   The degree to which a job requires a variety of different activities in carrying out the work and involves the use of a number of an individual's skills and talents.

skill-based pay   An alternative to job-based pay that sets pay levels on the basis of how many skills employees have or how many jobs they can do.

social-behaviorist theories   Theories that have a social and psychological origin. A cluster of explanations of behaviors that are intended to help understand why and how people work in organizational settings.

social security   The federally mandated pension fund designed to provide income to retired people to supplement savings, private pensions, and part-time work.

spot gainsharing   A gainsharing system that focuses on a specific problem in a specific department rather than on performance improvements for the whole organization.

standard-hour plan   An individual incentive plan that sets wages on the basis of completion of the job or task in some expected period of time.

straight piecework   An individual incentive plan where pay fluctuates on the basis of units of production per time period.

strategic human resource management   Placing a strategic perspective on the attraction, retention, and motivation of human resources.

strategic job analysis   A form of job analysis that tries to predict what a job will look like in the future.

strategic planning   In simple terms, the process of determining what an organization's mission is and how it plans to achieve the goals that are associated with the mission.

strategy   What an organization's key executives hope to accomplish in the long run.

stress   A person's physical, chemical, and mental reactions to stressors or stimuli in the environment—the boss, co-workers, HRM policies, and so on.

strike   An effort by employees to withhold their services from an employer in order to get greater concessions at the collective bargaining table.

structured employment interview   An interview that follows a prepared pattern of questions that were structured before the interview was conducted.

succession planning   Fills vacancies through a comprehensive career planning program.

suggestion system   A formal method of obtaining employees' advice for improvement in organizational effectiveness; it includes some kind of reward based on the successful application of the idea.

Sullivan Principles   When Leon Sullivan joined the Board of Directors of General Motors he used his position to promote equality among all workers and opposed apartheid in South Africa. His principles centered on nonsegregation of the races, equal pay, increasing the number of blacks in supervisory positions, and improving the quality of life of all workers at GM.

supplementary unemployment benefits (SUB)   The employer adds to unemployment compensation payments to help the employee achieve income security.

T

Taft-Hartley Act   A labor amendment of the Wagner Act, passed in 1947, that guaranteed employees' bargaining rights and also specified unfair labor union practices that would not be permitted.

task   A coordinated and aggregated series of work elements used to produce an output (units of production or service to a client).

task identity   The degree to which the job requires completion of a "whole" and identifiable piece of work— that is, doing a job from beginning to end with a visible outcome.

task significance   The degree to which the job has a substantial impact on the lives or work of other people, whether in the immediate organization or the external environment.

team building   A development method that helps organization members work more efficiently or effectively in groups.

telework   A work arrangement that permits a worker to perform tasks away from an office. The employee is connected through the use of e-mail, fax, computer, and/or teleconferencing.

third country national   An employee working for an international organization who is from a country other than the parent country of the organization or the host country in which the assignment is located.

360-degree feedback   A multi-source performance appraisal approach. Self and others (boss, subordinate, peers, customers) rate a person and data/information is fed back on his or her ratings.

total compensation approach   Total compensation is made up of base pay, variable pay, and indirect pay (benefits).

total quality management (TQM)   An approach that involves everyone in the firm in developing and fine-tuning processes that are customer-oriented, flexible, and responsive to improving the quality of every activity and function of the organization.

training   The systematic process of altering the behavior of employees in a direction that will achieve organizational goals.

two-tiered compensation plans   Compensation plans that protect the wages of workers hired before a certain date but start new workers at a lower pay rate.

type A behavior pattern   An action-emotion complex that can be observed in a person who is aggressive, in a struggle against time, competitive, and chronically impatient.

U

unemployment insurance   A state-mandated insurance benefit designed to provide a subsistence payment to employees between jobs.

union shop   A situation in which an employee is required to join a union after being hired.

union steward   A union representative who works at the job site to resolve disputes that arise in connection with the labor–management contract.

utility   Assessed using cost-benefit analysis, utility measures whether the use of a selection technique improves the quality of the people hired.

V

validity   Refers to the accuracy of a measure or a test. It states that a measure of a concept is accurate.

variable pay   Any compensation plan that emphasizes a share focus on organizational success, broadens the opportunities for incentives to nontraditional groups (such as nonexecutives or nonmanagers), and operates outside the base pay increase system.

vestibule training   A trainee learns a job in an environment that closely resembles the actual work environment. For example, pilots at United Airlines train in a jet simulation cockpit.

vesting   A guarantee that retirement benefits will be provided when a person leaves or retires from the firm.

virtual reality (VR)   A computer-based technology that enables users to learn in a three-dimensional environment.

W

wage   Pay calculated at an hourly rate.

Wagner Act   A labor law passed in 1935 that was designed to encourage the growth of trade unions and restrain management from interfering with that growth.

Web-based training   Online training that is delivered via the Internet or through a firm's intranet that is delivered on a Web browser.

weighted application blank   An application form designed to be scored and used in making selection decisions.

whistle-blowing   Stating or presenting a grievance complaint, or allegation to some person or entity outside the work organization or work unit.

wildcat strike   An unapproved strike that occurs because some segment of the union is not satisfied.

work group   Two or more people who work together to accomplish a goal and who communicate and interact with each other.

workers' compensation   Disability and death benefits mandated and administered by the states.

World Wide Web   An Internet service that links documents by providing links from server to server.

Y

yellow-dog contract   A contract (now illegal) that required that a person (such as a job applicant) would not join or form a union.

Name Index

Abate, Tom, 364
Abernathy, William, 353
Abosch, Kenan S., 321
Abram, T. G., 240
Abrams, Jim, 485
Ackroyd, S., 542
Adams, Amy, 31, 59
Adams, Jim, 436
Adamson, Jim, 83
Ades, Kim, 245
Adler, Nancy, 117
Adler, Roy D., 320
Agard, Adam, 542
Agochiya, Devendra, 436
Aichlmayr, Mary, 574
Aiken, Leona S., 145
Alavi, Seyyed Babak, 118
Albers, Susan, 437
Albrecht, Donna, 145
Alderfer, 304
Alexander, Ralph A., 240, 283
Alexander, Suzanne, 474
Allen, Douglas, 120
Allen, Everett, Jr., 383
Allen, James, 239
Allen, Keith, 120
Allen, M., 578
Alleyne, Sonia, 474
Alonzo, Vincent, 349
Alpin, John C., 460
Alvarez, Sharon, 120
Amar, A. D., 282
Anderson, Chris, 178
Anderson, Kirk, 146
Anderson, Sandy, 386
Anderson, Terry H., 90
Anhalt, Rebecca L., 282
Anten, Todd, 227
Anthes, Gary, 137
Apfelthaler, Gerhard, 61
Aquinis, Herman, 281
Arad, R., 437
Archer, Aurora, 51, 52
Armstrong, Michael, 320
Armstrong, Phillip M., 542
Arthur, Diane, 205
Arthur, Michael B., 447
Arthur, Winfred, Jr., 119
Ash, Ronald A., 177, 178, 180
Ashford, Blake E., 474
Asquith, Nancy, 179, 242
Aston, Anne, 119
Atchison, Thomas J., 177
Atkins, Paul W. B., 243
Atkinson, William, 573, 574
Augustine, Norman, 12
Austin, Marsha, 207
Avery, Simon, 511
Axelrod, Beth, 320

Babcock, David, 12
Babcock, Pamela, 23
Babic-Archer, Violeta, 52
Bacher, Jeffrey P., 348
Badham, Richard, 232
Bahis, Jane Easter, 541
Bahls, Jane, 242
Bailey, Alan, 259
Bailyn, Lotte, 44
Bainbridge, Stephen M., 350
Baldiga, Nancy R., 212
Baldwin, Peter, 89
Balkin, David B., 180
Bals, Daniel, 280–281
Baltes, Boris B., 180
Bandura, Albert, 218, 436
Barak, Michelle Mor, 61
Barbetta, Joanne, 93, 94
Barlow, Wayne E., 205
Barnett, Tim, 205
Barney, Jay, 117
Barnum, Darold T., 243
Baron, Helen, 118
Barrett, Colleen, 126
Barrett, Gerald V., 240, 281
Barrick, Murray, 240, 241
Barrier, Michael, 145, 240
Barsoux, Jean-Louis, 23
Bartholomew, Doug, 146
Bartmess, Andrew B., 436
Bates, Steve, 146, 321
Batterson, Robert, 485
Beam, Burton T., 382
Beamish, Paul W., 118
Beatty, Richard W., 24, 382
Beauregard, Russell S., 240
Bebchuk, Lucian A., 341, 343, 348, 350
Beck, Evelyn, 522
Becker, Brian E., 24, 382
Beehr, Terry A., 573
Beeler, Amanda, 212
Beeman, Don R., 120
Belohav, James A., 61
Bencivenga, Dominic, 574
Benedick, Clyde, 11
Benge, Eugene, 313
Benham, Philip O., Jr., 572
Bennett, Rita, 119
Bennett, Winston, Jr., 119
Bennis, Harry, 31, 56, 59
Benson, George, 437
Bentson, C. Cynthia, 243
Berckemeyer, Ricardo M., 53
Berger, Dr. Bradley C., 239
Bergman, Barbara R., 324
Bergman, Thoams J., 207
Bernal, David S., 240
Bernardin, H. J., 255
Bernstein, Aaron, 205

Bernstein, Ira, 240
Bernthal, Paul, 430
Bewayo, Edward D., 206
Beynon, Huh, 474
Bibbs, John, 436
Biersner, Robert J., 179
Bingham, Christopher, 120
Bingham, Clara, 89
Bishop, J. A., 320
Bitzer, Frank J., 61, 383
Bizot, Elizabeth B., 178
Black, J. Stewart, 118, 119, 120
Blahna, Mary Jo, 205
Blanchard, Ken, 145
Bland, Timothy S., 240
Blasi, J., 350
Blau, Gay, 321
Bledsoe, James, 322
Blencoe, Allyn, 179
Blimes, L., 24
Blossfield, Hans-Peter, 474
Bohl, Don L., 282
Boles, James S., 473
Bolles, Mark Emery, 449
Bolles, Richard N., 449, 473
Bols, Derick, 510
Bonnet, Adeline, 124
Bono, J. E., 240
Boone, Garrett, 479
Bordonaro, Frank, 437
Borman, Walter, 178
Bossard, Annette B., 120
Bossidy, Larry, 24
Bothell, Timothy, 437
Bott, Jennifer P., 240
Boudreau, John, 207, 240
Bowie, Vaughan, 573
Bowman, David, 206
Boynton, Albert, Jr., 145
Bracker, Jeffrey S., 474
Brady, Diane, 137, 146
Brady, Robert, 206
Brailov, Marc, 246
Brandt, William, 353
Branine, Mohamed, 180
Brannick, Michael T., 177, 178
Braverman, Mark, 530, 573
Breaugh, James A., 205, 208
Breen, Cindy, 575, 576
Breisch, Roger E., 254
Breisch, Walter E., 254
Bremmer, Brian, 155
Brice, Ray, 384
Briggs, Thomas E., 180
Brimm, Michael I., 120
Brinkmeyer, Kimberly, 242
Brisbee, Julie, 61
Briscoe, Dennis R., 120
Brokop, Don, 3, 4, 21

Bronte, Lydia, 474
Bross, Allon S., 119
Brown, Carolyn M., 474
Brown, David, 197
Brown, Duncan, 320
Bruce, Allison, 61
Bruch, Heike, 283
Bryant, Elizabeth, 479
Buchanan, David, 436
Buckingham, Marcus, 474
Buckley, M. Ronald, 178
Bucknall, Hugh, 24
Budd, John W., 510
Buell, Linda M., 474
Bunce, D., 573
Burck, Charles, 24
Burke, Lisa A., 180
Burke, Ronald J., 89, 573
Burnett, Jennifer R., 241
Burns, Meghan D., 242
Burris, Laura, 242
Burton, John, 363, 364
Bush, George H. W., 556
Bush, George W., 557, 577
Bush, Robert A. Baruch, 511
Butler, John E., 179
Buyinski, Theodore R., 350
Buzzanell, Patrice M., 184
Byrnes, N., 386

Cadrain, Diane, 242, 573
Cahn, Steven M., 90
Caligiuri, Paula M., 119
Callahan, C., 242
Camara, Wayne J., 542
Cameron, Andrew E., 382, 383
Cameron, Judy, 282
Cameron, Kim S., 61
Campbell, David, 450
Campbell, Mark, 572
Campbell, Robert B., 282
Campenello, Russell J., 3
Campion, James E., 241
Campion, Michael A., 180, 224, 241
Camuffo, Arnaldo, 147
Candler, Julie, 242
Capell, Perri, 207
Cardente, Charles, 339
Cardy, Robert L., 180, 282
Carel, Michael R., 511
Carey, D. J., 389
Carey, John, 567
Carl, Michael, 97, 114
Carnevale, Tony, 132
Carr, Linda, 180
Carroll, Stephen J., 283
Carter, Nancy, 148
Carter, Robert C., 179
Cascio, Wayne F., 144, 145, 179, 206, 207, 240, 255
Casebeer, Kenneth, 510
Casil, Amy Sterling, 510
Casio, Wayne F., 281
Casison, Jeannie, 349

Cason, Ann, 383
Cassity, Henry, 18
Castagenra, James, 510
Castro, Janice, 545
Catalano, R., 475
Caterinicchia, Dan, 146
Caudron, Shari, 205, 572
Cha, Ariana Eunjung, 232
Chadderhom, Lisa, 51
Chadwick, Ken, 205
Chaker, Anne Marie, 194
Chapman, Fern Schumer, 478
Charan, Ram, 24, 120
Charness, G., 349
Cheever, Ben, 3
Chen, Chien-Cheng, 206
Cherney, Elena, 113
Cherrington, David J., 118
Chiang, Harriet, 90
Chingos, Peter T., 349
Chiu, Su-Fen, 206
Chockalingam, Viswesvaran, 542
Christina, Sue-Chan, 241
Chu, Kathy, 120
Church, Mark, 540, 541
Cihon, Patrick J., 510
Clark, Kenneth B., 88
Clark, Kim, 478
Clay, Joan M., 242
Cleary, Pat, 577
Cleaver, Joanne, 206
Cleverly, William O., 382, 383
Clifton, Donald O., 474
Cline, Jim, 528
Clinton, Bill, 485, 556, 577
Cobb, Jeremy, 436
Cobb, S., 469–470, 475
Cobb-Clark, Deborah A., 205
Cobun, Jim, 290–292
Coe, Eugene, 87, 88
Cohen, Jacob, 145
Cohen, Patricia, 145
Cohen, Scott, 246
Cohen-Charash, Yochi, 321
Cole, Joanne, 125
Colquhoun, Tracy, 119
Colvin, Geoffrey, 61
Confucius, 479
Conley, Patrick R., 178
Conlin, Joseph, 145
Conlin, Michelle, 75
Connellan, Thomas K., 424, 437
Connelly, Rachel, 478
Connerly, Ward, 90
Conrad, Peter, 121
Converse, Patrick D., 178
Cook, Edmund, 90
Cooper, Cary L., 89, 573
Cooper, Charles, 322–324
Cooper, Christopher, 137
Cooper, Marc, 475
Coors, William, 560
Copeland, Bill, 146
Cornelius, Edwin T., III, 177, 179

Costa, Giovanni, 147
Coughlin, Dan, 89
Cox, Archibald S. S., 510
Coy, P., 51
Coye, Ray W., 61
Cron, D., 436
Cronshaw, Steven, 161, 178
Crosby, Philip B., 60
Crum, Kimberly Garts, 478
Culligan, John W., 455
Cunningham, Cynthia R., 179, 180
Custer, Bill, 393

Dale, David, 18
Dalkey, N., 145
Dalton, Dan, 242
Dane, Mark, 51
Darling, David, 239
Davenport, Thomas A., 281
Davidson, William H., 145
Davis, Curt, 26
Davis, Jean, 151, 159, 174
Davis, John H., 320
Dawes, Sheila, 575
Dawson, Chester, 155
De Corte, Wilfred, 180
De La Torre, Phillip, 282
De Paepe, Anneleen, 241
Deck, Steart, 207
Decker, Gary, 294
Decker, Kurt H., 382
DeFrank, Richard S., 562
DeGriff, Deborah, 478
DeGroot, Tim, 241
Del Pro, Amy, 282
Delpo, Amy, 542
Deming, W. Edwards, 254, 270, 353
Dence, Sue, 416
DeNisi, Angelo S., 179, 283
Dent, Harry S., Jr., 443
Derek, Thomas S., 455
Dessler, Gary, 382
Detlefs, Dale R., 382
deVries Kets, Manfred F. R., 437
Dierdorff, Erich C., 179
DiFulco, Denise, 52
Digh, Patricia, 44
Dillon, George, 572
Dipboye, Robert L., 207
Dobbins, Gregory H., 282
Dockery, Judy, 416
Dodd, Nancy G., 180
Domafrio, Howard, 473
Dona-Paras, Mary Cheryl, 458
Donne, Gary, 540
Donnelly, James H., 61
Donovan, John, 240
Dooley, C. D., 475
Doré, Timothy Lee, 320
Douglas, James A., 242
Dowling, P. J., 511
Downing, Neil, 383
Downs, Alan, 146
Drake, Andrea R., 349

Drake, St. Clair, 88
Drake, Susan, 61
Drobnic, Sonja, 474
Drucker, Peter F., 7, 269, 282, 503, 511
Druckman, Daniel, 24
Duarte, Deborah L., 61
Duckworth, Mark, 381
Duening, Thomas N., 246
Duffy, Shannon P., 90
Duffy, Tom, 179
Dulworth, Michael, 437
Dunlop, John, 36
Dunnette, Marvin D., 177, 242
Dutton, Gail, 118
Dwyer, Sean, 205

Eastmond, Daniel V., 435
Eaton, N. K., 242
Eddy, Erik, 147
Edelman, Karen A., 179
Eder, R. W., 241
Edmond, Alfred A., Jr., 474
Edmondson, Gail, 124
Eilbert, Henry, 23
Elk, Ellen, 435
Elkington, Tim, 207
Ellig, Bruce R., 319, 321
Ellis, Christine, 146
Ellis, Kristine, 436
Elly, Bruce R., 11
Elo, Anna-Liisa, 573
Emener, William G., 383
Eng, Lilly, 15
Engel, D. W., 389
Epstein, Lita, 382
Eren, Susan, 511
Erez, Miriam, 437
Espo, D., 578
Eugenio, Vince, 396
Evangelista, A. S., 180
Evans, Paul, 23
Fan, Chenche, 241
Farr, J. L., 266, 282, 283
Farr, Michael, 473
Fay, Charles H., 282, 321
Feeney, Sheila Anne, 146
Feild, Hubert S., 227, 243
Fein, Mitchell, 337
Feld, Daniel E., 179, 242
Feldman, Daniel C., 475
Feldman, Sally, 393, 418
Felin, Teppo, 120
Felsberg, Eric J., 177, 179
Ferris, Gerald R., 179, 241
Feuerstein, Aaron, 5, 6
Field, Hubert, 206
Field, Kevin A., 178
Fields, Dail L., 60
Filipzak, Bob, 320
Finan, Louis, 138
Fine, Sidney A., 161, 178
Fink, Laurence S., 435
Finkin, Matthew W., 510

Finley, Michael, 145
Fiorello, Conrad, 379
Fischer, Kurt, 145
Fisher, Anne, 206
Fisher, Bonnie, 573
Fishman, Shirley R., 118
Fister, Sarah, 245
Fitz-Enz, Jac, 12, 24, 146, 208
Fitzgerald, Louise F., 93
Flanagan, Alice K., 511
Fleetwood, Chad, 206
Fleischer, Charles H., 89, 281
Fleishman, Edwin, 178
Fletcher, Joyce K., 44
Flynn, Gillian, 181, 205, 206
Flynn, Jane, 181
Fogestrom, Marty, 3
Folger, Joseph P., 511
Ford, Kevin J., 240
Formby, J. P., 320
Forster, Julie, 113
Fossum, John A., 511, 512
Foster, Sally, 26
Foulkes, Fred K., 23
Foust, Dean, 205
Fox, Joyce, 455
France, Mike, 61
Francese, Peter, 205
Frank, Thomas, 511
Frase-Blunt, Martha, 207
Frazee, Valerie, 574
French, Michael T., 541
Fried, Jesse M., 341, 343, 348, 350
Friedman, L., 178
Fuerst, Donald E., 384
Fuller, Connie, 61
Fung, Helen, 118
Fung, Shirley, 348
Furchgott, Roy, 181
Furnham, Arian, 240
Fusaro, Roberta, 145

Gael, Sidney, 177
Gainey, Thomas, 208
Gainshaw, Damien, 474
Gale, Sarah F., 181
Galea, Christine, 321
Gallatin, Albert, 339
Galvin, Tammy, 402
Gamble, Louis G., 178
Ganci, Amy B., 117
Ganster, Daniel C., 180, 573
Garcia, Soccoro, 18
Garrety, Karin, 232
Garvin, David A., 435
Gatch, Robert M., 144
Gatewood, Robert D., 206, 227, 243
Gaughan, Lynn, 377
Gaugler, Barbara B., 243
Gay, Howard W., 473
Geoffrey, Lloyd, 349
George, Joey, 206
George, Tischelle, 138, 206

Gerbold, Hugo, 66, 85
Gerhart, Barry, 206, 349
Gerster, Darlene K., 460
Getkate, Maury, 178
Ghorpade, Jai, 177, 179
Ghoshal, Sumantra, 283
Gibbs, Michael J., 282
Gibson, James L., 61
Gilbert, Jacqueline, 205
Gilbert, Matthew, 283
Gillen, Terry, 321
Gillespie, Michael A., 178, 241
Gioia, Dennis A., 292
Gist, Marilyn E., 218
Glaser, Gary, 90
Gleason, John M., 243
Golden, Eve, 146
Golden, Lonnie, 474
Golden, Timothy D., 181
Goldstein, I. L., 400
Goldwasser, Donna, 435
Gollen, Paul, 60
Gomez-Meija, Luis R., 180, 349
Gompers, Samuel, 486
Gong, Sherrie, 281
Gontheir, Giovinella, 541
Good, Tom W., 282
Goodman, Scott A., 240
Goodridge, Elisabeth, 138
Goodwin, Larry K., 510
Gordon, Gloria C., 572
Gorman, Robert, 510
Gowan, Mary A., 119, 206, 475
Gowen, Charles P., III, 334
Graber, Jim M., 254
Grant, Joyce, 208
Grasshoff, Sven, 148
Gray, Matt J., 437
Green, Dot, 85
Greengard, Samuel, 148, 207
Greenhaus, Jeffrey H., 442, 473
Greer, Charles R., 121
Gregersen, Hal B., 118, 119, 120
Grene, Maureen T., 473
Grensing-Pophal, Lin, 573
Griffin, Ricky W., 180
Griffith, Richard, 242
Griffith, Rodger H., 474
Griggs, Willie, 71
Groshen, E., 349
Grossman, Robert J., 145, 146, 383
Grove, Steven E., 348
Guerin, Lisa, 88, 542
Guessford, Dennis, 145
Gueutal, Hal G., 146, 511
Guidard, Bertrand, 388
Guisti, Joseph, 145
Gulman, Michelle, 61
Gunsch, Dawn, 207
Gunsler, Laura Leedy, 89
Gurchiek, Kathy, 64, 542
Gustafson, Kristen, 398
Gutteridge, T. G., 442

Hackman, Dahlia, 121
Hackman, J. Richard, 171, 180, 437
Hagen, Sue, 18–19
Hagens, John, 377
Hahn, F. K., 389
Haka, Susan F., 349
Hale, C. H., 437
Hall, B. J., 350
Hall, Douglas T., 436
Hall, Graham, 119
Halpern, Michelle, 207
Hamilton, Tom, 290–292
Hamm, Steve, 113, 181
Hammer, Michael, 155
Hammonds, Keith, 181
Hand, Janice S., 321
Handfield-Jones, Helen, 320
Hanebury, Jean M., 576
Hanigan, Maury, 209
Hansen, Fay, 320, 348
Hansen, Mark, 569
Hanson, Bruce, 352
Hardison, Corrine, 209
Hardisty, Tom, 483, 503
Hardy, Cecil, 26
Hardy, David, 322–324
Harkavy, Alexandra, 206
Harrington, Harry, 573
Harris, Hilary, 104
Harris, Paul, 443
Harris, Philip R., 108
Harris-Bowlsbey, JoAnn, 474
Harrison, J. Kline, 119, 283
Hartmann, Linley C., 105
Hartwell, Tyler, 541
Harvey, Michael, 118
Harvey, Robert J., 165, 177, 178, 179
Harzing, Anne-Wil, 118
Haslberger, Arno, 119
Hatch, Diane D., 146, 205
Hatcher, Tim, 23
Hauser, Jacqueline, 120
Hauser, Reuben Z., 181
Hayden, Diana, 397, 398
Hayes, Theodore L., 179
Hays, Scott, 148
Heather, Hick, 541
Heavrin, Christina, 511
Hedge, Jerry, 436
Heifetz, Ronald A., 436
Heigesen, Sally, 41
Hein, Kenneth, 349
Heinemann, H., 349
Heisler, William J., 572
Heller, Daniel, 320
Helton, Tom, 178
Henderson, Richard I., 177
Heneman, Herbert, 177, 180
Heneman, Robert, 177, 180, 240
Henifin, Mary Sue, 572
Henneman, Todd, 83
Hequet, Marc, 206
Herberger, Carol, 475
Herman, Roger E., 205

Herzberg, Frederic, 171, 180, 304–305, 306, 320
Hesketh, Beryl, 180
Hiatt, Deidre, 524–525
Hilgert, Raymond L., 517
Hill, Anita, 72
Hill, Charles W. L., 117
Hill, Jacqueline, 18–19
Hintz, Heidi, 18
Hirschman, Carolyn, 61, 206
Hmurovic, Beverly L., 321
Hoffa, James, 36, 505
Hoffman, Matt, 479
Hofstede, Geert, 100, 118
Hogan, Joyce, 242
Holbeche, Linda, 23
Holihan, Richard, 540–541
Holland, John L., 448–449, 473
Hollenbeck, John R., 242
Holley, William W., Jr., 206, 321
Holm, Susan, 475
Holton, Elwood F., III, 62
Honoree, Andre, 348
Hood, Ray, 83
Hopkins, B. L., 321
Hopkins, Shirley A., 60
Hopkins, Willie E., 60
Horn, Peter W., 474, 573
Horney, Nicholas F., 181
Hornsby, Jeffrey S., 281
Hough, Leatta M., 177, 242
Hovland, Jane, 475
Howard, Julie, 351
Howell, Jane M., 436
Howell, Robert, 343
Howes, P. D., 389
Huber, V., 255
Hudson, Peter J., Jr., 241
Huff, Charlotte, 180
Huff, Joseph W., 180
Huffcutt, Allen I., 241
Huizenga, Betty, 473
Humphrey, Ed, 186–187, 202, 214, 236
Humphreys, N., 511, 512
Hunter, Sonia, 542
Hurtz, Gregory, 240
Huschman, Carolyn, 299, 475
Huselid, Mark A., 24, 382
Hutchison, William S., 383
Hyland, MaryAnne M., 119
Hyman, J. S., 389

Ibarra, Hermenia, 474
Immelt, Jeffrey, 341
Inglis, R. Evan, 383
Inness, Gregory, 66, 85
Ivancevich, John M., 60, 61, 117, 119, 205, 208, 218, 246, 437, 475, 562
Iwata, Kunihiko, 116–117

Jackson, Andrew, 493
Jackson, Carey, 474
Jackson, Douglas N., 240

Jackson, Susan, 179
Jacobires, Arleen, 474
Jacobs, S. L., 242
Jacobs, Sam, 393, 418
Jacobson, Mireille, 242
Jaffe, Greg, 137
James, Rick, 576
Janson, R., 180
Janz, T., 241
Jarvis, Tracey J., 541
Jauch, Lawrence, 178
Jeanneret, Paul R., 178, 179
Jeanneret, Richard, 178
Jeffers, Charles, 577
Jenkins, Margaret, 242
Jennings, Kenneth M., 321
Johns, Gary, 180
Johnson, Dennis L., 530
Johnson, Diane E., 23
Johnson, Florence, 460
Johnson, Glenn, 25
Johnson, Linda F., 572
Johnson, Lyndon B., 76
Johnson, Paul, 82
Joinson, Carla, 179
Jonathan, Jack, 383
Jones, Art, 393
Jones, Casey, 241
Jones, G. W., 123
Jones, J., 578
Jones, Laura Beth, 437
Jones, Melonie, 524
Jones, W. David, 572
Joseph, Jacob, 265
Joshi, Aparna, 119
Joshi, Ashwin, 180
Jossi, Frank, 321
Joyce, Diane, 82
Judge, Paul, 181
Judge, Timothy, 177, 180, 240, 320, 349
Juebbers, Lawrence A., 348
Junghae, Naomi, 567

Kamp, J. D., 242
Kandarian, Steven A., 384
Kane, Bob, 145
Kanin-Lovers, Jill, 320
Kanter, Rosabeth Moss, 61
Kantor, R. G., 389
Karp, Hank, 61
Karr, Angela, 474
Karr, Susan Schott, 416
Karren, Ronald J., 436
Kasl, S. V., 469–470, 475
Kasparek, Jorg, 377
Kaufman, B. E., 23
Kavanagh, Michael J., 146
Kearney, Robert P., 121
Kelleher, Herb, 125
Keller, Eric, 348
Keller, Shelley S., 23
Kelloware, Kevin E., 542
Kelly, Chuck, 12–13
Kendall, L. M., 282

Kenley, Osanna, 66
Kennedy, Shirley Duglin, 207
Kernan, Mary C., 281
Kerre, Paul, 138
Kershner, William F., 512
Kerwin, Kathleen, 155
Kessler, Steve, 525
Key, P., 246
Khoshaba, Deborah M., 320
Kiechet, Walter, III, 93
Kiehlbauch, John B., 530
Kiely, K., 578
Killing, J. Peter, 118
Kilpatrick, David, 348
Kim, Brian H., 241
Kim, Dong-One, 320
Kim, H., 320
Kim, W. Chan, 383
King, Dr. Martin Luther, Jr., 68
Kinicki, Angelo, 573
Kirby, Clark, 186–187, 202, 214, 215, 236
Kirchhoff, Sue, 386
Kirkpatrick, Donald, 431, 435, 437
Kizza, Joseph, 89
Klass, Brian, 208
Klehe, Ute-Christine, 241
Klein, Simone, 119
Kleiner, Brian, 121, 178, 350, 542
Kletzer, Lori G., 475
Klimoski, Richard J., 145
Kluge, Jurgen, 24, 282
Kluger, Jeffrey, 206
Kochin, Thomas A., 510
Koene, Bas, 208
Kollinger, Iris, 105
Konieczny, James, 138
Kono, Toyohiro, 147
Konopaske, Robert, 61, 105, 117, 119, 208, 218, 562
Konz, A. M., 178
Koonce, Richard, 181
Koprowski, Gene J., 207
Koretz, Gene, 475
Korman, Abraham K., 60
Koskoski, Mary, 350
Kossoudji, Sherrie, 205
Kotlyar, Igor, 245
Kovacevich, Richard, 7
Kraut, Allen I., 60
Kreps, Stacey, 524
Kreuger, A. B., 364
Kripalani, Manjeet, 113
Kruse, D., 350
Kuczynski, Sherry, 146
Kuhnhenn, J., 578
Kuriantcizk, J., 246
Kurutz, John G., 530
Kweskin, R., 206

La Fasto, Frank, 437
Laabs, Jennifer, 19, 146
Labadie, Tom, 428
LaBar, Gregg, 574
LaBarre, Polly, 41

Lachnit, Caroll, 118
Lakich, Pete, 356, 378
Lam, Simon, 145
LaMothe, Andre, 436
Landsberg, Richard D., 354
Landy, Frank L., 266, 282, 283
Langdon, Danny G., 179
Lareau, N. Peter, 88
Larson, Carl, 437
Latham, Gary P., 241, 265, 282, 429, 437
Latzko, William J., 177
Laubs, Jennifer, 125
Laudeman, Robert, 145
Lautenschlager, Gary J., 206
Lawler, Edward E., III, 23, 24, 180, 306, 320, 321, 437
Laws, Jerry, 557
Lawson, Karen, 396
Leana, Carrie R., 475
LeBlanc, Marion M., 542
Leblanc, Peter, 349
LeCraw, Donald J., 118
Lederer, Jules, 387
Ledford, Jerry, 349
Ledgerwood, D., 572
Lee, Chris, 435
Leibowitz, Z. B., 442
Lennox, Sam, 25–27
Leon, Eusebio, 472–473
Leonard, Bill, 62, 146, 206, 321, 436
Leonard, Sharon, 179
Lepak, David P., 117
Leppenen, Anneli, 573
Leung, Alicia S., 119
Levesque, Laurie, 206
Levi, Lennart, 573
Levine, David, 349
Levine, Edward L., 177, 178
Lewis, John L., 36, 486
Li, Dan, 146
Li Qiang, 506
Licht, Thomas, 282
Liden, Robert, 206
Lidwell, William, 61
Lievens, Filip, 180, 241
Ligons, Charles, 244
Lin, Zhiang, 146
Lincoln, James F., 335–336
Lincoln, John C., 335, 336
Linsky, Marty, 436
Lipow, Valerie, 227
Lissy, William E., 573
Litka, Michael, 120
Litz, Brett T., 437
Liu, Meina, 184
Locke, Edwin A., 218, 419–420, 425, 437
Locklear, Toni S., 178
London, Manuel, 283
Long, Susan, 543
Longenecker, Clinton O., 292, 435
Longley, Neil, 24
Lord, J. Scott, 206, 207, 209
Lorenz, Kate, 227
Lorenzi, Peter, 60, 436

Losey, Mike, 24, 350
Lovenheim, Peter, 511
Lowenfeld, Andreas F., 511
Lozada-Larsen, Susana R., 178
Lubin, Joann, 240
Lublin, J. S., 121
Lucas, Henry C., Jr., 61
Lucio, Jim, 441, 445, 455, 471
Luthans, Fred, 218, 436, 437
Luther, Nathan, 542
Lyman, J., 246
Lynn, Jacquelyn, 573

Macaleer, Bill, 144
Macan, Therese Hoff, 207
Macauley, Ann, 208
McCafferty, Joseph, 366
McCarthy, Joseph P., 283
McClean, Sally, 145
McClelland, Carol L., 180, 304
McClenahen, John S., 350
McClendon, John, 208
McCloy, R. A., 242
McCormick, Ernest J., 178, 179
McCormick, John, 118
McCormick, Steven, 148
McDermott, Jim, 349
MacDonald, Elizabeth, 354
McDowell, Wyatt, 542
Macedo Mourelle, Juiza de, 282
McElfresh, Steve, 15
McEnery, Jack, 387–389
McEvoy, Glenn, 205
McFadden, John J., 382
McFarland, Lynn, 118
McGarrah, Bob, 406, 418
McGarvey, Robert, 542
McGeachie, Sylvia, 387–389
McGregor, Douglas M., 269, 272, 282, 304
McGrne, Sally, 568
McInerney, Thomas, 52
McIsaac, Alison, 397
Mackenbach, Frederick W., 335
McKibben, Dave, 435
MacLaren, Vance, 242
McMahon, J. Timothy, 437
McRary, Bob, 544
McShulskis, Elaine, 206
McWilliams, Gary, 138
Madden, James, 24
Maddi, Salvatore R., 320
Madsen, Susan R., 572
Magill, Barbara Gamble, 89
Magnus, Margaret, 206, 209
Magnusen, Audrey, 90
Magnuson, Paul, 155
Maher, Kris, 23, 243
Mahoney, Dennis F., 383
Maidment, Fred, 485
Maira, Arun, 436
Majcen, Ken, 528
Majid, Nail, 75
Maljers, F. A., 145
Mallette, Paul, 60

Malone, Thomas M., 320
Malos, Stanley B., 241
Maltby, Lewis, 545
Mandell, Mel, 120
Manderscheid, Steven, 145
Mangen, Doreen, 349
Manley, Moriso, 93
Mannis, Nick, 151
Mantyla, Karen, 417
Marchiole, Nelson, 83
Marella, Dee, 383
Marett, Kent, 206
Mariani, Matthew, 206
Markowitz, Linda, 510, 511
Marmot, Michel, 89
Marquardt, M. J., 389
Marquez, Jessica, 146
Mars, Gerald, 542
Marschan, Rebecca, 119
Martin, Bob, 209
Martin, Carole, 227
Martin, Garry L., 320
Martin, Sandra E., 206
Martinez, Alfonso, 52
Martinez, Michelle Neely, 207
Martocchio, Joseph J., 319, 320, 382, 383
Maruca, Regina, 24
Maslach, Christina, 456
Maslow, Abraham, 304
Masters, Samantha, 483, 503
Mathieu, John E., 349
Matteson, Michael T., 60, 218, 475
Matthews, Harold, 393, 406, 418, 427
Matthews, Linda, 120
Mattick, Richard P., 541
Matusewitch, Eric, 89
Mauborgne, Renee, 383
Maurer, Harry, 471
Maurer, Todd J., 283
Mausner, B., 180
Mawhinney, Thomas, C., 321, 436
May, Karen E., 180
Mayerhofer, Helene, 105
Mayo, Elton, 7
Mazer, Robert F., 435
Mazin, Rebecca A., 382
Mecham, Robert C., 178, 179
Medsker, Gina J., 180
Meiners, Cary, 527
Meisinger, Sue, 24, 350
Melles, Rensia, 119
Mello, Jeffrey, 573
Melone, Joseph, 383
Melvina, Lenny, 31–32, 56, 59
Mendenhall, Mark E., 118, 120
Mento, Anthony J., 436
Mercer, William M., 351
Merchant, Kenneth A., 282
Mericle, Kenneth, 320
Meridith, Gwen, 393, 406, 418, 427, 432
Metzer, H., 572
Metzger, Michael, 242
Michaels, Ed, 320
Michalak, Donald, 404, 435

Michelitsch-Riedl, Gabriela, 105
Mickey, A. E., 349
Middleton, Laura Zaugg, 118
Miles, Jeffrey, 206
Milkman, Ruth, 60
Milkovich, George T., 109, 120, 319, 320, 348, 349, 350
Milliman, John F., 118
Minehan, Maureen, 89, 436
Miner, John, 541
Miners, Ian A., 545
Mintz, Jessica, 192
Mintzberg, Henry, 145
Mirkin, Morris, 387
Mitchell, Cynthia, 572
Mitchell, Terence R., 218, 349
Mitroff, Ian, 571
Mobley, Nancy, 138
Modrow-Thiel, Brita, 179
Moffatt, Susan, 118
Moffett, Matt, 362
Mohr, Alexander T., 119
Mohrman, Susan Albers, 437
Moltby, Lewis L., 545
Monk, Gerald, 511
Moore, R. Henry, 572
Moran, Robert T., 108
Moravec, Milan, 206
Morgenson, Frederick, 224, 241
Morgenstern, Marlene, 573
Morrigan, Viviane, 232
Morrison, Allen J., 118
Morrison, Ann M., 474
Morrissey, James A., 574
Morrissey, Kevin, 541
Moses, Lynne, 282
Motowidlo, Stephan J., 241
Mount, Michael K., 240, 241, 320
Mulcahey, David, 511
Muller, Helen J., 61
Mumford, Michael, 178, 241
Munniksma, Lisa, 206
Munsterberg, Hugo, 7, 23
Murphy, Betty Southard, 146, 205
Murphy, Kevin R., 282
Murray, Shelley S., 179, 180
Myers, Karen Kroman, 435
Myers, Robert J., 382
Myers, Steve, 541
Myrdal, Gunnar, 68, 88

Nadler, David A., 180
Naff, Katherine, 90
Napier, Nancy K., 179
Nariane, R., 246
Nash, James L., 574
Nassar-McMillan, Sylvia C., 475
Nathan, Barry, 240
Nathan, Maria, 118
Nathan, Sara, 83
Naumann, Earl, 119
Nedjah, Nadia, 282
Nelson, Alan E., 383
Nelson, Debra L., 572

Nelson, James, 456–458
Nelson, Linda S., 383
Neuman, George A., 180
Newman, Howard, 209
Newman, Jerry M., 109, 120, 319, 320, 348, 349, 350
Nichols, Tom, 326
Nickel, Tom, 416
Nickels, Bernard J., 241
Nickson, Stephen, 572
Niles, Spencer G., 474
Nixon, Richard, 298, 494
Nolan, Peter M., 18
Nord, G. Daryl, 146
Nord, Jeretta Horn, 146
Nord, Walter R., 572
Noren, Al, 25–26
Novicevic, Milorad M., 118
Nunnally, Jum C., 240
Nykodym, Nick, 545

Oaxaca, Ronald L., 145
O'Bannon, Douglas P., 349
Oberg, Kalervo, 119
O'Boyle, Thomas F., 437
O'Brien, Michael, 544, 545
Ochoa, Carlos, 119
Odiorne, George S., 208, 269, 282
Ogawa, Naohiro, 123
O'Keefe, Anne Marie, 545
Oldham, Greg R., 180
Oldham, R. G., 171
Olney, Peter B., Jr., 324
Olson, Madeline Hess, 349
Onder, Dr., 239
Ones, Deniz S., 242, 283, 542
Opdyke, Jeff D., 146
Ordonez de Pablos, Patricia, 23, 118
Orin, Rhoda D., 383
Orszag, Peter R., 384
O'Shaughnessy, K. C., 349
Oster, Emily, 567
Ostroff, C., 282
Oswald, Frederick L., 178, 241
Over, Paul, 542
Owens, William A., 241
Ozanian, Michael K., 354

Paderewski, Joe, 326–327, 345
Paetsch, Lauren, 573
Page, Ronald C., 118, 144, 145, 179
Palich, Leslie E., 474
Palmer, Helen, 178
Palmer, Ian, 145
Palmeri, Christopher, 155
Panaro, Gerald P., 177
Panelli, Guido, 326, 345
Parker, Glenn, 436
Parks, Rosa, 128
Parsons, Talcot, 88
Pasternack, A., 23
Pate, Carter, 24
Patton, Thomas, 319
Paunonen, Sampo V., 240

Pave, Irene, 478
Pavlov, Ivan P., 305
Pavlovic, Emily, 321
Peach, E. Brian, 321
Pear, Joseph, 320
Pearce, Craig L., 349
Pearlman, Sandra, 90
Peck, Sarah W., 348
Peikes, Lawrence, 242
Pelham, Denise, 138
Penner, Louis A., 320
Pepper, John, 110
Pereira, Joseph, 93
Perkins, Kathryn, 416
Perks, Ben, 351
Perry, Phillip M., 242
Pete, Lawrence H., 283
Peterson, Norman, 178
Peterson, Richard B., 120
Pfeffer, Jeffrey, 38, 39, 348
Phillips, Jack J., 24, 283, 437
Phillips, James S., 148, 240
Phillips, Jean M., 207
Phillips, Michael M., 113
Phillips, Patricia Pullman, 24
Piczak, Michael W., 181
Pieper, Rudiger, 121
Pierce, W. David, 282
Pinto, Patrick R., 179
Pisano, Leonard, 87–88
Piturro, Marlene, 207
Platt, Harlan, 24
Platt, Jake, 575
Po, Amy Del, 88
Poe, Andrea, 207
Poerio, Mark, 348
Polakoff, Phillip L., 366
Polaski, Sandra, 484
Polson, John, 208
Polzin, Michael J., 349
Pope, Ethan, 382
Popovich, P., 208
Porter, Kenneth, 343
Possett, Allison, 435
Posthuma, Richard, 224, 241
Potter, Edward E., 320
Poulsen, Kristen M., 447
Powel, Sarah, 437
Powell, Don R., 572
Premack, Steven L., 208
Prewitt, Kenneth, 61
Prezosi, Robert C., 24
Prien, Erich P., 178
Prien, Kristin O., 178
Prime, Michael, 541
Priz, Edward J., 382
Proctor, Stephen, 436
Pronk, Stephanie, 573
Prose, Donna Dee, 320
Pruit, Bettye H., 44
Pucik, Vladimir, 23, 120
Puetzer, Mary, 473
Pulakos, Elaine D., 241, 282, 436
Purdy, K., 180

Purpa, Philip H., 542
Pursell, Elliot D., 241

Quick, James Campbell, 572
Quick, Jonathan D., 572
Quinn, Robert E., 61
Quinn, Steve, 207
Quinones, Miguel A., 240

Rader, Mark, 241
Radhhakrishnan, Suresh, 474
Rafter, Michelle V., 207, 319
Raghavendra, B. G., 145
Ralston, Steven M., 206
Ramsay, Lauren J., 241
Randolf, David, 97, 114
Ransom, Michael, 145
Rapoport, Rhona, 44
Ravenscroft, Sue P., 349
Reagan, Ronald, 556
Reems, Carl, 356, 378
Reese, Shelly, 443, 572
Reeve, John M., 320
Regab, Marie, 93
Rehder, Robert R., 61
Reibstein, Larry, 207
Reich, Robert, 6
Reid, David M., 147
Reilly, Richard R., 282
Reingold, Jennifer, 137, 146
Remaekers, Stefan, 383
Remes, Jouko, 435
Renard, Monika K., 283
Renfro, Mary, 326–327, 345
Renn, Robert W., 180
Resnick, Rosalind, 208
Reville, Robert, 363
Reynolds, Douglas H., 282
Rhodes, Don, 243, 542
Rhone, Mel, 246
Ribark, Ronald F., 478
Riccardi, Joseph N., 437
Rice, Fay, 83
Richard, Michael A., 383
Richard, Orlando C., 205
Richardson, Helen L., 572
Richardson, Nancy, 573
Richter, Konstantin, 120
Ricks, Don M., 436
Rifkin, Will, 232
Ring, Peter Smith, 119
Rious, Sheila M., 320
Risher, Howard, 321, 350
Riusala, Kimmo, 119
Roberts, Bari-Ellen, 61
Roberts, Sally, 573
Roberts, Sara, 61
Robertson, Ivan, 177
Robins, Philip K., 382
Rodman, Nathaniel F., 541
Roelthisberger, Fritz, 7
Rogers, Carl, 412
Rogovsky, Nikolai, 117
Rorschach, H., 242

Rosenberg, Hilary, 354
Rosenbloom, Jerry S., 383
Rosenthal, Douglas B., 243
Ross, Randall, 63
Ross, Scott, 479
Rossmann, Giselind, 179
Roth, Philip L., 241
Rothstein, Mitchell G., 240
Rothwell, William, 146
Rout, Lawrence, 478
Rowen, Joshua, 474
Rowland, Kendrith, 118, 178
Rozek, Michael, 572
Rubenstein, Sidney P., 254
Rubery, Jill, 474
Rude, Andre, 148
Ryan, Ann Marie, 118, 242
Ryan, David, 572
Ryan, Thomas A., 436
Rynes, Sara, 206, 207, 349

Saari, Lise M., 241, 282, 437
Sackett, Paul R., 178, 242
Sagini, Meshack M., 281–282
Saks, Alan M., 474
Salgado, Jesus F., 240
Salvendy, G., 180
Samson, Harry, 418
Samuel, Leah, 511
Sanchez, Juan I., 180, 282
Sandberg, Jergen, 180
Sanders, Pete, 541
Sargent, John, 120
Sartain, Elizabeth Pedrich, 126
Sauter, Steven L., 573
Sawyer, Janet, 322–324
Sawyer, Salley B., 435
Scanlon, Joe, 336
Schaefer, Scott, 542
Scharf, Alan, 145
Schaubroeck, John, 145
Schay, Brigette W., 321
Schell, Michael S., 118
Schettler, Joel, 405
Schieber, Sylvester J., 384
Schmidt, Frank, 241, 242, 283
Schmidt, Veronica J., 478
Schmit, Mark J., 242
Schmitt, Neal W., 145, 241
Schneider, Alison, 90
Schneider, Benjamin, 178
Schneider, Dianne L., 542
Schoen, Sterling H., 517
Schuler, Randall, 117, 120, 179, 255
Schultz, Jeremy, 538
Schuster, J. R., 349
Schwartz, Joshua L., 542
Schwartz, Roger, 435
Schwarzenegger, Arnold, 363, 364
Scott, Clifton, 435
Scott, Miriam Basch, 180
Scott, Norman A., 478
Scott-Morgan, Peter, 436
Scoville, James G., 510

Seegart, Scott, 350
Segal, Jonathan A., 188, 469
Seidler, Susan M., 573
Sejen, Laury, 353
Sellers, Patricia, 145, 478
Selmer, Jan, 119
Seminario, Peg, 577
Senge, Peter M., 401, 405, 435
Senia, A., 475
Shand, Fiona, 541
Shaner, Robert, 434–435
Shank, Patti, 416
Shannon, Jones, 144
Shaver, Beverly, 544, 545
Shaw, James B., 179
Shaw, K. N., 437
Shaw, Sue, 120
Shechtman, Zipora, 243
Sheffi, Yossi, 60
Sheldon, Kendra, 435
Shelgren, Diane, 63
Shellenbarger, Sue, 184, 212, 474
Shelley, Kristina, 206
Shepard, Glen, 281
Sherman, Erik, 146
Shilling, Marvina, 119
Shimomitsu, Teruichi, 573
Shippmann, Jeffery, 180
Shirmeyer, Roslyn, 281
Shirouzu, Norishko, 268
Shore, J. E., 442
Shrivastava, Paul, 571
Shutta, James T., 473
Silverman, Charles, 88
Silverman, Rachel Emma, 245
Simeon, Robyn, 118
Simms, Jane, 119
Simms, Lynn, 290–292
Simons, Robert, 474
Simons, Tony, 306, 320
Simpson, Liz, 436
Sims, Doris M., 435
Sims, Henry P., Jr., 292, 436
Sims, Ronald R., 178
Singh, Sanjay, 145
Sirias, Danilo, 61
Sistrunk, Frank, 178
Skala, Kathy, 6
Skerry, Peter, 61
Skinner, B. F., 305, 421, 423
Skinner, Steven, 60
Slater, Joanna, 113
Slesnick, Twila, 382
Sloane, Ted, 129, 142
Slocum, J., 436
Smallwood, N., 23
Smart, Tim, 61
Smeltzer, Donald, 525, 542
Smith, Adam, 307, 321
Smith, Brien N., 281
Smith, Brooke E., 574
Smith, Constance Redley, 436
Smith, Geri, 117, 120
Smith, Harry, 557

Smith, Jennifer, 125
Smith, Matthew, 241
Smith, Mike, 177
Smith, Nashawn, 18
Smith, Patricia C., 282
Smith, S. L., 120
Smith, Sandy, 541
Smith, Shawn A., 382
Smith, Sheldon H., 350
Smither, James W., 282
Sneed, Lynne, 437
Snell, Scott A., 117
Snyder, Nancy Tennant, 61
Snyderman, B., 180
Solomon, Charlene Marmer, 83, 118, 120,
    146, 180
Solomon, Jay, 113
Somerdyke-Traband, Diane M., 545
Sommer, Steven M., 436
Sondenaa, Janna, 397, 398
Sorenson, Leslie E., 283
Sovio, Ulla, 435
Spelfogel, Evan J., 542, 543
Spiegelman, Robert G., 382
Spruell, Sarina, 474
Stafford, Diane, 207
Stajkovic, Alexander D., 218
Stalcup, Sue S., 240
Stambaugh, Robert, 138, 146
Stapel, Diederick A., 283
Stavrou-Costea, Eleni, 24
Staw, Barry M., 321
Stead, Bette Ann, 205
Steadman, Max, 290–292
Steel, Robert P., 436
Steele, Jacquelyn R., 240
Steele, Paul D., 541
Stein, Wolfram, 24, 282
Stephens, Elvis C., 242
Stephens, Gregory K., 121
Stephens, Thomas, 572
Sterling, Norman, 544, 545
Stern, Andy, 505
Sternlight, Jean R., 542
Stevens, Larry, 146
Stewart, Bob, 437
Stewart, Kim, 93, 209, 292, 324, 478, 545
Stewart, Thomas A., 24
Stokes, Garnett S., 241
Stone, Dianna L., 511
Stone-Romero, Eugene, 147
Stout, Hilary, 194
Stowers, James E., 383
Strauss, Susan, 206
Strazewski, Len, 525
Stroh, Linda, 104, 120, 148, 208
Sullivan, Rev. Leon, 112
Sullivan, Laura, 574
Summers, Joel, 474
Summers, Lynn, 348
Summers, Suzanne B., 179
Summers, Timothy P., 179
Sunoo, Brenda Paik, 208, 282
Surlcarrajan, P., 474

Sussen, Cheryl, 294, 311, 317
Sussman, Lyle, 542
Suttle, John C., 382
Suutari, Vesa, 119
Svyantec, Daniel J., 240
Swanson, Richard A., 62
Swartz, Jon, 207
Sweeney, John, 505
Swift, Harold, 528

Taft, P., 510
Tagliabue, John, 124
Takeuchi, Hiroraka, 120
Talbott, Shannon Peters, 120
Tannenbaum, Scott I., 146
Taoka, George M., 120
Tapscott, Don, 4
Tarter, Steve, 205
Taylor, Frederick W., 6–7, 23, 180, 304, 307,
    321, 331
Taylor, M. Susan, 207, 283
Teachout, Mark S., 240
Tebbutt, Jenny, 541
Tedeschi, Bob, 207
Teece, David J., 349
Teresko, John, 155
Terpstra, David, 207, 348
Tesluk, Paul E., 349
Tesone, Dana, 181
Tesser, Abraham, 283
Tett, Robert B., 240
Thackray, John, 155
Thakor, Mrugank V., 180
Thaler-Carter, Ruth, 207
Thelam, D. S., 572
Thibodeau, P., 578
Thiruvengadam, Meena, 117
Thomas, Barry W., 349
Thomas, Clarence, 72
Thomas, James N., 178
Thomlins, Christopher, 90
Thompson, Dennis, 573
Thompson, P., 542
Thompson, Stephanie, 61
Thorndike, Edward L., 305, 423, 437
Thornton, George C., III, 243
Tichy, Noel, 111, 120
Tierney, Robin, 117, 120
To, Siu-Ki Henty, 178
Tobin, Dan, 429
Tolzman, Kari, 178
Tornow, Walter W., 179
Torres, Jenice, 87–88
Tortarolo, John S., 366
Toufexis, Anostasic, 478
Tracy, Kay B., 283
Treanor, J. Robert, 382
Trieber, Edward, 525
Trost, Cathy, 93
Truman, Harry, 298
Trunko, Michael E., 349
Tsai, Wei-Chi, 206
Tubbs, Walter, 573

Tung, Rosalie, 107, 118, 119
Turner, Marlene E., 61
Tuscano, Guy, 572
Tye, Mary, 240
Tyler, Kathryn, 104

Udivactra, Firdaus, E., 571
Ulrich, Dave, 23, 24, 350
Useem, Jerry, 206
Utley, Kristine, 93

Valet, Will, 178
Valy-Durbin, Stacey, 104
Van De Voort, David M., 144, 145
Van Den Bergh, Nan, 541
Van der Heyden, Kees, 283
Van der Stede, Wim A., 282
Van Pelt, 120
van Riemsdijk, Maarten, 208
Van Yoder, Steven, 574
Vance, Charles M., 119
Vance, Robert J., 349
Vande Walle, D., 436
Vandenberg, Robert J., 180
Vardi, Yoav, 437, 541
Varghese, Anita, 206
Vargus, Mark E., 282
Varma, Arup, 104, 283
Vasilopoulos, Nicholas L., 282
Vega, Jorge, 472–473
Veiga, John F., 181
Velarde, Al, 347–348
Verduzco, Albert, 280–281
Veres, John G., III, 178
Vernon, Steven G., 382, 383
Viale, J. David, 435
Vinson, Mary N., 282
Visco, Albert J., 23
Viswesvaran, Chockalingam, 242, 283, 542
Voci, Elaine, 416
Vodanovich, Stephen J., 240
Von Glinow, Mary Ann, 118, 474
Voss, John, 362
Voss, Kim, 60
Vu, Uyen, 208

Wachter, Harmut, 179
Wah, Louisa, 205
Wahlquist, Richard, 246–247
Waldman, Adelle, 23
Walker, Alfred J., 146
Walker, Joe, 245
Wall, Jerry, 178
Wallace, J. Craig, 240

Wallace, Jerry, 307
Wallace, Julie, 443
Wallace, Marc J., Jr., 321
Walsh, David J., 542
Walters, C. F., 572
Wanek, James E., 242
Wanous, John P., 200, 208
Ward, Kevin, 474
Warner, David, 155
Warren, Susan, 572
Washington, Tracie L., 320
Watanabe, Hiroaki, 124
Waters, Donald, 435
Watson, Bibi S., 207
Watson, Hugh, 145
Watson, Mary, 182–183
Watson, Richard, 145
Watson, Roger, 572
Wayhan, Victor B., 146
Wayne, Sandy, 206
Weber, J., 61
Weekley, Jeff, 241
Weinberg, Carl, 352
Weiner, Ellis, 474
Weiss, Susan J., 147
Weitz, Eli, 437, 541
Welbourne, Thomas M., 349
Welch, D. E., 511
Welch, Denice, 119, 386
Welch, Jilly, 207
Welch, Lawrence, 119
Weldon, Elizabeth, 436
Wellner, Alison, 145
Wells, Susan J., 41, 240
Welsh, Dianne H. B., 436
Werner, Steve, 146
West, M. A., 573
West, Stephen G., 145
Wetzker, K., 24
Wetzstein, Cheryl, 11
Weyland, Orlene, 53
White, Erin, 23
White, Jack E., 61
White, Joseph B., 268
Whitener, Ellen M., 242
Whiteside, Kathleen S., 179
Whitford, David, 511
Whitman, Marina N., 319
Whitmore, Bob, 557
Whitmore, Paul G., 435
Whitney, David, 241
Whyte, Glen, 429
Whyte, William, 41
Wiesner, Willi, 241

Wilcox, Melynda, 137
Wiley, Joe, 208
Wilkes, Rog, 151
Williams, J. Spencer, 373
Williams, Joan C., 184
Williamson, J. G., 123
Williamson, Laura Gollub, 241
Willis, Rachel, 478
Wilson, Anne, 129, 142
Wilson, John P., 61
Wilson, Mark A., 179
Wilson, Martha, 31–33, 35, 56, 59
Windau, Janice, 572
Winslade, John, 511
Winters, Rebecca, 469
Wirt, Gary L., 542
Wiscombe, Janet, 181, 307, 542
Wisensale, Steven K., 382
Wislinski, Norbert, 441, 471
Witschger, Jim, 146
Witt, L. W., 241
Wood, Joanne V., 283
Wood, Robert E., 243
Woodward, Calvin, 320
Worthington, Patricia, 176–177
Wren, Daniel A., 321
Wright, Ann, 529
Wright, Bill, 557
Wright, Julie A., 180
Wright, Patrick M., 178

Xhonneux, P., 24
Xie, Jia Lin, 180

Yager, Edwin, 404, 435
Yates, Lois, 186
Yoshino, Kimi, 435
Young, Jeff, 377
Young, Lester, 432
Youngblood, S. A., 255
Youngman, Judith A., 320
Yukl, Gary A., 437
Yurdin, Donna, 430

Zachary, Louis J., 473
Zadell, Bill, 138
Zanko, Michael, 232
Zeller, Christian, 145
Zemke, Ron, 405
Zeyer, Ari, 349
Zhao, Wen, 547
Zingheim, Patricia K., 348, 349

Company Index

A. C. Nielsen, 189
A. E. Staley, 499, 500
Abbott Laboratories, 44
Aberdeen Group, 252
Abernathy & Associates, 353
Accenture, 198
Accenture HRM, 63
Acme Industrial Parts, 332
Adolph Coors Co., 460, 560–561
Advantica Restaurant Group, 83
Aetna Life and Casualty, 44, 52–53, 417, 426
Air Line Pilots Association, 36
Alcoa, 375, 458
Alcott Corp., 55
Allstate Insurance, 15, 190
American Airlines, 333, 384, 469
American Express, 113, 121, 455
American Home Products, 455
American Savings and Loan
    Association, 477
American Velvet Company, 339
American Woolmark Corp., 353
America's Job Bank, 195
Amoco (BP), 109, 193
AMP Inc., 136
Aon Consulting, 385
Apple Computer, 44, 140
Applied Materials, 397, 398
ARINC Inc., 416
Armstrong Floors and Ceiling, 409
Assurant Employee Benefits, 524
Atlantic Richfield, 375
AT&T, 83, 84, 140, 169, 173, 197, 198, 246,
    411, 417, 444, 469
Avon Products, 50

Bally Gaming International, 110
BankAmerica, 138, 173, 323, 561, 567
Baseball Players Association, 36
BAT Industries, 198
Bechtel Power Corporation, 244
Bell Helicopter, 139
Bell Telephone, 368–369
BellSouth, 245
Ben & Jerry's Ice Cream, 469
Berlitz International, 107
Best Buy, 63–64
Bethlehem Steel, 385
BF Goodrich, 411
Blockbuster, 245
Blue Cross/Blue Shield, 38, 370
Blue Shield of California, 561
Boeing Co., 3, 352
Boise Cascade, 411
Booz-Allen Hamilton, 194
Boston College Center for Work and Family, 3
Boswell Technologies, 97, 114
Brainbench, 252
Bridgestone/Firestone Tire & Rubber, 287–290

British Aerospace, 258
Broan Manufacturing Company,
    333–334
Budget Rent-a-Car, 387–389
Burger King, 301

Campbell Soup, 465
Canadian Imperial Bank of
    Commerce, 138
Canadian Life Assurance Company, 561
Canadian Pacific Railroad, 77
Career Connection Company, 211
Career Technologies, 211
CareerBuilder.com, 195, 196, 197
CareerPath.com, 196
Carnegie Corporation, 68
Castulon Corporation, 544–545
Catalytica, 45–46
Cendent Intercultural, 107
Center for Creative Leadership, 411
Ceridian Corporation, 528
Chaparral Steel, 14, 426
Charles Schwab Corp., 187
Chase Manhattan Bank, 476
Chemical Bank, 54, 477
Chemlawn, 93, 94
ChevronTexaco Corp., 113, 140, 174
Chicken Soup, 477
Children's Hospital Medical Center,
    Cincinnati, 194
Chrysler Corporation, 239, 371
Cigna, 212
Citibank, 148, 210
Citigroup, 113, 466
Coca-Cola, 101, 174
Colgate-Palmolive, 121
Colorado Memory Systems, 329–330
Com-Com Industries, 304
CompUSA, 428–429
Conference Board, 189
Container Store, 479
Continental Can, 459
Control Data, 563
Coopers & Lybrand, 174
Core States Financial Corporation,
    173, 470
Corning, 426
Coy Manufacturing, 356, 378
Cray Research, 465
Creative Staffing Solutions (CSS), 246–247
CVS Pharmacies, 4

Dana Corporation, 296
Decker Manufacturing, 294, 311, 317
Deere & Co., 385
Dell Computer, 110, 191
Deloitte Touche Tohmatsu, 34–35, 212
Delta Air Lines, 384
Denny's, 83

Development Dimension International,
    428, 429
Dice.com, 196
Disney, 366, 395
Dixie Chemical Company, 569
Dole Food Co., 18–19
Domino's Pizza, 438–439
Dow Jones & Co., 465
Drake Beam Morin, 141
Du Pont, 94, 416, 458
Duke Power Company, 71
Dunkin' Donuts, 438–439

Eaton, 461
Eckel Industries, 290–292
Eli Lilly & Co., 131, 173
Endicott Report, 189
Enron, 341
Ernst & Young, 44
e-Serve International Ltd., 113
EssentialAssist Plus, 524
Exxel/Atmos, 509–510
ExxonMobil, 409, 461

Farnam Castle, 107
Federal Express, 174, 426, 466
First Bank System, 477
First Tennessee National Corporation, 44
First Union Corporation, 470
FlipDog.com, 196
Ford Motor Company, 3, 51–52, 72, 197, 268,
    371, 417
Forrester Research, 195
Fort Technical System, 547, 569
Frito-Lay, 341

GAP, 4
GE Capital Services, 198
General Dynamics, 209
General Electric, 113, 121, 174, 191, 245,
    268, 323, 341, 401, 409, 411, 461,
    534
General Mills, 194, 341, 426
General Motors, 174, 197, 371, 469
Georgia Power Company, 81–82
Global Dynamics, 107
Goldman Sachs, 14, 51, 93–94
Gotham Furniture, 332
GTE Corporation, 195, 210, 366
Gulf Oil, 461
Gunther Manufacturing, 186–187, 202,
    214, 215, 236

Hardisty Manufacturing Company,
    483, 503
Harris Rothenberg, Inc., 525
Hazelden Foundation, 528
Hershey's, 246
Heublein, 459

Hewitt Associates, 138, 307
Hewlett-Packard, 52, 169, 173, 187, 212, 329,
    341, 469
HireSystems, Inc., 51
Hoffman Sports Association, 479
Home Depot, 245
Honda, 45, 121
Honeywell, 341
Hormel Meats, 344
Hospital Corporation of America, 430
HotJobs.com, 148, 195, 196, 479
Household International, 173
Houston Medical Center, 133–134
Hudson Manufacturing, 533
Humana, Inc., 148

IBM, 3, 4, 13, 45, 53, 113, 135, 366, 384,
    385–386, 411, 459–460, 461,
    477, 563
Infosys Technologies, Ltd., 113
Inland Steel Company, 280–281
Inroads Inc., 198
Integon, 11
Intel, 3, 14, 99, 417
International Paper Co., 138
ITT Hartford Group, 569

J. I. Case, 462
JC Penney, 409, 538
Job Stores Network, 211
Jobcentral.com, 196
JobNet, 211
Jobs.com, 196
John Alden Life Insurance Company,
    318–319
Johnsco Electronics, 123
Johnson & Johnson, 561
Judge Incorporated, 519, 538

Kaiser Corporation, 411
Kindred Communications, 416
Kmart, 131
Kodak Caribbean, Ltd., 472–473
Kraft, 173
Kroger Supermarkets, 4

Lehman Brothers, 459
Lenscrafters, 538
Levi Strauss & Co., 563
Lexington Memorial Hospital, 322–324
Liberty Bank, 416
Lincoln Electric Company, 335–336
Lockheed Martin, 246
Lockheed Missile & Space Company, 209
Los Angeles Lakers, 10
Lucky Stores, 540–541

McDonald's, 5, 77, 101
McDonnell Douglas, 523
McGraw-Hill, 537
Macy's, 210
Majcen & Associates, 528
Malden Mills, 5, 6
Managed Health Network, 524–525

Manville Corporation, 548
Martin Marietta, 12, 476
Matsumoto Medical Instruments,
    116–117
May Company, 12
MBTI Corporation, 151
MCI Telecommunications, 139
Melody Machine Product Corp., 3, 21
Mercer Human Resources Consulting, 341,
    351, 352, 384
Merck & Company, 139, 375
Merck-Medco, 4, 45
Merrill Lynch, 173, 212
MetLife, 306, 307
Metropolitan Property and Casualty Insurance
    Company, 277
Microsoft, 4, 14, 51, 55, 384
Midvale Steel Works, 6–7
Milacron, Inc., 144
Monsanto, 140, 199, 411, 469
Monster.com, 195, 196, 197
Morrison and Foerster, 567
Morton Salt Company, 344
Motorola, 110, 174, 417
Mutual Benefit Life Insurance, 155

Nabisco, 461
National Association of Colleges and
    Employers, 192
National Pancake House, 31–33, 35, 56, 59
National Semiconductor, 193, 395
NationJob.com, 196
NationsBank, 198
Navigant Consulting Inc., 351, 353
NCR, 198, 377
Neal Engineering Construction Company,
    441, 471
Nervewire, Inc., 3
Nestlé, 101
New Directions Behavioral Health, 524
New England Patriots, 10
New England Telephone and Telegraph
    Company, 567
New York University (NYU), 87–88
New York Yankees, 10
Northern Telecom, 103, 417
Northwest Airlines, 384
Northwestern Mutual Life Insurance, 564
Norwest, 9
Novell, 14
Nunn-Bush Shoe Company, 344
NYNEX, 54

Olin, 411
O'Melveny & Myers, 476
OmniTech Consulting Group, 417
Oracle, 113
Overnite Transportation, 504
Owens-Illinois, 451

PacifiCorp, 397–398
Partridge Enterprises, 251, 276, 278
Pearl Meyer & Partners, 341
Pearson Performance Solutions, 192

PepsiCo, 121, 138
Personnel Systems Associates, 309–310
Pfizer, Inc., 11, 169, 173, 212
Philip Morris, 94, 538
Phillips Petroleum, 140
Pittsburgh Plate Glass, 401
Polaroid Corporation, 340
Pratt & Whitney, 316, 381
PricewaterhouseCoopers, 352
Pritex, 407
Procter & Gamble, 4, 110, 135, 174, 340,
    344, 459
Prudential Financial Inc., 138
Prudential Insurance, 113, 140, 200, 454,
    561, 563
Psychological Corporation, 28

Quaker Oats, 561
Quick Wok, 210
Quiet Power Inc., 417

Ralston-Purina, 409
Rand Corporation, 132
Randstad North America, 396–397
RCA, 411
Reader's Digest, 3
Recruiting-Online.com, 189
Reid Psychological Systems, 192
Reliable Insurance, 66, 85
Rhino Foods, 469
Rialto Manufacturing Company, 330
Robert Shaw Controls Company, 553
Rugby Sporting Goods Company, 133

Saint Paul Medical Center, 209
Samsung, 16–17
Saratoga Institute, 12
Sealing Equipment Products Co.,
    347–348
Sears Roebuck & Co., 131, 469
Servo Corp of America, 55
Shell Oil Company, 148, 563
Sietar International, 107
SmithKline Beecham Corp., 522
Sony, 45
Southern New England Telephone, 200
Southern Pacific Railroad, 523
Southwest Airlines, 125–126, 384, 479
Sprowl Manufacturing, 151, 174
Starbucks, 191
State, Local, and Municipal Workers, 36
Stetord, 417
Stryker Corporation, 116–117
Superscape, 417
Supreme Textile Corporation, 25–27
Syntex, 461
Synthes, 434
Synygy Performance Management, 252

Tandem Computers, 12
Target, 245
Tata Counseling Services, 113
Taylor Group, 299
Tenneco, 563

Texaco, 53
Texas Instruments, 200, 210, 454
3M, 45, 462
Today's Fashion, 182–183
Towers Perrin, 3, 351, 352, 353
Toyota, 45, 124, 155
Trailmobile, 500
Travelers Insurance, 460
TRW, 461
Twin Oaks Hospital, 322–324

Ugly Duckling Rent-A-Car, 455
Unicru, 527
Unilever, 131
Union Carbide, 411, 548

United Airlines, 50, 384
United Parcel Service, 245
U.S. Military Academy, 200, 454
University of Houston, 374
University of Michigan, 139–140
USA Group, 416

Verizon, 195
Virtual Reality Institute, 417

Walgreens, 245
Wal-Mart, 74, 384, 505, 506
Washington Gas Light Company, 499
Washington University, 209
Watson Wyatt Worldwide, 252, 353, 384

Wells Fargo Bank, 9
Western Electric, 7, 458
Weyerhaeuser, 461
Whirlpool Corporation, 304
Wipro, Ltd., 113
Wisconsin Power and Light, 45
Workforce Magazine, 6
Wyeth Consumer Healthcare, 429–430

Xerox, 174, 341, 366, 401

Young Enterprises, 393, 406, 418, 432

Zacha Electronics, 314, 315
Zayre Corporation, 477

Subject Index

ABC analysis of behavior, 424–425
Abilities of employees, 56
Accident repeaters, 551
Accommodation tactic, 497
Accreditation Institute, 28
Adarand Constructors Inc. v. Peña, 84–85
Advancement phase of career, 444
Advertisements, recruitment, 194–195
   employees in, 209
   intangible benefits and, 209
   point-of-purchase, 209–210
Affirmative action, 66, 76, 82–86
   defined, 82
   at Denny's, 83
   involuntary plans, 82–84
   update on, 84–86
   voluntary plans, 82
AFL-CIO, 490
   conflict within, 505
   described, 489
   formation of, 486
   Local 201, 483, 503
   membership in, 504
African Americans; *see* Minorities
Age Discrimination in Employment Act
   (ADEA) of 1967, 71, 76–77,
   116–117, 139, 144, 217, 302,
   472–473, 538
Agency shop, 492
Aging workforce, 129
   baby boomers, 132
AIDS in the workplace, 566–568
Albermarle Paper Co. v. Moody, 71
Albertsons, Inc. v. Kirkingburg, 78
Alcoholic and substance-abusing
   employees, 521–523
   affecting performance, 528
   alcohol testing, 521–522
   drug testing, 522–523
   employee assistance programs, 523
   prevalence and cost, 521
Alexander v. Gardner-Denver Co., 538
Alternative Dispute Resolution (ADR), 80,
   537–539
Alternative-form reliability, 219
American Association for the Advancement
   of Science, 456
American Compensation Association, 344
American dream, 68
American Federation of Government
   Employees, 493
American Federation of Labor (AFL), 493
   formation of, 486
American Federation of State, County, and
   Municipal Employees, 493
American Institute of Stress, 562
American Management Association,
   49, 233, 461

American Society for Human Resource
   Management, 28
   Accreditation Program, 28–29
American Society for Training and
   Development, 29, 402–403
American Society of Safety Engineers,
   555–556
American Society of Training Directors
   (ASTD), 428
Americans with Disabilities Act (ADA) of
   1990, 3, 71, 77–79, 153, 165, 168
   covered entities and protected individuals
      and, 77–78
   employee discipline and, 522, 528, 531
   legal advisor, 176–177
   ongoing developments, 78–79
   reasonable accommodation and, 78
   safety and health and, 561, 565, 566,
      567, 569
   selection and, 233, 239
Anti-Injunction Act of 1932, 486
Anxiety reduction, 395
Application blanks, 221–224
   biographical information, 223
   clauses on, 222–223
   weighted, 223
Application cases
   Best Buy's approach to outsourcing, 63–64
   Campus Food Systems, 575–576
   comparable worth debate, 322–324
   drug testing, 544–545
   dual-career couples, 476–478
   evaluating store managers, 287–290
   human resource planning, 148–149
   job analysis, 182–184
   labor dilemma in a joint venture in
      Japan, 123
   managing multiple responsibilities,
      25–27
   politics of performance appraisal,
      290–292
   recruitment, 209–212
   resumes, 245
   selection, 244
   Toyota in France, 124
   training, 438–439
   unions, 515–517
   vanishing benefits, 384–386
   work-life balance, 211–212
Apprenticeship, 414
   as professional career stage, 445
Arbitration, 502–503
   as alternative dispute resolution
      method, 537
   interest, 500–501
Arbitration Act of 1888, 486
ARDM model for HRM, 33–35
   specific steps of, 34–35

Armed-truce tactic, 497
Artistic personality type, 448, 449
Assessment center, 234–235
Association of Certified Fraud Examiners
   (ACFE), 526, 527
Attitudes of employees, 56
Authorization card, 490

Baby boomers, 50, 132, 187
Bals v. Verduzco, 280–281
Bargaining unit, 490
Base pay, 330
Behavior description interview (BDI), 224
Behavior modeling, 411–412
Behavior modification, 421–425
   criticisms of, 425
   defined, 421–422
   extinction and, 423
   managerial perspective, 423–425
   negative reinforcement and, 422
   performance analysis and, 424–425
   positive reinforcement and, 422
   principles of, 422–423
   punishment and, 422–423
   as theory of motivation, 304–305
Behavioral expectation scale
   (BES), 264
Behavioral observation scale (BOS),
   265–266
   comments on, 271
Behaviorally anchored rating scale (BARS),
   264–265
   comments on, 271
Behaviorist learning techniques, 412–413
Best Corporate Citizen award, 13
Bhopal, India accident, 548
Big Five personality factors, 217
Biographical information blank (BIB),
   223
Boards of directors of global corporations,
   111
Bona fide occupational qualification
   (BFOQ), 70
Bonus pay plans, 351–354
Boycott, 499
Brito v. Zia Company, 255
Broadbanding, 316
*Brown v. Delaware and Hudson Railroad
   Co.,* 77
Bureau of Labor Statistics, 50, 55, 191, 298,
   344, 365, 503, 529, 548, 555, 575
Burlington Industries v. Ellerth, 73
Burnout, 456–458
Business plan gainsharing, 338
Business process outsourcing, 63–64, 138
Business streamlining, 50
Business Work-Life Study (BWLS), 44
BusinessWeek, 341

626

California Psychological Inventory, 231
California State University system, 86
California Test of Mental Maturity, 229
California's Proposition 209, 86
Campbell Interest and Skill Survey (CISS), 450–451
Career choice, 448–451
    personality and, 448–449
    skills examination and, 449–451
    video case, 479
    Vocational Preference Inventory and, 449
Career development, 451–460
    application case, 476–478
    commitment to, 451
    legal advisor, 472–473
    linking organizational needs with individual needs, 442
    during midcareer, 454–460
        alternatives, 458–459
        burnout, 456–458
        counseling, 458
        counteracting problems, 455
        midcareer plateau, 455
        minimizing retirement adjustment, 459–460
        preretirement problems, 459
    programs, 452, 463–471
        downsizing and job loss, 466, 469–471
        equal employment opportunity, 466–469
        managing dual careers, 464–466, 476–478
        workforce planning, 464
    for recent hires, 451–454
        causes of difficulties, 452–453
        counteracting early problems, 453–454
        demanding bosses, 454
        initial assignments, 454
        job challenge, 453
        job performance evaluation, 453
        job satisfaction, 453
        realistic job previews, 454
Career pathing, 460, 463
Career planning, 460, 593–602
    career basics and self-analysis, 593
    equal employment opportunity and, 466
    formal counseling, 461–463
    informal counseling, 461
    interviews, 599–601
    job offers, 602
    job search, 594–597
    process of, 460
    professional help for self-assessment, 594
    resumes, 597–599
    video case, 479
    visiting the company, 602
Career stages, 444–448
    advancement phase, 444
    establishment phase, 444

Career stages—Cont.
    important needs and, 444
    maintenance phase, 444
    of professionals; see Professionals, career stages of
    retirement phase, 444
CareerPath.com, 196
Careers, 440–478
    career challenge, 441, 471
    concept of, 442–444
    defined, 442–443
    generational differences, 443
    helping employees find their bearings, 446–447
    legal advisor, 472–473
Carpal tunnel syndrome (CTS), 568–569
Case method, 409
Census of Fatal Occupational Injuries (CFOI), 549
Centers for Disease Control and Prevention, 564, 567
Central American Free Trade Agreement (CAFTA), 484
Central tendency error, 274
Certification election, 490
Change management, 13
Change to Win Coalition, 505
Chief executive officer (CEO), 427
Child care, 375
Child labor, 301
China, unions in, 505, 506
Cincinnati Enquirer, 194
Civil Rights Act of 1964 (Title VII), 69–75, 117, 205, 302, 368, 466, 467, 565
    bona fide occupational qualification and, 70
    described, 69
    discrimination and, 69–70
    disparate impact and, 71
    disparate treatment and, 70
    English-only rules and, 74–75
    pregnancy discrimination and, 74
    religious minorities and, 74, 75
    retaliation and, 71–72
    sexual harassment and, 72–74
Civil Rights Act of 1991, 71, 75–76, 112, 117, 153, 165
Civil rights movement, 68
Civil Service Commission, 494
Civil Service Reform Act of 1978, 494
Classification system of job evaluation, 312–313
Clerical aptitude, 229
Closed shop, 492
Coaching-and-counseling training method, 413–414
Coal Mine Health and Safety Act of 1969, 553
COBRA, 370–371
Code of Hammurabi, 306
Cognitive ability tests, 229
Cognitive learning techniques, 412–413

Collective bargaining, 494–498
    concession, 495
    contract ratification, 498
    defined, 494
    developing a strategy, 496
    distributing, 494
    failure to reach agreement; see Impasse, bargaining
    forces influencing the process of, 494
    integrative, 494–495
    lack of good faith, 497
    prenegotiation stage, 495
    reaching a formal contractual agreement, 497–498
    selecting the negotiators, 495–496
    tactics and, 496–497
Collectivism, 100
College hire assimilation program (CHAP), 395
College recruiting, 198–200, 210–211
Commission, 332
Common metric questionnaire (CMR), 164
Commonwealth v. Hunt, 486
Communication
    of benefits, 378–379
    via e-mail, 208
    evaluation and, 253
    job analysis and, 154
    of policies, 12–13
Comparable benefits strategy, 378
Comparable-pay strategy, 308
Comparable worth, 301–302
    debate over, 322–324
Compensation, 293–354
    administration issues, 343–345
        open system, 343–344
        pay compression, 345
        pay security, 344–345
        secret system, 343–344
    application cases, 322–324, 351–354
    career challenges, 294, 311, 317, 326–327, 345
    current, 28, 29
    decisions; see Compensation decisions
    defined, 294
    executive, 341–343
    of expatriate managers, 109–110
        categories of allowances, 109
        sample of, 110
    external influences on, 295–303
        economic conditions, 298
        government policies; see Government policies, compensation and
        labor market, 295–298
        unions, 302–303
    financial, 295
    higher than required, 39
    incentive; see Incentive pay
    indirect financial; see Employee benefits
    internal influences on, 303–304
        decision makers and, 303–304
        labor budget, 303
    job analysis and, 154

Compensation—*Cont.*
    legal advisors, 318–319, 347–348
    motivation and, 304–307
        productivity and, 306–307
        satisfaction and, 306
        theories of, 304–305
    nonfinancial, 295
    objective of, 295
    payment methods; *see* Payment methods
Compensation decisions, 308–317
    broadbanding, 316
    delayering, 316
    determination of individual pay, 327–328
    individual, 316–317
    pay level, 308–309
    pay structure; *see* Pay structure
    pay surveys, 309–310
    payment methods; *see* Payment methods
Compensation for time off, 365
Competencies
    job analysis of, 169
    shifts in, 49
Competency alignment process (CAP), 174
Competency-based pay, 341
Competitive advantage, 38
    activities that enhance, 39
Competitiveness, 38
    compensation and degree of, 298
Computer databases, 211
Computer-assisted instruction (CAI), 415
Concession bargaining, 495
Conciliation, 500
Concurrent validity, 221
Conflict-based tactic, 497
Congress, U.S.
    civil rights and, 68, 71, 75
    employee benefits and, 384, 385
    labor relations and, 486–490
Congress of Industrial Organizations (CIO),
        486
Consolidated Omnibus Budget Reconciliation
        Act (COBRA) of 1985,
        370–371
Constitution, U.S., 522–523, 544–545
Construct validity, 220
Content validity, 219–220
Contingent workers, 54–55
Contract administration, 501–503
    arbitration, 502–503
    discipline, 501
    grievances, 501–502
Contract recruiting, 210
Contrast effect, 274–275
Conventional personality type, 448, 449
Cooperation tactic, 497
Cost-benefit analysis
    of recruiting, 202–203
    for the selection decision, 237
Cost-of-living adjustments (COLAS), 344
Cover letter, 192
Craft union, 483
Credential-based pay, 340
Criteria relevance, 256
Criteria sensitivity, 256
Criterion-related validity, 220–221

Critical incidents, 263
    comments on, 271
Cross-training, 39
Cross-utilization, 39
Culture and global HRM, 100–101
    cross-cultural training, 106–109
Culture shock, 105–106
    preparedness for, 108
    reverse, 106
Cumulative trauma disorders (CTDs),
        568–569
Cycle time management, 13–14

Data collection, 155–160
    choice among methods of, 159–160
    interviews, 156, 159
    job incumbent diary or log, 159
    observation, 156
    questionnaires, 159
Davis-Bacon Act of 1931, 302, 303
Decertification elections, 487
Defense Production Act of 1950, 298
Defined benefit pension plan, 374
Defined contribution plans, 339
    pensions, 374
Delayering, 316
Delphi technique, 132
Demanding bosses, 454
Demographics
    compensation and, 296
    work-family balance and, 172–174
    workforce, 129
Department of Commerce, U.S., 113
Department of Defense, U.S., 137, 210, 232,
        416, 417
Department of Energy, U.S., 232
Department of Health and Human Services,
        U.S., 555
Department of Justice, U.S., 84–85, 204–205,
        530, 564
Department of Labor, U.S., 36, 129, 161,
        189, 234, 299, 300, 465
Department of Transportation, U.S., 78, 233,
        521–522
Development; *see also* Training
    behavior modification; *see* Behavior
        modification
    career; *see* Career development
    defined, 393, 394
    diagnostic step in programs, 419
    evaluation of, 427–432
        criteria for, 430–431
        matrix guide for, 431–432
        strategic management, 428–430
    goal setting; *see* Goal setting development
        technique
    group techniques, 425–426
    individual techniques, 420–425
    management, 418–419
    organizational techniques, 426–427
    team building, 425–426
    total quality management, 426–427
Diagnostic approach to HRM
    ARDM model and, 33–35
    at Deloitte Touche Tohmatsu, 34–35

Diagnostic approach to HRM—*Cont.*
    diagnosis, 34, 35
    evaluation, 34, 35
    implementation, 34, 35
    people and, 56–57
        abilities, 56
        attitudes and preferences, 56
        motivation, 56–57
        personality, 57
    prescription, 34, 35
Diary, job incumbent, 159
Diaz v. Pan Am. World Airlines, 70
Dictionary of Occupational Titles (DOT),
        160, 161, 449
Differential Aptitude Test, 229
Differential pay levels, 296
Differential piece rate, 331–332
Direct financial compensation, 295
Disability income replacement insurance, 371
Discipline
    employee; *see* Employee discipline
    in labor contracts, 501
Discrimination, 69
    application blanks and, 222
    global HRM and, 112
    laws against; *see* Equal employment
        opportunity (EEO)
    recruitment and, 188–189, 194,
        204–205
Disequilibrium, state of, 562
Disparate impact, 71
Disparate treatment, 70
Distance training (distance learning),
        417–418
Distributive bargaining, 494
Distributive justice theory of motivation, 305
Diversity, 45
    goals and, 45
    labor force, 38–42
    location of organization and, 190
    recruitment and, 190, 195, 198
    strategic challenge of building, 50–53
Dothard v. Rawlinson, 70
Downsizing, 54, 77, 466, 469–471
Downward transfers, 458–459
Drug-testing program, 233–234, 522–523
    case for and against, 544–545
Dual careers, 464–466
    application case, 476–478

Economic conditions
    geography and, 43
    productivity, 37
    safety and health and, 552–553
    work sector of the organization, 37–38
Economic Stabilization Act of 1970, 298
Economic strike, 498
Education
    as an employee service, 375
    career planning and, 462
    earnings and, 297
    formal, as selection criterion, 216
    geography and, 42–43
Edwards Personal Preference
        Schedule, 231

EEOC v. Detroit Edison, 194
Egalitarianism, 39
Elder care, 375–376
E-mail, 208
Employee appraisal; *see* Performance
      evaluation
Employee assistance programs (EAPs), 523,
      524–525
Employee benefits, 355–390
   application case, 384–386
   career challenge, 356, 378
   changes in programs, 357
   cost-benefit analysis of, 379
   decisions about, 357–358
   defined, 356
   flexible benefits plans, 376–377
   health insurance; *see* Health insurance
   as indirect financial compensation, 356
   legal advisor, 381
   managing an effective program,
         377–379
      communication, 378–379
      involving participants and unions, 378
      monitoring costs, 379
      set objectives and strategy, 378
   mandated, 359–364
      in foreign countries, 387–389
      social security, 360–362
      unemployment insurance, 359–360
      workers' compensation, 362–364
   reasons for offering, 357
   reimbursement accounts, 376–377
   retirement income; *see* Retirement income
   services; *see* Employee services
   unions and, 357–358, 378
   vanishing, 384–386
   video case, 387–389
   voluntary; *see* Voluntary employee
         benefits
Employee discipline, 518–545
   application case, 544–545
   approaches to, 532–534
      hot stove rule, 532–533
      positive discipline, 534
      progressive pattern of discipline,
            533–534
   career challenge, 519, 538
   categories of difficult employees, 520–531
      alcoholic and substance-abusing
            employees, 521–523
      ineffective employees, 521
      possible causes for, 520
      rule violators, 529–531
      theft, fraud, and other illegal acts,
            523–528
   disciplinary interview, 534–535
   legal advisor, 540–541
   legal challenges to, 535–539
      alternative dispute resolution, 537–539
      employment at will, 536–537
   process of, 531–532
   rules and, 532
   types of misbehavior, 519
Employee evaluation; *see* Performance
      evaluation

Employee learning, 55
Employee ownership, 39
Employee Polygraph Protection Act of 1988,
      232, 527
Employee referrals, 194, 211
Employee services, 375–376; *see also*
      Employee benefits
   child care, 375
   defined, 356
   education programs, 375
   elder care, 375–376
   financial services, 376
   preretirement programs, 375
   reasons for offering, 357
   social and recreational programs, 376
   stock ownership plans, 375
Employee stock ownership plan (ESOP),
      339–340
Employees' attitudes about safety and health,
      552
Employment agencies, 196
Employment at will, 536–537
Employment Retirement Income Security Act
      (ERISA) of 1974, 373–374
Employment security, 39
Employment Service, U.S., 152, 187
Employment tests, 228–232
   cognitive ability tests, 229
   honesty, 231–232
   job sample performance tests, 228–229
   personality inventories, 231
   polygraph, 231–232
   psychomotor ability simulations, 230
   temperament tests, 231
Empowerment, 39
   job tasks and, 46
English-only rules, 74–75
Enterprising personality type, 448, 449
Environmental influences; *see* External
      environmental influences; Internal
      environmental influences
Environmental scanning, 131
Environmental unpleasantness, 46
Equal employment opportunity (EEO), 65–95
   affirmative action and; *see* Affirmative
         action
   Age Discrimination in Employment Act
         of 1967, 76–77
   Americans with Disabilities Act of 1990,
         77–79
   application case, 93–94
   career challenge, 66, 85
   Civil Rights Act of 1964; *see* Civil
         Rights Act of 1964 (Title VII)
   Civil Rights Act of 1991, 75–76
   content and career interpretation of
         laws, 69–79
   development of, 68–69
   economic status of minorities before
         1964 and, 69
   employment at will and, 536–537
   enforcing the law, 79–82
      the courts, 80–82
      Equal Employment Opportunity
            Commission, 79–80

Equal employment opportunity (EEO)—*Cont.*
   Equal Pay Act of 1963, 76
   evaluation and, 254
   Executive Order 11246, 76, 84–85
   government and, 69
   significance of, 66–67
   societal values and, 68
   state laws and, 79
   test of understanding of, 67, 95
Equal Employment Opportunity Commission
      (EEOC), 66, 71–74, 79–80, 302
   career planning and, 466
   Chrysler Corporation v., 239
   complaint steps and actions, 80
   performance evaluation and, 254–255
Equal pay, 301–302
Equal Pay Act (EPA) of 1963, 71, 76, 298,
      301–302
Equity theory of motivation, 305
E-recruiting, 195–196
   job seekers and, 197
Ergonomics, 568
   video case, 577–578
ERISA, 373–374
Essay evaluation, 262–263
   comments on, 271
Establishment phase of career, 444
Ethical policies, 13
   ethics hotlines, 527
   global HRM and, 111–112
Ethnocentric perspective, 102
European Trade Union
      Confederation, 115
European Union (EU), 98, 115
   compared to NAFTA, 484
Eustress, 562
*Everyday Revolutionaries: Working Women
      and the Transformation of American
      Life* (Heigesen), 41
Exchange theory of motivation, 305
Executive information systems
      (EISs), 140
Executive orders
   10988, 494
   11246, 76, 84–85
   11493, 494
   11823, 494
Executive pay, 341–343
Executive search firms, 196
Executives
   CEOs, 427
   succession planning, 140–141
Exempt employee, 300–301
Expatriate managers, 102
   compensating, 109–110
      categories of allowances, 109
      sample of, 110
   culture shock and, 105–106
   rapid response, 105
   repatriation of, 108–109
   selecting, 103–105
   self-awareness of, 108
   success and failure of, 104
   training the, 106–109
   women, 104

Expectancy (valance-instrumentality-expectancy) theory, 305, 306
Expectations, realistic, 395
Experience and past performance as selection criterion, 216
Experienced meaningfulness, 172
Experienced responsibility, 172
Expert estimate, 132–133
External environmental influences, 35–43
  competitiveness, 38, 39
  economic conditions, 36–38
  geographic location, 42–43
  government law and regulations, 35–36
  labor force composition and diversity, 38–42
  productivity, 37
  selection process and, 215
  unions, 36
  work sector of the organization, 37–38
Extinction, 423

Fact-finding, 500
Factor comparison method, 313–314
Fair Labor Standards Act (FLSA) of 1938, 174, 298–302
  child labor, 301
  Equal Pay Act, 301–302
  minimum wage, 299–300
  overtime pay, 300–301
Fallback positions, 459
Families and Work Institute, 44
Family and Medical Leave Act (FMLA) of 1993, 3, 368, 381
Family leave, 368
Faragher v. City of Boca Raton, 73
Fastest-growing occupations, 42
Federal Bankruptcy Code, 548
Federal Highway Administration, 521–522
Federal Labor Relations Authority (FLRA), 494
Federal Labor Relations Council (FLRC), 494
Federal Mediation and Conciliation Service, 500
Federal Pay Comparability Act of 1970, 308
Federal Register, 555
Federal Trade Commission (FTC), 141
Federal Wage Garnishment Act of 1970, 302
Feedback, 171, 172
Feedback interview, 276–279
Feedback pay, 341
Fifth Discipline: The Art and Practice of the Learning Organization, The (Senge), 405
Financial services, 376
Financial Services Industry game, 411
Finders fees, 194
"Fit" in global HRM, 101
Fitness-for-duty testing, 522
Flat rates, 328
Flexible (cafeteria) benefits plans, 376–377
Flexible spending accounts, 376–377
Flexible work arrangements, 173, 212

Flextime, 173, 174, 212
FMLA, 368, 381
Forced distribution, 267–268
Forced-choice format, 262
  comments on, 271
Forecasting demand for employees, 131–135
  expert estimate, 132–133
  modeling, 133–134
  multiple-predictive techniques, 134
  trend projection, 133
  unit-demand, 134–135
Foreign Corrupt Practices Act (FCPA) of 1977, 111–112
Foreign direct investment (FDI), 97, 99–100
Fortune, 191
Fortune v. National Cash Register, 536
Four-fifths rule, 71
401(k) plans, 372–373
  Web-centric, 373
France, 124
Fraternal Order of the Police, 493
Functional job analysis (FJA), 160–161

Gainsharing incentive plans, 334–339
  business plan, 338
  comparative analysis of, 337
  defined, 334
  ImproShare, 337
  Lincoln Electric, 335–336
  Rucker, 336–337
  Scanlon, 336
  spot, 338
  unsuccessful, 338–339
  winsharing, 338
Garcia v. Gloor, 74
Garcia v. Spun Steak, 75
Gatch v. Milacron, Inc., 144
Generation X, 296
  careers of, 443
Generation Y, 11
  careers of, 443
Geocentric orientation, 102
Geographic location, 42–43
  behavioral factors, 43
  economic factors, 43
  educational factors, 42–43
  legal-political factors, 43
  urban/rural, 42
Geographic transfers, 414–415
Germany, 114
Gilmer v. Interstate/Johnson Lane Corp., 538
Glass ceiling, 466, 467–469
Global corporations (GCs), 101–102
  boards of directors, 111
  host country nationals and, 110–111
Global Excellence Award, 429
Global human resource management (GHRM), 96–126
  application cases, 123–124
  career challenge, 97, 114
  cultural nature of, 100
  defined, 98
  developing, 121
  ethnocentric perspective and, 102

Global human resource management (GHRM)—*Cont.*
  expatriate managers and; *see* Expatriate managers
  "fit" and, 101
  geocentric orientation and, 102
  host country nationals and, 101, 110–111
  international comparisons of labor costs, 99
  labor relations and, 113–115
  legal advisor, 116–117
  legal and ethical climate of, 111–112
  outsourcing and, 113
  parent country nationals and, 102
  third country nationals and, 102
  video case, 125–126
Global Leadership Program (GLP), 111
Global market connection, 49
Global scanning, 131
Globalization, 97–98
Goal setting development technique, 419–421
  criticisms of, 421
  individual differences and, 421
  Locke on, 419–420
  process of, 420
  research on, 420
  steps in, 420
Goals
  helping organizational reach, 11
  human resource planning and, 129
  as internal environmental influence, 45
Good faith and fair dealing, covenant of, 536
Government Alliance for Training and Education (GATE), 418
Government Education and Training Network (GETN), 418
Government policies
  compensation and, 298–302
    other influences, 302
    other pay legislation, 302
    wage and hour regulations, 298–302
    wage controls and guidelines, 298
  employee shortage and, 137
  equal employment opportunity and, 69
  as external environmental influence, 35–36
  labor relations and, 485
  planning and, 129–130
  recruitment and, 188–189
Grading system of job evaluation, 312–313
Graduate Record Examination (GRE), 229
Graphic rating scale, 260–262
  example of, 261
Grievances, 501–502
Griggs v. Duke Power, 71
Guaranteed annual wage (GAW), 344

Halo error, 273–274
Harshness rating error, 274
Harvard Business Review, 155
Hawthorne effect, 455
Hawthorne studies, 7
Health, 559–562

Health benefits, 560
Health hazards, 547–550
Health insurance, 369–371
  Consolidated Omnibus Budget
      Reconciliation Act, 370–371
  health maintenance organizations, 370
  long-term-care legislation, 371
  preferred provider organizations, 370
  summarized, 369–370
Health Maintenance Act of 1973, 370
Health maintenance organization (HMO), 370
Hierarchy of human needs, 304
High-pay strategy, 308
HIV-AIDS in the workplace, 566–568
HMO, 370
Holidays, paid, 365
*Holihan v. Lucky Stores, Inc.,*540–541
Honesty tests, 231–232
Hopwood v. State of Texas, 85, 86
Host country nationals (HCNs), 101
  global corporations and, 110–111
Hot cargo agreement, 499
Hot stove rule, 532–533
HRMagazine, 329
Human factors engineering, 170
Human interaction, 46
Human relations movement, 7
Human relations specialists, 14, 15
Human resource information system (HRIS),
      129, 139–142
  defined, 139
  employees' privacy, identity theft, and,
      141–142
  executive information system, 140
  succession planning, 140–141
Human resource management (HRM), 1–29
  accreditation, 28–29
  as action-oriented, 5
  activities of, 5
  application case, 25–27
  career challenge, 3–4, 21
  careers in, 28–29
  defined, 1, 4
  department operations, 16–20
    meaningful objectives, 17, 19
    organization of, 19–20
    policy, 19
    procedures, 19
    strategy, 16–17
  equal employment and; *see* Equal
      employment opportunity (EEO)
  as future-oriented, 5
  global; *see* Global human resource
      management (GHRM)
  as globally-oriented, 5
  history of, 5–7
  measuring, 579–584
    basic principles, 580
    building blocks of, 580–581
    quantifying quality, 581–583
    summary, 584
  objectives of, 10–14
    achieving quality of work life, 12
    change management, 13

Human resource management (HRM)—*Cont.*
  objectives of—*Cont.*
    communicating policies, 12–13
    employment of workforce skills
        and abilities, 11
    ethical policies and socially
        responsible behavior, 13
    helping organizations reach goals, 11
    job satisfaction and self-actualization, 12
    managing urgency and faster cycle
        time, 13–14
    well-trained and well-motivated
        employees, 12
  organizational effectiveness and, 9–10
  outsourcing and, 14–15
  as people-oriented, 5
  performance of activities, 14–16
  place of, in management of the firm, 16
  planning; *see* Planning, human resource
  salaries in, 28, 29
  sources of information about, 585–591
  strategic importance of, 7–9
  strategic management approach; *see*
      Strategic management approach to HRM
Human Resource Planning Society, 49
Human resources accounting, 10
Human Resources Conference, 49
Humanist learning technique, 412–413
Hygiene theory of motivation, 304–305, 306

Identity theft, 141
Identity Theft and Assumption Deterrence
      Act of 1998, 141
Imitating models, 411–412
Immigration Reform and Control Act (IRCA)
      of 1986, 188–189
Impairment testing, 522, 523
Impasse, bargaining, 498–501
  lockouts and, 499–500
  permanent replacements, 500
  strikes and, 498–499
  third party intervention, 500–501
Implied contracts, 536
ImproShare gainsharing incentive plan, 337
In-basket technique, 410
Incentive pay, 39, 307, 329–339
  bonus pay plans, 351–354
  commission, 332
  design factors for, 329
  differential piece rate, 331–332
  example of, 329–330
  gainsharing plans; *see* Gainsharing
      incentive plans
  individual, 331–332
  merit, 330–331
  organizationwide, 333–339
  production bonus systems, 332
  productivity and, 307
  profit-sharing plans, 339
  standard-hour plan, 331
  straight piecework, 331
  Taylor plan, 331–332
  team, 333
  total compensation approach, 330

Incident method, 409
Independent contributor, 445
Indirect financial compensation, 295, 356;
      see also Employee benefits
Indirect pay, 330
Individual development techniques; *see*
      Behavior modification; Goal setting
      development technique
Individual evaluation methods, 260–266
  behavioral observation scale, 265–266
  behaviorally anchored rating scale,
      264–265
  checklists and weighted checklists, 264
  comments on, 271
  critical incident technique, 263
  essay evaluation, 262–263
  forced-choice format, 262
  graphic rating scale, 260–262
Individual retirement accounts (IRAs), 372
Individualism, 100
Indoor environmental quality (IEQ), 565–566
Industrial psychology, 6, 7
Industrial Revolution, 5, 50
Industrial union, 483
Ineffective employees, 521
Information sharing, 39
Information systems, 139–142
Information technology, 46
Initial assignments, 454
Initial job challenge, 453
Initial job performance evaluation, 453
Initial job satisfaction, 453
*Inland Steel v. National labor Relations
      Board,* 357
Innovation, quicker, 50
Inside moonlighting, 193–194
Institute for a Drug-Free Workplace, 234
Instructional methods, training and
      development, 402, 408–418
  behavior modeling, 411–412
  case method, 409
  in-basket technique, 410
  management games, 410–411
  off-the-job training; *see* Off-the-job training
  on-the-job training; *see* On-the-job training
  outdoor-oriented programs, 412
  role playing, 410
Instrumentality of goal-directed behavior, 305
Insurance
  disability income replacement, 371
  employer-purchased, 369
  health; *see* Health insurance
  life, 371
Integrative bargaining, 494–495
Interaction management, 411–412
Interest arbitration, 500–501
Internal environmental influences, 43–48
  goals, 45
  leader's style and experience, 48
  nature of the task, 46–47
  organization culture, 45–46
  selection process and, 214–215
  strategy, 44
  unions, 504–506

Internal environmental influences—*Cont.*
    work group, 47
    work-life balance, 44
International Association of Fire
        Fighters, 493
International Confederation of Free Trade
        Unions, 504
International Labor Organization, 115
International Longshore and Warehouse
        Union, 499
International Telework Association and
        Council (ITAC), 51
International Trade Secretariats, 115
International Union, UAW v. Johnson
        Controls, Inc., 70
International Union of Gas Workers, 499
Internet
    career planning and, 462, 594–597
    recruitment via, 189, 195–196, 208
    training and, 415, 416
    virtual human resource management
        and, 148
Internship programs, 197–198
Interrater reliability
    performance evaluation and, 256
    selection and, 219
Interviews
    behavioral description, 224
    as data collection device, 156, 159
    disciplinary, 534–535
    employment, 224–228
    errors that can occur in, 227
    feedback, 276–279
    job search and, 193
    situational, 224–225
    strategy for, 599–601
    structured, 224, 225
    training interviewers, 227–228
    unstructured, 224
    winning the interview game, 226–227
Intranets, 415
Investigative personality type, 448, 449
IRAs, 372

Japan
    global HRM and, 102–103
    labor dilemma in a joint venture in, 123
Job, 152
Job analysis, 150–169
    application cases, 182–184
    career challenge, 151
    charts, 154–155
    compensation and, 154
    conducting, 154
    data collection and; *see* Data collection
    defined, 152
    described, 151
    employee competencies and, 169
    functional, 160–161
    job descriptions and specifications, 165,
        167–169
    job design and; *see* Job design
    legal advisor, 176–177
    legally defensible, 153

Job analysis—*Cont.*
    management position description
        questionnaire, 164–167
    multimethod, 160
    position analysis questionnaire, 162–164
    quantitative techniques, 160–165
    recruitment and selection and, 153–154
    reengineering and, 155
    steps in, 152–153
    strategic HR management and, 168–169
    strategic planning and, 154
    training and career development and, 154
    uses of, 153–154
    vocabulary of, 152
    work oriented, 156
Job analysis information format (JAIF), 156
    example of, 157–158
Job challenge, initial, 453
Job characteristics model, 171–172
Job description, 152, 165, 167–169
    of a HR manager, 168
    job design and; *see* Job design
    legal advisor, 176–177
Job design, 39, 169–174
    categories of, 170
    job analysis and, 152–153
    job enrichment approach to, 171–172
    mechanistic approach to, 170–171
    motivational approach to, 171–172
    next challenge for, 174
    psychological states and, 172
    scientific management approach
        to, 170–171
    task differences and, 47
    work-family balance and, 172–174
Job enlargement, 171
Job enrichment, 171–172
Job evaluation, 311–314
    classification system, 312–313
    factor comparison, 313–314
    point system, 313
    ranking of jobs, 312
Job expectations, 395
Job fairs, 197
Job family, 152
Job instruction training (JIT) system,
        408–409
Job layoff, 469–471
Job loss, 466, 469–471
    effects of, 469–470
    managerial responses to, 470–471
Job orientation, 155–156
Job posting, 193
    career planning and, 462
Job preferences of recruits, 191
Job ranking, 312
Job sample performance tests,
        228–229
Job satisfaction, 12
    career development and, 453
Job search, 192–193
Job sharing, 173, 174, 477
Job specification, 152
Johnson v. Transportation Agency, 82, 467

Jorge Vega and Eusebio Leon v. Kodak
        Caribbean, Ltd., 472–473
Journal of College Placement, 189
Jurisdictional strike, 498

Knights of Labor, 486
Knowledge needs, 49
Knowledge of results, 172
Knowledge-based pay, 340

Labor costs, international, 99
Labor force composition, 38–42
    compensation and, 296–298
    minorities, 40
    older employees, 40–41
    projections of, 40, 42
    recruitment and, 190
    women, 39–40, 41
Labor Management Relations Act of 1947,
        488, 492, 498, 499, 500
Labor Management Reporting and Disclosure
        Act of 1959, 488, 492, 499
Labor market
    compensation and, 295–298
        international, 296–298
    recruitment and, 189
Labor market conditions, 485
Labor relations, 482–517; *see also* Labor
        unions
    application case, 515–517
    collective bargaining; *see* Collective
        bargaining
    contract administration, 501–503
        arbitration, 502–503
        discipline, 501
        grievances, 501–502
    defined, 483
    government and, 485
    international corporations and, 113–115
    labor legislation, 486–488
        early, 486
        Labor Management Relations Act, 488
        Labor-Management Reporting and
            Disclosure Act, 488
        National Labor Relations Act, 487–488
    labor market conditions and, 485
    legal advisor, 509–510
    public employee associations, 493–494
Labor unions, 485; *see also* Labor relations
    application case, 515–517
    business representatives, 489–490
    changing climate for, 503–507
        erosion of power, 504
        global unionization, 504–506
        membership trends, 504, 505
        organizing trends, 506–507
    collective bargaining; *see* Collective
        bargaining
    compensation and, 302–303
    defined, 483
    early collective action and, 486
    effects of, on HRM, 36
    employee benefits and, 357–358, 378
    federation of, 489

Labor unions—*Cont.*
    intermediate bodies, 489
    local, 489–490
    national, 489
    organizing campaign, 490–491
    public employee associations, 493–494
    safety and health issues, 553
    structure and management of, 489–490
    tactics of, 505
    union security; *see* Union security
    union steward, 490
Landrum-Griffith Act, 488, 492
Lateral transfers, 458
Law of effect, 423
Laws; *see also specific laws*
    application blanks and, 222
    enforcing, 79–82
    equal employment; *see* Equal employment
        opportunity (EEO)
    evaluation and, 253, 254–255
    as external environmental influence,
        35–36, 188–189
    foreign, 43
    global HRM and, 111–112
    labor relations, 486–488
        public sector, 493–494
    private pensions and, 373–374
    reference checks and, 233
Layoff criteria, 470
Leadership style and experience, 48
Learning, 399; *see also* Training
Learning organizations, 401
Learning theory and training, 400–401
Lecture-discussion approach, 415
Leniency, 274
Lie detectors, 231–232
Life insurance, 371
Life stages, 448
Lincoln Electric gainsharing incentive plan,
    335–336
Line managers, 15
Local nationals, 101
Location of organizations, 190
Lockouts, 499–500
Log, job incumbent, 159
Long-term orientation, 100
Long-term perspective, 39
Long-term-care legislation, 371
Looking Glass game, 411
Low-pay strategy, 308

McDonnell Douglas v. Green, 70
McNamara-O'Hara Service Contract Act, 302
Maintenance phase of career, 444
Management by objectives (MBO), 268–270
    comments on, 271
    evaluation examples, 269
    pitfalls and problems with, 270
    process of, 269
Management development, 418–419
Management games, 410–411
Management position description
        questionnaire (MPDQ), 164–165
    example of, 166–167

Managers
    CEOs, 427
    on-the-job training for, 413–415
    selection of, 234–237
    training expatriate, 106–109
Mandated benefits programs, 359–364
    in foreign countries, 387–389
    social security, 360–362
    unemployment insurance, 359–360
    workers' compensation, 362–364
Manifest Anxiety Scale, 231
Maquiladoras, 99, 112
*Mark Duckworth v. Pratt & Whitney,
    Inc.,* 381
Markov chain analysis, 133–134
Masculine cultures, 100
Maslach Burnout Inventory (MBI), 456
Maternity leave, 368–369
Measurement, 39
Mechanistic approach to job design,
    170–171
Media advertisements for recruiting; *see*
        Advertisements, recruitment
Mediation, 500
    as alternative dispute resolution method,
        537
Mediator, 500
Medicare, 38, 361, 385
Mental Measurement Yearbook, 228
Mental models, 405
Mentoring relationship, 445, 447
Mercer National Survey of Employer-
        Sponsored Health Plans, 524
Merit pay, 330–331
Merit ratings; *see* Performance evaluation
Meritor Savings Bank v. Vinson, 73
Mexico, 99, 112, 114
Midcareer crisis, 444
Midcareer plateau, 455
Minimum benefits strategy, 378
Minimum wage, 299–300
Minitrial, 537
Minnesota Clerical Test, 229
    example of, 230
Minnesota Counseling Inventory, 231
Minnesota Multiphase Personality Inventory,
    231
Minnesota Paper Form Board Test (MPFB),
    229
    excerpt from, 230
Minorities
    discrimination against; *see* Discrimination
    economic status of, before 1964, 69
    goal setting and, 421
    in the labor force, 40
    the law and; *see* Equal employment
        opportunity (EEO)
    religious, 74, 75
    safety and health and, 550
    union membership and, 504
Mixed standard scale, 261
Modeling, 133–134
Monster.com, 195, 196, 197
Monthly Labor Review, 189, 298

Moonlighting, 193–194
Motivation, 12
    compensation and, 304–307
        productivity and, 306–307
        satisfaction and, 306
        theories of, 304–305
    evaluation and, 253
    work, 56–57
Motivational approach to job design,
    171–172
Multimedia-based training (MBT), 147
Multimethod job analysis approach, 160
Multinational corporations (MNCs), 101–102
    expatriate managers in; *see* Expatriate
        managers
Multiple regression analysis, 134
Multiple-person evaluation methods, 266–268
    comments on, 271
    forced distribution, 267–268
    paired comparison, 266–267
    ranking, 266
Murphy v. United Parcel Service Inc., 78
Muslims, 74, 75
Myers-Briggs Type Indicators, 232

National Alliance of Businessmen, 68
National Association of Colleges and
        Employers, 192
National Association of Government
        Employees, 493
National Association of Letter Carriers, 493
National Association of Temporary and
        Staffing Services, 246
National Council on the Aging, 375
National Education Association, 493
National Federation of Government
        Employees, 493
National Fire Protection Association, 555
National Institute for Occupational Safety
        and Health (NIOSH), 550–551, 553,
        555, 559, 565, 568
National Institute on Drug Abuse, 521
National Labor Relations Act of 1935, 303,
        487, 500, 509
    unfair labor practices and, 487–488
National Labor Relations Board (NLRB),
        358, 487, 507, 509, 510
    union organizing campaigns and, 490–491
*National Labor Relations Board v. Jones and
        Laughlin Steel,* 487
National Mediation Board, 500
National Study of the Changing Workforce
        (NSCW), 44
National Teachers Association, 493
Nature of the task, 552
Needs assessment, 399, 403–404
Needs theorists, 304
Negative reinforcement, 422
"Negligent referrals," 233
Negotiators, 495–496; *see also* Collective
        bargaining
New York Times, The, 341
New York University, 87–88
Nominal group technique (NGT), 132–133

Nonexempt employee, 300–301
Norris-LaGuardia Act of 1932, 486
North American Free Trade Agreement
    (NAFTA), 97–98, 483
    success of, 484–485

Objectives, HRM, 17, 19
    relationship to other operations, 17
Occupational Information Network (O*NET),
    161
    Content Model, 161, 162
Occupational Safety and Health Act of 1970,
    174, 531, 547, 548, 553
    basic requirements of, 554
Occupational Safety and Health
    Administration (OSHA),
    553–558, 564
    Bloodborne Pathogen Standards, 567
    described, 550
    ergonomics and, 568, 577
    inspectors from, 555–556
    origin of, 553–555
    record keeping and reporting of,
        556–557
    report card on, 557–558
    safety standards of, 555
O'Connor Finger and Tweezer Dexterity
    Test, 230
    illustrated, 231
Office of Personnel Management, U.S.,
    20, 152
Offshoring, 297–298; *see also* Outsourcing
Off-the-job training, 415–418
    computer-assisted instruction, 415, 416
    distance training, 417–418
    lecture-discussion approach, 415
    multimedia-based training, 417
    virtual reality, 417
Oil, Chemical, and Atomic Workers' Union,
    553
Old-Age Survivors and Disability Insurance
    (OASDI) program, 360, 361
Older employees, 40–41, 132
Omnibus Budget Reconciliation Act (OBRA)
    of 1989, 371
Omnibus Transportation Employee Testing
    Act of 1991, 521
On-call pay, 299
Online recruiting, 189
Online training, 415, 416
On-the-job training, 408–409
    for managers, 413–415
        coaching and counseling, 413–414
        transfers and rotation, 414–415
        transitory anticipatory experiences, 414
Open shop, 491
Open system of compensation, 343–344
Operant conditioning; *see* Behavior
    modification
Operating managers, 14, 15
Organization chart, 155
Organization culture, 45–46
Organization Man (Whyte), 41
Organizational analysis, 399

Organizational behavior, 7
Organizational behavior modification; *see*
    Behavior modification
Organizational competitiveness, 38
Organizational effectiveness, 9–10
Organizational image, 191
Organizational preferences of recruits,
    191–192
Organizational socialization, 394
Organizational utility, 237
Organizationwide development technique,
    426–427
Orientation, 393–398
    defined, 393–394
    follow-up, 398
    goals of, 394–395
    guidelines for programs, 395, 398
    making new hires feel welcome, 396–398
    orienters, 395
    socialization and, 394
Outdoor-oriented programs, 412
Outplacement, 470
Outsourcing, 55
    as alternative to recruiting, 201
    Best Buy's approach to, 63–64
    business process, 63–64, 138
    compensation and, 296–298
    global HRM and, 113
    of HRM activities, 14–15
Outward Bound, 412, 427
Overarching philosophy, 39
Overtime, 201
Overtime pay, 300–301

Pacesetter strategy, 378
Pacesetters, 308
Pacific Maritime Association, 499
Paired comparison, 266–267
    comments on, 271
Parent country nationals (PCNs), 102
Parental leave, 368–369
Participation and empowerment, 39
Part-time workers, 55
Pay, 295; *see also* Compensation
Pay classes, 314, 315
Pay compression, 39, 345
Pay curve, 314
Pay equity, 301–302
Pay grade, 314, 315
Pay level, 308–309
Pay range, 315–316
Pay satisfaction, 306
Pay secrecy or openness, 343–344
Pay security, 344–345
Pay structure, 311–316
    broadbanding and, 316
    delayering and, 316
    job evaluation, 311–314
    pay class, 314, 315
    pay curves, 314
    pay range, 315–316
Pay surveys, 309–310
    sources of, 309–310
    usefulness of, 310

Payment methods, 328–343
    executive, 341–343
    flat rates, 328
    ownership, 339–340
    people-based, 340–341
    salaries, 328
    for time worked, 328
    variable pay; *see* Incentive pay
    wages, 328
Pease v. Alford Photo Industries, Inc., 73
Pension Benefit Guaranty Corp (PBGC),
    384, 385
Pensions, 373–374
People-based pay, 340–341
    competency-based, 341
    credential-based, 340
    feedback, 341
    knowledge-based, 340
    skill-based, 340
Perceived fairness, 305
Performance analysis, 404–407
Performance appraisal; *see* Performance
    evaluation
Performance evaluation, 250–292
    application cases, 287–292
    career challenge, 251, 276, 278
    career development and, 453
    case for using formal, 253–255
    defined, 253
    feedback interview, 276–279
    flawed, 254
    format of, 256–260
        established criteria, 256
        who, when, and how often to evaluate,
            257–260
    individual methods; *see* Individual
        evaluation methods
    interrater reliability and, 256
    the law and, 253, 254–255
    management by objectives, 268–270
    multiple person; *see* Multiple-person
        evaluation methods
    other terms for, 253
    potential problems in, 271–276
        avoiding employee problems,
            275–276
        eliminating rater errors, 275
        opposition to evaluation, 271–272
        rater problems; *see* Rater problems
        system design and operating
            problems, 272
    purposes of, 253–254
    relevance and, 256
    sensitivity and, 256
    techniques for, 260–271
        selection of, 270–271
    360-degree feedback system, 258–260
Performance management, 251–253
    making it work, 252
Performance review; *see* Performance
    evaluation
Performance-based testing, 522
Permanent replacements, 500
Person analysis, 399

Personal bias rating error, 275
Personal characteristics as selection
    criterion, 217–218
Personal mastery, 405
Personal rating; *see* Performance evaluation
Personality inventories, 231
Personality type, 57
    career choice and, 448–449
    as selection criterion, 217–218
Person-environment fit, 562–563
Personnel department; *see* Human resource
    management (HRM)
Personnel Journal, 209
Personnel ratio, 16
Peterman v. Teamsters, 536
Philadelphia Federal Society of Journeyman
    Cordwainers, 486
Physical characteristics as selection
    criterion, 217
Physical examinations, 233–234
Physical exertion, 46
Physical location of work, 46
Picketing, 499
Piecework, 331
Planning, human resource, 128–139; *see also*
    Human resource information system
    (HRIS)
    application case, 148–149
    career challenge, 129, 142
    defined, 129
    evaluation and, 253
    government policies and, 129–130
    legal advisor, 144
    management goals and, 129
    process of, 131–139
        forecasting; *see* Forecasting demand for
            employees
        action decisions, 137–139
        analyzing the current supply of
            employees, 135–137
        environmental scanning, 131
        model of, 130
        shortage of employees, 137
        situation analysis, 131
        surplus conditions, 137–139
    strategic planning and, 130–131
    virtual HR management and, 148–149
Point system of job evaluation plans, 313
Point-of-purchase recruiting, 209–210
Policy, HRM, 19
    recruitment and, 190–191
    relationship to other operations, 17
Polygraph tests, 231–232
Position, 152
Position analysis questionnaires (PAQ),
    162–164
    example of, 163
Positive discipline, 534
Positive reinforcement, 422
Postal Service, U.S., 529, 568–569
Power distance, 100
Power-bargaining tactic, 497
PPO, 370
Predictive validity, 220–221

Predictor, 220
Preferences of employees, 56
Preferential shop, 492
Preferred provider organization (PPO), 370
Pregnancy Discrimination Act of 1978,
    74, 368
Preretirement
    problems, 459
    programs, 375
Preventive health programs, 559–562
*Principles for the Validation and Use of
    Personnel Selection Procedures,* 219
Privacy of employees, 141–142
Private pensions, 373–374
    benefits of, 374
    government regulation of, 373–374
Private sector, 37–38
Procedures, HRM, 19
    relationship to other operations, 17
Process chart, 155
Production bonus systems, 332
Productivity, 37
    compensation and, 298, 306–307
    motivation and, 306–307
Professional employee organizations (PEOs),
    55, 201
Professionals, career stages of, 445–448
    apprenticeship, 445
    direction of the organization, 447–448
    independent contributor, 445
    mentoring relationship, 445, 447
Profit motive, 68
Profit-sharing plans, 339
    mandated, 387–388
Progressive pattern of discipline, 533–534
Promotion from within, 39, 190–191
Psychomotor ability simulations, 230
Public employee associations, 493–494
Public policy, violation of, 536
Public sector, 37–38
Pugh v. See Candies, Inc., 536
Punishment, 422–423

Quality improvement, 50
Quality of hire, 202–203
Quality of work life (QWL), 12
Questionnaires
    common metric, 164
    as data collection device, 159
    example of, 157–158
    management position description, 164–165
    position analysis, 162–164
Quota rating system, 268

Railway Labor Act of 1926, 486
Ranking as multiple-person evaluation
    method, 266
    comments on, 271
Ranking of jobs, 312
Rapid response, 50
    expatriate managers and, 105
Rater problems, 272–275
    central tendency error, 274
    contrast effect, 274–275

Rater problems—*Cont.*
    eliminating errors, 275
    employee problems, 275–276
    halo error, 273–274
    harshness rating error, 274
    leniency, 274
    personal bias rating error, 275
    "recency of events" rating error, 274
    standards of evaluation, 273
Realistic job previews (RJPs), 200–201
    career development and, 454
Realistic personality type, 448, 449
"Recency of events" rating error, 274
Recruiters, college, 198
    cost-benefit analysis of, 202–203
    effective, 199–200
Recruitment, 185–212
    alternatives to, 201–202
        outsourcing, 201
        overtime, 201
        temporary employment, 201–202
    application cases, 209–212
    career challenge, 186–187, 202
    cost-benefit analysis of, 202–203
    defined, 187
    e-mail and, 208
    external, 194–200
        college recruiting, 198–200, 210–211
        contract recruiting, 210
        employment agencies, 196
        e-recruiting, 195–196, 211
        executive search firms, 196
        media advertisements, 194–195,
            209–210
        special-events recruiting, 196–197
        summer internships, 197–198
    external influences, 188–190
        composition of work force, 190
        government restrictions, 188–189
        labor market conditions, 189
        location of organization, 190
    internal, 193–194, 215
        employee friends or relatives, 194, 211
        job posting, 193
        moonlighting, 193–194
    legal advisor, 204–205
    organizational view of, 190–191
        organizational image, 191
        policies and practices, 190–191
        recruiting requirements, 190
    potential employee's view of, 191–193
        job search, 192–193
        organizations and jobs, 191–192
        realistic job previews, 200–201
    selectivity in, 39
    via the Internet, 189
Reductions in force (RIFs), 77
Reengineering, 155
Reference checks, 232–233
Regression analysis, 134
Rehabilitation Act of 1973, 78
Reich v. John Alden Life Insurance Co.,
    318–319
Reimbursement accounts, 376–377

Reinforcement theory of motivation, 305
Relative deprivation theory, 306
Reliability
    of performance evaluation, 256
    of selection criteria, 218–219
Repatriation, 108–109
Repetitive stress injuries (RSIs), 568–569
Restricted shop, 491–492
Restructuring, 54
Resumes, 192–193
    personalizing, 597–599
    traditional, 245
Retaliation, 71–72
Retirement
    minimizing adjustment to, 459–460
    preretirement, 375, 459
Retirement income, 372–374
    401(k) plans, 372–375
    individual retirement accounts, 372
    private pensions, 373–374
    from savings and work, 372
    simplified employee pension accounts, 372
Retirement phase of career, 444
Return on investment (ROI), 429
    employee assistance programs and,
        524–525
Reverse culture shock, 106
Role playing, 410
Role pressures, 563
Rorschach Inkblot Test, 231
Rucker gainsharing incentive plan, 336–337
Rules for employee behavior, 532
    violators of, 529–531

Sabine Pilot Service, Inc. v. Hauck, 536
Safety and health, 546–578
    accident repeaters, 551
    application case, 575–576
    background, 547–550
    career challenge, 547, 569
    causes of accidents and illnesses, 550–551
    cumulative trauma disorders, 568–569
    economic conditions and, 552–553
    employees' attitudes and, 552
    ergonomics, 568, 577–578
    evaluation of programs, 569–570
    fatal occupational injuries, 549
    government responses to, 553–558; see also
        Occupational Safety and Health
        Administration (OSHA)
    HIV-AIDS, 566–568
    homicides in the workplace, 549–550
    indoor environmental quality, 565–566
    management goals and, 553
    nature of the task and, 552
    nonfatal occupational injuries, 548–549
    organizational responses to, 558–559
        inspection, reporting, and accident
            research, 558–559
        safety design and prevention, 558
        safety training and motivation, 559
    preventive health programs, 559–562
    responsibility for, 552–553
    stress management; see Stress management

Safety and health—Cont.
    unions and, 553
    video case, 577–578
    violence in the workplace, 549–550,
        564–565
    wellness approach, 559–562
Safety hazards, 547–550
Salary, 28, 29, 328; see also Compensation
Sarbanes-Oxley Act, 527
Scaling Equipment Products Co. Inc. v.
    Al Velarde, 347–348
Scanlon gainsharing incentive plan, 336
Scholastic Aptitude Test (SAT), 229
Scientific management, 6–7
    job design and, 170–171
Secret system of compensation, 343–344
Selection, 213–247
    application cases, 244–245
    career challenge, 214, 236
    cost-benefit analysis for, 237
    criteria, 216–221
        categories of, 216–218
        experience, 216
        formal education, 216
        past performance, 216
        personal characteristics, 217–218
        personality types, 217–218
        physical characteristics, 217
        reliability of, 218–219
        validity of; see Validity of selection
            criteria
    defined, 214
    environmental influences on
        external, 215
        internal, 214–215
    evaluation and, 253
    legal advisor, 239
    of managers, 234–237
    process of, 221–234
        employment tests; see Employment tests
        illustrated, 222
        interviews; see Interviews
        physical examinations, 233–234
        preliminary screening, 221–224
        reference checks and recommendations,
            232–233
    video case, 246–247
Selection ratio, 215
Self-actualization, 12
Self-assessment, 192
    professional help for, 594
Self-efficacy, 218
Self-evaluation, 258
Seniority, 345
September 11, 74
Service Employees International Union,
    505
Severance pay, 344
Sexual harassment, 72–74
    hostile work environment, 72, 73
    legal advisor concerning, 87–88
    meeting the challenge of, 93–94
    quid pro quo, 72, 73
    recent developments, 73–74

Shankle v. B-G Maintenance Management of
    Colorado, Inc., 538–539
Shared vision, 405
Shortage of employees, 137
Short-term orientation, 100
Sick leave, 367–368
Sick-building syndrome, 565–566
Significant other, 305
Simmons Simulator, Inc. game, 411
Simplified employee pension (SEP), 372
Singapore, 115
Sitdown strike, 499
Situation analysis, 131
Situational interview (SI), 224–225
Skill variety, 171
Skill-based pay, 340
Skills, essential and nonessential, 168
Skills and abilities of workforce, 11
Skills gap, 54
Skills inventory, 135–137
    contents of, 135–136
    defined, 135
    maintaining the, 136–137
Social and recreational programs, 376
Social comparison theories of motivation, 305
Social personality type, 448, 449
Social security, 360–362
    in foreign countries, 362
    probable changes in, 362
Social Security Act, 359
Social-behaviorist theories of motivation, 305
Socialization, 394
Socially responsible behavior, 13
Societal values, 68
Society for Industrial and Organizational
    Psychology (SIOP), 219
Society of Human Resource Management, 187
Society of Professional Benefit
    Administrators, 357
South Africa, 112
South Korea, 114–115
Spatial relations, 229
Special-events recruiting, 196–197
Spot gainsharing, 338
SRA Primary Mental Abilities Test, 229
Staff managers, 15
Staff sourcing, 201
Standard-hour plan, 331
Statistical utility, 237
Stock ownership plans, 375
Straight commission, 332
Straight piecework, 331
Strategic development, 428–430
Strategic human resource management
    (SHRM), 130–131
    job analysis and, 168–169
Strategic importance of HRM, 7–9
Strategic job analysis, 169
Strategic management approach to HRM,
    30–64
    activities by level, 48–49
    application case, 63–64
    career challenge, 31–33, 59
    challenges to, 49–55

Strategic management approach to HRM—*Cont.*
  challenges to—*Cont.*
    building a competitive workforce, 50–53
    caliber of workforce, 54
    contingent workforces, 54–55
    diversity, 50–53
    downsizing, 54
    organizational restructuring, 54
    outsourcing, 55
    technology, 49–50
  desirable end results, 57–58
  diagnostic approach; *see* Diagnostic approach to HRM
  external environmental influences; *see* External environmental influences
  internal environmental influences; *see* Internal environmental influences
  organization model, 33–35
  people and, 56–57
Strategic planning, 130–131
  job analysis and, 154
Strategy, HRM, 16–17
  collective bargaining, 496
  as internal environmental influence, 44
  relationship to other operations, 17
Stress, 562
Stress management, 562–564
  coping with, 563–564
  disease and, 562
  person-environment fit, 562–563
  role conflict and, 563
  stressors, 562, 563
  workload and, 563
Strikes, 498–499
Structural interview, 224
  form for, 225
Succession planning, 140–141
Suggestion systems, 333–335
Sullivan Principles, 112
Summary jury trial, 537
Supplementary unemployment benefits (SUB), 344
Supreme Court, U.S., 76, 359
  affirmative action and, 84, 86
  Civil Rights Act of 1964 and, 69–75, 93
  employee discipline and, 523
  job analysis and, 153
  labor relations and, 487, 492–493, 500–501, 502
Sutton et al v. United Airlines, 78
Systems thinking, 405

Tactics, collective bargaining, 496–497
Taft-Hartley Act, 488, 492, 498, 499, 500
Tailhook Association, 72
Task analysis, 399
Task identity, 47
  job enrichment and, 171
Task significance, 171, 172
Task to be performed, nature of, 46–47
Tasks, 152
Tax Reform Act of 1986, 372
Taxes and social security, 360–361

Taylor plan, 331–332
Team building, 425–426
Team incentives, 333
Team learning, 405
Teams, interdisciplinary, 39
Teamsters' Union, 489, 505, 553
Technology, 49–50
Telecommuting, 51
  job design and, 173, 174
Temperament tests, 231
Temporary employment, 201–202
Test-retest reliability, 219
Theft, fraud, and other illegal acts, 523–528
  deep bite of, 526–527
  ways to minimize, 525
Thematic Apperception Test, 231
Third country nationals (TCNs), 102
Third party intervention, 500–501
Third sector, 37–38
360-degree feedback, 258–260
Time dimension of work, 46
Time-off benefits, 365
Title VII; *see* Civil Rights Act of 1964 (Title VII)
Toll-free hotlines, 409
Torres v. Pisano, 87–88
Total compensation approach, 330
Total quality management (TQM), 426–427
Training, 392–439
  activities, 401–403
  application cases, 438–439
  career challenge, 393, 406, 418
  defined, 393, 394
  development and; *see* Development
  evaluation of, 253, 427–432
    criteria for, 430–431
    matrix guide for, 431–432
    strategic management, 428–430
  expatriate managers, 106–109
  goals of, 399–400
  important points about, 399
  instruction methods; *see* Instructional methods, training and development
  learning organizations and, 401
  learning theory and, 400–401
  legal advisor, 434–435
  managing the program, 403–407
    choosing trainers and trainees, 407
    needs assessment, 399, 403–404
    performance analysis, 404–407
  methods of providing, 403
  orientation; *see* Orientation
  safety, 539
  as skill development, 39
  systems model of, 400
  validity of, 399–400
Transfers and rotation, 414–415
Transitory anticipatory experiences, 414
Travel stress, 562
Trend projection, 133
True halo, 273–274
Tuition aid programs, 462
Turnover reduction, 395
Two-factor theory of motivation, 304–305, 306

Uncertainty avoidance, 100
Unemployment for African-Americans, 69
Unemployment insurance, 359–360
Unfair labor practices, 487–488
Uniform Guidelines on Employee Selection Procedures (UGESP) of 1978, 153, 156, 220, 254
Union security, 491–493
  agency shop, 492
  closed shop, 492
  levels of, 491–493
  open shop, 491
  preferential shop, 492
  restricted shop, 491–492
  right-to-work requirements, 493
  union shop, 492–493
Union shop, 492–493
Unions; *see* Labor unions
Unit-demand forecasting, 134–135
United Auto Workers, 371
United Brotherhood of Carpenters, 505
United Rubber Workers, 553
United States Office of Personnel Management General Schedule, 312
United Steelworkers of America v. Weber, 82
U.S. v. The City of Warren, Michigan, 204–205
University of Houston, 228
University of Texas, 85
Unstructured interview, 224
USA Today, 341
Utility, 237

Vacations, paid, 366
  in other countries, 366–367
Validity of selection criteria, 219–221
  construct, 220
  content, 219–220
  criterion-related, 220–221
  defined, 219
Validity of training, 399–400
Value and pay equity, 301–302
Values, 68
Variable pay, 330; *see also* Incentive pay
Vestibule training, 418
Video cases
  Budget Rent-a-Car and international compensation, 387–389
  Creative Staffing Solutions, 246–247
  Hotjobs.com, 479
  OSHA and unions versus manufacturers, 577–578
  Southwest Airlines: competing through people, 125–126
Violence in the workplace, 530–531
  as safety and health issue, 564–565
  warning signs of, 530
Virtual reality (VR), 417
Vocational Preference Inventory, 449
Voluntary employee benefits, 364–371
  compensation for time off, 365
  disability income replacement insurance, 371

Voluntary employee benefits—*Cont.*
  employer-purchased insurance, 369
  family leave, 368
  health insurance; *see* Health insurance
  life insurance, 371
  maternity leave, 368–369
  paid holidays, 365
  paid vacations, 366
    in other countries, 366–367
  parental leave, 368–369
  personal time off, 367
  sick leave, 367–368
  typical, 365

*W. W. Cross v. National Labor Relations
  Board,* 357
Wage and hour regulations, 298–302
Wage compression, 39, 345
Wage controls, 298
Wage freezes, 298
Wage guidelines, 298
Wage Stabilization Act of 1942, 298
Wages, 328; *see also* Compensation
Wagner Act, 303, 487
  unfair labor practices and, 487–488

Wall Street Journal, 189, 341
Walsh-Healy Act of 1936, 302
War Manpower Commission, 408–409
Wards Cove Packing Co. v. Antonio, 76
Watson v. Fort Worth Bank and Trust, 71
Wechsler Adult Intelligence Scale, 229
Weighted application blank, 223
Welfare Fund Disclosure Act, 358
Welfare secretaries, 7
Wellness approach, 559–562
Wildcat strike, 499
Winsharing, 338
Wisconsin State Employees' Association, 493
Women
  Equal Pay Act, 301–302
  as expatriate managers, 104
  glass ceiling, 466, 467–469
  in the labor force, 39–40
  maternity leave, 183–184
  recent successes of, 41
  returning to the workforce, 194
Wonderlic Personnel Test, 229
Work group, 47
Work motivation, 56–57
Work sector of the organization, 37–38

Worker Adjustment on Retraining
  Notification Act (WARN) of 1989,
  134
Worker function scale, 161
Workers' compensation, 362–364
  in California, 363–364
  managing claims, 366
Workforce
  baby boomers in, 132, 187
  building a competitive, 50–53
  caliber of, 54
  career development and, 464
  changing demographics of, 129
  diversity of; *see* Labor force composition
  shrinking, 187
Work-life balance, 44
  job design and, 172–174
  recruiting and, 211–212
Work-oriented job analysis, 156
World Health Organization, 566
Worthington v. City of New Haven, 176–177
*Wright v. Universal Maritime Serv.
  Corp.,* 502

Yellow-dog contracts, 486